Thru the Bible with J. Vernon McGee

By J. Vernon McGee

Thru the Bible with J. Vernon McGee

By J. Vernon McGee

VOLUME IV
Matthew—Romans

Thomas Nelson Publishers
Nashville

Compiled from previous publications by J. Vernon McGee.

Published in Nashville, Tennessee, by Thomas Nelson, Inc., Publishers and distributed in Canada by Lawson Falle, Ltd., Cambridge, Ontario.

Library of Congress Cataloging in Publication Data

McGee, J. Vernon (John Vernon), 1904–1988
Thru the Bible with J. Vernon McGee.

Based on the Thru the Bible radio program.
Includes bibliographies.
Contents: v. 1. Genesis—Deuteronomy—
v. 4 Matthew—Romans
1. Bible—Commentaries. I. Thru the Bible
(Radio program) II. Title.
BS491.2.M37 220.7′7 81-3930
ISBN 0-8407-4973-2 (Nelson) v. 1
ISBN 0-8407-4978-3 (Royal) v. 1
ISBN 0-8407-4976-7 (Nelson) v. 4
ISBN 0-8407-4981-3 (Royal) v. 4

Printed in the United States of America

26 - 03

TABLE OF CONTENTS

PREFACE

The radio broadcasts of the Thru the Bible Radio five-year program were transcribed, edited, and published first in single-volume paperbacks to accommodate the radio audience. From the beginning there was a demand that they be published in a more permanent form and in fewer volumes. This new hardback edition is an attempt to meet that need.

There has been a minimal amount of further editing for this publication. Therefore, these messages are not the word-for-word recording of the taped messages which went out over the air. The changes were necessary to accommodate a reading audience rather than a listening audience.

These are popular messages, prepared originally for a radio audience. They should not be considered a commentary on the entire Bible in any sense of that term. These messages are devoid of any attempt to present a theological or technical commentary on the Bible. Behind these messages is a great deal of research and study in order to interpret the Bible from a popular rather than from a scholarly (and too-often boring) viewpoint.

We have definitely and deliberately attempted "to put the cookies on the bottom shelf so that the kiddies could get them."

The fact that these messages have been translated into many languages for radio broadcasting and have been received with enthusiasm reveals the need for a simple teaching of the whole Bible for the masses of the world.

I am indebted to many people and to many sources for bringing this volume into existence. I should express my especial thanks to my secretary, Gertrude Cutler, who supervised the editorial work; to Dr. Elliott R. Cole, my associate, who handled all the detailed work with the publishers; and finally, to my wife Ruth for tenaciously encouraging me from the beginning to put my notes and messages into printed form.

Solomon wrote, ". . . of making many books there is no end; and much study is a weariness of the flesh" (Eccl. 12:12). On a sea of books that flood the marketplace, we launch this series of THRU THE BIBLE with the hope that it might draw many to the one Book, *The Bible.*

J. VERNON MCGEE

The Gospel According to

MATTHEW

INTRODUCTION

The Gospel of Matthew, although it is only twenty-eight chapters long, is a very important book. In fact, Genesis and Matthew are the two key books of the Bible.

As we come today to the Gospel of Matthew, I'd like to bridge the gap between the Old Testament and the New Testament because, in order to appreciate and to have a right understanding of the New Testament, it is almost essential to know something about this period of approximately four hundred years. This is the time span between the days of Nehemiah and Malachi and the birth of Jesus Christ in Bethlehem. You see, after Malachi had spoken, heaven went silent. Station G O D went off the air, and there was no broadcasting for four hundred years. Then one day the angel of the Lord broke in upon the time of prayer when there was a priest by the name of Zacharias standing at the altar in Jerusalem. The angel gave the announcement of the birth of John the Baptist who was the forerunner of the Lord Jesus. We shall see later how important John the Baptist is in the Gospel of Matthew.

We find that a great deal took place in this interval of four hundred years even though it is a silent period as far as Scripture is concerned. This period was a thrilling and exciting time in the history of these people, and in many ways it was also a tragic time. The internal condition of Judah experienced a radical transformation. A new culture, different institutions, and unfamiliar organizations arose in this period, and many of these new things appear in the New Testament.

World history had made tremendous strides in the interval between the Old and New Testaments. The Old Testament closed with the Medo-Persian Empire being the dominant power. Also, Egypt was still a power to be reckoned with in world politics. During the interval between the testaments, both faded from the scene as outstanding nations. World power shifted from the East to the West, from the Orient to the Occident, from Asia to Europe, and from Medo-Persia to Greece. When the New Testament opens, a new power, Rome, is the world ruler. A consideration of some important dates will give a bird's-eye view of this great transition period. (Because historians differ in their dating, consider these dates as approximate.)

480 B.C. Xerxes, the Persian, was victorious against the Greeks at Thermopylae but was defeated at the battle of Salamis. Actually, it was a storm that defeated him. This was the last bid of the East for world dominion.

333 B.C. Out of the West there came that "goat" which Daniel records in the eighth chapter of Daniel. This was Alexander the Great, the goat with the great horn. He led the united Greek forces to victory over the Persians at Issus.

332 B.C. Alexander the Great visited Jerusalem. He was shown the prophecy of Daniel which spoke of him; therefore he spared Jerusalem. Jerusalem was one of the few cities that he ever spared.

323 B.C. Alexander died way over in Persia. Apparently he had intended to move the seat of his empire there. Then the world empire of both East and West was divided among his four generals.

320 B.C. Judea was annexed to Egypt by Ptolemy Soter.

312 B.C. Seleucus founded the kingdom of the Seleucidae, which is Syria. He attempted to take Judea, and so Judea became the battleground between Syria and Egypt. This little country became a buffer state.

203 B.C. Antiochus the Great took Jerusalem, and Judea passed under the influence of Syria.

170 B.C. Antiochus Epiphanes took Jerusalem and defiled the temple. He had been mentioned in Daniel as the "little horn"(Dan. 8:9). He has been called the "Nero of Jewish history."

166 B.C. Mattathias, the priest of Judea, raised a revolt against Syria. This is the beginning of the Maccabean period. Probably the nation of Israel has never suffered more than during this era, and they were never more heroic than during this interval. Judas Maccabaeus, whose name

means "the hammer," was the leader who organized the revolt.

63 B.C. Pompey, the Roman, took Jerusalem, and the people of Israel passed under the rulership of a new world power. They were under Roman government at the time of the birth of Jesus and throughout the period of the New Testament.

40 B.C. The Roman senate appointed Herod to be king of Judea. There never has been a family or a man more wicked than this. One can talk about the terrible Mafia, but this family would exceed them all.

37 B.C. Herod took Jerusalem and slew Antigonus, the last of the Maccabean king-priests.

31 B.C. Caesar Augustus became emperor of Rome.

19 B.C. The construction of the Herodian temple was begun. The building had been going on quite awhile when our Lord was born and was still continuing during the time of the New Testament.

4 B.C. Our Lord Jesus was born in Bethlehem.

Radical changes took place in the internal life of the nation of Judea because of their experiences during the intertestamental period. After the Babylonian captivity, they turned from idolatry to a frantic striving for legal holiness. The Law became an idol to them. The classic Hebrew gave way to the Aramaic in their everyday speech, although the Hebrew was retained for their synagogues. The synagogue seems to have come into existence after the captivity. It became the center of their life in Judea and everywhere else they went in the world. Also, there arose among these people a group of parties which are mentioned in the New Testament and are never even heard of in the Old Testament:

1. *PHARISEES*—The Pharisees were the dominant party. They arose to defend the Jewish way of life against all foreign influences. They were strict legalists who believed in the Old Testament. They were nationalists in politics and wanted to restore the kingdom to the line of David. So they were a religio-political party. Today we would call them fundamental theologically and to the far right politically.

2. *SADDUCEES*—The Sadducees were made up of the wealthy and socially-minded who wanted to get rid of tradition. By the way, does that remind you of the present hour? Isn't it interesting that the rich families of this country are liberal? The crumbs still fall from the rich man's table. They are willing to give the crumbs, but they don't give their wealth, that is sure. The Sadducees were liberal in their theology, and they rejected the supernatural. Thus they were opposed to the Pharisees. The Sadducees were closely akin to the Greek Epicureans whose philosophy was "eat, drink, and be merry, for tomorrow we die." We may have a mistaken idea of the Sadducees. Actually, they were attempting to attain the "good life." They thought that they could overcome their bodily appetites by satisfying them, that by giving them unbridled reign, they would no longer need attention. In our day, a great many folk have this same philosophy. It did not work in the past; neither will it work today.

3. *SCRIBES*—The scribes were a group of professional expounders of the Law, stemming back from the days of Ezra. They became the hair-splitters. They were more concerned with the *letter* of the Law than with the *spirit* of the Law. When old Herod called in the scribes and asked where Jesus was to be born, they knew it was to be in Bethlehem. You would think that they would have hitchhiked a ride on the back of the camels to go down to Bethlehem to see Him, but they weren't interested. They were absorbed in the letter of the Law.

My friend, there is a danger of just wanting the information and the knowledge from the Bible but failing to translate it into shoe leather, not letting it become part of our lives. Through study we can learn the basic facts of Scripture, and all the theological truth contained in it, without allowing the Word of God to take possession of our hearts. The scribes fell into such a category. In our own day, I must confess that some of the most hard-hearted people I meet are fundamentalists. They are willing to rip a person apart in order to maintain some little point. It is important to know the Word of God—that is a laudable attainment—but also we are to translate it into life and pass it on to others.

4. *HERODIANS*—The Herodians were a party in the days of Jesus, and they were strictly political opportunists. They sought to maintain the Herods on the throne, because they wanted their party in power.

The intertestamental period was a time of great literary activity in spite of the fact there was no revelation from God. The Old Testament was translated into Greek in Alexandria, Egypt, during the period from 285 to 247 B.C. It was translated by six members from each of the twelve tribes; hence, the name given to this translation was *Septuagint*, meaning "seventy." This translation was used by Paul, and our Lord apparently quoted from it.

The Apocrypha of the Old Testament was written in this era. These are fourteen books which bear no marks of inspiration. There are two books classified as the Pseudepigrapha, *Psalter of Solomon* and the *Book of Enoch*. They bear the names of two characters of the Old Testament, but there is no evidence that these two men were the writers.

Although this was a period marked by the silence of God, it is evident that God was preparing the world for the coming of Christ. The Jewish people, the Greek civilization, the Roman Empire, and the seething multitudes of the Orient were all being prepared for the coming of a Savior, insomuch that they produced the scene which Paul labeled, in Galatians 4:4, "the fulness of time." The four Gospels are directed to the four major groups in the world of that day.

The Gospel of Matthew was written to the nation Israel. It was first written in Hebrew, and it was directed primarily to the religious man of that time.

The Gospel of Mark was directed to the Roman. The Roman was a man of action who believed that government, law, and order could control the world. A great many people feel that is the way it should be done today. It is true that there must be law and order, but the Romans soon learned that they couldn't rule the world with that alone. The world needed to hear about One who believed in law and order but who also offered the forgiveness of sins and the grace and the mercy of God. This is the Lord whom the Gospel of Mark presents to the Romans.

The Gospel of Luke was written to the Greek, to the thinking man.

The Gospel of John was written directly for believers but indirectly for the Orient where there were the mysterious millions, all crying out in that day for a deliverance.

There is still a crying out today from a world that needs a Deliverer. The religious man needs Christ and not religion. The man of power needs a Savior who has the power to save him. The thinking man needs One who can meet all his mental and spiritual needs. And certainly the wretched man needs to know about a Savior who not only can save him but build him up so that he can live for God.

The Gospel of Matthew was written by a publican whom the Lord Jesus had put His hand upon in a very definite way (see Matt. 9:9). He was a follower, a disciple, of the Lord Jesus. Papias says, Eusebius confirms, and other of the apostolic fathers agree, that this gospel was written originally by Matthew in Hebrew for the nation Israel, a religious people.

I don't have time to give the background of all this, but God has prepared this whole nation for the coming of Christ into the world. And He did come of this nation, as the Lord Jesus Himself said, ". . . salvation is of the Jews" (John 4:22). It was a great German historian who said that God prepared the Savior to come out of Israel—"salvation is of the Jews"—and He prepared the heathen for salvation, because they were lost and needed it.

This remarkable book is a key book of the Bible because it swings back into the Old Testament and gathers up more Old Testament prophecies than any other book. One might expect it to do this since it was first written to the Jews. But then, it moves farther into the New Testament than any of the other Gospels. For instance, no other gospel writer mentions the church by name; but Matthew does. He is the one who relates the Word of our Lord, ". . . upon this rock I will build my church . . ." (Matt. 16:18). Even Renan, the French skeptic, said of this gospel that it "is the most important book in Christendom, the most important that has ever been written." That is a remarkable statement coming from *him!* Matthew, a converted publican, was the choice of the Spirit of God to write this gospel primarily to the people of Israel.

The gospel of Matthew presents the program of God. The "kingdom of heaven" is an expression which is peculiar to this gospel. It occurs thirty-two times. The word *kingdom* occurs fifty times. A proper understanding of the phrase "kingdom of heaven" is essential to any interpretation of this gospel and of the Bible. May I make this statement right now, and I do make it categorically and dogmatically: The *kingdom* and the *church* are not the same. They are not synonymous terms. Although the church is in the kingdom, there is all the difference in the world.

For instance, Los Angeles is in California, but Los Angeles is not California. If you disagree, ask the people from San Francisco. California is not the United States, but it is in the United States. The Chamber of Commerce may think it is the United States, but it's not. It's only one fiftieth of it.

Likewise, the church is in the kingdom, but the kingdom of heaven, simply stated, is the reign of the heavens over the earth. The church is in this kingdom. Now I know that theologians have really clouded the atmosphere, and they certainly have made this a very complicated thing. Poor preachers like I am must come up with a simple explanation, and this is it: the kingdom of heaven is the reign of the heavens over the earth. The Jews to whom this gospel was directed understood the term to be the sum total of all the prophecies of the Old Testament concerning the coming of a King from heaven to set up a kingdom on this earth with heaven's standard. This term was not new to them (see Dan. 2:44; 7:14, 27).

The kingdom of heaven is the theme of this gospel. The One who is going to establish that kingdom on the earth is the Lord Jesus. The kingdom is all important. The Gospel of Matthew contains three major discourses concerning the kingdom.

1. *The Sermon on the Mount*. That is the *law* of the kingdom. I think it is only a partial list of what will be enforced in that day.

2. *The Mystery Parables*. These parables in Matthew 13 are about the kingdom. Our Lord tells us that the kingdom of heaven is like a sower, like a mustard seed, and so on.

3. *The Olivet Discourse*. This looks forward to the establishment of the kingdom here upon this earth.

It will be seen that the term "kingdom of heaven" is a progressive term in the Gospel of Matthew. This is very important for us to see. There is a movement in the Gospel of Matthew, and if we miss it, we've missed the gospel. It is like missing a turn-off on the freeway. You miss it, brother, and you're in trouble. So if we miss the movement in this marvelous gospel, we miss something very important.

This gospel is very much like the Book of Genesis. They are two key books of the Bible, and you really should be familiar enough with these two books so that you can *think* your way through them. I will be giving you chapter headings so you can learn to think your way through the book. I would tell my students in former days, "When you can't sleep at night, don't count sheep. Instead, think your way through Genesis. Then think your way through the Gospel of Matthew. Take it up chapter by chapter. Chapter One: what is it about? Chapter Two: what is it about? If you say to me that you don't like counting sheep or chapters, then talk to the Shepherd, but the finest way to talk to the Shepherd is to go through these two books. That will help you to get acquainted with Him and come to know Him." By the way, it's more important to have Him talk to us than for us to talk to Him. I don't know that I've got too much to tell Him, but He has a lot to tell me. I suggest that you learn the chapters of Matthew so that you don't miss the movement in them.

Now I want to give you one way of dividing the Gospel of Matthew. I'll follow a little different division, but this will help you to think it through. It is important to know Matthew in order to understand the Bible!

1. **Person** of the King
   Chapters 1–2
2. **Preparation** of the King
   Chapters 2–4:16
3. **Propaganda** of the King
   Chapters 4:17–9:35
4. **Program** of the King
   Chapters 9:36–16:20
5. **Passion** of the King
   Chapters 16:21–27:66
6. **Power** of the King
   Chapter 28

OUTLINE

CHAPTERS

1 Genealogy and Record of Virgin Birth of Jesus

2 Visit of Wise Men—Flight to Egypt—Return to Nazareth

3 John the Baptist, Forerunner of King, Announces Kingdom and Baptizes Jesus, the King

4 Testing of the King in Wilderness—Begins Public Ministry at Capernaum—Calls Disciples

5–7 Sermon on the Mount
- (1) Relationship of Subjects of Kingdom to Self, 5:1–16
- (2) Relationship of Subjects of Kingdom to Law, 5:17–48
- (3) Relationship of Subjects of Kingdom to God, 6:1–34
- (4) Relationship of Children of King to Each Other, 7:1–29

8 Six Miracles of King Demonstrate His Dynamic to Enforce Ethics of Sermon on Mount

9 Performs Six More Miracles—Calls Matthew—Contends with Pharisees

10 Jesus Commissions Twelve to Preach Gospel of the Kingdom to Nation Israel

11 Quizzed by Disciples of John—Rejects Unrepentant Cities—Issues New Invitation to Individuals

12 Conflict and Final Break of Jesus with Religious Rulers

13 Mystery Parables of Kingdom of Heaven

14 John the Baptist Beheaded—Jesus Feeds 5,000—Sends Disciples Into Storm at Sea—Walks on Water to Them

15 Jesus Denounces Scribes and Pharisees—Heals Daughter of Syrophoenician Woman and Multitudes—Feeds 4,000

16 Conflict with Pharisees and Sadducees—Confession from Disciples, Peter Spokesman—Jesus First Confronts Them with Church, His Death and Resurrection

17 Transfiguration—Demon Possessed Boy—Tax Money Provided by Miracle

18 Little Child—Lost Sheep—Conduct in Coming Church—Parable on Forgiveness

19 God's Standard for Marriage and Divorce—Little Children Blessed—Rich Young Ruler—Apostles' Position in Coming Kingdom

20 Parable of Laborers in Vineyard—Jesus Makes 4th and 5th Announcement of His Approaching Death—Mother Requests Places of Honor for James and John—Jesus Restores Sight to Two Men

21 King Offers Himself Publicly and Finally to Nation—Cleanses Temple—Curses Fig Tree—Condemns Religious Rulers with Parables of Two Sons and Householder

22 Parable of Marriage Feast for King's Son—Jesus Answers and Silences Herodians, Sadducees, Pharisees

23 Jesus Warns Against and Pronounces Woes Upon Scribes and Pharisees—Weeps over Jerusalem

24–25 Olivet Discourse

Jesus Answers Questions About Sign of End of Age and Sign of His Coming—Parable of Ten Virgins—Parable of Eight Talents—Judgment of Sheep and Goat Nations

26 Jesus Plotted Against—Anointed by Mary of Bethany—Sold by Judas—Observes Last Passover and First Lord's Supper—Agonizes in Gethsemane—Arrested and Tried by Religious Rulers—Disowned by Peter

27 Trial, Death and Burial of the King

28 Resurrection of the King—His Great Commission

CHAPTER 1

***THEME:** The genealogy of Jesus Christ and record of the virgin birth of Jesus*

THE GENEALOGY

The genealogy which opens the Gospel of Matthew and the New Testament is in many respects the most important document in the Scriptures. The entire Bible rests upon its accuracy. You will notice it has three divisions:

1. Genealogy from Abraham to David (vv. 1–6).
2. Genealogy from Solomon to the Babylonian captivity (vv. 7–11).
3. Genealogy from the Babylonian captivity to Joseph, the carpenter (vv. 12–17).

In our study of Genesis, we note the fact that it is a book about families. The genealogies there are very important, and we see them here as we start the New Testament.

Now I must confess that at first this looks rather boring. You give someone a New Testament, and they begin here in the Gospel of Matthew with a genealogy staring them in the face, and they're not going to get very far in it. A chaplain friend of mine told me that in World War II he gave out literally thousands of New Testaments to servicemen. He's seen the men in the bunks open the New Testament, read for a minute or two at the beginning of Matthew, start through that genealogy and come to the conclusion this Book wasn't for them. Can't blame them! My point is that we ought to use a little wisdom in giving out literature to people. The average person should start first in any one of the other three gospels, preferably Mark, rather than the Gospel of Matthew. But that doesn't lessen the importance of this genealogy.

The New Testament rests upon the accuracy of this genealogy because it establishes the fact that the Lord Jesus Christ is of the line of Abraham and of the line of David. Both are very important. The line of Abraham places Him in the nation, and the line of David puts Him on the throne—He is in that royal line.

The genealogies were very important to the nation Israel, and through them it could be established whether a person had a legitimate claim to a particular line. For example, when Israel returned from the captivity, we find in the Book of Ezra, "These sought their register among those that were reckoned by genealogy, but they were not found: therefore were they, as polluted, put from the priesthood" (Ezra 2:62). It was possible in Ezra's day to check the register of the tribe of Levi and remove those who made a false claim.

Evidently these genealogies were kept by the government and were accessible to the public. I have a notion they were kept in the temple because Israel was a theocracy, and actually the "church" and the state were one. This genealogy was obviously on display and could have been copied from the public records until the temple was destroyed in A.D. 70. The enemies of Jesus could have checked them and probably did. This is interesting and important because they challenged every move of the Lord Jesus, even offering a substitute explanation for the Resurrection, but they never did question His genealogy. The reason must be that they checked it out and found that it was accurate.

This is most important because it puts Jesus in a very unique position. You remember that He said the Shepherd of the sheep enters in by the door but the thief and the robber climb up some other way to get into the sheepfold (see John 10:1–2). That "fold" is the nation Israel. He didn't climb into the fold over a fence in the back, and He didn't come in through the alleyway. He came in through the gate. He was *born* in the line of David and in the line of Abraham. This is what Matthew is putting before us. He is the fulfillment of everything that had been mentioned in the Old Testament. So the enemies of Christ never could challenge Him in regard to His genealogy. They had to find some other ways to challenge Him, and, of course, they did.

When I was a teenager, I became interested in the Bible for the first time, and I went to a summer conference where the Lord spoke to my heart. Our Bible teacher thrilled my heart as he taught the Word of God. One morning he asked, "How many of you young people have read the Bible through in a year?" There were two to three hundred young people there, but not a hand went up. He asked the same question four times. Finally, one young man in the back put up his hand rather hesitatingly and said, "Well, I read it, but I only read the parts that were interesting. I didn't read the genealogies." Everybody laughed, and the teacher laughed, too, and admitted that he didn't read them either. At that very moment it occurred to me that since the Spirit of God has used so much printer's ink to give them to us, there must be some importance in them for us. So I'll have you note this genealogy now in Matthew because it is very important.

This is the genealogy of the Lord Jesus on Joseph's side. We'll have another when we get over to Luke, and that will be from Mary's side.

The book of the generation of Jesus Christ, the son of David, the son of Abraham [Matt. 1:1].

"The book of the generation" is a phrase which is peculiar to Matthew. It's a unique expression, and you won't find it anywhere else in the New Testament. If you start going back through the Old Testament, back through Malachi and Zechariah and Haggai and back to the Pentateuch, through Deuteronomy, Numbers, Leviticus, Exodus into Genesis, you'll almost come to the conclusion that it's nowhere else in the Bible except here in Matthew. Then all of a sudden, you come to the fifth chapter of Genesis and see "This is the book of the generations of Adam . . . ." (Gen. 5:1). There is that expression again. There are two books: the book of the generations of Adam and the book of the generation of Jesus Christ. How did you get into the family of Adam? You got in by a birth. You didn't perform it; in fact, you had nothing to do with it. But that's the way you and I got into the family of Adam. We got there by birth. But in Adam all die (Rom. 5:12). Adam's book is a book of death.

Then there is the other book, the book of the generation of Jesus Christ. How did you get into that family, into that genealogy? You got into it by a birth, the new birth. The Lord Jesus says we must be born again to see the kingdom of God (see John 3:3). That puts us in the Lamb's Book of Life, and we get there by trusting Christ. We all are in the first book, the book of the generations of Adam. I trust that you, my friend, are also in the Lamb's Book of Life.

Matthew says Jesus is "the son of David, the son of Abraham." Didn't Matthew know that Abraham came before David? Of course he did because he makes that clear in the rest of the genealogy. Then why did he put it this way? He is presenting the Lord Jesus as the Messiah, the One who is the King, the One who is to establish the kingdom of heaven on earth. And that comes first. He must be in the line of David in fulfillment of the prophecies that God made to David. He is the Son of David.

He is also the Son of Abraham and it is very important that He be the Son of Abraham, because God had said to Abraham, ". . . in thy seed shall all the nations of the earth be blessed . . ." (Gen. 22:18). And in Galatians 3:16 Paul explains who that "seed" is: "Now to Abraham and his seed were the promises made. He saith not, And to seeds, as of many; but as of one, And to thy seed, which is Christ." So Jesus Christ is the Son of Abraham.

Abraham begat Isaac; and Isaac begat Jacob; and Jacob begat Judas and his brethren;

And Judas begat Phares and Zara of Thamar; and Phares begat Esrom; and Esrom begat Aram;

And Aram begat Aminadab; and Aminadab begat Naasson; and Naasson begat Salmon;

And Salmon begat Booz of Rachab; and Booz begat Obed of Ruth; and Obed begat Jesse;

And Jesse begat David the king; and David the king begat Solomon of her that had been the wife of Urias [Matt. 1:2–6].

A careful look at the genealogy that follows is not only interesting; it is actually thrilling. Four names stand out as if they were in neon lights. It is startling to find them included in the genealogy of Christ. First, they are the names of women; second, they are the names of Gentiles.

Customarily, the names of women did not appear in Hebrew genealogies, but don't find fault with that for the very simple reason that today we have the same thing in marriage. In a marriage the name that the couple takes is the name of the man. They don't take the name of the woman. Her line ends; his goes on. That's the way we do it today, and that's the way they did it then.

Down through the years I have performed marriages in which the girl had a lovely name like Jones or Smith, and she wanted to exchange it for a name like Neuenschwander or Schicklegruber! You would think that she'd not want to surrender her name for one having four or five syllables, but that's the way they do it today. I have a clipping in my file of about ten years ago that tells of a couple in Pasadena who did the unusual thing of taking the name of the woman, which, I understand, can be legally done. But our custom is to take the name of the man, and it is the man's genealogy that is given.

In Jesus' day it was indeed unusual to find in a genealogy a woman's name—yet here we have four names. They are not only four women; they are four Gentiles. As you know, God in the Law said that His people were not to intermarry with tribes that were heathen and pagan. Even Abraham was instructed by God to send back to his people to get a bride for his son Isaac. Also, the same thing was done by Isaac for his son Jacob. It was God's arrangement that monotheism should be the prevailing belief of those who were in the line that was leading down to the Lord Jesus Christ. Yet in His genealogy are the names of four gentile women—two of them were Canaanites, one was a Moabite, and the fourth was a Hittite! You would naturally ask the question, "How did *they* get into the genealogy of Christ?"

"Thamar" is the first one, and she is mentioned in verse three. Her story is in Genesis 38, and there she is called Tamar. That chapter is one of the worst in the Bible. Thamar got into the genealogy because she was a sinner.

"Rachab" is the next one mentioned in verse five. She's not a very pretty character in her story back in Joshua chapter 2 where she is called Rahab. But she did become a wonderful person after she came to a knowledge of the living and true God. "By faith the harlot Rahab perished not with them that believed not, when she had received the spies with peace" (Heb. 11:31). She got into the genealogy of Christ for the simple reason that she *believed*. She had faith. Notice the progression here. Come as a *sinner*, and then reach out the hand of *faith*.

"Ruth" is the next one mentioned in verse five. She is a lovely person, and you won't find anything wrong with her. But at Ruth's time there was the Law which shut her out because it said that a Moabite or an Ammonite shall not enter into the congregation of the Lord (see Deut. 23:3). Although the Law kept her out, there was a man by the name of Boaz who came into his field one day and saw her. It was love at first sight.

Now, maybe you didn't know that I believe in love at first sight. I proposed to my wife on our second date, and the only reason I didn't propose on our first date was because I didn't want her to think I was in a hurry! I do believe in love at first sight. But don't misunderstand me—we waited a year before we were married, just to make sure. And I think that is always the wise thing to do.

Boaz loved Ruth at first sight, and he extended grace to her by putting his mantle around her and bringing her, a Gentile, into the congregation of Israel. She asked, ". . . Why have I found grace in thine eyes . . .?" (Ruth 2:10). You and I can ask that same question of God regarding His grace to us. Again, note the progression. We come as *sinners* and hold out the hand of *faith*, and He, by His marvelous grace, *saves* us.

"Bathsheba" is not mentioned by name but called "her that had been the wife of Urias" (v. 6). Her name isn't mentioned because it wasn't her sin. It was David's sin, and David was the one that really had to pay for it. And he did pay for it. She got into the genealogy of Christ because God does not throw overboard one of His children who sins. A sheep can get out of the fold and become a lost sheep, but we have a Shepherd who goes after sheep and always brings them back into the fold. He brought David back. So this is the whole story of salvation right here in this genealogy.

Now there are some more interesting things about this genealogy. If you will compare this genealogy with the one in 1 Chronicles 3 (some of the names are spelled differently), you will find that in verse eight of Matthew, the names of Ahaziah, Joash, and Amaziah are left out. This shows that genealogies are quoted to give us a view of a certain line of descendants and that every individual is not necessarily named in every genealogy of the Bible. I think we should remember this in the genealogies given to us in Genesis before the Flood. These are not necessarily complete genealogies, but they are given to trace a certain line for us. I personally think man has been on this earth a lot longer than Ussher's dating which is found in the margins of many editions of the Bible. Remember that these dates are by *Ussher* and are not part of the Bible. They are faulty and do not belong there.

And Ezekias begat Manasses; and Manasses begat Amon; and Amon begat Josias;

And Josias begat Jechonias and his brethren, about the time they were carried away to Babylon [Matt. 1:10–11].

In verse 11, we find that Matthew skips Jehoiakim but includes Jechonias. Jechonias deserves our special attention because God had said that none of his seed would sit on the throne. "As I live, saith the LORD, though Coniah [his name is Jeconiah, but God took the Je off his name because it is the prefix for

Jehovah, and this man was a wicked king] the son of Jehoiakim king of Judah were the signet upon my right hand, yet would I pluck thee thence . . . Thus saith the LORD, Write ye this man childless, a man that shall not prosper in his days: for no man of his seed shall prosper, sitting upon the throne of David, and ruling any more in Judah" (Jer. 22:24, 30). Because of the sin of this man Jechonias, no one in his line could ever sit on the throne of David. You see, Joseph is in this line, but Joseph is not the natural father of Jesus. This is one of the most remarkable facts in the Scriptures, and Matthew is trying to make it clear to us. Joseph gave to Jesus the title, the *legal* title, to the throne of David because Joseph was the husband of Mary who was the one who bore Jesus. Jesus Christ is not the seed of Joseph, nor is He the seed of Jeconiah. But both Joseph and Mary had to be from the line of David, and they were—through two different lines from two different sons of David. We'll find when we get to Luke that Mary's line comes from David through his son Nathan. Joseph's line comes through the royal line through Solomon. So Joseph and Mary both had to go to Bethlehem to be enrolled for taxation because they were both from the line of David. You see how interesting, fascinating, and important these genealogies are and how much they are worth our study.

Now the genealogy concludes with this verse—

And Jacob begat Joseph the husband of Mary, of whom was born Jesus, who is called Christ [Matt. 1:16].

You see that this breaks the pattern which began as far back as verse 2 where it says that Abraham *begat* Isaac. From then on it was just a whole lot of "begetting," and verse 16 begins by saying, "And Jacob begat Joseph." You would expect it to continue by saying that Joseph begat Jesus, but it does not say that. Instead, it says, "Jacob begat Joseph the husband of Mary, of whom was born Jesus, who is called Christ." Obviously, Matthew is making it clear that Joseph is not the father of Jesus. Although he is the husband of Mary, he is not the father of Jesus.

What is the explanation of this? Well, Matthew in the rest of this chapter will give us the explanation and will show how it fulfills Old Testament prophecy.

THE VIRGIN BIRTH OF JESUS CHRIST

Luke, who wrote the gospel bearing his name, was a Greek doctor. In his gospel, he goes into an extended section on obstetrics. Both gospels declare that Jesus was virgin born. Joseph was not His father, but Mary was not unfaithful to Joseph. Jesus is not an illegitimate child. This is something new: ". . . A woman shall compass a man" (Jer. 31:22).

Now, my friend, I have never objected to any man saying that he does not believe in the Virgin Birth. A man has the right to disbelieve. But I do have two very definite objections: I do not think that a *preacher* should deny the virgin birth of Jesus Christ. If he does, then he ought to get a job selling insurance and deal with births in a different way. And I do object to anyone saying that the *Bible* does not teach the virgin birth of Christ. The only Jesus that we have any historical record of is the One who was virgin born. If you want to take the position that He was not virgin born, where is your documentation? You will have to produce evidence—certainly more than the puny reasoning of man. It is so easy to sit in a swivel chair in some theological seminary and write a thesis on the impossibility of the Virgin Birth. You may write a very profound tome on the subject, but you haven't any documents to back up your denial. All you have is just rationalism. By the process of rationalizing you may say, "It couldn't have happened." Well, who are you to say that it couldn't have happened? A few years ago man said that it was impossible to go to the moon, but we have gone there, and we have gone there by using the laws of God. God is the Creator of natural laws. He can either use those natural laws or He can set them aside in order to accomplish His purposes. The record clearly states that Jesus Christ was virgin born.

In verse 17 we find a statement which will explain something in the genealogies.

So all the generations from Abraham to David are fourteen generations; and from David until the carrying away into Babylon are fourteen generations; and from the carrying away into Babylon unto Christ are fourteen generations [Matt. 1:17].

Matthew puts the genealogy into groupings to give an overall view of Old Testament history. One era extends from Abraham to David, another from David to the Babylonian captivity, and the third from the captivity in Babylon to the birth of Jesus Christ. Obviously, he has omitted some names from the genealogy in order to fit fourteen into each period. The question is, why did he do this? Apparently, the number fourteen (twice seven) offered some proof concerning the accuracy of this genealogy.

Now that Matthew has shown that Joseph is not the father of Jesus, he is going to give us an explanation. Already in the Old Testament, a supernatural birth has been predicted by God. Jeremiah is talking to the nation Israel when he says, "How long wilt thou go about, O thou backsliding daughter? for the LORD hath created a new thing in the earth, A woman shall compass a man" (Jer. 31:22). That's not the way it's done, my friend. That's not natural birth; it's supernatural. The virgin birth of the Lord Jesus is the "new thing" which God has done. And it is the fulfillment of Jeremiah's prophecy.

Now the birth of Jesus Christ was on this wise: When as his mother Mary was espoused to Joseph, before they came together, she was found with child of the Holy Ghost [Matt. 1:18].

"The birth of Jesus Christ was on this wise." Here's the way it happened, Matthew is telling us. When His mother, Mary, was espoused to Joseph, that is, she was engaged to him, before they came together—they had had no sexual relationship—she was found with child of the Holy Spirit.

Then Joseph her husband, being a just man, and not willing to make her a public example, was minded to put her away privily [Matt. 1:19].

The Mosaic Law was very specific at this point. It said that a woman who was guilty of being unfaithful should be stoned to death—that was the extreme penalty. But this man Joseph was a remarkable man. We devote a great deal of attention to Mary, and rightly so. Protestants should not let themselves be deterred from giving Mary a great deal of credit. She was a remarkable person. Remember that she was the one whom God chose to be the mother of our Lord, and God makes no mistakes. He picked the right girl. While all of this is true, we need to remember that God also chose Joseph. God made no mistake in choosing him either. A hotheaded man would immediately have had her stoned to death or would have made her a public example by exposing her. But Joseph was not that kind of man. He was a gentle person. He was in *love* with her, and he did not want to hurt her in any way, although he felt that she had been unfaithful to him.

But while he thought on these things, behold, the angel of the Lord appeared unto him in a dream, saying, Joseph, thou son of David, fear not to take unto thee Mary thy wife: for that which is conceived in her is of the Holy Ghost [Matt. 1:20].

In order to prevent a very tragic situation, the angel appeared to Joseph to make clear to him what was taking place.

And she shall bring forth a son, and thou shalt call his name JESUS: for he shall save his people from their sins [Matt. 1:21].

The name *Jesus* means "Savior." He shall have the name Jesus because He shall save His people from their sins.

Now all this was done, that it might be fulfilled which was spoken of the Lord by the prophet, saying [Matt. 1:22].

Matthew, who is writing for the nation Israel, points out that all this was done so that it might be fulfilled as the Lord had spoken. Matthew is appealing to the nation Israel to understand that this One who had come must be the fulfillment of the Old Testament prophecy.

It has been said that there are over three hundred prophecies concerning the first coming of Christ that have been literally fulfilled. I don't know how many of them are in Matthew, but I do know that Matthew quoted more from the Old Testament than the other three gospel writers all together. It seems he records things and substantiates them from the Old Testament because he is not primarily trying to give a "life of Christ" but is showing that this is the fulfillment of the Old Testament prophecies concerning Him.

Now he states the prophecy which was given in Isaiah 7:14:

Behold, a virgin shall be with child, and shall bring forth a son, and they shall call his name Emmanuel, which being interpreted is, God with us [Matt. 1:23].

Now let's look at this a moment because it is very important. The liberal theologian has, of course, denied the fact of the virgin birth of Christ, and he has denied that the Bible teaches His virgin birth. Very candidly, I suspect that the Revised Standard Version was published in order to try to maintain some of the theses of the liberals. In fact, I am sure of this because one of the doctrines they have denied is the Virgin Birth. In the New Testament of the Revised Standard Version, which was copyrighted in 1946, Matthew 1:23 reads thus: "All this took place to fulfill what the Lord had spoken by the prophet: 'Behold, a virgin shall conceive and bear a son, and his name shall be called Emmanuel' (which means, God with us)."

In the Old Testament of the Revised Standard Version, which was copyrighted in 1952, Isaiah 7:14 reads like this: "Therefore the Lord himself will give you a sign. Behold, a young woman shall conceive and bear a son, and shall call his name Immanuel." Notice that in Isaiah they substituted "young woman" for the word *virgin,* even though in Matthew 1:23 they had used the word *virgin,* which is a fulfillment of Isaiah 7:14!

The prophecy of Isaiah 7:14 was given as a *sign.* My friend, it is no sign at all for a young woman to conceive and bear a son. If that's a sign, then right here in Southern California a sign is taking place many times a day, every day. They translated it "young woman" to tone down that word *virgin.*

Let us look at Isaiah 7:14 in the original Hebrew language. The word used for "virgin" is *almah.* The translators of the RSV went to the writings of Gesenius, an outstanding scholar who has an exhaustive Hebrew lexicon. (I can testify that it's also exhausting to look at it!) Gesenius admitted that the common translation of the word is "virgin," but he said that it could be changed to "young woman." The reason he said that was because he rejected the miraculous. So this new translation and others who have followed him, have attempted to say that *almah* means "young woman" and not "virgin."

Let's turn back to Isaiah 7 and study the incident recorded there. This was during the time when Ahaz was on the throne. He was one of those who was far from God, and I list him as a bad king. God sent Isaiah to bring a message to him, and he wouldn't listen. So we read: "Moreover the LORD spake again unto Ahaz, saying, Ask thee a sign of the LORD thy God; ask it either in the depth, or in the height above. But Ahaz said, I will not ask, neither will I tempt the LORD" (Isa. 7:10–12). May I say, it was pious hypocrisy for him to say what he did. God had asked Isaiah to meet Ahaz on the way to deliver God's message to him that God would give victory to Ahaz. However, Ahaz wouldn't believe God and so, in order to encourage his faith, Isaiah tells him that God wants to give him a sign. In his super pious way Ahaz says, "Oh, I wouldn't ask a sign of the Lord." Isaiah answered him, "God is going to give you a sign whether you like it or not. The sign isn't just for you but for the whole house of David." Now here is the sign: ". . . Behold, a virgin shall conceive, and bear a son, and shall call his name Immanuel" (Isa. 7:14). Obviously, if this refers to a young woman, it would be no sign to Ahaz, or to the house of David, or to anybody else; but if a *virgin* conceives and bears a son, that, my friend, is a sign. And that's exactly what it means.

When the word *almah* is used in the Old Testament, it means a virgin. Rebekah was called an *almah* before she married Isaac. I asked a very fine Hebrew Christian, who is also a good Hebrew scholar, about that. He said, "Look at it this way. Suppose you went to visit a friend of yours who had three daughters and two of them were married and one was still single. He would say, 'These two are my married daughters, and this young lady is my third daughter.' Do you think he would mean a prostitute when he said 'young lady?' If you would imply that she was anything but a virgin, he would probably knock your block off." May I say, I would hate to be those who deny the virgin birth of Jesus Christ when they must come into the presence of the Son of God. I'm afraid they are going to wish they could somehow take back the things they have said to malign Him.

The fact that the word *almah* means "a virgin" is proven by the Septuagint. During the intertestamental period, seventy-two Hebrew scholars, six from each of the twelve tribes, worked down in Alexandria, Egypt, on the translation of the Hebrew Old Testament into the Greek language. When they came to this "sign" in Isaiah, those seventy-two men understood that it meant "virgin," and they translated it into the Greek word *parthenos.* That is the same word which Matthew uses in his gospel. My friend, *parthenos* does not mean "young woman"; it means "virgin." For example, Athena was the virgin goddess of Athens, and her temple was called the Parthenon because *parthenos* means "virgin." It is clear that the Word of God is saying precisely what it means.

HIS NAME

Notice something wonderful. "Behold, a virgin shall be with child, and shall bring forth a son, and they shall call his name Emmanuel, which being interpreted is, God with us." It looks as if there is a problem here. Can you tell me where Jesus was ever called Emmanuel? No, He is called Jesus because that is His name. He was given this name because He shall save His people from their sins. Christ, by the way, is His title; Jesus is His name. But it says here that He shall be called "Emmanuel, which being interpreted is, God with us."

Friend, here we have one of the most wonderful things in the entire Word of God. Let's look at this. Emmanuel means "God with us." He can't be Emmanuel, God with us, unless He is virgin born. That's the only way! And notice, unless He is Emmanuel, He cannot be Jesus, the Savior. The reason they call Him Jesus, Savior, is because He is God with us. This truth about the One who came down to this earth is one of the most wonderful things in the Bible.

"But we see Jesus, who was made a little lower than the angels for the suffering of death, crowned with glory and honour; that he by the grace of God should taste death for every man" (Heb. 2:9). He had to be a sacrifice that was acceptable. I couldn't die for the sins of the world. I can't even die a redemptive death for my own sins. But He can! How can Jesus be a Savior? Because He is Emmanuel, God with us. How did He get with us? He was virgin born. I say again, He was called Jesus. He was never called Emmanuel. But you cannot call Him Jesus unless He is Emmanuel, God with us. He must be Emmanuel to be the Savior of the world. That is how important the Virgin Birth is.

Can a person be a Christian and deny the Virgin Birth? Hear me very carefully: I believe that it is possible to accept Christ as your Savior without knowing much about Him. You may not even know that this record is in the Bible. But after you have become a child of God, you will not deny the Virgin Birth of the Lord Jesus. You may not have to know it to be saved, but as a child of God you cannot deny the virgin birth of Jesus Christ.

Do I sound dogmatic, friend? Well, I hope I do because I consider this to be all-important. I want a Savior who is able to reach down and save Vernon McGee. If He's just another man like I am, then He's not going to be able to help me very much. But if He is Emmanuel, God with us, virgin born, then He is my Savior. Is He your Savior today? He took upon Himself our humanity in this way so that He might taste death for us, that He might die a redemptive death on the cross for us.

CHAPTER 2

THEME: *The visit of the wise men after the birth of the Lord Jesus; the flight into Egypt; the return to Nazareth*

THE FULFILLMENT OF PROPHECY

All of this is an historical record of what took place, but back of it there is a tremendous truth being presented, and we don't want to miss that. We have said before that each gospel was directed to meet the needs of a particular group of people and that Matthew was written to the nation of Israel. It is for religious people. Recorded here is the fulfillment of four prophecies. To show how these Old Testament prophecies were fulfilled at the birth of Jesus is the purpose, I believe, of this chapter. I am sure there were many sincere students of the Scriptures living in Christ's day who wondered how all of these prophecies could be fulfilled. It seemed difficult, if not impossible. Let me list several here, then we will see how they were fulfilled at the time of Christ's birth: (1) He was to be born in Bethlehem (see Mic. 5:2); (2) He was to be called out of Egypt (see Hos. 11:1); (3) There was to be weeping in Ramah (see Jer. 31:15); and (4) He was a root from the stem of Jesse and therefore to be called a Nazarene (see Isa. 11:1).

Since Christ was to be born in Bethlehem, why should there be weeping in Ramah, which is about as far north of Jerusalem as Bethlehem is south of Jerusalem? And He was to be called a Nazarene although He would be born in Bethlehem and called out of Egypt. The question is: How could all of these prophecies be fulfilled in a little baby? Well, Matthew shows how literally, accurately, and easily all were fulfilled without any strain on prophecy or on history. It just came about as God said it would come about.

In our day when there are certain prophecies that relate to the second coming of

Christ, we may find it difficult to correlate them and to see the way in which they can all be fulfilled. I'm of the opinion we are coming to the time of their fulfillment, and we are going to find out that it all will take place in a normal, natural way. It looks like a jigsaw puzzle to us down here, but, when we get into His presence and it is all fulfilled, it will have been just as natural as the prophecies about His first coming. Every little piece in the jigsaw puzzle will fit into place, and we're going to wonder why in the world we didn't see it at the time.

THE VISIT OF THE WISE MEN

Now when Jesus was born in Bethlehem of Judaea in the days of Herod the king, behold, there came wise men from the east to Jerusalem [Matt. 2:1].

This is the historical record of the coming of the wise men. Notice that they came in the days of Herod the king. One thing that Herod did not want was competition. In fact, the one thing that Herod would not *tolerate* was competition. So the wise men coming to Jerusalem really alerted him.

"Behold, there came three wise men from the east to Jerusalem." Is that what your Bible says? You say, "No, you've inserted the number three." Well, isn't that what you've been taught by your Christmas cards? I think a great many people know more about the Christmas story from Christmas cards than from the Bible, and therefore they have many inaccurate impressions. I'll attempt to correct several of them in this chapter.

First, you will notice that the record doesn't tell us there were three wise men. I don't know how many there were, but I doubt whether three wise men would have disturbed Herod or have excited Jerusalem. I do believe that three hundred men would have done so. These wise men who came from the East evidently came from different areas. They had been studying the stars, and when this new star appeared, they joined forces and came to Jerusalem. I don't know how many there were, but I'm almost sure it wasn't three, and I believe three hundred would be more nearly true. But, please, don't say that I said there were three hundred!

But the wise men came—

Saying, Where is he that is born King of the Jews? for we have seen his star in the east, and are come to worship him [Matt. 2:2].

They were looking for a king, and that was the thing which disturbed Herod, the king.

"We have seen his star in the east." In poetry that is called the eastern star, and, actually, there is an organization by that name. The worthy matron of that group was a member of my church in Nashville, and she was greatly upset when she heard me say that it was not an eastern star. If they had seen His star in the east and it had been an eastern star, the wise men would have ended up in India or China. The star was in the west! The wise men were in the east. The star was in the west, and they followed it. They came west, not east. My question is this: How in the world did they associate a star with a king, and how did they identify it with Israel? All I know is that in that section of the East, the people had a prophecy given by Balaam, which is recorded in Numbers 24:17. (Remember that old Balaam gave this prophecy concerning the nation Israel.) "I shall see him, but not now: I shall behold him, but not nigh: there shall come a Star out of Jacob, and a Sceptre shall rise out of Israel, and shall smite the corners of Moab, and destroy all the children of Sheth."

Notice that the prophecy says a Star shall come out of Jacob—that is, the nation Israel. And a sceptre shall rise out of Israel. The star and the sceptre go together. That is the only place I know where they are put together in prophecy in the Old Testament. The wise men in the East had that prophecy, and so they came out of the mysterious East seeking a king.

This did disturb the city of Jerusalem and old king Herod.

When Herod the king had heard these things, he was troubled, and all Jerusalem with him [Matt. 2:3].

When there converged on the city of Jerusalem a very impressive delegation of wise men, asking a question like this, the whole city was disturbed.

Herod wanted to know about this. This man was Herod the Great, a very superstitious man. I hope that you have a good Bible dictionary and that you will take time to read about the Herod family. They were a bunch of rascals, much like the house of de'Medici. This family was a real first century Mafia. Herod the Great was the biggest rascal of them all. He was an Idumean who had bought his position from the Roman government; he was not of Israel at all. And he was really anxious to locate this One who appeared to be a rival for his throne.

And when he had gathered all the chief priests and scribes of the people together, he demanded of them where Christ should be born [Matt. 2:4].

He didn't ask; he *demanded.* He said, "I know that you have the Scriptures and in them you have a record of a Messiah that is coming. I want to know where He is to be born." One of the amazing things is that they were able to tell him.

And they said unto him, In Bethlehem of Judaea: for thus it is written by the prophet,

And thou Bethlehem, in the land of Juda, art not the least among the princes of Juda: for out of thee shall come a Governor, that shall rule my people Israel [Matt. 2:5–6].

When Herod asked the scribes this question, they didn't have to search the Scriptures for it; they knew where it was—Micah 5:2. As a matter of fact, they didn't need even to turn to it, because they had it in their minds. They could quote it. They knew all about the coming of the Messiah. The problem was that their knowledge was academic rather than vital. It was not personally meaningful to them. They are examples of folk who know the history contained in the Bible and they know certain factual truths, but these things carry no personal meaning for them. Since the scribes knew the Old Testament Scriptures so well, you would have thought that they would have gone to the wise men and said, "How about letting us ride down with you? We are looking for the Messiah, too!"

I wonder today how many people are really looking for the coming of the Lord. We talk about it, and we study a great deal about prophecy. Would you really like to see Him right now? Suppose He broke in right today where you are and into what you are doing. Would He interrupt anything? Would you like to say to Him, "I wish that You would postpone your visit to some other time"?

Herod got his information from the scribes—

Then Herod, when he had privily called the wise men, inquired of them diligently what time the star appeared [Matt. 2:7].

I am going to make a statement now and will try to prove it later: The star had appeared in the night sky sometime before the wise men appeared in Jerusalem. Remember that they made the trip by camel—not by jet plane. It is a long, hard trip by camel! I am of the opinion that they didn't arrive in Jerusalem until at least a year after the appearance of the star. This wasn't just a little Christmas celebration for them. As they traveled the long, weary miles, they had been hanging on to the hope of seeing Him and presenting their gifts to Him. Notice that Herod "inquired diligently" the *time* of the star's appearance in the sky. Keep that in mind. It will be an important fact later in the story.

So Herod sends the wise men on to Bethlehem—

And he sent them to Bethlehem, and said, Go and search diligently for the young child; and when ye have found him, bring me word again, that I may come and worship him also [Matt. 2:8].

He's being as subtle as an old serpent, and that's exactly what Herod was. Suppose he had said, "If there's a king born around here, I'm going to get rid of him," and then had sent soldiers down to Bethlehem. I can assure you that he would never have found the Child because He would have been hidden. He knew that the clever way and the best way was to let the wise men go down and find the child and then come back and tell him. He said he wanted to go down and worship Him, but of course what he really wanted to do was to kill Him.

When they had heard the king, they departed; and, lo, the star, which they saw in the east, went before them, till it came and stood over where the young child was.

When they saw the star, they rejoiced with exceeding great joy [Matt. 2:9–10].

Now the star appears again. I think they must have traveled a long time without seeing the star. That ought to answer the nonsense one hears today about there being a confluence of certain stars that happened at one particular time. Matthew makes it clear that this star was a very unusual star; in fact, it was a supernatural star. It was miraculous, and we needn't try to find an explanation for it. Now, it may be, as many astronomers think, that there was quite a movement in the heavens at that time. When He came, heaven and earth both responded to His coming into this world. I think such things did take place, but the wise men saw a supernatural star.

And when they were come into the house, they saw the young child with Mary his mother, and fell down, and worshipped him: and when they had opened their treasures, they presented unto him gifts; gold, and frankincense, and myrrh [Matt. 2:11].

When they arrived, Jesus was not in the stable behind an inn. The great movement of people in the city of Bethlehem had now all ceased. They had gone back to their homes because the enrollment was over. But this little Baby was newly born, and they couldn't move Him for a while. Probably such a trip for the Little One would have jeopardized His life. So they had stayed in Bethlehem and had moved into a house. The wise men found them in a *house*. Again, the Christmas cards show the wise men coming into the stable. Well, unless Joseph pointed out that stable to them, they never even knew where it was. They came to the *house*.

Please note that when they saw the young child with Mary His mother, they fell down and worshiped *Him*. If ever there was a time when Mary should have been worshiped, this was it. But they didn't worship her—they were *wise* men! They worshiped Him and presented to Him their treasures: gold and frankincense and myrrh.

It is very interesting to study the facts concerning His second coming as they are related to us in Isaiah 60:6: "The multitude of camels shall cover thee, the dromedaries of Midian and Ephah, all they from Sheba shall come: they shall bring gold and incense; and they shall shew forth the praises of the LORD." What gift is left out at His second coming? Myrrh! They do not bring myrrh because that speaks of His death. When He comes the second time, nothing will speak of His death. Gold speaks of His birth. He is born a King. Frankincense speaks of the fragrance of His life. Myrrh speaks of His death. All of this is indicated in the gifts that were brought to Him at His first coming. But at His next coming, myrrh will not be brought to Him. The next time He comes, He won't come to die upon a cross for the sins of the world. He will come as King of kings and Lord of lords.

And being warned of God in a dream that they should not return to Herod, they departed into their own country another way [Matt. 2:12].

The wise men had assumed that Herod was sincere and wanted to come down and worship Him. However, he would have killed the Child had not an angel of the Lord warned the wise men to go back to their own country by a different route. They may have continued south down to Hebron, then crossed over south of the Dead Sea, and thus they would be out of the range of Herod altogether.

THE FLIGHT INTO EGYPT

And when they were departed, behold, the angel of the Lord appeareth to Joseph in a dream, saying, Arise, and take the young child and his mother, and flee into Egypt, and be thou there until I bring thee word; for Herod will seek the young child to destroy him [Matt. 2:13].

The angel of the Lord appeared also to Joseph and told him that it was time to get the Child out of Bethlehem because Herod would attempt to murder Him.

When he arose, he took the young child and his mother by night, and departed into Egypt [Matt. 2:14].

Notice Joseph's instant obedience.

And was there until the death of Herod: that it might be fulfilled which was spoken of the Lord by the prophet, saying, Out of Egypt have I called my son [Matt. 2:15].

This is a quotation from Hosea 11:1. This is a marvelous prophecy because it has an historical basis. Out of Egypt the son was called, which was the *nation;* and out of Egypt the Son was called, who was a *Person*, this Child. So Joseph took the young Child and the mother to Egypt and stayed there until God called Him out.

Then Herod, when he saw that he was mocked of the wise men, was exceeding wroth, and sent forth, and slew all the children that were in Bethlehem, and in all the coasts thereof, from two years old and under, according to the time which he had diligently inquired of the wise men [Matt. 2:16].

Part of what I'm going to say now is supposition, and part is based on solid fact. As I mentioned before, the wise men did not arrive at the time the shepherds arrived at the stable. The wise men came later, and, according to verse 11, the family had moved into a house by then. When Herod had had his private session with the wise men, he "inquired of them diligently what time the star appeared." I suppose that the wise men said, "Well, it was about a year ago." If we are accurate in thinking that these wise men came from all quarters of the East and had met in a certain place from which they began their trek to Jerusalem, that would consume a great deal of time in a day when travel was by camel instead of by jet. It may have been a year, it may have been longer, but Herod was so infuriated that the wise men did not come back and report concerning the Child, that he probably said, "Well, if they said it was a year ago when they saw the star, I'll just double it and make it two years and kill all the children two years old and younger!" Herod was actually a madman.

Then was fulfilled that which was spoken by Jeremy the prophet, saying,

In Rama was there a voice heard, lamentation, and weeping, and great mourning, Rachel weeping for her children, and would not be comforted, because they are not [Matt. 2:17–18].

This is an unusual prophecy, also. Jeremiah didn't say that the weeping would be heard in Bethlehem. I'm sure there was great mourning in Bethlehem, too. But Jeremiah mentions Rama (spelled Ramah in the Old Testament), and Rama was about as far north of Jerusalem as Bethlehem was south of Jerusalem. And Rama was Jeremiah's country, by the way. I imagine that when the soldiers had been given their orders to slay the children, the captain said to Herod, "Where do you want me to begin?" And I think that old Herod said, "Well, just draw a circle around Jerusalem with the radius as far south as Bethlehem and as far north as Rama"—yet Rama was not in any way involved in it. So, you see, Herod slew a great many children. You can imagine the weeping all the way from Bethlehem to Rama, a radius of about ten to twelve miles, or twenty to twenty-five miles across the area. It must have been a heartbreaking time in the lives of these people when they lost their little ones. The prophecy given through Jeremiah was literally fulfilled.

THE RETURN TO NAZARETH

But when Herod was dead, behold, an angel of the Lord appeareth in a dream to Joseph in Egypt [Matt. 2:19].

I must call attention to this. We are told that *the* angel of the Lord appeared to Jacob at Peniel (see Gen. 32). Here it is *an* angel of the Lord. *The* angel of the Lord is the pre-incarnate Christ. Now Christ incarnate is down in Egypt.

Saying, Arise, and take the young child and his mother, and go into the land of Israel: for they are dead which sought the young child's life [Matt. 2:20].

It's essential to get Jesus out of the land of Egypt and back up into Israel. The most important reason is that He has been born under the Law, and He is to live under the Mosaic Law. He is the only One who really ever kept it. He must get out from under the influence of Egypt. He is not to be raised down there as Moses had been and as the children of Israel had been when they were becoming a nation down in Egypt.

And he arose, and took the young child and his mother, and came into the land of Israel.

But when he heard that Archelaus did reign in Judaea in the room of his father Herod, he was afraid to go thither: notwithstanding, being warned of God in a dream, he turned aside into the parts of Galilee [Matt. 2:21–22].

By the way, Archelaus was another Herod and very brutal.

And he came and dwelt in a city called Nazareth: that it might be fulfilled which was spoken by the prophets, He shall be called a Nazarene [Matt. 2:23].

"He shall be called a Nazarene." The Hebrew word for Nazareth was *Netzer*, meaning a branch or shoot. The city of Nazareth was so called because of its insignificance. The prophecies of Isaiah 11:1; Isaiah 53:2–3; and Psalm 22:6 are involved in the term *Nazarene*. But the Lord Jesus was given that term not only because He was a root out of the stem of Jesse, but because He grew up in the city of Nazareth, and He was called a Nazarene, which fulfilled the prophecies.

Now we have seen all four of the prophecies dealing with locations in the birth of Christ: born in Bethlehem, called out of Egypt, weeping in Rama, and called a Nazarene were fulfilled in a very normal way. He touched base in all of these places, and what seemed rather strange prophecies became very sane realities.

CHAPTER 3

***THEME:** John the Baptist, the forerunner of the King, announces the kingdom and baptizes Jesus, the King*

MINISTRY OF JOHN THE BAPTIST

In those days came John the Baptist, preaching in the wilderness of Judaea,

And saying, Repent ye: for the kingdom of heaven is at hand [Matt. 3:1–2].

Now, all of a sudden, John the Baptist walks onto the pages of Scripture. If we had Matthew's gospel only, we would ask, "Where did he come from, and what is his background?"—because Matthew gives us none of that, and the reason is obvious. The prophet Malachi had said that the messenger would come ahead to prepare the way for the coming of the King—"Behold, I will send my messenger, and he shall prepare the way before me. . ." (Mal. 3:1). This messenger was John the Baptist. You don't really need to know about the background of a messenger. When the Western Union boy delivers a message to your door, do you say to him, "Young man, did your ancestors come over on the Mayflower? What is your background?" You're not interested in that. You are interested in the message because the message is all-important, and that is what you want. So you thank him, give him a tip, and dismiss him. You are through with him.

John the Baptist made it very clear that he was just the messenger, and Matthew is making that clear, too. Therefore, he walks out onto the page of Scripture, preaching in the wilderness of Judea saying, "Repent ye: for the kingdom of heaven is at hand."

Now let's deal with these expressions: (1) "Repent ye"; (2) "the kingdom of heaven"; and (3) "is at hand." They are very important.

"Repent" is an expression that always has been given to God's people as a challenge to turn around. "Repent" in the original Greek is *metanoia*, meaning "to change your mind." You are going in one direction; turn around and go in another direction.

Repentance is primarily, I think, for saved people, that is, for God's people in any age. They are the ones who, when they become cold and indifferent, are to turn. That was the message to the seven churches of Asia Minor in Revelation 2 and 3, and it was the message of the Lord Jesus Himself.

Someone may ask whether the unsaved man is supposed to repent. The unsaved man is told that he is to *believe* on the Lord Jesus Christ. That was the message of Paul to the jailer at Philippi (see Acts 16:31). That old rascal needed to do some repenting; but when an unsaved man believes in Jesus, he is repenting. Faith means to turn to Christ, and when you turn to Christ, you must also turn from something. If you don't turn from something, then you aren't really turning to Christ. So repentance is really a part of believing, but the primary message that should be given to the lost today is that they should *believe* in the Lord Jesus Christ. We like to see folk come forward in a service to receive Christ or sign a card signifying that they have made that decision, but the important thing is to *trust* Christ as your Savior, and if you really turn *to* Him, you turn *from* something else.

The expression "kingdom of heaven" means the rule of the heavens over the earth. The Lord Jesus is the King. You can't have a kingdom without a king; neither can you have a king without a kingdom. Remember Richard III who said in the Shakespearean play, "My kingdom for a horse." If he had traded his kingdom for a horse, he wouldn't have been a king. He would have been only a man on horseback. A king must have a kingdom. So what did John the Baptist mean by "the kingdom of heaven is at hand"? He meant that the kingdom of heaven is present in the Person of the King.

Is there a present reality of the kingdom of heaven? Yes, there is. Those who come to Him as Savior and acknowledge Him are translated into the kingdom of His dear Son. They belong to Him now. And they have a much more intimate relationship than that of a subject with a king. Christ is the Bridegroom, and believers are part of His bride!

Then someone may ask whether we are like subjects in a kingdom because we are to carry out His commands. Again I say, there is more to it than that. We are to obey Him because we love Him. It is a love relationship. "If ye love me, keep my commandments" (John 14:15).

The "kingdom of heaven" is the rule of the heavens over the earth. That's not in existence today. Christ is not reigning over the world now. There must be something wrong with the thinking of those who insist that the kingdom of heaven is in existence in our day. Christ is not reigning in any form, shape or fashion—except in the hearts of those who have received Him. However, He is coming someday to establish His kingdom on the earth. When He does, He will put down rebellion. Believe me, He is really going to put it down.

The kingdom of heaven was at hand, or was present, in the Person of the King. That was the only way in which it was present.

Matthew now tells us that what he is recording is in fulfillment of prophecy—

For this is he that was spoken of by the prophet Esaias, saying, The voice of one crying in the wilderness, Prepare ye the way of the Lord, make his paths straight [Matt. 3:3].

"The prophet Esaias" is Isaiah, and the prophecy is in Isaiah 40:3.

"The voice of one crying in the wilderness"—all that John the Baptist claimed for himself was that he was a voice crying in the wilderness. And his purpose was to "prepare the way of the Lord."

And the same John had his raiment of camel's hair, and a leathern girdle about his loins; and his meat was locusts and wild honey [Matt. 3:4].

He's a strange individual, isn't he? He follows a strange diet and has an unusual way of dressing. I hate to say this, but today John would probably qualify in his looks as a vagrant. His raiment was of camel's hair, his leathern girdle was about his loins, his meat was locusts and wild honey. We're told that he never shaved and had long hair. Here's an unusual man, friend, a man with a mission. He's really an Old Testament character, walking out of the Old Testament onto the pages of the New Testament. He is the last of the Old Testament prophets.

Then went out to him Jerusalem, and all Judaea, and all the region round about Jordan [Matt. 3:5].

Notice that the crowds went out to him. John did not rent a stadium or an auditorium or a church, and there was no committee that invited him. In fact, he didn't come to town at all. If you wanted to hear John, you went out to where he was. Obviously, the Spirit of God was on this man.

And were baptized of him in Jordan, confessing their sins [Matt. 3:6].

In other words, all of this denoted a *change* in the lives of these people. The very fact that they submitted to John's baptism was an indication that they were leaving their old lives and turning to new lives.

THE PHARISEES AND SADDUCEES

But when he saw many of the Pharisees and Sadducees come to his baptism, he said unto them, O generation of vipers, who hath warned you to flee from the wrath to come?

Bring forth therefore fruits meet for repentance [Matt. 3:7–8].

Now see who is coming! Listen to the way he greets these dignified visitors. Suppose your preacher got up next Sunday morning and said, "O generation of vipers"! I imagine that the deacons would be looking for another preacher! This is really strong language. He's talking to the dignified Pharisees and Sadducees and is telling them, "There must be evidence of this new life. You can't just go through the *act* of baptism. There must be fruit in your life."

And think not to say within yourselves, We have Abraham to our father: for I say unto you, that God is able of these stones to raise up children unto Abraham [Matt. 3:9].

Friend, he's making a strong statement here! You can understand why he was not elected the most popular man of the year in Judea.

And now also the axe is laid unto the root of the trees: therefore every tree which bringeth not forth good fruit is hewn down, and cast into the fire [Matt. 3:10].

A great deal is said in the New Testament about fruit bearing. Fruit bearing is the result of having the right kind of tree. Only a fruit tree can produce fruit. He talks here about the axe being laid to the root of the tree, and the reason is that the tree is not bearing fruit. An apple tree will bear apples, and a plum tree will bear plums. But when a tree bears thorns, it is not an apple tree, and it must be cut down. The root and the fruit go together, by the way, and a tree must have the right kind of root to bear the right kind of fruit. That is exactly what John the Baptist is saying to them here. He is telling them that the wrong kind of tree is going to be taken down and cast into the fire.

I indeed baptize you with water unto repentance: but he that cometh after

me is mightier than I, whose shoes I am not worthy to bear: he shall baptize you with the Holy Ghost, and with fire [Matt. 3:11].

John is saying, "I baptize with water. But He is coming, and when He comes, He will baptize you with the Holy Ghost, *and* with fire"—that final "and" is already over nineteen hundred years long. You and I are living in the age of the Holy Spirit. Christ Jesus baptizes with the Holy Spirit in this present age. He will baptize with fire when He comes the second time, and fire means judgment. This distinction needs to be made.

Somebody will say, "I thought that on the Day of Pentecost, the believers were baptized with the Holy Spirit and with fire, because it says that tongues of fire sat upon each of them." Oh, my friend, you ought to read Acts 2:2–3 again. The record is this: "And suddenly there came a sound from heaven *as* of a rushing mighty wind, and it filled all the house where they were sitting. And there appeared unto them cloven tongues *like as* of fire, and it sat upon each of them" (italics mine). It wasn't wind and it wasn't fire; it was the coming of the Holy Spirit. But there was something to appeal to the eye-gate and to the ear-gate. Therefore, when the Holy Spirit came, there was not the fulfillment of the baptism of fire. Let me repeat that, the baptism of fire will take place at the *second* coming of Christ. In the present age of the Holy Spirit, the Holy Spirit comes upon every believer. Not just *some,* but *every* believer is baptized by the Holy Spirit, which means that the believer is identified with the body of Christ; that is, he becomes part of the body of Christ. This is one of the great truths in the Word of God.

John continues to speak of Christ's second coming—

Whose fan is in his hand, and he will throughly purge his floor, and gather his wheat into the garner; but he will burn up the chaff with unquenchable fire [Matt. 3:12].

JESUS IS BAPTIZED OF JOHN

Then cometh Jesus from Galilee to Jordan unto John, to be baptized of him [Matt. 3:13].

This is remarkable, and we are going to ask the question: "Why was Jesus baptized?" and try to answer it.

But John forbad him, saying, I have need to be baptized of thee, and comest thou to me?

And Jesus answering said unto him, Suffer it to be so now: for thus it becometh us to fulfil all righteousness. Then he suffered him [Matt. 3:14–15].

Why was Jesus baptized? There may be several answers, but the primary reason is stated right here: "For thus it becometh us to fulfil all righteousness." Jesus is identifying Himself *completely* with sinful mankind. Isaiah had prophesied that He would be numbered with the transgressors (see Isa. 53:12). Here is a King who identifies Himself with His subjects. Actually, baptism means identification, and I believe identification was the primary purpose for the baptism of the Lord Jesus. Again, the reason Jesus was baptized was not to set an example for us. It was not a pattern for us to follow. Christ was holy—He did not need to repent. You and I do need to repent. He was holy, harmless, undefiled, and separate from sinners. He was baptized to completely identify Himself with humanity.

There was a second reason Jesus was baptized. Water baptism is symbolic of death. His death was a baptism. You remember that He said to James and John when they wanted to be seated on His right hand and on His left hand in the kingdom, "Ye know not what ye ask. Are ye able to drink of the cup that I shall drink of, and to be baptized with the baptism that I am baptized with?" (Matt. 20:22). You see, Christ's death was a baptism. He entered into death for you and for me.

There is a third reason for the baptism of Jesus. At this time He was set aside for His office of priest. The Holy Spirit came upon Him for this priestly ministry. Everything that Jesus did, His every act, was done by the power of the Holy Spirit. "For he hath made him to be sin for us, who knew no sin; that we might be made the righteousness of God in him" (2 Cor. 5:21). There was sin *on* Him, but there was no sin *in* Him. My sin was put *on* Him, not *in* Him. That is an important distinction. Therefore, you and I are saved by being identified with Him. He identified Himself with us in baptism. And Peter says that we are saved by baptism (see 1 Pet. 3:21). In what way? By being identified with the Lord Jesus. To be saved is to be in Christ. How do we get into Christ? By the baptism of the Holy Spirit. I believe in water baptism because by it we declare that we are identified with Christ. The Lord Jesus said, ". . . him that cometh to me I will in no wise cast out" (John 6:37). We must recognize that we have to be identified with Christ, and that is accomplished by the Holy Spirit. Our water baptism is a testimony to this. One time an old salt said to a young sailor in trying to get him to accept Christ and be baptized, "Young man it is *duty* or *mutiny!*" And when you come to Christ, my friend, you are to be baptized because it is a duty. If you are not, it is mutiny.

This subject of baptism needs to be lifted out of the realm of argument to the high and lofty plane of standing for Christ. How we need to come out and stand for Christ!

Let me repeat verse 15: "And Jesus answering said unto him, Suffer it be so now: for thus it becometh us to fulfil all righteousness. Then he suffered him"—that is, John baptized Him.

And Jesus, when he was baptized, went up straightway out of the water: and, lo, the heavens were opened unto him, and he saw the Spirit of God descending like a dove, and lighting upon him:

And lo a voice from heaven, saying, This is my beloved Son, in whom I am well pleased [Matt. 3:16–17].

Here we have a manifestation of the Trinity. As the Lord Jesus is coming out of the water, the Spirit of God descends upon Him like a dove, and the Father speaks from heaven.

The Father says, "This is my beloved Son, in whom I am well pleased." The Lord Jesus is now identified with His people. What a King! Oh, what a King He is!

CHAPTER 4

***THEME:** The temptation of Jesus in the wilderness; the beginning of His public ministry at Capernaum; the calling of four of His disciples by the Sea of Galilee*

THE THREEFOLD TEMPTATION OF JESUS

Let us follow the movement of the Gospel of Matthew. Jesus came down to be born among us and so to be identified with us. He grew up as any other child would, except that He was harmless and without sin. Now, in His baptism, He has been identified with us. He has put on our sin. Now He is going to be tested because there are some real questions to be answered. Is the King able to withstand a test, and can He overcome?

The word *tempt* has a twofold meaning:

1. "Incite or entice to evil; seduce." There is something in each of us which causes us to yield to evil. This was not true of Jesus. ". . . the prince of this world cometh, and hath nothing in me" (John 14:30). He was ". . . holy, harmless, undefiled, separate from sinners . . ." (Heb. 7:26). So the temptation for Jesus had to be different from that which would cause me to fall, in that it needed to be a much greater temptation.

2. "Test." God does not tempt men with evil according to James 1:13. Yet, we are told ". . . God did tempt Abraham . . ." (Gen. 22:1). This means that God was testing the faith of Abraham.

Jesus is now to be tested. Could Jesus have fallen? I want to answer that with an emphatic *no!* He could not have fallen. If Jesus could have fallen, then you and I do not have a sure Savior at all.

Perhaps you are asking, "Well then, if Jesus could not have fallen, was His temptation a legitimate and genuine temptation?" May I say to you that His temptation was much greater than any that you and I have ever had. When a new model Chevrolet or Ford or Dodge is developed, it is thoroughly tested to prove it can stand the test. And every genuine diamond is tested to show that it is not a phony. In a similar way, the Lord Jesus Christ was tested to demonstrate that He was exactly who He claimed to be.

Let me illustrate with this little story. When I was a boy, I lived out in West Texas. It was a sparsely populated area in those days. The Santa Fe railroad came through our little town, but it went on by and stopped in the next little town. But it crossed the left fork of the Brazos River near our town. In the summertime there wasn't enough water in that river to rust a shingle nail, but in wintertime you could float a battleship on it. One winter we really had a flood, and it washed out the Santa Fe bridge. We were without a train for a long time. Finally, they put in a bridge. They worked a long time on it. Then one day they brought in two engines, stopped them on the bridge, and tied down their whistles. Believe me, that was more whistling than we had ever heard in our little town! All twenty-three of us ran down to see what was happening. As we were standing around, one brave citizen went up to the engineer in charge with our question, "What are you doing?" The engineer answered, "Testing the bridge." Our man said, "Are you trying to break it down?" The engineer almost sneered, "Of course not! We're testing it to *prove* that it can't be broken down."

May I say to you, that was the exact reason the Lord Jesus was tested. It was to prove, to demonstrate, that He could not be broken down. His testing, therefore, was greater than ours. There is a limit to what we can bear. You give me enough temptation, you build up the pressure, and finally I'll succumb to it. That is true of you, too. But Christ never gave in although the pressure continued to increase. In other words, a ten-pound fishing line will break when twenty pounds of pressure is put on it, but a hundred-pound line can bear more than twenty-five pounds of pressure. Now, I'm the ten-pound fishing line, and He is the one hundred-pound line.

Another really interesting feature of this temptation is the comparison and contrast with the testing of Eve in the Garden of Eden. To begin with, Christ was tested in a wilderness while Eve was tested in a garden. What a contrast!

Then was Jesus led up of the Spirit into the wilderness to be tempted of the devil [Matt. 4:1].

He was to be *tested* by the devil.

And when he had fasted forty days and forty nights, he was afterward an hungered.

And when the tempter came to him, he said, If thou be the Son of God, command that these stones be made bread [Matt. 4:2–3].

This is the same kind of temptation that came to Eve. The first one was *physical*. She saw that the tree was good for food (see Gen. 3:6). The Lord Jesus was told to turn stones to bread. First John 2:15–16 says that such temptation for the Christian is the ". . . lust of the flesh."

But he answered and said, It is written, Man shall not live by bread alone, but by every word that proceedeth out of the mouth of God [Matt. 4:4].

That is found in Deuteronomy 8:3. Jesus surely knew Deuteronomy, and He believed it was the inspired Word of God.

Now the second testing:

Then the devil taketh him up into the holy city, and setteth him on a pinnacle of the temple,

And saith unto him, If thou be the Son of God, cast thyself down: for it is written, He shall give his angels charge concerning thee: and in their hands they shall bear thee up, lest at any time thou dash thy foot against a stone [Matt. 4:5–6].

The Devil is quoting Psalm 91:11–12, although he does not quote it accurately. Now, this is the *spiritual* temptation. For Eve it was that she saw the fruit was ". . . to be desired to make one wise . . ." (Gen. 3:6). For the Christian, it is the ". . . pride of life . . ." (1 John 2:16).

Jesus said unto him, It is written again, Thou shalt not tempt the Lord thy God [Matt. 4:7].

He is quoting Deuteronomy 6:16.

The third testing is *psychological*.

Again, the devil taketh him up into an exceeding high mountain, and sheweth him all the kingdoms of the world, and the glory of them;

And saith unto him, All these things will I give thee, if thou wilt fall down and worship me [Matt. 4:8–9].

Satan showed Him the kingdoms of the world and their glory. This, you see, is a psychological temptation. Man lusts for power. Eve was subjected to the same temptation: ". . . ye shall be as gods, knowing good and evil" (Gen. 3:5). Many of us succumb to this test.

Notice the answer of the Lord Jesus—

Then saith Jesus unto him, Get thee hence, Satan: for it is written, Thou shalt worship the Lord thy God, and him only shalt thou serve [Matt. 4:10]

He is quoting Deuteronomy 6:13 and 10:20. Friend, we see that our Lord answered each time with Scripture. Certainly, that ought to have a message for all of us.

Why is it that many of us are having trouble living the Christian life? May I say this very kindly: It is *ignorance* of the Word of God. Notice that our Lord always answered by giving the Word of God. I believe that the Word of God has an answer for your particular problem. That doesn't mean that *I* know the answer for your problem. It doesn't mean that your psychologist or psychiatrist knows the answer for your problem. But God has an answer for your problem, and it is in His Word. That is the reason we should know the Book better than we do.

Let me repeat, the Lord Jesus answered Satan every time out of the Word. He did not say, "Well, *I* think this" or "*I* believe there is a better way of doing it." He said very definitely that the Word of God says thus and so. He used the Word of God for His answer. And for the child of God, that is enough.

By the way, the devil seemed to think it gave good answers because in the next verse we read—

Then the devil leaveth him, and behold, angels came and ministered unto him [Matt. 4:11].

Luke 4:13 tells us that the devil left Him for a little season. I think he was back the next day—and was testing Him throughout His life. Especially do we see the temptation of the devil in the Garden of Gethsemane where Jesus endured indescribable suffering.

Now let's make a very brief recapitulation of this episode in the life of our Lord and notice some things that it clearly teaches.

First of all, we have seen that Jesus was born a King, He was introduced as a King, He was baptized as a King, and now we have seen that He was tested as a King. All the way through Matthew's Gospel He is a King.

This testing revealed several things. One of them is that the devil is a person. In this contact with Jesus, he is treated as a person. This ought to answer any Bible believer who has questions about him, because there are those who insist that the devil is only an influence.

Also, we notice the very subtle insinuation of the devil. He first said, "*If* thou be the Son of God, command that these stones be made bread" (v. 3). In other words, *prove* it in a way which is not God's way. There was no attempt, of course, to tempt Jesus to commit a crime. For Him, that would not have been a real temptation because the inclination of Jesus was to do good. Since bread was the staff of life, to make stones into bread would be a very good thing. And later on in His ministry He fed the multitudes with bread. But the inherent evil of Satan's temptation was to get Jesus to go outside of the will of God for His life.

Also, we see that all the way through the temptations, the Lord Jesus answered the devil from the Word of God. In other words, He used the sword of the Spirit (see Eph. 6:17) to meet the enemy of God and man. *Every* time His answer was, "It is written." Oh, my friend, if only we were more adept at using the sword of the Spirit! It is our weapon in this day, and it is a very effective weapon.

Another interesting point is that Jesus quoted from the Book of Deuteronomy.

The second thing the devil wanted Jesus to do was to become a religious leader by a stupendous miracle rather than by offering His credentials in the manner that God had prescribed. The devil's way would miss the cross of Christ. Much of what is called Christianity today is "Devil-anity" or "Satan-anity" because it leaves the cross of Christ out altogether. The devil is asking Jesus to become a great religious leader by a miracle.

Friend, it's very dangerous today to be led astray by miracle workers. Right now many people are going after so-called faith healers. I don't know why so many folk go after that type of thing when a little investigation would reveal that there are no real miracles taking place in their services, although there is a great deal of emotion and folderol involved. In Southern California I have made an offer of one hundred dollars to anyone who will come forward and present their credentials and demonstrate that they were actually healed by a miracle worker, a healer. Frankly, I have been amazed that only two or three have come. These were very sincere folk who really believed that they had been healed. They thought that I was way out in left field because I didn't believe they had been healed—and I didn't. But don't misunderstand, I believe in miracle healing—that is, I believe that you go directly to the Great Physician. When you have something seriously wrong with you, you don't go to an intern or a quack doctor. What you do is go to a specialist in that particular field. I've taken my case to the Great Physician, and I can recommend Him. I believe in going directly to Him and not through some of these so-called miracle-workers. No man can perform miracles. Not even the Lord

Jesus would become a religious leader the way the Devil wanted Him to become one, and that is very interesting.

You'll notice that the Devil came back and quoted Scripture also. He said: "For he shall give his angels charge over thee . . . .They shall bear thee up in their hands, lest thou dash thy foot against a stone" (Ps. 91:11–12). The Devil was pretty good at quoting Scripture, but he wasn't quite accurate. Shakespeare said that the Devil could quote Scripture for his purpose; but, actually, the Devil can *misquote* Scripture for his purpose. Satan left out a very important phrase from the passage which he quoted from Psalm 91. He omitted ". . . to keep thee in all thy ways" (Ps. 91:11). That is the important part of the verse. Satan was attempting to get the Lord Jesus to ignore God's way. My friend, it is not always God's will to perform something in your life or in my life that is miraculous. There is an idea circulating in our contemporary society that we can *force* God to do something, that He is sort of a Western Union boy or that He is more or less working for you and is under your command to do what you desire Him to do. Oh, my friend, we can't do that! God is sovereign, and we happen to be the creature—He is the Creator. We must yield to the will of God. That may not be pleasant at times, but the will of God—not your will or my will—is that which is all important.

Another thing about this temptation which really raises a question is that the Devil offered the Lord Jesus the kingdoms of this world! Does the Devil have the kingdoms of the world to offer? Think that one over before you attempt to answer it. Well, let me give you my answer, and I have thought about it a great deal. The Lord Jesus did not challenge his statement that he had the kingdoms of the world to offer. Jesus didn't say to him, "You can't offer Me the kingdoms of the world because you don't have them to give." I assume that the Devil did have them to give. This fact gives us a little different viewpoint of the trouble we are having in the world today. The Devil is running everything! Some Christians tend to fight the evils of communism without realizing that behind communism is Satan and that behind the confusion and turmoil in the world is Satan. Let's remember who our enemy really is. He is a spiritual enemy. He wants to become God. Remember that he said to Jesus, "All these things will I give thee, if thou wilt fall down and *worship me*"!

In verse 11 we saw that after the third temptation, the Devil left the Lord Jesus for awhile. Certainly, he did not leave Him alone permanently.

JESUS BEGINS HIS PUBLIC MINISTRY AT CAPERNAUM

Now when Jesus had heard that John was cast into prison, he departed into Galilee;

And leaving Nazareth, he came and dwelt in Capernaum, which is upon the sea coast, in the borders of Zabulon and Nephthalim [Matt. 4:12–13].

Jesus withdrew from the Jerusalem area because John had been taken by Herod and put in prison. Now we have the Lord Jesus shifting His headquarters from the south to the north and from Nazareth, His hometown, over to Capernaum. Matthew does not give us the details of this move in his record. This is an example of the fact that the four gospel records do not attempt to parallel each other. One is not a carbon copy of any of the others. The attempt to harmonize the Gospels is a big mistake. I have written a booklet entitled *Why Four Gospels?* in which I attempt to show that each one is written for a definite purpose. Not one of them was intended to be a biography of the Lord Jesus—no one could write that. Each book presents its case to reach a certain segment of the human family. Matthew was written to reach the religious element and is primarily for the nation of Israel. Actually, it was written in Hebrew—Papias and Eusebius, church fathers, both say that, as well as others of that period.

Although Matthew gives us no details of the move to Capernaum, we learn from other gospels that Jesus had been rejected by His hometown. Capernaum became His headquarters and continued as such, as far as we can tell, until the hour that He went to Jerusalem for the final time to be crucified.

Matthew will give us the reason He moved His headquarters from Nazareth to Capernaum. The other gospel writers do not tell us this, but Matthew records it to show that in everything the Lord Jesus did, He was moving in fulfillment of the Old Testament prophecies—

That it might be fulfilled which was spoken by Esaias the prophet, saying,
The land of Zabulon, and the land of Nephthalim, by the way of the sea, beyond Jordan, Galilee of the Gentiles;

The people which sat in darkness saw great light; and to them which sat in the region and shadow of death light is sprung up [Matt. 4:14–16].

We find this prophecy in Isaiah 9:1–2 and Isaiah 42:6–7. I won't take the space to go into the background of this area called Galilee of the Gentiles, but if you want to do some research, you will find it very profitable to see the condition of that area at the time the Lord Jesus was there. Remember that He also spent His boyhood there. It was called Gentile country because out of the Roman Empire many folk had migrated to that area. There was a marvelous resort section around the Sea of Galilee, but it was very worldly and even wicked. The people in that area were very far from God.

The great light of the Lord Jesus broke upon them, and His very presence created a responsibility for them. They witnessed many of His miracles, but there was little response. Later, in Matthew 11:20–24, He pronounces judgment upon them when He says, "Woe unto thee, Chorazin!"

In Capernaum Jesus picked up right where John the Baptist left off.

From that time Jesus began to preach, and to say, Repent: for the kingdom of heaven is at hand [Matt. 4:17].

Jesus' message was, "Repent, turn around, come to Me, the kingdom of heaven is at hand." It was at hand in the person of the King, of course—they couldn't have the kingdom of heaven without Him. As we have seen the kingdom of heaven, simply stated, is the reign of the heavens over the earth. This is what the Lord Jesus will bring to this earth someday. This earth will become "heaven" for Israel, an earthly people, and they will go into eternity right down here. The church has a heavenly hope, but the earthly hope is also a marvelous hope, and it is the hope of the Old Testament.

JESUS BEGINS TO CALL HIS DISCIPLES

Now Jesus begins to gather disciples about Him. Notice the following verses.

And Jesus, walking by the sea of Galilee, saw two brethren, Simon called Peter, and Andrew his brother, casting a net into the sea: for they were fishers.

And he saith unto them, Follow me, and I will make you fishers of men [Matt. 4:18–19].

In the Gospels the Lord makes at least three calls to these men, or perhaps it would be more accurate to say that three meetings took place between Christ and these men. The first meeting took place in Jerusalem, as recorded in John 1:35–42. Their second meeting took place by the Sea of Galilee, and apparently this is the record of it. They had seen Him before this, but at that time He had not called them to be with Him. Now here at the Sea of Galilee when He meets them again, He calls them to follow Him. And then we will find that they went back to fishing—Mark and Luke give us that detail. And finally He called them again, and that was to apostleship.

The wonder of it all is that Jesus called men like this. I have always felt that since He called imperfect men like the disciples were, He may be able to use me, and He may be able to use you. It is encouraging to know that we don't have to be super-duper saints to be used by Him. He may not make you a fisher of men, if you are not in the fishing business. But whatever business you are engaged in, He can use you. Whatever your talent may be, if you will turn it over to Him, He can use it. Years ago a lady in my church was absolutely tongue-tied when it came to witnessing for Christ, but she could bake the most marvelous cakes! She used to deplore the fact of her inability to witness, and I said to her one day, "Did it ever occur to you that the Lord may want you in the church family to bake cakes?" That may seem ridiculous, but it is not. The important thing for us is to give ourselves to Him. Under His direction He won't have us all doing the same thing because He gives us separate gifts. The body of Christ has many members in it, and they all have different functions to perform.

And they straightway left their nets, and followed him.

And going on from thence, he saw other two brethren, James the son of Zebedee, and John his brother, in a ship with Zebedee their father, mending their nets; and he called them.

And they immediately left the ship and their father, and followed him [Matt. 4:20–22].

These are very interesting men, and we will get better acquainted with them as we move along, especially as we see them in the other gospel records.

Now remember that Jesus is in the northern section of Israel at this time—

And Jesus went about all Galilee, teaching in their synagogues, and preaching the gospel of the kingdom, and healing all manner of sickness and all manner of disease among the people [Matt. 4:23].

Notice that Jesus is *teaching* in their synagogues, and He is *preaching* the gospel of the kingdom. What is it? The gospel (Good News) of the kingdom is that it is at hand in the person of the King. They are to accept and receive Him. Also, He is healing their physical illnesses. Friend, there were thousands of people in that day whom Jesus healed. Matthew especially lets us know that. If we will pay attention to the text, we will find that there were not just a few isolated cases, but thousands of folk were healed. That is the reason the enemies of Jesus never questioned His miracles—there were too many of them walking around. By the way, I live in Southern California where many so-called faith healers claim the healing of thousands of people, but we don't see these purported miracles walking around, at least they don't come my way.

And his fame went throughout all Syria: and they brought unto him all sick people that were taken with divers diseases and torments, and those which were possessed with devils, and those which were lunatic, and those that had the palsy; and he healed them [Matt. 4:24].

Notice the multitudes.

And there followed him great multitudes of people from Galilee, and from Decapolis, and from Jerusalem, and from Judaea, and from beyond Jordan [Matt. 4:25].

Decapolis was a district containing ten cities in the northeastern part of Galilee, east of the Jordan River. (I have had the privilege of visiting one of those cities.) Also, folk came up from Jerusalem and from Judea, the southernmost division of Palestine, and from beyond Jordan, which means a long way off. Jesus is ministering there in the north of Palestine.

It should be kept in mind as we consider the Gospel of Matthew that Matthew is making no attempt to give us a chronological record of the life of Christ. He is presenting Jesus in his Gospel as King, and he follows a pattern which is a movement in bringing the King and His claims to the nation Israel. This is important to observe. If we miss the movement in Matthew, we miss the purpose of this Gospel.

CHAPTER 5

***THEME:** The beginning of the so-called Sermon on the Mount dealing with the relationship of the subjects of the kingdom to self and to law*

INTRODUCTION TO THE SERMON ON THE MOUNT

Although we will consider each chapter of the Sermon on the Mount separately, let's first consider it as a whole. The Lord Jesus gave four major discourses. Matthew records three of them: (1) the Sermon on the Mount, chapters 5–7; (2) the Mystery Parables Discourse, chapter 13; and (3) the Olivet Discourse, chapters 24–25. The Sermon on the Mount is the manifesto of the King. The Mystery Parables Discourse gives the direction that the kingdom of heaven will take after Christ's rejection. The Olivet Discourse is prophetic, looking toward the future. There is a fourth discourse, recorded in John's gospel, which deals with new truths and relationships in view of Christ's death, resurrection, ascension, and intercession. You and I are vitally connected with this latter discourse, by the way.

While the Sermon on the Mount is in Matthew 5–7, excerpts of it are in the other gospels, also. It is unlikely that our Lord gave it only one time. He repeated, as you know, a great deal of the truths that He gave and probably gave this message, which we call the Sermon on the Mount, on many occasions.

Luke records only a portion of it and mentions the fact that our Lord came down and stood on the plain, indicating that this was a different occasion. Frankly, Matthew's account is probably only a part of the Sermon on the Mount. I believe that our Lord gave a great deal more than we have here. However, this was given for our learning and our understanding today.

There are two things I would like to say by way of introduction to this section. One is that the far right and the far left are not confined to politics, but among theologians who expound Scripture we also have the far left and the far right. This is vividly revealed in the understanding of the Sermon on the Mount. The liberal theologian is to the far left. He treats the Sermon on the Mount as the gospel, the Good News. He acts (even if he doesn't say it) as if it were the only important part of Scripture.

Many years ago I played handball with a very liberal preacher who later became rather famous as a leader of the liberal wing. One day he told me that all he needed of the Bible was the Sermon on the Mount. He went even so far as to say that all he needed was the Golden Rule, as recorded in Matthew 7:12: "Therefore all things whatsoever ye would that men should do to you, do ye even so to them: for this is the law and the prophets." To say that this is all the Bible you need may sound good, but it is pious drivel. The question is not whether you feel that the Sermon on the Mount is your religion. The question is: Are you *living* it? That is the important thing, and we'll have more to say about that later.

Those who reduce the Christian message to the Sermon on the Mount represent a very large segment of liberalism in our day. But please notice that the content of the Christian gospel is not found in the Sermon on the Mount. For instance, there is absolutely no mention of the death and resurrection of Christ. Yet Paul said to the Corinthians, ". . . I declare unto you the *gospel*. . . ." What is the gospel? The Sermon on the Mount? No. Paul made it clear that the gospel is this: ". . . that Christ died for our sins according to the scriptures; And that he was buried, and that he rose again the third day according to the scriptures" (1 Cor. 15:1, 3–4, italics mine). My friend, the gospel is not in the Sermon on the Mount, and that is the reason a great many people like to claim it as their religion. The preaching of that doctrine has made more hypocrites in the church than anything else. It is nothing in the world but verbiage for men to say, "I live by the Sermon on the Mount." If a man is honest and will *read* the Sermon on the Mount, he will *know* that he is not living up to it.

My friend, if the Sermon on the Mount is God's standard (and it is) and you come short of it, what are you going to do? Do you have a Savior who can extend mercy to you? Do you know the One who can reach down in grace and save you when you put your faith in Him?

To reduce the Christian message to the Sermon on the Mount is a simplicity which the Scriptures would not permit under any circumstances whatsoever. To do so is the extreme left point of view.

There is also the extreme right point of view. This group treats the Sermon on the Mount as if it were the bubonic plague. They have nothing to do with it. They give the impression that there is something ethically wrong with it. This group is known as hyperdispensationalists. (Don't misunderstand, I am a dispensationalist but not a *hyper*-dispensationalist.) They maintain that we can't use the Sermon on the Mount at all. In fact, one of them told me that the Lord's Prayer has no meaning for us today. He was a prominent man, and after I heard him make that statement, I ran a sermon series on the Sermon on the Mount and the Lord's Prayer. In fact, I have a book entitled *Let Us Pray* which deals with the Lord's Prayer. The Lord's Prayer does have meaning for us in our day. It is *for* us, although it is not *to* us. But the extreme right want to rule it out entirely.

It is true that there is no gospel in the Sermon on the Mount, and it is tragic indeed to give it to unregenerate man as a standard of conduct, and to tell him that if he tries to measure up to it, he is a Christian.

The Sermon on the Mount is Law lifted to the nth degree. Man could not keep the Law in the Old Testament. So how in the world can he keep, in his own strength, the Sermon on the Mount which is elevated to an even higher degree?

It is likewise true that the modus operandi for Christian living is not really found in the Sermon on the Mount. It gives the ethic without supplying the dynamic. Living by the power of the indwelling Holy Spirit is just not one of the truths taught in the Sermon on the Mount. Paul says: "For what the law could not do, in that it was weak through the flesh, God sending his own Son in the likeness of sinful flesh, and for sin, condemned sin in the flesh: That the righteousness of the law might be fulfilled in us, who walk not after the flesh, but after the Spirit" (Rom. 8:3–4).

You don't find that teaching in the Sermon on the Mount. It contains nothing of the ministry of the Holy Spirit. However, it does contain high ethical standards and practices which are *not* contrary to Christian living; in fact, it expresses the mind of Christ which should be the mind of the Christian also. The great principles set down here are profitable for the Christian to study and learn, but he can never attain them in his own strength; he must go elsewhere to look for the *power.* What you have in the Sermon on the Mount is a marvelous electric light bulb, but you do not have the generator that produces the power that will make the light. And it is the light, not the bulb, that is all important.

The primary purpose of the Sermon on the Mount is to set before men the law of the kingdom. In Matthew we are talking about the King who has come to present Himself. John the Baptist was His forerunner, and the King called disciples to follow Him. Now He enunciates the law of the kingdom. This is the manifesto of the King and the platform of the Prince of Peace. And it's law! It will be the law of this world during the Millennium, and then it will find full fruition. Christ will reign on earth in person and will enforce every word of it. The Sermon on the Mount will finally prevail when He whose right it is to rule shall come. Now it's inconceivable to me that anyone who acknowledges Him today as Lord would despise this document or turn from it. The Christian who calls Jesus Christ *Lord,* will seek to do what He commands, but he can obey only in the power of the Holy Spirit. It is worse than futile to try to force the Sermon on the Mount on a gainsaying and rebellious world. Only the gospel of the grace of God can make men obedient to Christ, and it was given to bring men into *obedience* to God.

The Sermon on the Mount needs to be preached to bring conviction to the hearts of men. This document lets men know that they have sinned, and it reveals that none are righteous and that all have come short of God's glory.

The Christian can take the principles set down in the Sermon on the Mount and consider them in the light of other Scriptures. This will provide a wider view and a better understanding of the mind of Christ. For example, only here can you find Christ's definition of murder and adultery. Christ took two of the commandments and lifted them to the nth degree, "Thou shalt not kill" and "Thou shalt not commit adultery" (Exod. 20: 13–14). Are these the only two which He lifted to a higher level? The answer seems to be obvious. These are the only two which are recorded in Matthew. Apparently, He did or could lift each commandment to a much higher level of attainment. If it could be said of the Mosaic Law, ". . . for by the works of the law shall no flesh be justified" (Gal. 2:16), then it would be ten times more difficult for a man to be justified by the Sermon on the Mount.

Try putting down upon your own life these two commandments: "Thou shalt not kill" and "Thou shalt not commit adultery." Let me illustrate what I mean by a little story. This incident took place during my first pastorate when I was a lot more blunt than I am now. An elder in the church I served in Nashville, Tennessee, invited me to speak at a Chamber of Commerce luncheon. This elder was a very wonderful man. He was the vice-president of a bank in the city, a member of the Chamber of Commerce, and when he asked me to bring a brief message, he said, "You won't have but a few minutes, but I want you to give these businessmen the gospel." Well, I arrived at the place a little early, and there were several men standing around. I went up near the speaker's table, and there was a man there who shook hands with me and began to rip out oaths. I had never seen such a fine-looking, well-dressed man curse as this man did. Finally, he said to me, "What's your racket?" I told him that I was a preacher, and he began to cover up immediately. He apologized for his language. He didn't need to apologize to me; he needed to apologize to God because God heard him all the time—which I told him. Then he wanted me to know that he was an officer in a certain liberal church, and he boasted, "The Sermon on the Mount is my religion."

"It is?" I said, "Let's shake hands. I congratulate you—you've got a wonderful religion! By the way, how are you doing with it?"

"What do you mean?"

"You said that the Sermon on the Mount is your religion. Are you living by it?"

"Well, I try."

"That's not quite it. The Lord said that you are blessed if you *do* those things, not if you vote for them. Are you keeping it?"

"I think I am."

"Do you mind if we take a little test?"

"All right."

"The Sermon on the Mount says that if you are angry with your brother you are guilty of murder. Are you keeping that one?"

"Well, that's pretty strong, but I don't think I have been angry enough to kill anyone."

Then I quoted the one the Lord gave on adultery: "Whosoever looketh on a woman to lust after her hath committed adultery with her already in his heart" (v. 28), and asked him, "how about that one?"

"Oh, I guess that would get me!"

"Well, I imagine that there are several things in the Sermon on the Mount that would get you. Apparently you are not living by your religion. If I were you, I'd change my religion and get something that *works*."

Oh, how many people there are like that man! They very piously say that the Sermon on the Mount is their religion, but all they mean is that they think it is a good document and a very fine expression, but it doesn't affect them one whit. I found out later that the man I was talking with had two wives—one at home and one at his office. My friend, if the Sermon on the Mount is your religion, you had better make sure you are keeping it. It is loaded with law. But if you will look at the Sermon on the Mount honestly, it will bring you to a Savior who died for you on the cross. The Sermon on the Mount sets before us great principles and high goals. We need to know them, but they reveal how far we come short.

Matthew's record of the Sermon on the Mount is, I am sure, only a skeleton of Christ's actual message. I have divided it like this:

1. Relationship of the subjects of the kingdom to self (Matt. 5:1–16).
2. Relationship of the subjects of the kingdom to law (Matt. 5:17–48).
3. Relationship of the subjects of the kingdom to God (Matt. 6).
4. Relationship of the subjects of the kingdom to others (Matt. 7).

The Sermon on the Mount opens with the Beatitudes. It is well to note that they are *be*-atitudes, not *do*-attitudes. They state what the subjects of the kingdom *are*—they are the type of person described in the Beatitudes.

Verse 1 makes it clear why this discourse is called the Sermon on the Mount.

First it should be noted that the Lord did not actually give the Sermon on the Mount to the multitudes. He gave it to His disciples, those who were already His.

RELATIONSHIP OF THE SUBJECTS OF THE KINGDOM TO SELF

And seeing the multitudes, he went up into a mountain: and when he was set, his disciples came unto him:

And he opened his mouth, and taught them, saying [Matt. 5:1–2].

Although He did not actually give the Sermon on the Mount to the multitudes, He gave it to the disciples because He saw the multitudes and their need. Therefore, it was given to the multitudes indirectly.

In our day, men need first to come to Christ. While the kingdom is actually in abeyance, the present state of it is a place where the seed is being sown, and the seed is the Word of God. Our business in the world is to sow the seed, and the day is coming when Christ will establish His kingdom upon this earth.

Blessed are the poor in spirit: for theirs is the kingdom of heaven [Matt. 5:3].

This verse says, "Blessed are the poor in spirit." It doesn't tell you *how* to become poor in spirit; it just says, "Blessed are the poor in spirit." In these twelve verses, our Lord used the word *blessed* nine times. By the way, the Psalms open with the same word: "Blessed is the man . . ." (Ps. 1:1). This is in contrast to the curses of the Mosaic Law. You may remember that Joshua was told that when the people of Israel were come over Jordan, they were to stand on Mount Gerizim to bless the people. And then the curses were to be given from Mount Ebal. The blessings from the Sermon on the Mount are in sharp contrast to the curses from Mount Ebal, and they far exceed the blessings from Mount Gerizim, because Christ alone can bring those blessings. In our day only the saved sinner can know his poverty of spirit—"Blessed are the poor in spirit." The Sermon on the Mount, instead of making folk poor in spirit, makes them boast—like the man I referred to. He was boasting that the Sermon on the Mount was his religion, and he was trying to kid himself and kid me into thinking that he was keeping it. He wasn't keeping it at all; it was just making a hypocrite out of him. And there are a lot of those around.

I played golf one day in Tulsa, Oklahoma, with a very wealthy oil man. He told me, "I went to church just like the rest of the hypocrites, and I was one of them, talking about keeping the Sermon on the Mount. Then one day I found out that I was a lost sinner on the way to hell. I turned to Jesus Christ, and He saved me!" Oh, my friend, don't be deceived. Only the Spirit of God can reveal to you your poverty of spirit. The Lord Jesus in the Sermon on the Mount was not telling His disciples *how* to become citizens of the kingdom of heaven. They already were citizens of the kingdom.

We Christians today are actually very poor in spirit, we are spiritually bankrupt, but we have something to give which is more valuable than silver and gold. Paul expressed it this way: "As sorrowful, yet alway rejoicing; as poor, yet making many rich; as having nothing, and yet possessing all things" (2 Cor. 6:10). "As poor, yet making many rich" is referring to spiritual riches which are available to everyone who belongs to Christ.

The next beatitude is:

Blessed are they that mourn: for they shall be comforted [Matt. 5:4].

It is interesting to note that the same thoughts expressed in the Beatitudes can be found elsewhere in the Scriptures. The poor in spirit are referred to in Zephaniah 3:12. Micah is an example of those who mourn and are comforted (see ch. 7).

Blessed are the meek: for they shall inherit the earth [Matt. 5:5].

We find this in Psalm 37:11. The meek are not inheriting the earth in this day in which we live—I'm sure you recognize that. So apparently the Sermon on the Mount is not in effect today. However, when Christ is reigning, the meek will inherit the earth.

How do you become meek? Our Lord was meek and lowly, and He will inherit all things; we are the heirs of God and joint-heirs with Jesus Christ. We are told that the fruit of the Spirit is love, joy, peace, long-suffering, gentleness, goodness, faith, temperance, and meekness. Only the Spirit of God can break you and make you meek. If you could produce meekness by your own effort, you would be proud of yourself, wouldn't you? And out goes your meekness! Meekness is not produced by self-effort but by Spirit effort. Only the Holy Spirit can produce meekness in the heart of a yielded Christian. The Christian who has learned the secret of producing the fruit of the Holy Spirit can turn here to the Beatitudes and read, "Blessed are the meek: for they shall inherit the earth," and see that the rewards of meekness are still in the future. Paul asked the Corinthian believers, "Do ye not know that the saints shall judge the world? . . ." (1 Cor. 6:2).

The Beatitudes present goals which the child of God wants to realize in his own life, but he can't do it on his own. You may have heard of the preacher who had a message entitled "Meekness and How I Attained It." He said that he hadn't delivered his message yet, but as soon as he got an audience big enough, he was going to give it! Well, I have a notion that he had long since lost his meekness. Meekness can only be a fruit of the Holy Spirit.

Then in verse six we are told:

Blessed are they which do hunger and thirst after righteousness; for they shall be filled [Matt. 5:6].

What about the natural man; does he hunger and thirst for righteousness? The ones I meet do not! "But the natural man receiveth not the things of the Spirit of God: for they are foolishness unto him: neither can he know them, because they are spiritually discerned" (1 Cor. 2:14). The "natural man" is in contrast to the spiritual man who has found that Christ is his righteousness—". . . of him are ye in Christ Jesus, who of God is made unto us wisdom, and righteousness, and sanctification, and redemption" (1 Cor. 1:30).

Blessed are the merciful: for they shall obtain mercy [Matt. 5:7].

This beatitude is so misunderstood in our day because it makes our obtaining mercy conditional on our being merciful. This is not the condition on which *we* obtain mercy—"Not by works of righteousness which we have done, but according to his *mercy* he saved us, by the washing of regeneration, and renewing of the Holy Ghost" (Titus 3:5, italics mine). We should be merciful *because* we have obtained mercy. "But ye are a chosen generation, a royal priesthood, an holy nation, a peculiar people; that ye should shew forth the praises of him who hath called you out of darkness into his marvelous light: Which in time past were not a people, but are now the people of God: which had not obtained mercy, but now have obtained mercy" (1 Pet. 2:9–10).

Blessed are the pure in heart: for they shall see God [Matt. 5:8].

No honest man can say that his heart is pure. How can the heart of man, which is desperately wicked, be made clean? The Lord Jesus said, "Now ye are clean through the word which I have spoken unto you" (John 15:3). It is by the washing of regeneration that we are made clean. Only the blood of Christ can cleanse us from all sin (see 1 John 1:7).

Blessed are the peacemakers: for they shall be called the children of God [Matt. 5:9].

Can you name one peacemaker in the world right now? There is no one today who can make peace. Christ alone is the great Peacemaker. He made peace by His blood between a righteous God and an unrighteous sinner. "Therefore being justified by faith, we have peace with God through our Lord Jesus Christ" (Rom. 5:1).

Blessed are they which are persecuted for righteousness' sake: for theirs is the kingdom of heaven [Matt. 5:10].

The application of this beatitude to our day and to the remnant of Israel during the Great Tribulation is easy to see. But can it apply to the kingdom which is to be established? Won't all evil be removed in the kingdom? Well, many Scriptures show that in the millennial kingdom there will still be evil in the world because it will be a time of testing. The outbreak of rebellion at the end of the Millennium reveals that evil will be prevalent during the Millennium (see Rev. 20:7–9).

Ye are the salt of the earth: but if the salt have lost his savour, wherewith shall it be salted? it is thenceforth good for nothing, but to be cast out, and to be trodden under foot of men.

Ye are the light of the world. A city that is set on an hill cannot be hid [Matt. 5:13–14].

God's people in any age and under any condition are both salt and light in the world. The Scots translate "savour" by the more expressive word *tang*. I like their word much better. "If the salt has lost its tang." The problem today is that most church members have not only lost their tang as salt, but as pepper they have lost their pep also. We have very few salt and pepper Christians in our day. Now salt doesn't keep fermentation and that type of thing from taking place, but it will arrest it. You and I ought to be the salt in the earth and have an influence for good in the world.

Christians are also the light of the world. Certainly in the kingdom the believers are going to be the light of the world. This is a tremendous principle for us. We need to be a light in our neighborhood and wherever we go. We have no light within ourselves, but the Word of God is light. Being a light means giving out the Word of God in one way or another. This doesn't mean that you should be quoting Scripture all the time, but it does mean that you are to share the light that God has given you. It is very easy to cultivate some person, then quietly and graciously introduce them to a Bible-teaching church or radio program. There are many ways in which you can be light in the world.

Let your light so shine before men, that they may see your good works, and glorify your Father which is in heaven [Matt. 5:16].

There are those of the liberal persuasion that feel the Sermon on the Mount is anthropocentric, or man-centered, rather than theocentric, or God-centered. (Those are their terms.) But, obviously, the Sermon on the Mount is *not* anthropocentric, man-centered. It *is* theocentric. Does this verse say, "Let your light so shine before men, that they may see your good works, and glorify *you* and pat you on the back, and give you a gold medal and a loving cup?" No! This verse says that you and I are to let our light so shine in this world that we may glorify our Father which is in heaven. The Sermon on the Mount is God-centered. During the Millennium, during the kingdom here on earth, everything which is done and said will be God-centered. And in the present age, in this lost world in which you and I live today, our prime motivation should be to bring glory to God. This is something that every Christian should consider very seriously. The aim and purpose of our lives should be to glorify our God.

RELATIONSHIP OF THE SUBJECTS OF THE KINGDOM TO LAW

Think not that I am come to destroy the law, or the prophets: I am not come to destroy, but to fulfil [Matt. 5:17].

Remember that part of the Mosaic Law was the ceremonial law. Christ was the sacrifice for the sins of the world, the Lamb slain before the foundation of the earth. Christ came not to destroy the Law but to fulfill the Law. He fulfilled it in that He kept it during His earthly life. And the standard which was set before man *He* was able to attain, and now He is able to make over to you and me (and every believer) His own righteousness. God's standards have not changed, but you and I cannot attain them in our own strength. We need help; we need a Savior. We do need mercy, and we obtain mercy when we come to Christ.

For verily I say unto you, Till heaven and earth pass, one jot or one tittle shall in no wise pass from the law, till all be fulfilled [Matt. 5:18].

I hope you don't misinterpret what I am saying in this section which we call the Sermon on the Mount. I am not saying that we are free to break the Mosaic Law. The fact of the matter is that the Law is still a standard. It reveals to me that I cannot measure up to God's standard. This drives me to the cross of Christ. The only way I can fulfill the Law is by accepting the only One who could fulfill it—Jesus Christ.

Whosoever therefore shall break one of these least commandments, and shall teach men so, he shall be called the least in the kingdom of heaven: but whosoever shall do and teach them, the same shall be called great in the kingdom of heaven [Matt. 5:19].

You cannot break the commandments and get by with it. But you cannot keep them in your own strength. The only way you can keep them is to come to Jesus Christ for salvation, power, and strength. The commandments are not a *way* of salvation but a *means* to show you the way to salvation through the acceptance of the work of Jesus Christ.

For I say unto you, That except your righteousness shall exceed the righteousness of the scribes and Pharisees, ye shall in no case enter into the kingdom of heaven [Matt. 5:20].

It is very important to see His point right here. The Pharisees had a high degree of righteousness according to the Law, but that was not acceptable. How can you and I surpass their righteousness? It is impossible in our own efforts. We need Christ to do it for us.

Ye have heard that it was said by them of old time, Thou shalt not kill; and whosoever shall kill shall be in danger of the judgment:

But I say unto you, That whosoever is angry with his brother without a cause shall be in danger of the judgment: and whosoever shall say to his brother, Raca, shall be in danger of the council: but whosoever shall say, Thou fool, shall be in danger of hell fire [Matt. 5:21–22].

This is a tremendous statement! It means that if you are angry with your brother, you are a murderer! Do you claim to be keeping the Mosaic Law? You cannot break the Law and get by with it. You can't get by with mouthing the boast that the Sermon on the Mount is your religion and then break every part of it. My friend, both you and I need a Savior who has perfectly kept the Law and can impute to us His own righteousness.

Verily I say unto thee, Thou shalt by no means come out thence, till thou hast paid the uttermost farthing [Matt. 5:26].

Note that Jesus says, "Verily *I* say unto thee." He is lifting His teaching above the teaching of Moses. He is lifting Himself to the position of the Lawgiver and also the Interpreter, by the way.

Ye have heard that it was said by them of old time, Thou shalt not commit adultery:

But I say unto you, That whosoever looketh on a woman to lust after her hath committed adultery with her already in his heart [Matt. 5:27–28].

For many years I have publicly made the statement that nobody but the Lord Jesus has ever kept the Law. One Sunday morning I repeated it in my message, and afterward a big, burly, red-faced fellow came to me and said, "You always say that nobody keeps the Law. I want you to know that *I* keep the Law!" By the way, he belonged to a cult, although he attended services at the church I pastored. Since he claimed to keep the Law, I said, "All right, let's look at it," and I showed him verse 22 regarding hatred being the same as murder. He said that he kept that, although I don't believe that he did. So I gave him verse 28 and said, "It says here that if you so much as look upon a woman to lust after her, you have committed adultery. Now look me straight in the eye and tell me that you have never done that." He was red-faced to begin with, but you should have seen him then—he was really red-faced. He grunted some sort of epithet, turned on his heels, and walked out. Of course, he walked out! And I say to you, if you are honest, you will not claim to be keeping the Law. Remember that there were ten commandments. Although Matthew mentions only these two that Christ dealt with, I am of the opinion that He lifted all ten of them to the nth degree.

Oh, my friend, the Sermon on the Mount shows me that I have sinned and that I need to come to Him for mercy and help. To say that you are living by the Sermon on the Mount while all the time you are breaking it is to declare that the Law is not important.

In the following verses the Lord deals in a tremendous way with the Law and man's relationship to it.

And if thy right eye offend thee, pluck it out, and cast it from thee: for it is profitable for thee that one of thy members should perish, and not that thy whole body should be cast into hell.

And if thy right hand offend thee, cut it off, and cast it from thee: for it is profitable for thee that one of thy members should perish, and not that thy whole body should be cast into hell [Matt. 5:29–30].

This is severe, very severe, and it reveals, friends, that if you cannot meet God's standards, you need a Savior. Don't kid yourself and fool around with pretending that you are keeping the Law. You are only being a hypocrite. In Christian circles we are intent upon patting each other on the back and complimenting one another and giving each other credit for what we do when all the time we all are a pack of low-down, dirty, rotten sinners, not even fit for heaven. The Sermon on the Mount ought to drive you to the cross of Christ where you cry out for mercy. To do that is to honor the Law, my friend. Don't try to kid me into thinking that you are keeping it. I know you're not—because you are just like I am.

It hath been said, Whosoever shall put away his wife, let him give her a writing of divorcement:

But I say unto you, That whosoever shall put away his wife, saving for the cause of fornication, causeth her to commit adultery: and whosoever shall marry her that is divorced committeth adultery [Matt. 5:31–32].

Here the Lord gives the grounds for divorce. If someone is divorced for a reason not given in Scripture, that person is an adulterer. This is something that is entirely ignored today in Christian circles. This, however, will be the Law during the kingdom age because there will be men and women who will want to leave their mates during that period. We will deal with the divorce question in some detail when we get to chapter 19.

Again, ye have heard that it hath been said by them of old time, Thou shalt not forswear thyself, but shalt perform unto the Lord thine oaths:

But I say unto you, Swear not at all; neither by heaven; for it is God's throne:

Nor by the earth; for it is his footstool: neither by Jerusalem; for it is the city of the great King [Matt. 5:33–35].

The Lord Jesus is saying that we are to be the kind of persons who don't have to take an oath. As a boy, I can remember that my dad could go into the bank and borrow money, then come back a couple of days later to sign the note. Or he could call the bank by phone and have a certain amount of money credited to his account. Well, believe me, it is different in our day. Why? Because there are a lot more folk today who cannot be trusted. The Lord says that the child of God, under all circumstances, should be trustworthy. The Lord says:

But let your communication be, Yea, yea; Nay, nay: for whatsoever is more than these cometh of evil [Matt. 5:37].

When a man says to me, "I'd swear on a stack of Bibles a mile high," that is the fellow I do not believe because I think the lie he's telling is a mile high.

Ye have heard that it hath been said, An eye for an eye, and a tooth for a tooth [Matt. 5:38].

All of that will be changed when Christ is reigning in His kingdom.

But I say unto you, That ye resist not evil: but whosoever shall smite thee on thy right cheek, turn to him the other also [Matt. 5:39].

Do you live like this, or do you resist evil? There is a principle for us here, but we are living in a day when a wise man armed keepeth his house. And Paul could say, "Alexander the coppersmith did me much evil: the Lord reward him according to his works" (2 Tim. 4:14). In the kingdom you will be able to turn the other cheek. It reminds me of the Irishman whom someone hit on the cheek and knocked down. The Irishman got up and turned his other cheek. The fellow knocked him down again. This time the Irishman got up and beat the stuffin' out of that fellow. An observer asked, "Why did you do that?" "Well," replied the Irishman, "the Lord said to turn the other cheek and I did, but He never told me what to do after that."

And if any man will sue thee at the law, and take away thy coat, let him have thy cloak also.

And whosoever shall compel thee to go a mile, go with him twain.

Give to him that asketh thee, and from him that would borrow of thee turn not thou away [Matt. 5:40–42].

If you have a banker who says that he is living by the Sermon on the Mount, give this verse to him and see how far you get with it. Let's quit being hypocrites and realize that this is the law of the kingdom. When my Lord is on the throne down here on this earth, folk can live this way. In our day, business could not be conducted by this law. Years ago Archbishop McGee of Ireland said that it was impossible to conduct the affairs of the British nation on the basis of the Sermon on the Mount. I do not know whether I am related to Archbishop McGee or not, but I certainly find that I *think* as he did about the Sermon on the Mount. Although it contains great principles for the Christian in our day, it can be enforced only when Christ is on the throne. I think that ought to be quite obvious.

In our contemporary society many of the wealthy churches say that they follow the Sermon on the Mount. That is what the congregation gets as a steady diet on Sunday morning. However, if you go to the rich and try to get something from them, you won't get very far, I assure you. On Sunday they hear, "Give to him that asketh thee, and from him that would borrow of thee turn not thou away." It sounds great. They think the Sermon on the Mount is a great document, but on Monday morning it is cold-blooded business and cash on the barrelhead. That, of course, is the way the business world is set up today.

However, there is a great principle in these verses for us, and we should not miss that. Certainly we should be helpful to those who are in need. And there are many fine Christian acts that can be performed by believers. Historically, hospitals, orphan homes, and works of charity (which the Bible calls acts of love) have followed the preaching of the gospel. I do not know any place on earth where they preceded the gospel, but they always followed it. There should be the fruit of good works in a believer's life.

Ye have heard that it hath been said, Thou shalt love thy neighbour, and hate thine enemy.

But I say unto you, Love your enemies, bless them that curse you, do good to them that hate you, and pray for them which despitefully use you, and persecute you [Matt. 5:43–44].

This rule, I insist, is for the kingdom. The Lord Jesus lifts the Mosaic Law to the nth degree. He says that in the kingdom the enemy is to be loved instead of hated.

The believer today operates on a different principle. We are commanded to love all *believers,* and we express our love to our *enemies* by getting the gospel to them, giving them the message of God's saving grace that is able to bring them to heaven.

In concluding this chapter, our Lord says that we are to be perfect—

Be ye therefore perfect, even as your Father which is in heaven is perfect [Matt. 5:48].

How is it possible for you and me to be perfect? We are accepted in Christ, in the beloved.

There is no condemnation to them which are in Christ, and we get *in* Christ by faith in Him. The only way we can become perfect is through our faith in Christ—Christ imputes to us His righteousness. And then begins the slow process of sanctification in which God attempts to conform us to the image of His Son. This, of course, should be the goal of every believer. But seeking to attain perfection by our own efforts is absolutely futile. Do you think that you can go to God and say, "Look what I have done; look how wonderful I am," trying to get all the glory for yourself and to force God to save you on that basis? My friend, you are going to do nothing of the kind because you and I are not perfect. Most of us remember this:

Little Jack Horner
Sat in a corner
Eating a Christmas pie;
He put in his thumb,
And pulled out a plum,
And said, What a good boy am I!

We see a lot of that in religion today. Little folk sit around, reach in their thumb, and pull out a plum and say, "What a good boy am I!" My friend, you and I are not good by God's standards. We need a Savior.

As we have seen, in this chapter the King speaks of the righteousness which His subjects must possess. And it must be a righteousness to exceed the righteousness of the scribes and Pharisees. They had a religious righteousness. For instance, Nicodemus was an outstanding man, and he was religious. You can't find much to criticize about him. But our Lord said to him, "You have to be born again" (see John 3:1–8). Now we have to have a righteousness superior to that of the scribes and the Pharisees, and it can only come through trust in Christ.

CHAPTER 6

THEME: *The inner motives which govern external acts of righteousness, such as the giving of alms, prayer, fasting, and the getting of riches; the relationship of the subjects of the kingdom of heaven to God*

THE MOTIVE AND METHOD OF GIVING ALMS

Chapter 6 of Matthew deals with the external part of religion. We have seen in chapter 5 that the King speaks of the righteousness which His subjects must *possess*. It must be a righteousness to exceed the righteousness of the scribes and Pharisees, and that comes only through trust in Christ. In chapter 6 Matthew talks about the righteousness that the subjects of the kingdom are to *practice*. The motive, of course, is the important thing in what you do for God. No third party can enter into this relationship. These things are between the soul and God.

The items mentioned in this chapter—the giving of alms, prayer, fasting, money, and taking thought and care for the future—are very practical considerations.

First, our Lord talks about alms. Keep in mind that all of this has to do with externalities of religion or with ostentation in religion.

Take heed that ye do not your alms before men, to be seen of them: otherwise ye have no reward of your Father which is in heaven [Matt. 6:1].

Although the Lord Jesus is directing His remarks to the subjects of His coming kingdom, there is a great principle here for you and me.

Therefore when thou doest thine alms, do not sound a trumpet before thee, as the hypocrites do in the synagogues and in the streets, that they may have glory of men. Verily I say unto you, They have their reward [Matt. 6:2].

He is saying this with biting irony. Believe me, He knew how to use the rapier of sarcasm! When the Pharisees wanted to give something to the poor, it was their custom to go down to a busy street corner in Jerusalem and blow a trumpet. Although the purpose was to call the poor and needy together to receive the gifts, it afforded a fine opportunity to let others see their good works. Do you see parallels today in the way some Christians give? Our Lord said that when the Pharisees do it that way, they have their reward. What was their reward? Well, what was it that they were after? Jesus said they did it to have glory of men. They blew the trumpet, and everybody came running out to see how generously they gave, and that was their reward. Their giving was not between themselves and God.

Now, why do *you* give? There is more than one way to give. Several years ago I was asked to take an offering in a certain organization. I was told to be sure and give everybody an opportunity to stand up and tell how much he would give. For example, I was instructed to say, "How many will give one hundred dollars?" I asked, "Why in the world do you take an offering like that?" I was told that a certain man would attend who would give only one dollar if a regular offering was taken. However, if the question of how many would give one hundred dollars was asked, he would give that amount. May I say that he blew a trumpet. And I discovered when I came to know this man that this was the way he gave.

There are other people who give large checks but want to hand them to you personally. There was a man in my church who always gave me a check before I went into the pulpit. He thought this would excite me enough so that I would mention it. A friend of his came to me one day and said, "So-and-so is disturbed." He went on to explain that I did not acknowledge the very large check his friend had given me last Sunday. "That's right," I said, and told this man the reason why. "Your friend is a man of means and the check he gave me, in relationship to what he has, wasn't very much. Last Sunday a mail-carrier also handed me an envelope. He didn't want me to open it until after the service and did not want me to say a word to anyone about it. He gave me almost twice as much money as the man of means did. If I were going to acknowledge anybody, it would have to be the mail-carrier—but he didn't want me to do that."

May I say to you that giving is between you and God, and the very minute you get a third party involved, you don't get any credit in heaven.

There is a lot of so-called Christian giving today that isn't giving at all. For example, the college I graduated from played on human nature. While I was in school, beautiful architectural plans were drawn up for a tower to be put on an old hall. It was modestly announced that the tower would be named after the donor. At least a half dozen people wanted their names on that tower. Today it is called "So-and-so Tower" in honor of a certain man. His name is carved in stone which means that his trumpet is being blown all the time. A lot of people give like that. This kind of giving is worth nothing before God.

But when thou doest alms, let not thy left hand know what thy right hand doeth:

That thine alms may be in secret: and thy Father which seeth in secret himself shall reward thee openly [Matt. 6:3–4].

Don't reach in your pocket with one hand and then put the other hand in the air to let people know how much you are giving! Our Lord is saying that when you put your hand in your pocket to get something to give, be so secretive about it that the other hand doesn't know what you are doing. All of this is biting sarcasm.

Do our liberal friends really live by the Sermon on the Mount? I don't think they do!

THE MARKS OF GENUINE PRAYER

And when thou prayest, thou shalt not be as the hypocrites are: for they love to pray standing in the synagogues and in the corners of the streets, that they may be seen of men. Verily I say unto you, They have their reward [Matt. 6:5].

"Thou shalt not be as the *hypocrites* are"—my, our Lord used strong language, didn't He! "They have their reward." They pray so that they may be seen of men. A man might go wearing a prayer shawl, which advertises the fact that he is praying. Jesus said that when a man prays like that, he has his reward. He gets what he wants—that is, to be seen of men. But his prayer never gets above the rafters of the building.

But thou, when thou prayest, enter into thy closet, and when thou hast shut thy door, pray to thy Father which is in secret; and thy Father which seeth in secret shall reward thee openly [Matt. 6:6].

The concept we are dealing with here is revolutionary. Did you notice that the Lord uses the term *Father*? These are citizens of the kingdom that the Lord is talking about. How do you become a child of God today? John 1:12 gives us the answer: "But as many as received him, to them gave he power [the authority] to become the sons of God, even to them that [do no more or less than] believe on his name." Our Lord even said to Nicodemus, "You must be born again" (see John 3:3)—until then, you can't call God your Father. And in the Old Testament you will not find the word *Father* used in relation to a man with God. The nation Israel as a whole was called by God, ". . . Israel is my son . . ." (Exod. 4:22), but not an individual. The Lord Jesus is speaking of a new relationship.

Concerning the subject of prayer, we are told that it should be secret and sincere. Many an unknown saint of God will be revealed at the judgment seat of Christ as a real person of prayer.

But when ye pray, use not vain repetitions, as the heathen do: for they think that they shall be heard for their much speaking [Matt. 6:7].

I heard a fellow pray the other day, and he repeated his petition about a dozen times. The Lord Jesus says that if we ask the Father one time, He hears us.

Be not ye therefore like unto them: for your Father knoweth what things ye have need of, before ye ask him [Matt. 6:8].

Prayer should be marked by sincerity and simplicity:

1. Sincerity—Matthew 6:6. Go in and close the door—your prayer is between you and God.
2. Simplicity—Matthew 6:7. Don't use vain repetition. Get right down to the nitty-gritty and tell the Lord what you have on your mind. "Your Father knoweth what things ye have need of, before ye ask him" v. 8. Even though He already knows what we need, He wants us to come to Him and ask.

Now He gives us a sample prayer—"After this manner therefore pray ye."

Before we look at this so-called Lord's Prayer, let me say that I never use it in a public service. I don't think that a Sunday morning crowd should get up and pray, "Give us this day our daily bread" when they have a roast in the oven at home—they already have their meal. It is a very meaningful prayer for those who are hungry, but a well-fed Sunday morning congregation ought not to pray this because for them it is vain repetition.

However, it is a wonderful model prayer for believers of all conditions.

After this manner therefore pray ye: Our Father which art in heaven, Hallowed by thy name [Matt. 6:9].

Notice that this so-called Lord's Prayer could not be the prayer of the Lord Jesus. He couldn't pray this prayer. He couldn't join with you and me and say, "*Our* Father" because the relationship between the Father and the Son is the relationship in deity. It is a position, not a begetting. I became a son of God only through faith in Christ; therefore Christ couldn't join with me in saying, "Our Father."

"Which art in heaven." God is not a prisoner in this universe—He is beyond and above it. He is in the air spaces, in the stellar spaces, but He is far removed from His universe today. He is more than creation! He is the One sitting upon the throne of the universe, and He has it under His control!

"Hallowed be thy name," more correctly translated, would read, "Let thy name be made holy." The name of God stands for God, for all that God is. In what way can you and I make God's name holy? It is my conviction that by our lives we are to make God's name holy. When Abraham went into Canaan, a Canaanite passing by observed that they had a new neighbor, for he had seen Abraham's altar. Everywhere Abraham went he built an altar to God. And when Abraham began to do business with the Canaanites, they found him to be honest. They found that everything Abraham said invited their confidence. Finally, they reached the conclusion that the God whom Abraham worshiped was an holy God, and Abimelech said to Abraham, ". . . God is with thee in all that thou doest" (Gen. 21:22). The children of Heth said, ". . . thou art a mighty prince among us . . ." (Gen. 23:6). The entire life of Abraham revealed the reverence he felt for God. Surely the name of God was made holy in Canaan because of Abraham.

Thy kingdom come. Thy will be done in earth, as it is in heaven [Matt. 6:10].

"Thy kingdom come" is the kingdom about which Matthew has been speaking, the kingdom which Christ will establish on this earth. This is a worthy petition for all of us to pray.

Give us this day our daily bread [Matt. 6:11].

As I have indicated, this prayer is a model for our own prayers. Now I want you to notice this petition for a moment. It is a wonderful petition, so simple yet one that should come from our hearts with great enthusiasm. It speaks of our utter dependence upon God. Our bodily wants, our physical necessities, all are supplied by Him day by day. "Give us . . . our daily bread"—just as Israel gathered manna for the day, they gathered nothing for the morrow. They were not permitted to gather manna for the next week. They could not hoard it. This prayer gathers manna every day, "Give us this *day* our daily bread." It shows man that he lives from hand to mouth. It shows man that even his bodily necessities, his basic needs, come from God.

And forgive us our debts, as we forgive our debtors [Matt. 6:12].

Our Lord Jesus could not pray this—He had no sin to be forgiven. You see, it is not the Lord's prayer; it is the disciples' prayer.

"Forgive us our debts as we forgive those that are indebted to us" is legalistic; it is not grace. I thank God for another verse of Scripture, Ephesians 4:32, "And be ye kind one to another, tenderhearted, forgiving one another, even as God for Christ's sake hath forgiven you." Today God is forgiving us on the basis of what Christ has done for us, not on the basis by which we forgive—as touching the matter of our salvation. The redemption of God is in full view when God forgives us. It does not refer to our salvation when we read, "forgive us our debts, as we forgive our debtors." He is speaking here to those who are already saved, those who already have the nature of God. He does not wait for you to forgive before He forgives. This is not His method of settling the sin question. He gave His Son to die, and it is on this basis that God forgives.

In some churches today where there is formal religion, liturgy and ritual, they use "forgive us our debts" while others will use "forgive us our trespasses." Two little girls were talking about the Lord's Prayer as repeated in their churches. One said, "We have trespasses in our church," and the other said, "Well, in our church we have debts." (Probably they both were right as far as the churches of our day are concerned—they have both debts and trespasses.) So which phrase is accurate? There is no difficulty here at all since all of these words refer to the same thing, and that thing is sin.

And lead us not into temptation, but deliver us from evil: For thine is the kingdom, and the power, and the glory, for ever. Amen [Matt. 6:13].

"Lead us not into temptation." This word *lead* gives us the wrong impression because James says God does not tempt any man. That is true—God does not tempt any man. A better translation here would be, "Leave us not in temptation." It does not mean to keep us out of it, but when we are in it, do not leave us there.

"Deliver us from evil"—this deliverance is from the evil *one*. Deliver us from the evil one—deliver us from the Devil. Satan is today an awful reality. The world has tried many times to get rid of him. They laughed at Martin Luther who threw an inkwell at him. But recently we have had a turn in events. Any man who stands for God knows the awful reality of Satan. As we work in any church we become conscious of the presence of God and also dreadfully conscious of the presence of Satan. But we have this petition, "Deliver us from the evil one."

May I say that this is a marvelous prayer for a new believer to pray privately in learning to pray. My own mother was not saved until late in life. She didn't know how to pray, and she began by just repeating the Lord's Prayer. Finally she graduated from this, and she could pray her own prayer.

When we are teaching our children to pray, we begin them with, "Now I lay me down to sleep." Then one day little Willie adds, "God bless mama and God bless papa." That is a thrilling moment for us, because they are beginning to pray on their own. And our Lord gave the so-called Lord's Prayer as a model. It is a glorious, wonderful prayer, and it shows us what we should include in our own prayers. He would like us to learn to pray in our own words when we talk to Him.

As the Lord Jesus said in the verses preceding the Lord's Prayer, prayer is not to be done for display. It is a relationship between you and God, and the most effective prayer is when you enter into your closet—that is, a private place. I am not enthusiastic about public prayer meetings because of the fact that the deadest service of any in the church is the prayer meeting. As a pastor, I used to try to build up the prayer meeting, but I soon discovered that if you have fifty dead saints praying, you don't improve it by getting a hundred dead saints. It still is a pretty dead prayer meeting. What we need is a great deal more *private* prayer. It should take place between an individual and God.

THE MEANING OF FASTING

The Lord moves on now to the subject of fasting.

Moreover when ye fast, be not, as the hypocrites, of a sad countenance: for they disfigure their faces, that they may appear unto men to fast. Verily I say unto you, They have their reward [Matt. 6:16].

Fasting has a value for believers in our day, I am convinced of that, but only if it is done privately. It should be a personal matter between the soul and God.

But thou, when thou fastest, anoint thine head, and wash thy face;

That thou appear not unto men to fast, but unto thy Father which is in secret: and thy Father, which seeth in secret, shall reward thee openly [Matt. 6:17–18].

THE MAKING OF MONEY AND THE MEANING OF REAL RICHES

The Lord next turns to the subject of money. This is something many people don't like the preacher to talk about.

Lay not up for yourselves treasures upon earth, where moth and rust doth corrupt, and where thieves break through and steal:

But lay up for yourselves treasures in heaven, where neither moth nor rust

doth corrupt, and where thieves do not break through nor steal:

For where your treasure is, there will your heart be also [Matt. 6:19–21].

A great many folk think that money cannot be used in a spiritual way and that when you talk about money, you are talking about something that is only material. However, our Lord says that we are to lay up for ourselves treasure in heaven. How can we do that? Well, instead of putting it in a bank in Switzerland, put it in heaven by giving it to the Lord's work down here—but make sure it is in the *Lord's* work. You ought to investigate everything you give to. Make sure that you are giving to that which will accumulate treasure for you in heaven. If it is used for the propagation of the gospel and to get out the Word of God, it becomes legal tender in heaven, and that is how we gather treasure in heaven.

Perhaps you are saying, "But I don't give for *that* reason." You ought to, because our Lord said, "Lay up for yourselves treasures in heaven." That is a laudable motive for giving. And He gives the reason: "For where your treasure is, there will your heart be also." If you get enough treasure laid up in heaven, you are certainly going to think a lot about heaven. But if it is in the bank, your thoughts are going to be on the bank. There is an ever-present danger of worshiping mammon rather than God.

MATERIAL THINGS AND THE CHRISTIAN'S RELATIONSHIP TO THEM

Matthew 6 concludes with our Lord talking about other things that are material. He tells us that we are not to give much thought to our material needs. For example, the Lord says:

Behold the fowls of the air: for they sow not, neither do they reap, nor gather into barns; yet your heavenly Father feedeth them. Are ye not much better than they? [Matt. 6:26].

Birds cannot sow. Birds cannot reap. Birds cannot gather anything into barns, but you and I can. We are to sow, reap, and gather with the same abandon that a little bird has. The little bird is trusting God to take care of him, and we are to trust Him, also. "Are ye not much better than they?" This does not mean that we shouldn't exercise judgment, because God has given us this ability. Once a Christian asked me, "Do you think a Christian ought to have insurance?" My reply was, "Yes!" Insurance is one means we have today to put our minds at ease concerning the care of our families and ourselves. The important thing is that we are not to go through life with material things becoming a burden to us.

And why take ye thought for raiment? Consider the lilies of the field, how they grow; they toil not, neither do they spin [Matt. 6:28].

In this verse the question is asked, "why take ye thought for raiment?" Think of the time that is consumed by both men and women when it comes to buying clothes. And almost everyone has had the experience at some time of saying, "I can't go tonight, I don't have the right suit or dress to wear." Well, consider the lilies of the field. They cannot toil or spin, and yet God takes care of them. Of course, a Christian should dress as well as he can. To be slovenly in dress or in any action is not honoring to God. Our Lord called attention to the *beauty* of the flowers—

And yet I say unto you, That even Solomon in all his glory was not arrayed like one of these [Matt. 6:29].

I think He wants us to be as beautiful as possible. Some of us don't have much to work with, but we ought to do the best we can with what we've got.

Wherefore, if God so clothe the grass of the field, which to-day is, and to-morrow is cast into the oven, shall he not much more clothe you, O ye of little faith? [Matt. 6:30].

We are not to be overly anxious about the things of this world. Material things should not be the goal of our life.

But seek ye first the kingdom of God, and his righteousness; and all these things shall be added unto you.

Take therefore no thought for the morrow: for the morrow shall take thought for the things of itself. Sufficient unto the day is the evil thereof [Matt. 6:33–34].

"Take . . . no thought for the morrow" means no *anxious* thought. He takes care of the flowers and the birds, and He will take care of you. But the important thing is to put Him first in our life.

As someone has said, Today is the tomorrow that we worried about yesterday. How true that is for many of us!

CHAPTER 7

***THEME:** The relationship of the child of the King with other children of the King maintained by prayer; and final warnings about the two ways, false prophets, false profession, and the two foundations*

JUDGMENT OF OTHERS FORBIDDEN

Judge not, that ye be not judged.

For with what judgment ye judge, ye shall be judged: and with what measure ye mete, it shall be measured to you again [Matt. 7:1–2].

These verses have really been misunderstood. To *judge* can mean "to decide, to distinguish, to condemn, to avenge," and it actually can mean "to damn." These verses do not mean that a child of God is forbidden to judge others, but it does mean that we are not to judge the inward motives of others in the sense of condemning them. We do not know or understand why a brother in Christ does a certain thing. We see only outward acts. God doesn't forbid our judging wrong and evil actions, as we will see. The point is that if you are harsh in your judgments of others, you will be known as the type of person who is severe in his considerations of others. I know this type of person, and I am sure you do, also. Perhaps somebody has said to you, "Don't pay any attention to what he says; he never has a good word to say." You see, he is being judged by the way he judges. This is what our Lord is saying in these verses.

And why beholdest thou the mote that is in thy brother's eye, but considerest not the beam that is in thine own eye? [Matt. 7:3].

He is comparing a little piece of sawdust in your brother's eye to the great big redwood log in your own eye. The "log" is the spirit of criticism and prejudice. With that blocking your vision, you are in no position to judge the little sin of another.

Or how wilt thou say to thy brother, Let me pull out the mote out of thine eye; and, behold, a beam is in thine own eye?

Thou hypocrite, first cast out the beam out of thine own eye; and then shalt thou see clearly to cast out the mote out of thy brother's eye [Matt. 7:4–5].

This matter of harsh judgment is certainly something about which we need to be very careful. Although Jesus makes it clear that we are not to sit in harsh judgment upon another, He also said that by their fruits we would know them. The late Dr. James McGinley put it in his rather unique fashion, "I am no judge, but I am a fruit inspector." And we can really tell whether or not a Christian is producing fruit.

JUDGMENT OF OTHERS ENJOINED

Now He really puts us on the horns of a dilemma.

Give not that which is holy unto the dogs, neither cast ye your pearls before swine, lest they trample them under their feet, and turn again and rend you [Matt. 7:6].

We have to determine who the dogs are and who the pigs are, don't we? These are not four-legged animals He is talking about. We are not to give that which is holy unto dogs or cast our pearls before swine; therefore, there is a judgment that we need to make.

There are certain times and places where it is not worthwhile to say a word. This is a judgment you need to make. I remember a Tennessee legislator friend of mine who was a heavy drinker. He was wonderfully converted and is a choice servant of God today. The other members of the legislature knew how he drank. Then they heard he "got religion," as they called it. One day this fellow took his seat in the legislature, and his fellow-members looked him over. Finally, someone rose, addressed the chairman of the meeting and said, "I make a motion that we hear a sermon from Deacon So-and-So." Everyone laughed. But my friend was equal to the occasion. He got to his feet and said, "I'm sorry, I do not have anything to say. My Lord told me not to cast my pearls before swine." He sat down, and they never ridiculed him anymore.

A police inspector in the city of New York told me about certain apartments which were filled with no one but homosexuals. He told me, "They know I'm a Christian, and when they are brought into the station, they say to me, 'Preach us a sermon!' But I never cast my pearls before swine." He looked at me and said, "I guess you think I'm a little hard-boiled, but I was a flatfoot in that area, and I know those folk. I worked with them for years."

May I say to you, there are swine and there are dogs in our society. What are we to do? Jesus tells us that we are *not* to judge, and then He tells us we are to judge. Well, He tells us in the next verse what we are to do.

PRAYER, THE WAY OUT OF THE DILEMMA

Ask, and it shall be given you; seek, and ye shall find; knock, and it shall be opened unto you:

For every one that asketh receiveth; and he that seeketh findeth; and to him that knocketh it shall be opened [Matt. 7:7–8].

How to meet the people of this world is the greatest problem facing a child of God. Every day we rub shoulders with princes and paupers, gentlemen and scoundrels, truc and false professors. Some folk need our friendship and help, and we need them, and we ought to pull them to our hearts. Others are rascals and will destroy us, and we need to push them from us. How are we to know? To ask, seek, and knock definitely refers to this problem. These verses can be used for other situations also, but it is this situation that they have primary reference to.

While I was a pastor in downtown Los Angeles for twenty-one years, I met people from all walks of life. It took me thirty minutes to drive from my home to the church, and during that time I would tell the Lord I was going to meet some new people during the day and would ask Him to please tell me how I should act with each one. Some people would need my help, but others might try to put a knife in my back. You would be surprised how many times I have been fooled by people. Isn't it interesting that Peter, in the early church, knew Ananias and Sapphira were lying (Acts 5:1–11)? I can never tell when someone is lying. I do not have the spiritual discernment that they had in the early church. I believe it is a gift that only some people have today, and it is important to make discernment a matter of prayer. When you meet new friends, do you ever ask God to make it clear to you how to treat them? I have found out that it is a good idea to do this.

The next verses go on to say that God wants to help you in these matters.

Or what man is there of you, whom if his son ask bread, will he give him a stone?

Or if he ask a fish, will he give him a serpent?

If ye then, being evil, know how to give good gifts unto your children, how much more shall your Father which is in heaven give good things to them that ask him? [Matt. 7:9–11].

Now the so-called Golden Rule comes right in here—

Therefore all things whatsoever ye would that men should do to you, do ye even so to them: for this is the law and the prophets [Matt. 7:12].

All right, when you meet somebody new, how are you going to treat him? You don't know—you are not to judge—but if he is a dog or a swine, you had better know. You have to beware of phonies today. So what do you do? Make it a matter of prayer. "*Therefore* all things whatsoever ye would that men should do to you, do ye even so to them." This is the principle on which you should operate. "Therefore" is the most important word in the Golden Rule. It relates the Golden Rule to that which precedes it. That is, it postulates it on prayer. It all comes together in one package. Don't lift out the Golden Rule and say that you live by it. Understand what the Lord is talking about. Only as we "ask, seek, and knock" are we able to live in the light of the Golden Rule.

THE TWO WAYS

Enter ye in at the strait gate: for wide is the gate, and broad is the way, that leadeth to destruction, and many there be which go in thereat:

Because strait is the gate, and narrow is the way, which leadeth unto life, and few there be that find it [Matt. 7:13–14].

The picture which is given here is not that of a choice between a broad white way with lots of fun and a narrow, dark, uninviting alley. Actually, He is giving a picture of a funnel. If you enter the funnel at the broad end, it keeps narrowing down until you come to death, destruction, and hell. But you can enter the funnel at the narrow part. That's where Christ is—He is the way, the truth, and the life. He says, ". . . I am come that they might have life, and that they might have it more abundantly" (John 10:10). And the longer you walk with Him, the wider it gets. Remember that in Ezekiel's prophecy (ch. 47) there was a river flowing out from the throne of God which began as a little stream and widened out until it became a great river. That pictures the life of a child of God—it gets better every day. This is what our Lord was talking about.

Beware of false prophets, which come to you in sheep's clothing, but inwardly they are ravening wolves.

Ye shall know them by their fruits. Do men gather grapes of thorns, or figs of thistles? [Matt. 7:15–16].

Israel was warned against false prophets, and the church is warned against false teachers, but both classes come in sheep's clothing. "But there were false prophets also among the people, even as there shall be false teachers among you, who privily shall bring in damnable heresies, even denying the Lord that bought them, and bring upon themselves swift destruction" (2 Pet. 2:1). We are to recognize them by their fruits. That is what we are to watch for in their lives.

Not every one that saith unto me, Lord, Lord, shall enter into the kingdom of heaven; but he that doeth the will of my Father which is in heaven [Matt. 7:21].

You can run around and mouth about living by the Golden Rule, but the point is: Are you doing the will of the Father in heaven? If you are doing His will, you'll come to Christ, recognizing that you need a Savior.

Many will say to me in that day, Lord, Lord, have we not prophesied in thy name? and in thy name have cast out devils? and in thy name done many wonderful works?

And then will I profess unto them, I never knew you: depart from me, ye that work iniquity [Matt. 7:22–23].

Obviously these verses do not refer to believers today. Every believer, living or dead, will be caught up to meet the Lord in the air. None will hear the Lord say, "depart from me." This passage has particular reference to the Great Tribulation Period and the Millennium. This is the place to suggest that the Sermon on the Mount will have a particular meaning for the remnant during the Great Tribulation.

Also, there is a needed warning here for professing church members—in fact, for all believers. Folk talk enthusiastically about certain so-called miracle workers today, and they say to me, "You can tell God is with them." In light of these verses, can we be sure of that? The name of Christ is on the lips of many people who are leaders of cults and "isms." Just to use the name of Christ and the Bible is not proof that a system is genuine. It is not the outward profession but the inward relationship to a crucified but living Savior that is all-important.

THE TWO FOUNDATIONS

Therefore whosoever heareth these sayings of mine, and doeth them, I will liken him unto a wise man, which built his house upon a rock:

And the rain descended, and the floods came, and the winds blew, and beat upon that house; and it fell not: for it was founded upon a rock [Matt. 7:24–25].

If you have come to Christ, He is the foundation—"For other foundation can no man lay than that is laid, which is Jesus Christ" (1 Cor. 3:11). When you are resting on Christ, you can build on that foundation. By yielding to the Holy Spirit, you can build a life which the Bible likens to gold, silver, and precious stones.

But there is another kind of building—

And every one that heareth these sayings of mine, and doeth them not, shall be likened unto a foolish man, which built his house upon the sand:

And the rain descended, and the floods came, and the winds blew, and beat upon that house; and it fell: and great was the fall of it [Matt. 7:26–27].

What is that sand? It is human goodness and human effort. It is the old weakness of the flesh. My friend, I say to you that you need something better than the flesh has to offer.

Matthew concludes this section by saying—

And it came to pass, when Jesus had ended these sayings, the people were astonished at his doctrine:

For he taught them as one having authority, and not as the scribes [Matt. 7:28–29].

Our Lord Jesus was that kind of teacher—He taught with authority; He wasn't just repeating something He had read. And you and I need to recognize that we have nothing worthwhile to say unless it is with the authority of the Word of God and unless we *believe* it is the Word of *God*. I don't want to hear a man who gives me a string of theories, theories which he himself has never tried and actually knows nothing about. Today we have a gospel to give, a message of salvation. We know it works because it has worked in our case. And we have seen it work in the lives of others who have come to Christ.

My friend, the Sermon on the Mount is a glorious passage of Scripture. Don't bypass it. If you read it aright, it will bring you to the person of Jesus Christ. It will show you how you fail to measure up to its precepts. It will show you that you are weak and guilty. It will make you cry for mercy and will bring you to the person of Christ for salvation. When you accept Christ as Savior, He will give you the Holy Spirit who will enable you to live on this high standard.

THE SERMON ON THE MOUNT IN PERSPECTIVE

Now that we have concluded the Sermon on the Mount, I feel that we need to back off and get a perspective of it because many of my comments may have been new and strange to some folk. A great many people feel that the Sermon on the Mount states the way believers are to live in our contemporary society, that it is given to the church.

However, if we step back and look at the Word of God as a whole, we will see that God has given three great systems by which He is to govern and rule mankind.

The first one is the Mosaic system, the Law. As you know, early in Genesis (ch. 7) is the record that God had to destroy the entire human race (with the exception of one man and his family) because of their violence and because ". . . every imagination of the thoughts of his heart was only evil continually" (Gen. 6:5). The human family had departed from God, and He had to judge it. Out of the earth He could save only one man and his family, and from these God began a movement toward drawing out of this new population a man who would become the father of a people who would be a witness for Him. Actually, He was going to give them a land, and He was going to make them a great nation—numberless—and He was going to make them a blessing to the world. God, through them, was to reach the world. He gave them through Moses the Mosaic system, and it was a great sacrificial system. The Book of Exodus gives us the details of it and reveals that the very heart of it was the burnt altar where sacrifices were offered. That altar speaks of the cross of the Lord Jesus Christ, and God never forgave a sin apart from a sacrifice that was made, because, you see, Law did not save man. It only revealed to man that he was a sinner. It became a system of *condemnation*, not a system of *salvation*. Therefore, throughout the Old Testament the burnt offerings pointed to the coming of the Savior, the Lord Jesus Christ.

Jesus came and offered Himself as the King in order to fulfill the prophecies of the Old Testament. But His nation rejected Him.

The Gospel of Matthew presents Him as King. It is my personal conviction that everything in this gospel is to be understood in the light of the fact that He is the King. In the Gospel of Matthew, as we have indicated, He was born a King, He lived a King, He died a King, He rose again from the dead as a King, and He is coming again to this earth as a King.

One of the things that He did while He was here on earth was to enunciate a law that was different from the Mosaic Law. It was the so-called Sermon on the Mount, recorded in Matthew 5–7. Excerpts of it are found in the other gospels, but in Matthew it is given in its fullest extent. As I have mentioned, I am confident that it is an abridged edition, and the evidence of this is that He took two of the Mosaic commandments and lifted them to a higher degree of interpretation than they ever had been held in the Old Testament. For example, He said that if you are angry with your brother, you are guilty of murder. There is nothing about that in the Old Testament. Also, He said that if you so much as look upon a woman to commit adultery in your heart, that you are guilty of it. Believe me, friend, that involves half the human race today. There are very few men who are not guilty of breaking that commandment. Sometime ago a very fine looking woman, a wonderful Christian, and an excellent Bible teacher, told about meeting a certain man, and he happened to be a preacher. She said, "When he looked at me, I could tell what he was doing. He was undressing me, and I think he would have tried to rape me." The man never moved an eyelash, he was just sitting watching the woman approach him. According to the Sermon on the Mount, he was guilty of adultery.

The Sermon on the Mount lifts the Law to the nth degree. Somebody asks, "Isn't that what we are to live by today?" No, it is for the kingdom which is coming on the earth. At that time we will probably have the unabridged edition of the Sermon on the Mount. It will be the law of the kingdom, which Christ will set up in the future. There are great principles in it for us, but we have been given a different system. You and I are living in what is called the age of grace or the age of the Holy Spirit. It is a time when God saves by grace, not by keeping a law, not by following a law. We are not saved by anything that we do. Frankly, friend, you are not a Christian until you *believe* something, and that something is ". . . that Christ died for our sins according to the scriptures; And that he was buried, and that he rose again the third day according to the scriptures" (1 Cor. 15:3–4). That is the gospel; that is what saves you.

After you have been saved, God has a way for you to live, and that way is not the Mosaic Law, not the Ten Commandments. Oh, I know what all the great denominations teach. I was brought up and educated in one of them. My Shorter Catechism, when it comes to the subject of sanctification and how to live for God, drags in the Ten Commandments. Suppose you did keep all ten of the commandments (which you don't), that wouldn't save you, because that which saves you is faith in the Lord Jesus Christ. Therefore, the Law cannot save you.

Neither is the Law a way of life; it is not the Christian way of life. Immediately someone asks, "Does that mean you can break it?" Of course it does not give you freedom to break it. It merely means that we have a way of life which is much higher than the Ten Commandments. "But," you may argue, "you have just said that the Sermon on the Mount lifts the Law to the nth degree, so that must be our way of life." No, that's not it. Have you ever stopped to consider if you could keep the Sermon on the Mount?

Are you ready for some startling statements? The Sermon on the Mount has made more hypocrites in the church than anything else. I told you the story of a man who was a church member and an officer but who could cuss like a proverbial sailor, and he thought he was a Christian. When I turned on the light of the Sermon on the Mount, I found that all he did was vote for it; he just approved of it. He didn't keep it. He could not live by it. No one can live by it. You see, it provides a veneer of religion which a great many people assume when their heart is not changed. The *heart* of man has to be *changed*.

As a result, liberalism is not only found in politics, but liberalism in theology has played a great part. They talk about the fatherhood of God and the brotherhood of man. Well, the Lord Jesus contradicted that theory when He said even to the religious rulers of His day, "Ye are of your father the devil . . . ." (John 8:44). Evidently, there were some folk in that day who couldn't call God their Father. The universal fatherhood of God did not apply then, and it does not apply today. Since World War II, the United States has attempted to deal with the world in a spirit of brotherly love. We are hated by many of the nations of the world today and are envied by the rest of them. We have spent literally billions of dollars to buy peace, and we do not have peace in the world today. Why? Because, friend, you cannot run the world by the Sermon on the Mount. We have had politicians who have tried to put these principles to work. Well, aren't the principles good? Of course they are good, but there is something wrong. What is wrong? It is the *heart* of man that is wrong. Man is the problem.

A listener to our radio program wrote, saying, "Dr. McGee, I don't *have* problems; I *am* the problem!" That is the difficulty in the world. There is nothing wrong with the Ten Commandments. They have come from God. They reveal His mind, His will. The Sermon on the Mount reveals the mind and will of God as well. Certainly, there is nothing wrong with either of those. But there is something radically wrong with mankind.

Listen to the words of the Lord Jesus in the Gospel of Matthew; He will tell you where the problem is. He says, "But those things which proceed out of the mouth come forth from the heart; and they defile the man. For out of the heart proceed evil thoughts, murders, adulteries, fornications, thefts, false witness, blasphemies: These are the things which defile a man: but to eat with unwashen hands defileth not a man" (Matt. 15:18–20).

You can have a religion that requires the washing of hands and body, and you can go through any kind of ritual or liturgy, but the *heart* is the problem. Man has a desperate case of heart trouble today, and jogging won't help him. He needs Jesus, not jogging. The Lord Jesus Christ alone can change the heart by a miracle known as regeneration. He told even a nice, respectable Pharisee by the name of Nicodemus that he must be born again. Although the phrase *born again* is being misused and abused in our day, it is a marvelous, miraculous truth.

My friend, I say to you that you and I have

to be regenerated because we've got this old nature. When the Lord Jesus talked about what comes out of the heart, He was not talking about the heart of Joe Doaks, although his is included, He was talking about my heart and your heart. You see, the heart is the problem.

The apostle Paul enlarged upon this fact. He said, "Now the works of the flesh are manifest, which are these; Adultery, fornication, uncleanness, lasciviousness, idolatry, witchcraft, hatred, variance, emulations, wrath, strife, seditions, heresies, envyings, murders, drunkenness, revellings, and such like . . ." (Gal. 5:19–21).

Now we live in a day of situation ethics. We live in a day of gross immorality. People have thrown overboard the so-called Judeo-Christian ethic, and they do as they please. I heard a college professor being interviewed on television. He was asked the question: What is right in our day? His answer was: Anything is right if it makes you feel good. According to that, if it makes you feel good to kill your father and mother, it is perfectly all right.

God gave the Ten Commandments to control the old nature. But they didn't control the old nature, because the nation to whom God gave them departed from Him. They went far from God.

Nevertheless, man was not able to measure up to it—Paul repeatedly states this in his epistles.

Now how is man to live? He is not to live by his own effort, because he can't make it. The Word says, "But the fruit of the Spirit is love, joy, peace, longsuffering, gentleness, goodness, faith, meekness, temperance [self-control]: against such there is no law" (Gal. 5:22–23.). There is no law which can produce these things. It is not naturally in you or me to love—I am not referring to sexual love but to a real concern for others and a real love for God. That kind of love does not come naturally. There used to be a popular song entitled "Doing What Comes Naturally." Well, when man does what comes naturally, he produces our contemporary civilization which is as lawless and as violent as it can be. There is a question in the minds of many serious men in high places concerning whether or not our nation can survive. We cannot, my friend, apart from a restoration of control upon the old nature of man.

How can you produce these wonderful fruits of love, gentleness, meekness, etc.? Well, you cannot produce them by your own effort. Go back to the Sermon on the Mount where it says, "Blessed are the meek: for they shall inherit the earth" (Matt. 5:5). Talk to the Communists about that. Are they inheriting the world by being meek? Ask the people of Afghanistan if the Russian invaders came with meekness. And I received a letter from a missionary in Ethiopia which reveals that the meek are not inheriting the earth. Well, the meek are going to inherit the earth—but not until the King comes, the One who was the meekest Man who ever walked this earth. He is going to come in great power and glory, and He is going to put down unrighteousness upon this earth and establish His kingdom. When He does that, the Sermon on the Mount will be the law of the kingdom. But today, how are we to live? By the power of the Spirit; He is the One who produces these wonderful fruits in our lives: love, joy, peace. How about peace in your own heart? Do you have peace with God? Only the Spirit of God can give that to you. And joy—my friend, do you know what it is to have that real joy of the Lord? Then how about this business of meekness? You and I cannot be meek. We have a proud heart. I've got one—I enjoy having folk pat me on the back. Now don't tell me that you don't like it, because you like it, too. We are proud. That is the old nature manifesting itself. But the fruit of the Spirit is meekness. All through my ministry I have asked God to make me a meek man— "Oh, God, make me a meek man. Give me humility. Make me the kind of Christian that I ought to be!" I can't do it for myself. God wants to do it for us by the Holy Spirit.

My friend, this is a new way of living. This is not the Mosaic system, this is not the Sermon on the Mount, this is *new*! God has blessed us with all spiritual blessings in the heavenlies—it is spiritual blessings that He has given to us. And now we are to walk through this world in meekness, lowliness of mind and heart, by the power of the Spirit of God.

And today we are to be filled with the Holy Spirit which will enable us to live for God. It will produce fruit in our lives. It will enable us to *serve* God. This is the high plane to which we are called.

It is my hope that you now see the Sermon on the Mount in its true perspective.

Now we are ready to come down from the mount where He enunciated the ethic, and we will see that He also has the dynamic to enforce this law when He comes to rule upon this earth.

CHAPTER 8

***THEME:** Jesus demonstrates that He has the dynamic to enforce the ethic of the Sermon on the Mount*

INTRODUCTION

The previous chapter concluded the Sermon on the Mount. It has been conceded by friend and foe alike that there has been given no higher ethic than that in the Sermon on the Mount.

Now the question arises: How can one attain to that high ethic? To answer this question, Matthew brings together a series of miracles which demonstrate that the One who gave the ethic also has the dynamic for its accomplishment. Our Lord made it very clear to us who are believers that " . . . without me ye can do nothing" (John 15:5). I wish that we could keep that fact before us at all times. You and I, in and of ourselves, are unable to produce anything which is acceptable to God. Christ today works through the Holy Spirit, whom He sent into the world, to accomplish through us what we cannot do.

This reveals an important point: Matthew is not attempting to give us a biography of the Lord Jesus, nor is he attempting to put in chronological order the series of events that took place in His ministry. Rather, he is giving us a movement, which we must not miss. The King went to the mountain, enunciated His manifesto, the law of the kingdom; now He comes down from the mount, and we see twelve miracles that He performs. This demonstrates that when He rules on this earth, He will have the dynamic to enforce the laws of His kingdom.

As I have suggested previously, the Sermon on the Mount is probably in an abridged edition. In the Millennium we will have the unabridged, which means that there will be many more things to be carried out.

In chapters 8 and 9 Matthew tells us of twelve miracles. While he does not attempt to give all the miracles that demonstrate the King's power, he gives these in an organized, logical order. Let me call your attention to this in the six miracles recorded in the chapter before us:

1. Healing the leper, our Lord touches him. This is human disease at its worst.
2. Healing the centurion's servant is done from a distance—He has no physical contact with him.
3. Healing Peter's wife's mother, He touches her.
4. Casting out demons, He moves into the supernatural realm of spirits.
5. Stilling the winds and the sea is in the realm of nature and demonstrates His power over natural forces.
6. Casting out demons from the two Gergesenes is a very difficult case in the realm of the spirit world.

The King moves in all of these different areas, and Matthew lists them not in a chronological order but in a logical order. There is a definite movement in Matthew's record.

Now let us turn to the text.

When he was come down from the mountain, great multitudes followed him [Matt. 8:1].

Notice that "great multitudes followed him." There were not just a few folk. You see, He was up in Capernaum, where his headquarters were. And I am confident that the following miracle occurred there. Of course, this raises the question of where He had been when He gave the Sermon on the Mount. I have read many different theories, but I do not think the location is important for us to know. We are told that when He came down from the mountain, great crowds followed Him. Is the King who is able to enunciate the ethic also able to move with power among humanity? That is an important question.

When I was in college, I had a roommate who had gone through a rough year. He was attractive and popular and had fallen in with the wrong crowd. Finally, drinking forced him to quit his ministry. At graduation our speaker carried us into the clouds, telling us what we ought to do, which is what most graduation speakers do. Later, in our room, this fellow dropped down on his bed, dejected, and said, "Mac, I don't need anyone to tell me *what* to do. I need someone to tell me *how* to do it." That, my friend, is what all of us need, isn't it? Now the King has enunciated the ethic; does He have power?

JESUS HEALS A LEPER

And, behold, there came a leper and worshipped him, saying, Lord, if thou wilt, thou canst make me clean [Matt. 8:2].

Notice that Jesus came from the heights to the very depths. Leprosy, symbolic of sin in the Bible, was considered incurable; leprosy was the most loathsome disease. And when this leper came to Jesus, he did not ask, "Will You make me clean?" or "Are You able to make me clean?" This leper had faith. He recognized the lordship of Christ, and on that basis said, "If You will, You can make me clean." What we ask is not always the Lord's will, friend. But if it is His will, He can do it. It is most important that the will of God comes first. It may be easy for you, but it is difficult for me to put the will of God first. I put it like this, "Lord, will You do this because *I* want You to do it?" But the leper says, "I know You can, but will You?" That is, is it according to Your will?

This is a little different from what we hear folk pray today when they *demand* that the Lord do certain things. May I say to you, friend, let *Him* decide—and that's the way it is going to be done anyway.

And Jesus put forth his hand, and touched him, saying, I will; be thou clean. And immediately his leprosy was cleansed [Matt. 8:3].

"Jesus put forth his hand, and touched him." If *I* had touched a leper, what would have happened? Well, I might have contracted his disease, and I would not have healed him. But notice what happens. First of all, He did touch him.

Have you ever stopped to think that this man not only had the physical disease of leprosy but that he had a psychological hang-up that was terrible? I do not know this man's background, but I imagine that one day he noticed a breaking out on his hand. Perhaps he had been out plowing, came in, showed his wife, and she put some ointment on it. The next morning it was just as red as it could be, and he went out and plowed again. This went on for about a week, and his wife started getting uneasy. She suggested he visit the priest. He went to the priest who isolated him for fourteen days. At the end of this period of time the disease had spread. The priest told him he had leprosy.

The man asked the priest if he could go and tell his wife and children and say good-bye. The priest said, "I'm sorry, you cannot tell them good-bye. You cannot put your arm around your wife again or hold your children in your arms anymore. When anyone comes near you, you must cry out, 'Unclean, unclean.'" He saw his children grow up from a distance. They would leave food in a certain place, and he would come and get it after they withdrew. He could not touch them. In fact, he had been able to touch no one, and no one had been able to touch him. Then one day he came to Jesus and said, "Lord, if You will, You can make me clean." And what did the Lord Jesus do? He *touched* him. May I say to you that the touch of Jesus was one of the most wonderful things that ever had happened to the man. It not only cleansed his leprosy, but it brought him back into the family of mankind and into the family of God. "Immediately his leprosy was cleansed."

And Jesus saith unto him, See thou tell no man; but go thy way, shew thyself to the priest, and offer the gift that Moses commanded, for a testimony unto them [Matt. 8:4].

In Mark's record we find that this man was so overjoyed—and you can't blame him—that he went out and told everybody he met. He "blazed it abroad!" Consequently, the crowds pushed in on our Lord, and He was forced to retire from the city and stay in desert places.

JESUS HEALS THE CENTURION'S SERVANT

Jesus now enters into the city of Capernaum.

And when Jesus was entered into Capernaum, there came unto him a centurion, beseeching him [Matt. 8:5].

I'm sure the centurion had heard about the leper's healing. The centurion was a Gentile, a captain of sixty *centuries* (companies of one hundred men) in the Roman legion. Luke's record tells us that he had built a synagogue for the Jews. I have been in the ruins of that old synagogue. (If there is any place in existence where Jesus actually walked, it would be in that old synagogue.) Now hear the centurion's request—

And saying, Lord, my servant lieth at home sick of the palsy, grievously tormented [Matt. 8:6].

This servant was in a very serious condition.

And Jesus saith unto him, I will come and heal him.

The centurion answered and said, Lord, I am not worthy that thou shouldest come under my roof: but speak the word only, and my servant shall be healed.

For I am a man under authority, having soldiers under me: and I say to this man, Go, and he goeth; and to another, Come, and he cometh; and to my servant, Do this, and he doeth it [Matt. 8:7–9].

The centurion was in a position in which he recognized authority. He wore a Roman uniform and could say to a soldier under him, "Do this," and he did it. Why? Because of power, which is authority. He looked at Jesus and said, "You have that kind of power." He recognized that Jesus had that kind of authority over physical illness.

When Jesus heard it, he marvelled, and said to them that followed, Verily I say unto you, I have not found so great faith, no, not in Israel [Matt. 8:10].

It is recorded that on two occasions the Lord Jesus Christ marveled. One was at the unbelief of Israel, and the other was at the faith of this gentile centurion.

And I say unto you, That many shall come from the east and west, and shall sit down with Abraham, and Isaac, and Jacob, in the kingdom of heaven [Matt. 8:11].

It is interesting that He said that many should come from the "east and the west." At the time our Lord said this, my ancestors (and perhaps yours also) were in the west. Or perhaps your ancestors were in the east. Our Lord said that this message was going to get out to them also so that they could trust Him and could "sit down with Abraham, and Isaac, and Jacob, in the kingdom of heaven." What a tremendous statement!

Of course, each individual has to exercise personal faith in Christ. No individual can claim church membership, or family tradition, or the fact that his parents are Christian, for his own salvation.

And Jesus said unto the centurion, Go thy way; and as thou hast believed, so be it done unto thee. And his servant was healed in the selfsame hour [Matt. 8:13].

Although the afflicted servant was not in the presence of Jesus, the centurion's faith in Jesus Christ caused him to be healed. Jesus touched a leper, and he was healed. Now He heals the centurion's servant from a distance.

JESUS HEALS PETER'S WIFE'S MOTHER AND OTHERS

Next we come to the third miracle of healing.

And when Jesus was come into Peter's house, he saw his wife's mother laid, and sick of a fever.

And he touched her hand, and the fever left her: and she arose, and ministered unto them [Matt. 8:14–15].

Peter's mother-in-law was sick with a fever. He touched her and healed her. Notice these three types of diseases. One disease is leprosy, which is incurable. Another affliction is palsy, a paralysis. The other illness is a fever, possibly caused by a temporary illness.

The fourth miracle occurred in the evening.

When the even was come, they brought unto him many that were possessed with devils: and he cast out the spirits with his word, and healed all that were sick [Matt. 8:16].

The word translated "devils" should be *demons.* There are many demons, but there is only one Devil.

Let me call to your attention the fact that they brought "many" to Him. No isolated cases are given. Again I say that if you watch this gospel record carefully, you will see that Matthew makes it clear that there were literally thousands of people healed in that day. For instance there were thousands of blind men who could now see. There were thousands of crippled folk who were walking around normally. There were thousands of deaf folk who could now hear. This is the reason that the enemies of Jesus never questioned whether or not He had performed miracles. Instead, they asked how He had done them.

That it might be fulfilled which was spoken by Esaias the prophet, saying, Himself took our infirmities, and bare our sicknesses [Matt. 8:17].

This quotation is from Isaiah 53:4. Probably this verse is used by so-called faith healers more than any other verse. They claim that physical healing is in the Atonement, and they use this verse to support their position.

Let's turn the pages back to Isaiah and look at this verse, because I do not believe it gives sanction to the modern healing movement at all. "Surely he hath borne our griefs, and carried our sorrows: yet we did esteem him stricken, smitten of God, and afflicted. But he was wounded for our transgressions, he was bruised for our iniquities: the chastisement of our peace was upon him; and with his stripes we are healed" (Isa. 53:4–5). Of what are we healed? This passage from Isaiah clearly states that we are healed of our transgressions and iniquities. You say to me, "Are you sure about that?" I know this is what these verses are talking about because Peter says: "Who his own self bare our sins in his own body on the tree, that we, being dead to sins, should live unto righteousness: by whose stripes ye were healed" (1 Pet. 2:24). Healed of what? "Sins." Peter is making it very clear that he is talking about *sin*.

"All we like sheep have gone astray; we have turned every one to his own way; and the LORD hath laid on him the iniquity of us all" (Isa. 53:6). It was your *iniquity* and mine which was laid upon Him. Obviously, Isaiah is referring to the fact that Christ would grapple with the great fundamental problem of sin. To contend that healing is in the Atonement is beside the point. So is a glorified body in the Atonement, but I don't have mine yet. Do you? Also, a new earth with the curse removed is in the Atonement of Christ, but it is obvious that we do not have these yet. In this day when sin and Satan still hold sway, there is no release from sickness as an imperative of the Atonement. Why did Paul urge Timothy to take a little wine for his stomach? Why didn't he urge him to get his healing in the Atonement? Why didn't James urge the saints to claim the Atonement when he asked them to call in the elders to pray? (see James 5:13–15). Why didn't Paul claim healing in the Atonement when he mentioned the fact that there was given to him a thorn in the flesh?

"And lest I should be exalted above measure through the abundance of the revelations, there was given to me a thorn in the *flesh*, the messenger of Satan to buffet me, lest I should be exalted above measure. For this thing I besought the Lord thrice, that it might depart from me. And he said unto me, My grace is sufficient for thee: for my strength is made perfect in weakness. Most gladly therefore will I rather glory in my *infirmities*, that the power of Christ may rest upon me" (2 Cor. 12:7–9, italics mine).

There are other examples recorded concerning this subject. Paul, in Philippians, had a regular hospital on his hands. Epaphroditus had been ill (see Phil. 2:25–27), and Paul did not use the Atonement to claim healing.

My friend, we need to face the fact that it is not always God's will to heal. However, sometimes it *is* God's will to heal. Instead of going to a tent or an auditorium where healing services are advertised, why don't you go directly to the Great Physician, the Lord Jesus Christ? Find out if the healing is in His will for you. I believe in divine *healing* but not in so-called divine *healers*. Instead of going to an individual down here on earth who claims to have power, I prefer to take my case to the Great Physician and say with the leper, "If thou wilt, thou canst make me clean" (v. 2). Then whether we are healed or not healed, He gets the glory. And we want Him to have that.

Apparently, Paul knew nothing of this modern cultism of seeking healing in the Atonement. God can and does heal today, but not through so-called faith healers.

Now when Jesus saw great multitudes about him, he gave commandment to depart unto the other side [Matt. 8:18].

Notice the great multitudes of people about Him. Literally, He had healed thousands of afflicted people, and not just those individual cases recorded. John substantiated this fact in his Gospel of John when he wrote: "And many other signs truly did Jesus in the presence of his disciples, which are not written in this book: But these are written, that ye might believe that Jesus is the Christ, the Son of God; and that believing ye might have life through his name" (John 20:30–31).

TWO ASK PERMISSION TO FOLLOW JESUS

Just as Jesus was getting ready to cross to the other side, a man approached Him.

And a certain scribe came, and said unto him, Master, I will follow thee whithersoever thou goest [Matt. 8:19].

This scribe was probably a young man, because an older man most likely would not have acted in this manner. This scribe was in the crowd, toying with the decision to follow Him or not to follow Him. He did not know what to do. Then he saw Jesus preparing to go to the other side. The Lord and His disciples were moving toward the boat, and he had to make up his mind quickly. So he came out from the crowd, apparently fell down before the Lord and said, "I'll follow You wherever You go." The scribe had made his decision. The Lord looked at him and said frankly and candidly:

And Jesus saith unto him, The foxes have holes, and the birds of the air have

nests; but the Son of man hath not where to lay his head [Matt. 8:20].

In effect, the Lord Jesus was saying to this young man, "Have you counted the cost?" Our Lord was revealing His poverty when He was here upon this earth. The young man had opened his heart; so our Lord opens His heart. I imagine that He said something like this: It will cost you something to follow Me. When we go to a place, there are no reservations made for us at a Hilton Hotel or a Holiday Inn—we just don't have a place to stay. The birds of the air have nests, and the foxes have holes in the rocks where they can go, but the Son of man has nowhere to lay His head. The poverty of the Lord Jesus! Poverty is part of the curse that He bore.

We are not told that this young man followed Christ. I have always felt that he did. I think that when the boat pulled out, there was a young man in it who had made a decision for Him.

And another of his disciples said unto him, Lord, suffer me first to go and bury my father [Matt. 8:21].

Here is a young man who has made a decision to follow the Lord but wants to bury his father first. This incident has been greatly misunderstood. We get the impression that the old gentleman had just died and that the family was getting ready to hold the funeral service. Our Lord seems very harsh when He replies.

But Jesus said unto him, Follow me; and let the dead bury their dead [Matt. 8:22].

What does the Lord mean by this? How could the dead bury the dead?

Dr. Adam Smith, who was quite an authority on the Middle East, has written several helpful books. He tells of one incident where he wanted to hire an Arab guide. He explained where he wished to go and was told of a young man in a certain village who would be an excellent guide. Dr. Smith went to the village and asked the young man to be his guide and was told, "I first have to bury my father." And there, in front of his hut, sat the old gentleman as hale and hardy as you please. What the young Arab really meant was that he could not leave because he would have to care for his father until he died. The father was the son's responsibility.

The Lord Jesus told the young man who had come to Him to let someone else take care of his father or let the father take care of himself. Does He impress you as being unfeeling when He said this? I don't think He was. It is my conviction that our Lord was bringing this young man to make a decision. Was he going to put Christ first? When the young man made that decision, the Lord Jesus probably said to him, "Then you go back home and take care of your father."

Many years ago there was a young lady whose father was a demanding old man. She became a missionary, went to a field of service, and did a good work. When she came home after many years, she found her father absolutely helpless. There was no one else to care for him, and he accused her of deserting him and of not being a Christian. Her father had never made a decision for Christ; so she stayed home and made him comfortable and gave him companionship.

The old man was really shaken by it, and during that time he made a decision for Christ. I am confident that the Lord Jesus was leading her in all of that, but there was a day at the beginning when she had to decide whether she would go as a missionary and put Christ first.

That probably was the case of the young man whom Matthew tells us about here.

JESUS STILLS THE TEMPEST ON THE SEA OF GALILEE

And when he was entered into a ship, his disciples followed him [Matt. 8:23].

We have now come to the fifth miracle. It has nothing to do with healing a body but concerns a physical miracle over nature. Here the power of the Lord Jesus is demonstrated, and I believe that Adam had that same power before he lost his dominion. Now we see in the Lord Jesus, the last Adam, the manifestation of this dominion.

And, behold, there arose a great tempest in the sea, insomuch that the ship was covered with the waves: but he was asleep [Matt. 8:24].

This was no ordinary storm. We saw in the account of the temptation of Jesus that the Devil left Him for a little season—but not for long. I think this storm was actually satanic in its origin. This was an attempt of Satan to destroy the Lord.

Notice that our Lord was asleep. This is one of the most human scenes Matthew gives us. Jesus was so weary that even in a storm He could sleep! It reveals something else: He could sleep in a storm whereas I cannot. I'm a little nervous during storms, and so were the disciples—

And his disciples came to him, and awoke him, saying, Lord, save us: we perish [Matt. 8:25].

What little faith they had! Notice how He handled the situation—

And he saith unto them, Why are ye fearful, O ye of little faith? Then he arose, and rebuked the winds and the sea; and there was a great calm [Matt. 8:26].

He rebuked the disciples for their lack of faith, then He rebuked the winds and the sea. The word Luke uses for "rebuke" is *muzzle*. He controlled the waves like we would put a muzzle on a dog. And the waves just smoothed out!

Although it is true that these men exhibited very little faith at this time, there came a day when the storms of persecution broke over the bark of their little lives, and I can't find a record of any one of them crying out, "Carest thou not that we perish?" Rather, we read in Acts 4:29 that they said, "And now, Lord, behold their threatenings: and grant unto thy servants, that with all boldness they may speak thy word." That was the important thing to them. Oh, how we need that kind of courage and conviction in this day in which we live!

Note the profound impression made on His disciples by the miracle of stilling the storm.

But the men marvelled, saying, What manner of man is this, that even the winds and the sea obey him! [Matt. 8:27].

The One who could give the ethic is the One who can also demonstrate the dynamic.

JESUS CASTS THE DEMONS OUT OF TWO GERGESENES

The sixth miracle is a tremendous one. We will not go into detail, but it has to do with the casting out of demons.

And when he was come to the other side into the country of the Gergesenes, there met him two possessed with devils, coming out of the tombs, exceeding fierce, so that no man might pass by that way [Matt. 8:28].

Here Jesus is in Gadara, as it is called today. The people living here were from the tribe of Gad. In the Old Testament, when the land was being divided up among the tribes of Israel, the tribe of Gad stayed on the wrong side of the Jordan River. What happened to them? They went into the pig business, which, as Jews, they should not have done. Once you disobey the Lord, the next step of disobedience is not so difficult. Before long you are walking out of His way and His will altogether.

When Jesus entered into this country, He was met by two men possessed with devils. "Devils" is an unfortunate translation. The word properly and literally is *demons*. These were dangerous men, demon-possessed men.

And, behold, they cried out, saying, What have we to do with thee, Jesus, thou Son of God? art thou come hither to torment us before the time? [Matt. 8:29].

This miracle opens up a tremendous area that, unfortunately, we know so little about today. It is difficult for us to understand the import of this miracle because of our lack of understanding of demons. Personally, I believe the miracles involving demons are the greatest He performed.

And there was a good way off from them an herd of many swine feeding.

So the devils besought him, saying, If thou cast us out, suffer us to go away into the herd of swine [Matt. 8:30–31].

For some reason demons want to be brought into physical reality. They seem to be concerned about being materialized. They were even satisfied to indwell a herd of swine.

And he said unto them, Go. And when they were come out, they went into the herd of swine: and, behold, the whole herd of swine ran violently down a steep place into the sea, and perished in the waters [Matt. 8:32].

The herd of swine, however, would rather die than to have the demons possess them. Mankind is a little different. Many people are demon-possessed today. We had a real manifestation of the supernatural during the time of Moses, during the time of Elijah, and during the time of the Lord Jesus. Today we seem to be moving into an orbit where we are seeing more and more manifestations of that which is demonic. There are many evidences of it all about us. Many instances are difficult to pinpoint, and there is always a danger of going overboard and saying, "I believe So-

and-So is demon possessed." We need to be wary of doing this because it is sort of like witch-hunting. Nevertheless, there are many demon-possessed people today.

When I was in college, I attempted one time to major in abnormal psychology. I knew a man who worked with abnormal people. He was a medical doctor and a Christian, and he told me that he was fairly sure that many of his cases were actually in the realm of the supernatural, cases of demon possession.

It is interesting to note that the demons did not want to be confined. They knew something of the confinement of certain other demons, the fallen angels, as they are called in the Epistle of Jude. These demons wanted to materialize themselves in this world.

And they that kept them fled, and went their ways into the city, and told every thing, and what was befallen to the possessed of the devils.

And, behold, the whole city came out to meet Jesus: and when they saw him, they besought him that he would depart out of their coasts [Matt. 8:33–34].

This is certainly ironical, is it not? These people would rather have their pigs than Jesus. Believe me, this is not peculiar to the Gadarenes. There are a great many people today who prefer their "pigs" to the Lord Jesus Christ.

CHAPTER 9

***THEME:** Jesus performs six more miracles; calls Matthew; contends with the Pharisees; continues His ministry in Galilee*

In the previous chapter we have seen six miracles which demonstrate that the King has the dynamic, the power, to enforce the ethic He has pronounced, and the chapter before us continues the same thought. We see Him performing physical miracles of healing, one that I classify as supernatural (the raising of the dead) and the spiritual miracle of casting out a demon.

JESUS RETURNS TO CAPERNAUM

And he entered into a ship, and passed over, and came into his own city [Matt. 9:1].

Jesus left the country of the Gadarenes, who did not want Him, and returned to Capernaum.

And, behold, they brought to him a man sick of the palsy, lying on a bed: and Jesus seeing their faith said unto the sick of the palsy: Son, be of good cheer; thy sins be forgiven thee [Matt. 9:2].

We are given details in Mark's account concerning this event. Mark tells us how this man was let down through the roof of a house, and the Lord both healed him and forgave him his sins. Healing and the forgiveness of sins are related.

And, behold, certain of the scribes said within themselves, This man blasphemeth [Matt. 9:3].

The scribes were of the opinion that the Lord could not enable this sick man to walk. The Lord, knowing the thought of their minds and the evil in their hearts, asked them—

For whether is easier, to say, Thy sins be forgiven thee; or to say, Arise, and walk? [Matt. 9:5].

They wouldn't answer His question, but if they had answered, they would have had to say, "Well, for *us*, one is as great as the other."

But that ye may know that the Son of man hath power on earth to forgive sins, (then saith he to the sick of the palsy,) Arise, take up thy bed, and go unto thine house.

And he arose, and departed to his house [Matt. 9:6–7].

When this palsied man got up and walked, it meant that the One who could make him walk was the One who could forgive his sins.

My friend, you and I cannot forgive sins—only the Lord Jesus can do that. And since we cannot forgive sins, we cannot make a man walk. Satan is a deceiver, and we need to investigate the so-called healings we hear about today. Let's don't get in the way of what God does, and let's make sure that He receives the glory.

JESUS CALLS MATTHEW

And as Jesus passed forth from thence, he saw a man, named Matthew, sitting at the receipt of custom: and he saith unto him, Follow me. And he arose, and followed him [Matt. 9:9].

Matthew modestly passes over his call with only this verse. Luke tells us that Matthew made a great dinner in honor of Jesus (see Luke 5:27–29). Evidently the incident which follows took place at this dinner. Matthew invited many of his publican friends to this dinner because he wanted them to know the Lord Jesus Christ also.

And it came to pass, as Jesus sat at meat in the house, behold, many publicans and sinners came and sat down with him and his diciples.

And when the Pharisees saw it, they said unto his disciples, Why eateth your Master with publicans and sinners? [Matt. 9:10–11].

The Pharisees did not believe in eating with publicans and sinners. Many saints today still have the same idea. It doesn't hurt to invite sinners to dinner because they are the ones who need to be reached for Christ. We need to have some contact with sinners.

But when Jesus heard that, he said unto them, They that be whole need not a physician, but they that are sick [Matt. 9:12].

Jesus is the Great Physician. He has come to heal mankind of their basic problem, which is sin. This ought to be said to a lot of our little Christian groups who have their banquets and "fellowship" meetings and do not invite the unsaved. If the unsaved do come, the majority of the Christians freeze them out anyway. May I say to you that I think some of these so-called Christian groups are *sinful* in their very existence and in the way they meet today.

But go ye and learn what that meaneth, I will have mercy, and not sacrifice: for I am not come to call the righteous, but sinners to repentance [Matt. 9:13].

Matthew is at it again, quoting Hosea 6:6 from the Old Testament.

When Jesus said, "For I am not come to call the righteous, but sinners to repentance," He could have included the Pharisees, because they were sinners. In fact, all of us are included—"For *all* have sinned, and come short of the glory of God" (Rom. 3:23, italics mine).

PARABLE OF OLD GARMENT AND OLD BOTTLES

Then came to him the disciples of John, saying, Why do we and the Pharisees fast oft, but thy disciples fast not? [Matt. 9:14].

The disciples of John had been observing the Lord Jesus. After all, some of these men were originally disciples of John—we know that Andrew and Philip were. They had come and were following the Lord Jesus, and the other disciples of John said, "Look, here is something happening which is a little different from the way we do it, and we wonder why."

John, as has been indicated previously, was an Old Testament prophet. He walked out of the Old Testament into the New Testament to make the announcement, that the Messiah had come. Malachi had predicted, that a messenger would come to prepare the way for the Lord Jesus Christ. John said, "All I'm doing is getting the highway ready for the Lord. He will be here in a few minutes." And He did come as John had said.

Now our Lord is going to enunciate a great principle and reveal the fact that the dispensation is going to be changed.

And Jesus said unto them, Can the children of the bridechamber mourn, as long as the bridegroom is with them? but the days will come, when the bridegroom shall be taken from them, and then shall they fast [Matt. 9:15].

Although for believers today fasting has real value, we have been given no commandment to fast. Fasting should be done with the idea that we are prostrating ourselves before God because we are in need of His mercy and of His help. This is the thought behind fasting.

Now listen to the Lord as He explains the change of dispensations from the Old Testament of law to the New Testament of grace.

No man putteth a piece of new cloth unto an old garment, for that which is put in to fill it up taketh from the garment, and the rent is made worse.

Neither do men put new wine into old bottles: else the bottles break, and the

wine runneth out, and the bottles perish: but they put new wine into new bottles, and both are preserved [Matt. 9:16–17].

Our Lord is saying this: The old covenant, the old dispensation of law, was ending, and He had not come to project it or to continue under that dispensation. Actually, He had come to provide a new garment, and that new garment was the robe of righteousness which He gives to those who do nothing more than to trust Him.

The "bottles" were the wineskins of that day. They were fashioned of animal skin. You can see that when new wine would be put into a new wineskin, it would expand. But an old wineskin had reached the place of maximum expansion; when it was filled with new wine, it would naturally burst open and the wine would be lost.

Our Lord is saying this, "I haven't come to sew patches on an old garment. I have come to present a new garment, something which is altogether new." This was very radical. John summed it up in his gospel when he said, "For the law was given by Moses, but grace and truth came by Jesus Christ" (John 1:17).

JESUS HEALS A WOMAN AND RAISES A CHILD FROM THE DEAD

We come to the eighth and ninth miracles which, in a manner of speaking, are linked together. Both are miracles of healing, and it is a tremendous scene.

While he spake these things unto them, behold, there came a certain ruler, and worshipped him, saying, My daughter is even now dead: but come and lay thy hand upon her, and she shall live [Matt. 9:18.].

Luke in his gospel tells us that when this ruler first came to Jesus it was to ask Him to heal his daughter: "And, behold, there came a man named Jairus, and he was a ruler of the synagogue: and he fell down at Jesus' feet, and besought him that he would come into his house: For he had one only daughter, about twelve years of age, and she lay a-dying . . ." (Luke 8:41–42). The little girl was sick unto death, and while her father waited to talk with Jesus, a servant came and told him that the little girl had died.

And Jesus arose, and followed him, and so did his disciples [Matt. 9:19].

As Jesus and His disciples arose to follow Jairus to his home, a large crowd gathered around Him.

And, behold, a woman, which was diseased with an issue of blood twelve years, came behind him, and touched the hem of his garment [Matt. 9:20].

You cannot help but notice how striking this passage is. The little girl was twelve years old, and this woman had suffered with this issue of blood for twelve years. Here were twelve years of light going out of this child's life, and twelve years of darkness were coming to an end and light was breaking into this woman's life. Here is the contrast of light and darkness.

In the previous verse note what the woman did—Jesus did not touch her, as He did in many other miracles, but she touched Him. It was not the method, however, that brought about her healing; it was her faith.

For she said within herself, If I may but touch his garment, I shall be whole.

But Jesus turned him about, and when he saw her, he said, Daughter, be of good comfort; thy faith hath made thee whole. And the woman was made whole from that hour [Matt. 9:21–22].

Dr. Luke gives us much more detail about this miracle, recording our Lord's reaction to this woman's touch and her response. Jesus then moves from this woman and continues toward the house of Jairus.

And when Jesus came into the ruler's house, and saw the minstrels and the people making a noise,

He said unto them, Give place: for the maid is not dead, but sleepeth. And they laughed him to scorn [Matt. 9:23–24].

When Jesus arrived at the home, people were already mourning for the child. He told them the little girl was only sleeping and not dead, and they laughed at Him. None in the house believed Jesus could raise the dead, but He kept moving toward the child.

But when the people were put forth, he went in, and took her by the hand, and the maid arose [Matt. 9:25].

This is the first instance of raising the dead that we have in the Gospels. Three notable incidents of raising the dead are recorded. Again, Luke goes into more detail than Matthew. Luke adds that He spoke to the little girl in this lovely fashion, "Little lamb, wake up, I say." The method of Jesus in raising the dead was always the same. He spoke to the person directly.

After healing the woman with the issue of blood and raising Jairus' daughter from the dead, the fame of Jesus spread.

And the fame hereof went abroad into all that land [Matt. 9:26].

JESUS OPENS THE EYES OF TWO BLIND MEN

The tenth miracle concerns two blind men who followed the Lord Jesus—

And when Jesus departed thence, two blind men followed him, crying, and saying, Thou Son of David, have mercy on us [Matt. 9:27].

Note that the two blind men addressed Him as the "Son of David." This is significant in this gospel which presents Him as King.

And when he was come into the house, the blind men came to him: and Jesus saith unto them, Believe ye that I am able to do this? They said unto him, Yea, Lord.

Then touched he their eyes, saying, According to your faith be it unto you.

And their eyes were opened; and Jesus straitly charged them, saying, See that no man know it [Matt. 9:28–30].

This is another remarkable case where the Lord charges these men not to tell anyone about what happened to them. He said the same thing to the leper. There are several reasons for the Lord to ask this favor, but one is made clear in this passage. The publication of His miracles caused the crowds to press in upon Him and actually hindered Him at His work.

But they, when they were departed, spread abroad his fame in all that country [Matt. 9:31].

These two men whose sight was restored just couldn't contain their joy—"they . . . spread abroad his fame."

JESUS HEALS A MAN DUMB AND DEMON-POSSESSED

We now come to the eleventh miracle. Another demon-possessed man is healed. This is the third incident of demon possession recorded in chapters 8–9 of Matthew.

As they went out, behold, they brought to him a dumb man possessed with a devil.

And when the devil was cast out, the dumb spake: and the multitudes marvelled, saying, It was never so seen in Israel [Matt. 9:32–33].

Notice the reaction of the Pharisees—

But the Pharisees said, He casteth out devils through the prince of the devils [Matt. 9:34].

They did not deny that He had caused the dumb to speak and the blind to see and the crippled to walk. What they accused Him of was that He did these things by the power of Satan.

And Jesus went about all the cities and villages, teaching in their synagogues, and preaching the gospel of the kingdom, and healing every sickness and every disease among the people [Matt. 9:35].

"The gospel of the kingdom" is not the gospel of the grace of God. This does not mean to infer that there are *two* gospels. There is only one gospel, but there are many facets of it. The gospel of the kingdom was the announcement that the kingdom of the heavens was at hand. It meant to get ready for the King. It required a heart condition that would accept and follow the King who was then going to the cross.

"And healing every sickness and every disease among the people." We see again and again that Matthew inserts this information that there were thousands of folk who were healed in that day. This is the reason the enemy never questioned the fact that He performed miracles—it was too obvious.

Again let me say that in our day a great many people get excited about the claim of certain ones to have a gift of healing. Personally, I do not think that anyone in our day has that gift. As I mentioned previously, for many years I have offered one hundred dollars to anyone who would come forward and be able to prove that he had been healed by a so-called faith healer. You would think that out of literally hundreds of reported faith healings during the time of a sensational healing meeting, there would be one case that is genuine. I'll be honest with you—I did expect someone to come along that had had a psychological cure. No one has come.

I asked the leader of a certain denomination

who has offered one thousand dollars to anyone who could prove he had been cured by a faith healer what his experience had been. He told me about several lawsuits that had been filed against him by those who had tried to collect the money. No one, however, had ever been able to go into court and prove that he had been healed by a faith healer.

In contrast to this, there were thousands of folk who had been healed by our Lord when He was here. And I would think that there would be at least one today, wouldn't you think so? Let me ask you the question: Do you really *know* someone who has been healed by a man or woman? The point is that the Lord Jesus Christ is the Great Physician, and I believe—I *know*—that He can heal today as well as yesterday. I have great confidence in Him. Now let me make myself clear: We should seek the best medical help available to us, but we need to recognize that doctors are very limited. However, the Lord Jesus is not limited. We can be confident that He will deal with us according to His perfect will, and we need to give Him the credit for whatever happens.

But when he saw the multitudes, he was moved with compassion on them, because they fainted, and were scattered abroad, as sheep having no shepherd [Matt. 9:36].

The note of compassion which concludes this chapter is startling, isn't it?

God's ideal kings and rulers have been shepherds. Both Moses and David were shepherds before they led God's people. When we pray for the Lord to thrust forth laborers into His harvest, pray that He will give them *the heart of a shepherd.* Pray that the Lord will give you a heart of compassion for the lost.

Then saith he unto his disciples, The harvest truly is plenteous, but the labourers are few;

Pray ye therefore the Lord of the harvest, that he will send forth labourers into his harvest [Matt. 9:37–38].

Having said this to His disciples, He now sends them forth. My friend, when you pray for something, it is always well to be willing to do it yourself. When our Lord asked the disciples to pray for laborers, He sent into the harvest these very men whom He asked to pray about it. This is very interesting indeed. An old bishop in the Methodist church in Georgia years ago said, "When a man prays for a corn crop, the Lord expects him to say 'Amen' with a hoe." I have always believed that you should not pray about anything unless you are also willing to do it yourself.

CHAPTER 10

***THEME:** Jesus commissions the twelve apostles to go to the nation Israel and preach the gospel of the kingdom*

This chapter continues the movement we have seen in the gospel of Matthew. The Lord Jesus, having given the ethic, came down from the mountain, demonstrated His power in the twelve miracles which have been enumerated. Now He commissions the twelve apostles to go to the nation Israel and preach the gospel of the kingdom.

These men are to go, not as forerunners but as after-runners. Our Lord gave them power to perform miracles—this was their credential. (Have you ever noticed that John the Baptist never performed a miracle?) Note that their title is changed from disciple (learner) to apostle (delegate).

As we enter this chapter, keep in mind the number of cults which come to this chapter for their authority for some peculiar ministry or conduct. You see, the instructions for the Christian are not found in this chapter. We need to consider the instruction here in light of the circumstances and conditions under which they were given, and we should be able to interpret them accurately.

THE TWELVE COMMISSIONED AND NAMED

And when he had called unto him his twelve disciples, he gave them power against unclean spirits, to cast them out, and to heal all manner of sickness and all manner of disease [Matt. 10:1].

The power He gave to them was their credential as they went to the nation Israel. The prophets of the Old Testament had said that this would be the credentials of the Messiah. Having given them this power, they are no longer disciples but apostles.

Now the names of the twelve apostles are these; The first, Simon, who is called Peter, and Andrew his brother; James the son of Zebedee, and John his brother;

Philip, and Bartholomew; Thomas, and Matthew the publican; James the son of Alphaeus, and Lebbaeus, whose surname was Thaddaeus;

Simon the Canaanite, and Judas Iscariot, who also betrayed him [Matt. 10:2–4].

THE METHOD AND MESSAGE OF THE TWELVE

These twelve Jesus sent forth, and commanded them, saying, Go not into the way of the Gentiles, and into any city of the Samaritans enter ye not.

But go rather to the lost sheep of the house of Israel [Matt. 10:5–6].

Now if you are going to take your instructions from this chapter for your personal ministry, you will have to limit yourself to the nation Israel, because this is to be given to the "lost sheep of the house of Israel." Obviously, these verses do not contain our commission. Contrast it with our commission in Acts 1:8: ". . . and ye shall be witnesses unto me both in Jerusalem, and in all Judaea, and in Samaria, and unto the uttermost part of the earth." Notice that we are to include Samaria and the uttermost part of the earth, while Jesus instructed the twelve in this chapter to stay out of Samaria and not to go into the way of the Gentiles but only to "the lost sheep of the house of Israel."

And the message of the twelve was to be this:

And as ye go, preach, saying, The kingdom of heaven is at hand [Matt. 10:7].

How could it be "at hand"? It was at hand in the person of the King—He was in their midst.

At the turn of the century and at the conclusion of the Victorian era, there was a feeling of optimism throughout the so-called Christian world. All of the major denominations at that time took on the herculean task of "building the kingdom of heaven" here on this earth. Each group thought that they had a contract from God to accomplish this purpose. Of course, the church was never called to build the kingdom. The Lord Jesus Christ Himself will establish the kingdom when He returns to the earth. The church is a called-out body from the world to manifest Christ and to preach His gospel throughout the world. Kingdom business is none of our business.

The kingdom of heaven is within us when we receive Christ.

Now notice that our Lord sends out the twelve with the same credentials that He Himself has—

Heal the sick, cleanse the lepers, raise the dead, cast out devils: freely ye have received, freely give [Matt. 10:8].

Now I insist that if you are going to do one of the above things, you ought to be able to do all four of them. Note that raising the dead is included! Obviously, this was applicable to the time and circumstances under which it was given.

It is interesting to note that folk in our day who use verse 8 as their commission ignore the next verse—at least, I have never heard them use it—yet it all goes together in one package.

Provide neither gold, nor silver, nor brass in your purses [Matt. 10:9].

Some time ago I suggested to a so-called faith healer that he go to the hospitals where they really needed him. But it is interesting to see that these folk have to be in a place where an offering can be taken.

Obviously, we need to place this verse in its correct context. These were temporary instructions during our Lord's three-year ministry. There came a day at the end of His ministry when He gave different instructions to His apostles: "And he said unto them, When I sent you without purse, and scrip, and shoes, lacked ye any thing? And they said, Nothing. Then said he unto them, But now, he that hath a purse, let him take it, and likewise his scrip: and he that hath no sword, let him sell his garment, and buy one" (Luke 22:35–36).

And the apostle Paul wrote, "Even so hath the Lord ordained that they which preach the gospel should live of the gospel" (1 Cor. 9:14), and he deals at length with the matter of the preacher in 1 Corinthians 9. In our day, certainly God expects us to support Christian ministries.

My only suggestion is that if you are going to appropriate to yourself Matthew 10:8, be sure to take the next verse that goes along with it. I don't mean to be harsh, but it is important to interpret a verse in its context.

Now notice the further instructions our Lord gave to the twelve before He sent them out at this time—

And into whatsoever city or town ye shall enter, inquire who in it is worthy; and there abide till ye go thence [Matt. 10:11].

This certainly is not for our day. The best place for a visiting speaker to go is to a motel or hotel instead of causing an extra burden on folk when they are so busy. Some people still have a "prophet's chamber," and I know where many of them are in this country; they are delightful places. But in our day, I don't think our Lord would have us go into a town and ask, "Who is worthy in this town; who is your outstanding Christian?" then go and knock on his door and say, "Look, I'm here." Again, let's note that the Lord Jesus is giving His men temporary instructions under local circumstances for a three-year period. Let's interpret it in its correct context.

And when ye come into an house, salute it.

And if the house be worthy, let your peace come upon it: but if it be not worthy, let your peace return to you [Matt. 10:12–13].

The word *house* refers, of course, not to the building but to the people who live in it, the household.

And whosoever shall not receive you, nor hear your words, when ye depart out of that house or city, shake off the dust of your feet [Matt. 10:14].

This is not our commission today. This is not the attitude of modern missionaries. Certainly, when I have gone to other places to hold meetings, I have never gone outside the towns and shaken the dust off my feet. I won't say that I haven't felt like it in some places, but I have never done it. I feel that this instruction was given to these men for that particular time.

Verily I say unto you, It shall be more tolerable for the land of Sodom and Gomorrha in the day of judgment, than for that city [Matt. 10:15].

In the next chapter of Matthew we will find out what happened to some of these cities that fell under judgment.

WHAT THE TWELVE MUST EXPECT

Behold, I send you forth as sheep in the midst of wolves: be ye therefore wise as serpents, and harmless as doves [Matt. 10:16].

Having spoken about the local situation, the Lord now gives these men certain great principles by which they are to go as His witnesses. These *principles* are good for time and eternity, and they certainly are good for our day. The child of God should be wise as a serpent and harmless as a dove. It is dangerous to be one and not the other. I have met some who are wise as serpents—they are clever—but they are not harmless as doves. To use a common expression, they will *take* you. I know others who are quite gullible; they are harmless as doves, but they are not wise as serpents. A serpent is dangerous, and a dove is in danger, so that we need to combine both qualities.

But beware of men: for they will deliver you up to the councils, and they will scourge you in their synagogues [Matt. 10:17].

I have never been scourged in a synagogue, but I have been verbally scourged in some of our good churches.

And ye shall be brought before governors and kings for my sake, for a testimony against them and the Gentiles [Matt. 10:18].

In that day this certainly happened to those who were His. Also, it has happened subsequently to many in the church.

But when they deliver you up, take no thought how or what ye shall speak: for it shall be given you in that same hour what ye shall speak.

For it is not ye that speak, but the Spirit of your Father which speaketh in you [Matt. 10:19–20].

I believe these verses apply to those men who had no opportunity to prepare answers when they were arrested for doing the job Jesus sent them to do. These men sent out by the Lord made no preparation, and if we place these verses in the local situation, we will have no problem with them at all.

Unfortunately, there are many folk who apply these verses to themselves and make no preparation for their sermons! When I was in seminary, a fellow student, who was a little odd in more ways than one, believed that he should preach without any preparation. A friend and I decided one night that we would go and hear him preach. Well, it was painfully obvious that he had not prepared his message. On the way back to the seminary, my friend, who had even more nerve than I had, asked him, "Did you prepare that message tonight?"

"Of course, I didn't!"

"Well, how did you get it?"

"The Spirit of God gave it to me."

My friend said to him, "I don't think you ought to blame that message on the Holy Spirit!"

Another friend of mine was at Temple, Texas, years ago, when the trains were running through there, and he had to change trains there on a Sunday morning. As he waited for his connection, he was walking up and down with his notes in his hand because he was to preach that morning. He was wearing a long frock coat, and another man approached him who also was wearing a frock coat. The man asked him, "Are you a preacher?"

"Yes."

"What are you doing there?"

"I'm going over my notes for my sermon this morning."

"Do you mean to tell me that you *prepare* your sermons?"

"Yes, don't you?"

"No, I just get up and let the Holy Spirit speak through me."

"Well, suppose when you get up, the Holy Spirit doesn't give you the message immediately. Then what do you do?"

"Oh," he said, "I just mess around until He does!"

Unfortunately, there are a whole lot of preachers just messing around in our day and using as their excuse this instruction which our Lord gave to His apostles. That is really a misinterpretation of Scripture. If we put these verses back in their context and see them in their local situation, their meaning is crystal clear.

Jesus continues:

And the brother shall deliver up the brother to death, and the father the child: and the children shall rise up against their parents, and cause them to be put to death [Matt. 10:21].

The coming of Christ into the world divided man; it did not bring unity. When one person in a family accepts Christ and another family member does not, you have a division. Paul said it well in 1 Corinthians 1:18, "For the preaching of the cross is to them that perish foolishness; but unto us which are saved it is the power of God."

And ye shall be hated of all men for my name's sake: but he that endureth to the end shall be saved [Matt. 10:22].

This refers to the fact that the Lord will be able to keep His own for the three-year period of His ministry. Similarly, Matthew 24:13 means that the Lord will be able to keep His own during the Great Tribulation period, as we shall see when we come to chapter 24.

But when they persecute you in this city, flee ye into another: for verily I say unto you, Ye shall not have gone over the cities of Israel, till the Son of man be come [Matt. 10:23].

Notice that He says, "Ye shall not have gone over the cities of *Israel*"—not the world, but *Israel*—"till the Son of man be come," meaning until He is manifested before the nation. It is difficult for us to conceive of the fact that our Lord *covered* the nation of Israel. And there was a real division in the nation concerning Him. When He asked His disciples, ". . . Whom do men say that I the Son of man am?" (Matt. 16:13), they gave Him several answers. Everybody had his own opinion about Him. In our day He is still the most controversial Person who has ever been in the world.

PRINCIPLES THAT ARE TO GOVERN THE LIVES OF ALL DISCIPLES

Now the Lord Jesus gives His men general instructions. Again, these are great principles which you and I can certainly apply to ourselves, although the direct interpretation is to the twelve apostles.

The disciple is not above his master, nor the servant above his lord [Matt. 10:24].

We need to keep in mind that we are representing the Lord Jesus Christ, and He must come first. If we do not put Him first, we will have trouble—I mean trouble with *Him!*

It is enough for the disciple that he be as his master, and the servant as his lord. If they have called the master of the house Beelzebub, how much more

shall they call them of his household? [Matt. 10:25].

Don't worry about what people say about you if you are being faithful to Him. They did not say nice things about the Lord. If Jesus Himself received ill-treatment, His disciples could hardly expect to fare better.

Fear them not therefore: for there is nothing covered, that shall not be revealed; and hid, that shall not be known [Matt. 10:26].

Friend, your life is going to be turned wrong side out someday and so is mine. God's ultimate judgment will someday vindicate believers and deal with persecutors; so you had better have the inside of your life looking as attractive as the outside.

What I tell you in darkness, that speak ye in light: and what ye hear in the ear, that preach ye upon the housetops [Matt. 10:27].

I always think of a radio as being the best way of preaching from the housetops. Put an aerial on your rooftop and you can pick up even the most difficult radio stations. This is the way we preach from the housetops today, and I think it is an effective way.

And fear not them which kill the body, but are not able to kill the soul: but rather fear him which is able to destroy both soul and body in hell [Matt. 10:28].

In other words, fear God.

Someone asked Cromwell why he was such a brave man. Cromwell replied, "I've learned that when you fear God, you do not have any man to fear."

Are not two sparrows sold for a farthing? and one of them shall not fall on the ground without your Father [Matt. 10:29].

What a marvelous verse! The Lord takes care of the little sparrows. Have you ever watched a sparrow? I was in a hotel back East, in a downtown area, and there were hundreds of sparrows around a fountain on the grounds. I thought to myself, "There is not one of those birds that the Lord does not know about." How wonderful this is to remember.

But the very hairs of your head are all numbered [Matt. 10:30].

God loves you! The Lord Jesus loves you more than your mother loved you. Did your mother ever count the hairs on your head? But God knows the number!

Fear ye not therefore, ye are of more value than many sparrows [Matt. 10:31].

Think of that—if God knows where the sparrow is, my friend, He knows where you are. You will never get to the place where He doesn't know where you are.

Whosoever therefore shall confess me before men, him will I confess also before my Father which is in heaven.

But whosoever shall deny me before men, him will I also deny before my Father which is in heaven [Matt. 10:32–33].

It stands to reason that if we have accepted the Lord Jesus Christ as our personal Savior from sin, we will acknowledge it publicly or whenever it is deemed necessary to give a testimony. Therefore, the statement of verse 33 follows as day follows night. This verse alerts me to want to confess Him and never to deny Him. However, I don't want to make a fool of myself because there are times when I am not to cast my pearls before swine; that is, there are times when we do not honor Him by the use of His name in certain circles. Assuredly, we never want to deny Him—neither *will* we deny Him.

Think not that I am come to send peace on earth: I came not to send peace, but a sword [Matt. 10:34].

This is a verse with which the pacifist has had difficulty. However, until all unrighteousness is put down and suppressed, the Person of Christ will cause the enmity of Satan, and a battle will ensue.

I wish a little of this verse would get into the United Nations today and into the thinking of some liberal preachers. Christ did not come to bring peace at His first coming. Sin is still in the world; and, as long as it stays upon the earth, God says that there will be no peace for the wicked.

For I am come to set a man at variance against his father, and the daughter against her mother, and the daughter in law against her mother in law.

And a man's foes shall be they of his own household [Matt. 10:35–36].

Paul amplified the truth of this verse when he said, "For the preaching of the cross is to them that perish foolishness; but unto us which are saved it is the power of God" (1 Cor. 1:18). Actually, families have been divided by the preaching of the gospel. Also, brothers have been separated. There is a unity of believers, and that very unity makes a division with the unsaved world.

He that loveth father or mother more than me is not worthy of me: and he that loveth son or daughter more than me is not worthy of me [Matt. 10:37].

Unless you have really committed your life to Christ and paid a price, you cannot talk much about commitment. Personally, I do not brag about being a committed Christian, because I find that I am in Simon Peter's class. But, thank God, *He* is faithful. That's the wonder of it all!

And he that taketh not his cross, and followeth after me is not worthy of me [Matt. 10:38].

I wish that I could have heard Him use that expression, "not worthy of me." Many of us are not, and it means that He is not going to use us unless we are really committed to Him. But, thank God, He will not throw us overboard!

He that findeth his life shall lose it: and he that loseth his life for my sake shall find it [Matt. 10:39].

He is putting in contrast the life which we have here in the flesh with the gift of eternal life which comes through faith in the Lord Jesus Christ. It is possible that when a person comes to Christ, he may be put to death because of his faith. This is not true in the United States yet, but it is true in other parts of the world even in our day. A man who loses his physical life for Christ shall find eternal life which takes him into the presence of Christ. "We are confident, I say, and willing rather to be absent from the body, and to be present with the Lord" (2 Cor. 5:8).

He that receiveth you receiveth me, and he that receiveth me receiveth him that sent me.

He that receiveth a prophet in the name of a prophet shall receive a prophet's reward; and he that receiveth a righteous man in the name of a righteous man shall receive a righteous man's reward.

And whosoever shall give to drink unto one of these little ones a cup of cold water only in the name of a disciple, verily I say unto you, he shall in no wise lose his reward [Matt. 10:40–42].

In John 15 the Lord Jesus clarifies this section when He says that the world has hated Him and is going to hate His own. We ought not to be any more popular with the world than Jesus Christ is popular. The measure of our loyalty and faithfulness to Him is given in the prophet's reward and the righteous man's reward. If you defend the Lord Jesus as a prophet, you will receive a prophet's reward. If you receive Him as only a righteous man, you will receive a righteous man's reward. But if you acknowledge Him as Lord and Savior, you will receive a full reward. Our Lord makes it very clear that rewards are given on the basis of faithfulness.

CHAPTER 11

THEME: *Jesus continues His ministry; is quizzed by the disciples of John; rejects the cities where He has performed mighty works, and issues a new invitation to individuals*

The movement continues in this chapter. The Lord Jesus has enunciated the ethic, He has performed the miracles, and He has sent His disciples out to present His claims—they have gone down the highways and byways until they have covered all the cities of Israel. Now what is the reception? What is the reaction to His messianic claim? Let me give it to you in one word: *rejection!*

This chapter makes a turning point in the ministry of the Lord Jesus Christ. In verses 28–30 we will see that He gives a new message. It is a definite departure from the message of repentance in view of the presence of the King.

And it came to pass, when Jesus had made an end of commanding his twelve disciples, he departed thence to teach and to preach in their cities [Matt. 11:1].

Having sent out His disciples, He Himself goes out. How important it was to get the Word of God out to the people! And in our day it is equally important.

JESUS QUIZZED BY THE DISCIPLES OF JOHN

Now when John had heard in the prison the works of Christ, he sent two of his disciples [Matt. 11:2].

Back in Matthew 4:12 it is recorded that John the Baptist was put in prison. So he has been imprisoned for a while now, but he has been kept informed about the movements of the Lord Jesus. John's disciples have been watching Jesus and reporting to John. John is expecting any day for the door of his prison to be opened, because he believes that Jesus is coming immediately to the throne to establish His kingdom.

And said unto him, Art thou he that should come, or do we look for another? [Matt. 11:3].

John's question is a logical one. He has every reason to believe that the King would have assumed power by this time. He is definitely puzzled that the Lord is moving so slowly toward the throne.

Note the Lord's answer to John.

Jesus answered and said unto them, Go and shew John again those things which ye do hear and see:

The blind receive their sight, and the lame walk, the lepers are cleansed, and the deaf hear, the dead are raised up, and the poor have the gospel preached to them.

And blessed is he, whosoever shall not be offended in me [Matt. 11:4–6].

The answer of Jesus is remarkable and can be understood only in light of the credentials which the Old Testament said the Messiah would have. This is a direct reference to Isaiah 35:4–6: "Say to them that are of a fearful heart, Be strong, fear not: behold, your God will come with vengeance, even God with a recompence; he will come and save you. Then the eyes of the blind shall be opened, and the ears of the deaf shall be unstopped. Then shall the lame man leap as an hart, and the tongue of the dumb sing: for in the wilderness shall waters break out, and streams in the desert."

Now waters did not break out in the wilderness nor were there streams in the desert when Jesus came. Why? Because He did not establish the kingdom when He came the first time. But He was the King, and He had the credentials of the Messiah—that is all He is saying. John would recognize the credentials.

JESUS PAYS TRIBUTE TO JOHN THE BAPTIST

In the following verses the Lord Jesus defends John in case anyone wanted to criticize him.

And as they departed, Jesus began to say unto the multitudes concerning John, What went ye out into the wilderness to see? A reed shaken with the wind? [Matt. 11:7].

By the way, John was not the reed shaken with the wind; he was a wind shaking the reeds! In our day, the pulpit has become very weak because it is in subjection to somebody sitting out there in the pew who doesn't like the preacher. Or the message is tailored to suit a certain group in the church. Too often the pulpit is a reed that is shaken in the wind.

Thank God for John the Baptist, a wind shaking the reeds!

Our Lord continues His commendation of John the Baptist—

But what went ye out for to see? A man clothed in soft raiment? behold, they that wear soft clothing are in kings' houses [Matt. 11:8].

John the Baptist was rugged, a rugged individual!

But what went ye out for to see? A prophet? yea, I say unto you, and more than a prophet [Matt. 11:9].

He was a *prophet,* but he was more than a prophet.

For this is he, of whom it is written, Behold, I send my messenger before thy face, which shall prepare thy way before thee [Matt. 11:10].

The Lord declares clearly that John is the fulfillment of Malachi 3:1, which states: "Behold, I will send my messenger, and he shall prepare the way before me: and the Lord, whom ye seek, shall suddenly come to his temple, even the messenger of the covenant, whom ye delight in: behold, he shall come, saith the LORD of hosts." John was that messenger. John was specially chosen to introduce the Messiah to Israel. Note also John 1:21–23.

Verily I say unto you, Among them that are born of women there hath not risen a greater than John the Baptist: notwithstanding he that is least in the kingdom of heaven is greater than he [Matt. 11:11].

Sometimes we like to debate the question of who was greater: Abraham, Moses, or David. Jesus declares that John is greater than anyone in the past. No one topped John the Baptist.

"Notwithstanding he that is least in the kingdom of heaven is greater than he." When the Lord Jesus came, He began calling out a group of people who are even greater than John the Baptist. How can they be greater? Because they are in Christ and clothed with His righteousness.

And from the days of John the Baptist until now the kingdom of heaven suffereth violence, and the violent take it by force [Matt. 11:12].

This is a difficult verse to interpret because the "force" mentioned can be either internal or external. The forces of evil from without seek to destroy it, that is true. But also those who are committed wholeheartedly press into it; that is, they violently want to come in. There is a note of need and desperation. We have already seen that one young man ran and fell down at Jesus' feet, saying, "Master, I will follow you whithersoever thou goest!" (see Matt. 8:19). There are these two aspects. I am not clear in my own thinking as to what He meant. He may have been referring to both aspects.

For all the prophets and the law prophesied until John.

And if ye will receive it, this is Elias, which was for to come.

He that hath ears to hear, let him hear [Matt. 11:13–15].

John the Baptist fulfilled the prediction of the messenger to come, as recorded in Malachi 3:1. But the question arises: "If Israel had accepted Christ at His first coming, would He have established the kingdom immediately, and would John the Baptist have been Elijah?" The answer is *yes.* You say, "How can that be?" I have an answer for you: I don't know. I only know that this is what Jesus said, and He can do things which I cannot explain. In fact, He does a lot of things which I can't explain; I simply accept them.

There are those who argue, "Well, if Christ intended to go to the cross and die, His offer of Himself as King was not a sincere offer." But it *was* sincere. "But," they insist, "what if Israel had accepted Jesus as their King?" Well, the point is that they *didn't!* These are "if" questions we are asking, and the fact is that the Jews rejected the Lord. "Iffy" questions pose problems that don't exist. And there are enough problems that do exist without making up some!

The next two verses compose one of the Lord's parables that was loaded with biting sarcasm and irony. The Lord did not give this story to hurt or to harm but to illustrate a great truth.

But whereunto shall I liken this generation? It is like unto children sitting in the markets, and calling unto their fellows,

And saying, We have piped unto you, and ye have not danced; we have mourned unto you, and ye have not lamented [Matt. 11:16–17].

This is a picture of a group of children out playing in the streets. One group says, "Let's play funeral." They play funeral for a while, soon tire of it and then say, "Let's play wedding." Soon they grow tired of playing wedding. They go from one extreme to another. They are spoiled children. The generation Jesus was speaking to was like that, and our generation is, also.

For John came neither eating nor drinking, and they say, He hath a devil [Matt. 11:18].

John was both austere and severe. And they didn't feel comfortable with him.

The Son of man came eating and drinking, and they say, Behold a man gluttonous, and a winebibber, a friend of publicans and sinners. But wisdom is justified of her children [Matt. 11:19].

Jesus was friendly. What about Him? "Oh, He is gluttonous. He's too friendly with sinners!" They weren't pleased with John, nor were they pleased with Jesus.

There are some folk that you simply cannot please, and you are better off to forget about them. They don't like one preacher because he just stands up there and in a monotone gives his sermon. Then the next preacher they don't like because he is very demonstrative and pounds the pulpit. Or one is too profound, and they don't understand him, and the other is too simple—so they don't like him either. There are a lot of people whom no one can please, and that was certainly true in our Lord's day.

JESUS REJECTS UNREPENTANT CITIES

We have now come to a tremendous change. Remember that Jesus is the King. He has enunciated the ethic, He has presented His credentials by performing miracles, He has preached the gospel that the kingdom of heaven is at hand, He has presented Himself, but His people have rejected Him. Their rejection has caused Him to make a decision, and He rejects them. He is the King, and the King always has the last word.

Then began he to upbraid the cities wherein most of his mighty works were done, because they repented not:

Woe unto thee, Chorazin! woe unto thee, Bethsaida! for if the mighty works, which were done in you, had been done in Tyre and Sidon, they would have repented long ago in sackcloth and ashes [Matt. 11:20–21].

Chorazin and Bethsaida were cities in the north near Capernaum where the Lord had His headquarters. He had performed many miracles in this area. They rejected Him, and now He pronounces a judgment upon them.

But I say unto you, It shall be more tolerable for Tyre and Sidon at the day of judgment, than for you [Matt. 11:22].

Light creates responsibility. The Lord never had a ministry in Tyre or Sidon, nor did He have His headquarters there. But He spent a lot of time in the area of Chorazin and Bethsaida, and He holds them responsible for the light which He gave them. It is my understanding that there will be degrees of punishment as well as degrees of reward at the time of God's judgment. Even in our own day, there are many folk who have had a glorious opportunity to receive Christ, but they have turned their backs on Him.

Without going into detail, let me say this: I do not know what God will do with that person on a little island in the South Pacific who has never heard the gospel and bows down and worships an image. I *do* know what God is going to do with that person who comes and sits in church Sunday after Sunday and hears the gospel and does nothing about it.

Now the Lord speaks of Capernaum, His headquarters.

And thou, Capernaum, which art exalted unto heaven, shalt be brought down to hell: for if the mighty works, which have been done in thee, had been done in Sodom, it would have remained until this day [Matt 11:23].

What a privilege was theirs in having the headquarters of the Lord Jesus in their city! But they rejected Him. The Lord Jesus is saying that if the wicked city of Sodom had witnessed the miracles that He had performed in Capernaum, they would have turned from their wickedness and would not have merited the judgment that came upon them.

But I say unto you, That it shall be more tolerable for the land of Sodom in the day of judgment, than for thee [Matt. 11:24].

This is the harshest language of all. Remember it fell from the lips of the gentle Jesus. He speaks here as the Judge and King. This strong language ought to make us sit up and listen. I would much rather be a Hottentot in the darkness of a jungle without having heard the gospel than to be an officer in one of our modern churches, having a Bible but never truly having accepted Christ as Savior.

Although Sodom and Gomorrah were terrible places, it will be more tolerable for them in the day of judgment than for cities that heard the message of Jesus and rejected Him.

At that time Jesus answered and said, I thank thee, O Father, Lord of heaven and earth, because thou hast hid these things from the wise and prudent, and hast revealed them unto babes.

Even so, Father: for so it seemed good in thy sight [Matt. 11:25–26].

The phrase "Lord of heaven" takes you back to Genesis 14:19, where God is called by this name. He is the Lord of heaven and earth. Many wise people never learn this truth, but many babes understand it. Dr. Harry Ironside said many years ago, "Always put the cookies on the bottom shelf so the kiddos can get them." If you preach so children understand what you are saying, you can almost be sure the older folks will understand—but sometimes the children get it and the adults miss it.

All things are delivered unto me of my Father: and no man knoweth the Son, but the Father; neither knoweth any man the Father, save the Son, and he to whomsoever the Son will reveal him [Matt. 11:27].

This is another way of saying, ". . . no man cometh unto the Father, but by me" (John 14:6).

JESUS ISSUES NEW INVITATION TO INDIVIDUALS

These verses bring us to a definite break and change in the Lord's message. Up to this point the Lord taught, "Repent, the kingdom of heaven is at hand." He had presented His credentials and had been rejected as the Messiah. These cities which have been mentioned turned their backs upon Him, and so had Jerusalem. The Lord now turns His back upon the nation Israel, no longer presenting to them the kingdom. He is on His way to the cross, and His invitation is to the individual. Listen to Him:

Come unto me, all ye that labour and are heavy laden, and I will give you rest.

Take my yoke upon you, and learn of me; for I am meek and lowly in heart: and ye shall find rest unto your souls.

For my yoke is easy, and my burden is light [Matt. 11:28–30].

This language is in contrast to what has preceded it in this chapter. It is like coming out of a blizzard into the warmth of a spring day, like passing from a storm into a calm, like going from darkness into light. This is a new message from Jesus. He turns from the corporate nation to the individual. It is no longer the national announcement about a kingdom but a personal invitation to find the "rest" of salvation.

"I will give you rest" is literally, "I will rest you." When He speaks of being "heavy laden," He is referring to being burdened with sin. This same figure is used by Isaiah and the psalmist: "Ah sinful nation, a people laden with iniquity, a seed of evildoers, children that are corrupters: they have forsaken the LORD, they have provoked the Holy One of Israel unto anger, they are gone away backward" (Isa. 1:4). "For mine iniquities are gone over mine head: as an heavy burden they are too heavy for me" (Ps. 38:4).

My friend, sin is too heavy for you to carry—you'll really get a hernia if you try to carry your load of sin! The only place in the world to put that burden is at the cross of Christ. He bore it for you, and He invites you to come and bring your burden of sin to Him. He can forgive you because on the cross He bore the burden of your sin.

"Come unto me, all ye that labour and are heavy laden, and I will give you rest" refers to the salvation of the sinner through Jesus Christ. "Take my yoke upon you, and learn of me; for I am meek and lowly in heart: and ye shall find rest unto your souls" refers to the practical sanctification of the believer. There is a *rest* which Jesus gives, and it is the rest of redemption. There is also a *rest* which the believer experiences, and it comes through commitment and consecration to Christ. You don't have to worry about being recognized; you don't have to jockey for position if you are committed to Christ. Frankly, I quit joining organizations because I got so tired of watching ambitious men trying to be chairman of something or trying to be president of something. If you are committed to Christ, you don't have to worry about that. He will put you exactly where *He* wants you when you are yoked up to Him.

CHAPTER 12

***THEME:** Conflict and final break of Jesus with the religious rulers*

Again let me call your attention to the movement in the Gospel of Matthew. If you miss it, you miss the message that is here. Matthew is not trying to give a biography of the life of Jesus, nor is he recording the events in chronological order. He presents Christ as King—He was born a King and gave what we call the Sermon on the Mount, which was the ethic of the kingdom, the manifesto of the King. He demonstrated that He had the dynamic in the miracles He performed, then He sent out His apostles. The reaction was rejection! And then the King pronounced judgment on the cities.

Now there breaks out into the open a conflict between the Lord Jesus and the religious rulers of that day—the Pharisees in particular. Apparently, they were friendly to Him at first, but now they break with Him over the question of the Sabbath day.

We will see the Sabbath question in two places: on the outside in the field, then again on the inside in the synagogue.

JESUS CLAIMS TO BE LORD OF THE SABBATH

At that time Jesus went on the sabbath day through the corn; and his disciples were an hungered, and began to pluck the ears of corn, and to eat [Matt. 12:1].

We will see in this episode that Jesus asserts that He is Lord of the Sabbath day. But before we get involved in the sabbatic argument (which has been raging ever since!), let's look at the *reason* the disciples were pulling off and eating the grain. Why were they doing it? Because they were hungry. Why were they hungry? Because they were following Jesus. You remember that He had said to the young man who wanted to follow Him, "The foxes have holes, and the birds of the air have nests; but the Son of man hath not where to lay his head" (Matt. 8:20). And at this time, they were hungry. This is another reminder of the poverty that our Lord bore. And we will see Him defend His disciples' actions. This is where the break with the religious rulers came.

But when the Pharisees saw it, they said unto him, Behold, thy disciples do that which is not lawful to do upon the sabbath day [Matt. 12:2].

The Pharisees say to the Lord Jesus, "Why do You permit it?"

But he said unto them, Have ye not read what David did, when he was an hungered, and they that were with him [Matt. 12:3].

We find the record of this in 1 Samuel 21:1–6. It was during the days of David's rejection as king while Saul was ruling. Likewise, the Lord Jesus was being rejected as King; His messianic claim had not been acknowledged. Now He takes care of His men—regardless of the Sabbath day observance. And David took care of his men although it meant breaking the Mosaic Law.

How he entered into the house of God, and did eat the shewbread, which was not lawful for him to eat, neither for them which were with him, but only for the priests?

Or have ye not read in the law, how that on the sabbath days the priests in the temple profane the sabbath, and are blameless? [Matt. 12:4–5].

The priests worked on the Sabbath day.

But I say unto you, That in this place is one greater than the temple [Matt. 12:6].

The Lord Jesus here claimed superiority over the most holy center of their religious life, which was the temple. As far as the Pharisees were concerned, He had blasphemed. Not only had He broken the Sabbath, but He had blasphemed.

But if ye had known what this meaneth, I will have mercy, and not sacrifice, ye would not have condemned the guiltless [Matt. 12:7].

"I will have mercy, and not sacrifice" comes from Hosea 6:6. Our Lord defends His men by saying that they did not break the Sabbath day. Why?

For the Son of man is Lord even of the sabbath day [Matt. 12:8].

Believe me, He put His hand on the most sacred observance they had when He said that He was Lord of the Sabbath day. In the eyes of the Pharisees, He could make no greater claim. It certainly engendered their bitterness and their hatred.

Now we leave the fields where this encounter took place, and we go into the synagogue—but we are still faced with the same Sabbath question.

And when he was departed thence, he went into their synagogue [Matt. 12:9].

Notice that "he went into their synagogue"—not *ours* but *theirs*. He said something similar regarding the temple. At first it was *God's* temple, but He finally said, "*Your* house is left unto you desolate."

And, behold, there was a man which had his hand withered. And they asked him, saying, Is it lawful to heal on the sabbath days? that they might accuse him.

And he said unto them, What man shall there be among you, that shall have one sheep, and if it fall into a pit on the sabbath day, will he not lay hold on it, and lift it out? [Matt. 12:10–11].

Was this man with the withered hand "planted" there, deliberately, by the Pharisees to trap Jesus into healing him? If so, then there are two important admissions on the part of the enemies of Jesus:

1. They admitted He had power to heal the sick. As we have seen, the enemies of Jesus never questioned His ability to perform miracles. You have to be two thousand years away from it and working in a musty library on a master's or doctor's degree before you can question His miracles. The Pharisees freely admitted that He had power to heal the sick. This is why they planted this man with the withered hand.

2. They acknowledged that when a helpless man was placed in His pathway, He was moved by compassion to heal him, even on the Sabbath day. What an admission!

Their question about the legality of healing on the Sabbath day was designed to trap Him. But Jesus actually trapped His enemies. They conceded that a sheep should be rescued on the Sabbath day—in fact, the Mosaic Law made allowances for that.

How much then is a man better than a sheep? Wherefore it is lawful to do well on the sabbath days [Matt. 12:12].

This is the crux of the whole matter: Should He do good on the Sabbath day? Regardless of their answer—

Then saith he to the man, Stretch forth thine hand. And he stretched it forth; and it was restored whole, like as the other [Matt. 12:13].

Jesus healed the man on the Sabbath day. Did He break the Law? What is your answer? My answer is that He did *not* break the Law.

THE PHARISEES PLOT THE DEATH OF JESUS

This marks the break between the religious rulers and Jesus. Here is where they made the decision to destroy Him.

Then the Pharisees went out, and held a council against him, how they might destroy him [Matt. 12:14].

Up to this point the Pharisees had been friendly. They had wanted to hitch their wagon to His star and go with Him. But the Lord refused to go along with them, and they became His enemies. The break is made over the question of the Sabbath day, and the conflict comes out in the open. From here on these bloodhounds of hate get on His trail and never let up until they fold their arms beneath His cross. They begin now to plot His death, and they undoubtedly want to arrest Him at this time, but they are afraid of the crowds.

But when Jesus knew it, he withdrew himself from thence: and great multitudes followed him, and he healed them all [Matt. 12:15].

The action of the Pharisees led Jesus to withdraw temporarily because His hour had not yet come. They will not touch Him until the appointed time. It is interesting to note in this verse that Jesus did not heal only a few in the crowd—He healed them *all*. We cannot even conceive of the impression that this made in that day. It was something absolutely astounding. They had to accept or reject Him; it was impossible to be neutral.

He is still controversial today. The enemy is still after Him. New dirty plays and dirty books are blaspheming Him. You will either be His friend or His enemy. He will be your Savior or your Judge. You cannot get rid of Jesus Christ.

He healed the multitudes—

And charged them that they should not make him known [Matt. 12:16].

The Lord did not come to this earth as a thaumaturgist, that is, a wonder worker. He came to present His claims as Messiah. When

He was rejected, He continued on His course toward the cross to become the Savior of the world. His miracles caused crowds to press in upon Him so that He could not carry on His ministry as He wished.

That it might be fulfilled which was spoken by Esaias the prophet, saying,

Behold my servant, whom I have chosen; my beloved, in whom my soul is well pleased: I will put my spirit upon him, and he shall shew judgment to the Gentiles.

He shall not strive, nor cry; neither shall any man hear his voice in the streets.

A bruised reed shall he not break, and smoking flax shall he not quench, till he send forth judgment unto victory [Matt. 12:17–20].

"A bruised reed shall he not break"—no, He will instead bind up that "reed" who will let Him do so. "And smoking flax shall he not quench"—no, if that one continues to reject Him, the smoking flax will break out into the fire of judgment. The Lord won't quench it because man has a free will.

And in his name shall the Gentiles trust [Matt. 12:21].

In our day, friend, there is a definite moving out—not only toward the fulfillment of prophecy in general, but for the fulfillment of prophecy concerning the Gentiles. They are to be saved. Christ's rejection by His own people led to His gracious offer to the Gentiles. In the Book of Acts we read that He commissioned Paul to be a missionary to the Gentiles: "To open their eyes, and to turn them from darkness to light, and from the power of Satan unto God, that they may receive forgiveness of sins, and inheritance among them which are sanctified by faith that is in me" (Acts 26:18).

THE UNPARDONABLE SIN

Then was brought unto him one possessed with a devil, blind, and dumb: and he healed him, insomuch that the blind and dumb both spake and saw.

And all the people were amazed, and said, Is not this the son of David? [Matt. 12:22–23].

In other words, "This is our Messiah. He has the credentials." This was a tremendous miracle He performed, just as great as the raising of the dead if not greater. The continued miracles of Jesus in healing and casting out demons convinced the people that He was the Son of David, the Messiah. But what did the Pharisees say?

But when the Pharisees heard it, they said, This fellow doth not cast out devils, but by Beelzebub the prince of the devils [Matt. 12:24].

This is the question of the unpardonable sin. Follow this very carefully.

And Jesus knew their thoughts, and said unto them, Every kingdom divided against itself is brought to desolation; and every city or house divided against itself shall not stand:

And if Satan cast out Satan, he is divided against himself; how shall then his kingdom stand?

And if I by Beelzebub cast out devils, by whom do your children cast them out? therefore they shall be your judges [Matt. 12:25–27].

They would never say that their own people cast out demons by Beelzebub.

But if I cast out devils by the Spirit of God, then the kingdom of God is come unto you [Matt. 12:28].

"The kingdom of God is come unto you" in the presence of the Messiah. Christ is saying, "I am here! My power to cast out demons is My credential."

Or else how can one enter into a strong man's house, and spoil his goods, except he first bind the strong man? and then he will spoil his house.

He that is not with me is against me; and he that gathereth not with me scattereth abroad.

Wherefore I say unto you, All manner of sin and blasphemy shall be forgiven unto men: but the blasphemy against the Holy Ghost shall not be forgiven unto men.

And whosoever speaketh a word against the Son of man, it shall be forgiven him: but whosoever speaketh against the Holy Ghost, it shall not be forgiven him, neither in this world, neither in the world to come [Matt. 12:29–32].

There is no sin committed yesterday that the Lord would not forgive today because He died for *all* sin. The Holy Spirit came into the world to make real the salvation of Christ to the hearts of men. If you resist the working of the Spirit of God when He speaks to you, my friend, there is no forgiveness, of course. There is no forgiveness because you have rejected salvation made real to you by the Holy Spirit. And it is the work of the Spirit of God to regenerate you.

In Mark 3 the Lord amplifies the matter of the unpardonable sin by saying that it attributes the Spirit's work to Satan, that Christ had performed these miracles by Beelzebub when actually He was doing them by the power of the Spirit of God. You see, they were rejecting the witness of Himself and of the Holy Spirit.

In our day that particular sin cannot be committed because it could only be committed when Jesus was here upon the earth. There is no act of sin that you could commit for which there is no forgiveness. Of course, if you resist the Holy Spirit, there is no forgiveness because He is *bringing* forgiveness. It is like the man who is dying from a certain disease, and the doctor tells him there is a remedy for it. The man refuses to take the remedy and dies, not from the disease but from refusing to take the remedy. There is a remedy for the disease of sin, and the Holy Spirit applies it; but if you resist it, there is no remedy. That is the only way sin can be unpardonable today.

Now the Lord says:

O generation of vipers, how can ye, being evil, speak good things? for out of the abundance of the heart the mouth speaketh [Matt. 12:34].

"O generation of vipers"—you may remember that John the Baptist had called them the same thing.

A good man out of the good treasure of the heart bringeth forth good things: and an evil man out of the evil treasure bringeth forth evil things [Matt. 12:35].

"What is in the well of the heart will come out through the bucket of the mouth," someone has said. This scathing denunciation of the religious rulers by Jesus reveals that He has rejected them. Had they committed the unpardonable sin? At least the break with these enemies is final and the wound will not be healed.

But I say unto you, That every idle word that men shall speak, they shall give account thereof in the day of judgment [Matt. 12:36].

"Idle word" means blasphemies.

For by thy words thou shalt be justified, and by thy words thou shalt be condemned [Matt 12:37].

You will be "condemned" because you are speaking the thing which is in your heart.

THE SCRIBES AND PHARISEES DEMAND A SIGN

Then certain of the scribes and of the Pharisees answered, saying, Master, we would see a sign from thee [Matt. 12:38].

The scribes and Pharisees now use another subtle approach to Him. They appear to fall in step with His program by asking for a sign. They have no intention of believing because of a sign. They are trying to trap Him. Note how the Lord answers them.

But he answered and said unto them, An evil and adulterous generation seeketh after a sign; and there shall no sign be given to it, but the sign of the prophet Jonas [Matt. 12:39].

What was the sign of Jonah? Well, listen to Him—

For as Jonas was three days and three nights in the whale's belly; so shall the Son of man be three days and three nights in the heart of the earth [Matt. 12:40].

The Lord categorically refused to grant them a sign but directed them back to two incidents in the Old Testament. The first incident is the account of the prophet Jonah. Jonah was apparently raised from the dead when he was in the fish. God brought him out of darkness and death into light and life. Jonah's experience was typical of the coming interment and resurrection of Jesus Christ.

The men of Nineveh shall rise in judgment with this generation, and shall condemn it: because they repented at the preaching of Jonas; and, behold, a greater than Jonas is here [Matt. 12:41].

The Ninevites received Jonah and his preaching after his miraculous deliverance from the big fish, and they repented. The acts of Israel, as a nation, place her in a much worse position because she did not receive her Messiah and did not repent.

The second incident that Jesus referred them to concerns Solomon.

The queen of the south shall rise up in the judgment with this generation, and shall condemn it: for she came from the uttermost parts of the earth to hear the wisdom of Solomon; and, behold, a greater than Solomon is here [Matt 12:42].

Jesus was greater than Jonah and greater than Solomon. The queen of Sheba heard of Solomon and traveled from the ends of the earth to hear his wisdom. And the Lord Jesus Christ had come from heaven, but they would not turn to Him.

VALUELESS REFORMATION

Next Jesus gives one of the most profound and startling parables.

When the unclean spirit is gone out of a man, he walketh through dry places, seeking rest, and findeth none [Matt. 12:43].

A man has an unclean spirit, and the unclean spirit leaves him. The man thinks he is all cleaned up. Then what happens?

Then he saith, I will return into my house from whence I came out; and when he is come, he findeth it empty, swept, and garnished [Matt. 12:44].

In other words, reformation is no good. My friend, you can quit doing many things, but that won't make you a Christian. If everyone in the world would quit sinning right now, there wouldn't be any more Christians in the next minute or in the next day, because quitting sin doesn't make Christians. Reformation is not what we need.

Then goeth he, and taketh with himself seven other spirits more wicked than himself, and they enter in and dwell there: and the last state of that man is worse than the first. Even so shall it be also unto this wicked generation [Matt. 12:45].

This same situation is with us today. The hardest people in the world are unsaved church members because they think they are all right. They have undergone self-reformation—empty, swept, and garnished. They are like a vacant house, and all the evil spirits have to do is move in. The Devil owns them, and they don't recognize this fact. Reformation means death and destruction. Regeneration means life and liberty.

The final section of this chapter is even more startling, and it belongs with what has immediately preceded. There is a relationship that is greater than mother and son and even blood brothers! This is a relationship which is established with God through Jesus Christ by faith in Him.

While he yet talked to the people, behold, his mother and his brethren stood without, desiring to speak with him.

Then one said unto him, Behold, thy mother and thy brethren stand without, desiring to speak with thee.

But he answered and said unto him that told him, Who is my mother? and who are my brethren?

And he stretched forth his hand toward his disciples, and said, Behold my mother and my brethren! [Matt. 12:46–49].

The Lord is saying that the strongest relationship today is the relationship between Christ and a believer. Friend, if you are a child of God and you have unsaved family members, you are closer to Jesus Christ than you are to your own kin, including the mother that bore you. You are more closely related to other believers than you are to unsaved members of your family. This is tremendous! He is talking about a new relationship.

For whosoever shall do the will of my Father which is in heaven, the same is my brother, and sister, and mother [Matt. 12:50].

And what is the will of the Father? That you hear the Lord Jesus Christ, that you accept Him and trust Him.

CHAPTER 13

***THEME:** The parables of the kingdom of heaven show the direction of the kingdom after Israel's rejection of it until the King returns to establish the kingdom of heaven on the earth*

As we have said, the Gospel of Matthew is probably the key gospel to the Bible. It is the open door to both the Old and the New Testaments. If that is true, then chapter 13 is the key to the Gospel of Matthew. This makes chapter 13 all-important. It will give us a better understanding of what the kingdom of heaven is than any other place in the book. We call it the Mystery Parables Discourse, and it is one of the three major discourses in the Gospel of Matthew.

1. The Sermon on the Mount looks back to the past. It is the law for the land.
2. The Mystery Parables Discourse reveals the condition of the kingdom of heaven in the world during the present age.
3. The Olivet Discourse looks to the future, to the return of the King and the things beyond this age.

Let me remind you that our Lord followed John the Baptist in preaching, " . . . Repent: for the kingdom of heaven is at hand" (Matt. 4:17). And our Lord enunciated the law of that kingdom, the Sermon on the Mount. Then He demonstrated that He had the power, the dynamic, after which He sent His disciples out with the message. The messsge was met by rejection—Israel rejected its King. Therefore, our Lord hands down a judgment against the cities where His mighty works had been done and against the religious rulers. When they asked Him for a sign, He said that no sign would be given to them except that of Jonah. Jonah was a resurrection sign, and they were to have that fulfilled in Christ shortly after this. Finally, He gave that very personal invitation, "Come unto me, all ye that labour and are heavy laden, and I will give you rest (lit., "rest you")" (Matt. 11:28).

Now the question arises: What will happen to the kingdom of heaven? It is apparent that He will not establish it on the earth at His first coming. So what will happen to the kingdom of heaven during the interval between the suffering and the glory of Christ? Well, in the Mystery Parables Discourse our Lord sets before us kingdom-of-heaven conditions on earth during this interval, using seven or eight parables.

We call them Mystery Parables because in the Word of God a mystery is something hidden or secret up to a certain time and then revealed. The church is a mystery (according to this definition) since it was not a matter of revelation in the Old Testament. It was revealed after the death and resurrection of Christ. Actually, there could be no church until Christ died and rose again. Ephesians 5:25 says that ". . . Christ also loved the church, and gave himself for it."

It is important to note that the kingdom of heaven is not synonymous with the church nor is the church synonymous with the kingdom of heaven. The kingdom of heaven today is all Christendom (the portion of the world in which Christianity is predominant can be considered as Christendom). Obviously, the church is *in* Christendom, but it is not all of it by any means.

These Mystery Parables show the direction of the kingdom after it had been offered and rejected by Israel. They reveal what is going to take place between the time of Christ's rejection and the time when He returns to the earth as King. With these parables our Lord covers the entire period between His rejection by Israel and His return to the earth to establish His kingdom. I consider them very important.

As we begin this chapter, notice that the very actions of Jesus are interesting.

The same day went Jesus out of the house, and sat by the sea side.

And great multitudes were gathered together unto him, so that he went into a ship, and sat; and the whole multitude stood on the shore [Matt. 13:1–2].

Notice the symbolism here. "The same day went Jesus out of the house," which speaks of the house of Israel. "And sat by the sea side"—the sea represents the gentile nations (a symbolism used elsewhere in Scripture). Our Lord is leaving the nation of Israel and turning to the world. He is now speaking of what will take place in the world until He returns as King.

This act denotes a tremendous change that has taken place in His method. Great multitudes were gathered together to hear Him, and He went into a ship and began to talk to them as they stood on the shore.

PARABLE OF THE SOWER

Although our Lord gives several parables in this chapter, He interprets only two of them: the parable of the sower and the parable of the wheat and tares. His interpretation is a guide to the symbolism in the other parables. For instance, in this parable of the sower, the birds represent Satan. Now when He uses the symbol of birds in another parable, we may be sure that they do not represent something *good*. We need to be consistent and follow our Lord's interpretation.

The parable of the sower is the first of the Mystery Parables and may be considered as the foundation for all of them.

And he spake many things unto them in parables, saying, Behold, a sower went forth to sow [Matt. 13:3].

I'll just run ahead and give you our Lord's interpretation of the sower. He will tell us later that the sower is the Son of man and that the seed represents the Word of God.

And when he sowed, some seeds fell by the way side, and the fowls came and devoured them up:

Some fell upon stony places, where they had not much earth: and forthwith they sprung up, because they had no deepness of earth:

And when the sun was up, they were scorched; and because they had no root, they withered away.

And some fell among thorns; and the thorns sprung up, and choked them:

But other fell into good ground, and brought forth fruit, some an hundredfold, some sixtyfold, some thirtyfold [Matt. 13:4–8].

Sowing seed was a familiar sight in Palestine. They would sort of scratch the surface of the ground with a very crude plow. Sometimes they didn't even do that much. Then the sower would go out and fling the seeds upon the earth. Even today in our land in the springtime, all the way from Pocatello, Idaho, to Pensacola, Florida, and from Minnesota to Muleshoe, Texas, you will see farmers sowing wheat, corn, and cotton. It is a very familiar sight—of course, *we* use machines to sow the seed, while in that day it was sown by hand.

As I have mentioned, the sower represents the Lord Jesus—we learn this from the parable of the wheat and tares (v. 37). The Lord Jesus is the One sowing the seed, and I feel that this defines His work today in the world. He was the King, but He laid aside His regal robes, and today He is doing the work of a farmer, sowing seed—but He is still the King.

The *seed*, we learn from verse 19, represents the Word of God. The *field* symbolizes the world (v. 38). Notice that it is the world, not the church. We are talking about a world situation. I think the picture is something like this: Here is the church in the world, and outside there are multitudes of people who have not received Christ. The Word of God is given to this one, and the Word is given to that one, and the Word is given to another. One accepts, another does not accept. Our business is to sow the seed, although not everyone will receive it.

The Lord Jesus has charge of this great program of sowing seed. He has given me a little corner to work in, and my business is to sow seed. I want to be specific here. This is the day for sowing seed. I don't want to split hairs, but the "harvest" is *not* the picture for today. But someone says, "Didn't Christ say, 'Pray ye therefore the Lord of the harvest'?" Yes, and let's look at it again: "But when he saw the multitudes, he was moved with compassion on them because they fainted, and were scattered abroad, as sheep having no shepherd. Then saith he unto his disciples, The harvest truly is plenteous, but the labourers are few; Pray ye therefore the Lord of the harvest, that he will send forth labourers into his harvest" (Matt. 9:36–38).

This passage occurs just before the Lord sent out His apostles to the lost sheep of the house of Israel. The age of the Law was coming to an end. Harvesttime comes *after* seed has been sown. For fifteen hundred years, approximately, under Law, the seed had been sown. Then the harvest came, and a new age, a new dispensation, came in. At the close of one age there is a harvest, and at the beginning of another age is the sowing of seed. But I want to emphasize that the harvest at the end of an age is *judgment*. We will see that in some of the parables which follow.

However, in our day we are to be sowing the seed of the Word of God. I rejoice when I receive a letter from someone who has listened to my teaching of the Word by radio. Some folk listen for a year or more, and finally the seed germinates and brings forth fruit. It is my business to sow the seed while I am in the world, and it is *your* business also, my friend.

Now notice where the seed falls. It falls on four types of soil, and three-fourths of the seeds do not grow—they die. There was nothing wrong with the seed, but the soil was the problem. You can argue election all you want to, but in this parable there is a lot of free will exhibited. The condition of the soil is all-important as far as the seed is concerned.

Now let's look at our Lord's interpretation of the types of soil on which the seed fell. In verse 4 He says that some of it fell by the wayside, and the birds came and ate it up. In verse 19 He explains to His disciples the meaning of it—

When any one heareth the word of the kingdom, and understandeth it not, then cometh the wicked one, and catcheth away that which was sown in his heart. This is he which received seed by the way side [Matt. 13:19].

The birds represent the evil one—the Devil takes away the seed sown by the wayside. This is something which ought to cause every church member to examine his own heart. My friend, don't apply this to the other fellow, apply it to yourself. Someone has written a clever little poem which says:

When you get to heaven
You will likely view,
Many folk there
Who'll be a shock to you.

But don't act surprised,
Or even show a care,
For they might be a little shocked
To see you there.

The wayside soil apparently represents church members, professing Christians. They heard the Word of God, but it was not the hearing of faith. The Word was not mixed with faith—or if it was, it was a formal, intellectual faith which simply nodded the head. In other words, to folk like this, Christianity is a sideline. Belonging to the church is like belonging to a lodge or a club. These folk are in deep freeze. Not only do we find them in our churches, but some of them have fallen away from the church and are in cults and "isms."

The second group are represented by the rocky soil.

But he that received the seed into stony places, the same is he that heareth the word, and anon with joy receiveth it;

Yet hath he not root in himself, but dureth for a while: for when tribulation or persecution ariseth because of the word, by and by he is offended [Matt. 13:20–21].

These rocky-ground folk are the opposite of the first group. It was the Devil who took the Word away from the wayside hearers, but the flesh is the culprit with this group. Instead of being in deep freeze, they arc in the oven—warm, emotional, shedding tears, greatly moved. These are what I call Alka-Seltzer Christians. There is a lot of fizz in them. They make as much fuss during a service as a rocket on a launching pad, but they never get into orbit. I classify them as the Southern California type. They have great zeal and energy during special meetings, but they are like burned out Roman candles after the meetings are over.

I stood on the rear end of a train, years ago, going through Kansas. Someone had thrown a paper onto the railroad tracks. As our train sped past, the paper fluttered up into the air and went in every direction. As soon as the train had gone by, the paper settled down on the track and was soon dead still. As I looked way back at the paper lying there, I thought, "That is just like a lot of so-called Christians. When there is a sensational meeting in progress, they really get enthusiastic, but they have no real relationship with Christ. It is just an emotional high." They are the rocky-ground folk.

The third group of hearers is like thorny ground—

He also that received seed among the thorns is he that heareth the word; and the care of this world, and the deceitfulness of riches, choke the word, and he becometh unfruitful [Matt. 13:22].

With these folk the world crowds out the Word of God. The Devil got the wayside folk, and the flesh took care of the rocky-ground folk, but the world chokes out the Word for this class of hearers. The cares of the world move in. Sometimes it is poverty, and other times it is the deceitfulness of riches. It is quite interesting that folk at each end of the social spectrum—extreme poverty and extreme prosperity—are folk who are the most difficult to reach for Christ. I find that a great many people have let the cares of the world crowd out the Word of God. These three types of soil do not represent three types of believers—they are not believers at all! They have heard the Word and have only professed to receive it. My friend, it is well for all of us to examine ourselves to see whether or not we are really in the faith.

Thank God, some seed falls on good ground, and our Lord interprets this for us—

But he that received seed into the good ground is he that heareth the word, and understandeth it; which also beareth fruit, and bringeth forth, some an hundredfold, some sixty, some thirty [Matt. 13:23].

These are the hearers who receive the Word and understand it. Some of them don't bring forth much fruit—only thirtyfold, but some bring forth an hundredfold!

There must be an understanding of the Word. The Ethiopian eunuch, you remember, was reading the Word, but he didn't understand it—although he *wanted* to understand it. So the Spirit of God put Philip there as a hitchhiker. He took a ride with the Ethiopian and gave him a ticket to heaven. He explained the Word to him—that the One who was led as a sheep to the slaughter was the Lord Jesus Christ, that He was wounded for our transgressions and bruised for our iniquities. The Ethiopian believed and received Him.

Philip was sowing the seed of the Word of God. This is a kingdom-of-heaven situation as it reveals that the Sower, the Lord Jesus Christ, is sowing the seed of the Word of God in the world and that the Holy Spirit applies it to the hearts of those who want to believe.

After our Lord had given the parable of the sower, He said something quite interesting—

Who hath ears to hear, let him hear [Matt. 13:9].

Well, if we have these things on the side of our head called ears, can't we hear Him? Yes, but notice the question and His answer—

And the disciples came, and said unto him, Why speakest thou unto them in parables? [Matt 13:10].

Someone has said that a parable is an earthly story with a heavenly meaning. This is a good definition. But the word *parable* is from the Greek *parabolē*. We get our English word *ball* from it. You throw something down beside an object to measure it. For example, it's like putting a ruler down beside a table to measure it. That ruler is a parable; it is put down for the purpose of measuring. Our Lord gave parables to measure heavenly truth which He could set before us.

Why did He do it?

He answered and said unto them, Because it is given unto you to know the mysteries of the kingdom of heaven, but to them it is not given [Matt. 13:11].

If a man *wants* to know the Word of God, he can know it. He who wants to know the truth can know it. But you can shut your ears to it. There are multitudes of so-called broad-minded people who shut their ears to the Word of God. If you don't want to hear it, you won't hear it, my friend. Not only would you fail to hear it, but you wouldn't understand it if you did hear it. You must have the kind of ear that wants to hear the Word of God.

For whosoever hath, to him shall be given, and he shall have more abundance; but whosoever hath not, from him shall be taken away even that he hath [Matt. 13:12].

If you know a little truth and you want to know more, the Lord will add to it. If you don't want to know the truth, the Lord will see to it that you won't get it. You see, the Lord will never shut the door to one who wants to hear. He makes it very clear that this is His reason for speaking in parables. Those who don't want to hear will not understand them.

The Lord drew His parables from commonplace things, things that were at the fingertips of the people in that day. He gave them great spiritual truths illustrated by things they knew and could see. Someone has put this concept in verse—

He talked of grass and wind and rain
And fig trees and fair weather,
And made it His delight to bring
Heaven and earth together.

He spoke of lilies, vines and corn,
The sparrow and the raven.
And words so natural, yet so wise
Were on men's hearts engraven.

In the parable of the sower, we see what could be called a kingdom-of-heaven condition; that is, it exhibits God's present rulership over the entire earth as He calls out a people to His name. And God is carrying out His program today through the church, the called-out body, composed of every true believer. Therefore, we have a kingdom-of-heaven condition today as God is carrying on His program of bringing folk to a saving knowledge of Christ.

THE PARABLE OF THE TARES

Another parable put he forth unto them, saying, The kingdom of heaven is likened unto a man which sowed good seed in his field [Matt. 13:24].

In this parable our Lord picks up where He left off in the parable of the sower. He has told us that only one-fourth of the sown seed ever got into good ground. The other three-fourths never did produce anything because the folk who heard the Word did not respond to it. In other words, they were not saved. Of the people who heard the Word of God, only one-fourth were truly saved. Frankly, in my own ministry I have found the percentage even lower than that. If one out of ten responding to my invitation to receive Christ is genuine, I feel that my batting average is good. Other Christian workers tell me the same story. A member of the team of a very prominent evangelist has told me that only three percent of their inquirers can be considered genuine converts. So you see, our batting average is not too good, but we thank God for each person who does come to Christ. We are in a kingdom-of-heaven situation, giving out the Word of God—and this is what happens to it.

But now we see another facet of the kingdom-of-heaven condition in the world today. It is a picture of a man who sowed good seed in his field—

But while men slept, his enemy came and sowed tares among the wheat, and went his way [Matt. 13:25].

Notice *who* is asleep. While *men* slept, the enemy came. Remember, the sower is the Lord, and He neither slumbers nor sleeps. Satan is the enemy, and he sows tares among the wheat. The tares are false doctrine. There's a great deal of that type of sowing today.

But when the blade was sprung up, and brought forth fruit, then appeared the tares also [Matt. 13:26].

As wheat and tares first begin to grow, it is difficult to distinguish between them. Frankly, a lot of cults and "isms" also sound good at first. You cannot tell them from the real thing until about the twelfth or thirteenth lesson. Those are the lessons in which they introduce their false doctrine. Someone once said to me, "Dr. McGee, you should not criticize so-and-so. I listened to him, and he preached the gospel." Well, he does preach the gospel every now and then. But it is the other things he says that are in error. You see, he sows tares among the wheat.

Now we will see that the sower knew who was responsible for the tares—

So the servants of the householder came and said unto him, Sir, didst not thou sow good seed in thy field? from whence then hath it tares?

He said unto them, An enemy hath done this. The servants said unto him, Wilt thou then that we go and gather them up?

But he said, Nay; lest while ye gather up the tares, ye root up also the wheat with them.

Let both grow together until the harvest: and in the time of harvest I will say to the reapers, Gather ye together first the tares, and bind them in bundles to burn them: but gather the wheat into my barn [Matt. 13:27–30].

This is a very important picture to see and to interpret. Our Lord says, "Don't try to pull up the tares. Let them both grow together, and when they finally head up, you will be able to recognize which are tares and which are wheat."

Somebody comes to me and says, "Pastor McGee, do you think the world is getting better?" I reply that I do think it is getting better. Someone else asks me, "Do you think the world is getting worse?" I tell him that I do believe the world is getting worse. A third party who heard me give both answers, says, "What are you trying to do—ride the fence? It is not like you to try to please everybody." Right! But actually, both are true. The wheat is growing and the tares are growing. The world is getting better—the wheat is heading up. Never has there been so much Bible teaching as there is today. I thank God for that. And there are many wonderful saints of God who love His Word and who would die defending it. That wheat is growing, my friend!

However, the world is also getting worse. There are a lot of tares growing. I have been a pastor for a long time. When I began my ministry, I entered a denomination with the idea of cleaning it up. I was the one that just about got cleaned out. I found I could not straighten out my denomination. I was thankful to find out from this passage, and related passages, that my business was to preach the Word. I don't go around pulling up tares anymore because I found that when you pull up tares, you also pull up some wheat with them. But now I know that my business is not to pull up tares but to sow the wheat. Sowing the Word of God is my responsibility.

Both tares and wheat are growing in this

world. This is a kingdom-of-heaven situation in Christendom during this interval between Christ's rejection and His return to establish His kingdom upon the earth. It is not a picture of Christ's church. "Well," you say, "it certainly is a picture of the organized church." That is true, but the organized church is not *His* church. His church is composed of that invisible number of saints. When I say invisible, I mean that they are not confined to an organization. (Actually, I do not like the term *invisible* because I find out that a lot of the saints think it means that they are to be invisible Sunday night and at the midweek service. In fact, they are invisible many times.) The true church is made up of true believers, irrespective of any denomination. True believers are those who have trusted Christ as Savior, are resting in Him, and love His Word—this is the real test. Don't be disturbed that the wheat and tares are growing together. One day the Lord will put in His sickle and separate the tares and wheat. I am thankful it will not be my job because I am afraid I would pull up some of the wheat.

THE PARABLE OF THE MUSTARD SEED

This parable presents a different kind of seed.

Another parable put he forth unto them, saying, The kingdom of heaven is like to a grain of mustard seed, which a man took, and sowed in his field:

Which indeed is the least of all seeds: but when it is grown, it is the greatest among herbs, and becometh a tree, so that the birds of the air come and lodge in the branches thereof [Matt. 13:31–32].

The mustard tree is an unlikely symbol of the church or of individual Christians. Ordinarily, fruit-bearing trees are used to depict believers. Mustard is a condiment and has no food value. It's not wheat germ, loaded with vitamins; it's just good on hot dogs and hamburgers. Mustard is not a food you can live on.

The mustard seed does not grow into a mighty oak like the little acorn does. It is a shrub which thrives best in desert lands.

The mustard seed "is the least of all seeds." Several years ago a liberal preacher in our area made the discovery that the mustard seed is not the least of all seeds. He thought he had found an error in the Bible. What did our Lord mean by "the least of all seeds"? It was the least of all seeds that the people in His audience knew about. It is my understanding that it is least of all the seeds in the category of plants to which the mustard belongs. It is a very small seed.

"But when it is grown, it is the greatest among herbs, and becometh a tree, so that the birds of the air come and lodge in the branches thereof." This little seed, which should have become an herb, got to the fertilizer and became a tree large enough for birds to roost in.

This parable reveals the *outward* growth of Christendom as the parable of the leaven speaks of the *internal* condition of Christendom. The church has not converted the world, but it has had a tremendous influence on the world. Any place that Christianity has gone can be called Christendom.

This parable reveals the outward growth of the organized church. The church and the world have become horribly mixed. There has been real integration between man in the church and man in the world. They live and act very much alike in our day. The Christian should be *salt* in the world, not *mustard!*

"The birds of the air come and lodge in the branches thereof." Years ago I heard another liberal preacher interpret the birds as being different denominations. He spoke of the Baptist birds, the Presbyterian birds, the Methodist birds, and all other church groups as being birds. That, of course, is a contradiction of our Lord's own interpretation of the birds in the first parable. We can be sure that the birds in the parables of this discourse do not speak of anything good, but rather they represent evil. The birds are the ones that took the seed which fell by the wayside. Our Lord said that they represent the enemy who is Satan. I am afraid that Christendom today is a mustard tree filled with a lot of dirty birds!

THE PARABLE OF THE LEAVEN

The parable of the leaven is the key parable of this chapter. Let me try to help you realize the importance of it. First of all, the Gospel of Matthew is the key book of the Bible. Secondly, chapter 13 is the key chapter of Matthew. And thirdly, verse 33 is the key verse of chapter 13. So actually, what we have here is one of the key verses of the Bible!

Now notice the very important teaching in this verse—

Another parable spake he unto them; The kingdom of heaven is like unto leaven, which a woman took, and hid in

three measures of meal, till the whole was leavened [Matt. 13:33].

"The kingdom of heaven is like unto leaven"—but don't stop there—"which a woman took, and hid in three measures of meal." What does the leaven represent? There are those who interpret the leaven as the gospel, and they ought to know better! Nowhere is leaven used as a principle of good; it is always a principle of evil. The word *leaven* occurs ninety-eight times in the Bible—about seventy-five times in the Old Testament and about twenty-three times in the New Testament—and it is always used in a bad sense. The great scholar, Dr. Lightfoot, made the statement that rabbinical writers regularly used leaven as a symbol of evil. In the Old Testament it was forbidden to be used in the offerings made to God. In the New Testament our Lord warned to beware of the leaven of the Pharisees and of the Sadducees (see Matt. 16:6). And the apostle Paul spoke of the leaven of malice and wickedness (see 1 Cor. 5:8). Symbolism in Scripture does not contradict itself, and we may be certain that leaven is not used in a good sense here in Matthew 13. Leaven is not the gospel.

The gospel is represented by the three measures of meal. How do we know this? Because meal is made out of grain or seed, and our Lord has already told us in the parable of the sower that the seed represents the Word of God.

Remember that this parable is a picture of what happens to the Word of God on this earth during the interval between Christ's rejection and His exaltation when He will return to set up His kingdom. Note what happens to the Word of God represented by the meal. This woman comes along—I hope you ladies will forgive me for pointing this out—and when a woman is used in a doctrinal sense in Scripture, she is always used as a principle of *evil*. She takes the leaven and hides it in the meal. If the leaven represents the gospel, why in the world did she hide it? The gospel is to be shouted from the housetops and heralded to the very ends of the earth. Obviously, the leaven is a principle of evil, and the woman puts it in the meal, which represents the gospel, the Word of God.

We certainly see this in reality in our day. There is no cult or "ism" which ignores the Bible. I find that even those who worship the Devil, the demon worshipers, use the Bible. False teachers of every description put leaven in the meal, the Word of God.

What does leaven do? Well, leaven is a substance, such as yeast, used to produce fermentation. When it is put in bread dough, it causes it to rise. And it makes it tasty, also. That is the reason a great many people find a thrill in some of the cults. Unleavened bread is just blah as far as the natural taste is concerned. A little leaven really helps it. I grew up in the South, and my mother used to make delicious biscuits. She would put leaven in the dough and put them on the back of the stove to rise. If I came running into the kitchen, she would shush me because she didn't want those biscuits to fall. When they got to a certain height, she would stop the fermentation by putting them in the oven and baking them. Have you ever seen what happens when you let dough continue to rise? I tell you, it makes a pan of corruption—something you wouldn't want to eat! Leaven is a principle of evil.

This parable teaches that the intrusion of wrong doctrine into the church will finally lead to total apostasy—"The kingdom of heaven is like unto leaven, which a woman took, and hid in three measures of meal, *till the whole was leavened*." The Lord Jesus Christ Himself said, " . . . when the Son of man cometh, shall he find faith on the earth?" (Luke 18:8). The way the question is couched in the Greek, it demands a negative answer. In other words, he is saying that when He does return the world will be in total apostasy. And the apostle Paul, writing to a young man studying for the ministry, warns that the time will come when they will not endure sound doctrine (see 2 Tim. 4:3). The final, total apostasy of the church is revealed in the church of Laodicea (see Rev. 3:14–19).

All these things spake Jesus unto the multitude in parables; and without a parable spake he not unto them:

That it might be fulfilled which was spoken by the prophet, saying, I will open my mouth in parables; I will utter things which have been kept secret from the foundation of the world [Matt. 13:34–35].

"I will utter things which have been kept secret from the foundation of the world"—nail down that statement. Our Lord is giving us a brand-new truth. The things He is revealing now, in parables, have never been revealed like this in the Old Testament.

Then Jesus sent the multitude away, and went into the house: and his disciples came unto him, saying, Declare

unto us the parable of the tares of the field [Matt. 13:36].

Jesus has sent the multitude away and has gathered His disciples about Him. He is going to interpret the parable of the tares to them. We have already gone over it, but let's read it as the Scripture states it.

He answered and said unto them, He that soweth the good seed is the Son of man;

The field is the world; the good seed are the children of the kingdom; but the tares are the children of the wicked one;

The enemy that sowed them is the devil; the harvest is the end of the world; and the reapers are the angels.

As therefore the tares are gathered and burned in the fire; so shall it be in the end of this world [Matt. 13:37–40].

This is an exact picture of the condition in Christendom in our day. My Lord never missed His predictions. This has been fulfilled as accurately as anything possibly could be.

The Son of man shall send forth his angels, and they shall gather out of his kingdom all things that offend, and them which do iniquity [Matt. 13:41].

You see, in the kingdom during the Millennium there will be *evil* rearing its ugly head. But it will be taken out.

And shall cast them into a furnace of fire: there shall be wailing and gnashing of teeth.

Then shall the righteous shine forth as the sun in the kingdom of their Father. Who hath ears to hear, let him hear [Matt. 13:42–43].

These harsh words of Scripture came from the gentle lips of our wonderful Lord.

The last three parables are unusual in that they deal with certain different aspects of the kingdom of heaven as it is today.

THE PARABLE OF THE TREASURE HID IN A FIELD

Again, the kingdom of heaven is like unto treasure hid in a field; the which when a man hath found, he hideth, and for joy thereof goeth and selleth all that he hath, and buyeth that field [Matt. 13:44].

The "treasure" is Israel. The "field" is the world. The "man" is the Son of man who gave Himself to redeem the nation Israel. This is not a sinner buying the gospel because the gospel is not hidden in a field. Israel, however, is actually buried in the world today. Someone says, "Well, they are a nation right now." They are, but they certainly are having a struggle. They will not be able to enjoy their land until they receive it from the Lord Jesus Christ.

I was very much interested in reading a paper that came from Israel concerning a convention of certain scientists. In a picture I noted above the platform a great sign, printed in both Hebrew and English, which read something like this SCIENCE WILL BRING PEACE TO THIS LAND. May I say to you, friend, science will not bring peace to Israel—nor to any country. Only the Prince of Peace is able to do that.

Actually, Israel is buried throughout the world. The largest population of Jews is not in Israel but is in New York City. And Jewish people are scattered throughout the world. But God is not through with Israel as a nation. The apostle Paul wrote: "I say then, Hath God cast away his people? God forbid. For I also am an Israelite, of the seed of Abraham, of the tribe of Benjamin. God hath not cast away his people which he foreknew. . ." (Rom. 11:1–2).

Paul believed that the Lord was not through with Israel. Zechariah, one of the last writers in the Old Testament, wrote that a new day would come for Israel: "And I will pour upon the house of David, and upon the inhabitants of Jerusalem, the spirit of grace and of supplications: and they shall look upon me whom they have pierced, and they shall mourn for him, as one mourneth for his only son, and shall be in bitterness for him, as one that is in bitterness for his firstborn" (Zech. 12:10).

The prophet Jeremiah in many passages speaks of the regathering of the people of Israel and of God bringing them to their own land. That time is still future. When God regathers them, it will be by miracles so great that they will even forget their miraculous deliverance from Egypt which has been celebrated longer than any other religious holiday. God is not through with the nation Israel, and this parable makes that fact very clear. Israel is the treasure hid in a field, and Christ is the One who "for joy thereof goeth and selleth all that he hath, and buyeth that field." In fact, He gave *Himself* to redeem the nation. Our Lord purchased them with His blood, just as He bought your salvation and my salvation. Zechariah writes of the cleansing which will take place at the time of Christ's return to this earth: "In that day there shall be a fountain opened to the house of David and to the inhabitants of Jerusalem for sin and for uncleanness" (Zech. 13:1).

THE PARABLE OF THE PEARL OF GREAT PRICE

Again, the kingdom of heaven is like unto a merchant man, seeking goodly pearls:

Who, when he had found one pearl of great price, went and sold all that he had, and bought it [Matt. 13:45–46].

The popular interpretation of this parable says that the sinner is the merchantman and the pearl of great price is Christ. The sinner sells all that he has that he might buy Christ. One hymn says:

I have found the pearl of greatest price.
My heart doth sing for joy.
And sing I must for Christ is mine;
Christ shall my song employ.

I cannot accept this interpretation, and I have dismissed it as unworthy of thoughtful consideration. To begin with, *who* is looking for goodly pearls? Are sinners looking for salvation? My Bible does not read that way, nor has that been my experience as a minister. Sinners are not looking for salvation. The merchantman cannot be the sinner because he has nothing with which to pay. To begin with, he is not seeking Christ, and if he were, how could he buy Him? The merchantman sells all that he has—how can a sinner sell all that he has when he is *dead* in trespasses and sins (see Eph. 2:1)? Further, the Scriptures are very clear that Christ and salvation are not for sale. Salvation is a gift—"For God so loved the world, that he gave his only begotten Son, that whosoever believeth in him should not perish, but have everlasting life" (John 3:16). God so loved that He *gave*. And in Romans 6:23 we are told that "the *gift* of God is eternal life through Jesus Christ our Lord."

The correct interpretation of this parable reveals Christ as the merchantman. He left His heavenly home and came to this earth to find a pearl of great price. He found lost sinners and died for them by shedding His precious blood. He sold all that He had to buy us and redeem us to God. Paul told this to the Corinthians: "For ye know the grace of our Lord Jesus Christ, that, though he was rich, yet for your sakes he became poor, that ye through his poverty might be rich" (2 Cor. 8:9). He redeems us to God—He bought us.

Now let's look at the pearl for a moment. The pearl represents the church. A pearl is not a stone like the diamond. It is formed by a living organism. A grain of sand or other foreign matter intrudes itself into the shell of a small sea creature. It hurts and harms it. The response of the organism is to send out a secretion that coats over the foreign matter. That fluid builds up until a pearl is formed—not a ruby or a diamond, but a beautiful white pearl. A pearl is not like other gems. It cannot be cut to enhance its beauty. It is formed intact. The minute you cut it, you ruin it.

The pearl was never considered very valuable by the Israelites. Several verses of Scripture give us this impression. For example, in Job 28:18 pearls are classed with coral. Although the pearl was not considered valuable among the Hebrews, it was very valuable to the Gentiles. When Christ used the figure of "goodly pearls" (v. 45), I imagine that His disciples wondered why. Oriental people gave to the pearl a symbolic meaning of innocence and purity, fit only for kings and potentates.

With this information in our thinking, let's look again at the parable.

Christ came to this earth as the merchantman. He saw man in sin, and He took man's sin and bore it in His own body. Our sin was an intrusion upon Him—it was that foreign matter. And He was *made* sin for us. As someone has put it, I got into the heart of Christ by a spear wound. Christ ". . .was wounded for our transgressions, he was bruised for our iniquities . . ." (Isa. 53:5).

Notice Christ's response to the sinner. He puts around us His own righteousness. He covers us with His own white robe of righteousness. ". . . .we are his workmanship, created in Christ Jesus . . ." (Eph. 2:10). Christ sees us, not as we are now but as we shall be someday, presented to Him as ". . .a glorious church, not having spot, or wrinkle, or any such thing; but that it should be holy and without blemish" (Eph. 5:27). Christ sold all that He had in order that He might gain the church. "Beloved, now are we the sons of God, and it doth not yet appear what we shall be: but we know that, when he shall appear, we shall be like him; for we shall see him as he is" (1 John 3:2).

When we come to the last book of the Bible, the Book of the Revelation, we find a description of the New Jerusalem, the future home of the church. Notice the emblem on the outside of the city—the gates are made of *pearls!* That is no accident, friend; it is planned that way by Christ's design. He is the merchantman "Who, when he had found one pearl of great price, went and sold all that he had, and bought it."

THE PARABLE OF THE NET CAST INTO THE SEA

Again, the kingdom of heaven is like unto a net, that was cast into the sea, and gathered of every kind:

Which, when it was full, they drew to shore, and sat down, and gathered the goods into vessels, but cast the bad away.

So shall it be at the end of the world: the angels shall come forth, and sever the wicked from among the just [Matt. 13:47–49].

"So shall it be at the end of the world"—the word *world* is the Greek *aiōn*, meaning "age". The Bible does not teach the end of this world. It is true that time will be no more, but then eternity begins, and as far as I'm concerned, I can't tell the difference (and I have never met anyone else who could). The end of the age simply means the time when Christ will return to establish His kingdom on earth.

And shall cast them into the furnace of fire: there shall be wailing and gnashing of teeth [Matt. 13:50].

Our Lord makes it clear in this section that it is a terrible thing to be *lost.*

I was very much interested in reading a scientific paper written by men who were presenting certain scientific evidence in several different fields, and their point was that science was not sure of many things. For example, they were not sure exactly what the atom blast would do. They were not sure of the consequences of germ warfare. They were not sure about the effect of the birth control pill. And many other things were mentioned. Then one of the scientists said this, "It's just like this matter of eternity. You may not *know* whether there is a heaven or a hell, but you had better make sure that you are going to heaven because even if you happen to be wrong, you'll be all right. But if you are wrong, it is surely going to be bad." And our Lord made it very clear that it is indeed going to be very bad.

It is considered sophisticated in our day to be a suave person. Certainly, you will not be considered a square if you deny the existence of hell. But, my friend, in reality you don't know a thing about it, do you? You may say, "Well, you don't know either." Well, I know what is in this Book. And since the Bible has been accurate in everything it has predicted, and since in my own life I have proven it true, I take it for granted that it is accurate in its description of hell. And I work on that premise—and it's more than a premise.

If you were told that a hurricane was going to hit your town, what would you do? After you had been given the information, someone might come along and say, "Oh, they warned of a hurricane ten years ago, and no hurricane came." I think you would say, "Well, they might have been wrong ten years ago, but they could be right this time; so I think I'll go to a storm cellar." You would be a fool if you didn't. What about the man who rejects Christ's warning of hell? He says, "I'll take my chance." It will be too bad if he is wrong. Our Lord Jesus Himself makes this fact very clear in this parable when He says, "the angels shall come forth, and sever the wicked from among the just, And shall cast them into the furnace of fire: there shall be wailing and gnashing of teeth."

THE PARABLE OF THE HOUSEHOLDER

Some people call this verse a parable and others do not. Nevertheless, the content of this single verse has an important message for us.

Then said he unto them, Therefore every scribe which is instructed unto the kingdom of heaven is like unto a man that is an householder, which bringeth forth out of his treasure things new and old [Matt. 13:52].

This is a very personal verse, especially for those of us who teach and preach the Word of God. I am to bring forth both the old and new. Some folk say to me, "Oh, I've heard all of that before." Of course they have. But it is my business to bring forth old things, but I do hope to bring forth a few new thoughts, also.

JESUS RETURNS TO HIS OWN COUNTRY AND IS REJECTED

After teaching these parables, the Lord Jesus departed and headed toward Nazareth, His hometown.

And when he was come into his own country, he taught them in their syna-

gogue, insomuch that they were astonished, and said, Whence hath this man this wisdom, and these mighty works? [Matt. 13:54].

Let me call your attention again to the fact that in Christ's day they never questioned whether or not He could perform miracles. Their question was, "Whence hath this man this wisdom, and these mighty works?" Where does He get His wisdom, and how can He do these mighty works?

Is not this the carpenter's son? is not his mother called Mary? and his brethren, James, and Joses, and Simon, and Judas? [Matt. 13:55].

"Is not this the carpenter's son?" That was what confused them. They did not recognize who He really was. To them He was just a carpenter's son. And that is all He is to some folk in our day. They think He was a great teacher, a great man, a wonderful person, but to them He was only a carpenter's son.

And his sisters, are they not all with us? Whence then hath this man all these things? [Matt. 13:56].

It is obvious that the Lord Jesus had brothers and sisters—of course, they were half brothers and half sisters, younger than He was, and born of Mary and Joseph. They did not understand until after His resurrection that He was truly the Son of God.

And they were offended in him. But Jesus said unto them, A prophet is not without honour, save in his own country, and in his own house [Matt. 13:57].

You see, His hometown folk were so familiar with Him and with His family that they were "offended in him." That is, they took offense at Him. I suppose they said, "We know His family. He grew up among us. Where does He get the things He teaches?"

And he did not many mighty works there because of their unbelief [Matt. 13:58].

This is a tremendous revelation. Note what it was that limited the power of God when He was here. It was unbelief! "He did not many mighty works there because of their unbelief." It was not that He was unable to do them; but because of their *unbelief*, He did very few miracles there. My friend, the great problem with you and me is that we do not have faith to believe—and I'm talking about faith for the salvation of men and women. We need the kind of faith that believes Christ can save the lost. He is limited today in your own community, in your church, in your family, and in your own life by *unbelief*. And this is certainly true of me also. Our Lord states a great truth here. Let's not bypass it.

CHAPTER 14

THEME: *The forerunner, John the Baptist, is beheaded; Jesus withdraws but is followed by the multitude; He feeds the five thousand and sends His disciples over the sea into a storm, then walks on the water to them*

The movement in Matthew of the rejection of Jesus as King and His conflict with the religious rulers continues. This chapter reveals that events are moving to a crisis. John the Baptist is slain on the pretext that Herod must keep his oath. This is an overt act of antagonism toward light and right which must ultimately lay wicked hands on Jesus. Jesus withdraws in order not to force the wicked hand of Herod, for the hour of Jesus has not yet come.

The feeding of the five thousand is certainly the most important of the miracles of Jesus if we are to judge by the attention given to it by the gospel writers. It is the only miracle recorded by all the gospel writers.

THE MURDER OF JOHN THE BAPTIST

At that time Herod the tetrarch heard of the fame of Jesus,

And said unto his servants, This is John the Baptist; he is risen from the dead;

and therefore mighty works do shew forth themselves in him [Matt. 14:1–2].

If this sounds superstitious to you, you are right. It *is* superstitious, but it is not the superstition of the Bible nor of Jesus nor of His apostles, nor is it the superstition of Christianity. It is the superstition of old Herod and also of other ignorant people of that day. Somebody says, "Well, of course, in our contemporary society we are not superstitious like that." Aren't we? Notice how many people are following the horoscope and astrology charts. Also, religions of the Orient are having a tremendous influence in our modern culture. The human race is basically superstitious, my friend, and the minute you get away from the Word of God, you become superstitious. Even those who call themselves atheistic are turning to cults and "isms" and pagan religions, and we marvel that intelligent people could become involved in them.

The Person and the ministry of Jesus could not escape the notice of the king on the throne. Herod was a member of the family that you ought to look up in a good Bible dictionary. The whole family was a bunch of rascals and of the very darkest hue. They were the Mafia of the first century, and the Herod of this chapter was no exception.

The first several verses of this chapter are a flashback of what had already taken place. When Herod heard about the preaching of Jesus, he was immediately filled with fear and superstition. Herod had put John the Baptist to death, and he associated John with the Lord Jesus. Herod believed John had risen from the dead, and his fear changed to frenzy because he wanted to eliminate John altogether. Herod was a drunken, depraved, debased, weak man, and he was a killer. He had already murdered John, the forerunner of Christ, and he was prepared to murder the Lord Jesus Himself.

The following verses are part of the flashback describing the circumstances surrounding the death of John the Baptist.

For Herod had laid hold on John, and bound him, and put him in prison for Herodias' sake, his brother Philip's wife [Matt. 14:3].

Notice that it says that Herod *had* laid hold on John—it was a past action. Herod had imprisoned John "for Herodias' sake." Notice how Herod was influenced by others. Here it is by Herodias, and later on it will be by others. He was motivated like a politician. Everything he did was to gain the approval of others.

For John said unto him, It is not lawful for thee to have her [Matt. 14:4].

John the Baptist had spoken out against Herod's immorality—John wasn't a very good politician!

And when he would have put him to death, he feared the multitude, because they counted him as a prophet [Matt. 14:5].

Here we see that Herod was afraid of the crowd.

But when Herod's birthday was kept, the daughter of Herodias danced before them, and pleased Herod [Matt. 14:6].

Herod was a lascivious, lustful old creature, living with his brother's wife at the time, and John the Baptist had condemned him.

Whereupon he promised with an oath to give her whatsoever she would ask [Matt. 14:7].

He expected her to ask for some material thing, I suppose, and certainly something within reason.

And she, being before instructed of her mother, said, Give me here John Baptist's head in a charger [Matt. 14:8].

The mother, Herodias, lived up to the Herod name. Hers was a cruel and sadistic request, prompted by a brutal desire for revenge because of John's condemnation of her.

And the king was sorry: nevertheless for the oath's sake, and them which sat with him at meat, he commanded it to be given her [Matt. 14:9].

Imagine a man being motivated like that! He was afraid of what his guests might think of him for having made a promise and not making it good.

And he sent, and beheaded John in the prison.

And his head was brought in a charger, and given to the damsel: and she brought it to her mother [Matt. 14:10–11].

The sadistic, sad, and sordid account of what took place in that day reveals the type of society that existed then. John the Baptist was beheaded, and his head was given to the dancing girl on a platter! Human nature has not changed much. Lust and murder are part of contemporary society today.

And his disciples came, and took up the body, and buried it, and went and told Jesus [Matt 14:12].

The disciples of John claimed his body and tenderly and lovingly buried it.

JESUS WITHDRAWS

The Lord withdrew because He knew that Herod's fear would break out into a frenzy and cause him to do something rash. The Lord Jesus knew this man and wanted to avoid an incident because His hour had not yet come.

When Jesus heard of it, he departed thence by ship into a desert place apart: and when the people had heard thereof, they followed him on foot out of the cities [Matt. 14:13].

The Lord went by ship across the Sea of Galilee, but the crowd that had followed Him on foot out of the cities did not want Him to leave, so they walked around the shore of Galilee and met Him on the other side. This reveals how popular He was with the crowds.

And Jesus went forth, and saw a great multitude, and was moved with compassion toward them, and he healed their sick [Matt. 14:14].

Notice again that they brought their sick folk out to Him. He healed literally thousands of people in that day. To compare what He did to the healing cults of our day is blasphemous. It casts a reflection on Him—because what He did was above board and evident to everybody.

JESUS FEEDS THE HUNGRY

And when it was evening, his disciples came to him, saying, This is a desert place, and the time is now past; send the multitude away, that they may go into the villages and buy themselves victuals [Matt. 14:15].

Note that the disciples are attempting to advise Jesus what to do. Their advice was to send the people into the villages.

But Jesus said unto them, They need not depart; give ye them to eat [Matt. 14:16].

The feeding of the five thousand is the one miracle which is recorded in all four Gospels. For that reason alone it is an important miracle.

It was as if the disciples had appointed themselves to the board of directors to tell the Lord Jesus what to do. But He said to them, "They need not depart; give ye them to eat." It was an impossible command.

And they say unto him, We have here but five loaves, and two fishes [Matt. 14:17].

Having only five loaves and two fishes is typical of the sad state of the church in our day. Right now folk are saying that we need to send the multitudes away, that there are natural ways of caring for their needs. We send them to the psychiatrist for emotional help and to the government for physical relief. We do have spiritual bread to offer folk, although it may be only five loaves and two fishes, but the thing which is lacking is the power of the Lord Jesus. If we only had that power, we wouldn't need to send the multitudes away. We fail to realize that the solutions today are not in government nor in human imaginations but in God. No wonder the church is powerless.

He said, Bring them hither to me [Matt. 14:18].

I love that response! He is the Lord, my friend, and He says to us, "Bring what you have to Me." It is not what we have that counts with Him but actually what we don't have. The question is: Are we willing to release whatever we do have and let Him be the One to direct us in the disposition of it?

Don't get the impression that this little boy had five great big loaves of bread. They actually were little buns. There were over five thousand hungry people out there, and they had five little buns. This little boy had brought them—they were probably his lunch, and he could have eaten every bit of it. Five loaves and two small fish—and Jesus said, "Bring them hither to me."

And he commanded the multitude to sit down on the grass, and took the five loaves, and the two fishes, and looking up to heaven, he blessed, and brake, and gave the loaves to his disciples, and the disciples to the multitude [Matt. 14:19].

"He commanded the multitude to sit down on the grass." Someone has called our attention to something interesting here which most of us would have passed by. In Mark's account we are told that He made them sit down by companies or ranks, by hundreds and by fifties. These folk wore colorful clothing, and out there on the green grass they were seated probably by villages with each having its own distinct manner of dress. It must have been a thrilling sight to have seen this colorful group from the opposite hillside. They were probably wearing red, brown, blue, orange, and purple—probably a great deal of purple because purple dye was made in this area. It must have looked like one of those old-fashioned quilts. The Lord had them sit in order. The Lord did things orderly.

"And looking up to heaven, he blessed, and brake, and gave the loaves to his disciples, and the disciples to the multitude." These fellows who had appointed themselves to the board of directors in telling the Lord Jesus what to do find themselves now as waiters, serving the crowd. And that is really to be the particular ministry of apostles, disciples, ministers, evangelists, and all Christians in our day. We are to *feed* the multitude. There are too many people in our churches who want to tell how it should be done and too few who are willing to *do* it. A preacher said to me, "In my church we have all chiefs and no Indians. Everybody wants to be the head of something, chairman of a committee, or in another place of leadership." What the church needs is waiters to give out the Bread of Life, and the Bread is the Word of God. That's our business. All believers should be waiters passing it out.

And they did all eat, and were filled: and they took up of the fragments that remained twelve baskets full [Matt. 14:20].

I formerly thought that taking up the "fragments" meant that they picked up what we would call the garbage; that is, someone bit into a sandwich, then put it down when he saw a bigger one, and the half-eaten sandwich would be a fragment. However, I realize now that here were twelve baskets of bread and fish which were never touched. It is difficult for us who live in the midst of supermarkets to understand that many of the world's population went to bed hungry last night. Most people in that day never knew what it was to have a full meal, but twelve baskets of food left over indicates that everyone had a full tummy.

And they that had eaten were about five thousand men, beside women and children [Matt. 14:21].

There were five thousand men. This did not include the women and children. Is it too much to add one woman and one child to each man? The Lord actually fed closer to fifteen thousand than to five thousand people that day.

JESUS WALKS ON THE WATER

As soon as the multitude was fed, Jesus sent His disciples to the other side of the Sea of Galilee, and He went to pray.

And straightway Jesus constrained his disciples to get into a ship, and to go before him unto the other side, while he sent the multitudes away [Matt. 14:22].

"Straightway" is a word of urgency and swift movement. Matthew's record has a strange omission at the conclusion of the miracle of feeding the five thousand. He notes the urgency with which Jesus dismissed the multitudes and the haste in which He sent His disciples over the sea in the boat; however, he does not offer an explanation. John gives us the reason: "When Jesus therefore perceived that they would come and take him by force, to make him a king, he departed again into a mountain himself alone" (John 6:15). In view of the fact that Matthew is presenting that phase of the ministry of Jesus which has to do with His kingship, it may appear odd at first that he would ignore this attempt to make Jesus king. This is another evidence of the remarkable character of the claim of Jesus to be King. He is King by right and title. He will not become King by any democratic process. He is not "elected" King by the will of the people. He is King by the will of God. He will finally become King by force (see Ps. 2:8–9).

And when he had sent the multitudes away, he went up into a mountain apart to pray: and when the evening was come, he was there alone.

But the ship was now in the midst of the sea, tossed with waves: for the wind was contrary [Matt.14:23–24].

The Lord is in the mountains, in the place of prayer. The disciples are down on the Sea of Galilee in a storm and in darkness; they are in the place of peril. What a picture this is of our own day. Our Lord has gone on to the Father and is seated at the Father's right hand. We today are down here on a storm-tossed sea in the place of peril.

I love this next verse—

And in the fourth watch of the night Jesus went unto them, walking on the sea [Matt. 14:25].

The fourth watch is the morning watch, from three in the morning until daylight. This is the time the Lord walked on the sea, going to His disciples. And I think that will be the watch in which He will come for us at the Rapture. Christ is the bright and morning star for the church, and He will take the church out of the world. We don't know the date of His coming. There are men who would have us believe that they know the time, but they don't know. However, I believe that we are in the fourth watch of the night.

And when the disciples saw him walking on the sea, they were troubled, saying, It is a spirit; and they cried out for fear [Matt. 14:26].

This is the picture: Our Lord is up there on the mountain, and He sees the disciples in the storm, toiling and rowing, as Mark's record has it. Then He comes to them in the fourth watch. When they see Him, they say, "It is a spirit; and they cried out for fear." Somebody is going to say, "Well, they were superstitious." Yes, there may have been a certain amount of superstition in them, but what would *you* think if a man came to you walking on the water? Many years ago over in Tennessee a fellow said, "I didn't believe in ghosts either until I saw one!" And that is the position of the disciples. They had never seen a spirit before, but they think they are seeing one now!

But straightway Jesus spake unto them, saying, Be of good cheer; it is I; be not afraid [Matt. 14:27].

"Straightway Jesus spake unto them"—that is, *immediately* He reassured them that He was no ghost!

And Peter answered him and said, Lord, if it be thou, bid me come unto thee on the water [Matt. 14:28].

Peter has certainly been criticized for this. They say that he should not have asked to walk on water. Well, I rather admire the man. William Carey said, "Expect great things of God, and attempt great things for God." Certainly Peter did that! I am afraid that most of us are satisfied with little things from God.

Notice that Jesus did not rebuke Peter for asking—

And he said, Come. And when Peter was come down out of the ship, he walked on the water, to go to Jesus [Matt 14:29].

I hear people say that Peter failed to walk on the water, but that is not the way my Bible reads. My Bible says that Peter *walked* on the water to go to Jesus. This is not failure! Peter asked a tremendous thing of God. No wonder God used him in such a wonderful way during the days that followed. No wonder he was chosen to preach the sermon on the Day of Pentecost.

But when he saw the wind boisterous, he was afraid; and beginning to sink, he cried, saying, Lord, save me [Matt. 14:30].

Peter took his eyes off the Lord Jesus while he was walking on the water. When he began to sink, he prayed the shortest prayer in the Bible, "Lord, save me"! If Simon Peter had prayed this prayer like some of us preachers pray, "Lord, Thou who are omnipotent, omniscient, omnipresent . . . ," Peter would have been twenty-nine feet under water before he would have gotten to his request. Peter got right down to business, and you and I need to pray like that.

And immediately Jesus stretched forth his hand, and caught him, and said unto him, O thou of little faith, wherefore didst thou doubt? [Matt. 14:31].

Peter's problem was that he took his eyes off Jesus and looked at the waves rolling. You and I are in a world today where we see the waves rolling, and this is the time when we need to keep our eyes on the Lord Jesus Christ.

And when they were come into the ship, the wind ceased.

Then they that were in the ship came and worshipped him, saying, Of a truth thou art the Son of God [Matt. 14:32–33].

Our Lord performed this miracle for His own, that they might be brought into the place of faith. Even Simon Peter, who was audacious enough to say, "Lord, bid me come unto thee on the water" and actually walked on the water, which should have cemented his faith, got his eyes off Jesus, and his faith failed. I don't want to criticize Peter because that has been my problem, also. I have stepped out on faith many times and then have taken my eyes off Him. This is the tragedy of the hour for us in our day. But these things were done that the disciples might worship Him and *know* that He was the Son of God.

And when they were gone over, they came into the land of Gennesaret.

And when the men of that place had knowledge of him, they sent out into all that country round about, and brought unto him all that were diseased;

And besought him that they might only touch the hem of his garment: and as many as touched were made perfectly whole [Matt. 14:34–36].

After the storm He continued to minister to the needs of the people. Again, let me call your attention to the multitudes that were healed in that day. We have a detailed record of only a few healings, but thousands were made whole by the Lord.

CHAPTER 15

***THEME:** Jesus denounces scribes and Pharisees; rebukes His disciples; heals the daughter of the Syrophoenician woman and multitudes; feeds the four thousand*

This chapter continues the movement of the King, and He is beginning now to move toward the cross. We have already seen His rejection and conflict with the religious rulers. This chapter advances the ministry of Jesus to the very breaking point with the scribes and Pharisees. There is a lot of action here.

JESUS DENOUNCES THE SCRIBES AND PHARISEES

Then came to Jesus scribes and Pharisees, which were of Jerusalem, saying,

Why do thy disciples transgress the tradition of the elders? for they wash not their hands when they eat bread [Matt. 15:1–2].

The scribes and the Pharisees had come all the way from Jerusalem. In the previous chapter we saw that Jesus and His disciples were way out in a desert place where the crowds couldn't even get to a hamburger stand; so He had fed them. On the surface it may seem like a wonderful thing that the religious rulers had come all the way out to listen to Him. Well, frankly, they hadn't come all the way out to applaud Him or to accept His teaching; they had come to criticize Him. Immediately we recognize that this was not a friendly visit. They did not accuse Him of breaking the Scriptures but of violating the traditions which they considered to be on a par with the Scriptures. They wanted to know why His disciples did not wash their hands. They were referring to a ceremonial cleansing rather than to what we would consider a physical or sanitary washing. There are a great many people who feel that if you go through some sort of an outward ceremony and clean up on the outside, this is all that is necessary.

But he answered and said unto them, Why do ye also transgress the commandment of God by your tradition? [Matt. 15:3].

Jesus accuses them of breaking the commandment of God with their tradition. Their tradition, you see, permitted a man to disobey the Law, an amazing thing—and they had a very clever way of doing it.

For God commanded, saying, Honour thy father and mother: and, He that curseth father or mother, let him die the death.

But ye say, Whosoever shall say to his father or his mother, It is a gift, by whatsoever thou mightest be profited by me;

And honour not his father or his mother, he shall be free. Thus have ye made the commandment of God of none effect by your tradition [Matt. 15:4–6].

Our Lord is saying that honoring father and mother includes supporting them. The way they got around that responsibility was to dedicate their money as a gift to God, and that would relieve them of supporting their parents. This gave a pious way out for a man to break the Mosaic Law.

I still believe the best way to test a Christian is by his pocketbook. The barometer of the Christian today is how he handles his own money and how he handles God's money. The religious rulers of Jesus' day were helping men escape their responsibility.

I am of the opinion that God wants you to pay your honest debts before you give to Him. God wants you to take care of your personal responsibilities. He wants you to support your family before you give to Him. I once knew a man with a wild idea. This man came to me on payday and wanted to give me half his income while his family went hungry. When I found out, we had quite a little talk, and at first he was offended. Finally, he saw that he was neglecting his own family, which is a tragic thing to do. It is amazing how people try to escape a responsibility in a pious way.

Ye hypocrites, well did Esaias prophesy of you, saying,

This people draweth nigh unto me with their mouth, and honoureth me with their lips; but their heart is far from me [Matt. 15:7–8].

The Lord called the scribes and Pharisees *hypocrites*. This is the most frightful word in Scripture. Nothing quite corresponds to it, but it did not have quite the meaning in that day that it does today. To us it is a scorching word, but in Jesus' day it simply meant to answer back and was used of an actor in a play. It means that an actor would receive a cue and then answer back. Jesus accused the scribes and Pharisees of playing at religion.

The religious leaders were eager to have people go through the ceremony of washing their hands, but they ignored the condition of the heart, which was the important thing to God. In a very pious way they were breaking the Mosaic Law.

My friend, we also are pretty good at rationalizing. Parents say to their children, "You wash your hands before you come to the table," but they pay no attention to what their children see on television, which is the thing that is damaging the heart. Oh, of course, children should wash their hands, but what is on the inside is far more important.

Now our Lord will enlarge upon that statement—

And he called the multitude, and said unto them, Hear, and understand:

Not that which goeth into the mouth defileth a man; but that which cometh out of the mouth, this defileth a man [Matt. 15:10–11].

The great principle that Jesus was teaching is that moral defilement is spiritual, not physical.

Then came his disciples, and said unto him, Knowest thou that the Pharisees were offended, after they heard this saying? [Matt. 15:12].

The disciples are amazed that the Lord would offend the Pharisees. Up to this point there has been conflict between the religious leaders and Jesus, but this is the breaking point. The Lord continues to instruct His disciples.

But he answered and said, Every plant, which My heavenly Father hath not planted, shall be rooted up [Matt. 15:13].

The word *plant* here means "system". It is not too broad to interpret Jesus as saying, "Every religious system which My heavenly Father hath not planted shall be rooted up."

Let them alone: they be blind leaders of the blind. And if the blind lead the blind, both shall fall into the ditch [Matt. 15:14].

This to me is a humorous statement, and it is certainly biting sarcasm. The Pharisees were the blind leaders.

Then answered Peter and said unto him, Declare unto us this parable [Matt. 15:15].

The Lord has been speaking in parables to His disciples, but they had not gotten His point yet.

And Jesus said, Are ye also yet without understanding?

Do not ye yet understand, that whatsoever entereth in at the mouth goeth into the belly, and is cast out into the draught?

But those things which proceed out of the mouth come forth from the heart; and they defile the man [Matt. 15: 16–18].

This is a great principle. A person is not defiled by what goes into his mouth but by what comes out of his mouth. As someone has well said, what is in the well of the heart will come up in the bucket of the mouth sooner or later. Listen to Him—

For out of the heart proceed evil thoughts, murders, adulteries, fornica-

tions, thefts, false witness, blasphemies:

These are the things which defile a man: but to eat with unwashen hands defileth not a man [Matt. 15:19–20].

We are certainly seeing this working out in our contemporary culture. We are in the period of the "new morality" and have reached the day that Isaiah talked about when he said that they would ". . . call evil good, and good evil . . ." (Isa. 5:20). Those of us who believe the Bible are considered squares and entirely wrong. What do we have in this day of freedom, now that the lid has been taken off and man expresses what is in his heart? Do we have a new *morality?* No, we have the same old things—evil thoughts, murder, adultery, fornication, false witness, blasphemy, and thefts. We have really opened a Pandora's box, and we are in trouble.

Man has to be *controlled*. He is the most vicious animal on earth. We put other animals in cages, but man must be free to do his thing, and our Lord has told us what mankind will do, and He says that these things *defile*. All about us today is an emphasis on sex—in our schools, even in our churches, on television, on radio; it stares at you from billboards, from the covers of magazines, from newspaper headlines. My friend, these things *defile*. Don't tell me that you are immune to it; no one is immune to this type of thing. Our children and young people are being *defiled*—all in the lofty-sounding terminology of freedom of speech! The things that are in the heart are now coming out. Our Lord has made a tremendous statement here.

JESUS HEALS THE SYROPHOENICIAN WOMAN'S DAUGHTER

Then Jesus went thence, and departed into the coasts of Tyre and Sidon [Matt. 15:21].

Now our Lord leaves the land of Israel for the first time during His public ministry. This is interesting because He came to Israel as her King. When He sent His disciples out, He instructed them to go into the cities of Israel but not beyond her boundaries. Then the Lord was rejected by Israel, and there arose conflict. The breaking point between Jesus and the religious rulers came only a few verses ago. What happens? Jesus Himself steps over the boundaries of Israel and lays down another great principle. He will now receive the Gentiles. His invitation is, "Come unto me, all ye that labour and are heavy laden, and I will give you rest (lit., "rest you")" (Matt. 11:28).

And, behold, a woman of Canaan came out of the same coasts, and cried unto him, saying, Have mercy on me, O Lord, thou son of David; my daughter is grievously vexed with a devil.

But he answered her not a word. And his disciples came and besought him, saying, Send her away; for she crieth after us [Matt 15:22–23].

The Syrophoenician woman was a mixture of several races and a true Gentile (see Mark 7:26 for her nationality). She had no claim on Jesus as the Son of David, and when she addressed Him as such, He answered her not a word.

The disciples said, "Send her away, for she crieth after us." She was causing a disturbance and probably a little embarrassment.

But he answered and said, I am not sent but unto the lost sheep of the house of Israel [Matt 15:24].

This seems to be a harsh statement, but it was a statement of fact. Jesus was offering Himself first as the fulfillment of all the prophecies concerning the coming of the King in David's line. He was forcing this gentile woman to recognize that fact.

Jesus came as King of the Jews. You mark that down—it was the primary issue that had to be settled. He died with this superscription written over Him on the cross: THIS IS JESUS THE KING OF THE JEWS.

Now listen to this gentile woman—

Then came she and worshipped him, saying, Lord, help me [Matt. 15:25].

When she addressed Him as the Son of David, He said, "I am not sent but unto the lost sheep of the house of Israel." She as a Gentile had no claim upon Him as the Son of David. However, now she comes and worships Him, calling Him "Lord," and asks for help. Now she will get help, as we shall see.

But he answered and said, It is not meet to take the children's bread, and to cast it to dogs [Matt. 15:26].

That is a very strong statement! Such a rebuff would have driven many of us away. We would have turned on our heels and said, "You can't talk to us like that!"

And she said, Truth, Lord: yet the dogs eat of the crumbs which fall from their masters' table [Matt. 15:27].

You remember that our Lord told of a poor man who ate of the crumbs that fell from a rich man's table, and the dogs came and licked his sores. The Israelites used the word *dog* in reference to the Gentiles. This woman was willing to bear that reproach because she believed in the Lord Jesus.

Then Jesus answered and said unto her, O woman, great is thy faith: be it unto thee even as thou wilt. And her daughter was made whole from that very hour [Matt. 15:28].

Our Lord really marveled at the faith of this gentile woman. He had said, "Come unto me, all ye that labor and are heavy laden—I'll help you; I'll lift your burden," and that is what He did even for a Canaanite. Her answer had revealed a great faith, and to that our Lord responded.

JESUS CONTINUES TO HEAL

And Jesus departed from thence, and came nigh unto the sea of Galilee; and went up into a mountain, and sat down there.

And great multitudes came unto him, having with them those that were lame, blind, dumb, maimed, and many others, and cast them down at Jesus' feet; and he healed them [Matt. 15:29–30].

Again I call your attention to the multitudes of folk whom Jesus healed. There were not just a few isolated cases that could not be substantiated, but there were so many that nobody denied He performed miracles of healing.

Insomuch that the multitude wondered, when they saw the dumb to speak, the maimed to be whole, the lame to walk, and the blind to see: and they glorified the God of Israel [Matt. 15:31].

JESUS FEEDS THE FOUR THOUSAND

This miracle seems to be almost a duplication of the feeding of the five thousand.

Then Jesus called his disciples unto him, and said, I have compassion on the multitude, because they continue with me now three days, and have nothing to eat: and I will not send them away fasting, lest they faint in the way [Matt. 15:32].

Note again His compassion for people.

And his disciples say unto him, Whence should we have so much bread in the wilderness, as to fill so great a multitude? [Matt. 15:33].

Let's not miss the message that is here. Frankly, it seems like just a rerun of the feeding of the five thousand. It appears to be a repetition, and we wonder why Matthew included it since it doesn't seem to add any further advancement of the messianic claims of the Lord Jesus. However, we are in the section in which the emphasis is no longer upon Jesus pressing His messianic claim but the emphasis is on the *rejection* of His claim. And this miracle shows how slowly the disciples were to learn. They had already witnessed the feeding of the five thousand, and I think it took place only a few days before this; yet here they raise the same old objections of unbelief. Again His disciples say to Him, "Whence should we have so much bread in the wilderness, as to fill so great a multitude?"

And Jesus saith unto them, How many loaves have ye? And they said, Seven, and a few little fishes.

And he commanded the multitude to sit down on the ground.

And he took the seven loaves and the fishes, and gave thanks, and brake them, and gave to his disciples, and the disciples to the multitude [Matt. 15: 34–36].

Again He fed the multitudes. This is a revelation that the disciples had not really learned the lesson. Their reluctance to believe actually constitutes a form of rejection. My friend, unbelief is *sin*. In Romans 14:23 it says that ". . . whatsoever is not of faith is sin." In Hebrews 12:1 we are admonished to ". . . lay aside every weight, and the sin which doth so easily beset us. . . ." What is that weight? I think it is unbelief. Unbelief is *sin*. I am willing to make this confession: I wish that I believed Him more. He is worthy to be believed; I ought to believe Him fully, but the problem is with me. And I suspect that the problem is with you, also.

The Lord Jesus fed the multitude—

And they did all eat, and were filled: and they took up of the broken meat that was left seven baskets full.

And they that did eat were four thousand men, beside women and children [Matt. 15:37–38].

Notice that it was four thousand men plus women and children. In other words, families were there. Again, if we put one woman and one child with each man, the total fed would be twelve thousand.

And he sent away the multitude, and took ship, and came into the coasts of Magdala [Matt. 15:39].

This was part of the Lord's Galilean ministry. Magdala is on the Sea of Galilee and today lies in ruins.

This chapter reveals that our Lord's disciples are not keeping up. They are slow to believe and slow to understand. This is actually hindering the Lord Jesus. It seems at this point that, since He has reached the breaking point with the religious rulers, He is having a real problem with His disciples. He appears to be just marking time until they catch up.

Frankly, He is very patient with you and me, also. Many of us need to catch up; we are far behind in our belief and understanding. Oh, that we might *believe* Him!

CHAPTER 16

THEME: *Jesus continues the conflict with the Pharisees and Sadducees; Jesus calls for a confession from His disciples, and Peter speaks for the group; Jesus confronts them for the first time with the church, His death, and resurrection*

THE PHARISEES AND SADDUCEES ASK FOR A SIGN

For the second time the Pharisees and Sadducees ask for a sign from heaven, and again they are referred to Jonah.

The Pharisees also with the Sadducees came, and tempting desired him that he would shew them a sign from heaven.

He answered and said unto them, When it is evening, ye say, It will be fair weather: for the sky is red.

And in the morning, It will be foul weather to-day: for the sky is red and lowering. O ye hypocrites, ye can discern the face of the sky; but can ye not discern the signs of the times? [Matt. 16:1–3].

In Matthew 12:38 the scribes and Pharisees asked for a sign. At that time the Lord gave them the sign of Jonah. He is going to do that again, but first He calls their attention to the fact that, although they are very good at predicting the weather, they don't seem to be able to recognize the signs of the times.

Actually, the religious rulers are trying to trap the Lord Jesus, and He is going to warn His own men to beware of them. Notice that this is the second time He calls them "O ye hypocrites."

A wicked and adulterous generation seeketh after a sign; and there shall no sign be given unto it, but the sign of the prophet Jonas. And he left them, and departed [Matt. 16:4].

Our Lord had provided them with many signs, but they would not accept them. For the second time He predicts the sign of Jonah ("Jonas" is the Greek form of the Hebrew name *Jonah*). Back in chapter 12 verse 40 He had said, "For as Jonas was three days and three nights in the whale's belly; so shall the Son of man be three days and three nights in the heart of the earth." These Pharisees and Sadducees were not about to accept that as a sign.

In this chapter we will see three viewpoints concerning Jesus. The Pharisees and Sadducees consider Him an imposter and do not believe that He is the Messiah. The multitude thinks He is John the Baptist, Elijah, Jeremiah, or another of the prophets. In this, they were complimentary, although they missed the mark completely. His disciples present the third viewpoint. They believe that Jesus is the Messiah (Christ), the Son of the living God.

The Pharisees and Sadducees were asking for a sign. Jesus said that no sign would be given them but the sign of the prophet Jonah. "And he left them, and departed." There is a note of finality in His action as He turns and walks away from them. Then He warns His disciples of the leaven of these religious rulers.

JESUS WARNS HIS DISCIPLES

And when his disciples were come to the other side, they had forgotten to take bread.

Then Jesus said unto them, Take heed and beware of the leaven of the Pharisees and of the Sadducees.

And they reasoned among themselves, saying, It is because we have taken no bread [Matt. 16:5–7].

In Matthew 13 we learned that leaven is *always* a principle of evil and never a principle of good. The Lord says to beware of the leaven. If you are cautioned to beware of something, it will not be welcome or good. The disciples missed the understanding of the leaven at first, thinking it was bread.

Which when Jesus perceived, he said unto them, O ye of little faith, why reason ye among yourselves, because ye have brought no bread?

Do ye not yet understand, neither remember the five loaves of the five thousand, and how many baskets ye took up?

Neither the seven loaves of the four thousand, and how many baskets ye took up?

How is it that ye do not understand that I spake it not to you concerning bread, that ye should beware of the leaven of the Pharisees and of the Sadducees?

Then understood they how that he bade them not beware of the leaven of bread, but of the doctrine of the Pharisees and of the Sadducees [Matt. 16:8–12].

If it were a matter of material bread, the disciples should have remembered the two miracles of His—providing food for the five thousand and the four thousand—but it was not a matter of material bread. Leaven, according to our Lord's interpretation, is false *doctrine*. It is that which is evil. When people speak about the "leaven of the gospel," they are using a contradiction of terms. Leaven is never a picture of the gospel. Leaven always is symbolic of evil. If you accept the Lord Jesus Christ as an authority, this ought to clarify once and for all what leaven represents.

JESUS CALLS FOR A CONFESSION OF HIMSELF

All the way through the Gospel of Matthew we need to keep our thinking caps on because this gospel is the key to the rest of the Scriptures. We need to make sharp distinctions and note carefully what happens.

When Jesus came into the coasts of Caesarea Philippi, he asked his disciples, saying, Whom do men say that I the Son of man am? [Matt. 16:13].

If you look on a map, you will find three Caesareas. Caesarea Philippi is located to the north of the Sea of Galilee. The Lord Jesus is in the north, and He is in a position from which He is going to turn and begin a movement directly toward Jerusalem and the cross. Before He begins that journey, there are two things that must be clear in the minds of His disciples: (1) who He is, and (2) what He is going to do. My friend, these are the two things that all of us have to be clear on in order to be Christians. We have to know who He is, and we have to know what He did. We need to know these things in order that we might exercise faith and be saved.

Note our Lord's first question: "Whom do men say that I the Son of man am?" This is a question which He is still asking, and it is a question that is still being answered in our day. He still is the most controversial Person who has ever lived on the topside of this earth. Now we will hear the viewpoint of the multitudes, the crowds that followed Him. I believe that if you or I asked this question on a street corner of our own towns, we would probably get similar answers because folk are still confused about Him.

And they said, Some say that thou art John the Baptist: some, Elias; and others, Jeremias, or one of the prophets [Matt. 16:14].

"Some say that thou art John the Baptist." John the Baptist was a great man, and the people recognized him as such. In our day there are many folk who say that Jesus was a great teacher.

Some said regarding Jesus that He was "Elias." (The name *Elias* was the Greek form of "Elijah.") Elijah was certainly a great person, and there are those in our day who say that Jesus was a great person.

"And others, Jeremias." (Again, the Greek form is used.) Jeremiah was the weeping prophet, and the people saw our Lord weep. The crowds gave Him the credit for being a great prophet.

"Or one of the prophets." I suppose there was a variety of viewpoints as to which prophet Jesus was.

These, then, were the viewpoints of the average persons of that day.

A young preacher friend of mine, an extrovert, heard me speak of this; so he went out on the street corners and asked the question concerning Jesus Christ of folk who passed by. He got all sorts of viewpoints. Some said that He was the greatest teacher this world has ever seen. One person said that He was a founder of religion. Another felt that He was a *good* man. Another put Him in a class with other men who were famous in history—just "one of the prophets," you see.

Now the Lord Jesus turns to His apostles and asks them—

He saith unto them, But whom say ye that I am?

And Simon Peter answered and said, Thou art the Christ, the Son of the living God [Matt. 16:15–16].

The time has come for the disciples to make a decision and render a confession. Simon Peter was evidently the spokesman for the group. He said, "Thou art the Christ," which meant the Messiah, the Anointed One, the One who was predicted in the Old Testament, and the Lord Jesus was the fulfillment. Also—"the Son of the living God." Up to this point, that was the best confession and the highest tribute that could be made to Him. This is who Jesus is!

And Jesus answered and said unto him, Blessed art thou, Simon Bar-jona: for flesh and blood hath not revealed it unto thee, but my Father which is in heaven [Matt. 16:17].

Only the Holy Spirit can make Christ known to any person. No man today can call Jesus "Lord" but by the Holy Spirit. Only the Spirit of God can take the things of Christ and reveal them to us. Jesus said, "Flesh and blood hath not revealed it unto thee"; that is, "You didn't learn it by being with Me." I hear folk say, "Well, if I could have been with Jesus for three years [the apostles had been with Him about two and one half years now], then I would really know who He is." Would you? My friend, you can know Him just as well today because the Spirit of God has to make Him real to you.

And I say also unto thee, That thou art Peter, and upon this rock I will build my church; and the gates of hell shall not prevail against it [Matt. 16:18].

Let us look at this verse carefully. On what rock did Jesus build His church? There are those who say that it was built on Simon Peter. Well, obviously it was not, because there is a play upon words here. In the original Greek it is, "Thou art *Petros* [a little piece of rock], and upon this *petra* [bedrock] I will build my church." There are others who hold that Christ is building His church upon the confession that Simon Peter made. I don't agree with that at all.

Who is the Rock? The Rock is Christ. The church is built upon Christ. We have Simon Peter's own explanation of this. In 1 Peter 2:4, referring to Christ, he writes, "To whom coming, as unto a living stone, disallowed indeed of men, but chosen of God, and precious." And he remembers Isaiah 28:16, ". . . Behold, I lay in Sion a chief corner stone, elect, precious: and he that believeth on him shall not be confounded" (1 Pet. 2:6). The church is built upon Christ; He is the foundation. "For other foundation can no man lay than that is laid, which is Jesus Christ" (1 Cor. 3:11). Christ is the stone, and He says on this rock He *will build* His church. The church was still future when the Lord made this statement. And please don't tell me there was a church in the Old Testament because the church did not come into existence until after the death, resurrection, and ascension of Christ, and the sending of the Holy Spirit. There could not have been a church until all of these things had taken place. "I will build my church"—this was future.

The "gates of hell" refers to death. The word used for *hell* is the Greek word *hades*, the *sheol* of the Old Testament, which refers to the unseen world and means "death." The gates of *death* shall not prevail against Christ's church. One of these days the Lord Himself shall descend from heaven with a shout. That shout will be like the voice of an archangel and like a trumpet because the *dead* in Christ are to be raised. The gates of *death* shall not prevail against His church.

And I will give unto thee the keys of the kingdom of heaven: and whatsoever

thou shalt bind on earth shall be bound in heaven: and whatsoever thou shalt loose on earth shall be loosed in heaven [Matt. 16:19].

What are the keys of the kingdom of heaven? Were they given only to Simon Peter? No, Jesus gives them to those who make the same confession made by Peter, those who know Christ as Savior. If you are a child of God, you have the keys as well as any person has the keys. The keys were the badge of authority of the office of the scribes who interpreted the Scriptures to the people (see Neh. 8:2–8). Every Christian today has the Scriptures and, therefore, the keys. If we withhold the Word, we "bind on earth"; if we give the Word, we "loose on earth." No man or individual church has the keys—to the exclusion of all other believers. We have a responsibility today to give out the gospel because it is the only thing that can save people. This is a tremendous revelation. Who is sufficient for these things? You and I have a responsibility that is awesome indeed!

Then charged he his disciples that they should tell no man that he was Jesus the Christ [Matt. 16:20].

The Lord made this request because the mere knowledge of who He is will not save you. To find salvation you must know who He is and what He did and accept Him by faith.

JESUS ANNOUNCES HIS DEATH AND RESURRECTION

For the first time the Lord Jesus announces to His disciples His death and resurrection. The time was approximately six months before He was actually crucified. Why did He wait so long to make such an important announcement? Obviously, His disciples were not prepared for it, even at this time, judging from their reaction. He repeated five times the fact that He was going to Jerusalem to die (Matt. 17:12; 17:22–23; 20:18–19; 20:28). In spite of this intensive instruction, the disciples failed to grasp the significance of it all until after His resurrection.

From that time forth began Jesus to shew unto his disciples, how that he must go unto Jerusalem, and suffer many things of the elders and chief priests and scribes, and be killed, and be raised again the third day [Matt. 16:21].

This is what the Lord Jesus did for you and me. This is the gospel: that Christ died for our sins according to the Scriptures, was buried and raised again. You must know who He is. You must know what He did for you. If you know these two things, and by faith believe and receive them, you are saved. This had never been revealed before except to Nicodemus at the beginning of our Lord's ministry in John 3:1–16.

Then Peter took him, and began to rebuke him, saying, Be it far from thee, Lord: this shall not be unto thee [Matt. 16:22].

In essence Peter said, "You are the Messiah; You are the Son of God. You must not, You *cannot* go to the cross!" The cross was not in the thinking of the apostles at all, as you can see.

But he turned, and said unto Peter, Get thee behind me, Satan: thou art an offence unto me: for thou savourest not the things that be of God, but those that be of men [Matt. 16:23].

It is satanic for anyone to deny the facts of the gospel which are that Jesus died on the cross for our sins, was buried, and rose again from the dead. It is satanic when a man in the pulpit will deny these truths. The substitutionary death of Christ is the only thing that can save us, my friend. Later on Peter wrote this: "Who his own self bare our sins in his own body on the tree, that we, being dead to sins, should live unto righteousness: by whose stripes ye were healed." (1 Pet. 2:24). My, what a transformation had taken place in the mind of Peter!

Our Lord said to Peter, "Get thee behind me, Satan." Imagine this: Here is Peter by whom the Spirit of God could say that Jesus was the Son of God, and yet he could in the next moment let Satan deceive him!

Then said Jesus unto his disciples, If any man will come after me, let him deny himself, and take up his cross, and follow me [Matt. 16:24].

Many people interpret this verse, "Let him deny himself ice cream" or "Let him deny himself some luxury down here." What this verse says is "Let him deny *himself!*" You already know that the hardest person in the world to deny is yourself. To deny myself dessert is hard enough, but to deny *myself* is difficult indeed. To deny myself is to put self out of the picture and to put Christ in the place of self.

"And take up his cross, and follow me." We are not to take up Christ's cross but our own cross. There is a cross for you and a cross for me—that is, if we are going to *follow* Him.

For whosoever will save his life shall lose it: and whosoever will lose his life for my sake shall find it.

For what is a man profited, if he shall gain the whole world, and lose his own soul? or what shall a man give in exchange for his soul?

For the Son of man shall come in the glory of his Father with his angels; and then he shall reward every man according to his works [Matt. 16:25–27].

The person who will not assume the risks involved in becoming a disciple of the Lord Jesus Christ will, in the long run, lose his life eternally. The opposite is also true. At Christ's second coming all accounts will be settled and everyone will receive his proper rewards.

Verily I say unto you, There be some standing here, which shall not taste of death, till they see the Son of man coming in his kingdom [Matt. 16:28].

This verse belongs with chapter 17 because the account of the transfiguration of Jesus explains what He meant when He made this statement.

CHAPTER 17

THEME: *The Transfiguration; the demon-possessed boy and the faithless disciples; Jesus pays taxes by performing a miracle*

THE TRANSFIGURATION

As we noted at the conclusion of chapter 16, the final verse belongs to this chapter because it explains what our Lord meant when He made this statement:

Verily I say unto you, There be some standing here, which shall not taste of death, till they see the Son of man coming in his kingdom [Matt. 16:28].

This was fulfilled for the apostles in the Transfiguration of Jesus. The Transfiguration is that picture of the Son of man coming in His kingdom. Someone may say, "Can you be sure that the Lord Jesus had reference to His coming Transfiguration?" Well, Simon Peter was one of the apostles who was present at the Transfiguration, and in his second epistle he wrote of that experience: "For we have not followed cunningly devised fables, when we made known unto you the power and coming of our Lord Jesus Christ, but were eyewitnesses of his majesty. For he received from God the Father honour and glory, when there came such a voice to him from the excellent glory, This is my beloved Son, in whom I am well pleased. And this voice which came from heaven we heard, when we were with him in the holy mount" (2 Pet. 1:16–18). How was Jesus' statement fulfilled for the apostles in that day? When the Lord Jesus Christ was glorified on the Mount of Transfiguration with three of His disciples present, this statement was fulfilled. The Transfiguration was a miniature picture of the kingdom, and Simon Peter confirmed this for us.

The other gospels give the account of the Transfiguration, with the exception of the Gospel of John. This leads me to say something that may startle you. The Transfiguration does not prove, nor set forth, the *deity* of Christ. It sets forth the *humanity* of Christ. The Gospel of John emphasizes the deity of Christ and therefore omits the account of the Transfiguration, although the other three Gospels record it.

The Transfiguration of the Lord Jesus Christ is, in my judgment, not only the proof of His humanity but the *hope* of humanity. The Man whom you see glorified there, transfigured, is the kind of person that you, my friend, will be someday if you are a child of God. "Beloved, now are we the sons of God, and it doth not yet appear what we shall be: but we know that, when he shall appear, we shall be like him; for we shall see him as he is" (1 John 3:2). The glorious prospect of being like Christ is before every man.

The Lord Jesus Christ was glorified before His death and resurrection, and this is the picture which is given to us here. You will find that the Gospel of Luke presents details which neither Matthew nor Mark include, because Dr. Luke is the one who sets forth the perfect humanity of Jesus.

And after six days Jesus taketh Peter, James, and John his brother, and bringeth them up into an high mountain apart,

And was transfigured before them: and his face did shine as the sun, and his raiment was white as the light [Matt. 17:1–2].

"His face did shine as the sun." The light shone from within Him rather than upon Him from the outside like a spotlight. At this point let me make the suggestion that perhaps it was this sort of thing that clothed Adam and Eve in the Garden of Eden before their fall. After they sinned, they discovered that they were naked. The implication is that they were not naked before, which leads me to believe that they were clothed with this type of light. And it was the *humanity* of Jesus that was transfigured. The Transfiguration sets forth His perfect humanity.

The word *transfigured* is a very interesting word. It is the word *metamorphosis*, which means "a change of form or structure." The little woolly caterpillar will someday become a beautiful butterfly by the process of metamorphosis. This body that I have today, filled with infirmity and cancer, will someday be transfigured, and even those who are alive at the coming of Christ will be changed, transfigured. This is the hope of humanity.

And, behold, there appeared unto them Moses and Elias talking with him [Matt. 17:3].

Moses was the representative of the Law, and Elijah was the representative of the prophets. Moses had died, and Elijah had departed from this world in a chariot of fire. Luke tells us they were discussing Jesus' decease in Jerusalem—"And, behold, there talked with him two men, which were Moses and Elias: Who appeared in glory, and spake of his decease which he should accomplish at Jerusalem" (Luke 9:30–31). The Law and the prophets bore testimony to the death of the Lord Jesus Christ.

Then answered Peter, and said unto Jesus, Lord, it is good for us to be here: if thou wilt, let us make here three tabernacles; one for thee, and one for Moses, and one for Elias [Matt. 17:4].

Simon Peter could never resist an opportunity to make a speech. Every occasion was an auspicious one for him. He generally got to his feet to say something, and usually it was to say the wrong thing—that is, until the Day of Pentecost. But here it is the wrong thing; he should have kept quiet. God Himself rebukes him, as we shall see, because he was attempting to place Moses and Elijah on the same plane with the Lord Jesus. Luke offers the explanation for this indiscretion of Peter's by stating, ". . . not knowing what he said" (Luke 9:33). And there are a lot of folk who talk without knowing what they are saying! Peter was rebuked. He should have kept still.

While he yet spake, behold, a bright cloud overshadowed them: and behold a voice out of the cloud, which said, This is my beloved Son, in whom I am well pleased; hear ye him [Matt. 17:5].

This is God the Father's testimony to Jesus, the Son. Jesus is the final authority in matters of revelation. What Moses, Elijah and the prophets had to say was wonderful. The writer to the Hebrews says: "God, who at sundry times and in divers manners spake in time past unto the fathers by the prophets, Hath in these last days spoken unto us by his Son . . ." (Heb. 1:1–2). The *Son* is the One who came to earth as the final revelation of God to man.

Now notice this great statement by the Father—"This is my beloved Son, in whom I am well pleased; hear ye him." Have you ever heard a voice out of heaven commending you and saying that God was well pleased with you? Well, He has never said that to me either. In fact, He has never said it to anyone but this One. The Lord Jesus is the only One who ever has been well pleasing to God. And you and I well never get into God's presence until we are *in* Christ by faith. When we receive Christ as our Savior, then we are placed in the body of believers. Christ is the only One in whom God has been pleased, and we are accepted in the Beloved.

And when the disciples heard it, they fell on their face, and were sore afraid.

And Jesus came and touched them, and said, Arise, and be not afraid.

And when they had lifted up their eyes, they saw no man, save Jesus only [Matt. 17:6–8].

Do you want a good motto for your life? I suggest these two words: *Jesus only.* He is the One who is the authority. I hope you will mark those two words, *Jesus only,* in your Bible. They provide a good motto for all of us.

And as they came down from the mountain, Jesus charged them, saying, Tell the vision to no man, until the Son of man be risen again from the dead [Matt. 17:9].

Why wait until the Resurrection to tell it, and why should it be told at that time? Because it is part of the gospel story. It tells who Jesus is. He is the perfect Lamb of God. He has been tested for three years, and at this time He is on the way to the cross to die for the sins of the world. You see, God required a lamb without blemish, and the Lord Jesus Christ is the only One who could die a substitutionary death for mankind, because He was sinless. In His perfect humanity He was transfigured. He is the *hope* of mankind.

The hope of mankind is not in science or education. Both of them are letting us down today. They have created Frankenstein monsters, and we don't know what to do with them. For example, they have invented a little gasoline buggy in Detroit, Michigan, that is giving us a lot of trouble by polluting the air and clogging all the highways. Science cannot solve the problem. Believe me, friend, the hope of the world just happens to be in a Person by the name of Jesus Christ. Be sure you know Him; He is your only hope.

And his disciples asked him, saying, Why then say the scribes that Elias must first come? [Matt. 17:10].

Now this is a remarkable statement—

And Jesus answered and said unto them, Elias truly shall first come, and restore all things [Matt. 17:11].

Jesus confirms what was said in the prophecy of Malachi.

But I say unto you, That Elias is come already, and they knew him not, but have done unto him whatsoever they listed. Likewise shall also the Son of man suffer of them [Matt. 17:12].

This raises a question in the minds of a great many folk regarding John the Baptist. Was he really Elijah? We have covered the same problem in Matthew 11. What our Lord is doing in this chapter is trying to forestall the argument that Jesus had to die on the cross because John the Baptist was not Elijah—and Elijah has to come before Christ returns to establish His kingdom. Our Lord is saying that if they would receive Him as King, John would be Elijah. Don't ask me how that could be—I am only telling you what the Scriptures teach.

"Likewise shall also the Son of man suffer of them"—this is the second time the Lord Jesus mentions His approaching crucifixion.

Then the disciples understood that he spake unto them of John the Baptist [Matt. 17:13].

THE DEMON-POSSESSED BOY

In this scene we have a kingdom-of-heaven situation, as it is in today's world. Where does the church fit into it? Go with me now to the foot of the mountain where the other disciples (who were not with the Lord on the Mount of Transfiguration) are really in trouble.

And when they were come to the multitude, there came to him a certain man, kneeling down to him, and saying,

Lord, have mercy on my son: for he is lunatic, and sore vexed: for ofttimes he falleth into the fire, and oft into the water.

And I brought him to thy disciples, and they could not cure him [Matt. 17:14–16].

This was probably the worst case which had been brought to the attention of Jesus. It was also a sad situation because the disciples were impotent. This is a picture of the church today in a world that is demon-possessed and has gone crazy. Why is the church impotent in this crazy world? Because it doesn't have enough psychology or enough methods or enough money? It has all of those things, but they are not what the church really needs.

This man had to say to Jesus, "I brought him to Your disciples, but they could not heal him."

Then Jesus answered and said, O faithless and perverse generation, how long shall I be with you? how long shall I suffer you? bring him hither to me [Matt. 17:17].

"O faithless and perverse generation" would be His word to the church in our day and probably individually to you and to me. "Bring him hither to me." Jesus is the Great Physician. Take your case to Him, my friend.

And Jesus rebuked the devil; and he departed out of him: and the child was cured from that very hour [Matt. 17:18].

The Lord rebuked His disciples, and then He rebuked the demon. This is probably the worst case of demon possession our Lord dealt with.

Then came the disciples to Jesus apart, and said, Why could not we cast him out?

And Jesus said unto them, Because of your unbelief: for verily I say unto you, If ye have faith as a grain of mustard seed, ye shall say unto this mountain, Remove hence to yonder place; and it shall remove; and nothing shall be impossible unto you [Matt. 17:19–20].

"Nothing shall be impossible unto you"—that is, nothing that is according to the will of God for you. It was God's will that this boy be delivered from demon possession. Why couldn't the disciples deliver him? Because they didn't have the faith.

Howbeit this kind goeth not out but by prayer and fasting [Matt. 17:21].

This verse is not in the better manuscripts.

AGAIN JESUS ANNOUNCES HIS DEATH AND RESURRECTION

For the third time the Lord reminds His disciples that He would die and be raised again from the dead.

And while they abode in Galilee, Jesus said unto them, The Son of man shall be betrayed into the hands of men:

And they shall kill him, and the third day he shall be raised again. And they were exceeding sorry [Matt. 17:22–23].

This is the third time He speaks to His disciples of His death and Resurrection. The first time He mentioned it was when they were in Caesarea Philippi. Now He is in Galilee, on His way to Jerusalem, and He mentions it again. All that the disciples can do is to feel sorry.

TAX MONEY FROM THE FISH'S MOUTH

And when they were come to Capernaum, they that received tribute money came to Peter, and said, Doth not your master pay tribute? [Matt. 17:24].

"Tribute" was the assessment collected annually for the support of the temple.

He saith, Yes. And when he was come into the house, Jesus prevented him, saying, What thinkest thou, Simon? of whom do the kings of the earth take custom or tribute? of their own children, or of strangers? [Matt. 17:25].

"Jesus prevented him" means that Jesus went before him.

Peter saith unto him, Of strangers. Jesus saith unto him, Then are the children free [Matt. 17:26].

Jesus is trying to show Peter that just as the royal family is exempt from tax, so He, as the Son of God, would not be obligated to pay for the support of God's house.

Notwithstanding, lest we should offend them, go thou to the sea, and cast an hook, and take up the fish that first cometh up; and when thou hast opened his mouth, thou shalt find a piece of money: that take, and give unto them for me and thee [Matt. 17:27].

His method of getting the tax money was certainly novel, to say the least. Now our Lord demonstrates that He has recovered all that Adam lost. The creatures were obedient to Him. The fish as well as Peter followed His command. I believe that God had given to Adam the same dominion over all creation, but he lost it at the Fall. "And God said, Let us make man in our image, after our likeness: and let them have dominion over the fish of the sea, and over the fowl of the air, and over the cattle, and over all the earth, and over every creeping thing that creepeth upon the earth" (Gen. 1:26).

In the Transfiguration we see man restored to his original *purpose*. In the episode of the tribute money we see man restored to his original *performance*.

CHAPTER 18

THEME: *The little child, the lost sheep, conduct in the coming church, and the parable on forgiveness*

The next few chapters do not seem to further advance the movement in Matthew, but they do fill out many of the dark corners which have arisen because of the sudden digression in the kingdom of heaven due to the rejection of the King. Matthew 13 in the Mystery Parables Discourse has given us the overall outline of the kingdom of heaven in this age, but there are still questions to be answered. These chapters are helpful in answering many of them.

Now we find that the new birth is made essential in entering the kingdom.

A LITTLE CHILD BECOMES AN OBJECT LESSON

At the same time came the disciples unto Jesus, saying, Who is the greatest in the kingdom of heaven? [Matt. 18:1].

I wonder if you detect a note of fleshly ambition here? It may be that I just have a critical mind, but it seems to me that these men have been talking about this subject, and maybe two or three of them felt that they could reasonably be considered the greatest in the kingdom of heaven. So the Lord did a rather sensational thing.

And Jesus called a little child unto him, and set him in the midst of them [Matt. 18:2].

What does this tell us? It tells us that the little child came to the Lord without hesitation. In Mark 10:14 the Lord said, ". . . Suffer the little children to come unto me, and forbid them not. . . ." The problem was not in getting the little children to come to Him but in stopping the adults from hindering the little ones in coming to the Lord. This is a lovely picture we have here. Our Lord takes this little child and puts him in the midst of them.

And said, Verily I say unto you, Except ye be converted, and become as little children, ye shall not enter into the kingdom of heaven [Matt. 18:3].

This is a verse that has certainly been abused and misunderstood, but remember, the Lord Jesus is talking about *conversion* not *reversion*. Some people think this verse means that you must revert back to your childhood in some unusual fashion or that you are to become juvenile in your actions in order to enter the kingdom of heaven. The Lord is not talking about going back to a former childhood, but rather of going on to a new life. Here our Lord gives logic to the thinking of the disciples as He diverts their attention from the matter of holding an exalted place in the kingdom to that of primary importance; namely, of first being able to secure entrance into that kingdom. This is as radical as John 3:3, "Jesus answered and said unto him, Verily, verily, I say unto thee, Except a man be born again, he cannot see the kingdom of God." The important thing emphasized in this verse is the new birth. You must become a little child in the sense that you must be born again. When you are born again, you start out spiritually as a child.

Unfortunately, there are many folk who do not recognize their spiritual immaturity. When I was pastoring a large city church, you would be surprised at the number of requests that came to me from so-called new converts who wanted to come and give their testimonies. I feel that it was basically the same thing as the disciples' argument as to who would be the greatest in the kingdom of heaven. Our Lord says that if you have been converted, think of your spiritual age. You are to become a little child. Should a little child get up and blabber out a testimony immediately? Should a little child be an officer in the church? In listing qualifications for the office of bishop in the church, Paul rules out the novice: "Not a novice, lest being lifted up with pride he fall into the condemnation of the devil" (1 Tim. 3:6). I think that our Lord is saying something like that here.

Whosoever therefore shall humble himself as this little child, the same is greatest in the kingdom of heaven [Matt. 18:4].

When you go back and emphasize the *entrance* into the kingdom, the new birth, then you find that the one who humbles himself as a little child is the one who is greatest in the kingdom.

And whoso shall receive one such little child in my name receiveth me.

But whoso shall offend one of these little ones which believe in me, it were

better for him that a millstone were hanged about his neck, and that he were drowned in the depth of the sea [Matt. 18:5–6].

The word *offend* means "to cause to stumble"; that is, to lead into sin. Jesus warns against it in strong language! It seems to me that what He is doing in this section is making the evangelism of children a divine imperative. He gives top priority to winning the children to Christ. I commend anyone who is working with children today. There is nothing as important as that.

The story is told of Dwight L. Moody concerning his coming home one night after a meeting. His family asked him how many converts he had that night, and he said, "Two and a half." His family said, "Oh, you had two adults and one child who accepted the Lord as Savior." Moody replied, "No, no, two children and one adult accepted the Lord." He continued, "The adult was an old man and he had only half a life to give. He was just half of a convert." The little children are important.

A pastor of a Scottish church turned in his resignation years ago, and as he did so, the elders asked him why. "Well," he replied, "for this past year I've had but one convert, wee Bobby Moffat." Bobby Moffat was the man who opened up Africa to missionary work. It was the biggest year that preacher ever had! In these verses the Lord is putting a great emphasis upon children.

Woe unto the world because of offences! for it must needs be that offences come; but woe to that man by whom the offence cometh!

Wherefore if thy hand or thy foot offend thee, cut them off, and cast them from thee: it is better for thee to enter into life halt or maimed, rather than having two hands or two feet to be cast into everlasting fire [Matt. 18:7–8].

I can't think of anything more harsh than this!

And if thine eye offend thee, pluck it out, and cast it from thee: it is better for thee to enter into life with one eye, rather than having two eyes to be cast into hell fire.

Take heed that ye despise not one of these little ones; for I say unto you, That in heaven their angels do always behold the face of my Father which is in heaven [Matt. 18:9–10].

Our Lord says that we are not to despise one of the little ones. When one of them dies, his spirit goes immediately to be with God. All little ones go to heaven, my friend. If you have lost a little one, knowing this will be a great comfort to you. They go to heaven, not because they are innocent or because they are yours, but they go to heaven because Jesus *died* for them. That is what our Lord is talking about here. "Don't offend them; don't despise them. Let them come to Me. Even if they die, their spirits are going to be right there in the presence of My Father." So many parents wonder about the eternal state of their little ones.

King David knew about his. When his son by Bathsheba fell ill, he was greatly exercised about the life of the child. We have the record of this in 2 Samuel 12:15–23. He fasted and wept and lay all night upon the earth. But when the child was dead, he arose, bathed, changed his clothes, and went into the house of God and worshiped. His servants were baffled by his actions, and David's explanation was this " . . . While the child was yet alive, I fasted and wept: for I said, Who can tell whether GOD will be gracious to me, that the child may live? But now he is dead, wherefore should I fast? can I bring him back again? I shall go to him, but he shall not return to me." He had the confidence that one day he would be with him. This is a very precious truth. Many people have lost little ones, and I have lost a little one, also—my firstborn. She is buried here in Altadena in Southern California. Every now and then I go by there and put a few flowers on her grave. She's not there; she's with Him, but I go there because that is all I have left of her now. But someday, some golden tomorrow, I'm going to be there in heaven, and I am going to see my little one. She is saved. I have two children—one in heaven and one here on earth. I confess that I have worried more about the one here than the one in heaven. I know where my firstborn is, and someday I'll go to be with her.

The feeling of our Lord about children is very important to note, especially in our day when there are so many crimes committed against these little ones. Recently, I have been reading about a mother and a stepfather who left a precious little girl along the freeway. How shocking it was to read about this. They just wanted to get rid of her. Some folk believe there is no hell, but I want to say this: If there were no hell, there *ought* to be one for folk like that! And there *is* one. Our Lord uses the strongest language possible in warning us about offenses against children.

PARABLE OF THE LOST SHEEP

Now our Lord moves into the wonderful parable of the lost sheep.

For the Son of man is come to save that which was lost [Matt. 18:11].

This parable is different from the parable of the lost sheep in Luke 15. The key to this parable is the word *save*. In Luke 15 the emphasis is upon *finding* the lost, and in Matthew 18 it is upon *saving* the lost.

How think ye? if a man have an hundred sheep, and one of them be gone astray, doth he not leave the ninety and nine, and goeth into the mountains, and seeketh that which is gone astray?

And if so be that he find it, verily I say unto you, he rejoiceth more of that sheep, than of the ninety and nine which went not astray. [Matt. 18:12–13].

Notice how He closes this—He is still thinking in terms of the "little ones."

Even so it is not the will of your Father which is in heaven, that one of these little ones should perish [Matt. 18:14].

He will take care of them until they get to the age of accountability, but you, parent, are responsible for leading them to Christ. I am afraid that our school systems are using our children as guinea pigs for humanistic philosophies. Young people are paying an awful price in the contemporary schoolroom. My friend, we have a tremendous responsibility before God in this area.

PATTERN FOR CONDUCT IN THE CHURCH

Moreover if thy brother shall trespass against thee, go and tell him his fault between thee and him alone: if he shall hear thee, thou hast gained thy brother [Matt. 18:15].

If he sins against you, *you* are to go to him. This verse is speaking of sin committed by a believer. The obligation is upon the one who has been injured to approach his brother who has offended him and not vice versa.

But if he will not hear thee, then take with thee one or two more, that in the mouth of two or three witnesses every word may be established.

And if he shall neglect to hear them, tell it unto the church: but if he neglect to hear the church, let him be unto thee as an heathen man and a publican [Matt. 18:16–17].

There are some people who like to smother trouble and cover it up. This is not the way the Lord tells us to handle it. If there is a problem between two believers, it should be worked out in an amiable, peaceful, and quiet manner. If the individuals cannot work things out, take it to a group. If the group cannot work things out, the last resort is to take the problem to the church as the final authority. The Lord says in conclusion, concerning this subject:

Verily I say unto you, Whatsoever ye shall bind on earth shall be bound in heaven: and whatsoever ye shall loose on earth shall be loosed in heaven [Matt. 18:18].

We have already studied the contents of this verse in Matthew 16:19, where we learned that if we withhold the Word, we "bind on earth"; if we give the Word of God to others, we "loose on earth."

Again I say unto you, That if two of you shall agree on earth as touching any thing that they shall ask, it shall be done for them of my Father which is in heaven.

For where two or three are gathered together in my name, there am I in the midst of them [Matt. 18:19–20].

"If two of you shall agree on earth as touching any thing." Does He mean that if we agree on *anything*, He will hear us? Yes, but notice the condition: "where two or three are gathered together in *my name*." He will hear any request which is given in Christ's name—that is, a request that Christ Himself would make. Or, we could say that asking in His *name* is asking in His *will*.

"Where two or three are gathered together in my name, there am I in the midst of them" is the simplest form of church government. As verse 19 is a new basis for prayer, verse 20 is the new basis for the visible church. The early church began there: "And they continued stedfastly in the apostles' doctrine and fellowship, and in breaking of bread, and in prayers" (Acts 2:42).

JESUS' NEW PROVISO FOR FORGIVENESS

Then came Peter to him, and said, Lord, how oft shall my brother sin

against me, and I forgive him? till seven times? [Matt. 18:21].

Peter thought he was being magnanimous when he said this because two or three times was all you had to forgive according to the rabbis. Simon Peter was willing to forgive seven times. But Peter's generosity was parsimonious in comparison to the new estimation of Jesus—

Jesus saith unto him, I say not unto thee, Until seven times: but, Until seventy times seven [Matt. 18:22].

That is four hundred and ninety times! By that time, things might be pretty well worked out. If not, both of them would have reached old age to the extent that it wouldn't amount to much anyway! Four hundred and ninety times is going the limit—and that is the point our Lord is making.

Therefore is the kingdom of heaven likened unto a certain king, which would take account of his servants.

And when he had begun to reckon, one was brought unto him, which owed him ten thousand talents.

But forasmuch as he had not to pay, his lord commanded him to be sold, and his wife, and children, and all that he had, and payment to be made.

The servant therefore fell down, and worshipped him, saying, Lord, have patience with me, and I will pay thee all [Matt. 18:23–26].

I guess he was saying that he wanted to pay it back on the installment plan.

Then the lord of that servant was moved with compassion, and loosed him, and forgave him the debt [Matt. 18:27].

I think our Lord is using an outlandish illustration here to prove His point. The amount of money that this servant owed his lord was about twelve million dollars. That is a lot of money to forgive anyone!

But the same servant went out, and found one of his fellow-servants, which owed him an hundred pence: and he laid hands on him, and took him by the throat, saying, Pay me that thou owest [Matt. 18:28].

"An hundred pence" amounted to about seventeen dollars! Compare that to twelve million!

And his fellow-servant fell down at his feet, and besought him, saying, Have patience with me, and I will pay thee all.

And he would not: but went and cast him into prison, till he should pay the debt.

So when his fellow-servants saw what was done, they were very sorry, and came and told unto their lord all that was done.

Then his lord, after that he had called him, said unto him, O thou wicked servant, I forgave thee all that debt, because thou desiredst me:

Shouldest not thou also have had compassion on thy fellow-servant, even as I had pity on thee?

And his lord was wroth, and delivered him to the tormentors, till he should pay all that was due unto him.

So likewise shall my heavenly Father do also unto you, if ye from your hearts forgive not every one his brother their trespasses [Matt. 18:29–35].

This parable of the servant, who was forgiven but refused to forgive another, illustrates the *principle* of forgiveness. This is a new principle presented in this passage, but it is not quite the basis of forgiveness for believers which is set forth in Ephesians 4:32, "And be ye kind one to another, tenderhearted, forgiving one another, even as God for Christ's sake hath forgiven you." *Because* God has forgiven us, we are to forgive each other. If God forgave our sins in the same way we forgive others, none of us would be forgiven. But after we have become children of God, because we have been forgiven, we are to forgive. This is the principle of Christian conduct, of course.

CHAPTER 19

THEME: *Jesus enters Judea; proclaims God's standard for marriage and only grounds for divorce given; blesses little children; meets a rich young ruler; appoints the apostles to their position in the coming kingdom*

In the movement in Matthew, our attention is now directed to the geography of the gospel. Jesus again enters Judea as He moves to Jerusalem for the last time before His crucifixion. There is definite intention in all that He does and says.

JESUS RE-ENTERS JUDEA

And it came to pass, that when Jesus had finished these sayings, he departed from Galilee, and came into the coasts of Judaea beyond Jordan [Matt. 19:1].

"When Jesus had finished these sayings"—what sayings? The ones we have been considering in chapters 16–18. Having finished what He wanted to say in Galilee, He moved south and came into the borders of Judea, beyond Jordan, meaning the east bank of the Jordan River. The movement is in a physical and geographical sense now. Up yonder in Caesarea Philippi He announced that He was going to Jerusalem to die. He moved down into Galilee, and He spent time in that area around the Sea of Galilee. Capernaum was His headquarters, and He even crossed over into Gadara. Now He is on the border of Judea.

And great multitudes followed him; and he healed them there [Matt. 19:2].

I want to put two words together and emphasize what has been emphasized before several times. One word is *multitudes* and the other word is *healed*. It was not just a few people that were healed; multitudes were healed. I am more and more impressed by this as time goes on. If you are going to be a faith healer, brother, you ought to go to the hospitals and empty them. That is what our Lord did when He passed by; if anyone wanted to be healed, they could be healed. Multitudes were healed!

MARRIAGE AND DIVORCE

Now the religious rulers come to Him with a question regarding divorce. Our Lord restates God's ideal for marriage and the grounds for divorce.

The Pharisees also came unto him, tempting him, and saying unto him, Is it lawful for a man to put away his wife for every cause? [Matt. 19:3].

The Pharisees came to tempt or to *test* Him. They were after Him, trying to put Him in opposition to the Mosaic system. They brought a problem which is just as difficult today as it was then. "Is it lawful for a man to put away [divorce] his wife for every cause?" That is an equally live issue among Christians in our day.

Let me preface this a little by saying that God has given to all of mankind certain things for the welfare of the human family. For instance, He has given marriage for the protection of the home. Marriage is something which God has given to be a blessing to mankind whether saved or unsaved. Another example is that of capital punishment which God gave for the protection of a nation, to protect the lives of its citizens. Also God gave the sabbath law for the protection of the individual, that he might have one day of rest. God gave these laws to protect the individual, the family, and the nation. These were general laws which He gave to all mankind. Later on, He made them specific for His chosen people.

Now let's look at this question concerning marriage. Here it is in the smaller context of the nation Israel, of course. And we look at it today in the light of the contemporary Christian. "Is it lawful for a man to put away his wife for every cause?"

And he answered and said unto them, Have ye not read, that he which made them at the beginning made them male and female [Matt. 19:4].

The Lord Jesus took them back to the very beginning, back to God's ideal of marriage.

The Mosaic Law had permitted divorce on a broad basis: "When a man hath taken a wife, and married her, and it come to pass that she find no favour in his eyes, because he hath found some uncleanness in her: then let him write her a bill of divorcement, and give it in her hand, and send her out of his house" (Deut. 24:1).

As far as the Mosaic Law was concerned, a divorce was not as bad as was marriage to a stranger. For instance, if the priest's daughter married a stranger, she was shut out from the nation Israel. However, as time went on, the Mosaic Law was made meaningless, and the granting of divorce was done on the flimsiest pretexts, such as burning the bread. As a result, there was a great deal of discussion relative to divorce in our Lord's day.

And said, For this cause shall a man leave father and mother, and shall cleave to his wife: and they twain shall be one flesh?

Wherefore they are no more twain, but one flesh. What therefore God hath joined together, let not man put asunder [Matt. 19:5–6].

This was God's original plan for man and woman before sin entered the human family. Divorce was not in God's original plan. Why? Because *sin* was not in God's original plan, and divorce is always a result of sin. Regardless of what you may say, there is sin in the relationship somewhere which causes divorce. So our Lord took them back to the original plan of God.

They say unto him, Why did Moses then command to give a writing of divorcement, and to put her away? [Matt. 19:7].

You ought to read Deuteronomy 24:1–4 to get the background for their question. Why did Moses permit divorce?

He saith unto them, Moses because of the hardness of your hearts suffered you to put away your wives: but from the beginning it was not so [Matt. 19:8].

Why did Moses permit it? Because of the hardness of their hearts. You see, marriage was given to mankind, and it is the tenderest and the sweetest of human relationships. There is nothing like it. And, actually, marriage was to represent the relationship between Christ and the church. Therefore, only believers can set forth this high and holy relationship. However, when they fail, and bitterness and hardness of heart enter in, then that marriage becomes a hollow sham, and it is just a mockery of marriage. My friend, marriage is either made in heaven or in hell—there is no third place to make it. When marriage is made in the wrong place, it is in trouble to begin with. Even Christians find that marriage becomes a very shaky proposition.

Because of the hardness of the human heart, God permitted divorce. God is merciful to us—oh, how merciful! But His ideal is never divorce. I recognize that we are living in a culture which is very lax in this area. There are multitudes of divorced folk who will be reading this book. Let me repeat that the background of divorce is always sin. But, after all, all of us are sinners. Since God can forgive murderers, He can also forgive divorced folk. But we need to recognize that the root cause of divorce is sin.

Now our Lord is going to give something new—

And I say unto you, Whosoever shall put away his wife, except it be for fornication, and shall marry another, committeth adultery: and whoso marrieth her which is put away doth commit adultery [Matt. 19:9].

Adultery breaks the marriage relationship and provides the *one* ground for divorce. Somebody says to me, "Yes, but here is this poor Christian woman, married to a drunkard!" Or a fine Christian man is married to a godless woman. What about that? Well, believers may *separate* on other grounds, which seems to be the whole point of 1 Corinthians 7, but divorce is permitted on only one basis, adultery.

Divorce was granted for the purpose of permitting the innocent party to remarry. This rule is applicable only to believers; God is not regulating the lives of unbelievers but is holding them to the message of the cross first. God wants the unbeliever to come to Christ. He is lost whether he is married, divorced, or single. It makes no difference until he accepts Christ. The important thing to note is that for *believers* He puts down one ground for divorce: adultery.

Now suppose there is a believer whose spouse got a divorce on another ground. What about the innocent party? Well, if there has been adultery there, and in most cases there has been, then the innocent party is permitted to remarry. I believe that is the whole thought in this particular case.

Now, there is something else here that is important—

His disciples say unto him, If the case of the man be so with his wife, it is not good to marry [Matt. 19:10].

The disciples are saying, "Well, in that case it would be better to stay single." Well, you would avoid a lot of trouble—there is no question about that.

But he said unto them, All men cannot receive this saying, save they to whom it is given [Matt. 19:11].

This is so important, especially in our day. In the verse that follows, our Lord puts down a great principle. Even now the Roman Catholic church is wrestling with this problem.

For there are some eunuchs, which were so born from their mother's womb: and there are some eunuchs, which were made eunuchs of men: and there be eunuchs, which have made themselves eunuchs for the kingdom of heaven's sake. He that is able to receive it, let him receive it [Matt. 19:12].

"There are some eunuchs, which were so born from their mother's womb." There are some men and some women who do not need to marry. They get along very well by themselves, but that's not for everybody.

"And there are some eunuchs, which were made eunuchs of men." Some churches make a rule that folk in certain positions are not to marry. They have no right to do that.

"And there be eunuchs, which have made themselves eunuchs for the kingdom of heaven's sake." I know a person who went to the mission field, and before she left, I talked to her. I said, "Look, your chances are nil for getting married out there." She said, "I have thought that through, and I am willing to make that sacrifice." She made it voluntarily.

Somebody says, "Do you think that the preacher ought to get married? Or do you think the priest should be married?" May I say to you, this is a place where God puts down a principle. He says that it is up to the individual. We have to make that decision for ourselves.

Now here is something wonderful—

JESUS RECEIVES LITTLE CHILDREN

Then were there brought unto him little children, that he should put his hands on them, and pray: and the disciples rebuked them.

But Jesus said, Suffer little children, and forbid them not, to come unto me: for of such is the kingdom of heaven.

And he laid his hands on them, and departed thence [Matt. 19:13–15].

This passage is ample basis for the salvation of children who die in infancy. It is a fact that no child will reject Jesus if He is presented to the child on a Bible basis. This is one reason why we should get the gospel message to them. Someone might say, "Wait a minute—then everyone could be saved if we reach them as children." No, this is not true because they reach the age of accountability later. The reason for trying to get the gospel into the hearts of children is so that when they reach the age of accountability they will make a decision for Christ. It is *important* that this be followed through. Do not rest on the fact that your child made a decision when he was two, three, four, five, six, seven or eight years old, etc. My daughter made a decision for Christ when she was seven. Ever since that time I have asked her many times if she has really trusted the Lord as Savior. One day she said, "Daddy, why do you keep asking me that question?" I told her I just wanted to make sure. Actually, the decision will be made at the age of accountability. You say to me, "When is that age?" I don't know. I just know that it is important to get the gospel to our children. Instead of standing on a street corner and arguing about it, let's get it to them and then follow through when they reach the age of accountability by doing everything in our power to get them to trust Christ.

It is interesting that our Lord, having spoken about the issue of divorce, immediately begins to talk about children. The children are all important in any divorce. A woman once came to me wanting a divorce because she no longer loved her husband. She said, "Because of all the things he is doing, I no longer love him, and I have heard you say that when there is no love, there is no relationship. So I want to get a divorce." It is true that when there is no love there is no relationship, and that is tragic, but that is not the basis for divorce. I said to this woman, "You tell me that you don't love your husband, but do you love your children?" She said, "Of course I do, but what has that got to do with it?" I told her that it has everything to do with it. "You are to stay with him as long as you can if you love those children." My friend, the fact that our Lord said, "Let the little children come unto Me," ought to make any couple, especially a Christian couple, make every effort to hold their marriage together. A large percentage of children and young folk who are in trouble with the law come from broken homes. You would be surprised to learn the number of little ones who have been turned away from Christ because of the divorced parents. It is very significant that Jesus ties together the subject of divorce and His loving concern for little children.

THE RICH YOUNG RULER

And, behold, one came and said unto him, Good Master, what good thing shall I do, that I may have eternal life?

And he said unto him, Why callest thou me good? there is none good but one, that is, God: but if thou wilt enter into life, keep the commandments [Matt. 19:16–17].

Notice how this young man approaches the Lord Jesus. He addresses Him as Good Master. He is willing to concede that He is good, and probably the enemies of Jesus would not have gone that far.

"Why callest thou me good?" I am sure you can see what our Lord was after. When He said, "There is none good but one, that is, God," He was saying in effect, "If you see that I am good, it is because I am God." He is directing his thinking so that he might accept Him as the Christ, the Son of God. Then the Lord Jesus flashed on this young man's life the commandments that have to do with a man's relationship to his fellowman.

He saith unto him, Which? Jesus said, Thou shalt do no murder, Thou shalt not commit adultery, Thou shalt not steal, Thou shalt not bear false witness,

Honour thy father and thy mother: and, Thou shalt love thy neighbor as thyself.

The young man saith unto him, All these things have I kept from my youth up: what lack I yet? [Matt. 19:18–20].

This young man could say that he had kept these commandments, and yet he recognized a lack in his life. The commandments which our Lord gave him compose the last section of the Decalogue which has to do with a man's relationship to man. The first of the Ten Commandments have to do with man's relationship to God. Our Lord did not use those because He was leading this young man along in his thinking. However, now the Lord directs his thinking to his relationship to God—

Jesus said unto him, If thou wilt be perfect, go and sell that thou hast, and give to the poor, and thou shalt have treasure in heaven: and come and follow me [Matt. 19:21].

"If thou wilt be perfect," meaning *complete.* Following Jesus would have led him to see that he was not keeping the first commandments which have to do with a man's relationship to God. The Lord Jesus was on His way to the cross. If this man followed Jesus, it would be to the foot of a cross. Something, however, was preventing him from going after the Lord. His riches were his stumbling block. For you and for me it might be something entirely different.

But when the young man heard that saying, he went away sorrowful: for he had great possessions [Matt. 19:22].

It was his money that was keeping him from the Lord Jesus Christ. In our day there are many things that are keeping folk away from the Lord Jesus. Riches are only one thing; there are multitudes of other things. Actually, church membership is keeping many people from Christ because it puts them into a little cellophane bag that protects them from facing their sins. They feel secure because they have been through the ceremonies or have made their confession, and yet they may be as unconverted as any pagan in the darkest spot on topside of the earth. Today, is there something that is separating *you* from Christ? Is there anything in the way that is keeping you from Him?

Well, it was riches for this young man—

Then said Jesus unto his disciples, Verily I say unto you, That a rich man shall hardly enter into the kingdom of heaven [Matt. 19:23].

This is still true in our day—not many rich, not many noble, not many of the great ones of the earth are Christians.

And again I say unto you, It is easier for a camel to go through the eye of a needle, than for a rich man to enter into the kingdom of God [Matt. 19:24].

Many people miss the humor that our Lord sometimes used, and this passage is an example of it. There are some people who hold to the ridiculous explanation that there was a gate in Jerusalem called "The Eye of the Needle," that a camel had to kneel to pass through it, and that therefore the Lord was saying that a man had to become humble to enter the kingdom of heaven. Well, that misses the point altogether. Our Lord is talking about a real camel and a real needle with an eye. My friend, let me ask you a very plain question: Is it possible for a real camel to go through the eye of a real needle? I think you know the answer—he won't make it! It is impossible. But would it be possible for God to put a camel through a needle's eye? Well, God is not in that business, but He could do it. And only *God* can regenerate a man. That is the point our Lord is making here. It is easier for a camel to go through the eye of a needle than for a rich man to enter into the kingdom of God.

Many people today think they are going to be saved by who they are or by what they have. You are truly saved when you find out that you are a sinner, a beggar in God's sight, with nothing to offer Him for your salvation. As long as a person feels he can *do* something or *pay* God for salvation, he can no more be saved than a camel can be put through the eye of a needle.

When his disciples heard it, they were exceedingly amazed, saying, Who then can be saved? [Matt. 19:25].

Listen to Jesus' answer—

But Jesus beheld them, and said unto them, With men this is impossible; but with God all things are possible [Matt. 19:26].

This is the explanation. As far as any person is concerned—regardless of who you are—you are a candidate for salvation if you recognize that you have nothing to offer God but come to Him like a beggar with empty hands. When you come to Him like that, He can save you. With *God* all things are possible.

JESUS REWARDS HIS APOSTLE

Then answered Peter and said unto him, Behold, we have forsaken all, and followed thee; what shall we have therefore? [Matt. 19:27].

It is easy for us to think that Simon Peter is betraying a very selfish streak here. Did our Lord rebuke him?

And Jesus said unto them, Verily I say unto you, that ye which have followed me, in the regeneration when the Son of man shall sit in the throne of his glory, ye also shall sit upon twelve thrones, judging the twelve tribes of Israel [Matt. 19:28].

Our Lord did *not* rebuke him. Instead, He told him what a great reward would be his. Likewise, I believe that today, we as Christians ought to be working for a reward.

And everyone that hath forsaken houses, or brethren, or sisters, or father, or mother, or wife, or children, or lands, for my name's sake, shall receive an hundredfold, and shall inherit everlasting life.

But many that are first shall be last; and the last shall be first [Matt. 19: 29–30].

There is to be a reward for the saved ones who have sacrificed for Jesus' sake. Many an unknown saint, of whom the world has not heard, will be given first place in His presence someday. In that day I believe that many outstanding Christian leaders who receive wide acclaim in this life will be ignored while many unknown saints of God will be rewarded. What a glorious, wonderful picture this presents to us!

CHAPTER 20

***THEME:** Parable of the laborers in the vineyard; Jesus makes the fourth and fifth announcements of His approaching death, while the mother of James and John requests the places on the right and left for her sons; Jesus opens the eyes of two blind men along the roadside*

This chapter opens with the parable of the laborers in the vineyard, which is a continuation, begun in the last chapter, of Jesus' remarks on rewards. This chapter brings to an end the section that seems to mark time in the movement in Matthew. From this chapter on, the tempo of Matthew increases, and the Lord moves directly to the cross. This chapter also makes an important contribution to filling in some more of the dark corners of the present state of the kingdom of heaven. The principle for giving rewards is stated in this parable: Faithfulness to the task, rather than the amount of work done or the spectacular nature of the work, governs the giving of rewards.

PARABLE OF THE LABORERS IN THE VINEYARD

For the kingdom of heaven is like unto a man that is an householder, which went out early in the morning to hire labourers into his vineyard [Matt. 20:1].

This parable is closely related to the previous chapter. Matthew 19:30 says, "But many that are first shall be last; and the last shall be first." Verse 16 says, "So the last shall be first, and the first last: for many be called, but few chosen." So you see that at both the beginning and at the end of this parable the concept of the last being first and the first, last, forms sort of a parenthesis around it.

And when he had agreed with the labourers for a penny a day, he sent them into his vineyard.

And he went out about the third hour, and saw others standing idle in the marketplace,

And said unto them; Go ye also into the vineyard, and whatsoever is right I will give you. And they went their way.

Again he went out about the sixth and ninth hour, and did likewise [Matt. 20:2–5].

The "sixth" hour was high noon, and the "ninth" hour was three o'clock in the afternoon.

And about the eleventh hour he went out, and found others standing idle, and saith unto them, Why stand ye here all the day idle?

They say unto him, Because no man hath hired us. He saith unto them, Go ye also into the vineyard; and whatsoever is right, that shall ye receive.

So when even was come, the lord of the vineyard saith unto his steward, Call the labourers, and give them their hire, beginning from the last unto the first.

And when they came that were hired about the eleventh hour, they received every man a penny.

But when the first came, they supposed that they should have received more; and they likewise received every man a penny.

And when they had received it, they murmured against the goodman of the house,

Saying, These last have wrought but one hour, and thou hast made them equal unto us, which have borne the burden and heat of the day.

But he answered one of them, and said, Friend, I do thee no wrong: didst not thou agree with me for a penny?

Take that thine is, and go thy way: I will give unto this last, even as unto thee.

Is it not lawful for me to do what I will with mine own? Is thine eye evil, because I am good? [Matt. 20:6–15].

This is a tremendous parable which illustrates an important truth: It is not the amount of time which you serve nor the prominence or importance of your position which determines your reward. Rather, you will be rewarded for your faithfulness to the task which God has given you to perform, regardless of how small or how short or how insignificant it appears.

I have always felt that the Lord will someday reward a dear little lady who may have been a member of my church. I will turn to a member of my staff and say, "Do you know her?" He will say, "I have never heard of her. She did not sing in the choir, she was never president of any of our societies, and she never taught a Sunday school class. That woman didn't do anything, and look at the way the Lord is rewarding her!" We will probably find out that this dear lady was a widow with a young son. She never spoke to thousands of people like some evangelists and preachers, but she faithfully raised her one little boy, and he became a missionary who served God on a foreign field. The widow had been faithful in the task God had given her to do. Somebody might protest, "Well, she sure didn't work as hard as I did!" That might well be true, but God is not going to reward you for the *amount* of work you have done. He will reward you according to your faithfulness to the job which He called you to do. My friend, perhaps God has not called you to do something great for Him, but are you faithful in what He has assigned to you?

JESUS' FOURTH ANNOUNCEMENT OF HIS DEATH AND RESURRECTION

And Jesus going up to Jerusalem took the twelve disciples apart in the way, and said unto them [Matt. 20:17].

Notice the physical and geographical movement of this section. Jesus and His disciples are going up out of the Jordan Valley and are approaching Jerusalem where He is to die upon the cross.

Behold, we go up to Jerusalem; and the Son of man shall be betrayed unto the chief priests and unto the scribes, and they shall condemn him to death,

And shall deliver him to the Gentiles to mock, and to scourge, and to crucify him: and the third day he shall rise again [Matt. 20:18–19].

Our Lord couldn't spell it out any plainer than that. This is the fourth time He is telling them—in *detail* at this juncture—exactly what is going to happen to Him. Somehow or other the disciples didn't comprehend it—it just didn't fit into their program. However, as you and I read it now, we see very clearly that it was Christ's avowed intention to go to Jerusalem to die. Let's ponder the significance of this. He went there deliberately to die for you and for me. That is something to think about. The disciples of Jesus just couldn't believe it!

THE REQUEST OF THE MOTHER OF JAMES AND JOHN

At the time of Jesus' significant announcement of His pending death, the mother of James and John came to Jesus to ask Him a favor.

Then came to him the mother of Zebedee's children with her sons, worshipping him, and desiring a certain thing of him [Matt. 20:20].

There are a great many of us who worship Him with the same motive!

And he said unto her, What wilt thou? She saith unto him, Grant that these my two sons may sit, the one on thy right hand, and the other on the left, in thy kingdom [Matt. 20:21].

On any other occasion and at any other time, this request would be a natural one for a mother who was ambitious for her children. In this instance, however, she missed the atmosphere and the very understanding of what was really taking place at that time. The Lord will answer her, and in quoting the following Scripture, I am going to leave out a portion that is not in our better manuscripts.

But Jesus answered and said, Ye know not what ye ask. Are ye able to drink of the cup that I shall drink of. . . .They say unto him, We are able.

And he saith unto them, Ye shall drink indeed of my cup, . . . but to sit on my right hand, and on my left, is not mine to give, but it shall be given to them for whom it is prepared of my Father [Matt. 20:22–23].

When these two verses are read with omissions, the sense becomes clear. My friend, don't miss the meaning here because it is so important to Christians today. Our Lord is not saying that there is no place at His right hand and left hand for somebody. He is saying that He will not *arbitrarily* give the positions to James and John or to anyone else. Rather, the places are for those who prepare themselves for them.

Note this very carefully: Heaven is for the asking. You do nothing, *nothing*, for salvation. You are saved by faith in Christ through His marvelous grace. However, my friend, your position, your reward in heaven is determined by what you do down here on earth. That is very important, and Christians seem to have lost sight of it. What kind of a place are you preparing for yourself? Personally, I have no ambition for the places on Christ's right or left hand—I'm sure I have missed those—but I *am* working for a place. All of us should be doing this. In Philippians 3:14 Paul said, "I press toward the mark for the prize of the high calling of God in Christ Jesus." The trouble with Christians today is that too few are even trying to win anything. We need to recognize salvation as a free gift, but we need to get on the race course in order to receive a reward.

And when the ten heard it, they were moved with indignation against the two brethren [Matt. 20:24].

Do you know why they were moved with indignation? It was because *they* wanted the places at His right and left hands!

But Jesus called them unto him, and said, Ye know that the princes of the Gentiles exercise dominion over them, and they that are great exercise authority upon them.

But it shall not be so among you: but whosoever will be great among you, let him be your minister;

And whosoever will be chief among you, let him be your servant [Matt. 20:25–27].

This is a new approach to service and greatness, and it ought to be very clear in the minds of those who are engaged in Christian service. My friend, if you are going to sing for the Lord, please don't try to walk over all the other soloists. If you are trying to be a preacher of the gospel, don't try to push aside every other minister. If you are trying to be a church officer, don't do it at the expense of someone else. Our Lord makes it very clear that the way to be great and the way to serve Him is to take the lowest place.

Now, as Jesus and His disciples are very near to the city of Jerusalem, for the fifth time He tells them of His approaching death.

Even as the Son of man came not to be ministered unto, but to minister, and to give his life a ransom for many [Matt. 20:28].

This is a tremendous verse, and every Christian ought to memorize it. This verse should be at your fingertips so that when an opportunity to witness comes, you will be able to tell just why Jesus Christ came into the world and what His mission was, because there is still confusion at that point.

JESUS HEALS TWO BLIND MEN

And as they departed from Jericho, a great multitude followed him [Matt. 20:29].

Jesus and His disciples are going from Jericho to Jerusalem, which is the opposite direction from the man who went down from Jerusalem to Jericho and fell among thieves. The Lord is going from Jericho up to Jerusalem to *die* with thieves. That's on the other side of the freeway, and on that side you and I can never go. We can only come to Him in faith, for He died in our stead.

By the way, some folk think that because at His trial He did not defend Himself, He *never* defended Himself, and that Christians should follow the same policy. However, at other times He did defend Himself. When He went to Jerusalem to die, He did not defend Himself because He was taking *my* place, and I'm guilty. Believe me, there was no defense! That is the reason He did not open His mouth at that time. He was bearing my sin, and He was bearing your sin at that time.

And, behold, two blind men sitting by the way side, when they heard that Jesus passed by, cried out, saying, Have mercy on us, O Lord, thou son of David [Matt. 20:30].

I love these two fellows—no one could keep them quiet!

And the multitude rebuked them, because they should hold their peace: but they cried the more, saying, Have mercy on us, O Lord, thou son of David [Matt. 20:31].

Notice that they addressed Him accurately—"O Lord, thou son of David." They acknowledged His kingship. The Syrophoenician at first called Him the son of David, but the Lord reminded her that she had no claim on Him in this way. These men, however, were Jews and did have a claim on Him, and they exercised their claim!

And Jesus stood still, and called them, and said, What will ye that I shall do unto you?

They say unto him, Lord, that our eyes may be opened [Matt. 20:32–33].

The problem of these men seemed so obvious. Why did the Lord ask what He could do for them? My friend, when you come to the Lord Jesus Christ, you must tell Him your need. If you are coming to Him for salvation, you must tell Him that you are a sinner and need His salvation. If you don't, you will not be saved. That's the offense of the cross. Everybody would like to come to the cross if they could bring along the perfume of their self-righteousness and good deeds. But, my friend, you and I haven't any goodness at all, none whatsoever, to present to God. You can no more sweeten human character with training and psychology and education than you can sweeten a pile of fertilizer out in the barnyard with Chanel No. 5. We have to come to Him as sinners and receive Him as our Savior. And the blind men came to the Lord Jesus with their need, "Lord, that our eyes may be opened"!

So Jesus had compassion on them, and touched their eyes: and immediately their eyes received sight, and they followed him [Matt. 20:34].

Our Lord healed them, and they followed Him. Remember where He is going—He is on His way to the cross.

CHAPTER 21

***THEME:** Jesus enters Jerusalem officially, cleanses the temple, curses the fig tree, and when He is challenged by the chief priests and elders, He condemns them by parables of the two sons and the householder whose servants slew his son*

The movement in Matthew comes back into sharp focus in this chapter. Jesus comes to Jerusalem in a new role. Heretofore He had entered the city unobtrusively. Now He presses His claims as King upon the city of the King. Nothing could be more forward or daring. He cleanses the temple for the second time. This is presumption of the first order if He is not the One whom He claims to be. He curses the fig tree, which is a symbolic action. He meets the challenge of the religious rulers and by parable accuses them of plotting His death.

You will note the decisive and deliberate tone in the method of Jesus. He is forcing the issue now. He will force them to act when and how He chooses. He is in full control of the entire situation. He is never more kingly than when He approaches the cross.

THE SO-CALLED TRIUMPHAL ENTRY

And when they drew nigh unto Jerusalem, and were come to Bethphage, unto the mount of Olives, then sent Jesus two disciples,

Saying unto them, Go into the village over against you, and straightway ye shall find an ass tied, and a colt with her: loose them, and bring them unto me.

And if any man say aught unto you, ye shall say, The Lord hath need of them, and straightway he will send them [Matt. 21:1–3].

I see no point in reading a miracle into this incident, although many people do. I believe this is a normal, natural situation. Probably when our Lord was in Jerusalem the last time He made arrangements with some friends to use these animals the next time He came to the city. He may have disclosed to them what He intended to do, and they agreed to have them ready for Him at the Passover Feast. I think that He told them that He would send a couple of His disciples to get them and that He would tell them what to say—"The Lord hath need of them." I feel that this incident is much more wonderful if we look at it in this way.

All this was done, that it might be fulfilled which was spoken by the prophet, saying,

Tell ye the daughter of Sion, Behold, thy King cometh unto thee, meek, and sitting upon an ass, and a colt the foal of an ass [Matt. 21:4–5].

This is a quotation from Zechariah 9:9—"Rejoice greatly, O daughter of Zion; shout, O daughter of Jerusalem: behold, thy King cometh unto thee: he is just, and having salvation; lowly, and riding upon an ass, and upon a colt the foal of an ass."

There are certain important omissions in the quotation in Matthew which a careful comparison will reveal. "Rejoice greatly, O daughter of Zion" is omitted. Why? Because our Lord is not coming into Jerusalem for that time of rejoicing. That will take place at His second coming. Also omitted is "he is just, and having salvation"—the word *salvation* has the thought of victory, which will be fulfilled at His second coming. The conclusion to be drawn from these portions is that at His second coming there will be a true triumphal entry.

It is assumed that our Lord was displaying His meekness by riding upon this little donkey. That is not true. This little animal was ridden by kings. In our day it would be like riding into town in a Rolls Royce. The donkey was the animal of peace while the horse was the animal of war. When Jesus came into Jerusalem riding on this little animal of peace, He was offering Himself as King. In spite of the fact that He was doing that, the prophet says that He was humble. That is very important to see.

And the disciples went, and did as Jesus commanded them,

And brought the ass, and the colt, and put on them their clothes, and they set him thereon.

And a very great multitude spread their garments in the way; others cut down branches from the trees, and strawed them in the way.

And the multitudes that went before, and that followed, cried, saying, Hosanna to the son of David: Blessed is he that cometh in the name of the Lord; Hosanna in the highest [Matt. 21:6–9].

It is possible that He had never come into Jerusalem by this route before—we'll see that in the Gospel of John. I think that generally He came in by the sheep gate in a very unobtrusive manner, the gate through which the animals for sacrifice were brought. But not this time! Here He rides in as a King, and those who are with Him recognize Him as a King. It is their opportunity to accept Him or reject Him.

And when he was come into Jerusalem, all the city was moved, saying, Who is this?

And the multitude said, This is Jesus the prophet of Nazareth of Galilee [Matt. 21:10–11].

Our Lord forces Jerusalem to consider His claims for one final moment.

THE SECOND CLEANSING OF THE TEMPLE

And Jesus went into the temple of God, and cast out all them that sold and bought in the temple, and overthrew the tables of the moneychangers, and the seats of them that sold doves,

And said unto them, It is written, My house shall be called the house of prayer; but ye have made it a den of thieves [Matt. 21:12–13].

That is very strong language, is it not? Now let me call your attention to certain facts regarding the so-called triumphal entry. First of all, I do not think that "triumphal" entry is the proper name for it because, as we have seen, only certain portions of Zechariah's prophecy were fulfilled. Our Lord came into the city of Jerusalem in order that He might be the *Savior.* He was making the final public presentation of Himself to the people. When you consider the four Gospel records together, they present a composite picture. The obvious conclusion is that He did not enter the city on only one day but on three separate days.

The first time was on Saturday, the Sabbath day. There were no money changers on that day, and He looked around and left, "And Jesus entered into Jerusalem, and into the temple: and when he had looked round about upon all things, and now the eventide was come, he went out unto Bethany with the twelve" (Mark 11:11). He entered as *Priest.*

The second day He entered Jerusalem was on Sunday, the first day of the week. The money changers were there, and He cleansed the temple (vv. 12–13). On this day He entered as *King.*

The third day He entered Jerusalem was on Monday, the second day of the week. At that time He wept over Jerusalem, then entered the temple and taught and healed (see Luke 19:41–44; 47–48). He entered as a *Prophet* that day.

As we compare these three records in Matthew, Mark, and Luke, it becomes apparent that they record three different entries, and I believe that our Lord entered Jerusalem on three consecutive days and in three consecutive roles— as Priest, as King, as Prophet.

And He retired each day to Bethany. Apparently, He did not spend the night in the city until He was arrested.

Remember that the so-called triumphal entry ended at the cross. But He will come the second time in *triumph.* The writer to the Hebrews puts this together in a wonderful way: "So Christ was once offered to bear the sins of many; and unto them that look for him shall he appear the second time without sin unto salvation" (Heb. 9:28). We are told in Zechariah 14:4 that when He comes the next time to this earth, His feet will stand on the Mount of Olives—that's where He will touch down. Then when He enters the city of Jerusalem, that will be the triumphal entry! I cannot call these three entries into Jerusalem triumphal entries because He is on His way to the cross to die for your sin and my sin.

After the Lord cleansed the temple, many came to Him for help:

And the blind and the lame came to him in the temple; and he healed them [Matt. 21:14].

Notice how Matthew emphasizes the fact that multitudes of folk were healed.

And when the chief priests and scribes saw the wonderful things that he did, and the children crying in the temple, and saying, Hosanna to the son of David; they were sore displeased [Matt. 21:15].

They resented it.

And said unto him, Hearest thou what these say? And Jesus saith unto them, Yea; have ye never read, Out of the mouth of babes and sucklings thou hast perfected praise?

And he left them, and went out of the city into Bethany; and he lodged there [Matt. 21:16–17].

"And he left them" indicates His rejection of the religious leaders.

"And went out of the city into Bethany." As we have indicated, our Lord did not spend the night in Jerusalem until the night of His arrest. But we find Him coming back into the city the next day. This, I think, is the entry that Luke emphasizes for us, His third and last entry on Monday morning—

THE SCORCHED FIG TREE

Now in the morning as he returned into the city, he hungered.

And when he saw a fig tree in the way, he came to it, and found nothing thereon, but leaves only, and said unto it, Let no fruit grow on thee henceforward for ever. And presently the fig tree withered away [Matt. 21:18–19].

There has been a great deal of difficulty in attempting to interpret the fig tree incident. I have heard all sorts of ideas about what the fig tree represents. The fig tree, I believe, is symbolic of Israel as in Matthew 24, as we shall see. At least we can say with confidence that when our Lord came into the world, there was no fruit evidenced by the nation of Israel. There were only the outward leaves of a ritualistic, lifeless religion. This the Lord condemned. The nation of Israel went through a religious form, but they had no power. They had turned what God had given them into a dead, lifeless ritual without vitality and virility which no longer was accomplishing God's purpose. And I am of the opinion that God will deal the same way with the organized church which has turned its back upon the Person of Jesus Christ.

Again let me say that I feel His cursing of the fig tree is symbolic. Certainly He condemned the nation of Israel, and the nation suffered devastating judgment in A.D. 70.

And when the disciples saw it, they marvelled, saying, How soon is the fig tree withered away! [Matt. 21:20].

To them this was an amazing thing.

Jesus answered and said unto them, Verily I say unto you, If ye have faith, and doubt not, ye shall not only do this which is done to the fig tree, but also if ye shall say unto this mountain, Be thou removed, and be thou cast into the sea; it shall be done.

And all things, whatsoever ye shall ask in prayer, believing, ye shall receive [Matt. 21:21–22].

Our Lord is giving them a lesson in prayer, that there should be *faith* in prayer. They marvel that the fig tree was cursed, and He tells them that their problem is that they do not have faith to believe that God can move in such a miraculous way.

Frankly, I do not believe that our business is cursing fig trees or removing literal mountains. For many years I have lived in Southern California right along the foothills of the Sierra Madre mountains. To me they are lovely. I have never grown tired of them. I always enjoy looking at them, and there are never two days when they are alike. In Psalm 121 the psalmist says, "I will (lit., "Shall I . . .?") lift up mine eyes unto the hills, from whence cometh my help?" I don't think that he was implying that his help came from the hills, because he added, "My help cometh from the LORD, which made heaven and earth" (Ps. 121:1–2). Certainly, I do not look to those mountains for help, only for enjoyment, and I have never wanted to move them. I feel that there is something bigger and more important to do than mountain moving and fig tree cursing. To preach the gospel of Christ, to give out the Word of God so that the Spirit of God can use it—that, my friend, is a miracle! When these lips of clay can say something that the Spirit of God can use to transform a life, that involves the kind of faith that I want. What we need is faith to believe that God can and will use His Word.

THE SEARCHING QUESTION

Again Jesus is challenged by the religious authorities—

And when he was come into the temple, the chief priests and the elders of the people came unto him as he was teaching, and said, By what authority doest thou these things? and who gave thee this authority? [Matt. 21:23].

The religious rulers are becoming ugly and very hateful in their manner. They do not question what the Lord Jesus is doing. Do you notice that? They have no basis on which they can deny the miraculous things He does; they can only question His authority.

And Jesus answered and said unto them, I also will ask you one thing, which if ye tell me, I in like wise will tell you by what authority I do these things [Matt. 21:24].

Here is His question to them—

The baptism of John, whence was it? from heaven, or of men? And they reasoned with themselves, saying, If we shall say, From heaven; he will say unto us, Why did ye not then believe him?

But if we shall say, Of men; we fear the people; for all hold John as a prophet [Matt. 21:25–26].

You see, these religious rulers were attempting to trap Him by putting Him on the horns of a dilemma, but He immediately put them on the horns of a dilemma. He said, "I'll tell you by what authority I work if you will tell Me by what authority John the Baptist did his work. Was it from heaven or was it of men?" Of course, if they had said it was of heaven, our Lord would have said, "I move by the same authority." So they would not answer Him. They would not accept John's authority as being from heaven; so, of course, they would not accept Jesus' authority either.

And they answered Jesus, and said, We cannot tell. And he said unto them, Neither tell I you by what authority I do these things [Matt. 21:27].

You can sense the tension developing in this situation. The Lord is about to deliver a scathing denunciation of the religious rulers. He will give a parable that places publicans and harlots above them, and the charge of Jesus cannot be ignored. The Lord is moving against these two men.

PARABLE OF THE TWO SONS

But what think ye? A certain man had two sons; and he came to the first, and said, Son, go work to-day in my vineyard.

He answered and said, I will not; but afterward he repented, and went.

And he came to the second, and said likewise. And he answered and said, I go, sir: and went not.

Whether of them twain did the will of his father? They say unto him, The first. Jesus saith unto them, Verily I say unto you, That the publicans and the harlots go into the kingdom of God before you [Matt. 21:28–31].

This parable was a terrible insult to the religious rulers. Jesus likens them to the second son who said he would work for his father but did not. The Lord places publicans and harlots on a higher plane than these religious leaders.

This parable applies today. Many people have joined the church and are religious and think they are Christians, but they are not. They can perform their church rituals and give mental assent to the doctrines, but they are not genuine believers unless there has been a transformation in their lives. "Therefore if any man be in Christ, he is a new creature: old things are passed away; behold, all things are become new" (2 Cor. 5:17). The publicans and harlots recognized their sinfulness and came to Christ for salvation. They came late—at first they had said no to God, but they repented and came to Him, and He received them.

For John came unto you in the way of righteousness, and ye believed him not: but the publicans and the harlots believed him: and ye, when ye had seen it, repented not afterward, that ye might believe him [Matt. 21:32].

The religious rulers had a religion of exterior decorations with nothing real inside. When a person accepts Jesus Christ as Savior, the interior is not only redecorated, it is made new.

Now our Lord gives them another parable before they can get out of earshot—

PARABLE OF THE HOUSEHOLDER AND HIS VINEYARD

In this parable the householder represents God the Father, and the son is the Lord Jesus Christ. The husbandmen are a picture of Israel.

Hear another parable: There was a certain householder, which planted a vineyard, and hedged it round about, and digged a winepress in it, and built a tower, and let it out to husbandmen, and went into a far country:

And when the time of the fruit drew near, he sent his servants to the husbandmen, that they might receive the fruits of it.

And the husbandmen took his servants, and beat one, and killed another, and stoned another.

Again, he sent other servants more than the first: and they did unto them likewise.

But last of all he sent unto them his son, saying, They will reverence my son.

But when the husbandmen saw the son, they said among themselves, This is the heir; come, let us kill him, and let us seize on his inheritance [Matt. 21:33–38].

This is the most pointed parable that our Lord has given so far. It is His final warning to the religious rulers. When in the parable He said, "But last of all he sent unto them his son," the Son was standing before them, giving them the parable. What are they going to do with God's Son? He is telling them right now what is in their hearts.

And they caught him, and cast him out of the vineyard, and slew him [Matt. 21:39].

This was startling to these men!

When the lord therefore of the vineyard cometh, what will he do unto those husbandmen?

They say unto him, He will miserably destroy those wicked men, and will let out his vineyard unto other husbandmen, which shall render him the fruits in their seasons [Matt. 21:40–41].

Now He sends them back to the Old Testament for the analogy of the "stone" to Himself.

Jesus saith unto them, Did ye never read in the scriptures, The stone which the builders rejected, the same is become the head of the corner: this is the Lord's doing, and it is marvellous in our eyes?

Therefore say I unto you, The kingdom of God shall be taken from you, and given to a nation bringing forth the fruits thereof [Matt. 21:42–43].

It is interesting to note that the Lord changed the expression "kingdom of heaven" to "kingdom of God." I feel that He is using the larger term because He is getting ready to include the Gentiles and everybody that will come to Him.

"The kingdom of God shall be taken from you, and given to a nation bringing forth the fruits thereof"—that is, taken from the Jews and given to the church. "But ye are a chosen generation, a royal priesthood, an holy nation, a peculiar people; that ye should shew forth the praises of him who hath called you out of darkness into his marvellous light" (1 Pet. 2:9). The church is that "holy nation."

And whosoever shall fall on this stone shall be broken: but on whomsoever it shall fall, it will grind him to powder [Matt. 21:44].

"Whosoever shall fall on this stone shall be broken" relates to Christ's first coming. He is the Rock on which the church is built. "For other foundation can no man lay than that is laid, which is Jesus Christ" (1 Cor. 3:11). To fall on that Stone is to come to Christ for salvation in this day of grace. To reject Christ is to have the Stone fall later in the judgment about which Daniel prophesied (see Dan. 2:34,44–45), which relates to Christ's second coming.

And when the chief priests and Pharisees had heard his parables, they perceived that he spake of them [Matt. 21:45].

They knew what He was talking about. In our day, unfortunately, a great many folk don't see that there is also an application for themselves, especially for those in the church.

But when they sought to lay hands on him, they feared the multitude, because they took him for a prophet [Matt. 21:46].

Although the religious rulers had determined that Jesus should die, when they attempted to seize Him, they became fearful of the multitudes who considered Him a prophet of God.

CHAPTER 22

THEME: *Jesus gives the parable of the marriage feast for the king's son; Jesus answers and silences the Herodians, the Sadducees, and the Pharisees*

Chapter 21 closed with the religious rulers determined that Jesus would die. "They sought to lay hands on him" (Matt. 21:46), but they were afraid of the multitude at that time. The chapter before us continues the verbal clash our Lord is having with the religious rulers. He gives them first the parable of the king who made a marriage feast. This is His continuing answer to the chief priests and elders which He began in the previous chapter.

PARABLE OF THE MARRIAGE FEAST

This is one of the greatest parables Jesus gave for the period in which you and I live.

And Jesus answered and spake unto them again by parables, and said [Matt. 22:1].

Take note of the word *again*. This little word indicates that Jesus is still addressing the chief priests and elders mentioned in Matthew 21:23.

The kingdom of heaven is like unto a certain king, which made a marriage for his son [Matt. 22:2].

Obviously, "a certain king" is God the Father, and "his son" is the Lord Jesus. Notice that He resorts to the expression "kingdom of heaven" instead of kingdom of God which He used in the previous two parables. This parable parallels the Matthew 13 parables. But the emphasis here is upon how and why this age began rather than upon the conclusion of the age, which we saw in Matthew 13.

And sent forth his servants to call them that were bidden to the wedding: and they would not come [Matt. 22:3].

He "sent forth his servants to call them that were bidden to the wedding." Who were bidden? The lost sheep of the house of Israel—our Lord had sent His apostles to them, you recall. And the prophets had been the messengers back in the Old Testament.

Again, he sent forth other servants, saying, Tell them which are bidden, Behold, I have prepared my dinner: my oxen and my fatlings are killed, and all things are ready: come unto the marriage [Matt. 22:4].

What was the response?

But they made light of it, and went their ways, one to his farm, another to his merchandise:

And the remnant took his servants, and entreated them spitefully, and slew them [Matt. 22:5–6].

This was Israel's rejection of God's invitation. They killed His messengers, including the Lord Jesus Himself.

But when the king heard thereof, he was wroth: and he sent forth his armies, and destroyed those murderers, and burned up their city [Matt. 22:7].

This undoubtedly refers to the destruction of Jerusalem in A.D. 70 by Titus the Roman.

Then saith he to his servants, The wedding is ready, but they which were bidden were not worthy [Matt. 22:8].

Now we will see a definite change in the method and manner of the invitation, and it refers to the present age in which we live—

Go ye therefore into the highways, and as many as ye shall find, bid to the marriage.

So those servants went out into the highways, and gathered together all as many as they found, both bad and good: and the wedding was furnished with guests [Matt. 22:9–10].

But notice what happens—

And when the king came in to see the guests, he saw there a man which had not on a wedding garment [Matt. 22:11].

What is that wedding garment? The King's invitation is for everyone, but there is a danger of coming without meeting the demands of the King. That wedding garment is the righteousness of Christ which is absolutely essential for salvation, and it is supplied to all who believe. The apostle Paul speaks of this imputed righteousness: "But now the righteousness of God without the law [that is, apart from the law] is manifested, being witnessed by the law and the prophets; Even the righteousness of [from] God which is by faith of Jesus Christ unto all and upon all [it comes down upon all] them that believe: for there is no difference" (Rom. 3:21–22). *All* have to have a wedding garment.

And he saith unto him, Friend, how camest thou in hither not having a wedding garment? And he was speechless [Matt. 22:12].

Notice that he was speechless! I hear some folk say that they don't need to receive Christ, that they will take their chances before God, that they intend to argue their case. Well, our Lord said that this fellow without the wedding garment was *speechless*.

Then said the king to the servants, Bind him hand and foot, and take him away, and cast him into outer darkness; there shall be weeping and gnashing of teeth.

For many are called, but few are chosen [Matt. 22:13–14].

Whether or not you accept the wedding garment is up to you, but Christ has provided it for you. The invitation has gone out to everyone, but you will have to come on the King's terms.

Now the enemies of Christ will make their final onslaught, their final attack upon the Lord Jesus. The Herodians will come first, the Sadducees will come next, and finally the Pharisees will come. Then our Lord will question the Pharisees—and they will try to get away from Him as quickly as they can. That marks the final break, and in chapter 23 we will hear Him denounce them.

The Herodians will come with the question of paying tribute to Caesar. The Sadducees will come with a question regarding the resurrection. And the Pharisees will come with their question concerning the great commandment of the Law. We will see the marvelous way in which our Lord answers these men. May I say that I consider one of the proofs of His deity is the way in which He deals with the enemy.

JESUS ANSWERS THE HERODIANS

The Herodians come to Him with a question which is actually related to their particular position. They were a political party which favored the house of Herod and looked to those of that house to deliver them from the Roman yoke. I don't think the Herodians could be considered a religious party at all because they were strongly political. However, the Pharisees apparently used them, and it is quite possible that many of the Pharisees were Herodians as well.

Notice that the Pharisees instigate this first attack upon the Lord Jesus—

Then went the Pharisees, and took counsel how they might entangle him in his talk.

And they sent out unto him their disciples with the Herodians, saying, Master, we know that thou art true, and teachest the way of God in truth, neither carest thou for any man: for thou regardest not the person of men.

Tell us therefore, What thinkest thou? Is it lawful to give tribute unto Caesar, or not? [Matt. 22:15–17].

Obviously, they were not wanting His opinion. They had their own answer. It was a trick question. If He had said, "No, you are not to pay tribute to Caesar," He could be accused of being a traitor to Rome, and Rome was ruling over Israel at that time. If He had said, "Yes, you are to pay tribute to Caesar," He could not be the true Messiah. They thought that they had our Lord on the horns of a dilemma.

But Jesus perceived their wickedness, and said, Why tempt ye me, ye hypocrites? [Matt. 22:18].

Notice that He called them what they were—hypocrites.

Show me the tribute money. And they brought unto him a penny [Matt. 22:19].

It is notable that He used *their* coin. I have often wondered why He didn't use His own coin. I think it is because He didn't have one.

And he saith unto them, Whose is this image and superscription? [Matt. 22:20].

They were using the legal tender of the Roman government, and here it was a Roman coin.

They say unto him, Caesar's. Then saith he unto them, Render therefore unto Caesar the things which are Caesar's; and unto God the things that are God's [Matt. 22:21].

This is an amazing answer because it involves more than just answering their question—and He certainly did that. In addition, He is saying that they did owe something to Caesar. They were using his coins, they walked down Roman roads, and Rome did provide them with a measure of peace; so they did owe something to Rome. Therefore, render unto Caesar the things which are Caesar's. But there is another department: Render unto *God* the things that are *God's*.

When they had heard these words, they marvelled, and left him, and went their way [Matt. 22:22].

Obviously, this reveals that our Lord did not fall into their trap. Although they did owe Caesar something, that did not remove their responsibility to God.

The Herodians left Him, and now it's time for the Sadducees to come to bat, and they also attempt to trap Him—

JESUS ANSWERS THE SADDUCEES

The same day came to him the Sadducees, which say that there is no resurrection, and asked him,

Saying, Master, Moses said, If a man die, having no children, his brother shall marry his wife, and raise up seed unto his brother.

Now there were with us seven brethren: and the first, when he had married a wife, deceased, and, having no issue, left his wife unto his brother:

Likewise the second also, and the third, unto the seventh.

And last of all the woman died also.

Therefore in the resurrection whose wife shall she be of the seven? for they all had her [Matt. 22:23–28].

The Sadducees did not believe in the resurrection. They used a ridiculous illustration to try to trap the Lord. Imagine a woman who had had seven brothers for her husbands! She must have lived in Hollywood to accomplish this. Their question was, "Whose wife shall she be?" Now the Sadducees erred in two respects, and the Lord brings this to their attention.

Jesus answered and said unto them, Ye do err, not knowing the scriptures, nor the power of God [Matt. 22:29].

The Sadducees were ignorant in two spheres: ignorant of the Scriptures and ignorant of the power of God. Ignorance of the Scriptures and ignorance of the power of God caused them to bring up such a ridiculous illustration. The explanation is simple—

For in the resurrection they neither marry, nor are given in marriage, but are as the angels of God in heaven [Matt. 22:30].

He is not saying that they are angels. Neither will *we* be angels in heaven. But we will be like angels in that we will not marry in heaven. In other words, in heaven there will not be any necessity to continue the race by means of birth. This does not mean that a husband and wife who were very close down here cannot be together in heaven. If they want to be together, of course they can be together. But, my friend, think of the ones who wouldn't want to be together. They won't have to be together. However, they both will have new dispositions, and probably they will get along lots better up there than they did down here!

But as touching the resurrection of the dead, have ye not read that which was spoken unto you by God, saying,

I am the God of Abraham, and the God of Isaac, and the God of Jacob? God is

not the God of the dead, but of the living [Matt. 22:31–32].

This is a devastating statement! What about those who have gone before? What about Abraham today? Well, he is just as much Abraham today as he ever was. Abraham, Isaac, and Jacob have been simply transferred from earth to another place. They are not dead; they are alive. And this is true of your loved ones who are in Christ and are waiting in heaven for you. This is a glorious truth!

And when the multitude heard this, they were astonished at his doctrine [Matt. 22:33].

JESUS ANSWERS THE PHARISEES

Now the Herodians and the Sadducees have been silenced. The Pharisees have been watching Jesus and these two groups. The Pharisees were a religio-political party. They wanted to see the kingdom of David brought back into power in order to rid themselves of Rome. In restoring the kingdom they could join the Herodians, but as a religious party they opposed the Sadducees. The Pharisees would correspond to the conservative wing of the church today, and the Sadducees would correspond to the liberal wing of the church. The Pharisees, like the other two groups, were out to trap the Lord, and so their representative, a lawyer, posed a very interesting question.

But when the Pharisees had heard that he had put the Sadducees to silence, they were gathered together.

Then one of them, which was a lawyer, asked him a question, tempting him, and saying [Matt. 22:34–35].

The Pharisees have a huddle, then they plan a strategy and put forth this very clever lawyer, that is, a scribe, an expert in the Mosaic Law, to propound a question—

Master, which is the great commandment in the law? [Matt. 22:36].

Listen to the answer of the Lord Jesus—

Jesus said unto him, Thou shalt love the Lord thy God with all thy heart, and with all thy soul, and with all thy mind.

This is the first and great commandment [Matt. 22:37–38].

Notice that He did not pick any one of the Ten Commandments. He gives them a second one—

And the second is like unto it, Thou shalt love thy neighbour as thyself [Matt. 22:39].

When you put this down on your life, you will recognize that you are coming short of the glory of God.

Our Lord is very straightforward with this man. He says, "You want to know which is the greatest commandment. To love God is the greatest commandment, and to love your neighbor is the next greatest."

On these two commandments hang all the law and the prophets [Matt. 22:40].

These two commandments actually summarized the entire Mosaic Law. The answer of Jesus was so obviously accurate that if the Pharisees had been honest, they would have said, "We have fallen short. We cannot be saved by the Law; we do need a Savior." And at that time the Lord Jesus, the Savior, was almost under the shadow of the cross.

JESUS PUTS A QUESTION TO THE PHARISEES

The Pharisees huddle again to try to trap Him with another question, but He beats them to the punch and asks *them* a question—

While the Pharisees were gathered together, Jesus asked them,

Saying, What think ye of Christ? whose son is he? They say unto him, The son of David.

He saith unto them, How then doth David in spirit call him Lord, saying,

The LORD said unto my Lord, Sit thou on my right hand, till I make thine enemies thy footstool? [Matt. 22:41–44].

The Lord Jesus is quoting Psalm 110:1. How could David call his *son* his *Lord?* The Pharisees would have to say that the son would have to be supernaturally born for David to call him "my Lord."

If David then call him Lord, how is he his son? [Matt. 22:45].

This is the searching question which our Lord put to the Pharisees.

There are several implications in this question which are tremendous. Our Lord said that David wrote Psalm 110, that he wrote it by the Holy Spirit, and that he wrote it about the Messiah. "If David then call him Lord, how is he his son?" How could David call his son superior unless He was? The only logical answer to this question is the Virgin Birth. Jesus is David's son, but He is greater than David. A son of David cannot be greater than David unless there is something greater introduced into the line to make a greater son. The records of the supernatural birth of Jesus afford the only satisfactory answer. The *Lord* of David got into David's line, as stated in Luke's gospel, "And the angel answered and said unto her, The Holy Ghost shall come upon thee, and the power of the Highest shall overshadow thee: therefore also that holy thing which shall be born of thee shall be called the Son of God" (Luke 1:35). He is greater than David because He is the Lord from heaven.

The Lord Jesus was forcing the Pharisees to face up to the real issue and to acknowledge Him as David's son and as David's Lord.

This ended the verbal clash with the religious rulers.

And no man was able to answer him a word, neither durst any man from that day forth ask him any more questions [Matt. 22:46].

They made no verbal attack upon Him after this. They had determined His death, and that is the thing toward which they are going to move. They see that they cannot answer Him. This is one of the great proofs of His deity.

CHAPTER 23

***THEME:** Jesus warns the multitude against the scribes and Pharisees; pronounces woes upon the scribes and Pharisees; weeps over Jerusalem*

This chapter concludes the clash between the Lord Jesus and the religious rulers. He warns the multitudes about them and then denounces the religious rulers in unmistakable terms. No words that ever fell from the lips of our Lord were more scathing. It is a merciless condemnation. If you read this chapter carefully, it will blanch your own soul.

JESUS WARNS AGAINST THE SCRIBES AND PHARISEES

Jesus' public denunciation of the Pharisees took place at the temple, the stronghold of His enemies.

Then spake Jesus to the multitude, and to his disciples,

Saying, The scribes and the Pharisees sit in Moses' seat [Matt. 23:1–2].

These religious rulers were in the place of authority, and they controlled the Old Testament Scriptures. They usurped that which they had no right to usurp. They occupied very much the same position that church leaders occupy today. People looked to them for the interpretation of the truth.

All therefore whatsoever they bid you observe, that observe and do; but do not ye after their works: for they say, and do not [Matt. 23:3].

That is, do as the Scriptures teach, but don't follow the works of scribes and Pharisees because they are not following the Word of God.

Listen to His sad commentary upon the religious rulers—

For they bind heavy burdens and grievous to be borne, and lay them on men's shoulders; but they themselves will not move them with one of their fingers.

But all their works they do for to be seen of men: they make broad their phylacteries, and enlarge the borders of their garments,

And love the uppermost rooms at feasts, and the chief seats in the synagogues,

And greetings in the markets, and to be called of men, Rabbi, Rabbi [Matt. 23:4–7].

These men liked to have titles. These men liked to be recognized. They liked to wear certain religious garments and habits which set them apart from other people and drew attention to their high position. Our Lord is condemning all of this.

But be not ye called Rabbi: for one is your Master, even Christ; and all ye are brethren [Matt. 23:8].

"Be not ye called Rabbi"—meaning teacher. And in the church certain respect and honor belongs to a pastor, but he is no different from anyone else. He is just one of your brothers.

And call no man your father upon the earth: for one is your Father, which is in heaven.

Neither be ye called masters: for one is your Master, even Christ [Matt. 23:9–10].

A "father" is a life-giver. To call a man a "father" in spiritual matters is to put him in the place of God as the one who gives spiritual life. This is blasphemous. Only God the Father gives life. A "master" is one in a position of authority. Christ is the One in the position of authority as the head of the church today.

But he that is greatest among you shall be your servant.

And whosoever shall exalt himself shall be abased; and he that shall humble himself shall be exalted [Matt. 23:11–12].

If you want to be the greatest, then become the servant of all.

WOES PRONOUNCED AGAINST THE SCRIBES AND PHARISEES

Here we see the gentle Jesus using the harshest language that is in the entire Word of God. No prophet of the Old Testament denounced sin as the Lord Jesus denounces it.

Here in Southern California this section was called to the attention of a liberal preacher. He didn't even know it was in the Bible—he had never read the Bible! In our day there is a misunderstanding of who the Lord Jesus really is. Liberalism gives the impression that all He ever talked about was love. One of the banners that was carried about in a protest march in Berkeley a number of years ago bore the slogan "Jesus Yes, Church No." A senator from Oregon made a great deal of that, maintaining that the church is giving the wrong impression, that this generation wants Jesus, but that they don't want the church as it is. Well, I agree that the church in general is giving the wrong impression, but the main problem is that they have really misunderstood who Jesus is. He is not the "love-child" that the liberal thinks He is. Certainly it is true that He loves sinners and died for sinners, but also He is going to *judge* sinners. We need to have a correct perspective of Him. Therefore, *He* is the One who is misunderstood in our day.

The average conception of the Lord Jesus is not even biblical. For example, I asked a liberal preacher this: "Was the Jesus in whom you believe virgin born?"

He said, "No."

"Did he die on the cross for the sins of the world?"

"No."

"Did he rise bodily from the grave?"

"No!"

"Well, I'd like to know where *that* Jesus ever originated. There are no documents which give any information about *that* Jesus living in the first century. The only documents we have tell of One who was virgin born, who performed miracles, who died for the sins of the world, who rose from the dead, who ascended into heaven, and who is returning to this earth as the *Judge*."

My friend, *this* Jesus is not generally known today, and yet He is the only Jesus Christ who has ever lived. The other one is a figment of the imagination.

Listen to Him now as He pronounces woes upon the scribes and Pharisees. This is strong language.

But woe unto you, scribes and Pharisees, hypocrites! for ye shut up the kingdom of heaven against men: for ye neither go in yourselves, neither suffer ye them that are entering to go in [Matt. 23:13].

The Lord uses the term *woe* eight times in this section and calls scribes and Pharisees hypocrites seven times. He accuses them of blocking the way to heaven by their false leadership.

Woe unto you, scribes and Pharisees, hypocrites! for ye devour widows' houses, and for a pretence make long prayer: therefore ye shall receive the greater damnation [Matt. 23:14].

In other words, these men made long prayers, but they were heartless and crooked in their business dealings.

Woe unto you, scribes and Pharisees, hypocrites! for ye compass sea and land to make one proselyte, and when he is made, ye make him twofold more the child of hell than yourselves [Matt. 23:15].

Oh, they were great at going out and witnessing, but they were not bringing anyone to

God. None of their converts were actually born again.

Woe unto you, ye blind guides, which say, Whosoever shall swear by the temple, it is nothing; but whosoever shall swear by the gold of the temple, he is a debtor! [Matt. 23:16].

"He is a debtor!"—that is, his oath is binding.

Ye fools and blind: for whether is greater, the gold, or the temple that sanctifieth the gold?

And, Whosoever shall swear by the altar, it is nothing; but whosoever sweareth by the gift that is upon it, he is guilty [Matt. 23:17–18].

That is, he is guilty if he fails to carry out his oath.

Ye fools and blind: for whether is greater, the gift, or the altar that sanctifieth the gift?

Whoso therefore shall swear by the altar, sweareth by it, and by all things thereon.

And, whoso shall swear by the temple, sweareth by it, and by him that dwelleth therein.

And he that shall swear by heaven, sweareth by the throne of God, and by him that sitteth thereon [Matt. 23:19–22].

The Pharisees were teaching that if you swore by the temple or the altar, you were not bound to keep your oath. But if you swore by the *gold* of the temple or by the *gift* on the altar, the oath was binding. They were splitting hairs, of course, and they were placing the emphasis on material things rather than upon the spiritual purpose for which they were to be used.

Now listen to our Lord's strong denunciation—

Woe unto you, scribes and Pharisees, hypocrites! for ye pay tithe of mint and anise and cummin, and have omitted the weightier matters of the law, judgment, mercy, and faith: these ought ye to have done, and not to leave the other undone [Matt. 23:23].

They were very meticulous in tithing their little plants which produce condiments like mint, anise, and cummin. For instance, when I was a boy, my mother always grew a little patch of mint out in the backyard to put in iced tea in the summertime. Can you imagine one of these religious rulers measuring off a little patch of mint and taking a tenth of it to give to the Lord? Oh, they were so strict about those little matters! But our Lord says, "You have forgotten about the weightier matters of the law." And those weightier matters would have brought these men to the Person of Christ.

Ye blind guides, which strain at a gnat, and swallow a camel [Matt. 23:24].

Do you think this verse is humorous? I do, and if I had been present when Jesus said this, I would have laughed—unless, of course, I had been a Pharisee or a scribe. The Lord said this in a serious vein, but I am sure many in the crowd laughed, especially those who knew the old religious rulers.

There are a lot of folk who make so much of little things. I remember a dear lady who used to argue about the use of lipstick. She thought it was awful, and yet she had the meanest tongue of any person I know. She didn't think that was bad, but lipstick was terrible. Frankly, the paint of gossip on the end of the tongue—especially when it is used to blacken somebody's reputation—is lots worse than a little paint on the lips. It is amazing how people can strain at a gnat and swallow a camel!

Woe unto you, scribes and Pharisees, hypocrites! for ye make clean the outside of the cup and of the platter, but within they are full of extortion and excess [Matt. 23:25].

This fifth woe pictures the Pharisees with their emphasis on the externals. This is a picture of the average church today that is so busy making the outside of the cup and platter clean. They go through all the ceremonies. They want to have the best equipment. They talk so nice and piously on the outside, but inside they do not deal with sin. In most cases, they do not even like the word *sin*. But all of the external ceremonies cannot clean up their inner corruption. The Pharisees substituted ritual for reality, formality for faith, and liturgy for God.

Thou blind Pharisee, cleanse first that which is within the cup and platter, that the outside of them may be clean also [Matt. 23:26].

Don't misunderstand Him. He is not saying that the outside should not be clean. But you give a wrong impression when the inside is dirty and the outside is not. The place to start is on the inside.

Woe unto you, scribes and Pharisees, hypocrites! for ye are like unto whited sepulchres, which indeed appear beautiful outward, but are within full of dead men's bones, and of all uncleanness [Matt. 23:27].

To me this is the most frightening figure of speech which our Lord used. As I said previously, the cup and platter (saucer), clean on the outside and dirty on the inside, picture the average church in our day. But I am afraid that this simile of the tomb pictures the average church-goer—beautiful on the outside, but on the inside they are dead in trespasses and sins. They have a form of godliness, but they deny the power of it to make them new creations in Christ. My friend, until that happens to you, your church membership is null and void; it is nothing but hypocrisy. When I read that over half the population of the United States are church members, I wonder why in public places I see ninety-nine percent of the crowd drinking cocktails, using profanity, and telling dirty stories. We have a whole lot of marble tombs walking around, spiritual zombies, dead in trespasses and sins.

Even so ye also outwardly appear righteous unto men, but within ye are full of hypocrisy and iniquity [Matt. 23:28].

Oh, how He is denouncing religious leaders! And they *should* be denounced above everyone else. My friend, if you have a Bible-teaching church in your community and a preacher who believes the Book and is trying to teach it, for God's sake stand with him in these days. He needs you, and you need him. Oh, how we need men who believe the Word of God—and live it!

Woe unto you, scribes and Pharisees, hypocrites! because ye build the tombs of the prophets, and garnish the sepulchres of the righteous,

And say, If we had been in the days of our fathers, we would not have been partakers with them in the blood of the prophets.

Wherefore ye be witnesses unto yourselves, that ye are the children of them which killed the prophets.

Fill ye up then the measure of your fathers [Matt. 23:29–32].

And we are doing the same thing in our day. Great men of God, preachers, evangelists, missionaries, were denounced and ridiculed by their generations, but they are honored today. That was true of Spurgeon, Moody, Torrey, and many others. Our Lord sure did know human nature, and it has not changed. "You build the tombs to commemorate the prophets after they are gone, and you decorate the graves of the righteous!"

"Fill ye up then the measure of your fathers." These same religious leaders, who were honoring the prophets of the past, would soon force Rome to crucify the Son of God who was speaking to them.

Now this is something that will blanch your soul—

Ye serpents, ye generation of vipers, how can ye escape the damnation of hell? [Matt. 23:33].

Can you imagine stronger language than that? What does He mean by calling them a generation of vipers? He means that they are the offspring of snakes! This is devastating to that damnable doctrine of the universal brotherhood of man and the universal Fatherhood of God. God does not claim you if you have rejected Jesus Christ. The *only* way to become a child of God is to receive Christ. "But as many as received him, to them gave he power [the right] to become the sons of God, even to them that believe on his name" (John 1:12).

The Lord is speaking in harsh terms in these verses in Matthew. He is serving a cup of tea that is a little too strong for a great many of the liberal-minded folk of this present hour. Jesus Christ was no love child. He came to earth to die for your sins because He loved you, but if you reject Him, He becomes your Judge.

Wherefore, behold, I send unto you prophets, and wise men, and scribes: and some of them ye shall kill and crucify; and some of them shall ye scourge in your synagogues, and persecute them from city to city:

That upon you may come all the righteous blood shed upon the earth, from the blood of righteous Abel unto the blood of Zacharias son of Barachias, whom ye slew between the temple and the altar [Matt. 23:34–35].

Apparently the slaying of Zacharias was an incident which had taken place recently. Our Lord starts at the beginning with the murder of Abel and brings them down to the present hour. He makes it very clear that God will judge Israel for destroying the righteous. He is certainly contradicting our current philosophy that everyone will ultimately be saved. He says that they will not be saved.

Verily I say unto you, All these things shall come upon this generation [Matt. 23:36].

He is predicting the destruction of Jerusalem in A.D. 70. What does He do next? The One who made this strong denunciation will now *weep* over Jerusalem.

JESUS WEEPS OVER JERUSALEM

O Jerusalem, Jerusalem, thou that killest the prophets, and stonest them which are sent unto thee, how often would I have gathered thy children together, even as a hen gathereth her chickens under her wings, and ye would not!

Behold, your house is left unto you desolate [Matt. 23:37–38].

Jerusalem rejected Him in His so-called triumphal entry, and He has rejected Jerusalem, but now He weeps over this city. Yes, He denounced them, but He does love them. And knowing the judgment which must come, He weeps.

The statement was made in Dwight L. Moody's day that he was the only man living who should preach on hell because he did it with such compassion. And certainly our Lord pronounced these woes with a heart that was breaking. You remember that some of the people thought he was Jeremiah because, although Jeremiah gave the strongest denunciation in the Old Testament, he wept over it. I am of the opinion that we today should not make denunciations unless we are personally moved by them.

For I say unto you, Ye shall not see me henceforth, till ye shall say, Blessed is he that cometh in the name of the Lord [Matt. 23:39].

Not only were the religious rulers in shock, but His apostles were in shock, also. This seemed to them a strange turn of events. They expected Him to establish the kingdom, with Jerusalem as the capital. But now He says that their house is to be left desolate and that they will not see Him again until they say, "Blessed is he that cometh in the name of the Lord." You see, although He is on His way to the cross at this time, He gives them the assurance that He will return—and that will be His triumphal entry!

Obviously, the kingdom is going to be postponed. There are many who object to that teaching, but to do that, they must object to the language of our Lord. He tells His disciples that He will not establish the kingdom on earth at this time but that He will come again to establish it. That means that the kingdom is postponed, doesn't it? The apostles were surprised and disappointed at the idea of a postponement; so they come to Him with three questions, which we will see in the following chapter.

CHAPTER 24

***THEME:** The disciples ask Jesus three questions; He answers two about the sign of the end of the age and the sign of His coming*

Matthew 24 and 25, known as the Olivet Discourse, constitute the last of three major discourses in this gospel. They are called major discourses because of the extent, content, and intent of them.

JESUS PREDICTS THE DESTRUCTION OF JERUSALEM

Our Lord has now denounced the religious rulers. He has turned His back on Jerusalem and has told them that their house (temple) is left desolate.

And Jesus went out, and departed from the temple: and his disciples came to him for to shew him the buildings of the temple [Matt. 24:1].

The Lord Jesus has told them that His kingdom would be postponed and that the temple would be left desolate. (The temple was made up of many buildings. This was the temple that Herod was having built, and the construction was still in progress. It was made of white marble, and at this time it was very large and very beautiful.) The disciples are disturbed at the statement of Jesus that it is to be left desolate. So the disciples come to Him, wanting to show Him around the buildings.

And Jesus said unto them, See ye not all these things? verily I say unto you, There shall not be left here one stone upon another, that shall not be thrown down [Matt. 24:2].

"See ye not all these things?" The disciples thought they saw it, and they ask Him to take a look. So He says to them, "Do you really *see* it?" In our contemporary society, this is a good question for us to consider. Do we really *see* the world around us?

When my wife and I first came to Southern California, we spent every Monday, which was my day off, riding around looking at this fantastic place. (And it *was* fantastic in those days before everybody in the world tried to settle here!) After we had marveled at one beautiful spot after another, I would say to my wife, "But we really don't see it as it is. All of this is under God's judgment. It all will pass away." My friend, all these cultural centers, these great schools, these skyscrapers, these great cities which we see are going to pass away someday. It doesn't seem possible, and that is how the disciples felt.

Jesus continued by saying, "There shall not be left here one stone upon another, that shall not be thrown down." If His first statement put them in shock, this must have traumatized them.

When I was at the Wailing Wall in Jerusalem several years ago, the tour director tried to call my attention to the way the stones had been worn away by the people who had come there over the years to weep. That was certainly worth noting, but the thing that impressed me was that the wall was constructed of many kinds of stones. History tells us that the Wailing Wall was made up of stones which came from different buildings in different periods. At the pinnacle of the temple, which evidently was the corner of the temple area, recent excavations reveal the same thing—there are all kinds of stones from different periods. What does that mean? My friend, that means that not one stone was left upon another—the builders had to go and pick up stones from different places because in A.D. 70 Titus the Roman really destroyed that city!

Although this is ancient history to us, it was a shocking revelation to the disciples. They talked it over, I am sure, then came to Him with three questions.

And as he sat upon the mount of Olives, the disciples came unto him privately, saying, Tell us, when shall these things be? and what shall be the sign of thy coming, and of the end of the world? [Matt. 24:3].

(1) "When shall these things be?"—when one stone would not be left upon another; (2) "What shall be the sign of thy coming?"—The answer to this question is found in verses 23–51; and (3) "What shall be the sign . . . of the end of the world (completion of the age)?" The answer to this question is found in verses 9–22. The Lord Jesus is going to answer these three questions, and we call His answers the Olivet Discourse because it took place on the Mount of Olives.

JESUS ANSWERS THE DISCIPLES' QUESTIONS

The first question, "When shall these things be?"—when one stone shall not be left upon another, is not answered in the Gospel of Matthew. We find it in the Gospel of Luke, and we find segments of it in the Gospel of Mark. Why is it not included in Matthew's gospel? Because Matthew is the gospel of the kingdom; it presents the King. The destruction of Jerusalem in A.D. 70 has something to do with this age in which we live, but it has nothing to do with the distant future when the King is coming. Therefore, Matthew does not carry that part of the Olivet Discourse.

Let's look at our Lord's answer to the first question, as recorded in Luke's gospel: "And when ye shall see Jerusalem compassed with armies, then know that the desolation thereof is nigh. Then let them which are in Judaea flee to the mountains; and let them which are in the midst of it depart out; and let not them that are in the countries enter thereinto. For these be the days of vengeance, that all things which are written may be fulfilled. But woe unto them that are with child, and to them that give suck, in those days! for there shall be great distress in the land, and wrath upon this people. And they shall fall by the edge of the sword, and shall be led away captive into all nations: and Jerusalem shall be trodden down of the Gentiles, until the times of the Gentiles be fulfilled" (Luke 21:20–24).

Undoubtedly, many of those who heard the Lord Jesus say these things were present in A.D. 70 when the Roman armies surrounded the city, laid siege to it, cut it off from the rest of the world, then finally breached the wall and got in. What the Romans did was terrible.

They demolished the city. It was the worst destruction in its history, more devastating than that conducted by Nebuchadnezzar over six centuries earlier. When the Romans destroyed Jerusalem in A.D. 70, the first part of the Olivet Discourse was fulfilled.

The next two questions asked by the disciples were these: "What shall be the sign of thy coming, and of the end of the world [age]?"

The Lord is going to answer the disciples' questions in their chronological and logical order. He will answer their last question first and their second question last. The first thing the Lord deals with is the sign of the end of the world, or more accurately, the end of the age. The world will never come to an end. The old world will pass away and a new earth will be brought on the scene. It will be similar to trading in your old car for a new one. You don't say "This is the end of the car-age for me. I don't have a car anymore." You *do* have a car because you traded your old one in and got a new one. And the Lord is going to trade the old world in for a new one. The world will never come to an end. But it will be the end of an age, and that is the word the disciples are using in their question to the Lord Jesus.

In this Olivet Discourse, when Christ speaks of His coming, He is referring to His return to the earth to establish His kingdom. The church is not in the picture at all. In fact, by the end of the age, the church will have been removed, and it will be the last days of the nation Israel. He is speaking about the Great Tribulation Period and so labels it in this discourse.

JESUS TRACES THE CHARACTERISTICS OF THIS AGE

And Jesus answered and said unto them, Take heed that no man deceive you [Matt. 24:4].

The phrase "Take heed that no man deceive you" is characteristic of this entire age. The Lord gives this word of caution because there will be much deception, especially during the Tribulation Period when the Antichrist will appear. Peter warns us in 2 Peter 2:1, "But there were false prophets also among the people, even as there shall be false teachers among you, who privily shall bring in damnable heresies, even denying the Lord that bought them, and bring upon themselves swift destruction." We don't have to worry about false prophets, because if anybody starts prophesying in our day, we Christians can pooh-pooh him right off the scene because prophets are not for this period. However, we are to beware of false teachers, and there are a great many of those around. We must test them by Scripture. In this morning's mail a letter has come to me which illustrates this fact. It has come from a woman who apparently has an important position in an insurance company. She tells of a well-meaning friend who introduced her to a cult. After going to her friend's church for one year, she heard our Bible-teaching radio program, and the Scripture alerted her to the error of the cult. Then she tells of how she and her entire family went to a good church in her area. My friend, we need to beware of false teaching. There is a lot of it around in our day. Our Lord warns, "Take heed that no man deceive you."

For many shall come in my name, saying, I am Christ; and shall deceive many [Matt. 24:5].

Near the end of the age many people will claim to be Christ. We have such people present with us now. One man established a "holy city" in Northern California and expected any minute to be called to Washington, D.C., to solve the problems of the world. There are no "holy cities" on the face of the earth, but someday the Lord will come from the Holy of Holies in heaven to earth and solve the problems. It should be remembered that even now there are many antichrists, but at the end of the age there will come *one* Antichrist who will oppose Christ and set himself up as the only authority.

I believe that our Lord, up there on the Mount of Olives, looked down to the end of the age and to the Great Tribulation Period, but that at the beginning of His discourse, He bridged the gap by giving us a picture of the present age of the church. I recognize that there are many good Bible teachers, much better than I am, who take the position that in verses 5–8 He is speaking of the Tribulation Period, also; so if you want to disagree with me, you will be in very good company. However, it is my view that our Lord is not referring to the Great Tribulation until we reach verse 9 of this chapter.

And ye shall hear of wars and rumours of wars: see that ye be not troubled: for all these must come to pass, but the end is not yet [Matt. 24:6].

Wars and rumors of wars are not the sign that we are at the end of the age, by any means. The Lord is bridging the gap from where the disciples are to the end of the age. It is easy to think of major wars as indicative of the fact that we are at the end of the age. They are not! There have been many major wars in the past few thousand years and only about two hundred years of peace. When I was a little boy at the end of World War I, I remember hearing my dad and others talking about the books being printed declaring it was the end of the world. World War I caused this type of thinking. But after the war, we had a worldwide depression, World War II, and the atom bomb. By this time, I was a pastor in Pasadena, and I told my congregation that a wheelbarrow load of books would come out saying that we were at the end of the world because of World War II. You know something? I was wrong! Two wheelbarrow loads of books were printed, and they were sensational.

We have come a long way from World War II, and the end of the age still has not come. We should listen to the Lord and stop listening to false teachers. We will hear about wars and rumors of wars, but we should not be troubled because all these things will come to pass, and still it will not be the end of the age. Friend, we should also keep in mind that man will never solve the problem of war. The League of Nations could not solve this problem, and the United Nations will not be able to solve it either. There will be no peace until the Prince of Peace comes.

For nation shall rise against nation, and kingdom against kingdom: and there shall be famines, and pestilences, and earthquakes, in divers places.

All these are the beginning of sorrows [Matt. 24:7–8].

These are characteristics of the entire age and are therefore not signs of the end of the age, "but the end is not yet" (v. 6). False christs, rumors of wars, famines, pestilences, and earthquakes characterize the entire church age, but they will apparently be intensified as we draw near to the end of the age. Right now the population explosion has the world frightened and rightly so. People are starving to death by the thousands and the millions. And this situation is going to increase. The old black horse of famine (see Rev. 6:5–6) hasn't appeared yet, but at the end of the age the black horse and its rider will come forth. What we see today is just the beginning of sorrows.

The next verse begins with our first *time* word:

THE BEGINNING OF THE TRIBULATION WITH ITS SIGNS

Now the Lord begins to speak of the time of tribulation. You and I are living in the "age of the church" or the "age of the Holy Spirit," as some people like to speak of it. The Bible divides the world today into three groups of people: the Jews, the Gentiles, and the church of God (see 1 Cor. 10:32). In this age God is calling out a people to His name from both Jews and Gentiles to compose the third group, the church. It is this third group which will be taken out of the world at the time of the Rapture. Then the Great Tribulation will begin, and I believe that verse 9 speaks of this beginning—

Then shall they deliver you up to be afflicted, and shall kill you: and ye shall be hated of all nations for my name's sake [Matt. 24:9].

"Then shall they deliver you up to be afflicted"—who is the *you?* Obviously, He is not addressing the church but the nation Israel. The affliction He is talking about is anti-Semitism on a worldwide scale.

At this point let me inject an important fact for Christians in our day. As long as the true church is in the world, there could not be worldwide anti-Semitism because the church would resist it. No genuine believer in the Lord Jesus could hate the Jews; it is an impossibility. It is my feeling that the liberal wing of the church is presenting a false front to the Jews and that in the final analysis it will turn against them. But as long as the true church is in the world, there won't be worldwide anti-Semitism; it will break out *after* the church has been removed at the Rapture.

And then shall many be offended, and shall betray one another, and shall hate one another.

And many false prophets shall rise, and shall deceive many [Matt. 24:10–11].

As we saw earlier, the church is warned against false teachers while Israel is warned against false prophets. So here, after the church has been removed, again the warning is against false prophets.

And because iniquity shall abound, the love of many shall wax cold [Matt. 24:12].

This is a *principle,* and there are many principles in this Olivet Discourse which we can apply to our own day. Not long ago I met a preacher who had been a schoolmate of mine. He has become liberal in his theology; he drinks his cocktails, smokes his cigarettes, and lives just like the rest of the world lives. He told me, "McGee, you don't fight city hall; you join it!" He told me about how sinful practices had gotten into his church and how he is not planning to fight them. When iniquity abounds, the love of many grows cold, and this will be even more true at the end of the age.

This next verse is very startling to some folk—

But he that shall endure unto the end, the same shall be saved [Matt. 24:13].

The question is: Who endures to the end? Well, when I study the Book of Revelation, I find that God will stop all the forces of nature and of evil and even the forces of good while He seals a certain number of folk. So who is going to endure to the end? Those whom He seals at the beginning, of course. The Good Shepherd—in all ages—will bring His sheep through to the end. When He starts with an hundred sheep, He comes through with an hundred sheep.

When someone says to me, "So-and-so was very active in the church and has gone into sin. Is he saved?" I can only reply that I do not know. We will have to wait to see what happens. I tell people that the pigs will eventually end up in the pigpen, and the prodigal sons will all find their way back to the Father's house. It *is* confusing to find a son in a pigpen and a pig in the Father's house. Peter says, ". . . the sow that was washed [has returned] to her wallowing in the mire" (2 Pet. 2:22). Let's say that one of the little pigs went with the prodigal son to the father's house, that he was scrubbed clean, his teeth brushed with Pepsodent, and that a pink ribbon was tied around his neck. But he wouldn't stay in the father's house. Sooner or later he would go back to the pigpen where he belonged. "He that shall endure unto the end, the same shall be saved." You'll just have to wait and see. Sometimes a son, a Christian, will get into a pigpen, but since he is a son, he will get out someday. Why? Because he has a wonderful Shepherd. "The same shall be saved."

And this gospel of the kingdom shall be preached in all the world for a witness unto all nations; and then shall the end come [Matt. 24:14].

The gospel of the kingdom is what John the Baptist preached—"Repent ye: for the kingdom of heaven is at hand" (Matt. 3:2). And the Lord Jesus began His ministry with that message—"From that time Jesus began to preach, and to say, Repent: for the kingdom of heaven is at hand" (Matt. 4:17). Also, He sent His apostles out with that message (see Matt. 10). But in Matthew 11:28, we saw that our Lord's message changed to "Come unto me, all ye that labour and are heavy laden, and I will give you rest." And in Matthew 20:28 He said that He had come to give His life a ransom for many. But during the Tribulation Period the gospel of the kingdom will again be preached. It is not for our day, because we are to preach the gospel of the grace of God. Is the gospel of the kingdom another gospel? No, my friend, it is not. It is the same gospel with a different emphasis. We have no right to say that the kingdom of heaven is at hand because we don't know. But when the Great Tribulation Period begins, the people will know that they are close to the end, although they will not know the day nor the hour. Therefore, the message will be, "Repent: for the kingdom of heaven is at hand."

Now let me answer our critics who say that we who hold the dispensational view of Scripture teach that there are two or more ways of being saved. No, God has never had more than one basis on which He saves men, and that basis is the cross of Christ. Every offering before Christ came looked forward to the cross of Christ, and every commemoration since He has come looks back to the cross of Christ.

To illustrate this, let's go back to Genesis 4 and look at the offering which Abel brought to God. He brought a little lamb. If you had been there, you could have asked Abel, "Why are you bringing this little lamb? Do you think that a little lamb will take away your sins?" He would have said, "Of course not! I'm bringing this little lamb because God told me to do so. I am bringing it by faith." Then you could have asked him, "Well, if it won't take away your sins, why would He ask you to bring it?" Abel's answer would have been something like this: "This little lamb is pointing to One who is coming later, the seed of the woman, my mother. That One will take away our sins. I bring this little lamb by faith, recognizing that I am a sinner and need a substitute." You see, Abel was looking forward to the One who was coming.

John the Baptist not only said, "Repent ye: for the kingdom of heaven is at hand" (Matt. 3:2), but he also said, ". . . Behold the Lamb of God, which taketh away the sin of the world"

(John 1:29). John identified Him. Before the coming of Christ everyone who had come to God on *His* terms was saved on *credit.* And they were forgiven on the basis of the death of Christ. In the Old Testament God never saved anyone by Law. At the heart of the Mosaic system was the sacrificial system. They brought a lamb to God because the Law revealed that they were lawbreakers, that they were not obeying God, and that they did need to have a substitute to pay the penalty of their sins. The Law was given ". . . that every mouth may be stopped, and all the world may become guilty before God" (Rom. 3:19). My friend, you and I are lawbreakers, we are sinners needing a Savior. The thing to do is to receive Christ as your *Savior* before He comes as the Sovereign of this universe when He will be your *Judge*.

Now, going back to the verse we have been considering, "this gospel of the kingdom shall be preached in all the world for a witness unto all nations; and then shall the end come." This does not mean that while the church is here in the world the end can't come until the gospel of the grace of God is preached worldwide. I know there are those who use this verse to promote their Bible-teaching programs. While it is laudable to want to get the gospel to the ends of the earth, this is not the verse to use to promote it. You see, my friend, it is important to interpret Scripture in its context. Remember that our Lord is answering the question, "What is the sign of the end of the age?" (see v. 3). He is speaking of that end time.

THE GREAT TRIBULATION WITH ITS TROUBLE AND SORROWS

Now Jesus gives the sign that will identify this period of time.

When ye therefore shall see the abomination of desolation, spoken of by Daniel the prophet, stand in the holy place, (whoso readeth, let him understand:) [Matt. 24:15].

What is the abomination of desolation? Well, Daniel tells us about two of them. One of them was Antiochus Epiphanes, the Syrian, who came down and destroyed Jerusalem. In Daniel 11:31 we read: "And arms shall stand on his part, and they shall pollute the sanctuary of strength, and shall take away the daily sacrifice, and they shall place the abomination that maketh desolate." History bears out the fact that Antiochus Epiphanes came against Jerusalem in 170 B.C., at which time over one hundred thousand Jews were slain. He took away the daily sacrifice from the temple, offered the blood and broth of a swine upon the altar, and set up an image of Jupiter to be worshiped in the holy place.

However, our Lord is undoubtedly referring to the second abomination of desolation to which Daniel alludes (see Dan. 12:11), and I believe that it will be an image of Antichrist which will be set up in the temple. During the Tribulation the temple will be rebuilt and the nation of Israel will be back in Palestine. Obviously, our Lord is speaking of the temple rather than the church, because the church has no holy place. However, we cannot be certain that this is the abomination of desolation to which our Lord refers in the passage before us; this is just our surmising.

I am not looking for the abomination of desolation—I wouldn't know it if I met it on the street—but the people in the last days will be looking for it because it will be the sign to prove that they are in the Great Tribulation Period. Instead of our looking for Antichrist and his abominations, we are told to be "Looking for that blessed hope, and the glorious appearing of the great God and our Saviour Jesus Christ" (Titus 2:13).

Our Lord says, "(whoso readeth, let him understand:)," which means the people who are living at that time *will* understand. Since you and I won't be there, He hasn't given us many details.

Now we are given another *time* word. When the abomination of desolation appears, "Then"—

Then let them which be in Judaea flee into the mountains [Matt. 24:16].

You and I are not expecting to flee to the mountains of Judea. I live very near the San Gabriel Mountains, and my neighbor tells me that if an atom bomb is dropped in Southern California, he is going to head for a certain canyon up there (and I may follow him!), but that will not fulfill this prophecy. In fact, it has nothing whatever to do with it. Rather, it has to do with people who are in Judea. Our Lord is giving that prophecy to those people, not to us.

Let him which is on the housetop not come down to take any thing out of his house [Matt. 24:17].

The housetop in Palestine corresponds to our front porch or our patio. Again let me emphasize the fact that our Lord is speaking to the folk in Palestine, not to you and me. This warning is not applicable to us; we don't spend our time on our housetops!

Neither let him which is in the field return back to take his clothes [Matt. 24:18].

This refers to people engaged in agriculture. If a worker in the fields leaves his cloak at the end of the row in the early morning when it is cool, and the word comes that the abomination of desolation has appeared, he is not to go back and get his cloak, but he is to start running.

And woe unto them that are with child, and to them that give suck in those days! [Matt. 24:19].

This reveals His great care and concern for mothers and little children. It will be a time when one should not have children.

It is believed that there will be a great population explosion at the beginning of the Great Tribulation. The fact that this earth is becoming overweighted with people in our day may be another evidence that we are approaching the end of the age.

But pray ye that your flight be not in the winter, neither on the sabbath day [Matt. 24:20].

Again, these are people who are observing the Sabbath day, which is Saturday. This is another proof that Christ is speaking directly to the Jewish people. I don't go to church on the Sabbath but on Sunday because my Lord rose from the dead on that day.

For then shall be great tribulation, such as was not since the beginning of the world to this time, no, nor ever shall be [Matt. 24:21].

"For then shall be great tribulation"—in Revelation 7:14 the literal translation is "the tribulation the great one," placing the article before both the noun and the adjective for emphasis. In other words, this tribulation is unique; there has been nothing like it in the history of the world, and there will never again be anything like it. And notice that our Lord is the One who labels the end of the age as the Great Tribulation. (If you want to find fault with it, talk to Him, not to me.)

"Such as was not since the beginning of the world to this time, no, nor ever shall be." Since that is true, believe me, people will know it when it gets here! I hear people today talking about the church going through the Tribulation, and they don't seem to realize how severe it will be. In fact, some folk say that we are in the Great Tribulation at the present time! Well, things are bad in our day, I'll grant that, but this period can be matched with many other periods in history. When the Great Tribulation gets here, there will be nothing to match it in the past or in the future.

And except those days should be shortened, there should no flesh be saved: but for the elect's sake those days shall be shortened [Matt. 24:22].

We read in the Book of Revelation that during the Tribulation one third of the population of the earth will be destroyed. On another occasion one-fourth of the population will be destroyed. It is absolutely unique. Using the simile given to us in Revelation 6, the red horse of war, the black horse of famine, and then the pale horse of death will ride during that period, and the population of the earth will be decimated. There was a time when this seemed to be an exaggeration. Even some good commentators considered it hyperbole. However, now that several nations of the world have atom bombs, which could destroy the population of the world, it no longer appears to be exaggerated.

However, there is comfort in this verse—"but for the elect's sake those days shall be shortened." God will not let mankind commit suicide. That is the reason this will be such a brief period.

JESUS ASSURES THEM CONCERNING HIS COMING AGAIN

Now we come to what will be the sign of His coming.

Then if any man shall say unto you, Lo, here is Christ, or there; believe it not.

For there shall arise false Christs, and false prophets, and shall shew great signs and wonders; insomuch that, if it were possible, they shall deceive the very elect.

Behold, I have told you before [Matt. 24:23–25].

Don't miss what He is saying here. The ability to work miracles in our day should be looked upon with suspicion because the next great miracle worker will not be Christ; he will be Antichrist with his false prophets.

"If it were possible, they shall deceive the very elect." Who are the elect? In the Scriptures there are two elect groups: the elect of the nation Israel and the elect of the church.

We have to use common sense to determine which group is meant. Who has our Lord been talking about up to this point? Israel. All right, Israel is the elect in this verse, also. Jesus is not talking about the church. You can fool some of the people some of the time. You can fool all of the people some of the time. But you cannot fool God's children all of the time. It just can't be done. I have read many letters which testify of this. A recent letter is from a woman who has come out of a religious cult. She listened to our Bible-teaching radio program for months before she could see the error of the cult's teaching. It isn't possible to fool God's children all the time. They will come out of a cult eventually.

Wherefore if they shall say unto you, Behold, he is in the desert; go not forth: behold, he is in the secret chambers; believe it not.

For as the lightning cometh out of the east, and shineth even unto the west; so shall also the coming of the Son of man be [Matt. 24:26–27].

When He comes, there will not be any John the Baptist to announce Him. But when He comes, the whole world will know and it will be as public as lightning. Those of you that live in the Middle West know that a lightning storm is a public affair. When it comes, everybody knows about it, and sometimes it is a frightful experience. The Lord's second coming to the earth will be like that. No one will need to announce it. When our Lord comes the second time to establish His kingdom on earth, everyone will know He is coming. (Remember that His second coming to earth does not refer to the Rapture.)

For wheresoever the carcase is, there will the eagles be gathered together [Matt. 24:28].

This is the most difficult verse to understand in the entire Olivet Discourse. After speaking of His coming in glory like lightning out of heaven, then to speak of carrion-eating birds seems strange indeed. But I believe it refers to Christ's coming in judgment, because Revelation 19 tells us about an invitation that went out to the birds to come together for a great banquet, "And I saw an angel standing in the sun; and he cried with a loud voice, saying to all the fowls that fly in the midst of heaven, Come and gather yourselves together unto the supper of the great God; That ye may eat the flesh of kings, and the flesh of captains, and the flesh of mighty men, and the flesh of horses, and of them that sit on them, and the flesh of all men, both free and bond, both small and great. And I saw the beast, and the kings of the earth, and their armies, gathered together to make war against him that sat on the horse, and against his army" (Rev. 19:17–19). The birds that feed on carrion seem to be agents of divine judgment. When the Lord comes again, He will come in judgment.

Immediately after the tribulation of those days shall the sun be darkened, and the moon shall not give her light, and the stars shall fall from heaven, and the powers of the heavens shall be shaken [Matt. 24:29].

Notice that this is to be "Immediately *after* the tribulation of those days." It is my understanding that all of these things will take place at Christ's second coming to the earth.

And then shall appear the sign of the Son of man in heaven: and then shall all the tribes of the earth mourn, and they shall see the Son of man coming in the clouds of heaven with power and great glory [Matt. 24:30].

"Then shall appear the sign of the Son of man in heaven." What is that sign? Again I will have to speculate. Back in the Old Testament, you remember, the nation Israel was given the glory, the *shekinah* presence of God. No other nation or people has ever had that, nor does the church have it. The *shekinah* glory rested over the tabernacle and later the temple at Jerusalem. But because of Israel's sin, the *shekinah* glory left the nation. When Christ came the first time, He laid aside, not His deity, but His prerogative of deity, His glory—although John says, ". . . we beheld his glory . . ." (John 1:14), because there were times when it broke through. However, at His second coming, I believe that the *shekinah* glory will hover over the earth before He breaks through, and that will be the "sign of the Son of man in heaven."

"They shall see the Son of man coming in the clouds of heaven with power and great glory." This is His return to earth to set up His kingdom.

And he shall send his angels with a great sound of a trumpet, and they shall gather together his elect from the four winds, from one end of heaven to the other [Matt. 24:31].

The elect spoken of in this verse is still the nation Israel. The prophets in the Old Testament foretold of a miracle that would bring the Jews back into their land. (This is not the church which is going to be caught up out of this world to meet the Lord in the air. Angels are not connected with the Rapture.) The Lord will come in person to receive the church with the sound of a trumpet, and His voice will be like that of an archangel. He will not need any help to gather His church together. He died for the church, and He will bring it together. When He says that the "angels . . . shall gather together his elect from the four winds, from one end of heaven to the other," we can be sure that He is talking about the nation Israel—ministering angels have always been connected with Israel.

THE PARABLE OF THE FIG TREE AS A SIGN

Now learn a parable of the fig tree; When his branch is yet tender, and putteth forth leaves, ye know that summer is nigh:

So likewise ye, when ye shall see all these things, know that it is near, even at the doors [Matt. 24:32–33].

I do not see how the fig tree could represent anything other than the nation Israel (e.g., see Jer. 24; Hos. 9:10). There are certainly fig trees growing in abundance in Israel even in our day after all that has happened to that land. I was impressed with the fig orchards north of Jerusalem and the vineyards south of Jerusalem—the area south of Bethlehem is filled with vineyards. Fig trees and grapevines identify the land, and I believe that our Lord is using the fig tree as a symbol of that land.

Verily I say unto you, This generation shall not pass, till all these things be fulfilled [Matt. 24:34].

"This generation"—the Greek word can mean race and refer to the nation Israel. Or it could refer to the generation that will be living at the time these predictions come to pass. A generation is reckoned to be about twenty years, and certainly the predicted events of this section will take place in a much briefer time than twenty years. My feeling is that it could refer to either one, but I much prefer the interpretation that it refers to the preservation of the Jewish race. Haman was not able to destroy them, neither was Pharaoh, nor did Hitler succeed in his attempts. And no dictator in our day will be able to exterminate these people—God will see to that.

Heaven and earth shall pass away, but my words shall not pass away [Matt. 24:35].

He says, "You can just underscore what I've said, because heaven and earth will pass away, but My words will not." Heaven and earth will pass away; there will be a new heaven and a new earth (see Rev. 21:1), but He will not change His Word; it will stand throughout the eternal ages.

But of that day and hour knoweth no man, no, not the angels of heaven, but my Father only [Matt. 24:36].

Although they will know that this period is drawing near, they will not know the day nor the hour. Since there have been so many folk in our day who have tried to pinpoint the time of Christ's return, I'm of the opinion that in that future day there will be some folk who will try to figure it down to the very hour. But no one will know either the day or the hour. And He will use the illustration of Noah—

But as the days of Noe were, so shall also the coming of the Son of man be [Matt. 24:37].

Christ will come in a day which will be like the days of Noah.

For as in the days that were before the flood they were eating and drinking, marrying and giving in marriage, until the day that Noe entered into the ark,

And knew not until the flood came, and took them all away; so shall also the coming of the Son of man be [Matt. 24:38–39].

Now, the days of Noah were characterized by gross immorality—every thought and imagination of man's heart was only evil continually (see Gen. 6:5). But our Lord says that His coming will be in days like the days of Noah, and He mentions only that they were eating and drinking. Is there anything wrong with eating and drinking? No, we are told that whatever we do—whether we eat or drink, or whatsoever we do, we are to do all to the glory of God (see 1 Cor. 10:31). However, the people in Noah's day were not eating and drinking to the glory of God. In fact, they were living as though God did not exist.

A little boy was invited out to dinner for the first time in his life. He was just going next door, but to him it was a big event. So when the time came to go, he made a beeline for the house next door. When they sat down to the table to eat, the boy automatically bowed his head to offer thanks for the food because he came from a Christian home. Suddenly he realized he was the only one with a bowed head and the rest of the folks were passing food back and forth. He opened his eyes and, not having any inhibitions, said, "Don't you thank God for your food?" There was embarrassing silence for a moment, and then the lady of the house said, "No, we don't." The little fellow thought for a moment and then said, "You're like my dogs—they just start right in!"

In our day there are multitudes of people who receive a meal that comes from the hand of God three times a day while millions of people are starving to death, and they never think of thanking God. And in that future day, they will be right on the verge of the coming of Christ, and they will be living as though it will never take place.

Also, the people of Noah's day were "marrying and giving in marriage." Certainly our Lord is not saying that marriage is wrong. His point is that they rejected so completely God's warning through Noah that they went ahead and had their weddings—maybe even "church" weddings—right up to the day that Noah entered into the ark. They lived as though God did not exist. They did not believe that He would judge them and scorned the warning that a flood was imminent. "And knew not until the flood came, and took them all away; so shall also the coming of the Son of man be."

Then shall two be in the field; the one shall be taken, and the other left.

Two women shall be grinding at the mill; the one shall be taken, and the other left [Matt. 24:40–41].

I can hear someone saying to me, "Well, preacher, you have finally painted yourself into a corner. You said the church and the Rapture are not in the Olivet Discourse, but here they are. Two shall be in the field; one shall be taken, and the other shall be left."

Well, my friend, He still is not talking about the Rapture. After all, what is our Lord talking about here? "As the days of Noe were." Who was taken away in the days of Noah? "They knew not until the flood came, and took them *all* away." They perished in the Flood. This is not referring to the Rapture when the church will be taken out of the world. Rather, this pictures the removing from the earth by judgment those who are not going to enter the millennial kingdom.

Watch therefore: for ye know not what hour your Lord doth come [Matt. 24:42].

Watch is the important word, and it has a little different meaning from the watching that the child of God does now in waiting for the Rapture. Today we have a comforting hope. In that future day it will be watching with fear and anxiety. In the night they will say, "Would to God it were morning," and in the morning they will say, "Would to God it were evening." Today we are to wait and long for His coming. In that future day they will watch with anxiety for His return.

You may think that I am splitting hairs, but I'm not. I looked up the Greek word for *watch* and found that it had about eight different meanings. Although in English we have only the one word, it has several different meanings, also.

Let me illustrate this by a man who goes deer hunting. Every year this man goes into the woods to about the same spot. He puts up camp, and early in the morning he goes over the hogback on the hill and sits down by the trunk of an old tree and waits. After a while he hears a noise in the brush and thinks it might be a deer. He lifts his rifle and waits. He is watching for a deer.

Two weeks later you meet this same man down on the main street corner of town, and you see that he is looking intently down the street. You know that he is waiting for someone. You walk up to him and say, "Who are you watching for?" He replies, "I'm waiting for my wife; she is forty-five minutes late." He is watching for a dear again, but it is a different deer and he is watching in a little different way. Before, on the hill, he had his deer gun with him, and he sort of wishes he had it with him again, but it is against the law for him to shoot her! But he is watching, and watching in a different way, you see.

A month or two later you go to the hospital and you pass a room and see this man and his wife sitting by the bedside of a little child. The child has a burning fever, and the doctor has told them that the crisis will come about midnight. They are watching. My friend, that is a different type of watching than watching for a deer or waiting for a wife on the corner. This is watching with anxiety. And I think it will be somewhat with the same feeling that they will watch for our Lord's second coming.

But know this, that if the goodman of the house had known in what watch the thief would come, he would have

watched, and would not have suffered his house to be broken up.

Therefore be ye also ready: for in such an hour as ye think not the Son of man cometh.

Who then is a faithful and wise servant, whom his lord hath made ruler over his household, to give them meat in due season? [Matt. 24:43–45].

What our Lord is doing in the remainder of the Olivet Discourse is giving parables to illustrate the attitude of folk to His coming and what will happen when He does come.

Blessed is that servant, whom his lord when he cometh shall find so doing.

Verily I say unto you, That he shall make him ruler over all his goods.

But and if that evil servant shall say in his heart, My lord delayeth his coming;

And shall begin to smite his fellow-servants, and to eat and drink with the drunken;

The lord of that servant shall come in a day when he looketh not for him, and in an hour that he is not aware of,

And shall cut him asunder, and appoint him his portion with the hypocrites: there shall be weeping and gnashing of teeth [Matt. 24:46–51].

This parable reflects the attitude of some folk in that future day. They shall say, "Well, the Lord delays His coming—so I'll just go on living carelessly." When Christ returns, He will judge that man.

This is a great principle which is applicable to every age. You and I ought to live our lives in the light of the fact that we are to stand in the presence of Christ. Note that I didn't say in the light of the *coming* of Christ but in the light of the *presence* of Christ. Regardless of whether Christ comes an hundred years from today or a thousand years, you and I will stand in His presence. Whether you are saved or lost, you will stand in His presence. If you are saved, you will have to give Him an account of your life to see if you receive a reward. If you are lost, you will stand there to be judged. Therefore, every person should live his life in light of the fact that he is to stand in the presence of the Lord. This is the great emphasis in the Olivet Discourse. Therefore, it has applications to us, although the interpretation is specifically to folk living at the time of Christ's return as King.

CHART OF OLIVET DISCOURSE

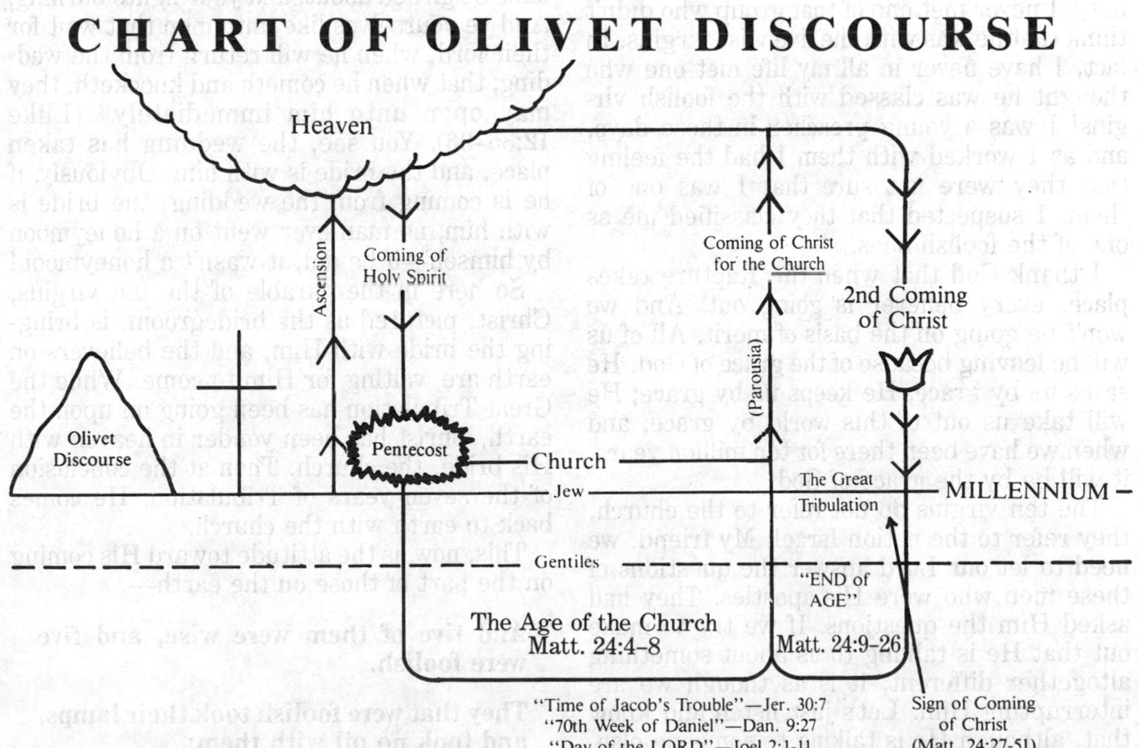

CHAPTER 25

***THEME:** Olivet Discourse continued—the parable of the ten virgins, the talents, and the judgment of the gentile nations*

This chapter enlarges upon the answer of Jesus to the question, "What shall be the sign of thy coming?" (Matt. 24:3). There is the parable of the ten virgins, which tests the genuineness of the faith of Israel; the parable of the talents, which tests the faithfulness of His servants; and the judgment of the gentile nations, which tests their right of admission into the kingdom. This chapter shows the significance of the coming of Christ as it relates to these groups that shall then be in the world. A close analysis of each group will reveal that it can be stripped down to a personal attitude and relationship to Jesus Christ.

The parable of the ten virgins is the basis for those who believe in what is known as the partial rapture, where only some will be taken out of the world. The "partial rapture" group is made up of very fine people. When I first became pastor in Nashville, Tennessee, there was a wonderful Bible class there, and they supported me in getting Bible conferences into Nashville. From the beginning, the class had been taught by a teacher who believed in a partial rapture. Candidly, I feel that the partial rapture theory ministers to spiritual snobbery. I never met one of that group who didn't think that he was with the five wise virgins. In fact, I have never in all my life met one who thought he was classed with the foolish virgins! I was a young preacher in those days, and as I worked with them I had the feeling that they were not sure that I was one of them. I suspected that they classified me as one of the foolish ones.

I thank God that when the Rapture takes place, every believer is going out. And we won't be going on the basis of merit. All of us will be leaving because of the grace of God. He saves us by grace; He keeps us by grace; He will take us out of this world by grace; and when we have been there for ten million years, it will be by the grace of God.

The ten virgins do not refer to the church, they refer to the nation Israel. My friend, we need to let our Lord answer the questions of these men who were His apostles. They had asked Him the questions. If we try to make out that He is talking to us about something altogether different, it is as though we are interrupting Him. Let's just listen and know that, although He is talking to someone else, we can make application of these wonderful parables to our own lives.

PARABLE OF THE TEN VIRGINS

Then shall the kingdom of heaven be likened unto ten virgins, which took their lamps, and went forth to meet the bridegroom [Matt. 25:1].

To better understand the customs in Israel during the New Testament period, we refer to the Peshitta, which is a Syriac version of the Bible. Although it is not a text to be recommended, it does shed light on some of the customs of the day. The Peshitta translation of the verse before us indicates that the virgins went forth to meet the bridegroom *and the bride,* which means that the bridegroom is coming from the marriage to the marriage supper. It is my understanding that, although the marriage of Christ and the church takes place in heaven, the marriage supper takes place on this earth. A passage in the Gospel of Luke substantiates this. As our Lord is giving warnings and parables, He says, "Let your loins be girded about, and your lights burning; And ye yourselves like unto men that wait for their lord, when he will return from the wedding; that when he cometh and knocketh, they may open unto him immediately" (Luke 12:35–36). You see, the wedding has taken place, and the bride is with him. Obviously, if he is coming from the wedding, the bride is with him; no man ever went on a honeymoon by himself—if he did, it wasn't a honeymoon!

So here in the parable of the ten virgins, Christ, pictured as the bridegroom, is bringing the bride with Him, and the believers on earth are waiting for Him to come. While the Great Tribulation has been going on upon the earth, Christ has been yonder in heaven with His bride, the church. Then at the conclusion of the seven years of Tribulation, He comes back to earth with the church.

This, now, is the attitude toward His coming on the part of those on the earth—

And five of them were wise, and five were foolish.

They that were foolish took their lamps, and took no oil with them:

But the wise took oil in their vessels with their lamps [Matt. 25:2–4].

Oil is symbolic of the Spirit of God. In that day I think there will be phonies as there were at His first coming. Jesus called them hypocrites. They will have lamps but no oil.

While the bridegroom tarried, they all slumbered and slept.

And at midnight there was a cry made, Behold, the bridegroom cometh; go ye out to meet him.

Then all those virgins arose, and trimmed their lamps [Matt. 25:5–7].

Notice that *both* the wise and the foolish virgins slept. The difference in them was that some had the Holy Spirit (represented by the oil) and some did not—because they were not genuine believers.

Our Lord concludes this parable with a warning—

Watch therefore, for ye know neither the day nor the hour wherein the Son of man cometh [Matt. 25:13].

Notice that it is "the day nor the hour" rather than the century or the year, as it is from our perspective. The attitude for His own during this future period is to *watch*. That is the important thing for them to do.

PARABLE OF THE TALENTS

This is another parable for that future generation that will be waiting for our Lord's return to earth.

For the kingdom of heaven is as a man travelling into a far country, who called his own servants, and delivered unto them his goods.

And unto one he gave five talents, to another two, and to another one; to every man according to his several ability; and straightway took his journey [Matt. 25:14–15].

Notice that the master gave to his servants responsibilities according to their individual abilities.

Then he that had received the five talents went and traded with the same, and made them other five talents.

And likewise he that had received two, he also gained other two [Matt. 25:16–17].

Notice that the "talents" were sums of money. They do not represent talents in the sense of the natural endowments of a person such as a musical talent. The application to us is that whatever God has given to us, we are to use for Him.

But he that had received one went and digged in the earth, and hid his lord's money [Matt. 25:18].

All were given a certain sum of money and told to use it profitably. But one buried the talent he had been given. He was not faithful to his master.

After a long time the lord of those servants cometh, and reckoneth with them.

And so he that had received five talents came and brought other five talents, saying, Lord, thou deliveredst unto me five talents: behold, I have gained beside them five talents more.

His lord said unto him, Well done, thou good and faithful servant: thou hast been faithful over a few things, I will make thee ruler over many things: enter thou into the joy of thy lord.

He also that had received two talents came and said, Lord, thou deliveredst unto me two talents: behold, I have gained two other talents beside them.

His lord said unto him, Well done, good and faithful servant; thou hast been faithful over a few things, I will make thee ruler over many things: enter thou into the joy of thy lord.

Then he which had received the one talent came and said, Lord, I knew thee that thou art an hard man, reaping where thou hast not sown, and gathering where thou hast not strawed:

And I was afraid, and went and hid thy talent in the earth: lo, there thou hast that is thine [Matt. 25:19–25].

The response of his master was this—

His lord answered and said unto him, Thou wicked and slothful servant, thou knewest, that I reap where I sowed not, and gather where I have not strawed:

Thou oughtest therefore to have put my money to the exchangers, and then at my coming I should have received mine own with usury.

Take therefore the talent from him, and give it unto him which hath ten talents.

For unto every one that hath shall be given, and he shall have abundance: but from him that hath not shall be taken away even that which he hath.

And cast ye the unprofitable servant into outer darkness: there shall be weeping and gnashing of teeth [Matt. 25:26–30].

There is a great principle in this parable for us. And it was given in the light of the fact that all of us—you and I included—are going to have to stand in the presence of God and give an account of how we have used what He has given to us. The Lord is not going to ask us how *much* we have done for Him but how *faithful* we have been to that which He wanted us to do.

For the child of God there are two important things: (1) Find out what God wants us to do; that is, determine what the talent is that He has given us, and then (2) be faithful in the use of it. To some of us God gives a very small ministry, and that may be upsetting to us; but if we are one-talent people, God expects us to be *faithful* with that.

JUDGMENT OF THE NATIONS

In this chapter our Lord is alerting God's people to the fact that we are to ready ourselves for His coming. This is certainly true in the next few verses.

During the Tribulation Period all nations will have the opportunity to hear and receive God's message. The gospel of the kingdom will be preached among all nations, we are told. But some will reject God's messengers, Christ's brethren, and thereby reject Christ.

When the Son of man shall come in his glory, and all the holy angels with him, then shall he sit upon the throne of his glory [Matt. 25:31].

The polarization of all of the Olivet Discourse is moving toward the placing of Jesus Christ on the throne of this world. This is the message of the Gospel of Matthew—in fact, it is the message of the entire Word of God.

Now we will see that the nations will be judged. You may ask, "Doesn't it mean individuals?" Yes, you can consider it as individuals composing the nations. But nations are responsible to God.

And before him shall be gathered all nations: and he shall separate them one from another, as a shepherd divideth his sheep from the goats.

And he shall set the sheep on his right hand, but the goats on the left [Matt. 25:32–33].

These are all Gentiles who have lived through the Great Tribulation and appear as a mingling of sheep and goats, which our Lord will separate and judge as two distinct groups.

Then shall the King say unto them on his right hand, Come, ye blessed of my Father, inherit the kingdom prepared for you from the foundation of the world:

For I was an hungered, and ye gave me meat: I was thirsty, and ye gave me drink: I was a stranger, and ye took me in:

Naked, and ye clothed me: I was sick, and ye visited me: I was in prison, and ye came unto me.

Then shall the righteous answer him, saying, Lord, when saw we thee an hungered, and fed thee? or thirsty, and gave thee drink?

When saw we thee a stranger, and took thee in? or naked, and clothed thee?

Or when saw we thee sick, or in prison, and came unto thee?

And the King shall answer and say unto them, Verily I say unto you, Inasmuch as ye have done it unto one of the least of these my brethren, ye have done it unto me [Matt. 25:34–40].

The 144,000 Jews sealed at the time of the Great Tribulation will go out over the entire world to preach the message of the gospel of the kingdom, which is to receive Christ as the sacrifice for their sins and to be ready for His immediate coming. Some nations will reject Christ. Antichrist will have God's messengers butchered and slain, and anyone who would give them a cup of cold water will do so at the risk of his life. To hand out a cup of cold water has little value in our day, but in the Great Tribulation it will have tremendous value. It will mean taking a stand for Jesus Christ. The basis on which the nations will be judged is their acceptance or rejection of Jesus Christ. He says, "Inasmuch as ye have done it unto one of the least of these my brethren, ye have done it unto me"—because the messengers were representing Him. That will be the way they evidence faith in the message that the kingdom of heaven is at hand and that they are to repent and turn to Christ to be saved.

For those who reject, symbolized as goats, there is only judgment—

Then shall he answer them, saying, Verily I say unto you, Inasmuch as ye did it not to one of the least of these, ye did it not to me.

And these shall go away into everlasting punishment: but the righteous into life eternal [Matt. 25:45–46].

Entire nations will enter the millennial kingdom. Out of these will be some individuals who will reject Christ. But the judgment of the nations at the second coming of Christ is to determine what nations are to enter the millennial kingdom. This judgment is separate and distinct from all other judgments.

CHAPTER 26

***THEME:** Final events in the life of Jesus immediately before the cross; the plot to arrest Him; the anointing by Mary of Bethany; the selling by Judas Iscariot; the celebration of the first Lord's Supper; the predicted denial by Peter; the agony in the Garden of Gethsemane; the betrayal by Judas; the arrest by the chief priests; the trial before Caiaphas and the Sanhedrin; the denial by Peter*

This is the longest chapter in the Gospel of Matthew. There is a break at the conclusion of verse 30. The events recorded in John 15–17 could be inserted here. Another natural break would be at the beginning of verse 57. A chapter division here would set the trial before the religious rulers in a separate category. Perhaps those who divided the Scriptures included so many events in one chapter to give the reader something of the scope and rapidity of these significant happenings.

Every incident and detail in this chapter points to the cross. There is a trip-hammer precision here that may give the reader the impression that Jesus is caught in the vortex of circumstances over which He has no control. A careful examination and consideration, however, will reveal that He is the master of circumstances, and He is never more kingly than when He draws near the cross.

All things recorded in this chapter and chapter 27 should be studied in the light of His determination at Caesarea Philippi—six months previously—to go to Jerusalem to die: "From that time forth began Jesus to shew unto his disciples, how that he must go unto Jerusalem, and suffer many things of the elders and chief priests and scribes, and be killed, and be raised again the third day" (Matt. 16:21).

He is moving according to God's timetable, and He is forcing the issue. He is *not* the helpless victim caught between the upper millstone of religious intrigue and the nether millstone of Roman power. A reverence should pervade our thinking as we consider these things written in this chapter, for they are vitally related to our salvation.

PLAN TO KILL JESUS

And it came to pass, when Jesus had finished all these sayings, he said unto his disciples [Matt. 26:1].

"When Jesus had finished all these sayings"—what sayings? The Olivet Discourse. He has answered their questions regarding the end of the age, and now He has something else for them—

Ye know that after two days is the feast of the passover, and the Son of man is betrayed to be crucified [Matt. 26:2].

Now let's read ahead to verse 5 and see something very interesting here—

Then assembled together the chief priests, and the scribes, and the elders of the people, unto the palace of the high priest, who was called Caiaphas,

And consulted that they might take Jesus by subtilty, and kill him.

But they said, Not on the feast day, lest there be an uproar among the people [Matt 26:3–5].

In verse 2 Jesus tells His disciples that He is going to die. According to the record, this is the sixth time He has told them. Six months before this, beginning at Caesarea Philippi, He announced His impending death. And now He sets the *time* of His death. He tells them that He will die during the Passover. But the religious rulers had other plans—notice verse 5: "But *they* said, Not on the feast day, lest there be an uproar among the people." The very ones who put Him to death said that they would *not* crucify Him during the Passover; *He* said that He would die during the Passover. When did He die? He died during the Passover. You see, Jesus, not His enemies, set the time of His execution. He is in command; He is the King in Matthew's gospel, and when He seems more helpless and weak than at any other time, He still is in charge. The bitter hatred of His enemies had led them to plot His murder, and they wanted to do it their way, but they will not be permitted to do that. The closer Jesus gets to the cross, the more kingly He becomes.

We pass from that incident to one of marvelous light.

JESUS IS ANOINTED BY MARY OF BETHANY

Now when Jesus was in Bethany, in the house of Simon the leper,

There came unto him a woman having an alabaster box of very precious ointment, and poured it on his head, as he sat at meat [Matt. 26:6–7].

Bethany was the place of love, as Jerusalem was the place of hate. He stayed in Bethany during His last hours before His death. This incident took place in the home of Simon the leper. Why did they call him Simon the leper? Did he have leprosy? There was a time when he had this disease, but Jesus had undoubtedly healed him. Now he is able to sit down and have fellowship with the Lord Jesus and others who are having dinner with him at his home.

This is a wonderful scene, my friend. The Lord's enemies today do not know Him. They do not know the Lord who healed, who loved, who wept and judged. In fact, some of His enemies of today recently presented a play in a local college in which Jesus and His disciples were characterized as sinful men! Our laws have banned prayer and Bible reading in schools, but they permit the dirtiest, filthiest portrayals of our Lord, and outright blasphemy! Of course, those who produce such things are ignorant; they don't know our Lord. In fact, they are spiritual lepers. If they told the truth, they would have to say of themselves, "Unclean, unclean!"

When you have come to the Lord Jesus and have been cleansed by Him, you can sit down and have fellowship with Him. This is the scene we have in this passage. As they were having dinner, a woman (John 12:3 tells us that it was Mary) came to Jesus with an alabaster box of precious ointment and anointed both His head and His feet with fragrant ointment. John also tells us that it was Judas Iscariot who led the agitation against her, although all the disciples agreed with him.

But when his disciples saw it, they had indignation, saying, To what purpose is this waste? [Matt. 26:8].

I wonder how much they really cared about the poor. They remind me of folk in our contemporary society who are always talking about taking care of the poor but are doing nothing about it themselves. In our government there are quite a few legislators who are millionaires and are always talking about a poverty program and other aid for the poor. Have you ever attempted to find out how much they personally have done for the poor? I don't care for that kind of hypocrisy! The evidence of the sincerity of your concern is always in what you yourself are doing. Are you trying to make an impression, or are you really trying to help folk?

For this ointment might have been sold for much, and given to the poor [Matt. 26:9].

That is accurate—it could have been. It is estimated that the cost of it equalled a year's salary for a rural worker.

When Jesus understood it, he said unto them, Why trouble ye the woman? for

she hath wrought a good work upon me [Matt. 26:10].

As far as Christians are concerned, they should not give to anything nor do anything that does not glorify the name of the Lord Jesus Christ. Personally, I refuse to participate in any so-called good works in the community unless Christ is glorified in them, unless they are done in His name. And I am amazed at how little they really accomplish. How much do they really give that brings blessing to people? It makes me sick when I hear of the corruption among the politicians in the poverty programs. However, when loving assistance is given in the name of the Lord Jesus, He Himself said that it was a *good* work.

For ye have the poor always with you; but me ye have not always [Matt. 26:11].

Those of us who say we trust Christ and want to honor and glorify Him ought to be doing *more* in His name today.

For in that she hath poured this ointment on my body, she did it for my burial.

Verily I say unto you, Wheresoever this gospel shall be preached in the whole world, there shall also this, that this woman hath done, be told for a memorial of her [Matt. 26:12–13].

That home of Simon the leper in Bethany was a place of light and friendship for the Lord Jesus. In contrast, Jerusalem was the place of hatred. He did not spend a night in the city of Jerusalem during that final week, but He went out to Bethany and stayed with these folk who loved Him. Those who want Him, who love Him, are the ones He fellowships with in our day. My friend, you can have Him if you want Him.

The beautiful story of the broken alabaster box has filled the world with its fragrance. Our Lord said, "Wheresoever this gospel shall be preached in the whole world, there shall also this, that this woman hath done, be told for a memorial of her." And we are telling it right now. I hear folk speak about being in the apostolic succession, but I would like to be in the succession of Mary. Mary alone, of all Christ's followers, understood and entered into His death, while the apostles missed the point completely. Although she stood on the fringe of things, she understood, and to let Him know, she anointed Him. Did she waste her ointment? In the gospel records I read that on the morning of that first day of the week other women came to the tomb of Jesus to anoint His body for burial. I have a question to ask you: Did they put their ointment on the body of Jesus? No, He wasn't in that tomb—He was risen. Mary alone had the privilege of anointing Him. My friend, you and I need to break our alabaster box of ointment in the name of the Lord Jesus. The world outside doesn't know Him; so we ought to be very careful that what we do brings glory, not to ourselves, but to Him.

Now we turn from that beautiful scene of light to another dark scene.

PLOT OF JUDAS TO SELL JESUS

Then one of the twelve, called Judas Iscariot, went unto the chief priests,

And said unto them, What will ye give me, and I will deliver him unto you? And they covenanted with him for thirty pieces of silver.

And from that time he sought opportunity to betray him [Matt. 26:14–16].

This deed of Judas Iscariot is dark and dastardly in contrast to Mary's act of spiritual perception. Dante gave Judas and Brutus the lowest place in *The Inferno*, and no one since then has said he was wrong. These men did the lowest and basest thing men could do when they betrayed one to whom they should have been loyal.

"He sought opportunity to betray him." You see, the arrest had to take place when Jesus was alone—that is, when the crowds were gone. Judas waited for such a time.

THE PASSOVER AND THE LAST SUPPER

Now the first day of the feast of unleavened bread the disciples came to Jesus, saying unto him, Where wilt thou that we prepare for thee to eat the passover?

And he said, Go into the city to such a man, and say unto him, The Master saith, My time is at hand; I will keep the passover at thy house with my disciples.

And the disciples did as Jesus had appointed them; and they made ready the passover [Matt. 26:17–19].

Now the Lord Jesus will go with His own into the Upper Room, and there He will make the announcement that one will betray Him.

Now when the even was come, he sat down with the twelve.

And as they did eat, he said, Verily I say unto you, that one of you shall betray me.

And they were exceeding sorrowful, and began every one of them to say unto him, Lord, is it I? [Matt. 26:20–22].

Every one of those men knew that he had it within his heart to betray Christ. Have you discovered that in your own heart and life? My friend, you and I are just that low. You may say, "Oh, I wouldn't do that!" Are you sure? I would betray Him within the next five minutes if He didn't keep His hand on me—and you would, too. That ought to keep us close to Him.

And he answered and said, He that dippeth his hand with me in the dish, the same shall betray me.

The Son of man goeth as it is written of him: but woe unto that man by whom the Son of man is betrayed! it had been good for that man if he had not been born.

Then Judas, which betrayed him, answered and said, Master, is it I? He said unto him, Thou hast said [Matt. 26:23–25].

It is interesting to note that Judas did not call Him *Lord* as the other disciples did (see v. 22). At this juncture Judas left the room, according to John's record: "He then having received the sop went immediately out: and it was night" (John 13:30).

And as they were eating, Jesus took bread, and blessed it, and brake it, and gave it to the disciples, and said, Take, eat; this is my body.

And he took the cup, and gave thanks, and gave it to them, saying, Drink ye all of it;

For this is my blood of the new testament, which is shed for many for the remission of sins [Matt. 26:26–28].

Here we see the Lord instituting the Lord's Supper over the dying ashes of a fading feast, the Passover. The cup circulated seven times during the Passover. It was evidently at the last time that Jesus instituted the Lord's Supper. During the feast they sang the Hallel Psalms—Psalms 111 to 118. When you read them for your own spiritual profit, keep in mind that our Lord sang them on that auspicious night. At that last supper, He reared a new monument to Himself. It was not made of marble or bronze but was made of the temporary elements of bread and wine. *Both speak of His death until He comes again.*

But I say unto you, I will not drink henceforth of this fruit of the vine, until that day when I drink it new with you in my Father's kingdom [Matt. 26:29].

The Passover will be reinstituted in the Millennium. The Lord said that He would drink the fruit of the vine again in the kingdom. This means that apparently the Passover during that time will look back to His death on the cross. The Passover, which had looked forward for centuries to His coming, will also during the Millennium look back to His coming.

And when they had sung an hymn, they went out into the mount of Olives [Matt. 26:30].

PREDICTION OF PETER'S DENIAL

Then saith Jesus unto them, All ye shall be offended because of me this night: for it is written, I will smite the shepherd, and the sheep of the flock shall be scattered abroad [Matt. 26:31].

This is a quotation from Zechariah's prophecy (see Zech. 13:7).

But after I am risen again, I will go before you into Galilee.

Peter answered and said unto him, Though all men shall be offended because of thee, yet will I never be offended [Matt. 26:32–33].

Peter's answer suggested that he did not trust the other disciples either but that the Lord could sure depend upon him! Peter's problem was that he didn't know himself, and that is the problem many of us have today.

Jesus said unto him, Verily I say unto thee, That this night, before the cock crow, thou shalt deny me thrice.

Peter said unto him, Though I should die with thee, yet will I not deny thee. Likewise also said all the disciples [Matt. 26:34–35].

It was early in the evening that Peter said he would not deny our Lord. Yes, he was even ready to die with the Lord. That same night before the cock crowed Peter denied Him, not once, but three times.

GETHSEMANE

Then cometh Jesus with them unto a place called Gethsemane, and saith unto the disciples, Sit ye here, while I go and pray yonder.

And he took with him Peter and the two sons of Zebedee, and began to be sorrowful and very heavy.

Then saith he unto them, My soul is exceeding sorrowful, even unto death: tarry ye here, and watch with me.

And he went a little farther, and fell on his face, and prayed, saying, O my Father, if it be possible, let this cup pass from me: nevertheless not as I will, but as thou wilt [Matt. 26:36–39].

We need to pay attention to the prayer that our Lord is praying here. "This cup" evidently represents His cross, and the contents are the sins of the whole world. More than the death itself and the terrible suffering of crucifixion is something else that we do not seem to realize. It is this: Jesus, holy, harmless, and separate from sinners, was made *sin* for us. There on the cross the sin of humanity was put on Him—not in some forensic or academic manner, but in reality. We cannot even imagine the *horror* He felt when that sin was placed upon Him. It was a horrendous experience for this One who was holy. Notice that He was not asking to escape the cross, but He was praying that God's will be done. It is impossible for you and me to enter into the full significance of Gethsemane, but I think it was there that He won the victory of Calvary. Undoubtedly, He was tempted by Satan in Gethsemane as truly as He was in the wilderness. Notice verse 42: "He went away again the second time, and prayed, saying, O my Father, if this cup may not pass away from me, except I drink it, thy will be done." He was accepting it. To say that our Lord was trying to avoid going to the cross is not exactly true. In His humanity He felt a repugnance and the awful horror of having the sins of the world placed upon Himself, and He recoiled for a moment from it. But He committed Himself to the Father. He came to do the Father's will.

Now let's look at the disciples who were in the garden with Him—Peter, James, and John. After His first prayer, He came back to them and found them sleeping—

And he cometh unto the disciples, and findeth them asleep, and saith unto Peter, What, could ye not watch with me one hour?

Watch and pray, that ye enter not into temptation: the spirit indeed is willing, but the flesh is weak [Matt. 26:40–41].

"Watch"—stay awake, be alert—"and pray, that ye enter not into temptation." What was the temptation? Who was going to tempt them? Satan was there. Jesus wrestled with an unseen foe—that is obvious. He overcame the enemy there in Gethsemane. The victory of Calvary was won in Gethsemane.

He went away again the second time, and prayed, saying, O my Father, if this cup may not pass away from me, except I drink it, thy will be done [Matt. 26:42].

He commits Himself to the Father's will.

And he came and found them asleep again: for their eyes were heavy.

And he left them, and went away again, and prayed the third time, saying the same words.

Then cometh he to his disciples, and saith unto them, Sleep on now, and take your rest: behold, the hour is at hand, and the Son of man is betrayed into the hands of sinners [Matt. 26:43–45].

"Sleep on now, and take your rest." Obviously, there is an interval of time between this and the next verse. He didn't tell them to go to sleep and in the next breath tell them to get up. There was time for their nap, and they needed this rest. Notice how our Lord pays attention to the needs of their bodies. After they had slept awhile, He said—

Rise, let us be going: behold, he is at hand that doth betray me.

And while he yet spake, lo, Judas, one of the twelve, came, and with him a great multitude with swords and staves, from the chief priests and elders of the people [Matt. 26:46–47].

The fact that Judas, and also the enemies of Jesus, had witnessed many miracles makes them realize that Jesus has supernatural power and that He might use it. So when they come to arrest Him, they bring a whole crowd of armed men. Possibly the whole guard came to arrest Him.

Now he that betrayed him gave them a sign, saying, Whomsoever I shall kiss, that same is he: hold him fast [Matt. 26:48].

That hot kiss of betrayal is one of the worst things in recorded history.

And forthwith he came to Jesus, and said, Hail, master; and kissed him.

And Jesus said unto him, Friend, wherefore art thou come? Then came they, and laid hands on Jesus, and took him [Matt. 26:49–50].

A kiss can either be a sign of acceptance or rejection (see Ps. 2:12.) In this instance Judas bestowed a kiss of betrayal upon the Lord Jesus, and it was one of the most despicable acts of man. Some theologians contend that Judas was predestined to betray Jesus and could do nothing else. If this were true, Judas was nothing more than a robot. I believe Judas made up his own mind to betray our Lord and had every opportunity to change his plans. You may say, "Yes, but it was prophesied that he would betray Jesus." I have to agree with you. It was prophesied, and our Lord marked him out as the man. However, after Judas had fulfilled the prophecy, after Jesus was betrayed, Judas could have repented. Jesus gave Judas one final opportunity to repent and accept Him. Even after he gave Jesus that hot kiss of betrayal, Jesus called him, "Friend." Later, when Judas went to the temple and threw down the silver given to him to betray the Lord, he could have changed his mind. As the priests were taking Jesus to Pilate, Judas could have fallen down before Him and said, "Forgive me, Lord, I did not know what I was doing." The Lord would have forgiven him.

And, behold, one of them which were with Jesus stretched out his hand, and drew his sword, and struck a servant of the high priest's, and smote off his ear [Matt. 26:51].

We know who that was; it was Simon Peter. I think that he was trying to prove something. Earlier Peter had boasted that he would die protecting Jesus, but Jesus told him that he would deny Him that very night. Well, Peter got a sword somewhere, and he intended to protect his Lord. But Peter was a fisherman, not a swordsman. He sliced off the man's ear; but he wasn't after ears, he was after his head. He intended to lop off the man's head, but he almost missed him!

Then said Jesus unto him, Put up again thy sword into his place: for all they that take the sword shall perish with the sword.

Thinkest thou that I cannot now pray to my Father, and he shall presently give me more than twelve legions of angels? [Matt. 26:52–53].

In other words, "I don't need your little sword, Peter. I haven't come to put up a battle against the religious rulers. I have come to die for the sins of the world."

But how then shall the scriptures be fulfilled, that thus it must be? [Matt. 26:54].

You see, our Lord is fulfilling Scripture. Matthew makes this very clear.

In that same hour said Jesus to the multitudes, Are ye come out as against a thief with swords and staves for to take me? I sat daily with you teaching in the temple, and ye laid no hold on me [Matt. 26:55].

Previously, His hour had not yet come. But now His hour *has* come—

But all this was done, that the scriptures of the prophets might be fulfilled. Then all the disciples forsook him, and fled [Matt. 26:56].

Jesus had predicted this. All of the disciples leave Him now.

PALACE OF THE HIGH PRIEST

And they that had laid hold on Jesus led him away to Caiaphas the high priest, where the scribes and the elders were assembled [Matt. 26:57].

We find out later that the father-in-law of Caiaphas was really the instigator of all this. But Jesus must be brought to Caiaphas, the high priest, for the first charge. Because the religious rulers are going to ask Rome for the death penalty, they must determine that night what charge against Jesus they can bring when they go to Pilate in the morning.

But Peter followed him afar off unto the high priest's palace, and went in, and sat with the servants, to see the end [Matt. 26:58].

Simon Peter followed afar off. It is dangerous for any of us to follow Jesus afar off. We are told in John 18:15–16 that with the aid of John, Peter gained entrance to the courtyard. He waited there to "see the end," and in just a short while he would deny the Lord.

Now the chief priests, and elders, and all the council, sought false witness against Jesus, to put him to death;

But found none: yea, though many false witnesses came, yet found they none. At the last came two false witnesses [Matt. 26:59–60].

You see, because the religious rulers had no charge against the Lord Jesus, they had to find *false* witnesses. And the trouble with getting false witnesses was in finding one that could stand up under investigation. Pilate might be a little inquisitive (which he was) and ask a few annoying questions. Finally, they found two witnesses—

And said, This fellow said, I am able to destroy the temple of God, and to build it in three days [Matt. 26:61].

According to John 2:19–22, even the disciples misunderstood Jesus when He made the statement: ". . . Destroy this temple, and in three days I will raise it up." They didn't understand it until after Jesus' resurrection. Evidently the false witness was a man who had been present at the time Jesus made the statement, but notice that he doesn't quote Him accurately.

And the high priest arose, and said unto him, Answerest thou nothing? what is it which these witness against thee? [Matt. 26:62].

He tries to get the Lord Jesus to answer so the Sanhedrin will know what kind of an argument to use. The accusation is so absolutely farfetched that our Lord does not answer it.

But Jesus held his peace. And the high priest answered and said unto him, I adjure thee by the living God, that thou tell us whether thou be the Christ, the Son of God [Matt. 26:63].

Now the high priest puts Him on oath and asks Him the specific question, "Are you the Christ, the Son of God?"

Jesus saith unto him, Thou hast said: nevertheless I say unto you, Hereafter shall ye see the Son of man sitting on the right hand of power, and coming in the clouds of heaven [Matt. 26:64].

"Jesus saith unto him, Thou hast said"—this is tantamount to saying, "Yes, you have said who I am." Jesus claims for Himself the title "Son of man." Dr. Warfield said that this is the highest title the Lord had. This is a title the prophets used (see Daniel and Ezekiel). It was an epithet of deity. He could have claimed no greater position than to have said He was "the Son of man sitting on the right hand of power, and coming in the clouds of heaven."

Then the high priest rent his clothes, saying, He hath spoken blasphemy; what further need have we of witnesses? behold, now ye have heard his blasphemy [Matt. 26:65].

"Then the high priest rent his clothes"—that is, he tears his robes, signifying extreme grief at hearing blasphemy. They think that they have a charge against Jesus now.

What think ye? They answered and said, He is guilty of death.

Then did they spit in his face, and buffeted him; and others smote him with the palms of their hands,

Saying, Prophesy unto us, thou Christ, Who is he that smote thee? [Matt. 26:66–68].

How they hated the Lord Jesus! This is the natural antagonism of the human heart to His goodness, His righteousness, His holiness, and the fact that He is God. Do you realize, my friend, that if you and I had only our old natures, we would try to knock God off His throne? A few years ago a crowd was saying that God was dead! Do you know why they said that? Because they would like to get Him off His throne. Human nature hates Him.

Here in the Sanhedrin He was slapped, spit upon, beaten with fists, and ridiculed.

"Saying, Prophesy unto us, thou Christ, Who is he that smote thee?" They played a game with Him. They apparently blindfolded Him, then hit Him on the face, and He was to guess who did it. They would never have let Him guess right, of course.

PETER'S DENIAL OF JESUS

We will look at this in more detail in the other gospel records.

Now Peter sat without in the palace: and a damsel came unto him, saying, Thou also wast with Jesus of Galilee.

But he denied before them all, saying, I know not what thou sayest.

And when he was gone out into the porch, another maid saw him, and said unto them that were there, This fellow was also with Jesus of Nazareth.

And again he denied with an oath, I do not know the man.

And after a while came unto him they that stood by, and said to Peter, Surely thou also art one of them; for thy speech bewrayeth thee [Matt. 26:69–73].

Galilean pronunciations were a little different from those used in Judea. Peter had a Galilean accent!

Then began he to curse and to swear, saying, I know not the man. And immediately the cock crew [Matt. 26:74].

The poor man did not realize how weak he really was! But our Lord had prayed that his faith would not fail, and it did not.

And Peter remembered the word of Jesus, which said unto him, Before the cock crow, thou shalt deny me thrice. And he went out, and wept bitterly [Matt. 26:75].

Simon Peter was in the wrong place. For him, it was the place of temptation. No alibi can be offered for his base denial. He was guilty of an heinous act. However, Peter did repent and come back into fellowship with the Lord he loved. In fact, Peter was the one to whom He gave the privilege of preaching the first sermon after the coming of the Holy Spirit at Pentecost, and *three thousand* people were saved!

CHAPTER 27

THEME: *Events surrounding the crucifixion of Jesus; Sanhedrin delivers Jesus to Pilate; repentance of Judas; trial before Pilate; release of Barabbas; crucifixion, death, and burial of Jesus; the tomb sealed and a watch set*

We have come to the central fact of the gospel message: the crucifixion of Christ. When Paul defined the gospel to the Corinthians, he said, "For I delivered unto you first of all that which I also received, how that Christ *died* for our sins according to the scriptures" (1 Cor. 15:3, italics mine). We have now come to the record of that tremendous event.

We will see that Matthew does not give a record of the actual crucifixion. In fact, no gospel writer does that. They merely tell what went on around the cross. I know that there are men who depict in graphic terms how the nails were driven into the quivering flesh and how the blood spurted out, but that is not in the Bible. In the inspired record it is as if God placed the mantle of darkness over the last three hours of the life of Jesus on the cross and said, "This is something you cannot look at. It is beyond human comprehension. The suffering cannot be fathomed." It was a transaction between the Father in heaven and the Son on the cross. The cross became an altar upon which the Lamb of God, who takes away the sin of the world, was offered.

The simple statement of Matthew is, "And they crucified him."

This chapter begins with the morning after Jesus had been arrested in the Garden of Gethsemane, after He had been brought before Caiaphas and the Sanhedrin, after false witnesses had testified against Him, after He had been beaten and ridiculed, and after Peter had denied Him.

THE SANHEDRIN DELIVERS JESUS TO PILATE

When the morning was come, all the chief priests and elders of the people took counsel against Jesus to put him to death [Matt. 27:1].

They have formulated a charge against Jesus and will take Him now to the supreme court. They think they have a case which will stand up before the Roman court.

And when they had bound him, they led him away, and delivered him to Pontius Pilate the governor [Matt. 27:2].

Pilate had a palace in Jerusalem, although his headquarters were in Caesarea on the Mediterranean Sea. He was in Jerusalem at the Passover season because the city was crowded with Jews who had come to the feast, and generally there were riots on such occasions.

Then Judas, which had betrayed him, when he saw that he was condemned, repented himself, and brought again the thirty pieces of silver to the chief priests and elders [Matt. 27:3].

You see, the Lord Jesus was there when Judas came. As the chief priests and elders were leading Him through that hall to take Him to Pilate, here comes Judas. Why doesn't Judas turn to the Lord Jesus and ask forgiveness? Instead of doing that, he addressed the religious rulers—

Saying, I have sinned in that I have betrayed the innocent blood. And they said, What is that to us? see thou to that [Matt. 27:4].

In other words, "You did the job, and it's over with. We have the One we were after. We have paid you off, and we have no need of you any further."

And he cast down the pieces of silver in the temple, and departed, and went and hanged himself [Matt. 27:5].

This man leaves the temple area, goes out, and hangs himself. He could have turned to the Lord Jesus and would have been forgiven!

And the chief priests took the silver pieces, and said, It is not lawful for to put them into the treasury, because it is the price of blood [Matt. 27:6].

How pious they are! They can't put it in the temple treasury because it is blood money.

And they took counsel, and bought with them the potter's field, to bury strangers in.

Wherefore that field was called, The field of blood, unto this day [Matt. 27:7–8].

This was a remarkable fulfillment of prophecy—

Then was fulfilled that which was spoken by Jeremy the prophet, saying, And they took the thirty pieces of silver, the price of him that was valued, whom they of the children of Israel did value;

And gave them for the potter's field, as the Lord appointed me [Matt. 27:9–10].

You will find this prophecy alluded to in Jeremiah 18:1–4 and evidently quoted from Zechariah 11:12–13. It is credited to Jeremiah simply because in Jesus' day Jeremiah was the first of the books of the prophets, and that section was identified by the name of the first book.

The significant thing is that Jesus was present when Judas returned with his thirty pieces of silver. In fact, Jesus was on His way to die—even for Judas. Our Lord had given him an opportunity to come back to Him there in the Garden of Gethsemane, and He had said, "Friend, wherefore art thou come?" And even at this eleventh hour, Judas could have turned to the Lord Jesus and would have been forgiven.

PILATE QUESTIONS JESUS

And Jesus stood before the governor: and the governor asked him, saying, Art thou the King of the Jews? And Jesus said unto him, Thou sayest [Matt. 27:11].

You see, the religious rulers wanted to get rid of Jesus because of what they considered blasphemy. You remember that when the high priest put Him on oath and asked Him if He was the Christ, the Son of God, Jesus said that He was. And further He said, "Hereafter shall ye see the Son of man sitting on the right hand of power, and coming in the clouds of heaven" (Matt. 26:64). To the religious rulers that was blasphemy, and they would have stoned Him on that charge, but Rome did not allow the Jews to carry out the death penalty. So they had to deliver Jesus to Pilate with a charge that would stick in a Roman court. Treason would be one that would stick, and so Jesus was charged with claiming to be the King of the Jews.

The answer of Jesus to the charge was, "Thou sayest"—or, "It is as you say."

And when he was accused of the chief priests and elders, he answered nothing [Matt. 27:12].

They made certain false charges against Him, and our Lord didn't bother to answer them.

Then said Pilate unto him, Hearest thou not how many things they witness against thee?

And he answered him to never a word; insomuch that the governor marvelled greatly [Matt. 27:13–14].

He was the Lamb of God, you see, who before the shearers was dumb (see Isa. 53:7).

Now at that feast the governor was wont to release unto the people a prisoner, whom they would.

And they had then a notable prisoner, called Barabbas [Matt. 27:15–16].

Matthew does not give us the byplay that took place. All the other gospel writers add a great deal to this account, but Matthew simply states the bare facts.

Obviously, Pilate felt that the religious rulers had no basis for requesting the death penalty. Jesus had not incited rebellion against Rome. Others had, but Jesus had not. Pilate had a problem on his hands. He wanted to please the religious leaders in order to maintain peace in Jerusalem, but he felt that he could not arbitrarily sentence the Lord Jesus to death. So he hit upon a solution to the problem. Since it was his habit to release a Jewish prisoner during the Passover celebration, he would offer the crowd a choice: Jesus; or a very notorious prisoner called Barabbas, who was guilty of murder, robbery, treason—the whole bit.

Therefore when they were gathered together, Pilate said unto them, Whom will ye that I release unto you? Barabbas, or Jesus which is called Christ? [Matt. 27:17].

Pilate thought that the crowd would certainly ask that Jesus be released—the contrast between Him and Barabbas was so evident.

For he knew that for envy they had delivered him [Matt. 27:18].

Pilate was a clever politician. He could see what was taking place, and he was sure that the crowd would ask for Barabbas to be crucified and Jesus to be released. This would give him a happy "out" to this situation.

When he was set down on the judgment seat, his wife sent unto him, saying, Have thou nothing to do with that just man: for I have suffered many things this day in a dream because of him [Matt. 27:19].

Pilate's wife was as superstitious as could be. Perhaps she was tied up in a mystery religion, and this sort of thing could have been satanic. I do not believe that this warning came from God. If she had been a just woman, she would have investigated Jesus and found out more about Him. She did not, however. She was simply superstitious and asked her husband to have nothing to do with Him.

But the chief priests and elders persuaded the multitude that they should ask Barabbas, and destroy Jesus [Matt. 27:20].

You see, the religious rulers were clever politicians themselves. They circulated among the crowd saying, "Ask that Barabbas be delivered and Jesus be destroyed."

The governor answered and said unto them, Whether of the twain will ye that I release unto you? They said, Barabbas [Matt. 27:21].

Pilate was taken aback. He had not known how low religion would stoop.

Pilate saith unto them, What shall I do then with Jesus which is called Christ? They all say unto him, Let him be crucified [Matt. 27:22].

Imagine a Roman judge asking a crowd what he should do with a prisoner! Pilate was the judge, and he should make the decision. The Gospel of John tells us that Pilate repeatedly called Jesus inside the judgment hall and questioned Him privately. His thought seemed to be, "Jesus, if You will cooperate with me, I can get You out of this, and it will get me off this hot seat I'm on!" But the Lord Jesus would not defend Himself. When we analyze this mock trial, we come to the conclusion that Pilate was the one on trial and, actually, that Jesus was the Judge.

Pilate had to make a decision relative to Him; so he asked the crowd, "What shall I do then with Jesus which is called Christ?" The answer came back to him—it was flung in his face—"Let him be crucified!"

And the governor said, Why, what evil hath he done? But they cried out the more, saying, Let him be crucified [Matt. 27:23].

A mob never has a reason.

When Pilate saw that he could prevail nothing, but that rather a tumult was made, he took water, and washed his hands before the multitude, saying, I am innocent of the blood of this just person: see ye to it [Matt. 27:24].

Pilate called for a basin of water and washed his hands, declaring that he would have nothing to do with the execution of Jesus. But it was not that easy. He had to make a decision—every man does. It was John Newton who wrote:

"What think ye of Christ?" is the test,
To try both your state and your scheme;
You cannot be right in the rest,
Unless you think rightly of Him.

Although Pilate washed his hands, the bitter irony of it is that in the oldest creed of the church stand these words: ". . . crucified under Pontius Pilate." The blood of Jesus was on his hands no matter how much he washed them.

Then answered all the people, and said, His blood be on us, and on our children [Matt. 27:25].

Unfortunately, that has been the case, and it can be so demonstrated.

Then released he Barabbas unto them: and when he had scourged Jesus, he delivered him to be crucified [Matt. 27:26].

Pilate was willing to stoop this low himself! He had to make a decision, and his decision, of course, was one of rejection.

Then the soldiers of the governor took Jesus into the common hall, and gathered unto him the whole band of soldiers [Matt. 27:27].

The soldiers were free to do with Him as they pleased. He became a plaything for this brutal, cruel, crowd.

And they stripped him, and put on him a scarlet robe.

And when they had platted a crown of thorns, they put it upon his head, and a reed in his right hand: and they bowed the knee before him, and mocked him, saying, Hail, King of the Jews! [Matt. 27:28–29].

It is frightful what they did to Him—

And they spit upon him, and took the reed, and smote him on the head [Matt. 27:30].

The soldiers took this opportunity to have their fun with Him before He was crucified. Since He was going to die anyway, they could mutilate Him and do anything they wished with Him. They played a cruel Roman game known as "hot-hand" with their prisoners. All the soldiers would show the prisoner their fists. Then they would blindfold the prisoner, and all but one would hit him as hard as they could. Then they would remove the blindfold, and if the prisoner was still conscious, he was to guess which soldier did not hit him. Obviously, the prisoner could never guess the right one. They would continue this until they had beaten the prisoner to a pulp. I believe that the Lord Jesus was so mutilated that you would not have recognized Him. "As many were astonied at thee; his visage was so marred more than any man, and his form more than the sons of men" (Isa. 52:14).

And after that they had mocked him, they took the robe off from him, and put his own raiment on him, and led him away to crucify him.

And as they came out, they found a man of Cyrene, Simon by name: him they compelled to bear his cross [Matt. 27:31–32].

Jesus was subjected to abject humiliation and untold suffering. We are given the impression here that He was too weak to carry His cross because of the ordeal to which the soldiers had subjected Him.

THE CRUCIFIXION

And when they were come unto a place called Golgotha, that is to say, a place of a skull [Matt. 27:33].

That place can be identified, I believe, as Gordon's Calvary (named for General Gordon who selected it as the probable site of Golgotha). I have looked around that area. After all these years and the things that have happened to the city Jerusalem, it is difficult to make a judgment, but certainly the topography of Gordon's choice is close to the biblical description of Golgotha. It is a place that resembles a skull.

They gave him vinegar to drink mingled with gall: and when he had tasted thereof, he would not drink [Matt. 27:34].

This is a fulfillment of Psalm 69:21: "They gave me also gall for my meat; and in my thirst they gave me vinegar to drink."

And they crucified him, and parted his garments, casting lots: that it might be fulfilled which was spoken by the prophet, They parted my garments among them, and upon my vesture did they cast lots [Matt. 27:35].

The prophecy is from Psalm 22, which presents a graphic picture of death by crucifixion: "They part my garments among them, and cast lots upon my vesture" (Ps. 22:18).

And sitting down they watched him there [Matt. 27:36].

In my opinion it is here that we see humanity which has reached its lowest depth. You don't need to go to skid row or to a prison to see man at his lowest, you can see him here—"sitting down they watched him there." I believe that in this crowd was Saul of Tarsus. Later on when he wrote to Timothy, he called himself the chief of sinners (see 1 Tim. 1:15), and I believe he called himself that because he *was* the chief of sinners.

And set up over his head his accusation written, THIS IS JESUS THE KING OF THE JEWS.

Then were there two thieves crucified with him, one on the right hand, and another on the left.

And they that passed by reviled him, wagging their heads,

And saying, Thou that destroyest the temple, and buildest it in three days, save thyself. If thou be the Son of God, come down from the cross [Matt. 27:37–40].

"If thou be the Son of God, come down from the cross." Notice that they raise the doubt—"*If* thou be the Son of God. . . ." Little did they know that since He is the Son of God, He will not come down from the cross. He doesn't have to prove anything at this point. He is now dying for the sins of the world.

Likewise also the chief priests mocking him, with the scribes and elders, said [Matt. 27:41].

You would think that after this pack of bloodhounds had succeeded in getting Him on the cross, they would go home and let Him die in peace, but they didn't. They stayed there taunting Him while there was still life in His body.

He saved others; himself he cannot save. If he be the King of Israel, let him now come down from the cross, and we will believe him [Matt. 27:42].

That is a true statement—"He saved others; himself he cannot save." If He were to save you and me, He would have had to die on that cross. If He had come down from the cross, you and I would have to be executed for our sins. *We* deserve it; we are hell-doomed sinners. Christ was taking our place there. As surely as He took the place of Barabbas, He took our place.

"Let him now come down from the cross, and we will believe him." Would they have believed Him? I don't think so.

He trusted in God; let him deliver him now, if he will have him: for he said, I am the Son of God [Matt. 27:43].

You can see that the crowd understood that Jesus claimed deity.

The thieves also, which were crucified with him, cast the same in his teeth [Matt. 27:44].

Matthew calls our attention to the thieves who were crucified with Him and the fact that they joined with the religious rulers in mocking Him. He does *not* call our attention to the fact that one of the thieves finally turned to Jesus. The kingdom presented in Matthew will be on this earth, and the thief who repented went with Christ to paradise that very day.

Now from the sixth hour there was darkness over all the land unto the ninth hour [Matt. 27:45].

Our Lord was put on the cross at the third hour, which would be nine o'clock in the morning. By twelve noon, man had done all he could to the Son of God. Then at the noon hour, darkness settled down, and that cross became an altar on which the Lamb who taketh away the sin of the world was offered.

And about the ninth hour Jesus cried with a loud voice, saying, Eli, Eli, lama sabachthani? that is to say, My God, my God, why hast thou forsaken me? [Matt. 27:46].

We find the answer to that question in Psalm 22. It opens with these words: "My God, my God, why hast thou forsaken me? why art thou so far from helping me, and from the words of my roaring?" Then we read the answer in verse 3: "*But thou art holy . . .*" (Ps. 22:1, 3, italics mine). When my sin is put upon Jesus, God has to withdraw. Our Savior had to be executed if He were going to take my sin and yours.

Some of them that stood there, when they heard that, said, This man calleth for Elias.

And straightway one of them ran, and took a sponge, and filled it with vinegar, and put it on a reed, and gave him to drink [Matt. 27:47–48].

Why? To fulfill prophecy—"They gave me also gall for my meat; and in my thirst they gave me vinegar to drink" (Ps. 69:21).

The rest said, Let be, let us see whether Elias will come to save him.

Jesus, when he had cried again with a loud voice, yielded up the ghost [Matt. 27:49–50].

Notice how He died: He "yielded up the ghost"—that is, He dismissed His spirit. As a pastor I have often heard the death rattle, the gasp for that last breath which we all want so badly. Our Lord didn't go that way. He dismissed His spirit. He went willingly.

INCIDENTS CONNECTED WITH HIS DEATH

At the death of Christ several very notable things took place. One was an earthquake. Another was that the veil in the temple, the curtain which separated the Holy of Holies from the rest of the temple, was torn in two—

And, behold, the veil of the temple was rent in twain from the top to the bottom; and the earth did quake, and the rocks rent [Matt. 27:51].

Notice that the veil was torn, not from the bottom to the top but from top to bottom. It was rent by God, not by man. The veil symbolizes the body of Jesus. When His body was rent upon the cross—when He had paid the penalty for your sin and my sin in His own body—then the way was opened into the presence of God. Therefore, you and I don't have to have a priest or a preacher go into the presence of God for us; we can go directly to the throne of God *through Christ*. Let's emphasize that the *only* way to the Father is through His Son. "For there is one God, and one mediator between God and men, the man Christ Jesus" (1 Tim. 2:5).

And the graves were opened; and many bodies of the saints which slept arose,

And came out of the graves after his resurrection and went into the holy city, and appeared unto many [Matt. 27:52–53].

This is an event that is mentioned only by Matthew. We wish more had been told. I can only say that I believe it happened just the way Matthew tells it and that those who arose were part of that great company who went to heaven when Christ led captivity captive at His ascension (see Eph. 4:8–10). The earthquake mentioned in verse 51 was an intelligent quake, not haphazard, because the graves were opened by it, and "many bodies of the saints which slept arose"—just certain ones.

"And [they] appeared unto many." There were many witnesses who saw these certain folk because, according to Matthew, they "went into the holy city, and appeared unto many." There is a very excellent treatment of this, and the other miracles which occurred at this time, in a little booklet entitled *The Six Miracles of Calvary,* written by Bishop Nicholson. If you are interested in pursuing this study, I recommend it to you. It is a rich little book.

Now when the centurion, and they that were with him, watching Jesus, saw the earthquake, and those things that were done, they feared greatly, saying, Truly this was the Son of God [Matt. 27:54].

In Mark's account it says this: "And when the centurion, which stood over against him, saw that he so cried out, and gave up the ghost, he said, Truly this man was the Son of God" (Mark 15:39). Apparently, that Roman centurion, who was in charge of the actual crucifixion, stood beneath Christ's cross. As he witnessed some of the miraculous events during this time and as he saw the Lord Jesus dismiss His spirit, the fact was confirmed to him that this was the Son of God. I believe that the centurion became a saved man. He probably did not know a great deal; he had never read Strong's theology or Hodges' theology, nor Augustine's *City of God*, nor any of *my* books, but he knew enough to take his place beneath the cross of Christ. And that is all that God asks of any sinner.

And many women were there beholding afar off, which followed Jesus from Galilee, ministering unto him:

Among which was Mary Magdalene, and Mary the mother of James and

Joses, and the mother of Zebedee's children [Matt. 27:55–56].

JESUS BURIED IN JOSEPH'S TOMB

When the even was come, there came a rich man of Arimathaea, named Joseph, who also himself was Jesus' disciple [Matt. 27:57].

We did not know that he was a disciple until this event. It is interesting to see that the very thing which caused the apostles to scatter seems to have drawn into the open others who, up to this time, would have been called secret disciples. Joseph of the town of Arimathaea stepped out and declared his faith.

He went to Pilate, and begged the body of Jesus. Then Pilate commanded the body to be delivered [Matt. 27:58].

Joseph went to Pilate on the basis that he was a disciple of Jesus.

And when Joseph had taken the body, he wrapped it in a clean linen cloth [Matt. 27:59].

John tells us that Nicodemus worked with Joseph in preparing the body of Jesus for burial—"And there came also Nicodemus, which at the first came to Jesus by night, and brought a mixture of myrrh and aloes, about an hundred pound weight. Then took they the body of Jesus, and wound it in linen clothes with the spices, as the manner of the Jews is to bury" (John 19:39–40). These two men, who apparently had been in the background, now came out in the open as the disciples of Jesus. It is interesting to note that only loving hands touched the body of Jesus after His death.

And laid it in his own new tomb, which he had hewn out in the rock: and he rolled a great stone to the door of the sepulchre, and departed.

And there was Mary Magdalene, and the other Mary, sitting over against the sepulchre [Matt. 27:60–61].

Note this one tender incident in connection with the death of Jesus. Several women were faithful and stayed at the cross. They were loyal when the apostles had fled.

Near the hill, which we designate as Gordon's Calvary, is a tomb which is pointed out as the tomb in which Jesus was buried. It is called the Garden Tomb. We have no way of knowing if this was the tomb of Jesus; frankly, I have my doubts. There are many sepulchres in that area, and it could have been any one of them. I feel sure that His tomb is in that area, and the Garden Tomb is as good a choice as any of them. But to determine the exact location of Golgotha and of the tomb and to make them sacred shrines is not Christ's intention. I saw a woman go into the tomb and on hands and knees kiss the floor where the bodies were placed! That has no value. What our Lord wants us to do is to believe the gospel—that He died for our sins, was buried, and rose again—and to take that good news to the whole world.

THE SEPULCHRE IS SEALED AND THE WATCH SET

Now the next day, that followed the day of the preparation, the chief priests and Pharisees came together unto Pilate,

Saying, Sir, we remember that that deceiver said, while he was yet alive, After three days I will rise again.

Command therefore that the sepulchre be made sure until the third day, lest his disciples come by night, and steal him away, and say unto the people, He is risen from the dead: so the last error shall be worse than the first.

Pilate said unto them, Ye have a watch: go your way, make it as sure as ye can.

So they went, and made the sepulchre sure, sealing the stone, and setting a watch [Matt. 27:62–66]

The zeal of the enemy actually gives a confirmation of Jesus' resurrection! If they had gone off and left that tomb as it was, their later explanation for the tomb's being empty might be plausible. But, my friend, when you've got a tomb that is sealed and a Roman guard around it watching it, their claim that the apostles stole away the body of Jesus sounds pretty silly. The enemies of Jesus went to a lot of trouble to make the sepulchre sure, and that fact furnishes a marvelous confirmation of His resurrection.

Another interesting point is that when our Lord had told His disciples that He would rise again the third day, they had told a great many people, and the religious rulers got word of it. As soon as they could get another audience with Pilate, they said, "Look, Jesus made the statement that He would rise again the third day, and we want to make sure His body stays in that tomb." Of course, they did not believe He would be resurrected, but neither did the apostles believe that He would come out of that tomb alive.

CHAPTER 28

THEME: *The resurrection of Jesus; the giving of the Great Commission*

The arch of the gospel rests upon two great pillars: (1) the death of Christ, and (2) the resurrection of Christ. Listen to the apostle Paul as he defines the gospel: "For I delivered unto you first of all that which I also received, how that Christ died for our sins according to the scriptures; And that he was buried, and that he rose again the third day according to the scriptures" (1 Cor. 15:3–4).

In the previous chapter we have seen the death and burial of the Lord Jesus, and in this chapter we will see His Resurrection. Both are essential to my salvation and yours. "Who [Jesus] was delivered for our offences, and was raised again for our justification" (Rom. 4:25). He was made sin for us that we might be made the righteousness of God in Him.

The unique fact of the gospel is the Resurrection. All other religions record the death of their leader. *Only* the Christian faith records the Resurrection of its Founder. All other religious leaders are dead. *Only Jesus is alive.* This is important and imperative to know.

No gospel writer gives the complete details which concern the Resurrection. Each records that aspect of the Resurrection which contributes to the furtherance of the purpose which the Spirit had in mind. Therefore the four Gospels present a composite picture. No writer is seeking to give the entire and complete record but only that which serves his purpose. All the gospel accounts need to be put together to get the total picture, and no conflict or contradiction will appear among them.

Regarding the order of events connected with the resurrection of Christ, I would like to share with you a very fine note found in *The Scofield Reference Bible* on page 1043:

> The order of *events,* combining the four narratives, is as follows: Three women, Mary Magdalene, and Mary the mother of James, and Salome, start for the sepulchre, followed by other women bearing spices. The three find the stone rolled away, and Mary Magdalene goes to tell the disciples (Lk. 23:55–24:9; John 20:1,2). Mary, the mother of James and Joses, draws nearer the tomb and sees the angel of the Lord (Mt. 28:2). She goes back to meet the other women following with the spices. Meanwhile Peter and John, warned by Mary Magdalene, arrive, look in, and go away (John 20:3–10). Mary Magdalene returns weeping, sees the two angels and then Jesus (John 20:11–18), and goes as He bade her to tell the disciples. Mary (mother of James and Joses), meanwhile, has met the women with the spices and, returning with them, they see the *two* angels (Lk 24:4,5; Mk. 16:5). They also receive the angelic message, and, going to seek the disciples, are met by Jesus (Mt. 28:8–10).
>
> The order of our Lord's *appearances* would seem to be: On the day of His resurrection: (1) To Mary Magdalene (John 20:14–18). (2) To the women returning from the tomb with the angelic message (Mt. 28:8–10). (3) To Peter, probably in the afternoon (Lk. 24:34; 1 Cor. 15:5). (4) To the Emmaus disciples toward evening (Lk. 24:13–31). (5) To the apostles, except Thomas (Lk. 24:36–43; John 20:19–24). Eight days afterward: (1) To the apostles, Thomas being present (John 20:24–29). In Galilee: (1) To the seven by the Lake of Tiberias (John 21:1–23). (2) On a mountain, to the apostles and five hundred brethren (1 Cor. 15:6). At Jerusalem and Bethany again: (1) To James (1 Cor. 15:7). (2) To the eleven (Mt. 28:16–20;Mk. 16:14–20; Lk. 24:33–53; Acts 1:3–12). To Paul: (1) Near Damascus (Acts 9:3–6; 1 Cor. 15:8). (2) In the temple (Acts 22:17–21; 23:11). To Stephen, outside Jerusalem (Acts 7:55). To John on Patmos (Rev. 1:10–19).

Matthew presents Jesus as the King. The features of the resurrection story which contain the element of the spectacular and sensational are given. There is a fanfare of trumpets in the account given in Matthew. He was born a King. He lived as a King. He died a King, and He arose from the dead a King. Matthew tells of the earthquake, of the angel's descent, of the stone rolled away, of the frightened guards, and of the effort by the religious rulers to cover up the fact of the empty tomb.

Compare Luke's gospel with Matthew's account. There is quietness and a subdued tone which characterizes Luke's purpose. The women come in the stillness of the early morning, and the stone is already rolled away. The Lord Jesus appears to two unknown disciples on an obscure road leading to Emmaus and then to the disciples in a secret room of a house of unknown address. Luke is recording the human story while Matthew is presenting Him in His kingly office. Both records are accurate, as are the records in the other two gospels, but they are presented from four different viewpoints.

APPROACH OF THE TWO MARYS TO THE TOMB

In the end of the sabbath, as it began to dawn toward the first day of the week, came Mary Magdalene and the other Mary to see the sepulchre [Matt. 28:1].

The other gospel records tell us that they were bringing sweet spices to anoint the body of Jesus. It is difficult to identify the "other Mary." Tradition states that she was the mother of James and Joses.

And, behold, there was a great earthquake: for the angel of the Lord descended from heaven, and came and rolled back the stone from the door, and sat upon it [Matt. 28:2].

Why was it necessary to roll back the stone? To let Jesus out? No, He was gone when the stone was rolled back. The tomb was not opened to let Him out but to let *them* in.

His countenance was like lightning, and his raiment white as snow [Matt 28:3].

It is interesting to note the description of the angel because this is very unusual in Scripture (see Dan. 10:6; Rev. 10:1 for other descriptions).

And for fear of him the keepers did shake, and became as dead men [Matt. 28:4].

I can imagine that the guards were very happy to leave after this episode! They were helpless in the presence of the angel.

And the angel answered and said unto the women, Fear not ye: for I know that ye seek Jesus, which was crucified [Matt. 28:5].

"Fear not"—when the supernatural touches the natural, it is always with a word to allay fear.

He is not here: for he is risen, as he said. Come, see the place where the Lord lay [Matt. 28:6].

This is the divine announcement of the Resurrection. Jesus had left the tomb before the stone had been rolled away. Later He would enter a room with a locked door. The glorified body of Jesus was radically different from the body with which He was born.

And go quickly, and tell his disciples that he is risen from the dead; and, behold, he goeth before you into Galilee; there shall ye see him: lo, I have told you [Matt. 28:7].

The angelic announcement ceased at this point. From here on the message would be told by human lips—"Come, see. . . . go quickly, and tell." But before any individual attempts to witness, he must first have an unshakable conviction of the truth of the Resurrection. He must have it settled in his own mind that Christ died for his sins and was buried—"Come, see the place where the Lord lay"—and that Christ rose again—"He is not here: for he is risen." Then with these convictions, he can "go quickly, and tell." My friend, you and I are to *go*, and we are to *tell*.

APPEARANCE OF JESUS TO THE TWO MARYS

And they departed quickly from the sepulchre with fear and great joy; and did run to bring his disciples word [Matt. 28:8].

Note the mingled feelings of the women—fear and great joy.

And as they went to tell his disciples, behold, Jesus met them, saying, All hail. And they came and held him by

the feet, and worshipped him [Matt. 28:9].

This seems to contradict the encounter of Mary Magdalene with her resurrected Lord. In John 20:17 we find this: "Jesus saith unto her, Touch me not; for I am not yet ascended to my Father: but go to my brethren, and say unto them, I ascend unto my Father, and your Father; and to my God, and your God." The explanation is that between these two encounters Jesus had ascended to His Father and had presented His precious blood in heaven's Holy of Holies.

Then said Jesus unto them, Be not afraid: go tell my brethren that they go into Galilee, and there shall they see me [Matt. 28:10].

He made an appointment to see them in Galilee.

ALIBI OF THE KEEPERS

Now when they were going, behold, some of the watch came into the city, and shewed unto the chief priests all the things that were done [Matt. 28:11].

These soldiers who were on guard duty went into the city and reported to the chief priests. They didn't know when Jesus left the tomb. All they knew was that after the stone was rolled away, they took a look inside the tomb, and the body wasn't there! The entire episode had nearly frightened them to death. They could have been executed for allowing the body of Jesus to disappear under their very eyes.

And when they were assembled with the elders, and had taken counsel, they gave large money unto the soldiers,

Saying, Say ye, His disciples came by night, and stole him away while we slept [Matt. 28:12–13].

This is not a very plausible explanation! Imagine a soldier, especially a Roman soldier, assigned guard duty in a certain place and given strict orders to stand guard over a certain thing and to prohibit all trespassing. Suppose someone did come and take away the thing he was assigned to guard. And suppose that his explanation to his commanding officer was, "I went to sleep." What do you think would happen to him?

And if this come to the governor's ears, we will persuade him, and secure you [Matt. 28:14].

In others words, "Don't worry if this reaches the ears of the governor. We won't let him put you before a firing squad."

So they took the money, and did as they were taught: and this saying is commonly reported among the Jews until this day [Matt. 28:15].

A bribe aided in persuading them to offer this feeble excuse. This was the first century alibi to explain away the resurrection of Christ. Unbelief has now had nineteen centuries to think it over, and there are other alibis. However, none yet have been offered that can explain away the documentary evidence.

THE GREAT COMMISSION

In our contemporary society we have two opposing viewpoints regarding this so-called Great Commission. Frankly, I think both of them are extreme. Our Lord's commission to His disciples as recorded by Matthew is a source of controversy. One extreme group feels that the Great Commission contains the *only* command for the church. That is *it*, and they hang on to it. The other extreme group feels that it has no meaning for our day and that it should be excluded from the church program. It seems to me that both of these groups are in error.

We have endeavored to show that Matthew has direct *application* for us, and certainly the Great Commission has an application for us in our day. This does not mean that it will not find a final and full meaning in the future—I think it will. But, as it is obvious that Matthew did not give the *total* record of the Resurrection, neither did he give us the total commission. I feel that everything our Lord said on any subject should be put together and given as a composite in order to give a full-orbed command for the present day as well as for the future. The commission in Matthew should be considered with the commission recorded in the other gospel records and especially with Acts 1:8: "But ye shall receive power, after that the Holy Ghost is come upon you: and ye shall be witnesses unto me both in Jerusalem, and in all Judaea, and in Samaria, and unto the uttermost part of the earth." We are to be His witnesses, and we are to be endued with power from on high.

Then the eleven disciples went away into Galilee, into a mountain where Jesus had appointed them.

And when they saw him, they worshipped him: but some doubted [Matt. 28:16–17].

Some worshiped and some doubted—that is how it has been for over nineteen hundred years! And, my friend, *you* are in one category or the other.

And Jesus came and spake unto them, saying, All power is given unto me in heaven and in earth [Matt. 28:18].

He was speaking as the King.

Go ye therefore, and teach all nations, baptizing them in the name of the Father, and of the Son, and of the Holy Ghost [Matt. 28:19].

This, I am confident, will have a real application during the Great Tribulation Period and even during the Millennium. But, my friend, it has an application for us today, also.

"Baptizing them in the name of the Father, and of the Son, and of the Holy Ghost [Spirit]." Baptism by water in the name of the Trinity has been practiced by the church from its beginning. Even Paul, who was not sent to baptize (see 1 Cor. 1:14–17), practiced this rite of the early church. "The name of the Father, and of the Son, and of the Holy Ghost [Spirit]" is evidence for the Trinity of the Godhead.

Teaching them to observe all things whatsoever I have commanded you: and, lo, I am with you alway, even unto the end of the world. Amen [Matt. 28:20].

Notice that teaching is part of the work of the church (see Eph. 4:11). The teachings of Jesus are found not only in the Gospels but in the Epistles (see 1 Thess. 4:2).

"Lo, I am with you alway, even unto the end of the world." The word *world* is the Greek *aiōn,* meaning age. Our Lord promises to be with us right on through to the very end of the age. In His *power* the Great Commission can be carried out.

We have looked at the Great Commission, now let's consider the great omission. Do you see what Matthew has omitted from his record? There is no *ascension* of Christ here. Why? The obvious reason is that the kingdom will be here upon this earth, and Matthew leaves the King here on earth because this is where the King is to be. Luke 24:49–53 and Acts 1:6–11 record the ascension of Christ. At the time of the Rapture of the church, the Lord Jesus will take His own out of the world to be with Himself, and the Ascension is essential for that event.

However, Matthew is the Gospel of the King. Jesus was born a King. He lived as a King. He died as a King. He rose again as a King. And, my friend, He will be coming again to this earth as King of kings and Lord of lords! I hope you will bow to Him today.

BIBLIOGRAPHY

(Recommended for Further Study)

Frank, Harry Thomas, editor. *Hammond's Atlas of the Bible Lands*. Maplewood, New Jersey: Hammond Inc., 1977. (Excellent and inexpensive.)

Gaebelein, Arno C. *The Gospel of Matthew.* Neptune, New Jersey: Loizeaux Brothers, Inc., 1910.

Ironside, H. A. *Expository Notes on the Gospel of Matthew.* Neptune, New Jersey: Loizeaux Brothers, Inc., n.d. (Especially good for young Christians.)

Kelly, William. *Lectures on the Gospel of Matthew.* Neptune, New Jersey: Loizeaux Brothers, Inc., 1868.

McGee, J. Vernon. *Moving Thru Matthew.* Pasadena, California: Thru the Bible Books, 1955. (An outline study.)

Pentecost, J. Dwight. *The Parables of Our Lord.* Grand Rapids, Michigan: Zondervan Publishing House, 1982.

Pentecost, J. Dwight. *The Words and Works of Jesus Christ.* Grand Rapids, Michigan: Zondervan Publishing House, 1981.

Scroggie, W. Graham. *A Guide to the Gospels.* London: Pickering & Inglis, 1948. (Excellent for personal or group study.)

Thomas, W. H. Griffith. *Outline Studies in Matthew.* Grand Rapids, Michigan: Eerdmans, 1961.

Toussaint, Stanley D. *Matthew: Behold the King.* Portland, Oregon: Multnomah Press, 1980.

Vos, Howard F. *Matthew: A Study Guide Commentary.* Grand Rapids, Michigan: Zondervan Publishing House, 1979.

Vos, Howard F. *Beginnings in the Life of Christ.* Chicago, Illinois: Moody Press, 1975.

Walvoord, John F. *Gospel of Matthew.* Chicago, Illinois: Moody Press, 1975.

The Gospel According to

MARK

INTRODUCTION

The Gospel of Mark is chronologically the first gospel that was written. It was actually one of the first books written in the New Testament—not the first, but one of the first. It was probably written from Rome prior to A.D. 63.

This man Mark was one of the writers of the New Testament who was not actually an apostle. Matthew was an apostle, of course, and so was John. Luke was a very close friend and an intimate of Paul the apostle.

John Mark—*John* was his Jewish name, while *Mark* was his Latin surname (Acts 12:12): "And when he had considered the thing, he came to the house of Mary the mother of John, whose surname was Mark; where many were gathered together praying." (This is referring to the time when Simon Peter was released from prison.) Actually, this is the first historical reference to John Mark that we have in Scripture. Obviously, his mother was a wealthy and prominent Christian in the Jerusalem church, and evidently the church there met in her home.

Mark was one who went with Paul on the first missionary journey. He was a nephew of Barnabas. Paul tells us that in Colossians 4:10. He evidently was the spiritual son of Simon Peter, because Peter, writing in 1 Peter 5:13, says, "The church that is at Babylon, elected together with you, saluteth you; and so doth Marcus my son." The Gospel of Mark has long been considered Simon Peter's gospel. I think there is evidence for that; we'll look at that a little more closely in a moment.

John Mark joined Paul and Barnabas before the first missionary journey. We're told in Acts 13:5: "And when they were at Salamis, they preached the word of God in the synagogues of the Jews: and they had also John to their minister." But this man turned back at Perga in Pamphylia, and apparently it was a fact that he was maybe a little "yellow" or "chicken," as we would say today. I don't think we need to defend John Mark for turning back. He may have had an excuse, but Paul didn't want to take him on the second missionary journey, although Uncle Barnabas did. Barnabas was a great fellow and was ready to forgive; but not Paul. In Acts 15:37–38 I read, "And Barnabas determined to take with them John, whose surname was Mark. But Paul thought not good to take him with them, who departed from them from Pamphylia, and went not with them to the work." Now, that looks to me like Paul thought Mark had failed. We're told in verse 39 of that chapter, "And the contention was so sharp between them, that they departed asunder one from the other: and so Barnabas took Mark, and sailed unto Cyprus." As far as we are concerned, he sails right off the pages of Scripture. We know very little about the ministry of John Mark.

We do know that John Mark made good. When Paul wrote his swan song in 2 Timothy 4:11 he says, "Only Luke is with me. Take Mark, and bring him with thee: for he is profitable to me for the ministry."

There has always been a question of whether he is mentioned somewhere in the gospel record. While I call attention to it, I personally do not think that there is any basis to that supposition at all.

We are told that this man, Mark, got his *facts* of the gospel from Peter. Others say that he got the *explanation* of the gospel from Paul. I'm willing to accept that.

Why are there four Gospels? One reason is that they were written to different people. Matthew was written for the nation Israel; it was written for the religious man. Mark was written specifically for the Roman, and it was suited for the Roman times. It was written for the strong man. The Romans ruled the world for a millennium. The Gospel of Mark was written for such people. The Romans actually had subjugated the world; they had brought peace and justice, good roads, law and order, protection; but it was a forced peace. The iron heel of Rome was on mankind, and it had to pay a price. Rome was a strong dictatorship. Dr. D. S. Gregory has expressed it like this: "[The Roman] was to try whether human power, taking the form of law, regulated by political principles of which a regard for law and justice was most conspicuous, could perfect humanity by subordinating the individual to the state and making the state universal" (Gregory, *Key to the Gospels*, p. 53). Dr. Robert D. Culver, in his book *Daniel and the Latter Days*, says that the Roman gave to the world the kind of peace that the League of

Nations and now the United Nations tries to give to the world. This kind of peace has already been tried by the Romans, and it must be a peace that is pushed down on the world, forced on the world, and held in the hands of a very strong man. The world today, of course, is looking again for that strong man to come along.

Rome represented active, human power in the ancient world, and it led to dictatorship. The power was actually vested in one man, which, of course, was the thing that was dangerous. Again that is the danger today, as we are moving in that direction. I'd like to quote Dr. D. S. Gregory (*Key to the Gospels*, p. 161) again in this connection. "The grandest Roman, the ideal man of the race, was therefore the mightiest worker, conqueror, organizer, and ruler,—the man who as *Caesar* could sway the sceptre of the universal empire. Caesar and Caesarism were the inevitable result of Roman development. . . . When [the Roman] had been made to feel most deeply that natural justice in the hands of a human despot is a dreadful thing for sinful man,—the Holy Ghost proposes to commend to his acceptance Jesus of Nazareth as his Sovereign and Saviour, the expected deliverer of the world." We're moving into a position today where there will come a police state, ruled by one man. He'll be satanic, ruling over sinful men so that they will cry out for deliverance. The only One who will be able to deliver will be the Lord Jesus Christ when He comes!

Paul wrote to the Romans, ". . . I am not ashamed of the gospel of Christ: for it is the power of God unto salvation to every one that believeth . . ." (Rom. 1:16). That power is the power that can extend mercy. In the days when the Caesars ruled, the world longed for mercy and all they got was power. It was a day in which no man dared to resist that power because to resist it was fatal. To flee from it was impossible—one could never get beyond it. It was in that day that God sent a message to that segment of the population, and John Mark is the writer.

John Mark is giving Simon Peter's account of the gospel. The early church felt that this was true and took that position. For example, Papias, one of the early church fathers, recorded that John Mark got his gospel from Simon Peter: "Mark, the interpreter of Peter, wrote carefully down all that he recollected, but not according to the order of Christ's speaking or working." Eusebius says that "such a light of piety shone into the minds of those who heard Peter that they were not satisfied with once hearing, nor with the unwritten doctrine that was delivered, but earnestly besought Mark (whose gospel is now spread abroad) that he would leave in writing for them the doctrine which they had received by preaching." So it was, therefore, that we got Simon Peter's gospel through John Mark.

It is a gospel of action because Simon Peter was that kind of man. It is a gospel of action, written to the Roman who was also a man of action.

In Mark's gospel, Jesus lays aside the regal robes of kingship and girds Himself with the towel of service. He is King in Matthew's gospel; He is the Servant in the Gospel of Mark. But He is not man's servant; He is God's Servant. Mark expresses it by stating the words of our Lord, "For even the Son of man came not to be ministered unto, but to minister, and to give his life a ransom for many" (Mark 10:45).

In Mark's gospel Jesus is presented as the Servant of Jehovah. This fulfills Isaiah 42:1–2: "Behold my servant, whom I uphold; mine elect, in whom my soul delighteth; I have put my spirit upon him: he shall bring forth judgment to the Gentiles. He shall not cry, nor lift up, nor cause his voice to be heard in the street."

Bernard, way back in 1864, said of the Gospel of Mark: "St. Peter's saying to Cornelius has been well noticed as a fit motto for this gospel: 'God anointed Jesus of Nazareth with the Holy Ghost and with power; who went about doing good and healing all those who were oppressed of the devil.' "

Someone has put it like this:

I read
In a book
Where a man called
Christ
Went about doing good.
It is very disconcerting
To me
That I am so easily
Satisfied
With just
Going about.

We read a great deal today about protesting and marches, and we hear about do-gooders, both the politicians and the preachers. They all *talk* about doing good, but they are just going about. The Lord Jesus came in the winsomeness of His humanity and the fulness of His deity doing good. This was only the beginning of the gospel. He died and rose again. Then He said to His own, "Go." The gospel was then completed. This is the gospel today.

The style of Mark is brief and blunt, pertinent and pithy, short and sweet. Mark is stripped of excess verbiage and goes right to the point. This is the gospel of action and accomplishment. Here Jesus is not adorned with words and narrative, but He is stripped and girded for action.

Mark is written in a simple style. It is designed for the masses of the street. It is interesting to note that the connective *and* occurs more than any other word in the gospel. It is said to occur 1,331 times. I didn't count that, friend, but if you doubt that statement, you count them. Very frankly, if I had turned in a college English paper with that many *and*s in it, I would have been flunked. Yet it is a potent word when it is used correctly. It is a word of action, and it means something must follow. I've heard a lot of speakers, especially young preachers, and when they are reaching for something to say they will use the word *and*. The minute they say that, my friend, they've got to say something else. No sentence can end with *and*. *And* always leads to further action.

Mark wrote this gospel, I believe, in Rome, evidently for Romans, because they were a busy people and believed in power and action. They wanted the answer to this question: *Is Jesus able to do the job?* This gospel is brief enough for a busy man to read. Few Old Testament Scriptures are quoted and Jewish customs are explained, which give additional proof that it was written for foreigners.

Matthew gives us a genealogy because a king must have a genealogy. Mark does not give one because a servant doesn't need a genealogy, he needs references. A servant needs to do the job. We're going to see that in this gospel because that is the way Jesus is presented.

OUTLINE

The Credentials of Christ

I. John Introduces the Servant, Chapter 1:1–8
(Death of John, 6:14–29)

II. God the Father Identifies the Servant, Chapter 1:9–11
(Transfiguration, 9:1–8)

III. The Temptation Initiates the Servant, Chapter 1:12–13

IV. Works and Words Illustrate (Illumine) the Servant, Chapters 1:14–13:37

A. Miracles
1. *Healing (Physical)*
   a. Peter's Wife's Mother (Fever), and Others, Chapter 1:29–34
   b. Leper, Chapter 1:40–45
   c. Palsied Man Let down through Roof, Chapter 2:1–12
   d. Man with Withered Hand, Chapter 3:1–5
   e. Many Healed by Sea of Galilee, Chapter 3:6–10
   f. Woman with Issue of Blood, Chapter 5:21–34
   g. Sick at Nazareth, Chapter 6:5–6
   h. Disciples Heal, Chapter 6:13
   i. Sick in Land of Gennesaret, Chapter 6:53–56
   j. Deaf and Dumb of Decapolis, Chapter 7:31–37
   k. Blind Man of Bethsaida, Chapter 8:22–26
   l. Blind Bartimaeus, Chapter 10:46–52
2. *Nature (Natural)*
   a. Stills the Storm, Chapter 4:35–41
   b. Five Thousand Fed, Chapter 6:32–44
   c. Walks on Sea, Chapter 6:45–52
   d. Four Thousand Fed, Chapter 8:1–9
   e. Fig Tree Cursed, Chapter 11:12–14
3. *Demons (Spiritual)*
   a. Man in Synagogue, Chapter 1:21–27
   b. Many Demons in Capernaum, Chapter 1:32–34
   c. Demons in Galilee, Chapter 1:39
   d. Unclean Spirits by Sea of Galilee, Chapter 3:11–12
   e. Scribes Charge that He Casts out Demons by Beelzebub, Chapter 3:22–30
   f. Demoniac of Gadara, Chapter 5:1–20
   g. Syrophenician's Demon-possessed Daughter, Chapter 7:24–30
   h. Demon-possessed Boy, Chapter 9:14–29
4. *Raised from Dead (Supernatural)*
   Daughter of Jairus, Chapter 5:35–43

B. Parables and Teaching
1. *Parables*
   a. No Fasting with the Bridegroom Present, Chapter 2:19–20
   b. New Cloth on Old Garment, Chapter 2:21
   c. New Wine in Old Bottles, Chapter 2:22
   d. Sower, Chapter 4:1–20
   e. Candle and Bushel, Chapter 4:21–25
   f. Seed Growing, Chapter 4:26–29
   g. Mustard Seed, Chapter 4:30–34
   h. Man Demanding Fruit from Vineyard, Chapter 12:1–12

i. Fig Tree, Chapter 13:28–33
j. Man on Trip, Chapter 13:34–37

2. *Miscellaneous Teachings*
   a. Preaching the Gospel of the Kingdom, Chapter 1:14–15
   b. Preaching in Galilee, Chapter 1:28, 35–39
   c. Sabbath, Chapter 2:23–28
   d. New Relationship, Chapter 3:31–35
   e. Synagogue in Nazareth, Chapter 6:1–4
   f. The Twelve Sent out, Chapter 6:7–12
   g. The Twelve Return, Chapter 6:30–31
   h. Pharisees Denounced, Chapter 7:1–23
   i. Leaven Explained, Chapter 8:10–21
   j. Death of Christ, Chapters 8:27–38; 9:30–32; 10:32–34
   k. Mark of Greatness, Chapter 9:33–37
   l. Rebuke of Sectarianism, Chapter 9:38–41
   m. Hell, Chapter 9:42–50
   n. Marriage, Chapter 10:1–16
   o. Riches, Chapter 10:23–31
   p. Prayer, Chapter 11:22–26
   q. Authority of Jesus, Chapter 11:27–33
   r. Taxes, Chapter 12:13–17
   s. Resurrection, Chapter 12:18–27
   t. The Great Commandment, Chapter 12:28–34
   u. Messiah, Chapter 12:35–40
   v. Olivet Discourse, Chapter 13:1–27
3. *Incidents*
   a. Call of Disciples, Chapters 1:16–20; 2:13–18; 3:13–21
   b. Death of John the Baptist, Chapter 6:14–29
   c. Transfiguration, Chapter 9:1–13
   d. Rich Young Ruler, Chapter 10:17–22
   e. Ambition of James and John, Chapter 10:35–45
   f. Triumphal Entry, Chapter 11:1–11
   g. Jesus Cleanses Temple, Chapter 11:15–18
   h. Fig Tree Withered, Chapter 11:19–21
   i. Widow's Mite, Chapter 12:41–44

V. Death, Burial and Resurrection Insure the Servant, Chapters 14:1–16:20
   A. Plot to Put Jesus to Death, Chapter 14:1–2
   B. Jesus at Supper in Bethany, Chapter 14:3–9
   C. Judas Bargains to Betray Jesus, Chapter 14:10–11
   D. The Passover, Chapter 14:12–26
   E. The Garden of Gethsemane, Chapter 14:27–42
   F. The Arrest of Jesus, Chapter 14:43–52
   G. The Trial of Jesus, Chapters 14:53–15:15
   H. The Crucifixion of Jesus, Chapter 15:16–41
   I. The Burial, Chapter 15:42–47
   J. The Resurrection, Chapter 16:1–18
   K. The Ascension, Chapter 16:19–20

CHAPTER 1

***THEME:** John introduces the Servant; God the Father identifies the Servant; the temptation initiates the Servant; works and words illustrate (illumine) the Servant; preaching the gospel of the kingdom; call of disciples; man in synagogue; preaching in Galilee; Peter's wife's mother (fever), and others healed; demons in Galilee; leper healed*

There probably is more content in this first chapter of Mark than any other chapter in the Bible (with the exception of Gen. 1). It covers the ministry of John the Baptist, after going back to the prophecies of Isaiah and Malachi. It takes in the first year's ministry of Jesus and follows Him through a busy Sabbath day. It concludes with the mighty work of cleansing the leper. In spite of the pressure of a busy life, Jesus took time to pray.

This chapter of crowded content is made striking by the absence of genealogy which is so prominent in Matthew. We have already stated why. A king must have a genealogy. A servant needs references, not a "birth certificate." It is not a question as to His ancestors, rather as to His actions—can He do the job? Jehovah's Servant is marked out here by His accomplishments. Besides this, the Romans or other outsiders would not be concerned with the genealogy of Jesus, which is traced back to Abraham.

As we begin the text of this gospel, let us ask God to bring us into vital relationship with Jesus. We are going to behold the Lord Jesus Christ. Dr. A. J. Gordon wrote: "The look saves but the gaze sanctifies."

JOHN INTRODUCES THE SERVANT

The beginning of the gospel of Jesus Christ, the Son of God;

As it is written in the prophets, Behold, I send my messenger before thy face, which shall prepare thy way before thee.

The voice of one crying in the wilderness, Prepare ye the way of the Lord, make his paths straight [Mark 1:1–3].

This is not the beginning of either John or Jesus. It is the beginning of the gospel when the Lord Jesus came to this earth and died upon a cross and rose again. That, my friend, is the gospel.

There are three beginnings recorded in Scripture. Let us put them down in chronological order:

1. "In the beginning was the Word" (John 1:1). This goes back to a dateless beginning, a beginning before all time. Here the human mind can only grope. It is logical rather than chronological because in my thinking, I must put my peg somewhere in the past in order to take off. If I see an airplane in the air, I assume there is an airport somewhere. I may not know where it is, but I know the plane took off from some place. So when I look around at the universe, I know that it took off from somewhere and that somewhere there is a God. But I don't know anything about that beginning. God comes out of eternity to meet us. I just have to put down the peg at the point where He does meet us, back as far as I can think, and realize He was there before that.

2. "In the beginning God created the heaven and the earth" (Gen. 1:1). This is where we move out of eternity into time. However, although many people have been attempting to date this universe, no man so far knows. Man's guesses have ranged from six thousand to three billions of years. We know so little but, when we come into His presence and begin to know even as we are known, then we will realize how we saw through a glass darkly. I'm sure we will marvel at our stupidity and our ignorance. Our God is a great God. He has plenty of time.

3. "The beginning of the gospel . . ." (v. 1) is the same as "That which was from the beginning . . ." (1 John 1:1). This is dated. It goes back to Jesus Christ at the precise moment He took upon Himself human flesh. Jesus Christ is the gospel!

Then Mark, who has very few quotations from the Old Testament, quotes two prophecies. The Romans knew very little about prophecy. He does this to show them that this One whom he is talking about doesn't need a genealogy, but He does need references. So Mark shows that His references go back to Isaiah and to Malachi. Both John and Mark declare that the coming of John the Baptist fulfilled the prophecies of the one who would be the forerunner of Christ.

John did baptize in the wilderness, and preach the baptism of repentance for the remission of sins [Mark 1:4].

I want to change the wording so that we can get the meaning of this verse. John preached repentance and baptized *unto* remission for sins, not *for* remission of sins. The Greek preposition *eis* is used with *remission* and is translated "unto" or "into." His ministry was preparatory. It was preparing them for the coming of the Lord Jesus Christ into the world. Jesus Christ is the One who remits sins.

And there went out unto him all the land of Judaea, and they of Jerusalem, and were all baptized of him in the river of Jordan, confessing their sins.

And John was clothed with camel's hair, and with a girdle of a skin about his loins; and he did eat locusts and wild honey [Mark 1:5–6].

John the Baptist was remarkable, not only in his message, but remarkable in his dress and in his diet. This man was one who had been set aside for this ministry. He was of the order of the priests, a Levite, and was expected to minister in the temple in Jerusalem. But God had called him as a prophet, and he is out in the wilderness preaching. And the people come out to hear him!

Today, we like to put a church in a location where people live or where they can congregate and come together. We feel that the church should be accessible. John didn't work on that theory at all. He was way out yonder in the wilderness and the multitudes went out to him.

And preached, saying, There cometh one mightier than I after me, the latchet of whose shoes I am not worthy to stoop down and unloose [Mark 1:7].

This reveals something of how remarkable this man really was. He stirred the multitudes. He was a strange and a strong man, but his was a solo voice. Notice his humility. John the Baptist was an humble man.

I indeed have baptized you with water: but he shall baptize you with the Holy Ghost [Mark 1:8].

This is the great distinction between John and Jesus. The *real* baptism is the baptism with the Holy Spirit. *Ritual* baptism is by water. Water baptism is very important today because it is a testimony. In the Gospel of Matthew we learned that the reason the Lord Jesus was baptized was actually to identify Himself with mankind.

GOD THE FATHER IDENTIFIES THE SERVANT

And it came to pass in those days, that Jesus came from Nazareth of Galilee, and was baptized of John in Jordan [Mark 1:9].

Notice Mark's headline—"JESUS CAME." What a thrill! Jesus is coming again someday. That's another wonderful headline. But here, the Lord Jesus came from the obscurity of thirty years of quiet training in little Nazareth. He comes now and identifies Himself with the human family in His baptism. You remember that Jesus had said to John, ". . . Suffer it to be so now . . ." (Matt. 3:15), because John didn't think he should baptize Jesus.

Notice also that His name *Jesus* is used here. Jesus came. We will find that it is His common name that is used in this gospel. The name *Jesus* is used more frequently in Mark than any other name.

And straightway coming up out of the water, he saw the heavens opened, and the Spirit like a dove descending upon him:

And there came a voice from heaven, saying, Thou art my beloved Son, in whom I am well pleased [Mark 1:10–11].

Here we see the Trinity brought together in a very definite way. We see the Lord Jesus, the second Person of the Godhead; the Spirit of God who descends like a dove upon Him—the Spirit is the third Person of the Godhead; and the voice from heaven saying, "Thou art my beloved Son" is that of the Father, the first Person of the Godhead. So the Trinity is brought to our attention. And this, by the way, is heaven's seal upon the Person and dedication of Jesus.

You will notice that things are happening very fast here. He is the Servant. John the Baptist is the one who introduces Him, and then God the Father identifies Him and puts His seal upon Him. Next the temptation will initiate Him.

THE TEMPTATION INITIATES THE SERVANT

And immediately the spirit driveth him into the wilderness [Mark 1:12].

Driveth is a word of fierceness and seriousness. The Spirit of God moved Him right out into the wilderness that He might be tempted. This is something that is very important for us to see. We come again to that question: Can He do the job? Other men had failed; they couldn't stand up under temptation. Adam failed. Noah got through the Flood, and then he miserably fell on his face. We saw that Abraham failed. Moses failed—he led the children of Israel out of Egypt, but he wasn't permitted to enter the Promised Land. And poor David failed. So we see that the temptation initiates Him into His work.

And he was there in the wilderness forty days, tempted of Satan; and was with the wild beasts; and the angels ministered unto him [Mark 1:13].

We do not have the detail given here that we find in Matthew and in Luke. He was in the wilderness forty days, tempted of Satan. He was tempted during the whole forty days. Some people seem to have the impression that He fasted forty days and then Satan tempted Him. My friend, He was being tempted all the time.

Some people have the idea that He was there tempted of Satan and that the wild beasts more or less contributed to the temptation. Mark is saying here that He was with the wild beasts and the angels and they both ministered to Him. The beasts are a part of creation put under the dominion of man. That's the reason God created these creatures. Remember in Genesis we learned that everything was a preparation to make a home for man. As far as we know, this earth is the only place in which there is mankind and which is habitable for man. Here, the beasts which were below the Man Christ Jesus ministered to Him, and the angels above Him ministered to Him. That is what Mark is saying here.

PREACHING THE GOSPEL OF THE KINGDOM

Now after that John was put in prison, Jesus came into Galilee, preaching the gospel of the kingdom of God,

And saying, The time is fulfilled, and the kingdom of God is at hand: repent ye, and believe the gospel [Mark 1:14–15].

After the temptation, we find Jesus beginning His ministry. Notice again Mark's flaming headline: JESUS CAME. After John the Baptist was imprisoned, Jesus came into Galilee. He begins His ministry now, preaching the gospel of God, saying, "The time is fulfilled, and the kingdom of God is at hand."

"Of the kingdom" is not in the better manuscripts and I, personally, think it should be "preaching the *gospel of God* and saying, The time is fulfilled." The gospel of God is that the kingdom of God is at hand. In Matthew it was the "kingdom of heaven." Is there a distinction between the two? Yes, there is, and there is also an overlapping. The kingdom of heaven is God's rule over the earth; the kingdom of God includes His entire universe, even beyond the bounds of this earth. So the kingdom of heaven is *in* the kingdom of God. Matthew is applying God's rule specifically to this earth. Mark is reaching out and including a wider area because the kingdom of God includes the entire universe with all of His creatures. As far as the earth is concerned, to say "the kingdom of heaven is at hand" or "the kingdom of God is at hand" would be synonymous. But the kingdom of God would include regions beyond the earth while the kingdom of heaven means the reign of the heavens over the earth.

"Repent ye, and believe the gospel." The message of Jesus is the same as the message of John the Baptist in Matthew's gospel. "Repent ye: for the kingdom of heaven is at hand" (Matt. 3:2; 4:17). I believe that in our day, the message is really turned around—that is, we put faith before repentance. When you turn to Jesus Christ in faith, you are actually turning *to* Him *from* something else, and that turning *from* something is repentance. If there was not that turning *from* something, then apparently there was not a real turning *to* Christ. It is true that if there is a real turning to Christ, there will be a manifestation of a change in the life showing that the believer is turning from something. So there is no contradiction at all. The important thing is for the people to believe in the gospel.

We are seeing fast action here, but, remember, this gospel is written for the Romans who were men of action. They were men of power who ruled the world. Matthew is directed to the religious man. Mark was written to the strong man. Luke is addressed to the thinking man. The Gospel of John is directed to the wretched man, the man who needs salvation.

CALL OF DISCIPLES

Now as he walked by the sea of Galilee, he saw Simon and Andrew his brother casting a net into the sea: for they were fishers.

And Jesus said unto them, Come ye after me, and I will make you to become fishers of men.

And straightway they forsook their nets, and followed him.

And when he had gone a little farther thence, he saw James the son of Zebedee, and John his brother, who also were in the ship mending their nets.

And straightway he called them: and they left their father Zebedee in the ship with the hired servants, and went after him [Mark 1:16–20].

There were three separate and distinct calls made to the apostles:

1. In John 1:35–51 we are told that when Jesus went up to Jerusalem He met these men and gave them a general call, informal and casual. They wanted to know where He lived because John the Baptist had marked Him out, and some of John's disciples followed Him. But they didn't stay with Him—He didn't ask them to at this time. They went back to their fishing in Galilee.

2. Now, we find here in Mark that at the beginning of His ministry, He walks along the sea and finds the disciples fishing, and He calls them to discipleship. They are to be "fishers of men." However, we find in Luke 5:1–11 that again they went back to their fishing.

3. The final call was a call to apostleship. It is recorded in Mark 3; Matthew 10; and Luke 6. They had gone back to fishing, and Simon Peter said to Him, ". . . Depart from me; for I am a sinful man, O Lord" (Luke 5:8). What he is really saying is, "Why don't you go and get somebody else. Let me alone because I have failed you so—I'm a sinful man." But the Lord didn't give him up; thank God for that. So the Lord came to them the third time and appointed them to apostleship.

MAN IN SYNAGOGUE

And they went into Capernaum; and straightway on the sabbath day he entered into the synagogue, and taught [Mark 1:21].

You will remember that when the religious leaders would question Him about what He did on the Sabbath day, He would make it very clear, ". . . My Father worketh hitherto, and I work" (John 5:17). We are going to see that He didn't work an eight-hour day—"Behold, he that keepeth Israel shall neither slumber nor sleep" (Ps. 121:4). This Sabbath day starts out early in the morning when He entered into the synagogue and taught. This synagogue in Capernaum was not a center of vital religion in that day. It seems that He left Nazareth because His own people would not receive Him and He went down to Capernaum, which He made His headquarters all during His earthly ministry.

And they were astonished at his doctrine: for he taught them as one that had authority, and not as the scribes [Mark 1:22].

Here we see the effect of the potency of truth and the manner of this Man. The criticism against the church today and against the ministry is that we do not speak with authority. The reason the ministry does not speak with authority is that we have lost our faith. When I say "we," I do not mean I have lost my faith. I mean that, as a class, the ministry today does not attempt to preach and to teach the Word of God. There is a departure from the truth and a tremendous bifurcation between the pulpit and the Word of God. The synagogue offered nothing vital in that day, and as a result, when our Lord spoke, they were astonished at His doctrine.

And there was in their synagogue a man with an unclean spirit; and he cried out,

Saying, Let us alone; what have we to do with thee, thou Jesus of Nazareth? art thou come to destroy us? I know thee who thou art, the Holy One of God [Mark 1:23–24].

This first miracle in the Gospel of Mark is in the spiritual realm. Only God is in control in the spiritual realm; He is in control of the demons. There is a great deal of historical evidence that demonism was rampant in the entire Roman Empire. The only way demonism can be met is by the Lord Jesus because He, and He alone, is able to move in this realm. That is the reason Mark gives this as the first miracle. He brings this miracle first because if Jesus has power in this realm, then there are two things that are implied. First, He has power in any realm. Second, only God could do such a thing. This was a part of His credentials, you see. He had authority; He had power. He taught as One who had authority, and now He demonstrates that He has power.

If you are aware of what is taking place in our contemporary culture today, you recognize that Satan worship has become very prominent. There are things happening today in the realm of the occult that can be explained only on the basis that it is satanic and that it is supernatural. You cannot explain reasonably why young people today will leave homes where they are loved, join a vagrant band, and then go out and murder! That seems unbelievable. That's satanic, friend. And we're going to see actual demon possession if this continues.

Christian friend, there is only one way to deal with this, and that is in the name of the Lord Jesus Christ. He alone can control the demons. That is the first miracle that is given to us in Mark.

And Jesus rebuked him, saying, Hold thy peace, and come out of him.

And when the unclean spirit had torn him, and cried with a loud voice, he came out of him.

And they were all amazed, insomuch that they questioned among themselves, saying, What thing is this? what new doctrine is this? for with authority commandeth he even the unclean spirits, and they do obey him [Mark 1:25–27].

Notice, friend, He is demonstrating His power and His authority in His teaching and in His miracles and they cannot understand it. He has authority which they cannot comprehend.

PREACHING IN GALILEE

And immediately his fame spread abroad throughout all the region round about Galilee [Mark 1:28].

Mark takes us on to the next incident which evidently took place the same day but sometime in the afternoon.

PETER'S WIFE'S MOTHER AND OTHERS HEALED

And forthwith, when they were come out of the synagogue, they entered into the house of Simon and Andrew, with James and John.

But Simon's wife's mother lay sick of a fever, and anon they tell him of her.

And he came and took her by the hand, and lifted her up; and immediately the fever left her, and she ministered unto them [Mark 1:29–31].

She's not called a mother-in-law, she's called Simon's wife's mother. My own mother-in-law used to call this to my attention. She thought this was a nice way of saying it, and I'm sure it is. So here was another miracle which He performed that same day. Then we follow Him on into the evening.

And at even, when the sun did set, they brought unto him all that were diseased, and them that were possessed with devils [demons] [Mark 1:32].

I am sure you recognize that "devils" in the King James Version should be translated *demons*. There is only one Devil, who is Satan, but there are many demons, as we shall see.

And all the city was gathered together at the door.

And he healed many that were sick of divers diseases, and cast out many devils [demons]; and suffered not the devils [demons] to speak, because they knew him [Mark 1:33–34].

Now Mark is doing precisely the same thing that Matthew did. He calls our attention to the fact that he tells us only very few incidents of Jesus' healing. He literally healed hundreds and hundreds of people, but only a few isolated incidents are recorded for us.

It is interesting to note that the demon world recognized Him. They knew and believed who He was, and yet they are not saved, of course.

We've gone through a busy day with Him, and you would think that after such an exhausting Sabbath day, He would sleep late the next morning. But we read:

PREACHING IN GALILEE

And in the morning, rising up a great while before day, he went out, and departed into a solitary place, and there prayed [Mark 1:35].

I know a lot of preachers take Monday off after a busy Sunday. I don't blame them for that. I formerly did it myself, but I haven't done it for quite a few years now. No, we see Jesus rising up early to go to a solitary place to pray. What a lesson this is for us.

And Simon and they that were with him followed after him.

And when they had found him, they said unto him, All men seek for thee.

And he said unto them, Let us go into the next towns, that I may preach there also: for therefore came I forth.

And he preached in their synagogues throughout all Galilee, and cast out devils [Mark 1:36–39].

This is the beginning of the gospel, you see, for by His teaching He is preparing them for that which is salvation; that is, His death and His resurrection. His teaching will not save you, friend, but rather it is His work on the cross that saves us.

Notice that He preached in their synagogues and cast out demons throughout all Galilee. He covers that entire territory in His three years of ministry.

Again we note that there was a great manifestation of demon power at this time. There are three such periods: one was during the time of Moses, one was during the time of Elijah, and one was during the time of our Lord here on earth.

We come, now, to the last miracle of the chapter. All of these have been hard cases, and they all have been different. This one is a leper. Leprosy was not incurable, as we see in Leviticus, but it was a disease that could be fatal. It was certainly a tragic disease as it deformed and mutilated the victim and barred him from society.

LEPER HEALED

And there came a leper to him, beseeching him, and kneeling down to him, and saying unto him, If thou wilt, thou canst make me clean.

And Jesus, moved with compassion, put forth his hand, and touched him, and saith unto him, I will; be thou clean [Mark 1:40–41].

There is a tremendous psychological side to this miracle. One doesn't touch a leper. This man hadn't been touched in many years. Nor had he been able to touch anyone. I imagine his family brought out the food and drink for him, left it, and after they had retired he would come up and get it. He probably could wave to them, but he could never come to them again, never hold them in his arms, never touch them. But now the Lord *touches* this man, and He cleanses him!

And as soon as he had spoken, immediately the leprosy departed from him, and he was cleansed.

And he straitly charged him, and forthwith sent him away;

And saith unto him, See thou say nothing to any man: but go thy way, shew thyself to the priest, and offer for thy cleansing those things which Moses commanded, for a testimony unto them [Mark 1:42–44].

The cleansing of a leper was to follow a Mosaic ritual. Our Lord did not break the Mosaic Law.

But he went out, and began to publish it much, and to blaze abroad the matter, insomuch that Jesus could no more openly enter into the city, but was without in desert places: and they came to him from every quarter [Mark 1:45].

This man, instead of keeping quiet about it, went out and published it. If you want to get a thing out, publish it, put it in the paper or on the radio. That's what this man did. To "blaze" abroad means to set something on fire like a forest fire. Friends, if you are having trouble getting your neighbors to listen to you, just set your place on fire! I can assure you that the whole neighborhood will come around you.

Some years ago I was holding meetings in a church in Prescott, Arizona, and I jokingly remarked to the preacher, "If you want to get a crowd here this week, set the place on fire." Do you know that when I was preaching on Sunday night he got up, walked out in the Sunday School department, came back in, pushed me aside, and said, "Friends, the church is on fire." He asked them to file out in an orderly way, and by then we could hear the sirens and the fire engines coming. Now I tell you, we had a good crowd all week. The announcement of the meeting had been on the back pages of the newspaper, but on Monday, it was on the front page with the account of the fire at the church and the assurance that the meetings would go on. So the crowds came all week. After that I facetiously recommended to every preacher who was going to hold meetings that he set the place on fire! That's one way to get a crowd.

So this healed man blazed abroad the news. He disobeyed our Lord, however. I used to go over after I had finished preaching, to help preach for a black man, a very wonderful preacher in Texas. I got over there one evening before he had finished preaching, and I want to tell you, he said one of the wisest things I've heard about this. Preaching on this section of the Gospel of Mark, he said, "The Lord told him not to tell anybody and he told everybody. He tells us to tell everybody and we tell nobody." I thought that was good. I want to say, friend, the disobedience of this cleansed leper is not as bad as our disobedience today. We are to tell everybody and we tell nobody.

However, because he blazed abroad the news, the crowds came, and our Lord had to withdraw from Capernaum for a time.

CHAPTER 2

THEME: *Palsied man let down through roof; call of disciples; no fasting with the bridegroom present; new cloth on old garment; new wine in old bottles; the Sabbath*

Chapter 2 is another chapter filled with action. It is really a continuation of chapter 1, beginning with that marvelous connective "and" that Mark uses so often. It's the little word that is the cement that holds this gospel together. It always joins what has gone before with what is to follow.

PALSIED MAN LET DOWN THROUGH ROOF

And again he entered into Capernaum after some days; and it was noised that he was in the house [Mark 2:1].

We see that He entered into Capernaum after some days. As we have said before, He had moved His headquarters from His hometown of Nazareth down to Capernaum. The best I can tell is that Capernaum remained the headquarters for our Lord's earthly ministry of three years.

We saw in chapter 1 that He had to withdraw into desert places because the leper whom He had healed didn't obey what Jesus had requested him to do, but had gone out and told everyone. So then the crowds pushed upon Him and our Lord couldn't do His work.

This is one of several reasons why the Lord Jesus did not come as a thaumaturgist, a wonder worker. He didn't want that to be the thing that would characterize Him. He didn't want this man and others to tell about His miracles because He had come for a spiritual ministry. He had come to die upon the cross for the sins of the world. This type of publicity obscures the gospel.

Very candidly, and I want to be fair and frank, one of the reasons that I object so vociferously today to these people who put the emphasis on healing or tongues or something like that is that, even if these were gifts for this age in which we are living, it is getting the cart before the horse. Someone said to me some time ago, "Well, Dr. McGee, So-and-So preaches the gospel, just like you do, and he has a healing ministry too." Yes, but is he known for preaching the gospel? Is that the reason people go to the meetings? Do they go to hear the gospel to be saved, or is the emphasis upon healing or some other emotional experience? I think we need to whittle this down to a very fine point. Our business is primarily to preach the gospel. We see here in Mark's gospel that our Lord was hindered so much because of this sensation over the leper that He left Capernaum for a while (we don't know for how long) and then came back again.

When He came back, it says it was noised that He was in the house. The little Greek word *the* is really an adjective in the Greek and it is so declined. It is a modifier to the word *house* and refers to a very definite, particular house. So the question is: Which house is mentioned in the first chapter of this gospel? In the first chapter we are told that after He had been to the synagogue that morning, He entered into the house of Simon and Andrew. This leads us to believe that when these fellows start taking off the roof, they are taking the roof off Simon Peter's house! It's hard to imagine Peter being docile and standing aside to let them do it. Not Simon Peter! I have a notion that he even threatened them with the police. It was his house.

The word got around that our Lord had come back to Capernaum and that He was at Simon Peter's house.

And straightway many were gathered together, insomuch that there was no room to receive them, no, not so much as about the door: and he preached the word unto them [Mark 2:2].

The ministry of our Lord was to preach the Word of God, and that is the emphasis that we feel should be made today. It is the emphasis upon the Word of God, upon the integrity and inerrancy of the Word of God. My prayer for myself in this connection is, "Oh, God, give me more confidence in the Word of God." I see what it is doing today in hearts and lives, and I know what it has done for me. As a result, I should have even more confidence than I have. I'll be very frank with you; sometimes I wonder whether it is going to have any influence in any heart or life. I must confess that I don't have the faith that I should have. We must remember that this is the Word of God and it will never return unto Him void (Isa. 55:11). So I rejoice to read here that our Lord preached the Word unto them.

Now our attention is directed to another group. It consists of a little delegation of five.

They are coming down the dusty road to Capernaum.

And they come unto him, bringing one sick of the palsy, which was borne of four.

And when they could not come nigh unto him for the press, they uncovered the roof where he was: and when they had broken it up, they let down the bed wherein the sick of the palsy lay [Mark 2:3–4].

Our attention is directed to this little group of five and this is how they look. One man is sick with the palsy, poor fellow. He couldn't even have made it there because he's in that stretcher. The other four make a kind of quartet, one at each corner of the stretcher. And here they come. They can't get in because of the crowd which actually fills the doors and the windows.

Now, I've found in church work today that the thing that is done more than anything else is to designate committees. The committee is what the pastor of a church often depends on. Church work, today, is done largely by the committees of various organizations. Someone has said that a committee is made up of those who take down minutes and waste hours. Another has said that a committee is made up of a group of people who individually can do nothing, but together they can decide that nothing can be done. And that is generally what they do.

If they did it like we do it, this little group had a committee. They had a door committee who came up and looked around and then went back and said. "You can't get in the door." Then they had the window committee who went up and looked around and came back and said, "You can't get in a window." Fortunately, they had a roof committee, and the roof committee came back and said, "We think we can get him down through the roof." So, maybe, if you have enough committees, there will be one that will function.

Anyway, they decided to let him down through the roof, and so these men tackle the job of taking off the roof. When they get him down into the presence of Christ, I think they are embarrassed because they see they have broken up the meeting. You can imagine what it did for the meeting in progress! We have no notion what the Lord was teaching on this occasion, but it came to a sudden halt. But our Lord must have looked at them and smiled—I'm almost sure that He did.

When Jesus saw their faith, he said unto the sick of the palsy, Son, thy sins be forgiven thee [Mark 2:5].

Whose faith? It was the faith of these men. That disturbed me for quite a few years whenever I looked at this verse. It seemed to me that it was the faith of these men that was responsible for his being saved. "Thy sins be forgiven thee." But as I studied it, I realized that it was not *their* faith that saved him.

It's wonderful to have a godly mother, but you are not going to heaven tied to your mamma's apron strings. It's wonderful to have a godly father, but your godly father won't save you. You will have to exert faith yourself. *You* must be the believing one.

On closer examination we see that it is not the faith of these four men that saved this man. It was the faith of these men that brought him to the place where he could hear the Lord Jesus deal with him individually and personally. "When Jesus saw their faith" means their faith to bring the palsied man to Him. When He saw this, then He dealt personally with the man and said, "Son, thy sins be forgiven thee."

What we need in the church today is stretcher-bearers—men and women with that kind of faith to go out and bring in the unsaved so they can hear the gospel. There are many people today who are paralyzed with a palsy of sin, a palsy of indifference, or a palsy of prejudice. A great many people are not going to come into church where the gospel is preached unless you take a corner of the stretcher and bring them in. That's what these men did. They had the faith to bring this poor man to hear the Lord Jesus deal with him personally and say, "Son, thy sins be forgiven thee."

But there were certain of the scribes sitting there, and reasoning in their hearts,

Why doth this man thus speak blasphemies? who can forgive sins but God only? [Mark 2:6–7]

Here's the enemy and they don't speak out but just think their thoughts. In their thinking, they are wrong on the first question, but they are right in the second question. This Man was not speaking blasphemies. But it is true that only God can forgive sin.

No judge has any right to let a criminal off. His business is to enforce the law. God is the moral ruler of this universe, and He must defend His own laws. God cannot be lawless. He can't be, because He is righteous. Having made the laws, He obeys those laws, and His laws are inexorable. They are not changed at all, and by them you and I are guilty before God. We need forgiveness of our sins and He does forgive. Let us never make the mistake of thinking He forgives because He is bighearted. He forgives us because Christ paid the penalty for our sins! The Lord Jesus was not speaking blasphemies—He *is* God. And He could forgive sins because He came to this earth to provide a salvation for you and me and for the man with the palsy.

And immediately when Jesus perceived in his spirit that they so reasoned within themselves, he said unto them, Why reason ye these things in your hearts? [Mark 2:8].

These men didn't speak out, you see, but they thought this in their hearts. He tries to draw them out, but these men had had a run-in with Him before and they had always come away with a bloody nose. So they decided the best thing to do here was to keep quiet, and they did. So our Lord said to them,

Whether is it easier to say to the sick of the palsy, Thy sins be forgiven thee; or to say, Arise, and take up thy bed, and walk? [Mark 2:9].

By the way, they're not about to answer that one at all. They're quiet and since they are quiet, He is still going to deal with them. He knew what they were thinking. In John 2:25 it says: "[Jesus] . . . needed not that any should testify of man: for he knew what was in man." Now the Lord Jesus really puts them on the spot. Is it easier to forgive the sins of this man or to make him arise and walk? Even though they didn't answer, I'm sure they would have said it is just as impossible to do one as the other. Only God could do either. That answer is right and that is why the Lord Jesus told the man to take up his bed and walk.

But that ye may know that the Son of man hath power on earth to forgive sins, (he saith to the sick of the palsy,)

I say unto thee, Arise, and take up thy bed, and go thy way into thine house [Mark 2:10–11].

An old Scottish commentator said that the reason He told the man to take up his bed and walk was because he would not have a relapse. He wouldn't be back on that bed, and he wouldn't be coming back to the stretcher. He's going to walk from now on. When our Lord healed, He did a good job of it.

And immediately he arose, took up the bed, and went forth before them all; insomuch that they were all amazed, and glorified God, saying, We never saw it on this fashion [Mark 2:12].

You see, this is a gospel of action and here is one of the miracles of action.

And he went forth again by the sea side; and all the multitude resorted unto him, and he taught them.

And as he passed by, he saw Levi the son of Alphaeus sitting at the receipt of custom, and said unto him, Follow me. And he arose and followed him [Mark 2:13–14].

CALL OF DISCIPLES

We have continuing action here, although this is not a miracle. We see a lot of action in this gospel.

This is the call of Levi, or Matthew. Matthew, by the way, belonged to the tribe of Levi. Imagine that! He belonged to the priestly tribe and here he has become a publican, of all things. And, by the way, this should answer the question about the ten lost tribes. This is one of the many places where we find an individual who belongs to another tribe besides Judah. When anyone tries to say there are the ten *lost* tribes today, they must be on an Easter-egg hunt. Friend, those tribes were not lost. Here is one of them right here, a man of the tribe of Levi becoming one of the disciples of our Lord. Our Lord is calling him here in this remarkable incident. You may remember that Matthew, in his gospel record, told us nothing about the fact that he gave a great dinner and invited some of his friends—the only kind of friends he had were sinners, by the way.

And it came to pass, that, as Jesus sat at meat in his house, many publicans and sinners sat also together with Jesus and his disciples: for there were many, and they followed him.

And when the scribes and Pharisees saw him eat with publicans and sinners, they said unto his disciples, How is it that he eateth and drinketh with publicans and sinners? [Mark 2:15–16].

Did you notice that three times here the statement is made that the guests there were publicans and sinners? Apparently there wasn't a good man on the list. None of the elite of the town were there. Notice that the publicans come ahead of the sinners. These were the tax collectors of that day.

When Jesus heard it, he saith unto them, They that are whole have no need of the physician, but they that are sick: I came not to call the righteous, but sinners to repentance [Mark 2:17].

That is a tremendous answer. You don't call for the doctor when everybody is well. It's when you are sick that you want the doctor to come over. The Lord Jesus said that He hadn't come to call the righteous but to call sinners. The reason He said that, actually, was because there were only sinners there. There was only one kind of folk there that day. There was no righteous person there, by any means, but the Pharisees thought *they* were!

And the disciples of John and of the Pharisees used to fast: and they come and say unto him, Why do the disciples of John and of the Pharisees fast, but thy disciples fast not? [Mark 2:18].

They were under the Law, but under the Law there was no instruction given for fasting. God had given seven feasts for His people, not fast days.

NO FASTING WITH THE BRIDEGROOM PRESENT

And Jesus said unto them, Can the children of the bridechamber fast, while the bridegroom is with them? as long as they have the bridegroom with them, they cannot fast.

But the days will come, when the bridegroom shall be taken away from them, and then shall they fast in those days [Mark 2:19–20].

What He is saying to them is that it is more important to be related to Him and to have fellowship with Him than it is to fast. It is the same today, friend. It is one thing to be religious and to put up a front, but it's another thing to enjoy fellowship with the Lord Jesus and to love Him.

NEW CLOTH ON OLD GARMENT—NEW WINE IN OLD BOTTLES

No man also seweth a piece of new cloth on an old garment: else the new piece that filled it up taketh away from the old, and the rent is made worse.

And no man putteth new wine into old bottles: else the new wine doth burst the bottles, and the wine is spilled, and the bottles will be marred: but new wine must be put into new bottles [Mark 2:21–22].

The Lord is giving two illustrations about this new life of love and fellowship with Him. He is saying that He did not come to polish up the Law. He didn't come to add to the Mosaic system. He didn't come to add a refinement or a development to it. He came to do something new. He didn't come to patch up an old garment but to give us a new garment.

Under the Law men worked, and their works were like an old moth-eaten garment. Our Lord came to provide a new robe of righteousness that comes down onto a sinner who will trust Christ. This will enable him to stand before Almighty God. This is the glorious, wonderful thing that He is saying here, friend. Our Lord didn't come to extend or project the Law of the Old Testament system or of religion. He came to introduce something new. And that which is new will be the fact that He will die for the sins of the world. New wine goes into new wine skins. A new garment goes onto a new man. That robe of righteousness comes down on one who through faith has become a son of God. This is a tremendous thing!

THE SABBATH

In the last part of this chapter we come to a Sabbath day in the fields. Then in chapter 3, it begins with the Sabbath day inside the synagogue. We see these two incidents in Matthew and in Luke. It is very important because it was on this question of the Sabbath day that He broke with the religious rulers. From this time on, they sought His death.

He claims in this incident that He is the Lord of the Sabbath day. In the synagogue, He does good on the Sabbath day. The question, of course, arises: Did He really break the Sabbath in either instance? When He healed the poor man with the withered hand, did He break the Sabbath law? Absolutely He did not. He came to fulfill the Law. But here we find that He is giving an interpretation of this. He reveals that He is the Lord of the Sabbath day, and that doing good was the thing that was all important.

And it came to pass, that he went through the corn fields on the sabbath day; and his disciples began, as they went, to pluck the ears of corn [Mark 2:23].

The "corn" is the Greek *sporima*, meaning sown fields of grain. It may have been barley, or it could have been wheat. The disciples were plucking the grain and eating, which the Pharisees interpreted as harvesting grain and threshing it on the Sabbath. The Law permitted people to pull the grain. We read in Deuteronomy 23:24–25: "When thou comest into thy neighbour's vineyard, then thou mayest eat grapes thy fill at thine own pleasure; but thou shalt not put any in thy vessel. When thou comest into the standing corn of thy neighbour, then thou mayest pluck the ears with thine hand; but thou shalt not move a sickle unto thy neighbour's standing corn." Actually, they were following the Law. If they had put in a sickle, they would have been harvesting. But the Pharisees had put their own interpretation to it and would, therefore, interpret the action as breaking the Law.

And the Pharisees said unto him, Behold, why do they on the sabbath day that which is not lawful?

And he said unto them, Have ye never read what David did, when he had need, and was an hungered, he, and they that were with him? [Mark 2:24–25].

He did not insist that they had not broken the Sabbath. Actually, He refused to argue the issue with them. Now He goes into the life of David, their king, and He cites an incident in the life of David where he had definitely broken the Mosaic Law and was justified. You see, the letter of the Law was not to be imposed when it wrought hardship upon one of God's servants who was attempting to serve Him. And that, of course, is the story concerning David, and our Lord uses that illustration.

How he went into the house of God in the days of Abiathar the high priest, and did eat the shewbread, which is not lawful to eat but for the priests, and gave also to them which were with him?

And he said unto them, The sabbath was made for man, and not man for the sabbath:

Therefore the Son of man is Lord also of the sabbath [Mark 2:26–28].

This is a great principle in respect to the Sabbath day and its meaning. The Law was really made for man and not man for the Sabbath. Another great principle is, that the Lord Jesus is the Lord of the Sabbath. Both those things are very important. By the way, I have a little booklet entitled, *The Sabbath Day or the Lord's Day, Which?* This is a very important question today. Remember that we are not under the old Mosaic system concerning the Sabbath day because it was a part of the covenant between the nation Israel and God (Exod. 31:12–17).

This Sabbath incident in the field and the Sabbath incident which we find at the beginning of chapter 3 should go together; so even though there is a chapter break in the Bible, let us go right on in our study of the incidents that relate to the Sabbath day.

CHAPTER 3

THEME: *Man with withered hand; many healed by Sea of Galilee; unclean spirits by Sea of Galilee; call of disciples; scribes charge that He casts out demons by Beelzebub; new relationship*

This chapter continues the Sabbath day discussion which led to a final break with the religious rulers.

It is obvious from this chapter that Jesus healed multitudes whose stories could be recorded separately, like that of the man let down through the roof. Mark impresses us in this chapter, not by placing the microscope down on certain incidents, but by letting us look through the telescope at the multitudes He healed. This raises the question as to the number that Jesus probably dealt with personally. Any attempt to compute the number would be mere speculation. Evidently Mark would have us believe that it was extensive.

MAN WITH WITHERED HAND

And he entered again into the synagogue; and there was a man there which had a withered hand.

And they watched him, whether he would heal him on the sabbath day; that they might accuse him [Mark 3:1–2].

The question arises here: was this man, this cripple, planted there purposely? I think the answer is absolutely yes. The other incident was out in the fields, the Sabbath in the corn fields, and that was a *secular* spot. Here it is the Sabbath in the synagogue and this is a *sacred* spot. The Lord Jesus had been healing the multitudes. They knew that, if they planted this crippled man right in the way of our Lord, Jesus would heal him when He came into the synagogue. Actually, what they did was a compliment to the Lord Jesus. They knew He was compassionate. But, of course, they were interested in being able to say that He broke the Sabbath by healing the man on the Sabbath day. So I believe the man was placed there, and we are told that the enemy was there, watching.

Our Lord's enemies are beginning to watch for some little flimsy excuse whereby they might bring a charge against Him. And they are not going to have long to wait, because notice what He did.

And he saith unto the man which had the withered hand, Stand forth [Mark 3:3].

The Lord is going to do something here. I think maybe the Wycliffe translation is better here: "Rise, come into the midst and stand there." In other words, He asked this man to come and stand in the midst because He wants to say something.

And he saith unto them, Is it lawful to do good on the sabbath days, or to do evil? to save life, or to kill? But they held their peace [Mark 3:4].

They had learned not to answer Him because they always got into trouble when they did.

And when he had looked round about on them with anger, being grieved for the hardness of their hearts, he saith unto the man, Stretch forth thine hand. And he stretched it out: and his hand was restored whole as the other [Mark 3:5].

Now the Lord Jesus broke through all of this red tape of their traditions, and He got to the heart of God's purpose in giving the Sabbath day to Israel originally. They wouldn't answer Him because they knew they would incriminate themselves. Notice that here the Lord Jesus looks around with anger. You can put it down in your memory that Jesus could get angry.

Dr. Graham Scroggie notes that the word for "anger" here is in the aorist tense in the Greek and it carries the sense of momentary anger. The Greek word for "grieve" here is used in the present tense in the sense of a continuing grief. So what we find here is this: "When He had looked round about on them with anger"—just a flash of anger, not a grudge or with malice aforethought. But "being *grieved* for the hardness of their hearts" was something that He carried with Him. He always had that awful grief because of the hardness of their hearts.

Jesus heals the man. It was the Sabbath; but because the Sabbath is made for man and because He is the Lord of the Sabbath, Jesus healed the man on the Sabbath day. The incident in the last part of chapter 2 and this incident must be considered together. These two incidents brought about the break with the religious rulers.

MANY HEALED BY SEA OF GALILEE

And the Pharisees went forth, and straightway took counsel with the Herodians against him, how they might destroy him [Mark 3:6].

Because of these two incidents, both pertaining to the Sabbath day, these bloodhounds of hate got on His trail and they never let up until they folded their arms beneath the cross of Christ. This is the beginning of a plan and plot to put Him to death.

But Jesus withdrew himself with his disciples to the sea: and a great multitude from Galilee followed him, and from Judaea,

And from Jerusalem, and from Idumaea, and from beyond Jordan; and they about Tyre and Sidon, a great multitude, when they had heard what great things he did, came unto him [Mark 3:7–8].

You will notice people are coming from various areas now and are following Him. Our Lord withdrew tactfully at this time because as He said, ". . . mine hour is not yet come." (John 2:4). Later on He did move into the face of all the opposition in Jerusalem, but now He withdraws and the crowd follows Him. If you note these places and look them up on a map, you will find they cover that entire area. From all these places folk are coming to hear the Lord Jesus Christ.

Now He is in another danger. This time it is not from the religious rulers because they are afraid of the crowd. He is in danger of being overwhelmed by the mob. You know today that a celebrity has to be protected from the mob—so notice what Jesus does.

And he spake to his disciples, that a small ship should wait on him because of the multitude, lest they should throng him.

For he had healed many; insomuch that they pressed upon him for to touch him, as many as had plagues [Mark 3:9–10].

The crowds were not only hindering Him but were actually endangering Him. They were pressing in from every side. And we're told that He healed many. You can't reduce "many" to round figures, but many means *many.* The Gospels relate to us only a few of the specific examples of His healing of "many." The desperation of the people is also significant. You know, friends, the human family is a needy family. We all belong to this family.

UNCLEAN SPIRITS BY SEA OF GALILEE

And unclean spirits, when they saw him, fell down before him, and cried, saying, Thou art the Son of God.

And he straitly charged them that they should not make him known [Mark 3:11–12].

Now we see that the unclean spirits acknowledged Him. We're going to hold that subject for a little later because I want to put an emphasis at the right time upon the matter of demon possession. We are seeing that again today in what is known as Satan worship, and there is a great deal of that going on today. But we see that He did not want the testimony of the underworld. The demons acknowledged who He was, but He didn't want their testimony.

CALL OF DISCIPLES

We now begin to see the sovereign purpose of God in choosing and ordaining the twelve apostles.

And he goeth up into a mountain, and calleth unto him whom he would: and they came unto him [Mark 3:13].

This is something I would have you note. He does the choosing here. Whether we like it or not, He does the choosing. "Ye have not chosen me, but I have chosen you, and ordained you, that ye should go and bring forth fruit, and that your fruit should remain: that whatsoever ye shall ask of the Father in my name, he may give it you" (John 15:16). It is not irreverent to say that since He chose them and they did not choose Him, He's responsible for them. That's a real comfort to know. God has saved you, begun a good work in you, and He's going to stick right with you, friend. He's going to see you through. That is what this means. And when the Lord Jesus calls, they respond.

And he ordained twelve, that they should be with him, and that he might send them forth to preach,

And to have power to heal sicknesses, and to cast out devils [Mark 3:14–15].

This is His final call to the apostles. Here is where they actually become apostles, and here is where they are sent out on a ministry set apart for Him. They are also set apart from Him in that He will not go with them physically. Mark does not furnish the details here, but in Matthew 10:5–42 there is recorded for us the message and method for them at this particular time.

In verses 16 through 19 the names of the apostles are listed. I would like to run through the list of the twelve: 1. Simon Peter (He is the first in all the lists of the apostles.); 2. James, son of Zebedee; 3. John, the brother of James; 4. Andrew, brother of Simon Peter (He is customarily listed with his brother.); 5. Philip; 6. Bartholomew, (also called Nathanael); 7. Matthew; 8. Thomas; 9. James the less, son of Alphaeus; 10. Thaddaeus, who is also called Lebbaeus and Jude; 11. Simon, the Canaanite; and 12. Judas Iscariot.

I have a book called *Marching Through Mark* in which I compare the lists of apostles as they are given in the four Gospels and in the Book of Acts. It is interesting to make this comparison of how they are listed and the different names that are used. These are the men that He chose.

And the multitude cometh together again, so that they could not so much as eat bread.

And when his friends heard of it, they went out to lay hold on him: for they said, He is beside himself [Mark 3:20–21].

Mark will impress us how busy Jesus really was. Note the reaction of His friends. If a man devotes his life to some noble but earthly cause, he is applauded. The musician, the athlete, the businessman, the artist, the statesman who gives himself to his work is recognized for his total devotion. But if a man gives himself in total dedication to the cause of God, he is branded as a fanatic.

SCRIBES CHARGE THAT HE CASTS OUT DEMONS BY BEELZEBUB

And the scribes which came down from Jerusalem said, He hath Beelzebub, and by the prince of the devils casteth he out devils [Mark 3:22].

Beelzebub was a heathen deity to whom the Jews ascribed supremacy among evil spirits.

And he called them unto him, and said unto them in parables, How can Satan cast out Satan?

And if a kingdom be divided against itself, that kingdom cannot stand.

And if a house be divided against itself, that house cannot stand.

And if Satan rise up against himself, and be divided, he cannot stand, but hath an end [Mark 3:23–26].

What He is saying is simply this: He could not be casting out demons by the power of the demons for the very simple reason that then a house would be divided against itself.

No man can enter into a strong man's house, and spoil his goods, except he will first bind the strong man; and then he will spoil his house [Mark 3:27].

You first have to bind a strong man before you can rob his house. And that is the truth here. The Lord Jesus is not doing this by the power of Satan because then Satan would be divided and would be against himself.

Verily I say unto you, All sins shall be forgiven unto the sons of men, and blasphemies wherewith soever they shall blaspheme:

But he that shall blaspheme against the Holy Ghost hath never forgiveness, but is in danger of eternal damnation:

Because they said, He hath an unclean spirit [Mark 3:28–30].

That was the unpardonable sin then. It could not be committed today in that way. To begin with they have Him, the second Person of the Godhead, present with them, and they accuse Him of casting out demons by Beelzebub when He is doing it by the power of the Holy Spirit. So they were actually rejecting the works of two Persons of the Godhead, the testimony of the Son and the testimony of the Holy Spirit. They were expressing an attitude of unbelief which was permanent rejection of Christ. They were resisting the Holy Spirit. That was unpardonable.

It is impossible to commit an unpardonable sin today—if by that you mean one can commit a sin today, come under conviction because of it tomorrow, come to God in repentance, and He would not forgive you. You see, Christ died for *all* sin, not just some sin. He didn't die for all sin but *one*, the unpardonable sin. There is no such thing as being able to commit a sin today that He will not forgive. The attitude and state of the unbeliever is unpardonable—not the act. When a man blasphemes with his mouth, that is not the thing that condemns him; it is the attitude of his heart, which is a permanent condition—unless he stops resisting. This is the sin against the Holy Spirit: to resist the convicting work of the Holy Spirit in the heart and life.

NEW RELATIONSHIP

There came then his brethren and his mother, and, standing without, sent unto him, calling him.

And the multitude sat about him, and they said unto him, Behold, thy mother and thy brethren without seek for thee.

And he answered them, saying, Who is my mother, or my brethren?

And he looked round about on them which sat about him, and said, Behold my mother and my brethren!

For whosoever shall do the will of God, the same is my brother, and my sister, and mother [Mark 3:31–35].

The half brothers of Jesus—James and Jude—both wrote Epistles, and they never mention that Jesus was their half brother. You see, anyone who is in Christ Jesus is closer to Him than His physical mother and His physical brothers were in that day. That is the reason He could look around and say that these "are closer kin to Me than even My mother and My brothers." The important thing is to be rightly related to God in Christ Jesus by having received Him as Savior, which gives us the right of being the sons of God. That is bringing us wonderfully close to Him, my friend.

CHAPTER 4

***THEME:** The Sower; candle and bushel; seed growing; mustard seed; stills the storm*

In this chapter of Mark we find several parables and then the miracle of stopping the storm. This has all been in the Gospel of Matthew, except for one particular parable, which is given here that is not found in Matthew, and it is the only part that makes it different and outstanding, as we shall see. First we find the parable of the sower as a *declaration* and then we have the *exposition* of the parable of the sower. This is followed by other parables and then one miracle.

We said in the beginning of the Gospel of Mark that this is a gospel of action; yet here the emphasis is upon parables with only one miracle. But you will notice that the parables which Mark gives are parables of action. Each one of these parables is really a very moving thing. That's why we titled our booklet on Mark, *Marching Through Mark*. The emphasis is still upon action, even when Mark is giving the parables.

And he began again to teach by the sea side: and there was gathered unto him a great multitude, so that he entered into a ship, and sat in the sea; and the whole multitude was by the sea on the land [Mark 4:1].

Matthew gives us quite an emphasis at this point for he says that Jesus went out of the house and He entered into a ship on the sea. This action as recorded by Matthew is very symbolic. The house generally illustrates the house of Israel, and the seas represent the nations of the Gentiles. His very action is that He turns from His people and He goes to the world. That actually is the background of these parables, and they need to be looked at in the context of global situations. I think this is very important for us to see.

These took place, by the way, during the height of His ministry. He was very busy, the pressure was upon Him, and He was physically weary. In fact, He was so tired, as we shall see in this chapter, that He fell asleep in the ship at sea. He was asleep because He was weary.

And he taught them many things by parables, and said unto them in his doctrine [Mark 4:2].

Jesus adopted the use of parables as a way to teach the people many things. At this point He is about halfway through His three years of ministry. He had used certain symbolic illustrations before, such as telling the woman at the well about the water of life; He had told His disciples that He would make them fishers of men and that the fields were white unto harvest. Also He had talked about salt and light and foundations of rock and sand in the Sermon on the Mount. But these are not parables. Now He has adopted the parabolic method and tells the parable of the sower.

THE SOWER

Hearken; Behold, there went out a sower to sow:

And it came to pass, as he sowed, some fell by the way side, and the fowls of the air came and devoured it up.

And some fell on stony ground, where it had not much earth; and immediately it sprang up, because it had no depth of earth:

But when the sun was up, it was scorched; and because it had no root, it withered away.

And some fell among thorns, and the thorns grew up, and choked it, and it yielded no fruit [Mark 4:3–7].

These are the three areas where the seeds fell and they represent the unsaved that do not accept the gospel. They do not accept the Word of God. Their lives are like the wayside where the birds devour the seed—the Devil takes away the Word. Others are like the stony ground where the sun withers it because there is no depth of soil for it. On the thorny ground the thorns choke it.

But then there is the good ground.

And other fell on good ground, and did yield fruit that sprang up and increased; and brought forth, some thirty, and some sixty, and some an hundred [Mark 4:8].

Now here we have only a fourth of it falling on good ground, which represents the ones who are saved, the ones who receive the Word. But there are different degrees of fruit-bearing here: thirty, sixty, and an hundredfold. You remember that the Lord said to His own in that Upper Room Discourse as He was going out on the way to the Garden of Gethsemane, "I am the genuine vine." Then He told them that He wanted them to bring forth fruit, more fruit, and much fruit. There are three degrees of fruit-bearing in those who are His own in that instance, just as we find three degrees in this parable.

And he said unto them, He that hath ears to hear, let him hear [Mark 4:9].

He puts up a danger signal. It's like the "Stop—Look—Listen" sign at a railroad crossing. Even so, it is obvious some missed it because we find in the next verse:

And when he was alone, they that were about him with the twelve asked of him the parable.

And he said unto them, Unto you it is given to know the mystery of the kingdom of God: but unto them that are without, all these things are done in parables:

That seeing they may see, and not perceive; and hearing they may hear, and not understand; lest at any time they should be converted, and their sins should be forgiven them [Mark 4:10–12].

There were obviously some who didn't understand the parable at all. When they ask Him, He answers with these verses that have a certain degree of ambiguity. Let me give you an explanation that might be helpful. The reason that Jesus resorted to parables from this point to the end of His ministry is arresting. His enemies rejected His teachings, and the multitudes had become indifferent to spiritual truths. They were actively interested in His miracles but not in the spiritual application. He now resorts to the use of parables to enlist their interest. The antagonistic attitude of His enemies and the lethargy, indifference and incomprehension of the multitudes necessitated a change to the use of parables so that those who hungered and thirsted after righteousness would be filled and those who wanted spiritual truth could have their eyes opened.

We find the same thought in the second chapter of 1 Corinthians, where Paul writes: "But as it is written, Eye hath not seen, nor ear heard, neither have entered into the heart of man, the things which God hath prepared for them that love him. But God hath revealed them unto us by his Spirit: for the Spirit searcheth all things, yea, the deep things of God." Then he goes on in verse 13, "Which things also we speak, not in the words which man's wisdom teacheth, but which the Holy Ghost teacheth; comparing spiritual things with spiritual. But the natural man receiveth not the things of the Spirit of God: for they are foolishness unto him: neither can he know them, because they are spiritually discerned" (1 Cor. 2:9–10, 13–14).

This is a great principle that Paul put down, and it is still applicable today. We can use every means to try to get people to understand spiritual truth, but they must want to understand them before these things can be made real to them. I would like to make this statement: If a person's heart and eyes are open and he wants to know, then the Spirit of God is going to bring in the great truth to his heart. He will make these things quite real and living for that person.

We sometimes use the expression—I know I say it rather carelessly—that you'll be lost if you do not accept Christ as your Savior. That is not really the truth, friend. The truth is that you are *already* lost. The point that should be accurately stated is that you will continue to be lost if you do not receive Christ as your Savior. You're not on trial, my friend. If you are a lost person, you are *lost.* Now it is your reaction and reception to the Word of God that is going to determine whether you will be saved or not. Will you accept Him as your Savior?

Somebody may say that this is beginning to move into a philosophical realm and this is not reality. This is asking a person to do something that is rather spooky, rather superstitious. I don't think it is at all, my friend. Let me illustrate it.

Mrs. McGee and I were down in Florida and found that we had bought tickets from an airline that was out on strike. We had to go back to Los Angeles on another airline, but we could use our original tickets. When I called the girl at the airport, she was able to confirm the fact that we had tickets with the airline that was on strike, and she assured us our tickets were good, our plane would leave the next morning at a certain time, and we should get to the airport about thirty minutes ahead of that time. You know, friends, I have never met this girl—not even to this good day—but I believed her. Mrs. McGee and I were there at the airport the next morning. Our tickets were good. The plane was there and we boarded it. We believed every bit of the information about that plane, and don't try to tell me that plane was not a reality. In just such a way God has given His Word. He asks you to trust Christ.

God's Word is the seed that falls. What kind of soil are you today? Are you the one with the thorns so the seed falls by the wayside or on thorny ground? Or does God's Word fall on good ground? That is the important thing. All of us are lost, and it is our *reception* of the Word of God that determines whether we are saved or whether we remain lost.

Now He gives the exposition of the parable up through verse 20.

And he said unto them, Know ye not this parable? and how then will ye know all parables?

The sower soweth the word.

And these are they by the way side, where the word is sown; but when they have heard, Satan cometh immediately, and taketh away the word that was sown in their hearts.

And these are they likewise which are sown on stony ground; who, when they have heard the word, immediately receive it with gladness;

And have no root in themselves, and so endure but for a time: afterward, when affliction or persecution ariseth for the word's sake, immediately they are offended.

And these are they which are sown among thorns; such as hear the word,

And the cares of this world, and the deceitfulness of riches, and the lusts of other things entering in, choke the word, and it becometh unfruitful.

And these are they which are sown on good ground; such as hear the word, and receive it, and bring forth fruit, some thirtyfold, some sixty, and some an hundred [Mark 4:13–20].

I'll go over it quickly. The sower is the Son of Man and the seed is the Word of God. The birds by the wayside are Satan. The stony-ground hearers are those who let affliction and persecution turn them from God. That is the flesh, and many people today are letting the flesh keep them from God. Then there are the thorny-ground hearers, those who let the cares of the world distract them. That is the world today. So many people today are letting the world shut them out from God. Then the good-ground hearers are those who are converted genuinely by the Word of God. They bring forth only percentages of fruit and only one third of these bring forth an hundredfold. So we see that we have here a parable with real action.

CANDLE AND BUSHEL

And he said unto them, Is a candle brought to be put under a bushel, or under a bed? and not to be set on a candlestick?

For there is nothing hid, which shall not be manifested; neither was any thing kept secret, but that it should come abroad [Mark 4:21–22].

What we have here is a parable of the candle and its action. Light creates responsibility. A man who receives the truth must act. We are held responsible to the degree to which we have had light given us. The light is shining, and your response to the light is all important. The point is, you and I were in darkness until the light of the gospel got through to us. We get the impression that man is a sinner because of his weakness or because of his ignorance. But Paul says very candidly (in Rom. 1) that men, when they knew God, glorified Him not as God. Man is a *willful* sinner. That's the kind of sinners all of us are, and the light that comes in will create a responsibility. We are lost, and if we do not accept the Light, if we do not accept Him, we remain lost.

If any man have ears to hear, let him hear [Mark 4:23].

This is action. God demands this action. Faith is action. Faith is acting upon what God has said. How important that is today.

I come back to the illustration of our plane trip. You must act on the fact that you have a ticket. You must believe and trust that there is a plane and that it is going to carry you right to the place you wish to go. But just sitting there in the airport *believing it* won't get you there. You must believe it enough to board the plane. That is what it means to believe.

SEED GROWING

And he said, So is the kingdom of God, as if a man should cast seed into the ground;

And should sleep, and rise night and day, and the seed should spring and grow up, he knoweth not how.

For the earth bringeth forth fruit of herself; first the blade, then the ear, after that the full corn in the ear.

But when the fruit is brought forth, immediately he putteth in the sickle, because the harvest is come [Mark 4:26–29].

Here is an unusual parable that our Lord gave and only Mark records it. It is another parable of action. It is about the "kingdom of God." Remember that I said the kingdom of God and the kingdom of heaven are two terms that are used. Actually, here they are synonymous, but the kingdom of God is not identical with the kingdom of heaven. The kingdom of God is the larger term including the whole universe; the kingdom of heaven is God's rule over the earth, which is, of course, in the kingdom of God. For instance, the state of California is in the United States, but it is not the United States. It is *in* it. So when I am in California, I am also in the United States.

Our Lord talks about the growing of the seed here. Even today we still don't know too much about the growing of a seed into a plant, then producing fruit. It is a mystery to this day. This is another parable of power and action. The old bromide is true: "Great oaks from little acorns grow." After all of the years of scientific progress, there is not much more men can add to this. The label of osmosis adds little to our understanding, although the reservoir of knowledge has been increased.

During the month of March I traveled by train from Atlanta, Georgia, to Los Angeles, California. Spring had already come to the southern section of our country. Trees were budding, flowers were blooming—the azaleas in Mississippi were gorgeous, and the farmers everywhere were plowing and planting. No one could tell just what was happening, but everyone was reacting to it and accepting it with full enjoyment and happy anticipation of the future harvest. Tremendous power was being released in nature as nitrogen took on the garment of green. If God let it go at once it would make a hydrogen bomb sound like a Chinese firecracker.

This parable illustrates the power of the Word of God working in our hearts and lives. What a marvelous parable it is.

Now we have the third parable about seed in this chapter.

MUSTARD SEED

And he said, Whereunto shall we liken the kingdom of God? or with what comparison shall we compare it?

It is like a grain of mustard seed, which, when it is sown in the earth, is less than all the seeds that be in the earth:

But when it is sown, it groweth up, and becometh greater than all herbs, and shooteth out great branches; so that the fowls of the air may lodge under the shadow of it.

And with many such parables spake he the word unto them, as they were able to hear it.

But without a parable spake he not unto them: and when they were alone, he expounded all things to his disciples [Mark 4:30–34].

Mustard is not food; it is a condiment. And the growth of a mustard seed into a tree is unnatural. This pictures the outward growth of Christendom into great organizations, big churches, large programs, all produced by human energy and not by the Holy Spirit. The birds in the branches are not even good. They represent Satan.

STILLS THE STORM

Now we find here that when our Lord leaves off teaching, they go out into the sea. He wants a rest because He's tired. He goes to sleep. And then we find this miracle of His quieting the sea.

And the same day, when the even was come, he saith unto them, Let us pass over unto the other side.

And when they had sent away the multitude, they took him even as he was in the ship. And there were also with him other little ships.

And there arose a great storm of wind, and the waves beat into the ship, so that it was now full.

And he was in the hinder part of the ship, asleep on a pillow: and they awake him, and say unto him, Master, carest thou not that we perish?

And he arose, and rebuked the wind, and said unto the sea, Peace, be still. And the wind ceased, and there was a great calm.

And he said unto them, Why are ye so fearful? how is it that ye have no faith?

And they feared exceedingly, and said one to another, What manner of man is

this, that even the wind and the sea obey him? [Mark 4:35–41].

Do you know what made them fear? It was not so much the fact that He quieted the storm but that it responded immediately. It just leveled out; there was a sudden calm. This miracle was so great that it made these men afraid.

What a wonderful lesson we learn here. He puts us into the storms of life in order that we might grow closer to Him and that we might know Him better.

Jesus, Savior, pilot me
Over life's tempestuous sea:
Unknown waves before me roll,
Hiding rocks and treach'rous shoal;
Chart and compass come from Thee—
Jesus, Savior, pilot me!

"Jesus, Savior, Pilot Me"
—Edward Hooper

CHAPTER 5

***THEME:** Demoniac of Gadara; woman with issue of blood; daughter of Jairus raised from dead (supernatural)*

We come now to one of the most important chapters in the Gospel of Mark. I'm sure some of you are smiling now, because I think I say that about every chapter we study. Well, every chapter *is* the most important chapter when you are studying it! But this one is important because the Gospel of Mark is a gospel of action. There are more of the miracles given in this gospel than in any other, and in this chapter there are three outstanding miracles related. They could be performed only by the hand of Omnipotence. That is why I think this is a remarkable chapter.

Let me say just a word today about demon possession. We promised it on several occasions in Matthew, and when we began Mark we said that we'd have something a little more detailed to say concerning it. This is the place.

DEMONIAC OF GADARA

And they came over unto the other side of the sea, into the country of the Gadarenes [Mark 5:1].

Our Lord had taught on the other side and had given them parables. He was weary and so had crossed the sea. The Gadarenes were the inhabitants of Gadara, and this is the land that was given to the tribe of Gad on the east side of the Jordan River. Remember, Gad chose the wrong side of Jordan. They were the ones who stayed on the east side, and now we find them in the pig business. You see, when you start away from God, you just keep going away from Him.

And when he was come out of the ship, immediately there met him out of the tombs a man with an unclean spirit [Mark 5:2].

He's "a man," a human being. Note that first of all and write it down. He is in a desperate condition, but he is still a man. That is what the Lord Jesus saw—a man. In spite of his condition, Jesus saw the man. His conduct suggests that the man was a maniac. Notice what it says about him.

Who had his dwelling among the tombs; and no man could bind him, no, not with chains:

Because that he had been often bound with fetters and chains, and the chains had been plucked usunder by him, and the fetters broken in pieces: neither could any man tame him.

And always, night and day, he was in the mountains, and in the tombs, crying, and cutting himself with stones [Mark 5:3–5].

This is a desperate case of a man possessed with this unclean spirit. He dwelt, which means he settled down, among the tombs. This is where he lived; this was his ghetto. The tombs were unclean places. The dead were there, and sometimes the bodies were exposed. He no longer enjoyed the society of normal men but he lived among the dead. We find from Matthew that there was another man, but Mark and Luke center on this one. We gather that the other man was no companion to this man, nor, of course, were the dead any company to him. He was alone. Yet we are told that he possessed superhuman power; so they could not bind him. Just because a man demonstrates power which is supernatural does not prove that God gave it to him. This case is a typical example. He was a wild man; no one could confine him. He was miserable. He suffered great physical harm which he inflicted on himself. He's a creature of pathos and pity, and on the human plane he is a hopeless case. He's inarticulate and just crying out. What an awful condition! And all due to demon possession!

But when he saw Jesus afar off, he ran and worshipped him,

And cried with a loud voice, and said, What have I to do with thee, Jesus, thou Son of the most high God? I adjure thee by God, that thou torment me not.

For he said unto him, Come out of the man, thou unclean spirit [Mark 5:6–8].

It was the man who worshiped Him, not the demon. He was afraid of Jesus. He suffered from what I suppose would be called spiritual schizophrenia, a split personality. Sometimes it is the man and sometimes it is the demon speaking. In verse 7 it literally says, "What is there to thee and me?" That is, "What have we in common?" This poor man—possessed by demons!

And he asked him, What is thy name? And he answered, saying, My name is Legion: for we are many [Mark 5:9].

The answer of this man is baffling but it's not bad grammar. He says, "My name is . . . " indicating that the man was trying to speak, but then the demons take over and they say, "We are many."

And he besought him much that he would not send them away out of the country.

Now there was there nigh unto the mountains a great herd of swine feeding.

And all the devils besought him, saying, Send us into the swine, that we may enter into them.

And forthwith Jesus gave them leave. And the unclean spirits went out, and entered into the swine: and the herd ran violently down a steep place into the sea, (they were about two thousand;) and were choked in the sea [Mark 5:10–13].

There is a tremendous occurrence presented to us here. The demons made a very peculiar request. They preferred swine to the abyss. The permission of Jesus here has been severely criticized by men who are liberal in their theology. Their objection has been that He would not destroy the swine, as the "gentle Jesus" wouldn't do things like that. That's nonsense, of course. I was having breakfast in Chicago with a man who had gone into liberalism. I had known him in school, and he had been sound then, but the way he was talking about Jesus and describing Him was totally fictitious. And he used this illustration, saying he didn't believe Jesus would destroy swine because that was such a terrible thing. Well, to begin with, these people shouldn't have been in the pig business. The Mosaic Law forbade it. And then I reminded this fellow that the two thousand pigs destroyed here were insignificant compared to the pigs that were destroyed in the Flood at the time of Noah. And the third interesting thing was that as we were having breakfast together, he was eating bacon. "Oh, my!" I said to him, "I wish the little piggie that you are eating this morning were here to tell you what he thinks of you, for you weep like the walrus and the carpenter." (You remember, they just kept on eating the oysters but they wept because there was a lot of sand, not because they were eating the oysters. They wept for the wrong thing.) Well, I think we have a lot of that type of thinking about us today.

Now let me come back and say some things about this matter of demon possession:

1. Not only Mark but all of the Scriptures bear definite witness to the reality of demons. For those who accept the authority of Scripture, there must be an acceptance of the reality of demons.

2. They were especially evident during the ministry of Jesus but, of course, were not confined to that period. By the way, we're living in a day right now when there is a resurgence and a manifestation of demonism again. Many illustrations of this could be given.

3. For some strange reason they seek to indwell mankind. They seek to manifest their evil nature through human beings. They are extremely restless. This description is clear. "When the unclean spirit is gone out of a man, he walketh through dry places, seeking rest;

and finding none, he saith, I will return unto my house whence I came out" (Luke 11:24). Is this not the characteristic of all evil, even evil men? There is the restlessness of seeking expression of the evil nature.

Good spirits never seek to take possession of men. The Holy Spirit is the one exception, and He only indwells believers. But as truly as He indwells believers so demons can possess the unsaved. Demons cannot possess the saved. We are told that greater is He that is in us (the Holy Spirit) than he that is in the world (Satan) (1 John 4:4). Therefore, a child of God cannot be demon-possessed.

4. In this incident the demons would rather go into a herd of swine than the abyss. That is interesting to note.

5. They should be called demons and not devils. There is only one Devil. Our translation is faulty here. They are called "unclean spirits" because of their nature.

6. Scripture does not give us the origin of them. Anything I would say today would be highly speculative.

7. There seems to be many of them.

8. They are under the control of Satan. Now I said I would not speculate, but here I go. I'm of the opinion that when Satan fell, these were the angels that followed him. Now having said that, let's not say any more.

9. Their purpose is the final undoing of man. They are certainly working on Satan's program.

10. There are present-day examples of demon possession. We have Satan worship right in our own neighborhoods, and there are a lot of college students and professors who are engaged in it. They say they find reality in it. I think they do, by the way. I think that Satan is prepared to give reality to those who worship him. The all-important question is: what kind of reality do they find?

11. The Lord Jesus Christ has power over demons. That, I think, is the great lesson for us to learn.

There is no reason for any believer to be afraid of demons or to adopt some superstition or spooky notion concerning them. If you feel that you are bothered with them, then just ask the Lord Jesus to deliver you. They have been cast out in His name, and it is a lack of faith in the Lord Jesus to walk in fear of them today. If you feel that they can control you in any way, or possess you, or direct you, then you need counselling. Remember that the Lord Jesus Christ has power over demons.

There is a very pertinent poem written by Joseph Odell about this incident. You know that the people of Gadara came and asked the Lord Jesus to leave their coast. The reason was that they would rather have swine than have *Him.* That's a rather heart-searching question for the present day because there are a lot of people who would rather have other things—that are just as bad as pigs—than to have Christ.

Rabbi, begone! Thy powers
Bring loss to us and ours.
Our ways are not as Thine,
Thou lovest men, we—swine.
Oh, get Thee hence, Omnipotence!
And take this fool of Thine!
His soul? What care we for his soul?
What good to us that Thou has made him whole?
Since we have lost our swine.
And Christ went sadly,
He had wrought for them a sign
Of love and hope and tenderness divine—
They wanted swine.

Christ stands without your door and gently knocks,
But if your gold or swine the entrance blocks,
He forces no man's hold—he will depart
And leave you to the treasures of your heart.
No cumbered chamber will the Master share,
But one swept bare
By cleansing fires, then plenished fresh and fair
With meekness and humility and prayer.
There he will come, yet coming, even there
He stands and waits and will no entrance win
Until the latch be lifted from within.
—Joseph H. Odell

WOMAN WITH ISSUE OF BLOOD

The next miracle is closely connected with the miracle of the raising of the daughter of Jairus.

And when Jesus was passed over again by ship unto the other side, much people gathered unto him: and he was nigh unto the sea.

And, behold, there cometh one of the rulers of the synagogue, Jairus by name; and when he saw him, he fell at his feet,

And besought him greatly, saying, My little daughter lieth at the point of

death: I pray thee, come and lay thy hands on her, that she may be healed; and she shall live.

And Jesus went with him; and much people followed him, and thronged him.

And a certain woman, which had an issue of blood twelve years,

And had suffered many things of many physicians, and had spent all that she had, and was nothing bettered, but rather grew worse,

When she had heard of Jesus, came in the press behind, and touched his garment.

For she said, If I may touch but his clothes, I shall be whole [Mark 5:21–28].

Now Jesus has returned again to His land. In telling this incident, it is interesting that Luke, who was a physician, said she couldn't be healed. Mark says that she had suffered many things of the physicians, and she had spent all that she had. So we see that this matter of medical expense being so great today is not new at all.

And straightway the fountain of her blood was dried up; and she felt in her body that she was healed of that plague.

And Jesus, immediately knowing in himself that virtue had gone out of him, turned him about in the press, and said, Who touched my clothes?

And his disciples said unto him, Thou seest the multitude thronging thee, and sayest thou, Who touched me? [Mark 5:29–31].

The disciples thought it was a very peculiar question since the whole crowd was pressing in on Him. But only one touched Him in faith for healing!

The situation is the same today. I think we have a lot of folk around who use the name of Jesus freely. They are running around saying that it is Jesus this, and Jesus that, and people think they certainly know Him. Surely they know Him, but they have touched Him as the crowd touched Him—not like this woman touched Him, for she touched Him in faith for healing.

And he looked round about to see her that had done this thing.

But the woman fearing and trembling, knowing what was done in her, came and fell down before him, and told him all the truth.

And he said unto her, Daughter, thy faith hath made thee whole; go in peace, and be whole of thy plague [Mark 5:32–34].

She had been in this condition for twelve years. Did you notice that the little girl was twelve years old? Twelve years of suffering coming to an end and twelve years light entering into darkness, the darkness of death. The father who had come, when he saw our Lord talking to this woman and dealing with her, I'm sure thought, *Oh, why doesn't He hurry. Doesn't He know that my little girl is so sick at home that she'll die unless He moves?* Our Lord purposely did not move. He healed this woman, and while He is dealing with her one comes with a message, which is whispered to the father.

RAISED FROM DEAD (SUPERNATURAL) DAUGHTER OF JAIRUS

While he yet spake, there came from the ruler of the synagogue's house certain which said, Thy daughter is dead: why troublest thou the Master any further?

As soon as Jesus heard the word that was spoken, he saith unto the ruler of the synagogue, Be not afraid, only believe.

And he suffered no man to follow him, save Peter, and James, and John the brother of James.

And he cometh to the house of the ruler of the synagogue, and seeth the tumult, and them that wept and wailed greatly.

And when he was come in, he saith unto them, Why make ye this ado, and weep? the damsel is not dead, but sleepeth.

And they laughed him to scorn. But when he had put them all out, he taketh the father and the mother of the damsel, and them that were with him, and entereth in where the damsel was lying [Mark 5:35–40].

So Jesus goes to the home and puts out those who don't believe. When they were out, He goes in and the record tells us:

And he took the damsel by the hand, and said unto her, Talitha cumi; which

is, being interpreted, Damsel, I say unto thee, arise [Mark 5:41].

"Talitha cumi" was an expression of the Aramaic that the little girl would have understood. It was her native tongue and I think it could be translated "Little lamb, wake up!" That's what He said to her and that is a sweet, lovely thing. We find that our Lord raised a little girl, He raised a man in the vigor of young manhood (the widow's son at Nain), and then probably a mature man or even a senior citizen, Lazarus. He raised them all the same way. He spoke to them!

I think this little girl represents the little folks, those little ones before they reach the age of accountability. And He said to her in this lovely way, "Little lamb, wake up." I know right now I'm speaking to a lot of folk who have lost little ones. When we lost our first little one, what a sad thing it was for us. It's wonderful for me to know that although she has been in His presence for many years, one of these days He's going to speak those words again, "Little lamb, wake up!" He'll be talking to my little lamb and to your little lamb. Then that little form that we laid away will be raised from the grave, the spirit joined to the glorified body, and we will again have our little ones some day. What a wonderful, beautiful thing this is. It is a demonstration of His power.

And straightway the damsel arose, and walked; for she was of the age of twelve years. And they were astonished with a great astonishment.

And he charged them straitly that no man should know it; and commanded that something should be given her to eat [Mark 5:42–43].

Isn't that practical? If a twelve-year-old girl, or boy for that matter, were waked up from sleep and were made well, what would they want? Food, of course. So He told them to feed the little one. How practical this is and how wonderful it is.

These are the three great miracles that to my judgment demonstrate the great message of the Gospel of Mark. He is God's Servant with God's power. He is a Man of action and He has come not to be ministered unto but to minister and to give His life a ransom for many. Here we see Him in this chapter doing three wonderful miracles. He casts out demons from the man in Gadara. He heals the woman with an issue of blood. He raises this little twelve-year-old daughter of Jairus.

CHAPTER 6

THEME: *Synagogue in Nazareth; healing the sick at Nazareth; the Twelve sent out; disciples heal; death of John the Baptist; the Twelve return; five thousand fed; walks on sea; sick in land of Gennesaret healed*

This is the second longest chapter in the Gospel of Mark. Mark follows his usual style of presenting the action in the ministry of Jesus with machine-gun-like rapidity, but in the first twenty-nine verses there is a lull in the intense activity. Jesus returns to Nazareth. He sends out the Twelve to preach and they report back to Him. Then He feeds the five thousand, walks on the water, and heals in the land of Gennesaret. The chapter closes with the ministry of Jesus around the Sea of Galilee in the locality of the western shore. Jesus is tremendously popular at this time. It is the peak of His ministry.

SYNAGOGUE IN NAZARETH

And he went out from thence, and came into his own country; and his disciples follow him.

And when the sabbath day was come, he began to teach in the synagogue: and many hearing him were astonished, saying, From whence hath this man these things? and what wisdom is this which is given unto him, that even such mighty works are wrought by his hands?

Is not this the carpenter, the son of Mary, the brother of James, and Joses, and of Juda, and Simon? and are not his sisters here with us? And they were offended at him [Mark 6:1–3].

When this incident has been compared with the fourth chapter of Luke, the critics say that it reveals a contradiction in the Bible. They say the two accounts conflict one with the other. The fact of the matter is that we have the record of two visits that our Lord made to His hometown of Nazareth. I think He probably made other visits to Nazareth, but these are the two that are recorded. Luke 4 relates the first visit and He went there alone. He performed no miracle and He left suddenly when they tried to kill Him. On the second visit, which is recorded here in Mark 6, we find His disciples are with Him, that He healed "a few sick folk," and that He remained in this area. This is based on information from Matthew 13:53–58 as well as this chapter of Mark 6. On both occasions He entered the synagogue and taught, and on both occasions He was rejected by His fellow townspeople. So this is not a conflict, but rather two records of two visits that He made to His hometown. The first time He left, He went down to Capernaum and made that His headquarters. But He returned because He wanted to reach His hometown people.

In the first verse when it says "his country," it literally means His fatherland. It was the custom of our Lord to go to the synagogue on the Sabbath day wherever He was. I think He felt the need to worship God in this way and, also, it was the place to reach the people of that day. His teaching amazed those who had known Him. His words, His works, His wonders all occasioned a consternation on the part of His fellow citizens, which prompted their questions. They actually did not believe that Nazareth could produce anyone like Jesus. They were looking at themselves, of course, and judging Nazareth by themselves. Nazareth hadn't done too well by them—so they figured there couldn't be One like the Lord Jesus. They had no faith in One of their own, and they had no faith in themselves.

This passage also reveals that Mary had other children. These were half brothers and sisters of Jesus. I think the Jude who is mentioned here is the author of the Epistle of Jude. And they were *scandalized* because of Him. They thought that they knew Him, which was, of course, their stumbling stone. I think there is a danger in getting familiar with Jesus. He is One with whom we don't get familiar at all. That was their problem. They thought they knew Him, but they did not. They had seen Him as a boy grow up in the town.

But Jesus said unto them, A prophet is not without honour, but in his own country, and among his own kin, and in his own house [Mark 6:4].

I think the common colloquialism of the day is apropos here, "An expert is an ordinary fellow from another town." We think that whoever comes from afar knows more than our crowd knows. I guess maybe that is the reason some of us go up and down and through the country ministering elsewhere. Sometimes many of us are more effective away from home than we are at home.

HEALING THE SICK AT NAZARETH

And he could there do no mighty work, save that he laid his hands upon a few sick folk, and healed them.

And he marvelled because of their unbelief. And he went round about the villages, teaching [Mark 6:5–6].

You see that He did not leave this area at this time but stayed in the vicinity. The first time He had been practically run out of town and had gone down to Capernaum to make His headquarters there. This is a remarkable passage because it tells us He couldn't perform any mighty works there because of their unbelief.

The only limitation to omnipotence is unbelief. Faith is the one requirement to release the power of God in salvation. In the great chapter of Isaiah 53 that reveals God's great salvation, the prophet opens the chapter with: "Who hath believed our report? and to whom is the arm of the Lord revealed?" (Isa. 53:1). Who will believe it? My friend, unbelief shuts off Omnipotence. Unbelief insulates and isolates the power of God. It still does that today!

He marvelled at their unbelief (v. 6). This is not the only time we notice that He marvels. In Matthew 8:10—"When Jesus heard it, he marvelled, and said to them that followed, Verily I say unto you, I have not found so great faith, no, not in Israel"—He was speaking of the faith of the centurion.

Now we notice that He went round about the villages teaching. This is a wonderful lesson for Christian workers. There are certain men in God's work who do not want to go to a small place to minister. I've actually been criticized by some ministers and Christian workers for going to certain small churches instead of going to the larger ones. My feeling is that our Lord set us a tremendous example here when it says that He went about their villages. Imagine, friends, the Lord of Glory, the Son of God here on this earth ministering in little villages. He could have sent a telegram over to Rome and hired the Colosseum for a big meeting! Today we have men who are suffering from megalomania. They feel they have to have a big crowd. All of us need to learn a lesson from Jesus.

There is a story about Dr. C. I. Scofield, the man who was responsible for *The Scofield Reference Bible*. He had been invited to speak in a church in North Carolina. Because it was a rainy night, about twenty-five people came to the meeting. The young preacher leaned over and apologized to Dr. Scofield for the small number who had come to hear his preaching and teaching. Dr. Scofield replied, "Young man, my Lord had only twelve men in His school and in His congregation most of the time. If He had only twelve, who is C. I. Scofield to be concerned about a big crowd?"

THE TWELVE SENT OUT

And he called unto him the twelve, and began to send them forth by two and two; and gave them power over unclean spirits [Mark 6:7].

He is now sending out His disciples, and He sends them with the message of repentance, which is the same message He has been preaching. He sends them two by two. It's interesting that neither Matthew nor Luke told us that when they recorded this incident. He gave them power over unclean spirits, which seems to be the very highest power they could exercise.

And commanded them that they should take nothing for their journey, save a staff only; no scrip, no bread, no money in their purse:

But be shod with sandals; and not put on two coats [Mark 6:8–9].

Why such a command? Well, they were to travel light. This is to indicate the urgency and the lateness of the hour, the importance of their mission, and their total dependence upon God. Later on, we shall find that they were told to take these things because they were going on a longer journey. Matthew makes it clear that this time they were to go only to the lost sheep of the house of Israel, and they were to accept the hospitality that was offered to them.

And he said unto them, In what place soever ye enter into an house, there abide till ye depart from that place.

And whosoever shall not receive you, nor hear you, when ye depart thence, shake off the dust under your feet for a testimony against them. Verily I say unto you, It shall be more tolerable for Sodom and Gomorrha in the day of judgment, than for that city [Mark 6:10–11].

This is a serious and a solemn trip they are to take. Light creates responsibility. To reject the grace of God invited His judgment. The same is still true today.

DISCIPLES HEAL

And they went out, and preached that men should repent.

And they cast out many devils, and anointed with oil many that were sick, and healed them [Mark 6:12–13].

They preached a message of repentance, and the miracles authenticated their message. This commission was limited to the lost sheep of the house of Israel. It is not the pattern for today. Repentance is part of the gospel message, however; it is contained in the command to *believe*.

The record of this incident is longer in the Gospel of Matthew and we go into more detail in our study of it in that Gospel. The fame of Jesus had spread throughout that area. Not only the common people but even Herod on the throne had heard of Jesus. Now we find this strange reaction on the part of King Herod. The murder of John the Baptist had taken place sometime before. I think it is recorded here to explain Herod's strange and superstitious reaction.

DEATH OF JOHN THE BAPTIST

And king Herod heard of him; (for his name was spread abroad:) and he said, That John the Baptist was risen from the dead, and therefore mighty works do shew forth themselves in him.

Others said, That it is Elias. And others said, That it is a prophet, or as one of the prophets [Mark 6:14–15].

We can see that this man Herod was very superstitious. But there was a great deal of mingled reaction among the people about the Lord Jesus as to who He was. There is that same reaction today, by the way. We find that different people have different viewpoints and different explanations of the Person, the presence, and the power of the Lord Jesus. So there was this confusion, and Herod was definitely afraid.

But when Herod heard thereof, he said, It is John, whom I beheaded: he is risen from the dead [Mark 6:16].

Herod was afraid.

For Herod himself had sent forth and laid hold upon John, and bound him in prison for Herodias' sake, his brother Philip's wife: for he had married her.

For John had said unto Herod, It is not lawful for thee to have thy brother's wife [Mark 6:17–18].

The murder of John had taken place previous to this point in the ministry of Jesus. Notice that John boldly denounced sin in high places. He had denounced Herod for taking Herodias, his brother's wife. This enraged her and caused her to plot John's death.

Therefore Herodias had a quarrel against him, and would have killed him; but she could not:

For Herod feared John, knowing that he was a just man and an holy, and observed him; and when he heard him, he did many things, and heard him gladly [Mark 6:19–20].

Did Herodias keep Herod from turning to God?

And when a convenient day was come, that Herod on his birthday made a supper to his lords, high captains, and chief estates of Galilee;

And when the daughter of the said Herodias came in, and danced, and pleased Herod and them that sat with him, the king said unto the damsel, Ask of me whatsoever thou wilt, and I will give it thee [Mark 6:21–22].

Herodias had asked her daughter to dance before him because she knew what a lecherous, lustful old man he was. He gave the daughter a blank check and she could ask anything she wanted.

And he sware unto her, Whatsoever thou shalt ask of me, I will give it thee, unto the half of my kingdom.

And she went forth, and said unto her mother, What shall I ask? And she said, The head of John the Baptist [Mark 6:23–24].

The mother was prepared for this. The brutality of this woman boggles the mind.

And she came in straightway with haste unto the king, and asked, saying, I will that thou give me by and by in a charger the head of John the Baptist.

And the king was exceeding sorry; yet for his oath's sake, and for their sakes which sat with him, he would not reject her [Mark 6:25–26].

Another weakness of Herod is revealed here. He was afraid of what his friends might think and say. He had a false sense of values about an oath.

And immediately the king sent an executioner, and commanded his head to be brought: and he went and beheaded him in the prison,

And brought his head in a charger, and gave it to the damsel: and the damsel gave it to her mother [Mark 6:27–28].

This was cold-blooded murder!

And when his disciples heard of it, they came and took up his corpse, and laid it in a tomb [Mark 6:29].

The disciples of John took up the decapitated body of John and tenderly buried it.

THE TWELVE RETURN

Mark now returns the narrative to the ministry of Jesus. The apostles make their first report. Note the absence of details.

And the apostles gathered themselves together unto Jesus, and told him all things, both what they had done, and what they had taught.

And he said unto them, Come ye yourselves apart into a desert place, and rest a while: for there were many coming and going, and they had no leisure so much as to eat [Mark 6:30–31].

It is impossible for us to understand how really busy the Lord Jesus was and how great the demands were upon Him. He had to withdraw to an uninhabited place in an attempt to rest and let His apostles rest.

FIVE THOUSAND FED

And they departed into a desert place by ship privately.

And the people saw them departing, and many knew him, and ran afoot thither out of all cities, and outwent them, and came together unto him.

And Jesus, when he came out, saw much people, and was moved with compassion toward them, because they were as sheep not having a shepherd: and he began to teach them many things [Mark 6:32–34].

It was futile to try to find a place to be alone. The crowd followed around the shore of the Sea of Galilee, and they were there to meet Jesus and the disciples when they landed. The reaction of Jesus was one of complete sympathy. All people are sheep to Him. He alone is the true Shepherd. This is the reason He fed them. He first met their spiritual needs by teaching them. Then He met their physical needs by feeding them.

And when the day was now far spent, his disciples came unto him, and said, This is a desert place, and now the time is far passed:

Send them away, that they may go into the country round about, and into the villages, and buy themselves bread: for they have nothing to eat.

He answered and said unto them, Give ye them to eat. And they say unto him, Shall we go and buy two hundred pennyworth of bread, and give them to eat? [Mark 6:35–37].

He commands them to do an impossible task. They must learn, as we must learn, that He always commands the impossible. The reason is obvious. He intends to do the work.

He saith unto them, How many loaves have ye? go and see. And when they knew, they say, Five, and two fishes.

And he commanded them to make all sit down by companies upon the green grass.

And they sat down in ranks, by hundreds, and by fifties.

And when he had taken the five loaves and the two fishes, he looked up to heaven, and blessed, and brake the loaves, and gave them to his disciples to set before them; and the two fishes divided he among them all.

And they did all eat, and were filled.

And they took up twelve baskets full of the fragments, and of the fishes.

And they that did eat of the loaves were about five thousand men [Mark 6:38–44].

This is a miracle. The Creator who made the fish at the beginning and caused the grain to multiply in the field, now by His fiat word creates food for the crowd. This may have been the first time many in this crowd ever were filled.

WALKS ON SEA

And straightway he constrained his disciples to get into the ship, and to go to the other side before unto Bethsaida, while he sent away the people [Mark 6:45].

There is an urgency expressed in the two words *straightway* and *constrained*. The explanation is found in John 6:15. Jesus perceived that they would try by force to make Him a king.

And when he had sent them away, he departed into a mountain to pray.

And when even was come, the ship was in the midst of the sea, and he alone on the land.

And he saw them toiling in rowing; for the wind was contrary unto them: and about the fourth watch of the night he cometh unto them, walking upon the sea, and would have passed by them.

But when they saw him walking upon the sea, they supposed it had been a spirit, and cried out:

For they all saw him, and were troubled. And immediately he talked with them, and saith unto them, Be of good cheer: it is I; be not afraid.

And he went up unto them into the ship; and the wind ceased: and they were sore amazed in themselves beyond measure, and wondered.

For they considered not the miracle of the loaves: for their heart was hardened [Mark 6:46–52].

Note that here we find no record of Simon Peter coming to Him walking on the water. After all, Mark got his information on the human plane from Simon Peter, and Peter just left out his part of the story. It is Matthew who gives us that detail.

I do want to call your attention to verse 48 where it says, "And he saw them toiling in rowing." Those men were in the boat that night and they were mingling their sweat with the waves whose salt water was breaking over their little boat. They were straining at the oars and they actually thought they were going down. But He saw them toiling and rowing. I love that! I don't know where you are today or what position you are in. You may be in a hard spot right now; you may be sitting alone in a corner of darkness. You may be facing temptations and problems that are too great to bear. You may find yourself out on a stormy sea and you feel as if your little boat is going down.

I have some good news for you, Christian friend. "He saw them toiling in rowing." He sees you. He knows your problems. You don't have to send up a flare to let Him know. He already knows. Oh, that today you might commit your way to Him in a very definite way. That is something that so many of us need to do in times of darkness—just commit our way unto Him. "He saw them toiling in rowing." Only Mark, by the way, records that. Then we find that He came to them and He entered into the ship with them. And Mark says that they were "amazed in themselves beyond measure."

In the conclusion of this chapter we find that He went over to the land of Gennesaret.

SICK IN LAND OF GENNESARET HEALED

And when they had passed over, they came into the land of Gennesarct, and drew to the shore.

And when they were come out of the ship, straightway they knew him,

And ran through that whole region round about, and began to carry about in beds those that were sick, where they heard he was.

And whithersoever he entered, into villages, or cities, or country, they laid the sick in the streets, and besought him that they might touch if it were but the border of his garment: and as many as touched him were made whole [Mark 6:53–56].

You and I today can't even envisage the number of sick people that He had healed. I understand there is one denomination that has offered one thousand dollars to anybody who will come forward and show that he has been healed by a "faith healer." I understand the thousand dollars has never been taken. It's amazing, isn't it, when you hear all this propaganda today that is going around. In Jesus' day one could have brought together thousands of people that He had healed. My friend, He was genuine. It was real. That is the reason the enemy never denied that He performed miracles.

CHAPTER 7

***THEME:** Pharisees denounced; Syrophoenician's demon-possessed daughter; deaf and dumb of Decapolis*

This chapter carries out the theme of Mark, which is to show that the Lord Jesus is God's Servant who is doing God's will. He is a Man of action and He is doing the things that would appeal to the Roman of that day and to any person who is interested in getting a job done. That is the wonderful thing about Him as a Savior; He can save, and He is the only One who can.

The intertestamental period is that time between the close of the Old Testament and the opening of the New Testament in which many changes took place. It was one of the most eventful periods in the history of the nation Israel. During the time of their captivity and in this period between the Testaments after they had returned to the land, there was a development of new groups and parties not mentioned in the Old Testament. There were the Pharisees, the Sadducees, the scribes, and the Herodians.

Scribes—the scribes had a good beginning. Evidently Ezra was a scribe and the founder of that group. They were the professional expounders of the Law. However, by the time of our Lord they had become "hair-splitters" and were more concerned with the *letter* of the Law than with the *spirit* of the Law.

That, I think, is one of the great problems we have today. There has been put into the interpretation of the laws in this country this "hair-splitting" method and the philosophical interpretation that was never intended in the law. I believe that is what has come out of certain law schools in the East. As a result, our legal system and our political system are in the mess we find today. That is what had happened to religion in our Lord's day.

Pharisees—the Pharisees also had a good beginning. They arose to defend the Jewish way of life against all foreign influences. They were strict legalists, they believed in the Old Testament, and they were nationalists in politics. They wanted to bring in the coming of the kingdom of heaven (or the kingdom of God) upon the earth.

Sadducees—the Sadducees were made up of the wealthy and socially-minded. They had no spiritual depth. They wanted to get rid of tradition. They rejected the supernatural and were opposed to the Pharisees who accepted the supernatural and accepted the Old Testament. They were closely akin to the Greek Epicureans.

Herodians—the Herodians were a party in the days of Jesus who arose as political opportunists. They were strictly a party to try to keep the Herods on the throne.

This background will help us understand the incident before us.

PHARISEES DENOUNCED

Then came together unto him the Pharisees, and certain of the scribes, which came from Jerusalem [Mark 7:1].

You will notice that our Lord has made such an impression that these men are drawn out of Jerusalem, and they have come to the place where He is ministering in Galilee. Also they will come across the Jordan River into the area of the Decapolis, that is, the area of ten cities. We'll see that in a moment.

And when they saw some of his disciples eat bread with defiled, that is to say, with unwashen, hands, they found fault.

For the Pharisees, and all the Jews, except they wash their hands oft, eat not, holding the tradition of the elders.

And when they come from the market, except they wash, they eat not. And many other things there be, which they have received to hold, as the washing of cups, and pots, brasen vessels, and of tables [Mark 7:2–4].

Let us stop to look at this for just a moment because it is quite interesting. There is a crisis arising about the Person of Jesus. Back in Mark 6:30 we read that the apostles had gathered themselves around Jesus and had told Him all the things that they had done after He had sent them out. They had come back and reported to Him. Now also the scribes and the Pharisees are coming out and gathering about Him. There is bound to be a confrontation here between the Lord Jesus and His followers and the Pharisees and their followers. One group is made up of His friends, His followers, who love Him. The second group is comprised of His enemies who seek to destroy Him.

It has always been this way. There are two groups: those who trust Him and those who reject Him. To be personal, which group are you in? That makes all the difference in the world. The question is not whether you are a member of a church or have been through some ceremony; rather it is what is your relationship to Jesus Christ? That is the all-important question.

Now this obviously was a special delegation from Jerusalem. They had been sent to Galilee to spy on Jesus. They were the intellectual opponents sent to trap the Lord Jesus. The way that our Lord defended Himself is to me another proof of His deity— ". . . Never man spake like this man" was the testimony of His enemies (John 7:46). Of course, it wasn't difficult for them to find some fault because the Lord Jesus entirely ignored their traditions.

Now what was their tradition? They were not simply criticizing the disciples because of a breach of etiquette, but for the fact that the Lord was not having them keep the traditions, which were their interpretation of the Old Testament. This referred to a ceremonial cleansing and hadn't anything to do with sanitary measures. Mark explains for the benefit of the Romans that this custom of ceremonial cleansing was peculiar to Israel; and it was.

God had given to Israel a great deal of information about cleansing. In the Old Testament, in the Book of Leviticus, there is a great deal of instruction about cleansing. It was very important because God was teaching them the great lesson that a sinner had to be cleansed before he could enjoy fellowship with a holy God. But the Pharisees had built a great tradition that was supposed to be an interpretation of the Mosaic Law, and some of them even contended that Moses had given them the traditions when he gave them the Law. In time, these traditions became the interpretation of the Law, and eventually there was a wide departure in the traditions from what had been the intent of the Law.

In our passage here, some of this tradition is given in detail. They would ceremonially wash the cups and pots and brasen vessels and the tables. All of this was a burdensome sort of thing and was an entirely outward performance. The word used for "washing" is *baptism*. They baptized cups, pots, religious objects, even tables. Now this is religion with a vengeance, friend, and you can see that one could get so involved in going through a ritual of religion that one would forget the whole purpose—which is that a person must be made *right* with God before a relationship can be established. We find the same kind of thing today. So many people will argue points of religion when it is the Person of Jesus Christ that should be our concern. Now let's go on:

Then the Pharisees and scribes asked him, Why walk not thy disciples according to the tradition of the elders, but eat bread with unwashen hands? [Mark 7:5].

This accusation which they lodge against His disciples was, of course, really an accusation against Him personally, because these were His followers. Now notice how our Lord deals with them—and it isn't tenderly at all!

He answered and said unto them, Well hath Esaias prophesied of you hypocrites, as it is written, This people honoureth me with their lips, but their heart is far from me [Mark 7:6].

I wouldn't say that is gentle. A hypocrite is one who is just acting a part; it is a word used for actors on the stage. They were going through a religious ritual without experiencing any reality at all. The lips and the heart might as well have belonged to two separate persons. They had no more heart experience than a wooden dummy upon the knee of a ventriloquist.

My friend, there are a lot of people who are just going through a ritual in church today. The heart must be involved if it is genuine. "That if thou shalt confess with thy mouth the Lord Jesus, and shalt believe in thine heart that God hath raised him from the dead, thou shalt be saved. For with the heart man believeth unto righteousness; and with the mouth confession is made unto salvation" (Rom. 10:9–10). Oh, people get involved today in creeds and church confessions and public worship, dress and even "separation." All of this can become a matter of tradition and not a direct and personal dealing with the Lord Jesus Christ.

Howbeit in vain do they worship me, teaching for doctrines the commandments of men [Mark 7:7].

Worship is empty when the rules of men are substituted for the Word of God. So now we come to the very heart of the matter.

For laying aside the commandment of God, ye hold the tradition of men, as the washing of pots and cups: and many other such like things ye do.

And he said unto them, Full well ye reject the commandment of God, that ye may keep your own tradition [Mark 7:8–9].

Here was the whole issue. They were substituting traditions of men for the Word of God. A tradition may actually be good and may be established for a very good reason. However, it becomes evil when it is a substitute for the Word of God in later generations. And that is what has happened to these people here.

I think this is the reason that so many denominations today have departed from the Word of God. They first substituted a creed for the Word of God. Then they began to substitute the word of men and the thinking of men and their own little ritual and their own little denomination. Before long, the Word of God went out the window. This has happened again and again.

For Moses said, Honour thy father and thy mother; and, Whoso curseth father or mother, let him die the death:

But ye say, If a man shall say to his father or mother, It is Corban, that is to say, a gift, by whatsoever thou mightest be profited by me; he shall be free [Mark 7:10–11].

Now He is giving them an example of what they were doing. Moses had said in the Law that they were to honor their father and their mother. But their tradition permitted them to escape the responsibility to their parents. If a man did not want to help his father and mother when they became old and needy, he would dedicate his possessions to the priest in the temple and it was called *Corban* which means "a gift." At the man's death, his estate went to the temple and he was relieved of his responsibility to his parents.

And ye suffer him no more to do aught for his futher or his mother;

Making the word of God of none effect through your tradition, which ye have delivered: and many such like things do ye [Mark 7:12–13].

He's saying that this tradition was pernicious and it directly contradicted the intent of the Law of God, which was to honor their father and mother.

There is a great danger today that people will give to any group or organization that has appealed to them. There are literally thousands of Christian organizations that have men out in the field, combing the highways and byways to find people to give to their organization. There is a grave danger in that. There are certain personal responsibilities that people must fulfill.

As we go on down the passage before us we see He goes into detail.

And when he had called all the people unto him, he said unto them, Hearken unto me every one of you, and understand:

There is nothing from without a man, that entering into him can defile him: but the things which come out of him, those are they that defile the man [Mark 7:14–15].

He is differentiating that which is external and that which is internal and is pointing out what is real. He shows here that religion is not something that you can rub on as you do a salve. It is not something that you eat or refrain from eating.

You'll notice then that He went into the house and his disciples came to Him and asked Him about the parable.

And he saith unto them, Are ye so without understanding also? Do ye not perceive, that whatsoever thing from without entereth into the man, it cannot defile him;

Because it entereth not into his heart, but into the belly, and goeth out into the draught, purging all meats?

And he said, That which cometh out of the man, that defileth the man [Mark 7:18–20].

Let's really take a look at what does come out of man:

For from within, out of the heart of men, proceed evil thoughts, adulteries, fornications, murders,

Thefts, covetousness, wickedness, deceit, lasciviousness, an evil eye, blasphemy, pride, foolishness:

All these evil things come from within, and defile the man [Mark 7:21–23].

I'll guarantee you that if you will buy the morning paper wherever you live and will read it through, you will find that this is what came out of man during the last twenty-four hours:

Evil thoughts
Adulteries and fornications—unlawful sex relations
Murders (anger is also murder)
Thefts (loafing on the job is also stealing)

Covetousness—grasping and greediness for material things and positions
Wickedness—all the acts that are intended to hurt people
Deceit—the pretense that people put up
Lasciviousness—sensuality
Evil eye—envy
Blasphemy—slander against God or man
Pride (God hates this above all else)
Foolishness—acts done without any respect of God or man

These all come out of the heart of man and that is why the Lord Jesus says, "Ye must be born again."

SYROPHOENICIAN'S DEMON-POSSESSED DAUGHTER

And from thence he arose, and went into the borders of Tyre and Sidon, and entered into an house, and would have no man know it: but he could not be hid.

For a certain woman, whose young daughter had an unclean spirit, heard of him, and came and fell at his feet:

The woman was a Greek, a Syrophenician by nation; and she besought him that he would cast forth the devil out of her daughter.

But Jesus said unto her, Let the children first be filled: for it is not meet to take the children's bread, and to cast it unto the dogs.

And she answered and said unto him, Yes, Lord: yet the dogs under the table eat of the children's crumbs.

And he said unto her, For this saying go thy way; the devil is gone out of thy daughter.

And when she was come to her house, she found the devil gone out, and her daughter laid upon the bed [Mark 7:24–30].

We have had this incident before. You will recall that our Lord stepped out of His own land and met this woman who was a Greek and a citizen of Tyre. She came to Jesus in faith. And the word *daughter* here is the diminutive form which means she was just a little girl. At first, our Lord's treatment of her may appear brutal, but you will remember that when we studied this in the Gospel of Matthew, we showed the dispensational interpretation which is actually the revelation of a tremendous truth. And I think here something else tremendous is also revealed and that is the accuracy of the four Gospels. This woman is an outstanding example of faith in one who lives outside His land. And our Lord answered her petition. One wonders whether He came to that area for the specific purpose of answering the faith of this woman.

DEAF AND DUMB OF DECAPOLIS

And again, departing from the coasts of Tyre and Sidon, he came unto the sea of Galilee, through the midst of the coasts of Decapolis [Mark 7:31].

Jesus leaves Tyre and Sidon, and goes through Decapolis on His way to the Sea of Galilee. *Decapolis* translated is "ten cities," a district containing ten cities, mostly on the east of the Jordan, in the area near the Sea of Galilee. The list includes the following:

Scythopolis	Gerasa	Dion
Hippos	Gadara	Canatha
Pella	Raphana	Philadelphia
Damascus		

I was at the ruins of Gerasa or Jerish, as it is called today. I thought, "My, this is one of the places where my Lord came and He taught." He had a tremendous ministry in this area. The crowds came into those cities.

And they bring unto him one that was deaf, and had an impediment in his speech; and they beseech him to put his hand upon him.

And he took him aside from the multitude, and put his fingers into his ears, and he spit, and touched his tongue;

And looking up to heaven, he sighed, and saith unto him, Ephphatha, that is, Be opened.

And straightway his ears were opened, and the string of his tongue was loosed, and he spake plain.

And he charged them that they should tell no man: but the more he charged them, so much the more a great deal they published it;

And were beyond measure astonished, saying, He hath done all things well: he maketh both the deaf to hear, and the dumb to speak [Mark 7:32–37].

All the things He did were done as aids to

faith. The whole thought here reveals the fact that the condition of this man caused Jesus to use this method. His ears were first opened so that he could hear. After this it apparently was useless to try to get the crowd to remain silent. It was this miracle which brought about a great impetus in enlarging the ministry of Jesus, which had already broken all bounds.

At this time pressure upon Jesus was humanly unbearable. In spite of the pressure put upon Jesus, the burdens of the multitudes, the tensions of the times, the long busy days, and the weariness of the body, the crowd could say, "He hath done all things well." We just add our word of agreement to this and say a hearty amen.

Friend, He still does all things well today!

CHAPTER 8

***THEME:** Four thousand fed; leaven explained; blind man of Bethsaida; death of Christ*

The eighth chapter is about the same length as the seventh chapter. It still carries out the great theme of Mark with the emphasis upon action. Jesus feeds the four thousand in the coasts of Decapolis, the Pharisees ask for a sign at Dalmanutha, the friends of a blind man ask Jesus to touch his eyes at Bethsaida, and Peter makes his confession of faith in Caesarea Philippi. What the Lord Jesus did was important to the Romans, and it is important to us today. Is the Lord Jesus able to save to the uttermost? Can He do the job? He is the Servant of Jehovah, and we find that He can do the job.

We find in this chapter that our Lord does a lot of moving around, and there weren't good highways in that day. That land is a small land, but when you reduce the speed down to walking speed, it's a pretty sizable land. And He traveled by walking.

FOUR THOUSAND FED

Some people feel that the feeding of the four thousand, which opens this chapter, is a duplication of the feeding of the five thousand, and they practically ignore it. This has caused some to say that the feeding of the four thousand is the neglected miracle of Jesus.

When the critic comes to this parable, in his usual way he seeks to rid the Bible of the supernatural. His explanation of this miracle is that it was included after the feeding of the five thousand to strengthen the claim of the apostles that Jesus was a miracle worker. Obviously, if this were true, the second miracle would be greater than the first—instead of four thousand, it would be nearer ten thousand—because when men fabricate, they exaggerate. But here it is restraint, by the way.

The two miracles of feeding the multitudes are strikingly similar in several features. He feeds the thousands, one time it is five and the next time it is four. But there are seven points of dissimilarity that we need to call to your attention:

1. In the first instance the multitude had been with the Lord one day; in the second instance it had been three days.

2. Upon the first occasion the disciples were told to "go and see" what supplies were available, while upon the other they were ready with the information before they were asked.

3. When the five thousand were fed there were five loaves and two fishes, while for the four thousand there were seven loaves and a few fishes.

4. The first time, which was near the Passover, the multitude was told to sit in companies "upon the green grass," while the second time, later in the year when the green of the Near East would be burnt by the oriental sun, they were instructed to sit "on the ground" (lit., "on the earth").

5. In the first instance our Lord is said to have "blessed . . . the loaves," while upon the second occasion He is said to have given thanks, first for the loaves, and later to have "blessed" the fish.

6. After the five thousand were fed twelve baskets of fragments remained, but when the four thousand were satisfied there were seven baskets over.

7. Obviously, the number that was fed was different in each instance.

It seems that the sharp contrast between the two is found in the time that Jesus fed the multitudes. In the feeding of the five thousand, it was at the conclusion of the first day. Jesus had been teaching them, but according to John, He followed the feeding of the five thousand with the discourse of the Bread of Life. This important discourse was sort of an after-dinner speech, you see. In the feeding of the four thousand, the multitude had been with Jesus for three days listening to His teaching. The physical food followed the teaching. In other words, the crowd had not come out to eat but to hear the teaching of Jesus.

I think this is an important lesson for us. Are we using church dinners to get the crowd? If so, then our motive is wrong. Many churches can get people out in the middle of the week only if they have a banquet. Some Bible classes depend upon the food to draw people in for the message. Can God bless such efforts regardless of how pure the motive? Well, I'll let you answer it. The end does not always justify the means.

As we begin to read now, notice that "in those days" places this incident during the time He was in the Decapolis. The multitude evidently had followed Jesus into a desert place which was convenient for teaching but not readily accessible to supplies. *Great* multitudes are following Him now.

In those days the multitude being very great, and having nothing to eat, Jesus called his disciples unto him, and saith unto them,

I have compassion on the multitude, because they have now been with me three days, and have nothing to eat:

And if I send them away fasting to their own houses, they will faint by the way: for divers of them came from far.

And his disciples answered him, From whence can a man satisfy these men with bread here in the wilderness?

And he asked them How many loaves have ye? And they said, Seven.

And he commanded the people to sit down on the ground: and he took the seven loaves, and gave thanks, and brake, and gave to his disciples to set before them; and they did set them before the people [Mark 8:1–6].

There is something quite interesting here. It looks as though the disciples had forgotten about His feeding of the five thousand. I'm of the opinion that many of us have the same kind of experience. God does some very gracious and good things for us, and we forget it by the next time. When a new emergency arises, we find ourselves neophytes; that is, it is all brand new to us again. That has been my experience as I have periodic X-rays made of my lungs to see whether the cancer has spread. And every time it is a new experience for me and I must confess that every time I am frightened. So I have really a fellow-feeling for these disciples.

They had made an inventory of the crowd, though, because they knew how many loaves there were. Maybe they were expecting Jesus to repeat the miracle of the five thousand. This time there were more loaves for fewer people but it was still true, "What are these among so many?" And who had the loaves this time? We don't know. Some unknown person had them and even though *we* don't know who he was, he will have his reward someday.

In this instance they sat on the bare ground, while at the feeding of the five thousand they had been told to sit on the grass, as I had mentioned. And how many fish? It just says "a few small fishes." The number really is unimportant, and He's not counting the fish. When God is in it, you will notice, there is always a surplus. Whether He feeds five or four thousand, He doesn't give them just a snack; He gives them a full dinner. Incidentally, if we add one woman and one child for each of the men, we probably would be nearer to the actual number of people who were fed—about twelve thousand.

And straightway he entered into a ship with his disciples, and came into the parts of Dalmanutha [Mark 8:10].

The location of Dalmanutha cannot be ascertained accurately. Apparently it was on the coast of the Sea of Galilee and they had to cross the sea to get to it, which means they came to the west side. They traveled by boat and evidently the spot was somewhere on the northwest coast. Now the bloodhounds of hate are on His trail again.

LEAVEN EXPLAINED

And the Pharisees came forth, and began to question with him, seeking of him a sign from heaven, tempting him.

And he sighed deeply in his spirit, and saith, Why doth this generation seek after a sign? verily I say unto you, There shall no sign be given unto this generation.

And he left them, and entering into the ship again departed to the other side.

Now the disciples had forgotten to take bread, neither had they in the ship with them more than one loaf.

And he charged them saying, Take heed, beware of the leaven of the Pharisees, and of the leaven of Herod [Mark 8:11–15].

In the Scriptures leaven represents wrong or evil teaching; it never means the gospel. One of the fallacious things that is being taught today is that leaven represents the gospel in the parable of the woman who hid leaven in three measures of meal (Matt. 13:33). The meal symbolizes the gospel, and the leaven, which represents wrong teaching, was hidden in it. It is the process of making something taste good to the natural man. Actually, what is liberalism? It all came into existence by the pulpit trying to please the unsaved church members. And today we have a lot of men trying to please the congregation, even when they are unsaved. And that, may I say, is putting leaven in—that is, mixing wrong eaching with the truth of the gospel. The only kind of bread they will eat is that which has leaven because leaven makes bread taste good. I was brought up on hot biscuits, friend, and the natural man likes them. Leaven is the evil that is put in. And here He is warning them about the wrong teaching of the Pharisees and Herod.

Having eyes, see ye not? and having ears, hear ye not? and do ye not remember? [Mark 8:18].

I've been a preacher for a long time, and sometimes I discover something that startles me. There will be some person whom I think knows spiritual truth; yet they have missed the entire thought. They don't get it at all and one wonders where they have been. There are people who have been studying the Bible for years and who are like that. They are like these apostles who have ears, yet hear not.

When I brake the five loaves among five thousand, how many baskets full of fragments took ye up? They say unto him, Twelve.

And when the seven among four thousand, how many baskets full of fragments took ye up? And they said, Seven.

And he said unto them, How is it that ye do not understand? [Mark 8:19–21].

The Word of God is the Bread of Life because the Word of God reveals Him. We are to feed on the Bible and to beware of false teaching. I think that ought to be clear to us here in the teaching that He gives.

BLIND MAN OF BETHSAIDA HEALED

And he cometh to Bethsaida; and they bring a blind man unto him, and besought him to touch him [Mark 8:22].

Here is another one of these remarkable miracles of our Lord. He assented to their request by touching his eyes. But you notice that He led the blind man out of town. Had Bethsaida, where many of His mighty works had been performed, become like Nazareth where He could no longer perform mighty works? Surely there is no medicinal value in saliva, but the Lord uses this to increase the faith of this man. Let us read this and learn the spiritual truth for us here.

And he took the blind man by the hand, and led him out of the town; and when he had spit on his eyes, and put his hands upon him, he asked him if he saw aught.

And he looked up, and said, I see men as trees, walking.

After that he put his hands again upon his eyes, and made him look up: and he was restored, and saw every man clearly.

And he sent him away to his house, saying, Neither go into the town, nor tell it to any in the town [Mark 8:23–26].

This place of Bethsaida had already had judgment pronounced upon it (Matt. 11:21). Now there's something in this miracle we want to look at very carefully. Why did He use this method? Couldn't He have opened the eyes of this man as He did in other instances? Of course, He could have. He could have made this man see clearly at the very beginning. But there is a lesson for the man and a lesson here for us.

There are three stages in this case:

1. Blindness. We are all first spiritually blind. Like the blind man we can say, "Once I was blind, but now I can see." But you'll notice that He gained only partial sight, and only Mark tells us this.

2. Partial sight. Is this not our condition today? "For now we see through a glass darkly; but then face to face . . ." (1 Cor. 13:12). Every now and then I get a letter from some person who gives me to understand that

they have great spiritual discernment. They are way up there with the upper ten, and sometimes they say they think that's where I am. But I have a confession to make to you. I only see through a glass darkly. There are many things I don't understand.

There are some people who don't feel that way. They think that they know all there is to know about everything. That is one of the curses of some of our good Bible-teaching churches. I was a pastor for a great many years, and I had members who never bothered to come to mid-week Bible study. Do you know why? They already knew more than I know. While that may be true, the tragic thing was that they thought they knew more than they actually knew.

Socrates, in his day, made the statement that he was the wisest of the Athenians. That shocked everybody because he was a very humble man. So they asked him what he meant. And he said something like this, "Well there are a great many of the Athenians who think they know, and I know I do not know. And since I know that I do not know, I am the wisest of the Athenians."

May I say to you that there are a lot of the saints today who think they know. But Paul says that we see through a glass darkly, and that is our state in this life. But eventually when we come into His presence we shall know as we are known. I'll surely be glad when I get over there where I'm going to know something!

3. Perfect sight. The third stage is perfect vision. We'll get our 20-20 spiritual vision when we come into His presence, and that's when we'll really be able to see. You'll notice that when our Lord had finished, He had healed this man perfectly.

There is something here that I don't have time to develop fully today, but have you ever noticed the different methods that our Lord used in opening eyes of the blind? Here at Bethsaida when He healed the blind man, he touched his eyes. So this man had an experience. I imagine that he would have organized the "Metho-rene" church and they would sing "The Touch of His Hand on Mine." When Jesus healed blind Bartimaeus, He didn't touch him at all but just told him from a distance, and faith alone opened his eyes. I suppose he would have organized the "Congreterian" church and they would sing, of course, "Only Believe." But the man who had been born blind was told to go and wash in the pool of Siloam and that's an entirely different method according to John, chapter 9. So this man would have organized a "Siloam-Baptian" church and they would sing, "Shall We Gather at the River." You say that that is absurd. Sure is. Absurd for that day, but today that is exactly what is being done. May I say to you that here is a lesson for us.

DEATH OF CHRIST

And Jesus went out, and his disciples, into the towns of Caesarea Philippi: and by the way he asked his disciples, saying unto them, Whom do men say that I am? [Mark 8:27].

The important thing here is, who is Jesus? Jesus wanted to know men's estimate of Him.

WHAT THINK YE OF CHRIST?

"What think ye of Christ" is the test
To try both your state and your scheme;
You cannot be right in the rest,
Unless you think rightly of Him.

Friend, to be united to Him, joined to Him, is the important thing. We are to enjoy a right relationship with Jesus Christ.

If you look on a map, you will find three Caesareas. Caesarea Philippi is located to the north of the Sea of Galilee. The Lord Jesus was in the north and He was in a position from which He was going to turn and begin a movement directly toward Jerusalem and the Cross.

And they answered, John the Baptist: but some say, Elias; and others, One of the prophets [Mark 8:28].

There was much confusion regarding His person. All opinions were high but fell short of who He is.

And he saith unto them, But whom say ye that I am? And Peter answereth and saith unto him, Thou art the Christ [Mark 8:29].

This was their final examination for the first phase of His ministry. They were within six months now of the Cross.

This is the finest thing that Simon Peter ever said. He spoke for the group. Mark gives us only a fragment of the confession. *Christ* is not a name. *Jesus* is His name. *Christ* is a title—in the Hebrew, it was the *Messiah,* which means the "Anointed One." This title gathers up all the rich meaning of the Old Testament. It is a fragment with fullness (cf. Mic. 5:2; Isa. 7:14; Ps. 2:2; Ps. 45:6–7; and Mal.

3:1). These are but a few of the many Old Testament references. Jesus came to reveal God.

And he charged them that they should tell no man of him [Mark 8:30].

Why this strange admonition? They were to wait until the gospel story was complete. Notice the next verse.

And he began to teach them, that the Son of man must suffer many things, and be rejected of the elders, and of the chief priests, and scribes, and be killed, and after three days rise again [Mark 8:31].

Jesus did not reveal His Person apart from His work of redemption. Salvation depends on who He is and what He did.

The final phase of their training begins here. It was at Caesarea Philippi that He first revealed His cross to them.

And he spake that saying openly. And Peter took him, and began to rebuke him [Mark 8:32].

Even now they were unprepared to receive it. This is the worst thing Simon Peter ever said.

But when he had turned about and looked on his disciples, he rebuked Peter, saying, Get thee behind me, Satan: for thou savourest not the things that be of God, but the things that be of men [Mark 8:33].

Jesus attributed this statement to Satan. Satan denies the value of the death of Jesus.

And when he had called the people unto him with his disciples also, he said unto them, Whosoever will come after me, let him deny himself, and take up his cross, and follow me.

For whosoever will save his life shall lose it; but whosoever shall lose his life for my sake and the gospel's, the same shall save it.

For what shall it profit a man, if he shall gain the whole world, and lose his own soul?

Or what shall a man give in exchange for his soul?

Whosoever therefore shall be ashamed of me and of my words in this adulterous and sinful generation; of him also shall the Son of man be ashamed, when he cometh in the glory of his Father with the holy angels [Mark 8:34–38].

The Lord does not reveal His Person apart from His work of redemption. After Peter confessed who He is and they truly recognized Him, He immediately told them, ". . . the Son of man must suffer many things, and be rejected of the elders, and of the chief priests, and scribes, and be killed, and after three days rise again" (Mark 8:31). And then He gives the passage we have quoted. Here He is not putting down a condition of salvation, but stating the position of those who are saved. This is what He is talking about. "Whosoever therefore shall be ashamed of me." What kind of a Christian are *you* today? Are you one who acknowledges Him and serves Him and attempts to glorify Him? My friend, this is all important in these days in which we live.

CHAPTER 9

THEME: *Transfiguration; demon-possessed boy; death of Christ; mark of greatness; rebuke of sectarianism; teaching about hell*

TRANSFIGURATION

We come now to the ninth chapter of the Gospel of Mark, and we have again the account of the Transfiguration. This can be found in the first three Gospels, the synoptic Gospels. Then Mark tells us in detail that while the Transfiguration was going on at the top of the mountain, there was complete failure of the disciples at the foot of the mountain. They could not cast the demon out of the boy. Then Jesus again announces His death, and the disciples dispute as to who should be greatest among them. Jesus rebukes their party spirit and warns against hell. So this is another chapter just loaded with dynamite in the gospel of action.

Mark is customarily briefer in his account than the other evangelists, but he gives the longest account of the Transfiguration. It is interesting to ponder why he would emphasize it. It is our judgment that the Transfiguration sets forth the perfect humanity of Christ and was not given to set forth His deity. As we said, the synoptic Gospels all relate it, but John does not. John's gospel, which sets forth the deity of Christ, does not give the account of the Transfiguration.

You will remember that in the last verse of chapter 16 in Matthew, Jesus said, ". . . There be some standing here, which shall not taste of death, till they see the Son of man coming in his kingdom." There are all sorts of interpretations of that, but I think it is very clear that our Lord had definite reference to His transfiguration. Two men who were there, Peter and John, make reference to it. Peter says in 2 Peter 1:16–18: "For we have not followed cunningly devised fables, when we made known unto you the power and coming of our Lord Jesus Christ, but were eyewitnesses of his majesty. For he received from God the Father honour and glory, when there came such a voice to him from the excellent glory, This is my beloved Son, in whom I am well pleased. And this voice which came from heaven we heard, when we were with him in the holy mount." He is saying that they were witnesses of the power and coming of our Lord Jesus Christ. When? At the Transfiguration!

And he said unto them, Verily I say unto you, That there be some of them that stand here, which shall not taste of death, till they have seen the kingdom of God come with power [Mark 9:1].

I believe that the reason this is stated at this particular juncture before His death and resurrection was for us to understand that whether He went to the cross or not, the kingdom is in His hands. He could have stepped off this earth back to heaven and He would have been the sovereign Ruler of the universe. But that way He couldn't have saved you and He couldn't have saved me. I'm not going to develop that further, but that is important.

And after six days Jesus taketh with him Peter, and James, and John, and leadeth them up into an high mountain apart by themselves: and he was transfigured before them [Mark 9:2].

Of course, the question arises as to why He took these three men. Let me say first that He didn't take them because they were His little pets or that they were superior to the others. I think that they were the weakest of the apostles, and He had to carry them along with Him like babies or they would not have come along at all.

I was noticing a mother go down the street who had three children with her. She was carrying one, she was leading one by the hand, and one was walking behind her. She'd have to stop every now and then for him to catch up. I watched them as they made very slow progress down the street. I thought to myself, *That little fellow following her surely is taking a lot of time.* But then I realized that the one she was carrying couldn't go along at all unless she carried him. I feel that Peter, James, and John are rather like that. They seemed to be an exclusive group, but I think they were just babies, and He had to carry them. So He took them in for the Transfiguration.

Peter says that they were eyewitnesses of His majesty. This is it. This is the glorified Christ as He will come some day to this earth. This also, friend, is a picture of what you and I will be someday. We are told that we shall be like Him (see 1 John 3:2). You will recall that John says, ". . . we beheld his glory, the glory as of the only begotten of the Father" (John 1:14).

The word *transfigured* here is the Greek word *metamorphoom*, or *metamorphose* in English. The Transfiguration took place in the body of Jesus—it wasn't just a light or some effect produced from the outside. The Transfiguration was the light that shone from within. I rather think that Adam and Eve were clothed like that, with a light from within. The Transfiguration teaches, therefore, the perfect humanity of Jesus and not His deity.

And his raiment became shining, exceeding white as snow; so as no fuller on earth can white them [Mark 9:3].

His raiment became white. It was whiter than was even believable, because the light came from within, you see. The word *fuller* means a cloth dresser and refers to the laundry. In other words, no modern washday miracle could have produced such brightness. All of it came from within.

And there appeared unto them Elias with Moses: and they were talking with Jesus [Mark 9:4].

Elias is the Greek form of *Elijah*. Elijah was the representative of the prophets. Moses was the representative of the Law. We are told that both the Law and the prophets bore testimony of the death of Jesus. Luke tells us that they talked about the decease of Jesus. We know that Moses knew of Christ because we are told in Hebrews 11:26 concerning Moses: "Esteeming the reproach of Christ greater riches than the treasures in Egypt: for he had respect unto the recompence of the reward." Moses knew He was coming. All of the prophets spoke of His suffering and the glory that should follow.

And Peter answered and said to Jesus, Master, it is good for us to be here: and let us make three tabernacles; one for thee, and one for Moses, and one for Elias.

For he wist not what to say; for they were sore afraid [Mark 9:5–6].

Peter was the spokesman for them here just as he always was the spokesman. And Simon Peter generally spoke when he didn't know what to say. I think that Simon Peter put his foot in his mouth time and time again and he certainly did it here.

And there was a cloud that overshadowed them: and a voice came out of the cloud, saying, This is my beloved Son: hear him [Mark 9:7].

All attention now is focused on the Lord Jesus Christ. His Word is final. We don't put Moses or Elijah on a par with Him.

And suddenly, when they had looked round about, they saw no man any more, save Jesus only with themselves [Mark 9:8].

By the way, that "Jesus Only" is a marvelous headline, is it not? "Jesus Only" is not only a headline in Mark's gospel, but it ought to be a headline in the lives of believers today. In a brief way he states such great and weighty words—Jesus Only!

And as they came down from the mountain, he charged them that they should tell no man what things they had seen, till the Son of man were risen from the dead [Mark 9:9].

You see, the death and resurrection of Christ must go along with this story. The Transfiguration saves no man. It presents the ideal or the goal. But that goal can only come through the death of Christ upon the cross and through His resurrection from the dead. And you will notice that He always puts His death and resurrection together.

And they kept that saying with themselves, questioning one with another what the rising from the dead should mean [Mark 9:10].

They were entirely ignorant of the Resurrection. At the time of Jesus' resurrection they rushed to the cemetery, but they did not expect to see a living Savior. You don't go to the graveyard to see the living, but to pay respect to the dead.

And they asked him, saying, Why say the scribes that Elias must first come?

And he answered and told them, Elias verily cometh first, and restoreth all things; and how it is written of the Son of man, that he must suffer many things, and be set at nought.

But I say unto you, That Elias is indeed come, and they have done unto him whatsoever they listed, as it is written of him [Mark 9:11–13].

Our Lord made it clear that when anyone would say, "Well, after all, Jesus could not establish the kingdom because the prophet said that Elijah must come first," that John the Baptist had come in the spirit of Elijah. If they had accepted Jesus as the Messiah, John would have been the fulfillment of the prophecy. However, since they did not accept Jesus as their Messiah at His first coming, the prophecy of Elijah as His forerunner would be fulfilled at His second coming.

Now, from this glorious scene on the mountain top, we go down to the total defeat of the disciples at the foot of the mountain.

DEMON-POSSESSED BOY

And when he came to his disciples, he saw a great multitude about them, and the scribes questioning with them.

And straightway all the people, when they beheld him, were greatly amazed, and running to him saluted him.

And he asked the scribes, What question ye with them?

And one of the multitude answered and said, Master, I have brought unto thee my son, which hath a dumb spirit;

And wheresoever he taketh him, he teareth him: and he foameth, and gnasheth with his teeth, and pineth away: and I spake to thy disciples that they should cast him out; and they could not [Mark 9:14–18].

This is actually a picture of Christendom today. The Lord Jesus has already gone into the presence of the Father and is there in His glorified body. His apostles are there with Him. They have already gone on, and most of the church has already gone on. Moses and Elijah are there today. The Mount of Transfiguration pictures heaven today.

But look at this poor earth and see the problem down here. This boy represents a mad earth today. I tell you, I believe that if we could get off and look at this earth and behold it as God looks at it, and probably as the angels look at it, we would come to the conclusion that man on this earth must be mad. He appears to be demon-possessed by the way he is acting and the things he is doing down here. The sad thing is that the man brought the boy to the disciples, but they couldn't do anything. And the tragic thing about this hour is that the church is helpless in the presence of the world's need.

Right now, the organized church in desperation is reaching out, protesting and marching and getting involved in all kinds of things, and the world is actually criticizing the church because they feel it should get even more involved. But social matters are not our business! We ought to be able to help a poor demon-possessed boy today by presenting a Savior to him who will make him rational and who will bring him into a right relationship with God. Unfortunately, the same thing has to be said of the church, "They could not." The disciples could not and we cannot.

He answereth him, and saith, O faithless generation, how long shall I be with you? how long shall I suffer you? bring him unto me [Mark 9:19].

What a wonderful statement! Bring him unto Me! We are attempting to do everything except bring lost men to Jesus Christ.

And they brought him unto him: and when he saw him, straightway the spirit tare him; and he fell on the ground, and wallowed foaming.

And he asked his father, How long is it ago since this came unto him? And he said, Of a child.

And ofttimes it hath cast him into the fire, and into the waters, to destroy him: but if thou canst do any thing, have compassion on us, and help us [Mark 9:20–22].

This case, friend, is a bad case. It may not have been quite as bad as the case of the man among the tombs over in Gadara because he was a grown man and had been demon-possessed for a long time. This was a boy but had he gone on in this state he would probably have been as bad, if not worse, than the other case. So this father just casts himself upon the Lord Jesus on behalf of his tortured son. When we do that, friend, He'll do something to help.

Jesus said unto him, If thou canst believe, all things are possible to him that believeth [Mark 9:23].

The thought here is that Jesus turned to the father and asked him to believe—could the father have been responsible in any way for the condition of the boy? It is not a question of "if Thou canst do anything"—the Lord Jesus can do everything. The question is, "If thou canst believe." What about the father? The Lord Jesus told him that all things are possible to him that believeth.

And straightway the father of the child cried out, and said with tears, Lord, I

believe; help thou mine unbelief [Mark 9:24].

Here is the father's desperate plea of faith!

When Jesus saw that the people came running together, he rebuked the foul spirit, saying unto him, Thou dumb and deaf spirit, I charge thee, come out of him, and enter no more into him.

And the spirit cried, and rent him sore, and came out of him: and he was as one dead; insomuch that many said, He is dead.

But Jesus took him by the hand, and lifted him up; and he arose [Mark 9:25–27].

The question arises here whether this also is a case of our Lord raising the dead. I am of the opinion it is, but I don't want to labor that point.

And when he was come into the house, his disciples asked him privately, Why could not we cast him out?

And he said unto them, This kind can come forth by nothing, but by prayer and fasting [Mark 9:28–29].

Now, in the Lord's answer to the disciples, we find that the word *fasting* is not in the better manuscripts. The emphasis is upon prayer. And today, friend, the church is weak because prayer is weak in the church.

DEATH OF CHRIST

And they departed thence, and passed through Galilee; and he would not that any man should know it.

For he taught his disciples, and said unto them, The Son of man is delivered into the hands of men, and they shall kill him; and after that he is killed, he shall rise the third day [Mark 9:30–31].

You will notice that He always puts His death and resurrection together.

But they understood not that saying, and were afraid to ask him [Mark 9:32].

They didn't quite understand this matter of being raised from the dead. Here He is talking about His own death for them and you would think that these men might have at least made some inquiry. They dared to dispute among themselves who would be greatest in the kingdom after He had just announced His death. They should have been ashamed of their conduct here. This is not the first time He has announced His death and resurrection to them, and still they do not understand.

MARK OF GREATNESS

And he came to Capernaum: and being in the house he asked them, What was it that ye disputed among yourselves by the way?

But they held their peace: for by the way they had disputed among themselves, who should be the greatest.

And he sat down, and called the twelve, and saith unto them, If any man desire to be first, the same shall be last of all, and servant of all [Mark 9:33–35].

This is the profound spiritual principle of greatness.

And he took a child, and set him in the midst of them: and when he had taken him in his arms, he said unto them,

Whosoever shall receive one of such children in my name, receiveth me: and whosoever shall receive me, receiveth not me, but him that sent me [Mark 9:36–37].

He illustrates this principle with the child. Note that Jesus took the child in His arms.

REBUKE OF SECTARIANISM

And John answered him, saying, Master, we saw one casting out devils in thy name, and he followeth not us: and we forbad him, because he followeth not us.

But Jesus said, Forbid him not: for there is no man which shall do a miracle in my name, that can lightly speak evil of me.

For he that is not against us is on our part.

For whosoever shall give you a cup of water to drink in my name, because ye belong to Christ, verily I say unto you, he shall not lose his reward [Mark 9:38–41].

John is always thought of as a ladylike apostle but notice his fiery disposition here. Jesus rebukes any kind of sectarian spirit. You will notice that the basis of unity which Jesus made is "in My name." That which is done in the name of Jesus cannot be denied by any follower. However, the label of "Jesus" is put on much today that actually is not "in His name."

TEACHING ABOUT HELL

Now notice that in verse 42, He comes back to the child that He has taken into His arms. This is tender, but it is severe upon those who offend a little child.

And whosoever shall offend one of these little ones that believe in me, it is better for him that a millstone were hanged about his neck, and he were cast into the sea [Mark 9:42].

Then He adds this:

And if thy hand offend thee, cut it off: it is better for thee to enter into life maimed, than having two hands to go into hell, into the fire that never shall be quenched [Mark 9:43].

Do you realize who it is here that is talking about hell? There are those today who say that He is the gentle Jesus. Friend, He is the only One who talked about hell. Paul never talked about it, but Jesus did. And since He did, it would be well for us to listen to Him. He said that there is a place, and it is called hell. I'm confident that it is a *place*, and it is a place just like He describes it.

Verses 44 and 46 are not in the better manuscripts. It might be well if we omit them.

Jesus talks about the hand, the foot, the eye.

And if thy foot offend thee, cut it off: it is better for thee to enter halt into life, than having two feet to be cast into hell, into the fire that never shall be quenched:

And if thine eye offend thee, pluck it out: it is better for thee to enter into the kingdom of God with one eye, than having two eyes to be cast into hell fire [Mark 9:45,47].

The eye can lead to sin. Think of Eve who first saw the tree was good for food.

For every one shall be salted with fire, and every sacrifice shall be salted with salt.

Salt is good: but if the salt have lost his saltness, wherewith will ye season it? Have salt in yourselves, and have peace one with another [Mark 9:49–50].

These are strange statements. The thought is that both fire and salt purify. Fire purifies by burning away the dross and impurities. Salt penetrates and burns out the corruption and stays the spread of impurities. If we have salt—the cleansing work of the Word of God—working within us, it sanctifies and brings peace.

CHAPTER 10

THEME: *Teaching about marriage; rich young ruler; teaching about riches; death of Christ; ambition of James and John; blind Bartimaeus*

The first verse tells us that "he arose from thence, and cometh into the coasts of Judaea by the farther side of Jordan." You will notice that there is a movement here in Mark. In fact, the geography in Mark is quite interesting. In Mark 9:30 we read that, "they departed thence, and passed through Galilee; and he would not that any man should know it." He was making His final departure from there and He certainly didn't want a big send-off. Now He comes "into the coasts of Judaea by the farther side of Jordan," which means on the east side. That was in the area called Decapolis after the ten cities which were there. So we find Him by the farther side of Jordan. The people are coming to Him again, and He taught them "as he was wont." He's now making His final ascent to Jerusalem. The enemies, those bloodhounds of hate, are on His trail.

TEACHING ABOUT MARRIAGE

And he arose from thence, and cometh into the coasts of Judaea by the farther side of Jordan: and the people resort

unto him again; and, as he was wont, he taught them again.

And the Pharisees came to him, and asked him, Is it lawful for a man to put away his wife? tempting him [Mark 10:1–2].

We need to understand that they do not ask this question because they want an answer. They are asking Him the question in order to trap Him. They had their own viewpoint concerning marriage and divorce; so they pose this trick question: "Is it lawful for a man to put away his wife?" It's a clever question and was really a live issue at this time because Herod had put away his wife and married his brother Philip's wife. John the Baptist had been beheaded because he had spoken out against it. So if Jesus answered no to their question, it would not only make Him contradict Moses, but it would bring Him into conflict with Herod. The death of Jesus was not to be determined on this issue. That's very important to see. On the other hand, if He said yes to their question, they could accuse Him of being lax in His teaching. So now notice His method. It always was His method and it was a good one. He countered with a question.

And he answered and said unto them, What did Moses command you?

And they said, Moses suffered to write a bill of divorcement, and to put her away [Mark 10:3–4].

He knew they would have to say that because back in Deuteronomy 24:1–2 there was the Mosaic Law: "When a man hath taken a wife, and married her, and it come to pass that she find no favour in his eyes, because he hath found some uncleanness in her: then let him write her a bill of divorcement, and give it in her hand, and send her out of his house. And when she is departed out of his house, she may go and be another man's wife."

Moses permitted divorce, as you can see. Actually, it was not Moses' intention nor was it God's intention for a man or a woman to get a divorce over some little picayunish excuse. However, in time, the religious rulers interpreted it so that the wife's burning the biscuits would be grounds for divorce.

Now our Lord goes back to that which is fundamental, and this is important to see. He turns it from a discussion of divorce to a discussion of marriage. And today that is the area into which we should move. I have so many questions from people asking about the grounds for divorce. When they are ready to get married, they never talk to the preacher. They are not interested in finding out whether he would approve or not; their only question is whether he will marry them. That is all they are concerned about.

The important thing to see here is that our Lord is going to discuss marriage with them. Notice how He handles it. He gives the reason God permitted divorce. It was because of sin that God granted divorce under the Mosaic Law.

And Jesus answered and said unto them, For the hardness of your heart he wrote you this precept.

But from the beginning of the creation God made them male and female.

For this cause shall a man leave his father and mother, and cleave to his wife;

And they twain shall be one flesh: so then they are no more twain, but one flesh.

What therefore God hath joined together, let not man put asunder [Mark 10:5–9].

What Jesus is saying here takes them back to God's ideal at the creation before sin entered the world. Divorce was not in His plan and program at that time. He had something better for man. It may likewise be said that murder was not in His plan, but murderers have been forgiven. Divorce is a sin, but divorced people can be forgiven. And I think that under certain circumstances divorced people can be remarried; that is, from a scriptural viewpoint. I don't know why we will forgive a murderer but often refuse to forgive a divorced person. We act almost as if he has committed the unpardonable sin. People who are saved after securing a divorce ought not to bear the stigma any more than any other sinner who has been saved. We are all sinners saved by grace. It just happens that divorce is their sin.

What He is saying in this section here is that marriage is a stronger tie than that of parent and child. A child may be disowned, and marriage may be broken by unfaithfulness. Jesus is showing here that marriage is something that God makes. God joins a couple together. This was the original intention of the Creator. Any violation of this is sin, but it is not the unpardonable sin, I can assure you.

The basic problem is marrying the wrong person. It looks to me like we are locking the stable after the horse is gone. There are people getting married who ought not to get married. This is the problem. The sin was that they got married in the first place. My Christian friend, marriage is something that God wants to arrange for you, if you will let Him.

And in the house his disciples asked him again of the same matter.

And he saith unto them, Whosoever shall put away his wife, and marry another, committeth adultery against her.

And if a woman shall put away her husband, and be married to another, she committeth adultery [Mark 10:10–12].

This is the strongest statement against divorce that is found in the Scripture. How is it to be interpreted? All the Scriptures on divorce should be brought together and considered before a proper induction can be made. The parallel passage in Matthew lists fornication as the one basis for divorce. Why did Mark omit this? Mark was writing to the Romans who did not know the Mosaic Law, while Matthew was writing for Israel who had and knew the Mosaic Law of divorce. So it must be considered in that light.

Romans 7:2 does not apply to the problem of divorce: "For the woman which hath an husband is bound by the law to her husband so long as he liveth; but if the husband be dead, she is loosed from the law of her husband." In this passage Paul is using a well-established law, that a wife is bound to a living husband until death frees her, as an illustration of the believer's relationship to the principle of law. The Mosaic system took care of the unfaithful wife or husband. They were stoned to death according to Deuteronomy 22:22–24. Now today we don't stone them to death. If we did, there would be so many rock piles we wouldn't be able to get around them.

According to the Mosaic Law, a husband or wife who is guilty of adultery may be treated as dead by the other mate. Scripture does recognize one ground for divorce—unfaithfulness. The innocent party is free to marry, it would seem, from Christ's words.

The discussion of divorce and the blessing of the little children are brought together by both Matthew and Mark. It seems to me the Spirit of God is trying to tell us something here. The child is the innocent product of the marriage, and a divorce becomes doubly evil because the little children suffer so in the divorce. It is amazing to see the number of young people from broken homes who get into trouble today. That is no accident, by any means. That is the way it works out.

And they brought young children to him, that he should touch them: and his disciples rebuked those that brought them.

But when Jesus saw it, he was much displeased, and said unto them, Suffer the little children to come unto me, and forbid them not: for of such is the kingdom of God.

Verily I say unto you, Whosoever shall not receive the kingdom of God as a little child, he shall not enter therein.

And he took them up in his arms, put his hands upon them, and blessed them [Mark 10:13–16].

The children would not have to become adults to come to Him. We wait for little Willie to grow up and maybe then he'll make a decision for Christ. Our Lord says that He wishes the adults would become little children. We hear so much today about going on and growing and developing. That's wonderful—after you have become a child of God. But, actually, most of us are going the wrong way. We need to leave our cleverness and our sophistication and our great knowledge that we boast of today and return to the simplicity of childhood—with simple, childlike faith, trust Christ Jesus.

Our Lord took the children up in His arms, put His hands upon them, and blessed them. He never did take anybody else up in His arms like that, friend. He took the little children, because they are the ones He will receive. When they die in infancy, before the age of accountability, they go to be with Him.

RICH YOUNG RULER

And when he was gone forth into the way, there came one running, and kneeled to him, and asked him, Good Master, what shall I do that I may inherit eternal life?

And Jesus said unto him, Why callest thou me good? there is none good but one, that is, God [Mark 10:17–18].

In this day of crass materialism, this incident of the rich young ruler and the teaching of our Lord about riches are certainly very applicable. Matthew tells us that the ruler was young, and this was a normal question for a man under the Law to ask. He is living under the Mosaic system and is asking what he must do to inherit eternal life.

Jesus tries to get the young man to think. Why should he call Jesus *good?* There is only One who is good and that is God. If he is calling Jesus good, then Jesus is God. Now notice that Jesus gives the young man the commandments which are in the second section of the Ten Commandments.

Thou knowest the commandments, Do not commit adultery, Do not kill, Do not steal, Do not bear false witness, Defraud not, Honour thy father and mother.

And he answered and said unto him, Master, all these have I observed from my youth [Mark 10:19–20].

The first section of the commandments is labeled *pietas* and has to do with man's relationship to God. The second section is labeled *probitas* and has to do with man's relationship with man. Our Lord did not speak of the man's relationship to God but of his relationship to man. He could meet the standard of the second section and said he had kept them all.

Then Jesus beholding him loved him, and said unto him, One thing thou lackest: go thy way, sell whatsoever thou hast, and give to the poor, and thou shalt have treasure in heaven: and come, take up the cross, and follow me.

And he was sad at that saying, and went away grieved: for he had great possessions [Mark 10:21–22].

Jesus told him he lacked one thing. What was that? It was his relationship to God. The thing that was hindering him was his riches. He had called Jesus good; and if he will follow Jesus, he'll find out that the reason Jesus is good is because He is God. Jesus asked him to separate himself from his riches and follow Him. Where would this lead him? Well, at this time the Lord Jesus is on the way to die for the sins of this man. Had he followed Jesus, he would have come to the cross for redemption. But the young man "was sad at that saying, and went away grieved: for he had great possessions."

TEACHING ABOUT RICHES

There is a great message here. Paul says that ". . . the love of money is the root of all evil" (1 Tim. 6:10). He was merely repeating what our Lord said in this discourse. Money will buy anything except the most valuable thing—eternal life. This discourse reveals the impossibility of a rich man entering into heaven by means of his riches. It is impossible for any man to enter heaven by his own means.

And Jesus looked round about, and saith unto his disciples, How hardly shall they that have riches enter into the kingdom of God!

And the disciples were astonished at his words. But Jesus answereth again, and saith unto them, Children, how hard is it for them that trust in riches to enter into the kingdom of God!

It is easier for a camel to go through the eye of a needle, than for a rich man to enter into the kingdom of God [Mark 10:23–25].

Well, a camel can't go through the eye of a needle. That's humanly impossible, or should we say "camel" impossible. But for God all things are possible.

And they were astonished out of measure, saying among themselves, Who then can be saved?

And Jesus looking upon them saith, With men it is impossible, but not with God: for with God all things are possible [Mark 10:26–27].

The man can't do it; only the Lord Jesus can. We have the idea today that money can buy everything. Someone has written these lines about money that we do well to think over:

Money will buy a bed, but it will not buy sleep.
Money will buy food, but it will not buy an appetite.
Money will buy medicine, but it will not buy health.
Money will buy a house, but it will not buy a home.
Money will buy a diamond, but it will not buy love.
Money will buy a church pew, but it will not buy salvation.

Jesus invited this young man to get rid of that which stood between him and God. If he had followed the Lord Jesus, he would have learned that the reason Jesus is good is because Jesus is God.

Then Peter began to say unto him, Lo, we have left all, and have followed thee.

And Jesus answered and said, Verily I say unto you, There is no man that hath left house, or brethren, or sisters, or father, or mother, or wife, or children, or lands, for my sake, and the gospel's,

But he shall receive an hundredfold now in this time, houses, and brethren, and sisters, and mothers, and children, and lands, with persecutions; and in the world to come eternal life [Mark 10:28–30].

Instead of rebuking Peter, Jesus promised a reward for those who sacrifice for Him.

But many that are first shall be last; and the last first [Mark 10:31].

This is a principle which will operate in giving out rewards.

DEATH OF CHRIST

And they were in the way going up to Jerusalem; and Jesus went before them: and they were amazed; and as they followed, they were afraid. And he took again the twelve, and began to tell them what things should happen unto him,

Saying, Behold, we go up to Jerusalem; and the Son of man shall be delivered unto the chief priests, and unto the scribes; and they shall condemn him to death, and shall deliver him to the Gentiles:

And they shall mock him, and shall scourge him, and shall spit upon him, and shall kill him: and the third day he shall rise again [Mark 10:32–34].

You see, He's moving now toward Jerusalem. He knows and is telling them that He is going there to die. Notice again that, with His death, He always mentions His resurrection.

AMBITION OF JAMES AND JOHN

And James and John, the sons of Zebedee, come unto him saying, Master, we would that thou shouldest do for us whatsoever we shall desire.

And he said unto them, What would ye that I should do for you?

They said unto him, Grant unto us that we may sit, one on thy right hand, and the other on thy left hand, in thy glory.

But Jesus said unto them, Ye know not what ye ask: can ye drink of the cup that I drink of? and be baptized with the baptism that I am baptized with? [Mark 10:35–38].

We had this story in Matthew, you will remember. The mother had come to Jesus and asked this privilege for her sons. So when Jesus asked them whether they could be baptized with the same baptism that He would suffer, they answered that they could.

And they said unto him, We can. And Jesus said unto them, Ye shall indeed drink of the cup that I drink of; and with the baptism that I am baptized withal shall ye be baptized:

But to sit on my right hand and on my left hand is not mine to give; but it shall be given to them for whom it is prepared [Mark 10:39–40].

We know that James became a martyr. John was exiled on the Isle of Patmos. Although it is not believed that he was martyred, he may have been executed; we do not know.

Our Lord did not say that there is not a place on His right hand and left hand. He said the place is not given arbitrarily to anyone He wants to give it to. But those who will receive it are preparing themselves for that place. Friend, you get heaven as a gift. But your place in heaven—you work for that. Salvation is free, but we work for a reward. If you are going to be rewarded of Him, you won't get it by twiddling your thumbs or wringing your hands or sitting in a rocking chair. You'll have to work to receive that.

And when the ten heard it, they began to be much displeased with James and John [Mark 10:41].

They were displeased because *they* wanted the best positions.

So the Lord must teach them another principle. The method this world uses is not God's method.

But Jesus called them to him, and saith unto them, Ye know that they which are accounted to rule over the Gentiles exercise lordship over them; and their great ones exercise authority upon them.

But so shall it not be among you: but whosoever will be great among you, shall be your minister:

And whosoever of you will be the chiefest, shall be servant of all [Mark 10:42–44].

God's method is to take those who are humble and make themselves small by serving and place them as the leaders. The chief must be the servant of all. Then He states the key to this gospel:

For even the Son of man came not to be ministered unto, but to minister, and to give his life a ransom for many [Mark 10:45].

BLIND BARTIMAEUS

This account appears in Matthew and again in Luke. There are people who deny the inerrancy of Scripture because they can't reconcile the accounts of the Gospels here. Matthew mentions two blind men, but Mark centers his attention on Bartimaeus because he was the one who spoke out. I think the critic who tries to tear apart the accounts in the Gospels is the third blind man!

And they came to Jericho: and as he went out of Jericho with his disciples and a great number of people, blind Bartimaeus, the son of Timaeus, sat by the highway side begging.

And when he heard that it was Jesus of Nazareth, he began to cry out, and say, Jesus, thou son of David, have mercy on me.

And many charged him that he should hold his peace: but he cried the more a great deal, Thou son of David, have mercy on me.

And Jesus stood still, and commanded him to be called. And they call the blind man, saying unto him, Be of good comfort, rise; he calleth thee.

And he, casting away his garment, rose, and came to Jesus.

And Jesus answered and said unto him, What wilt thou that I should do unto thee? The blind man said unto him, Lord, that I might receive my sight.

And Jesus said unto him, Go thy way; thy faith hath made thee whole. And immediately he received his sight, and followed Jesus in the way [Mark 10:46–52].

It is thrilling to think that Bartimaeus followed Jesus now with his eyes open. In a few days he will see Jesus dying on the cross.

Are you blind? Or have you, too, seen Jesus dying for you? Look and live!

CHAPTER 11

***THEME:** Triumphal entry; fig tree cursed; Jesus cleanses temple; fig tree withered; prayer; authority of Jesus*

We are coming now to the last days in the earthly life of our Lord. I have divided this chapter in this way:

1. Jesus presents Himself publicly to His nation as the Messiah (vv. 1–11).
2. Jesus pronounces a blight on the fig tree (vv. 12–14).
3. Jesus purifies the temple (vv. 15–21).
4. Jesus' prayer discourse (vv. 22–26).
5. Jesus perturbs the religious rulers (vv. 27–33).

This eleventh chapter deals with the three days that He came into Jerusalem. I take the position that His so-called triumphal entry really wasn't that at all. It was the Lord Jesus coming to Jerusalem in a public manner at the conclusion of His earthly ministry and presenting Himself. Actually, it amounted to a rejection of His overture. He really came in on three separate days, and not on just one day. I think that each gospel is presenting a different aspect of His coming into Jerusalem. The first day He came was a Sabbath day, Saturday. He returned on Sunday and cleansed the temple. Then He returned on Monday and wept over the city.

TRIUMPHAL ENTRY

And when they came nigh to Jerusalem, unto Bethphage and Bethany, at the mount of Olives, he sendeth forth two of his disciples [Mark 11:1].

We have seen in the last few chapters that Jesus is moving toward Jerusalem. He's moving geographically and He's moving chronologically closer to His death. This is the last week of His earthly life. Bethany and Bethphage are two little towns on the other side of the Mount of Olives from Jerusalem. (I intended to walk over there and back myself, but I never got around to it the few days that I was in Jerusalem. If I ever go there again, I want to do that. The fact of the matter is that I want to spend more time walking through that land. It's one thing to get in a bus or a car and ride along and have these places pointed out, but it's another thing to take a map and walk along, stopping along the way and having a conversation with anyone who could understand English. I know one could discover many things which the average tourist does not see at all today.)

Now the Lord Jesus is giving directions to two of His men.

And saith unto them, Go your way into the village over against you: and as soon as ye be entered into it, ye shall find a colt tied, whereon never man sat; loose him, and bring him.

And if any man say unto you, Why do ye this? say ye that the Lord hath need of him; and straightway he will send him hither [Mark 11:2–3].

There are two possible explanations regarding the colt that Jesus was to ride into Jerusalem. The Lord Jesus could have known about it since He is God and, therefore, omniscient. This could have been a miracle from beginning to end. On the other hand, all of this could have been arranged beforehand, and it would therefore be entirely human. It doesn't seem necessary to read a miracle in here when the natural explanation is in order. I believe our Lord had arranged for this beforehand, and I think you will find greater meaning if you look at it that way. The important feature is that Jesus is asserting His authority. Notice that if anyone questions them about loosing the colt, they are to say that the Lord has need of it. That is asserting authority.

While some are plotting His death, others are yielding allegiance to Him. "Straightway he will send him hither." There were those who were obeying Him. Now that has been true for over nineteen hundred years. There are these two classes of people even today. As we read on, we find that they went into the town and found things just as the Lord had said.

And they went their way, and found the colt tied by the door without in a place where two ways met; and they loose him.

And certain of them that stood there said unto them, What do ye, loosing the colt?

And they said unto them even as Jesus had commanded: and they let them go [Mark 11:4–6].

You will notice that they merely follow His instructions and return with the colt.

And they brought the colt to Jesus, and cast their garments on him; and he sat upon him.

And many spread their garments in the way: and others cut down branches off the trees, and strawed them in the way.

And they that went before, and they that followed, cried, saying, Hosanna; Blessed is he that cometh in the name of the Lord [Mark 11:7–9].

I'm not sure that this was very impressive to those in Jerusalem. I'm sure it would not have been impressive to anyone who had been in Rome at the time that one of the Caesars returned from a campaign and had a great triumphal entry, a victorious return of a Caesar. It is said that so much booty and so many captives were brought back that the parade would go on for two or three days and nights. That would be triumphal, you see.

Here it was just a few Galileans, peasants, but the impressive thing and the important thing is that the Lord Jesus is offering Himself publicly.

And Jesus entered into Jerusalem, and into the temple: and when he had looked round about upon all things, and now the eventide was come, he went out unto Bethany with the twelve [Mark 11:11].

There are two things here that are important to see. It was obviously the Sabbath day and the money changers and the oxen were not there. On this first day He came in as the Priest, and He was the sacrifice. He came in as the Great High Priest to offer the sacrifice that is acceptable to God for your sins and for my sins.

And note that He did not spend the night in Jerusalem but returned to Bethany for the evening. Jesus had thrust Himself before the city publicly and was demanding a decision. As far as we can tell, He did not spend a night in the city that rejected Him.

FIG TREE CURSED

And on the morrow, when they were come from Bethany, he was hungry:

And seeing a fig tree afar off having leaves, he came, if haply he might find any thing thereon: and when he came to it, he found nothing but leaves; for the time of figs was not yet.

And Jesus answered and said unto it, No man eat fruit of thee hereafter for ever. And his disciples heard it [Mark 11:12–14].

And this is "on the morrow," the second day, and they were coming from Bethany. This is the second day He entered in triumph. This little incident has caused great controversy. On this day He cleansed the temple and He cursed the fig tree.

The nation Israel, in my opinion, is represented by the fig tree. I recognize there are others who will take exception to that, and I don't want to be controversial. What I'm interested in is that there is a great spiritual lesson here. Israel had the outward leaves of a God-given religion, but there was no spiritual fruit. I wonder if we could say that of the church today? This would be His message to the church of Laodicea. They didn't have anything—they were poor and blind and needed to have ointment to open their eyes. This means that the Holy Spirit was not there. I believe this is the same thing that Isaiah was talking about in Isaiah 29:13: "Wherefore the Lord said, Forasmuch as this people draw near me with their mouth, and with their lips do honour me, but have removed their heart far from me, and their fear toward me is taught by the precept of men." I would consider this the condition of the church today.

The Lord Jesus cursed the fig tree, and the fig tree withered away.

JESUS CLEANSES TEMPLE

And they come to Jerusalem: and Jesus went into the temple, and began to cast out them that sold and bought in the temple, and overthrew the tables of the moneychangers, and the seats of them that sold doves [Mark 11:15].

Here He cleanses the temple. John tells us that He cleansed it at the beginning of His ministry and now He cleanses it at the end of His ministry. This took place on the second day, and this was not the Sabbath day; it was Sunday. The money changers were now in the temple. They had a seat on the stock market and were there so that when strangers came from other countries they could exchange coins. The strangers couldn't use their foreign coins but needed the legal coin of the temple. When these moneychangers would make the exchange, they, of course, charged the people a certain percentage. It served a good purpose in a way, but the trouble of it was that our Lord said it had become a den of thieves. It had become a religious racket.

Friend, this is always a danger in any Christian enterprise. That is the reason folks ought to check on religious organizations before they support them.

You see, His public presentation of Himself as the Messiah was not a triumphal entry into Jerusalem. He was *rejected.* I don't like the term, and it is not scriptural to call it "triumphal." Wait until you see Him someday when He comes and the ". . . dead in Christ shall rise first: Then we which are alive and remain shall be caught up together with them . . ."(1 Thess. 4:16–17). You will see that tremendous throng of folk who have trusted Christ during more than nineteen hundred years—millions of saints going out. My friend, that will really be a triumphal entry. I think it's going to take place over a long period of time. The raising will be in a moment, in the twinkling of an eye, but the parade has a long way to go. He's going to lead them into a new place, a new creation, a new home for this new group. It will not be just to the moon, but to the New Jerusalem. What a glorious thing that will be! That will be triumphant!

We have come now to the third day.

FIG TREE WITHERED

And in the morning, as they passed by, they saw the fig tree dried up from the roots.

And Peter calling to remembrance saith unto him, Master, behold, the fig tree which thou cursedst is withered away [Mark 11:20–21].

This causes our Lord to give this discourse on prayer. They marvelled at the fig tree, and this causes Him to give the discourse.

TEACHING ABOUT PRAYER

And Jesus answering saith unto them, Have faith in God [Mark 11:22].

It's interesting that this discourse on the prayer of faith grew out of Peter's calling attention to the blighted fig tree. You see, the first step in prayer must be faith in God. The writer to the Hebrews stated this same principle: "But without faith it is impossible to please him; for he that cometh to God must believe that he is, and that he is a rewarder of them that diligently seek him" (Heb. 11:6).

If you don't believe in God, friend, then the skeptic is certainly correct when he says that prayer is a madman talking to himself. Having faith in God is the first step.

For verily I say unto you, That whosoever shall say unto this mountain, Be thou removed, and be thou cast into the sea; and shall not doubt in his heart, but shall believe that those things which he saith shall come to pass; he shall have whatsoever he saith [Mark 11:23].

This is a verse that is so misunderstood today. The Christian does not need to throw mountains around literally, but he needs power for living and meeting the daily mountains of cares and problems. This is why Paul could pray for the Ephesians, "That he would grant you, according to the riches of his glory, to be strengthened with might by his Spirit in the inner man" (Eph. 3:16). Don't pray for me that I'll be able to move the mountains that are behind our headquarters here in Pasadena. Frankly, I see no point in moving the mountains. And if I did move them, where in the world would I put them? I don't want to put them out in the ocean because they look pretty up where they are. But I want to tell you very candidly that I would like to be strengthened with might by the Holy Spirit in the inner man. That, my friend, would be greater than moving a mountain. That's the thing that is important and is, I feel, what He is talking about as He gives them this visible illustration to show what prayer can do.

Therefore I say unto you, What things soever ye desire, when ye pray, believe that ye receive them, and ye shall have them [Mark 11:24].

Have faith in God. This does not give you the ability to satisfy your own selfish desires but have faith in God that His will might be done in your life.

And when ye stand praying, forgive, if ye have aught against any: that your Father also which is in heaven may forgive you your trespasses.

But if ye do not forgive, neither will your Father which is in heaven forgive your trespasses [Mark 11:25–26].

Here is a condition that the individual must meet before prayer is heard and answered. An unforgiving spirit will short-circuit the power of prayer, and that's important to understand. God forgives us for Christ's sake (Eph. 4:32). That is the way we are saved. But if you and I are going to have power in our lives, there must be forgiveness. That is very important.

Now we find the chief priests coming out to try to trap Him.

AUTHORITY OF JESUS

And they come again to Jerusalem: and as he was walking in the temple, there come to him the chief priests, and the scribes, and the elders,

And say unto him, By what authority doest thou these things? and who gave thee this authority to do these things? [Mark 11:27–28].

They are still on His trail, you see, these bloodhounds of hate. They are resisting Him at every turn. They challenged His authority. They were the religious rulers; they were the official representatives of religion in their day, and they had delegated no authority to Him. So they want to know where He got His authority.

And Jesus answered and said unto them, I will also ask of you one question, and answer me, and I will tell you by what authority I do these things.

The baptism of John, was it from heaven, or of men? answer me [Mark 11:29–30].

That was a good question, by the way, and it was a devastating question to the religious rulers. You see, if they said that John's baptism was from heaven, then the obvious follow-up would be, "Then why didn't you accept it?" If they repudiated John, then the people would be antagonized, for they accepted John.

And they reasoned with themselves, saying, If we shall say, From heaven; he will say, Why then did ye not believe him?

But if we shall say, Of men; they feared the people: for all men counted John, that he was a prophet indeed.

And they answered and said unto Jesus, We cannot tell. And Jesus answering saith unto them, Neither do I tell you by what authority I do these things [Mark 11:31–33].

They had to wiggle out of answering the question of Jesus by claiming ignorance. It might be argued that this did not afford Jesus a sufficient ground for not answering their question. My friend, they were not seeking an answer. They were trying to trap Him. They had no intention of following His teaching if He had told them. He does not answer them because He is not falling into their trap. This, to me, is one of the great proofs of His deity—the way He handled His enemies.

Remember that when men and women came to our Lord with sincere questions as sincere seekers, they received a sincere and genuine answer to their inquiries.

CHAPTER 12

THEME: *Man demanding fruit from vineyard; question of taxes; the Resurrection; the Great Commandment; the Messiah; the widow's mite*

Note in this chapter and in succeeding chapters that there are no miracles. We have stated before that Mark is the gospel of action with the emphasis on miracles. According to this premise, it would seem that the action is slowing down now to a standstill. Actually, this is the lull before the storm. And we'll see a lot of action coming up.

Now I've made a little outline of this chapter that I'll give you:

(1) Jesus quickens the battle with the religious rulers with the parable of the vineyard (vv. 1–12);

(2) Jesus queers the plot of the Pharisees and Herodians about paying taxes to Caesar (vv. 13–17);

(3) Jesus quells the skepticism of the Sadducees concerning the Resurrection (vv. 18–27);

(4) Jesus quiets the mind of the scribe about the greatest commandment (vv. 28–34);

(5) Jesus questions the Pharisees about the Messiah and quotes Psalm 110 (vv. 35–40);

(6) Jesus qualifies scriptural giving by evaluating the two mites of the widow (vv. 41–44).

We are coming to a great deal of action, but a different kind. The Lord Jesus is the Passover Lamb and He is put up for close inspection now before He is to be slaughtered. (You remember that the Passover lamb was kept up and closely observed to make sure it was without blemish.) All the waves of men's wrath will roll over His head in a few days now. This is not a period of quiet and inaction, but it is the fiercest encounter with the religious rulers. Both sides bring up their heavy artillery and make every arrangement and preparation for the battle of heaven and hell, light and darkness, God and Satan. This could hardly be called a period of inaction or cessation of hostilities.

The three years of periodic skirmishes of Jesus with the religious rulers break out in a bitter verbal encounter. He takes the initiative, wins a victory in the verbal area, and they cease trying to trap Him in that way. They had hoped to force Him to say something that would turn the people against Him. All the questions they asked Him were loaded.

He precipitated this action by giving the most pointed, plain, and direct parable of His ministry—the vineyard. The meaning is obvious. The chapter opens with this parable.

MAN DEMANDING FRUIT FROM VINEYARD

And he began to speak unto them by parables. A certain man planted a vineyard, and set an hedge about it, and digged a place for the winevat, and built a tower, and let it out to husbandmen, and went into a far country [Mark 12:1].

The vineyard is the nation Israel according to Isaiah 5:1–7. He brought that "vine" out of Egypt; He planted it (the nation of Israel). He gave to them a God-given religion. They are the only people that ever had a God-given religion and the visible presence of God. Churches have never had that. Now He gives a parable for the religious rulers of His day.

And at the season he sent to the husbandmen a servant, that he might receive from the husbandmen of the fruit of the vineyard.

And they caught him, and beat him, and sent him away empty.

And again he sent unto them another servant; and at him they cast stones, and wounded him in the head, and sent him away shamefully handled.

And again he sent another; and him they killed, and many others; beating some, and killing some.

Having yet therefore one son, his wellbeloved, he sent him also last unto them, saying, They will reverence my son.

But those husbandmen said among themselves, This is the heir; come, let us kill him, and the inheritance shall be ours.

And they took him, and killed him, and cast him out of the vineyard.

What shall therefore the lord of the vineyard do? he will come and destroy the husbandmen, and will give the vineyard unto others.

And have ye not read this scripture; The stone which the builders rejected is become the head of the corner:

This was the Lord's doing, and it is marvellous in our eyes?

And they sought to lay hold on him, but feared the people: for they knew that he had spoken the parable against them: and they left him, and went their way [Mark 12:2–12].

It is quite obvious what He is talking about in this parable. The servants that God sent were the prophets. The "certain man" who had the vineyard is God the Father. The vineyard is the nation Israel. God had chosen and protected this nation. The husbandmen were the religious rulers. Finally, He sent His Son; and that, of course, is the Lord Jesus, the beloved Son of the Father. In a special way, Jesus came to the nation Israel first. ". . .I am not sent but unto the lost sheep of the house of Israel" (Matt. 15:24). But He also came for the entire world, according to John 3:16. But here our Lord is making a deliberate and direct thrust at the religious rulers who stood before Him. They had already plotted His death and He brings their plans out into the light. "He knew what was in man." He tells the religious rulers what they will do. He prophesies their every step and anticipates their every move. He charges them with murder before they kill Him. This is a remarkable incident, friend. Then He predicts the judgment of the religious rulers. We can see the fulfillment of that in A.D. 70 when Titus the Roman destroyed that city and took them into captivity. We can look at the Colosseum in Rome. It was Jewish slave labor that built it.

Now let us notice something wonderful here. "The stone which the builders rejected is become the head of the corner." This is like a two-in-one parable of the vineyard and the stone. Christ was a stumbling stone and a rock of offense to the religious rulers, but many of the people turned to Him and He became the headstone of the corner. This will ultimately be fulfilled in the future when He comes again to the earth. We find this described in Zechariah 4:7 "Who art thou, O great mountain? before Zerubbabel thou shalt become a plain: and he shall bring forth the headstone thereof with shoutings, crying, Grace, grace unto it."

The religious rulers would have taken the Lord Jesus at this time and executed Him, but they were afraid of the people, you see. This parable of the vineyard set off a verbal war, and they send further delegations to Him.

QUESTION OF TAXES

And they send unto him certain of the Pharisees and of the Herodians, to catch him in his words.

And when they were come, they say unto him, Master, we know that thou art true, and carest for no man: for thou regardest not the person of men, but teachest the way of God in truth: Is it lawful to give tribute to Caesar, or not?

Shall we give, or shall we not give? But he, knowing their hypocrisy, said unto them, Why tempt ye me? bring me a penny, that I may see it [Mark 12:13–15].

Their question is a masterpiece. They flattered Him, but He called them hypocrites. He didn't accept their flattery. (By the way, He did accept what Nicodemus had said to Him because he was sincere.) My, but they were hypocrites!

Why did He ask them for a penny? He is going to use their own coin, it is true, but I think that He didn't have one Himself. Just think of that. The Lord of Glory was in this world and He didn't have a dime in His pocket, friend. Can you imagine that? How wonderful He was! He didn't have a coin, and He didn't have a lot of credit cards in His pocket either. So He just asked them for a coin, and they gave Him one.

And they brought it. And he saith unto them, Whose is this image and superscription? And they said unto him, Caesar's.

And Jesus answering said unto them, Render to Caesar the things that are Caesar's, and to God the things that are God's. And they marvelled at him [Mark 12:16–17].

They gave Him a coin, and He asked them the question. You see, if He had answered them that they were to pay tribute to Caesar, then that would have meant that He put Caesar ahead of Moses and ahead of the Messiah. And if He said they were not to pay tribute, He would have been guilty of insurrection against Caesar. They thought they had Him in a trap, but they didn't have Him at all. They had to marvel at His answer.

His answer reveals that a child of God has a twofold responsibility and, in fact, maybe even more than twofold. Someone told me some time ago that his father was in the hospital and his mother was sick but that he had some money set aside as a church contribution. When I inquired further, he said his parents were really in dire need and would have to accept charity if he didn't help them. So I told him that his responsibility was to them. We get some strange, pious notions today.

We do have a responsibility to our government. When I see my income tax, sometimes I think I have too much responsibility. It pinches and hurts me when I see the way some of our senators are living and when I see the corruption that is taking place in all areas of government today. I must confess that then I resent paying the income tax. But that does not mean that I ought not to pay some. We have a definite responsibility to government.

Also, we have a responsibility to our loved ones. We have a responsibility to our church. I have a responsibility to you, today, to give the Word of God to you. We all have our responsibilities, and that is what the Lord is saying. You have a responsibility to Caesar. Discharge it. But that doesn't relieve you of your responsibility to God. My, what a marvellous incident!

Actually, He takes this incident and turns it into a parable. "Give me a coin." With that coin, He illustrated a great truth. The coin has two sides. These are two areas of life in which we have a responsibility. Man has both an earthly or physical and a heavenly or spiritual obligation. Citizens of heaven pay taxes down here. Pilgrims down here should deposit eternal wealth in heaven. So you see how He silenced these Herodians who wanted to put the house of Herod into power.

Then come unto him the Sadducees, which say there is no resurrection; and they asked him, saying,

Master, Moses wrote unto us, If a man's brother die, and leave his wife behind him, and leave no children, that his brother should take his wife, and raise up seed unto his brother [Mark 12:18–19].

The Sadducees, you will remember, were the liberals of the day. They denied the supernatural. What they stated was accurate, by the way. They referred to the law of the kinsman-redeemer which is illustrated in the Book of Ruth. They knew what the Scripture said.

Now there were seven brethren: and the first took a wife, and dying left no seed.

And the second took her, and died, neither left he any seed: and the third likewise.

And the seven had her, and left no seed: last of all the woman died also [Mark 12:20–22].

This is a ridiculous illustration, isn't it? Well, it could be duplicated today in Hollywood or in our contemporary society perhaps, but it is ridiculous. So their question is:

In the resurrection therefore, when they shall rise, whose wife shall she be of them? for the seven had her to wife.

And Jesus answering said unto them, Do ye not therefore err, because ye know not the scriptures, neither the power of God? [Mark 12:23–24].

I would say that this is the difficulty today with those who are so critical of the Scriptures—they do not know the Scriptures nor the power of God. I notice that right now there is a promotion to cut down the population explosion and some folk say this is contrary to the Bible. God said to Adam, "Be fruitful and multiply." It is true that God did say that to Adam, but He didn't say that to the "Adamses" today. He wasn't talking to this present generation. If you and your spouse were the only couple on earth, I imagine that is what He would say to you. He did repeat it again to Noah when Noah was very much alone with his family and there was no one else on earth. But He didn't repeat that for us today. This is not even stated for Christians to do. It shows a woeful ignorance of the Bible; yet today such people spout off about the Bible when they should not be heard.

The Lord told the Sadducees that they were ignorant of two things: (1) They did not know the Scriptures and (2) they did not know the power of God.

For when they shall rise from the dead, they neither marry, nor are given in marriage; but are as the angels which are in heaven [Mark 12:25].

This doesn't mean that a man and a woman who were together down here can't be together in heaven. They won't be together as man and wife. They are not establishing a home up there, nor are they raising children. That's the thing that He's saying to them here.

And as touching the dead, that they rise: have ye not read in the book of Moses, how in the bush God spake unto him, saying, I am the God of Abraham, and the God of Isaac, and the God of Jacob?

He is not the God of the dead, but the God of the living: ye therefore do greatly err [Mark 12:26–27].

They do not know the power of God. Abraham is not dead; Isaac is not dead, Jacob is not dead. Their bodies were buried there in Hebron, but they are not dead. They have gone to be with Him, and that is where Christians are today that die in the Lord, friend. He is devastating in His answers to these religious rulers. Now we have another person coming to our Lord, after hearing the discussion with the Sadducees.

THE GREAT COMMANDMENT

And one of the scribes came, and having heard them reasoning together, and perceiving that he had answered them well, asked him, Which is the first commandment of all?

And Jesus answered him, The first of all the commandments is, Hear, O Israel; The Lord our God is one Lord [Mark 12:28–29].

This is a quotation from Deuteronomy 6:4. It is not one of the Ten Commandments, but it is the greatest doctrinal statement in the Old Testament. Literally it should read, "Jehovah our Elohim [plural] is one Jehovah." Israel was to witness to a world of polytheism and idolatry concerning the unity of the Godhead. The church is to witness to a world of atheism and unitarianism concerning the Trinity.

And thou shalt love the Lord thy God with all thy heart, and with all thy soul, and with all thy mind, and with all thy strength: this is the first commandment [Mark 12:30].

By the way, do you keep this commandment, my friend? If you say that you don't need Christ as a Savior, that you obey God, then I ask you this question, "Do you love God with all your heart and mind and soul?" If you don't, then you are breaking His commandment and you need a Savior. I *know* I need a Savior. I don't measure up here. I wish I did. I love Him but not as I should.

And the second is like, namely this, Thou shalt love thy neighbor as thyself. There is none other commandment greater than these [Mark 12:31].

Now, if you can measure up here, maybe you could apply for salvation on your own merit. Until you do you need a Savior.

And the scribe said unto him, Well, Master, thou hast said the truth: for there is one God; and there is none other but he:

And to love him with all the heart, and with all the understanding, and with all the soul, and with all the strength, and to love his neighbour as himself, is more than all whole burnt offerings and sacrifices.

And when Jesus saw that he answered discreetly, he said unto him, Thou art not far from the kingdom of God. And no man after that durst ask him any question [Mark 12:32–34].

What the scribe said is certainly true. To love God and to love our neighbor is more than all offerings and sacrifices. Friend, may I say again, if you don't measure up to loving God with all your heart and understanding and soul and strength and to loving your neighbor as yourself, then you need a Savior. Turn to Him!

Now this ended the question period as far as men asking Jesus questions was concerned. The enemy could not trap Him. Now Jesus is going to do the questioning.

THE MESSIAH

And Jesus answered and said, while he taught in the temple, How say the scribes that Christ is the son of David?

For David himself said by the Holy Ghost, The LORD said to my Lord, Sit thou on my right hand, till I make thine enemies thy footstool.

David therefore himself calleth him Lord; and whence is he then his son? And the common people heard him gladly [Mark 12:35–37].

Right here Jesus is teaching His own virgin birth. How could David, in Psalm 110 where he is speaking of a future descendant of his, call his own great-great-great-great-grandson his Lord? Well, the only way he can call him his Lord is for Him to be The LORD, friend. The only way He can be The LORD is to be more than David's son. He must be virgin born to be the Son of God. This is a great thought that our Lord is teaching here.

Notice also that here Jesus definitely ascribes Psalm 110 to David. He says that David wrote this psalm by the Holy Spirit. And Jesus says that this psalm is speaking concerning Him, the Messiah.

And he said unto them in his doctrine, Beware of the scribes, which love to go in long clothing, and love salutations in the marketplaces,

And the chief seats in the synagogues, and the uppermost rooms at feasts:

Which devour widows' houses, and for a pretence make long prayers: these shall receive greater damnation [Mark 12:38–40].

Jesus is teaching that privilege creates responsibility. He denounces the scribes because their lives contradicted the Scriptures they taught. Their judgment will be more severe than those who have not heard the Scriptures.

THE WIDOW'S MITE

The final incident in this chapter shows Jesus doing an audacious thing that only God should do. He watched how the people gave.

And Jesus sat over against the treasury, and beheld how the people cast money into the treasury: and many that were rich cast in much [Mark 12:41].

He has the authority today to stand over the taking of the offering in your church or whenever you are asked to give to some cause; that is, for God's work. He's there to watch you, friend. He doesn't watch what you give. He watches how much you keep for yourself.

And there came a certain poor widow, and she threw in two mites, which make a farthing [Mark 12:42].

He had noted that the rich cast in much. They were the big givers. Oh, my, how we love the big givers. The rich gave generously. But He didn't commend that. He watched that widow, and she gave two mites. Compared to the wealth of that temple, friend, what she gave wasn't worth a snap of your fingers. But do you know what He did? He took those two mites, and He just kissed them into the coin and the gold of heaven and made them more valuable than anything any rich man ever gave. Do you know why? Because He saw that she kept nothing for herself but gave all to Him. Her love and devotion were in the gift. I tell you, that is the way He measures.

Some folk ask whether they should give a tenth to God. My friend, how much do you keep for yourself? It's not how much you give to Him. You're not required to give a certain amount or a certain percentage. The question is, how much do you really love Him? The Lord is the One who watches how people give. It's not what they put in. The widow didn't give anything of great value, friend. I doubt that the treasurer paid much attention to it. But the Lord takes the two coppers of the widow and exchanges them for the gold of heaven.

CHAPTER 13

THEME: *Olivet Discourse; parable of the fig tree; parable of the man on a trip*

Again in this chapter we will find that there are no miracles, but there is a great deal of action. Mark's gospel is a gospel of action and has placed much emphasis on miracles. But in this chapter the action is *future* action. The action really hasn't come to a standstill, but it is still future. It records the eschatological events which will end this age. The catastrophic events of the Great Tribulation are given, and the second coming of Christ is graphically described. This is action geared to the divine power, and that, my friend, is greater than atomic power.

The Olivet Discourse, which we find in this chapter, is a parallel account with Matthew. It is much briefer here than in Matthew; in fact, it is an abridged edition. This has been generally true of Mark, except in some notable instances where he gives the longest account of an incident. In general, his policy is to abbreviate everything and give rapid action.

This is my outline of the chapter:

1. Presentation of questions by disciples to Jesus on top of the Mount of Olives (vv. 1–4);
2. Panorama of this age (vv. 5–7);
3. Persecution preceding the Great Tribulation (vv. 8–13);
4. Prophecy of the Great Tribulation (vv. 14–23);
5. Proclamation of the second coming of Christ (vv. 24–27);
6. Parable of the fig tree (vv. 28–33);
7. Program for God's people (vv. 34–37).

There are a lot of "P's" in that pod, don't you think? That's what we have in this chapter before us.

OLIVET DISCOURSE

And as he went out of the temple, one of his disciples saith unto him, Master, see what manner of stones and what buildings are here! [Mark 13:1].

Now here, I think, is an example of how there can be a misunderstanding of a passage of Scripture. One naturally asks the question, "What's back of all this?" We have no indication why the disciples should make such a statement. Actually, we must go back to Matthew 23:38 to find out. Jesus had pronounced a coming desolation upon the temple. The disciples were puzzled because there was a grandeur and a glory about the temple and the surrounding buildings. They wanted to be sure that He noted it. So one of them said, "Master, see what manner of stones and what buildings are here!"

And Jesus answering said unto him, Seest thou these great buildings? there shall not be left one stone upon another, that shall not be thrown down [Mark 13:2].

He asks them a question. They had asked Him to see the buildings because they wanted to make sure that He hadn't missed them. Now He asks them, "Do you really see them?"

Jesus is teaching a great spiritual lesson here. During the last few years of my pastorate in downtown Los Angeles, a forty-two story building went up right next door to the church. Across the way, within a block and a half is a forty-story building, two fifty-story buildings within a block of us, and diagonally across the street from us will be a sixty-story building. Down the street from us they plan the greatest downtown shopping area in America. There will be several skyscrapers, a big shopping mall, a great department store, two hotels. My friend, we could ask that question today. Don't you see all these beautiful buildings? They are brand new, and they are beautiful. But what do we really see? We see their beauty, strength, stability, and permanence. It looks to me as if they are here for a long time unless a bad earthquake comes along. Really, these buildings are temporary. They are passing away. A true perspective would allow us to see that not one stone is going to be left upon another. Actually, these are of steel and concrete but still they are all coming down. Paul stated the spiritual truth this way: "While we look not at the things which are seen, but at the things which are not seen: for the things which are seen are temporal; but the things which are not seen are eternal" (2 Cor. 4:18).

My friend, that is the great truth. Did you know that Nebuchadnezzar walked through great Babylon in his day and saw all the glory of Babylon. As he walked through, he said, "Is not this great Babylon that I built?" Have you seen a picture of the ruins of Babylon today? Nothing to brag about there. It's all gone, friend; the glory has disappeared. And the skyscrapers of Los Angeles are all coming down, too, by the way. He says it will all come down. These things are passing away.

My friend, do you see the things that are eternal?

And as he sat upon the mount of Olives over against the temple, Peter and James and John and Andrew asked him privately,

Tell us, when shall these things be? and what shall be the sign when all these things shall be fulfilled? [Mark 13:3–4].

Mark is always putting in a little something that we don't get in the other Gospels. We wouldn't have known it was these four men who actually were delegated as the committee who waited on Jesus with the questions, but here they are named. Remember, this is Peter's gospel. Peter told Mark that these four men were in the group that asked Him privately.

Mark states two of the questions. Matthew states three questions that they asked. Luke gives part of the answer. When we put it all together, we find that Matthew records all three questions put to our Lord by the disciples: (1) ". . . Tell us, when shall these things be?" This refers to when one stone will not be left on another, and Luke gives our Lord's answer to this question; (2) "and what shall be the sign of thy coming, and" (3) what shall be the sign "of the end of the world?" (Matt. 24:3). Matthew and Mark give our Lord's answer to the last two questions. Matthew has it in a great deal more detail than Mark, but we will look at Mark's emphasis. Remember that he is writing to the Romans, and he is going to call attention to that which reveals power and action and drama.

And Jesus answering them began to say, Take heed lest any man deceive you:

For many shall come in my name, saying, I am Christ; and shall deceive many [Mark 13:5–6].

We find this is a constant warning—a warning against false Christs. Some may think that this is not a danger today. I think it is very pertinent right now. For example, the Christ of liberalism is an antichrist—he is not the real Christ! Some of you may think that they preach the Christ of the Bible. They do not. According to their statements, the Christ they preach was not virgin born, never performed a miracle, did not shed his blood for the sins of the world, was not raised bodily from the grave, did not ascend into heaven, and is not coming again bodily. Do you know there is no Jesus like that in the Bible? The Jesus of the Bible was virgin born and did perform miracles and did shed His blood for the sins of the world. He was raised bodily from the grave and ascended into heaven and is coming again. That is what the Bible says, and the Bible contains the only documents of an historical nature concerning Him. The Bible claims all these great cardinal facts of the faith. Evidently the liberal is talking about another Christ, another Jesus. And any other Christ, friend, is antichrist. Listen to the apostle John: "Little children, it is the last time: and as ye have heard that antichrist shall come, even now are there many antichrists; whereby we know that it is the last time" (1 John 2:18).

There are a lot of antichrists. I have called your attention to the one of liberalism, but there are a lot of phonies around today claiming to be Christ. I understand that a founder of a religion here in Southern California is claiming today that he can do what Christ could not do. One of the Beatles claimed that their group was more popular than Christ and that they were able to do more than He was able to do for our day. There are a lot of antichrists around. Our Lord did well to warn us about that.

And when ye shall hear of wars and rumours of wars, be ye not troubled: for such things must needs be; but the end shall not be yet [Mark 13:7].

And then wars, like false Christs, characterize the whole age. No believer should be disturbed by wars. They are not the sign of the end of the age. Neither antichrists nor wars indicate that we are at the end of the age. When I say "antichrists" I am not referring to *the* Antichrist, although all of these false Christs are pointing to him, the final Antichrist.

For nation shall rise against nation, and kingdom against kingdom: and there shall be earthquakes in divers places, and there shall be famines and troubles: these are the beginnings of sorrows [Mark 13:8].

Today man feels he is so civilized because he has so many gadgets, and he thinks he is making the world such a wonderful place. Then all of a sudden he discovers that he is polluting the earth and that he is going to make it uninhabitable. And before long, unless he cuts down the population explosion, he's going to starve to death. The Bible says, friend, that troubles and famines would come. It is interesting that this Book, which men have despised, is so accurate about it all. A few years ago men thought science would solve the problems of the world. Now we know it has made problems that neither science nor the world can solve.

Even Bernard Shaw had to say, "The science to which I pinned my faith has failed, and you are beholding an atheist who has lost his faith." What a tragedy! May I say to you, these are the things that characterize the end of the age.

But take heed to yourselves: for they shall deliver you up to councils; and in the synagogues ye shall be beaten: and ye shall be brought before rulers and kings for my sake, for a testimony against them.

And the gospel must first be published among all nations [Mark 13:9–10].

Now I don't think He's talking about the church here. By "gospel" He means the gospel of the kingdom. This is also the gospel of grace. There are not two gospels. The gospel of the kingdom is actually a facet of the gospel of grace. All salvation is by the grace of God, and God has never had but one way to save sinners and that is by the blood of Jesus Christ. But the gospel of the kingdom will emphasize "Repent for the kingdom of heaven is at hand." In other words, "He is coming." And when they say it in that day, it will be in the Great Tribulation Period, and it will be accurate.

But when they shall lead you, and deliver you up, take no thought beforehand what ye shall speak, neither do ye premeditate: but whatsoever shall be given you in that hour, that speak ye: for it is not ye that speak, but the Holy Ghost [Mark 13:11].

This is no verse for a lazy preacher to use as an excuse for not preparing a sermon. I remember a friend of mine down in Texas told me that he was in Temple, Texas, one morning. He had changed trains there as he was going out to a little town to preach. Another preacher there was watching him and saw him walking up and down and going over his notes for his sermon. "Are you a preacher?" my friend was asked.

"Yes."

"What are you doing?"

"I'm going over my notes for my sermon."

"You mean that you prepare your sermon beforehand?"

"Of course, don't you?"

"No, I don't. I wait until I get up there and the Spirit of God gives me a message."

"Well, suppose the Spirit of God doesn't give you the message immediately. What do you do then?"

"Oh, I just mess around until He does."

Friend, I'm afraid there is a lot of messing around today. This verse is not talking about anything like that. This refers to the day when the 144,000 of the nation Israel are witnesses. This is a message for them in that day. This is not an excuse for you and me not to prepare our Sunday school lesson.

Now the brother shall betray the brother to death, and the father the son; and children shall rise up against their parents, and shall cause them to be put to death [Mark 13:12].

There shall be base betrayal.

And ye shall be hated of all men for my name's sake: but he that shall endure unto the end, the same shall be saved [Mark 13:13].

There will be worldwide anti-Semitism in that day. But when God puts His seal upon them in that day, they are going to make it through to the end.

And now we come to a very dramatic part.

But when ye shall see the abomination of desolation, spoken of by Daniel the prophet, standing where it ought not, (let him that readeth understand,) then let them that be in Judaea flee to the mountains [Mark 13:14].

This is the beginning of the Great Tribulation. The first three and a half years of it are comparatively quiet; it is the false peace of the Antichrist. Then, in the midst of it, there appears this "abomination of desolation" spoken of by Daniel the prophet. It will stand where it ought not, that is, in the Holy Place. You see if Mark had said to the Romans that the abomination of desolation would stand in the Holy Place, they would have said, "Where is that?" He says it will stand where it shouldn't stand. That's more understandable to many of us too. We need to understand that the Holy Place was given only to the nation Israel. It was a specific place in the temple on earth. The church has no Holy Place.

And let him that is on the housetop not go down into the house, neither enter therein, to take any thing out of his house:

And let him that is in the field not turn back again for to take up his garment [Mark 13:15–16].

Note the urgency. They are not to go back and get their belongings but to start running.

But woe to them that are with child, and to them that give suck in those days!

And pray ye that your flight be not in the winter [Mark 13:17–18].

This is the beginning of the Great Tribulation.

For in those days shall be affliction, such as was not from the beginning of the creation which God created unto this time, neither shall be.

And except that the Lord had shortened those days, no flesh should be saved: but for the elect's sake, whom he hath chosen, he hath shortened the days.

And then if any man shall say to you, Lo, here is Christ; or, lo, he is there; believe him not [Mark 13:19–21].

Those will be terrible days.

For false Christs and false prophets shall rise, and shall shew signs and wonders, to seduce, if it were possible, even the elect.

But take ye heed: behold, I have foretold you all things [Mark 13:22–23].

False Christs and false prophets will perform genuine wonders by the power of Satan.

The second coming of Christ is introduced by the darkening of the universe and a universal display of heavenly fireworks, a fulfillment of Joel 2:28–32.

But in those days, after that tribulation, the sun shall be darkened, and the moon shall not give her light,

And the stars of heaven shall fall, and the powers that are in heaven shall be shaken.

And then shall they see the Son of man coming in the clouds with great power and glory [Mark 13:24–26].

Those are not rain clouds that He is describing. They are the glory clouds, the *shekinah* glory. I believe that is the sign of the Son of Man in heaven.

And then shall he send his angels, and shall gather together his elect from the four winds, from the uttermost part of the earth to the uttermost part of heaven [Mark 13:27].

This is not the Rapture of the church. Christ will not send angels to gather out His own, but they will be caught up to meet Him in the air (see 1 Thess. 4:13–18). Rather, this section is describing events which will take place after the Tribulation (see v. 24) when Christ will return to the earth in glory and judgment.

PARABLE OF THE FIG TREE

Now learn a parable of the fig tree; When her branch is yet tender, and putteth forth leaves, ye know that summer is near:

So ye in like manner, when ye shall see these things come to pass, know that it is nigh, even at the doors [Mark 13:28–29].

The fig tree speaks of the nation Israel. I recognize that there is disagreement here, and I don't mind folk disagreeing with me and thinking the fig tree means something else. But I personally believe there is Scripture to make it clear. After all, the nation Israel is God's timepiece. He says we are to look to the fig tree. God's timepiece is not G-R-U-E-N, nor is it B-U-L-O-V-A; God's timepiece is I-S-R-A-E-L.

Verily I say unto you, that this generation shall not pass, till all these things be done [Mark 13:30].

"This generation" could refer to the race of Israel. It would then teach the indestructibility of this people. Or "this generation" could refer to a generation of people and their total life span. In that case it would mean that those who saw the beginning of these events would see the conclusion of them also. The latter is the more likely meaning, it seems to me.

The emphasis appears to be on the rapidity in which these events transpire rather than upon the permanence of the nation Israel. However, both facts are sustained by Scripture.

Heaven and earth shall pass away: but my words shall not pass away.

But of that day and that hour knoweth no man, no, not the angels which are in heaven, neither the Son, but the Father [Mark 13:31–32].

This verse is admittedly difficult. If Jesus is God, it is difficult to account for this lack of omniscience. "Neither the Son" is added by Mark (cf. Matt. 24:36). Mark presents Jesus as "the servant, and the servant knoweth not what his Lord doeth." The servant character of Jesus represents His most typical and true humanity. He "took upon him the form of a servant." When He became a man, He limited Himself in order to be made like us. He was not omnipresent when He became man. Martha rebuked Jesus, "Lord, if thou hadst been here, my brother had not died." It is reasonable to assume that there was a self-limitation relative to His omniscience.

Take ye heed, watch and pray: for ye know not when the time is [Mark 13:33].

The proper attitude of God's people in all ages as they face the prophetic future is one of watching and praying.

PARABLE OF THE MAN ON A TRIP

For the Son of man is as a man taking a far journey, who left his house, and gave authority to his servants, and to every man his work, and commanded the porter to watch.

Watch ye therefore: for ye know not when the master of the house cometh, at even, or at midnight, or at the cock-crowing, or in the morning:

Lest coming suddenly he find you sleeping.

And what I say unto you I say unto all, Watch [Mark 13:34–37].

This parable concludes Mark's account of the Olivet Discourse. Jesus applied this parable to Himself in relationship to His second coming. There is a responsibility of God's people in view of the fact that Jesus will demand a report at His return. Added to praying and watching is the task of working.

This instruction is for you and me today also, although the watching is different. One can watch in anxiety and one can watch in fear. But the child of God is to be watching, looking for that blessed hope and the glorious appearing. That is joyful anticipation.

CHAPTER 14

THEME: *Plot to put Jesus to death; Jesus at supper in Bethany; Judas bargains to betray Jesus; the Passover; the garden of Gethsemane; the arrest of Jesus; the trial of Jesus*

Now, friend, we come to the longest chapter in the Gospel of Mark; it has seventy-two verses. We are certainly in a chapter of action now. However, Jesus is no longer the one performing the action. He is being acted upon by others—both friends and enemies. The time has come for Him to be delivered up. His earthly ministry is concluded in the fulfillment of prophecy. "He is brought as a lamb to the slaughter . . ." (Isa. 53:7). He is delivering Himself into the hands of men. Mary anoints Him, Judas betrays Him, Peter denies Him, and the Sanhedrin arrests Him. He delivers Himself into the will of the Father.

As we come into the shadow of the cross, the reverent heart realizes we are on holy ground. There are depths that have not been plumbed and heights that have not been scaled. The action of this moment involves the anguish and agony of His soul. His hour has come! Do you remember that at the wedding of Cana He had said to His mother, "mine hour is not yet come" (John 2:4)? But now it has come!

In this chapter and the one that follows there is a strange agreement of heaven and hell. Light and darkness are going together in the same direction. Righteousness and sin are going to the cross, and God and Satan have decided that Jesus shall be crucified. And there are individual decisions converging upon the cross—as there are even to this day.

Here is my outline of the chapter:

1. Chief priests and scribes plot to kill Jesus (vv. 1–2).
2. Mary of Bethany pours ointment upon the head of Jesus (vv. 3–9).
3. Judas plans to betray Jesus (vv.10–11).
4. Jesus prepares for last Passover and first Lord's Supper (vv. 12–25).
5. Peter pledges his allegiance (vv. 26–31).
6. Jesus prays in Garden of Gethsemane (vv. 32–42).
7. Jesus placed under arrest (vv. 43–52).
8. Jesus put on trial before the Sanhedrin (vv. 53–65).
9. Peter protests that he does not know Jesus (vv. 66–72).

PLOT TO PUT JESUS TO DEATH

After two days was the feast of the passover, and of unleavened bread: and the chief priests and the scribes sought how they might take him by craft, and put him to death.

But they said, Not on the feast day, lest there be an uproar of the people [Mark 14:1–2].

The Passover was observed on the fourteenth day of the first month which is the Jewish month Nisan and corresponds to our April. "In the fourteenth day of the first month at even is the LORD'S passover" (Lev. 23:5). Then the Feast of Unleavened Bread was on the fifteenth day of the same month, and it continued for seven days thereafter. "And on the fifteenth day of the same month is the feast of unleavened bread unto the LORD: seven days ye must eat unleavened bread" (Lev. 23:6). It was, I think, the intention of these eleven rulers to take Jesus at the end of the Passover season, after the crowds had left Jerusalem, and then put Him to death.

They decided they would not do it on the feast day—that is, during the Passover season, which is the Feast of Unleavened Bread and which extended for seven days. You see, at the end of that seven days the people would begin to leave Jerusalem and then they would reach out and put their hands upon Him. The reason they didn't want to touch Him during the feast days was that they feared an uproar or a riot. The crowds were in Jerusalem for the feast and the people held Jesus in high esteem. The common people heard Him gladly. He fed and healed them.

JESUS AT SUPPER IN BETHANY

And being in Bethany in the house of Simon the leper, as he sat at meat, there came a woman having an alabaster box of ointment of spikenard very precious; and she brake the box, and poured it on his head [Mark 14:3].

Here is a lovely thing. John's gospel places this incident six days before the Passover (see John 12:1). Then have Matthew and Mark erred in placing this incident just before the Passover? No. We must remember that neither Matthew nor Mark is attempting to give a chronological order. Their obvious purpose is to place this lovely incident next to the dark deed of Judas—that is, the plot to betray Jesus. They are portraying a vivid contrast and conflict of light and darkness, and that is the reason they are brought together like this. Matthew and Mark do not attempt to give a chronological biography of Christ. Both friend and foe are moving toward the cross but by different routes. Mary of Bethany is coming the way of light and love. Judas is moved by foul and dark motives. And, by the way, it is John who tells us that this woman was Mary, the sister of Martha and Lazarus (see John 12:3).

And there were some that had indignation within themselves, and said, Why was this waste of the ointment made?

For it might have been sold for more than three hundred pence, and have been given to the poor. And they murmured against her [Mark 14:4–5].

John also tells us in his account that it was Judas who led in the defection and caused the others to follow along. The pious suggestion that the proceeds be used for charitable purposes has covered up the real reason. Judas wanted to appropriate it for his own selfish ends. Sad to say, sometimes we find the same sort of thing today in Christian work. If they had given the money to Judas, where do you think it would have gone?

And Jesus said, Let her alone; why trouble ye her? she hath wrought a good work on me.

For ye have the poor with you always, and whensoever ye will ye may do them good: but me ye have not always [Mark 14:6–7].

If they were sincere, there would be many opportunities to help the poor, and they could avail themselves of those opportunities. The presence of the poor is one of the characteristics of this age. There will be no elimination of poverty until Jesus comes. This idea today that you can eliminate poverty by handing out dollars is a big mistake. There are so many other things that are wrong in the world that must be corrected first.

She hath done what she could: she is come aforehand to anoint my body to the burying.

Verily I say unto you, Wheresoever this gospel shall be preached throughout the whole world, this also that she hath done shall be spoken of for a memorial of her [Mark 14:8–9].

She had done what she could. That is all that God has ever asked of any person to do. But the important thing to notice here is that Mary had a spiritual discernment which was sadly lacking even in the apostles at this particular time. She anointed His body for the burial. Just think of it. This frail woman stood on the fringe of the events which were leading to the cross, and she let the Lord Jesus know that she understood. None of the apostles sensed this, but she did. The fragrance of the box of ointment she broke that day has been borne across the centuries by the Holy Spirit unto our day. It still fills hearts with its sweetness even at the present hour. Here in the shadow of His suffering there was one who understood.

It is so easy to read this, and it may become meaningless to us. Have any of us broken our alabaster box upon Jesus so that there might be a fragrance in our lives and it might be a blessing to others? I think that maybe if some broke their alabaster boxes of ointment it would be to help the poor. I'm wondering today if those who are God's people are really doing what they could do.

Now notice that right next to this lovely thing she did, the light of it and the love of it, we have the plan of Judas to betray our Lord.

JUDAS BARGAINS TO BETRAY JESUS

And Judas Iscariot, one of the twelve, went unto the chief priests, to betray him unto them.

And when they heard it, they were glad, and promised to give him money. And he sought how he might conveniently betray him [Mark 14:10–11].

Here we see Judas in his act of darkness. This man is now plotting to put Jesus to death. The plot was to wait for a convenient time to betray Him. But, you see, the Lord upset the apple cart. We find in the Gospel of John that the Lord said to Judas, ". . . That thou doest, do quickly" (John 13:27). So Judas must have rushed out to the Pharisees and said, "You'd better go get Him now because our plot has been discovered. He told me to do quickly that which I planned to do. He may leave town." So they got the officers immediately, and they went out to arrest Him.

THE PASSOVER

Going back to the Gospel of Mark, we find the next thing mentioned is our Lord preparing for the Passover.

And the first day of unleavened bread, when they killed the passover, his disciples said unto him, Where wilt thou that we go and prepare that thou mayest eat the passover? [Mark 14:12].

The Passover was to be eaten with unleavened bread, and then there were seven days of unleavened bread to follow (Exod. 12:14–20). On one occasion I was in Israel at the time of the Passover, and I was staying in a hotel in Haifa. We had unleavened bread for seven days, and I want to tell you, friend, I got pretty tired of that bread. The rest of the food was delicious, but that bread got very monotonous.

Now the disciples here were meticulous in following the letter of the Mosaic Law. They wanted to know where they were going to eat the Passover. They were going to do it right. In a few hours Jesus was to fulfill the meaning of the Passover.

And he sendeth forth two of his disciples, and saith unto them, Go ye into the city, and there shall meet you a man bearing a pitcher of water: follow him.

And wheresoever he shall go in, say ye to the goodman of the house, The Master saith, Where is the guestchamber, where I shall eat the passover with my disciples? [Mark 14:13–14].

Now again, I think this reveals the human side of our Lord, and it also reveals the fact that there were those who loved Him at this time and were preparing the Passover for Him. It also reveals the fact that our Lord was the omniscient God. Apparently the "goodman of the house" was some unnamed follower of the Lord. There is no reason to doubt that there had been a previous offer of the guest room to Jesus. I'm of the opinion that sometime during those three years of His public ministry this man had come to the Lord Jesus and had offered this room. I think he told Jesus, "Now, when You come up to Jerusalem to the Passover, I have this room for You and it will be prepared just for You." I tell you, this was a wonderful service which he performed. There are many things which we can do for the Lord Jesus, and this is what this man did.

And he will shew you a large upper room furnished and prepared: there make ready for us.

And his disciples went forth, and came into the city, and found as he had said unto them: and they made ready the passover [Mark 14:15–16].

Notice that Jesus celebrated the Passover in a borrowed room. Obviously the room had been made ready for Jesus; so I think there had been a previous commitment on this. I don't think that the host of this occasion should be blamed for not being there to wash the feet of the disciples, either. It was to be a private Passover. The Lord has said, "I shall eat the passover with my disciples" (v. 14). It would be private, and the host would not interfere.

You will recall that we noted a former experience like this when Jesus sent the disciples for a donkey for Him to ride into Jerusalem. They found it as He said they would. I think there had been a previous arrangement made for the little donkey. I think our Lord was making arrangements as He went along.

And in the evening he cometh with the twelve [Mark 14:17].

Notice that He came in the evening. The Passover begins at sundown, and I think He came in under cover of darkness. He is not going to force their hand until He is ready, but at the proper time He will deliver Himself into their hands and they will crucify Him. It will not be according to *their* schedule but according to *His* schedule, by the way. This is a marvelous thing.

This was a lovely occasion. He ate the Passover with them in a leisurely and informal way. We've made our observance of the Lord's Supper on Sunday mornings a very formal service. You'll find that He ate the Passover supper here with them, and the next meal that He had with them was breakfast on the shores of the Sea of Galilee after His resurrection. I think this time was a wonderful time of fellowship.

I personally do not criticize church dinners in and of themselves. I think they can serve a wonderful purpose, but the type of church dinners we have today are often not quite what they should be. It is wonderful for people to meet and have fellowship around the person of Christ. If He is not the center, and we're just having a grand old time, though we call it fellowship, we have missed the point. A church dinner should be an occasion to meet around the person of Christ. That was the purpose of this Passover feast, by the way.

And as they sat and did eat, Jesus said, Verily I say unto you, One of you which eateth with me shall betray me.

And they began to be sorrowful, and to say unto him one by one, Is it I? and another said, Is it I? [Mark 14:18–19].

All of them knew they were capable of doing it, friend. If you have not discovered that you are totally depraved, that you are not a good person but a sinner, that you are thoroughly capable of turning your back on God, you haven't discovered very much.

Unfortunately there are people in the church who don't recognize that they are sinners and are lost. And there are saved people in the church who don't realize they are capable of turning their backs on God. Each of us could ask, "Is it I?"

And he answered and said unto them, It is one of the twelve, that dippeth with me in the dish.

The Son of man indeed goeth, as it is written of him: but woe to that man by whom the Son of man is betrayed! good were it for that man if he had never been born [Mark 14:20–21].

It was Judas Iscariot who had made the decision to betray Him. The responsibility of Judas was great for he had the opportunity of being with Jesus for three years. The psalmist had written: "Yea, mine own familiar friend, in whom I trusted, which did eat of my bread, hath lifted up his heel against me" (Ps. 41:9). He pointed out Judas Iscariot, and I think that Judas Iscariot left at this particular juncture.

Jesus instituted a new feast on the dying embers of the old, the Passover feast. He reared a new monument, not a monument of brass or marble but one that takes these elements that perish so easily, bread and wine. The Passover had looked forward to His coming as the Passover Lamb, and now the Lord's Supper looks back to His death. The bread speaks of His *body* that was broken. (Remember that not a *bone* in His body was broken.)

And as they did eat, Jesus took bread,and blessed, and brake it, and gave to them, and said, Take, eat: this is my body.

And he took the cup, and when he had given thanks, he gave it to them: and they all drank of it.

And he said unto them, This is my blood of the new testament, which is shed for many.

Verily I say unto you, I will drink no more of the fruit of the vine, until that day that I drink it new in the kingdom of God [Mark 14:22–25].

There are several things here that I think are interesting and important. The Passover cup went around seven times during the Passover feast. During that time they would sing one of the great Hallel Psalms. Apparently it was the seventh time around when He did not drink but instituted the Lord's Supper with them. The Lord's Supper now looks back to what He did for us on the cross more than nineteen hundred years ago.

The Passover looked forward to His coming, but the Passover will be restored for the millennial kingdom (as we learn in Ezekiel). And the reason for it, I think, is that during the Millennium there will be a remembrance of His coming; when it was first instituted, it had looked forward to His coming. I see no reason why it couldn't look forward and also look backward. And, by the way, that would bring out the real meaning of the Passover during the millennial kingdom. Paul says, ". . . For even Christ our passover is sacrificed for us" (1 Cor. 5:7).

THE GARDEN OF GETHSEMANE

And when they had sung an hymn, they went out into the mount of Olives.

And Jesus saith unto them, All ye shall be offended because of me this night: for it is written, I will smite the shepherd, and the sheep shall be scattered.

But after that I am risen, I will go before you into Galilee.

But Peter said unto him, Although all shall be offended, yet will not I.

And Jesus saith unto him, Verily I say unto thee, That this day, even in this night, before the cock crow twice, thou shalt deny me thrice.

But he spake the more vehemently, If I should die with thee, I will not deny thee in any wise. Likewise also said they all [Mark 14:26–31].

We find here first that Simon Peter pledges his allegiance. He was sincere, of course, but he did not know his own weakness. That is the problem with most of us today. We don't know our own weakness. And I personally believe that you don't find out about this in psychology. I think the only place that you can really see yourself is in the Word of God. That is the only mirror that you have.

Let me quote a little excerpt of material that is being printed by a Christian organization, which, I think, gives the wrong impression. It talks about a girl with a problem who went to her pastor. "After several talks together the pastor realized he was not equipped to help her as much as she could be helped. He referred Betty to a competent, Christian psychologist; one who as a professional counselor led Betty into a deeper understanding of the sources of her anxiety, many of them stemming from childhood experiences long since forgotten but recalled and understood under the guidance of a skilled helper. The result: a Christian teen released from the grip of emotional problems and given a new relationship with herself, others, and the Lord." May I say, that type of thing reads like Grimm's fairy stories—"They lived happily ever after."

Now, I happen to know that the Christian psychologist is no more competent to solve these problems today than the average pastor. I think we've been deluded today into believing that the Christian psychologist is able to say, "Hocus-pocus, abracadabra," and somehow or another the problems are solved.

My friend, may I say to you, none of us knows the depths of the human heart. Only the Word of God can let us see what sinners we are. That was the problem with Betty in the article; that is the problem with me, and that is the problem with you. When we recognize that, we see that anyone who truly knows the Word of God is able to help us. If we take the emphasis away from the Word of God, we can find that people get one problem solved with the help of the psychologist and come away with two more problems. Then the last estate of the man is worse than the first. Let's be very clear. The only solution to a problem is the Lord. You don't solve the problem so that you are enabled to go to the Lord. No, you go to the Lord and *He* is the chief and the great

Physician. By the way, He is the great Psychologist and He alone knows us. In the final analysis, He is the *only* One. I am insistent in saying this, as you can see, because I think it is important today for somebody to say it. We are finding that a great many today are making merchandise of the ills of folk when actually only the Word of God can solve their ills. God Himself must do it, if we'd only learn to go to Him and cast ourselves upon Him. Maybe we recognize that we have had a bad childhood—friend, we've had a bad everything! But we have a Savior who loves us, and we can go to Him. How wonderful it is to have Someone to go to.

We find the Lord Jesus now telling them that He is going before them into Galilee. He announces His resurrection. He tells them the sheep are going to be scattered but He will go on into Galilee after His resurrection. He promises to meet them there. But Simon Peter couldn't let it go at that. He declares that he will not be offended even if the others are. Here again we see that he just doesn't know what he is saying. So our Lord prepares him for what is coming. And He lets Peter know that He is going to stand by him.

My friend, the Lord will stand by you in times like this. He will be there in our most desperate and dastardly hour. He certainly was with this man Peter.

And they came to a place which was named Gethsemane: and he saith to his disciples, Sit ye here, while I shall pray.

And he taketh with him Peter and James and John, and began to be sore amazed, and to be very heavy;

And saith unto them, My soul is exceeding sorrowful unto death: tarry ye here, and watch [Mark 14:32–34].

The Garden of Gethsemane must have been a familiar spot to which they came rather frequently. Whether it is the "Garden of Gethsemane" as it is known today we do not know. I am of the opinion that it should be on the other side of the mountain—but the location is really immaterial. Since they came here rather frequently, it was a place that Judas knew. Our Lord never spent a night inside the city of Jerusalem. He went out to this place.

There are only eleven disciples now. He leaves an outer circle of eight. He takes three of them, Peter, James, and John, a step closer to Him in this hour. He went to pray. The language indicates that He faced a sore ordeal in the garden. "Began to be sore *amazed*" is actually *startled* or more intense—we would say *stunned*. It says that He was very "heavy" (lit. *distressed)*.

He faces here a travail of soul that was as great, if not greater, than the suffering of the body on the cross. Did He face the tempter again here in the garden? I think He did. I must be very frank and say that we can only stand here on the fringe. There are mysteries in the garden that we cannot understand. I think it is audacious and actually borders on the blasphemous for people to sing, "I'll go with Him through the garden." I'm sorry, friend, if you don't mind, I'll beg off. I can't go with Him through the garden. You don't know how weak and stumbling and bumbling I really am. I can't go with Him through the garden, but I will stand at the edge and watch Him pray. He asked us to watch and pray so that we enter not into temptation.

And he went forward a little, and fell on the ground, and prayed that, if it were possible, the hour might pass from him.

And he said, Abba, Father, all things are possible unto thee; take away this cup from me: nevertheless not what I will, but what thou wilt [Mark 14:35–36].

Mark says that He prayed that the hour might pass from Him. It was not *death* He dreaded but rather the *hour* of the cross—that moment when sin was to be put upon Him. He was made sin for us (see 2 Cor. 5:21). Mark makes the "hour" and the "cup" synonymous.

Listen to the writer to the Hebrews: "Who in the days of his flesh, when he had offered up prayers and supplications with strong crying and tears unto him that was able to save him from death, and was heard in that he feared; Though he were a Son, yet learned he obedience by the things which he suffered" (Heb. 5:7–8).

Now He returns to the place where He had stationed the three disciples.

And he cometh, and findeth them sleeping, and saith unto Peter, Simon, sleepest thou? couldest not thou watch one hour?

Watch ye and pray, lest ye enter into temptation. The spirit truly is ready, but the flesh is weak [Mark 14:37–38].

The three disciples were not at all alarmed. In fact, they could sleep through it all. This man, Peter, wasn't even disturbed that he was going to deny Christ. He should have been watching and praying, but he just went off to sleep. Watching and praying is the way for us to avoid temptation today, friend.

Now you'll notice that Jesus goes back and He repeats the first prayer.

And again he went away, and prayed, and spake the same words [Mark 14:39].

And the disciples went to sleep again.

And when he returned, he found them asleep again, (for their eyes were heavy,) neither wist they what to answer him [Mark 14:40].

They had no explanation for their failure. We certainly learn here that the flesh cannot be trusted.

And he cometh the third time, and saith unto them, Sleep on now, and take your rest: it is enough, the hour is come; behold, the Son of man is betrayed into the hands of sinners.

Rise up, let us go; lo, he that betrayeth me is at hand [Mark 14:41–42].

Apparently there was a lapse of time in here so that they had a brief sleep before He was arrested.

THE ARREST OF JESUS

And immediately, while he yet spake, cometh Judas, one of the twelve, and with him a great multitude with swords and staves, from the chief priests and the scribes and the elders [Mark 14:43].

Now you see that they have come out to do the thing that they said they would not do. They had said, "Not during the feast days."

And he that betrayed him had given them a token, saying, Whomsoever I shall kiss, that same is he; take him, and lead him away safely [Mark 14:44].

Here we have recorded one of the basest acts of treachery. It is foul and loathsome. Judas knew our Lord's accustomed place of retirement, and he led the enemy there.

A kiss is a badge of love and affection, but Judas used it to betray Christ. This makes his act even more dastardly and repugnant. Incidentally, we learn here that our Lord in His humanity looked no different from other men. He needed to be identified in a crowd.

And as soon as he was come, he goeth straightway to him, and saith, Master, master; and kissed him [Mark 14:45].

You will notice that Judas calls Him, "Master." He does not call Him "Lord." ". . . no man can say that Jesus is the Lord, but by the Holy Ghost" (1 Cor. 12:3).

And they laid their hands on him, and took him [Mark 14:46].

This marks the moment that Jesus was delivered into the hands of sinful men. He yields Himself now to go to the cross.

Simon Peter attempts to come to His rescue:

And one of them that stood by drew a sword, and smote a servant of the high priest, and cut off his ear.

And Jesus answered and said unto them, Are ye come out, as against a thief, with swords and with staves to take me?

I was daily with you in the temple teaching, and ye took me not: but the scriptures must be fulfilled [Mark 14:47–49].

Jesus points out that this fulfills prophecy. If these people had believed their own Scriptures, they might have hesitated or even changed their minds.

And they all forsook him, and fled [Mark 14:50].

As we suspected, it was Peter who cut off the man's ear with his sword. John also tells us that the man's name was Malchus. Simon Peter was a pretty good fisherman but a pretty sorry swordsman. He had intended to get the neck, but he missed it and got an ear.

"They all forsook him, and fled" is a fulfillment of prophecy.

Then we have this incident of a certain young man.

And there followed him a certain young man, having a linen cloth cast about his naked body; and the young men laid hold on him:

And he left the linen cloth, and fled from them naked [Mark 14:51–52].

There has always been speculation as to who this is. Some think it may have been the apostle Paul. Some think it may have been John Mark. I personally think it would be more apt to have been John Mark.

THE TRIAL OF JESUS

And they led Jesus away to the high priest: and with him were assembled all

the chief priests and the elders and the scribes [Mark 14:53].

Jesus is now brought before Caiaphas, the high priest who was acceptable to Rome. Annas, his father-in-law, was actually the high priest according to the Mosaic Law. Jesus was first brought before Annas, which John records. Some believe that Annas was the real rascal behind the plot to kill Jesus. This is a meeting of the Sanhedrin.

And Peter followed him afar off, even into the palace of the high priest: and he sat with the servants, and warmed himself at the fire [Mark 14:54].

Peter is moving toward his shameful fall. He followed afar off and then sits with the wrong crowd.

And the chief priests and all the council sought for witness against Jesus to put him to death; and found none [Mark 14:55].

The meeting of the Sanhedrin was illegal since it was at night. Their method was likewise illegal. They heard only witnesses who were against Jesus.

For many bare false witness against him, but their witness agreed not together.

And there arose certain, and bare false witness against him, saying,

We heard him say, I will destroy this temple that is made with hands, and within three days I will build another made without hands.

But neither so did their witness agree together [Mark 14:56–59].

Many were willing to bear false witness, but no two agreed. A charge had to be established in the mouth of at least two witnesses. Of course Jesus did not say that He would destroy the temple and then raise it up in three days. He said, "Destroy this temple"; that is, *you* destroy this temple, and John explains, "But he spake of the temple of his body" (John 2:21).

And the high priest stood up in the midst, and asked Jesus, saying, Answerest thou nothing? what is it which these witness against thee?

But he held his peace, and answered nothing. Again the high priest asked him, and said unto him, Art thou the Christ, the Son of the Blessed?

And Jesus said, I am: and ye shall see the Son of man sitting on the right hand of power, and coming in the clouds of heaven [Mark 14:60–62].

Jesus did not defend Himself against such obvious falsehood. Again He was fulfilling prophecy: ". . . as a sheep before her shearers is dumb, so he openeth not his mouth" (Isa. 53:7). The silence of Jesus surprised and annoyed the high priest. He wanted Jesus to answer to see if He might condemn Himself. Finally, the high priest put Him under oath. Under oath Jesus claimed to be the Messiah, the Son of God. He could make no higher claim. He added a claim that could pertain only to the Son of God: "I saw in the night visions, and, behold, one like the Son of man came with the clouds of heaven, and came to the Ancient of days, and they brought him near before him. And there was given him dominion, and glory, and a kingdom, that all people, nations, and languages, should serve him: his dominion is an everlasting dominion, which shall not pass away, and his kingdom that which shall not be destroyed" (Dan. 7:13–14).

The high priest understood what He said and all the implications of it. He displayed his intense emotion by tearing his garment. In doing this, he broke the Mosaic Law, as the garment of the high priest was not to be torn.

Then the high priest rent his clothes, and saith, What need we any further witnesses?

Ye have heard the blasphemy: what think ye? And they all condemned him to be guilty of death.

And some began to spit on him, and to cover his face, and to buffet him, and to say unto him, Prophesy: and the servants did strike him with the palms of their hands [Mark 14:63–65].

They condemned Him to die because He claimed to be the Messiah. The charge was changed when they went before Pilate (see Mark 15:3). Their treatment of Him was the worst indignity He could endure. Imagine spitting in the face of the Son of God!

While the farce of the trial of Jesus was in progress, Simon Peter was in the place of great temptation.

And as Peter was beneath in the palace, there cometh one of the maids of the high priest:

And when she saw Peter warming himself, she looked upon him, and said, And thou also wast with Jesus of Nazareth.

But he denied, saying, I know not, neither understand I what thou sayest. And he went out into the porch; and the cock crew.

And a maid saw him again, and began to say to them that stood by, This is one of them.

And he denied it again. And a little after, they that stood by said again to Peter, Surely thou art one of them: for thou art a Galilaean, and thy speech agreeth thereto [Mark 14:66–70].

A little wisp of a maid caused him to deny His Lord. Peter was ashamed to be known as a follower of Jesus at this time. Have we ever been in a similar position? May God forgive our cowardice and weakness as He did that of Peter.

On the third encounter notice that Peter's weakness in wanting to talk too much got him into trouble. His speech gave him away.

But he began to curse and to swear, saying, I know not this man of whom ye speak.

And the second time the cock crew. And Peter called to mind the word that Jesus said unto him, Before the cock crow twice, thou shalt deny me thrice. And when he thought thereon, he wept [Mark 14:71–72].

This man had not known his own weakness. Simon Peter loved Jesus, and he was sincere when he promised to be loyal to Him. But he did not know himself. He had not yet come to the place where he saw no good in the flesh at all.

However, Peter could repent of his sin, and that is the real test of a genuine believer. These were tears of heartbroken repentance. Years later in his epistle he wrote, "Who are kept by the power of God through faith unto salvation ready to be revealed in the last time" (1 Pet. 1:5). Peter knew that the Lord Jesus had kept him!

We close this chapter with Jesus in the hands of His enemies. His own are scattered. One has betrayed Him; another has denied Him. It is the night of sin!

CHAPTER 15

***THEME:** The trial of Jesus; the crucifixion of Jesus; the burial*

We are now in the study of the crucifixion of Christ. I know that all Scripture is given by inspiration of God and it is profitable (see 2 Tim. 3:16), but this portion that describes the death and resurrection of Christ has particular meaning for us today. We closed the last chapter with Jesus in the hands of His enemies. His own are scattered. One has betrayed Him. Another has denied Him.

Sin is the issue this night in two different ways. Sin is trying to destroy Him. And He is doing something about sin—He is dying for your sin and my sin. I suppose it can be said that the cross is one of the many paradoxes of the Christian faith for that reason. It is at once the greatest tragedy of the ages and the most glorious victory of earth and heaven. Therefore, we should not come to this chapter with a feeling of defeat or sympathy for the Sufferer. We should walk softly and reverently through these scenes with a heart welling up to God in thanksgiving for providing so great salvation (see Heb. 2:3).

The tragic note is inescapable in these scenes with the cruel injustice and bitter suffering inflicted upon Jesus. It is no wonder that Clovis, the barbarian, when he first heard the gospel read, exclaimed, "If I had only been there with my soldiers." But remember, it is not our sympathy that the Son of God wants. He wants our *faith*. Believe on the Lord Jesus Christ. "That if thou shalt confess with thy mouth the Lord Jesus, and shalt believe in thine heart that God hath raised him from the dead, thou shalt be saved. For with the heart man believeth unto righteousness; and with the mouth confession is made unto salvation" (Rom. 10:9–10). He wants the *faith* of your heart, not the *sympathy* of your heart.

Mark is the gospel of action, and this fifteenth chapter sets forth the supreme nature of the action. The Crucifixion is the climactic point and crowning event of this action. It is the Crucifixion toward which all creation and the purposes of God were moving from all eternity, for He was the "Lamb slain from the foundation of the world." The gospel is now translated into action! Paul could say later on, "For I delivered unto you first of all that which I also received, how that Christ died for our sins according to the scriptures; And that he was buried, and that he rose again the third day according to the scriptures" (1 Cor. 15:3–4).

You see, the gospel is what *He* did. It is not what God is asking *you* to do. It is *His* action, not your action or mine. You and I are in no position to do anything that would be acceptable to God. Your righteousness and my righteousness are not acceptable for salvation. God must, and does, provide that righteousness in Christ. He ". . . was delivered for our offences, and was raised again for our justification," for our righteousness (Rom. 4:25).

Now I will give an outline for this fifteenth chapter:

1. Jesus carried before Pilate (vv. 1–6).
2. Jesus condemned—Barabbas released (vv. 7–15).
3. Jesus crowned with thorns (vv. 16–23).
4. Jesus crucified (vv. 24–41).
5. Jesus committed to Joseph—new tomb (vv. 42–47).

THE TRIAL OF JESUS

And straightway in the morning the chief priests held a consultation with the elders and scribes and the whole council, and bound Jesus, and carried him away, and delivered him to Pilate [Mark 15:1].

The reason that they did this was that the Sanhedrin could condemn Jesus to die, but they could not carry out the execution. Only Rome could do that. Therefore, this body had to appeal to the Roman court for the execution of the death penalty that they had decided upon. Now the charge which they had brought against Him in the Sanhedrin would never stand up before Pilate. So they met early the next morning to formulate charges that would stand up before the Roman court and would make *legal* the illegal action of the night before.

You see, Pilate is the Roman governor who is in Jerusalem at this time. His headquarters were down at Caesarea because he liked that place—it was on the seacoast and had a delightful climate. He didn't like Jerusalem. He came up there only at feast times to keep down any riots. The Roman government didn't permit riots and protest marches and that type of thing, which is one reason Rome stood for about one thousand years as a great world empire. I think that present-day nations need to take note of this.

Pilate was a politician. Expediency rather than Roman justice was the motivating force in his life. He actually sought to release Jesus when he discovered He was innocent, but at the same time he wanted to please the religious rulers. Yet, if you will notice here, he couldn't really get the cooperation from Jesus that he hoped to get. He thought that, if Jesus would cooperate, he could please the religious rulers, too. Pilate is a typical example of a cheap politician who is unloosed from the noble moorings of honesty and integrity and "carries water on both shoulders," seeking to compromise and to please all sides. And when you try to do that, you please no one.

And Pilate asked him, Art thou the King of the Jews? And he answering said unto him, Thou sayest it [Mark 15:2].

That would be the same as saying, "You're right. I am."

And the chief priests accused him of many things: but he answered nothing.

And Pilate asked him again, saying, Answerest thou nothing? behold how many things they witness against thee.

But Jesus yet answered nothing; so that Pilate marvelled.

Now at that feast he released unto them one prisoner, whomsoever they desired [Mark 15:3–6].

Pilate was amazed and shocked at a prisoner who would stand before him and not defend himself. I imagine that other prisoners went to great lengths to defend themselves, but this Prisoner was different. He didn't defend Himself and Pilate wanted to know the reason.

Now, when we compare the Gospel of John, we will find that there was a great deal of interplay between Pilate and the religious rulers as Pilate actually sought to deliver Jesus. He took Him on the inside to talk to Him. Then he came back out and then took Him in again, hoping to get His cooperation. But Pilate found out that he had to stand on his own two feet and make a decision relative to Jesus Christ. For that matter, that is exactly what every man and every woman has to do.

Pilate then thought he could get off the hook by releasing a prisoner. This man just couldn't believe that anyone would ask for Barabbas to be delivered and for Jesus to be crucified. He really thought that he had found a solution for the dilemma in which he found himself.

And there was one named Barabbas, which lay bound with them that had made insurrection with him, who had committed murder in the insurrection [Mark 15:7].

Here was a man guilty of murder and guilty of leading an insurrection. He was the chief prisoner at that time. He was actually to be crucified along with the others. I think the Lord Jesus was crucified on the cross intended for Barabbas.

But Pilate answered them, saying, Will ye that I release unto you the King of the Jews?

For he knew that the chief priests had delivered him for envy.

But the chief priests moved the people, that he should rather release Barabbas unto them.

And Pilate answered and said again unto them, What will ye then that I shall do unto him whom ye call the King of the Jews?

And they cried out again, Crucify him [Mark 15:9–13].

A very remarkable and unheard of thing is taking place here. It was evident to Pilate that the charges brought against Jesus were false. Here he had on his hands a prisoner who was an outstanding criminal, and so he makes the comparison between Jesus and Barabbas. He was so shocked when they asked for Barabbas to be released that he, the judge, asked the people in consternation what he should do then with Jesus.

Then Pilate said unto them, Why, what evil hath he done? And they cried out the more exceedingly, Crucify him [Mark 15:14].

The mob had been instructed to demand that Jesus be crucified. Here we see mob rule with a vengeance. When Pilate asked what evil Jesus had done, they simply cried out more and more, "Crucify him." No mob is prepared to reason or to use its head or use good judgment. All they can do is cry out, "Crucify him."

And so Pilate, willing to content the people, released Barabbas unto them, and delivered Jesus, when he had scourged him, to be crucified [Mark 15:15].

Pilate obviously was a weak, vacillating politician. He yielded to the cry of the mob, and he delivered the Lord Jesus to be crucified. Roman justice certainly went awry here. An innocent man is to die. But wait a minute—He is taking my place and I am *not* innocent. He's taking your place also.

THE CRUCIFIXION OF JESUS

And the soldiers led him away into the hall, called Praetorium; and they call together the whole band [Mark 15:16].

When any criminal was to be crucified, he was turned over to these soldiers. They were a brutal lot, and they could do as they pleased with the prisoner. They, of course, humiliated their prisoners, tortured them, and made them a plaything for their sadistic appetites. This is the thing they do now with the Lord Jesus.

I've suggested that they played a game, a Roman game called "hot hand." Each would stick up a fist in the face of Jesus; then they would blindfold Him and all but one would hit Him. They beat His face into a pulp until I don't think He looked like a man. Of course, when they would take the blindfold off, He had to pick out the fist that had not hit Him. The prisoner never could pick out the right one. Even if He did, they wouldn't admit it was the right one because they were going to play that game again and again. It was a vicious beating, which is probably the reason we are told that they had to get this man Simon of Cyrene to carry the cross. Our Lord was thirty-three years old—He still had the strength of youth. I'm confident He was muscular. He had walked up and down that country. He'd been a carpenter, and He'd been able to drive the moneychangers out. But they had beaten Him unmercifully.

And they clothed him with purple, and platted a crown of thorns, and put it about his head,

And began to salute him, Hail, King of the Jews! [Mark 15:17–18].

The act of putting a purple robe and crown of thorns on Him was mere mockery.

And they smote him on the head with a reed, and did spit upon him, and bowing their knees worshipped him [Mark 15:19].

This was vicious. The imperfect tense of the verbs indicates that they kept on smiting Him and spitting on Him. This was more than ordinary human hatred. This was brutal and cruel, revealing the degradation of the human heart. Do you see what He endured when He took your place? The cross was still before Him.

And when they had mocked him, they took off the purple from him, and put his own clothes on him, and led him out to crucify him.

And they compel one Simon a Cyrenian, who passed by, coming out of the country, the father of Alexander and Rufus, to bear his cross [Mark 15:20–21].

After a morning of inhuman suffering they led Him away to be crucified. Simon was from Cyrene in North Africa. He probably was attending the Passover in Jerusalem. It appears that he was picked out of the crowd by chance to help carry the cross. It is believed that Jesus carried the cross to the city gates.

And they bring him unto the place Golgotha, which is, being interpreted, The place of a skull [Mark 15:22].

Golgotha means "the place of a skull." Our word is *Calvary*.

And they gave him to drink wine mingled with myrrh: but he received it not [Mark 15:23].

The wine mingled with myrrh was a drug to help deaden the awful ordeal of the cross for those about to die. It is interesting to note that when He was born, wise men brought Him myrrh. When He died, He was offered myrrh. Myrrh speaks of His death.

And when they had crucified him, they parted his garments, casting lots upon them, what every man should take [Mark 15:24].

Actually a better translation here would be "*after* they crucified him." No gospel writer records the details of the Crucifixion; they give us only incidents around the Crucifixion. The Spirit of God drew a veil over it as if to say, "There is nothing here to satisfy sadistic gossip. There is nothing here with which an idle mind should be occupied. It is too horrible."

The parting of His garments was in fulfillment of the prophecy in Psalm 22:18.

And it was the third hour, and they crucified him.

And the superscription of his accusation was written over, THE KING OF THE JEWS [Mark 15:25–26].

Now we are told here that it was the third hour when they crucified Him, which was nine o'clock in the morning. (Mark uses the Hebrew computation of time, while John uses the Roman.) We must put all the gospel writing together to get the full superscription. John tells us that it was written in Hebrew, Greek, and Latin. No gospel writer is intending to give us the whole story.

The charge for which they crucified Him was this:

"THE KING OF THE JEWS"

It may seem an anomalous statement to say that it was true. It was not true in the way they meant it. He had led no insurrection against Rome. He offered Himself to Israel and was rejected.

And with him they crucify two thieves; the one on his right hand, and the other on his left.

And the scripture was fulfilled, which saith, And he was numbered with the transgressors [Mark 15:27–28].

Jesus was crucified, we are told, with two thieves—the one on His right hand and the other on His left. And that was done, Mark says, so that the Scripture might be fulfilled. Then he quotes Isaiah 53:12, ". . . and he was numbered with the transgressors. . . ."

And they that passed by railed on him, wagging their heads, and saying, Ah, thou that destroyest the temple, and buildest it in three days,

Save thyself, and come down from the cross.

Likewise also the chief priests mocking said among themselves with the scribes, He saved others; himself he cannot save [Mark 15:29–31].

This was true. He could not save others and at the same time save Himself. He gave Himself for others—this is the great principle of redemption.

Let Christ the King of Israel descend now from the cross, that we may see and believe. And they that were crucified with him reviled him.

And when the sixth hour was come, there was darkness over the whole land until the ninth hour.

And at the ninth hour Jesus cried with a loud voice, saying, Eloi, Eloi, lama sabachthani? which is, being interpreted, My God, my God, why hast thou forsaken me? [Mark 15:32–34].

I want you to notice here that Mark gives us the Crucifixion by the clock. On the third hour He was put on the cross, and at the sixth hour (which would be twelve noon) darkness came down. The high noon sun was covered, and darkness came down over the cross. From the sixth hour to the ninth hour, that would be until three o'clock in the afternoon, there was darkness.

Now will you notice this: the first three hours were from 9:00 A.M. until 12 noon; the second three hours were from 12 noon to 3:00 P.M. Jesus hung on the cross for six hours. In the first three hours there was physical light; in the second three hours there was physical darkness. But in the first three hours there was spiritual darkness; in the second three hours there was spiritual light. Why? Because in those first three hours man did his worst. They crucified Him and they reviled Him. Even those who were hanging with Him on the cross reviled Him. At least at the first, both thieves did. At that time the enemy, marching around down beneath the cross, were wagging their heads and ridiculing Him. In the first three hours man was working, doing his very worst; in the second three hours God was working. He was suffering at the hands of man in the first three hours; He was suffering *for* man in the last three hours. In the first three hours He was dying because of sin; in the second three hours He was dying for the sin of the world. So during the time of the physical darkness, there was actually spiritual light and God was working. In those first three hours sin was doing all it could to destroy Him; in the second three hours He is making His soul an offering for sin. In those last three hours He is paying for the sins of the world. It was during this period that He was made sin for us; He became sin for us. He was forsaken of God and yet, even at that time, God was in Christ, reconciling the world unto Himself (see 2 Cor. 5:19). What a paradox we find here.

And some of them that stood by, when they heard it, said, Behold, he calleth Elias.

And one ran and filled a sponge full of vinegar, and put it on a reed, and gave him to drink, saying, Let alone; let us see whether Elias will come to take him down [Mark 15:35–36].

The crowd misunderstood what He said. They probably thought that He had called for Elijah because of the similarity of the words, and they said, "Let us see whether Elijah will come." You wonder whether they didn't halfway suspect that He really was the Messiah. I think there is something in the human heart that would tell them—and did tell them—this was the Messiah.

Then they gave Him some wine to quench His thirst. This was not the drug that they offered Him earlier. He took this in order to fulfill the prophecy: "They gave me also gall for my meat; and in my thirst they gave me vinegar to drink" (Ps. 69:21).

And Jesus cried with a loud voice, and gave up the ghost.

And the veil of the temple was rent in twain from the top to the bottom [Mark 15:37–38].

He did not die because the bodily organs refused to function. He surrendered up His spirit.

The rending of the veil was evidently witnessed by many priests. Three o'clock was the time of the evening sacrifice and they were serving in the temple at that very moment. This must have had some effect on them. At any rate, we note later on that many of the priests came to a saving knowledge of Christ. "And the word of God increased; and the number of the disciples multiplied in Jerusalem greatly; and a great company of the priests were obedient to the faith" (Acts 6:7). This reveals that many of the priests believed on the Lord Jesus Christ, and we have every reason to believe that some of them were serving in the temple at the time of the Crucifixion.

The fact that the very moment when He gave up the ghost was the moment that the veil was rent in twain is not accidental by any means. They are specifically stated together.

Jesus gave up the ghost. He could not die

until He had given up His spirit. He did not die because His bodily organs refused to function, which means He died differently, of course, from any of us. I've been in the presence of quite a few people when they have died. These folk, I've always noticed, have a death rattle. The last thing we do is try to draw in our breath. The one thing we want is that final breath. He didn't do that. He dismissed His spirit. So that certainly made His death different even in a physical sense.

At that very instant, the veil was torn in two. The veil speaks of the humanity of Christ. The Book of Leviticus gives us more understanding of the veil because the Book of Leviticus has to do with the service in the tabernacle. That veil, you will recall, speaks of the humanity of Christ, and this carries a tremendous message. You see, the humanity of Christ, or the life of Christ, shuts us out from God. His sinless life shows how sinful ours are. The minute He died, the veil was rent. It is His death that brings us to God, friend, not His life.

And when the centurion, which stood over against him, saw that he so cried out, and gave up the ghost, he said, Truly this man was the Son of God [Mark 15:39].

I believe that this was the confession of faith in this centurion and this was as far as he could go at this time. He couldn't have said anything that would have revealed his faith more than this. He acknowledged that Jesus is God's Son. He acknowledged who He was and certainly what He was doing. I do not believe that this man had all the details of theology. This man had never read Strong's theology or any of my books, but this man knew enough to take his place beneath the cross of Christ. And, you know, that is all God has ever asked any sinner to do. He asks us to come in faith to Him. That is what this man is doing. We must remember that he was a pagan Roman, and he had the cruel job of crucifying men. He was certainly made very tender at this time.

Now we are told about the women who were present.

There were also women looking on afar off: among whom was Mary Magdalene, and Mary the mother of James the less and of Joses, and Salome;

(Who also, when he was in Galilee, followed him, and ministered unto him;) and many other women which came up with him unto Jerusalem [Mark 15:40–41].

It is interesting to note, by the way, that the women were the last to leave the cross and the first to arrive at the tomb. These stood afar off, we're told here. They remained faithful. They were the ones who were faithful to the very end. His disciples and apostles were scattered at this time. There are other women who are not named here at all for it says, "and many other women which came up with him unto Jerusalem."

THE BURIAL

And now when the even was come, because it was the preparation, that is, the day before the sabbath,

Joseph of Arimathaea, an honourable counsellor, which also waited for the kingdom of God, came, and went in boldly unto Pilate, and craved the body of Jesus.

And Pilate marvelled if he were already dead: and calling unto him the centurion, he asked him whether he had been any while dead.

And when he knew it of the centurion, he gave the body to Joseph [Mark 15:42–45].

This is something that is quite interesting to note. Joseph of Arimathaea is a little-known follower of Jesus. He actually had charge of the burial, and he had the courage to step out in the open here. He was a member of the Sanhedrin (see Luke 23:51–52), and this man had not consented to the counsel and the deed of that group. He was of Arimathaea, a city of that land. He also was waiting for the kingdom of God. This man now steps out as a follower of the Lord Jesus when the apostles were scattered, gone under cover, and he asks for the body of Jesus.

We're told here that Pilate marveled that He was so soon dead. The reason is that customarily a person who was crucified would linger alive on a cross, sometimes for days. His life would just gradually expire. It was a cruel and inhuman mode of torture. This is the reason Pilate marveled and made special inquiry. Jesus gave up the ghost. That is important for us to see. During the last hours of dying, a prisoner on the cross had his legs broken to hasten his death. But Jesus was already dead, and it was not necessary to break His legs. That, you know, was a fulfillment of prophecy that not a bone of His body would be broken.

Pilate, we are told, gave the body to Joseph. It is interesting to note that there are two words used for *body* in this section.

Joseph asked for the body—*soma* is the Greek word.

Pilate gave him the body—*ptoma* is the Greek word.

The first speaks of the total personality, and it is a word of care and tenderness. The word used when Pilate gave the body just means the corpse or the carcass. It is a different viewpoint and attitude toward death and toward the bodies of those that are dead. The word Joseph used was a word of tenderness for the body. He wanted Jesus. All Pilate did was to give him a carcass. What a difference that is!

Friend, only the Lord Jesus can put any value on you. You and I are not worth very much, but He paid a tremendous price for our redemption. We groan within these bodies, but even our bodies are to be redeemed. There is a day coming when we will experience the redemption of our bodies. That is just a little added insight here.

Notice that Joseph is called a rich man, and he put away the body tenderly into his new tomb.

And he bought fine linen, and took him down, and wrapped him in the linen, and laid him in a sepulchre which was hewn out of a rock, and rolled a stone unto the door of the sepulchre [Mark 15:46].

That door was sealed. The Romans sealed the rock and guarded it with Roman soldiers (see Matt. 27:66).

And Mary Magdalene and Mary the mother of Joses beheld where he was laid [Mark 15:47].

The women were the only mourners. They were with Him to the very end. God bless the women.

CHAPTER 16

THEME: *The Resurrection; the Ascension*

Now we come to the resurrection and ascension of Jesus. The bodily resurrection of Jesus is one of the cardinal doctrines of the Christian faith. It is the heart of the primitive gospel. Every sermon in the Book of Acts is a message on the Resurrection—every speaker got to this subject. The early church dwelt upon it constantly. Today there is scant reference to the Resurrection, and in many churches there is one sermon preached each year on Easter Sunday with the message of the Resurrection. "He is risen!" That is the thrilling message which electrified a lethargic and sinful generation in the Roman Empire. It turned them upside down, wrong side out, and right side up; and they went out to tell the world about it. There would be hope today if the church would preach this truth with much *assurance*.

Let me mention here that this chapter has been under severe criticism by the higher critics. I mention this so someone doesn't wonder why I do not mention the textual problem here. Verses 9–20 have been called in question by the textual scholars of both the conservative and liberal groups. Wescott and Hort omit it from their Greek text, but they do include it in smaller type. Nestle follows the same procedure by separating it from the regular text. Some, from the liberal wing, omit it altogether.

It is true that two of the better manuscripts omit it entirely. Aleph and the Vatican manuscripts end Mark's gospel at verse 8 of chapter 16.

It is not my intention to go into a discussion in the field of New Testament Introduction. Rather, I am interested in giving attention to the meaning of the text. I believe that these last twelve verses are a part of the inspired Scripture and shall treat them as any other portion of the Word of God. The omission of this portion from two of our better manuscripts is not sufficient grounds to remove it from Scripture, especially when all the other manuscripts and uncials contain it. The internal evidence is not enough to dismiss it either, as the style is still that of Mark—brief and blunt.

Here is my outline of the last chapter of the Gospel of Mark:

1. The arrival of the women at the empty tomb (vv. 1–4).
2. The announcement of the angel that Jesus had risen (vv. 5–8).
3. The appearances of Jesus (vv. 9–18).
4. The ascension of Jesus (vv. 19–20).

THE RESURRECTION

And when the sabbath was past, Mary Magdalene, and Mary the mother of James, and Salome, had bought sweet spices, that they might come and anoint him [Mark 16:1].

This was now early on Sunday morning, the first day of the week. They were never able to anoint His body. It was not Mary of Bethany who wasted her ointment, but these women wasted theirs because, when they brought it to the tomb, Jesus was gone—He was alive again.

And very early in the morning the first day of the week, they came unto the sepulchre at the rising of the sun.

And they said among themselves, Who shall roll us away the stone from the door of the sepulchre?

And when they looked, they saw that the stone was rolled away: for it was very great [Mark 16:2–4].

The Sabbath had ended at sundown on Saturday. They had secured the spices sometime after that in order to make the trip to the tomb so early on Sunday morning. The same women who were present at the cross came to the tomb. I think it is accurate to state that the women were the last at the cross and the first at the tomb.

The attitude of the disciples was that, since Jesus was dead it was better to stay under cover until after all the excitement had died down and they were no longer in danger. Did they intend to go to the tomb? There is no evidence to support such an intention. It seems that none of them intended to visit that tomb.

Now it was very early, sunrise, and these women intended to anoint the body of Jesus with the spices they had bought. They were presented with the difficulty of getting into the tomb because of the stone at the door. They found that their difficulty was dissolved by the fact that the stone had been rolled away. The body of Jesus was gone. There was a heavenly messenger with the first announcement of the Resurrection. The fact that the tomb was empty has been well attested and established. The evidence is such that it would be acceptable in a court of law.

And entering into the sepulchre, they saw a young man sitting on the right side, clothed in a long white garment; and they were affrighted.

And he saith unto them, Be not affrighted: Ye seek Jesus of Nazareth, which was crucified: he is risen; he is not here: behold the place where they laid him.

But go your way, tell his disciples and Peter that he goeth before you into Galilee; there shall ye see him, as he said unto you [Mark 16:5–7].

To study the facts of the empty tomb we need to put the four gospel records together. Some of the facts are in Matthew and others are in John's gospel. Right here I want to quote a statement given by Lord Lyndhurst, High Chancellor of Great Britain (1846) and High Steward of Cambridge, the highest honor which they confer. This man said, "I know pretty well what evidence is; and, I tell you, such evidence as that for the Resurrection has never broken down yet."

The women were specifically told to go and report to the disciples. (The angel surely was not waiting for some disciple to come by, as we can see from the message he sends to them. Jesus will meet them in Galilee as He had promised them. John 21 tells us of that remarkable meeting.) You can imagine the amazement of these women. They were speechless. And this, frankly, doesn't seem to me to be an appropriate place for Mark to end his gospel, as some of the critics claim.

And they went out quickly, and fled from the sepulchre; for they trembled and were amazed: neither said they any thing to any man; for they were afraid [Mark 16:8].

Now we come to the section that is not included in all the manuscripts but which we believe is the Word of God.

Now when Jesus was risen early the first day of the week, he appeared first to Mary Magdalene, out of whom he had cast seven devils.

And she went and told them that had been with him, as they mourned and wept.

And they, when they had heard that he was alive, and had been seen of her, believed not.

After that he appeared in another form unto two of them, as they walked, and went into the country [Mark 16:9–12].

Mark makes it very clear to us that he hadn't been following a chronological order in his gospel. But now he says that this is the order. He is being chronological. He appeared first to Mary Magdalene. The disciples didn't believe Mary Magdalene at all. After that He appeared to two others, walking in the country. Luke gives us the account of that walk on the road to Emmaus.

And they went and told it unto the residue: neither believed they them.

Afterward he appeared unto the eleven as they sat at meat, and upbraided them with their unbelief and hardness of heart, because they believed not them which had seen him after he was risen [Mark 16:13–14].

You see that Mark does not include all the details, but he does state the order of the events which he reports.

And he said unto them, Go ye into all the world, and preach the gospel to every creature [Mark 16:15].

This has been a gospel of action. Now He's telling them to get into action! They are to go. And, by the way, He is saying to us today that we should be men and women of action for God. What are you doing today to get out the Word of God? That is our business, friend. You should be having some part in getting the Word of God *out* today.

He that believeth and is baptized shall be saved; but he that believeth not shall be damned [Mark 16:16].

He does not say that if you are not baptized you will be damned. He is not saying that baptism is necessary to salvation, but that the person who is saved will be baptized. It is the rejection of Christ which brings eternal damnation. "He that believeth on the Son hath everlasting life: and he that believeth not the Son shall not see life; but the wrath of God abideth on him" (John 3:36).

And these signs shall follow them that believe; In my name shall they cast out devils; they shall speak with new tongues;

They shall take up serpents; and if they drink any deadly thing, it shall not hurt them; they shall lay hands on the sick, and they shall recover [Mark 16:17–18].

If you want to accept any of these sign gifts, then you must take them all, brother. I'll be glad to prepare a formaldehyde cocktail if you think you can drink it. What am I trying to say? These signs have followed the preaching of the gospel. But they are not signs to continue the preaching of the gospel. They disappeared even in the early church, but they do manifest themselves on some primitive mission frontiers even today. But if someone maintains that they are injunctions for today, then one must accept them all, even the drinking of a deadly poison. Even before the end of the first century, the sign gifts were no longer the credentials of the apostles. The test was correct doctrine (see 2 John 10). It is the Word of God that is the great sign in this hour.

THE ASCENSION

So then after the Lord had spoken unto them, he was received up into heaven, and sat on the right hand of God.

And they went forth, and preached everywhere, the Lord working with them, and confirming the word with signs following. Amen [Mark 16:19–20].

This is Mark's brief statement of the great fact of the Ascension and the present ministry of Jesus at the right hand of God. The disciples *did* go out to carry the gospel to every creature, and the Lord *did* work with them and confirmed the Word with signs which they performed.

This is the gospel of action. May we be men and women of *action* for God!

BIBLIOGRAPHY

(Recommended for Further Study)

Alexander, J. A. *Commentary on the Gospel of Mark.* Carlisle, Pennsylvania: The Banner of Truth Trust, 1858.

Earle, Ralph. *Mark: Gospel of Action.* Chicago, Illinois: Moody Press, n.d.

English, E. Schuyler. *Studies in Mark's Gospel.* New York, New York: Our Hope Publishers, 1943.

Hendriksen, William. *Exposition of the Gospel According to Mark.* Grand Rapids, Michigan: Baker Book House, 1975. (Comprehensive for advanced study.)

Hiebert, D. Edmond. *Mark: A Portrait of a Servant.* Chicago, Illinois: Moody Press, 1974. (An excellent comprehensive treatment.)

Ironside, H. A. *Addresses on the Gospel of Mark.* Neptune, New Jersey: Loizeaux Brothers. (Especially good for young Christians.)

Morgan, G. Campbell. *The Gospel According to Mark.* Old Tappan, New Jersey: Fleming H. Revell Co., 1927.

Scroggie, W. Graham. *The Gospel of Mark.* Grand Rapids, Michigan: Zondervan Publishing House, n.d. (Splendid outlines.)

Van Ryn, August. *Meditations in Mark.* Neptune, New Jersey: Loizeaux, 1957.

Vos, Howard F. *Mark, A Study Guide Commentary.* Grand Rapids, Michigan: Zondervan Publishing House, 1978. (Excellent for personal or group study.)

Wuest, Kenneth S. *Mark in the Greek New Testament for English Readers.* Grand Rapids, Michigan: William B. Eerdmans Publishing Co., 1950.

The Gospel According to

LUKE

INTRODUCTION

Luke was the beloved physician of Colossians 4:14, "Luke, the beloved physician, and Demas, greet you." He used more medical terms than Hippocrates, the father of medicine. The choice of Luke by the Holy Spirit to write the third gospel reveals that there are no accidental writers of Scripture. There was a supernatural selection of Luke. There were "not many wise" called, but Luke belongs to that category. He and Paul were evidently on a very high intellectual level as well as a high spiritual level. This explains partially why they traveled together and obviously became fast friends in the Lord. Dr. Luke would rank as a scientist of his day. Also he wrote the best Greek of any of the New Testament writers, including Paul. He was an accurate historian, as we shall see. Luke was a poet—he alone records the lovely songs of Christmas. Luke was an artist; he sketches for us Christ's marvelous, matchless parables.

A great deal of tradition surrounds the life of Dr. Luke. He writes his gospel from Mary's viewpoint, which confirms the tradition that he received his information for his gospel from her. Surely he conferred with her. Also, there is every reason to believe that he was a Gentile. Most scholars concur in this position. Paul, in the fourth chapter of Colossians, distinguishes between those "who are of the circumcision" and the others who are obviously Gentiles, in which group he mentions Luke. Sir William Ramsay and J. M. Stifler affirm without reservation that Luke was a Gentile. This makes it quite interesting to those of us who are Gentiles, doesn't it?

Remember that Luke wrote the Book of Acts where we learn that he was a companion of the apostle Paul. In Acts 16:10 he says, "And after he had seen the vision, immediately we endeavoured to go into Macedonia. . . ." He was with Paul on the second and, I think, the third missionary journeys. From this verse on he writes in the first person—it is the "we" section of the Book of Acts. Prior to this verse he writes in the third person. So we can conclude from Acts 16 that Luke was with Paul on that historical crossing over into Europe. He probably was a convert of Paul, then went with him on this second missionary journey, and stayed with him to the end. When Paul was writing his "swan song" to Timothy, he says, "Only Luke is with me . . ." (2 Tim. 4:11). All this explains why Paul calls him the *beloved* physician.

Jesus is the *second* man, but the *last* Adam. "And so it is written, The first man Adam was made a living soul; the last Adam was made a quickening spirit. . . . The first man is of the earth, earthy: the second man is the Lord from heaven" (1 Cor. 15:45, 47). God is making men like Jesus: "Beloved, now are we the sons of God, and it doth not yet appear what we shall be: but we know that, when he shall appear, we shall be like him; for we shall see him as he is" (1 John 3:2). Therefore, Jesus is the *second* man—for there will be the third and the fourth—and the millionth. However, He is the *last* Adam. There will *not* be another head of the human family. Jesus was ". . . made like unto his brethren . . ." (Heb. 2:17) that His brethren might be made like unto Him.

At the close of the nineteenth century there was a wave of skepticism that swept over Europe and the British Isles. There was delusion and disappointment with the optimism which the Victorian era had produced. There was, on the lighter side, a rebellion against it which produced the Gay Nineties. Also it caused many scholars to begin a more serious investigation of the Bible, which had been the handbook of the Victorian era. They were skeptical before they began. Among them was a very brilliant young scholar at Cambridge by the name of William Ramsay. He was an agnostic, who wanted to disprove the accuracy of the Bible. He knew that Luke had written an historical record of Jesus in his gospel and that he had written of the missionary journeys of Paul in the Book of Acts. He also knew that all historians make mistakes and that many of them are liars.

Contemporary authors Will and Ariel Durant, who spent forty years studying twenty civilizations covering a four thousand year period, made the following statement in their book, *The Lessons of History*: "Our knowledge of the past is always incomplete, probably inaccurate, beclouded by ambivalent evidence and biased historians, and perhaps distorted by our own patriotic or religious partisanship.

Most history is guessing; the rest is prejudice."

It is safe to say that this was also the attitude of Sir William Ramsay when he went as an archaeologist into Asia Minor to disprove Dr. Luke as an historian. He carefully followed the journeys of Paul and made a thorough study of Asia Minor. He came to the conclusion that Dr. Luke had not made one historical inaccuracy. This discovery caused William Ramsay to become a believer, and he has written some outstanding books on the journeys of Paul and on the churches of Asia Minor.

Dr. Luke wrote his gospel with a twofold purpose. First, his purpose was literary and historical. Of the four Gospels, Luke's gospel is the most complete historical narrative. There are more wide-reaching references to institutions, customs, geography, and history of that period than arc found in any of the other gospels. Secondly, his purpose was spiritual. He presented the person of Jesus Christ as the perfect, divine Man and Savior of the world. Jesus was God manifest in the flesh.

Matthew emphasizes that Jesus was born the Messiah.

Mark emphasizes that Jesus was the Servant of Jehovah.

Luke stresses the fact that Jesus was the perfect Man.

John presents the fact that God became a Man.

However, it is interesting to note that John did not use the scientific approach. Dr. Luke states that he examined Jesus of Nazareth, and his findings are that Jesus is God. He came to the same conclusion as John did, but his procedure and technique were different.

Matthew presents the Lord Jesus as the Messiah, King, and Redeemer.

Mark presents Christ as the mighty Conqueror and Ruler of the world.

John presents Christ as the Son of God.

Luke presents the perfect, divine Son of God as our great High Priest, touched with the feeling of our infirmities, able to extend help, mercy, and love to us.

Luke wrote to his countrymen, just as Matthew wrote to his. Luke wrote to the Greek mind and to the intellectual community.

In the fourth century B.C. the Greeks placed on the horizon of history the most brilliant and scintillating display of human genius the world has ever seen. It was called the Periclean Age, pertaining to Pericles and the period of the intellectual and material preeminence of Athens. The Greeks attempted to perfect humanity and to develop the perfect man. This attempted perfection of man is found in the physical realm in such work as the statues of Phidias, as well as in the mental realm. They were striving for a beautiful as well as a thinking man. The literary works of Plato, Aristotle, Homer, Aeschylus, Sophocles, Euripides, Aristophanes, and Thucydides all move toward the picture of perfect man and strive to obtain the universal man.

The Greeks made their gods in the likeness of men. In fact, their gods were but projections of man. The magnificent statues of Apollo, Venus, Athena, and Diana were not the ugly representations that have come out of the paganism of the Orient. They deified man with his noble qualities and base passions. Other Greek gods include Pan, Cupid, Bacchus (the god of wine and revelry), and Aphrodite. Not all of their gods were graces; some of them were the avenging Furies because they were making a projection of mankind.

Alexander the Great scattered this gripping culture, language, and philosophy throughout the lands which he conquered. Greek became the universal language. In Alexandria, Egypt, the Old Testament was translated into Greek. We call that translation the Septuagint. It is one of the finest translations of the Old Testament that we have. The New Testament was written in Greek. The Greek language provided the vehicle for the expression and communication of the gospel to all of mankind. It has been the finest language to express a fact or communicate a thought.

Even though Greek culture, language, and philosophy were the finest ever developed, the Greeks fell short of perfecting humanity. The Greeks did not find Utopia. They never came upon the Elysian fields, and they lost sight of the spiritual realm. This world became their home, playground, schoolroom, workshop, and grave.

Dr. F. W. Robertson said this of the Greeks: "The more the Greek attached himself to this world, the more the unseen became a dim world." This is the reason the Greeks made an image to the UNKNOWN GOD, and when the apostle Paul preached the gospel to them, this is where he began. The cultivated Athenians were skeptics, and they called Paul a "babbler" and mocked him as he endeavored to give them the truth.

Paul declared that the gospel is foolishness to the Greeks, but he also wrote to the Greek mind. He told them that in times past they were Gentiles, having no hope and without God in the world. That is the picture of the

Greek, friend. But Paul also told them that when the right time had come, God sent forth His Son, made of a woman, made under the Law, and that this Son of God died for them. Paul walked the Roman roads with a universal language, preaching a global gospel about the perfect Man who had died for the men of the world. The religion of Israel could produce only a Pharisee, the power of Rome could produce only a Caesar, and the philosophy of Greece could produce only a global giant like Alexander the Great who was merely an infant at heart. It was to this Greek mind that Luke wrote. He presented Jesus Christ as the perfect Man, the universal Man, the very person the Greeks were looking for.

Note these special features of Luke's gospel:

1. Although the Gospel of Luke is one of the synoptic gospels, it contains many features omitted by Matthew and Mark.

2. Dr. Luke gives us the songs of Christmas.

3. Dr. Luke has the longest account of the virgin birth of Jesus of any of the Gospels. In the first two chapters, he gives us an unabashed record of obstetrics. A clear and candid statement of the Virgin Birth is given by Dr. Luke. All the way from Dr. Luke to Dr. Howard Kelly, a gynecologist at Johns Hopkins, there is a mighty affirmation of the Virgin Birth, which makes the statements of pseudo-theologians seem rather puerile when they unblushingly state that the Virgin Birth is a biological impossibility.

4. Dr. Luke gives us twenty miracles of which six are recorded in no other gospel.

5. He likewise gives us twenty-three parables, and eighteen of them are found nowhere else. The parables of the Prodigal Son and the Good Samaritan are peculiar to this third Gospel.

6. He also gives us the very human account of the walk to Emmaus of our resurrected Lord. This proves that Jesus was still human after His resurrection. Dr. Luke demonstrates that the Resurrection was not of the spirit, but of the body. Jesus was ". . . sown a natural body . . . raised a spiritual body . . ." (1 Cor. 15:44).

7. A definite human sympathy pervades this gospel, which reveals the truly human nature of Jesus, as well as the big-hearted sympathy of this physician of the first century who knew firsthand a great deal about the suffering of humanity.

8. Dr. Luke uses more medical terms than Hippocrates, the father of medicine.

OUTLINE

I. Birth of the Perfect Man; His Family, Chapters 1–3

A. Announcement of the Births of John and Jesus; the Birth of John, Chapter 1

1. Purpose of Gospel, Chapter 1:1–4
   (Periodic sentence)
2. Gabriel Appears to Zacharias and Announces the Birth of John, Chapter 1:5–25
3. Gabriel Appears to Mary and Announces the Virgin Birth of Jesus, Chapter 1:26–38
4. Mary Visits Elisabeth, Chapter 1:39–56
   (Hail Mary and *Magnificat)*
5. Birth of John (Zacharias' *Benedictus*), Chapter 1:57-80

B. Birth of Jesus; His Reception; His Circumcision; His Journey to Jerusalem at Twelve Years of Age, Chapter 2

1. Birth of Jesus at Bethlehem in a Stable, Chapter 2:1–7
2. Reception of Jesus: Angels Announce His Birth to Shepherds; Shepherds Visit Stable, Chapter 2:8–20
3. Circumcision of Jesus and Purification of Mary, Chapter 2:21–24
4. Incident in Temple Concerning Simeon, Chapter 2:25-35
   (*Nunc Dimittis*, vv. 29–32)
5. Incident in Temple Concerning Anna; Return to Nazareth, Chapter 2:36–40
6. Visit of Joseph, Mary, and Jesus to Jerusalem When Jesus Was Twelve, Chapter 2:41–52
   (*Dr. Luke says He was growing normally in body, mind, and spirit*—v. 52.)

C. Ministry of John the Baptist; Baptism of Jesus; Genealogy of Mary, Chapter 3

1. Ministry of John, Chapter 3:1–20
2. Baptism of Jesus, Chapter 3:21–22
   (*Trinity*—v. 22)
3. Genealogy of Mary, Chapter 3:23–38
   (Mary was also descended from David, v. 31—see Matt. 1.)

II. Testing of the Perfect Man; Rejection by His Hometown, Chapter 4
"Tempted like as we are" (Heb. 4:15).

A. Temptation of Jesus, Chapter 4:1–13

B. Jesus Returns to Galilee and Nazareth; Rejected by His Hometown, Chapter 4:14–30
(Jesus quotes from Isaiah 61:1–2 in v. 18.)

C. Jesus Moves His Headquarters to Capernaum; Continues His Ministry, Chapter 4:31–44

III. Ministry of the Perfect Man in Area of Galilee, Chapters 5–9

A. Jesus Calls Disciples for the Second Time; Cleanses Lepers; Heals Man with Palsy; Calls Matthew; Gives Parables on New Garment and Wine Skins, Chapter 5

B. Jesus Defends Disciples for Plucking Grain on Sabbath; Heals Paralyzed Man on Sabbath; Chooses Twelve; Gives Sermon on the Plain, Chapter 6

C. Jesus Heals Centurion's Servant; Restores to Life Son of Widow of Nain; Commends John the Baptist; Goes to Dinner at Pharisee's House; Gives Parable of Two Debtors, Chapter 7

D. Jesus Gives Parables: Sower, Lighted Candle, Personal Relationships; Stills Storm; Casts out Demons at Gadara; Heals

Woman with Issue of Blood; Restores to Life Daughter of Jairus, Chapter 8

E. Jesus Commissions and Sends Forth the Twelve; Feeds 5000; Announces Death and Resurrection; Transfigured; Casts Out Demons from an Only Son; Sets His Face Toward Jerusalem; Puts Down Test for Discipleship, Chapter 9

IV. Ministry of the Perfect Man on Way to Jerusalem, Chapters 10–18

A. Jesus Sends Forth the Seventy; Pronounces Judgment on Chorazin, Bethsaida, and Capernaum; Gives Parable of Good Samaritan; Enters Home of Mary and Martha, Chapter 10

B. Jesus Teaches Disciples to Pray by Using Parables of the Persistent Friend and a Good Father; Accused of Casting Out Demons by Beelzebub; Gives Parables—Unclean Spirit Leaving a Man, Sign of Jonah, Lighted Candle; Denounces Pharisees, Chapter 11

C. Jesus Warns of Leaven of Pharisees; Gives Parables of Rich Fool, Return from Wedding, Testing of Servants in Light of Coming of Christ; States He Is a Divider of Men, Chapter 12

D. Jesus Teaches Men Not to Judge but Repent; Gives Parable of Fig Tree; Heals Woman with Infirmity; Gives Parables of Mustard Seed and Leaven; Continues to Teach as He Goes Toward Jerusalem; Weeps over Jerusalem, Chapter 13

E. Jesus Goes to Dinner at Home of Pharisee; Gives Parables of Impolite Guests, the Great Supper, Building a Tower, King Going to War, Salt That Loses Its Tang, Chapter 14

F. Jesus Gives Parable of Lost Sheep, Lost Coin, Two Lost Sons (Prodigal Son), Chapter 15
(The obedient Son is the One who is giving the parable.)

G. Jesus Gives Parable About Unjust Steward; Answers Covetous Pharisees; Speaks on Divorce; Recounts Incident of Rich Man and Lazarus (Poor Man), Chapter 16

H. Jesus Instructs His Disciples on Forgiveness, Faithful Service; Heals Ten Lepers (One Samaritan Returns to Give Thanks); Speaks on Spiritual Nature of Kingdom and His Coming Again, Chapter 17

I. Jesus Gives Two Parables on Prayer; Blesses Little Children; Confronts Rich Young Ruler with Five of Ten Commandments; Heals Blind Man on Entering Jericho, Chapter 18

V. Ministry of the Perfect Man in Jericho and Jerusalem, Chapters 19–21

A. Jesus Enters Jericho and Home of Zacchaeus; Conversion of Zacchaeus; Gives Parable of Ten Pounds; Enters Jerusalem; Weeps over City; Cleanses Temple, Chapter 19

B. Jesus' Authority Challenged; Gives Parable of Vineyard; Questioned about Paying Tribute to Caesar; Silences Sadducees about Resurrection; Questions Scribes, Chapter 20

C. Jesus Notes How People Give, Commends Widow; Answers Question in Olivet Discourse, "When Shall These Things Be?", Chapter 21

VI. Betrayal, Trial and Death of the Perfect Man, Chapters 22–23
(Our Kinsman-Redeemer)

A. Judas Plots with Chief Priests to Betray Jesus; Jesus Plans for Last Passover and Institutes Lord's Supper; Announces His Betrayal, Position of Apostles in Future Kingdom; Peter's Denial; Warns Disciples of Future; Goes to Gethsemane; Betrayed by Judas; Arrested and Led to High Priest's House; Denied by Peter; Mocked, Beaten, Brought Before Sanhedrin, Chapter 22

B. Jesus Brought before Pilate and Herod; Barabbas Released; Jesus Foretells Destruction of Jerusalem and Prays for His Enemies; Jesus Crucified; Mocked by Rulers, Soldiers, One Thief; Other Thief Turns to Jesus and Is Accepted by Him; Dismisses His Spirit; Placed in New Tomb of Joseph of Arimathaea, Chapter 23

VII. Resurrection of the Perfect Man, Chapter 24:1–48

A. Jesus Raised from the Dead; Leaves Joseph's Tomb, Chapter 24:1–12
B. Jesus Goes Down Road to Emmaus, Reveals Himself to Two Disciples Chapter 24:13–34
C. Jesus Goes to the Assembled Disciples, Reveals Himself to the Eleven; Gives Commission to Go, Chapter 24:35–48
(He is still a Man; emphasizes the importance of the Word of God.)

VIII. Ascension of the Perfect Man, Chapter 24:49–53

Jesus Promises to Send Holy Spirit; Ascends to Heaven in Attitude of Blessing His Own, Chapter 24:49–53

CHAPTER 1

***THEME:** The purpose of the gospel; Gabriel appears to Zacharias and announces the birth of John; Gabriel appears to Mary and announces the virgin birth of Jesus; Mary visits Elisabeth; birth of John*

Historically Dr. Luke begins his gospel before the other synoptic Gospels. Heaven had been silent for over four hundred years when the angel Gabriel broke through the blue at the golden altar of prayer to announce the birth of John the Baptist. Luke gives us the background as well as the births of John and Jesus.

Three songs are in this chapter: (1) Elisabeth's greeting of Mary—verses 42–45; (2) Mary's magnificat—verses 46–55; and (3) Zacharias' prophecy—verses 68–79.

THE PURPOSE OF THE GOSPEL

Forasmuch as many have taken in hand to set forth in order a declaration of those things which are most surely believed among us,

Even as they delivered them unto us, which from the beginning were eyewitnesses, and ministers of the word;

It seemed good to me also, having had perfect understanding of all things from the very first, to write unto thee in order, most excellent Theophilus,

That thou mightest know the certainty of those things, wherein thou hast been instructed [Luke 1:1–4].

Two words are important in this passage and should not be passed over. "Eyewitness" is the Greek word *autoptai—auto* meaning "that which is of itself," and *opsomai* meaning "to see." "To see for yourself" would be an eyewitness. It is a medical term which means to make an autopsy. In fact, what Dr. Luke is trying to say is, "We are eyewitnesses who made an autopsy, and I am writing to you about what we found."

The second important word Dr. Luke uses is *ministers*, which is the Greek *huperatai*, meaning "an under-rower on a boat." In a hospital the "under-rower" is the intern. Dr. Luke is saying that all of them were just interns under the Great Physician. What Dr. Luke is telling us is that as a physician and a scholar, he made an autopsy of the records of those who had been eyewitnesses.

The first four verses of this chapter form a tremendous beginning. Luke wrote his gospel to give people certainty and assurance about the Lord Jesus Christ.

My friend, how much assurance do you have? Do you *know* that you are a child of God through faith in Jesus Christ? Do you *know* that the Bible is the Word of God? I feel sorry for the person who is not sure about these things. Do you wobble back and forth and say, "I am not sure about my salvation or the Bible. I guess I do not have enough faith." Not having enough faith may not be your problem. Your problem may be that you do not *know* enough. You see, ". . . faith cometh by hearing, and hearing by the word of God" (Rom. 10:17). If you really knew the Word of God, you would believe it. Those who are ignorant of the Bible have the problems. The problem is not with the Bible or with the Lord Jesus Christ; the problem lies with us.

GABRIEL APPEARS TO ZACHARIAS AND ANNOUNCES THE BIRTH OF JOHN

There was in the days of Herod, the king of Judaea, a certain priest named Zacharias, of the course of Abia: and his wife was of the daughters of Aaron, and her name was Elisabeth [Luke 1:5].

God breaks through after 400 years of silence. Chronologically Dr. Luke begins the New Testament. He goes back to the birth of John the Baptist, to where the angel Gabriel appeared to John's father as he served in the temple. John's parents were Zacharias and Elisabeth. *Zacharias* means "God remembers," and *Elisabeth* means "His oath." Together their names mean, "God remembers His oath." When did God take an oath? Psalm 89:34–37 records God's oath: "My covenant will I not break, nor alter the thing that is gone out of my lips. Once have I sworn by my holiness that I will not lie unto David. His seed shall endure for ever, and his throne as the sun before me. It shall be established for ever as the moon, and as a faithful witness in heaven. Selah." God swore an oath to David that one of his descendants would have an eternal reign. Christ is that descendant. "God remembers His oath!" God is ready to break through into human history after 400 years of silence.

Notice that the Scripture tells us both Zacharias and Elisabeth were righteous. That is, they were right. How were they right? They recognized they were sinners and brought the necessary sacrifices.

And they were both righteous before God, walking in all the commandments and ordinances of the Lord blameless [Luke 1:6].

Their walk commended their salvation. When they committed a sin or made a mistake, they brought the proper sacrifice.

However, there was tragedy in their lives because they had no child.

And they had no child, because that Elisabeth was barren, and they both were now well stricken in years [Luke 1:7].

Here was an old couple who did not have a child. To be childless was practically a disgrace for a Hebrew woman, and Elisabeth had no children.

Zacharias, belonging to the tribe of Levi, served in the temple.

And it came to pass, that while he executed the priest's office before God in the order of his course,

According to the custom of the priest's office, his lot was to burn incense when he went into the temple of the Lord.

And the whole multitude of the people were praying without at the time of incense.

And there appeared unto him an angel of the Lord standing on the right side of the altar of incense.

And when Zacharias saw him, he was troubled, and fear fell upon him [Luke 1:8–12].

Zacharias was serving at the golden altar, the place of prayer. It was the time of the evening sacrifice, and in this particular part of the service he placed incense upon the altar. Suddenly an angel appeared. If you saw an angel, what would you do? Your reaction would be the same as this man's. You would be troubled and fearful.

But the angel said unto him, Fear not, Zacharias: for thy prayer is heard; and thy wife Elisabeth shall bear thee a son, and thou shalt call his name John [Luke 1:13].

Zacharias was praying for a son. Elisabeth was praying for a son. I think that many people were praying that they would have a son. How do I know he is praying for a son? Because the angel said, "Your prayer is heard."

And thou shalt have joy and gladness; and many shall rejoice at his birth.

For he shall be great in the sight of the Lord, and shall drink neither wine nor strong drink; and he shall be filled with the Holy Ghost, even from his mother's womb [Luke 1:14–15].

The son of Elisabeth and Zacharias was to be a Nazarite. One of the things the Nazarite vowed was that he would not drink strong drink or wine. He was to find his joy in the Holy Spirit and in God. That is the reason Paul, in Ephesians 5:18, says, "And be not drunk with wine, wherein is excess; but be filled with the Spirit." Get your joy from God, not from a bottle. There are a lot of bottle-babies today. I am not speaking of crib babies but of adult babies hanging over a bar. And there are some Christians today who have to be pepped up and hepped up in order to face life. We need to recognize that the Holy Spirit of God can give us the strength to face life.

And many of the children of Israel shall he turn to the Lord their God.

And he shall go before him in the spirit and power of Elias, to turn the hearts of the fathers to the children, and the disobedient to the wisdom of the just; to make ready a people prepared for the Lord [Luke 1:16–17].

Let us understand clearly that although John the Baptist went forth in the spirit and power of Elijah, he was not Elijah. John would turn the hearts of the fathers to the children. He was to bridge the generation gap. Our problem today is not so much that there is a gap between the adults and youth but that there is a gap between adults and God. If adults had a proper relationship with God, they would not have the problem with young people that exists.

And Zacharias said unto the angel, Whereby shall I know this? for I am an old man, and my wife well stricken in years [Luke 1:18].

I cannot help but laugh at a verse like this. A great many people do not find humor in the Bible, but there is—and this verse gives us a taste of it. Here is a man, a priest, who has gone to God in prayer. At the altar of incense he says, "Oh, God, give me a son." Now when God says through the angel Gabriel, "I am going to give you a son," Zacharias replies, "How do I know?" He says, "My wife is old and I am old, and I do not think we can have a child." Yet he was praying for a son!

Have you ever prayed like that? You ask God for something, but you really do not believe He is going to give it to you. This is one reason we do not receive answers to our prayers. We have no faith at all. This man Zacharias is quite human, and I cannot help but laugh at him because that's the way I pray sometimes.

And the angel answering said unto him, I am Gabriel, that stand in the presence of God; and am sent to speak unto thee, and to shew thee these glad tidings [Luke 1:19].

The Word of God has the seal of God upon it. The Word of God carries authority. What Vernon McGee says is not important, but what the Word of God says is important. God speaks to us through His Word.

And, behold, thou shalt be dumb, and not able to speak, until the day that these things shall be performed, because thou believest not my words, which shall be fulfilled in their season [Luke 1:20].

Zacharias, who has been so vocal, will be dumb for a period of time. Unbelief is always dumb. That is, it never has a message. I agree with Elizabeth Barrett Browning who said that one without faith should be silent. There are many babblers around who are everlastingly spouting off about their unbelief. If they haven't anything to say, they should keep quiet. Let the man speak who believes in God and has something to say.

And the people waited for Zacharias, and marvelled that he tarried so long in the temple.

And when he came out, he could not speak unto them: and they perceived that he had seen a vision in the temple: for he beckoned unto them, and remained speechless [Luke 1:21–22].

This passage also strikes me as being funny. God, after 400 years of silence, once again breaks through to the human race, but the very man that He communicates with does not believe Him. And now he is made dumb. Can you imagine his trying to explain to the people that he is dumb? How would you make known to people that you had seen an angel and could not talk? It would not be easy. Think about the gyrations Zacharias must have used trying to make known his predicament. It must have been comical.

And it came to pass, that, as soon as the days of his ministration were accomplished, he departed to his own house [Luke 1:23].

Long ago King David had arranged that the priests in the temple would serve a certain period of time, then have a vacation. One priest would serve, then have some time off, and another priest would serve. This is what happened with Zacharias, but he had to finish his term of office without speaking. When his vacation time came, he still had to keep quiet; so I imagine he went home and listened to Elisabeth.

And after those days his wife Elisabeth conceived, and hid herself five months, saying,

Thus hath the Lord dealt with me in the days wherein he looked on me, to take away my reproach among men [Luke 1:24–25].

This is an interesting situation. Zacharias cannot talk. Elisabeth, because of her condition, remains in seclusion for several months. I imagine she talked his arm off for that period of time and constantly reminded him, "Zacharias, we are going to have a son!"

GABRIEL APPEARS TO MARY AND ANNOUNCES THE VIRGIN BIRTH OF JESUS

And in the sixth month the angel Gabriel was sent from God unto a city of Galilee, named Nazareth,

To a virgin espoused to a man whose name was Joseph, of the house of David; and the virgin's name was Mary [Luke 1:26–27].

We move now from Jerusalem to Nazareth. Six months after the angel Gabriel appeared to Zacharias, he appears to Mary.

Two times in one verse she is called a virgin. Do you know what a virgin is? I ask this because many folks do not seem to know. A virgin is a woman who could never have a child in a natural way because she has never had a relationship with a man that would make the birth of a child possible. Someone needs to talk rather plainly today because there are men saying that the Virgin Birth is biologically impossible. When I hear a man make that statement, I always feel like calling him up and saying, "I would like to have lunch with you and tell you about the birds and the bees because you do not seem to know much about them." The Scripture makes it clear that the Lord Jesus Christ was virgin born.

I do not object to an unbeliever saying that he does not believe in the Virgin Birth, but when he makes the statement that the *Bible* does not teach it, I object. I say very plainly that one who makes this statement must have something wrong with his intellect or is ignorant of the birds and the bees. It should be remembered that Luke was a doctor and he gives the most extended account of the Virgin Birth.

And the angel came in unto her, and said, Hail, thou that art highly favoured, the Lord is with thee: blessed art thou among women [Luke 1:28].

There is a tendency among Protestants to play down the role of Mary, but this verse tells us that she was highly favored. In the same breath, however, let me say that she was blessed *among* women, not *above* women. She is not lifted above women; she lifted up womanhood. This is the role she played. It is so easy to say that a woman brought sin into the world, but remember, it was a woman, and not a man, who brought the Savior into the world.

And when she saw him, she was troubled at his saying, and cast in her mind what manner of salutation this should be [Luke 1:29].

Mary was troubled at the sayings of the angel. When the supernatural touches the natural, it always creates fear. Mary also "cast in her mind what manner of salutation this should be." I cannot resist saying this, but Mary's reaction was similar to a black friend of mine in Memphis, Tennessee. Years ago he said to me, "You know, I never believed in ghosts either, until I saw one!" Believe me, friends, when you have seen an angel, you have a right to be afraid. I think I would be afraid if I saw one.

And the angel said unto her, Fear not, Mary: for thou hast found favour with God.

And, behold, thou shalt conceive in thy womb, and bring forth a son, and shalt call his name JESUS.

He shall be great, and shall be called the Son of the Highest: and the Lord God shall give unto him the throne of his father David:

And he shall reign over the house of Jacob for ever; and of his kingdom there shall be no end [Luke 1:30–33].

This is plain language. There is no way of misinterpreting it. This passage is quite literal. Those folks who deny the Virgin Birth also do not believe that the Lord is going to sit on the throne of His father David. Apparently it was understood that what Luke is writing about is literal. The virgin's womb is literal and the throne of David is literal. He shall literally reign over the house of Jacob and of His kingdom there shall be no end. That kingdom is also a reality.

Then said Mary unto the angel, How shall this be, seeing I know not a man? [Luke 1:34].

Mary was the first one to question the Virgin Birth. She said, "How can it be?" This is still a good question. Dr. Luke quotes the angel Gabriel and gives us the answer.

And the angel answered and said unto her, The Holy Ghost shall come upon thee, and the power of the Highest shall overshadow thee: therefore also that holy thing which shall be born of thee shall be called the Son of God [Luke 1:35].

No man had anything to do with the birth of Jesus Christ. We are told in the Book of Leviticus that the birth of a child caused a woman to be unclean because she brought a sinner into the world. Mary is told that she is *not* bringing a sinner into the world; He is holy. The union of man and woman can only produce a child with a sin nature. By the Virgin Birth is the only way God could get that "holy thing" into the human family. In Psalm 51:5 David said, "Behold, I was shapen in iniquity; and in sin did my mother conceive me." Mary's Son would be different. He would be virgin born.

You can deny the Virgin Birth if you want to. If you are an unbeliever, I would expect you to deny it. If, however, you write and tell me that you are not a Christian but you believe the Virgin Birth, I will be terribly upset. If you are not a Christian, of course you don't believe it. However, you cannot say that the Bible does not teach the Virgin Birth, because it does.

Do you know why this Baby is going to be

called the Son of God? Because He *is* the Son of God. Remember that Dr. Luke approaches his gospel from the scientific point of view. He states that he examined Jesus of Nazareth, and his findings are that Jesus is God. Luke came to the same conclusion that John came to in his gospel, but his procedure and technique were different. Dr. Luke has used plain, simple language to present his findings and if we cannot understand his message, we need to go back and learn our ABCs again.

And, behold, thy cousin Elisabeth, she hath also conceived a son in her old age: and this is the sixth month with her, who was called barren.

For with God nothing shall be impossible [Luke 1:36–37].

The birth of John the Baptist is also miraculous, but it is not a virgin birth. The statement of the angel "For with God nothing shall be impossible" is a good one and something we need to hold onto during these days. I want to emphasize, however, that there are folk who have taken this statement and twisted and distorted its meaning. There is nothing impossible with God when He has determined to do it, but He will not necessarily do the impossible we ask of Him. Many people use this verse as a cliché to cover up the fact that they want their own selfish desires. Nothing is impossible with God but there is a great deal that is impossible with you and me. When a man says, "Nothing is impossible with God" and fails at some task he claims the Lord gave him to do, it causes unbelievers to ridicule God. Anything God determines to do He can accomplish, because there is nothing impossible with God. But that does not mean He will do everything believers want Him to do, because some things are not included in His plan. Let us put everything in proper perspective before we do a lot of talking that will hurt and harm the cause of Jesus Christ rather than help it.

And Mary said, Behold the handmaid of the Lord; be it unto me according to thy word. And the angel departed from her [Luke 1:38].

This verse reveals Mary's submission to the will of God. She told the angel, "Be it unto me according to thy word." At that very moment a cloud came over her life, and that cloud was there until the Lord Jesus Christ came back from the dead. The resurrection of Christ proves His virgin birth. It was questioned until then. You cannot deny the Virgin Birth and believe the Resurrection, or vice versa. The Virgin Birth and the Resurrection go together; they stand or fall together.

MARY VISITS ELISABETH

After a time Mary decided to visit Elisabeth up in the hill country of Judea.

And Mary arose in those days, and went into the hill country with haste, into a city of Juda;

And entered into the house of Zacharias, and saluted Elisabeth.

And it came to pass, that, when Elisabeth heard the salutation of Mary, the babe leaped in her womb; and Elisabeth was filled with the Holy Ghost [Luke 1:39–41].

What we are dealing with here is miraculous, and there is no use trying to offer a natural explanation. You either believe what happened in these verses or you do not. I am so weary of people today, especially preachers, who try to appear intellectual by attempting to explain away the miracles in the Bible. You either accept the miracles of the Bible or you do not, and what took place in these verses was a miracle. This woman is filled with the Holy Spirit, and the babe leaps in her womb.

And she spake out with a loud voice, and said, Blessed art thou among women, and blessed is the fruit of thy womb [Luke 1:42].

This begins the first song given to us in Luke's gospel, and it is lovely. Dr. Luke was the poet who gives us all the songs of Christmas; this is the first one, and it comes from Elisabeth.

And whence is this to me, that the mother of my Lord should come to me?

For, lo, as soon as the voice of thy salutation sounded in mine ears, the babe leaped in my womb for joy.

And blessed is she that believed: for there shall be a performance of those things which were told her from the Lord [Luke 1:43–45].

Little is said in Scripture about Elisabeth. She sang the first song of the New Testament, and when you have a soloist like this, you should not ignore her. She is a remarkable person. She had faith while her husband Zacharias did not. He was struck dumb because of his unbelief, but Elisabeth was not. She believed God. Now she encourages Mary. Mary is a young woman and Elisabeth is an old woman. Elisabeth had walked with God for many years and she assures her that there would be a performance of those things which had been revealed to her. I would like to give Elisabeth a little credit along with the others. She should not be deified, of course. She was only a woman, just as Mary was only a woman. And Mary needed the encouragement that Elisabeth could give.

And Mary said, My soul doth magnify the Lord,

And my spirit hath rejoiced in God my Saviour.

For he hath regarded the low estate of his handmaiden: for, behold, from henceforth all generations shall call me blessed [Luke 1:46–48].

Now Mary sings a song. This is known as the *Magnificat.* This song teaches us several interesting things. Mary tells us in her song that she needed a Savior and that she rejoiced in Him. Protestant friend, let us call her blessed. We don't make her a goddess and kneel before her, but we do need to call her blessed. It was her glorious privilege to be the mother of the Son of God, to bring Him into the world. We should not play it down, but we should not play it up either. She was a wonderful person, and it was no accident that she was chosen by God. It was, His definite decision, and God makes no mistakes.

Listen as Mary continues to sing her song:

For he that is mighty hath done to me great things; and holy is his name.

And his mercy is on them that fear him from generation to generation.

He hath shewed strength with his arm; he hath scattered the proud in the imagination of their hearts.

He hath put down the mighty from their seats, and exalted them of low degree.

He hath filled the hungry with good things; and the rich he hath sent empty away.

He hath holpen his servant Israel, in remembrance of his mercy;

As he spake to our fathers, to Abraham, and to his seed for ever [Luke 1:49–55].

Mary sings, "He hath shewed strength with his arm." In Isaiah 53:1 the prophet Isaiah said, ". . . to whom is the arm of the LORD revealed?" Then Isaiah begins immediately to reveal the Lamb of God that takes away the sin of the world. God has shown the strength of His arm and revealed His power and love in the salvation He has given to mankind.

Mary also mentions Abraham in her song. There is more reference to Abraham than to any other person in the Old Testament. In fact, there is more about Abraham on the human plane than about anyone else in the Bible.

And Mary abode with her about three months, and returned to her own house [Luke 1:56].

BIRTH OF JOHN

The remainder of this chapter records the birth of John the Baptist and the song of Zacharias. I will lift out some of the high points.

Now Elisabeth's full time came that she should be delivered; and she brought forth a son.

And her neighbours and her cousins heard how the Lord had shewed great mercy upon her; and they rejoiced with her.

And it came to pass, that on the eighth day they came to circumcise the child; and they called him Zacharias, after the name of his father.

And his mother answered and said, Not so; but he shall be called John [Luke 1:57–60].

They named the baby after his father at first. Elisabeth, however, set the record straight and said that he was to be called John.

And they said unto her, There is none of thy kindred that is called by this name.

And they made signs to his father, how he would have him called.

And he asked for a writing table, and wrote, saying, His name is John. And they marvelled all.

And his mouth was opened immediately, and his tongue loosed, and he spake, and praised God [Luke 1:61–64].

In those days a family name was usually given to a new baby. When the question of naming the baby came along, the relatives assumed he would be called Zacharias—Zacharias Jr., I guess. Elisabeth made the correction, but they appealed to Zacharias. Since he could not speak, he wrote for them, "His name *is* John." He had already been named by God. Those present marveled at the name.

After this, Zacharias was able to speak again and he immediately began to sing praises to God. Although he did not have much faith, when the baby was born he could rejoice in God. Again, the lack of faith displayed by Zacharias is a quality many of us have. When God hears and answers prayer, we really get up and rejoice. I sometimes think that the reason God answers prayer for some of us weaker saints is so that we will have something to rejoice about. As a rule, weaker saints do not do much rejoicing. The stronger saints, with more faith, rejoice in all circumstances.

And fear came on all that dwelt round about them: and all these sayings were noised abroad throughout all the hill country of Judaea.

And all they that heard them laid them up in their hearts, saying, What manner of child shall this be! And the hand of the Lord was with him.

And his father Zacharias was filled with the Holy Ghost, and prophesied saying,

Blessed be the Lord God of Israel; for he hath visited and redeemed his people,

And hath raised up an horn of salvation for us in the house of his servant David [Luke 1:65–69].

It was quite obvious that John was going to be an unusual child.

At John's birth, Zacharias, who has been dumb for about nine months, is not only able to speak, but he will sing a solo. Elisabeth sang the first song, Mary sang the second one, and now it is quite proper that Zacharias sing a song. His song is one of prophecy. Although Zacharias is not in the line of David, he does recognize that his son is going to be the forerunner of Jesus Christ, as foretold by Malachi and Isaiah. John is to be the one to announce the coming of the Messiah. The presence of the forerunner indicates that the Messiah is not far behind. He is coming soon.

As he spake by the mouth of his holy prophets, which have been since the world began:

That we should be saved from our enemies, and from the hand of all that hate us;

To perform the mercy promised to our fathers, and to remember his holy covenant;

The oath which he sware to our father Abraham,

That he would grant unto us, that we being delivered out of the hand of our enemies might serve him without fear,

In holiness and righteousness before him, all the days of our life [Luke 1:70–75].

God made these promises to Abraham. Mary, Elisabeth, and Zacharias still believed that the promises made to Abraham would be fulfilled. There are some today who have given up and do not believe God will make good His promises to Abraham. Friends, if you believe God is going to make good John 3:16 to you, you have no right to discount the promises God made to Abraham.

And thou, child, shalt be called the prophet of the Highest: for thou shalt go before the face of the Lord to prepare his ways;

To give knowledge of salvation unto his people by the remission of their sins,

Through the tender mercy of our God; whereby the dayspring from on high hath visited us,

To give light to them that sit in darkness and in the shadow of death, to guide our feet into the way of peace.

And the child grew, and waxed strong in spirit, and was in the deserts till the day of his shewing unto Israel [Luke 1:76–80].

John was to be called a prophet of the Highest. He was to go before the face of the Lord to prepare His ways. John knew that the Messiah was in their midst. John the Baptist was a very unusual person. He was prepared to do a special task for God.

CHAPTER 2

THEME: *Birth of Jesus at Bethlehem in a stable; reception of Jesus: angels announce His birth to shepherds; shepherds visit stable; circumcision of Jesus and purification of Mary; incident in temple concerning Simeon; incident in temple concerning Anna; return to Nazareth; visit of Joseph, Mary, and Jesus to Jerusalem when Jesus was twelve*

Jesus was brought to the temple when He was eight days old to be circumcised according to Mosaic Law: "But when the fulness of the time was come, God sent forth his Son, made of a woman, made under the law, To redeem them that were under the law, that we might receive the adoption of sons" (Gal. 4:4–5). As a result of this visit to Jerusalem, we have the songs of Simeon and Anna.

The one isolated incident from the boyhood of Jesus is recorded by Dr. Luke to let us know that Jesus had a normal human childhood (see v. 52). "Jesus increased in wisdom (mental) and stature (physical), and in favor with God and man (spiritual)."

Before we look at the text, it is necessary to consider some background material. As you recall, Luke's gospel is historical and written especially for the Greek and the thinking man. It also has a great spiritual purpose which is to present the Son of God. Neander, one of the great saints of the past, made this statement: "The three great historical nations had to contribute, each in its own peculiar way, to prepare the soil for the planting of Christianity,—the Jews on the side of the religious element; the Greeks on the side of science and art; the Romans, as masters of the world, on the side of the political element." The Gospels of Matthew, Mark, and Luke were each directed to a particular segment of humanity. Matthew was written to the Jew, Mark was written to the Roman, and Luke was written to the Greek.

Dr. Gregory wrote: "The Greeks are clearly distinguished from the other great historic races by certain marked characteristics. They were the representatives of reason and humanity in the ancient world. They looked upon themselves as having the mission of perfecting men" (*Key to the Gospels*, p. 211). They were the cosmopolitans of that age. They made their gods in the likeness of men, as well as in their own likeness, and therefore joined to human culture utter worldliness and godlessness.

Paul was the right person to go to Athens to enlighten the Greeks about their altar to the "UNKNOWN GOD." Dr. Luke, a Gentile, went with Paul.

The mission of the Greeks was thus evidently a part of the preparation for the coming of the Lord Jesus Christ into the world. It forced the thinking men of that age to feel and confess the insufficiency of human reason (even in its most perfect development) for the deliverance and perfection of mankind. It left them waiting and longing for one who could accomplish this work.

The Greek language became a vehicle for getting the Word of God out. The gospel was communicated to the world in the Greek language. God used Alexander the Great to make it possible.

Of Alexander the Great it has been written: "He took up the meshes of the net of civilization, which were lying in disorder on the edges of the Asiatic shore, and spread them over all other countries which he traversed in his wonderful campaigns. The East and the West were suddenly brought together. Separated tribes were united under a common government. New cities were built, as the centres of political life. New lines of communication were opened, as the channels of commercial activity. The new culture penetrated the mountain ranges of Pisidia and Lycaonia. The Tigris and Euphrates became Greek rivers. The language of Athens was heard among the Jewish colonies of Babylonia; and a Grecian Babylon was built by the conqueror in Egypt and called by his name" (Conybeare and Howson, *Life, Times, and Travels of St. Paul*, vol. 1, p. 9). That city was Alexandria; it still bears this name.

Keep this background in mind as we look at the birth of the Lord Jesus Christ.

BIRTH OF JESUS AT BETHLEHEM IN A STABLE

And it came to pass in those days, that there went out a decree from Caesar Augustus, that all the world should be taxed.

(And this taxing was first made when Cyrenius was governor of Syria.) [Luke 2:1–2].

Someone might think when they read the phrase, "all the world should be taxed" that the Roman Empire was taxing the United States of America too. The Greek word for *world, oikoumene,* means "inhabited earth" and referred to the civilized world of that day. My uncivilized ancestors in northern Europe in those days were not even included in this taxing, although Caesar Augustus would have loved to have taxed everybody if he could have gotten to them.

Who was Caesar Augustus? He was the adopted son of Julius Caesar. Actually his name was Octavianus and he took the name Caesar—I think he had a right to it. Now the name *Augustus* was not a name at all but a title. When the senate submitted to him certain titles like king, emperor, and dictator, he was not satisfied. Instead he chose the title *Augustus*. It had a religious significance, and it was an attempt to deify himself.

It was no accident that Dr. Luke mentioned the name of Caesar Augustus. This man signed a tax bill that the whole world (of that day) be taxed. He needed money to raise an army to control his vast empire and to live in luxury himself. Notice Luke's historical reference that this taxing was first made when Cyrenius was governor of Syria.

And all went to be taxed, every one into his own city.

And Joseph also went up from Galilee, out of the city of Nazareth, into Judaea, unto the city of David, which is called Bethlehem; (because he was of the house and lineage of David:)

To be taxed with Mary his espoused wife, being great with child.

And so it was, that, while they were there, the days were accomplished that she should be delivered.

And she brought forth her firstborn son, and wrapped him in swaddling clothes, and laid him in a manger; because there was no room for them in the inn [Luke 2:3–7].

Joseph and Mary came out of Nazareth in Galilee and went into Judea to Bethlehem, the city of David. Joseph did this because he was of the house and lineage of David. Why did Mary have to go to Bethlehem? She also was of the lineage of David.

I am thrilled when I read this simple, historically accurate passage with tremendous spiritual truth behind it. Caesar Augustus attempted to make himself a god. He wanted to be worshiped. He signed a tax bill which caused a woman and man, peasants, living in Nazareth, to journey to Bethlehem to enroll. That woman was carrying in her womb the Son of God! This is tremendous! This Caesar Augustus tried to make himself God, but nobody today reverences him or pays taxes to him. But that little baby in Mary's womb—many of us worship Him today and call Him our Savior.

Caesar Augustus was merely the tool in God's hand to bring to pass the prophecy "But thou, Beth-lehem Ephratah, though thou be little among the thousands of Judah, yet out of thee shall he come forth unto me that is to be ruler in Israel; whose goings forth have been from of old, from everlasting" (Mic. 5:2). This is a remarkable account.

Everything that happened was arranged by God. If anyone had said to Caesar, "Wait a minute; women about to give birth are going to have to be moved in order for you to get your taxes," I think he would have replied, "I do not care about babies or their mothers; I am only interested in taxes, armies, money and luxury." Well, that is all gone now, including Caesar.

Dr. Luke gets right down to the little human details in this passage. He is saying that Mary put swaddling clothes on this little child—baby clothes and diapers on the Son of God! How perfectly human He was—God manifest in the flesh!

RECEPTION OF JESUS: ANGELS ANNOUNCE HIS BIRTH TO SHEPHERDS; SHEPHERDS VISIT STABLE

And there were in the same country shepherds abiding in the field, keeping watch over their flock by night [Luke 2:8].

Many people ask the question, "When was Jesus Christ born?" It could not have been in the dead of winter or the shepherds would not have been out at night with their sheep. But the date of His birth is irrelevant, just as the day upon which He was crucified is irrelevant. The Scripture does not say *when* He was born; the important thing is that He was born. The Scripture does not say *when* He was crucified; the important thing is that He died for our sins.

And, lo, the angel of the Lord came upon them, and the glory of the Lord

shone round about them: and they were sore afraid.

And the angel said unto them, Fear not: for, behold, I bring you good tidings of great joy, which shall be to all people.

For unto you is born this day in the city of David a Saviour, which is Christ the Lord [Luke 2:9–11].

It is wonderful to see a little baby come into the world, and your heart goes out to him; there is a sympathy that goes from you to him. That is the way God entered the world. He could have entered—as He will when He comes to earth the second time—in power and great glory. Instead, He came in the weakest way possible, as a baby. George Macdonald put it this way:

They all were looking for a King
  To slay their foes and lift them high:
Thou cam'st, a little baby thing
  That made a woman cry.

That is the way the Saviour came into the world. He did not lay aside His deity; He laid aside His glory. There should have been more than just a few shepherds and angels to welcome Him—all of creation should have been there. Instead of collecting taxes, that fellow Caesar should have been in Bethlehem to worship Him. Jesus Christ could have forced him to do that very thing, but He did not. He laid aside, not His deity, but His prerogatives of deity. He came a little baby thing.

And this shall be a sign unto you; Ye shall find the babe wrapped in swaddling clothes, lying in a manger [Luke 2:12].

Again Dr. Luke is emphasizing His humanity. He came into this world as a human being. He is touched with the feeling of our infirmities.

God knows about mankind. He knows you, and He knows me. He understands us because He came into this world a human being. This also means that we can know something about God, because He took upon Himself our humanity.

And suddenly there was with the angel a multitude of the heavenly host praising God, and saying,

Glory to God in the highest and on earth peace, good will toward men [Luke 2:13–14].

Our Authorized Version gives the wrong impression here. The angels did not say, "on earth peace, good will toward men." What they actually said was, "peace to men of good will," or "peace among men with whom He is pleased." The angels did not make the asinine statement that many men make today which goes, "Let's have peace, peace, peace." My friend, "There is no peace, saith the LORD, unto the wicked" (Isa. 48:22). We live in a day when we need to beat our plowshares into swords—not the other way around. We live in a wicked world. We live in a Satan-dominated world, and therefore there is no peace. There is, however, peace to men of good will. If you are one of those who has come to Christ and taken him as Savior, you can know this peace of God. Romans 5:1 states: "Therefore being justified by faith, we have peace with God through our Lord Jesus Christ." When Christ came the first time, this is the kind of peace He brought. At His second coming He will come as the Prince of Peace; at that time He will put down unrighteousness and rebellion in the world. He will establish peace on the earth. But until He comes again, there will be no peace on this earth.

And it came to pass, as the angels were gone away from them into heaven, the shepherds said one to another, Let us now go even unto Bethlehem, and see this thing which is come to pass, which the Lord hath made known unto us.

And they came with haste, and found Mary, and Joseph, and the babe lying in a manger [Luke 2:15–16].

The shepherds hurried to Bethlehem. There they found Mary, Joseph, and the baby Jesus. They were probably the first to visit the Babe since Matthew tells us that the wise men did not arrive until much later. In fact, when the wise men finally found the Lord Jesus, He was living in a house and probably many months had elapsed.

And when they had seen it, they made known abroad the saying which was told them concerning this child.

And all they that heard it wondered at those things which were told them by the shepherds.

But Mary kept all these things, and pondered them in her heart.

And the shepherds returned, glorifying and praising God for all the things that they had heard and seen, as it was told unto them [Luke 2:17–20].

Mary pondered many things in her heart as a mother would do. Because of danger to His life, Mary and Joseph took the young child into Egypt for a time and later returned to Nazareth.

Since He had come into the human family, and since He had been born under the Mosaic Law, He followed the Law.

CIRCUMCISION OF JESUS AND PURIFICATION OF MARY

And when eight days were accomplished for the circumcising of the child, his name was called JESUS, which was so named of the angel before he was conceived in the womb.

And when the days of her purification according to the law of Moses were accomplished, they brought him to Jerusalem, to present him to the Lord [Luke 2:21–22].

For forty days a woman was considered unclean after the birth of a child, according to the Mosaic Law. Mary as a sinner had to bring a sacrifice to the Lord. She needed a Savior as she said.

(As it is written in the law of the Lord, Every male that openeth the womb shall be called holy to the Lord;)

And to offer a sacrifice according to that which is said in the law of the Lord, A pair of turtledoves, or two young pigeons [Luke 2:23–24].

Mary and Joseph offered turtledoves as a sacrifice, which were an evidence of their poverty. The sacrifice was for Mary and not for the Child. As far as we know, Jesus never offered a sacrifice.

INCIDENT IN TEMPLE CONCERNING SIMEON

And, behold, there was a man in Jerusalem, whose name was Simeon; and the same man was just and devout, waiting for the consolation of Israel: and the Holy Ghost was upon him.

And it was revealed unto him by the Holy Ghost, that he should not see death, before he had seen the Lord's Christ.

And he came by the Spirit into the temple: and when the parents brought in the child Jesus, to do for him after the custom of the law,

Then took he him up in his arms, and blessed God, and said [Luke 2:25–28].

There was a man by the name of Simeon who by the Holy Spirit was in the temple when the Lord Jesus was brought in to fulfill the Mosaic Law. God had promised Simeon that he would *see* the salvation of God. What did he see? He saw a little Baby. Salvation is a Person, and not something that you *do*. Salvation is a Person, and that Person is the Lord Jesus Christ. You either have Him, or you don't have Him. You either trust Him, or you don't trust Him. Do *you* have Him today?

Now here is another solo, and Simeon is singing it for us.

Lord, now lettest thou thy servant depart in peace, according to thy word:

For mine eyes have seen thy salvation,

Which thou hast prepared before the face of all people;

A light to lighten the Gentiles, and the glory of thy people Israel [Luke 2:29–32].

This is a remarkable statement coming from a man who was limited in his outlook upon life—that is, he was limited to a particular area geographically. Yet he saw the One who was to be the Savior of the *world*. This is to me one of the amazing things about the Word of God, especially the New Testament. Although given to a certain people, it is certainly directed to the world. No other religion pointed that way. You will notice that the religions of the world are generally localized for a peculiar people, generally a race or nation. But Christianity has been from the outset for all people everywhere.

And Joseph and his mother marvelled at those things which were spoken of him.

And Simeon blessed them, and said unto Mary his mother, Behold, this child is set for the fall and rising again of many in Israel; and for a sign which shall be spoken against;

(Yea, a sword shall pierce through thy own soul also,) that the thoughts of many hearts may be revealed [Luke 2:33–35].

Notice that Luke calls them "Joseph and his mother," not His father and mother.

Mary paid a tremendous price to bring the Savior into the world. She paid an awful price to stand beneath the cross of the Lord Jesus and watch Him die.

The cross of Christ has moved many people—artists have painted the picture, songwriters have written music about it, and authors and preachers have sketched those moments with words. There is a danger of dwelling on His death in a sympathetic way. Christ did not die to elicit anyone's sympathy. He does not want your sympathy, He wants your faith. Later in the Gospel of Luke, when the Lord is on the way to the cross, some women began to weep. Jesus turned to them and said, "Daughters of Jerusalem, weep not for me, but weep for yourselves, and for your children" (Luke 23:28). If you have tears for Jesus, save them for yourself and your family. Do not weep for Him, because He does not want your sympathy. Jesus Christ wants your faith.

However, when Mary stood beneath that cross and watched Jesus die, it was with a broken heart. Of course her suffering had nothing to do with *your* salvation; her suffering had nothing to do with *her* salvation. Her suffering was due to a human relationship. She was His human mother. She had brought Him into the world and raised Him. He was her son. You see, when our Lord looked down from the cross and said, ". . .Woman, behold thy son!" (John 19:26), a human relationship was there that no one else had. She was suffering as His mother. And at that time the prophecy of Simeon was fulfilled—the sword pierced through her soul also.

INCIDENT IN TEMPLE CONCERNING ANNA

There are many solos in this gospel and now here is another one.

And there was one Anna, a prophetess, the daughter of Phanuel, of the tribe of Aser: she was of a great age, and had lived with an husband seven years from her virginity;

And she was a widow of about fourscore and four years, which departed not from the temple, but served God with fastings and prayers night and day.

And she coming in that instant gave thanks likewise unto the Lord, and spake of him to all them that looked for redemption in Jerusalem [Luke 2:36–38].

Anna, like Simeon, was living very close to God; and He granted to her also the gracious insight of recognizing His Son, her Messiah. She gave thanks. Although her song is not recorded, it is a song of praise.

I cannot refrain from saying that there are those who say there are ten lost tribes of Israel (that is, that the ten tribes which went into Assyrian captivity in the eighth century B.C. migrated north rather than returning to the land of Israel). If you search through the Bible from the time Israel returned to the land after the captivity, you can pick up practically all of the tribes. Here Anna is mentioned as a member of the tribe of Asher. Evidently Anna did not get lost!

The account of Matthew tells us that the next event in the life of Jesus was a trip to Egypt. Luke omits this account entirely. It is well to remember again the purpose for writing each gospel is different. Matthew presents the Lord Jesus Christ as King, and Luke presents Him as the perfect Man. The coming of the wise men does not fit into Luke's purpose for writing. The wise men came looking for a king, not for the ideal of the Greek race. Luke presents Him as the perfect Man, and notice how he carries out his purpose even at this point.

RETURN TO NAZARETH

And when they had performed all things according to the law of the Lord, they returned into Galilee, to their own city Nazareth.

And the child grew, and waxed strong in spirit, filled with wisdom: and the grace of God was upon him [Luke 2:39–40].

Luke is presenting the perfect Man. Dr. Luke looks at the Boy not only through the eyes of an obstetrician but through the watchful eye of a pediatrician. The Lord Jesus grew (physically), waxed strong in spirit (spiritually), and was filled with wisdom (mentally). The grace of God was upon this Boy and He grew physically, spiritually, and mentally.

VISIT OF JOSEPH, MARY, AND JESUS TO JERUSALEM WHEN JESUS WAS TWELVE

Next is recorded an incident that only Dr. Luke relates. Luke does this because he is a pediatrician and is interested in the Lord as a boy as well as a man. Luke lifts one scene out of the boyhood of Jesus when He was twelve years old. Since nothing is recorded in the Gospels about the early life of Jesus, some people call this segment of His life the "silent years." I do not consider them silent years; I believe that the Old Testament Scriptures fill in these years if you look closely. Luke's account is a detailed, isolated incident that took place when Jesus was twelve years old.

Now his parents went to Jerusalem every year at the feast of the passover.

And when he was twelve years old, they went up to Jerusalem after the custom of the feast.

And when they had fulfilled the days, as they returned, the child Jesus tarried behind in Jerusalem; and Joseph and his mother knew not of it.

But they, supposing him to have been in the company, went a day's journey; and they sought him among their kinsfolk and acquaintance.

And when they found him not, they turned back again to Jerusalem, seeking him [Luke 2:41–45].

Mary and Joseph were raising a normal, healthy child. He did not run around wearing a halo, friend. The artists of the Middle Ages had some strange conceptions about the Lord Jesus, both as a child and as an adult. I do not believe He looked like any of their ideas. He was just a normal boy.

In those days people traveled in companies. When the time came to leave Jerusalem, the folk going to Galilee gathered together at a little town right north of Jerusalem to begin the journey home. That is where they missed Him. Joseph probably said, "Where is Jesus?" And Mary replied, "I thought He was with you." They looked for Him among all the people they knew, and when they discovered that He was missing, they returned to Jerusalem. They looked for Jesus for three days, and where do you suppose they found Him? He was in the temple.

And it came to pass, that after three days they found him in the temple, sitting in the midst of the doctors, both hearing them, and asking them questions.

And all that heard him were astonished at his understanding and answers.

And when they saw him, they were amazed: and his mother said unto him, Son, why hast thou thus dealt with us? behold, thy father and I have sought thee sorrowing.

And he said unto them, How is it that ye sought me? wist ye not that I must be about my Father's business?

And they understood not the saying which he spake unto them [Luke 2:46–50].

When Mary and Joseph finally found Jesus in the temple, He was standing in the midst of the learned doctors of that day, both hearing them and asking them questions. Apparently He was asking them questions they could not answer. And they were astonished at His answers—remember, He was only twelve! I think it is clear that Mary and Joseph were a little provoked with Him.

The answer of Jesus revealed His surprise that they did not realize He should be about His Father's business. Now, if Joseph were the father, he could have stepped up and said, "Well, what are you trying to do—get some carpenter work here in Jerusalem?" No—His Father was not Joseph. He was speaking of the business of His heavenly Father. Mary, at this point, did not exactly appreciate who He was and what His work entailed, but she pondered these things in her heart.

And he went down with them, and came to Nazareth, and was subject unto them: but his mother kept all these sayings in her heart.

And Jesus increased in wisdom and stature, and in favour with God and man [Luke 2:51–52].

Jesus was subject unto His parents. This is interesting in the light of the fact that young people today are rebelling and are demanding to be heard. They say we ought to listen to them. I have listened to them, and I have not heard them say anything yet, regardless of all the publicity they are given on the television and radio. I personally do not think a college student has much to say. He is still green behind his ears, regardless of his I.Q. The information he has been given is limited and biased, and he does not have the experience to evaluate it. It is remarkable to see that this Boy, Jesus, the Son of God, obeyed His parents and was subject unto them!

Dr. Luke gives us a report about those silent years when Jesus was growing to adulthood. He grew in wisdom (mentally), in stature (physically), in favor with God (spiritually) and man (socially). In every area the Lord Jesus Christ was growing into perfect manhood.

CHAPTER 3

***THEME:** Ministry of John the Baptist; baptism of Jesus; genealogy of Mary*

Luke, with a true historian's approach, dates the ministry of John the Baptist with secular history. He places the emphasis upon John's message of repentance as the condition for the coming of the Messiah. From the Mosaic system of washing in water, which was a common custom of immersion in that day, John baptized those who came to him as merely a preparation (a moral reformation) for the coming of Christ. Christ would baptize by the Holy Spirit—a real transformation.

The genealogy in this chapter is Mary's, which reveals two facts. First, it goes back to Adam, the father of the human family. Jesus was truly human. Matthew, in presenting Jesus as king, traces the genealogy back only as far as Abraham. Luke, in presenting Jesus as man, goes back to Adam. In the second place, Mary was descended from David through another than Solomon—David's son Nathan (cf. v. 31; 1 Chron. 3:5).

MINISTRY OF JOHN THE BAPTIST

This chapter contains a great deal of detail; Luke is a stickler for accuracy.

Now in the fifteenth year of the reign of Tiberius Caesar, Pontius Pilate being governor of Judaea, and Herod being tetrarch of Galilee, and his brother Philip tetrarch of Ituraea and of the region of Trachonitis, and Lysanias the tetrarch of Abilene [Luke 3:1].

Six characters are identified in this verse which allow us to date the time. Caesar Augustus was emperor when the Lord Jesus Christ was born, but when John began his ministry Tiberius Caesar was emperor. Secular history, which must supply us with the details, tells us that Tiberius was brilliant but brutal. He was clever but cunning. He was inhuman and profane. He attempted to master the world.

Next the names of the puppet rulers are given.

Annas and Caiaphas being the high priests, the word of God came unto John the son of Zacharias in the wilderness [Luke 3:2].

Annas and Caiaphas were the high priests. Why were there *two* high priests? Two high priests reveals the power of Rome over the religion of Jerusalem in that day. Annas was the power behind the throne, but Caiaphas was the one Rome put out in front.

The normal experience for John would have been to serve in the temple as his father had. He should have been a leader in the temple, but he despised it. Instead he went into the wilderness and renounced his priesthood. He did not wish to serve in a corrupt system, and so he became a prophet. That is the picture: John was a priest and he became a prophet.

John the Baptist is one of those striking characters who appear from time to time. He reminded the people of Elijah because of certain similarities in their methods. He also reminded the people of One who was one day going to appear—the Messiah. John the Baptist was a paradoxical person. He was truly an unusual man. Luke has told us of his miraculous birth. It was attended by a visitation from the angel Gabriel. His entire boyhood was passed over, and the next event in his life was the beginning of his ministry. He was a priest, a prophet, and a preacher. He was a priest by birth because he was the son of Zacharias, but he was called by God to be a prophet.

And he came into all the country about Jordan, preaching the baptism of repentance for the remission of sins [Luke 3:3].

John preaches the baptism of repentance. He is the last of the prophets. He is actually an Old Testament character who walks out onto the pages of the New Testament. He is picturesque, unshaven, and shaggy, wearing camel's hair clothes. He is different in his dress, his diet, and his looks. He will receive the same reception that many prophets received—he will be put to death.

The most unwelcome message, even today, is the voice of the prophet. The world will not receive a man who contradicts its philosophy of life. If you want to be popular, and this is also true of preachers, you have to sing in unison with the crowd. God have mercy on the pulpit that is nothing in the world but a sounding board for what the congregation is saying. The world does not want to hear the voice of God, especially when that voice speaks of judgment. John's message was very strong.

As it is written in the book of the words of Esaias the prophet, saying, The voice of one crying in the wilderness, Prepare ye the way of the Lord, make his paths straight.

Every valley shall be filled, and every mountain and hill shall be brought low; and the crooked shall be made straight, and the rough ways shall be made smooth;

And all flesh shall see the salvation of God.

Then said he to the multitude that came forth to be baptized of him, O generation of vipers, who hath warned you to flee from the wrath to come? [Luke 3:4–7].

I wonder how long a preacher would last in any church if he began his Sunday sermon by saying, "O generation of vipers"? I do not think he would be in the pulpit the following Sunday. The people would soon get rid of him. I do not recommend using John's unusual introduction for a sermon, but I do think it would be appropriate in many churches.

Bring forth therefore fruits worthy of repentance, and begin not to say within yourselves, We have Abraham to our father: for I say unto you, That God is able of these stones to raise up children unto Abraham [Luke 3:8].

John's message was one of repentance. That is not exactly our message today, although repentance is included in faith. Paul said to the Thessalonian believers that they had ". . . turned to God from idols to serve the living and true God" (1 Thess. 1:9). You can't turn *to* God without turning *from* something. (When you turn *to* anything, you turn *from* something else.) When you turn to God, you turn from sin—and that is repentance. When you accept Christ as your Savior, you are going to turn from the things of the world. Perhaps you have heard about the love of God, but you have not been moved by it and you have wondered why. You need to hear that voice crying in the wilderness, "Repent." Repentance is a part of saving faith. Repentance is not the message of the hour; we preach the grace of God, but if you have been a recipient of God's grace and have turned *to* Him, you are going to have to turn *from* your sins. If you do not turn from your sins, you have not really turned to God. Repentance is involved in salvation, but today God's message is, ". . . Believe on the Lord Jesus Christ, and thou shalt be saved . . ." (Acts 16:31).

And now also the axe is laid unto the root of the trees: every tree therefore which bringeth not forth good fruit is hewn down, and cast into the fire [Luke 3:9].

In John's day, trees that did not produce were useless. They were cut down and used for firewood. John's message is strong. John never brought the message of the redeeming love of God. He wasn't called to give that message. His was a message of impending judgment. We need to recognize that this is one of the facets of the message from God for our day also. The nation of Israel had not been productive, as God had expected, and judgment was going to be their portion. John was telling Israel that if they did not bring forth fruit, the axe would come down on the root of the tree. The Lord Jesus Christ is saying the same thing to the church today.

And the people asked him, saying, What shall we do then?

He answereth and saith unto them, He that hath two coats, let him impart to him that hath none; and he that hath meat, let him do likewise [Luke 3:10–11].

John was telling Israel in plain, understandable language that they were living for "self" and not attempting to share what they had with others.

Then came also publicans to be baptized, and said unto him, Master, what shall we do?

And he said unto them, Exact no more than that which is appointed you [Luke 3:12–13].

The publicans were tax collectors and were well known for their greediness. They turned, however, to John and asked, "What shall we do?" They also turned to the Lord.

And the soldiers likewise demanded of him, saying, And what shall we do? And he said unto them, Do violence to no man, neither accuse any falsely; and be content with your wages [Luke 3:14].

This is a practical message that John gave to these people who came from different classes and conditions. My friend, if you are a printer, you reveal that you are a Christian by the way you print. If you are a soldier, you reveal your

Christianity by the way you soldier. If you are a housewife, you reveal your Christianity by the way you are a housewife. You reveal what you are. "Wherefore by their fruits ye shall know them" (Matt. 7:20).

And as the people were in expectation, and all men mused in their hearts of John, whether he were the Christ, or not;

John answered, saying unto them all, I indeed baptize you with water; but one mightier than I cometh, the latchet of whose shoes I am not worthy to unloose: he shall baptize you with the Holy Ghost and with fire:

Whose fan is in his hand, and he will throughly purge his floor, and will gather the wheat into his garner; but the chaff he will burn with fire unquenchable [Luke 3:15–17].

John makes it clear that his message is not the final one. He is preparing the way for the One to come.

John baptized with water. Jesus has been baptizing with the Holy Spirit for over nineteen hundred years now. He shall also baptize with fire at His second coming. Fire speaks of judgment.

Some folk think that this is a reference to the Day of Pentecost when the Holy Spirit came, and there was the appearance of fire on the heads of those assembled. However, it is important to notice that in Acts 2:3 it was ". . . *like as of* fire . . ." (italics mine)—it was not fire. The coming of the Holy Spirit was not the fulfillment of the baptism of fire. That will take place at the second coming of our Lord.

But Herod the tetrarch, being reproved by him for Herodias his brother Philip's wife, and for all the evils which Herod had done,

Added yet this above all, that he shut up John in prison [Luke 3:19–20].

John had reproved Herod publicly because he had married Herodias, the wife of his brother Philip. Herodias had been furious over this and demanded that John be put in prison. Herod fulfilled her desire and had John arrested and imprisoned.

THE BAPTISM OF JESUS

Now when all the people were baptized, it came to pass, that Jesus also being baptized, and praying, the heaven was opened,

And the Holy Ghost descended in a bodily shape like a dove upon him, and a voice came from heaven, which said, Thou art my beloved Son; in thee I am well pleased [Luke 3:21–22].

Luke is not attempting to give a chronological order of events. If he were, he would have recorded the baptism of Jesus before the arrest of John the Baptist.

At the baptism of Jesus, the Trinity is revealed. The Holy Spirit descends upon Jesus, who is also a member of the Trinity, and the heavenly Father speaks from heaven.

GENEALOGY OF MARY

The rest of this chapter deals with the genealogy of Mary, not Joseph. The genealogy of Joseph is found in Matthew's gospel. Matthew's genealogy begins with Abraham and comes down to the Lord Jesus Christ through David and through Solomon. The *legal* title to the throne came through Joseph.

Luke's genealogy is different. It is given in reverse order from Matthew's. Luke goes back to David and then back to Adam. Luke gives Mary's story, and this is clearly her genealogy. The royal blood of David flowed through her veins also, and Jesus' *blood* title to the throne of David came through her.

Two things about this genealogy should be noted. First, Dr. Luke makes it clear that Joseph was *not* the father of the Lord Jesus Christ.

And Jesus himself began to be about thirty years of age, being (as was supposed) the son of Joseph, which was the son of Heli [Luke 3:23].

The word *son* as it is used in this genealogy is not in the better manuscripts. Joseph was not the son of Heli. The word *son* is added to indicate the lineage through the father (the man) who was the head of the house. In other words, the genealogy is listed according to the man's name. In Matthew, where it is giving the genealogy through Joseph, it states that Jacob *begat* Joseph.

The second important thing to notice is verse 31 which reads:

Which was the son of Melea, which was the son of Menan, which was the son of Mattatha, which was the son of Nathan, which was the son of David [Luke 3:31].

Matthew traces the line of Christ through David's son, Solomon. That is the royal line. Luke traces the line of Christ through David's son, Nathan. Mary had the blood of David in her veins. Jesus Christ is the Son of David.

Luke reveals Jesus Christ as the Son of Man and the Savior of the *world*. His line does not stop with Abraham, but goes all the way back to Adam who was the first "son" of God—the created son of God. But he fell from that lofty position when he sinned. Jesus Christ, the last Adam and the Son of God, is come to bring mankind back into that relationship with God which Adam formerly had and lost. This relationship is accomplished through faith in the Lord Jesus Christ.

CHAPTER 4

THEME: *The temptation of Jesus; Jesus returns to Galilee and Nazareth—rejected by His hometown; Jesus moves His headquarters to Capernaum and continues His ministry*

Jesus is tempted as a man by Satan. They were human temptations such as come to all of us. They cover the entire spectrum of human temptations and are threefold:

1. Satan asks Jesus to make stones into bread to satisfy needs of the body. There is nothing wrong with bread. Bread is the staff of life. The body has need of bread, and Jesus was starving. What is wrong? To use His great powers to minister to Himself would be selfish. He must demonstrate the truth of the great principle, ". . . Man shall not live by bread alone . . ." (Matt. 4:4). This is contrary to the thinking of this crass materialistic age that lives only to satisfy the whims of the body. Modern man in our secular society says, "Eat, drink, and be merry, for tomorrow we die." And as far as man is concerned, that ends it all. Selfishness is the curse of a creedless, secular society. Our Lord, in meeting this temptation, refuted the popular philosophy of the world.

2. Satan offers Jesus the nations of the world. Nations derive their power through brute force and political intrigue. War is a way of life. Hate and fear are the whips to motivate the mob. This is satanic, and Satan offers the kingdoms of the world on these terms. Men must be changed in order to enter God's kingdom: "Jesus answered and said unto him, Verily, verily, I say unto thee, Except a man be born again, he cannot see the kingdom of God" (John 3:3). The answer of Jesus has a note of finality, ". . . Thou shalt worship the Lord thy God, and him only shalt thou serve" (Matt. 4:10). Then the apostle Paul tells us, "For though we walk in the flesh, we do not war after the flesh: (For the weapons of our warfare are not carnal, but mighty through God to the pulling down of strong holds;) Casting down imaginations, and every high thing that exalteth itself against the knowledge of God, and bringing into captivity every thought to the obedience of Christ" (2 Cor. 10:3–5).

3. Satan tempts Jesus to cast Himself down from the temple. It would seem a logical procedure for Jesus to impress the crowd as to His person and mission. But Jesus will follow no easy way to the throne. He must wear the crown of thorns before He wears the crown of glory. Stifler states succinctly, "There are two ways of despising God, one is to ignore His power, the other is to presume upon it." Both are sin. It is easy to do nothing and then mouth pious platitudes about God providing for the sparrows and that He will take care of us. But God says, "In the sweat of thy face shalt thou eat bread . . ." (Gen. 3:19).

For example, the missionary to a foreign land will have to study to learn the language, and then God will help him. We are partners of God, not puppets. Dr. Edward Judson, after considering what his father, Adoniram Judson, suffered in Burma said, "If we succeed without suffering, it is because others have suffered before us. If we suffer without success, it is that others may succeed after us." Jesus rejected a false and phony spiritual stance. His answer was devastating: "Ye shall not tempt the LORD your God, as ye tempted him in Massah" (Deut. 6:16).

Actually, Jesus began His public ministry in His hometown of Nazareth where He was rejected and ejected. It was in the synagogue where He announced the fulfillment of Isaiah 61:1–2 in a remarkable way.

THE TEMPTATION OF JESUS

And Jesus being full of the Holy Ghost returned from Jordan, and was led by the Spirit into the wilderness,

Being forty days tempted of the devil. And in those days he did eat nothing: and when they were ended, he afterward hungered [Luke 4:1–2].

We have before us the testing of the Lord Jesus Christ. The synoptic Gospels—Matthew, Mark, and Luke—all record this testing. John does not record this incident because he is presenting the Lord Jesus as the Son of God with the emphasis upon His deity. The synoptic Gospels place the emphasis upon the humanity of the Lord Jesus. He was tempted as a man. In the Gospel of Luke He is presented as the Son of Man. Luke 3:38 says, "Which was the son of Enos, which was the son of Seth, which was the son of Adam, which was the son of God." This is the genealogy of Mary which traces the line of Christ back to Adam. Being a son of Adam takes Him right back to the beginning of the race of which we are members. It was as a human being that He was tempted in all *points* like we are; yet He was without sin.

There is a frightful and fearful darkness about the temptation of our Lord that is an appalling enigma. I must confess that I cannot explain it, but I will take you to the very edge, and at the fringe I hope we can learn something. There were unseen and hidden forces of evil all about Him. He was surrounded by powers of darkness and destruction. He grappled with the basic problems of mankind, that which is earthy, and He won a victory for mankind. He won a victory for you and me.

There are several preliminary considerations we need to have in mind as we look at the testing of our Lord. We are told that He was filled with the Holy Spirit. As man, the Son of God needed to be filled with the Spirit in order to meet the temptation. And, friend, *I* cannot face the temptations of this world in my own strength. In Romans 7:21 Paul tells us, "I find then a law, that, when I would do good, evil is present with me." Haven't you found that to be true? In Romans 8:3–4 Paul continues, "For what the law could not do, in that it was weak through the flesh, God sending his own Son in the likeness of sinful flesh, and for sin, condemned sin in the flesh: That the righteousness of the law might be fulfilled in us, who walk not after the flesh, but after the Spirit." So in Galatians 5:16 Paul concludes, "This I say then, Walk in the Spirit, and ye shall not fulfil the lust of the flesh." We *need* the Holy Spirit.

In Deuteronomy 8:2 God told the Israelites, "And thou shalt remember all the way which the LORD thy God led thee these forty years in the wilderness, to humble thee, and to prove thee, to know what was in thine heart, whether thou wouldest keep his commandments, or no." In other words, God was *testing* the Israelites. God never tests anyone with evil.

We are told that, before the Lord was tested, He was led (Mark says *driven*) by the Holy Spirit into the wilderness. In other words, the Lord did not *seek* the temptation. Even at the Garden of Gethsemane He prayed, "Let this cup pass from me" (see Luke 22:42).

The Lord's temptation did not begin at the end of the forty days; rather, Luke is telling us that after the temptation He was hungry. He was tempted of the Devil all during those forty days. Satan did not stop tempting the Lord after the wilderness temptation either. At the Garden of Gethsemane was another onslaught of Satan. In verse 13 of this chapter Luke tells us, "And when the devil had ended all the temptation, he departed from him for a *season*."

Something else we need to understand is that Satan is a person. I understand that from thirty percent to ninety percent of the ministers say that he is not a person. The Scripture, however, makes it quite clear that the Devil is a person. When he tempted the Lord Jesus, did he come in bodily form? Did he come as a spirit or did he come as an angel of light? The Bible tells us that the Lord met him face-to-face. We need to realize that Satan is subtle—one time he is a roaring lion seeking whom he may devour, and the next time he is an angel of light deceiving even the elect if he could do so (see 1 Pet. 5:8; 2 Cor. 11:14).

What is the meaning of the Lord's temptation? The word *tempt* has a twofold meaning. To tempt means "to incite and entice to evil," and it means "to seduce." If a person can be seduced to do evil, that means there is something in the individual that causes him to yield. It would not be a temptation unless something in a person could yield to it. However, this was not true of the Lord Jesus Christ. He could say, "Hereafter I will not talk much with you: for the prince of this world cometh, and hath nothing in me" (John 14:30). I do not know about you, friend, but every time Satan comes to me he always finds some place to take hold of. Our Lord was holy, harmless, undefiled and separate from sinners (see Heb. 7:26). The temptation of Christ was not a temptation to do evil.

Then the word *tempt* is used in another way. Genesis 22:1 tells us that ". . . God did tempt Abraham . . ." in that God *tested* Abraham. Also He proved, or tested, Israel for forty years in the wilderness. This raises a question. Could the Lord Jesus Christ have fallen? *No*, Christ could not have fallen. Then was it a legitimate temptation? It was a *test*. All new articles are tested. For example, tires and automobiles are tested. On television commercials the manufacturers show you the new model car and drive it through purgatory to show you the amount of punishment it can take. Everything is tested, and for anything to break down would be pretty embarrassing for the manufacturer. The Lord Jesus Christ could not have fallen; so was this a legitimate test? It was, and let me illustrate this fact with a simple story.

When I was a boy in west Texas, we lived on the west fork of the Brazos River. In the summertime there was not enough water in the stream to rust a shingle nail. It was dry. In wintertime, however, you could have kept a battleship afloat in it. One year we had a flood, and it washed out a railroad bridge over the river. Santa Fe railroad workers came immediately to build a new bridge. When the bridge was completed, they put two engines on the bridge and tied down the whistles. In our little town we had never heard two engine whistles blow at the same time; so everyone raced to the bridge, all twenty-seven of us. One brave fellow in the crowd asked, "What are you doing?" The engineer replied, "We are testing the bridge." "Do you think it will break?" the young man queried. "Of course it won't break," the engineer said with almost a sneer. "If you know it won't break, why are you putting the engines on the bridge?" the young man wondered. "Just to *prove* that it won't break," said the engineer.

That is what the Lord's temptation was. It showed us that we have a Savior who is holy, harmless, undefiled, separate from sinners, and able to save to the uttermost those who come unto God through Him (see Heb. 7:25–26).

The Lord was tested in a way that we could never have been tested. When we are tested, there is always a breaking point. When we reach the breaking point, we break and then the pressure is removed. The pressure was never removed from our Lord.

His was a threefold temptation: physical, psychological, and spiritual.

The Lord was tested in the physical realm.

And the devil said unto him, If thou be the Son of God, command this stone that it be made bread [Luke 4:3].

The Devil did not ask the Lord to commit a crime. Bread is the staff of life and is a necessity. On one occasion the Lord fed a multitude of five thousand persons, and four thousand persons at another time. Eve looked at the tree in the midst of the Garden of Eden and saw that it was good for food and ate of it. John calls this test the lust or the desire of the flesh (see 1 John 2:16). A man must live, you know, and in order to live he must eat. That is the philosophy of most people today. The clamor of the crowd, the medley of the mob is, "What shall we eat, and drink and wherewithal shall we be clothed?" That is just about all that life is for most people. Men will become dishonest, steal, gamble, sell liquor, and resort to almost anything to obtain something for their bodies. Women will sell their virtue for a mink coat or a diamond ring. Satan revealed his low estimate of mankind when he told the Lord, ". . . Skin for skin, yea, all that a man hath will he give for his life" (Job 2:4). That is not true because Job did not yield. And our Lord used the sword of the Spirit, which is the Word of God, to defeat Satan.

And Jesus answered him, saying, It is written, That man shall not live by bread alone, but by every word of God [Luke 4:4].

Next Satan tested the Lord in the psychological realm.

And the devil, taking him up into an high mountain, shewed unto him all the kingdoms of the world in a moment of time.

And the devil said unto him, All this power will I give thee, and the glory of them: for that is delivered unto me; and to whomsoever I will I give it.

If thou therefore wilt worship me, all shall be thine.

And Jesus answered and said unto him, Get thee behind me, Satan: for it is written, Thou shalt worship the Lord thy God, and him only shalt thou serve [Luke 4:5–8].

This test had to do with what John calls the lust of the eyes. In the Garden of Eden, Eve looked at the fruit on the tree in the midst of the garden and saw that it was pleasant to the eyes. Satan took Christ high on a mountain and showed Him the kingdoms of the world and offered them to Him. The "kingdoms of the world" encompassed the great Roman Empire. But Christ was on His way to the throne by way of the cross. Satan was saying, "Let's miss the cross." Paul tells us, "For the preaching of the cross is to them that perish foolishness . . ." (1 Cor. 1:18)—how foolish to take that route of suffering when Satan offered an easy way to the throne! Now let me say something that may shock you. It is satanic to try and build a kingdom here on earth without Jesus Christ! There are only two rulers: the Lord Jesus and Satan. If you are not taking the Lord into account, you must take the other. Paul said, "For I determined not to know any thing among you, save Jesus Christ, and him crucified" (1 Cor. 2:2).

Finally the Lord was tested in the spiritual realm.

And he brought him to Jerusalem, and set him on a pinnacle of the temple, and said unto him, If thou be the Son of God, cast thyself down from hence:

For it is written, He shall give his angels charge over thee, to keep thee:

And in their hands they shall bear thee up, lest at any time thou dash thy foot against a stone.

And Jesus answering said unto him, It is said, Thou shalt not tempt the Lord thy God.

And when the devil had ended all the temptation, he departed from him for a season [Luke 4:9–13].

Eve desired the fruit of the tree in the midst of the garden because it could make one wise. John calls this testing ". . . the pride of life . . ." (1 John 2:16). This deals with the realm of the spirit and faith. Satan wanted the Lord to demonstrate that He was the Son of God—"Show them, prove it, then they will accept you." It was not faith; it was presumption. It was daring God. Faith is quietly waiting upon God, doing His will. It is interesting to note that when Satan quoted from Psalm 91:11–12, he misquoted Scripture, just as he misquoted God's word in the garden to Eve.

Why was Jesus Christ tempted? To demonstrate that you and I have a sinless Savior. He is sinless, impeccable, and able to save. He proved that all power had been given to Him. There is a Man in glory today, friend, who understands us and is able to sympathize with us. It is wonderful to have a Savior like that! John writes, "My little children, these things write I unto you, that ye sin not. And if any man sin, we have an advocate with the Father, Jesus Christ the righteous: And he is the propitiation for our sins: and not for ours only, but also for the sins of the whole world" (1 John 2:1–2). The Lord Jesus can be depended upon in every circumstance of life.

JESUS RETURNS TO GALILEE AND NAZARETH—REJECTED BY HIS HOMETOWN

After Satan tested the Lord Jesus Christ, He was strengthened.

And Jesus returned in the power of the Spirit into Galilee: and there went out a fame of him through all the region round about [Luke 4:14].

After the temptation the Lord comes forth in the power of the Holy Spirit. Temptation will do one of two things for an individual: it will either strengthen or weaken him. It is like the army, which will make you or break you. Whether this is actually true of the army, I do not know. This I do know, however, that suffering and testing will either sweeten or sour you, soften or harden you. There is an old familiar illustration which says that the same sun will melt the wax but harden the clay. It is the character of, or the condition of, the element and not the sun that melts the wax and hardens the clay. God is not going to harden you. He did not harden Pharaoh's heart. Pharaoh already possessed a hard heart, and God only brought that fact out into the open. Our Lord identified Himself with mankind. Scripture confirms this fact: "Wherefore in all things it behooved him to be made like unto his brethren, that he might be a merciful and faithful priest in things pertaining to God, to make reconciliation for the sins of the people" (Heb. 2:17). The Lord Jesus Christ became a man and so after His ordeal He needed the strengthening of the Holy Spirit. And if our Lord needed the strengthening of the Holy Spirit after His testing, how much more do we need Him!

And he taught in their synagogues, being glorified of all [Luke 4:15].

After the temptation the Lord returned to Galilee and taught in the synagogues. He was glorified by the people; He was praised and complimented. This verse sounds like a doxology. You know, it is possible to praise Him and still reject Him. It is possible to sing the doxology and turn down His claims. The same crowd that sang "Hosanna" and wanted to crown Him, the next day joined the mob to crucify Him. I think of a picture of the Crucifixion with the empty cross in the foreground and in the background is the donkey feeding on withered palm branches. That is the way it was. One day the Lord was praised, and the next day He was crucified.

Now we come to one of the most beautiful incidents recorded in God's Word. It is a scintillating story that flashes with light. It is fragrant with meaning. It is lovely to look at, and this is the way Dr. Luke tells it:

And he came to Nazareth, where he had been brought up: and, as his custom was, he went into the synagogue on the sabbath day, and stood up for to read.

And there was delivered unto him the book of the prophet Esaias. And when he had opened the book, he found the place where it was written,

The Spirit of the Lord is upon me, because he hath anointed me to preach the gospel to the poor; he hath sent me to heal the broken hearted, to preach deliverance to the captives, and recovering of sight to the blind, to set at liberty them that are bruised,

To preach the acceptable year of the Lord.

And he closed the book, and he gave it again to the minister, and sat down. And the eyes of all them that were in the synagogue were fastened on him.

And he began to say unto them, This day is this scripture fulfilled in your ears [Luke 4:16–21].

This incident is recorded only by Dr. Luke and is so remarkable that we cannot pass it by. We are told that after the temptation, the Lord returned to His hometown. Generally the hometown is proud of the local boy who has become famous. As was His custom on the Sabbath, He went to the synagogue in Nazareth.

Notice that He never entertained the false notion that you can worship God in nature as well as in the appointed place. Although I enjoy playing golf, I get a little weary of hearing some men say very piously that they can worship God just as easily on the golf course on Sunday as they can in church. What they say is true, but the question I always ask them is, "When you take your golf bag out on the course on Sunday morning, do you go out to worship God or to play golf?" The fact of the matter is, they have no intention of worshiping God on the golf course. You go to church on Sunday morning to worship God, and you go out on the golf course to play golf. It was the custom of our Lord to go to the synagogue on the Sabbath day.

The synagogue was one of the most important religious institutions of the Jews in the time of our Lord. It must have come into existence during the time of the Babylonian captivity. The Jews were far from their native land, from the temple and the altar. They no doubt felt drawn to gather round those who were especially pious and God-fearing in order to listen to the Word of God and engage in some kind of worship. In Ezekiel 14:1 and 20:1 it is mentioned that the elders gathered around Ezekiel, and it may have been in such a setting as the synagogue.

After the exile, the synagogue remained. At first it was meant only for the exposition of the Mosaic Law. Later, a time of prayer and preaching was added. However, primarily, the synagogue was for instruction in the Law for all classes of people. At the time of our Lord there were synagogues in all the larger towns.

I can now fill in one day of the silent years of Christ's earthly life. I do not know much about the other six days of each week, other than He was a carpenter and worked on those days. But I know that every seventh day He went to the synagogue. He went to the appointed place to worship because He could witness there.

Now He has come home for awhile and is in the synagogue. He is handed the Book, and He begins to read from it. He reads from Isaiah. In those days the Bible was not divided into chapters and verses, but had it been, He would have read Isaiah 61:1–2. The important thing to notice is where He broke off reading. He did not read, ". . . and the day of vengeance of our God. . . ." He closed the Book and gave it back to the minister. The amazing thing is that He did not stop reading at the end of a sentence but stopped before finishing it. In our translation, He stopped reading at the comma, but there was no comma in the text He was reading. He made absolutely no mention of the phrase, "the day of vengeance of our God." He made no mention of any of the text that followed this phrase. Do you know why? He looked at that crowd and said: "This day is this scripture fulfilled in your ears."

Here is a passage of Scripture that was going to be fulfilled down to a comma, and the rest of the passage would not be fulfilled until He came back the second time. The day of vengeance had not yet come. What is the day of vengeance? It is that time of which God said, "Ask of me, and I shall give thee the heathen for thine inheritance, and the uttermost parts of the earth for thy possession" (Ps. 2:8). How is the Lord going to get the heathen for His inheritance? "Thou shalt break them with a rod of iron; thou shalt dash them in pieces like a potter's vessel" (Ps. 2:9). That is the way the Lord will come to power. That will be the day of vengeance. That is the great Day of the Lord, and it will take place when Christ comes the second time. He came the first time to preach the gospel to the poor that they might be saved. He came anointed by the Holy Spirit to bring the glorious message of salvation. We are still living in that wonderful day, the day of the gospel. When He comes the second time, it will be the day of vengeance.

And all bare him witness, and wondered at the gracious words which proceeded out of his mouth. And they said, Is not this Joseph's son? [Luke 4:22].

The people looked at Him and remembered Him as Joseph's son, a carpenter. That seemed to spoil it all. How could He be the Messiah? Luke is making it very clear that He took upon Himself our frail humanity.

And he said unto them, Ye will surely say unto me this proverb, Physician, heal thyself: whatsoever we have heard done in Capernaum, do also here in thy country.

And he said, Verily I say unto you, No prophet is accepted in his own country.

But I tell you of a truth, many widows were in Israel in the days of Elias, when the heaven was shut up three years and six months, when great famine was throughout all the land;

But unto none of them was Elias sent, save unto Sarepta, a city of Sidon, unto a woman that was a widow.

And many lepers were in Israel in the time of Eliseus the prophet; and none of them was cleansed, saving Naaman the Syrian [Luke 4:23–27].

The Lord is illustrating this in a marvelous way. He cited two Gentiles who lived outside of the land of Israel—the widow of Sarepta and Naaman of Syria—in whose lives God worked miraculously. He is trying to show them that they, His own people, were apt to miss a great blessing because they would not accept who He was. They would be like the many widows and the many lepers of Israel who were not healed during the time of Elijah.

And all they in the synagogue, when they heard these things, were filled with wrath,

And rose up, and thrust him out of the city, and led him unto the brow of the hill whereon their city was built, that they might cast him down headlong.

But he passing through the midst of them went his way [Luke 4:28–30].

The people of Jesus' hometown rejected Him. The country around Nazareth is rough country, and they led Him to the brow of a hill, intending to push Him off to His death. His escape from this mob was a miracle.

JESUS MOVES HIS HEADQUARTERS TO CAPERNAUM AND CONTINUES HIS MINISTRY

And came down to Capernaum, a city of Galilee, and taught them on the sabbath days [Luke 4:31].

From this verse through the rest of the chapter we have one day with the Lord Jesus. Many of us would have loved to have spent a day with Him when He was on earth. Luke makes this possible for us.

Both Matthew and Mark record the fact that the Lord Jesus moved His headquarters from His hometown of Nazareth to Capernaum on the Sea of Galilee. He did this because the people from His own town would not receive Him. There came a day when He told the people of Capernaum, "And thou, Capernaum, which art exalted to heaven, shalt be thrust down to hell" (Luke 10:15). Because His headquarters were there, what an opportunity they had! Light creates responsibility.

And they were astonished at his doctrine: for his word was with power [Luke 4:32].

As the Lord taught in the synagogue on the Sabbath, He did not speak as a scribe or a Pharisee but as one who had authority.

And in the synagogue there was a man, which had a spirit of an unclean devil, and cried out with a loud voice,

Saying, Let us alone; what have we to do with thee, thou Jesus of Nazareth? art thou come to destroy us? I know thee who thou art; the Holy One of God.

And Jesus rebuked him, saying, Hold thy peace, and come out of him. And when the devil had thrown him in the midst, he came out of him, and hurt him not.

And they were all amazed, and spake among themselves, saying, What a word is this! for with authority and power he commandeth the unclean spirits, and they come out.

And the fame of him went out into every place of the country round about [Luke 4:33–37].

We are living in a day when demonism has lifted its ugly head again, and Satan worship is a reality. Demons were working in the days of our Lord, and they are working now. Our Lord cast a demon out of an individual. Even considering the use of drugs, it is difficult to explain some of the actions and awful crimes being committed unless the perpetrator is under the power and control of Satan.

And he arose out of the synagogue, and entered into Simon's house. And Simon's wife's mother was taken with a great fever; and they besought him for her.

And he stood over her, and rebuked the fever; and it left her: and immediately she arose and ministered unto them [Luke 4:38–39].

After leaving the synagogue, it seems that the Lord went to Simon Peter's house, probably for the noonday meal. While He was in Peter's house, He healed "Simon's wife's mother," Peter's mother-in-law, who had a great fever. The severity of diseases was indicated by saying one had a small or a great fever. This evidently was a serious illness. Our Lord rebuked the fever, using Luke's medical terminology, "be muzzled." The fever was like a wild dog that had broken the leash. Our Lord also dealt with sin like that. Immediately she arose and ministered unto them. When the Lord Jesus Christ healed someone, healing did not come gradually but took place immediately. It was an amazing thing.

I heard about a meeting conducted by a "faith healer" not long ago. It was reported that a cripple was led up to the platform where he was declared healed then led away, still limping. Then someone came to the platform who said he had internal cancer, and the faith healer declared that he was immediately healed of cancer. It is amazing how people will accept that type of testimony. Why wasn't the crippled man healed immediately? If our Lord had done it, the cure would have been immediate. I can hear someone asking, "Don't you believe in divine healing?" My answer is, "What other kind of healing is there?" All healing is divine. This is what Dr. Luke is telling us. Doctors do not always recognize this fact.

A wonderful doctor who was a member of my church in Texas once said to me, "I send the bill, but God does the healing. I take out that part that is offending the body, but God will have to be the Healer." What a great testimony. God, and not an individual, does the healing.

Now when the sun was setting, all they that had any sick with divers diseases brought them unto him; and he laid his hands on every one of them, and healed them.

And devils also came out of many, crying out, and saying, Thou art Christ the Son of God. And he rebuking them suffered them not to speak: for they knew that he was Christ.

And when it was day, he departed and went into a desert place: and the people sought him, and came unto him, and stayed him, that he should not depart from them.

And he said unto them, I must preach the kingdom of God to other cities also: for therefore am I sent.

And he preached in the synagogues of Galilee [Luke 4:40–44].

His day had started in the morning, teaching in the synagogue. Now it is late in the evening. The Lord goes outside to the multitude that had gathered, and He moves from one to another, touching and healing them. Matthew in recording this incident quotes from the prophet Isaiah: "That it might be fulfilled which was spoken by Esaias the prophet, saying, Himself took our infirmities, and bare our sicknesses" (Matt. 8:17). The Lord healed in a wonderful way. "Surely he hath borne our griefs, and carried our sorrows: yet we did esteem him stricken, smitten of God, and afflicted" (Isa. 53:4). The Lord bore the sicknesses and diseases of the people sympathetically, in spite of the fact that the nation Israel in that day esteemed Him stricken. That is the way we also esteem Him. You see, He did not heal these people on the basis of their faith as far as we know, but His great heart of sympathy caused Him to move in their behalf.

We are told to have such a heart of sympathy today. "Bear ye one another's burdens, and so fulfil the law of Christ" (Gal. 6:2).

CHAPTER 5

THEME: *Jesus calls the disciples for the second time; Jesus cleanses the lepers; Jesus heals man with palsy; Jesus calls Matthew; Jesus gives parables on new garment and wine skins*

JESUS CALLS THE DISCIPLES FOR THE SECOND TIME

And it came to pass, that, as the people pressed upon him to hear the word of God, he stood by the lake of Gennesaret,

And saw two ships standing by the lake: but the fishermen were gone out of them, and were washing their nets.

And he entered into one of the ships, which was Simon's, and prayed him that he would thrust out a little from the land. And he sat down, and taught the people out of the ship [Luke 5:1–3].

The Lake of Gennesaret is the Sea of Galilee. The fishermen there had left their boats and were washing their nets. The Lord climbed into Simon Peter's boat and asked him to push the boat out a little from the land. What a pulpit! I believe this illustration is both figurative and suggestive. Every pulpit is a "fishing boat," a place to give out the Word of God and attempt to catch fish. He had told these men that He would make them fishers of men. This does not mean that you and I will catch fish every time we give out the Word—the disciples didn't—but it does mean that the one on board must not forget the supreme business of life which is to fish for the souls of men.

Now when he had left speaking, he said unto Simon, Launch out into the deep, and let down your nets for a draught [Luke 5:4].

After the Lord had finished speaking to the people, He said, "Now we'll leave off fishing for men, and we're going to fish for fish." Matthew and Mark tell us that the first time the Lord called these men He was walking by the Sea of Galilee and saw Simon Peter and his brother Andrew casting a net into the sea—they were fishermen—and the Lord said to them, ". . . Follow me, and I will make you fishers of men" (cf. Matt. 4:19; Mark 1:17). Now these men have returned to their occupation of fishing. The Lord evidently made three calls to His disciples. He *met* most of them in Jerusalem. John tells us about it in John chapter one. When John the Baptist marked Him out, several of his disciples wanted to know where Jesus dwelt. Among those who followed John were Philip, Nathanael, Simon Peter, and Andrew. The Lord did not call these men to be disciples at this time; He just *met* them. Later on, the Lord passed by the Sea of Galilee, saw them fishing, and called them to follow Him. They left their nets and followed Him. Now they had returned to the fishing business. Later on, Dr. Luke will tell us that once again the Lord called them to go fishing for men and at that time made them apostles.

As our Lord had been speaking to the crowd from his boat, Simon Peter had been sitting in the boat listening. When He finished speaking, He told Simon, "Launch out into the deep, and let your net down. You quit fishing with Me; now I am going to fish with you."

And Simon answering said unto him, Master, we have toiled all the night, and have taken nothing: nevertheless at thy word I will let down the net [Luke 5:5].

"*Nevertheless* at thy word I will let down the net," indicates that Simon Peter had put up an argument. These men were expert fishermen, and thought they knew all about fishing in the Sea of Galilee—and they did. Peter makes it very clear that they had fished all night without catching anything.

The story is told that when Wellington once gave a command to one of his generals, he answered that it was impossible to execute the command. Wellington told him, "You go ahead and do it, because I don't give impossible commands." When the Lord Jesus Christ gives a command, you do not need to argue with Him and say, "We've tried it before and it cannot be done." He does not give impossible commands.

And when they had this done, they enclosed a great multitude of fishes: and their net brake [Luke 5:6].

Fishing must be done according to His directions. There are many lessons for us here. Fishing is an art. You must go where the fish are; you must use the right kind of bait; you must be patient; but the important lesson He is teaching us is that we must fish according to His instructions. If we are ever going to win men for Him, we must fish according to His instructions.

In this instance the net broke. Later on, in the Gospel of John, a net overloaded with fish does *not* break. The fisherman's net illustrates a truth. At this point there is no net that can hold the fish for the simple reason that He has not yet died and risen from the dead—that is the gospel. The "net" which will hold fish must be one that rests upon the death and resurrection of Christ—at this time there had been no death and resurrection. The net broke. After His death and resurrection, He told them how to fish and the net did not break (see John 21:1–11). Here He tells them to go out and preach the gospel to the very ends of the earth.

And they beckoned unto their partners, which were in the other ship, that they should come and help them. And they came, and filled both the ships, so that they began to sink.

When Simon Peter saw it, he fell down at Jesus' knees, saying, Depart from me; for I am a sinful man, O Lord [Luke 5:7–8].

Notice that this is a tremendous catch of fish!

Peter confesses his failure; he is not even a good fisherman of fish due to his lack of faith. When Simon said, "Depart from me; for I am a sinful man, O Lord," he was saying, "Lord, you called me to be a fisher of men and I failed. I went back to fishing for fish—I thought I knew that kind of fishing better, but I find that I don't! Depart from me. Let me alone. I am a sinful man. You should find someone upon whom you can depend." The Lord, however, did not intend to get rid of Simon Peter. He was going to use him, and this applies to us also. All we have to do is recognize that we are not very good fishermen—recognize our failures and faithlessness. When we are willing to depend on Him, He will not put us out of the fishing business, and He will not throw us overboard. He will *use* us. This is an encouraging truth!

For he was astonished, and all that were with him, at the draught of the fishes which they had taken:

And so was also James, and John, the sons of Zebedee, which were partners with Simon. And Jesus said unto Simon, Fear not; from henceforth thou shalt catch men [Luke 5:9–10].

Simon Peter did catch men. Remember how well he did on the Day of Pentecost—the Lord's answer to Peter is certainly significant. Three thousand souls came to Christ after his first sermon! Peter was fishing according to God's instructions.

There is another lesson here. Do you know there is another fisherman? Do you know that Satan also is a fisherman? Paul tells us that in 2 Timothy 2:26, which says, "And that they may recover themselves out of the snare of the devil, who are taken captive by him at his will." Satan has his hook out in the water too. God is fishing for your soul, and Satan also is fishing for your soul with a hook baited with the things of the world. You might say God's hook is a cross. The son of God died upon that cross for *you*. This is God's message for you. By the way, whose hook are you on today? You are either on God's hook or Satan's hook. Either the Devil has you or God has you. There is no third fisherman!

JESUS CLEANSES THE LEPERS

And it came to pass, when he was in a certain city, behold a man full of leprosy: who seeing Jesus fell on his face, and besought him, saying Lord, if thou wilt, thou canst make me clean.

And he put forth his hand, and touched him, saying, I will: be thou clean. And immediately the leprosy departed from him [Luke 5:12–13].

In verses 12–15 we have the story of the healing of a leper. Luke was a good doctor. He recognized a psychological implication in the healing of this leper that was not much understood in that day.

We are not told how the man discovered that he had leprosy, but it could have happened in the following manner. One day he came in from plowing and said to his wife, "I have a little sore on the palm of my hand. It bothers me when I am plowing. Could you put a poultice on it and wrap it for me?" His wife bandaged his hand, but the next day the sore was worse. In a few days they both became alarmed. His wife said, "You should go to the priest." He went to the priest who put him in isolation for fourteen days. When he was brought out the priest looked him over and found the leprosy had spread. The priest told him he was a leper. The heartbroken man said to the priest "Let me go to my wife and children and tell them goodbye." The priest replied, "You cannot tell them goodbye. You will never be able to take your lovely wife in your arms again. You will never be able to put your arms around those precious children of yours." The man went off, alone. His family brought his food to a certain place and then withdrew when he came to get it. In the distance he could see his wife and observe his children growing day by day.

Then one day the Lord Jesus Christ came by. The leper declared, "If You will, You can heal me." The King of kings replied, "I will, be thou clean." But notice *how* the Lord healed him. He put forth His hand and touched this man afflicted with leprosy. This poor man had not felt anyone's touch for years. Can you imagine what it must have meant to him to have the touch of Christ's hand upon him?

Has the Lord Jesus touched your life? There are so many lives that need to be touched. If you are His, and you are fishing at His command, I am confident that you can reach someone for the Lord. You need to reach out your hand and touch some soul whom only you can touch for Him today.

JESUS HEALS MAN WITH PALSY

And it came to pass on a certain day, as he was teaching, that there were Pharisees and doctors of the law sitting by, which were come out of every town of Galilee, and Judaea, and Jerusalem: and the power of the Lord was present to heal them.

And, behold, men brought in a bed a man which was taken with a palsy: and they sought means to bring him in, and to lay him before him.

And when they could not find by what way they might bring him in because of the multitude, they went upon the housetop, and let him down through the tiling with his couch into the midst before Jesus.

And when he saw their faith, he said unto him, Man, thy sins are forgiven thee [Luke 5:17–20].

This is the account of the paralytic in Capernaum who was healed. Some friends of this man let him down through the roof of a house in order for the Lord Jesus Christ to see him. Both Matthew and Mark record this incident. Mark gives the longest account, though his is the shortest gospel. The Lord healed this man because these four men brought him into His presence where the poor fellow could hear, "Man, thy sins are forgiven thee." It was a wonderful word that came to this man.

There are many people who are not going to receive the message of salvation unless you lift a corner of their stretcher and carry them to the place where they can hear the Word of the Lord. They are paralyzed—immobilized by sin and by many other things the world holds for them. Some are paralyzed by prejudice and others by indifference. They are never going to hear Jesus say to them, "Thy sins are forgiven thee," unless you take the corner of their stretcher and bring them to Him.

All of these incidents reveal the fact that the Lord Jesus Christ wants us to spread the message of salvation to others. This is why I preach the Word of God—and remember that one man cannot carry a stretcher alone. It took four men to carry the stretcher of the paralyzed man. More men and women are needed today to help get the Word of God out to those who need Him.

JESUS CALLS MATTHEW

And after these things he went forth, and saw a publican, named Levi, sitting at the receipt of custom: and he said unto him, Follow me.

And he left all, rose up, and followed him [Luke 5:27–28].

Matthew gives us this much information in his Gospel, and Mark gives a little more detail; but Luke shares even more.

And Levi made him a great feast in his own house: and there was a great company of publicans and of others that sat down with them [Luke 5:29].

This dinner was given by Levi as a way of trying to win people to the Lord Jesus Christ. Levi had not been trained in a theological seminary. He was a tax gatherer and a rascal. When he came to the Lord Jesus, he did what he could. He was a rich publican—so he gave a dinner and invited all his rascal friends to it so that they could meet Jesus Christ.

The scribes and Pharisees who were there had a difficult time keeping their mouths shut and finally they came to Him.

But their scribes and Pharisees murmured against his disciples, saying, Why do ye eat and drink with publicans and sinners? [Luke 5:30].

The scribes and Pharisees criticize with a question, and the Lord Jesus has a good answer for it. Our Lord protects His own men.

And Jesus answering said unto them, They that are whole need not a physician; but they that are sick.

I came not to call the righteous, but sinners to repentance [Luke 5:31–32].

The scribes and Pharisees asked the disciples why they ate with publicans and sinners. The Lord's answer was simple and wonderful. He was the Great Physician and He did not go around healing people that were well! He came to minister to those who were sick with sin. The gospel is really for those who recognize their need. There are some people who think they are too good to be saved. They are not aware of their need. If you recognize that you have a need, then the gospel is for you. Christ can and will save you. If you are self-sufficient, recognize no personal need, and go in your self-chosen pathway, it will lead you to destruction. I am sorry. The Great Physician can do nothing for those who think they are not sick.

And they said unto him, Why do the disciples of John fast often, and make prayers, and likewise the disciples of the Pharisees; but thine eat and drink? [Luke 5:33].

The scribes and Pharisees then ask why John's disciples and the disciples of the Pharisees fast while the disciples of Jesus are having a good time.

And he said unto them, Can ye make the children of the bridechamber fast, while the bridegroom is with them?

But the days will come, when the bridegroom shall be taken away from them, and then shall they fast in those days [Luke 5:34–35].

We today are to have a good time, but fasting is also beneficial, recognizing that our Lord is in heaven and we are in a world that has rejected Him. The point is that, whether we feast or fast, our business is to get the Word out to people who need Him.

JESUS GIVES PARABLES ON NEW GARMENT AND WINE SKINS

This is the first parable in the Gospel of Luke.

And he spake also a parable unto them; No man putteth a piece of a new garment upon an old; if otherwise, then both the new maketh a rent, and the piece that was taken out of the new agreeth not with the old.

And no man putteth new wine into old bottles; else the new wine will burst the bottles, and be spilled, and the bottles shall perish.

But new wine must be put into new bottles; and both are preserved.

No man also having drunk old wine straightway desireth new: for he saith, The old is better [Luke 5:36–39].

The natural man likes his old ways. He likes his old wine—that is, his old religion. The important thing is to recognize that our Lord brought something new to mankind—the gospel. He did not come into the world to do any patching of the old garment. He did not come to patch up the Law. He came to pay the penalty of sin by dying on the cross. But He did more than that. He arose from the dead so that He could place upon us His robe of righteousness. He gives us the new wine of the gospel. The new wine of the gospel must be placed in the new wineskin of grace, not into the old one of law. "And be not drunk with wine, wherein is excess; but be filled with the Spirit" (Eph. 5:18). This is the message that the Lord gives out today. He came to give us something new. He came to save us by faith in Him.

This entire chapter points in one direction, and that is to present the glorious gospel of the Lord Jesus Christ in as many ways as possible so that men might hear and have an opportunity to choose whether they will accept Him or reject Him.

All of us must make this decision for ourselves.

CHAPTER 6

***THEME:** Jesus defends disciples for plucking grain on Sabbath; Jesus chooses the Twelve; Jesus gives sermon on the plain*

JESUS DEFENDS DISCIPLES FOR PLUCKING GRAIN ON SABBATH

The first part of this chapter is almost a repetition of the other synoptic Gospels. It begins with the action of Christ on the Sabbath day. The first incident is in the fields on the Sabbath day.

And it came to pass on the second sabbath after the first, that he went through the corn fields; and his disciples plucked the ears of corn, and did eat, rubbing them in their hands.

And certain of the Pharisees said unto them, Why do ye that which is not lawful to do on the sabbath days?

And Jesus answering them said, Have ye not read so much as this, what David did, when himself was an hungered, and they which were with him;

How he went into the house of God, and did take and eat the shewbread, and gave also to them that were with him; which it is not lawful to eat but for the priests alone?

And he said unto them, That the Son of man is Lord also of the sabbath [Luke 6:1–5].

As the disciples plucked the grain and rubbed it in their hands, the Pharisees accused them of threshing the grain on the Sabbath day. Of course they were not breaking the Mosaic Law, as it permitted people to pull the grain (see Deut. 23:24–25). If they had been cutting it with a sickle, they would have been harvesting. But the Pharisees had their own interpretation, and therefore they interpret the action as breaking the Law.

Our Lord did not insist that they had not broken the Sabbath; He refused to argue the issue with them. He cited an incident in the life of David where he had definitely broken the Mosaic Law and was justified. His point was that the letter of the Law was not to be imposed when it wrought hardship upon one of God's servants. Obviously the disciples were hungry. It cost them something to follow Jesus.

Then we have the incident of the Sabbath day in the synagogue.

And it came to pass also on another sabbath, that he entered into the synagogue and taught: and there was a man whose right hand was withered.

And the scribes and Pharisees watched him, whether he would heal on the sabbath day; that they might find an accusation against him.

But he knew their thoughts, and said to the man which had the withered hand, Rise up, and stand forth in the midst. And he arose and stood forth.

Then said Jesus unto them, I will ask you one thing; Is it lawful on the sabbath days to do good, or to do evil? to save life, or to destroy it?

And looking round about upon them all, he said unto the man, Stretch forth thy hand. And he did so: and his hand was restored whole as the other.

And they were filled with madness; and communed one with another what they might do to Jesus [Luke 6:6–11].

The man with the withered hand was planted there, you may be sure. In doing this they really paid our Lord a wonderful compliment. They believed He could heal him, and they believed He would heal him. They knew He was both powerful and compassionate. They were exactly correct in their estimation of Him. Our Lord healed the man. Then His enemies used the occasion to accuse Him of breaking the Sabbath day. Matthew tells us that they plotted His death from that moment on.

JESUS CHOOSES THE TWELVE

As I mentioned previously, some of the disciples were introduced to our Lord when He went to Jerusalem. Later, walking by the Sea of Galilee, He called those men to follow Him. Then they went back to fishing. And He went by and called them again, at which time, the record tells us, "they forsook all, and followed him" (Luke 5:11). Now we have come to the third stage. Out of an unspecified number of disciples, He chose twelve men to be His apostles.

And it came to pass in those days, that he went out into a mountain to pray, and continued all night in prayer to God.

And when it was day, he called unto him his disciples: and of them he chose twelve, whom also he named apostles;

Simon, (whom he also named Peter,) and Andrew his brother, James and John, Philip and Bartholomew,

Matthew and Thomas, James the son of Alphaeus, and Simon called Zelotes,

And Judas the brother of James, and Judas Iscariot, which also was the traitor [Luke 6:12–16].

Notice that Jesus prayed all night to God. Why? He was going to choose twelve men to be His apostles. He spent the entire night in prayer before making His choice. One of the apostles turned out to be a traitor. Another apostle denied Him but later repented. Notice, however, that God's men were always *chosen.* There are many candidates, to be sure, but consider what John 15:16 says: "Ye have not chosen me, but I have chosen you." This has been a great comfort to me. I was a clerk in a bank when the Lord called me to be a preacher. I never dreamed of becoming a preacher; in fact, I actually looked down on preachers. I did not call Him, but He called me. I've always felt good about it, because since He called me, He is responsible. That is wonderful. It gives me comfort. The Lord found it essential and practical to spend the entire night in prayer before selecting the twelve apostles. Men chosen for God's work should be selected on the basis of much prayer. The robe of Elijah did not fall by accident upon Elisha; it fell providentially. The present-day procedure by the church for choosing men to fill an office is far from God's standard. We follow our feelings and consult our own selfish desires. We use human measuring rods rather than God's measuring stick. We should spend time with God before making our decisions.

JESUS GIVES SERMON ON THE PLAIN

And he came down with them, and stood in the plain, and the company of his disciples, and a great multitude of people out of all Judaea and Jerusalem, and from the sea coast of Tyre and Sidon, which came to hear him, and to be healed of their diseases;

And they that were vexed with unclean spirits: and they were healed.

And the whole multitude sought to touch him: for there went virtue out of him, and healed them all [Luke 6:17–19].

As I have said many times before, multitudes were healed on this occasion. In our Lord's day literally thousands of people were healed. There were no healing lines, no slapping of this one and patting of that one, no having people fall backwards and forwards. The people whom the Lord healed did not have to do anything. Our Lord would even heal them at a distance. The healings performed by the Lord were genuine, and we have Dr. Luke's statement to prove it. I do not believe in faith *healers* but I do believe in faith *healing.* Take your problem to the Great Physician. He is the best doctor you can consult, and He does not send you a bill; nor do you have to be on Medicare to get Him to take your case.

Now we come to the so-called "Sermon on the Mount," which is not a sermon on the *mount* as it was delivered on a *plain.* Of course the Sermon on the Mount was delivered on a mountain, as recorded in Matthew. The similarity in content indicates that the Lord gave His teachings again and again. We do not need a harmony of the Gospels as much as we need a contrast of the Gospels. The remarkable thing about this sermon in Luke is its dissimilarity to the sermon in Matthew. There are omissions, certain inclusions, blessings and woes, attitudes and judgments.

And he lifted up his eyes on his disciples, and said, Blessed be ye poor: for yours is the kingdom of God.

Blessed are ye that hunger now: for ye shall be filled. Blessed are ye that weep now: for ye shall laugh.

Blessed are ye, when men shall hate you, and when they shall separate you from their company, and shall reproach you, and cast out your name as evil, for the Son of man's sake [Luke 6:20–22].

Up to this point the content of the Sermon on the Plain is similar to Matthew's Sermon on the Mount. The Lord gave the same teaching in many places but in a different form. Beginning with verse 23, a new thought is introduced.

Rejoice ye in that day, and leap for joy: for, behold, your reward is great in heaven: for in the like manner did their fathers unto the prophets [Luke 6:23].

This verse speaks about the reception of, and attitude toward, God's prophets by mankind. The true prophet speaks for God and is persecuted. The false prophet misrepresents God and is patronized by men. The true prophet must have faith in God and maintain a quiet confidence which looks beyond the things which are seen to the things which are eternal. This is what keeps a man true to God.

Verses 20–22 speak about the poor, hungry and weak, who are hated, reproached, considered outcasts, and called evil. All you have to do is look back into the Old Testament to see that this is true. It is true today. The man who preaches the Word of God is going to have a rough time. If he does not have a rough time, something is wrong. The false prophets were (and *are*) rich and had plenty to eat. They could laugh and were considered good fellows. God has something to say to them.

But woe unto you that are rich! for ye have received your consolation.

Woe unto you that are full! for ye shall hunger. Woe unto you that laugh now! for ye shall mourn and weep.

Woe unto you, when all men shall speak well of you! for so did their fathers to the false prophets.

But I say unto you which hear, Love your enemies, do good to them which hate you,

Bless them that curse you, and pray for them which despitefully use you [Luke 6:24–28].

We find that the false prophet is patronized by the world, and if he will say the right thing, the world will pay him well. The Lord Jesus Christ makes it clear, however, that he needn't expect God to pay him. The false prophet may become popular with the world, but he will be notorious with God. He may have a lot of fun on earth, but he will cause heaven to weep. He may be well fed, but he has a starved soul.

Very little is said today about the godless rich. The Lord had a great deal to say about the godless rich in Scripture: "Woe unto you that are rich! for ye have received your consolation." Everyone seems to be after the poor criminal who stole $25.00, or a suit of clothes, or a $50.00 ring. The godless poor, however, are not nearly as dangerous as the godless rich. The godless rich give glamour to godlessness. There is probably more hypocrisy among the rich than any other group. They will pay a false prophet to preach in their church—they own the church and the property. No rich church has the reputation of being an evangelical church; the gospel will not be preached there. There may be a few exceptions to this, but if there are, I do not know about them.

In New York City there is a church that bears the name of a rich man. The church will not have a gospel minister preach there because a gospel preacher would condemn this rich man just as James did when he said: "Go to now, ye rich men, weep and howl for your miseries that shall come upon you. Your riches are corrupted, and your garments are motheaten. Your gold and silver is cankered; and the rust of them shall be a witness against you, and shall eat your flesh as it were fire. Ye have heaped treasure together for the last days" (James 5:1–3).

I wonder when Christians in this country are going to wake up to the fact that these rich politicians are throwing crumbs from their tables down to the poor. They are not interested in the poor or in the rights of an individual. They want to be able to keep their riches and enjoy them in selfishness, and they are willing to give a few crumbs to the poor in order to do it. As far as civil rights go, I am not concerned about the color of a man's skin but about the color of his heart. Has his heart been washed in the blood of the Lord Jesus Christ? If it has, then he is my brother. I am going to be living with him for eternity and I had better start learning to live with him now—and I am. A man's heart may be as black as ink and his skin white as snow; yet he is not my brother. I am sorry to have to say that, but it is true.

What I am saying may sound revolutionary, and it is, but it is what Jesus Christ said, friend. There are those who tell me that they are following Jesus. They do not dare to follow Him. Read what He says in this chapter and, believe me, it will remove the cloak of hypocrisy and peel off the skin of any man. Try on the Sermon on the Plain for size and find out if you are keeping it.

And as ye would that men should do to you, do ye also to them likewise.

For if ye love them which love you, what thank have ye? for sinners also love those that love them.

And if ye do good to them which do good to you, what thank have ye? for sinners also do even the same.

And if ye lend to them of whom ye hope to receive, what thank have ye? for sinners also lend to sinners, to receive as much again.

But love ye your enemies, and do good, and lend, hoping for nothing again; and your reward shall be great, and ye shall be the children of the Highest: for he is kind unto the unthankful and to the evil.

Be ye therefore merciful, as your Father also is merciful.

Judge not, and ye shall not be judged: condemn not, and ye shall not be condemned: forgive, and ye shall be forgiven:

Give, and it shall be given unto you; good measure, pressed down, and shaken together, and running over, shall men give into your bosom. For with the same measure that ye mete withal it shall be measured to you again.

And he spake a parable unto them, Can the blind lead the blind? shall they not both fall into the ditch?

The disciple is not above his master: but every one that is perfect shall be as his master.

And why beholdest thou the mote that is in thy brother's eye, but perceivest not the beam that is in thine own eye?

Either how canst thou say to thy brother, Brother, let me pull out the mote that is in thine eye, when thou thyself beholdest not the beam that is in thine own eye? Thou hypocrite, cast out first the beam out of thine own eye, and then shalt thou see clearly to pull out the mote that is in thy brother's eye.

For a good tree bringeth not forth corrupt fruit; neither doth a corrupt tree bring forth good fruit.

For every tree is known by his own fruit. For of thorns men do not gather figs, nor of a bramble bush gather they grapes.

A good man out of the good treasure of his heart bringeth forth that which is good; and an evil man out of the evil treasure of his heart bringeth forth that which is evil: for of the abundance of the heart his mouth speaketh.

And why call ye me, Lord, Lord, and do not the things which I say? [Luke 6:31–46].

The minister of a church who is seeking popularity does not dare mention sin. Some use the gyration of psychoanalysis to explain away the exceeding sinfulness of sin. It is called a relic of a theological jungle. Sin is not a crime against God, according to many modern preachers. They are afraid to say that God hates sin and that Jehovah is a Man of War.

To be right in God's sight you cannot compliment the ego, pat the pride, smile upon sin, and put cold cream on the cancer of sin. You cannot write a prescription on philosophy and have it filled in the pleasures of the world. The only place you can go is to the foot of the cross. There God performs an operation, major surgery, and makes you a new creature in Christ Jesus. That is the message we have in the Sermon on the Plain. It complements the Sermon on the Mount. It is a message the Lord gave many times to many different groups of people.

The Lord concludes this with a parable.

Whosoever cometh to me, and heareth my sayings, and doeth them, I will shew you to whom he is like:

He is like a man which built an house, and digged deep, and laid the foundation on a rock: and when the flood arose, the stream beat vehemently upon that house, and could not shake it: for it was founded upon a rock.

But he that heareth, and doeth not, is like a man that without a foundation

built an house upon the earth; against which the stream did beat vehemently, and immediately it fell; and the ruin of that house was great [Luke 6:47–49].

The house that was built on the rock—stood. The house that was built on the sand was absolutely washed away.

This chapter reveals to me that I am a sinner before God, and it almost takes my skin off! There is a Rock, though, upon which I can build a foundation that will stand. That Rock is Christ Jesus. Paul said, "For other foundation can no man lay than that is laid, which is Jesus Christ" (1 Cor. 3:11). My friend, where are you building your foundation? Where is your house? Is it built on the Rock which is Christ Jesus, or is it built on sand?

If you can read the Sermon on the Plain and not see that you are a lost and hell-doomed sinner, I feel sorry for you. I feel sorry for the poor rich man who has not heard the gospel. Whoever will may get on the Solid Rock which is Christ. He will save without money and without price. Come to Him in simple faith, and trust Him.

CHAPTER 7

***THEME:** Jesus heals the centurion's servant; Jesus restores to life the son of the widow of Nain; Jesus commends John the Baptist; Jesus goes to dinner at a Pharisee's house; Jesus gives parable of two debtors*

This chapter opens with another meticulous record of healing. In this case it is the centurion's servant. Although Jesus had no personal contact with the servant, he was made well.

Dr. Luke alone records the raising from the dead of the son of the widow of Nain. He is the only gospel writer who records Jesus raising from the dead two persons (the other was Jairus' daughter, Luke 8:54–55).

Also in this chapter is the first of eighteen parables that Luke alone records. It grew out of Jesus' visit to the home of a Pharisee where a woman anointed His feet with ointment. The simple parable of the two debtors revealed that this woman of the street was better than Simon, the Pharisee.

JESUS HEALS THE CENTURION'S SERVANT

Now when he had ended all his sayings in the audience of the people, he entered into Capernaum.

And a certain centurion's servant, who was dear unto him, was sick, and ready to die.

And when he heard of Jesus, he sent unto him the elders of the Jews, beseeching him that he would come and heal his servant.

And when they came to Jesus, they besought him instantly, saying, That he was worthy for whom he should do this:

For he loveth our nation, and he hath built us a synagogue.

Then Jesus went with them. And when he was now not far from the house, the centurion sent friends to him, saying unto him, Lord, trouble not thyself: for I am not worthy that thou shouldest enter under my roof:

Wherefore neither thought I myself worthy to come unto thee: but say in a word, and my servant shall be healed.

For I also am a man set under authority, having under me soldiers, and I say unto one, Go, and he goeth; and to another, Come, and he cometh; and to my servant, Do this, and he doeth it.

When Jesus heard these things, he marvelled at him, and turned him about, and said unto the people that followed him, I say unto you, I have not found so great faith, no, not in Israel.

And they that were sent, returning to the house, found the servant whole that had been sick [Luke 7:1–10].

There were many Roman soldiers in this city. A centurion was a Roman officer who commanded one hundred men. Apparently this officer was a man of faith. His love for the Jewish nation was evidenced by his building a synagogue for them at Capernaum. In his position he was an officer with authority. He could say to a soldier, "Do this, or "Go there," and the soldier would obey. He recognized that Jesus had that kind of power and that He had only to speak the word in order that his servant might be healed. Jesus marveled at the faith of this man. It is recorded that only on two occasions Jesus marveled. He marveled at the faith of the centurion and at the unbelief of Israel.

JESUS RESTORES TO LIFE THE SON OF THE WIDOW OF NAIN

And it came to pass the day after, that he went into a city called Nain; and many of his disciples went with him, and much people.

Now when he came nigh to the gate of the city, behold, there was a dead man carried out, the only son of his mother, and she was a widow: and much people of the city was with her.

And when the Lord saw her, he had compassion on her, and said unto her, Weep not.

And he came and touched the bier: and they that bare him stood still. And he said, Young man, I say unto thee, Arise.

And he that was dead sat up, and began to speak. And he delivered him to his mother.

And there came a fear on all: and they glorified God, saying, That a great prophet is risen up among us; and, That God hath visited his people [Luke 7:11–16].

Only Dr. Luke records this incident. It concerns a restoration to life or, as some would call it, a resurrection. The instances recorded of Jesus raising people from the dead technically are not resurrections as we think of them. All the Lord did was restore life back into the old bodies. Tradition says that after the Lord raised Lazarus from the dead, Lazarus asked Him if he would have to die again. Our Lord told him he would have to die again, and Lazarus never smiled from that day on. Whether or not that tradition is accurate, I can imagine that going through the doorway of death once would be enough!

Up to this day only one Person has been raised from the dead in resurrection, and that is the Lord Jesus Christ. He is the firstfruits of them that sleep. He is the only one raised from the dead in a glorified body. One of these days, in the event we call the Rapture, the dead in Christ and the living believers will be changed into resurrected and glorified bodies, and will be caught up to be with the Lord. That resurrected body will never die.

The account of the dead son of the widow of Nain is indeed sad. He was the *only* son of a widowed mother which made his death twice as tragic. While passing through the village of Nain, the Lord met the funeral procession. Someone has said that He broke up every funeral He met. I am of the opinion that He raised from the dead more than the three people who are recorded in the Bible. These three instances are examples, probably from three age groups: a child, a young man, and an adult man.

Jesus raised this young man from the dead for the sake of this lonely mother. He had compassion for this woman and her situation. He touched the casket in which the young man lay and spoke to him. He always used the same method in raising people from the dead. He spoke directly to them. Also at the Rapture, it will be His voice. Scripture tells us, "For the Lord himself shall descend from heaven with a shout, with the voice of the archangel, and with the trump of God: and the dead in Christ shall rise first: Then we which are alive and remain shall be caught up together with them in the clouds, to meet the Lord in the air: and so shall we ever be with the Lord" (1 Thess. 4:16–17). He is coming for us with a shout. His voice will be like the voice of the archangel and the trump of God. His one solo voice will call His own back from the dead. He always used the same method in restoring life. He did not, however, use the same method in other miracles. But to raise the dead He always spoke directly to them.

JESUS COMMENDS JOHN THE BAPTIST

At this juncture John the Baptist sent some of his disciples to the Lord Jesus to ask a few questions because John was puzzled.

And John calling unto him two of his disciples sent them to Jesus, saying, Art thou he that should come? or look we for another?

When the men were come unto him, they said, John Baptist hath sent us unto thee, saying, Art thou he that should come? or look we for another? [Luke 7:19–20].

We have met John the Baptist before in Matthew and Mark. His dress was quite picturesque and unusual. There are those today who adopt a peculiar dress which may indicate a religious crank or a religious nut. While it is true that John the Baptist used an unusual dress, that is not what made him unusual. It was his message and ministry that set him apart. He was called of God—and we had better be sure we are called of God if we are going to wear religious garb. Many people think that by adopting the outward trappings of Christianity they will become Christians.

Not long ago a young woman was in front of our radio headquarters, taking a survey, and asked me what my occupation was. I told her that I was a minister and then asked her what a person had to do to become a Christian. She replied that to be a Christian you had to be good to your neighbors, not criticize anyone, and be friendly rather than harsh. She went on with quite a list of things that one should do to become a Christian. I told her, "You think Christianity is something you do on the outside. It is not. Christianity is a personal relationship with Jesus Christ. It is more than trying to imitate Christ, or wearing certain religious garb. You must be born again. To be a Christian means to have an experience with Christ. 'If any man be in Christ, he is a new creation'" (see 2 Cor. 5:17).

John the Baptist seems to be misplaced in the New Testament; he does not belong in the New Testament at all. He is the last of the illustrious Old Testament prophets. He is the bridge over the yawning chasm between the Old and New Testaments. He ranks with such notables as Samuel, Elijah, Isaiah, and Jeremiah. Christ told that generation to whom He preached, "Woe unto you, scribes and Pharisees, hypocrites! because ye build the tombs of the prophets, and garnish the sepulchres of the righteous, And say, If we had been in the days of our fathers, we would not have been partakers with them in the blood of the prophets. Wherefore ye be witnesses unto yourselves, that ye are the children of them which killed the prophets" (Matt. 23:29–31). They proved themselves genuine children who inherited the nature of their fathers because John the Baptist, last of the Old Testament prophets, was at that time in prison, and his voice was soon to be silenced in death.

While John was in prison, doubt had captivated his mind.

There are those who try and give a psychological explanation for the question John the Baptist asked, "Art thou he that should come?" John was looking for the Messiah and wanted to know if Christ was the one. To try and psychologically explain it away is rather amusing. They say that because he was in prison, he was depressed, discouraged, and dejected. I don't believe a word of it. John had announced the kingdom and denounced the nation. He had pronounced the coming of the King. He was a highway builder for the King. John identified the Messiah and said, "He shall baptize you with the Holy Ghost and with fire: Whose fan is in his hand, and he will throughly purge his floor, and will gather the wheat into his garner; but the chaff he will burn with fire unquenchable" (Luke 3:16–17). This is strong language. John was not expecting a Sunday school picnic. John was expecting Christ to establish the kingdom in all of its glory and power. Since this had not happened, John sent some of his disciples to ask if Christ was the One they were looking for, or were they to look for another?

Notice that the Lord Jesus received the messengers cordially, but He kept them waiting.

And in that same hour he cured many of their infirmities and plagues, and of evil spirits; and unto many that were blind he gave sight.

Then Jesus answering said unto them, Go your way, and tell John what things ye have seen and heard; how that the blind see, the lame walk, the lepers are cleansed, the deaf hear, the dead are raised, to the poor the gospel is preached.

And blessed is he, whosoever shall not be offended in me [Luke 7:21–23].

Jesus kept John's disciples waiting while He performed many miracles so that they could go back to tell John that they had seen the fulfillment of prophecy concerning the Messiah. Isaiah 35:5–6 predicts His first coming: "Then the eyes of the blind shall be opened, and the ears of the deaf shall be unstopped. Then shall the lame man leap as an hart, and the tongue of the dumb sing . . . ." Jesus told John's disciples to tell him that they had seen the credentials of the Messiah. Actually John had fulfilled his mission. And Jesus realized that He was not moving as fast as John wanted Him to, but in the presence of intellectual difficulties, He is asking John to trust Him.

He is asking the same thing of you and me. He asks for our faith when we cannot understand. "For the preaching of the cross is to them that perish foolishness; but unto us which are saved it is the power of God" (1 Cor. 1:18). Doubts are not a sign that you are smart. On the contrary, they are a sign that you are very foolish and do not know everything. They signal the fact that you belong to a group which is perishing. Many learned professors sit in swivel chairs in dusty, musty libraries, far removed from life and human need, and write about the intellectual difficulties of accepting the Bible, the deity of Jesus Christ, and redemption by the blood of Christ. I believe the *Word* of *God*, friend, and I hope you do.

And when the messengers of John were departed, he began to speak unto the people concerning John. What went ye out into the wilderness for to see? A reed shaken with the wind?

But what went ye out for to see? A man clothed in soft raiment? Behold, they which are gorgeously apparelled, and live delicately, are in kings' courts [Luke 7:24–25].

Was John the Baptist a reed shaken with the wind? Indeed, he was not. John was rough and rugged. He was unshakable.

But what went ye out for to see? A prophet? Yea, I say unto you, and much more than a prophet.

This is he, of whom it is written, Behold, I send my messenger before thy face, which shall prepare thy way before thee [Luke 7:26–27].

This is a quotation from Malachi 3:1 and establishes John the Baptist as the forerunner of the Messiah.

For I say unto you, Among those that are born of women there is not a greater prophet than John the Baptist: but he that is least in the kingdom of God is greater than he.

And all the people that heard him, and the publicans, justified God, being baptized with the baptism of John [Luke 7:28–29].

This is a tremendous tribute that Jesus gives to John the Baptist.

But the Pharisees and lawyers rejected the counsel of God against themselves, being not baptized of him.

And the Lord said, Whereunto then shall I liken the men of this generation? and to what are they like?

They are like unto children sitting in the marketplace, and calling one to another, and saying, We have piped unto you, and ye have not danced; we have mourned to you, and ye have not wept [Luke 7:30–32].

In other words, they were like a bunch of spoiled brats. A lot of folks are that way. I was a pastor for almost forty years, and a great deal of that time was spent as a wet nurse, burping spiritual babies—which is what these religious rulers were in Christ's day. The Lord said they were like children playing in a marketplace. One of the children says, "Let's play wedding." The others say, "No, that's too jolly." "Then let's play funeral." No, they don't want to play funeral because it is too sad. Our Lord said these petulant children were exactly like that religious generation. And I wonder if this is an accurate picture of the average church today.

For John the Baptist came neither eating bread nor drinking wine; and ye say, He hath a devil.

The Son of man is come eating and drinking; and ye say, Behold a gluttonous man, and a winebibber, a friend of publicans and sinners!

But wisdom is justified of all her children [Luke 7:33–35].

I hear people say, "I do not like that preacher because he is too intellectual, and his tone is monotonous." And the same folk say, "I do not like that preacher because he pounds the pulpit and yells at the top of his voice." The problem is not with these two types of preachers. The problem is with the spoiled baby who complains. That is what the Lord said in His day, and it is still applicable today.

JESUS GOES TO DINNER AT A PHARISEE'S HOUSE

And one of the Pharisees desired him that he would eat with him. And he went into the Pharisee's house, and sat down to meat. [Luke 7:36].

This is one of the notable occasions when the Lord Jesus Christ went out to dinner. When He went out to dinner, it was never a dull affair. Remember, He had been denouncing these Pharisees. He called them spoiled brats; so it is difficult to believe that the invitation to dinner from this Pharisee was a friendly one. The Pharisee invited Him to dinner so that he could spy on Him and find something wrong with Him.

And, behold, a woman in the city, which was a sinner, when she knew that Jesus sat at meat in the Pharisee's house, brought an alabaster box of ointment,

And stood at his feet behind him weeping, and began to wash his feet with tears, and did wipe them with the hairs of her head, and kissed his feet, and anointed them with the ointment.

Now when the Pharisee which had bidden him saw it, he spake within himself, saying, This man, if he were a prophet, would have known who and what manner of woman this is that toucheth him: for she is a sinner [Luke 7:37–39].

While Christ was in the home of the Pharisee, a woman came. She brought an alabaster box of ointment and entered the house of the Pharisee. When you had guests in that day, your neighbors had a perfect right to come in and stand along the wall or sit on their haunches and watch. They did not come to comment, only to watch. This woman came in and took her place behind the Lord Jesus. In those days they didn't sit on chairs at the table; they reclined on couches. So Jesus was reclining on a couch, with His feet sticking out in back, leaning on His arm, as He talked across the table to His host. As she stood by the feet of the Lord Jesus, weeping, because her sins had been forgiven, she began to wet His feet with tears and wipe His feet with the hairs of her head. Then she kissed His feet and anointed them with the costly ointment.

Now this old Pharisee would not have spoken to this type of woman on the street. He might have done business with her after dark when no one could see, but he would not have anything to do with a woman of her reputation during daylight hours. When he saw her wiping and kissing the Lord's feet, he thought, *He must not be a prophet or he would know the kind of woman she is and have nothing to do with her.*

JESUS GIVES PARABLE OF TWO DEBTORS

And Jesus answering said unto him, Simon, I have somewhat to say unto thee. And he saith, Master, say on.

There was a certain creditor which had two debtors: the one owed five hundred pence, and the other fifty.

And when they had nothing to pay, he frankly forgave them both. Tell me therefore, which of them will love him most?

Simon answered and said, I suppose that he, to whom he forgave most. And he said unto him, Thou hast rightly judged [Luke 7:40–43].

Jesus said, "Simon, I want to talk to you." Simon said, "Go ahead." This is one of the delightful parables Dr. Luke records. You can see from the content of this story the direction the Lord Jesus is taking.

And he turned to the woman, and said unto Simon, Seest thou this woman? I entered into thine house, thou gavest me no water for my feet: but she hath washed my feet with tears, and wiped them with the hairs of her head [Luke 7:44].

For the first time the Lord acknowledges this woman. He has not paid a bit of attention to her up to this time, but now He turns and looks at her. While He is looking at her, He says to Simon, who is on the other side of the table, "Seest thou this woman?" Simon had already said within himself that he did not think the Lord knew what kind of woman she was or He would not have permitted her to touch Him. Now our Lord says, "Simon, do you really know this woman? Look at her. You think you see her but you do not at all." The Lord is really rubbing this Pharisee the wrong way. This is the reason I believe that the Lord was not invited to dinner as a friendly gesture, but so that the Pharisee could spy upon Him. Now the Lord Jesus says:

Thou gavest me no kiss: but this woman since the time I came in hath not ceased to kiss my feet.

My head with oil thou didst not anoint: but this woman hath anointed my feet with ointment.

Wherefore I say unto thee, Her sins, which are many, are forgiven; for she

loved much: but to whom little is forgiven, the same loveth little.

And he said unto her, Thy sins are forgiven [Luke 7:45–48].

The Lord is saying, "You did not even exercise the common courtesies of the day." The Lord declares he did not have good manners. If Simon had been the proper kind of host, he would have washed the Lord's feet. He would have anointed the Lord's head and kissed Him. That was the custom of the day, but Simon did none of these things. (Unfortunately, the same thing could be said about a lot of Christians; they may read Emily Post, but they do not have good manners.)

I wish I had been present at this dinner. Our Lord was tops as an after-dinner speaker! What He said blanched the soul of Simon. This poor woman from the streets, without hope, wanted forgiveness. The God of heaven is there and He has forgiven her. Now He tells Simon, "You have judged correctly. You said that the one who owed the most would naturally be the one who would love him most. Well, she was a great sinner and has been forgiven a whole lot. But you, because you don't think you are a sinner, have not even asked for forgiveness." And that hypocritical old Pharisee sat there—an unforgiven sinner.

And they that sat at meat with him began to say within themselves, Who is this that forgiveth sins also?

And he said to the woman, Thy faith hath saved thee; go in peace [Luke 7:49–50].

This is very pertinent for our day. If you are a church member and have never asked the Lord Jesus for forgiveness, you are lost. This woman did not have any good works to her credit, but she believed in the Lord, she trusted Christ, she asked for forgiveness.

CHAPTER 8

THEME: *Jesus gives parables; parable of the sower; parable of the lighted candle; personal relationships; stills the storm; Jesus casts out demons at Gadara; Jesus heals woman with issue of blood; restores to life daughter of Jairus*

JESUS GIVES PARABLES

As our Lord continued His ministry, many people were turning to Him, and some of them were officials in high places.

And it came to pass afterward, that he went throughout every city and village, preaching and shewing the glad tidings of the kingdom of God: and the twelve were with him,

And certain women, which had been healed of evil spirits and infirmities, Mary called Magdalene, out of whom went seven devils,

And Joanna the wife of Chuza Herod's steward, and Susanna, and many others, which ministered unto him of their substance [Luke 8:1–3].

PARABLE OF THE SOWER

And when much people were gathered together, and were come to him out of every city, he spake by a parable:

A sower went out to sow his seed: and as he sowed, some fell by the way side; and it was trodden down, and the fowls of the air devoured it.

And some fell upon a rock; and as soon as it sprung up, it withered away, because it lacked moisture.

And some fell among thorns; and the thorns sprang up with it, and choked it.

And other fell on good ground, and sprang up, and bare fruit an hundredfold. And when he had said these things, he cried, He that hath ears to hear, let him hear.

And his disciples asked him, saying, What might this parable be?

And he said, Unto you it is given to know the mysteries of the kingdom of God: but to others in parables; that seeing they might not see, and hearing they might not understand.

Now the parable is this: The seed is the word of God.

Those by the way side are they that hear; then cometh the devil, and taketh away the word out of their hearts, lest they should believe and be saved.

They on the rock are they, which, when they hear, receive the word with joy; and these have no root, which for a while believe, and in time of temptation fall away.

And that which fell among thorns are they, which, when they have heard, go forth, and are choked with cares and riches and pleasures of this life, and bring no fruit to perfection.

But that on the good ground are they, which in an honest and good heart, having heard the word, keep it, and bring forth fruit with patience [Luke 8:4–15].

The Sower is Jesus. The seed is His Word. The birds are a symbol of the Devil. The "rocky places" are those who receive the Word of God in the enthusiasm of the flesh. Trouble and persecution dampen the interest. For a time fleshly hearers of the Word manifest great interest and zeal, but a little trouble reveals their lack of true faith. Only some of the seed falls on good ground and brings forth a full harvest. These are the hearers who are genuinely converted by the Word of God.

PARABLE OF THE LIGHTED CANDLE

No man, when he hath lighted a candle, covereth it with a vessel, or putteth it under a bed; but setteth it on a candlestick, that they which enter in may see the light.

For nothing is secret, that shall not be made manifest; neither any thing hid, that shall not be known and come abroad.

Take heed therefore how ye hear: for whosoever hath, to him shall be given; and whosoever hath not, from him shall be taken even that which he seemeth to have [Luke 8:16–18].

The parable of the candle is one of action. Light creates responsibility. A man who receives the truth must act. We are held responsible to the degree that light has been given us. The point is that you and I were in darkness until the light of the gospel got through to us. Sometimes we are given the impression that man is a sinner because of his weakness or because of his ignorance. But Paul says very candidly (see Rom. 1) that men, when they knew God, glorifed Him not as God. Man is a willful sinner. That is the kind of sinners all of us are, and the light that comes in will create a responsibility. We come into this world lost, and if we do not accept the Light, who is Christ, we remain lost. We are held responsible for the light we have received.

PERSONAL RELATIONSHIPS

Then came to him his mother and his brethren, and could not come at him for the press.

And it was told him by certain which said, Thy mother and thy brethren stand without, desiring to see thee.

And he answered and said unto them, My mother and my brethren are these which hear the word of God, and do it [Luke 8:19–21].

Christ is declaring a new relationship in this passage. He was not denying His family relationship but was getting ready to declare one infinitely deeper, higher, and more permanent, transcending by far any blood relationship. This brings a believer mighty close to Him.

STILLS THE STORM

Now it came to pass on a certain day, that he went into a ship with his disciples: and he said unto them, Let us go over unto the other side of the lake. And they launched forth.

But as they sailed he fell asleep: and there came down a storm of wind on the lake; and they were filled with water, and were in jeopardy.

And they came to him, and awoke him, saying, Master, master, we perish. Then he arose, and rebuked the wind and the raging of the water: and they ceased, and there was a calm.

And he said unto them, Where is your faith? And they being afraid wondered,

saying one to another, What manner of man is this! for he commandeth even the winds and water, and they obey him [Luke 8:22–25].

Jesus gave a command to cross the sea. An unordinary storm arose. The intensity of the storm suggests the savagery of Satan. The Lord went to sleep because He was weary—so weary that the violent storm did not disturb Him. The disciples became frightened and felt that everyone in the boat would perish. The storm did not disturb the Lord, but the attitude of His disciples did. He rebuked the wind and the sea as one would speak to dogs on a leash. Literally His command was, "Be muzzled." The miracle lies in the fact that the wind ceased immediately, and the sea, which would have rolled for hours, instantly became as smooth as glass. How often He puts us in the storms of life in order that we might come closer to Him and learn what manner of Man He really is.

JESUS CASTS OUT DEMONS AT GADARA

Now our Lord arrives at Gadara where a maniac lived who was possessed by demons. Because of his profession Dr. Luke goes into this story more thoroughly than do the other writers.

And they arrived at the country of the Gadarenes, which is over against Galilee.

And when he went forth to land, there met him out of the city a certain man, which had devils long time, and ware no clothes, neither abode in any house, but in the tombs [Luke 8:26–27].

Apparently there were two demoniacs, and Luke selects only one for a definite purpose. Why? Luke is a doctor, and he is attempting to give an illustration. Concerning this matter of demons, there are those who think they belong to the category of ghosts, goblins, gnomes, sylvan satyrs, and stygian shades, fables and fairies. For many years the average Christian viewpoint on demons was that *if* they ever existed, they no longer exist today. However, I believe we are seeing a manifestation and resurgence of demon possession in our day. It is difficult to explain what is taking place in our contemporary society without believing in the existence of demons.

Dr. Luke treats demonism with remarkable insight from a doctor's viewpoint in a rather scientific way. Matthew's account of this story is matter-of-fact. Mark's account is more emotional and spectacular. Earlier in his gospel Luke has dealt with demonism, making it clear that demonism and diseases are different. Demon possession is just as real as cancer or leprosy. Demons disturb men physically, mentally, and spiritually. They can destroy the souls of men and be the eternal doom of men. Dr. Luke tells us in the next chapter that demons are synonymous with unclean spirits.

The case of the demon-possessed man at Gadara is one of the worst on record. There are some facts that we need to consider in connection with this account. The tribe of Gad inhabited the country of Gadara. This tribe did not cross over the river Jordan with Joshua when Israel inhabited the land. This man who was demon-possessed wore no clothes. I think there is a relationship between nudity and demon possession. He did not dwell in a house like normal people, but he dwelt among the tombs and caves. The personality of this man was degraded, debased, and destroyed. He had no will of his own; he was in the possession of demons.

When he saw Jesus, he cried out, and fell down before him, and with a loud voice said, What have I to do with thee, Jesus, thou Son of God most high? I beseech thee, torment me not.

(For he had commanded the unclean spirit to come out of the man. For oftentimes it had caught him: and he was kept bound with chains and in fetters; and he brake the bands, and was driven of the devil into the wilderness.) [Luke 8:28–29].

The demon recognized Jesus. James tells us, "Thou believest that there is one God; thou doest well: the devils also believe, and tremble" (James 2:19). Demons are the enemies of God and they are going to be judged.

What is the origin of demons? We cannot be dogmatic. The physical world has something in it that cannot be seen—it is the atom. They exist and have made an impact on our day and generation. Likewise in the spiritual world there are certain things we cannot see. Angels are real, but we cannot see them. There are two classes of angels: those that are with God and serve Him and those that fell with Satan at the beginning. Homer speaks of *daimon* and *Theos* as being synonymous. Hesiod, a Greek philosopher, says that all demons are good, while another Greek philosopher, Empedocles, declares that demons are both bad and good. Behind all idolatry and ancient religions was demonism.

Demons control a man so that he cannot do what he wants to do. Demons cause people to do frightful and terrifying acts. They cause people to perform soul-destroying acts. They cause mothers to kill their children, husbands to kill their wives, and children to kill their parents. People commit senseless acts, and they do not know why they do such terrible things. These things are happening in our day, and mankind is blaming everything but demons as the cause.

And Jesus asked him, saying, What is thy name? And he said, Legion: because many devils were entered into him.

And they besought him that he would not command them to go out into the deep.

And there was there an herd of many swine feeding on the mountain: and they besought him that he would suffer them to enter into them. And he suffered them.

Then went the devils out of the man, and entered into the swine: and the herd ran violently down a steep place into the lake, and were choked [Luke 8:30–33].

This man was not possessed by *one* demon but by a legion of demons. There are three thousand to six thousand men in a Roman legion of soldiers. The word *legion* was used like the word *mob*. There was a *mob* of demons in this man, and they did not want to go "out into the deep." That "deep" is the bottomless pit, or the abyss, where the other fallen angels are incarcerated. Jude tells us about it in Jude 6: "And the angels which kept not their first estate, but left their own habitation, he hath reserved in everlasting chains under darkness unto the judgment of the great day." Demons want to inhabit the body of a person. When a demon is cast out of a person, he will wander around and come back to try to enter that person again; or, if he cannot gain entrance, he will go to another person. He does not want to be without a body. When the Lord cast the demons out of this man, they were willing to go into the bodies of the swine which were feeding on the hillside rather than go into the abyss. Notice that the pigs would rather be dead than have the demons indwell them!

When they that fed them saw what was done, they fled, and went and told it in the city and in the country.

Then they went out to see what was done; and came to Jesus, and found the man, out of whom the devils were departed, sitting at the feet of Jesus, clothed, and in his right mind: and they were afraid.

They also which saw it told them by what means he that was possessed of the devils was healed [Luke 8:34–36].

A marvelous transformation had taken place in this man. Only Christ can deliver from the power of Satan. We are seeing a resurgence of demonism in our day. It is a frightful, ugly thing, and we need to call upon God for help.

Then the whole multitude of the country of the Gadarenes round about besought him to depart from them; for they were taken with great fear: and he went up into the ship, and returned back again.

Now the man out of whom the devils were departed besought him that he might be with him: but Jesus sent him away, saying,

Return to thine own house, and shew how great things God hath done unto thee. And he went his way and published throughout the whole city how great things Jesus had done unto him.

And it came to pass, that, when Jesus was returned, the people gladly received him: for they were all waiting for him [Luke 8:37–40].

It is startling to read that the people of Gadara came and asked the Lord Jesus to leave their coasts. The reason was that they would rather have the swine than have *Him*. That's a rather heart-searching question for the present day because there are a lot of people who would rather have other things—which are just as bad as pigs—than to have Christ!

JESUS HEALS WOMAN WITH ISSUE OF BLOOD; RESTORES TO LIFE DAUGHTER OF JAIRUS

When Jesus returned to the other side of the Sea of Galilee, crowds gathered around Him. There were two desperate people in the crowd.

And, behold, there came a man named Jairus, and he was a ruler of the synagogue: and he fell down at Jesus' feet, and besought him that he would come into his house:

For he had one only daughter, about twelve years of age, and she lay a-dying. But as he went the people thronged him.

And a woman having an issue of blood twelve years, which had spent all her living upon physicians, neither could be healed of any,

Came behind him, and touched the border of his garment: and immediately her issue of blood stanched [Luke 8:41–44].

Jairus came to get Jesus to heal his daughter, not to raise her from the dead. His faith was small, but his situation was desperate. He believed that Jesus would have to touch her. As Jesus began to deal with Jairus, He was interrupted by the woman with the issue of blood. The woman had been suffering with the affliction for twelve years. The daughter of Jairus was twelve years old. Twelve years of darkness were ending and twelve years of light were fading.

And Jesus said, Who touched me? When all denied, Peter and they that were with him said, Master, the multitude throng thee and press thee, and sayest thou, Who touched me?

And Jesus said, Somebody hath touched me: for I perceive that virtue is gone out of me.

And when the woman saw that she was not hid, she came trembling, and falling down before him, she declared unto him before all the people for what cause she had touched him, and how she was healed immediately.

And he said unto her, Daughter, be of good comfort: thy faith hath made thee whole; go in peace [Luke 8:45–48].

Jesus did not touch the woman; she touched Him and was healed instantly. Remember that a crowd was all about Jesus. The disciples, seeing the crowd pressing in on Him, knew that He was being touched by scores of people; yet only the woman was healed.

While he yet spake, there cometh one from the ruler of the synagogue's house, saying to him, Thy daughter is dead; trouble not the Master.

But when Jesus heard it, he answered him, saying, Fear not: believe only, and she shall be made whole.

And when he came into the house, he suffered no man to go in, save Peter, and James, and John, and the father and the mother of the maiden [Luke 8:49–51].

When they reached the home of Jairus, the paid mourners had already gone to work. They stopped weeping long enough to laugh at Jesus in their unbelief.

And all wept, and bewailed her: but he said, Weep not; she is not dead, but sleepeth.

And they laughed him to scorn, knowing that she was dead [Luke 8:52–53].

The Lord took Peter, James, John, and the father and mother of the girl inside with Him to where the little girl lay. Dr. Luke tells us that He spoke to the little girl in this lovely fashion, "Maid, arise." It could be translated, "Little lamb, wake up." The child arose. He brought her back to a world of suffering for the sake of her parents, not for her sake.

And he put them all out, and took her by the hand, and called, saying, Maid, arise.

And her spirit came again, and she arose straightway: and he commanded to give her meat.

And her parents were astonished: but he charged them that they should tell no man what was done [Luke 8:54–56].

My friend, notice again that the method Jesus uses in raising the dead is always the same. He calls them and they hear His voice! Once again our Lord demonstrated that He is indeed God.

CHAPTER 9

***THEME:** Jesus commissions and sends forth the Twelve; Jesus feeds the five thousand; Jesus announces His death and resurrection; transfigured; Jesus casts out demons from an only son; Jesus sets His face toward Jerusalem; Jesus puts down test for discipleship*

JESUS COMMISSIONS AND SENDS FORTH THE TWELVE

Then he called his twelve disciples together, and gave them power and authority over all devils, and to cure diseases [Luke 9:1].

When our Lord was here on earth, He gave the gift of healing to His apostles. It was one of the "sign" gifts. It served as the credential of the apostles—to demonstrate that they were who they claimed to be. When the church got under way (before the New Testament was in written form), the sign of an apostle was the fact that he had the "sign" gifts. Peter could heal the sick and raise the dead. Paul could heal the sick and raise the dead. To do this was proof that they were true apostles of the Lord Jesus Christ.

Jesus sent His disciples out to preach the kingdom of God and to heal the sick. This took place *before* He died upon the cross. Today the important thing is not healing. If you will read the Epistles carefully, you will see that even though Paul had the gift of healing, toward the end of his ministry he apparently did not exercise it at all. He told Timothy to take a little wine for his stomach's sake (see 1 Tim. 5:23) but did not heal him. Paul himself had a ". . . thorn in the flesh . . ." (2 Cor. 12:7), and though he asked God to remove it, God did not remove it. Also he wrote to Timothy, ". . . Trophimus have I left at Miletum sick" (2 Tim. 4:20). Why did not Paul heal his friend Trophimus? Paul, you see, had come to the end of his ministry, and the sign gifts even then were beginning to disappear from the church. Apparently when Scripture became a part of the church, the gift of healing passed from the scene. Authority moved from a *person* to the *page* of Scripture, the Word of God. Toward the end of his life John warned that correct doctrine was a man's credential. "If there come any unto you, and bring not this *doctrine*, receive him not into your house, neither bid him God speed" (2 John 10, italics mine). Paul said, "But though we, or an angel from heaven, preach any other gospel unto you than that which we have preached unto you, let him be accursed" (Gal. 1:8). The word *accursed* is the Greek word *anathema* and means "damned." That is very strong language which places absolute authority in the Scriptures.

And he sent them to preach the kingdom of God, and to heal the sick.

And he said unto them, Take nothing for your journey, neither staves, nor scrip, neither bread, neither money; neither have two coats apiece [Luke 9:2–3].

Some people use this passage as a basis for their ministry today. Watch such a preacher, and see if he takes an offering. See if he takes anything with him when he goes on a journey—scrip (which means a suitcase), food, or money. Our Lord gave these instructions to His twelve disciples, not to us.

And whatsoever house ye enter into, there abide, and thence depart [Luke 9:4].

Of course today the laborer is worthy of his hire. I feel that any man who is giving out the Word of God should be supported. In the days of Christ the situation was different. The disciples had to stay in private homes because there were no Holiday Inns or Hilton Hotels. All entertaining was done in private homes.

And whosoever will not receive you, when ye go out of that city, shake off the very dust from your feet for a testimony against them [Luke 9:5].

The impact of their ministry affected even Herod.

Now Herod the tetrarch heard of all that was done by him: and he was perplexed, because that it was said of some, that John was risen from the dead;

And of some, that Elias had appeared; and of others, that one of the old prophets was risen again.

And Herod said, John have I beheaded: but who is this, of whom I hear such

things? And he desired to see him [Luke 9:7–9].

Herod was the ruler who had been responsible for the imprisonment and execution of John the Baptist. Mark tells us that Herod was afraid Jesus was John the Baptist come back to life. The curiosity of Herod caused him to want to see Jesus.

And the apostles, when they were returned, told him all that they had done. And he took them, and went aside privately into a desert place belonging to the city called Bethsaida.

And the people, when they knew it, followed him: and he received them, and spake unto them of the kingdom of God, and healed them that had need of healing [Luke 9:10–11].

This furnishes the setting for feeding the five thousand. He had taken them aside to rest—but there was no opportunity for that. Certainly the crowd was inconsiderate; yet our Lord graciously received them—taught them and healed those who were ill.

JESUS FEEDS THE FIVE THOUSAND

They put themselves in the unlovely position of being advisors of Christ—telling Him what to do. Unfortunately, many of us are guilty of doing this today. Friend, He doesn't need our suggestions.

And when the day began to wear away, then came the twelve, and said unto him, Send the multitude away, that they may go into the towns and country round about, and lodge, and get victuals: for we are here in a desert place.

But he said unto them, Give ye them to eat. And they said, We have no more but five loaves and two fishes; except we should go and buy meat for all this people [Luke 9:12–13].

Now they become financial advisors, economic experts.

For they were about five thousand men. And he said to his disciples, Make them sit down by fifties in a company.

And they did so, and made them all sit down [Luke 9:14–15].

At last they are in their rightful place, obeying Christ.

Then he took the five loaves and the two fishes, and looking up to heaven, he blessed them, and brake, and gave to the disciples to set before the multitude.

And they did eat, and were all filled: and there was taken up of fragments that remained to them twelve baskets [Luke 9:16–17].

Matthew, Mark, and John also record the feeding of the five thousand. Notice that our Lord assigns His disciples an impossible task. They must learn, as we must learn, that He always commands the impossible. The reason is obvious—He intends to do the work. The Creator, who made the fish in the beginning and causes the grain to multiply in the fields, now by His fiat word creates food for the crowd. This may have been the first time many in this crowd ever were filled. The "fragments" which were left do not refer to what we might put in the garbage can. Rather, they were pieces of food which had not been served. God always provides a surplus.

JESUS ANNOUNCES HIS DEATH AND RESURRECTION

And it came to pass, as he was alone praying, his disciples were with him: and he asked them, saying, Whom say the people that I am?

They answering said, John the Baptist; but some say, Elias; and others say, that one of the old prophets is risen again.

He said unto them, But whom say ye that I am? Peter answering said, The Christ of God.

And he straitly charged them, and commanded them to tell no man that thing [Luke 9:18–21].

The important question here is, who is Jesus? Jesus wanted to know men's estimate of Him. I am sure His purpose in asking this question of them was to crystalize in their thinking who He actually was. There was much confusion regarding His person. Notice that all opinions were high, but all fell short of who He was and is. The finest thing Peter ever said was, ". . . Thou art the Christ, the Son of the living God" (see Matt. 16:16 for his entire statement).

Saying, The Son of man must suffer many things, and be rejected of the elders and chief priests and scribes, and be slain, and be raised the third day [Luke 9:22].

Again Jesus prepares them for His approaching death. But notice that He never mentions His death without also mentioning His resurrection.

And he said to them all, If any man will come after me, let him deny himself, and take up his cross daily, and follow me.

For whosoever will save his life shall lose it: but whosoever will lose his life for my sake, the same shall save it.

For what is a man advantaged, if he gain the whole world, and lose himself, or be cast away?

For whosoever shall be ashamed of me and of my words, of him shall the Son of man be ashamed, when he shall come in his own glory, and in his Father's, and of the holy angels [Luke 9:23–26].

Here He is not putting down a condition of salvation but stating the position of those who are saved. This is what He is talking about. "Whosoever shall be ashamed of me and of my words, of him shall the Son of man be ashamed." What kind of Christian are *you* today? Are you one who acknowledges Him and serves Him and attempts to glorify Him? My friend, this is all important in these days in which we live.

TRANSFIGURED

In dealing with the Transfiguration, Dr. Luke adds something that the other gospel writers leave out.

But I tell you of a truth, there be some standing here, which shall not taste of death, till they see the kingdom of God [Luke 9:27].

Simon Peter interprets this verse for us. He said that he saw the kingdom. Where did he see it? Peter was with the Lord on the holy mount and was an eyewitness of it. He tells us about it in 2 Peter 1:16–18 which says, "For we have not followed cunningly devised fables, when we made known unto you the power and coming of our Lord Jesus Christ, but were eyewitnesses of his majesty. For he received from God the Father honour and glory, when there came such a voice to him from the excellent glory, This is my beloved Son, in whom I am well pleased. And this voice which came from heaven we heard, when we were with him in the holy mount." This is the explanation Simon Peter gives, and that is good enough for me. I think the man who was there ought to know more about it than some of these modern scholars who were not present.

And it came to pass about an eight days after these sayings, he took Peter and John and James, and went up into a mountain to pray [Luke 9:28].

The Lord took Peter, James, and John up into a mountain to pray. While He prayed, the Lord's countenance was altered. The fashion of His countenance was "transfigured"—this word is from the Greek *metamorphoom—metamorphosis* in English. That which took place is like the experience of the caterpillar; first you have the caterpillar, then it encases itself in the cocoon, and out comes a beautiful butterfly. The Transfiguration does not set forth the deity of Christ, but the humanity of Christ. Transfiguration is the goal of humanity. When you see the Lord Jesus Christ transfigured there on the mount, you are seeing exactly what is going to take place in that day when we are translated. The dead shall be raised, and those who are alive shall be *changed;* that is, they shall undergo metamorphosis. Then they will all be translated and brought into the presence of God.

And as he prayed, the fashion of his countenance was altered, and his raiment was white and glistering [Luke 9:29].

This verse does not mean that a light, as a spotlight, shone on Him, but that a light came from within His body and shone outwardly. Some people ask the silly question, "Are we going to wear clothes in heaven?" I think we will, but I do not believe we will need them because we will be clothed in this glory-light such as clothed our Lord.

And behold, there talked with him two men, which were Moses and Elias:

Who appeared in glory, and spake of his decease which he should accomplish at Jerusalem [Luke 9:30–31].

Two men appeared on the mount: Moses, the representative of the Law, and Elijah, the representative of the prophets, and they were bearing witness to Him. What did they talk about? They spoke about the approaching death of Christ. Paul says that the gospel he preached was one to which both the Law and prophets bore testimony. The gospel is *not* contrary to the Old Testament at all. Paul put it like this: "But now the righteousness of God without the law is manifested, being witnessed by the law and the prophets" (Rom. 3:21). The Law and the prophets reveal that the *only* way God could save us is through the righteousness that we obtain by faith. In the Old Testament this was done by bringing a sacrifice. The sacrificial system was the very heart of the Mosaic system. That little lamb that was offered on the altar is symbolic of Christ who died for our sins. And the prophets spoke of the Lamb of God that would take away the sin of the world.

But Peter and they that were with him were heavy with sleep: and when they were awake, they saw his glory, and the two men that stood with him.

And it came to pass, as they departed from him, Peter said unto Jesus, Master, it is good for us to be here: and let us make three tabernacles; one for thee, and one for Moses, and one for Elias: not knowing what he said [Luke 9:32–33].

Good old Simon Peter just has to say something. He should have kept his mouth closed at this time, but he has to speak up, and I guess he thinks he is saying something important. But Luke adds, "not knowing what he said." Many people, like Peter, speak pious words without knowing what they say. Peter suggests they build three tabernacles, which puts Moses and Elijah on a par with Jesus Christ, although he puts the Lord at the head of the list. Many anthologies of religion list Buddha, Mohammed, Moses, and Christ as founders of religion. It may seem strange to you, but Jesus Christ is not the founder of any religion. He did not found a religion; He died on a cross for the sins of the world. He is the *Savior*, and that is why we are not saved by religion; we are saved by Christ. I remember Dr. Carrol said many times, "When I came to Christ, I lost my religion." A great many people need to lose their religion and find Christ.

While he thus spake, there came a cloud, and overshadowed them: and they feared as they entered into the cloud.

And there came a voice out of the cloud, saying, This is my beloved Son: hear him.

And when the voice was past, Jesus was found alone. And they kept it close, and told no man in those days any of those things which they had seen [Luke 9:34–36].

CASTS OUT DEMONS FROM AN ONLY SON

And it came to pass, that on the next day, when they were come down from the hill, much people met him.

And, behold, a man of the company cried out, saying, Master, I beseech thee, look upon my son: for he is mine only child.

And, lo, a spirit taketh him, and he suddenly crieth out: and it teareth him that he foameth again, and bruising him hardly departeth from him.

And I besought thy disciples to cast him out; and they could not.

And Jesus answering said, O faithless and perverse generation, how long shall I be with you, and suffer you? Bring thy son hither.

And as he was yet a-coming, the devil threw him down, and tare him. And Jesus rebuked the unclean spirit, and healed the child, and delivered him again to his father.

And they were all amazed at the mighty power of God. But while they wondered every one at all things which Jesus did, he said unto his disciples [Luke 9:37–43].

This entire scene is a picture of today. Jesus has passed on into the glory. His disciples are with Him. We are down here in this world at the foot of the mountain where there is confusion, compromise, and impotence. The world today acts like a demon-possessed man, and the church is helpless in the presence of the world's need. When Jesus spoke to the crowd, He rebuked them for their lack of faith concerning this boy, and apparently the disciples and skeptics were included.

The condition of this boy was pitiful. Jesus turned to the father and asked him to believe. The father made a desperate plea for faith, the other gospel writers tell us. The disciples were puzzled because they had cast out demons previously but could not cast out this one. Our Lord confirms that this case was different because of its seriousness. The Lord rebuked the demon, healed the child, and delivered him to his father. The process of casting out the demon revealed again the seriousness of the case.

JESUS SETS HIS FACE TOWARD JERUSALEM

After delivering the demon-possessed boy, the Lord and His disciples head for Jerusalem. Once again our Lord speaks about His impending death.

Let these sayings sink down into your ears: for the Son of man shall be delivered into the hands of men.

But they understood not this saying, and it was hid from them, that they perceived it not: and they feared to ask him of that saying [Luke 9:44–45].

They didn't quite understand this matter of being raised from the dead. Here He is talking about His own death for them, and you would think that these men might have at least made some inquiry.

Then there arose a reasoning among them, which of them should be greatest [Luke 9:46].

After the Transfiguration you would think they would be humbled and obedient to His will. On the contrary, they became ambitious. They were thinking of the crown and ignored the cross. They were desirous of vainglory. This has been the curse of His disciples from that day to this. It is one of the curses of the church. In Paul's letter to the Galatian Christians he wrote, "Let us not be desirous of vain glory, provoking one another, envying one another" (Gal. 5:26).

And Jesus, perceiving the thought of their heart, took a child, and set him by him,

And said unto them, Whosoever shall receive this child in my name receiveth me: and whosoever shall receive me receiveth him that sent me: for he that is least among you all, the same shall be great [Luke 9:47–48].

This is a great principle. It is my conviction that the greatest saints are the unknown folk in our churches who quietly and faithfully serve Him.

And John answered and said, Master, we saw one casting out devils in thy name; and we forbad him, because he followeth not with us.

And Jesus said unto him, Forbid him not: for he that is not against us is for us.

And it came to pass, when the time was come that he should be received up, he stedfastly set his face to go to Jerusalem,

And sent messengers before his face: and they went, and entered into a village of the Samaritans, to make ready for him.

And they did not receive him, because his face was as though he would go to Jerusalem [Luke 9:49–53].

Notice the rejection by the Samaritans. We think of the "good" Samaritans because of the parable, but they were no more lovely than the Jews—both rejected Him.

And when his disciples James and John saw this, they said, Lord, wilt thou that we command fire to come down from heaven, and consume them, even as Elias did? [Luke 9:54].

John is always thought of as a ladylike apostle, but notice his fiery disposition here.

But he turned, and rebuked them, and said, Ye know not what manner of spirit ye are of.

For the Son of man is not come to destroy men's lives, but to save them. And they went to another village [Luke 9:55–56].

Jesus rebukes any kind of sectarian spirit. What a stinging rebuke: "The Son of man is not come to destroy men's lives, but to save." At another occasion He said, "For the Son of man is come to seek and to save that which was lost" (Luke 19:10). John entirely misunderstood the purpose of Christ's first coming.

JESUS PUTS DOWN TEST FOR DISCIPLESHIP

In this section we see three applicants who want to become disciples of the Lord Jesus. Notice this is not giving the way of salvation. The question, ". . . what must I do to be saved?" (Acts 16:30), is not asked here. Rather this is what is required to become a follower, a disciple of Christ.

The first applicant is an impetuous and impulsive young man.

And it came to pass, that, as they went in the way, a certain man said unto him, Lord, I will follow thee whithersoever thou goest.

And Jesus said unto him, Foxes have holes, and birds of the air have nests;

but the Son of man hath not where to lay his head [Luke 9:57–58].

Our Lord's answer to him revealed His own poverty when He was on earth. When they traveled, there would be no reservations for them at a motel. Poverty was part of the curse that He bore. Did the young man follow Him? We are not told. I like to think that he did.

And he said unto another, Follow me. But he said, Lord, suffer me first to go and bury my father.

Jesus said unto him, Let the dead bury their dead: but go thou and preach the kingdom of God [Luke 9:59–60].

The next applicant had made a decision to follow the Lord Jesus, but he wanted to first bury his father. This verse has been greatly misunderstood. Jesus was not forbidding this boy to attend the funeral of his father. Rather, the boy is saying that he would have to take care of his father until he died. After his father was gone, he would be free to follow Jesus.

When it comes to discipleship, human affection takes second place to His will. When a conflict arises between human affections and Christ, He claims the first place. However, His will and human affection may not always conflict.

And another also said, Lord, I will follow thee; but let me first go bid them farewell, which are at home at my house.

And Jesus said unto him, No man, having put his hand to the plough, and looking back, is fit for the kingdom of God [Luke 9:61–62].

This third applicant wanted a furlough to bid loved ones good-bye. He was a halfway and halfhearted follower of Christ. He wanted to be a disciple, but he did not want to make any sacrifice. He was not impelled by the urgency, the importance of the mission. Remember that the Lord Jesus Christ was even then on His way to the Cross. He had steadfastly set His face to go to Jerusalem.

Friend, the cost of discipleship is high. It demands all we have to give. The apostle Paul wrote, "Brethren, I count not myself to have apprehended: but this one thing I do, forgetting those things which are behind, and reaching forth unto those things which are before, I press toward the mark for the prize of the high calling of God in Christ Jesus" (Phil. 3:13–14).

CHAPTER 10

THEME: *Jesus sends forth the seventy; Jesus pronounces judgment on Chorazin, Bethsaida and Capernaum; Jesus gives parable of the good Samaritan; Jesus enters the home of Mary and Martha*

JESUS SENDS FORTH THE SEVENTY

After these things the Lord appointed other seventy also, and sent them two and two before his face into every city and place, whither he himself would come.

Therefore said he unto them, The harvest truly is great, but the labourers are few: pray ye therefore the Lord of the harvest, that he would send forth labourers into his harvest [Luke 10:1–2].

The Lord sent out seventy disciples who were to prepare the way for the ministry of Jesus. Only Luke tells us of this. The work was for a limited time, and their office was temporary because Jesus was journeying toward Jerusalem.

We hear a great deal today about "praying the Lord of the harvest to send forth laborers into the harvest"—that the Lord looks out upon the world which is ripe unto harvest, and our business today is to gather in the harvest. This may sound strange to you, but I do not consider it my business to harvest. My business is sowing. If you have ever been a farmer, you know there is a vast difference between sowing seed and harvesting the crop after the seed has matured. Someone counters, "But the Lord said that the harvest is great and the laborers few." We must remember *where*

Jesus was when He made that statement. He was on the other side of the cross at the time, and an age was coming to an end. At the end of every age is judgment. The judgment that ends an age is a harvest, and the age itself is for the sowing of seed. I believe that we are sowing seed today, and that at the end of this age there will be a harvest. In the parable of the tares and wheat the Lord said, "Let both grow together until the harvest: and in the time of harvest I will say to the reapers, Gather ye together first the tares, and bind them in bundles to burn them: but gather the wheat into my barn" (Matt. 13:30). My business is to sow the seed which is the Word of God. That is the business of every Christian.

Go your ways: behold, I send you forth as lambs among wolves.

Carry neither purse, nor scrip, nor shoes: and salute no man by the way.

And into whatsoever house ye enter, first say, Peace be to this house.

And if the son of peace be there, your peace shall rest upon it: if not, it shall turn to you again.

And in the same house remain, eating and drinking such things as they give: for the labourer is worthy of his hire. Go not from house to house.

And into whatsoever city ye enter, and they receive you, eat such things as are set before you:

And heal the sick that are therein, and say unto them, The kingdom of God is come nigh unto you [Luke 10:3–9].

Jesus warns them that they can expect hardship and danger—they will be "lambs among wolves." They are to travel light and waste no time in idle conversations. They are to be men impelled by one supreme motive—to prepare hearts for the coming of Christ personally.

JESUS PRONOUNCES JUDGMENT ON CHORAZIN, BETHSAIDA, AND CAPERNAUM

But into whatsoever city ye enter, and they receive you not, go your ways out into the streets of the same, and say,

Even the very dust of your city, which cleaveth on us, we do wipe off against you: notwithstanding be ye sure of this, that the kingdom of God is come nigh unto you.

But I say unto you, that it shall be more tolerable in that day for Sodom, than for that city.

Woe unto thee, Chorazin! woe unto thee, Bethsaida! for if the mighty works had been done in Tyre and Sidon, which have been done in you, they had a great while ago repented, sitting in sackcloth and ashes.

But it shall be more tolerable for Tyre and Sidon at the judgment, than for you.

And thou, Capernaum, which art exalted to heaven, shalt be thrust down to hell.

He that heareth you heareth me; and he that despiseth you despiseth me; and he that despiseth me despiseth him that sent me [Luke 10:10–16].

Our Lord solemnly speaks of the seriousness of rejecting His messengers—to reject them was to reject Him.

And the seventy returned again with joy, saying, Lord, even the devils are subject unto us through thy name.

And he said unto them, I beheld Satan as lightning fall from heaven.

Behold, I give unto you power to tread on serpents and scorpions, and over all the power of the enemy: and nothing shall by any means hurt you.

Notwithstanding in this rejoice not, that the spirits are subject unto you; but rather rejoice, because your names are written in heaven [Luke 10:17–20].

In order to complete the story of the seventy, Luke describes their return. They came back thrilled and excited. This is the same experience we have when we give out the Word of God, and someone comes to Christ. How glorious we feel! What a lesson for us to remember the words of Jesus, "rejoice not, that the spirits are subject unto you; but rather rejoice, because your names are written in heaven." When there is success in our ministry, it is His work, not ours.

In that hour Jesus rejoiced in spirit, and said, I thank thee, O Father, Lord of heaven and earth, that thou hast hid these things from the wise and prudent, and hast revealed them unto babes: even so, Father; for so it seemed good in thy sight.

All things are delivered to me of my Father: and no man knoweth who the Son is, but the Father; and who the Father is, but the Son, and he to whom the Son will reveal him.

And he turned him unto his disciples, and said privately, Blessed are the eyes which see the things that ye see:

For I tell you, that many prophets and kings have desired to see those things which ye see, and have not seen them; and to hear those things which ye hear, and have not heard them [Luke 10: 21–24].

JESUS GIVES PARABLE OF THE GOOD SAMARITAN

Now we come to one of the things that characterizes the Gospel of Luke—parables. Dr. Luke majors in parables just as Mark majors in miracles. Dr. Luke records certain parables that are among some of the most familiar parts of the Bible. The parable of the Good Samaritan is probably the best-known story. Some literary critics consider it the greatest story ever told.

And, behold, a certain lawyer stood up, and tempted him, saying, Master, what shall I do to inherit eternal life? [Luke 10:25].

The parable of the Good Samaritan came about as an answer to a question about eternal life. It was not an honest question, but it was a good question and a stock question. A "certain lawyer" asked the question—but he was not a lawyer in the sense we think of it.

I heard a little story about lawyers in our judicial system. Two lawyers were in court. It was a difficult case, and there was a great deal of controversy. The court opened and lawyer number one jumped up and called the other lawyer a liar. The second lawyer jumped up to retaliate and called the first lawyer a thief. The judge rapped for silence, and said, "Now that the lawyers have identified themselves, we will begin the case."

However, the lawyer in this parable was not part of a judicial system; but rather, he was an interpreter of the Mosaic Law, and in that sense he was a lawyer.

Now our Lord had a very wonderful way of dealing with questions. He answered a question by asking a question. It is known, by the way, as the Socratic method because Socrates used it: answer a question with a question. It lets a man answer his own question. So the lawyer tries to put Jesus on the witness stand, and He turns around and puts *him* on the witness stand.

He said unto him, What is written in the law? how readest thou? [Luke 10:26].

Jesus knew that he was an expert in the Mosaic Law.

And he answering said, Thou shalt love the Lord thy God with all thy heart, and with all thy soul, and with all thy strength, and with all thy mind; and thy neighbour as thyself.

And he said unto him, Thou hast answered right: this do, and thou shalt live [Luke 10:27–28].

I wonder if you notice the barb that is in this.

But he, willing to justify himself, said unto Jesus, And who is my neighbour? [Luke 10:29].

Notice that our Lord said, "You have answered right." Remember that this took place before Christ died on the cross. Does it mean a man can be saved by keeping the Law? Yes, but let's follow through on this. It is not the hearers of the Law, but the doers of the Law that are justified. If you say you can keep it, I'll have to remind you that God contradicts you. He says it is impossible to be justified by the Law because no one can keep the Law—". . . by the works of the law shall no flesh be justified" (Gal. 2:16). "For what the law could not do, in that it was weak through the flesh, God sending his own Son in the likeness of sinful flesh, and for sin, condemned sin in the flesh: That the righteousness of the law might be fulfilled in us, who walk not after the flesh, but after the Spirit" (Rom. 8:3–4).

Now if the lawyer had been honest, which he was not, he would have said, "Master, I've sincerely tried to love God with all my heart, soul, strength, and mind, and my neighbor as myself. But I can't do it. I've miserably failed. So how can I inherit eternal life?" But instead of being honest, he adopted this evasive method and said, "And who is my neighbour?"

Now Christ gave him an answer to this question, and it is the parable of the Good Samaritan. It is a simple story but a marvelous one.

And Jesus answering said, A certain man went down from Jerusalem to Jericho, and fell among thieves, which stripped him of his raiment, and

wounded him, and departed, leaving him half dead.

And by chance there came down a certain priest that way: and when he saw him, he passed by on the other side.

And likewise a Levite, when he was at the place, came and looked on him, and passed by on the other side [Luke 10:30–32].

It is possible that this lawyer was a Levite and that he squirmed at this point because it touched him in a personal way.

But a certain Samaritan, as he journeyed, came where he was: and when he saw him, he had compassion on him,

And went to him, and bound up his wounds, pouring in oil and wine, and set him on his own beast, and brought him to an inn, and took care of him.

And on the morrow when he departed, he took out two pence, and gave them to the host, and said unto him, Take care of him; and whatsoever thou spendest more, when I come again, I will repay thee.

Which now of these three, thinkest thou, was neighbour unto him that fell among the thieves?

And he said, He that shewed mercy on him. Then said Jesus unto him, Go, and do thou likewise [Luke 10:33–37].

Dean Brown of Yale University has said that three classes of men that represent three philosophies of life are brought before us in this parable.

1. The Thief: His philosophy of life says, "What you have is mine." This is socialism or communism.

2. The Priest and Levite: His philosophy of life says, "What I have is mine." This is rugged individualism that has gone to seed. His cry is, "Let the world be damned, I will get mine." This is godless capitalism.

3. The Good Samaritan: His philosophy says, "What I have belongs to you." This is a Christian philosophy of life. "What I have is yours if I can help you." Folk who talk about "Christian socialism" don't recognize that they are two distinct philosophies.

Now our Lord intended that we bring this parable right down to where we live. We are told that a certain man went down from Jerusalem to Jericho and fell among thieves. That is a picture of humanity. That is the race that has come from Adam. Mankind came from Jerusalem, the place where they approached God, to Jericho, the accursed city. Humanity, you see, fell. Humanity found itself helpless, hopeless, and unable to save itself. Mankind was dead in trespasses and sin—this man who had fallen among thieves was half dead. The thieves are a picture of the Devil who, John 8:44 tells us, was a murderer from the beginning. Concerning this subject our Lord said, "All that ever came before me are thieves and robbers . . ." (John 10:8). When the multitude came to arrest Christ, He said to them, ". . . Are ye come out as against a thief with swords and staves for to take me? I sat daily with you teaching in the temple, and ye laid no hold on me" (Matt. 26:55). The Devil is a thief, and our Lord was crucified between two thieves—this is quite interesting, is it not?

Then we are told that a certain priest passed by on the other side. He represents ritualism and ceremonialism which cannot save a person. Someone has said that the reason the priest passed by on the other side was because he saw that the man had already been robbed! Next a Levite came by, and he too passed by on the other side. He represents legalism. Neither ritualism, ceremonialism, nor legalism can save. Then a "certain" Samaritan passed by. Whom did the "certain Samaritan" represent? He is the One who told the parable. When ritualism, ceremonialism, legalism, and religion could not do anything to help man, *Christ* came. He is able to bind up the broken-hearted. He is able to take the lost sinner, half-dead, lost in trespasses and sins, and help him.

This parable has a practical application for you and me today. Any person you can help is your neighbor. It does not mean that only the person living next to you is your neighbor. People need Christ, the Good Samaritan. There is a great deal of talk about getting the gospel out to the world, but not much of an effort is made to see that people know about Christ. It is like the young fellow who was courting a girl. He wrote her a letter and said to her, "I would climb the highest mountain for you, swim the deepest river for you, cross the widest sea for you, and cross the burning desert for you!" Then he added a P.S.: "If it does not rain next Wednesday, I will come to see you." That sounds like the average Christian's commitment to Christ!

The world today is like the man that fell among thieves and needs our help. The world needs Christ. Christ can not only rescue us from drowning, but He can teach us to swim.

Ritualism and formalism see mankind drowning and say, "Swim, brother, swim." But man cannot swim. Legalism and liberalism push across toward man and say, "Hang on, brother, hang on." But man cannot hang on. There is a song which says, "I was sinking deep in sin far from the peaceful shore, very deeply stained within, sinking to rise no more; but the Master of the sea heard my despairing cry, from the waters lifted me, now safe am I." Christ lifted me, my friend, and He can lift you too. That is the message of the Good Samaritan.

JESUS ENTERS THE HOME OF MARY AND MARTHA

Now it came to pass, as they went, that he entered into a certain village: and a certain woman named Martha received him into her house.

And she had a sister called Mary, which also sat at Jesus' feet, and heard his word.

But Martha was cumbered about much serving, and came to him, and said, Lord, dost thou not care that my sister hath left me to serve alone? bid her therefore that she help me.

And Jesus answered and said unto her, Martha, Martha, thou art careful and troubled about many things:

But one thing is needful: and Mary hath chosen that good part, which shall not be taken away from her [Luke 10:38–42].

Without going into a lot of detail, suffice it to say that Mary had done her part; then she went to sit at the feet of Jesus. Martha, her sister, was a dear soul and if it had not been for her they would not have had that lovely dinner. She got busy, however, and became frustrated. Possibly she reached for a pan, thought it was not big enough, then reached for another, and a pan fell off the top shelf. It was too much for her and she came walking out of the kitchen, and said something which she would not have said under normal conditions. Our Lord was very gentle with her, but said, "Mary has chosen the best part."

My frustrated, confused friend, are you at that corner of life where you do not know which way to turn? Then, for goodness sake, sit down. Sit at Jesus' feet. Look in His Word and see what He has to say. It will help you with your housework. It will make you a better dishwasher. It will help you sweep the floors cleaner. You will dig a better ditch, mow a better lawn, and study your lesson better. Your work at the office will be easier, and you will be able to drive your car better. Just take *time* to sit at the feet of Jesus. Mary chose the best part.

CHAPTER 11

THEME: *Jesus teaches disciples to pray by using parables of the persistent friend and a good father; Jesus accused of casting out demons by Beelzebub; parable of unclean spirit leaving a man; the sign of Jonah; parable of the lighted candle; Jesus denounces the Pharisees*

JESUS TEACHES DISCIPLES TO PRAY BY USING PARABLES OF THE PERSISTENT FRIEND AND A GOOD FATHER

And it came to pass, that, as he was praying in a certain place, when he ceased, one of his disciples said unto him, Lord, teach us to pray, as John also taught his disciples.

And he said unto them, When ye pray, say, Our Father which art in heaven, Hallowed be thy name. Thy kingdom come. Thy will be done, as in heaven, so in earth.

Give us day by day our daily bread.

And forgive us our sins; for we also forgive every one that is indebted to us.

And lead us not into temptation; but deliver us from evil [Luke 11:1–4].

This important section deals with prayer as it is found nowhere else in the Gospels. It may sound similar to other portions in the Gospels, but it is actually different. There are those who feel that this passage is an insertion, an intrusion, in the chronological account of the ministry of Christ. It is true that it does not follow the movement, but it introduces many interesting implications.

The reason His disciple wanted to know how to pray was that he had seen and heard Christ pray. It was the custom of our Lord to retire alone to pray. A disciple evidently overheard His prayer, and a desire was born in his heart to pray like Christ prayed.

At this moment, friend, the Lord Jesus Christ is at God's right hand making intercession for us. He is our great Intercessor. And it is still a good idea to ask Him to teach us to pray. An appropriate petition is, "Lord, teach me to pray."

This disciple was not just asking *how* to pray. The Lord had given the Sermon on the Mount which outlined how one should pray. This disciple was not asking for a technique, a system, an art form, or a ritual to follow. It was not a matter of *how* to do it, but he wanted to pray like Christ prayed.

Many folks *say* their prayers. It is sort of an amen to tag on the end of the day when you put on your pajamas. I was brought up in a home where I never heard prayer nor ever saw a Bible. The first time I ever engaged in prayer was at a conference when I was a boy. I stayed in a dormitory with other boys, and at night the one in charge told us to put on our pajamas and gather together for prayer. I got the impression, at the very beginning, that in order to pray you had to put on your pajamas; you could not pray any other time. Your pajamas were sort of your prayer clothes. Of course that was a ridiculous conception, but, frankly, we need someone to teach us to pray—not just to say prayers, but to get through to God.

This disciple asked the Lord, "Teach us to pray, as John also taught his disciples." This is an unexpected glimpse into the life of John the Baptist—sort of a farewell look at him because this is the last we'll see him. In this last picture, what do we see? We see John as a man of prayer. "Teach us to pray, as John also taught his disciples." Is anyone going to say that about you or me? All great servants of God have been men of prayer. The barren lives of Christians and the deadness of the church today are the result of prayerlessness. That is our problem.

In answer to their request the Lord gives them this. I do not believe He intended it to become the prayer I hear so often in public services. It is not to be a stilted form for public services, but a spontaneous, personal prayer, like a son talks to his father. God the Father *knows* me and I do not think He wants me to put on airs, assume an unnatural voice, and use flowery language. I think He wants me to talk like Vernon McGee. Nor does He want me to be "wordy." I get so weary of "wordy" prayers—and I think God does also.

Let us look at some of the elements of prayer. The first part is worship—"Hallowed be thy name." "Thy kingdom come" is praying for God's will to be done on earth. It involves the putting down of evil and the putting up of good. It means you have a desire for God's will in your life. It is useless to mouth the words of this prayer without meaning them. This prayer is for the believer; it is not for the unsaved. There is a prayer for the unsaved which is, "God be merciful to me a sinner" (Luke 18:13), but it can be even simpler than that. God *is* merciful and is able to extend mercy to you. You do not have to beg Him to save you; He will save you if you will come to Him.

Part of this prayer is for physical provision, "Give us day by day our daily bread." Then we are told to pray, "And forgive us our sins; for we also forgive every one that is indebted to us." I do not believe that I can measure up to this standard; I hope you can. Do you forgive everyone? Well, my friend, God wants us to forgive others. Our standard is set for us in Ephesians 4:32 which says, "And be ye kind one to another, tenderhearted, forgiving one another, even as God for Christ's sake hath forgiven you."

God help us to be men and women of prayer. We do not need more preachers, churches, or missionaries, but we do need more people who know how to pray.

God is not through with the subject of prayer in this chapter. Only Luke records this next parable, and it sheds a different light upon the subject of prayer. It is a parable of contrast.

And he said unto them, Which of you shall have a friend, and shall go unto him at midnight, and say unto him, Friend, lend me three loaves;

For a friend of mine in his journey is

come to me, and I have nothing to set before him?

And he from within shall answer and say, Trouble me not: the door is now shut, and my children are with me in bed; I cannot rise and give thee [Luke 11:5–7].

I want to bring this parable right up to date. Suppose a man and his wife and children live in California. They receive a letter from her mother saying that she is coming for a visit. She says that she will arrive on a certain day in the middle of the afternoon. The family decides that they will take her out to dinner when she comes. The big day arrives and the mother-in-law does not show up. The afternoon passes into evening and finally they receive a telephone call, and the mother-in-law explains that she has been delayed by car trouble. They are sure she will have dinner before she comes. At midnight here she is. The son-in-law casually inquires, "Have you had dinner?" She replies that she has not and is very hungry! Since there is nothing in the house to eat, the son-in-law decides to go next door to his good neighbor and borrow some food. His neighbor says, "Wait until morning. You are not starving. I am in bed and so are my children. Go home."

I say unto you, Though he will not rise and give him, because he is his friend, yet because of his importunity he will rise and give him as many as he needeth [Luke 11:8].

The man says, "Neighbor, you do not know my mother-in-law. Please get up." So he continues to pound on the door, and finally the neighbor gets up and gives him what he is asking for.

Now this is a parable by contrast.

And I say unto you, Ask, and it shall be given you; seek, and ye shall find; knock, and it shall be opened unto you.

For every one that asketh receiveth; and he that seeketh findeth; and to him that knocketh it shall be opened [Luke 11:9–10].

My friend, do you think that God is asleep? Do you feel that He has gone to bed when you pray, and you cannot get Him up? Do you believe that He does not want to answer your prayers? God *does* want to answer your prayers and He will. That is what this parable is saying. It is a parable by contrast and not by comparison. You do not have to storm the gates of heaven or knock down the door of heaven in order to attract God's attention. God is not reluctant to hear and answer you. God tells us in Isaiah 65:24, "And it shall come to pass, that before they call, I will answer; and while they are yet speaking, I will hear." God wants to hear and answer.

Some people think that God does not hear and answer their prayers. Maybe they do not get the message—sometimes God says, "No!" Our problem is that we do not like to take no for an answer. God *always* hears the prayers of His own, and answers them, but when He says no it is because we are not praying for that which is best for us. I have learned over the years that the best answer God has given to some of my requests has been no.

As a young preacher I prayed for God to open up the door to a certain church where I wanted to serve as pastor. I was asked to candidate, which I did. The machinery of the church and the political bigwigs met behind closed doors to decide if I would be pastor. They decided not to accept me because I was not a church politician, and theirs was a strategic church in that day. I went to the Lord and cried about it and told Him how He had let me down. Today I am ashamed of myself, and I have asked Him to forgive me for my attitude. He did not let me down. He knew what was best for me. He had something much better in store for me. Many times since then I have thanked Him for that no. You do not have to storm the gate of heaven to get God to answer your prayer. God has not gone to bed. The door is wide open and He says, "Knock, seek, and ask." Take everything to God in prayer, and He will give you His very best.

If a son shall ask bread of any of you that is a father, will he give him a stone? or if he ask a fish, will he for a fish give him a serpent? [Luke 11:11].

Before you go to God in prayer, make sure He is really your Father. "But as many as received him, to them gave he power to become the sons of God, even to them that believe on his name" (John 1:12). Believing that the Lord Jesus Christ died for you and rose again for your justification makes you a son of God. When you trust Christ as your Savior, you are baptized by the Spirit of God into the body of Christ, and you are a son who can go to God and say, "Father." If you ask your earthly father for bread, will he give you a stone? If you ask him for a fish, will he give you a serpent? Can you imagine a father doing that?

Or if he shall ask an egg, will he offer him a scorpion?

If ye then, being evil, know how to give good gifts unto your children: how much more shall your heavenly Father give the Holy Spirit to them that ask him? [Luke 11:12–13].

At that time He told His disciples to ask for the Holy Spirit. As far as I can tell, they never did ask for the Spirit. Later on Christ said, ". . . Receive ye the Holy Ghost" (John 20:22). They needed the Holy Spirit during those intervening days before Pentecost. Then on the great Day of Pentecost He came and baptized them into the body of believers, which put them *in* Christ. They were filled on that day with the Holy Spirit. That filling is something all of us need. All believers have been baptized into the body of Christ—"For by one Spirit are we all baptized into one body, whether we be Jews or Gentiles, whether we be bond or free; and have been all made to drink into one Spirit" (1 Cor. 12:13).

JESUS ACCUSED OF CASTING OUT DEMONS BY BEELZEBUB

This incident is also recorded in Matthew 12:24–30 and Mark 3:22–30. From this account has come the notion of the so-called unpardonable sin.

And he was casting out a devil, and it was dumb. And it came to pass, when the devil was gone out, the dumb spake; and the people wondered.

But some of them said, He casteth out devils through Beelzebub the chief of the devils [Luke 11:14–15].

The convincing nature of Jesus' miracles forced the Pharisees to offer some explanation for them. They could not deny the existence of miracles when they were happening before their eyes. They resorted to the basest and most blasphemous explanation for the miracles of Jesus. They did not deny that they took place but claimed that they were done by the power of the Devil.

And others, tempting him, sought of him a sign from heaven.

But he, knowing their thoughts, said unto them, Every kingdom divided against itself is brought to desolation; and a house divided against a house falleth.

If Satan also be divided against himself, how shall his kingdom stand? because ye say that I cast out devils through Beelzebub.

And if I by Beelzebub cast out devils, by whom do your sons cast them out? therefore shall they be your judges [Luke 11:16–19].

Christ showed them the utter absurdity of their line of reasoning.

But if I with the finger of God cast out devils, no doubt the kingdom of God is come upon you [Luke 11:20].

"The kingdom of God is come upon you" means that it was among them in the presence of the person of Jesus who had the credentials of the King.

When a strong man armed keepeth his palace, his goods are in peace:

But when a stronger than he shall come upon him, and overcome him, he taketh from him all his armour wherein he trusted, and divideth his spoils [Luke 11:21–22].

The "strong man armed" is Satan. The demon-possessed man was an evidence of his power. But, you see, Jesus is stronger than Satan, which was the reason He could cast out the demon.

"A strong man armed keepeth his palace" is a verse that has a message for us. There are those who want to disarm us—disarm us as a nation and disarm us in our homes. But "a strong man armed keepeth his palace." There are wicked men abroad. And Satan is abroad. As long as there is a strong enemy, we do well to be armed.

PARABLE OF UNCLEAN SPIRIT LEAVING A MAN

When the unclean spirit is gone out of a man, he walketh through dry places, seeking rest; and finding none, he saith, I will return unto my house whence I came out.

And when he cometh, he findeth it swept and garnished.

Then goeth he, and taketh to him seven other spirits more wicked than himself; and they enter in, and dwell there: and the last state of that man is worse than the first [Luke 11:24–26].

This parable pictures the precarious position of Israel and the Pharisees. The parable speaks of a man with an unclean spirit. The demon leaves the man, and the man feels that he is clean—empty, swept, and garnished. Reformation is no good, friends. If everyone in the world would quit sinning right now, there would not be more Christians. To stop sinning does not make a Christian. Reformation is not what is needed. Regeneration is what is needed. Israel had swept her house clean through the ministries of John the Baptist and Jesus, but she would not invite the Lord Jesus Christ to occupy it. So this wicked generation of Jews would reach an even worse state, as described in the parable.

THE SIGN OF JONAH

And when the people were gathered thick together, he began to say, This is an evil generation: they seek a sign; and there shall no sign be given it, but the sign of Jonas the prophet.

For as Jonas was a sign unto the Ninevites, so shall also the Son of man be to this generation.

The queen of the south shall rise up in the judgment with the men of this generation, and condemn them: for she came from the utmost parts of the earth to hear the wisdom of Solomon; and, behold, a greater than Solomon is here.

The men of Nineve shall rise up in the judgment with this generation, and shall condemn it: for they repented at the preaching of Jonas; and, behold, a greater than Jonas is here [Luke 11: 29–32].

The "sign" would be His own resurrection, of course. He directs them back to two incidents in the Old Testament. The first is the account of the prophet Jonah. Jonah was apparently raised from the dead when he was in the fish. God brought him out of darkness and death into light and life. Jonah's experience was typical of the coming death and resurrection of Jesus Christ. The Ninevites received Jonah and his preaching after his miraculous deliverance, and they repented. The acts of Israel, as a nation, place her in a much worse position because she did not receive her Messiah and did not repent.

PARABLE OF THE LIGHTED CANDLE

No man, when he hath lighted a candle, putteth it in a secret place, neither under a bushel, but on a candlestick, that they which come in may see the light.

The light of the body is the eye: therefore when thine eye is single, thy whole body also is full of light; but when thine eye is evil, thy body also is full of darkness.

Take heed therefore that the light which is in thee be not darkness.

If thy whole body therefore be full of light, having no part dark, the whole shall be full of light, as when the bright shining of a candle doth give thee light [Luke 11:33–36].

Our Lord gives a simple explanation on the purpose of a candle. It is a light giver; its purpose is to transmit light. The resurrection of Christ is the light. The resurrection of Christ is the one ray of light in this world. You and I are in a world bounded by birth and death—we are boxed in by these two events. The resurrection of Christ is that which brings hope from the outside. What will men do with the light?

To see an object, two things are essential: light to make the object visible, and eyes to behold the object. A light is of no use to the blind. A man who can see but has no light and a blind man with a light are in the same predicament. A light and an eye are essential for sight.

Even in the presence of Christ, men were obviously not seeing Him; they were stumbling over Him. That did not mean that He was not the Light of the World; it meant that men were blind.

DENOUNCES THE PHARISEES

And as he spake, a certain Pharisee besought him to dine with him: and he went in, and sat down to meat.

And when the Pharisee saw it, he marvelled that he had not first washed before dinner [Luke 11:37–38].

He omitted ceremonial cleansing, which was a religious rite.

And the Lord said unto him, Now do ye Pharisees make clean the outside of the cup and the platter; but your inward part is full of ravening and wickedness.

Ye fools, did not he that made that which is without make that which is within also? [Luke 11:39–40].

Religion is not a matter of externalities. It is a heart affair. This is a great principle.

He pronounces three woes which illustrate this principle.

But rather give alms of such things as ye have; and, behold, all things are clean unto you.

But woe unto you, Pharisees! for ye tithe mint and rue and all manner of herbs, and pass over judgment and the love of God: these ought ye to have done, and not to leave the other undone [Luke 11:41–42].

They had false values. He is not saying that it was wrong to tithe, but their wrong was in what they had left undone. And, friend, giving of your substance will not make you a Christian. However, if you love Christ, you *will* give of your substance.

Woe unto you, Pharisees! for ye love the uppermost seats in the synagogues, and greetings in the markets.

Woe unto you, scribes and Pharisees, hypocrites! for ye are as graves which appear not, and the men that walk over them are not aware of them [Luke 11:43–44].

In other words, they were a bad influence.

Then answered one of the lawyers, and said unto him, Master, thus saying thou reproachest us also [Luke 11:45].

The shoe was beginning to fit. The Pharisees were occupied with externalities. The sin of the scribes was insincerity. They were adding to the Law, making it more difficult, yet not attempting to follow it themselves.

And he said, Woe unto you also, ye lawyers! for ye lade men with burdens grievous to be borne, and ye yourselves touch not the burdens with one of your fingers.

Woe unto you! for ye build the sepulchres of the prophets, and your fathers killed them.

Truly ye bear witness that ye allow the deeds of your fathers: for they indeed killed them, and ye build their sepulchres.

Therefore also said the wisdom of God, I will send them prophets and apostles, and some of them they shall slay and persecute:

That the blood of all the prophets, which was shed from the foundation of the world, may be required of this generation;

From the blood of Abel unto the blood of Zacharias, which perished between the altar and the temple: verily I say unto you, It shall be required of this generation.

Woe unto you, lawyers! for ye have taken away the key of knowledge: ye entered not in yourselves, and them that were entering in ye hindered [Luke 11:46–52].

These religious rulers occupied very much the same position that church leaders occupy today. People looked to them for the interpretation of the truth. They placed the emphasis on material things rather than on the spiritual purpose for which those things were to be used. And they themselves were not living according to the Scriptures.

Unfortunately, the greatest hindrance to the cause of Christ today is the professed believer. We need to examine our own lives in the light of this Scripture!

And as he said these things unto them, the scribes and the Pharisees began to urge him vehemently, and to provoke him to speak of many things:

Laying wait for him, and seeking to catch something out of his mouth, that they might accuse him [Luke 11:53–54].

CHAPTER 12

***THEME:** Jesus warns of the leaven of the Pharisees; parable of the rich fool; parable of the return from the wedding; the testing of servants in light of the coming of Christ; Jesus states He is a divider of men*

JESUS WARNS OF THE LEAVEN OF THE PHARISEES

The twelfth chapter continues to record the tremendous ministry of our Lord. Luke adds some new things which I shall emphasize.

In the mean time, when there were gathered together an innumerable multitude of people, insomuch that they trode one upon another, he began to say unto his disciples first of all, Beware ye of the leaven of the Pharisees, which is hypocrisy [Luke 12:1].

This is the period of time when Christ's ministry peaked. Great crowds of people were following Him. It was at this time that He performed so many miracles. There were litterally thousands of blind who had their eyes opened, thousands of lame that were made to walk, and thousands of dumb that were made to speak. Christ healed multitudes. In fact, this crowd was so large it was impossible to number them. The people were pushing against one another, and actually some were being trampled. It was a dangerous place to be.

Christ warns the crowd about the leaven of the Pharisees. If leaven symbolized the gospel, as many people think it does, why would the Lord warn His disciples about the *leaven* of the Pharisees? Leaven is a principle of evil, and the leaven of the Pharisees was hypocrisy. There is a great deal of leaven about today!

For there is nothing covered, that shall not be revealed; neither hid, that shall not be known.

Therefore whatsoever ye have spoken in darkness shall be heard in the light; and that which ye have spoken in the ear in closets shall be proclaimed upon the housetops.

And I say unto you my friends, Be not afraid of them that kill the body, and after that have no more that they can do.

But I will forewarn you whom ye shall fear: Fear him, which after he hath killed hath power to cast into hell; yea, I say unto you, Fear him [Luke 12:2–5].

It was upon this principle that both Cromwell and, I believe, Martin Luther based the statement, "Fear God and you will have no one else to fear." Let me repeat that when Cromwell was asked the basis for his courage and fearlessness, he replied that he had learned that if he feared God he would fear no man. That is exactly what our Lord is saying in this passage.

Are not five sparrows sold for two farthings, and not one of them is forgotten before God?

But even the very hairs of your head are all numbered. Fear not therefore: ye are of more value than many sparrows.

Also I say unto you, Whosoever shall confess me before men, him shall the Son of man also confess before the angels of God:

But he that denieth me before men shall be denied before the angels of God [Luke 12:6–9].

Our Lord's public rebuke of the religious leaders would, of course, bring their wrath down upon His head. And His disciples could expect the same kind of treatment from them. The Lord Jesus gives them these words of comfort and assurance of God's care for them. Since He sees the fall of a sparrow, He is fully aware of the needs of those who are teaching and preaching His Word.

And whosoever shall speak a word against the Son of man, it shall be forgiven him: but unto him that blasphemeth against the Holy Ghost it shall not be forgiven [Luke 12:10].

When a man blasphemes with his mouth, that is not the thing that condemns him; it is the attitude of his heart. Blasphemy against the Holy Spirit is to resist His convicting work in the heart and life. This is a permanent condition—unless he stops resisting.

And when they bring you unto the synagogues, and unto magistrates, and

powers, take ye no thought how or what thing ye shall answer, or what ye shall say:

For the Holy Ghost shall teach you in the same hour what ye ought to say [Luke 12:11–12].

This is not intended to be an excuse for a lazy preacher or Sunday school teacher failing to make preparation. Rather, it was assurance to His own men that the Holy Spirit, whom He would send, would give them courage and wisdom as they faithfully witnessed for Him. We have many examples of this in the Book of Acts.

And one of the company said unto him, Master, speak to my brother, that he divide the inheritance with me.

And he said unto him, Man, who made me a judge or a divider over you?[Luke 12:13–14].

Our Lord absolutely refused to sit in judgment in a case like this. I wish, today, those of us who attempt to counsel might take this position. Counselors are so quick to judge and tell folk what they should do. The Lord Jesus would not sit in judgment. Now, of course, when the Lord came to earth the first time, He did not come as a judge but as a Savior. The next time He comes it will be as Judge. The Father has committed all judgment unto His Son (see John 5:22).

Out of this incident our Lord made this statement, then gave a parable of the "rich fool."

And he said unto them, Take heed, and beware of covetousness: for a man's life consisteth not in the abundance of the things which he possesseth [Luke 12:15].

This is certainly a good verse for many Christians in this age of crass materialism, when it seems that "things" are so important and occupy so much of our time. Covetousness is one of the outstanding sins of this hour. This is not a sin that others can see you commit, and at times you may not even be aware you are committing it. St. Francis of Assisi once said, "Men have confessed to me every known sin except the sin of covetousness."

The judgment sometimes made of Americans is quite interesting. Several years ago the *Sunday Pictorial* in London gave an assessment of America in which it said: "You shock us by your belief that the almighty dollar and armed might alone can save the world." I am wondering if America is not in this position today: overcome by covetousness.

PARABLE OF THE RICH FOOL

And he spake a parable unto them, saying, The ground of a certain rich man brought forth plentifully:

And he thought within himself, saying, What shall I do, because I have no room where to bestow my fruits? [Luke 12:16–17].

Notice the emphasis on the word *I* in this passage. This man had a bad case of perpendicular "I-itis"—"What shall *I* do, because *I* have no room where to bestow *my* fruits."

And he said, This will I do: I will pull down my barns, and build greater; and there will I bestow all my fruits and my goods.

And I will say to my soul, Soul, thou hast much goods laid up for many years; take thine ease, eat, drink, and be merry.

But God said unto him, Thou fool, this night thy soul shall be required of thee: then whose shall those things be, which thou hast provided?

So is he that layeth up treasure for himself, and is not rich toward God [Luke 12:18–21].

This man had gathered all of his treasure on earth but had stored none in heaven. The same idea is expressed in this epitaph:

Here lies John Racket
In his wooden jacket.
He kept neither horses nor mules.
He lived like a hog.
He died like a dog.
And left all his money to fools.

Our Lord called the man in this parable a fool, but notice what kind of man he was, apparently. All outward appearances indicate that he was a good man. He was a law-abiding citizen. He was a good neighbor. He was a fine family man. He was above suspicion. He was living the good life in suburbia in the best residential area of the city. He was not a wicked man or a member of the Mafia. He was not in crooked politics. He was not engaged in shady business. He was not an alcoholic or keeping a woman on the side. This man seems to be all right; yet our Lord called him a fool.

Why? This man gave all of his thought to himself, and he was covetous.

I had a little tea party
This afternoon at three.
'Twas very small—
Three guests in all

Just I, Myself, and Me.
Myself ate all the sandwiches,
While I drank up the tea.
'Twas also I who ate the pie
And passed the cake to Me.

This is the way many people live. The parable of the rich fool is one of the most pungent paragraphs in the Word of God. The philosophy of the world today is "Eat, drink and be merry, for tomorrow we die." Our Lord said, "That's the problem, that's what makes a man a fool." If you live as though this life is all there is, and you live just for self, and as though there is nothing beyond death, you are a fool.

And he said unto his disciples, Therefore I say unto you, Take no thought for your life, what ye shall eat; neither for the body, what ye shall put on.

The life is more than meat, and the body is more than raiment.

Consider the ravens: for they neither sow nor reap; which neither have storehouse nor barn; and God feedeth them: how much more are ye better than the fowls? [Luke 12:22–24].

Now, of course it is not wrong to store up things. The problem with the rich fool was covetousness. He was trying to get more, more, and more. That is the curse of godless capitalism. Have you noticed the strong judgment that is pronounced upon the rich in the last days? James 5:1 describes it: "Go to now, ye rich men, weep and howl for your miseries that shall come upon you." Riches have become a curse.

Our great nation thought that the almighty dollar would solve the problems of the world, and we are in a bigger mess than ever. We are arguing about whether or not "In God we trust" should remain on our money. Let's take it off because it is hypocrisy anyway. We are not trusting in God but in the dollar. To have a slogan on money means nothing at all. America needs to turn back to reality and truth and quit mouthing religion. We should search our hearts and ask ourselves, "Am I living for this life only?" Our Lord said, "Go look at the birds. Learn something from them."

If ye then be not able to do that thing which is least, why take ye thought for the rest?

Consider the lilies how they grow: they toil not, they spin not; and yet I say unto you, that Solomon in all his glory was not arrayed like one of these [Luke 12:26–27].

When I go to the Hawaiian Islands, I look for the hibiscus. It is one of my favorite flowers. I wonder what God had in mind when He made the hibiscus. It is a careless flower. The rose is a careful flower that holds its petals tightly and opens them up gradually. The hibiscus, however, flings open the door and great big petals wave at you. It is a beautiful and colorful flower.

Our Lord said, "Consider the lilies, how they grow." Flowers are saying a lot to us today: "My, you human beings certainly go to a great deal of trouble to take care of your bodies. You use lotions, sprays, ointments, and perfume, among other things upon your bodies, and then you clothe them. Even after you are all perfumed and dressed up, you cannot compare to the beauty of a flower." What a message, friend. Some of us need to depend upon God a little bit more.

If then God so clothe the grass, which is to-day in the field, and to-morrow is cast into the oven; how much more will he clothe you, O ye of little faith? [Luke 12:28].

This is not to encourage indolence. Birds cannot build barns; flowers cannot spin. But man can. God intends him to use the ability He gave him—but not to live as if the exercise of these abilities is all there is to life.

And seek not ye what ye shall eat, or what ye shall drink, neither be ye of doubtful mind.

For all these things do the nations of the world seek after: and your Father knoweth that ye have need of these things.

But rather seek ye the kingdom of God; and all these things shall be added unto you [Luke 12:29–31].

Our world is engaged in commerce. Half of the world will spend its heart's blood in building a better mouse trap while the other half will go to the ends of the earth to buy the mouse trap. Both groups are forgetting there is a God in heaven and that all men have an eternal soul.

Fear not, little flock; for it is your Father's good pleasure to give you the kingdom.

Sell that ye have, and give alms; provide yourselves bags which wax not old, a treasure in the heavens that faileth not, where no thief approacheth, neither moth corrupteth.

For where your treasure is, there will your heart be also [Luke 12:32–34].

All men will one day stand before the awful presence of God, stripped of the "things" that occupied his life on earth. He will have no treasure up there. He lived without God; he will die without God.

PARABLE OF THE RETURN FROM THE WEDDING

Now we have two parables which Christ gave in connection with His return.

Let your loins be girded about, and your lights burning;

And ye yourselves like unto men that wait for their lord, when he will return from the wedding; that when he cometh and knocketh, they may open unto him immediately.

Blessed are those servants, whom the lord when he cometh shall find watching: verily I say unto you, that he shall gird himself, and make them to sit down to meat, and will come forth and serve them.

And if he shall come in the second watch, or come in the third watch, and find them so, blessed are those servants.

And this know, that if the goodman of the house had known what hour the thief would come, he would have watched, and not have suffered his house to be broken through.

Be ye therefore ready also: for the Son of man cometh at an hour when ye think not [Luke 12:35–40].

Although this parable primarily applies to Israel and the second coming of Christ to set up His kingdom on earth, the *principle* applies to the church as we anticipate His coming at the Rapture.

In the Orient a groom had a wedding supper with his friends and then went to claim his bride at her home. The servants of the groom were expected to be dressed for work and have their lamps lighted for the return procession. The attitude of the believer to the return of Christ is to be one of readiness, having "the loins . . . girded"—doing all we can for Him, and living in expectation of His return.

When the figure changes from the "bridegroom" to the "thief," it is to emphasize the element of an unexpected appearance. Paul used the same figure of speech for Christ's second coming in 1 Thessalonians 5:2 which says, "For yourselves know perfectly that the day of the Lord so cometh as a thief in the night." However, the Lord does not come as a *thief* to Rapture the church. Rather, we shall arise to meet Him in the air.

THE TESTING OF SERVANTS IN LIGHT OF THE COMING OF CHRIST

And the Lord said, Who then is that faithful and wise steward, whom his lord shall make ruler over his household, to give them their portion of meat in due season?

Blessed is that servant, whom his lord when he cometh shall find so doing [Luke 12:42–43].

This is one of the outstanding parables that teaches our responsibility in light of our Lord's coming. Again, this parable is primarily for Israel, but the principle applies to us as believers, as we anticipate the Rapture. Many people feel that the Lord is coming soon, so they are waiting instead of working. We should work as though the Lord was not coming for another one thousand years. Let's quit all this business of trying to set a date for His coming and get ready. The blessed hope is the coming of Christ, and we should be filling our "hope chests" with works that we can one day lay at His feet.

Of a truth I say unto you, that he will make him ruler over all that he hath.

But and if that servant say in his heart, My lord delayeth his coming; and shall begin to beat the menservants and maidens, and to eat and drink, and to be drunken;

The lord of that servant will come in a day when he looketh not for him, and at an hour when he is not aware, and will cut him in sunder, and will appoint him his portion with the unbelievers [Luke 12:44–46].

This parable teaches us two important lessons. Skepticism about the Lord's coming again produces (1) the mishandling of authority and (2) laziness in one's conduct. We are to live in the expectancy of His return. Our lives should be lived as if the Lord is going to appear the next moment, and we will have to give an account of ourselves to Him. In truth, we will have to account for ourselves in that day when He comes.

And that servant, which knew his lord's will, and prepared not himself, neither did according to his will, shall be beaten with many stripes.

But he that knew not, and did commit things worthy of stripes, shall be beaten with few stripes. For unto whomsoever much is given, of him shall be much required: and to whom men have committed much, of him they will ask the more [Luke 12:47–48].

Maybe He will not come today or tomorrow, but He is going to come. Our tendency is to let things slip because He has not yet appeared. We feel like we get by with things, but in reality we get by with nothing. In that day when He comes, we will be judged. "For we must all appear before the judgment seat of Christ; that every one may receive the things done in his body, according to that he hath done, whether it be good or bad" (2 Cor. 5:10). Who is "we"? We Christians are to appear before the judgment seat of Christ. Our judgment will not determine whether or not we will be saved. This will not be a criminal court, but a circuit court where our property will be in danger. He will judge us in order to see if we are worthy or not to receive rewards. There will be degrees of rewards for the believer just as there will be degrees of punishment for the unbeliever.

JESUS STATES HE IS A DIVIDER OF MEN

I am come to send fire on the earth; and what will I, if it be already kindled? [Luke 12:49].

Even at this hour when the world is experiencing the deepest darkness we've had in nineteen hundred years, the Lord Jesus Christ is being blasphemed! The fire has been thrown out on the earth today!

But I have a baptism to be baptized with; and how am I straitened till it be accomplished! [Luke 12:50].

This verse is speaking of Christ's death upon the cross.

Suppose ye that I am come to give peace on the earth? I tell you, Nay; but rather division:

For from henceforth there shall be five in one house divided, three against two, and two against three.

The father shall be divided against the son, and the son against the father; the mother against the daughter, and the daughter against the mother; the mother in law against her daughter in law, and the daughter in law against her mother in law [Luke 12:51–53].

When a person receives Jesus Christ as his Savior, he is immediately separated from the unbelievers around him. This will be true whether they be his relatives or his friends.

And he said also to the people, When ye see a cloud rise out of the west, straightway ye say, There cometh a shower; and so it is.

And when ye see the south wind blow, ye say, There will be heat; and it cometh to pass.

Ye hypocrites, ye can discern the face of the sky and of the earth; but how is it that ye do not discern this time? [Luke 12:54–56].

We need to realize and recognize what kind of world we are living in. Man thinks he is big enough and good enough to bring peace on the earth. This is a fallacy—man is a warmonger. The United Nations was formed to bring peace and to keep peace on earth. May I say, the United Nations is one of the best *fighting* arenas in the world today! We need to realize that until Christ comes there can be no real peace.

CHAPTER 13

THEME: *Jesus teaches men not to judge but repent; parable of the fig tree; Jesus heals woman with infirmity; parables of the mustard seed and leaven; continues to teach as He goes toward Jerusalem; Jesus weeps over Jerusalem*

JESUS TEACHES MEN NOT TO JUDGE BUT REPENT

There were present at that season some that told him of the Galilaeans, whose blood Pilate had mingled with their sacrifices.

And Jesus answering said unto them, Suppose ye that these Galilaeans were sinners above all the Galilaeans, because they suffered such things?

I tell you, Nay: but, except ye repent, ye shall all likewise perish.

Or those eighteen, upon whom the tower in Siloam fell, and slew them, think ye that they were sinners above all men that dwelt in Jerusalem?

I tell you, Nay: but, except ye repent, ye shall all likewise perish [Luke 13:1–5].

The victims of Pilate and the men who were killed when the tower fell were not judged of God. God does nothing in spite. But Christ was telling the religious crowd of His day that unless they repented, they would also perish.

This passage has several fine lessons for us. The first one teaches us that when some Christian has trouble beyond the average amount (and many do), we are not to interpret it to mean that he is a greater sinner than others. Trouble does not always come to a person because of his sins.

The other side of the coin is that just becoming a Christian does not automatically inoculate you against trouble. You will miss the Great Tribulation, but you will not miss the *little* tribulation if you are a Christian. You are going to have a little of it right down here.

Another thing we should see is that when trouble comes to someone else and not to you, it does not indicate that you are superior to that individual. Perhaps God is permitting you to see the other fellow's trouble in order to bring you to Himself.

PARABLE OF THE FIG TREE

The parable of the fig tree grew out of the previous discussion.

He spake also this parable; A certain man had a fig tree planted in his vineyard; and he came and sought fruit thereon, and found none.

Then said he unto the dresser of his vineyard, Behold, these three years I come seeking fruit on this fig tree, and find none: cut it down; why cumbereth it the ground?

And he answering said unto him, Lord, let it alone this year also, till I shall dig about it, and dung it:

And if it bear fruit, well: and if not, then after that thou shalt cut it down [Luke 13:6–9].

The fig tree without fruit is symbolic, in my opinion, of the nation Israel. The owner of the fig tree expected it to bear fruit and was disappointed when it was barren. He had the unquestioned right to take the fruit and to act in judgment by cutting down the tree. Israel had been promised blessings if they walked in the light God had given them and curses if they rejected the light. The nation was given special attention—cultivated and fertilized. It should have produced fruit, but it did not. Israel rejected Christ, even saying, ". . . His blood be on us, and on our children" (Matt. 27:25). Israel did experience God's judgment and was scattered among the nations of the world.

It is interesting to note that Israel cannot live in her land today and have peace while she continues to reject God. It is not Russia or the Arabs that are giving Israel so much trouble; it is God. Israel is God's chosen people. He is going to bring them back to their land someday in faith and belief. They are returning to the land today in unbelief, and they do not have peace. This is the evidence of the hand of God in the affairs of the world.

JESUS HEALS THE WOMAN WITH THE INFIRMITY

And he was teaching in one of the synagogues on the sabbath.

And, behold, there was a woman which had a spirit of infirmity eighteen years, and was bowed together, and could in no wise lift up herself.

And when Jesus saw her, he called her to him, and said unto her, Woman, thou art loosed from thine infirmity.

And he laid his hands on her: and immediately she was made straight, and glorified God.

And the ruler of the synagogue answered with indignation, because that Jesus had healed on the sabbath day, and said unto the people, There are six days in which men ought to work: in them therefore come and be healed, and not on the sabbath day [Luke 13:10–14].

This woman had one of the worst cases of illness recorded in the Bible. She had a severe malady. The problem arose not because our Lord healed her, but because He healed her on the Sabbath day. The Lord healing people on the Sabbath day was a recurring source of contention between Himself and the religious rulers.

This woman had a spirit of infirmity that had plagued her for eighteen years. It is difficult to translate into English the terminology that Dr. Luke uses to describe her condition. They are medical terms. Her illness was chronic. Because of it she was bowed down or, as Weymouth translates it, "bent double." This poor woman could not lift herself up. Here was a woman in a desperate condition. She was an unfortunate wretch who was an object of pity. This was probably one of the most terrible cases of physical infirmity that the Lord dealt with on earth.

The Lord then answered him, and said, Thou hypocrite, doth not each one of you on the sabbath loose his ox or his ass from the stall, and lead him away to watering?

And ought not this woman, being a daughter of Abraham, whom Satan hath bound, lo, these eighteen years, be loosed from this bond on the sabbath day? [Luke 13:15–16].

I must confess that I do not understand why this woman had been bound by Satan. She apparently was not an immoral person, as she was a regular attendant at the synagogue even in her condition. It was in the synagogue that the Great Physician said to her, "Be loosed." He laid His hands on her, and immediately she was made straight and glorified God. His touch upon her was not essential but was an aid to her faith. It was personal contact. And personal contact with Him is the important thing for us also.

The ruler of the synagogue rebuked her sharply—yet this woman had not come to the synagogue with any intention of being healed. The reaction of the religious ruler was strange indeed. He was more interested in the rule than he was in the fact that a poor woman, who had been shackled for eighteen years with a grievous infirmity, had been freed. The Sabbath question was the most important issue to these religious rulers. Yet Sabbath prohibitions had become a burden too great to be borne. The Sabbath question is still one of heated debate today. The important thing is not to argue about religion, but to learn to live it.

And when he had said these things, all his adversaries were ashamed: and all the people rejoiced for all the glorious things that were done by him [Luke 13:17].

The people, though they heard Him gladly, seemed to go no farther with Him. It is possible to become so religious and callous that you can exclude Jesus from your life too. You may know all the answers and be an expert in argument, but the real question is, "Have you ever let Christ into your heart?" There is no substitute for that. Are you filled with doubts? Are you puzzled or troubled? Are you bent double with the burdens of life? Then come to the Lord Jesus Christ with your burdens and sins. You can come to Him anytime. He is ready and waiting to meet your need.

PARABLES OF THE MUSTARD SEED AND LEAVEN

Then said he, Unto what is the kingdom of God like? and whereunto shall I resemble it?

It is like a grain of mustard seed, which a man took, and cast into his garden; and it grew, and waxed a great tree; and the fowls of the air lodged in the branches of it.

And again he said, Whereunto shall I liken the kingdom of God?

It is like leaven, which a woman took and hid in three measures of meal, till the whole was leavened [Luke 13:18–21].

The mustard seed is symbolic of the outward aspect of Christendom with its multiplied organizations and denominations. The mustard seed is to become an herb and not a tree. Instead of church organizations lagging behind, there is actually an abnormal growth which has been too fast. They have lost their true character as they have become great. The "birds" are the key of this parable. They represent the Devil who is active in Christendom and in many so-called churches.

Leaven represents not the gospel but a principle of evil. Leaven never represents good as used in the Bible. Leaven occurs about ninety-eight times in the Bible—about seventy-five times in the Old Testament and about twenty-three times in the New Testament. It is always used in a bad sense. Although many sincere folk think of leaven as representing the gospel, which will spread over the entire world and convert the world, they are doomed to disappointment. There will be no kingdom and no peace until Christ returns to establish His kingdom on this earth. The organized church cannot bring in His kingdom. In His own good time Christ Himself will come and establish His kingdom.

JESUS CONTINUES TO TEACH AS HE GOES TOWARD JERUSALEM

And he went through the cities and villages, teaching, and journeying toward Jerusalem [Luke 13:22].

Jesus is continuing to move toward Jerusalem. Luke has already told us, "And it came to pass, when the time was come that he should be received up, he stedfastly set his face to go to Jerusalem" (Luke 9:51). He is on His way there, on His way to die in Jerusalem. This was to be our Savior's last journey.

Then said one unto him, Lord, are there few that be saved? and he said unto them,

Strive to enter in at the strait gate: for many, I say unto you, will seek to enter in, and shall not be able.

When once the master of the house is risen up, and hath shut to the door, and ye begin to stand without, and to knock at the door, saying, Lord, Lord, open unto us; and he shall answer and say unto you, I know you not whence ye are:

Then shall ye begin to say, We have eaten and drunk in thy presence, and thou hast taught in our streets.

But he shall say, I tell you, I know you not whence ye are; depart from me, all ye workers of iniquity.

There shall be weeping and gnashing of teeth, when ye shall see Abraham, and Isaac, and Jacob, and all the prophets, in the kingdom of God, and you yourselves thrust out.

And they shall come from the east, and from the west, and from the north, and from the south, and shall sit down in the kingdom of God.

And, behold, there are last which shall be first, and there are first which shall be last [Luke 13:23–30].

Why this question was asked is difficult to discern. Perhaps it was sincere. The charisma of Christ drew the multitudes, but they soon discovered that it cost to follow Him. There were those coming and going all the time. As He approached Jerusalem this last time it was noticeable. There came a day when it was written, "And they all forsook him, and fled" (Mark 14:50). He made it abundantly clear that it would *cost* to follow Him. That we in our sophisticated and soft affluency think otherwise is heresy!

Since this was a speculative question, Jesus did not answer it directly. He is saying to this man, "Make sure *you* are saved." In the rest of this brief discourse, the Lord made it clear that many will be saved who are not sons of Abraham, Isaac, and Jacob.

The same day there came certain of the Pharisees, saying unto him, Get thee out, and depart hence: for Herod will kill thee.

And he said unto them, Go ye, and tell that fox, Behold, I cast out devils, and I do cures to-day and to-morrow, and the third day I shall be perfected.

Nevertheless I must walk to-day, and to-morrow, and the day following: for it cannot be that a prophet perish out of Jerusalem [Luke 13:31–33].

In this warning from the Pharisees, the Lord Jesus labeled Herod a *fox*. Man has not ascended from the animal; but sometimes he descends to the animal plane in living. Our Lord gives here the veiled program of His redemption and resurrection.

JESUS WEEPS OVER JERUSALEM

O Jerusalem, Jerusalem, which killest the prophets, and stonest them that are

sent unto thee; how often would I have gathered thy children together, as a hen doth gather her brood under her wings, and ye would not!

Behold, your house is left unto you desolate: and verily I say unto you, Ye shall not see me, until the time come when ye shall say, Blessed is he that cometh in the name of the Lord [Luke 13:34–35].

Again He expresses His love and concern for Jerusalem, the city where He was to die. He also pronounces judgment upon the ". . . city of the great King" (Matt. 5:35). Also He announces that He is coming again. The next time will be the real Triumphal Entry.

CHAPTER 14

THEME: *Jesus goes to dinner at home of Pharisee; parable of the impolite guests; parable of the great supper; parable about building a tower; parable of a king going to war; parable about salt that loses its tang*

Luke alone records the delightful occasion of the Lord Jesus going out to dinner at the home of one of the chief Pharisees, and of His giving His host and guests a lesson in etiquette in the devastating parable of the ambitious guest. Also there are two other parables in this chapter that are in no other Gospel—the building of a tower and a king preparing to make war, which both relate to discipleship. He concludes with the parable of the salt that loses its tang.

JESUS GOES TO DINNER AT HOME OF PHARISEE

Jesus is going out to dinner again, and this time we are going to have some fun.

And it came to pass, as he went into the house of one of the chief Pharisees to eat bread on the sabbath day, that they watched him [Luke 14:1].

I must confess that if a Pharisee had asked me to come to dinner for the purpose of spying on me, I would have refused. The Pharisee was watching for something that would discredit our Lord. This first verse provides the atmosphere, tone, and color of the situation. It was the prelude before the dinner that produced the tenseness.

And, behold, there was a certain man before him which had the dropsy [Luke 14:2].

A trap was laid to ensnare the Lord. I believe this man was deliberately planted to motivate our Lord to break the Sabbath by healing him. Notice what He did. The Lord asked the question first, and they were afraid to answer Him.

And Jesus answering spake unto the lawyers and Pharisees, saying, Is it lawful to heal on the sabbath day?

And they held their peace. And he took him, and healed him, and let him go;

And answered them, saying, Which of you shall have an ass or an ox fallen into a pit, and will not straightway pull him out on the sabbath day? [Luke 14:3–5].

If their ox or donkey fell into something, they would rescue it. In other words, if any of those rascals had had a flat tire on the Sabbath, they would have fixed it, and the Lord knew it. "That's the reason I'm fixing up this fellow here—he's in trouble."

And they could not answer him again to these things [Luke 14:6].

This incident created a rather tense situation for dinner.

PARABLE OF THE IMPOLITE GUESTS

And he put forth a parable to those which were bidden, when he marked how they chose out the chief rooms; saying unto them [Luke 14:7].

This scene is as rich as it can be. In that day they did not have place cards at the table. Place cards must have been originated by some hostess who wanted to preserve her furniture! Without place cards at the table, there was a mad rush to get to the best seats. At the table in that day there were four chief places. When the cook said, "Soup's on," everyone made a beeline for the table. In that day couches rather than chairs were used so that the guests reclined at the table. There were three places to recline on each side; the center place was the seat of honor which made four chief places. At the head table there would be seats one, two and three on one side; seat number two, the center seat, would be the place of honor. Around on the other side would be seats four, five, and six, with number five as the seat of honor. Around on the other side are seats seven, eight, and nine, with seat number eight the seat of honor. On the fourth side of the table number eleven would be the seat of honor.

It is understandable that one of these old Pharisees could not move as fast as some of the younger Pharisees. When the cook called, "Soup's on," the old Pharisee, who had moved as close as possible to the dining area, ran for seat number two. One of the younger Pharisees got there before he did; so he turned the corner fast and tried to reach number five seat. He was too late again because someone was already sitting there. Quickly he tried for seat number eight, but he did not make it to that seat in time either. He turned the corner and made a dive for seat number eleven and made it. It was the lowest seat, but still a seat of honor. He reclined there out of breath.

Can you imagine what a hilarious picture it must have been to see these men running as fast as they could for the seats of honor? Now our Lord will correct their manners.

When thou art bidden of any man to a wedding, sit not down in the highest room; lest a more honourable man than thou be bidden of him;

And he that bade thee and him come and say to thee, Give this man place; and thou begin with shame to take the lowest room.

But when thou art bidden, go and sit down in the lowest room; that when he that bade thee cometh, he may say unto thee, Friend, go up higher: then shalt thou have worship in the presence of them that sit at meat with thee [Luke 14:8–10].

The Lord Jesus said, "When you are invited to dinner, don't rush to get the seat of honor. The host may have someone else in mind for that seat. He would have to come to you and say, 'Move over to the lowest seat so my guest of honor can sit here.'" To get to the lowest seat, all you have to do is move over one seat, but it is embarrassing.

"When you are invited to a dinner, always go to the lowest seat. You will not have any trouble getting it because no one else will be trying for it. Then when the host comes in and sees where you are sitting, he will say, 'You are to be my guest of honor. Please sit in the seat of honor.' Then someone else will have to move." This is good manners and just the opposite of the demonstration this group had just put on.

Our Lord draws a great principle from this incident:

For whosoever exalteth himself shall be abased; and he that humbleth himself shall be exalted [Luke 14:11].

This is an important principle for us as believers.

Next our Lord corrects the host.

Then said he also to him that bade him, When thou makest a dinner or a supper, call not thy friends, nor thy brethren, neither thy kinsmen, nor thy rich neighbours; lest they also bid thee again, and a recompence be made thee.

But when thou makest a feast, call the poor, the maimed, the lame, the blind:

And thou shalt be blessed; for they cannot recompense thee: for thou shalt be recompensed at the resurrection of the just [Luke 14:12–14].

Our Lord is setting forth another great principle. Most of us have the same guests over to dinner one time, and the next time we go to one of their homes, and so it goes week after week. It is sort of a round-robin situation. The Lord is condemning that practice. There is nothing wrong with having your group in once in a while, but have you ever thought about doing something for those who have nothing? They cannot pay you back; they will not be able to invite you to dinner next week. Do a few things where you will be the giver with no thought of ever being paid back.

PARABLE OF THE GREAT SUPPER

Can you imagine the tenseness at this dinner? It started with our Lord healing the man with dropsy—in the face of their disapproval. Then He looked the guests straight in the eyes and corrected their manners. Then He corrected the host. Believe me, the atmosphere was tense. Nobody was saying a word.

And when one of them that sat at meat with him heard these things, he said unto him, Blessed is he that shall eat bread in the kingdom of God [Luke 14:15].

This is, without a doubt, one of the pious platitudes that this man is used to giving. In that awkward moment of silence, when no one was saying anything, one old rascal speaks out and says, "Blessed is he that shall eat bread in the kingdom of God." I wish I could have been there. I would have asked him, "What do you mean by that?" I doubt that he could have told me what he really meant. At least I have never found a commentator who could explain what he meant. His statement was nothing more than a pious cliché. You hear a lot of pious platitudes in our conservative circles today. I get so tired of hearing them. One of the most common clichés is, "Praise the Lord." It is a wonderful thing to praise the Lord, but sometimes it becomes a little boring when a person uses that phrase constantly, but does not praise the Lord in his heart. Let us steer clear of pious clichés.

The Lord did not let this rascal get by with his cliché. He turned to him, and I think His eyes flashed with anger as He spoke to him.

Then said he unto him, A certain man made a great supper, and bade many:

And sent his servant at supper time to say to them that were bidden, Come; for all things are now ready [Luke 14:16–17].

It was the custom to send out invitations to such a dinner a long time in advance, but as the actual day for the dinner arrived, a personal invitation was extended. God has issued an invitation. What is man going to do with it? God's invitation is for salvation. You cannot buy your way in to this feast. You cannot elbow your way in. You come to this dinner by the grace of God. "For by grace are ye saved through faith; and that not of yourselves: it is the gift of God: Not of works, lest any man should boast" (Eph. 2:8–9). You get into this dinner by receiving a gift. The only thing that will exclude any human being from heaven is a refusal to accept the invitation.

The Lord Jesus said, "You say, 'Blessed is he that eateth bread in the kingdom'; that is pious nonsense. Here is what men are doing with God's invitation:"

And they all with one consent began to make excuse. The first said unto him, I have bought a piece of ground, and I must needs go and see it: I pray thee have me excused [Luke 14:18].

This is not an excuse, it is an alibi. Someone has said, "An alibi is a lie stuffed in the skin of an excuse." No one who was invited said, "I will not come to the dinner." They were simply making excuses to cover up the fact that they did not want to come.

The first man to give an excuse was either a liar or a fool. Can you imagine buying property without first looking at it?

And another said, I have bought five yoke of oxen, and I go to prove them: I pray thee have me excused [Luke 14:19].

The first man let possessions keep him away. The second man let business keep him away. Again I have to say of this second man that he is either a liar or a fool. How could this man plow at night? In those days they did not have flood lights. This man was making excuses. "I must make a living," is a phrase I hear often. People are so busy with their business they have no time for God. One day you are going to die, and you will discover that business will go on as usual without you.

And another said, I have married a wife, and therefore I cannot come [Luke 14:20].

There was a law in Israel that excused a man from going to war if he had taken a new wife. This man had the weakest excuse of all. Why didn't he bring his wife with him and come to the dinner? His natural affection kept him away from the dinner. How many times I have heard a man say, "I don't come to church because Sunday is the only day I can spend with my family."

These things keep more people from God than anything else: possessions, business, and natural affection. How many people today are kept from God because of these things? Well, God has an engraved invitation for you. It is written in the blood of Jesus Christ and invites you to the great table of salvation.

So that servant came, and shewed his lord these things. Then the master of the house being angry said to his servant, Go out quickly into the streets and lanes of the city, and bring in hither the poor, and the maimed, and the halt, and the blind.

And the servant said, Lord, it is done as thou hast commanded, and yet there is room.

And the lord said unto the servant, Go out into the highways and hedges, and compel them to come in, that my house may be filled.

For I say unto you, That none of those men which were bidden shall taste of my supper [Luke 14:21–24].

This is a severe statement. If you reject God's invitation, He has to reject you. You are excluded because of your refusal to accept His invitation.

And there went great multitudes with him: and he turned, and said unto them,

If any man come to me, and hate not his father, and mother, and wife, and children, and brethren, and sisters, yea, and his own life also, he cannot be my disciple.

And whosoever doth not bear his cross, and come after me, cannot be my disciple [Luke 14:25–27].

These verses are simply saying that we should put God first. A believer's devotedness to Jesus Christ should be such that, by comparison, it looks as if everything else is hated. All terms which define affections are comparative.

PARABLE ABOUT BUILDING A TOWER

For which of you, intending to build a tower, sitteth not down first, and counteth the cost, whether he have sufficient to finish it?

Lest haply, after he hath laid the foundation, and is not able to finish it, all that behold it begin to mock him,

Saying, This man began to build, and was not able to finish [Luke 14:28–30].

It will cost something to make a decision for Christ. It will cost something to be His disciple. Think it over, friend. You should count the cost before you make the decision.

PARABLE OF A KING GOING TO WAR

Or what king, going to make war against another king, sitteth not down first, and consulteth whether he be able with ten thousand to meet him that cometh against him with twenty thousand?

Or else, while the other is yet a great way off, he sendeth an ambassage, and desireth conditions of peace.

So likewise, whosoever he be of you that forsaketh not all that he hath, he cannot be my disciple [Luke 14:31–33].

A person can be saved by accepting Jesus Christ as Savior, but a person will never follow and serve Him until he is willing to make a sacrifice. That is what this passage is teaching. There is a difference between being a believer and being a disciple. Unfortunately, not all believers are disciples.

PARABLE ABOUT SALT THAT LOSES ITS TANG

Salt is good: but if the salt have lost his savour, wherewith shall it be seasoned?

It is neither fit for the land, nor yet for the dunghill; but men cast it out. He that hath ears to hear, let him hear [Luke 14:34–35].

Nothing is more worthless than salt that has lost its saltiness. May the Lord deliver *us* from being useless Christians!

CHAPTER 15

THEME: Parable of the lost sheep; parable of the lost coin; parable of two lost sons

Now we come to probably the best-loved parable that our Lord told; we call it the parable of the Prodigal Son.

The background for this parable is that the publicans and sinners came in to hear the Lord Jesus by multitudes. The Pharisees and scribes began to murmur, to criticize Him because of this. They were scandalized that He would receive them and even eat with them.

His answer to the murmuring of the Pharisees and scribes is a parable. Customarily it is called three parables: the parable of the lost sheep, the parable of the lost coin, and the parable of the lost son. Actually, it is three parts of one parable; it is three pictures in a single frame.

When I was a youngster, I used to visit my aunt, and I remember seeing a picture called a triptych, which she kept in the attic—that's where she let me sleep when the house was filled up with relatives. I liked to look at that picture because it was three pictures in one frame. This is what our Lord gives us here, three pictures that belong together. It is a triptych.

Then drew near unto him all the publicans and sinners for to hear him.

And the Pharisees and scribes murmured, saying, This man receiveth sinners, and eateth with them [Luke 15:1–2].

I can't resist telling the story of a little girl who heard this verse read. On a cold London night, she stepped, shivering, into the shelter of a church where a service was in progress. After the service, when the congregation had gone, she approached the rector, "Sir, I never knew my name was in the Bible!" He smiled, "Well, little girl, what is your name?" "My name," she answered excitedly, "is *Edith*." "Oh, I'm sorry to disappoint you, but *Edith* does not appear in the Bible." She insisted, "Yes, it does. I heard you read it tonight. It said, 'Jesus receiveth sinners, and *Edith* with them!'"

Certainly our Lord receives Edith—and Mary and John and all the rest of us. Thank God, He does receive sinners!

PARABLE OF THE LOST SHEEP

Now in this wonderful parable we see the first picture, that of a lost sheep.

And he spake this parable unto them, saying,

What man of you, having an hundred sheep, if he lose one of them, doth not leave the ninety and nine in the wilderness, and go after that which is lost, until he find it?

And when he hath found it, he layeth it on his shoulders, rejoicing.

And when he cometh home, he calleth together his friends and neighbours, saying unto them, Rejoice with me; for I have found my sheep which was lost.

I say unto you, that likewise joy shall be in heaven over one sinner that repenteth, more than over ninety and nine just persons, which need no repentance [Luke 15:3–7].

The shepherd in this parable is the Great Shepherd, Jesus Christ. We are the sheep. He had one hundred sheep, and one of them got lost. Frankly, that would be a pretty good percentage, to start out with one hundred sheep and end up with ninety-nine. This Shepherd, however, would not be satisfied with just ninety-nine sheep. When one sheep got lost, He went out and looked for it. When He found it, He put it on His shoulders, the place of strength. He is able to save to the uttermost. The high priest of the children of Israel wore an ephod. On the shoulders of the ephod were two stones. On them were engraved the names of the twelve tribes—six tribes on one stone and six on the other. The high priest carried the children of Israel on his shoulders. Our great High Priest carries us on His shoulders, and we will not become lost. When He starts out with one hundred sheep, He will come through with one hundred sheep—not ninety-nine. This is a picture of the Lord Jesus Christ out looking for those who are His own.

PARABLE OF THE LOST COIN

The second picture in this triptych is that of the lost coin.

Either what woman having ten pieces of silver, if she lose one piece, doth not light a candle, and sweep the house, and seek diligently till she find it?

And when she hath found it, she calleth her friends and her neighbours together, saying, Rejoice with me; for I have found the piece which I had lost.

Likewise, I say unto you, there is joy in the presence of the angels of God over one sinner that repenteth [Luke 15:8–10].

The coin was probably part of the row of coins which formed a headpiece, signifying her married state. To lose a part of it was like losing a stone out of one's wedding ring. The woman depicts the Holy Spirit whose ministry is to make sure that each one who belongs to the Bridegroom will be present for the wedding. Every coin will be in place. Every one is valuable to Him.

PARABLE OF TWO LOST SONS

As I mentioned previously, Dr. Luke, a medical doctor and a scientist, was also an artist. And he is the one who records our Lord's glorious parables which no other gospel writer gives us.

And he said, A certain man had two sons [Luke 15:11].

Immediately our Lord begins to put the background on the canvas. And I see a lovely home (because this will represent the home of the Father, the heavenly Father) and it's a glorious home. It's a home that has all of the comforts and all of the joys and all of the love that ever went into a home. In that home there's the "certain man," and that is God the Father. And this Father had two sons. He has more sons than that, but these are representative, you see. One of these boys is called the elder and the other is called the younger. We see the lovely home, and out in front there stand the Father and two boys.

Now let's watch our Lord put some more in the picture for us.

And the younger of them said to his father, Father, give me the portion of goods that falleth to me. And he divided unto them his living.

And not many days after the younger son gathered all together, and took his journey into a far country, and there wasted his substance with riotous living [Luke 15:12–13].

Here in this lovely home, a home in which there was everything in the world that the heart of man could want—love, joy, fellowship, comforts—this younger boy does a very strange thing. He says, "I'm tired of the discipline. I don't like it here. I'd like to stretch my wings. I've been looking over the pasture, and the grass over in the other field looks to me like it's lots greener." And I do not know why that's true, but to you and me the grass in the next pasture always looks greener. The boy looked out from home and said, "If I could only get away off yonder on my own, it would be wonderful." He didn't like it at home; he fell out with his father and lost fellowship with him. And so the father gave to him his living, and the boy left with his pockets full of money—which he did not earn with work that he'd done himself. Every bit that came to him, his father had given to him. He didn't get it by his ability, he didn't get it because he was clever, and he didn't get it because he had worked hard. The money he had in his pocket was there because he had a very generous father. And so the boy starts out for the far country.

Now our scene shifts, and we've got to put in another picture here, and the picture is the far country; you can paint it any way you want to. May I say to you, you can paint it in lurid colors, and many have attempted to paint it that way. I do not think it's exaggerated to paint it in lurid colors. This boy found out what it was to have what the world calls a good time. He made all of the nightclubs; he knew café society; he had money. And when you have money, you can get fair-weather friends. For a time he lived it up. He enjoyed the pleasures of sin for a season there in the far country. You paint your own picture there. Our Lord didn't put in any details of what the boy did. But we can well imagine some of the things that he did. However, there did come a day when he'd finished living it up; he reached into his pocket and there wasn't anything left.

And when he had spent all, there arose a mighty famine in that land; and he began to be in want [Luke 15:14].

Not only is he in a very bad way financially, but the country is also in a bad way. You see, in that country where he thought the grass was greener, the grass has now dried up. They're having a famine in that land, and this boy does not know what to do. If you want to know the truth, he's afraid to go home. He should not have been afraid, but he was afraid to go home. Now he's desperate. He is so desperate that he's going to do something that no Jew would ever have done unless he'd hit the bottom. This boy has hit the bottom. He can't get a job. He goes around to see some of these fair-weather friends, and he says, "Bill, do you remember how you used to come to the banquets I gave and the dinners, and that I always picked up the check and I paid for the liquor and I paid for the girls? Do you remember that? Now I'm in a bad way. I wonder if you couldn't tide me over or maybe you could give me a job." And the fair-weather friend says, "I'm sorry. You say you've lost all your money? Well, I'm through with you. I'm not interested in you anymore. My secretary will show you to the door." And the boy found, after going from place to place, that he didn't have any real friends in the far country. Finally he ended up by going out to the edge of town where there was a man who was raising pigs, and you could tell it a mile away. And the boy went over to him and said, "I'd like to have a job." The man says, "Well, I can't pay you. You know, we're having a lot of difficulty, but if you can beat the pigs to it, you can eat here at least." That's exactly the point to which he had sunk. And when our Lord said that this man "would fain have filled his belly with the husks that the swine did eat," every Israelite, both Pharisee and publican, who was listening to Him that day, winced because a Hebrew couldn't go any lower than that—he was to have nothing to do with swine (the Mosaic Law had shut him off from them), but to stoop to the place where he'd go down and live with them was horrifying! That's the picture, and it's a black picture. You see, this boy has hit the very bottom.

Somebody is immediately going to say, "Well, this is the fellow who is a sinner, and he is going to get saved." No, I'm sorry to tell you that such is not the picture that's given to us here. This is not the picture of a sinner that gets saved. May I say to you, and say it very carefully, that when this boy was living at home with the father and was in fellowship with him, he was a son, and there was never any question about that. When this boy got to the far country and was out there throwing his money around, he was still a son. That is never questioned. And when this boy went down and hit the bottom and was out there with the pigs (and if you'd been a half-mile away looking over there among the pigs, I don't think you could have told him from a pig), he was not a pig—he was a son. In this story that our Lord told there was never any question as to whether the boy was a son or not. He was a son all the time.

Somebody says, "Then this is not the gospel." Yes, it is the gospel also. And I will hold to that for the very simple reason that an evangelist in southern Oklahoma many years ago used this parable to present the gospel. People said he imitated Billy Sunday, but I had never heard of Billy Sunday; so it didn't make any difference to me whom he imitated. He was a little short fellow, holding services under a brush arbor. And the thing that interested us boys was the fact he could jump as high as the pulpit. He'd just stand flat right there and up he'd go—a little short fellow. And we'd sit out there and watch him, and the next day we'd practice to see if we could jump that high. May I say to you, one night he preached on the Prodigal Son, and that's the night I went forward. Don't tell me the gospel is not there. It is there.

However, let's understand what the parable is primarily about. The parable is not how a sinner gets saved; it reveals the heart of a Father who will not only save a sinner but will also take back a son that sins.

And he went and joined himself to a citizen of that country; and he sent him into his fields to feed swine.

And he would fain have filled his belly with the husks that the swine did eat: and no man gave unto him [Luke 15:15–16].

Maybe you thought a moment ago I was exaggerating when I said his fair-weather friends wouldn't help him. Our Lord made it very clear that they wouldn't help him—"no man gave unto him." Why is it today that Christians sometimes get the impression that the man of the world is really his friend when he's trying to lead him into sin and lead him away from God? Well, believers do get that impression. This boy got that impression also. He was being led away from home, from his father, farther and farther away. And he thought these folks were his friends.

Now we don't have any letters that he wrote back to some of his friends at home. But if we had one, I think that it would have said, "Say, you ought to come over here. You know, there are some real people over here where I am. I tell you, I'm having a big time. You ought to come over." But, may I say to you, the day came when he found out these were not his friends. "No man gave unto him."

Now that's the black part of the picture, and I think it's about time for us to see some of the bright colors our Lord painted into the picture, for our Lord always, always put down a black background and then put the bright colors in the foreground of the picture. Have you ever noticed that God paints that way? And so, on the black background of this boy's sin—down in the pigpen, out of fellowship with his father, having left home in a huff—our Lord begins to put the bright color.

And when he came to himself, he said, How many hired servants of my father's have bread enough and to spare, and I perish with hunger! [Luke 15:17].

He came to himself. Sin does an awful thing for us. It makes us see the world incorrectly. It makes us see ourselves in the wrong light. It makes us see the pleasures of this world in the wrong perspective, and we just don't see clearly when we're in sin. This boy, when he was at home, looked out yonder at the far country, and it all looked so good—the grass was so green and the fun was so keen; but now he came to himself. And the first thing he did was a little reasoning. He began to use his intelligence. He said, "You know, I'm a son of my father, and here I am in a far country. I'm down here in a pigpen with pigs, and back in my father's home the servants are better off than I am, and I'm his son." When he began to think like that, he began to make sense. And this young man now acts like he's intelligent.

I will arise and go to my father, and will say unto him, Father, I have sinned against heaven, and before thee,

And am no more worthy to be called thy son: make me as one of thy hired servants [Luke 15:18-19].

Now we get to a really bright picture. This is the brightest one of all, and it's the picture of that lovely home we were telling you about. Oh, it's a beautiful home. It's the father's house. The Lord Jesus said, "In my Father's house there are many abiding places . . ." (John 14:2, translation mine). This is the house. The house is there in the background, and I see a father looking out the window. He's been looking out the window every day since his boy left. And do you know why he's been looking out the window? He knew that one day that boy would be trudging down the road coming home.

Somebody asks, "Do you believe that if you're once saved you're always saved?" Yes. Somebody asks, "Do you believe that a Christian can get into sin?" Yes. "Can a Christian stay in sin?" No. Because in the Father's house the Father is watching, and He says, "All my sons are coming home. My sons don't like pigpens because they do not have the nature of a pig. They have the nature of a son. They have My nature, and they won't be happy except in the Father's house. The only place in the world where they will be content is the Father's house. And every one of My sons that goes out to the far country and gets into a pigpen—regardless of how dirty he gets, or how low he sinks—if he's My son, one day he'll say, 'I'll arise, and I'll go to my Father.'" And the reason he'll say, "I'll go to my Father," is because the Man who lives in the big house is his Father. Up until now, after at least 6,000 years of recorded human history, there never yet has been a human pig that has said, "I will arise and go to my Father's house." Never, never. Pigs love it down there. They don't want to go to the Father's house. The only one who wants to go to the Father's house is a son; and one day the son will say, "I will arise and I will go to my Father."

Now the son starts home. Maybe you thought a moment ago that I was exaggerating when I said that this father had been looking out the window every day. But he had, and now he sees him coming. He has compassion, and runs, and says to his servant, "Go down to the tree and cut me about a half a dozen hickory limbs. I'm going to switch this boy within an inch of his life." Is that the way your Bible reads? Well, mine doesn't either. It ought to read that way. Under the Mosaic Law a father had a perfect right to bring a disobedient son before the elders and have him stoned to death. This father had a perfect right to say, "This boy took my name and my money, my substance, and he squandered it. He disgraced my name. I'll whip him within an inch of his life." He had a right to do this. But this father, rather, did something amazing. And when our Lord got to this part of the parable, and when He put this bright color on, it caused all those that were present to blink their eyes. They said, "We can't believe that. It's bad enough to see him hit the bottom and go down yonder with the pigs, but it's worse for the father to take him back home without doing something. He ought to punish him. That's the thing that we don't like. He ought to be punished." Will you notice what the father did. Let me read it accurately now.

And he arose, and came to his father. But when he was yet a great way off, his father saw him, and had compassion, and ran, and fell on his neck, and kissed him [Luke 15:20].

He's in rags, and you can almost smell him—

oh, that pig smell! There stands the boy, and the father goes and puts his arms around him and kisses him.

And the son said unto him, Father,I have sinned against heaven, and in thy sight, and am no more worthy to be called thy son [Luke 15:21].

Now he'd memorized a little speech, you see. He's saying the thing he'd planned in the far country. I think he repeated that little speech all the way home. I think every step of the way he said, "When I get home, I'm going to say to him, 'Father, I have sinned against heaven, and before thee, and am no more worthy to be called thy son: make me as one of thy hired servants.'" He started to say this to his father but he didn't get very far. He got as far as, "I am no more worthy to be called thy son" when he was interrupted.

But the father said to his servants. Bring forth the best robe, and put it on him; and put a ring on his hand, and shoes on his feet:

And bring hither the fatted calf, and kill it; and let us eat, and be merry:

For this my son was dead, and is alive again; he was lost, and is found. And they began to be merry [Luke 15:22–24].

If you really want to have a ball, you can't do it in the far country. If you're God's child, you can't sin and get by with it. You may even go to the pigpen, but, my friend, you can never enjoy it. If you're a son of the Father, there'll come a day when you're going to say, "I will arise and go to my Father, " and you will go. And when you go, you will confess to Him. "If we confess our sins, he is faithful and just to forgive us our sins, and to cleanse us from all unrighteousness" (1 John 1:9). That's the way a sinning child gets back into the fellowship of the Father's house. In fact, the only way back is by confession.

Have you ever noticed the things the father says he's going to do for the son? He says, "Get a robe." Now a robe was clean clothing that went on him after he'd been washed. "If we confess our sins, he is faithful and just to forgive us our sins, and to cleanse us from all unrighteousness." Our Lord washes us. The One who girded Himself with a towel is the One who will wash one of His sons who comes back to Him; he has to be cleansed when he's been to the far country. And that robe is the robe of the righteousness of Christ that covers the believer after he is cleansed. The ring is the insignia of the full-grown son, with all rights pertaining thereto. He's brought back into his original position. Nothing is taken from him. He's brought back into his place in the Father's house.

Christ right now is at God's right hand, still girded with the towel of service for one of His who gets soiled feet or soiled hands by being in the far country. When we confess to Him, He is faithful and just to forgive us our sins and to cleanse us from all unrighteousness. We have to come like the Prodigal Son came. "Father, I have sinned, and I'm no longer worthy to be called your son. Make me a hired servant." And the Father will say, "I'd never make you a hired servant. You're my son. I'll cleanse you, I'll forgive you, I'll bring you back into the place of fellowship and usefulness."

A son is a son forever.

There is another Prodigal Son in this parable.

Now his elder son was in the field: and as he came and drew nigh to the house, he heard music and dancing.

And he called one of the servants, and asked what these things meant.

And he said unto him, Thy brother is come; and thy father hath killed the fatted calf, because he hath received him safe and sound.

And he was angry, and would not go in: therefore came his father out, and entreated him [Luke 15:25–28].

Listen to this boy—what a complainer and a griper he is! This is the *real* Prodigal Son. He was angry when he heard that his brother had returned and a party was being given in his honor. He would not go in and join the others at the feast. His father came out and entreated his son to come to the banquet.

And he answering said to his father, Lo, these many years do I serve thee, neither transgressed I at any time thy commandment: and yet thou never gavest me a kid, that I might make merry with my friends:

But as soon as this thy son was come, which hath devoured thy living with harlots, thou hast killed for him the fatted calf.

And he said unto him, Son, thou art ever with me, and all that I have is thine.

It was meet that we should make merry, and be glad: for this thy brother was dead, and is alive again; and was lost, and is found [Luke 15:29–32].

There are many Christians who are not living in a far country; they are trying to live for God, but they are as poor as Job's turkey. Why? They are blessed with all spiritual blessings, but they will not lay hold upon them. God says, "It is all yours; everything that I have belongs to you—take it." Our heavenly Father is rich in spiritual blessings and they belong to us, but He will not force them upon us. We must reach out and take them for ourselves. The story closes with the elder son out of fellowship with his Father. The Father, however, left the door to fellowship wide open.

Years ago Dr. Chadwick made the statement that there is a third son in the parable of the Prodigal Son. The younger son broke the Father's heart, the elder son was out of fellowship, and the third Son is the One who uttered the parable. He is Jesus Christ, the Son of God. He is the ideal Son without sin. He came *to* a far country, not to run away, but to do the will of His Father. He did not spend His life in riotous living but in sacrificial dying. He was not a Prodigal Son but a Prince of Peace who shed His blood for the sins of the world. He was not a wayward son but a willing sacrifice. He says, "But as many as received him, to them gave he power to become the sons of God, even to them that believe on his name" (John 1:12). Salvation comes to those who simply believe on His name.

If you are the son who went away to a far country, you can come back to the Father by confessing your sins to Him. Perhaps you are like the elder son who was out of fellowship. He had no concern or love for his brother. He thought he was serving God; he had never transgressed as his brother had. Yet he had never enjoyed a feast with his friends. The Father says to you, "All that I have is thine." How wonderful to have a Father like this!

Sinner friend, if you have never trusted Jesus Christ as your Savior, you are not the Father's son. You can become a son only by putting your faith and trust in Christ who died for you. If you accept Christ and come to Him, God becomes your Father and He will never throw you overboard. If you leave Him and one day return, He will be waiting to put His arms around you. How wonderful He is!

CHAPTER 16

***THEME:** Parable of the unjust steward; Jesus answers the covetous Pharisees; Jesus speaks on divorce; Jesus recounts the incident of the rich man and Lazarus (poor man)*

PARABLE OF THE UNJUST STEWARD

This parable has been greatly misunderstood, and one of the reasons is because it looks as though our Lord is commending a crook. This steward is an out-and-out crook. Some folk assume that anyone whom the Lord Jesus mentioned in a parable is a hero and an example of the noblest character. If this is your assumption, then prepare to make a change because you will have difficulty with this parable. This man is a scoundrel. When I was a pastor, I attempted one summer to run a series of sermons on rascals of revelation, scoundrels of Scripture, thieves of theology, bad men of the Bible, and crooks of Christianity. It was a long series because there were so many rogues! This steward is one of them.

I have already called attention to the fact that Luke gives parables by contrast. He is the only gospel writer that does this. Most parables are parables by comparison.

In this parable the Lord uses as an example a man who followed the principles of the world. We are told in the Word of God that the world loves its own but hates those who belong to God. "If the world hate you, ye know that it hated me before it hated you. If ye were of the world, the world would love his own: but because ye are not of the world, but I have chosen you out of the world, therefore the world hateth you" (John 15:18–19). A child of God does not belong to this world and does not live by the principles of this world. In Galatians 1:3–4 Paul says, ". . . our Lord Jesus Christ, Who gave himself for our sins, that he might deliver us from this present evil world, according to the will of God and our Father." Again in Romans 12:2 Paul says, "And be not conformed to this world: but be ye transformed by the renewing of your mind, that ye may prove what is that good, and acceptable, and perfect, will of God." Finally, "Love not the world, neither the things that are in the world . . ." (1 John 2:15). Now, in the world is what we call the "law of life" and the unjust steward is a man who operates by that law.

The first commandment of the world is "self-preservation." A shady business deal is winked at, questionable practices countenanced, and a clever crook is commended by the world. The law is on the side of the crook and the criminal many times. Every man, according to the world's law, is considered innocent until he is proven guilty. The Word of God takes the opposite approach. God says that man is guilty until he is proven innocent. He says, "For all have sinned, and come short of the glory of God" (Rom. 3:23). A man can never be innocent before God, but he certainly can become justified before Him. "There is therefore now no condemnation to them which are in Christ Jesus . . ." (Rom. 8:1). When a man trusts Jesus Christ as his Savior, he is justified by faith. This is the *only way* a man can be justified.

And he said also unto his disciples, There was a certain rich man, which had a steward; and the same was accused unto him that he had wasted his goods [Luke 16:1].

This is the story of a rich man and his unjust steward. A steward is a man who has charge of another man's goods. Abraham had a steward, you remember, who had charge of all his possessions. It was Abraham's steward who went on a trip to Haran to find a bride for Abraham's son Isaac. David had stewards, mentioned in 1 Chronicles 28:1. David's stewards had charge over all of the king's possessions, including his children. Paul tells us, "Moreover it is required in stewards, that a man be found faithful" (1 Cor. 4:2).

The steward in this parable would correspond to the president of a corporation. He had charge of this rich man's goods. He was guilty of malfeasance in office and misappropriation of funds. He was like the bank president who absconds with bank funds. The unjust steward wasted the goods of his master.

And he called him, and said unto him, How is it that I hear this of thee? give an account of thy stewardship; for thou mayest be no longer steward [Luke 16:2].

The day of reckoning had come for this man. He had to give an account. Now since he had the signet ring of his master and was the paymaster, instead of drawing up a financial statement, he decided to use the law of the world which is self-preservation.

Then the steward said within himself, What shall I do? for my lord taketh away from me the stewardship: I cannot dig; to beg I am ashamed [Luke 16:3].

This man had soft hands and felt he could not be a common laborer. And he was ashamed to beg. It makes you smile to read this verse—the man may have been ashamed to beg, but he was not ashamed to steal! Unfortunately, there are a lot of people like that today.

I am resolved what to do, that, when I am put out of the stewardship, they may receive me into their houses [Luke 16:4].

This man did not repent; he had no regret or remorse for his actions. This man was crooked—called clever by the world's standards. He had no training for other work, and his age was probably against him. He was too proud to beg, but he was not ashamed to be dishonest.

So he called every one of his lord's debtors unto him, and said unto the first, How much owest thou unto my lord?

And he said, An hundred measures of oil. And he said unto him, Take thy bill, and sit down quickly, and write fifty [Luke 16:5–6].

The steward was asking, "How much do you owe my master?" This man owed his master one hundred barrels of oil. "Well," the steward said, "oil is about one dollar a barrel now. I will tell you what we will do. We will let you have it for fifty cents a barrel." The man only had to pay half of what he owed.

Then said he to another, And how much owest thou? And he said, An hundred measures of wheat. And he said unto him, Take thy bill, and write fourscore [Luke 16:7].

I do not know why he did not give this fellow the same discount that he gave the other fellow, but this man had to pay eighty cents on the dollar. The unjust steward is just as big a crook at the end as he was at the beginning of his career.

He is not being punished.

And the lord commended the unjust steward, because he had done wisely: for the children of this world are in their generation wiser than the children of light [Luke 16:8].

This is a shocking statement. Who made it? The lord of the steward, meaning his employer, the rich man. Apparently this man got rich using the same kind of principles that his unjust steward used. He tells him he has done wisely. In what way? According to the principles of the world. This is the world that hates Christ. It makes its own rules. The law of the world is "dog eat dog." The worldly lord commended his worldly steward for his worldly wisdom according to his worldly dealings.

The Lord Jesus said, "For the children of this world are in their generation wiser than the children of light." That is, the children of this world, of this age, use their money more wisely than do the children of light.

And I say unto you, Make to yourselves friends of the mammon of unrighteousness; that, when ye fail, they may receive you into everlasting habitations [Luke 16:9].

The most shocking and startling statement of all concerns the relationship of the believer to the "mammon of unrighteousness." What is the "mammon of unrighteousness?" It is riches, money. Money is not evil in itself; money is amoral. It is the *love of money* that is the root of all evil. For believers money is to be spiritual. Our Lord said that we should lay up for ourselves treasures in heaven. We should be wise in the way we use our money. Then when we "fail" or come to the end of life, we will be welcomed into heaven.

He that is faithful in that which is least is faithful also in much: and he that is unjust in the least is unjust also in much.

If therefore ye have not been faithful in the unrighteous mammon, who will commit to your trust the true riches?

And if ye have not been faithful in that which is another man's, who shall give you that which is your own? [Luke 16:10–12].

We are stewards of that which is material. We own nothing as believers. We are responsible to God for how we use His goods. He says that the men of this world are wiser than the children of light in their stewardship. For years I was pastor of a church in downtown Los Angeles which was near the financial district. Through the years I watched many of the men go into a broker's office and watch the fluctuation of the stock market. They would sit down in the morning and figure out what they were going to do. They would not invest in any stock unless they thought it was going to go up in value, or they would play the market. A Christian man once told me that he had made his money by playing the stock market. For this reason he would not accept an office in the church—I do not know how he reconciled to himself the fact that he was a church member. He was clever at making money.

How many Christians today are smart in the use of the mammon of unrighteousness—money? Do they use it to gather spiritual wealth? God will hold you responsible for the misuse of the material wealth He gives you. I personally know of a program that is run just for the self-interest of one individual. In another organization ninety percent of what is given to that program supports a tremendous overhead that keeps men driving Cadillac automobiles. That means you would have to give one hundred dollars to get ten dollars to the poor folk they are telling you about. There is something wrong with the *way* Christians give their money. This would not happen if Christians were as smart as the men of the world. How smart are you, Christian friend, in money matters? Are you using your money to see that the Word of God reaches those who need it?

In the parable of the unjust steward the Lord Jesus is saying, "Do you think God is going to trust you with heavenly riches if you are not using properly that which He has given you on earth?" Money is a spiritual matter. You are responsible not only for giving it, but for investing it where it will yield the highest dividends in folk reached for Christ.

No servant can serve two masters: for either he will hate the one, and love the other; or else he will hold to the one, and despise the other. Ye cannot serve God and mammon [Luke 16:13].

What are you doing with your money? Are you making money? If you are, what are you doing with it? This is a pertinent question. Are you using it for the things of the world? If you are, you are serving mammon; that is your master. Are you serving God or mammon? You cannot serve them both.

JESUS ANSWERS THE COVETOUS PHARISEES

The Pharisees heard Jesus and began to feel convicted.

And the Pharisees also, who were covetous, heard all these things: and they derided him.

And he said unto them, Ye are they which justify yourselves before men; but God knoweth your hearts: for that which is highly esteemed among men is abomination in the sight of God.

The law and the prophets were until John: since that time the kingdom of God is preached, and every man presseth into it.

And it is easier for heaven and earth to pass, than one tittle of the law to fail [Luke 16:14–17].

God knew the hearts of the Pharisees. God knows your heart. God knows my heart. We can put up a front with each other but not with God. We cannot measure up to God's standard.

JESUS SPEAKS ON DIVORCE

Whosoever putteth away his wife, and marrieth another, committeth adultery: and whosoever marrieth her that is put away from her husband committeth adultery [Luke 16:18].

If this were the only verse of Scripture on the subject of divorce, there would be no divorce for a Christian. This verse should be compared with Matthew 19 and 1 Corinthians 7. All of Scripture must be considered on a certain subject to ascertain its truth. Our Lord spoke on this subject, to these men who were under the Law, because they were making light of the Law of God.

JESUS RECOUNTS THE INCIDENT OF THE RICH MAN AND LAZARUS (POOR MAN)

Now we come to another great parable that only Luke presents. I do not believe this is a fictitious story. I believe He drew this story from real life just as He did His other parables. Jesus used illustrations that were familiar to His hearers. They knew exactly what He was talking about. He uses the name of one of the individuals involved in this parable; the Lord would not have given the name of someone who did not exist.

There was a certain rich man, which was clothed in purple and fine linen, and fared sumptuously every day [Luke 16:19].

This is the story of a rich man who lived and died without God. It moves into a realm that we know nothing about. In this parable the Lord passes from this world to the next without making any break at all. Although we cannot penetrate the curtain between this life and the next life, our Lord speaks of the next world as naturally as He speaks of this life.

When man is left to his own imagination, he seeks out many inventions and out of his wildest dreams he makes unlimited speculations. When man uses his imagination, he gets into trouble. In this parable we learn what the Word of God says. There were only four men who ever spoke with authority concerning the other side of death: the Lord Jesus; Lazarus; John, who was given the Revelation; and Paul, who was ". . . caught up to the third heaven" (2 Cor. 12:2).

And there was a certain beggar named Lazarus, which was laid at his gate, full of sores.

And desiring to be fed with the crumbs which fell from the rich man's table: moreover the dogs came and licked his sores [Luke 16:20–21].

Here are two men at the opposite ends of the social and financial ladder—and, I suppose, every other ladder. One man represents the top echelon in riches, and the other man represents the lowest extreme of poverty. No two men could be farther apart in every way. This poor man was dependent upon the crumbs that fell from the rich man's table. He never was invited to sit at the rich man's table; he had to be kept in a menial place. The dogs came and licked his sores. In a few words our Lord pictures the depths of the terrible degradation and despair into which this man had fallen. I am sure had you lived in that town you might have gotten the impression that poor Lazarus, dressed in rags, did not have much in the way of any spiritual discernment or spiritual riches. I am sure all of us would have written him off as a hopeless case. On the other hand, I am sure that the rich man had several buildings named after him—perhaps a church, a school, or a mission enterprise. I am sure he had a wonderful name in the town in which these two men lived. However, all that the people in the town could see were the outward appearances of the rich man and the beggar whose sores were licked by dogs. This is a picture of abject poverty and extreme riches. Two men could not have been farther apart.

And it came to pass, that the beggar died, and was carried by the angels into Abraham's bosom: the rich man also died, and was buried [Luke 16:22].

Our Lord comes right to the door of death and passes through it as if it were nothing unusual. When the beggar died, there was no funeral. They just took his body out and threw it into the Valley of Gehenna where refuse was thrown and burned; this is the place where they threw the bodies of the poor in that day. The minute the beggar stepped through the doorway of death, angels became his pallbearers and he was carried by them into Abraham's Bosom.

The rich man also died and was buried. He had a big funeral, and the preacher pushed him all the way to the top spot in heaven. The only trouble is that the preacher got his directions mixed up; the rich man went the other way.

And in hell he lift up his eyes, being in torments, and seeth Abraham afar off, and Lazarus in his bosom [Luke 16:23].

Notice two things here: The lost go to a place of conscious torment. Also, people know each other after death. We do not lose our identities.

The word *hell* is in the Greek *hadēs*, meaning "the unseen world." Actually, *hell*, as we think of it, is a place that has not yet been opened up for business; we don't read of it until we get to Revelation 20:10, where it tells us that hell's first occupants will be the Antichrist and the false prophet. When they died, Lazarus and the rich man went to the unseen world, the place of the departed dead.

Death is separation; it never means extinction. Adam, in the day that he ate of the forbidden fruit, died. Physically he did not die until about nine hundred years later, but the day that he ate of the fruit he was separated from God. Jesus spoke of it when He said, ". . . I am the resurrection, and the life: he that believeth in me, though he were dead, yet shall he live: And whosoever liveth and believeth in me shall never die . . ." (John 11:25–26). Man is separated from God by sin. People are dead while they live. Paul told the Ephesians, "And you hath he quickened, who were dead in trespasses and sins" (Eph. 2:1).

Certain spots in a big city are really alive and jumping at night. If you want to see a lot of zombies and dead people, look in on one of these nightclubs. That is where you will find them. They are beating the drums, blaring out the music, getting the beat, drinking all they can, and getting high on drugs because they are dead and want to live.

There is a second death, which is spiritual death, and it means eternal separation from God. At physical death the body becomes inert and lifeless because the person's spirit has moved out. The body is put into the grave, and the elements return to the dust: ". . . for dust thou art, and unto dust shalt thou return" (Gen. 3:19). Therefore, death means separation.

It will help us understand this parable if we realize that Sheol or hades (translated hell in the New Testament) is divided into two compartments: paradise (which is called Abraham's Bosom in this parable) and the place of torment. Paradise was emptied when Christ took with Him at His ascension the Old Testament believers (see Eph. 4:8–10). The place of torment will deliver up the lost for judgment at the Great White Throne (see Rev. 20:11–15). All who stand at this judgment are lost, and they will be cast into the lake of fire, which is the second death.

Now when the rich man died, his spirit went to the place of torment, the compartment where the lost go. The beggar went to the compartment called paradise or Abraham's Bosom.

Note that our Lord is not saying that the rich man went to the place of torment because he was rich and that the poor man went to Abraham's Bosom because he was poor. Going through the doorway of death certainly changed their status, but it was due to what was in the hearts of these two men. This is what our Lord has been saying through this entire section—man cannot judge by the outward appearance.

There are some other things revealed in this story that we would not know if our Lord had not revealed them.

And he cried and said, Father Abraham, have mercy on me, and send Lazarus, that he may dip the tip of his finger in water, and cool my tongue; for I am tormented in this flame [Luke 16:24].

The rich man becomes the beggar, while the beggar is now the rich man.

But Abraham said, Son, remember that thou in thy lifetime receivedst thy good things, and likewise Lazarus evil things: but now he is comforted, and thou art tormented.

And beside all this, between us and you there is a great gulf fixed: so that they which would pass from hence to you cannot; neither can they pass to us, that would come from thence [Luke 16:25–26].

The bodies of believers today, since the resurrection of Jesus Christ, go into the grave and return to dust, but their spirits go to be with Christ. "We are confident, I say, and willing rather to be absent from the body, and to be present with the Lord" (2 Cor. 5:8). The lost today still go to the place of torment in hades. Ephesians 4:8–10 gives us the following picture, "Wherefore he saith, When he ascended up on high, he led captivity captive, and gave gifts unto men. (Now that he ascended, what is it but that he also descended first into the lower parts of the earth? He that descended is the same also that ascended up far above all heavens, that he might fill all things.)" In other words, when our Lord descended into hades after His crucifixion on the cross, He entered the paradise section, emptied it, and took everyone into God's presence. No one occupies the paradise section of hades today. The only part of hades still occupied is the place of torment where unbelievers go when they die. The day is coming when hades will be cast into the lake of fire and men will no longer go there at all (see Rev. 20:14).

The body is merely the physical house in which we live. At death we move out of our old homes. You can do anything you want to with the old house after it is deserted, but the important thing is what happens to the spirit after it has left the body. Where is it going?

Heaven is a place, friend, and the moment you die you will either go there to be with Christ, or you will go to the place of torment where you will ultimately be judged and then cast into the lake of fire. The point is that God never intended the latter as an end for anyone of the human family. The lake of fire was made for the Devil and his angels (see Matt. 25:41). You *choose* your final destination.

"There is a great gulf fixed:" our Lord made that clear. You must make the decision in this life where you will go after your death. You do not get a second chance after death.

Then he said, I pray thee therefore, father, that thou wouldest send him to my father's house [Luke 16:27].

Notice his concern for his living brothers. He wanted them to repent, change their minds before it was too late. Friend, if the lost could come back, they would preach the gospel to us.

For I have five brethren; that he may testify unto them, lest they also come into this place of torment.

Abraham saith unto him, They have Moses and the prophets; let them hear them.

And he said, Nay, father Abraham: but if one went unto them from the dead, they will repent.

And he said unto him, If they hear not Moses and the prophets, neither will they be persuaded, though one rose from the dead [Luke 16:28–31].

Many people believe that multitudes would repent if someone returned from the dead to tell them what it was like. Well, Someone *has* come back from the dead. His name is Jesus Christ. They did not believe Him any more than they believed Moses and the prophets. Friend, do not delay in making your choice. There will be no opportunity after death.

CHAPTER 17

THEME: *Jesus instructs His disciples on forgiveness; Jesus instructs His disciples on faithful service; Jesus heals ten lepers; Jesus speaks on the spiritual nature of God's kingdom; Jesus speaks of His coming again*

JESUS INSTRUCTS HIS DISCIPLES ON FORGIVENESS

Then said he unto the disciples, It is impossible but that offences will come: but woe unto him, through whom they come!

It were better for him that a millstone were hanged about his neck, and he cast into the sea, than that he should offend one of these little ones [Luke 17:1–2].

What the Lord says here is very severe. I will be honest with you; I think I would rather be most any person than the one selling drugs to young people today. I believe that the punishment for one who sells drugs will be greater than for some others. It is serious business to cause someone, especially a youngster, to offend. There is one thing worse than going to hell; it is going to hell and having a son or daughter say to you, "Dad, I am here because I followed you." That is the worst thing that can happen to a person.

Take heed to yourselves: If thy brother trespass against thee, rebuke him; and if he repent, forgive him.

And if he trespass against thee seven times in a day, and seven times in a day turn again to thee, saying, I repent; thou shalt forgive him.

And the apostles said unto the Lord, Increase our faith.

And the Lord said, If ye had faith as a grain of mustard seed, ye might say unto this sycamine tree, Be thou plucked up by the root, and be thou planted in the sea; and it should obey you [Luke 17:3–6].

In other words, His disciples should be ready always to forgive. He does not say that the one who offends should not be rebuked. He should be made to appreciate his fault, but when he sincerely repents, he should be forgiven—even if he repeats his sin over and over.

JESUS INSTRUCTS HIS DISCIPLES ON FAITHFUL SERVICE

Once again Jesus is severe. There are those who talk about the gentle Jesus, but if you read some of these passages, you will find that He was not always gentle. He was gentle with children, but not with those who offended them.

But which of you, having a servant plowing or feeding cattle, will say unto him by and by, when he is come from the field, Go and sit down to meat?

And will not rather say unto him, Make ready wherewith I may sup, and gird thyself, and serve me, till I have eaten and drunken; and afterward thou shalt eat and drink?

Doth he thank that servant because he did the things that were commanded him? I trow not [Luke 17:7–9].

Let me make an application of this passage. There are people who believe that because they try to follow the Sermon on the Mount and are good neighbors and try to love people, that someday God is going to pat them on the back and say, "What a fine person you are. You have earned your way to heaven." If you keep the Ten Commandments and the Sermon on the Mount, which you cannot, you are doing only what you are supposed to do. Do you think you would receive salvation for that? My friend, that's what you are supposed to do as one of His creatures. We need to recognize that salvation is a *gift*; you cannot work for it. Keeping God's Law is a duty.

So likewise ye, when ye shall have done all those things which are commanded you, say, We are unprofitable servants: we have done that which was our duty to do [Luke 17:10].

JESUS HEALS TEN LEPERS (ONE SAMARITAN RETURNS TO GIVE THANKS)

And it came to pass, as he went to Jerusalem, that he passed through the midst of Samaria and Galilee [Luke 17:11].

Remember, our Lord is on His way to Jerusalem.

And as he entered into a certain village, there met him ten men that were lepers, which stood afar off:

And they lifted up their voices, and said, Jesus, Master, have mercy on us.

And when he saw them, he said unto them, Go shew yourselves unto the priests, And it came to pass, that, as they went, they were cleansed.

And one of them, when he saw that he was healed, turned back, and with a loud voice glorified God,

And fell down on his face at his feet, giving him thanks: and he was a Samaritan [Luke 17:12–16].

The Pharisees winced at this one!

And Jesus answering said, Were there not ten cleansed? but where are the nine?

There are not found that returned to give glory to God, save this stranger.

And he said unto him, Arise, go thy way; thy faith hath made thee whole [Luke 17:17–19].

Jesus healed ten lepers. Only one of the ten, who was a Samaritan, returned to thank Jesus for what He had done. Jesus then did a second thing for him—He forgave his sins. The other nine lepers were healed but were not saved. Thankfulness should be in the Christian's heart. Why do you go to church on Sunday? Do you go there to worship God and thank Him for all He has done for you? Part of your worship is to thank Him. About the only thing we can give to God is our thanksgiving. How wonderful it is just to thank Him. We are even to make our requests to God *with thanksgiving.* We ought to have a thankful heart toward Him.

JESUS SPEAKS ON THE SPIRITUAL NATURE OF GOD'S KINGDOM

And when he was demanded of the Pharisees, when the kingdom of God should come, he answered them and said, The kingdom of God cometh not with observation:

Neither shall they say, Lo here! or, lo there! for, behold, the kingdom of God is within you [Luke 17:20–21].

Jesus speaks of the fact that the "kingdom of God cometh not with observation." To whom is He talking? He is answering the Pharisees who are demanding that He tell them when the kingdom will come. He is not saying that the kingdom of God is inside the hearts of these godless and hostile Pharisees. Rather, the kingdom of God was in their midst, in the person of the King, the Lord Jesus Christ. He was right then standing among them.

JESUS SPEAKS OF HIS COMING AGAIN

One of the greatest delusions of our time is that man is going to improve himself and his world; that he is going to build the kingdom of God without God. He expects to bring in the Millennium without Christ.

Now the glorious day of the kingdom was the subject of much of what Christ had to say. In fact, He emphasized the future—the change coming and His return. A liberal theologian of the past, who had been teaching that Jesus was an ethical teacher, got tired of being a parrot, and began to study the words of the Lord Jesus Christ. He made the discovery (and he wrote a book on it) that Christ was an eschatological teacher, that His main subject was the future, His coming to earth again.

In this important section before us, our Lord warns His disciples not to be deceived concerning His return.

Now the return of Christ is in two phases. The first phase is what we call the "Rapture of the church" which is the taking away of true believers (detailed for us in 1 Thess. 4:13–18). But in this passage He is talking about the second phase of His return, which is returning to the earth to establish His kingdom. This will take place after the Rapture and after the Great Tribulation.

And he said unto the disciples, The days will come, when ye shall desire to see one of the days of the Son of man, and ye shall not see it.

And they shall say to you, See here; or see there: go not after them, nor follow them [Luke 17:22–23].

The first time He came, they failed to recognize Him because they were looking for a conquering Messiah to come and deliver them from Rome. Instead He came as a baby and lived as a peasant. The next time He comes it will not be in an isolated place like Bethlehem, but He will come in glory. Therefore He warns them not to pay any attention to those who say

He is here or there—or who say He is coming at a certain time. This is one reason you cannot set the date of the coming of Christ.

For as the lightning, that lighteneth out of the one part under heaven, shineth unto the other part under heaven; so shall also the Son of man be in his day [Luke 17:24].

When He comes to this earth to establish His kingdom, it will be as public as lightning. Compare this with His extensive discourse in Matthew 24.

But first must he suffer many things, and be rejected of this generation [Luke 17:25].

The cross was in the program of God. He went by way of the cross to get you and me. He outlined His program very clearly: He would suffer and be rejected by His people.

And as it was in the days of Noe, so shall it be also in the days of the Son of man [Luke 17:26].

How was it in the days of Noah? What does He have reference to?

They did eat, they drank, they married wives, they were given in marriage, until the day that Noe entered into the ark, and the flood came, and destroyed them all [Luke 17:27].

What is wrong with these things? Marriage is not wrong—it is right. What is wrong with eating and drinking? We must do this to live. Why does Jesus mention these things? Well, the generation of Noah was living as if God did not exist when judgment was imminent. Today men and women are eating and drinking (and not even marrying though living together), and they do not recognize that the judgment of God is out there in the future—when, we do not know.

Likewise also as it was in the days of Lot; they did eat, they drank, they bought, they sold, they planted, they builded;

But the same day that Lot went out of Sodom it rained fire and brimstone from heaven, and destroyed them all [Luke 17:28–29].

This is a tremendous thing our Lord says at this juncture. Lot is altogether different from Noah; yet there are similarities. None in Sodom were panicking, selling out their property and getting out of town. The stock market did not collapse because Lot said that judgment was coming. They simply didn't believe it.

God would not destroy the city until Lot had been taken out of it. Neither will He bring the Great Tribulation upon this earth (which immediately precedes the coming of Christ to the earth) until He takes His own out of the world. It is interesting that He uses Lot as an example here, which He does not do in the Olivet Discourse in Matthew 24. The reason is that in Matthew He is answering their question about His coming to earth to establish His kingdom. Here in Luke it is a wider subject. Sodom, because of her sin, stood on the brink of destruction, and the moment Lot left town, judgment fell. I believe that the minute believers leave this earth in the Rapture, the Great Tribulation will begin.

Even thus shall it be in the day when the Son of man is revealed [Luke 17:30].

God has a people in the world today who are just like Lot in many respects. Although they have trusted Christ as Savior, they compromise with the world. Yet as believers they will be taken out of the world before the day of judgment comes. Today the world doesn't listen to the church. As in Lot's day, they think we are mocking.

In that day, he which shall be upon the housetop, and his stuff in the house, let him not come down to take it away: and he that is in the field, let him likewise not return back [Luke 17:31].

In Matthew's account of the Olivet Discourse, the Lord Jesus labels this period the Great Tribulation.

Remember Lot's wife [Luke 17:32].

She is an example of one who did not believe God. She had daughters and friends in Sodom. Probably they were having a bridge party that afternoon. She kept saying, "Let's go back." Why did she look back? She didn't believe God would destroy that city. Therefore we are to remember Lot's wife. To believe God is the important thing for us.

Whosoever shall seek to save his life shall lose it; and whosoever shall lose his life shall preserve it [Luke 17:33].

This is one of those great paradoxes of Scripture. In that day there will be a great scramble to save their lives, but it will be too late. They are to be willing to lose their lives and just turn them over to Jesus Christ. Any attempt to save life in that day will avail nothing.

I tell you, in that night there shall be two men in one bed; the one shall be taken, and the other shall be left.

Two women shall be grinding together, the one shall be taken, and the other left.

Two men shall be in the field; the one shall be taken, and the other left [Luke 17:34–36].

In the days of Noah, who was taken out of the world? Who was left in the world? This is not the Rapture He is talking about. This is, as in the Olivet Discourse in Matthew 24:37–41, a direct reference to taking away the ungodly in judgment and leaving on earth those who will enter the millennial kingdom.

Notice that Christ implied that the earth was round—one will be in bed and another working out in the field. There will be night on one side of the earth and day on the other side.

And they answered and said unto him, Where, Lord? And he said unto them, Wheresoever the body is, thither will the eagles be gathered together [Luke 17:37].

Compare this verse with Revelation 19:17. This is what we call the Battle of Armageddon, which is actually the *war* of Armageddon, and will be ended when Christ comes to establish His kingdom upon the earth.

CHAPTER 18

***THEME:** Parable of the unjust judge; parable of the Pharisee and the publican; Jesus blesses the little children; Jesus confronts the rich young ruler with five of the Ten Commandments; Jesus heals the blind man on entering Jericho*

Before we begin this chapter, I want to say a word about our Lord personally. I believe that He was God manifest in the flesh. I also believe that He was not any less God because He was man. On the other hand, I believe He was not any more man because He was God. He was a perfect man—a real man. Frankly, if you had been there in that day, you would have enjoyed His company. It would have been a real privilege to be in His company and to hear His laughter. I don't like any picture I see of Him; the artists never picture Him laughing, and I think He laughed many times. Our Lord was so human. In His presence you would have the best time you ever had. You know folk, I am sure, whom you love to be with. I know several preachers whose company I especially enjoy. They sharpen my wits and my mental powers; yet they tell the funniest jokes I've ever heard. I think our Lord was good at that. We are coming to an incident that I am confident made many people smile.

And he spake a parable unto them to this end, that men ought always to pray, and not to faint [Luke 18:1].

He concluded chapter 17 with a discourse on the last days and the fact that He would be coming again. And He likened the last days to the days of Noah, that they would be difficult days—days that would not be conducive to faith. So now He talks to them about a life of faith in days that are devoid of faith. That is the reason it is so pertinent for this hour. We are living in days, as He indicated, when men's hearts are failing them for fear. What we have in this first parable is a pertinent paragraph on prayer for the present hour. Notice that He says He spoke a parable to them to this end; that is, for this *purpose*, that men should always pray, and not to faint.

He opens two alternatives to any man who is living in difficult days. You and I will have to do one of the two. You will have to make up your mind which you are going to do. Men in difficult days will either faint or they will pray. Either there will be days of fear or days of faith.

During World War II, when the bombing was so intense on the city of London, a sign appeared in front of one of the churches in London that read, "If your knees knock together, kneel on them!" That is practically a restatement of what our Lord has said, "Men ought always to pray, and not to faint."

It is the same thought that Paul put a little differently, "Pray without ceasing" (1 Thess.

5:17). This does not mean you are to go to an all-day or all-night prayer meeting. Prayer is an attitude of the life. It is more an attitude of life than an action of the lips. Remember that Paul said to the Romans, ". . . the Spirit itself maketh intercession for us with groanings which cannot be uttered" (Rom. 8:26). That is, they cannot be put into our *words*. And many times we do not have the words to pray, but we are praying nonetheless. And it is the entire life that is behind the words which are spoken that makes prayer effective.

There was a famous preacher, years ago in the state of Georgia, who had many very unusual expressions. One of them was this, "When a man prays for a corn crop, God expects him to say Amen with a hoe." You can't just stay on your knees all the time and pray for a corn crop. That's pious nonsense. But to pray for the corn crop and then go to work is the thing our Lord is talking about in days when men's hearts are failing them. "Men ought always to pray, and not to faint."

PARABLE OF THE UNJUST JUDGE

When He told this story about the unjust judge and the widow, it probably was well known to the hearers of that day. They knew exactly what He was talking about. The story goes like this:

Saying, there was in a city a judge, which feared not God, neither regarded man,

And there was a widow in that city; and she came unto him, saying, Avenge me of mine adversary [Luke 18:2–3].

Now in this city there was a judge who was a godless fellow. He was an unscrupulous politician, scheming, cold, and calculating. Everything he did was for himself, as we shall see. Everything he did had to minister to his own advancement and satisfy his own ambition. He did not fear God. God had no place in this man's thinking. And since he did not fear God, he had no regard for man. He had no respect for this widow at all.

The widow likely was being beaten out of her little home. The mortgage was being foreclosed, and she was being treated unjustly. She went to this prominent judge, took her place in his office, and asked the secretary if she might talk to the judge. The secretary told her, "He's very busy. If you will just tell me the nature of your complaint. . . ."

So the widow told her, "I'm just a poor widow. I live out here at the edge of town, and I'm about to lose my place. It is unfair and unjust, and I want to appeal to the judge."

The secretary went into the judge's office and said, "There is a widow out there. . . ."

"Well, I can get rid of her in three minutes. I'm a politician, I know how to handle her. Let her come in."

She came in. He listened to her for three minutes. Then he said, "I'm sorry, but that's out of my realm. I'd *love* to do something for you, but I am unable to do anything. Good day."

The next day when he came into the office, there was the widow. He hurried into his office, called his secretary in, and asked, "What's that widow doing back?"

"She says she wants to see you."

"You go back and tell her I am busy until lunch time."

"I've already told her that. But she brought her lunch. She says she will stay here as long as necessary."

She stayed all that day and didn't get to see him. He thought he had gotten rid of her. But the next morning when he came in, there she was! She did that for several days, and finally he said, "I'll have to do something about this. I can't go on like this." Notice that our Lord records what he said "within himself."

And he would not for a while: but afterward he said within himself, Though I fear not God, nor regard man:

Yet because this widow troubleth me, I will avenge her, lest by her continual coming she weary me [Luke 18:4–5].

The word *weary* is a very poor translation. I only wish it were translated literally. What he said was this, "I must see her lest she give me a black eye!"

You see, he was thinking of himself. I don't know if he meant a literal black eye—we are not told that the widow had threatened him! But the very fact that a widow is sitting in the judge's office every day doesn't look good. He had gotten into office by saying, "I'm thinking of the poor people," but he wasn't—he was thinking of himself. "And lest she give me a black eye, I'd better hear her." To his secretary he said, "Bring her in." This time he said to the widow, "I'll give you legal protection." That's the parable.

And the Lord said, Hear what the unjust judge saith.

And shall not God avenge his own elect, which cry day and night unto him,

though he bear long with them? [Luke 18:6–7].

Now, I have heard many Bible teachers say that this parable teaches the value of importunate prayer. Although I don't like to disagree with men who are greater than I, that isn't so. This is not a parable on the persistency or the pertinacity of prayer—as though somehow God will hear if you hold on long enough.

This is a parable by *contrast*, not by comparison.

Parables were stories given by our Lord to illustrate truths. The word *parable* comes from two Greek words. *Para* means "beside" and *ballo* is the verb, meaning "to throw"—(we get our word *ball* from it). A parable means something that is thrown beside something else to tell you something about it. For instance, a yardstick placed beside a table is a parable to the table—it tells you how high it is. A parable is a story our Lord told to illustrate divine truth. There are two ways He did this. One is by comparison, but the other is by *contrast*.

Our Lord is saying, "When you come to God in prayer, do you think that God is an *unjust judge*? When you come to Him in prayer, do you think He is a cheap politician? Do you think God is doing things just for political reasons?" My friend, if you think this, you are wrong. God is not an unjust judge.

If this unjust judge would hear a poor widow because she kept coming continually, then why do you get discouraged going to God who is *not* an unjust judge, but who actually *wants* to hear and answer prayer? Why are God's people today so discouraged in their prayer life? Don't you know, my friend, He is not an unjust judge? You don't have to hang onto His coattail and beg Him and plead with Him. God *wants* to act in your behalf! If we had that attitude, it would change our prayer life—to come into His presence knowing He wants to hear. We act as if He is an unjust judge, and we have to hold onto Him or He will not hear us at all. God is not an unjust judge.

PARABLE OF THE PHARISEE AND THE PUBLICAN

Now our Lord gives another parable on prayer.

And he spake this parable unto certain which trusted in themselves that they were righteous, and despised others:

Two men went up into the temple to pray; the one a Pharisee, and the other a publican [Luke 18:9–10].

This is a parable that is familiar to all of us. Oh, with what trenchant and biting satire He gave them this! But He didn't do it to hurt them; He did it to help them. He said that two men went up to the temple to pray—a Pharisee and a publican. You could not get any two as far apart as those two men were. The Pharisee was at the top of the religious ladder. The publican was at the bottom. His parable wasn't about publicans and sinners—publicans were right down there with the sinners. The Pharisee was at the top, supposedly the most acceptable one to God. He went into the temple to pray, he had access to the temple, he brought the appointed sacrifice. As he stood and prayed, his priest was yonder in the Holy Place putting incense on the altar. This old Pharisee had it made.

The Pharisee stood and prayed thus with himself, God, I thank thee, that I am not as other men are, extortioners, unjust, adulterers, or even as this publican [Luke 18:11].

Isn't that an awful way to begin a prayer! And that is the way many of us do. You say, "I don't do *that*." Yes, you do. I hear prayers like that. Oh, we don't say it exactly that way. We are fundamental—we have learned to say it better than that. We have our own way of putting it, "Lord, I thank You I can give You my time and my service." How I hear that! What a compliment that is for the Lord! Friend, we don't get anywhere in prayer when we pray like that. God doesn't need our service.

The Pharisee said, "I thank thee, that I am not as other men"; then he began to enumerate what he wasn't. "I'm not an extortioner"—evidently there was somebody around who was an extortioner. "I am not unjust. I am not an adulterer." Then he spied that publican way outside, and said, "And, believe me, Lord, I'm not like that publican. I'm not like that sinner out there."

Then he began to tell the Lord what he did:

I fast twice in the week, I give tithes of all that I possess [Luke 18:12].

My, isn't he a wonderful fellow! Wouldn't we love to have him in our church!

Our Lord said he "prayed thus *with himself*." In other words, he was doing a Hamlet soliloquy. Hamlet, you know, goes off and stands talking to himself—and Hamlet is "off," by the way; he is a mental case. Hamlet says, "To be, or not to be, that is the question." And this old Pharisee is out there talking to himself—he thinks he is talking to God, but his prayer never got out of the rafters. All he did was have a pep talk; he patted himself on the back and went out proud as a peacock. God never heard that prayer.

The old publican—oh, he was a rascal. He was a sinner; he was as low as they come. He had sold his nation down the river when he had become a tax collector. When he became a tax gatherer, he denied his nation. When he denied his nation, as a Jew, he denied his religion. He turned his back on God. He took a one-way street, never to come back to God. Why did he do it? It was lucrative. He said, "There's money down this way." He became rich as a publican. But it did not satisfy his heart. Read the story of Levi; read the story of Zacchaeus in Luke 19—a publican's heart was *empty*. This poor publican in his misery and desperation, knowing that he had no access to the mercy seat in the temple, cried out to God.

And the publican, standing afar off, would not lift up so much as his eyes unto heaven, but smote upon his breast, saying, God be merciful to me a sinner [Luke 18:13].

"God be merciful to me a sinner" does not adequately express it. Let me give it to you in the language that he used. He would not so much as lift up his eyes unto heaven, but he smote on his breast, and said, "O God, I'm a poor publican. I have no access to that mercy seat yonder in the Holy of Holies. Oh, if you could only make a mercy seat for *me*! I want to come."

Our Lord said *that* man was heard. Do you know why he was heard? Because Jesus Christ right there and then was on the way to the cross to make a mercy seat for him. John writes: "And he is the propitiation for our sins: and not for ours only, but also for the sins of the whole world" (1 John 2:2). *Propitiation* means "mercy seat." Christ is the mercy seat for our sins, and not for ours only, but also for the sins of the *whole world*.

The publican's prayer has been answered. Actually, today you don't have to ask God to be merciful. He *is* merciful. Many people say, "We have to beg Him to be merciful." My friend, what do you want Him to do? He gave His Son to die for you. He says to the worst sinner you know, "*You* can come. There is a mercy seat for you." I have to admit to you that I had to come to that mercy seat. And if you are God's child, you have come to that mercy seat where He died yonder on the cross for your sins and my sins. The penalty has been paid. The holy God is able to hold His arms outstretched. You don't have to beg Him; you don't have to promise Him anything because He knows your weakness; you do not have to join something; you do not even have to *be* somebody. You can be like a poor publican. You can come and trust Him, and He will save you. God is merciful.

I tell you, this man went down to his house justified rather than the other: for every one that exalteth himself shall be abased; and he that humbleth himself shall be exalted [Luke 18:14].

JESUS BLESSES THE LITTLE CHILDREN

The little children loved to be with the Lord Jesus.

And they brought unto him also infants, that he would touch them: but when his disciples saw it, they rebuked them [Luke 18:15].

Even the disciples said, "Do not bring the little children to Him. Do not bother Him."

But Jesus called them unto him, and said, Suffer little children to come unto me, and forbid them not: for of such is the kingdom of God [Luke 18:16].

The feeling was that small children were not too important. The Lord Jesus felt differently about children. They were not a bother to Him.

Verily I say unto you, Whosoever shall not receive the kingdom of God as a little child shall in no wise enter therein [Luke 18:17].

Children normally and naturally came to the Lord. He did not want the adults to keep them away from Him. God have mercy on any adult who keeps little children away from God. Concerning this subject, Luke has already said, "It were better for him that a millstone were hanged about his neck, and he cast into the sea, than that he should offend one of these little ones" (Luke 17:2). You see, the little ones will follow you. They have complete trust in you. They will do anything you want them to do. God have mercy on you if you don't bring them to God! Children would normally come to Him.

Someone may object, "But children have a fallen nature." Yes, they do. But that little one has not reached the age of accountability; the only decision he can make is the decision that is suggested to him. That's the nature of the little child. Of course, the little one will grow up and develop a will of his own. Then that's when the trouble begins! But while he is still pliable, make sure that he comes to Christ.

JESUS CONFRONTS THE RICH YOUNG RULER WITH FIVE OF THE TEN COMMANDMENTS

The account of the rich young ruler is also given in Matthew 19:16–30 and in Mark 10:17–31. It is a wonderful story. In this account our Lord made inquiry into the conduct of the rich young ruler.

And a certain ruler asked him, saying, Good Master, what shall I do to inherit eternal life?

And Jesus said unto him, Why callest thou me good? none is good, save one, that is, God [Luke 18:18–19].

The Lord Jesus Christ was leading this young man to see that if he recognized goodness in Jesus, it was because He was God. That is the reason Jesus urged him to follow. It would have led him to accept Jesus as the disciples had—". . . the Christ, the Son of the living God" (Matt. 16:16).

Thou knowest the commandments, Do not commit adultery, Do not kill, Do not steal, Do not bear false witness, Honour thy father and thy mother.

And he said, All these have I kept from my youth up.

Now when Jesus heard these things, he said unto him, Yet lackest thou one thing: sell all that thou hast, and distribute unto the poor, and thou shalt have treasure in heaven: and come, follow me [Luke 18:20–22].

Jesus flashed on the young ruler the second section of the Ten Commandments which is labeled "probitas." This section deals with man's relationship with man. The first section has to do with man's relationship to God and is labeled "pietas." This young man could meet the second section, but not the first. He needed a relationship with God, which he evidently lacked. Riches stood in the way of this. The Law condemned this attractive young man. Riches were the stumbling block for him. For another man it might be something else. It is impossible for any man to get into the kingdom of heaven by riches or by any human means. Only God could put a camel through a needle's eye, and only God can *regenerate*.

And when he heard this, he was very sorrowful: for he was very rich.

And when Jesus saw that he was very sorrowful, he said, How hardly shall they that have riches enter into the kingdom of God!

For it is easier for a camel to go through a needle's eye, than for a rich man to enter into the kingdom of God.

And they that heard it said, Who then can be saved?

And he said, The things which are impossible with men are possible with God.

Then Peter said, Lo, we have left all, and followed thee.

And he said unto them, Verily I say unto you, There is no man that hath left house, or parents, or brethren, or wife, or children, for the kingdom of God's sake,

Who shall not receive manifold more in this present time, and in the world to come life everlasting [Luke 18:23–30].

In spite of the lack and unwillingness in his life, it is said that Jesus loved him. Riches separated this young man from Jesus. Had he followed Jesus, he would have come to the cross for redemption, for Jesus was very close to the cross at this time. Who was this young man? I do not know who he was. You may be like him today, I do not know. Did he follow the Lord later on? We hope so. Will you follow the Lord? He loves you.

JESUS HEALS THE BLIND MAN ON ENTERING JERICHO

Before we look at this incident, I should mention that critics of the Bible find in this a contradiction, because Matthew speaks of two blind men, while Mark and Luke mention only one. However, if you will read this passage carefully, you will see that Matthew and Mark obviously refer to a work of healing as Jesus *departed* from Jericho. Bartimaeus, the active one of the two, the one who cried, ". . . Jesus, thou son of David . . . ," is specifically mentioned in Mark 10:46. The healing described by Luke, in verses 40–43, occurred before Jesus *entered* Jericho. This man also used the familiar form of address, "son of David."

And it came to pass, that as he was come nigh unto Jericho, a certain blind man sat by the way side begging:

And hearing the multitude pass by, he asked what it meant.

And they told him, that Jesus of Nazareth passeth by [Luke 18:35–37].

By addressing Jesus as the "son of David," he acknowledged His kingship. He knew Jesus was able to heal him and so it was impossible to keep him quiet. He knew what he wanted, and he had great faith in Jesus. Jesus' dealing with this blind man is tender and thrilling.

And he cried, saying, Jesus, thou son of David, have mercy on me.

And they which went before rebuked him, that he should hold his peace: but he cried so much the more, Thou son of David, have mercy on me.

And Jesus stood, and commanded him to be brought unto him: and when he was come near, he asked him,

Saying, What wilt thou that I shall do unto thee? And he said, Lord, that I may receive my sight.

And Jesus said unto him, Receive thy sight: thy faith hath saved thee.

And immediately he received his sight, and followed him, glorifying God: and all the people, when they saw it, gave praise unto God [Luke 18:38–43].

After he was healed, he followed Jesus with his eyes open. What will he see in a few days? He will see Jesus dying on the cross. Multitudes of people today with 20-20 vision have not yet seen Jesus' death on the cross related to their lives and the forgiveness of their sins. If you have not yet done so—*look* and *live!*

CHAPTER 19

THEME: *Jesus enters Jericho and home of Zacchaeus; the conversion of Zacchaeus; parable of ten pounds; Jesus enters Jerusalem; Jesus weeps over the city; Jesus cleanses the temple*

JESUS ENTERS JERICHO AND HOME OF ZACCHAEUS

Remember that at the time of this incident, the Lord Jesus Christ is on His way to Jerusalem to die on the cross. On His way, He goes through Jericho.

And Jesus entered and passed through Jericho [Luke 19:1].

Luke tells us that Jesus had been over in Samaritan country. When He left Samaria, He headed toward Jerusalem. He seems to be off the beaten path—but is He? He goes to Jericho because there is a sinner there. In fact, there are two or three sinners in Jericho. The Lord is going after them. If you miss the movement here, you will miss the entire message of this passage.

Jericho was the city that God had given into the hand of Joshua. A curse was placed on whoever would rebuild it. The man who rebuilt it in the days of Ahab reaped the curse in all its fulness. In Jesus' day it was like a resort area, the Las Vegas of that time. Many people spent their vacations there. Here the publicans lived. The publicans were like the modern Mafia. They were tax gatherers and were despised.

We are told that Jesus "entered and passed through Jericho." He also entered and passed through this world. He did not come to earth to stay but to die. I entered this world to live, and I would like to live a long time. But Jesus' only purpose in coming to earth was to die for the sins of the world. This tremendous movement is mirrored in the fact that He entered and passed through Jericho. Do not miss that.

THE CONVERSION OF ZACCHAEUS

And, behold, there was a man named Zacchaeus, which was the chief among the publicans, and he was rich [Luke 19:2].

Three things are said about this man in verse two. The Spirit of God has a way—with one flourish of the pen—of telling us all we need to know about a person. The first thing we learn about this man is that his name is Zacchaeus. When I found out that his name meant "pure," I began to laugh, and my wife came into my study to find out what was so funny. Imagine a publican who was pure! He was given that name as a baby. His father and mother looked down at him and thought he was the most precious little fellow in the world. When he grew up, I think there was a lot of fun in Jericho when he was called by his name. They would say, "Hello, Pure." What a name for a tax gatherer!

Zacchaeus was a chief among publicans. His parents never dreamed he would turn out this way. One dark night he had to decide whether or not he would sell out to Rome. As a publican he would have to pay Rome a stated amount for a certain territory in which he would gather taxes. Then, of course, he would gather *more* taxes than he paid Rome, which made him rich. Zacchaeus was the leader among the publicans. He had given up his religion. He had no more access to the temple. He was probably the publican who stood afar off, and smote his breast, as he said, "God be merciful to me a sinner" (Luke 18:13). Zacchaeus wanted a mercy seat to which he could come as a poor sinner. He wanted to come back to God.

Zacchaeus was rich. He made his profession pay. He did not conduct his business halfheartedly. If he went to collect taxes from a widow who could not pay, he would put her out of the house. If a man could not pay enough, he would take out a mortgage on the place. He had robbed many people. Although he had once made a decision to become a publican, he found out that all the wealth in the world would not satisfy his heart. He wished he could go back and start over. He had gone down a one-way street and he knew of no way to get back to the mercy seat. He wanted mercy, and our Lord knew that. The Lord went to Jericho for the purpose of helping this man. He wanted to take Zacchaeus with Him, not to Jerusalem, but to the cross for salvation.

And he sought to see Jesus who he was; and could not for the press, because he was little of stature [Luke 19:3].

A friend of mine who is a seminary professor is puzzled about whether there was one blind man or two blind men in Jericho. (His problem is that Matthew tells of two blind men who were healed in Jericho, while Luke speaks of only one.) I kiddingly told him once that there were two blind men and that I could prove it from the Bible. The second blind man was Zacchaeus because the Bible says, "He could not see for the press." He was a small man. He had eyes but they were too close to the ground. He did what I used to do every New Year's day at the Rose Parade. I would climb up a ladder and look over the heads of everyone in front of me at the parade. Zacchaeus was not able to find a ladder; so he climbed up into a sycamore tree.

And he ran before, and climbed up into a sycomore tree to see him: for he was to pass that way [Luke 19:4].

When I was in Jericho, I took a good look at a sycamore tree. It has a slick bark, and it is always a long way to the first limb. This is a difficult tree to climb, and I think this little man had a hard time climbing a tree like this. Zacchaeus sweated it out but finally got up the tree and settled down on a limb among the leaves. He thought he was secluded there, and he had a private box for the parade. He waited. Sure enough, Jesus came by. Our Lord knew he was there. Jesus was passing through Jericho to reach him.

And when Jesus came to the place, he looked up, and saw him, and said unto him, Zacchaeus, make haste, and come down; for to-day I must abide at thy house [Luke 19:5].

When our Lord looked up into that sycamore tree and saw Zacchaeus, I think He laughed. It is true that the text does not say that He did, but it is difficult to read this account without seeing the humor in it. The Lord looked into that tree as if to say, "Well, Zacchaeus, you wanted to see Me. You really worked hard to get up into that tree. Now make haste and come down." Make haste? This poor fellow had spent half a day getting up into the tree! But it did not take long for him to get down. It is always easier to come down than to go up. Our Lord said to him, "I must abide at thy house." Our Lord did not stop at the mayor's house; He did not stop at the home of a Pharisee; He did not stop at the home of any prominent person. He was going home with a publican!

And he made haste, and came down, and received him joyfully.

And when they saw it, they all murmured, saying, That he was gone to be guest with a man that is a sinner [Luke 19:6–7].

Zacchaeus was having fun now. For him it was a joyful occasion, but "they" murmured. Who are "they"? They are the gossiping crowd. They were saying, "Can you imagine that He is going to dinner at the house of a man who is a sinner?"

There was a lapse of time—how much, we are not told. Jesus had dinner with Zacchaeus, but He did not stay all night. They shut the door and the crowd milled around outside and gossiped, but no one knew what went on inside. Finally the door opened, and there stood Zacchaeus.

And Zacchaeus stood, and said unto the Lord; Behold, Lord, the half of my goods I give to the poor; and if I have taken any thing from any man by false accusation, I restore him fourfold [Luke 19:8].

Something had happened to this man! He admitted that he had been robbing the poor and promised to give half of his goods to the poor and to restore fourfold to those whom he had falsely taxed. He was acting according to the Mosaic Law (see Exod. 22). Something had happened inside Zacchaeus, and he was a new man.

We are not given an account of the conversation between Zacchaeus and our Lord. For some reason the Holy Spirit did not give us an account of what transpired between these two men. However, when our Lord talked to men He usually spoke of two things: (1) man's need and (2) God's ability to meet that need. He did not have to tell Zacchaeus that he was a sinner. Zacchaeus knew he was a sinner, and so did everyone else. The Lord told him there was a remedy for sin. He said, "I am going to Jerusalem to die on the cross so that there will be a mercy seat for you, Zacchaeus."

And Jesus said unto him, This day is salvation come to this house, forsomuch as he also is a son of Abraham [Luke 19:9].

Zacchaeus was shut out from the mercy seat in the temple when he became a publican. That mercy seat pointed to the Lord Jesus Christ and to His blood that He shed for us on the cross. The Lord wanted this hated man to know that He was going to Jerusalem to die, and His death would provide for him a mercy seat. This publican made a decision for Christ and became a new man.

For the Son of man is come to seek and to save that which was lost [Luke 19:10].

Note that Zacchaeus did not come to the door and say, "I want to give my testimony: Jesus saves and keeps and satisfies." Rather he said, "Half my goods I will give to the poor, and I will make right the things that have been wrong." By this I know he has been converted. And, friend, this is the only way the world will know that *you* are converted. They do not know it by testimony; they know it only by what they see in your life. If it were not for his changed life, I would never know that this old publican got converted.

The experience of Zacchaeus is a good illustration of what James says: "Yea, a man may say, Thou hast faith, and I have works: shew me thy faith without thy works, and I will shew thee my faith by my works" (James 2:18). Zacchaeus showed his faith by his works. He did not talk about his faith; he demonstrated it. The world is not *listening* for something today; it is *looking* for something. Zacchaeus had what the world is looking for. Jesus had dinner with him and his life changed.

Jesus is still entering and passing through your town wherever it is, and He wants to have dinner with those who do not know Him. He wants to talk about your soul and salvation. What about it? Has He passed through your home? Has He knocked on your heart's door? Have you let Him in?

PARABLE OF TEN POUNDS

And as they heard these things, he added and spake a parable, because he was nigh to Jerusalem, and because they thought that the kingdom of God should immediately appear [Luke 19:11].

Jesus now is approaching Jerusalem. Many of His followers, including His apostles, think that He was about to set up His kingdom on earth. But He is coming to Jerusalem to *die.* He is showing them that the kingdom is going to be postponed.

He said therefore, A certain nobleman went into a far country to receive for himself a kingdom, and to return [Luke 19:12].

The "certain nobleman" represents the Lord Jesus Christ. He will receive the kingdom from His Father—not from us. He is not asking anyone to vote for Him the next time He comes. People will either receive Him or they will be destroyed. He came the first time as a Savior. Next time He will come as King.

And he called his ten servants, and delivered them ten pounds, and said unto them, Occupy till I come.

But his citizens hated him, and sent a message after him, saying, We will not have this man to reign over us [Luke 19:13–14].

This is the message the world has for the Lord Jesus Christ today. This, however, will not keep God from sending His Son back to earth. They rebelled against God and His Messiah. They did not want Him to rule over them; so they nailed Him to a cross.

And it came to pass, that when he was returned, having received the kingdom, then he commanded these servants to be called unto him, to whom he had given the money, that he might know how much every man had gained by trading.

Then came the first, saying, Lord, thy pound hath gained ten pounds.

And he said unto him, Well, thou good servant: because thou hast been faithful in a very little, have thou authority over ten cities [Luke 19:15–17].

While He is away, friend, He has given you a pound. He has given every one of His servants an opportunity, and that opportunity is the pound. You are to be faithful to that over which He has made you steward. Your pound may be an entire city, a handful of people, or a home. Whatever it is, you are to be *faithful*. Some may gain five pounds and some may gain ten pounds while the Lord is away but when He comes again, He will reward you according to your faithfulness.

And the second came, saying, Lord, thy pound hath gained five pounds.

And he said likewise to him, Be thou also over five cities.

And another came, saying, Lord, behold, here is thy pound, which I have kept laid up in a napkin:

For I feared thee, because thou art an austere man: thou takest up that thou layedst not down, and reapest that thou didst not sow.

And he saith unto him, Out of thine own mouth will I judge thee, thou wicked servant. Thou knewest that I was an austere man, taking up that I laid not down, and reaping that I did not sow:

Wherefore then gavest not thou my money into the bank, that at my coming I might have required mine own with usury?

And he said unto them that stood by, Take from him the pound, and give it to him that hath ten pounds.

(And they said unto him, Lord, he hath ten pounds.)

For I say unto you, That unto every one which hath shall be given; and from him that hath not, even that he hath shall be taken away from him.

But those mine enemies, which would not that I should reign over them, bring hither, and slay them before me [Luke 19:18–27].

When He returns, He will reward them according to their faithfulness, you see. The important thing is *faithfulness*.

And when he had thus spoken, he went before, ascending up to Jerusalem [Luke 19:28].

He continues on His way to Jerusalem to deliver Himself up into the hands of His enemies.

JESUS ENTERS JERUSALEM

The Gospels present a composite picture of the so-called triumphal entry. By piecing the Gospels together, the conclusion is obvious that He entered Jerusalem three times, once a day on three separate days:

First—Saturday (the Sabbath day). There were no money changers on that day, and He looked around and left, "And Jesus entered into Jerusalem, and into the temple: and when he had looked round about upon all things, and now the eventide was come, he went out unto Bethany with the twelve" (Mark 11:11). *He entered as Priest.*

Second—Sunday (first day of week). The money changers were there and He cleansed the temple (see Matt. 21:12–13). *He entered as King.*

Third—Monday (second day of week). He wept over Jerusalem and entered the temple and taught and healed (see vv. 41–44, 47–48). *He entered as Prophet.*

And it came to pass, when he was come nigh to Bethphage and Bethany, at the mount called the mount of Olives, he sent two of his disciples,

Saying, Go ye into the village over against you; in the which at your entering ye shall find a colt tied, whereon yet never man sat: loose him, and bring him hither.

And if any man ask you, Why do ye loose him? thus shall ye say unto him, Because the Lord hath need of him.

And they that were sent went their way, and found even as he had said unto them.

And as they were loosing the colt, the owners thereof said unto them, Why loose ye the colt?

And they said, The Lord hath need of him [Luke 19:29–34].

I see no point in reading a miracle into this incident, although many people do so. I believe this is a normal, natural situation. Probably when our Lord was in Jerusalem previously He made arrangements with some friends to use these animals the next time He came to the city. His friends agreed to let Him use the animals at the time of the Passover Feast. The owners of these animals were expecting the Lord and had them tied outside for Him. He told His disciples what to say in case anyone asked, so that they would know the Lord had sent them on this errand. The important thing in this passage is that Jesus asserts His authority, "The Lord hath need of him."

And they brought him to Jesus: and they cast their garments upon the colt, and they set Jesus thereon.

And as he went, they spread their clothes in the way.

And when he was come nigh, even now at the descent of the mount of Olives, the whole multitude of the disciples began to rejoice and praise God with a loud voice for all the mighty works that they had seen;

Saying, Blessed be the King that cometh in the name of the Lord: peace in heaven, and glory in the highest [Luke 19:35–38].

The crowd did not know the full significance of this action. A few days later the crowd cried, "Crucify Him!"

Even the disciples did not know the significance until later: "These things understood not his disciples at the first: but when Jesus was glorified, then remembered they that these things were written of him, and that they had done these things unto him" (John 12:16).

And some of the Pharisees from among the multitude said unto him, Master, rebuke thy disciples.

And he answered and said unto them, I tell you that, if these should hold their peace, the stones would immediately cry out [Luke 19:39–40].

This episode of coming into Jerusalem as the Lord Jesus Christ did, was bound to incite the Roman rulers to act because of two things that He did. First, He accepted the reverence and loyalty of these followers. In the second place, He did not silence them.

The Lord Jesus Christ recognized that eternal and significant issues were at stake and that to rebuke His followers would force the silent stones to cry out. In fact, they *were* crying out, for when Nehemiah had rebuilt the walls and gates of the city, there was a message in the stones. Those very stones and walls were proclaiming the gospel message, and the gates were fairly shouting, "Lift up your heads, O ye gates; and be ye lift up, ye everlasting doors; and the King of glory shall come in" (Ps. 24:7). (For amplification of this, see the author's booklet, *The Gospel in the Gates of Jerusalem.*)

It should be remembered that the so-called triumphal entry ended at the cross. Christ will come the second time in triumph. Hebrews 9:28 says, "So Christ was once offered to bear the sins of many; and unto them that look for him shall he appear the second time without sin unto salvation." The second time the Lord will come to this earth, His feet will stand on the Mount of Olives (see Zech. 14:4). Then the Lord will enter Jerusalem. His *true* Triumphal Entry will be at His second coming. His first entry into Jerusalem took Him to the cross to die for our sins. By His death and resurrection, salvation is offered unto us.

JESUS WEEPS OVER THE CITY

And when he was come near, he beheld the city, and wept over it,

Saying, If thou hadst known, even thou, at least in this thy day, the things which belong unto thy peace! but now they are hid from thine eyes [Luke 19:41–42].

And, friend, they are still hidden from their eyes. I saw a picture of a convention they were having in Jerusalem some time ago. Stretched across the auditorium was a huge motto which read: "Science Will Give Us Peace In Our Day." Well, science has not brought them peace. It has produced sophisticated weapons and the atom bomb, but it has not brought peace.

For the days shall come upon thee, that thine enemies shall cast a trench about thee, and compass thee round, and keep thee in on every side,

And shall lay thee even with the ground, and thy children within thee; and they shall not leave in thee one stone upon another; because thou knewest not the time of thy visitation [Luke 19:43–44].

The fulfillment of this prophecy is written in history. In A.D. 70, Titus the Roman leveled Jerusalem and slaughtered the inhabitants without mercy.

JESUS CLEANSES THE TEMPLE

And he went into the temple, and began to cast out them that sold therein, and them that bought;

Saying unto them, It is written, My house is the house of prayer: but ye have made it a den of thieves.

And he taught daily in the temple. But the chief priests and the scribes and the chief of the people sought to destroy him,

And could not find what they might do: for all the people were very attentive to hear him [Luke 19:45–48].

Our Lord uses very strong language as He cleans up the temple for the second time. This action of Jesus officially closes His ministry to the nation.

CHAPTER 20

THEME: *Jesus' authority challenged; parable of the vineyard; Jesus is questioned about paying tribute to Caesar; Jesus silences the Sadducees about resurrection; Jesus questions the scribes*

JESUS' AUTHORITY CHALLENGED

And it came to pass, that on one of those days, as he taught the people in the temple, and preached the gospel, the chief priests and the scribes came upon him with the elders,

And spake unto him, saying, Tell us, by what authority doest thou these things? or who is he that gave thee this authority?

And he answered and said unto them, I will also ask you one thing; and answer me [Luke 20:1–3].

Jesus came into the temple every day and taught until He was arrested at the time of the Passover. He used the Socratic method of answering a question with a question. This was His question:

The baptism of John, was it from heaven, or of men? [Luke 20:4].

This was one question the religious rulers could not answer without condemning themselves. They had to go off in a huddle to decide on an answer.

And they reasoned with themselves, saying, If we shall say, From heaven; he will say, Why then believed ye him not?

But and if we say, Of men; all the people will stone us: for they be persuaded that John was a prophet.

And they answered, that they could not tell whence it was.

And Jesus said unto them, Neither tell I you by what authority I do these things [Luke 20:5–8].

Their question was not honest and sincere. If they had been willing to accept John, they would have been willing to accept the Lord Jesus Christ also. If they had believed John, they would have never questioned the authority of the Lord Jesus.

PARABLE OF THE VINEYARD

The parable of the vineyard is recorded in Matthew and Mark.

Then began he to speak to the people this parable; A certain man planted a vineyard, and let it forth to husbandmen, and went into a far country for a long time.

And at the season he sent a servant to the husbandmen, that they should give him of the fruit of the vineyard: but the husbandmen beat him, and sent him away empty [Luke 20:9–10].

The owner of the vineyard kept sending servants to the husbandmen to see how things were going. One by one the servants were beaten. God sent prophet after prophet to Israel, and they were absolutely rejected. Many of them were stoned and killed. Finally the Father sent His Son.

Jesus Christ was the Son and He was telling these religious rulers exactly what was in their hearts and minds to do with Him. They were going to crucify Him, and God was going to permit it.

And he beheld them, and said, What is this then that is written, The stone which the builders rejected, the same is become the head of the corner? [Luke 20:17].

The Lord was telling them they could kill Him but could not destroy the purpose of God. The Stone that they reject will become the head of the corner. This is a clear prediction of the Lord's rejection and subsequent triumph.

Whosoever shall fall upon that stone shall be broken; but on whomsoever it shall fall, it will grind him to powder [Luke 20:18].

Today you and I can fall on that Stone, who is Christ Jesus, and be saved—that is, we have to come to Him as a sinner, broken in spirit, broken in heart. When we do this, we are on the foundation that no *man* can lay, which is Jesus Christ the Stone. "For other foundation can no man lay than that is laid, which is Jesus Christ" (1 Cor. 3:11). Daniel tells of that Stone which will fall in judgment someday and "grind to powder" the nations that reject Him (see Dan. 2). What the Lord is saying in this parable is as clear as the noonday sun. It could not have been misunderstood.

JESUS IS QUESTIONED ABOUT PAYING TRIBUTE TO CAESAR

And the chief priests and the scribes the same hour sought to lay hands on him; and they feared the people: for they perceived that he had spoken this parable against them [Luke 20:19].

We can see that the religious rulers certainly got the point of His parable. The problem is that too many people in our churches today miss the point.

And they asked him, saying Master, we know that thou sayest and teachest rightly, neither acceptest thou the person of any, but teachest the way of God truly [Luke 20:21].

This was spoken like the true hypocrites these men were.

Is it lawful for us to give tribute unto Caesar, or no? [Luke 20:22].

The Herodians are the ones who posed this question because they wanted to get rid of Caesar and put the house of Herod over Israel.

But he perceived their craftiness, and said unto them, Why tempt ye me?

Shew me a penny. Whose image and superscription hath it? They answered and said, Caesar's [Luke 20:23–24].

The question of the Herodians was a loaded one designed to trap Jesus. Had He said "Yes"—to pay tribute to Caesar, then He would have put Caesar ahead of Moses and ahead of their Messiah. If He had said "No"—not to pay tribute to Caesar, then He would have been subject to arrest by Rome.

The method Jesus adopted in dealing with this question is a masterpiece. He asked for the Roman denarius. Does this mean that Jesus did not have any money? At least He made them produce the coin.

And he said unto them, Render therefore unto Caesar the things which be Caesar's and unto God the things which be God's [Luke 20:25].

They were using the legal tender of the Roman Empire. Rome did provide certain advantages and privileges. Rome maintained law and order by her standards and provided protection. Rome made and maintained roads and kept the sea lanes open. She had a universal currency system which was an aid to business. The Jews owed Rome something for the use of coins, roads, and law and order. Caesar had something coming to him.

God had something coming to Him also. He provided all the utilities: lights, air, water, and the elements from which roads and coins are made. There are two areas of life in which we have a responsibility. Man has both an earthly and an heavenly obligation. He has both a physical and a spiritual responsibility. Citizens of heaven pay taxes down here. Pilgrims down here should deposit eternal wealth in heaven.

JESUS SILENCES THE SADDUCEES ABOUT RESURRECTION

Then came to him certain of the Sadducees, which deny that there is any resurrection; and they asked him,

Saying, Master, Moses wrote unto us, If any man's brother die, having a wife, and he die without children, that his brother should take his wife, and raise up seed unto his brother [Luke 20:27–28].

You find this in Deuteronomy 25:5–6. It was an unusual law, but we see it in action in the Book of Ruth.

There were therefore seven brethren: and the first took a wife, and died without children.

And the second took her to wife, and he died childless.

And the third took her; and in like manner the seven also: and they left no children, and died.

Last of all the woman died also.

Therefore in the resurrection whose wife of them is she? for seven had her to wife [Luke 20:29–33].

Of course their question was ridiculous.

And Jesus answering said unto them, The children of this world marry, and are given in marriage:

But they which shall be accounted worthy to obtain that world, and the resurrection from the dead, neither marry, nor are given in marriage:

Neither can they die any more: for they are equal unto the angels; and are the children of God, being the children of the resurrection [Luke 20:34–36].

According to both Matthew and Mark, He told them their problem was that they knew neither the Scriptures nor the power of God.

Now that the dead are raised, even Moses shewed at the bush, when he calleth the Lord the God of Abraham, and the God of Isaac, and the God of Jacob.

For he is not a God of the dead, but of the living: for all live unto him [Luke 20:37–38].

You see, after Jesus had answered the Herodians and the Pharisees soundly, the Sadducees bring this old cliché to Him with the thought that anyone answering their question would be ridiculous. The Sadducees would correspond to the liberal section of the contemporary church, while the Pharisees could be equated with the conservatives. The Sadducees rejected the supernatural. They, therefore, did not believe in the Resurrection.

Their question grows out of a situation created by the Mosaic system. The Sadducees attempted to make it preposterous by saying that the woman married seven times. That in itself is not likely, but it could happen. In our day there are examples of those who have been married as often, but they are more concerned about the present life than anything beyond.

The Sadducees, as a sect, arose about 300 B.C. Most of the high priests and temple politicians were Sadducees. They were prominent and rich. Isn't it interesting that today most of the church politicians and the *rich* churches are liberal? That tells us that human nature has not changed down through the centuries.

The Sadducees denied the miraculous. They stripped the Scriptures of the supernatural. (They were in direct conflict with the Pharisees who were supernaturalists.) They never accepted the inerrancy of Scripture. There is a striking similarity between the beliefs of the Sadducees and liberalism today. Liberalism is a departure from historic Christianity. Concerning conservatism and liberalism, Dr. Louis Berkhof said, "The difference is so great between them that one of them will have to surrender the term *Christian.*" I have decided that the liberal is not Christian at all. Many churches should call themselves the "Boulevard Religious Club" or the "First" or "Second Religious Club" because they are not Christian.

There was a time when those who were

unregenerate were outside the church. They denied the authority of Scripture, the deity of Christ, and the supernatural. They were called infidels and skeptics. When I first came to Southern California, you could see them on soap boxes in front of downtown churches or in the city parks. Now they are in the pulpits of the city. They are still infidels and skeptics; they still deny the deity of Christ and the supernatural. They have crept into the church unawares.

The Sadducees were the greatest enemies which Christ had and were the main instigators of the first persecution of the church. The Pharisees with the Sadducees were the leaders in the persecution of the Lord Jesus. After the death of the Lord, the Pharisees dropped the entire affair. They were no longer interested in persecuting Him or His followers; in fact, many of them became Christians. The Sadducees, however, went on with the persecution of the church. You can read about it in the third and fourth chapters of Acts.

The Resurrection was the acid test of the Sadducees, and it is the acid test of the liberal. They do not believe in a literal resurrection. It is interesting that there is no account in Scripture of a Sadducee ever coming to Christ for salvation. A Pharisee named Nicodemus was converted, and Acts 6:7 tells us, ". . . a great company of the priests were obedient to the faith." Many priests became believers, but there is no record of a Sadducee being converted.

Every young minister soon discovers that the preaching of the cross is an offense. He will never be voted the most outstanding citizen in his town. He will never find himself in a great political position, nor will he be on television very often. The subtle temptation is to throw overboard the gospel of the Lord Jesus Christ and become a popular preacher. Judas sold out the Lord. Peter denied Him but loved Him and came back to Him. When a man sells Christ for popularity, he will never come back. "Can the Ethiopian change his skin, or the leopard his spots? . . ." (Jer. 13:23). The next time some starry-eyed optimist tells you that the liberals are coming back to Christ, forget it. The Sadducees were the worst enemies that the gospel of Christ ever had—whether in the first or the twentieth centuries.

JESUS QUESTIONS THE SCRIBES

The Lord concludes this question-and-answer period by asking the scribes a question.

Then certain of the scribes answering said, Master, thou hast well said.

And after that they durst not ask him any question at all.

And he said unto them, How say they that Christ is David's son?

And David himself saith in the book of Psalms, The LORD said unto my Lord, Sit thou on my right hand,

Till I make thine enemies thy footstool.

David therefore calleth him Lord, how is he then his son?

Then in the audience of all the people he said unto his disciples,

Beware of the scribes, which desire to walk in long robes, and love greetings in the markets, and the highest seats in the synagogues, and the chief rooms at feasts;

Which devour widows' houses, and for a shew make long prayers: the same shall receive greater damnation [Luke 20:39–47].

Right here, Jesus is teaching His own virgin birth. How could David, in Psalm 110 where he is speaking of a future descendant call his own great-great-great-great-grandson his Lord? Well, the only way he can call Him his Lord is for Him to be The Lord, friend. The only way He can be The Lord is to be more than David's son. He must be virgin born to be the Son of God. This is a great thought that our Lord is teaching here.

Notice also that here Jesus definitely ascribes Psalm 110 to David. He says that David wrote this psalm by the Holy Spirit. And Jesus says that this psalm is speaking concerning Him, the Messiah.

CHAPTER 21

***THEME:** Jesus notes how people give and commends the widow; Jesus answers question in Olivet Discourse "When shall these things be?"*

Now we come to the prophetic section of Luke's gospel. Although it corresponds to the Olivet Discourse in Matthew and Mark, there is a contrast with the similarity. Matthew's gospel gives us the three questions which the disciples asked the Lord Jesus: (1) When shall these things be?—that is, one stone not left upon another; (2) What shall be the sign of thy coming? (3) And of the end of the age? (see Matt. 24:3). In the chapter before us He answers the first question. Luke deals with one of the most practical aspects of the prophecy, and there is no mystery or speculation to his meaning, because most of Luke's record is no longer prophecy; it is history. It was fulfilled in A.D. 70. After all, "prophecy is the mold into which history is poured," and there has already been some pouring done here.

JESUS NOTES HOW PEOPLE GIVE AND COMMENDS THE WIDOW

And he looked up, and saw the rich men casting their gifts into the treasury.

And he saw also a certain poor widow casting in thither two mites.

And he said, Of a truth I say unto you, that this poor widow hath cast in more than they all:

For all these have of their abundance cast in unto the offerings of God: but she of her penury hath cast in all the living that she had [Luke 21:1–4].

Compared to the wealth of that temple (and it was a wealthy temple), the widow's gift did not amount to very much. Her two little coppers did not do much to help in the upkeep of the temple. Our Lord, however, does not measure giving that way. He measures it, not by what you give, but by what you keep for yourself. We are not living under the tithe system because that dictates what you must give. What you keep for yourself is "grace" giving. There are many people who should be giving more than one tenth to the Lord because of the way He has blessed them. One man told me, "If I gave only one tenth of my substance to the Lord, I would feel as though I was stealing from Him." God looks at the sacrifice of the giver. Generally it is the one who cannot give much who is making the real sacrifice. God looks at what you keep for yourself.

Next Sunday morning someone may observe what you give, and say, "My, he gives a whole lot to the Lord's work!" But what does *God* say? He is looking at what you are keeping for yourself.

JESUS ANSWERS QUESTION IN OLIVET DISCOURSE "WHEN SHALL THESE THINGS BE?"

And as some spake of the temple, how it was adorned with goodly stones and gifts, he said,

As for these things which ye behold, the days will come, in the which there shall not be left one stone upon another, that shall not be thrown down [Luke 21:5–6].

When the Lord mentioned that the poor widow gave more than all the rich, the disciples said, "Look at this temple, the riches in it, the valuable stones in its construction!" The wealth was impressive. But did they really *see* it? Its magnificence would soon be gone. It would soon lie in rubble, not one stone left upon another. And, friend, that is the way you and I should see the wealth of this world. It won't be here long; it will soon pass away.

And they asked him, saying, Master, but when shall these things be? and what sign will there be when these things shall come to pass? [Luke 21:7].

You will find that in Matthew's and Mark's gospels the emphasis is put upon the last two questions asked of the Lord Jesus: "What is the sign of Your coming?" and "the end of the age?" The return of Christ is the more important thing in Matthew, and He answers questions that relate to it. Now here in Luke He emphasizes when "there shall not be left one stone upon another"; that is, the destruction of Jerusalem. Although this is part of the Olivet Discourse, our Lord probably answered the first question of the disciples; then later, as they came to the Mount of Olives and asked Him in detail, He gave the more formal and complete statement which we find in Matthew's gospel. Undoubtedly, our Lord gave

His teachings over and over again. After all, repetition is the way we all learn.

And he said, Take heed that ye be not deceived: for many shall come in my name, saying, I am Christ; and the time draweth near: go ye not therefore after them [Luke 21:8].

The characteristic of the times would be that there would be false Christs, which is a feature of the age in which we live, and has been since He was here. There were false messiahs in His day, and today there are those who claim supernatural power. Although they talk a great deal about Jesus, they move themselves into His place and take to themselves the glory that should be His. I think there are quite a few false Christs walking about, and certainly false religions abound.

But when ye shall hear of wars and commotions, be not terrified: for these things must first come to pass; but the end is not by and by.

Then said he unto them, Nation shall rise against nation, and kingdom against kingdom [Luke 21:9–10].

War is another characteristic of the age. War will be intensified toward the end of the age. Although pacifism is growing, the Word of God says, "For when they shall say, Peace and safety; then sudden destruction cometh upon them, as travail upon a woman with child; and they shall not escape" (1 Thess. 5:3). We are right now in that position. Wars identify the entire period until the Lord returns.

And great earthquakes shall be in divers places, and famines, and pestilences; and fearful sights and great signs shall there be from heaven [Luke 21:11].

These are another feature of the age, probably intensified toward the end.

But before all these, they shall lay their hands on you, and persecute you, delivering you up to the synagogues, and into prisons, being brought before kings and rulers for my name's sake.

And it shall turn to you for a testimony.

Settle it therefore in your hearts, not to meditate before what ye shall answer:

For I will give you a mouth and wisdom, which all your adversaries shall not be able to gainsay nor resist [Luke 21:12–15].

The Lord is speaking to the nation Israel in these verses. All of these things apply specifically to the Jews. John 15:18–19 tell us, "If the world hate you, ye know that it hated me before it hated you. If ye were of the world, the world would love his own: but because ye are not of the world, but I have chosen you out of the world, therefore the world hateth you." If you are a follower of the Lord Jesus Christ, you are not going to win any popularity contest, I can assure you.

And ye shall be betrayed both by parents, and brethren, and kinsfolks, and friends; and some of you shall they cause to be put to death.

And ye shall be hated of all men for my name's sake.

But there shall not an hair of your head perish.

In your patience possess ye your souls [Luke 21:16–19].

These verses apply directly to the 144,000 Jews who will be indestructible during the time of the Great Tribulation Period. The suffering of these Jews will be much greater during the Tribulation than it was under the German persecution with the ovens and concentration camps.

And when ye shall see Jerusalem compassed with armies, then know that the desolation thereof is nigh [Luke 21:20].

Remember they had asked Him, "When shall these things be?" (v. 7)—that is, when one stone would not be left upon another. Well, that took place when Titus the Roman besieged Jerusalem in A.D. 70. I am of the opinion that many of these men, about forty years later, remembered Christ's words when they looked over the battlements of the walls of Jerusalem and saw the banners of Titus' army unfurled, and said, "This is the day the Lord talked about." (This same thing will happen again during the last days.)

Then let them which are in Judaea flee to the mountains; and let them which are in the midst of it depart out; and let not them that are in the countries enter thereinto [Luke 21:21].

They were to do *then* what they are to do in the Great Tribulation Period. They were to get out of Jerusalem as quickly as possible. The great Jewish historian Josephus tells us about the horrible siege of Jerusalem. During the extended blockage of the city, mothers ate their own children. People died like flies, and the dead were thrown over the walls. Those who stayed either died of starvation or were sold as slaves. Again the Lord is drawing a miniature picture of what it is going to be like in the last days. There are those who claim that it could never happen a second time. It happened once, friend; that is a matter of history. The Lord said it would happen, and it did. He said it will happen again, and I believe He is right.

For these be the days of vengeance, that all things which are written may be fulfilled.

But woe unto them that are with child, and to them that give suck, in those days! for there shall be great distress in the land, and wrath upon this people.

And they shall fall by the edge of the sword, and shall be led away captive into all nations: and Jerusalem shall be trodden down of the Gentiles, until the times of the Gentiles be fulfilled [Luke 21:22–24].

The Jews were scattered. Titus put them in slavery. They built the great Colosseum in Rome. Great distress and wrath fell upon the nation of Israel. From the day that Titus entered that city, about 1900 years ago, the Jews have never been able to get the Gentiles out of Jerusalem. Gentiles have controlled Jerusalem from the day Titus conquered it until the present day. "Holy places" in Jerusalem are held by Gentiles. And there stands the Mosque of Omar where their temple should stand. Our Lord said Jerusalem would be trodden down of the Gentiles until the time of the Gentiles is fulfilled. I have watched Jerusalem for a long time, and it is still trodden down by the Gentiles. The Gentiles are still in Jerusalem. Isn't it amazing how accurate the Word of God is?

And there shall be signs in the sun, and in the moon, and in the stars; and upon the earth distress of nations, with perplexity; the sea and the waves roaring [Luke 21:25].

I think this has reference to the last days before Christ returns to the earth. This is the way it is going to be in the last days.

Men's hearts failing them for fear, and for looking after those things which are coming on the earth: for the powers of heaven shall be shaken [Luke 21:26].

There are people who quote this verse and say it is a picture of today. My friend, if I may use a common colloquialism of the streets, "You ain't seen nothin' yet." If you think we are seeing a fulfillment of this verse now, you are wrong. Things are bad today, I agree. Political crises and social distress are cause for great concern. Physical disturbances are overwhelming, but they are going to get much worse in the last days.

And then shall they see the Son of man coming in a cloud with power and great glory [Luke 21:27].

Christ could return at any moment. Things are happening so fast today that the church, the body of Christ, could be taken from this earth before you have finished reading this paragraph. If it is, I hope you will be with me in His presence.

And when these things begin to come to pass, then look up, and lift up your heads; for your redemption draweth nigh [Luke 21:28].

Are these things beginning to come to pass? I am not in a position to know. I have no inside information. All I can say is that my salvation and redemption is nearer now than when I first believed. I know that He is coming back and that is what is important to me.

And he spake to them a parable; Behold the fig tree, and all the trees;

When they now shoot forth, ye see and know of your own selves that summer is now nigh at hand.

So likewise ye, when ye see these things come to pass, know ye that the kingdom of God is nigh at hand [Luke 21:29–31].

I still consider the fig tree symbolic of the nation Israel. God's timepiece is not Gruen or Bulova, but Israel. The fig tree represents Israel (see Jer. 24:1-5; Hos. 9:10).

Verily I say unto you, This generation shall not pass away, till all be fulfilled [Luke 21:32].

"This generation" could refer to the race of Israel. It would then teach the indestructibility of this people. Or it could refer to a generation of people and their total life span. In that case it would mean that those who saw the beginning of these events would see the conclusion of them also. Because the emphasis appears to be on the rapidity in which these events transpire, rather than upon the permanence of the nation Israel, I favor the second explanation.

Heaven and earth shall pass away: but my words shall not pass away.

And take heed to yourselves, lest at any time your hearts be overcharged with surfeiting, and drunkenness, and cares of this life, and so that day come upon you unawares.

For as a snare shall it come on all them that dwell on the face of the whole earth [Luke 21:33–35].

Don't let down your guard today, friend. Don't give up. These are great days to live for God! I am not called upon to reform the world, or change the world. That is God's business, not my business. He has asked me to live for Him, and He has asked me to get His Word out. That is what I am attempting to do, and I hope you are doing this also. It is very comfortable to be in the will of God.

Watch ye therefore, and pray always, that ye may be accounted worthy to escape all these things that shall come to pass, and to stand before the Son of man [Luke 21:36].

How are you going to be worthy? The only thing that will make me worthy is my position in Christ. Therefore, I have trusted Him as my Savior, and I have committed my way to Him, so that if I am alive at the time of the Rapture, I'll be going to meet Him in the air by the grace of God.

And in the day time he was teaching in the temple; and at night he went out, and abode in the mount that is called the mount of Olives.

And all the people came early in the morning to him in the temple, for to hear him [Luke 21:37–38].

Many of us would like to have been with the group to hear Him.

CHAPTER 22

THEME: *Judas plots with the chief priests to betray Jesus; Jesus plans for the last Passover and institutes the Lord's Supper; Jesus announces His betrayal; position of the apostles in the future kingdom; Peter's denial; Jesus warns the disciples of the future; Jesus goes to Gethsemane; Jesus betrayed by Judas; Jesus arrested and led to the High Priest's house; Jesus denied by Peter; Jesus is mocked and beaten; Jesus is brought before the Sanhedrin*

JUDAS PLOTS WITH THE CHIEF PRIESTS TO BETRAY JESUS

Now the feast of unleavened bread drew nigh, which is called the Passover [Luke 22:1].

Jesus has come to Jerusalem. Six months before, in Caesarea Philippi, He had steadfastly set His face to go to Jerusalem to die. Everything He did from then on was a movement toward Jerusalem. The Mount of Transfiguration and the so-called triumphal entry are behind Him. It is the time of the Passover and He, the Lamb of God which taketh away the sins of the world, is going to die.

And the chief priests and scribes sought how they might kill him; for they feared the people [Luke 22:2].

The religious rulers would have taken Him immediately and slain Him, but they were afraid of the people. It was the Passover, which meant that people from everywhere were in the city; and they were *for* Him. They were the silent majority.

Then entered Satan into Judas surnamed Iscariot, being of the number of the twelve [Luke 22:3].

Is it possible for a Christian to be demon-possessed? Is it possible for Satan or a demon to enter a Christian? The answer, of course, is no. It is possible, however, for a church member who is not a Christian to be possessed. Some of the meanest people I have met were not in the Mafia or in jail but were members of a church. I have met some people in the church that I am confident were demon-possessed. It would be difficult to explain their conduct on any other basis. My friend, if you are going to stand on the sidelines and listen to the preaching of the gospel and do nothing about it but mix and mingle with God's people, the day will come when Satan will move into the vacant house, as we saw in Luke 11:24–26. One of Satan's demons will take up residence. That is what happened to Judas who had rejected Jesus.

And he went his way, and communed with the chief priests and captains how he might betray him unto them.

And they were glad, and covenanted to give him money [Luke 22:4–5].

The religious rulers had been wondering how they were going to take Him. Now one of His own men comes along and offers to betray Him.

And he promised, and sought opportunity to betray him unto them in the absence of the multitude [Luke 22:6].

The plot was: Wait until the crowd leaves Jerusalem. Wait until we can get Him alone so people will not know what we are doing. They planned to take Him secretly. Judas was to bide his time and let the religious rulers know when the time was right. Actually that time never came, because Jesus forced them to act immediately. Jesus, as recorded in the Gospel of John, gave Judas that sop in the Upper Room at the Last Supper and told him, "What you do, do quickly. The time has come. You are going to have to move hurriedly." And Judas did just that.

JESUS PLANS FOR THE LAST PASSOVER AND INSTITUTES THE LORD'S SUPPER

Jesus and His disciples now plan the last Passover.

Then came the day of unleavened bread, when the passover must be killed.

And he sent Peter and John, saying, Go and prepare us the passover, that we may eat.

And they said unto him, Where wilt thou that we prepare?

And he said unto them, Behold, when ye are entered into the city, there shall a man meet you, bearing a pitcher of water; follow him into the house where he entereth in.

And ye shall say unto the goodman of the house, The Master saith unto thee, Where is the guestchamber, where I shall eat the passover with my disciples?

And he shall shew you a large upper room furnished: there make ready.

And they went, and found as he had said unto them: and they made ready the passover [Luke 22:7–13].

I see no reason to read a miracle into this passage. Our Lord had been to Jerusalem many times. He knew the man who had this upper room. I am sure he had said to our Lord, "When you are in Jerusalem, bring your disciples here." Probably the Lord had already made arrangements with him to use the room and was letting him know that He needed it at this time.

And when the hour was come, he sat down, and the twelve apostles with him [Luke 22:14].

This is the time of the Last Supper, and Judas was present.

And he said unto them, With desire I have desired to eat this passover with you before I suffer:

For I say unto you, I will not any more eat thereof, until it be fulfilled in the kingdom of God.

And he took the cup, and gave thanks, and said, Take this, and divide it among yourselves:

For I say unto you, I will not drink of the fruit of the vine, until the kingdom of God shall come [Luke 22:15–18].

At the Passover the cup circulated several times, and I think the Lord participated up to the last cup. That was the cup of joy. He did not drink it. The question arises, "Did He ever drink that cup?" I think He did. On the cross they gave Him vinegar to drink, and in Hebrews it says, ". . . for the joy that was set before him [he] endured the cross . . ." (Heb. 12:2).

On the dying embers of the fading feast of Passover, the Lord Jesus Christ fanned into flame the new feast of the Lord's Supper.

And he took bread, and gave thanks, and brake it, and gave unto them, saying, This is my body which is given for you: this do in remembrance of me.

Likewise also the cup after supper, saying, This cup is the new testament in my blood, which is shed for you [Luke 22:19–20].

The Lord took two of the most frail elements in the world as symbols of His body and blood. Bread and wine—both will spoil in a few days. When He raised a monument, it was not made of brass or marble, but of two frail elements that perish. He declared that the bread spoke of His body and the wine spoke of His blood. The bread speaks of His body broken—not a *bone* broken but a broken *body* because He was made sin for us (see 2 Cor. 5:21). I do not believe He even looked human when He was taken down from that cross. Isaiah had said of Him, ". . . his visage was so marred more than any man, and his form more than the sons of men" (Isa. 52:14); and ". . . there is no beauty that we should desire him" (Isa. 53:2).

For centuries the Passover feast had looked forward to the Lord's coming and His death. Now He is in the shadow of the cross, and this is the last Passover. The Passover feast has now been fulfilled. We gather about the Lord's Table and search our hearts. What we do at this Table is in remembrance of Him. We look back to what He did for us on the cross, and we look forward to His coming again. "For as often as ye eat this bread, and drink this cup ye do shew the Lord's death till he come" (1 Cor. 11:26).

JESUS ANNOUNCES HIS BETRAYAL

But, behold, the hand of him that betrayeth me is with me on the table [Luke 22:21].

The one who was going to betray Him was in their midst. There are those who believe that Judas actually left before the institution of the Lord's Supper. I think that is accurate. Luke doesn't give the chronological order; he gives us those facts necessary to the purpose of his commentary. John makes it clear that during the Passover our Lord took the sop, gave it to Judas, and said, "That thou doest, do quickly" (see John 13:26–30). Then Judas left.

And truly the Son of man goeth, as it was determined: but woe unto that man by whom he is betrayed!

And they began to inquire among themselves, which of them it was that should do this thing [Luke 22:22–23].

Every one of the disciples believed he was capable of denying and betraying the Lord. If you are honest, you know that you also could betray Him. If He did not keep His hand on me, I could deny Him in the next five minutes. Thank God, however, He will not take His hand off me, and I rejoice in that.

POSITION OF THE APOSTLES IN THE FUTURE KINGDOM

And there was also a strife among them, which of them should be accounted the greatest [Luke 22:24].

These men who had recognized how low they could stoop also had ambitions to be the greatest. Can you imagine that? Right in the shadow of the cross these men are grasping for position. We see that in the church today. The saints today are not much of an improvement over the apostles.

And he said unto them, The kings of the Gentiles exercise lordship over them; and they that exercise authority upon them are called benefactors.

But ye shall not be so: but he that is greatest among you, let him be as the younger; and he that is chief, as he that doth serve.

For whether is greater, he that sitteth at meat, or he that serveth? is not he that sitteth at meat? but I am among you as he that serveth [Luke 22:25–27].

The Lord is telling them that He has taken the lower position. That is what He did when He took my place on the cross. It is like a master getting up from the table and telling his servant, "You sit down and eat, and I will serve you." When Jesus Christ came to earth, all mankind should have been His servant! Instead, He served mankind. He set a table of salvation and has invited us to this great feast of salvation.

Ye are they which have continued with me in my temptations [Luke 22:28].

The Lord is gracious to His disciples and commends them for continuing with Him through His testings here on earth.

And I appoint unto you a kingdom, as my Father hath appointed unto me;

That ye may eat and drink at my table in my kingdom, and sit on thrones judging the twelve tribes of Israel [Luke 22:29–30].

I am sure the apostles will have a special place in the kingdom. They bridged the gap between the Old and New Testaments. They came out of the Old Testament economy and moved into the New Testament economy. You and I are not in that position today. None of us fits into that particular place because chronologically they bridged the gap. They will be given a prominent position and will not only eat and drink at the Lord's table but will also sit on thrones and judge the twelve tribes of Israel. That will be their position.

The child of God has some great things in store for the future. The redeemed are going to occupy exalted positions. I wonder if you are working for a place in heaven. I do not mean to say that you should work for your salvation. You do not work for salvation, but you do work for your *place* in heaven. You are going to heaven by the grace of God, but you are going to be judged according to your works to see what position will be yours. Are you interested in your good works? You should be!

Now I believe that the only thing God will judge is the exercise of the gift He gave us. He gives us a gift when we are put into the body of believers at the time of salvation, and there are literally thousands of gifts. The subject of gifts is an interesting one. Do you know what one of the gifts was in the early church? There was a woman named Dorcas who sewed. Sewing was her gift. She made clothes for widows who otherwise would not have had any clothes. You will be rewarded according to your faithfulness in exercising the gift God has given to you. The way you live your Christian life is important before God, my beloved.

PETER'S DENIAL

And the Lord said, Simon, Simon, behold, Satan hath desired to have you, that he may sift you as wheat:

But I have prayed for thee, that thy faith fail not: and when thou art converted, strengthen thy brethren [Luke 22:31–32].

The word *converted* in this passage does not mean conversion as we think of it. The Lord is speaking about the time when Peter will have a change of heart and mind and his faith will be increased. At that time such a tremendous change would be wrought in Peter that he would be able to strengthen his brethren. The Lord knew that Peter would deny Him, and yet He said, "I have prayed for thee, that thy faith fail not."

The Lord today is our intercessor. He knows when you are moving toward the place of failure and stumbling. If you belong to Him, my friend, He has already prayed for you that your faith fail not. You may fail Him, but if you belong to Him, your *faith* will not fail. The reason your faith will not fail is because He has prayed for you. My, what a picture of His love!

In John 17:9 our Lord prayed to the Father, "I pray for them: I pray not for the world, but for them which thou hast given me; for they are thine." The Lord does not pray for the world. He died for the world, and you cannot ask Him to do any more than that. He died for the world, but He prays for His own that they will be kept while they are in the world. The Lord Jesus Christ prayed for you today. It may be that you did not pray for yourself but He has prayed for you.

Peter was later able to strengthen his brethren. The man who has been tested is the man who is really able to help others, even if he has failed and has come back to the Lord. This is the reason I always send a converted drunkard to talk to a drunkard. When I was a young preacher, one drunkard whom I tried to help just patted me on the knee and said, "Vernon, you are a good boy." However, he did not think I could understand his case. He was right; I could not. I found a man who had been an old drunken bum before coming to Christ and asked him to see this man. He went to his home, sat down beside him, and said, "Bill, you know you and I used to drink together. Jesus has saved me, and He can save you too." And He did—He saved Bill too. The man who has been through the experience himself is the one who can help.

And he said unto him, Lord, I am ready to go with thee, both into prison, and to death [Luke 22:33].

Peter meant every word of this, but he did not know himself, Many of us do not really know how weak we are.

And he said, I tell thee, Peter, the cock shall not crow this day, before that thou shalt thrice deny that thou knowest me [Luke 22:34].

Simon Peter simply did not believe that he could deny his Lord, but he did—before that night was over.

JESUS WARNS THE DISCIPLES OF THE FUTURE

And he said unto them, When I sent you without purse, and scrip, and shoes,

lacked ye any thing? And they said, Nothing [Luke 22:35].

It is marvelous the way the disciples were provided for during that particular period of time when the Lord sent them to the lost sheep of the house of Israel. He is now going to send them on a new mission with a new message. They will actually have a new audience because they will not be confined to Israel but will carry the message to the world.

Then said he unto them, But now, he that hath a purse, let him take it, and likewise his scrip; and he that hath no sword, let him sell his garment, and buy one [Luke 22:36].

You had better pack your suitcase and get your traveler's checks if you are going out for the Lord today and give out the gospel. You had better be prepared to protect yourself and your loved ones. We are living in difficult days. The Lord said, "He that hath no sword, let him sell his garment, and buy one." Why? For self protection, of course. They were living in days that required a sword. We need to recognize that fact also. If we do not resist evil today, all kinds of evil will befall us. We could end up in the hospital or have some of our loved ones slain.

For I say unto you, that this that is written must yet be accomplished in me, And he was reckoned among the transgressors: for the things concerning me have an end [Luke 22:37].

When the enemies of the Lord Jesus Christ put Him to death on the cross, that ended His payment for the sins of the world.

And they said, Lord, behold, here are two swords. And he said unto them, It is enough [Luke 22:38].

You do not need to overdo this thing and make your home an armed garrison, but you do need to protect yourself.

JESUS GOES TO GETHSEMANE

Gethsemane is holy ground, so I need to remove my spiritual shoes as I stand on this sacred spot, and remove my spiritual hat as I gaze in rapture upon Him. Many people glibly sing, "I'll go with Him through the garden." I cannot go with Him through the garden. The Lord Jesus left His disciples outside the garden. I will stay outside with them and peer over the wall into the darkness and listen to the travail of His soul. If our hearts are sensible, we shall thank God for the One who pressed the cup of our sorrow and suffering to His lips and drank to the very dregs. We cannot penetrate the darkness of the garden, but we can understand more fully the significance of the cup as He gave it to His own in the Upper Room. Everywhere I have tasted the cup, it has been sweet. He drank the bitter cup that my cup might be sweet. There is a mystery and a depth in that garden but not ambiguity or obscurity. We will do well to worship as we behold Him in the garden and catch the note of His voice.

Now we see through a glass darkly. It was Gregory of Nazianzen who years ago wrote: "I love God because I know Him. I adore Him, because I cannot comprehend Him." So I worship at the Garden of Gethsemane, and I do not try to have all the answers.

And he came out, and went, as he was wont, to the mount of Olives; and his disciples also followed him.

And when he was at the place, he said unto them, Pray that ye enter not into temptation [Luke 22:39–40].

There are two expressions in this passage that are quite interesting. The first one is "as he was wont" and the second one is "at the place." Apparently the Lord did not stay in the city of Jerusalem at night. We have seen this to be true in the so-called triumphal entry. He had been rejected by the city, and so He rejected the city. It is thought that He spent every night for the final week of His life either in the garden or in Bethany.

After the Lord's Supper He went to the garden. On that last night an unfamiliar transaction took place there. Although I don't know all about it, it is obvious that He wrestled with an unseen foe. He overcame the enemy there and gained the victory The victory of Calvary was won in Gethsemane. You see, at the beginning of our Lord's ministry, Satan came and tempted Him. Satan offered our Lord the kingdoms of the world if He would worship him but He would have to miss the cross, of course. Then we are told, by Dr. Luke, that Satan left Him ". . . for a season" (Luke 4:13). When did Satan return? I presume Satan returned many times, but there was a special effort at the beginning of the Lord's ministry to get Him to avoid the cross, and now at the end of the Lord's ministry this is the temptation of Satan again.

You will recall that during His ministry the Lord told His disciples that He would suffer many things and that His enemies would put

Him to death. Peter replied, ". . . Be it far from thee, Lord: this shall not be unto thee" (Matt. 16:22). Do you remember the Lord's answer to Peter? The Lord said, ". . . Get thee behind me, Satan: thou art an offence unto me: for thou savourest not the things that be of God, but those that be of men" (Matt. 16:23). Satan's theology has no place for the cross of Christ. It was Satan who came to Him in the garden. It was at this time that the Lord said to His disciples, "Pray that ye enter not into temptation."

And he was withdrawn from them about a stone's cast, and kneeled down, and prayed,
Saying, Father, if thou be willing, remove this cup from me: nevertheless not my will, but thine, be done [Luke 22: 41–42].

How far can you throw a stone? That is how far our Lord went ahead of His disciples before He kneeled down to pray. He prayed that the cup might be removed. This is a topic that has caused quite a bit of discussion. There are those who believe that He was afraid He would die before He got to the cross. I do not wish to be dogmatic, but I do not see the sense of that theory. There is no merit in a Roman cross. There is no merit in the wood. The merit is in the One who died. If He had died on the gallows or in the electric chair, His death would have had just as much value. If Christ had died in the Garden of Gethsemane, it still would have been His death that had the merit.

The cup, I think, was the cross, and I do not mean the suffering of death. The cup was that He was made sin for us. He is the Holy One of God. When my sin was put upon Him, it was repulsive. I do not know why we think we are so attractive to God. My sin put upon Christ was repulsive and awful. It was terrible, and for a moment He rebelled against it. It was in the Garden of Gethsemane under the shadow of the cross that the Tempter came to offer the Lord once again the crown without the cross. The Lord, however, had come to do His Father's will and so He could say "nevertheless not my will, but thine, be done." He committed Himself to His Father's will, although bearing your sin and mine was so repulsive to Him.

And there appeared an angel unto him from heaven, strengthening him [Luke 22:43].

There was an angelic ministry at the time of our Lord's temptation in the desert. Now there is an angelic ministry in the garden when Satan comes to tempt Him again. Luke alone recalls this fact.

And being in an agony he prayed more earnestly: and his sweat was as it were great drops of blood falling down to the ground [Luke 22:44].

Only Dr. Luke tells us that the Lord sweat great drops of blood. The Lord showed a tremendous physical reaction to the agony and conflict that confronted Him. I cannot explain what happened and do not propose to try. I am not, however, impressed by the biological explanations offered today. I realize there are some wonderful Christian doctors that have come up with some interesting explanations, but I still am not impressed. He shed His blood for me and I bow in reverence and worship.

But none of the ransomed ever knew
How deep were the waters crossed,
Nor how dark was the night that the Lord
passed through,
Ere He found His sheep that was lost:

From "The Ninety and Nine"
—Elizabeth C. Clephane

One of the tragic things of the moment is all of the American boys who have bled and died on various battlefields around the world to keep America free. How many Americans appreciate what they have done? I am not impressed with the crowd that protests war while they are living it up in pleasure-mad America. However, there is a worse tragedy than this. Christ's heart was broken because of our lost condition. He bled and died for our eternal liberty. He said, ". . . I am come that they might have life, and that they might have it more abundantly" (John 10:10). He loved a lost world so much that He went to the very depths of hell itself to offer it salvation. And the world spurns the Holy One of God, the spotless Savior who was made sin for us. Let me ask you a question. Have you rejected Him? Have you spurned Him? Are you ungrateful for what He did for you?

Stand in the hush of Gethsemane and listen. Do you hear the sob of His soul? Do you hear the falling drops of blood? Look yonder in the garden by an olive tree and see, bending low in agonizing prayer, the Savior who took upon Himself your humanity and mine. The next day He went to the cross.

JESUS BETRAYED BY JUDAS

And when he rose up from prayer, and was come to his disciples, he found them sleeping for sorrow,

And said unto them, Why sleep ye? rise and pray, lest ye enter into temptation.

And while he yet spake, behold a multitude, and he that was called Judas, one of the twelve, went before them, and drew near unto Jesus to kiss him.

But Jesus said unto him, Judas, betrayest thou the Son of man with a kiss? [Luke 22:45–48].

This is the basest act of treachery ever recorded. It is foul and loathsome. Judas knew our Lord's accustomed place of retirement, and he led the enemy there. A kiss is a badge of love and affection. Judas used it to betray Christ, which makes his act more dastardly and repugnant. It is well to observe that our Lord in His humanity was not different from other men. He needed to be identified in a crowd. This marks the moment that Jesus was delivered into the hands of sinful men.

When they which were about him saw what would follow, they said unto him, Lord, shall we smite with the sword?

And one of them smote the servant of the high priest, and cut off his right ear.

And Jesus answered and said, Suffer ye thus far. And he touched his ear, and healed him.

Then Jesus said unto the chief priests, and captains of the temple, and the elders, which were come to him, Be ye come out, as against a thief, with swords and staves?

When I was daily with you in the temple, ye stretched forth no hands against me: but this is your hour, and the power of darkness [Luke 22:49–53].

The disciples thought it was time to use that sword. It was not the time to use the sword, however, because Jesus was now on His way to the cross. The sword was for their personal defense after He was gone. Darkness and light met at the cross of Christ.

JESUS ARRESTED AND LED TO THE HIGH PRIEST'S HOUSE

Then took they him, and led him, and brought him into the high priest's house. And Peter followed afar off [Luke 22:54].

It is a dangerous thing to follow the Lord afar off. This is what Peter did. Jesus is arrested and brought before Caiaphas, the high priest acceptable to Rome. Annas, his father-in-law, was actually the high priest according to the Mosaic Law. Jesus was first brought before Annas which is recorded by John. Some believe Annas was the real rascal in back of the plot to kill Jesus. This was a meeting of the Sanhedrin. Peter was moving toward his shameful fall as he followed afar off and then sat with the wrong crowd.

JESUS DENIED BY PETER

And when they had kindled a fire in the midst of the hall, and were set down together, Peter sat down among them.

But a certain maid beheld him as he sat by the fire, and earnestly looked upon him, and said, This man was also with him.

And he denied him, saying, Woman, I know him not [Luke 22:55–57].

While the farce of the trial of Jesus was in progress, Simon Peter was in the place of great temptation. A little wisp of a maid caused Him to deny His Lord. Peter was ashamed to be known as a follower of Jesus at this time. Have we ever been in a similar position? May God forgive our cowardice and weakness as He did that of Peter.

And after a little while another saw him, and said, Thou art also of them. And Peter said, Man, I am not.

And about the space of one hour after another confidently affirmed, saying, Of a truth this fellow also was with him: for he is a Galilaean [Luke 22:58–59].

Another person pointed him out as a follower of Jesus when he attempted to get in with a different crowd. Again Simon Peter denied it and withdrew to a different spot. This time his weakness in wanting to talk too much got him into trouble. His speech gave him away as a Galilaean.

And Peter said, Man, I know not what thou sayest. And immediately, while he yet spake, the cock crew [Luke 22:60].

Friend, if Peter had left things like this, it would have been his finish. He would have ended like Judas Iscariot, but notice what happened:

And the Lord turned, and looked upon Peter. And Peter remembered the word of the Lord, how he had said unto him, Before the cock crow, thou shalt deny me thrice.

And Peter went out, and wept bitterly [Luke 22:61–62].

Simon Peter loved Jesus, and he was sincere when he promised to be loyal to Him, but he did not know his own weakness. He had not yet come to the place where he saw no good in the flesh at all. Peter wept. These were tears of genuine repentance.

Any child of God can come back to Him. "If we confess our sins, he is faithful and just to forgive us our sins, and to cleanse us from all unrighteousness" (1 John 1:9). Simon Peter was as bad as Judas—he did not sell Him, but he denied Him. The difference between Judas and Peter is that Peter repented. Our Lord prayed that Peter's faith would not fail.

JESUS IS MOCKED AND BEATEN

And the men that held Jesus mocked him, and smote him.

And when they had blindfolded him, they struck him on the face, and asked him, saying, Prophesy, who is it that smote thee?

And many other things blasphemously spake they against him [Luke22: 63–65].

The chief priests and elders took Jesus to the home of Annas. It was illegal to hold Christ without a charge, but they held Him until they could formulate one in a meeting of the Sanhedrin. You see, they arrested Him before they had a plan. The interesting thing is that they did not intend to take Him as quickly as they did. Probably Judas had come to them and said, "You better get Him while you can," thinking He might leave the city. The Lord, of course, had no intention of leaving. Have you ever noticed the many things that were illegal in the trial of Jesus? The religious rulers arrested Him for breaking the Mosaic Law; yet they broke the Law by trying Him at night and by rendering a decision the same day He was tried, which too was illegal. Also the high priest tore his garment, which was specifically prohibited by the Law.

The religious rulers put Jesus into the hands of soldiers until a charge was made against Him. If the death sentence was going to be brought against a prisoner, the soldiers played games with him. The game they played with the Lord was called "hot hand." Each soldier would double up his fist in front of the blindfolded prisoner and hit him. Only one soldier would not hit him. Then the blindfold was removed and the prisoner was to guess which soldier had not hit him. They played the game again and again until I think they beat the face of Christ to a pulp. I doubt that anyone could have recognized Him. There was no form left to His face. ". . . his visage was so marred more than any man, and his form more than the sons of men" (Isa. 52:14). The Lord must have been a frightful sight after they got through with Him. This is one of the reasons He could not carry His cross.

JESUS IS BROUGHT BEFORE THE SANHEDRIN

And as soon as it was day, the elders of the people and the chief priests and the scribes came together, and led him into their council, saying,

Art thou the Christ? tell us. And he said unto them, If I tell you, ye will not believe:

And if I also ask you, ye will not answer me, nor let me go.

Hereafter shall the Son of man sit on the right hand of the power of God [Luke 22:66–69].

The Sanhedrin asked Jesus two questions. The first one was, "Art thou the Christ?" If the Lord had answered yes, He could have been charged with treason because anyone claiming to be a messiah was regarded by Rome as potentially dangerous. In Psalm 110:1 the Father says to the Son, ". . . Sit thou at my right hand, until I make thine enemies thy footstool." He is King of kings and Lord of lords.

Then said they all, Art thou then the Son of God? And he said unto them, Ye say that I am [Luke 22:70].

This is their second charge.

And they said, What need we any further witness? for we ourselves have heard of his own mouth [Luke 22:71].

This is the basis on which they agreed to have Him crucified. Notice, however, it is not the charge they brought before the Roman court. When they moved from the Jewish court to a Roman court they changed the charges.

CHAPTER 23

***THEME:** Jesus is brought before Pilate; Jesus is brought before Herod and Barabbas is released; Jesus foretells destruction of Jerusalem and prays for His enemies; Jesus is crucified; Jesus mocked by rulers and soldiers; Jesus mocked by one thief—the other thief turns to Jesus and is accepted by Him; Jesus dismisses His spirit; Jesus is placed in the new tomb of Joseph of Arimathaea*

JESUS IS BROUGHT BEFORE PILATE

And the whole multitude of them arose, and led him unto Pilate.

And they began to accuse him, saying, We found this fellow perverting the nation, and forbidding to give tribute to Caesar, saying that he himself is Christ a King [Luke 23:1–2].

Pilate was the Roman governor of Palestine. He usually came to Jerusalem during the time of the Passover to keep an eye on the crowds that came to celebrate the feast. Since a violation of the Mosaic Law would carry absolutely no weight with a Roman, they accused Him of treason which was utterly absurd.

And Pilate asked him, saying, Art thou the King of the Jews? And he answered him and said, Thou sayest it [Luke 23:3].

Imagine this scene. Here is a carpenter in peasant garment standing before Pilate. The Jewish religious leaders have arrested Him. Pilate asks Him a question that I'm sure seemed preposterous, "Art thou the King of the Jews?" Jesus answered, "Thou sayest it." Or, "It is as you say." It was a clear statement of fact. And Pilate wanted to let Him go.

Then said Pilate to the chief priests and to the people, I find no fault in this man [Luke 23:4].

Pilate is saying that Jesus had committed no crime for which He could be charged.

And they were the more fierce, saying, He stirreth up the people, teaching throughout all Jewry, beginning from Galilee to this place [Luke 23:5].

Now the religious rulers accuse Jesus of leading a revolution. They say that He had rebelled against constituted authority.

JESUS IS BROUGHT BEFORE HEROD AND BARABBAS IS RELEASED

When Pilate heard of Galilee, he asked whether the man were a Galilaean.

And as soon as he knew that he belonged unto Herod's jurisdiction, he sent him to Herod, who himself also was at Jerusalem at that time [Luke 23:6–7].

Pilate wanted to get off the hook. Since Galilee was under Herod's jurisdiction and Herod was also in Jerusalem, Pilate sent Jesus to him. I do not believe it was an accident that Herod was in Jerusalem.

And when Herod saw Jesus, he was exceeding glad: for he was desirous to see him of a long season, because he had heard many things of him; and he hoped to have seen some miracle done by him [Luke 23:8].

Prior to this time Jesus had told the Pharisees to deliver a message to Herod which was, "Go ye, and tell that fox, Behold, I cast out devils [demons], and I do cures to-day and to-morrow, and the third day I shall be perfected" (Luke 13:32). Herod's curiosity was excited about Jesus and he wanted to see Him.

Then he questioned with him in many words; but he answered him nothing [Luke 23:9].

Our Lord did not have one word for Herod. He was an old fox. He had gone past the point of no return; he was on his way to a lost eternity. He was a member of the notorious Herod family, and our Lord made no effort to reach him.

And the chief priests and scribes stood and vehemently accused him.

And Herod with his men of war set him at nought, and mocked him, and arrayed him in a gorgeous robe, and sent him again to Pilate.

And the same day Pilate and Herod were made friends together: for before they were at enmity between themselves [Luke 23:10–12].

Can't you see the religious rulers jumping up and down and doing everything they could to see that Jesus was convicted? Herod could see that he was not going to get anywhere with Jesus; so with his men of war he decided to mock Him. The "gorgeous robe" they put upon Him was undoubtedly one of Herod's cast-off robes which they used to mock Jesus' claims of royalty. Since there was nothing else Herod could do, he decided to send Jesus back to Pilate. Here is the beginning of an ecumenical movement! Before this problem of Jesus arose, Herod and Pilate had been enemies. Now they come together because they are both opposed to Jesus.

And Pilate, when he had called together the chief priests and the rulers and the people,

Said unto them, Ye have brought this man unto me, as one that perverteth the people: and, behold, I, having examined him before you, have found no fault in this man touching those things whereof ye accuse him:

No, nor yet Herod: for I sent you to him; and, lo, nothing worthy of death is done unto him [Luke 23:13–15].

Pilate felt that there was nothing with which they could accuse Jesus. Herod had done nothing but mock Him, put a robe on Him, and send Him back to Pilate. The charges were not worth considering.

I will therefore chastise him, and release him [Luke 23:16].

Wait a minute! That is wrong. If Jesus is guilty of something, He should be punished. If He is innocent, He should be set free. To chastise Him and let Him go is compromise. I agree with Marlowe, the Englishman, that compromise is the most immoral word in the English language.

(For of necessity he must release one unto them at the feast.)

And they cried out all at once, saying, Away with this man, and release unto us Barabbas:

(Who for a certain sedition made in the city, and for murder, was cast into prison.)

Pilate therefore, willing to release Jesus, spake again to them.

But they cried, saying, Crucify him, crucify him.

And he said unto them the third time, Why, what evil hath he done? I have found no cause of death in him: I will therefore chastise him, and let him go.

And they were instant with loud voices, requiring that he might be crucified. And the voices of them and of the chief priests prevailed.

And Pilate gave sentence that it should be as they required.

And he released unto them him that for sedition and murder was cast into prison, whom they had desired; but he delivered Jesus to their will.

And as they led him away, they laid hold upon one Simon, a Cyrenian, coming out of the country, and on him they laid the cross, that he might bear it after Jesus [Luke 23:17–26].

Pilate is trying to escape making a decision about Jesus, but he cannot. Careful analysis of Pilate's part in the trial will reveal that *he* is on trial and Jesus is the Judge. Jesus is not trying to escape, but Pilate is. Pilate sought for an easy escape from these astute religious politicians. He hit upon giving them a choice between Barabbas and Jesus. To him the decision was obvious. He detected that they wanted Jesus dead because of envy. Pilate did not reckon with the depth to which religion can sink when it goes wrong. Matthew tells us that the chief priests and elders persuaded the multitude to ask for Barabbas. Pilate was startled when the crowd demanded Barabbas to be released. Imagine a judge asking a crowd for their decision as to what should be done with a man on trial! He decided that Jesus was innocent; yet he handed Jesus over to be crucified. What Roman justice!

Pilate finally had to make a decision, just as every man today has to make a decision relative to Jesus Christ. What have *you* decided about Him?

JESUS FORETELLS DESTRUCTION OF JERUSALEM AND PRAYS FOR HIS ENEMIES

And there followed him a great company of people, and of women, which also bewailed and lamented him.

But Jesus turning unto them said, Daughters of Jerusalem, weep not for me, but weep for yourselves, and for your children.

For, behold, the days are coming, in the which they shall say, Blessed are the barren, and the wombs that never bare, and the paps which never gave suck.

Then shall they begin to say to the mountains, Fall on us; and to the hills, Cover us [Luke 23:27–30].

On His way to the cross He spoke to women who were crying about Him. He said there was a day coming when it would be better not to bring children into the world, referring to the time of the Great Tribulation. Then He told the women not to weep for Him. He does not want our sympathy; He wants our faith. He did not have to die, and He did not die to gain our sympathy.

JESUS IS CRUCIFIED

And when they were come to the place, which is called Calvary, there they crucified him, and the malefactors, one on the right hand, and the other on the left [Luke 23:33].

Two criminals were crucified with the Lord.

Then said Jesus, Father, forgive them; for they know not what they do. And they parted his raiment, and cast lots [Luke 23:34].

The Lord asked His Father to forgive the crowd for crucifying Him. If He had not done this, the crowd would have been guilty of committing the unpardonable sin of putting to death the Son of God.

JESUS MOCKED BY RULERS AND SOLDIERS

And the people stood beholding. And the rulers also with them derided him, saying, He saved others; let him save himself, if he be Christ, the chosen of God [Luke 23:35].

If Jesus had come down from the cross, He would not have been the Christ. He would not have fulfilled all of Isaiah 53 which speaks of His death. "He was taken from prison and from judgment: and who shall declare his generation? for he was cut off out of the land of the living: for the transgression of my people was he stricken" (Isa. 53:8). Because Jesus Christ stayed on the cross, we can be healed of sin, the awful plague of mankind.

And the soldiers also mocked him, coming to him, and offering him vinegar,

And saying, If thou be the king of the Jews, save thyself.

And a superscription also was written over him in letters of Greek, and Latin, and Hebrew, THIS IS THE KING OF THE JEWS [Luke 23:36–38].

When Jesus was crucified, they put a superscription over Him in Greek, Latin, and Hebrew. Greek was the language of intelligence, of education, of literature, and of science. Latin was the language of law and order, of the military and of government. Hebrew was the language of religion. When Christ returns to set up His kingdom, He will be the political ruler, the educational ruler, and the spiritual ruler of this universe. How accurate the superscription was!

By the way, to get the full superscription, we have to put together all four gospel records.

JESUS MOCKED BY ONE THIEF—THE OTHER THIEF TURNS TO JESUS AND IS ACCEPTED BY HIM

And one of the malefactors which were hanged railed on him, saying, If thou be Christ, save thyself and us.

But the other answering rebuked him, saying, Dost not thou fear God, seeing thou art in the same condemnation?

And we indeed justly; for we receive the due reward of our deeds: but this man

hath done nothing amiss [Luke 23: 39–41].

Both Matthew and Mark tell us that in the beginning both thieves ridiculed the Lord Jesus. But during the six hours that they were on the cross, especially the last three hours, one thief saw that something unusual was taking place. He recognized that this One dying on the cross was not dying for Himself but for another. Although he knew Barabbas should be on that cross, he also seemed to realize He was dying for *him*. He recognized that this was a transaction between God and the Man on the cross, and the Man on the cross was *God*. Then he turned to Him in faith.

And he said unto Jesus, Lord, remember me when thou comest into thy kingdom.

And Jesus said unto him, Verily I say unto thee, To-day shalt thou be with me in paradise [Luke 23:42–43].

That very day this thief who was not fit to live on earth, according to the Roman government, went to be with the Lord. This man was a *bad* thief, not a good one, but because of his faith in the Son of God he became a saved thief. This man had faith to believe that the Lord Jesus was coming into a kingdom, and it would come after His death! Obviously, this thief had come a long way theologically while hanging on that cross.

Our Lord made the remarkable statement that this thief would be in paradise with Him that very day. These two thieves had been arrested for the same crime, tried for the same crime, condemned for the same crime, and were dying for the same crime. What was the difference between them? There wasn't any—both were thieves. The difference lies in the fact that one thief believed in Jesus Christ and one did not.

Many years ago I was playing tennis with a friend of mine who was liberal in his theology. I asked him, "What would you tell the thief on the cross? Would you tell him to run on errands of mercy? Would you tell him to use his hands for deeds of kindness?" He looked at me rather startled. I said, "Well, come on, that's what you tell your people to do." "Yes," he said, "but they can do those things." "But what are you going to tell this poor thief? What could he do? His hands and feet are not coming down from that cross until they come down in death. And, by the way, what church would you ask him to join? What ceremony would you ask him to go through?"

Friend, our Lord said to that thief, "Today you'll be with Me in paradise." He went into the presence of God because of His faith in Christ.

JESUS DISMISSES HIS SPIRIT

And it was about the sixth hour, and there was a darkness over all the earth until the ninth hour.

And the sun was darkened, and the veil of the temple was rent in the midst [Luke 23:44–45].

Christ's life was symbolized by the veil which actually shut out man from God in the Old Testament economy. When Christ died on the cross, the veil was torn in two so that the way to the Father was open!

And when Jesus had cried with a loud voice, he said, Father, into thy hands I commend my spirit: and having said thus, he gave up the ghost [Luke 23:46].

Remember, once again, that this is Dr. Luke speaking from a doctor's viewpoint. He had been in the presence of many people who had died. He knew how they died, and He knew how our Lord died. Our Lord's death was different. It has been my unpleasant duty to be in the presence of folk who are dying. There is what is commonly known as the "death rattle" when one draws his last breath. It is always with a struggle and with great effort. The two thieves on their crosses undoubtedly died that way, but the Lord Jesus did not. He voluntarily died. He dismissed His spirit. Did you notice what He said? "Father, into thy hands I commend my spirit," with a loud voice; it doesn't sound like a man whose life is ebbing away. John adds that His final word was a shout of victory—*"Tetelestai!"* It is finished!

Now when the centurion saw what was done, he glorified God, saying, Certainly this was a righteous man [Luke 23:47].

The centurion, I believe, became a saved man. He had charge of the crucifixion of Christ. At the foot of the cross he looked up and saw that something unusual was taking place, and he could glorify God. He saw that Christ was a righteous man. The other gospel writers add to Luke's account that the centurion said that He was the Son of God. I realize that the centurion's confession of faith was not enough to join the average Bible church, but let us put him back where he stands. He is at the Crucifixion. He knew nothing about the death and resurrection of Jesus Christ. He had never read any books on theology. This poor fellow was in the dark, but he couldn't have said anything that revealed his faith more than this.

And all the people that came together to that sight, beholding the things which were done, smote their breasts, and returned [Luke 23:48].

There was an ominous and fearful sort of atmosphere about the death of Christ. No gospel writer describes the death of Christ in detail. It is as if the Spirit of God pulled down the veil because the Crucifixion was too horrible to gaze upon. There is nothing here to satisfy your curiosity. Mankind was shut out from what happened on the cross. Just as we had to stand on the fringe at the Garden of Gethsemane, certainly we have to stand on the fringe of what happened at the cross. We can only look up and trust the One who is dying there for us.

And all his acquaintance, and the women that followed him from Galilee, stood afar off, beholding these things [Luke 23:49].

JESUS IS PLACED IN THE NEW TOMB OF JOSEPH OF ARIMATHAEA

The final section of this chapter deals with the burial and resurrection of Jesus Christ, which belong together. Paul wrote, "For I delivered unto you first of all that which I also received, how that Christ died for our sins according to the scriptures; And that he was buried, and that he rose again the third day according to the scriptures" (1 Cor. 15:3–4). These are the facts of the gospel. What is your relationship to these facts? Jesus died. He was buried. He rose again from the dead. What does that mean to you? Do you believe He died for you? Do you believe that when He was buried your sins were absolutely buried too, so that the sin question was settled? Do you believe that He rose again, and you rose with Him? To believe this puts us *in* Christ. God sees us in Christ. His righteousness becomes our righteousness; His standing becomes our standing, which is all that you and I have of which we can boast today.

And, behold, there was a man named Joseph, a counsellor; and he was a good man, and a just [Luke 23:50].

This man Joseph was obviously a very prominent man. He was a member of the Sanhedrin. He apparently exercised a lot of influence. He was, however, a man who stood alone when he took a stand for Christ.

(The same had not consented to the counsel and deed of them;) he was of Arimathaea, a city of the Jews: who also himself waited for the kingdom of God [Luke 23:51].

Although Joseph was a member of the Sanhedrin, he did not agree with the action they took, which tells us that the Sanhedrin did not act unanimously when they put down the edict to have the Lord Jesus Christ crucified. He was what could be called a pious, religious man; then having come face-to-face with Christ, he had taken a stand for Him. Apparently there were many believers in the Lord who were not open about it like the disciples were. However at the time of the Crucifixion the disciples went underground, and those that had been underground came out in the open. Joseph and Nicodemus were two prominent men who finally openly declared their trust in the Savior. John's gospel tells us that Nicodemus joined with Joseph in burying the Lord Jesus. They were the undertakers who had charge of His burial.

This man went unto Pilate, and begged the body of Jesus [Luke 23:52].

The faith of Joseph is out in the open now. As a man of means and influence he asks for the body of Jesus.

And he took it down, and wrapped it in linen, and laid it in a sepulchre that was hewn in stone, wherein never man before was laid [Luke 23:53].

The question arises, "Where was the tomb in which Jesus was laid?" There are two places today that are said to be that tomb. One place has a Roman Catholic church built over it, and the other one is outside the city wall. I, personally, do not believe that either place is where Jesus was buried. There were several groups that so hated Christ and Christianity that they would have removed every vestige and reminder of Him. The forces of Rome under Titus, in A.D. 70, destroyed and actually plowed the city of Jerusalem. The tomb known as the Garden Tomb, which is shown to tourists, somehow escaped destruction. I am sure it is *not* the tomb in which the body of Jesus was placed, although His tomb was undoubtedly somewhere in that area. God would not leave anything like the tomb intact, because certain people would make it a fetish rather than making the Lord Jesus the object of worship. When I was in Jerusalem at the Garden Tomb, one lady in our tour got down on her hands and knees and began to kiss the floor of the tomb; then she began to weep and howl! There is no value in that! Even if it were the tomb in which He was buried, the value is not in the tomb but in the One who is at God's right hand today, the living Savior. Let us turn our attention to Him.

And that day was the preparation, and the sabbath drew on.

And the women also, which came with him from Galilee, followed after, and beheld the sepulchre, and how his body was laid [Luke 23:54–55].

This little group of loyal women, who probably performed the menial tasks for our Lord and His disciples, were with Him to the very end.

As to the actual day of His death, the Bible does not say that He died for our sins on Wednesday, Thursday, or Friday. The Bible simply says that Jesus died for our sins. We should not waste time arguing about which day it was. I do think, however, that since it says the Sabbath drew on, it was Friday.

The women saw how the body of Jesus was laid. In other words, it was not a finished burial. Later Nicodemus and Joseph wrapped the linen around the body in mummy fashion. John's gospel adds that they wound it in linen clothes with the spices (about one hundred pounds of myrrh and aloes), as ". . . the manner of the Jews is to bury" (John 19:40).

And they returned, and prepared spices and ointments; and rested the sabbath day according to the commandment [Luke 23:56].

Because the Sabbath day was a day of rest, they did not come to the tomb. They prepared the spices to put on the Lord's body, but they wasted their spices because by the time they came to do it, His body was no longer in the tomb. Mary of Bethany, you recall, had anointed His body while He was alive and was criticized for wasting the precious ointment. But hers was not wasted.

CHAPTER 24

THEME: *Jesus is raised from the dead—leaves Joseph's tomb; Jesus goes down the road to Emmaus—reveals Himself to two disciples; Jesus goes to the assembled disciples—reveals Himself to the Eleven; Jesus gives commission to go; Jesus promises to send the Holy Spirit; Jesus ascends to heaven in the attitude of blessing His own*

JESUS IS RAISED FROM THE DEAD—LEAVES JOSEPH'S TOMB

Now upon the first day of the week, very early in the morning, they came unto the sepulchre, bringing the spices which they had prepared, and certain others with them [Luke 24:1].

The women came bringing their spices. I have always wanted to ask those women what they did with those spices. Mary was rebuked when she anointed the living Lord, "Why are you wasting this expensive ointment?" (see John 12:5). But her ointment was not wasted. The spices of these women were not used, and I think they went to waste. The women were probably so excited that they just left the spices at the tomb.

And they found the stone rolled away from the sepulchre [Luke 24:2].

The stone was not rolled away to let the Lord Jesus out but to let them in.

And they entered in, and found not the body of the Lord Jesus [Luke 24:3].

He had already left.

And it came to pass, as they were much perplexed thereabout, behold, two men stood by them in shining garments:

And as they were afraid, and bowed down their faces to the earth, they said unto them, Why seek ye the living among the dead?

He is not here, but is risen: remember how he spake unto you when he was yet in Galilee,

Saying, The Son of man must be delivered into the hands of sinful men, and be crucified, and the third day rise again.

And they remembered his words [Luke 24:4–8].

The question, "Why do you seek the living among the dead?" was a good one. Why did the women come, and why did Peter (and John) come running to the tomb? They were seeking the dead among the dead; they were not seeking the living. They did not believe that the Lord Jesus Christ would come back from the dead.

Some people feel there is conflict among the Gospels concerning the morning of the Resurrection and the events which took place. A thorough study of the Gospels will reveal that there is no conflict at all. Each writer is presenting a different facet of the Resurrection. Luke tells us about the coming of the women to the tomb and dwells on that. The women remembered these words of Jesus when the angels reminded them. Sometimes you can hear something—and almost know it is true—but do not believe it. That is the way a lot of people treat the Word of God today. All of the gospel writers make it abundantly clear that the Lord Jesus told His disciples again and again that He was going to Jerusalem to die, and be raised again on the third day. They heard what He said but somehow they really did not believe it.

And returned from the sepulchre, and told all these things unto the eleven, and to all the rest.

It was Mary Magdalene, and Joanna, and Mary the mother of James, and other women that were with them, which told these things unto the apostles [Luke 24:9–10].

You would think the apostles would be greatly impressed by what the women told them, but notice their reaction:

And their words seemed to them as idle tales, and they believed them not [Luke 24:11].

You would have thought that these women would have been considered credible witnesses and their testimony would have been accepted. The first disbelievers of the Resurrection were the apostles themselves. Yet our Lord had told them over and over what was going to happen concerning His death and resurrection.

Then arose Peter, and ran unto the sepulchre; and stooping down, he beheld the linen clothes laid by themselves, and departed, wondering in himself at that which was come to pass [Luke 24:12].

Simon Peter had to turn over in his mind all the evidence before he came to a decision about what had happened. I do not think he was quite as alert mentally as was John the apostle. John tells us in his gospel that when he went to the tomb and looked in, he believed. John was convinced about the Lord's resurrection immediately, but Simon Peter had to think about it for awhile.

JESUS GOES DOWN THE ROAD TO EMMAUS—REVEALS HIMSELF TO TWO DISCIPLES

Now we come to the road to Emmaus. The Emmaus road is an interesting one to be on. We hear a lot today about being on the Jericho road—but that's where you fall among thieves. I would much rather take the Emmaus road where we meet our resurrected Lord.

And, behold, two of them went that same day to a village called Emmaus, which was from Jerusalem about threescore furlongs [Luke 24:13].

There is some question as to the distance of Emmaus from Jerusalem. It was probably about seven miles.

And they talked together of all these things which had happened.

And it came to pass, that, while they communed together and reasoned, Jesus himself drew near, and went with them.

But their eyes were holden that they should not know him [Luke 24:14–16].

On the road to Emmaus the Lord joined two disciples who were talking about Him. They had not seen the Lord, and candidly, they did not believe that He had risen from the dead. They did not believe that the One who had joined them on the road was the resurrected Christ. To begin with, they were not looking for Him at all.

And he said unto them, What manner of communications are these that ye have one to another, as ye walk, and are sad? [Luke 24:17].

Jesus raised the question.

And the one of them, whose name was Cleopas, answering said unto him, Art thou only a stranger in Jerusalem, and hast not known the things which are come to pass there in these days? [Luke 24:18].

This question, raised by Cleopas, reveals a sidelight not given by anyone but Dr. Luke. The arrest, Crucifixion, and purported Resurrection from the dead had stirred Jerusalem. These two men could not believe that there was anyone in the area that did not know about it. It would be like walking down the street in your hometown with a friend and discussing the trip to the moon. A stranger joins you and says, "You mean someone has been to the moon?" You would naturally react. It would be difficult for someone to live in this day and age and not know that someone has been to the moon and back to earth. It was just as incredible to these disciples that someone had not heard about the events of the past few days. Paul, in his defense before King Agrippa, said that he was persuaded that none of these things were hidden from him ". . . for this thing was not done in a corner" (Acts 26:26). It was not something that was done secretly. It was public news, and everyone in the area was talking about it.

And he said unto them, What things? And they said unto him, Concerning Jesus of Nazareth, which was a prophet mighty in deed and word before God and all the people [Luke 24:19].

Did you notice what they said? They said that He "*was* a prophet." They thought He was dead. They did not believe that He had come back from the dead.

And how the chief priests and our rulers delivered him to be condemned to death, and have crucified him [Luke 24:20].

Now they gave a witness to the death of Christ.

But we trusted that it had been he which should have redeemed Israel: and beside all this, to-day is the third day since these things were done [Luke 24:21].

These men were saying that they had hoped Jesus Christ was the Prophet that would redeem Israel, but now it was too late. He had been crucified. He was dead. They did not have much faith in what this Prophet had said, you can be sure of that.

Yea, and certain women also of our company made us astonished, which were early at the sepulchre;

And when they found not his body, they came, saying, that they had also seen a vision of angels, which said that he was alive [Luke 24:22–23].

These men did not believe the report of the women. They did not believe the tomb was empty. You can see how much unbelief there was in the Resurrection at this time. But there is a little hope and a little light that breaks upon the thinking of these two men.

And certain of them which were with us went to the sepulchre, and found it even so as the women had said: but him they saw not [Luke 24:24].

Just as it seemed their faith ballooned up, they put a pin in it—"but him they saw not." They did not know what had happened, but somehow the body had been taken away. They were not prepared to explain what had taken place, but the fact remained that no one had seen the Lord.

Then he said unto them, O fools, and slow of heart to believe all that the prophets have spoken [Luke 24:25].

This is a very important section, friend. The Lord, in speaking about His resurrection, did not show them the prints of the nails in His hands to prove it. He referred them to the Scriptures rather than to the nail prints. He told them, "You should have believed what the prophets said." It is well to note the Lord's attitude toward the Bible. The day in which we live is a day of doubt. There are people who are actually saying that you cannot be intelligent and believe the Bible. Many people are afraid that they will not be considered intelligent; so they don't come out flat-footed and say whether they believe the Bible or not. I suppose it is the most subtle and satanic trap of our day to discount the inerrancy and integrity of the Word of God. Christ says a man is a *fool* not to believe it. He gave an unanimous and wholehearted acceptance of the Bible's statements, with no ifs, ands, or buts.

The other day I picked up a seminary professor and took him to a filling station, because he had car trouble. As we rode along, I asked him about his school's viewpoint of the inerrancy of Scripture. "Well," he said, "you mean the infallibility of the Bible?" I replied, "Wait a minute, you are arguing semantics. You know what I mean, and I know what you mean. Do you or do you not believe in the inerrancy of Scripture?" Well, he wouldn't make a forthright declaration whether or not he believed it. He wanted to appear intelligent. Frankly, a lot of these men do not have the intestinal fortitude to stand for the Word of God. I think their problem is more intestinal than intellectual!

Now notice that the Lord puts the emphasis upon the Word of God.

Ought not Christ to have suffered these things, and to enter into his glory?

And beginning at Moses and all the prophets, he expounded unto them in all the scriptures the things concerning himself [Luke 24:26–27].

He began with Moses and the prophets. Moses and the prophets had spoken of *Him*. His death and resurrection had fulfilled their prophecies. I'd love to have been there that evening, listening to Him, wouldn't you? Christ says that there are two things which are essential to the understanding of the Word of God. They are simple but important. First, as verse 25 indicates, we must have faith in the Bible. Christ said, "O fools, and slow of heart to believe all that the prophets have spoken." Pascal said, "Human knowledge must be understood to be believed, but divine knowledge must be believed to be understood." I think the Bible is a closed book to the critic and the infidel. He can learn a few facts, but he misses the message. On the other hand, some simple soul whose heart is turned in humble faith to God will be enlightened by the Holy Spirit of God. The eyes of his understanding will be opened. Great men of the past have come to the pages of Scripture for light and life in the hours of darkness or crisis. It is not smart to ridicule the Bible. The Lord said, "You are a *fool* not to believe it." I would rather lack sophistication and subtlety than to be a fool.

Then the Lord says that the Bible can only be divinely understood. Human intellect is simply not enough to comprehend its truths. Verse 45 tells us: "Then opened he their understanding, that they might understand the scriptures." Then in 1 Corinthians 2:14 Paul declares, "But the natural man receiveth not the things of the Spirit of God: for they are foolishness unto him: neither can he know them, because they are spiritually discerned." There are things that are above and beyond human comprehension, and only the Holy Spirit of God can make them real to us. Our prayer ought to be, "Open Thou mine eyes that I may behold wondrous things out of Thy Word." We should come with a humble attitude to the Word of God. Just because you read the Bible does not mean that you know it. The Holy Spirit of God will have to make it real to you.

And they drew nigh unto the village, whither they went: and he made as though he would have gone further.

But they constrained him, saying, Abide with us: for it is toward evening, and the day is far spent. And he went in to tarry with them.

And it came to pass, as he sat at meat with them, he took bread, and blessed it, and brake, and gave to them.

And their eyes were opened, and they knew him; and he vanished out of their sight [Luke 24:28–31].

The resurrected, glorified Christ wants to fellowship with those who are His own. He only fellowships with those who believe in Him. They wanted Him to stay with them, and He was known to them at the table in the breaking of the bread.

Eating around a table is a wonderful time to share the things of Christ. There is nothing wrong with a church banquet, provided it is not all given over to hearing some soloist, or watching a magician, or some type of entertainment. We have too many church programs that leave Jesus Christ out. To have true fellowship and blessing, He must be in the midst breaking the bread.

And they said one to another, Did not our heart burn within us, while he talked with us by the way, and while he opened to us the scriptures?

And they rose up the same hour, and returned to Jerusalem, and found the eleven gathered together, and them that were with them [Luke 24:32–33].

Late as it is, they hurry back over the miles with the wonderful news.

Saying, The Lord is risen indeed, and hath appeared to Simon [Luke 24:34].

The Lord Jesus Christ appeared to Simon Peter privately because there was something that needed to be straightened out. Remember that Peter had denied Him. The restoration to fellowship was a personal and private transaction between Peter and his Lord.

JESUS GOES TO THE ASSEMBLED DISCIPLES—REVEALS HIMSELF TO THE ELEVEN

And they told what things were done in the way, and how he was known of them in breaking of bread.

And as they thus spake, Jesus himself stood in the midst of them, and saith unto them, Peace be unto you.

But they were terrified and affrighted, and supposed that they had seen a spirit [Luke 24:35–37].

I am sure our reaction would have been the same if we had been there.

And he said unto them, Why are ye troubled? and why do thoughts arise in your hearts?

Behold my hands and my feet, that it is I myself: handle me, and see; for a spirit hath not flesh and bones, as ye see me have [Luke 24:38–39].

I do not want to labor this point, but the glorified body of our Lord was flesh and *bones* and not flesh and blood. His blood had been shed on the cross.

And when he had thus spoken, he shewed them his hands and his feet.

And while they yet believed not for joy, and wondered, he said unto them, Have ye here any meat?

And they gave him a piece of a broiled fish, and of an honeycomb.

And he took it, and did eat before them [Luke 24:40–43].

This is a master stroke and Dr. Luke shares it with us. The proof that He, our Lord and Savior, is a human being is that He could eat food.

And he said unto them, These are the words which I spake unto you, while I was yet with you, that all things must be fulfilled, which were written in the law of Moses, and in the prophets, and in the psalms, concerning me.

Then opened he their understanding, that they might understand the scriptures [Luke 24:44–45].

They simply had not believed His Word. In order to understand the Bible you have to have the Spirit of God open your mind and heart. Only the Spirit can make Bible study real to you.

JESUS GIVES COMMISSION TO GO

And said unto them, Thus it is written, and thus it behoved Christ to suffer, and to rise from the dead the third day:

And that repentance and remission of sins should be preached in his name among all nations, beginning at Jerusalem [Luke 24:46–47].

Notice the global outlook of these verses. The viewpoint here is worldwide. This gospel is to go to the ends of the earth.

JESUS PROMISES TO SEND THE HOLY SPIRIT

And ye are witnesses of these things.

And, behold, I send the promise of my Father upon you: but tarry ye in the city of Jerusalem, until ye be endued with power from on high [Luke 24:48–49].

Men witnessing to the world was His method. And the message was that He died and rose again from the dead, and that, by trusting Him, sinners could be saved. The power to carry the witness to the world is the Holy Spirit.

JESUS ASCENDS TO HEAVEN IN THE ATTITUDE OF BLESSING HIS OWN

And he led them out as far as to Bethany, and he lifted up his hands, and blessed them.

And it came to pass, while he blessed them, he was parted from them, and carried up into heaven [Luke 24:50–51].

The last time the disciples saw the Lord He was in the attitude of blessing. When He comes the next time He will come in judgment upon the world. He will not come in judgment for the church; He will come in blessing. We are to look with great joy and anticipation for His coming.

And they worshipped him, and returned to Jerusalem with great joy:

And were continually in the temple, praising and blessing God. Amen [Luke 24:52–53].

This is the testimony of the Gospel of Luke. I trust that it has been a blessing to you. My own heart has been blessed, my mind enriched, and my will strengthened. Because I have studied again this marvelous Gospel of Luke, I want to know Him better. I hope you do too.

BIBLIOGRAPHY

(Recommended for Further Study)

Geldenhuys, Norval. *Commentary on the Gospel of Luke.* Grand Rapids, Michigan: Wm. B. Eerdmans Publishing Co., 1951.

Hendriksen, William. *Exposition of the Gospel of Luke.* Grand Rapids, Michigan: Baker Book House, 1978. (Very comprehensive.)

Ironside, H. A. *Addresses on the Gospel of Luke.* Neptune, New Jersey: Loizeaux Brothers, 1947.

Kelly, William. *An Exposition of the Gospel of Luke.* Addison, Illinois: Bible Truth Publishers, n.d.

Luck, G. Coleman. *Luke.* Chicago, Illinois: Moody Press, n.d. (Concise survey.)

Morgan, G. Campbell. *The Gospel According to Luke.* Old Tappan, New Jersey: Fleming H. Revell Company, n.d.

Morris, Leon. *The Gospel According to St. Luke.* Grand Rapids, Michigan: Wm. B. Eerdmans Publishing Co., 1975.

Pentecost, J. Dwight. *The Words and Works of Jesus Christ.* Chicago, Illinois: Moody Press, 1981.

Thomas, W. H. Griffith. *Outline Studies in the Gospel of St. Luke.* Grand Rapids, Michigan: Wm. B. Eerdmans Publishing Co., 1950.

Van Ryn, August. *Meditations in Luke.* Neptune, New Jersey: Loizeaux Brothers. n.d.

Vos, Howard F. *Beginnings in the Life of Christ.* Chicago, Illinois: Moody Press, 1975.

The Gospel According to

JOHN

INTRODUCTION

It is generally assumed that the Gospel of John is easy to understand. Often you hear the cliché, "The Gospel of John is the *simple* gospel." And the simplicity of the language has deceived a great many folk. It is written in monosyllabic and disyllabic words. Let me lift out a couple of verses to illustrate. Notice how simple these words are: "He came unto his own, and his own received him not. But as many as received him, to them gave he power to become the sons of God, even to them that believe on his name" (John 1:11–12).

We have no problem with the words themselves, but actually, we're dealing here with the most profound gospel. Take an expression like this: "ye in me, and I in you" which appears in John 14:20. Seven words—one conjunction, two prepositions and four pronouns—and you could ask any child in the fourth grade the meaning of any one of those words and he could give you a definition. But you put them together—"ye in me, and I in you"—and neither the most profound theologian nor the greatest philosopher has ever been able to probe the depths of their meaning. "Ye in me" we know means salvation; "and I in you" means sanctification, but beyond that none of us can go very far. We think, sometimes, because we know the meaning of words that we know what is being said. The words are simple, but the meaning is deep.

Jerome said of John's gospel, "John excels in the depths of divine mysteries." And no truer statement was ever made. Dr. A. T. Pierson put it like this, "It touches the heart of Christ."

Though it is assumed that John is the simple gospel, it's not always assumed that the apostle John is the author of it. The Baur-Tubingen School in Germany years ago began an attack upon the Gospel of John. And this has been a place where the liberal has really had a field day. I took a course in seminary (even in my day) on the authorship of the Gospel of John. The professor finally concluded the course by saying he thought John was the author. A wag in the class remarked, "Well, I believed John wrote it before I started the class and I believe it now; so I just wasted a semester!" Let me assure you that we are not going to waste time here relative to the authorship of this gospel other than to mention two statements that make it quite obvious that John is the writer of it.

One of the reasons it was felt that John might not be the writer was because Papias (I've quoted him now for each of the Gospels) was thought to have never mentioned the authorship of John. But Professor Tischendorf, the German who found the Codex Sinaiticus, which is probably our best manuscript of the Old Testament, down in Saint Catherine's Monastery in the Sinaitic peninsula, was working in the Vatican library when he came upon an old manuscript that has a quotation from Papias in which it was made clear that John was the author of this gospel. I personally wouldn't want any better authority than that. Also, Clement of Alexandria, who lived about A.D. 200, makes the statement that John was persuaded by friends and also moved by the Spirit of God to write a spiritual gospel. And I believe that the Gospel of John is that spiritual gospel. In my mind there's not a shadow of a doubt that John is the author.

However, the more significant question is: *Why* did John write his gospel? It was the last one written, probably close to A.D. 100. All the other apostles were dead, the writers of the New Testament were all gone, and he alone was left. In an attempt to answer this question we find again a diversity of theories. There are those who say that it was written to meet the first heresy of the church which was Gnosticism. The Gnostics believed that Jesus was God but not man at all, that the apostles only thought they saw Him, but actually did not. And Irenaeus expressly makes the statement that the purpose of John was to confute the Gnostic Cerinthus. But Tholuck makes it very clear that this is not a polemic gospel at all and he is not attempting to meet that issue. Also, there are those who say that it is a supplement to what the others had written, that he merely added other material. But Hase answers that by saying, "This Gospel is no mere patchwork to fill up a vacant space."

You see, these theories do not give an adequate answer to account for all the peculiar facts that are in this gospel which a true explanation must do. And, in my judgment, the only satisfactory explanation is that John wrote at the request of the church which already had three Gospels (Matthew, Mark, and Luke were being circulated) and wanted something more spiritual and deep, something that would enable them to grow. That's exactly what Augustine, the great saint of the early church, said:

> In the four Gospels, or rather in the four books of the one Gospel, the Apostle St. John not undeservedly with reference to his spiritual understanding compared to an eagle, has lifted higher, and far more sublimely than the other three, his proclamation, and in lifting it up he has wished our hearts also to be lifted (Gregory, *Key to the Gospels*, pp. 285-286).

That is the purpose of the Gospel of John. That is the reason that he wrote it.

Accordingly, therefore, when we come to the Gospel of John, we find that he does not take us to Bethlehem. We will never grow spiritually by singing "O Little Town of Bethlehem" umpteen times at Christmas. John won't take us to Bethlehem because he wants you and me to grow as believers. John takes us down the silent corridors of eternity, through the vast emptiness of space, to a beginning that is not a beginning at all. "In the beginning was the Word" (John 1:1). Some say that this world came into being three billion years ago. I think they're pikers. I think it has been around a lot longer than that. What do you think God has been doing in eternity past, twiddling His thumbs? May I say to you, He had a great deal to do in the past, and He has eternity behind Him. So when you read, "In the beginning," go as far back as your little mind can go into eternity past, put down your peg—and Jesus Christ comes out of eternity to meet you. "In the beginning was [not is] the Word, and the Word was with God, and the Word was God" (John 1:1). Then come on down many more billions of years. "All things were made by him; and without him was not any thing made that was made" (John 1:3). Then John, in the fourteenth verse, takes another step: "And the Word was made flesh, and dwelt among us" (John 1:14).

The Greek philosophers and the Greek mind for which Luke wrote would stop right there and say, "We're through with you. We can't follow you." But John was not writing for them, and he goes even further. "No man hath seen God at any time; the only begotten Son, which is in the bosom of the Father, he hath declared him" (John 1:18). "Declared him" is *exegeted* Him, led Him out in the open where man can see Him and come to know Him. The Man who had no origin is the Son who comes out of eternity.

Luke, who was a medical doctor, looked at Him under a "microscope." Though John's method is altogether different, he comes to the same conclusion as did Luke. You could never call John's method scientific. The Christian who has come to a knowledge of Christ and faith in Him doesn't need to have the Virgin Birth gone over again; he already believes that. Therefore, when he comes to the Gospel of John, he finds sheer delight and joy unspeakable as he reads and studies it.

Unfortunately, though, he thinks the unbeliever ought to have it also. And you'll find it is used in personal work more than any other gospel. After all, doesn't the average Christian consider it the simple gospel? Is it simple? It's profound. It's for believers. It enables them to grow.

When I was a pastor in Pasadena, I had a doctor friend who, because of his position, was able to get together students at Cal Tech for a Bible class. Do you know what he taught? You're right, the Gospel of John. He told me, "You know, I really shook that bunch of boys with the first chapter." I met him several weeks after that and asked him how the class was getting on. "Oh," he said, "they quit coming." Well, after all, they had been in a school where you pour things into a test tube, where you look at things under a microscope. I said, "Why didn't you take the Gospel of Luke?" "Because," he said, "I wanted to give them the simple gospel." Well, he didn't. John is not simple; it's profound. It is for believers.

Also there was a seminary professor in this area not long ago who was asked to teach the Bible to a group of businessmen at a noon luncheon. Guess what book he taught. You're right! He said, "They don't know very much, so I'll give them the Gospel of John." I wish he'd given them the Gospel of Mark. That's the gospel of action, the gospel of power, the gospel for the strong man. But he gave them the Gospel of John.

The Gospel of John is for those who already believe. When you come to chapters thirteen through seventeen you can write a sign over it, *For Believers Only* and you could put under that, *All Others Stay Out*. I don't think that section was ever meant for an unbeliever. Jesus took His own into the Upper Room and revealed to them things that enabled them to grow. And no other gospel writer gives us that. Why? Because they're the evangelists who are presenting Christ as the Savior of the world. Somebody asks, "But doesn't John do that?" Yes, he does, but he is primarily writing for the growth of believers.

John gives more about the resurrected Christ than does any other gospel writer; in fact, more than all the others put together. Paul said that, though we have known Christ after the flesh, we don't know Him that way anymore. Rather, we know Him as the resurrected Christ. For this reason John attempts to give the appearances of Jesus after His resurrection, and he mentions seven of them.

The first was one of the most dramatic as He appeared to Mary Magdalene there in the garden. The second was to the disciples in the Upper Room, Thomas being absent. The third appearance was again to the disciples in the Upper Room with Thomas present (these three appearances are recorded in ch. 20). Then we see Him appearing by the Sea of Galilee. Several disciples were out fishing. He called to them from the shore, "Do you have any fish?" (see John 21:5).

He is going to ask you that some day, and He's going to ask me. Have you been doing any fishing recently? Well, you catch them only the way He tells you. You have to fish by His instructions.

And then He prepared breakfast for them. I wish I had been there for that outdoor breakfast. That was a real cookout. And friend, He still wants to feed you in the morning—also during the day and in the evening—with spiritual food. Then He commissioned Simon Peter: "Simon, do you love Me?" (see John 21:15–17). Jesus did not say that you have to be a graduate of a seminary to be able to serve Him. He asked, "Do you love Me?" That's the one condition. Don't misunderstand me. If you love Him, you will want training to prepare you for the ministry He has for you, but He wants to know that you love Him. The reason multitudes of folk are not serving Him today is that they do not love Him. And then Peter was told that he was to be a martyr; but John, no, he will live on in order to write this gospel, three epistles, and the Book of Revelation. There are the seven appearances that John records, and all of them are for believers; they minister to us today.

At the time of the birth of Christ there was a great expectation throughout the heathen world. That was a strange thing.

> Suetonius relates that "an ancient and definite expectation had spread throughout the East, that a ruler of the world would, at about that time, arise in Judaea." Tacitus makes a similar statement. Schlegel mentions that Buddhist missionaries traveling to China met Chinese sages going to seek the Messiah about 33 A.D. (*Life of Vespasian*, c. iv.).

There was an expectation throughout the world at that time that He might come. And it was out of the mysterious East that the wise men came to Jerusalem, "Saying, Where is he that is born King of the Jews? . . ." (Matt. 2:2).

The marvel is that this Gospel of John, so definitely designed to meet the need of believers, is also designed for the Oriental mind as is no other. Whom do I mean by Orientals? The Egyptians, the Babylonians, the Persians, the uncounted millions in India and in China. Even to this good day we know so little about that area of the world. What about Tibet or Outer Mongolia? It is still the mysterious East. We do know this: there is fabulous wealth there, and right next to it is abject poverty. Out of this land of mystery came the wise men. They were bringing gifts—gold, frankincense, and myrrh for Him. There are a lot of questions to be answered there. Out of that land of mystery they came. That Oriental splendor that we've heard so much about reveals unbelievable wealth, and it is still there—ornate palaces, gaudy grandeur, priceless gems. It has so entranced the West that, when Columbus started out for this country (we give him credit for discovering America, but he wasn't looking for our continent), he was trying to find a new route to the East in order to bring back something of the wealth that was there.

However, by the side of that wealth there is extreme poverty of the basest sort, dire destitution, millions living in squalor and misery. Their worldly goods consist of the rags they have on their backs. One hundred million will die of starvation in this next decade, we're told. You may ask, "Well, why don't we send food for them?" There's not enough to go around. Our decision is what hundred million will starve? Will it be these or those? But the thing that arrests us is that the poor were crying for help, and the wealthy had found no solution to the problems of life. The Orient gave freest reign to human desires. Although they had this freedom, there was no satisfaction. They've had the great pagan religions—Buddhism, Shintoism, Hinduism, Confucianism, and Mohammedanism. Yet out of that area, with all that they had, their wise men came asking, ". . . Where is he that is born King of the Jews? for we have seen his star in the east, and are come to worship him" (Matt. 2:2). They needed salvation. They had none; no religion ever gave that to them. And this is the reason people in the mysterious East have reveled in the Gospel of John as no others have. It is a mind today that will revel in the Gospel of John. The Lord Jesus can meet the need of this type of mind, as John reveals.

Out of heaven's glory He came, that One who was before any beginning that we can envision. "And the Word was made flesh" and walked down here among men. The Orient had religion. After all, Israel belonged to that area of the world. The Orient had all kinds of religion. They had temples—ornate, hideous, with degrading rituals. They had cults of the occult. And John tells us that the first public act of the Lord Jesus was to go into the temple of that day and cleanse it. By this He is telling them something, these people who worshiped in their degrading temples, that God is *holy.* If you're going to worship God you'll have to be cleansed; the temple will have to be cleansed; there can be no compromise with evil or wrong.

A religious ruler came to Jesus one night—John alone tells us this. Our Lord that night said to this religious ruler, who had everything and was religious to his fingertips, "You must be born again" (see John 3:3). He needed to have a new life and get rid of the old religion. Jesus said that He had not come to sew a patch on the old garment, but He came to give them the robe of righteousness that would enable them to stand before a holy God. This is what that area of the world needed.

Womanhood was degraded in the Orient. Our Lord ennobled womanhood because He came, born of a woman. He went to a wedding to answer the mockery that they'd made of marriage with the harems of the East. Christ went to a wedding and put His blessing upon it. Also Jesus sat down at a well and had a conversation with a woman of very questionable character. But she was a woman for whom He later died. The soul of a woman was as precious to Him as the soul of a man.

Christ fed the multitudes, followed the meal with a discourse on the Bread of Life, and then escaped because He did not want them to make Him king of their stomachs.

The Oriental mind would understand Jesus' discourse on the Bread of Life. It is unfortunate that the managers of our supermarkets don't understand it—they think it's bread and beans on the shelf that's important, and He said it's not. A man in the Orient who hasn't bread and beans will understand that. I am afraid some of us miss it today.

The Lord Jesus said in this gospel, "I am the light of the world; I am the bread of life; I am the way, the truth and the life." And the Orient was wretched and perishing in that day, as it is today. John says: "And many other signs truly did Jesus in the presence of his disciples, which are not written in this book: But these are written, that ye might believe that Jesus is the Christ, the Son of God; and that believing ye might have life through his name" (John 20:30–31). The thing that they needed above everything else was life. And, friend, this is what the whole world needs today—not religion, but life!

Now before we begin our study of this magnificent gospel, let me call your attention to some striking features.

The first three Gospels are called the Synoptic Gospels because they are written from the same viewpoint with a similar pattern. The fourth Gospel is different.

1. Matthew and Mark emphasize the miracles of Jesus, and Luke gives attention to the parables. John does neither.

2. The miracles in John are given as signs and were chosen with a great deal of discrimination in order to interpret certain great truths. (For example, the discourse on the Bread of Life follows the feeding of the five thousand.) There are eleven specific signs in the Gospel of John.

3. There are no parables in the fourth gospel. The word *parable* does occur one time in John 10:6, but it is not the regular Greek word *parabolē* but *paroimia.* This word ought not to be translated "parable" at all. The story of the Good Shepherd is not a parable; it is a discourse.

John gives us a chronological order which is well to note. The fact of the matter is, if you will follow it along, it will give you a ladder on which you can fit the three-year ministry of Christ. (For example, in John 1:29, 35 he says, "The next day . . . , the next day.") He's giving not only a logical but also a chronological sequence in his gospel. He also gives attention to places and cities—for example, "Bethabara beyond Jordan" (John 1:28); "Cana of Galilee" (John 2:1).

The deity of Christ is emphasized in this gospel and is actually in the foreground. But the humanity of Christ is not lost sight of. Do you notice it is only John who tells about His trip through Samaria, and that He sat down at the well, and that He was weary with His journey? Can you think of anything more human than that? Well, I can think of one thing—Jesus wept. And it is John who tells us that, by the way.

The name *Jesus* is used almost entirely to the exclusion of *Christ* in this gospel. That is strange because the emphasis is upon the deity of Christ, and you'd think that he would use the name *Christ*. Then why does he use the name *Jesus?* It is because God became a man.

There is a mighty movement in this gospel and it is stated in John 16:28. "I came forth from the Father, and am come into the world: again, I leave the world, and go to the Father." God became a man; this is the simple statement of the sublime fact.

OUTLINE

I. Prologue—Incarnation, Chapter 1:1–18
   A. Word Is God, Chapter 1:1–3
   B. Word Became Flesh, Chapter 1:14
   C. Word Revealed God, Chapter 1:18

II. Introduction, Chapter 1:19–51
   A. Witness of John the Baptist, Chapter 1:19–36
   B. Witness of Andrew, Chapter 1:37–42
   C. Witness of Philip, Chapter 1:43–46
   D. Witness of Nathanael, Chapter 1:47–51

III. Witness of Works and Words, Chapters 2–12
   A. Jesus at Marriage in Cana (First Work), Chapter 2:1–12
   B. Jesus Cleanses Temple During Passover in Jerusalem (First Word), Chapter 2:13–22
   C. Jesus Interviews Nicodemus in Jerusalem (Second Word), Chapter 2:23–3:36
   D. Jesus Interviews Woman at Well in Sychar (Third Word), Chapter 4:1–45
   E. Jesus Heals Nobleman's Son in Capernaum (Second Work), Chapter 4:46–54
   F. Jesus Heals Man at Pool of Bethesda (Third Work), Chapter 5
   G. Jesus Feeds Five Thousand on East of Sea of Galilee (Fourth Work and Word), Chapter 6
   H. Jesus Teaches at Feast of Tabernacles in Temple (Fifth Word), Chapter 7
   I. Jesus in Temple Forgives Woman Taken in Adultery (Sixth Word), Chapter 8
   J. Jesus Opens Eyes of Man Born Blind in Jerusalem (Fifth Work), Chapter 9
      1. Record of Miracle, Chapter 9:1–7
      2. Reaction to Miracle, Chapter 9:8–41
   K. Jesus Is the Good Shepherd (Seventh Word), Chapter 10
      1. Humanity—Christ in Form of Servant, Chapter 10:1–21
      2. Deity—Christ Equal with God, Chapter 10:22–42
   L. Jesus Raises Lazarus from Dead in Bethany (Sixth Work), Chapter 11
   M. Witness of Jew and Gentile to Jesus, Chapter 12
      1. Jesus Comes to Bethany for Supper, Chapter 12:1–11
      2. Jesus Comes to Jerusalem—Tearful Entry, Chapter 12:12–19
      3. Jesus Comes to Greeks, Chapter 12:20–26
      4. Jesus Comes to His Hour, Chapter 12:27–36
      5. Jesus Comes to End of Public Ministry, Chapter 12:37–50

IV. Witness of Jesus to His Witnesses, Upper Room Discourse, Chapters 13–17
   A. Jesus Washes Feet of Disciples, Chapter 13
   B. Jesus Comforts His Disciples, Chapter 14
   C. Jesus Is Genuine Vine; Disciples Are Branches, Chapter 15
   D. Jesus Will Send Holy Spirit During His Absence, Chapter 16
   E. The Lord's Prayer, Chapter 17
      1. Jesus Prays for Himself, Chapter 17:1–5
      2. Jesus Prays for Disciples, Chapter 17:6–19
      3. Jesus Prays for His Church, Chapter 17:20–26

V. Witness to World, Chapters 18–20
   A. Arrest and Trial of Jesus, Chapter 18

1. Arrest in Gethsemane; Trial before Annas, Chapter 18:1–14
2. First Denial by Simon Peter, Chapter 18:15–18
3. Trial before High Priest, Chapter 18:19–24
4. Second Denial by Simon Peter, Chapter 18:25–27
5. Trial before Pilate, Chapter 18:28–40

B. Death of Jesus at Golgotha; Burial in Tomb of Joseph, Chapter 19

C. Resurrection of Jesus; Appearances to Mary, Disciples, Thomas, Chapter 20

VI. Epilogue—Glorification, Chapter 21

The Resurrected Jesus Is Still God

Lord of Our Wills—Directs our Service (v. 6)

Lord of Our Hearts—Motive for Service (vv. 15–17)

Lord of Our Minds—Lack of Knowledge No Excuse from Service (v. 22)

Another division of the Gospel of John:

LIGHT—John 1–12
LOVE—John 13–17
LIFE—John 18–21

CHAPTER 1

THEME: *Prologue—Incarnation; Word is God, Word became Flesh, Word revealed God; witness of John the Baptist; witness of Andrew; witness of Philip, witness of Nathanael*

WORD IS GOD—WORD BECAME FLESH—WORD REVEALED GOD

In the beginning was the Word, and the Word was with God, and the Word was God [John 1:1].

The Gospel of John introduces the Lord Jesus Christ with three tremendous statements:

"In the beginning was the Word,"
"And the Word was with God,"
"And the Word was God."

"The Word" is one of the highest and most profound titles of the Lord Jesus Christ. To determine the exact meaning is not easy. Obviously the Lord Jesus Christ is not the *logos* of Greek philosophy; rather He is the *memra* of the Hebrew Scriptures. Notice how important the Word is in the Old Testament. For instance, the name for Jehovah was never pronounced. It was such a holy word that they never used it at all. But this is the One who is the Word and, gathering up everything that was said of Him in the Old Testament, He is now presented as the One "In the beginning." This beginning antedates the very first words in the Bible, "In the beginning God created the heaven and the earth." That beginning can be dated, although I do not believe that anyone can date it accurately—it is nonsense to say that it is 4004 B.C., as Ussher's dating has it. It probably goes back billions and billions of years. You see, you and I are dealing with the God of eternity. When you go back to creation He is already there, and that is exactly the way this is used—"in the beginning *was* the Word." Notice it is not *is* the Word; it was not in the beginning that the Word started out or was begotten. *Was* (as Dr. Lenske points out) is known as a durative imperfect, meaning continued action. It means that the Word was in the beginning. What beginning? Just as far back as you want to go. The Bible says, "In the beginning God created the heaven and the earth" (Gen. 1:1). Does that begin God? No, just keep on going back billions and trillions and "squillions" of years. I can think back to billions of years back of creation—maybe you can go beyond that—but let's put down a point there, billions of years back of creation. He already was; He comes out of eternity to meet us. He did not begin. "In the beginning *was* the Word"—He was already there when the beginning was. "Well," somebody says, "there has to be a beginning somewhere." All right, wherever you begin, He is there to meet you, He is already past tense. "In the beginning was the Word"—five words in the original language, and there is not a man on topside of this earth who can put a date on it or understand it or fathom it. This first tremendous statement starts us off in space, you see.

The second statement is this, "and the Word was with God." This makes it abundantly clear that He is separate and distinct from God the Father. You cannot identify Him as God the Father because He is *with* God. "But," someone says, "if He is with God, He is not God." The third statement sets us straight, "and the Word was God." This is a clear, emphatic declaration that the Lord Jesus Christ is God. In fact, the Greek is more specific than this, because in the Greek language the important word is placed at the beginning of the sentence and it reads, "God was the Word." That is emphatic; you cannot get it more emphatic than that. Do you want to get rid of the deity of Christ? My friend, you cannot get rid of it. The first three statements in John's gospel tie the thing down. "In the beginning was the Word, and the Word was with God, and the Word was God."

Let's move on down to verse 14 and notice the three statements there.

And the Word was made flesh, and dwelt among us, (and we beheld his glory, the glory as of the only begotten of the Father,) full of grace and truth [John 1:14].

"And the Word was made flesh,"
"And the Word dwelt among us,"
"He was full of grace and truth."

The Greek philosopher probably would have stayed with us through verse one, but he leaves us here. He would never agree that the Word was made flesh. The Greek language allows us to put it more specifically and, I think, more accurately: "The Word was *born* flesh." Turn this over in your mind for a moment. Here comes God out of eternity, already the Ancient of days; but He also came to Bethlehem, a little baby thing that made a woman cry. And notice that John's gospel does not even mention His birth in Bethlehem. Do you know why? He is talking about One who is too big for Bethlehem. Out of eternity, the Word became flesh.

"And [the Word] dwelt among us" is the second statement in verse 14. "Dwelt" is from *skenoo;* it means "He pitched His tent among us." Our human bodies are merely little tents in which we live. The apostle Paul used the same imagery: ". . . we know that if . . . this tabernacle were dissolved . . ." (2 Cor. 5:1). This house in which we live is a tabernacle, a tent, that can be blown over in a night; it can be snuffed out in an instant. Because you and I live in these little tents, the God of eternity took upon Himself a human body and thus pitched His tent down here among us. Such is the second tremendous statement.

Notice the third, "(and we beheld his glory, the glory as of the only begotten of the Father,) full of grace and truth." Now John is saying something else. The question I would naturally ask at this point is, "If He was made flesh, He certainly limited Himself." John says, "Wait a minute–He was full of grace and truth." The word "full" means that you just could not have any more. He brought all the deity with Him, and He was full of grace and full of truth when He came down here.

Now we move to verse 18 to find three statements again.

No man hath seen God at any time; the only begotten Son, which is in the bosom of the Father, he hath declared him [John 1:18].

"No man hath seen God at any time;"
"The only begotten Son, which is in the bosom of the Father,"
"He hath declared him."

Notice the first: "No man hath seen God at any time." Why? He will explain it in this gospel; the Lord Jesus will tell the woman at the well, "God is a Spirit: and they that worship him must worship him in spirit and in truth" (John 4:24)—for God is spirit. No man has seen God at any time. What about the appearances in the Old Testament? God never revealed himself in the Old Testament to the eyes of man. What, then, did they see? Well, go back and read the record. For instance, Jacob said that he saw God, but what he saw was the angel of the Lord who wrestled with him. That was a manifestation, but he did not see God, because God is a Spirit. "No man hath seen God at any time."

The second statement is, "the only begotten Son." The best Greek text is that of Nestle, the German scholar. He has come to the definite conclusion that it is not the only begotten Son, but the only begotten *God*. I prefer that also. "Which is in the bosom of the Father" tells us a great deal. He did not come from the head of God to reveal the wisdom of God; He did not come from the foot of God to be a servant of man. (Have you ever noticed that although we speak of the fact He was a servant, whose shoes did He ever shine? Did He ever run an errand for anybody? He did not. He said, "For I came down from heaven, not to do mine own will, but the will of him that sent me" (John 6:38). He was God's servant—He came to serve Him, and as He served the Father, He served men.) He did not come from the feet; He did not come from the head; it was from the bosom of the Father that He came. He came to reveal the heart of God: He was "the only begotten Son, which is in the bosom of the Father."

The third statement completes verse eighteen: "he hath declared him." The Greek word here is *exegesato*. *Ago* is "to lead" and *ex* is "out." It means that what Jesus Christ did was to lead God out into the open. Do you know anything bigger than that? A little trip to the moon is nothing in comparison. Here He comes out of eternity past, the God of this universe, the Creator of everything, taking upon Himself human flesh, and bringing God out into the open so that men can know Him. My friend, the only way in the world you can know God is through this One, Jesus Christ. Jesus Christ came to reveal God because He is God.

I am not through with these statements; there is something else here. Let's put together the first verse in each of these three groups and see what we come up with:

"In the beginning was the Word,"
"And the Word was made flesh,"
"No man hath seen God at any time."

You could not see God—God is spirit. He had to become flesh; He had to become one of us in order for us to know Him. We could not go up there to understand Him; He had to come down here and bring God down where we are.

Now let's put the second statements together from each of the three groups:

"The Word was with God,"
"And dwelt among us,"
"The only begotten Son, which is in the bosom of the Father."

Consider this One for a moment—the angels bowed before Him, He was with God, on an equality with God. The apostle Paul wrote of Him, He ". . . thought it not robbery to be equal with God" (Phil. 2:6). That is, He did not go to school to become God; it was not something He worked overtime to attain. It was not a degree that He earned. He did not *try* to be God; He *was* God. I do not mean to be irreverent, but He did not say to the Father when He came to this earth, "Keep your eye on Gabriel; he is after My job; watch him while I'm gone." He did not have to do that—nobody could take His place. He was God. Here He comes: born in Bethlehem, a few little shepherds there, not many; He goes up to Nazareth, thirty years hidden away in Nazareth. God, out of eternity coming down and going to Nazareth, working in a carpenter shop. Why? So you can know God. The only way you will ever know Him, my friend, is to know this One. "The only begotten Son, which is in the bosom of the Father" is the only One who can reveal God to us.

Now notice the third statement in each group:

"The Word was God"
"And we beheld his glory, the glory as of the only begotten of the Father, full of grace and truth"
"He hath declared him."

When He was down here, He was still God, full of grace and truth. And He declared Him; He is the only one who can lead Him out in the open where we can get acquainted with Him.

We are not through with this. I want you to see something else. How do you divide up this universe? I sat with a man who designed the shield that has been on all these space crafts to make their re-entry. He is a scientist who is an authority on heat. As we had lunch together in New Jersey, he said, "You know, this universe is made up of just three things. I believe that God has put His fingerprints on everything—the Trinity is everywhere." Then he explained what he meant. The universe is divided up into time, space, and matter. Can you think of a fourth? The very interesting thing is that time, space, and matter include everything that is in this universe as you and I know it. Then time can be divided into just three parts: past, present, and future. Can you think of a fourth? And what about space? Length, breadth, and height. Is there another direction? Also there is in matter energy, motion, and phenomena. Those are the three divisions of the three divisions. The universe in which we live bears the mark of the Trinity.

Now notice the way in which the Incarnation is geared into this observation. Verse 1:

Time: "In the beginning was the Word, and the Word was with God."

Space: "The Word was made flesh"—became flesh, came down into space. Where? To Bethlehem, a little geographical spot—and even this earth was a pretty small spot for Him to come to—and He pitched His tent here among us. We beheld His glory, full of grace and truth.

Matter: "No man hath seen God at any time; the only begotten Son, which is in the bosom of the Father, he hath declared him." Because He became matter, became a man, took upon Himself humanity, men could see and know God. This is the time, space, and matter of the Incarnation. Let's divide each of these into three.

Past: "In the beginning *was* the Word."

Present: "The Word was made (became) flesh" (in our day).

Future: "No man hath seen God at any time; the only begotten Son . . . hath declared him." The apostle Paul, at the end of his life, said, "That I may know him, and the power of his resurrection . . ." (Phil. 3:10). That will be for the future—to really know Him; today we actually know so little because we are finite.

Then look at space, divided into length, breadth and height.

Length: "In the beginning was the Word."

Breadth: He came down to this earth and was made flesh.

Height: No man has seen God at any time; the only begotten Son, who is in the bosom of the Father—He has come from the heights to set Him before us.

Consider the divisions of matter: energy, motion, and phenomena.

Energy: In the beginning was the *Word*, and the *Word* was with God—that's energy. How did this universe come into existence? God spoke. Every rational person has to confront this problem of how this universe began. That is the reason evolution has been popular—it offers to the natural man an explanation for the origin of the universe. You must have an explanation for it if you do any thinking at all. Where did it come from? Well, here is the answer: "In the beginning was the Word." God spoke. That is the first thing that happened. When God speaks, when the Word speaks, energy is translated into matter. What is atomic fission? It is matter translated back into energy—poof! it disappears. Creation began with energy. In the beginning was the *Word*. The *Word* was with God. The *Word* was God.

Motion: The Word was made flesh. He came out of heaven's glory and He came to this earth.

Phenomena: The greatest phenomenon in this world is Jesus Christ. The wonders of the ancient world, the wonders to see in our day are nothing in comparison to the wonder of the Incarnation—God became man!

These statements are bigger than any of us, and yet they are so simple. We have read them, probably memorized them, yet no man can plumb the depths of them. "In the beginning was the Word, and the Word was with God, and the Word was God. . . . And the Word was made flesh, and dwelt among us, (and we beheld his glory, the glory as of the only begotten of the Father,) full of grace and truth. . . . No man hath seen God at any time; the only begotten Son, which is in the bosom of the Father, he hath declared him" (vv. 1, 14, 18).

These three verses are the great building blocks; now let us consider some of the cement that holds them together.

All things were made by him; and without him was not any thing made that was made [John 1:3].

The Lord Jesus Christ is the Creator. Not only did He exist before Bethlehem, but He created the vast universe including the material out of which man constructed Bethlehem. All things were made by Him; He is the instrument of creation. Nothing came into existence without Him.

In him was life; and the life was the light of men [John 1:4].

Now we are confronted with something else—two of the simplest things in the world: light and life. *Zoe* and *phos* are the two words in the original language. From *zoe* we get zoology, the study of life; and from *phos* we get photo or anything that is built on it, such as photograph—it is light. These two things are so common that we take them for granted. Life—we see it everywhere. There may be a great deal of life right where you are at this moment. You go out in the woods and you see the same thing—life. It greets you on every hand, but can you explain it? You see in the Sunday pictorials and the sensational magazines that men now have discovered the source of life. But if you read them, you find that they have not found the source at all, though they think they are close to it. They put the microscope down on a green leaf. One moment they see that a little cell is arranged one way and is dead as a doornail. The next moment the thing is rearranged in another way, and it is alive. And then the thing starts growing and doubling, dividing and multiplying itself. Why does it do that? Life.

The other common thing is light. What is light? I listened to Irwin Moon try to explain it (and Irwin gave the best explanation I have heard), but when he got through I was not sure if light is a real something or if it is just waves, because they can cut the thing off and still light will go through. As you know, certain kinds of light will go through objects that would stop waves. What in the world is light?

You see, we are dealing with things that are fundamental, though men today with all their scientific gadgets know so little about them.

"In him was life"—all life is in Jesus Christ. "In him was life; and the life was the light of men." You and I live in a universe that is spiritually dark. The fact of the matter is, it is physically dark to a certain degree. But God said, ". . . Let there be light . . ." (Gen. 1:3) and these light holders are placed about throughout His universe like street lights in a big city. We are told that when a man gets away from this earth a short distance, he is in total, absolute darkness, and it is frightening to be out where there is nothing from which the sun can be reflected. Our little globe is out in a dark universe, yet that is nothing compared to the spiritual darkness that envelops it. When the sun disappears, there is physical darkness over the land; but twenty-four hours a day there is spiritual darkness here, awful spiritual darkness. Man does not know God; man is in rebellion against God; man is in sin that blinds him to God. In the Lord Jesus Christ there is life, and the life that He gives is the *light* of men. In fact, His life is the only thing that can kindle light in the heart of an individual. An unregenerate man has no spiritual life within him. This is the reason that when you present to him Jesus Christ, he says, "I don't get it. I don't understand that at all."

I used to go down to the jail in Cleburne, Texas, and speak to the men. It was not a large jail and I could talk to them in a conversational tone. I would start off talking about football (because in Texas football is a religion!), and those hardened men would get enthusiastic about it. I talked also of other things and they were interested. Then I would turn the conversation to something spiritual, and I could see the darkness come over their faces. I might just as well have been talking to corpses. And that is what they were—men dead in trespasses and sins. This world today is in spiritual darkness, and the Lord Jesus Christ has brought the only light there is in the world. He is the light. "In him was life; and the life was the light of men."

And the light shineth in darkness; and the darkness comprehended it not [John 1:5].

That word "comprehend" is an unfortunate translation. And a wiseacre did not help it by rendering it, "and the darkness was not able to put it out." That is no translation at all. The word in the Greek is *katelaben*, meaning actually "to take down." It is the picture of a secretary to whom the boss is giving dictation, and she stops and says, "I can't take that down. I am not able to take it down." The light shines in darkness and the darkness is not able to take it in. That is it exactly. Someone said to me, "Boy, was I in darkness before I received Christ! And I don't know why I didn't see." Well, that is it: you were in darkness and you did not see. The darkness just cannot take it in.

Now this is something quite interesting, and it is not true of physical light. You go into a dark room, and the minute you switch on the light, the darkness leaves, it disappears. Darkness and light cannot exist together physically. The moment you bring light in, darkness is gone. The minute light is taken out, darkness will come right back in. But *spiritual* light and darkness exist together. Sometimes there is a husband who is saved and a wife who is unsaved—or vice versa. Here is a believer working next to another man who says, "What do you mean when you talk about being a Christian? I do the best I can. Am I not a Christian?" There you have light and darkness side by side and the darkness just cannot take it in. That is exactly what is said here, "The light shineth in darkness; and the darkness comprehended it not."

He was in the world, and the world was made by him, and the world knew him not [John 1:10].

That was the tragedy—the world was in darkness, spiritual darkness, and did not know Him. Even today we are seeing the rise of atheism and unbelief, and we will see it more and more in the days that lie ahead. A great many people do not seem to recognize that unbelief and atheism go naturally with the natural man. Somebody says to me, "Oh, did you read in the paper what Dr. So-and-So of a certain seminary wrote?" Yes, I read it. "Well, isn't it awful?" No, I do not think so. He would upset my apple cart if he said that he believed the Bible, because he is an unbeliever by his own statement. He says that he does not believe in being born again, that he does not believe he has to receive Christ in order to be saved. Now I do not expect that man to say he believes the Bible. That would be absolutely contrary to his statements. The so-called theologians and theological professors who espouse the "God is dead movement," present us with the preposterous, untenable claim that they are Christian atheists! Obviously atheism precludes the possibility of being Christian, yet unbelief has moved into our seminaries and pulpits across the land. The world does not know Him.

He came unto his own [his own things], and his own [people] received him not [John 1:11].

He came into His own universe but His own people did not receive Him.

But as many as received him, to them gave he power to become the sons of God, even to them that believe on his name [John 1:12].

"But as many as received him, to them gave he power." The word *power* is not *dunamis* power like dynamite, physical power, but *exousian* power which is delegated power, authority. "But as many as received him, to them gave he the *authority* to become the sons of God [children, *tekna* of God], even to them that believe on his name."

Notice that this is for "them that *believe* on his name." And always with the word "believe" there is a preposition. You see, faith, as the Bible uses it, is not just head knowledge. Many people ask, "You mean all that I have to do is to say I believe?" Yes, that is all you have to do, but let's see what that implies. With the verb "to believe" there is always a preposition—sometimes *en* (in), sometimes *eis* (into) or sometimes *epi* (upon). You must believe into, in, or upon Jesus Christ. Let me illustrate with a chair. I am standing beside a chair and I believe it will hold me up, but it is not holding me up. Why? Because I have only a head knowledge. I just say, "Yes, it will hold me up." Now suppose I believe into the chair by sitting in it. See what I mean? I am committing my entire weight to it and it is holding me up. Is Christ holding you up? Is He your Savior? It is not a question of standing to the side and saying, "Oh, yes, I believe Jesus is the Son of God." The question is have you trusted Him, have you believed into Him, are you resting in Him? This chair is holding me up completely. And at this moment Christ is my complete Savior. I am depending on Him; I am resting in Him.

THE WITNESS OF JOHN THE BAPTIST

And this is the record of John, when the Jews sent priests and Levites from Jerusalem to ask him, Who art thou? [John 1:19].

This is the first incident in the life of John the Baptist which John gives us in his gospel record. He does not give us the story of the beginning of this man. We find out about his birth in the Gospel of Luke, but here the record of John the Baptist begins when a delegation from Jerusalem comes to question him. They come out to ask him, "Who art thou?"

In this question there is a subtle temptation, because this offered John an opportunity to make something of himself. In John 3:30 we find his response when his disciples wanted him to make something of himself. He said, "He must increase, but I must decrease." What a statement that is! That is a statement that every believer should make. But every believer should live it, too. "He must increase, but I must decrease." Friend, both can't be on top. Either Christ is primary in your life and occupies first place, or you (that is, the selfish "I") will be on top. You can't have both. He must increase and I must decrease, or else it will be the other way around.

Now note the answer that he gives to the religious rulers:

And he confessed, and denied not; but confessed, I am not the Christ [John 1:20].

You see, they cleverly suggest that he might be the Messiah—they have a messianic hope. But he makes it very clear that he is not the Christ; he is not the Messiah. They are looking to the wrong man. So, if he is not the Christ, what great person is he?

And they asked him, What then? Art thou Elias? And he saith, I am not. Art thou that prophet? And he answered, No [John 1:21].

You notice how brief and matter-of-fact John is here. His answers are terse, and they get briefer as the religious rulers continue to question him. If he's not the Christ, he must be Elijah. If he's not Elijah, he must be "that prophet." They are referring to a prophet "like unto Moses" who had been promised back in Deuteronomy 18:15. John gives an emphatic "No!" He is not the predicted prophet of Deuteronomy.

Then said they unto him, Who art thou? that we may give an answer to them that sent us. What sayest thou of thyself? [John 1:22].

They insist that he must tell them who he is. They can't take back a report of just a string of negatives. So John does identify himself.

He said, I am the voice of one crying in the wilderness, Make straight the way of the Lord, as said the prophet Esaias [John 1:23].

Notice that he is a voice. You see, Christ is the Word! John is the voice! A voice is all John wants to be. He has a grand message to give, a message much greater than he is. Frankly, we should be satisfied to be only a voice, because certainly the message we have to give is greater than the individual. And that voice should, of course, declare the glories of Christ.

Notice the grand message that he gives. "Make straight the way of the Lord." In other words, "Get ready for the coming of the Lord." I take it that he means the kingdom of heaven is at hand. It was at hand in the person of the King, you see. And he tells them to "Make straight the way." This would be the same as telling them to get the crooked things out of their lives; to deal with the things that are wrong. This we need to do also. When we do that, there is opened for us fellowship with God. "If we say that we have fellowship with him, and walk in darkness, we lie, and do not the truth" (1 John 1:6). We need to get our lives straight, and we can get them straight by confession, as we are taught in 1 John 1:8–9.

You will notice that he says he is quoting the prophet Isaiah. ". . . Prepare ye the way of the LORD, make straight in the desert a highway for our God" (Isa. 40:3).

And they which were sent were of the Pharisees.

And they asked him, and said unto him, Why baptizest thou then, if thou be not

that Christ, nor Elias, neither that prophet? [John 1:24–25].

They are now presenting him with a technical point. "If you are none of these, then why do you baptize?"

John answered them, saying, I baptize with water: but there standeth one among you, whom ye know not;

He it is, who coming after me is preferred before me, whose shoe's latchet I am not worthy to unloose [John 1:26–27].

Today, we call this man John the Baptist. But he said that he merely used water. There was One coming after him, who would baptize with fire and with the Holy Spirit. That fire is the baptism of judgment which is to come upon the earth. The baptism of the Holy Spirit took place at Pentecost. One wonders whether Christ was in the crowd that day. We don't know. But He might have been.

"He . . . coming after me is preferred before me, whose shoe's latchet I am not worthy to unloose." A servant must do every task of his master. A disciple, however, must do every task except take the thong out of the teacher's shoes. That was the rule of that day. John is saying that he is a servant. He is not even a disciple; he is merely a servant. And he is not even worthy to be that servant, although that is what he is.

These things were done in Bethabara beyond Jordan, where John was baptizing [John 1:28].

I called attention in the Introduction to the fact that the apostle John gears us into the geography and to the calendar. Here we have a geographical location given to us. And then notice that the following verse begins, "The next day." John is showing to us that the One who came from out of eternity, the Word made flesh, is now geared into geography and into our calendar down here.

The next day John seeth Jesus coming unto him, and saith, Behold the Lamb of God, which taketh away the sin of the world [John 1:29].

John marks Him out here. He is the Savior. He is not only the Messiah; He is also the Savior. He is a very great Savior for He is the Lamb of God. He is the complete Savior because He takes away sin. He is the almighty Savior because He takes away the sin of the world. He is the perpetual Savior because He "taketh" away—present tense. Anyone can come to Him at any time.

Here we find the fulfillment of the answer that Abraham had given to Isaac those many years ago. Isaac had said, ". . . Behold the fire and the wood: but where is the lamb for a burnt offering? And Abraham said, My son, God will provide himself a lamb for a burnt offering . . ." (Gen. 22:7–8). John tells us that Jesus is the Lamb.

This proves that Cain was wrong and Abel was right. Abel brought a little lamb. All the lambs that were slain on Jewish altars down through the ages now find their fulfillment in Him. John marks Him out. "Behold the Lamb of God, which taketh away the sin of the world."

This is he of whom I said, After me cometh a man which is preferred before me: for he was before me.

And I knew him not: but that he should be made manifest to Israel, therefore am I come baptizing with water [John 1:30–31].

John is saying that Jesus is the real Baptizer. We might call Him Jesus the Baptizer. He is the One who will baptize with the Holy Spirit and with fire.

And John bare record, saying, I saw the Spirit descending from heaven like a dove, and it abode upon him.

And I knew him not: but he that sent me to baptize with water, the same said unto me, Upon whom thou shalt see the Spirit descending, and remaining on him, the same is he which baptizeth with the Holy Ghost.

And I saw, and bare record that this is the Son of God.

Again the next day after John stood, and two of his disciples;

And looking upon Jesus as he walked, he saith, Behold the Lamb of God! [John 1:32–36].

Before it was the Lamb of God that taketh away the sin of the world. That is the *work* of Christ. Now it is "Behold the Lamb of God!" He is the Lamb in His *Person*. We see that John baptized Jesus and that Jesus was identified by the Holy Spirit. So, looking upon Jesus as He walked, John says, "Behold the Lamb of God!"

WITNESS OF ANDREW

And the two disciples heard him speak, and they followed Jesus.

Then Jesus turned, and saw them following, and saith unto them, What seek ye? They said unto him, Rabbi, (which is to say, being interpreted, Master,) where dwellest thou?

He saith unto them, Come and see. They came and saw where he dwelt, and abode with him that day: for it was about the tenth hour [John 1:37–39].

He extends the same invitation to you today, "Come and see." Taste of the Lord and see whether or not He is good (see Ps. 34:8).

Notice again how specifically John gears this into time— it was late in the evening.

One of these two who had been disciples of John the Baptist was Andrew, and the very first thing that he does is to go after his own brother, Simon.

One of the two which heard John speak, and followed him, was Andrew, Simon Peter's brother.

He first findeth his own brother Simon, and saith unto him, We have found the Messias, which is, being interpreted, the Christ.

And he brought him to Jesus. And when Jesus beheld him, he said, Thou art Simon the son of Jona: thou shalt be called Cephas, which is by interpretation, A stone [John 1:40–42].

This man, Simon, was as weak as water. Our Lord told him that he would be a stone man. I think everybody laughed there that day because nobody believed he could become the rock man, the man who would stand up on the Day of Pentecost and give the first sermon, which would be used to sweep three thousand persons into the church (see Acts 2:40–41).

WITNESS OF PHILIP

The day following Jesus would go forth into Galilee, and findeth Philip, and saith unto him, Follow me.

Now Philip was of Bethsaida, the city of Andrew and Peter [John 1:43–44].

Again we are dealing with geography. Bethsaida is up on the Sea of Galilee. We know that Peter and Andrew and Philip lived up there. They were fishermen.

Philip findeth Nathanael, and saith unto him, We have found him, of whom Moses in the law, and the prophets, did write, Jesus of Nazareth, the son of Joseph.

And Nathanael said unto him, Can there any good thing come out of Nazareth? Philip saith unto him, Come and see [John 1:45–46].

WITNESS OF NATHANAEL

This Nathanael is a wiseacre, and he makes a wisecrack here. Can any good thing come out of Nazareth? And I think he laughed at his own joke, by the way. But Philip didn't laugh. He just said, "Come and see." That is the really important thing—come and see.

Jesus saw Nathanael coming to him, and saith of him, Behold an Israelite indeed, in whom is no guile! [John 1:47].

Here is an Israelite in whom there is no Jacob. You see, although this man is a wisecracker, he is not deceitful or cunning. There is nothing of the old Jacob in him. He is an Israelite in whom there is no Jacob.

Nathanael saith unto him, Whence knowest thou me? Jesus answered and said unto him, Before that Philip called thee, when thou wast under the fig tree, I saw thee.

Nathanael answered and saith unto him, Rabbi, thou art the Son of God; thou art the King of Israel [John 1:48–49].

The Lord Jesus had two doubters among His apostles. The one at the beginning was Nathanael; the one at the end was Thomas. This man, this skeptic, this one who wonders whether any good can come out of Nazareth, confesses before the interview is over that Jesus is the Son of God, the King of Israel.

When Nathanael confessed that the Lord Jesus is the Son of God and the King of Israel, it reveals that something very important did come out of Nazareth.

Jesus answered and said unto him, Because I said unto thee, I saw thee under the fig tree, believest thou? thou shalt see greater things than these [John 1:50].

The Lord more or less rebuked him and asked whether it was just because He saw him under the fig tree that he believed. Jesus promises him that he will see greater things. Indeed during the next three years, Nathanael did see much greater things than these.

And he saith unto him, Verily, verily, I say unto you, Hereafter ye shall see heaven open, and the angels of God ascending and descending upon the Son of man [John 1:51].

Our Lord had said to this man, "Behold, an Israelite in whom there is no Jacob." Now He follows up on this by referring to the incident in the life of the patriarch Jacob when, as a young man, he had run away from home. In fact, he had to leave home because his brother Esau was after him to murder him. His first night away from home was at Beth-el, and there the Lord appeared to him. A ladder was let down from heaven, and on that ladder the angels were ascending and descending. The meaning for Jacob was that God had not lost contact with him. He had thought that when he left home, he had left God back there. He had a limited view of God, of course. At Beth-el he learned that God would be with him.

Our Lord picks that up here and says that the ladder was Himself. You'll see now the angels of God ascending and descending upon the Son of Man. The angels ministered to Him, and the angels were subject to Him. Here He was given charge over the angels. He could send them as messengers to heaven, and they would return also. So Jesus says that Nathanael will see heaven opened and the angels of God ascending and descending upon the Son of Man. He is going to see that the Father from the top of that ladder will speak of this One, saying, ". . . This is my beloved Son, in whom I am well pleased" (Matt. 3:17).

The ladder is Christ, and only by Him can you and I make contact with God. The Lord Jesus said, ". . . I am the way, the truth, and the life: no man cometh unto the Father, but by me" (John 14:6). He is the ladder—not one that you climb, but One that you trust, One that you rest upon and believe in. That is the important thing to see here.

This first chapter of John's gospel has been lengthy and extremely important. The prologue presents the incarnation of the Word—He is God, He became flesh, He reveals the Father. Then He is introduced by witnesses. John the Baptist testifies that Jesus is the revealer of God. Andrew testifies that Jesus is the Messiah. Philip testifies that Jesus fulfills the Old Testament. Nathanael witnesses that Jesus is the Son of God, the King of Israel.

CHAPTER 2

THEME: *Jesus at marriage in Cana (first work); Jesus cleanses temple during Passover in Jerusalem (first word); Jesus interviews Nicodemus in Jerusalem (second word)*

JESUS AT MARRIAGE IN CANA (First Work)

The important incident in this chapter is when Jesus, invited to the marriage in Cana, performed His first miracle. We are told in the eleventh verse, "This beginning of miracles did Jesus." This, then, is the answer to those who teach that the Lord Jesus, as a little boy down in Egypt making clay pigeons with the other little boys, would touch the clay pigeons and they would fly away. That makes a pretty good story, but there is no fact in it. This record makes it very clear that He did not perform miracles in Egypt, but that His first miracle was at Cana of Galilee.

The wonder of all this is that here is the One who is in the beginning with God and is God. He came out of eternity. He was made flesh and for his first thirty years lived in Nazareth of Galilee. Then He walks over a hill to attend a wedding in Cana.

Notice that again John gears this in with time and space. "And the third day." Our Lord is now going out into His ministry.

And the third day there was a marriage in Cana of Galilee; and the mother of Jesus was there:

And both Jesus was called, and his disciples, to the marriage [John 2:1–2].

Many Bible teachers believe that she was there because she was related to the individuals who were getting married, or at least to one of the families. This is largely a supposition, but it could well be true. The Lord Jesus and His disciples were also invited.

The time is given here as the third day. It is thought that this was probably late February or early March in the year A.D. 27. The very interesting thing is that John carefully gives the places. In the previous chapter we were back in Bethsaida, and now the scene shifts to Cana of Galilee. Then it will move to Capernaum in verse 12 and to Jerusalem in verse 13. John gives us the chronological sequence and the geography.

It says that "the mother of Jesus" was there. She is never called Mary in the Gospel of John. She comes to Jesus with a very unusual request. Notice what she says to Him.

And when they wanted wine, the mother of Jesus saith unto him, They have no wine [John 2:3].

The question comes up about the wine. I read recently of a liberal who called Jesus a bootlegger. Such sacrilege! In that day, wine was a staple article of diet. However, drunkenness was absolutely condemned. There was no thought of drunkenness connected with this. A wedding was a religious occasion, by the way, and these were folk who believed the Old Testament. You can put it down that there was no intoxication at this wedding.

The wedding is a picture of another wedding that is coming. Christ began His ministry on this earth at a wedding. He will conclude it, as far as the church is concerned, with a wedding. At the marriage supper of the Lamb the church will be presented to Him as a bride.

This is the first miracle which He performed. Moses' first miracle was turning water into blood. Christ's first miracle was turning water into wine. The Law was given by Moses, but grace and truth came by Jesus Christ. What a contrast!

What did Mary mean by her statement? First of all, it is well to call attention to the fact that this was a very poor family. They simply didn't have enough refreshments. Bengal in his commentary said that, when she told the Lord there was no wine, it was a gentle hint for Him and His disciples to depart. Calvin writes that it was a suggestion for Him to occupy the minds of the guests with a discourse. It would be just like John Calvin to suggest that, by the way. If you have ever read Calvin's *Institutes*, you know they are profound, but boring. If Calvin had been there, *he* would have given them a discourse and probably put them all to sleep! However, I do not think that the context here would permit either interpretation. I don't believe it was a hint for Him to leave nor a suggestion to occupy the minds of the guests. I think that very candidly she is saying, "Perform a miracle. This would be an appropriate occasion."

You will recall that when the angel Gabriel appeared to her and told her that she was the one who was to bring forth the Messiah, Mary raised the question about the Virgin Birth, ". . . How shall this be, seeing I know not a man?" (Luke 1:34). Gabriel made it very clear that the Holy Spirit would come upon her and that which was conceived in her was holy. She showed her faith and submission when she said, ". . . Behold the handmaid of the Lord . . ." (Luke 1:38). From that moment, and during the intervening years, there was always a question about her virginity. People actually raised questions about Jesus. She is really saying, "Here is Your opportunity to perform a miracle and demonstrate that I am accurate when I said that You were virgin born and that You are the One whom I have claimed You are." Jesus gives her a very clear answer.

Jesus saith unto her, Woman, what have I to do with thee? mine hour is not yet come [John 2:4].

His implication is, "This is not the occasion. I'll clear your name, but not here."

When He was hanging on the cross and the mother of Jesus was standing beneath that cross, you remember that He looked down and said to her, "Woman, behold thy son!" (John 19:26). At that time His hour had come. In three days He would come back from the dead. When the disciples met in an upper room after His resurrection and ascension, Mary could look around, for she was there, and she could say to each of those disciples, "I told you that He was the Son of God!" Paul says that He is ". . . declared to be the Son of God with power, according to the spirit of holiness, by the resurrection from the dead" (Rom. 1:4).

Here she is asking Him to do something that will demonstrate who He is to clear her name. He tells her that He is going to do just that—He will clear her name—but that the hour has not yet come. That hour did come! His resurrection proves who He is. And don't forget that the Resurrection proves the Virgin Birth of Christ. We tend to look at the Virgin Birth at Christmas time as an isolated fact. It is connected with His resurrection, friend, because He is who He claimed to be.

His mother saith unto the servants, Whatsoever he saith unto you, do it [John 2:5].

What good advice! I've always wanted to preach a Mother's Day sermon on this text, "Whatsoever he saith unto you, do it." My subject would be "A Mother's Advice." I never got around to it as a pastor, but it is good advice.

And there were set there six waterpots of stone, after the manner of the purifying of the Jews, containing two or three firkins apiece.

Jesus saith unto them, Fill the waterpots with water. And they filled them up to the brim [John 2:6–7].

Our attention is now drawn to these six water pots. They were used in ceremonial cleansing. Because this was a poor family, the pots were evidently beaten and battered, and probably had been pushed in the back somewhere. They hoped when the wedding guests came that no one would notice them. I think our Lord must have embarrassed the family when He asked for those pots to be brought out. Then He tells them the exact procedure to follow and they filled them to the brim.

And he saith unto them, Draw out now, and bear unto the governor of the feast. And they bare it.

When the ruler of the feast had tasted the water that was made wine, and knew not whence it was: (but the servants which drew the water knew;) the governor of the feast called the bridegroom,

And saith unto him, Every man at the beginning doth set forth good wine; and when men have well drunk, then that which is worse: but thou hast kept the good wine until now [John 2:8–10].

We don't want to get diverted here by arguing whether this wine was intoxicating or not. Very candidly, that is not the issue here at all. If you think you can make something out of this, you're entirely wrong.

Notice there is something omitted here. Where is the bride? I don't find her anywhere. And what did the bride wear? That's the most important part of our weddings. Now I've officiated at many weddings, hundreds of weddings during my ministry, and I've seen many brides come down the aisle. I've learned in the course of time that when I come in at the beginning, nobody is particularly interested in the preacher. Then the bridegroom comes in, and, very candidly, not many are interested in him. The only one who smiles at him is his mother. Then the bride comes down the aisle, and everybody looks. Now what did this bride at Cana wear? We don't know. Why? Because Jesus and those empty water pots are the important things here.

Friend, here is something wonderful. He took empty water pots and He had them filled with water. Then as they ladled out the water, I think the miracle took place. When they took the water and served it to the guests, it became wine.

This holds a great spiritual lesson for you and me. Jesus uses us as water pots today. We're just beaten and battered water pots. We're not attractive and ought to be pushed to the side and covered up. But He wants to use us. He wants to fill us with water. What is the water? The water is the Word of God, friend. He wants to fill you and me with the water of the Word of God. Then, after He fills us with the water of the Word of God, He wants us to ladle it out. When we ladle it out—I don't know how to explain it—but when the water leaves the water pots and gets to those for whom it is destined, it becomes wine. It becomes the wine of joy through the working of the Holy Spirit. We are told, "And be not drunk with wine, wherein is excess; but be filled with the Spirit" (Eph. 5:18). The Holy Spirit takes that water and performs a miracle in the life of an individual. Although I cannot explain it, I often see it take place. I have right here on my desk a dozen letters that have come in recently from people who have been saved by just hearing the Word of God through my radio program. Now, I don't understand it. I'm just an old water pot, and I've got a little of the water of the Word inside me. As I ladle it out, it becomes the wine of joy to folk who receive it.

Years ago when I was speaking to the Hollywood Christian group, there was a couple there who had been saved out of a night club. They said they were going to use their talent for Jesus. Well, I didn't like that. I asked them afterward what kind of a talent they used in a night club that Jesus could use. They stumbled around with an answer; so I said, "Look, when you and I came to Jesus, He didn't get anything but sinners. He got old battered water pots." So I told them about these water pots at Cana. I told them Jesus wanted to fill their lives with the Word of God, the water, and then wanted to ladle it out. I said that when the Holy Spirit ladled it out, it would become the wine of joy in their own lives and would bring a new desire and the joy of life into the life of any believer who would trust Him. They accepted that advice, and we remained good friends. Several years ago I met them on a street in Chicago. We saw each other coming. When they got within earshot, he said to me, "Here come a couple of old beaten up water pots." I want to say this: God has used them but not with the talent that was used in the night club. He filled them with the water of the Word of Life.

Friend, this is the great message that is here for you and me. He wants to fill us with the Word of God and then ladle it out.

After this he went down to Capernaum, he, and his mother, and his brethren, and his disciples: and they continued there not many days [John 2:12].

This is probably referring to that time when His home town would not accept Him. When He went into the synagogue and read from Isaiah, they said, ". . . Is not this Joseph's son?" (Luke 4:22). They probably would have destroyed Him at that time. So He moved His headquarters down to Capernaum and, as far as I can tell, that continued to be His headquarters during His ministry of three years.

JESUS CLEANSES THE TEMPLE DURING PASSOVER IN JERUSALEM (First Word)

And the Jews' passover was at hand, and Jesus went up to Jerusalem [John 2:13].

Here we have another geographical point. He started out at Cana of Galilee, went to Capernaum, and is now in Jerusalem.

Notice that John labels this feast the "Jews' passover." It is no longer the ". . . LORD'S passover . . ." (Exod. 12:27). It is the Jews' passover—merely a religious feast, quite meaningless, just a ritual to go through. The One of whom the Passover speaks has now come. ". . . For even Christ our passover is sacrificed for us" (1 Cor. 5:7).

Our Lord went up to Jerusalem. This was not at the beginning of His public ministry but probably at the end of the first year. All males were required to go to Jerusalem three times a year, at the time of the Feast of Passover, at the Feast of Pentecost, and at the Feast of Tabernacles. He went up for the Passover which was about April the fourteenth. So you see that John gears this into the geography and into the calendar.

Now we find that He cleanses the temple. He did this twice. One cleansing was at the beginning of His ministry and one again at the end of His ministry.

And found in the temple those that sold oxen and sheep and doves, and the changers of money sitting [John 2:14].

They were selling animals and selling doves and changing money. It is quite interesting that they would not accept any kind of money except the temple money there; no other kind could be used or offered. So they had an exchange place, and they made a good profit by making the exchange of coins. When I came back from Venezuela some time ago, I came back with some Venezuelan money that I wanted to get rid of because I couldn't spend it here. There was an exchange place in the airport and I went up there and told them that I wanted to change it for American money. Believe me, friend, I didn't get as much as when I made the trade the other way around; that is, exchanging American money for the Venezuelan money. Now that is the way they did here at the temple, you see.

Why did they have such a system? Why did they do this? Because they were making religion easy. They would take the Roman coinage, which had an effigy of Caesar and the imprint of paganism on it, and they would exchange that for Jewish coinage which could be used in the temple. So they were there for the convenience of the worshipers. Also, they changed large coins into smaller ones. Not only did they make religion easy, but they also made religion cheap. I recognize that we ought not to overemphasize money in the church and should not beg, but I'll tell you something that is more intolerable than that. Some people treat the church and the cause of Christ as something so cheap that at times it becomes necessary to sound an alarm.

They were also selling animals. There was a lot of traffic in those sacrificial animals. It was work and expense to raise those sheep and oxen, and somebody would have to do it for a price. It was very easy for all this to become a religious racket. Today we have that problem with us also.

And when he had made a scourge of small cords, he drove them all out of the temple, and the sheep, and the oxen;

and poured out the changers' money, and overthrew the tables;

And said unto them that sold doves, Take these things hence; make not my Father's house an house of merchandise.

And his disciples remembered that it was written, The zeal of thine house hath eaten me up [John 2:15–17].

I tell you, the Lord was rough. There is no question about that. I don't like the pictures we have of an anemic-looking Christ. The artists don't seem to realize who He was.

The disciples remembered the verse from Psalm 69:9. This psalm is quoted seventeen times in the New Testament and is one of the six most quoted psalms in the New Testament. It is quoted again in John 15:25 and 19:28–29. The other psalms which are frequently quoted are Psalms 2, 22, 89, 110, and 118.

Then answered the Jews and said unto him, What sign shewest thou unto us, seeing that thou doest these things?

Jesus answered and said unto them, Destroy this temple, and in three days I will raise it up [John 2:18–19].

The word that He used for destroy is *luo* which means "to untie." He is, of course, referring to His own human body.

Then said the Jews, Forty and six years was this temple in building, and wilt thou rear it up in three days? [John 2:20].

The temple at that time was Herod's temple. It was still in the process of being built, and it had already been under construction for forty-six years.

There is a specific use of words in the Greek here that I want you to see. In verses 14 and 15, when it tells of Jesus cleansing the temple, the word used for temple is *hieron* which refers to the temple as a whole. Specifically, it was the outer court of the temple which Jesus cleansed. The word Jesus uses in verse 19 and the Jews repeat in verse 20 is *naos* which refers to the inner sanctuary of the temple. This word can also be used in reference to the body as Paul does in 1 Corinthians 6:19 when he says that the holy place today is not a temple made with hands but that our body is the temple *(naos)* of the Holy Spirit. The Jews were asking the Lord whether He really meant that He would destroy this temple, but, of course, our Lord meant the temple of His body.

But he spake of the temple of his body [John 2:21].

Jesus said that if they destroyed this temple, He would "raise it up." The word He used was *egeirō,* which John uses five times in his gospel. Its actual meaning is "to wake up" and, each time the word is used, it refers to awaking from the dead. Paul used the same word in his sermon in Antioch of Pisidia where he used it four times. It refers to the resurrection of Christ, and it refers to the resurrection of believers, also. It is used in reference to the restoration to life of Lazarus. It was a "waking up." That is the picture which we have in this word *egeirō*. That is precisely what He meant when He spoke of the temple of His body. But His disciples didn't understand that, and it was not until after His resurrection that they recalled it and referred to it.

When therefore he was risen from the dead, his disciples remembered that he had said this unto them; and they believed the scripture, and the word which Jesus had said [John 2:22].

JESUS INTERVIEWS NICODEMUS IN JERUSALEM (Second Word)

Now we are coming to something that is intensely interesting. Actually, we should read from verse 23 right on into chapter 3 where we have the story of Nicodemus. All of this took place in Jerusalem during the time of the Passover.

Now when he was in Jerusalem at the passover, in the feast day, many believed in his name, when they saw the miracles which he did [John 2:23].

A great many folk read that and say, "My, isn't it wonderful that people were believing on Him." But it wasn't wonderful, friend, because theirs was not saving faith at all. They merely nodded in assent when they saw the miracles that He did. So notice what follows.

But Jesus did not commit himself unto them, because he knew all men,

And needed not that any should testify of man: for he knew what was in man [John 2:24–25].

The language that is used here is saying that He did not believe in them. You see, they believed in Him, but He didn't believe in them. In other words, to put it very frankly, their faith was not a saving faith, which He realized, of course. He knew what was in their hearts.

This is always a grave danger today for those who say they believe in Jesus. What do you *mean* when you say you believe in Jesus? Do you mean that you believe in the facts of the gospel? The important question is: Do you *trust Him* as your Savior who died for your sins? Was He raised for *your* justification? Is He your only hope of heaven?

This crowd was interested, and when they saw Him perform miracles, they believed. They had to—they *saw* the miracles. But Jesus didn't believe in them. He knew their belief was not genuine "because he knew all men." He knew what was in the human heart. He didn't need anyone to testify to Him of man because He knew what was in man.

In other words, the Lord Jesus didn't commit Himself unto the mob there. The great company believed on Him, but He didn't entrust Himself to them. When Nicodemus came to Him at night, our Lord did commit Himself unto him because this man's faith was genuine.

It is unfortunate that the movement here is broken by a chapter break.

CHAPTER 3

THEME: *Jesus interviews Nicodemus in Jerusalem (second word)*

JESUS INTERVIEWS NICODEMUS IN JERUSALEM (Second Word)

This is an instance where the chapter break is unfortunate; so we will put it together without the break.

> **But Jesus did not commit himself unto them, because he knew all men,**
>
> **And needed not that any should testify of man: for he knew what was in man.**
>
> **There was a man of the Pharisees, named Nicodemus, a ruler of the Jews [John 2:24–3:1].**

This man is set apart from the mob. Our Lord didn't trust the mob because He knew their faith was not genuine. But this man Nicodemus is a genuine man. Let's get acquainted with him.

Three things are said about him here. The first thing is that he was a man of the Pharisees. That means that he belonged to the best group in Israel. They believed in the inspiration of the Old Testament, they believed in the coming of the Messiah, they believed in miracles, and they believed in the Resurrection. He was a man of the Pharisees, and his name was Nicodemus—we are given his name. And he was a ruler of the Jews. This tells us of the three masks that this man wore.

This is a picture of modern man if there ever was one. Nicodemus was a man of the Pharisees when he met with them. When he was in their midst, he was just one of them. He more or less let down his guard. Then, when he went out from the Pharisees and walked down the street, people would see him coming and would step off the sidewalk. He would be wearing his robe and his phylacteries and prayer shawl, and they would say, "My, that is the ruler, Nicodemus. He's an outstanding man. He's a ruler of the Jews." So he would adopt an altogether different attitude with them. But his name was Nicodemus, and down underneath these two masks that he wore, he was just plain, little old "Nicky."

There are many men who live like this today. There's many a man who is a businessman and president of a corporation. He goes into the office in the morning and those in the office speak to him and they call him, "Mister," and they bow and scrape to him. Although they think they know him, they don't really. Then he leaves his office and sees several of his customers that morning and when they ask him about business, he says, "Oh, business is great." Then he goes to his club at noon for lunch. The minute he steps inside the club, he's a different man. He's not Mister So-and-So, the president of a corporation, but now he's just plain old Joe Dokes. They play golf with him, they think they know him, and they call him by his first name. He adopts a different attitude with them. It is a different relationship. They ask him about business and he tells them, "Oh, business is great." Then in the evening, when the work is done, he goes home. He opens the door to his home, steps in and takes off his coat, and drops down into a chair. He's an altogether different man. His wife comes in and looks at him as he sits there dejected with both of his masks off now. He's no longer the businessman, the head of a corporation, and he's no longer one of the fellows at the club. Now he's just plain little old "Joe." His wife asks him, "What's the matter, Joe? Is business bad?" He replies, "Business is rotten." This is who he really is.

The same came to Jesus by night, and said unto him, Rabbi, we know that thou art a teacher come from God: for no man can do these miracles that thou doest, except God be with him [John 3:2].

This man, Nicodemus, comes to the Lord Jesus with a mask on. He says, "*we* know." Who is we? The Pharisees. He comes as a man of the Pharisees. He is wearing that mask.

He comes with a genuine compliment. He's no hypocrite. He says that we Pharisees have agreed that You are a teacher come from God. I think that he came to talk about the kingdom of God. The Pharisees wanted to establish the kingdom and throw off the yoke of Rome, but they had no way of doing it. Here comes this One who is popular—with the multitudes following Him wherever He goes—so the Pharisees want to hitch their little wagon to His star. Since He has come from the country up in Galilee and they think He doesn't know how to deal with these politicians as they do, they want to combine forces. So Nicodemus comes, acknowledging that Jesus is a teacher come from God.

The proof that he points to are the miracles Jesus performed. He had to recognize the miracles. Please notice that no one doubted the miracles of our Lord—not in that day! You've got to be a professor in a seminary today, removed by two thousand years and several thousand miles from the land where it all took place, and then you can doubt the miracles. But you will not find that either the friends of Jesus or His enemies ever doubted His miracles.

Jesus answered and said unto him, Verily, verily, I say unto thee, Except a man be born again, he cannot see the kingdom of God [John 3:3].

This is the reason I think he came to talk about the kingdom of God. I see no other reason why our Lord would almost abruptly interrupt him and say to him, "The thing is, you can't even *see* the kingdom of God except you've been born again." Now here is a man, a Pharisee, who is religious to his fingertips, and yet our Lord told him he couldn't see the kingdom of God except he be born again. If this man came to talk about the kingdom and the establishing of it, which I think he did, then certainly this statement of our Lord detoured him. So now he drops the mask of the man of the Pharisees, but he is still a ruler of the Jews.

Nicodemus saith unto him, How can a man be born when he is old? can he enter the second time into his mother's womb, and be born? [John 3:4].

Jesus had said he must be born again. The Greek word for "again" is *anothen* which means "from above." This man Nicodemus couldn't think of anything but a physical birth. He immediately dropped the condescending mask of the Pharisee and asked how this could be. Our Lord wasn't speaking of a physical birth at all. He was speaking about a spiritual birth. But Nicodemus couldn't understand about a spiritual birth. The reason was that he had no spiritual capacity to comprehend it.

Jesus answered, Verily, verily, I say unto thee, Except a man be born of water and of the Spirit, he cannot enter into the kingdom of God [John 3:5].

Now what does it mean to be born of water and of the Spirit? There are those who think that to be born of water is a reference to water baptism. But this would be a strange expression if it did refer to that. Then, there have been several very fine Christian doctors who interpret "born of water" as the physical birth which is a birth in water; that is, the child in the womb is in water. I don't think that is what is meant here at all. He wasn't talking about the difference between natural birth and spiritual birth, but He was talking about *how* a man could be born "from above" or "born again."

As we saw in chapter 2, water is symbolic of the Word of God. We will find later in this book that Jesus says, "Sanctify them through thy truth: *thy word* is truth" (John 17:17, italics mine). There is a cleansing, sanctifying power in the Word. In John 15:3 Jesus says, "Now ye are clean through the *word* which I have spoken unto you" (italics mine). The Word of God is likened unto water again and again. We believe that "born of water and of the Spirit" means that a person must be born again by the Holy Spirit using the Scripture. We believe, very definitely, that no one could be born again without the Word of God applied by the Spirit of God. One today is born from above by the use of water, which is the Word of God, and the Spirit, the Holy Spirit, making it real to the heart.

There are three outstanding conversions in the Book of Acts. They have been given to us, I think, primarily as illustrations. There is the conversion of the Ethiopian eunuch, the conversion of Cornelius, and the conversion of Paul. These three men are representatives of the three families of Noah: the son of Shem, the son of Ham, and the son of Japheth. In each of these three cases, the Word of God was used by the Spirit of God for their conversions. God's method seems to be the Word of God, used by the Spirit of God, given through a man of God. I am confident that our Lord, saying that one must be born of water and of the Spirit, referred to the Spirit of God using the Word of God. Without this, Nicodemus could not enter into the kingdom of God.

That which is born of the flesh is flesh; and that which is born of the Spirit is spirit [John 3:6].

God does not intend to change the flesh, meaning this old nature which you and I have. The fact of the matter is that it can't be changed. The Word of God has much to say about this. The old nature is at war with God. "Because the carnal mind is enmity against God: for it is not subject to the law of God, neither indeed can be. So then they that are in the flesh cannot please God" (Rom. 8:7–8). God has no program for our old nature to retrieve it, or improve it, or develop it, or save it. That old nature is to go down into the grave with us. And, if the Lord comes before we go down into the grave, we are to be *changed* in the twinkling of an eye, which means we will get rid of that old nature. It can never be made obedient to God. "That which is born of the flesh is flesh." That is an axiom. God does not intend to save the flesh at all. This old nature must be replaced by the new nature. The spiritual birth is necessary so that you and I may be given a new nature, friend.

Now notice that Nicodemus who had been hiding behind the mask, "ruler of the Jews," will be losing it.

Marvel not that I said unto thee, Ye must be born again.

The wind bloweth where it listeth, and thou hearest the sound thereof, but canst not tell whence it cometh, and whither it goeth: so is every one that is born of the Spirit [John 3:7–8].

Jesus is saying, "You can't tell where the wind comes from and you can't tell where it is going." The air currents and the winds are something that man still doesn't control. The wind blows where it wills. We can't detour it, and we can't change it. There is an attempt being made to seed down the hurricanes in the Gulf of Mexico and the Caribbean area, but so far we haven't tamed the wind.

Although we can't control the wind, we surely can tell when it's blowing. You and I can be standing out on the street and you can say to me, "The wind is blowing!" I answer, "How do you know?" You would reply, "Look at that tree up there, see how the leaves are blowing, and notice how the tree is bending over." We can tell when the wind is blowing.

Now, friend, I don't know how to explain to you the spiritual birth. I know there are a lot of books being published that claim to explain it, but the difference between the authors and me is that they don't seem to know that they don't know, while I am willing to admit that I don't know. "The wind bloweth where it listeth . . . so is every one that is born of the Spirit." Although we don't quite understand it, it illustrates the way one is born of the Spirit. I can't tell you exactly how the Spirit of God operates, but I can surely tell when He is moving in the lives and hearts of His people. That's exactly what our Lord is saying here.

Our Lord has gotten rid of the two masks. The man who stands before Him is no longer the man of the Pharisees and he is no longer the ruler of the Jews. Who is he? Let's see what the verse says.

Nicodemus answered and said unto him, How can these things be? [John 3:9].

Now he stands there, just plain, little old "Nicky." He's wondering how these things can be and our Lord is going to talk to him very plainly. By the way, you and I can put up our masks before each other and there are many people today who use them. When they are with a certain crowd, they act a certain way. The mask, friend, hides just what we really are. When we come to the Lord Jesus, we have to take off all our masks. We can't use them there. You have to be the real "you." You have to come just as you are; then Jesus will deal with you that way. And this is the way He will deal with this man Nicodemus.

Jesus answered and said unto him, Art thou a master of Israel, and knowest not these things? [John 3:10].

That's gentle satire that our Lord is using here. He is saying to this man, "You are a ruler in Israel and acting as if I were telling you something that couldn't be true, because if it were true, you would have known about it." And then Jesus asks, "Don't you know these things, Nicodemus?"

Verily, verily, I say unto thee, We speak that we do know, and testify that we have seen; and ye receive not our witness.

If I have told you earthly things, and ye believe not, how shall ye believe, if I tell you of heavenly things?

And no man hath ascended up to heaven, but he that came down from heaven, even the Son of man which is in heaven [John 3:11–13].

He tells Nicodemus that he hasn't received His witness even as it was spoken to him.

Then He goes on to show that there is a tremendous movement which is set forth here in the Gospel of John. I called attention in the Introduction to the saying of our Lord in John 16:28, "I came forth from the Father, and am come into the world: again, I leave the world, and go to the Father." And now He says, "No man hath ascended up to heaven." That is the answer to those today who feel that Elijah and Enoch went to heaven when they were translated. I don't think so because up to this point the Lord Jesus says that no man hath ascended up to heaven, but He that came down from heaven, even the Son of Man which is in heaven. In other words, He is saying that He is the only One who can speak about heaven because He is the only One who has ascended up to heaven. Now it is true that there are a host of folk who have gone to heaven after Christ, but in the Old Testament, when a saint of God died, one of God's own, he went to a place that is called Paradise or Abraham's Bosom—our Lord called it that (see Luke 16:22). It was not until after Christ died and ascended to heaven and led captivity captive that He took those who were in Paradise into the presence of God in heaven. Since then, for the child of God, it has always been ". . . absent from the body . . . present with the Lord" (2 Cor. 5:8). But when Jesus was here, no other man had ascended to heaven.

And as Moses lifted up the serpent in the wilderness, even so must the Son of man be lifted up:

That whosoever believeth in him should not perish, but have eternal life [John 3:14–15].

When Moses lifted up that brass serpent on a pole, because of God's judgment upon the sin of the people, all they had to do for healing was to look to it. As Moses lifted up the serpent, so Christ is going to be lifted up. That serpent, you see, represented the sin of the people. And Christ was made sin for us on the cross because He bore our sin there. As Moses lifted up the serpent in the wilderness, even so must the Son of Man be lifted up.

Now our Lord repeats to Nicodemus probably the most familiar words we have in the Bible:

For God so loved the world, that he gave his only begotten Son, that whosoever believeth in him should not perish, but have everlasting life [John 3:16].

There are two things that we need to note here. One is that we *must* be born again. The other is that the Son of Man *must* be lifted up. They are related. It takes the death of Christ and the resurrection of Christ—He must be lifted up. Since He has been lifted up, since He bore our penalty, the Spirit of God can regenerate us. And we *must* be born again—that is the only way God can receive us.

The motivation for all of this is that God so *loved* the world. God never saved the world by love, which is the mistaken thinking of today. It doesn't say that God's love saved the world, because the love of God could never save a sinner. God does not save by love, friends. *God saves by grace!* "For by grace are ye saved through faith; and that not of yourselves: it is the gift of God: Not of works, lest any man should boast" (Eph. 2:8–9). Now, how does God save? God saves by grace. But God so *loved* the world, that He *gave* His only begotten Son that whoever (you can write your name in here and I can write mine) believes in Him should not perish, but have everlasting life. Notice that with the word *believe* is the little preposition *in* which means to believe *in* Christ. That is, we trust Him as the One who bore the penalty for our sins. This is a personal thing. We must each believe that He died in our place and in our stead. My friend, you must believe that He died for you.

For God sent not his Son into the world to condemn the world; but that the world through him might be saved.

He that believeth on him is not condemned: but he that believeth not is condemned already, because he hath not believed in the name of the only begotten Son of God [John 3:17–18].

We see here that, when Jesus came the first time, He was not a judge. He made that very clear to the man who wanted Him to give a judgment between himself and his brother. He said, ". . . Man, who made me a judge or a divider over you?" (Luke 12:14). He didn't come as a Judge the first time. He came as the Savior. He will come the next time as the Judge. But now He says that God didn't send Him into the world to condemn the world, but that the world through Him might be saved. Whoever does not believe in Him is condemned. Friend, if you don't believe, you are already condemned. Why? Because "he hath not believed in the name of the only begotten Son of God." That wonderful name is Jesus—His name is Jesus because He is the Savior of the world. Anyone who will believe in that name is no longer under condemnation but has everlasting life.

Remember that He is talking to Nicodemus, a Pharisee. The Pharisees believed that the Messiah, when He came, would be a judge. The Old Testament presented two aspects of the coming of the Messiah. One was His coming as a Savior, coming to die, coming to pay a penalty; the other was His coming as the Judge. They reasoned that the Messiah would be a judge when He came because the Old Testament presents that aspect. In Psalm 2:9 we read, "Thou shalt break them with a rod of iron. . . ." Daniel speaks of Him as a judge of the whole world (Dan. 7:13–14). Psalm 45 talks about His ruling the world in righteousness, and Isaiah 11 and Isaiah 42 speak of His judgments in righteousness. The Lord Jesus is making it very clear to Nicodemus that God sent not His Son *this time* to judge the world, but that the world through Him might be saved. The "world" is the Greek word *kosmos*—God's redemptive purpose embraces the entire world. He did not come to condemn or to judge the world but to save the world.

In Christ there is no condemnation. Those who are not in Christ are *already* condemned. There are a great many who feel that the world is on trial today. It is not. The world is lost. You and I live in a lost world, and we'll not wait until the final judgment to see that we are lost. Our position is something like a man who is in prison being asked whether or not he will accept a pardon. That is the gospel. It is not telling a man that he is on trial. He is already condemned. He is already in prison waiting for execution. But the gospel tells him a pardon is offered to him. The point is, will you accept the pardon? How wonderfully clear that is. The gospel is to save those who are already lost.

And this is the condemnation, that light is come into the world, and men loved darkness rather than light, because their deeds were evil.

For every one that doeth evil hateth the light, neither cometh to the light, lest his deeds should be reproved.

But he that doeth truth cometh to the light, that his deeds may be made manifest, that they are wrought in God [John 3:19–21].

This is the judgment, you see, of the world. The day that the world crucified Christ—on that day the world made a decision. It must now be judged by God. The condemnation, or the judgment, is that light is come into the world, but because men's deeds were habitually evil, they loved the darkness. Rats always scurry for a dark corner when light enters a room. Today I received a letter from a girl who said that, before she was saved, she never cared for our Bible-teaching program. Naturally, she did not want the light at all. Only those who turn to Christ want the light.

Notice that in this verse our Lord approaches so many things from the negative point. "For every one that doeth evil hateth the light, neither cometh to the light, lest his deeds should be reproved." We hear today of the power of positive thinking. Believe me, friend, there is a lot of power in negative thinking and negative speaking. Listen to other things He said. ". . . I came *not* to call the righteous, but sinners to repentance" and ". . . the Son of man came *not* to be ministered unto, but to minister, and to give his life a ransom for many" (Mark 2:17; 10:45, italics mine). "God sent *not* his Son into the world to condemn the world." And He says that every one that doeth evil hateth the light. In other words, whoever habitually practices what is wrong hates the light. "Light" and "truth" are used in the same way. "He that doeth truth cometh to the light." Error and darkness are always in contrast to light and truth. This ends His interview with Nicodemus.

TESTIMONY OF JOHN THE BAPTIST

After these things came Jesus and his disciples into the land of Judaea; and there he tarried with them, and baptized.

And John also was baptizing in Aenon near to Salim, because there was much water there: and they came, and were baptized.

For John was not yet cast into prison [John 3:22–24].

At this time, John was still able to preach ". . . the kingdom of heaven is at hand" (Matt. 3:2). It was after the Lord's temptation that John was cast into prison. The other Gospels tell us that.

Then there arose a question between some of John's disciples and the Jews about purifying.

And they came unto John, and said unto him, Rabbi, he that was with thee beyond Jordan, to whom thou barest witness, behold, the same baptizeth, and all men come to him [John 3:25–26].

This is a very interesting statement. The disciples of John, I would assume, are jealous. They are suggesting that he should not mention the name of Jesus. They feel it would be best if he didn't. And then they imply that he should not have borne witness to Him to begin with because all are going to Him—well, now, that is hyperbole—but it reveals they were jealous and were afraid John was going to lose all his followers.

Now this man John makes a very clear statement. There is not a jealous bone in the body of John.

John answered and said, A man can receive nothing, except it be given him from heaven.

Ye yourselves bear me witness, that I said, I am not the Christ, but that I am sent before him.

He that hath the bride is the bridegroom: but the friend of the bridegroom, which standeth and heareth him, rejoiceth greatly because of the bridegroom's voice: this my joy therefore is fulfilled.

He must increase, but I must decrease [John 3:27–30].

One cannot escape the tremendous force of this, friend. John the Baptist is the last of the Old Testament prophets. He is actually not in the church. He makes it clear here. "He that hath the bride." Who is the bride? The church. "He that hath the bride is the bridegroom." Then who is John? He is the friend of the Bridegroom. He will be present at the marriage supper of the Lamb, but he is not a part of the church by any means. He is the last of the Old Testament prophets who walks out of the Old Testament onto the pages of the New Testament to announce the coming of the Messiah.

"A man can receive nothing, except it be given him from heaven." Again and again this truth will come out. Jesus said, "No man can come unto me, except it were given unto him of my Father" (John 6:65). How tremendous these statements are! And then John says that Christ must increase but that John must decrease. His ministry is now coming to an end.

He that cometh from above is above all: he that is of the earth is earthly, and speaketh of the earth: he that cometh from heaven is above all.

And what he hath seen and heard, that he testifieth; and no man receiveth his testimony.

He that hath received his testimony hath set to his seal that God is true.

For he whom God hath sent speaketh the words of God: for God giveth not the Spirit by measure unto him.

The Father loveth the Son, and hath given all things into his hand.

He that believeth on the Son hath everlasting life: and he that believeth not the Son shall not see life; but the wrath of God abideth on him [John 3:31–36].

John makes it very clear that the Lord Jesus Christ is superior, and he gives them this wonderful testimony concerning the Lord Jesus.

"He that believeth on the Son *hath* everlasting life." You have it right now! Friend, you couldn't have it any clearer than that. John the Baptist preached the gospel, as you can see. He told the message that men are lost without Christ, but they have everlasting life through faith in Christ. What a testimony this man had. What a tremendous witness to the Lord Jesus Christ!

CHAPTER 4

***THEME:** Jesus interviews the woman at the well in Sychar (third word); Jesus heals the nobleman's son in Capernaum (second work)*

Chapter 4 brings us to the very important incident in the ministry of our Lord as He goes through Samaria.

When therefore the Lord knew how the Pharisees had heard that Jesus made and baptized more disciples than John,

(Though Jesus himself baptized not, but his disciples,)

He left Judaea, and departed again into Galilee [John 4:1–3].

This, apparently, was immediately after the incident in chapter 3. It was in the month of December and probably near December 27. This was the time that John the Baptist was in prison. When John was imprisoned, Jesus left Judaea and went back into Galilee.

Why did He retire from Judaea? Well, He did not want to precipitate a crisis. You see, the Lord Jesus was moving according to schedule, a heavenly schedule set by the Father. He has made it very clear that He came to do the Father's will. Speaking of His own life, He said, "No man taketh it from me, but I lay it down of myself. I have power to lay it down, and I have power to take it again. This commandment have I received of my Father" (John 10:18). They can't touch Him until His time has come. When we reach the thirteenth chapter of John, we will see that His time had then come. "Now before the feast of the passover, when Jesus knew that his hour was come that he should depart out of this world unto the Father" (John 13:1)—you see He's moving on His Father's schedule, friend; He has come to do the Father's will.

So He departed again into Galilee. He went back up where His headquarters were, which, we believe, were in the city of Capernaum.

JESUS INTERVIEWS THE WOMAN AT THE WELL IN SYCHAR (Third Word)

And he must needs go through Samaria [John 4:4].

That word *must* attracts our attention. Why *must* He go through Samaria? In order to reach a certain woman. Listen to Him in verse 34, "My meat is to do the will of him that sent me, and to finish his work." He must go through Samaria because it is the Father's will for Him to go through Samaria. His destination, apparently, was Cana of Galilee where He had made the water into wine. There was a certain nobleman whose son was sick and He is headed in that direction. But He must go through Samaria.

There were three routes He could have taken. He could have gone along the coast. There was a route there, and it is still there today, by the way. He could have gone through Peraea which is up at the other side of Jordan. Or He could go through Samaria. Josephus tells us that, although the most direct route was through Samaria, the Jews didn't go that route due to the antipathy between the Jews and the Samaritans. However, our Lord went through Samaria.

Then cometh he to a city of Samaria, which is called Sychar, near to the parcel of ground that Jacob gave to his son Joseph [John 4:5].

Joseph's tomb is near by. At the fork of the old Roman road south of Sychar He meets the woman at the well. Mount Gerizim is to the northwest, and the synagogue of the Samaritans is on the slope of Mount Gerizim. I've been at that spot and have taken pictures there. This is the place to which our Lord comes.

Now Jacob's well was there. Jesus therefore, being wearied with his journey, sat thus on the well: and it was about the sixth hour [John 4:6].

The sixth hour according to Roman time would be six o'clock in the evening, but we are following Jewish time here and the sixth hour was twelve noon. He was weary with His journey. How perfectly human He was. You see, John presents Him as the Son of God, as God manifest in the flesh. "The Word was made flesh" (John 1:14). Friend, although the language is simple, it expresses something that is overwhelming. Think of it! The God of eternity came down to this earth. The Word was made flesh and dwelled among us—He pitched His tent here among us. He went through Samaria and sat down at a well in order that He might reach this woman of Samaria!

The Samaritans were a group of poor people in that day.

There cometh a woman of Samaria to draw water: Jesus saith unto her, Give me to drink [John 4:7].

This woman is obviously a dissolute woman. I think she is probably as common as pig tracks. She's rude and immoral. We would call her today a hussy or a broad, if you please.

What a contrast she is to the man, Nicodemus, we saw in the preceding chapter. And notice how differently our Lord deals with her. With Nicodemus, a man who was religious to his fingertips, our Lord was harsh and blunt, but see how gentle He is with this woman. He asks a favor of her. He appeals to her sympathy—He is thirsty and asks for a drink. What condescension on His part! He is the Water of Life and He asks her for water.

(For his disciples were gone away unto the city to buy meat.) [John 4:8].

It is noon and His disciples have gone to the city to buy food. The fact that they were buying the Samaritans' food also reveals Jesus' total rejection of the Jewish prejudice which considered Samaritan food unclean, even as swine's flesh.

Then saith the woman of Samaria unto him, How is it that thou, being a Jew, askest drink of me, which am a woman of Samaria? for the Jews have no dealings with the Samaritans [John 4:9].

Twice she refuses His request. She's rude here, and insolent, impudent, and impertinent—she tosses her pert and saucy head. She makes this racial distinction. It is said that the Samaritans would sell to the Jews, but they wouldn't drink from the same vessel with them.

You see what our Lord is doing here. He is coming to the very lowest place to which He can come. But watch how the Lord deals with her. He is very skillful and sympathetic, but He also talks with her forcefully, faithfully, and factually. He doesn't give her a lecture on integration or civil rights. He isn't a candidate for some office. He just appeals to her womanly curiosity. He creates an interest and a thirst.

Jesus answered and said unto her, If thou knewest the gift of God, and who it is that saith to thee, Give me to drink; thou wouldest have asked of him, and he would have given thee living water [John 4:10].

As He appeals to her curiosity, her attitude immediately changes.

The woman saith unto him, Sir, thou hast nothing to draw with, and the well is deep: from whence then hast thou that living water?

Art thou greater than our father Jacob, which gave us the well, and drank thereof himself, and his children, and his cattle? [John 4:11–12].

The woman calls Him "Sir" which she had left out before. Then she was impudent and rude, but now there is a difference. The whole point here is that this woman is thinking in terms of the physical; her thinking could get no higher than the water level down in the well.

Notice that she identifies herself with Jacob. She does this purposely, as racially the Samaritans were Jacob's descendants who had intermarried with peoples from the north following the Assyrian Captivity of Israel in 721 B.C.

Jesus answered and said unto her, Whosoever drinketh of this water shall thirst again:

But whosoever drinketh of the water that I shall give him shall never thirst; but the water that I shall give him shall be in him a well of water springing up into everlasting life [John 4:13–14].

Jesus makes it clear that He is not talking about water in Jacob's well. Rather, He is making a contrast, you see. Today the crowds are going to the water holes of this world, seeking satisfaction. They also are constantly looking for the physical, not the spiritual satisfaction. But now Jesus has created a desire in this woman's heart for the spiritual water.

The woman saith unto him, Sir, give me this water, that I thirst not, neither come hither to draw [John 4:15].

She's thirsty for spiritual water, but then her thinking goes right back down into that well again.

Jesus saith unto her, Go, call thy husband, and come hither [John 4:16].

This is the master stroke. Although the water is available for all, there is a condition to be met—there must be a thirst, a need. She must, therefore, recognize that she is a sinner. So our Lord says to her, "Go call your husband." That is a touchy subject. She becomes flippant again.

The woman answered and said, I have no husband. Jesus said unto her, Thou hast well said, I have no husband:

For thou hast had five husbands; and he whom thou now hast is not thy husband: in that saidst thou truly [John 4:17–18].

She was accurate about that. She had had five husbands, but she didn't have one then. She was living with a man in adultery. Our Lord insists that, when you come to Him, you must deal with sin. All secrets must come out before Him. Here was a sinner. One of the reasons she was not so popular with the women of the town was because she was too popular with the men of the town.

The woman was actually shocked into reverence. But then she wanted to change the subject by opening a religious argument.

The woman saith unto him, Sir, I perceive that thou art a prophet.

Our fathers worshipped in this mountain; and ye say, that in Jerusalem is the place where men ought to worship [John 4:19–20].

Now that will make a good religious argument, friend. Where are you going to worship? In this mountain or in Jerusalem? That caused many an argument in that day.

There are many people today who want to argue religion, but they don't want to live it. I'm convinced that most of the superficiality in our churches today is there as a cover-up of sin. Unfortunately our churches are honeycombed with hypocrisy, a compromise with evil, and a refusal to face up to sin. You know, it's easy to preach about the sin of the Moabites which they committed about 4,000 years ago, but what about our sins today? It was the brother of Henry Ward Beecher who said, "I like a sermon where one man is the preacher and one man is the congregation so that when the preacher says, 'Thou art the man,' there's no mistaking whom he's talking about." There are many ministers today who are afraid to preach on the sins of Christians. This was confirmed to me several years ago. I was speaking in a summer conference on the first eight chapters of Romans. This is not often used as a subject because Paul deals with sin. At first I could actually feel a resentment. By the middle of the week, the Holy Spirit began to break up hard hearts and a fellow who seemed to be the most pompous and pious saint came to me wanting to confess his sins. I told him not to confess them to me, but to go to the great High Priest, the Lord Jesus. He would hear him when he confessed, and He would forgive him. What a change took place in this man! At that same conference two ministers came to me, personally and privately, asking, "Do you preach like this in your own church?" Well, I did preach like that, but I found out there was a little cell of super-duper saints, who liked to criticize the preacher so as to take the attention off themselves. They really wanted to be active—in fact, they wanted to run the church—but they did not want to deal with sin in their lives.

Our Lord did not avoid or sidestep the issue of personal sin. I believe that if you really have honest questions or doubts, the Lord will reveal the solution to you. And our Lord dealt with this woman on the question she had raised.

Jesus saith unto her, Woman, believe me, the hour cometh, when ye shall neither in this mountain, nor yet at Jerusalem, worship the Father.

Ye worship ye know not what: we know what we worship: for salvation is of the Jews [John 4:21–22].

The thing that was important to this woman was whether she should worship God in this mountain where the Samaritans worship Him, or should she worship Him in Jerusalem. Jesus told her the day was coming when He would not be worshiped in either place. Why?

But the hour cometh, and now is, when the true worshippers shall worship the Father in spirit and in truth: for the Father seeketh such to worship him.

God is a Spirit: and they that worship him must worship him in spirit and in truth [John 4:23–24].

It is irrelevant, therefore, where you worship God. It is not *where* but *how* you worship Him that is important. Our Lord answered her very adequately. God is a Spirit. You don't have to run to this place or that place. True worshipers worship Him in spirit and in truth.

The woman saith unto him, I know that Messias cometh, which is called Christ: when he is come, he will tell us all things [John 4:25].

Even the Samaritans were looking for the Messiah to come. That is something that is very interesting. Today the second coming of Christ is believed and loved by those who are

His. Those who are not really His, though church members, have a nagging feeling that He might come. Although they say they don't believe in His second coming, it still disturbs them.

An atheist in London several years ago made the statement that the thing that disturbed him was that the Bible might be true and that Jesus might come again. If He did, this man realized he would be in trouble. Believe me, he surely will be in trouble!

The woman now is profoundly interested, and there is a wistful longing in her heart.

The woman saith unto him, I know that Messias cometh, which is called Christ: when he is come, he will tell us all things.

Jesus saith unto her, I that speak unto thee am he [John 4:25–26].

How majestic and sublime this statement is! This woman is brought face to face now with the Savior of the world, the Messiah. Friend, this is my question to you today, whoever you are, wherever you are, and however you are: Have you come face to face with the Lord Jesus Christ as this woman did? I tell you, she found herself in His presence. "I that speak unto thee am he!"

And upon this came his disciples, and marvelled that he talked with the woman: yet no man said, What seekest thou? or, Why talkest thou with her?

The woman then left her waterpot, and went her way into the city, and saith to the men,

Come, see a man, which told me all things that ever I did: is not this the Christ? [John 4:27–29].

The woman had turned in faith to the Lord Jesus; so now she rushes into the city to tell others. Notice that she does not talk to the women because she's not on speaking terms with them. Some of those men were involved with her, and they are very much interested in knowing whether He could tell all things that she had done. So here is what happened.

Then they went out of the city, and came unto him [John 4:30].

The men came because of her witness. That is very important for us to see. The fact that she witnessed to others is evidence of her faith.

In the mean while his disciples prayed him, saying, Master, eat.

But he said unto them, I have meat to eat that ye know not of.

Therefore said the disciples one to another, Hath any man brought him aught to eat?

Jesus saith unto them, My meat is to do the will of him that sent me, and to finish his work [John 4:31–34].

The reason that He went through Samaria was to do the Father's will by reaching this woman.

Say not ye, There are yet four months, and then cometh harvest? behold, I say unto you, Lift up your eyes, and look on the fields; for they are white already to harvest.

And he that reapeth receiveth wages, and gathereth fruit unto life eternal: that both he that soweth and he that reapeth may rejoice together.

And herein is that saying true, One soweth, and another reapeth.

I sent you to reap that whereon ye bestowed no labour: other men laboured, and ye are entered into their labours [John 4:35–38].

Remember that this took place in December, and harvest in that area would be in April.

In this age in which we are living today, our business is to sow. I am attempting through the radio media to sow the Word of God. I hope that good churches will reap because I have sown. One pastor told me that because of the radio messages, he had received into his church over one hundred members. We are reaching a great many people who are members of liberal churches, but they want to know where to go to be taught the Word of God. This pastor said that because folk had listened to the broadcast and then realized that they wanted the Word of God, they had come to his church. They will join churches where the Word is taught. One sows and another reaps. I rejoice in that.

And many of the Samaritans of that city believed on him for the saying of the woman, which testified, He told me all that ever I did [John 4:39].

A great company was reached in Samaria through this woman with the "shady" past!

So when the Samaritans were come unto him, they besought him that he would tarry with them: and he abode there two days.

And many more believed because of his own word;

And said unto the woman, Now we believe, not because of thy saying: for we have heard him ourselves, and know that this is indeed the Christ, the Saviour of the world [John 4:40–42].

What a wonderful thing we see here. They came to the Living Water and they drank. The only condition was for them to thirst. You will never know that you thirst until you know that you are a sinner, friend. Isaiah cried, "Ho, every one that thirsteth, come ye to the waters . . ." (Isa. 55:1). Our Lord gave the same invitation: "If any man thirst, let him come unto me, and drink" (John 7:37). The Water of Life is for "any man." But the one condition is thirst. Many of the Samaritans came to Him, and they drank.

As many men came to Christ through the witness of the woman at Samaria, today many people are led to know Christ through the influence of another. In fact, it is the effect of one life upon other lives, the impact of one personality upon another, which often leads people to Christ. Some young people have remarkable parents, or one remarkable parent, and because of the influence of the parent they may come to Christ. They live in the light of that parent with no personal contact with Christ Himself. Then later they stumble and fall when the influence of the parent is gone. I've seen that happen again and again during my years as a pastor. It is a wonderful thing to exercise an influence on another for Christ, but don't let it stand there! See that the individual gets through to Christ in a personal relationship for himself. The Samaritans said, "Now we believe, not because of thy saying: for we have heard him ourselves, and know that this is indeed the Christ, the Saviour of the world."

JESUS HEALS THE NOBLEMAN'S SON IN CAPERNAUM (Second Work)

Now after two days he departed thence, and went into Galilee.

For Jesus himself testified, that a prophet hath no honour in his own country.

Then when he was come into Galilee, the Galilaeans received him, having seen all the things that he did at Jerusalem at the feast: for they also went unto the feast.

So Jesus came again into Cana of Galilee, where he made the water wine. And there was a certain nobleman, whose son was sick at Capernaum [John 4:43–46].

Notice the geography John gives us here again. Jesus leaves Samaria and goes into Galilee, and many Galilaeans believe on Him because they had seen Him at the feast and had watched the things He had done. Then He goes specifically to Cana of Galilee because there is a certain nobleman there whose son is way down in Capernaum.

When he heard that Jesus was come out of Judaea into Galilee, he went unto him, and besought him that he would come down, and heal his son: for he was at the point of death [John 4:47].

Here is a father who exercised faith in behalf of his son. This illustrates the thing we have just been saying. Make sure your own child has a *personal* contact with Jesus Christ. The essential thing would have been for the father to have brought the boy to Christ. I think that we have a right to claim our loved ones for Christ. We should exercise our own influence upon the lives of others. I believe that you've got to be a witness to your loved ones and that you've got to reveal in your own life that you have a living faith in Christ and that it works.

A man who was a member of the church I served in Los Angeles came to me one day, asking me to pray for the salvation of his son. Unfortunately, although he was an officer of the church, his life wasn't very good. The boy had walked out of the house, and I honestly couldn't blame the boy for it at all. The father wanted me to counsel with the boy and attempt to lead him to Christ. I very candidly told him that I wouldn't talk with the boy. I said, "You've served that boy 'roast preacher' for so long that he hasn't any use for me. You've done nothing but criticize. Now you've lost your influence with him, and I will pray that someone else will exert an influence on your boy and bring him to the Lord." Friend, if you are a parent, remember that your life exerts a powerful influence upon your children, both good and bad.

The nobleman came to Jesus asking Him to come down and heal his son who was at the point of death.

Then said Jesus unto him, Except ye see signs and wonders, ye will not believe.

The nobleman saith unto him, Sir, come down ere my child die.

Jesus saith unto him, Go thy way; thy son liveth. And the man believed the word that Jesus had spoken unto him, and he went his way [John 4:48–50].

This man protested that he was not just looking for signs and wonders; he wanted his boy. That was all-important to him. Jesus responded to this man's faith and He did heal the boy. That is wonderful.

However, it's too bad he didn't bring the boy into the presence of Christ. That was of the utmost importance. We hope he did so after the boy was well. The Samaritan woman, even though she had been a bad woman, brought the men face to face with the Lord Jesus.

You can influence someone that no preacher can reach. In fact, nobody else can reach that individual but you. You have that influence over that individual. Be very sure that you bring him face to face with Christ.

And as he was now going down, his servants met him, and told him, saying, Thy son liveth.

Then inquired he of them the hour when he began to amend. And they said unto him, Yesterday at the seventh hour the fever left him [John 4:51–52].

It's difficult to be sure just what time John is using. According to Roman time this would have been about seven in the evening.

So the father knew that it was at the same hour, in the which Jesus said unto him, Thy son liveth: and himself believed, and his whole house.

This is again the second miracle that Jesus did, when he was come out of Judaea into Galilee [John 4:53–54].

The father claimed his whole household for Christ. They would each have to exert faith personally, but this man claimed them and would exert his influence for Christ.

The word for *miracle* here is actually the word *sign*. This is the second sign that Jesus did.

CHAPTER 5

THEME: *Jesus heals man at Pool of Bethesda (third work)*

JESUS HEALS MAN AT POOL OF BETHESDA (Third Work)

Chapter 5 brings us to this very wonderful incident of the healing of the impotent man at the pool of Bethesda. Actually, in a sense, this miracle is the turning point in the ministry of Christ. You see, this miracle set the bloodhounds of hate on His track, and they never let up until they put Him to death on the cross.

Notice verse 16:

And therefore did the Jews persecute Jesus, and sought to slay him, because he had done these things on the sabbath day.

But Jesus answered them, My Father worketh hitherto, and I work.

Therefore the Jews sought the more to kill him, because he not only had broken the sabbath, but said also that God was his Father, making himself equal with God [John 5:16–18].

You see, the clash with them was over the Sabbath day; they never forgave Him for what He did on the Sabbath. They hated Him because He said, ". . . The sabbath was made for man, and not man for the sabbath" (Mark 2:27). The miracle that our Lord performed here really put murder into their hearts. They hated Him because of the Sabbath and because He made Himself equal with God.

"Making himself equal with God" is a clear-cut claim to deity. I have heard the liberals say that the Bible does not teach the deity of Christ. I don't know what those men are talking about. I feel they are either woefully ignorant or they are absolutely dishonest. You may disagree with the Lord Jesus, and you may disagree with the Bible, but how can you put any other construction on these plain words, "making himself equal with God"? If that isn't claiming deity, then I do not know how a person would be able to claim deity.

Now let's go back to the beginning of the chapter. It starts with a feast of the Jews. The question arises as to which feast this is. It is probably the Passover. There are three great feasts of the Jews: "Three times in a year shall all thy males appear before the LORD thy God in the place which he shall choose; in the feast of unleavened bread, and in the feast of weeks, and in the feast of tabernacles. . ." (Deut. 16:16). Since in John 2 we find the Passover, and in John 7 we find the Feast of Tabernacles, many have assumed that this feast is Pentecost. We are not told because that is not really the important thing here. I rather think it could be the Feast of Passover again.

After this there was a feast of the Jews; and Jesus went up to Jerusalem.

Now there is at Jerusalem by the sheep market a pool, which is called in the Hebrew tongue Bethesda, having five porches.

In these lay a great multitude of impotent folk, of blind, halt, withered, waiting for the moving of the water [John 5:1–3].

Now it was really the sheep gate, not a market, where the pool was. The name of the pool was Bethesda which means, "house of olives" or "house of mercy." It had five porches. In these lay a great multitude. The word *great* is not in the better manuscripts, but it doesn't change the meaning because a multitude is a great number anyway. "A multitude of *impotent* folk" means people without strength.

Many years ago, when I was pastor in Pasadena, I went up one year to speak at the Preventorium where little fellows and girls who had weak lungs or tuberculosis were cared for. They presented an Easter program. There was one little fellow there who quoted this entire fifth chapter of John, all forty-seven verses. He made only one error and I always felt it wasn't much of an error. In verse 3, he quoted it like this, "In these lay a great multitude of *important* folk." Quite a few people smiled when he said that. I got to thinking about it, and realized he was correct. They were important. One of them caused the Lord Jesus to come to this place and any of the others could have turned to Him. They were important to Him.

The fourth verse of this chapter is not in the better manuscripts. To say this, does not mean that I don't believe in the inerrancy of Scripture. I want to assure you that I do believe in the inerrancy of Scripture. Why in the world do you think that I teach the entire Bible? But I do think we should heed scholarship—fundamental, conservative scholarship which suggests that because it is not in the better manuscripts, it was put in by a scribe as a word of explanation. I believe it is factual and it helps me understand why this crowd of impotent folk were here. But whether it belongs in Scripture or not is not worth an argument. To me it is not the essential thing because there is something far more important here. However, I did want to give this word of explanation.

For an angel went down at a certain season into the pool, and troubled the water: whosoever then first after the troubling of the water stepped in was made whole of whatsoever disease he had [John 5:4].

This is the explanation of why they were there. The belief was that an angel stirred the water at a certain season. I personally feel that a great many cures took place there that were psychological cures. There are a number of people today, just as there were then, who are sick in their minds, ignorant, and superstitious. There are quite a few who go to faith healers today who believe they get healed. There is always a question whether or not they were ever really sick. Another question is whether they stay permanently healed. My point is that the Lord Jesus Christ heals today just as He did at the pool of Bethesda, and that one is not healed by some moving of the water.

And a certain man was there, which had an infirmity thirty and eight years [John 5:5].

Our attention is directed to one man here. Whether he had been at the pool all that time we do not know. We are told that he was infirm for thirty-eight years and that apparently he moved with difficulty. I would judge he was the worst case there. Think of how frustrating it was for this poor fellow! Even if he hadn't been there for the thirty-eight years, he must have been there for several years. He must have been much older than thirty-eight years, and his condition was the result of his own sin. In verse 14 the Lord Jesus said to him, "Behold, thou art made whole: sin no more, lest a worse thing come unto thee." You can well imagine this poor fellow lying there, keeping his eyes on the water, waiting for the moving of the water. He would hope somehow or other to be the first one to get down in the water. But there had been disappointment after disappointment. He was in such a bad state that the others would always get into the water first. I'm sure he saw many cures there. People who were sick in their minds would be healed in their minds.

Our Lord apparently knew that he had been impotent for a long time and that he had waited at the pool for a long time. Notice His approach to him.

When Jesus saw him lie, and knew that he had been now a long time in that case, he saith unto him, Wilt thou be made whole? [John 5:6].

That's a peculiar question to ask a sick man. It seems rather absurd, doesn't it? Of course, he wanted to be made whole, but the Lord asked him the question for two reasons. First, to beget hope in the man. His case was hopeless, and I think the light of hope had pretty much gone out of his life, and he was in despair. Secondly, and this is the most important, Jesus wanted to get the man's eyes off the pool. Jesus wanted him to look to Him. I think this man had never noticed anybody else who came up there. He never watched anything else but just kept his eyes on the pool. So our Lord startled him with the question, "Do you earnestly desire to be made whole?" I think the man normally and naturally would look up. Who would ask a question like that? His answer was, "Of course, I want to be made whole. But that's not my problem. What I need is somebody to put me in the water."

The condition of so many people today is just like that man who was watching that pool, waiting for something to happen. I'm bold enough to say that it is the condition of all of us in these days. We are waiting. Just think of the people in our churches, waiting for some great, sweeping emotion to engulf them. Then there are those who are postponing making a decision for Christ. They are not willing to turn to Him because they are looking for an emotion; they are looking for something to happen. Another great group of people today have their eyes on business and they are waiting for something to happen to get rich quick. I was pastor in Texas in a place where they drilled for oil, and I knew a lot of my folk who just sat around watching a dry well. There wasn't any moving of water or anything else. It was dry. They wanted that to become an oil well and they had their eyes on the physical. Because they were entranced by the material, they lost sight of Jesus Christ. Then there are some people today who are looking to some individual. They've heard of the experience of someone else and they are waiting for something like that to happen in their lives. But they are doomed to bitter disappointment. I've talked to many of these people. They come under all of these categories. They are all waiting with their eyes fixed on some *thing*. Unfortunately, they have their eyes fixed on the wrong thing, or the wrong individual, or the wrong happening. I'll ask you a question. Are you waiting for something to happen these days? If you tell me what it is, I could write your biography. The Thessalonians ". . . turned to God from idols to serve the living and true God" (1 Thess. 1:9). They took their eyes off things in Thessalonica, and they turned to the Lord Jesus Christ.

I'm sure this man looked up rather amazed that anyone would ask him that question.

The impotent man answered him, Sir, I have no man, when the water is troubled, to put me into the pool: but while I am coming, another steppeth down before me [John 5:7].

What a sad story that tells. This poor, helpless, hopeless, homeless, lonely fellow is really saying, "Would I be made whole? Of course, I would. But I haven't anybody to put me in the pool. Would *You* put me in the pool?" The Lord Jesus has no notion of getting that man into the pool. He is going to get him out of it and away from it. The minute the man gets his eye on the Lord Jesus, something will happen.

Jesus saith unto him, Rise, take up thy bed, and walk [John 5:8].

He told him to rise (get up), take up his bed, and walk. He was to give up his place there at the pool to somebody else. He's to take his bed because no arrangements will be made for a relapse. There isn't going to be any relapse!

And immediately the man was made whole, and took up his bed, and walked: and on the same day was the sabbath.

The Jews therefore said unto him that was cured, It is the sabbath day: it is not lawful for thee to carry thy bed.

He answered them, He that made me whole, the same said unto me, Take up thy bed, and walk.

Then asked they him, What man is that which said unto thee, Take up thy bed, and walk?

And he that was healed wist not who it was: for Jesus had conveyed himself away, a multitude being in that place [John 5:9–13].

The next thing that happens is that the enemies accuse the man of carrying his bed on the Sabbath day. Well, that was the proof that he was healed. Can you imagine how ridiculous these religious rulers were to be upset because he carried his bed on the Sabbath day?

Our Lord seemed to use a miraculous way of getting away from the crowd there that day because the man really didn't know who it was that had healed him.

Afterward Jesus findeth him in the temple, and said unto him, Behold, thou art made whole: sin no more, lest a worse thing come unto thee.

The man departed, and told the Jews that it was Jesus, which had made him whole.

And therefore did the Jews persecute Jesus, and sought to slay him, because he had done these things on the sabbath day [John 5:14–16].

What actually happened was simply this: the Lord healed him physically at the pool of Bethesda but He healed his soul there in the temple. Sin had caused the man's trouble. First, he got a well body, and then he got a well soul. He came to know Jesus, you see. Then he was able to tell who He was. This impotent man was waiting and waiting, looking at the pool, and one day Jesus, the Lamb of God, came by and saw him. Then the man saw Jesus. The impotent man met the Omnipotent Man. The thing that is amazing to me is that there were multitudes left in those porches and they were not healed. Today there are multitudes who are not saved. Isn't Jesus willing to save them? Yes, but they haven't looked at Jesus. They're just waiting, friend, waiting for something to happen.

This is the incident that put those bloodhounds of hate on the trail of Jesus. (When John says the "Jews," he is actually referring to the religious rulers of the Jews.) This is the point at which they began to persecute Jesus and sought to slay Him.

But Jesus answered them, My Father worketh hitherto, and I work [John 5:17].

When that man got down into the ditch of sin, the Lord Jesus and the Father could no longer rest on the Sabbath Day. Although God rested after the creation of the physical universe, after the fall of man He didn't rest, because man, like an ox, had gotten down into the ditch.

Therefore the Jews sought the more to kill him, because he not only had broken the sabbath, but said also that God was his Father, making himself equal with God [John 5:18].

These men never let up until they folded their arms beneath His cross.

THE CLAIMS OF JESUS

Our Lord now goes on to make three tremendous claims concerning Himself. It is on the basis of these claims that we can use John 5:24 in presenting the gospel. We will try to put it all together here.

The first claim:

Then answered Jesus and said unto them, Verily, verily, I say unto you, The Son can do nothing of himself, but what he seeth the Father do: for what things soever he doeth, these also doeth the Son likewise [John 5:19].

The Lord Jesus is saying that He is God and that He can do what God does. There is a perfect correspondence and harmony between the Father and the Son. Therefore, the charge that was made against Him was absurd. The Son does not contradict the Father, nor does the Father contradict the Son. Jesus does what God does. Jesus can forgive sins. Then He goes on to say that there is a personal and intimate relationship between the Father and the Son.

For the Father loveth the Son, and sheweth him all things that himself doeth: and he will shew him greater works than these, that ye may marvel [John 5:20].

The second claim:

For as the Father raiseth up the dead, and quickeneth them; even so the Son quickeneth whom he will [John 5:21].

Jesus imparts life, gives life, to whom He will. If the Father raises the dead, the Son will raise the dead. Today we hear a great deal being said about the gift of healing, but with that gift went the ability to raise the dead. Paul raised the dead, and so did Simon Peter. Our Lord gave them that gift. It was an apostolic gift of healing and raising the dead, which disappeared with the apostles. The Lord Jesus raised the dead. He raised the dead because He was God. These other men did it in the name of the Lord Jesus.

The third claim:

For the Father judgeth no man, but hath committed all judgment unto the Son [John 5:22].

A literal reading would be, "For not even the Father judgeth anyone, but He hath given all judgment unto the Son." You can have everlasting life if you hear His word and believe it. Why? Because the Lord Jesus does what God does, because He raises the dead, and because He is going to judge all men someday. Whether saved or lost, they are going to appear before Him. The believers will appear before Him at the judgment which we call the Bema seat of Christ to see whether they receive a reward (see 2 Cor. 5:10). The lost will come before Him at the Great White Throne (see Rev. 20:11). Remember that the Lord Jesus did not come to judge the first time, but He will come as Judge the next time, and *all* judgment is committed to Him.

Jesus definitely puts Himself on a par with God the Father.

That all men should honour the Son, even as they honour the Father. He that honoureth not the Son honoureth not the Father which hath sent him [John 5:23].

It is on the basis of these three claims, these three great principles, that He goes on to this wonderful statement in verse 24 which is used so much in personal work today. It is right that we should use it, but we need to remember to back it up with the claims Jesus has just made.

Verily, verily, I say unto you, He that heareth my word, and believeth on him that sent me, hath everlasting life, and shall not come into condemnation; but is passed from death unto life [John 5:24].

Notice that He says, "*hath* everlasting life" which is right now—present tense. The believer does not come into *condemnation*, which is another word for judgment. He is passed out of death into life.

Now who is saying this? This is a tremendous promise, but who is making it? That is the important thing.

Years ago, in a cotton patch in my southland, a man stood up and read to those that were weary from picking cotton and were lying on their sacks. He read, "Come unto me, all ye that labour and are heavy laden, and I will give you rest" (Matt. 11:28). One man raised himself from off his cotton sack and said, "Them's good words, but who said them?"

Well, these are good words: "He that heareth my word, and believeth on him that sent me, hath everlasting life, and shall not come into condemnation; but is passed from death unto life." Who said them? Christ has given us the three statements concerning Himself which are the foundation for this verse. Jesus is God (v. 19); He raises the dead (v. 21); and He is going to judge (v. 22). Who He is makes these words truly wonderful words.

Now Jesus goes on with another great statement.

Verily, verily, I say unto you, The hour is coming, and now is, when the dead shall hear the voice of the Son of God: and they that hear shall live.

Marvel not at this: for the hour is coming, in the which all that are in the graves shall hear his voice [John 5:25, 28].

What does He mean in verse 25 when He says "the hour . . . now is"? Well, we're in that period of the hour that is coming. Verse 28 makes it clear that the hour has not yet arrived, but "the hour is coming." The whole thought is that we are living in the period or the age or the dispensation that is moving to the time when "the dead shall hear the voice of the Son of God: and they that hear shall live."

If we are in the period of the "hour that is coming," then what does He mean that it also "now is"? Who are the dead who hear His voice now? In John 11 where we have the incident in which Jesus raised Lazarus from the dead, you will remember that He said to the two sisters at the time of the death of Lazarus, "I am the resurrection, and the life: he that believeth in me, *though he were dead*, yet shall he live: And whosoever liveth and believeth in me shall never die" (John 11:25–26, italics mine). "Though he were dead." Does this mean the person that is in the grave hears? No, no, this is referring to spiritual death! Death means separation from God. The hour *is coming* when those who are in the grave shall hear His voice and shall live, but the hour *is now* when those who are spiritually dead hear His voice and live. Paul wrote to the Ephesian believers that they had been dead in trespasses and sins. That is the spiritual condition of everyone. But then, "he that heareth my word, and believeth on him that sent me, hath everlasting life, and shall not come into condemnation; but is passed from death [out of spiritual death] unto life," the life that He gives. So in verses 25 and 28 He is talking about two separate things. The time is now when Christ gives spiritual life. The hour is coming when He will raise the dead out of the grave.

For as the Father hath life in himself; so hath he given to the Son to have life in himself;

And hath given him authority to execute judgment also, because he is the Son of man [John 5:26–27].

The Lord Jesus is a life giver, you see. Not only does He have life, but He gives life. He also has the right to execute judgment. He came the first time as the Savior and not to judge, but He is coming the next time as the Judge. At that time, those in the graves will hear His voice.

Marvel not at this: for the hour is coming, in the which all that are in the graves shall hear his voice,

And shall come forth; they that have done good, unto the resurrection of life; and they that have done evil, unto the resurrection of damnation [John 5:28–29].

A better translation for the word *damnation* would be "judgment."

There are two resurrections mentioned here. The Book of Revelation is even more specific and describes the completion of the first resurrection (Rev. 20:4–6) and the second resurrection (Rev. 20:11–15). The first resurrection is the resurrection of all the saved—the first phase of which is the next thing on the agenda of God. We call it the Rapture of the church. "Rapture" is a good translation of the Greek *harpazō*. Paul used it in 1 Thessalonians 4:17 where he says we shall be "caught up," which means "to be raptured." The Rapture takes place at some time in the future. It is not dated and there are no signs given for it. It could happen at any moment. He is going to call His own out of this world, both the living and the dead. That is part of the first resurrection. Then, during the Tribulation Period, a great many believers will become martyrs. They will be raised at the end of the Great Tribulation Period together with the Old Testament saints. That also is part of the first resurrection. They will be raised to live forever here upon this earth. That is the first resurrection. It is the resurrection of life, as our Lord called it.

Then the resurrection of judgment is the Great White Throne judgment when all the unsaved, of all the ages, will be raised. They wanted to be judged by their works, and they will be! They will stand before God who is just and righteous; they will have an opportunity to stand before a Holy God and to plead their case. But God has already warned them; there is no one saved in that judgment. It is only the lost who are brought there, and they will be judged according to their works, because there are degrees in punishment (see Luke 12:47–48).

I can of mine own self do nothing: as I hear, I judge: and my judgment is just; because I seek not mine own will, but the will of the Father which hath sent me [John 5:30].

Jesus says, "I can of mine own self do nothing." That is His self-limitation when He came down to this earth and took upon Himself our humanity. He came down as a man, not to do His own will but the Father's will.

This is the example for us today. You and I have a will, an old nature, that is not obedient to God. We can't be obedient to God because we are actually in rebellion against God. That is the natural state of every man. That is the reason our Lord had to tell Nicodemus that he must be born again. Those who are in the flesh cannot please God. "That which is born of the flesh is flesh; and that which is born of the Spirit is spirit" (John 3:6). You and I have to have the new birth because this old nature is incorrigible, my friend. It is in rebellion against God. It has been carrying a protest banner before the gates of heaven ever since man came out through the gates of paradise in the Garden of Eden.

Now our Lord is going to show that there are witnesses to the fact that His claims are true.

If I bear witness of myself, my witness is not true.

There is another that beareth witness of me; and I know that the witness which he witnesseth of me is true [John 5:31–32].

The Scripture teaches that in the mouth of two or three witnesses a thing is established. "I bear witness of myself"—that would not stand up in court. But "There is another that beareth witness of me." The witness He is referring to here is not John the Baptist. They would immediately think that is the one to whom He is referring, but He makes it clear that He is not referring to a human witness at all.

Ye sent unto John, and he bare witness unto the truth [John 5:33].

Now, He is saying that John the Baptist did bare witness to Him. So that is one witness whom they knew. But He is referring to still another Witness, not a human witness, and that makes two witnesses for them to recognize.

But I receive not testimony from man: but these things I say, that ye might be saved [John 5:34].

He claims a higher Witness than the witness of man. Yet, He does give a testimony to John the Baptist. In our King James Version He calls John a "light." A more accurate translation is "lamp." You see, Jesus is the Light; John was His witness, His light bearer, His lamp, if you please.

He was a burning and a shining light: and ye were willing for a season to rejoice in his light.

But I have greater witness than that of John: for the works which the Father hath given me to finish, the same works that I do, bear witness of me, that the Father hath sent me [John 5:35–36].

Here we see that the credentials that the Lord Jesus had were the miracles that He performed. This idea today that there are those who have the same power that Jesus had is, to my judgment, blasphemy. You see, these miracles which He performed attested that He was who He claimed to be. And, friend, there weren't just a few isolated instances of healing. He didn't put on healing services. He took no offerings. He didn't have people get in a line and come by Him. He moved out into the crowds, into the highways and the byways. And as He moved along, people were healed. I've called attention to this in the Gospels again and again, and it is important to refresh our memories concerning this. Friend, there were not just half a dozen, or even a hundred or two whom He had healed; there were literally thousands of people whom He had healed. It was openly demonstrated. Nobody in that day contradicted the fact that He healed—he would have been a fool if he had. It is over nineteen hundred years later in a musty library in New York City, thousands of miles removed, that scholars can sit down and write books declaring that they don't believe Jesus performed miracles. But that doesn't prove a thing, friend. His miracles were His credentials. His works bore witness that the Father had sent Him.

And the Father himself, which hath sent me, hath borne witness of me. Ye have neither heard his voice at any time, nor seen his shape.

And ye have not his word abiding in you: for whom he hath sent, him ye believe not.

Search the scriptures; for in them ye think ye have eternal life: and they are they which testify of me [John 5:37–39].

This last verse is so frequently misunderstood. It is not an imperative but is an indicative. Let me put it like this: "You search the Scriptures." He's making a statement; He is not urging them to do something. He tells them that they search the Scriptures thinking that in them they will find eternal life, but they don't understand that the Scriptures testify of Jesus. Friend, you had better be careful so that you find Jesus in the Bible. If you don't, then your search is in vain.

And ye will not come to me, that ye might have life [John 5:40].

The Scriptures speak of Him, but the religious rulers are unwilling to come to Him. They are missing the point.

But I know you, that ye have not the love of God in you.

I am come in my Father's name, and ye receive me not: if another shall come in his own name, him ye will receive [John 5:42–43].

Someday the Antichrist is coming, and the world will receive him. They rejected Christ. The Antichrist will come in his own name, will have an image made of himself, and they will accept him.

How can ye believe, which receive honour one of another, and seek not the honour that cometh from God only? [John 5:44].

They looked for the applause of men. Back scratching is still the curse today in our churches, even our good churches. There are teachers with itching ears. Each one wants to compliment the other rather than tell the truth of the Word of God. They "seek not the honour that cometh from God only."

Do not think that I will accuse you to the Father: there is one that accuseth you, even Moses, in whom ye trust.

For had ye believed Moses, ye would have believed me: for he wrote of me.

But if ye believe not his writings, how shall ye believe my words? [John 5:45–47].

Friend, that is so important. Back in the books of the Pentateuch which I have recently taught, I have attempted to point out the Lord Jesus. Although *I* don't find Him on every page, I believe He *is* on every page of the Pentateuch. He says, "Moses . . . wrote of me." I think He is on every page of the Bible.

When a man begins to make an attack upon the Old Testament, watch out! He really is making a subtle attack on the Lord Jesus Christ. I'm afraid there are many men who very foolishly begin to question the Old Testament and don't realize what they are doing. It is like the man at the insane asylum who was digging at the foundation. A man came by and asked, "Why are you trying to dig out the foundation? Don't you live in the building?" "Yes," he answered, "but I live upstairs!" I'm afraid that a great many foolish people say, "But I live in the New Testament." My friend, the Old Testament is the foundation. Our Lord said, "If you believe not his writings, how shall you believe my words?" They both go together.

CHAPTER 6

THEME: *Jesus feeds five thousand near Sea of Galilee (fourth work and word)*

We come now to the miraculous feeding of the five thousand—a miracle recorded in all four Gospels. In the Gospel of John, Jesus follows this miracle with a discourse on the Bread of Life. John records only certain miracles, and he calls the miracles *signs* because signs are for a purpose. You will remember that he said, "And many other signs truly did Jesus in the presence of his disciples, which are not written in this book: But these are written, that ye might believe that Jesus is the Christ, the Son of God; and that believing ye might have life through his name" (John 20:30–31). This is an important verse because it is actually the key to this entire gospel.

Now we find Jesus feeding the five thousand, and out of this grows His great discourse on the fact that He is the true Bread of God.

JESUS FEEDS THE FIVE THOUSAND (Fourth Work and Word)

After these things Jesus went over the sea of Galilee, which is the sea of Tiberias [John 6:1].

After what things? Well, the things that were recorded back in the fifth chapter. He had left Jerusalem and probably had come up on the east side of the Jordan River. Now He crosses over the Sea of Galilee and, apparently, comes to the north section. This took place about six months to a year after the events of chapter 5. It was about one year before His crucifixion, by the way.

The way the events are dated is by the feasts that John mentions. As we have said, John ties his gospel down to a calendar and to a map. The One who came out of heaven's glory, the Word who was made flesh, the One who pitched His tent here among us, that One walked by the Sea of Galilee, went to Cana, and to Nazareth, Capernaum, Bethsaida, Jerusalem, Decapolis, etc. So we read that "after these things Jesus went over the sea of Galilee." John says, "And the passover, a feast of the Jews, was nigh" (v. 4). So apparently He had been back in the land of Galilee because in chapter 5 He had been in Jerusalem and had gone in the sheep gate. This indicates a time lapse between chapters 5 and 6 when He went over the Sea of Galilee.

And a great multitude followed him, because they saw his miracles which he did on them that were diseased [John 6:2].

The tense of the verb would be more accurate if it were translated, "And a great multitude was following Him" and "because they were seeing His miracles."

This great multitude didn't actually believe in Him in a saving way. They didn't trust Him. They were interested in His miracles. They wanted Him because He could make them well.

Friend, the mission of Jesus was not to restore our physical bodies. He wants to be Lord of our hearts. This is why John had said at the very beginning that He "needed not that any should testify of man; for he knew what was in man" (John 2:25). He didn't commit Himself to that crowd back there at Jerusalem, and He's not about to commit Himself to this crowd that is gathering around now. They simply want to see the miracles that He can perform.

And Jesus went up into a mountain, and there he sat with his disciples [John 6:3].

The place that is pointed out to tourists visiting Israel is not what we would call a mountain. Actually, in that land three thousand feet is about as high as they go, but the hills are very rugged. The one they point out is a very lovely spot and could well be the place where He fed the five thousand. It's near Capernaum, by the way.

Jesus went up into the mountain and sat there with His disciples. The Passover was near.

When Jesus then lifted up his eyes, and saw a great company come unto him, he saith unto Philip, Whence shall we buy bread, that these may eat? [John 6:5].

Philip was the quiet one; he never had much to say. Our Lord was drawing him out at this particular time. You will find in verse 8 that Philip and Andrew seem to have gotten together. Andrew and Philip evidently were quite active men, very busy, but just not speakers. You don't hear either one of them. Yet Andrew is the one who brought Simon Peter to the Lord, and the Greeks came to Philip and Andrew when they wanted to see Jesus. Philip got together with Andrew to find out what to do. So we find them together here.

Is our Lord asking for advice in His question to Philip? May I say to you, He never asked for advice. Then why did He ask Philip the question?

And this he said to prove him: for he himself knew what he would do [John 6:6].

He was testing Philip. Philip looked over that crowd that was coming—five thousand men besides women and children. I estimate it must have been at least fifteen thousand people. Friend, that's a pretty good-sized crowd, especially for that land and in that day. When Philip saw them coming, he wasn't thinking of a miracle at all.

Philip answered him, Two hundred pennyworth of bread is not sufficient for them, that every one of them may take a little [John 6:7].

Why did Philip light upon that fixed sum of two hundred denarii? I think that is what they had in the treasury at that time. Probably Judas had made a treasurer's report that morning, and that was the total. Philip looked at the crowd, then thought of what they had in the treasury bag, and said that two hundred pennyworth of bread would not be sufficient for them. The "penny" was the Roman coin *denarius*. One denarius represented a day's wages for a common laborer.

The other gospel writers tell us that the disciples advised the Lord Jesus. They wanted to be on the board of directors. They said, "Why don't You send the multitude away?" Our Lord answered, "We're not going to send them away. We're going to have them sit down and we're going to feed them" (cf. Luke 9:12–15). These men who had elected themselves to the board of directors found themselves waiters, serving the crowd. And that is what they should have been doing all the time.

By the way, this leads me to say that there are too many men in the church today who want position. They want to have an office; they want to be on the board of directors. They like to tell the preacher what to do. Yet they do not have all the necessary information to begin with, nor do they have spiritual discernment. They don't realize that they are the ones who ought to be out doing the work of the ministry. They ought to be out witnessing for the Lord—passing the bread to the hungry multitudes. But generally they would rather advise the pastor how to do it.

So here our Lord is drawing out Philip, and Philip says they don't have enough money to buy sufficient bread. Since Philip and Andrew are together, Andrew speaks up.

There is a lad here, which hath five barley loaves, and two small fishes: but what are they among so many? [John 6:9].

Andrew, you see, had been circulating around through the crowd, making a survey. Surveys are important, I guess, but they are seldom very helpful. You can see Andrew and Philip there together. Philip says the money in the treasury won't feed them. Andrew says all he's found is a little lad with five barley loaves and two small fish. Remember, these five barley loaves were not big commercial loaves of bread or family loaves. They were more like a hamburger bun. They were just big enough to put with the fish. That's all this man Andrew could produce. It was a hopeless project—"What are they among so many?"

And Jesus said, Make the men sit down. Now there was much grass in the place. So the men sat down, in number about five thousand [John 6:10].

I would call your attention to the fact that there were five thousand men. I think a woman and one child with each man would be a reasonable estimate of the crowd, which would be fifteen thousand people. Now the Lord Jesus is going to feed that multitude. Here is something, I think, that is interesting to note. If you have fifteen thousand people to feed, that is certainly a liability. If you have five loaves and two fish and also the two hundred denarii, then, friend, these are your total assets. May I say that if a committee would have handed in a report with those assets and those liabilities, they would have said, "There's nothing you can do about it." Someone has called a committee a group of people who individually can do nothing, and collectively they can decide that nothing can be done. Or, a committee is a group of people who take down minutes and waste hours. So here is the committee report: to feed them would be impossible.

You see, what you need in this equation is what I call the mathematics of a miracle. You need Jesus. I tell you, if you have the five loaves plus the two fishes plus Jesus, then you've got something, friend. Without Him, you don't have anything at all.

Jesus told them to make the men sit down and they sat down. Mark emphasizes the fact that they sat down by companies; that is, each of the groups of people which had come from a certain section sat down together. They may have been distinguished by robes of a certain color from their area. Everything that our Lord did was done decently and in order. Each little group was color on the background of green grass. I am of the opinion that if you could have been on the hill on the opposite side from where these people were sitting, you would have seen something that would have been as beautiful as a patchwork quilt. It would have been very orderly, because our Lord was doing it.

And Jesus took the loaves; and when he had given thanks, he distributed to the disciples, and the disciples to them that were set down; and likewise of the fishes as much as they would.

When they were filled, he said unto his disciples, Gather up the fragments that remain, that nothing be lost.

Therefore they gathered them together, and filled twelve baskets with the fragments of the five barley loaves, which remained over and above unto them that had eaten [John 6:11–13].

As a student in a liberal college, I never shall forget how the professor explained away this miracle. What he said was that the disciples had gathered together these loaves and fishes ahead of time and had stored them up in a cave. Then the Lord Jesus just backed up to that cave, and the disciples just sort of slipped them out under His arm, concealed by a flowing robe! It was sort of like hocus-pocus, abracadabra. The only thing wrong with that explanation is that it won't work. You would have to have more faith to believe *that* than to believe it just like it is, my friend. To begin with, where would they find a bakery in that area that could provide that many loaves? And where would they get that many fish for this particular occasion at this time? We have no record that Andrew and Peter had been out fishing! This explanation is utterly preposterous and ridiculous, as you can see.

The obvious explanation is that a miracle was performed here. When you add Jesus to the side of the assets, you have more than enough. In fact, you have twelve baskets of leftovers. That doesn't mean they were scraps. I used to think that a fellow would bite on a sandwich, then when he would see a bigger one, he would put the first one down and reach over and get the new sandwich so that the fragments were that which had been partially eaten. That's not true. There were twelve baskets of sandwiches that weren't even touched, my friend. Do you know what this means? It means that the crowd got all they wanted to eat. And people in that land and in that day were often hungry. There were many people in the crowd there that day who for the first time in their lives had their tummies filled. You see, when the Lord Jesus does anything, He does a good job of it.

Then those men, when they had seen the miracle that Jesus did, said, This is of a truth that prophet that should come into the world.

When Jesus therefore perceived that they would come and take him by force, to make him a king, he departed again into a mountain himself alone [John 6:14–15].

You see, they are following Him because He's a miracle worker. And I'm almost sure that He had to perform another miracle to get free from the crowd. The reason He got free from them was because they wanted to make Him a king. "Well," someone says, "isn't He a King?" Yes, it is true that He was born a King. But this is not the route by which He is coming to kingship.

JESUS WALKS ON THE WATER

And when even was now come, his disciples went down unto the sea,

And entered into a ship, and went over the sea toward Capernaum. And it was now dark, and Jesus was not come to them.

And the sea arose by reason of a great wind that blew.

So when they had rowed about five and twenty or thirty furlongs, they see Jesus walking on the sea, and drawing nigh unto the ship: and they were afraid.

But he saith unto them, It is I; be not afraid.

Then they willingly received him into the ship: and immediately the ship was at the land whither they went [John 6:16–21].

The other gospels tell us that He hurried the disciples down to the Sea of Galilee and put them on a boat to go across while He went up into the mountain to pray. Since those mountains are about three thousand feet high, a storm from them will break suddenly upon the Sea of Galilee—and this was a real storm! When they were twenty-five or thirty furlongs out on the sea, they were halfway across. It was in the middle of this inland sea that they saw Jesus walking on the water. They were afraid because they didn't recognize Him.

The same liberal professor who explained away the feeding of the five thousand tried to explain away this miracle, too. He said the ship was at the land, so Jesus was actually walking on the shore—but the disciples *thought* that He was walking on the water. May I say that John had been a fisherman on this Sea of Galilee, and he knew it well. He specifically mentions their position in the lake so we would know they were not at the shore.

Jesus came to them in the storm. And that is a time He comes to His own today. He makes Himself more real to us in a time of trouble and sorrow. I don't know why He waits until midnight, until the waves are rolling, but perhaps that is the only time we will listen to Him. When the storms of life are beating upon our little bark, our hearts are ready for His presence.

"Immediately the ship was at the land whither they went." This may be another miracle, or John may mean that with no delay they reached the other side since the water was now calm. Or it may be the language of love—with Him in the boat it didn't seem far to the other side.

JESUS GIVES A DISCOURSE ON THE BREAD OF LIFE

We find now that the crowd is beginning to look for Him and they are disappointed. They discover that both the Lord Jesus and the disciples are gone.

The day following, when the people which stood on the other side of the sea

saw that there was none other boat there, save that one whereinto his disciples were entered, and that Jesus went not with his disciples into the boat, but that his disciples were gone away alone;

(Howbeit there came other boats from Tiberias nigh unto the place where they did eat bread, after that the Lord had given thanks:)

When the people therefore saw that Jesus was not there, neither his disciples, they also took shipping, and came to Capernaum, seeking for Jesus [John 6:22–24].

They apparently had come up from the southern part of the Sea of Galilee, and He had fed them there near Tiberias. Then they had come on by boat to Capernaum. That seems to be the way that we have it here.

This is the first time John used the title *Lord*—"after that the Lord had given thanks." As we have seen, the common name John uses for Him is *Jesus* because He is "the Word . . . made flesh" (John 1:14). Who is that Word? It is Jesus. ". . . thou shalt call his name JESUS: for he shall save his people from their sins" (Matt. 1:21).

The crowd was really wanting to know how He had been able to get away as He did.

And when they had found him on the other side of the sea, they said unto him, Rabbi, when camest thou hither?

Jesus answered them and said, Verily, verily, I say unto you, Ye seek me, not because ye saw the miracles, but because ye did eat of the loaves, and were filled [John 6:25–26].

Jesus doesn't really answer their question directly. He penetrated beneath the surface to their motive for seeking Him. Actually, the word He used was not literally "loaves" but a word that means fodder. You ate the fodder and were filled. Your only interest was that your tummies were full.

Labour not for the meat which perisheth, but for that meat which endureth unto everlasting life, which the Son of man shall give unto you: for him hath God the Father sealed [John 6:27].

Let me put this into our language of today (this is not a translation but only an attempt to bring out the meaning): stop working for food that perishes, but work for food that endures for everlasting life, which food the Son of Man will give you, for on Him, God the Father has set His seal.

You will recall that this is the same approach which our Lord made to the woman at the well. For her it was water that she wanted; for these folk it is bread. These are two essential things. Bread and water are very important to maintain life. Jesus is both Bread and Water. Notice that He uses these commonplace symbols. He is the *Word,* and the Word became flesh. How can we explain that? Jesus, the Word, is reaching down and communicating where we can understand it. He said that He is Water and that He gives Living Water. He said that He is Bread. We know what water is and we know what bread is.

Then said they unto him, What shall we do, that we might work the works of God? [John 6:28].

In other words, they are asking what they can *do* to be saved. Man has always felt that if he could just work at it, he could be saved. Man feels thoroughly capable of working out his own salvation. He feels competent to do it, and he feels that God must accept his works. Notice carefully what the work of God is.

Jesus answered and said unto them, This is the work of God, that ye believe on him whom he hath sent [John 6:29].

You see, the work of God is not that which is commanded by God, but it is that which has been wrought by God. In other words, it is what God has done and not what you do. It is the work of God and not the works of man. "This is the work of God, that ye *believe* on him whom he hath sent." He is saying that God provided food. He is the One who has provided that for us today, and we are to partake of it. The invitation He gives is to a banquet. Go out on the byways and highways and tell them they are invited to come. It is a free meal, by the way, but it happens to be spiritual food.

They said therefore unto him, What sign shewest thou then, that we may see, and believe thee? what dost thou work? [John 6:30].

May I say that this reveals the hardness of the human heart. Here are the men who had been fed miraculously by our Lord when He fed the five thousand and they say, "Show us a sign. What dost Thou work?" In other words, they did not want to believe at all. And they take their conversation right back to the dinner table.

Our fathers did eat manna in the desert; as it is written, He gave them bread from heaven to eat.

Then Jesus said unto them, Verily, verily, I say unto you, Moses gave you not that bread from heaven; but my Father giveth you the true bread from heaven.

For the bread of God is he which cometh down from heaven, and giveth life unto the world [John 6:31–33].

They are still thinking of physical food and say, "Moses gave our people manna." Actually it wasn't Moses who gave the manna; God did that. And it wasn't a one-time deal. God fed them every day for forty years. They want to be fed, and that is what they are after. Manna gave life in that day, and it was a gift from God. The manna gave physical life to them out there in the wilderness, but the Lord Jesus gives spiritual life. "My Father giveth you the true bread from heaven."

Then said they unto him, Lord, evermore give us this bread [John 6:34].

They are just like the woman at the well who asked for water but was thinking of physical water so she wouldn't need to come and draw water at the well anymore. It took our Lord quite a while to lift her thinking out of that well to the spiritual Water. And it takes Him a long time to get these folk away from the dinner table and get them to see the spiritual Bread that gives spiritual life.

And Jesus said unto them, I am the bread of life: he that cometh to me shall never hunger; and he that believeth on me shall never thirst [John 6:35].

He joins the two together. Christ is the manna. He is the One who came down from heaven and gave His life for the world that we might have life. That is salvation. We will also see that He is the Bread that we are to feed upon constantly so that we might grow spiritually. After all, manna was miracle food, and it was thrilling. When the children of Israel got into the Promised Land, they were given the "old corn of the land" which symbolizes the Word of God. Believe me, lots of people don't like the "old corn."

But I said unto you, That ye also have seen me, and believe not.

All that the Father giveth me shall come to me; and him that cometh to me I will in no wise cast out [John 6:36–37].

"You want bread? Well, I am the Bread of Life. But you have seen Me, and you do not believe. All that the Father gives Me shall come to Me; and him that comes to Me I will in no wise cast out."

This thirty-seventh verse is a very important verse. There is a theological argument that rages today on election or free will. There are some people who put all their eggs in the basket of election. There are others who put all their eggs in the basket of free will. I'm not proposing to reconcile the two because I have discovered that I cannot. If you had met me the year that I entered seminary, or the year I graduated, I could have reconciled them for you. I never have been as smart as I was my first year and my last year in seminary. I knew it all then. I could reconcile election and free will, and it was a marvelous explanation. Now I've even forgotten what it was. It was pretty silly, if you want to know the truth.

Election and free will are both in this verse. "All that the Father giveth me shall come to me" states a truth, and that is election. But wait a minute! "And him that cometh to me I will in no wise cast out" is also true, and "him that cometh to me" is free will. I don't know how to reconcile them, but they are both true. The Father gives men to Christ, but men have to come. And the ones that come are the ones, apparently, whom the Father gives to Him. You and I are down here, and we don't see into the machinery of heaven. I don't know how God runs that computer of election, but I know that He has given to you and to me a free will and we have to exercise it.

Because Spurgeon preached a "whosoever will" gospel, someone said to him, "If I believed like you do about election, I wouldn't preach like you do." Spurgeon's answer was something like this, "If the Lord had put a yellow stripe down the backs of the elect, I'd go up and down the street lifting up shirttails, finding out who had the yellow stripe, and then I'd give them the gospel. But God didn't do it that way. He told me to preach the gospel to every creature that 'whosoever will may come.'" Jesus says, "and him that cometh to me I will in no wise cast out." So, my friend, you can argue about election all you want to, but you can come. And if you come, He'll not cast you out.

Someone may ask, "You mean that if I'm not the elect I can still come?" My friend, if you come, you will be the elect. How tremendous this is!

For I came down from heaven, not to do mine own will, but the will of him that sent me [John 6:38].

How wonderful it is that the *will* of God is for you to come to Him. Jesus came down from heaven because "the Son of man must be lifted up." He came to do the Father's will in that, and it is the Father's will that you be born again. But you will have to come to Him, friend; that is the only way. You must come to the Lord Jesus by faith.

And this is the Father's will which hath sent me, that of all which he hath given me I should lose nothing, but should raise it up again at the last day [John 6:39].

The term *predestination* applies only to the saved. It means just exactly what He is saying here. When a person accepts Christ, he is justified; and just as surely as he is justified, he is going to be glorified. When Jesus starts out with one hundred sheep, He's going to come through with one hundred sheep. He will not lose one. That is what this means. Everyone who believes and receives Christ has everlasting life and will be raised up again at the last day.

The Jews then murmured at him, because he said, I am the bread which came down from heaven.

And they said, Is not this Jesus, the son of Joseph, whose father and mother we know? how is it then that he saith, I came down from heaven? [John 6:41–42].

You see, He taught that He was God and that He came down from heaven. May I say to you, in this section here He is teaching His Virgin Birth. There are those who say the Lord Jesus never taught that He was virgin born. What do you think He is saying here, friend? The Jews understood what He was saying. They asked how this could be when they knew His father and His mother. Well, it's by the Virgin Birth. As the angel told Mary, it was the Holy Spirit who conceived that "holy thing" in Mary (see Luke 1:35). This section right here (beginning with v. 38) is a complement or a counterpart of the Virgin Birth and needs to be added to the other portions of Scripture which deal with it. "I came down from heaven"—that's the Christmas story. "Out of the ivory palaces into a world of woe." He came down from heaven's glory; He stepped down from the throne to ascend the cross for you and for me. He did it by way of the Virgin Birth. You can have the jingle of bells and all the Ho, Ho, Ho's—but that is not Christmas. The Virgin Birth of the Lord Jesus Christ is the Christmas story.

They got the message immediately and asked, "Is not this Jesus, the son of Joseph"? They thought they knew His father and His mother, but He is not the son of Joseph. He came down from heaven.

Jesus therefore answered and said unto them, Murmur not among yourselves.

No man can come to me, except the Father which hath sent me draw him: and I will raise him up at the last day [John 6:43–44].

Actually, the word translated "draw" is *drag*. That is divine election. You ask me to explain it? I can't explain it at all, friend; I just know that you have a free will and you can exercise it. God holds you responsible for it, and you know you are responsible. You know right now you can come or not come. It's up to you.

It is written in the prophets, And they shall be all taught of God. Every man therefore that hath heard, and hath learned of the Father, cometh unto me [John 6:45].

There is Scripture after Scripture in the Old Testament that refers to this. For instance, Isaiah 54:13: "And all thy children shall be taught of the LORD; and great shall be the peace of thy children." Isaiah 60:2–3: "For, behold, the darkness shall cover the earth, and gross darkness the people: but the LORD shall arise upon thee, and his glory shall be seen upon thee. And the Gentiles shall come to thy light, and kings to the brightness of thy rising." There are these statements that they will come to Him, and *you* can come to Him. These things are made so wonderfully clear. There are many references to it. Malachi 4:2 is another: "But unto you that fear my name shall the Sun of righteousness arise with healing in his wings; and ye shall go forth, and grow up as calves of the stall." Every man that listens to the Father and learns of Him will come to Me is what He is saying. You see, if you listen to the Word of God, then you'll come to Christ. That is where the great emphasis is being placed here.

Not that any man hath seen the Father, save he which is of God, he hath seen the Father.

Verily, verily, I say unto you, He that believeth on me hath everlasting life [John 6:46–47].

The One who has seen the Father is the Lord Jesus Christ. "He who believes on Me has everlasting life." It can't be said any more clearly.

I am that bread of life.

Your fathers did eat manna in the wilderness, and are dead.

This is the bread which cometh down from heaven, that a man may eat thereof, and not die.

I am the living bread which came down from heaven: if any man eat of this bread, he shall live for ever: and the bread that I will give is my flesh, which I will give for the life of the world [John 6:48–51].

He came down to this earth: "the Word was made flesh" (John 1:14). He is going to the cross to lay that human life down there as a sacrifice to pay for your sins and my sins. Friend, when you partake of that, that is, when you *accept* that, you are saved. Someone may say, "Oh, that's so vivid and so strong." That's what they said in that day, too.

The Jews therefore strove among themselves, saying, How can this man give us his flesh to eat? [John 6:52].

They were thinking of His literal flesh, of course.

Then Jesus said unto them, Verily, verily, I say unto you, Except ye eat the flesh of the Son of man, and drink his blood, ye have no life in you [John 6:53].

That means to partake of Him spiritually, which is more real than a physical partaking.

Whoso eateth my flesh, and drinketh my blood, hath eternal life; and I will raise him up at the last day.

For my flesh is meat indeed, and my blood is drink indeed.

He that eateth my flesh, and drinketh my blood, dwelleth in me, and I in him.

As the living Father hath sent me, and I live by the Father: so he that eateth me, even he shall live by me.

This is that bread which came down from heaven: not as your fathers did eat manna, and are dead: he that eateth of this bread shall live for ever [John 6:54–58].

Friend, this is an amazing statement. Our Lord is preparing these men for that Last Supper and the institution of the Lord's Supper. This, obviously, is something that is not to be taken literally because He was right there before them. He is not saying for them to begin to eat Him and to drink His blood! What He is saying is that He is going to give His life. In that Upper Room He made it very clear that the blood is the symbol of life. "For the life of the flesh is in the blood . . ." (Lev. 17:11). God had taught the Israelites that truth from the very beginning when He called them out of the land of Egypt. There at Mount Sinai Moses gives them this great axiom, "the life of the flesh is in the blood," which is also medically true, by the way. The life of the flesh *is* in the blood. And Jesus is giving His life. He will shed His blood upon the cross and give His life. Salvation is by accepting and receiving Him in a most intimate way.

This is the basis for the sacrament of the Lord's Supper. Friend, there has been just as much disagreement among believers in the churches down through the ages over the interpretation of the Lord's Supper as there has been over baptism. I don't think they have fought over it quite as much, but the disagreement is there.

Hoc est meus corpus—"This is my body." When He gave them the bread at the supper in the Upper Room, He said, " . . . This is my body . . . " (Luke 22:19). Now there have been different emphases put on that.

The Roman Catholic church puts the emphasis upon *this*. *This* is My body. They say that transubstantiation takes place, that the bread becomes the flesh of Christ. Well, I don't think our Lord taught cannibalism in any form, shape, or fashion. I think, of course, that is a wrong emphasis. Then there are those who have taken the position of the Lutheran church, which is consubstantiation. This means that *by*, *with*, *in*, *through*, and *under* the bread you get the body of Christ. Again, may I say, I think that falls short of what our Lord really means. Then there are those who take Zwingli's position. He was the Swiss Reformation leader who gave it a spiritual interpretation. He felt it was just a symbol, just a religious ritual, and that is all. I think that is probably the interpretation that most of Protestantism gives to it today. Frankly, I feel that falls as far short of the interpretation of the Lord's Supper as the other two do. Calvin put the emphasis on *is*—"This *is* my body." The Reformed faith has always put the emphasis there, and the early church put the emphasis there. The bread is bread, and it always will be bread. It cannot be changed. The wine is always just what it is, and there is no miracle that takes place there. You don't get the body of Christ by going through the ritual. And yet, it is more than a ritual. I had a seminary professor who taught us that in the Lord's Supper it is bread in your mouth, but it is Christ in your heart. Friend, I believe that there is a spiritual blessing that comes in observing the Lord's Supper. I think that He ministers to you spiritually through your obedience in observing the Lord's Supper. There is no such thing as a hocus-pocus there. Nor is it just an idle ritual that we go through. It is meaningful, and it has a spiritual blessing for the heart.

I think that is what our Lord is saying to them here. An intimate, real relationship with Him is the important thing. When they ate manna in the wilderness it was only a temporary thing. Jesus has something that is eternal—*life* which is eternal. We are told at the beginning of this gospel, "In him was life; and the life was the light of men" (John 1:4).

These things said he in the synagogue, as he taught in Capernaum.

Many therefore of his disciples, when they had heard this, said, This is an hard saying; who can hear it?

When Jesus knew in himself that his disciples murmured at it, he said unto them, Doth this offend you?

What and if ye shall see the Son of man ascend up where he was before?

It is the spirit that quickeneth; the flesh profiteth nothing: the words that I speak unto you, they are spirit, and they are life [John 6:59–63].

There was definite reaction to what Jesus had said and differences of opinion. Jesus tells them that they are not going to eat Him literally because He is going back to heaven. It is the Spirit that makes alive; the flesh profits nothing. So obviously, friend, He is not talking about His literal body. We are to appropriate the Lord's Supper by faith. The juice in the cup is sweet, and I always taste the sweetness, remembering that He bore the bitter cup for me on the cross so that I might have this sweet cup. That sweet cup is to remind me that He shed His blood for me, and there is a spiritual blessing there.

"The words that I speak unto you, they are spirit, and they are life." During my ministry, I have always read to the congregation from the Word of God during the Lord's Supper. I find that the Word of God ministers to the hearts of the people. Why? Because the words of the Lord Jesus are spirit and they are life.

But there are some of you that believe not. For Jesus knew from the beginning who they were that believed not, and who should betray him.

And he said, Therefore said I unto you, that no man can come unto me, except it were given unto him of my Father [John 6:64–65].

But remember now, you have to put with that "whosoever will may come." It's up to you, you see.

From that time many of his disciples went back, and walked no more with him [John 6:66].

You can see that in the group there that day were the hostile leaders, the religious leaders. Also there was an undesignated number of disciples in addition to the twelve. And in the twelve was Judas. So you actually find four opinions concerning Him at this time. Many of these disciples—not the twelve—but many of the other disciples turned and went back.

Then said Jesus unto the twelve, Will ye also go away?

Then Simon Peter answered him, Lord, to whom shall we go? thou hast the words of eternal life [John 6:67–68].

This is a marvelous statement on the part of Simon Peter. And the question he asks is pertinent to us today. If you say that the Lord Jesus is not a Savior to you and that He doesn't meet your needs at all, then may I ask you where you are going? I saw a group of young people on the island of Maui, out in the Hawaiian Islands. They had a picture of Krishna in front of them and they were going over and over a monotonous song. Poor little folk! They weren't finding any satisfaction in that. What disillusionment is coming to so many today! There are those who are turning in every direction for light. Let me ask you the question of Simon Peter: "To whom shall we go?" The Lord Jesus is the One, and the only One, who has the Words of eternal life.

And we believe and are sure that thou art that Christ, the Son of the living God.

Jesus answered them, Have not I chosen you twelve, and one of you is a devil?

He spake of Judas Iscariot the son of Simon: for he it was that should betray him, being one of the twelve [John 6:69–71].

This man, Judas Iscariot, is really a great mystery. Here our Lord numbers him with the twelve and He said that He had chosen him. Yet he was a demon, which probably means demon-possessed, and this is the man who is going to betray Him. All the way through our Lord gave him every opportunity to make a decision for Him. It is difficult to interpret evil like this, friend. It is one of the mysteries.

Evil is always a mystery, which is one of the things that makes it so attractive. Suppose right now I would say to you that I am holding two sticks. One stick is perfectly straight because it is a ruler. You can easily imagine how that ruler looks because it can be straight only one way. Then suppose that I say that I am also holding in my hand a crooked stick. I'm of the opinion that if each one of you drew a picture of how you think that stick looks, everyone would draw it differently. That's because it can be crooked in a million different ways. You see, evil has a mystery to it. I must confess that, as this man Judas Iscariot walks across the pages of Scripture, it's difficult to interpret him. And here our Lord says this amazing thing about him: he is a demon!

What a contrast is the testimony of Simon Peter—"we believe and are sure that thou art that Christ, the Son of the living God."

CHAPTER 7

THEME: *Jesus teaches at Feast of Tabernacles in temple (fifth word)*

This chapter contains the wonderful truths that Jesus is the Water of Life and that He promises to give the Holy Spirit to those who believe on Him.

JESUS TEACHES AT FEAST OF TABERNACLES IN TEMPLE (Fith Word)

After these things Jesus walked in Galilee: for he would not walk in Jewry, because the Jews sought to kill him [John 7:1].

"After these things." This is a common expression with John who is giving us a chronological picture. The events of chapter 6 took place in Galilee at the Sea of Galilee; but before that, Jesus had been in Jerusalem where there had arisen the controversy concerning Him at the pool of Bethesda. It seems that the events of chapter 6 transpired about one year before the cross in April; the events in chapter 7 occur about six months later, in October. Matthew 15–18 and Mark 7–9 and Luke 9 relate incidents which transpired during this period.

During the last year of His ministry, Jesus confined His activities to Galilee. It says that He walked no longer in Jewry, that means in Judaea, because the religious rulers there had a plot to kill Him. Jesus is following a divine schedule which His Father had given Him. These men could not touch Him until His time was come. We are now entering the last six months of His life, and the first incident which John records in that period is this occurrence of the Feast of Tabernacles.

Verse 1 reveals that a storm is gathering about the Person of Christ. Six months later that storm will break in all its fury upon Jesus on the cross. Friend, that storm is still going on. There is more difference of opinion about Him than about any other person who has ever lived. They blaspheme Him and say the worst things about Him that ever have been said. He's controversial today.

Although the storm is gathering, Jesus chose this time to abandon His method of staying away, and He went up to Jerusalem because it was the Feast of Tabernacles.

Now the Jews' feast of tabernacles was at hand [John 7:2].

There were three feasts which every male Jew was required to attend in Jerusalem. Our Lord kept the Law; He had to go up to Jerusalem during the feasts of Passover, Tabernacles, and Pentecost. The Feast of Tabernacles is described in Leviticus 23. This was a feast of great joy to celebrate Israel's wonderful deliverance out of the land of Egypt. Because they had lived in tents during the wilderness journey, this is a feast of tents, or booths. They didn't have campers, you see, but they did camp out in booths. There was the blowing of trumpets and seventy bullocks were offered. There was the pouring out of water in the temple, with a double portion on the last day of the feast to remind them that God gave them water from the rock in the wilderness. They brought the water from the pool of Siloam and poured out literally barrels of water. During this festival, they illuminated the inner court with a regular torch parade. This was commemorating the pillar of fire that guided the children of Israel by night as they wandered in the wilderness. Now we can understand that the pillar of cloud and the pillar of fire that led the children of Israel were both pictures of our Lord Jesus Christ.

All the feasts of Jehovah in the Old Testament have been fulfilled except the Feast of Tabernacles. This will be fulfilled when our Lord returns to the earth. Thus it symbolizes the great joy of that time.

His brethren therefore said unto him, Depart hence, and go into Judaea, that thy disciples also may see the works that thou doest.

For there is no man that doeth any thing in secret, and he himself seeketh to be known openly. If thou do these things, shew thyself to the world.

For neither did his brethren believe in him [John 7:3–5].

These brethren are not His disciples but are His half-brothers. Their names are given to us in Matthew 13:55: James, Joses, Simon, and Judas. His half-brother, James, is the one who wrote the Epistle of James; His half-brother, Judas, probably is the one who wrote the Epistle of Jude. That was much later, of course, and at this point His brothers do not believe in Him. They are giving Him advice that He can't use at all.

Then Jesus said unto them, My time is not yet come: but your time is alway ready [John 7:6].

They are advising Jesus out of their unbelief, but Jesus does not take their advice. He is moving according to schedule, but it is His Father's schedule. He is not following the wisdom of the world, nor did He ever appeal to His own mind—it isn't that He doesn't think it is the right time to go. He is on a definite schedule from the Father; He is doing His will.

Notice the little word *yet* in "My time is not *yet* come." Jesus did not say that He would not go down to the feast, but He was not going down with them publicly to win public favor by something spectacular, or whatever they wanted Him to do. He would go at His Father's appointed time and in His Father's way.

The world cannot hate you; but me it hateth, because I testify of it, that the works thereof are evil.

Go ye up unto this feast: I go not up yet unto this feast; for my time is not yet full come.

When he had said these words unto them, he abode still in Galilee [John 7:7–9].

The world is hostile to Christ. The reason is that our Lord Jesus Christ is the Light of the World. He turns on that Light, and that Light reveals everything that is wrong; it reveals sin. He condemns sin. That is the reason He is hated even today. He condemns sin by His very presence, by His very life. This raises a hostility in man because the heart of man is evil. Christ went to the cross because He loved the human family. Redeeming love is what has broken the heart of hostile man.

We see this so clearly in the life of Saul of Tarsus. He was breathing out threatenings. He hated the Lord Jesus and anyone who followed Him. But, when he came to know the Lord Jesus as his Savior, it broke his heart, and he could say, "He loved me, and gave himself for me" (see Gal. 3:20).

But when his brethren were gone up, then went he also up unto the feast, not openly, but as it were in secret [John 7:10].

He probably traveled with His disciples on a back road and entered into the city through the sheep gate. I believe He always entered Jerusalem through the sheep gate until the time of His so-called triumphal entry when He appeared publicly, offering Himself to the nation and actually demanding that they either accept or reject Him.

Then the Jews sought him at the feast, and said, Where is he?

And there was much murmuring among the people concerning him: for some said, He is a good man: others said, Nay; but he deceiveth the people.

Howbeit no man spake openly of him for fear of the Jews [John 7:11–13].

The "Jews" are the religious rulers—they were looking for Him and expecting Him because the Law required that He come to the feast. There was a lot of discussion concerning Him, but it was all done quite secretly because anyone would be attacked for making any statement that would be inclined in His favor and would be in danger of arrest.

Now about the midst of the feast Jesus went up into the temple, and taught [John 7:14].

Quite suddenly, He appeared in the temple. This Feast of Tabernacles is in the calendar of God and sets before us the coming of Christ in His return to earth and the events and stages which lead up to that. This feast speaks of the consummation of all things. He will appear suddenly. ". . . and the Lord, whom ye seek, shall suddenly come to his temple . . ." (Mal. 3:1). This will be fulfilled in His return to the earth.

And the Jews marvelled, saying, How knoweth this man letters, having never learned? [John 7:15].

Have you noticed how often we find Jesus teaching? Note the priority which He gave to the Word of God. The Jews (these would be the religious leaders) were astounded because He had no formal training in the rabbinical schools. They marveled that He could speak as He did. Even His enemies were forced to admit, "Never man spake like this man" (v. 46).

Jesus answered them, and said, My doctrine is not mine, but his that sent me [John 7:16].

To reject the message of Jesus is to reject the message of God. In chapters 4 and 5, He has insisted that to reject Him is to reject God. Don't ever tell me that He didn't make Himself equal with God. You may reject that He is, but you can never say that the Bible does not declare Him to be equal with God.

If any man will do his will, he shall know of the doctrine, whether it be of God, or whether I speak of myself [John 7:17].

"If anyone is willing to do His will" is the way Weymouth translates this. The Old Testament invites, "O taste and see that the LORD is good . . ." (Ps. 34:8). We have an adage that says, "The proof of the pudding is in the eating of it." Jesus invites you; come and make a laboratory test. "If any man will do his will, he shall know of the doctrine." There must be an attitude of love for the Word of God. Someone has said that human knowledge must be known to be loved, but divine knowledge must be loved to be understood. Here we have the steps: knowledge, love, obedience. That is what He asks you to do.

It's so easy to sit on the sidelines and be a Monday morning quarterback. We love to tell others how it should have been done or to speak our mind without really knowing. Jesus says, "Taste the Lord!" "If any man will do his will, he shall know of the doctrine, whether it be of God, or whether I speak of myself." That is the wonder of the Word of God. Friend, if you are willing, God will make it real to you. The Holy Spirit will confirm it to you.

He that speaketh of himself seeketh his own glory: but he that seeketh his glory that sent him, the same is true, and no unrighteousness is in him [John 7:18].

The question is whether men want to hear God. If they do, then God will speak to them in His Word. Then they will accept Jesus Christ who came to speak for the Father. Unfortunately, men are often more interested in a man who is seeking his own glory. If Jesus Christ had been trying to found some new cult, these men would have listened. But Jesus was not glorifying Himself; rather, He was giving all the glory to the Father and so ". . . the natural man receiveth not the things of the Spirit of God: for they are foolishness unto him: neither can he know them, because they are spiritually discerned" (1 Cor. 2:14). Therefore, some people read the Bible and get nothing out of it.

Did not Moses give you the law, and yet none of you keepeth the law? Why go ye about to kill me? [John 7:19].

Here is the hypocrisy of the legalist, the person who says the Sermon on the Mount is his religion or the person who says he lives by the Ten Commandments. The Lord Jesus says, "none of you keepeth the law." The Law is a mirror to let us see that we are lost sinners.

The Law is important—don't misunderstand me—you don't kick the Law out the door. It expresses the will of God. But the purpose of the Law is to show us that we are sinners and that we need a Savior. The Law is a schoolmaster to bring us to Christ (see Gal. 3:24).

The people answered and said, Thou hast a devil: who goeth about to kill thee?

Jesus answered and said unto them, I have done one work, and ye all marvel [John 7:20–21].

Possibly they did not realize that there was a plot to put Jesus to death. Jesus refers to His work when He healed the man at the pool of Bethesda. This had aroused antagonism.

Moses therefore gave unto you circumcision; (not because it is of Moses, but of the fathers;) and ye on the sabbath day circumcise a man.

If a man on the sabbath day receive circumcision, that the law of Moses should not be broken; are ye angry at me, because I have made a man every whit whole on the sabbath day?

Judge not according to the appearance, but judge righteous judgment [John 7:22–24].

Circumcision is a rite which goes back to Abraham and is older than the Mosaic Law. He is showing them their own inconsistency in their practice. In trying to keep the Law, they broke the Law. If a child was eight days old on the Sabbath day, they would break the Sabbath Law and circumcise the child. They have no reply to this! Then Jesus warns them against making superficial judgments. That is still a difficulty with most of us today. We make superficial judgments because we don't have all the facts.

Then said some of them of Jerusalem, Is not this he, whom they seek to kill?

But, lo, he speaketh boldly, and they say nothing unto him. Do the rulers know indeed that this is the very Christ?

Howbeit we know this man whence he is: but when Christ cometh, no man knoweth whence he is [John 7:25–27].

Again we note that there was a division concerning who Jesus is.

Then cried Jesus in the temple as he taught, saying, Ye both know me, and ye know whence I am: and I am not come of myself, but he that sent me is true, whom ye know not.

But I know him: for I am from him, and he hath sent me [John 7:28–29].

This is quite oratorical. Jesus is saying, "Do you really know Me? You *think* you know Me, you see Me, but you don't really know Me. You think you know where I have come from, but you don't really know."

Then they sought to take him: but no man laid hands on him, because his hour was not yet come [John 7:30].

It's interesting that even though they were anxious to take Jesus, they couldn't touch Him until His hour had come.

And many of the people believed on him, and said, When Christ cometh, will he do more miracles than these which this man hath done?

The Pharisees heard that the people murmured such things concerning him; and the Pharisees and the chief priests sent officers to take him.

Then said Jesus unto them, Yet a little while am I with you, and then I go unto him that sent me.

Ye shall seek me, and shall not find me: and where I am, thither ye cannot come [John 7:31–34].

Our Lord answered the Pharisees that they would take Him at the proper time—not until then. Then He tells them He will leave them. He is speaking of His resurrection and His ascension. They would never be able to touch Him again. Have you ever noticed that after His death upon the cross, none but loving hands touched Him? None but loving eyes saw Him.

Then said the Jews among themselves, Whither will he go, that we shall not find him? will he go unto the dispersed among the Gentiles, and teach the Gentiles?

What manner of saying is this that he said, Ye shall seek me, and shall not find me: and where I am, thither ye cannot come? [John 7:35–36].

I think this is ridicule. They didn't think that Jesus could hide from them.

We come now to the last day of the feast, and it was on that day that they poured out a double portion of water in the temple. I think He could have been standing ankle deep in water when He said these words. They were celebrating the fact that God had given them water from the rock during the long trek of Israel through the wilderness. Paul tells us that the Rock was Christ (see 1 Cor. 10:4). He is the One who gives the real water, the Water of Life.

In the last day, that great day of the feast, Jesus stood and cried, saying, If any man thirst, let him come unto me, and drink [John 7:37].

This is free will, friend. "If *any* man." That means you. God is offering a gift to you. Also here is election: "If any man thirst." The question is, "Are you thirsty?" Have you perhaps been drinking at the mud holes of the world, and have you been finding that they are not satisfying? "If any man thirst, let him come unto me, and drink." You can come to Him and receive Him as your Savior.

He that believeth on me, as the scripture hath said, out of his belly shall flow rivers of living water.

(But this spake he of the Spirit, which they that believe on him should receive: for the Holy Ghost was not yet given; because that Jesus was not yet glorified.) [John 7:38–39].

The Holy Spirit had not yet been given because Jesus was not yet glorified. The Holy Spirit did not come until the Day of Pentecost. Then He came to indwell believers and to form them into one body. The coming of the Holy Spirit on that day assures us that Jesus had arrived back at the Father's throne.

Many of the people therefore, when they heard this saying, said, Of a truth this is the Prophet [John 7:40].

Some of the people believed and turned to Him. They drank and were satisfied.

Others said, This is the Christ. But some said, Shall Christ come out of Galilee? [John 7:41].

We have the same thing today. Some believe, and some do not believe.

Hath not the scripture said, That Christ cometh of the seed of David, and out of the town of Bethlehem, where David was?

So there was a division among the people because of him [John 7:42–43].

He *was* of the seed of David and out of the town of Bethlehem. That was where He first touched down on this earth. It was "splashdown" for Him in that miserable little stable in that miserable little town. It's not like the pretty pictures you see on Christmas cards. He began in Bethlehem, but He didn't stay there for His earthly ministry. If these people had really wanted to know, they could have learned that His birth took place in Bethlehem and that He did fulfill the prophecies. He is the One who is giving them the invitation to come and drink, but they put up this objection. There will always be a division among the people over who He is until He comes to reign.

And some of them would have taken him; but no man laid hands on him [John 7:44].

They couldn't. His hour was not yet come.

Then came the officers to the chief priests and Pharisees; and they said unto them, Why have ye not brought him?

The officers answered, Never man spake like this man [John 7:45–46].

What a testimony these men gave about Jesus, "Never man spake like this man." He was *the* great teacher, but it is not by His teaching that we are saved. He saves us by His death and resurrection.

Then answered them the Pharisees, Are ye also deceived?

Have any of the rulers or of the Pharisees believed on him?

But this people who knoweth not the law are cursed.

Nicodemus saith unto them, (he that came to Jesus by night, being one of them,)

Doth our law judge any man, before it hear him, and know what he doeth?

They answered and said unto him, Art thou also of Galilee? Search, and look: for out of Galilee ariseth no prophet.

And every man went unto his own house [John 7:47–53].

This is the Nicodemus who came to Jesus by night. I think that Nicodemus trusted the Lord that night. He is a Pharisee, and he defends Jesus. They ridicule him with a joke, "Art thou also of Galilee?" That was a disgrace to them. It was like city folk making fun of the country folk. It is interesting to note that they did know the facts of their Scripture: "Out of Galilee ariseth no prophet." In the true sense He hadn't come out of Galilee, nor had He come out of Bethlehem. He had come out of glory. "Unto us a child is born, unto us a son is given" (Isa. 9:6)—the Son came out from heaven.

"Every man went unto his own house." No one invited Jesus into his home. It was a feast night, but Jesus went out to the Mount of Olives. As far as we know, He never spent a night in Jerusalem.

How about you, my friend? Do you go to your own home and leave Jesus out in the cold? Or have you accepted His wonderful invitation so that you live in the love and light of His presence?

CHAPTER 8

THEME: *Jesus in temple forgives woman taken in adultery (sixth word)*

The chapter opens with the episode of the woman taken in adultery. John uses his customary method of following an incident with a discourse. There was a sharp conflict between our Lord and the religious rulers relative to this woman and what should be done with her. Arising from this came the marvelous discourse on Jesus the Light of the World.

The episode of the woman, covering the first eleven verses, is not found in some of the better manuscripts. As I am sure you know, our English Bibles are translated from the original languages. The New Testament was first written in the Greek language. Extant manuscripts were used to compile a Greek New Testament; then our English translations were made from that. The Greek text of Westcott and Hort omits the incident of the woman taken in adultery from its position in the eighth chapter of John but inserts it at the end of that gospel. Nestle's Greek text includes it but encloses it in brackets. Augustine writes that it was omitted because of a prudish fear that it would encourage adultery. However, if we read the account carefully, we will see that it does not condone sin. Rather, it condemns sin. We have both a scholarly and moral basis for considering it part of the inspired Word of God.

JESUS IN TEMPLE FORGIVES WOMAN TAKEN IN ADULTERY (Sixth Word)

Jesus went unto the mount of Olives.

And early in the morning he came again into the temple, and all the people came unto him; and he sat down, and taught them [John 8:1–2].

Remember that the night before there had been a meeting of the Sanhedrin and that people were divided in their opinion as to whether or not Jesus was the Messiah. Nicodemus defended Him. Everyone had gone home, and not one had invited Jesus to his house. Early in the morning, He came back into Jerusalem, went back to the temple, and sat down to teach.

And the scribes and Pharisees brought unto him a woman taken in adultery; and when they had set her in the midst,

They say unto him, Master, this woman was taken in adultery, in the very act [John 8:3–4].

What could be more crude and rude and brutal than this act of these religious rulers? As our Lord was sitting in the temple area teaching the people, there is a hullabaloo outside. Then here come these religious rulers dragging a woman with her clothes in disarray, her hair all disheveled, defiant, and resisting them. The crowd would naturally turn and look to see what in the world was happening. The religious rulers bring her right into the midst of the group that the Lord Jesus is teaching! They fling her down on the ground there and make their crude charge. "This woman was taken in adultery, in the very act."

She is guilty, there is no doubt about that. And what she did was sin. Our Lord called it *sin*—He finally said to her, "Go, and *sin* no more." They knew the Law perfectly well: "And the man that committeth adultery with another man's wife, even he that committeth adultery with his neighbour's wife, the adulterer and the adulteress shall surely be put to death" (Lev. 20:10). Where was the man? The very fact that they did not produce the man also makes it apparent that they were not interested in enforcing the Law. They had another motive.

Now Moses in the law commanded us, that such should be stoned: but what sayest thou?

This they said, tempting him, that they might have to accuse him. But Jesus stooped down, and with his finger wrote on the ground, as though he heard them not [John 8:5–6].

They are right about the Law of Moses; there is no way of toning it down. She should be stoned. They are putting Him on the horns of a dilemma. Will He contradict Moses? Will He say something else, offer some other explanation? They did this to trap Him so that they might accuse Him. They didn't really want to stone the woman. They wanted to stone *Him*. Our Lord knew that, of course—He "needed not that any should testify of man: for he knew what was in man" (John 2:25).

This scene is very interesting. The defiant woman is flung before Him. The crowd has no respect for her embarrassment, her feelings, and they leer at her and crane their necks to see her, adding to her humiliation.

Jesus stoops and writes on the ground. In effect, He dismisses the case. He will not join with her accusers. He will not so much as look at her to add to her embarrassment. He stoops down and writes as though He doesn't even hear them.

This is the only record that we have of His writing anything. He is the One about whom more books have been written, pro and con, than about any other person who has ever lived; yet He never wrote anything except this in the sands of the temple floor, which the wind or the feet of the crowd erased.

What did He write? Of course we don't know, but I can make a suggestion. Turning back to the prophets, we pick up something quite interesting: "O LORD, the hope of Israel, all that forsake thee shall be ashamed, and they that depart from me shall be written in the earth, because they have forsaken the LORD, the fountain of living waters" (Jer. 17:13). Now, who had forsaken the Lord? This woman? Yes, she had. The religious rulers? Yes, they had. Their names shall be written in the earth. This is what I think He wrote, linking their names with sins of their past. Perhaps He wrote the name of a woman living in Rome. One old pious Pharisee had had an affair in Rome when he was a young fellow. His wife didn't know about it; no one in Jerusalem knew about it; but our Lord knew that old rascal. As He just wrote the name of the woman, the old Pharisee came over and saw it—and suddenly remembered that he had another appointment. Perhaps one of the scribes made regular trips to Ephesus, a great sinning place, to a certain address over there which Jesus wrote in the sand. The scribe looked at it and said, "Oh, my gracious!" He left hurriedly. Another scribe may have left a girl in Galilee who was pregnant. He didn't marry her, and he didn't think anyone knew. Our Lord wrote the name of the girl and the scribe's name with it.

"Thou hast set our iniquities before thee, our secret sins in the light of thy countenance." (Ps. 90:8). Secret sin on earth is open scandal in heaven.

So when they continued asking him, he lifted up himself, and said unto them, He that is without sin among you, let him first cast a stone at her.

And again he stooped down, and wrote on the ground.

And they which heard it, being convicted by their own conscience, went out one by one, beginning at the eldest, even unto the last: and Jesus was left alone, and the woman standing in the midst [John 8:7–9].

Jesus gives the requirements for being a judge, which is something for all of us to hear. We have the right to be the judge of others provided we meet the requirement. That requirement is *sinlessness*. May I say to you, my friend, I don't know about you, but that takes me out of the stone-throwing business.

An old Scottish commentator says that the elder ones left first because they had more sense than the younger ones. The younger ones hung around until they saw their own names come up and then they finally caught on and left also. So there was not a person left there who could throw a stone at her except One. Only Jesus could have thrown the stone at her. All the others had slinked away. What hypocrites they were!

When Jesus had lifted up himself, and saw none but the woman, he said unto her, Woman, where are those thine accusers? hath no man condemned thee?

She said, No man, Lord. And Jesus said unto her, Neither do I condemn thee: go, and sin no more [John 8:10–11].

This woman was guilty of sin, and according to the Law of Moses an adulteress was to be put to death. Is Jesus reversing the Mosaic system? No. He is placing His cross between that woman and her sin. This One who is the Son of the virgin, who Himself was under a cloud all of His life, is going to the cross to pay the penalty for even the sin of this woman. He did not come into the world to condemn the world. He did not come to judge this woman. He came into the world to be a Savior!

A great many people think they are lost because they have committed a certain sin. I have news for you. One is not lost because he is a murderer, or a liar, or a thief, or an adulterer, or because he has borne false witness or committed other sins. A person does these things because he is lost and does not believe in Jesus Christ. Jesus Christ forgives sins. He is the Savior. He died for the sins of the whole world. Any person who comes to the Lord Jesus Christ is forgiven.

JESUS IS THE LIGHT OF THE WORLD (Sixth Word)

We notice that Jesus often follows this method. After an incident or a miracle, He gives a discourse on that subject.

Then spake Jesus again unto them, saying, I am the light of the world: he that followeth me shall not walk in darkness, but shall have the light of life [John 8:12].

Notice He says, "I am"—this "I am" occurs again and again. In the Old Testament, Jehovah is the ". . . I AM THAT I AM . . ." (Exod. 3:14). Very frankly, we are told very little about God. We know He is the self-existing One, that He has all wisdom and all power. The Lord Jesus came to this earth not only to redeem man but also to reveal God to man. Jesus greatly expands our understanding by using the commonplace things like bread, light, and water, to symbolize Himself. He uses the ordinary to speak of the extraordinary, the physical to speak of the spiritual, the temporal to speak of the eternal, the here-and-now to speak of the hereafter, the earthly to speak of the heavenly, the limited to speak of the unlimited, and the finite to speak of the infinite. Jesus gives us a revelation of God when He tells us that He is Bread, He is Water, He is Life. Then we understand that not only is God self-existing, but that He also meets our every need. Jesus said, "I am the bread of life" (John 6:35), "I am the light of the world" (John 8:12), "I am the door" (John 10:9), "I am the good shepherd" (John 10:11), "I am the resurrection, and the life" (John 11:25), "I am the way, the truth, and the life" (John 14:6), and "I am the vine, ye are the branches" (John 15:5).

Here Jesus is saying, "I am the light of the world." He has just exposed the sin of the scribes and the Pharisees who brought the woman guilty of adultery. Because they were just as guilty as she, they had to flee. When one turns on the light, all the rats, the bats, and the bedbugs crawl away. Light exposes sin, which is the reason the scribes and the Pharisees had to leave.

"I am the light of the world" is the highest claim that He has made so far in the Gospel of John. One of the definitions of God is that He is Light (see 1 John 1:5). He is absolute in His holiness and in His justice. Even physical light is one of the most complicated things as well as one of the most essential things for us. Who really knows what it is? In some ways it acts like waves and in some ways it acts like particles of matter. The startling thing is that men, acting on both of these definitions or principles, have been able to make remarkable inventions and discoveries. Some say that both are true and yet others say both can't be true. Is light the absence of darkness? Is darkness the absence of light? We say a room is filled with light. What do we mean? Does it weigh any more when it is filled with light? There could be no such thing as color without light. The red rose is red because it has absorbed every other part of light except red. That is the reason we see red in the red rose.

We don't understand light and certainly a child doesn't understand light, but he does know enough about it to turn on the light switch when he enters a dark room. Jesus Christ is the Light of the World. Just as the sun is the physical light of this world, He is spiritual Light. Just as a little child can have enough sense to come into the presence of light, so any sinner today, though he be "a fool and a wayfaring man" (see Isa. 35:8), can come into the presence of the Lord Jesus Christ.

There are those who deny that Christ is the Light of the World. They are walking in a lesser light. As the moon has no light of its own, but reflects light from the sun, so this civilization that we live in today owes everything to Christ. We have hospitals, charities, orphans' homes, consideration for the poor, rights of labor because the Lord Jesus came to this earth. The reason we have problems in these areas today is that we have wandered too far from the Light. The world is just walking in moonlight, as it were. How this poor old world needs to get back to the Light which is Christ.

"He that followeth me shall not walk in darkness, but shall have the light of life." There are those who have attempted to liken Jesus the Light to the headlights of a car. Friend, the headlights of a car do not lead anywhere. Who does the leading?—The fellow at the steering wheel. Unfortunately, this is the way many Christians try to live their lives. I don't consider this an apt illustration of Christ.

During this Feast of Tabernacles, Israel was remembering the deliverance when the pillar of fire led the children of Israel through the wilderness. They were celebrating this with a torch parade. When Jesus said, "I am the light of the world," this is what He was referring to. Whenever and wherever the pillar of fire led, the children of Israel followed. We are to follow Him in like manner, looking to Him as the Light of the World.

The Pharisees therefore said unto him, Thou bearest record of thyself; thy record is not true.

Jesus answered and said unto them, Though I bear record of myself, yet my record is true; for I know whence I came, and whither I go; but ye cannot tell whence I come, and whither I go [John 8:13–14].

There is now a sharp conflict between the religious rulers and Christ. They are really accusing Him of boasting when He claimed to be the Light. Jesus gives them a threefold reason why His testimony is true.

First, He says, "I know whence I came." He says He knows where He came from and, hence, He knows Himself. By the way, folks on this earth can't tell you where they came from. Scientists try to tell us what has happened millions of years ago; yet none of them was here even one hundred years ago. They don't *know* where they came from; they can only speculate. But the Lord Jesus knew from where He came.

Ye judge after the flesh; I judge no man.

And yet if I judge, my judgment is true: for I am not alone, but I and the Father that sent me [John 8:15–16].

His second statement is that He judges no man after the flesh. Any judgment that you or I make is after the flesh. Our judgment is limited because we simply do not have all the facts. The theory of evolution is an example of this. Because our judgments are based on very fragmentary facts, they really are speculation. Either man accepts speculation or he accepts revelation. If one judges according to the flesh, he will naturally follow speculation. The Lord Jesus says that *He* does not judge according to the flesh. He gives the judgment that comes from heaven. He gives God's viewpoint, God's estimation. This is revelation, and it differs from man's point of view. That is why the hostility of these religious rulers is mounting.

It is also written in your law, that the testimony of two men is true.

I am one that bear witness of myself, and the Father that sent me beareth witness of me [John 8:17–18].

Here is the third reason that His testimony is true. The Father had borne witness to Him. They had heard the Father's voice out of heaven.

Then said they unto him, Where is thy Father? Jesus answered, Ye neither know me, nor my Father: if ye had known me, ye should have known my Father also [John 8:19].

They are reflecting on His birth again. Notice that Jesus calls God "my Father" in a different relationship from what you and I have with Him through faith in Christ. Remember, He said to Mary after His resurrection, "I ascend unto my Father, and your Father" (John 20:17). We become children of God through faith in Jesus Christ, but Jesus is His Son because of His position in the Trinity. He is God the Son, and He addresses God the Father. This has nothing to do with generation or regeneration, but it has everything to do with His position in the Trinity.

"If ye had known me, ye should have known

my Father also." Here is the cleavage. Here is the real issue. There is no middle ground. If you are going to know God the Father, you must come through Jesus Christ. There is no other way.

These words spake Jesus in the treasury, as he taught in the temple: and no man laid hands on him; for his hour was not yet come.

Then said Jesus again unto them, I go my way, and ye shall seek me, and shall die in your sins: whither I go, ye cannot come.

Then said the Jews, Will he kill himself? because he saith, Whither I go, ye cannot come [John 8:20–22].

The treasury was in the women's court. This was where they had brought the woman taken in adultery. You will notice how much these Jews were in the dark. First they ask, "Where is thy Father?" Now they ask, "Will he kill himself?" They know nothing about the fact that He has been instructing His own that He is going to Jerusalem to die at the hands of the Gentiles, that He will be delivered up to die by these very same religious rulers, and that He will die a redemptive death for the sins of the world. Will He kill Himself? No! He will *give* Himself a ransom for many.

And he said unto them, Ye are from beneath; I am from above: ye are of this world; I am not of this world [John 8:23].

We find this same thought in 1 Corinthians 2:14. Human knowledge can be understood by any other man who has a human nature—if his IQ is high enough. But divine knowledge is different. Only the Spirit of God can take the things of Christ and show them to us. That's what He is saying here.

I said therefore unto you, that ye shall die in your sins: for if ye believe not that I am he, ye shall die in your sins [John 8:24].

People die because they are sinners. That is the natural consequence of sin. "If ye believe not that I am he, ye shall die in your sins." Can a person be saved on his deathbed? Yes, if he accepts the Lord Jesus Christ as his Savior. But a person can reject Christ too long, just as these Jews did. There comes a time when one has rejected Christ too long and then will not want ever to accept Him.

Then said they unto him, Who art thou? And Jesus saith unto them, Even the same that I said unto you from the beginning [John 8:25].

These Jews did not know what His mission was, His work was, nor did they know Him. "Where is thy Father?" "Will He kill Himself?" "Who art Thou?" Jesus answers that His statement concerning Himself is always the same. He consistently claims that He is the Messiah, the Savior of the world.

I have many things to say and to judge of you: but he that sent me is true; and I speak to the world those things which I have heard of him [John 8:26].

Our Lord always maintained that what He was doing and saying was what the Father wanted Him to do and say. He claimed that God the Father had sent Him and that He was doing the Father's will. He never appealed to His own mind or His own intellect. This is an example for us who are preachers. It is God's Word that we are to be giving out rather than messages that are the product of our own intellects.

They understood not that he spake to them of the Father [John 8:27].

They missed the whole point. They are of the earth; they do not understand heavenly things.

Then said Jesus unto them, When ye have lifted up the Son of man, then shall ye know that I am he, and that I do nothing of myself; but as my Father hath taught me, I speak these things [John 8:28].

When Jesus calls Himself the Son of Man, He is referring to Daniel 7:13–14. The Son of Man comes to the Ancient of Days to be made ruler of this universe. So the Lord Jesus is referring here to His crucifixion and also to His crowning that is yet to come.

After the death and resurrection of Christ, many of these religious rulers believed. We are told in the Book of Acts that many of the priests in Jerusalem believed. This is what He is saying to them now. Afterwards they would know that He is the One He claims to be. It is the redemptive death of Christ that explains Him, why He came, and who He is. One cannot really know who He is until one knows what He has done.

And he that sent me is with me: the Father hath not left me alone; for I do always those things that please him.

As he spake these words, many believed on him [John 8:29–30].

Have you ever finished a day without looking back on it and wishing that you had done some things a little differently? Our Lord never finished a day with a regret. He always did those things that pleased His Father. He is making it abundantly clear that He has come to do the Father's will.

Then said Jesus to those Jews which believed on him, If ye continue in my word, then are ye my disciples indeed;

And ye shall know the truth, and the truth shall make you free [John 8:31–32].

Faith alone saves, but the faith that saves is not alone. It will produce something. After a person believes on the Lord Jesus Christ, he will want to "continue in His Word." The proof of faith is continuing with the Savior. As the pastor of a church, I learned to watch out for the person who is active in the church but is not interested in the study of the Word of God. Such a one is dangerous to a church.

The truth shall make you free. The truth is that Jesus Christ is the Savior of the world. He is the Truth. First we come to Him as our Savior. Then as we go on with Him, we know by experience that we are free. We are free from the penalty of sin—we don't need to lie awake at night worrying about going to hell. He doesn't even ask us to live the Christian life. He asks us to trust Him and let Him live His life through us. When we yield to Him, we are free.

They answered him, We be Abraham's seed, and were never in bondage to any man: how sayest thou, Ye shall be made free? [John 8:33].

They lied when they said that. They had been in bondage in Egypt and in Babylon, and as they spoke they were under the iron heel of Rome. What a misrepresentation that was.

Jesus answered them, Verily, verily, I say unto you, Whosoever committeth sin is the servant of sin.

And the servant abideth not in the house for ever: but the Son abideth ever.

If the Son therefore shall make you free, ye shall be free indeed.

I know that ye are Abraham's seed; but ye seek to kill me, because my word hath no place in you.

I speak that which I have seen with my Father: and ye do that which ye have seen with your father [John 8:34–38].

They were not free physically, and they were not free spiritually. They claimed to be Abraham's seed; yet they sought to kill Jesus.

"Whosoever committeth sin is the servant of sin" is in the present tense. If you continue in a life of sin, you are a servant of sin. I doubt if any of us go through one day without sinning, but the child of God comes to the Father every day and confesses his sin. The child of the Devil will never do that. This is the thought of Romans 6:16, "Know ye not, that to whom ye yield yourselves servants to obey, his servants ye are to whom ye obey . . . ?"

Jesus gets rather subtle now. A servant may come and work for you during the day, but when evening comes, he gets his hat and goes home. The son comes in, pitches his hat in a corner, sits down and relaxes, because he is the son. The Lord was telling these rulers that they are not really God's children. They were in the temple then, but they wouldn't be there long. In A.D. 70 Titus came and took every one of them away and sold them into slavery. The five o'clock whistle had blown, and the servants left the house.

The Son makes us free indeed. We do not have to be the servant of sin. Many Christians accept defeat and failure as a normal Christian life. God never intended us to live like that. He intends us to live for Him by the power of the Holy Spirit.

They answered and said unto him, Abraham is our father. Jesus saith unto them, If ye were Abraham's children, ye would do the works of Abraham.

But now ye seek to kill me, a man that hath told you the truth, which I have heard of God: this did not Abraham.

Ye do the deeds of your father. Then said they to him, We be not born of fornication; we have one Father, even God.

Jesus said unto them, If God were your Father, ye would love me: for I proceeded forth and came from God; neither came I of myself, but he sent me.

Why do ye not understand my speech? even because ye cannot hear my word.

Ye are of your father the devil, and the lusts of your father ye will do. He was a murderer from the beginning, and abode not in the truth, because there is no truth in him. When he speaketh a lie, he speaketh of his own: for he is a liar, and the father of it [John 8:39–44].

The old adage says, "Like father, like son." Although they claim that they are the children of Abraham, Jesus tells these men that if they were truly the children of Abraham, they would act like Abraham. Instead, they are trying to kill Him. So instead of being the children of Abraham, they are, in fact, the children of the Devil. Satan is the originator of murder and of lying, and they were being his imitators, his children. "Ye do the deeds of your father."

Notice that they again bring up the subject, "We be not born of fornication." When I first entered the ministry, I took the position that one could deny the Virgin Birth and still be a Christian. I don't do so today. If we deny the Virgin Birth of Christ, I believe we are joining this taunting crowd who said, "We be not born of fornication." Yet, this crowd want to claim that God is their Father. Jesus says, "If God were your Father, ye would love me: for I proceeded forth and came from God; neither came I of myself, but he sent me."

How do *we* know that God is our Father? John, in his epistle, gives us this answer: "Whosoever believeth that Jesus is the Christ is born of God: and every one that loveth him that begat loveth him also that is begotten of him" (1 John 5:1).

These Jews thought they were the children of God when they were actually the children of the Devil. We find the same idea today. This doctrine of the universal Fatherhood of God and the universal brotherhood of man has brought us into a lot of trouble. It has shaped the philosophy of our nation. We sit down at a conference table with the children of the Devil, and we call them the children of God. I am afraid that our nation has been deceived by other nations of the world because our wise diplomats and smart politicians are simply working on the wrong premise. The Bible does not teach the universal Fatherhood of God and the universal brotherhood of man. Obviously Jesus did not teach the universal Fatherhood of God because He was saying to these religious rulers that they were children of the *Devil*. Apparently, there are some people who are not the children of God! One becomes a child of God only through faith in the Lord Jesus Christ.

The words of Jesus antagonized these men. Yet, Jesus insisted that His words are truth. He also insisted that none of them could convince Him of sin. Jesus is from God, and anyone who is a child of God will listen to Jesus Christ. People still don't like to hear that today. Folks try to think we're all nice, sweet brothers to each other, and they talk of love, love, love. My friend, if you are going to stand for the *truth* today, then you will denounce the evil just as our Lord did. That is going to bring antagonism.

And because I tell you the truth, ye believe me not [John 8:45].

Isn't it interesting that Jesus can tell people the truth and they will not believe. It arouses their intense antagonism. Yet people will believe the wildest rumors and the biggest lies. Dictators have learned that. Hitler was very frank about this in his book when he said that if a big lie is told again and again and again, finally the people will believe it. Today advertisers and the news media have learned this also.

Which of you convinceth me of sin? And if I say the truth, why do ye not believe me?

He that is of God heareth God's words: ye therefore hear them not, because ye are not of God.

Then answered the Jews, and said unto him, Say we not well that thou art a Samaritan, and hast a devil? [John 8:46–48].

Jesus put His very life on the line when He asked, "Which of you convinceth me of sin?" This is one of the great proofs of the deity of Christ. Believe me, if any of His enemies had had one shred of evidence against Him, they would have used it. They have no logical answers for His questions. So what do they do? They come up with ridicule. I learned this method long ago when I was on a debate team. When they have no logical answer, they resort to ridicule. Listen to the Jews. "You're a Samaritan; you have a demon"—as I'm sure you know, *demon* is the correct translation. This is name-calling and pure ridicule.

Jesus answered, I have not a devil; but I honour my Father, and ye do dishonour me.

And I seek not mine own glory: there is one that seeketh and judgeth.

Verily, verily, I say unto you, If a man keep my saying, he shall never see death [John 8:49–51].

I wish we could see Him standing in that crowd. They hate Him so much that they want to kill Him. They have murder in their hearts, and He has nothing but love in His. He is going to go to the cross to die for them. They are thinking of death for Him, but He is offering them life. "If a man keep my saying, he shall never see death." He is offering them eternal life, spiritual life. My friend, this Jesus is more than a man.

Then said the Jews unto him, Now we know that thou hast a devil. Abraham is dead, and the prophets; and thou sayest, If a man keep my saying, he shall never taste of death.

Art thou greater than our father Abraham, which is dead? and the prophets are dead: whom makest thou thyself?

Jesus answered, If I honour myself, my honour is nothing: it is my Father that honoureth me; of whom ye say, that he is your God:

Yet ye have not known him; but I know him: and if I should say, I know him not, I shall be a liar like unto you: but I know him, and keep his saying.

Your father Abraham rejoiced to see my day: and he saw it, and was glad.

Then said the Jews unto him, Thou art not yet fifty years old, and hast thou seen Abraham?

Jesus said unto them, Verily, verily, I say unto you, Before Abraham was, I am.

Then took they up stones to cast at him: but Jesus hid himself, and went out of the temple, going through the midst of them, and so passed by [John 8:52–59].

Did Abraham ever see Christ? He certainly did. The appearances of God to people in the Old Testament was an appearance of Jesus Christ to these people. "No man hath seen God at any time; the only begotten Son, which is in the bosom of the Father, he hath declared him" (John 1:18). Then, too, although Abraham's body was buried there, yet Abraham was really not dead but was in the presence of God. Jesus makes this very clear, as recorded in Luke 20:38. "For he is not a God of the dead, but of the living: for all live unto him."

The liberal theologian today teaches that Jesus Christ was a great teacher, but that He never really claimed to be God. My friend, listen to this. "Before Abraham was, I am." Not, I *was*—I *AM*. He is the Jehovah, the I AM, God. The Jews understood perfectly. Because they knew precisely what He was claiming, they took up stones to kill Him for blasphemy.

The issue is Jesus Christ. He put these Jews on the spot. They had to make a decision concerning Him. You must make a decision concerning Him. Either He is the Truth or He is a liar. Either He is God and Savior, or He is not. You must decide. Either you accept Him or you reject Him. Remember that your decision does not in any way change who He is. He is the great I AM, Jehovah, the eternal God. Your decision is to accept or deny this.

CHAPTER 9

***THEME:** Jesus opens the eyes of a man born blind in Jerusalem (fifth work); record of the miracle; reaction to the miracle*

The Lord has been giving His discourse on the Light of the World. Because He claimed that He is God, the Jews wanted to kill Him. Jesus "hid" Himself as He went out of the temple, "going through the midst of them" (John 8:59). It was a miracle that He could escape this angry mob. His time had not yet come, and so they could not lay their hands on Him.

The incident which now follows is still really a continuation of the discourse on the Light of the World. The enemies of the Lord Jesus could not see because they were spiritually blind. The blind man also could not see, even when the Light of the World stood before him, but Jesus is going to reveal Himself to him. Before the blind man can see, he must have his eyes restored. Light must be received. There must be a receiver as well as a sender of light.

We used to argue the question about noise. If a tree falls in the forest and nobody is there to hear it, is there a noise? The obvious answer is that there are sound waves, but if there is no ear there to pick up the sound and interpret it, no one hears it as noise. There must be a receiver.

The lack of sight does not mean that light is not there. Light reveals the condition of the eye. The Light of the World reveals the condition of the soul. The Pharisees thought they saw, but they were blind.

There is a story of a mining explosion in West Virginia. The explosion plunged the trapped men into total darkness. When the rescue team managed to get a light through to them, one of the young men finally said, "Well, why don't they turn on the light?" They all looked at him in amazement, and then they realized that the explosion had blinded him. In the darkness, he did not know that he was blind. The light revealed to him and to them that he was blind.

This is what Jesus means in verse 39 of this chapter: "For judgment I am come into this world, that they which see not might see; and that they which see might be made blind." Light reveals the true condition. Those who are blind, but do not realize it, can know that they are truly blind.

A prominent member of the English Parliament took Mr. Edmund Burke, who was a statesman and a great orator, to hear Dr. Hugh Black, one of the great preachers of Scotland. Dr. Black preached a powerful sermon exalting the Lord Jesus Christ. After the service the friend waited for Mr. Burke's reaction to the message. Finally he said, "He is a great orator, but what was he talking about?" Here was a brilliant man who was blind.

It is our responsibility to get out the Word of God, and there our responsibility ends. It is the work of the Holy Spirit to open the heart of the listener and cause him to obey the Word. We should present the Light of the World to people, but the Holy Spirit must open the eyes. This is what is meant in 2 Corinthians 2:15–16: "For we are unto God a sweet savour of Christ, in them that are saved, and in them that perish: To the one we are the savour of death unto death; and to the other the savour of life unto life. . . ." We are equally as "successful" when we do not win a convert as when we do. We are simply to shine the light, to hold up Jesus Christ, the Light of the World. One fellow will say to us, "Where is the light? That doesn't make sense to me." We will look at him and say, "Poor fellow, he is blind." Another fellow will say to us, "Thank you for showing me the light. I was blind but now I see."

JESUS OPENS THE EYES OF A MAN BORN BLIND IN JERUSALEM (Fifth Work)

And as Jesus passed by, he saw a man which was blind from his birth [John 9:1].

Logically this episode of the blind man follows the wonderful statement of our Lord, "I am the light of the world" (John 8:12). There evidently was a lapse of time between chapter 8 and the opening of chapter 9 because He is moving in a more leisurely manner—"as Jesus passed by."

RECORD OF THE MIRACLE

This is the only record of our Lord healing a man with congenital blindness.

And his disciples asked him, saying, Master, who did sin, this man, or his parents, that he was born blind? [John 9:2].

The disciples want to establish the cause of his disease. They want to discuss who is at fault, who it is that sinned. In their day there were probably four answers they would have given. The pagans of that day, as many of today also, believed in reincarnation and held that congenital disease could be the result of sins committed during a former existence. The Jews never did accept this explanation. Then there is the argument of heredity, that the sins of the fathers are visited upon the children to the third and fourth generations (see Exod. 20:5). We know that this is possible and that blindness in some cases can be the result of the sin of the parent. Then, there was the explanation that the sin of Adam was passed to each member of the human family so that all are subject to death and disease. And finally, the Jewish rabbis believed that a child in the womb could sin.

Jesus answered, Neither hath this man sinned, nor his parents: but that the works of God should be made manifest in him.

I must work the works of him that sent me, while it is day: the night cometh, when no man can work.

As long as I am in the world, I am the light of the world [John 9:3–5].

Jesus doesn't give them the answer they wanted. He says the important thing is not to probe around in the past and try to find out who is guilty. The thing to do is to cure the man. It may be true that an ounce of prevention is worth a pound of cure, but after a man is sick, it's pretty important to get that pound of cure for him.

God has His own wise reasons for permitting sickness, disease, suffering, and trouble. When I went to the hospital for surgery, I received letters from hundreds of people. Out of those letters, there were several who proposed to tell me why God let this happen to me. The only trouble was, I don't think that any one of them knew. God doesn't always reveal to us why He permits things. I believe this:

God never does, nor suffers to be done
But what we would ourselves,
Could we but see through all events of things
As well as He.

God has His way, and He doesn't propose to tell us all His reasons. He does ask us to walk with Him by faith through the dark times of our lives.

I think, frankly, that we need to understand that our Lord is not saying for one minute that this man was sort of a spiritual guinea pig. I believe the punctuation of the verse misleads us. Jesus is saying, "Neither hath this man sinned, nor his parents. But that the works of God should be made manifest in him, I must work the works of Him that sent me, while it is day."

God has created you and me for His glory. He did not create us that we might try to be a somebody down here. He created us for *His* glory. If we miss that, we miss the entire purpose of our creation. These trials and sufferings come to us because they bring about the glory of God. This blind man, through the healing of his blindness, will bring about the glory of God. Not only will this blind man see (and think how much he would *enjoy* seeing all the rest of his life), but also he will see Jesus Christ and come to know Him as his Savior.

Now Jesus reverts to His original statement. "I am the light of the world." The night makes all of mankind blind. No one can see. Christ is the spiritual Light of the World, and without Him everyone is blind. But as long as He is in the world, He is the Light of the World. He is still in the world today, my friend. He comes to us in the person of the Holy Spirit. Unless the Son of God, by means of the Holy Spirit, opens our eyes so that we can see spiritual things, we will remain blind as bats.

When he had thus spoken, he spat on the ground, and made clay of the spittle, and he anointed the eyes of the blind man with the clay,

And said unto him, Go, wash in the pool of Siloam, (which is by interpretation, Sent.) He went his way therefore, and washed, and came seeing [John 9:6–7].

Christ had to touch the blind man, and the blind man had to obey Christ. Christ must touch our spiritual vision and bring new life to the dead spiritual optic nerve. It is not a question of who sinned. "For all have sinned, and come short of the glory of God" (Rom. 3:23). If Christ has not touched your eyes, you are not seeing.

There are so many people right in our churches today who are blind and don't know it. People write to me and say they listened to our Bible-teaching program for months; then all of a sudden their eyes were opened and they saw. Like the poor young man in the mine explosion, there are people standing in the light of the Word of God who say, "Why doesn't someone turn on the light?" That is exactly what Pontius Pilate did. He asked, "What is truth?" (John 18:38) as he was standing right in the presence of the One who said, "I am the way, the truth, and the life" (John 14:6). We need to let Christ touch our eyes so that we can see.

You will notice that Christ touched this man, although the man still could not see Him. Then Jesus asked him to go wash, and the man obeyed. We may ask why Jesus used this method to heal the man. I think there are several reasons: (1) This gospel sets forth the deity of Christ, but it also sets forth Jesus as a man. Jesus had just claimed His deity and now He touches the blind man, man to man. (2) The blind man must obey the Lord Jesus Christ if he is to see. (3) The Lord sent him to the pool which is called Siloam, and John makes a point of telling us *Siloam* means "Sent." Even the name of the pool bears testimony that Jesus is *sent* from the Father. Jesus may be implying to this man that He has been sent from the Father, and in the same way He is sending him. (4) The blind man needed the water to make him see. The water represents the Word of God in many passages of Scripture. It is my firm conviction that there never can be a conversion without the Word of God. "The entrance of thy words giveth light; it giveth understanding unto the simple" (Ps. 119:130). (5) The Jews needed this testimony because in verse 29 they say, "We know that God spake unto Moses: as for this fellow, we know not from whence he is." They must see by this healing of the blind man that Jesus is the God-man who is sent from the Father.

May I point out that the *method* of healing this man is not the important issue. The *Person* who heals is the important issue. It is Christ who opened his eyes. The blind man's part was to trust and obey.

Jesus used different methods of healing people. If the method was the touch, the man healed would insist everyone would need the same experience that he had. He would go away singing, "The Touch of His Hand on Mine." When Jesus healed others by not touching them at all, they would insist that one doesn't need to experience anything, not even His touch. They would say that all one needs is the Word of Jesus. They would go away singing, "Only Believe." Then, this blind man here would say to all of them that they are wrong. He'd say you've got to be touched and then you must go to the pool and wash; so he would be singing, "Shall We Gather at the River?" You are going to tell me that is perfectly absurd, silly, and ridiculous. It sure is, but I know a lot of "blind" folk today who will argue about the necessity of a certain ceremony or an experience to be saved. However, the all-important thing is to come to Christ, to believe Him, to obey Him. "Him that cometh to me I will in no wise cast out" (John 6:37). It is the person of the Lord Jesus Christ that is important.

I want to stop here and show how the condition of the blind man parallels our condition as sinners before we were saved.

1. The blind man was outside the temple, shut out from God. Remember that Paul says in Ephesians 2:12 that *we* were strangers from the covenants of promise, that we had no hope; we were without God in the world. That is the condition of everyone before he is saved. Without God, without hope, shut out!

2. The man was blind. He was unable to see the Savior. John Hancock heard a sermon of John Witherspoon on the text "I am the door: by me if any man enter in, he shall be saved" (John 10:9). As he walked home he thought to himself, "I have always admired John Witherspoon but tonight I didn't follow him. He impresses me as being a great preacher, but tonight I couldn't understand him." When he got home he put the key in the lock and pushed open the big door of his colonial home. He said, "Oh, I *see!*" His family laughed and said, "Of course, you see. You were out in the dark and now you have come into the light." He answered, "Yes, but I mean that I now see that Jesus is the door, and faith is the key that turns the lock, I now trust Christ, and I see Him."

We were blind without Christ. Did you see Him as your Savior before you were saved? Was He the wonderful One to you then? No. We were blind.

3. The man had been blind from birth. We were born in sin. We came into this world as sinners.

4. The blind man was beyond human help. Nobody had a cure for his blindness. We were helpless sinners in this world and no one had a cure for us.

5. He was a beggar. This is what hurts a lot of people. They hate to admit they are beggars. They would be willing to pay for salvation, but it is not for sale. You have to come to God for salvation as this beggar did. God *gives* it away. This beggar could never have bought salvation because he had nothing with which to buy it. "Ho, every one that thirsteth, come ye to the waters, and he that hath no money; come ye, buy, and eat; yea, come, buy wine

and milk without money and without price" (Isa. 55:1).

6. He made no appeal to Jesus. Blind Bartimaeus was loud and insistent, but this man just sat there. He didn't know Jesus. It took him a long time to grow in grace and in the knowledge of Jesus Christ. Friend, did you really want to get saved? Were you looking for salvation? Were you looking for the Lord Jesus? If you are the average person, you were not. You were not looking for Him, but He was looking for you. That is the story of man and his salvation.

7. There was no pity shown to him by others. The Jews passed him by on their way to the temple. The disciples wanted to argue about him. They had no intention of showing any mercy to this man, and they were not prepared to do anything for him. This is a picture of the human family. Christ feels compassion for us, and Christ alone can help us.

REACTION TO THE MIRACLE

There is a change in a man who had been blind. He no longer must feel his way home every day but walks home *seeing*. I think this man was shouting, "Hallelujah, I can see!"

1. The neighbors—

The neighbours therefore, and they which before had seen him that he was blind, said, Is not this he that sat and begged?

Some said, This is he: others said, He is like him: but he said, I am he [John 9:8–9].

Can't you picture the neighborhood? Someone stands at the window and says, "Look, there's the blind man." His wife goes to the door to look and says, "That's not the blind man. He looks like the blind man but he's not blind." So the man must identify himself to his own neighbors.

The neighbors knew something had happened to him. I do not believe that if you are truly converted, if you have changed from blindness to seeing, you can go on without people noticing that you have changed. If there is no evidence of a change, then something is wrong, radically wrong.

Therefore said they unto him, How were thine eyes opened?

He answered and said, A man that is called Jesus made clay, and anointed mine eyes, and said unto me, Go to the pool of Siloam, and wash: and I went and washed, and I received sight.

Then said they unto him, Where is he? He said, I know not [John 9:10–12].

I love the testimony of this man. He told only what he knew—a good, honest, sincere testimony. He grew in perception every time he gave his testimony. Notice how accurate the Word of God is. He didn't say Jesus took spittle and made clay. In his blindness he didn't know that. All he knew was that he felt clay rubbed on his eyes. His testimony is honest, not elaborated or glamorized.

Salvation is really a simple matter. It is coming to the Lord Jesus and experiencing the power of God. This man hadn't even seen Jesus and yet the Lord Jesus had opened his eyes. The important thing for us is not to see Jesus but to believe in Him.

2. The Pharisees—

They brought to the Pharisees him that aforetime was blind.

And it was the sabbath day when Jesus made the clay, and opened his eyes.

Then again the Pharisees also asked him how he had received his sight. He said unto them, He put clay upon mine eyes, and I washed, and do see [John 9:13–15].

Again, the man's testimony is very simple. You would think these Pharisees would have rejoiced that a blind man could now see. You'd think they would break out in a "Hallelujah Chorus." Not this cold-blooded crowd! Now notice the reaction of the Pharisees. They just don't know what to do about a man born blind who is now walking around seeing.

Therefore said some of the Pharisees, This man is not of God, because he keepeth not the sabbath day. Others said, How can a man that is a sinner do such miracles? And there was a division among them [John 9:16].

These men were undoubtedly some of the cleverest men on earth. I believe beyond a shadow of a doubt that they would have been more than a match for the Greek philosophers. They were experts at arguing. They are going to use a syllogistic method of arguing. They have a major premise, a minor premise, and then a conclusion. If both the premises are true, the conclusion will be true. But if either of the premises is false, the conclusion will be false. Here is their reasoning:

Major premise—all people from God keep the Sabbath.

Minor premise—Jesus does not keep the Sabbath.

Conclusion—Jesus is not from God.

Their false major premise kept people from coming to the true conclusion. If both premises had been true, their conclusion would have been true.

Major premise—Only people from God can open the eyes of a man born blind.

Minor premise—Jesus opened the eyes of the blind man.

Conclusion—Jesus is from God.

Unfortunately, we find similar controversies going on in our churches today. There are arguments over nonessentials while the world outside is dying and going to hell, blind to the gospel. There is still the same old argument. "He doesn't keep the Sabbath"—which means "He doesn't do it our way."

They say unto the blind man again, What sayest thou of him, that he hath opened thine eyes? He said, He is a prophet.

But the Jews did not believe concerning him, that he had been blind, and received his sight, until they called the parents of him that had received his sight [John 9:17–18].

In their argumentation they ask, "How can a man that is a sinner do such miracles?" This is the very thing which helped the blind man to grow in his perception. If a sinner can't do such miracles, yet because of Him he can see, then this One must be a *prophet*! He must be from God. The blind man has taken another step.

"But the Jews did not believe concerning him." When men don't want to believe a thing, it is amazing what little peccadilloes they will attempt to dig up to really get away from the truth. Because they won't accept the man's testimony, they call in his parents.

3. The parents—

And they asked them, saying, Is this your son, who ye say was born blind? how then doth he now see?

His parents answered them and said, We know that this is our son, and that he was born blind:

But by what means he now seeth, we know not; or who hath opened his eyes, we know not: he is of age; ask him: he shall speak for himself.

These words spake his parents, because they feared the Jews: for the Jews had agreed already, that if any man did confess that he was Christ, he should be put out of the synagogue [John 9:19–22].

Here is religious conniving, and it is one of the most pernicious things that is imaginable. The religious rulers are trying to find somebody they can hang this on, and the parents want to get off the hook. These rulers never contested the fact that the man had been blind and now could see. It's only professors in swivel chairs in universities who doubt the miracles Jesus performed. The people who were present never denied that a miracle had been performed.

Therefore said his parents, He is of age; ask him [John 9:23].

The parents knew that a miracle had been done. But they were not prepared to explain *how* the miracle had been done. They did not want to be excommunicated because that would completely ostracize them, and they didn't want to get into that kind of trouble. Since the religious rulers cannot deny the miracle, they will try to keep the Lord Jesus from receiving the credit for it.

Then again called they the man that was blind, and said unto him, Give God the praise: we know that this man is a sinner [John 9:24].

The Jews now go back to their first argument: this Man is a sinner because He broke the Sabbath. Don't give glory to this Man, the Lord Jesus. Give the glory to God. My, doesn't that sound nice and pious!

He answered and said, Whether he be a sinner or no, I know not: one thing I know, that, whereas I was blind, now I see [John 9:25].

He hasn't seen the Lord Jesus yet. This is the second time they have brought him into court, and he is a little weary of the whole thing. Yet, listen to his testimony. "One thing I know, that, whereas I was blind, now I see."

That is the testimony of any sinner who has been saved. Once I was blind but now I see. Once I was in spiritual darkness but now I am in spiritual light. Once I did not know Christ, but now I know Him as my Savior. I don't know about you, but I get a little weary of long-winded testimonies. I suspect that many of them are padded and embellished and polished up to make them attractive. Sometimes the emphasis is placed on the past, so much so that the people actually come out as heroes in their testimony. They were leaders in crime, they were rubbing shoulders with the gang leaders, they knew all the great ones, they were the worst alcoholics, the worst gamblers, and on and on. Then they heard the gospel and were converted. The people who hear such testimonies go home and call their friends, "My, have you heard the testimony of So-and-So?"—and they are so busy telling about So-and-So and all the things he had done that they hardly even mention Christ. Friend, the important part of any testimony that I want to hear is simply this, "Once I was blind; now I see."

Then said they to him again, What did he to thee? how opened he thine eyes? [John 9:26].

The Pharisees are really up against it. They're trying their best to find some little flaw that they can seize upon to explain away the miracle that has been performed. They cannot simply dismiss it as theologians and professors try to do today. The man is there, and he can see.

He answered them, I have told you already, and ye did not hear: wherefore would ye hear it again? will ye also be his disciples?

Then they reviled him, and said, Thou art his disciple; but we are Moses' disciples [John 9:27–28].

The man who had been blind is beginning to understand what they are doing, and he gets a little sarcastic with them, "Will you also be His disciples?" He makes another interesting observation, "Will you hear it again?" Not only are the Pharisees blind so they cannot see the Light of the World, they are also deaf so they cannot hear.

We know that God spake unto Moses: as for this fellow, we know not from whence he is.

The man answered and said unto them, Why herein is a marvellous thing, that ye know not from whence he is, and yet he hath opened mine eyes.

Now we know that God heareth not sinners: but if any man be a worshipper of God, and doeth his will, him he heareth.

Since the world began was it not heard that any man opened the eyes of one that was born blind.

If this man were not of God, he could do nothing.

They answered and said unto him, Thou wast altogether born in sins, and dost thou teach us? And they cast him out [John 9:29–34].

The religious rulers revile him. You can notice again that, when men do not have an answer, they will resort to ridicule. Inadvertently they have slowly moved the healed blind man into a line of logic so that he knows only a man from God could do such a miracle: there is no doubt that he had been healed, so this Man must be from God. Remember, he still has never seen Jesus.

These rulers have no answer. They cannot meet the argument or give a satisfactory explanation. The facts confound and contradict them. What do they do? They cast the man out. This excommunication shut him out of the temple. It also shut him out of business. It made him an outcast, almost like a leper. He would be shut out of everything religious and social.

4. The blind man meets Jesus—

Jesus heard that they had cast him out; and when he had found him, he said unto him, Dost thou believe on the Son of God?

He answered and said, Who is he, Lord, that I might believe on him?

And Jesus said unto him, Thou hast both seen him, and it is he that talketh with thee.

And he said, Lord, I believe. And he worshipped him [John 9:35–38].

The Lord Jesus comes on the scene. This man has defended the Lord Jesus, has come out the winner in the argument, but has been cast out by the religious rulers. It is quite wonderful that the Lord Jesus comes to him. Friend, it is always Jesus who looks for the man. The Lord has prepared this man all along the way. Now the man must put his faith in the Son of God. Our Lord now comes to him with that crucial question: "Dost thou believe on the Son of God?" The experiences through which he has gone have strengthened his faith and clarified his thinking. The Lord knows that he is ready for this final step. This man is so very open, so honest and sincere. He asks who the

Son of God is so that he might believe. You can see the eagerness of this man. He wants to go farther. He wants to come to know Him. Our Lord responds in this lovely way, "Thou hast both seen him, and it is he that talketh with thee." The man believes Him and worships Him. This is one of the finest instances of faith that we have in the entire Word of God. Our Lord took this blind man step by step and brought him to His feet where he could say, "Lord, I believe," and he worshiped Him.

It is so with the steps of every sinner. We are blind at first. We are lost sinners, and we don't even see our lost condition. Then we come to Christ. He reveals Himself to us; our eyes are opened and we see who He is and what He has done for us. Then the question is: "Will you believe?" This man's answer can also be your answer, "Lord, I believe." And you will fall at His feet and worship Him.

And Jesus said, For judgment I am come into this world, that they which see not might see; and that they which see might be made blind [John 9:39].

This seems to be a strange statement. The Lord says that there are those who have eyes and see not. They have physical eyes and physical sight, but they are blind spiritually. If a man will admit he is blind and will come to Jesus as a blind man, Jesus will give him spiritual insight. Paul writes: "But the natural man receiveth not the things of the Spirit of God: for they are foolishness unto him: neither can he know them, because they are spiritually discerned" (1 Cor. 2:14).

My friend, if you have come into the presence of the Lord Jesus, the Light of the World, and still say, "What is truth?" or "I just don't see that He is my Savior," or "I don't understand what this is about," then you are not seeing. You are spiritually blind. The Pharisees had eyes; they thought they saw; they were religious people, zealous people, and yet they were blind.

The heathen are lost. They are in darkness. Yet the Lord puts each man through a series of steps. If there is any man today out yonder in heathenism who wants to know about Jesus, the Lord will get the gospel to him. The man who sits in the church pew and hears the preaching of the Word of God and the giving out of the gospel is in the presence of the Light. That Light reveals his blindness. Jesus said, ". . . If therefore the light that is in thee be darkness, how great is that darkness!" (Matt. 6:23). If you know the facts about Jesus Christ, the Light of the World, but you will not believe, then, my friend, you are spiritually blind and there is nothing else to offer you. If you have been in the presence of the Savior of the world and have rejected Him, there is no other Savior to offer to you.

And some of the Pharisees which were with him heard these words, and said unto him, Are we blind also?

Jesus said unto them, If ye were blind, ye should have no sin: but now ye say, We see; therefore your sin remaineth [John 9:40–41].

We began with a blind man who was healed so that he saw, both physically and spiritually. We end with religious rulers who were terribly, tragically blind, yet who thought they could see. In the presence of Christ, in the presence of the Light, in the presence of the revelation of God, they said they had no sin.

Some of the most dogmatic people today are the atheists and the cultists. They say they see, but they are blind. They reject the Lord Jesus Christ, and so their sin remains. Although they are not walking around with a white walking stick, they are blind.

CHAPTER 10

***THEME:** Jesus is the Good Shepherd (seventh word); humanity—Christ in form of servant; deity—Christ equal with God*

HUMANITY—CHRIST IN FORM OF SERVANT

The ancient sheepfold of that day still exists in many towns in that land. It was a public sheepfold. In the evening all the shepherds who lived in that town would bring their sheep to the sheepfold and turn them in for the night. They would entrust them to the porter who kept the sheep; then they would go to their homes for the night. The next morning the shepherds would identify themselves to the porter, and he would let them in the door to get their sheep.

1. "Door into the sheepfold"—

Verily, verily, I say unto you, He that entereth not by the door into the sheepfold, but climbeth up some other way, the same is a thief and a robber.

But he that entereth in by the door is the shepherd of the sheep [John 10:1–2].

The sheepfold represents the nation Israel. Jesus is telling them that He came in by the door. He goes on to say that anyone who doesn't come by the door, but climbs in some other way, is a thief and a robber. This is a tremendous claim that He is making here. He came in by the door. He came in legally. That is, He came in fulfillment of the prophecies of the Old Testament. He came in under the Law. "But when the fulness of the time was come, God sent forth his Son, made of a woman, made under the law" (Gal. 4:4). He came in the line of David according to prophecy (see Luke 1:32). He was born in Bethlehem according to prophecy (see Mic. 5:2). Not only was He in the line of David, but He was born of a virgin according to prophecy (see Isa. 7:14). At the time that He was born, He was a rod out of the stem of Jesse (see Isa. 11:1). Now this is interesting. By the time Jesus came, the royal line of David had dropped back to the level of the peasant. There was no royalty anymore. Jesse had been a farmer down in Bethlehem. In fact, he raised sheep. His son, David, had the anointing oil poured on him, and that line became the kingly line. But when the Lord Jesus was born, He was just a branch out of the stem of Jesse, the peasant. Jesus was simply a carpenter and wore a carpenter's robe. How accurately the prophecies were fulfilled!

He is the Messiah, and He came in through the door. No one else could have had the credentials that He had. Anyone else would have been a thief and a robber. They would not have had the credentials of the Messiah and would have had to climb over the fence. You see, in the preceding chapter, the man healed of his blindness had been excommunicated, put out of the temple. The religious rulers are rejecting the Lord Jesus, and now they are challenging Him. Remember they said, "Are we blind also?" Our Lord made it very clear that they were blind. Now He presents His credentials. This is a tremendous claim He is making in this chapter: Israel is the sheepfold; Jesus is the Good Shepherd.

To him the porter openeth; and the sheep hear his voice; and he calleth his own sheep by name, and leadeth them out [John 10:3].

Whom does the porter represent? The porter is the Holy Spirit. The Spirit of God came upon Jesus, and everything that He did, He did by the power of the Spirit of God. The Holy Spirit was opening the ears of His sheep to hear His voice. His sheep have responded. This ties in with the preceding chapter. Those religious rulers were blind spiritually and, what is more, they were deaf. They didn't even hear His voice. But He calls His own sheep by name and leads them out. The blind man heard Him call. Simon heard His call, and Jesus changed his name to Peter, which means a stone. He called James and John, Nathanael and Philip. He stopped under a tree in Jericho and called Zacchaeus. He calls His sheep by name.

Let me digress for a moment to say that when the Lord Jesus calls His own out of the world at the time of the Rapture, I believe that His call will have every believer's name in it. I think I'll hear Him say personally, "Vernon McGee." That will be wonderful! He knows my name, you see, and He'll call it at that time. And He'll call *you* if you are one of His sheep. You will hear your name in His shout!

He leads His sheep out of the sheepfold, out of Judaism. You see, the religious rulers had excommunicated the man whose sight Jesus had restored. Jesus is going to lead this sheep out of Judaism.

And when he putteth forth his own sheep, he goeth before them, and the sheep follow him: for they know his voice [John 10:4].

When I was near Bethlehem, I spent some time looking over a sheepfold that was still in use. A sheepfold is an enclosure where shepherds put their sheep for the night. The porter has charge of it. Then the shepherd spends the night in his own bed. When he comes to the sheepfold in the morning, his sheep are all mixed up with somebody else's sheep—there is no brand or marking on the sheep. How does he get the sheep that are his? He calls them by name. The sheep don't have to be identified; they know their shepherd's voice. When he starts out over the hill, his own sheep come out of the fold and follow him. They know him. Our Lord says, "The sheep will follow him because they know his voice."

It is the most wonderful thing in the world to know that, when we give out the Word of God, Jesus is calling His sheep. The Spirit of God is the Porter who does the opening, and the sheep will hear. Our Lord will lead His sheep out of a legal system, perhaps even out of a church where they're not being fed. They will follow Him. You cannot permanently fool God's sheep. It is true that the sheep may get into a cult or an "ism" for a while, but the sheep will recognize the voice of the Shepherd. Unfortunately, many preachers are afraid to stand up for the truth; however, when a man preaches the Word of God, the sheep will hear it. We can depend on that because our Lord said, "My sheep hear my voice" (v. 27).

And a stranger will they not follow, but will flee from him: for they know not the voice of strangers [John 10:5].

I believe that you can fool some of God's people some of the time, but I don't think you can fool God's people all the time. For a time, God's sheep may *think* they hear Him but eventually discover that it is not His voice. Then they will turn to the teaching of the Word of God because they know their Shepherd. It is amazing. I have been teaching the Word of God for about forty years and have learned again and again that when His sheep hear His voice, they will follow Him.

For a long time I worried about those who will not listen to the message. I have reached the point that I don't worry about them. The reason they don't hear His voice is that they are not His sheep. Wherever we find people who are eager for the Word of God, we know they are His sheep.

This parable spake Jesus unto them: but they understood not what things they were which he spake unto them [John 10:6].

The word *parable* is really not an accurate translation. The Greek word for parable is *parabolē* and the word in this verse is *paroimia,* which really means "an allegory." The Gospel of John does not record any of the parables of our Lord. It records the metaphors and allegories such as "I am the light of the world" (John 8:12) and "I am the bread of life" (John 6:35). These are not parables but are figures of speech to let us know something about God. They are intended to give us light on the subject so that we can see. So it should actually read, "This allegory spake Jesus unto them." They didn't understand what He was saying because, as He had said, they were blind.

Our Lord also said, "Who hath ears to hear, let him hear" (Matt. 13:9). It is possible to have ears and yet not hear. They hear it all right, but they don't hear it as the Word of God. That is the important thing. Beloved, how do you hear it? It is this important difference in hearing to which our Lord referred when He quoted Isaiah, ". . . By hearing ye shall hear, and shall not understand; and seeing ye shall see, and shall not perceive" (Matt. 13:14).

2. "Door of the sheep"—

Then said Jesus unto them again, Verily, verily, I say unto you, I am the door of the sheep.

All that ever came before me are thieves and robbers: but the sheep did not hear them [John 10:7–8].

Here He gives another allegory. He has spoken about the door of the sheepfold, but now He moves one more step and says that He is the *Door* of the sheep. The Lord Jesus is the Door for those coming out of Israel. They had just cast the blind man out of the synagogue, out of the sheepfold. Immediately the Lord Jesus had come to this man and revealed Himself to him. When the Lord revealed Himself to the man, He became the Door for this man. The man had been brought out of the sheepfold and to the Lord Jesus Christ to follow

Him. This is the second great truth which our Lord is stating in this chapter.

Our Lord will state this same principle in John 15 when He says, "I am the true vine. . . . ye are the branches" (John 15:1, 5). The vine in the Old Testament is a picture of the nation Israel. Jesus is saying that it is no longer the connection with the nation Israel but the relationship with Him which is the joining of the branches with the Vine. They must come out from Judaism, come out from ritualism, and come to Him. He is saying that He is the Door. Remember, He is talking to the religious rulers. By the way, some of them did come to Him after His resurrection.

3. "The Door"—

I am the door: by me if any man enter in, he shall be saved, and shall go in and out, and find pasture.

The thief cometh not, but for to steal, and to kill, and to destroy: I am come that they might have life, and that they might have it more abundantly [John 10:9–10].

Jesus Christ is the Way. He is the only Way. He is the Way *out* for you and He is the Way *in* for you. He has come to bring us an abundant life.

The thief comes to steal, to kill, and to destroy. I think this is a test you can apply to a church, a religious organization, a radio or television program. Is it a religious racket? Is somebody getting rich out of it? Compare it to the Good Shepherd who came to save sinners and to give us life, abundant life.

Here is a brief review of this passage:

1. "Door into the sheepfold" (v. 1). The sheepfold is the nation Israel. Jesus will lead His sheep out of Judaism, out from under a legalistic system.

2. "Door of the sheep" (v. 7). Jesus is the Door for those coming out of Judaism (e.g., the excommunicated man who had been blind); He has called them out. ". . . Save yourselves from this untoward generation" (Acts 2:40).

3. "The Door" (v. 9). Jesus Christ is the Door for both Jew and Gentile. He is the Door of salvation. Freedom to go in and out and find pasture is the liberty of the sons of God in Christ Jesus.

4. "The Good Shepherd"—

I am the good shepherd: the good shepherd giveth his life for the sheep.

But he that is an hireling, and not the shepherd, whose own the sheep are not, seeth the wolf coming, and leaveth the sheep, and fleeth: and the wolf catcheth them, and scattereth the sheep.

The hireling fleeth, because he is an hireling, and careth not for the sheep [John 10:11–13].

How can Jesus be the Door and the Shepherd at the same time? Actually, there was no door that swung on hinges and had a padlock to secure the sheepfold. The man who was guarding it slept across the doorway so that he himself was the door. Jesus is not only the Door but He is also the Good Shepherd, the One who stays in the doorway. He is the Door which opens to eternal life; He is the One who protects His own; He is also the Good Shepherd.

Jesus is also called the Lamb of God. How can He be the Lamb of God and at the same time be the Good Shepherd? This may sound like mixed metaphors, but it is one of the most glorious truths in Scripture. He is the "Lamb of God, which taketh away the sin of the world" (John 1:29). He came down and identified Himself with us who are the sheep—but He is the Shepherd also. The fact that He became a Lamb emphasizes the humanity of Jesus Christ. The fact that He is the Good Shepherd emphasizes the deity of Christ. He alone was worthy and able to save us. No other human being could do this; He had to be God.

The Lord Jesus Christ has a threefold relationship to this flock which is known as His church. First of all He is the *Good Shepherd*, and He defines the Good Shepherd in verse 11: "I am the good shepherd: the good shepherd giveth his life for the sheep." Then He is the *Great Shepherd*, for we read in the magnificent benediction given in Hebrews 13:20: "Now the God of peace, who brought again from the dead the great shepherd of the sheep with the blood of an eternal covenant, even our Lord Jesus, make you perfect in every good thing to do his will . . ." (ASV). So today He is the Great Shepherd of the sheep, as seen in Psalm 23. But wait, that does not give the total picture. He is also the *Chief Shepherd*. This speaks of the future. Peter says in his first epistle, "And when the chief Shepherd shall appear, ye shall receive a crown of glory that fadeth not away" (1 Pet. 5:4).

The hireling does not care for the sheep. Founders of some of the world religions did very little for their followers. Modern cult leaders actually get rich off the people. In contrast to this, the Good Shepherd gives His life for the sheep, and He protects His own.

I am the good shepherd, and know my sheep, and am known of mine.

As the Father knoweth me, even so know I the Father: and I lay down my life for the sheep [John 10:14–15].

Here is a wonderful relationship. He knows His sheep, and His sheep know Him. Paul wrote, "That I may know him, and the power of his resurrection . . . " (Phil. 3:10). To know Him is to love Him. In this connection one should read what God says about shepherds in His message through Ezekiel, chapter 34.

Notice that this is the third time that He says His sheep know Him. To know Jesus Christ is all important and everything else becomes secondary. That is one reason I have given up arguing about nonessentials. Let's stop arguing about religion and about details. The important issue is to know Jesus Christ. Do you hear His voice; do you know the Shepherd?

There is no shepherd like this One. David risked his life to save his sheep from a bear and from a lion. The Son of David gave His life for His sheep.

And other sheep I have, which are not of this fold: them also I must bring, and they shall hear my voice; and there shall be one fold, and one shepherd [John 10:16].

There are other sheep which are not of this fold—the fold is Israel—but others will also hear His voice, and there shall be one flock and one Shepherd. It is really "flock" (*poimnē*), not "fold" *(aulē)* in this second phrase. You see, there is to be one flock and one Shepherd. There is to be the one flock containing Jew and Gentile, rich and poor, bond and free, male and female, black and white, people from every nation, and out of every tongue and tribe.

Therefore doth my Father love me, because I lay down my life, that I might take it again.

No man taketh it from me, but I lay it down of myself. I have power to lay it down, and I have power to take it again. This commandment have I received of my Father [John 10:17–18].

He says that all of this is the will of the Father. The Father loves Him because He died for us. We also ought to love Him because He died for us. He made His soul an offering for sin. On the cross during those three hours of darkness, God the Father put upon Him the sin of the world, and He went through hell for you and me. The Good Shepherd gave His life for the sheep.

He makes it very clear that He gave His life willingly. He was in full control at His trial. Also He set the time of His death. The Jews said it shouldn't be on a feast day lest there be an uproar, a riot, of the people, but He *was* crucified on the feast day. He was never more kingly than when He went to the cross. If one reads the Gospels carefully, one is aware that actually the Roman government was on trial, the nation Israel was on trial, you and I were on trial. Although He didn't have to die, He did it willingly for the sins of the world. "Looking unto Jesus the author and finisher of our faith; who for the joy that was set before him endured the cross, despising the shame . . ." (Heb. 12:2). No man could take His life from Him. He claimed power to lay down His life and to take it again.

There was a division therefore again among the Jews for these sayings.

And many of them said, He hath a devil, and is mad; why hear ye him?

Others said, These are not the words of him that hath a devil. Can a devil open the eyes of the blind? [John 10:19–21].

This refers to the fact that He opened the eyes of the man who was born blind. The crowd there that day said, "Well, a demon could never have done what He did!" There is a division. Why? Because some are sheep and some are not. Sheep will hear and the others will not hear.

The issue is still the same today as it was then. Either the Lord Jesus Christ was a mad man or He is the Savior of the world. Either He has a demon or He is the Son of God. There has always been that division. When Paul preached at Athens, some believed and some did not. When I preach, some believe and some do not. We cannot expect it to be any different.

The so-called liberal theologians are the most inconsistent and illogical people. Jesus Christ cannot be only a good teacher and a great example. He is either a fraud or He is the Son of God. Jesus Christ puts you on the horns of a dilemma, my friend. He is a mad man or He is your God and your Savior.

DEITY—CHRIST EQUAL WITH GOD

And it was at Jerusalem the feast of the dedication, and it was winter [John 10:22].

The Feast of Tabernacles was in the last part of October; the Feast of Dedication was in the last part of December—so there was a two-month interval. This feast celebrated the time when Judas Maccabaeus delivered the temple from Antiochus Epiphanes, the Syrian, who had polluted it. This took place in 167 B.C. and was still celebrated in our Lord's day.

"And it was winter." Jesus is through with the nation. From here on, in the Gospel of John, He talks to His own. He will not make another public call. It is now too late for the harvest. The Lamb of God is being shut up in preparation to go to the cross and die for the sins of the world.

Friend, may I remind you that you can play at this thing too long. Winter is coming for you. There will come a day when you won't be able to witness. If you are going to do anything for Him, you had better do it now. If you have never sincerely accepted Jesus Christ as your Savior, may I remind you that winter can come for that, too. There does come a time when it is too late, my beloved, too late to be saved. You can persist in rejecting the Lord Jesus Christ so long that finally you will be unable to accept Him. The prophet spoke of this eventuality: "The harvest is past, the summer is ended, and we are not saved" (Jer. 8:20).

And Jesus walked in the temple in Solomon's porch.

Then came the Jews round about him, and said unto him, How long dost thou make us to doubt? If thou be the Christ, tell us plainly [John 10:23–24].

There was a big porch out there which was for the Gentiles, for those who were outside the nation Israel. Our Lord was no longer coming into the temple. It was winter, and He walked in Solomon's porch.

Jesus had made His identity very clear, and those who accepted Him understood that He was the Messiah, the Christ. Remember that Andrew had told his brother, "We have found the Messiah" (see John 1:41). Nathanael recognized Him, "Rabbi, thou art the Son of God; thou art the King of Israel" (John 1:49). The Samaritan woman understood who He was; and the Samaritan men said, "Now we believe, not because of thy saying: for we have heard him ourselves, and know that this is indeed the Christ, the Saviour of the world" (John 4:42). Also the man healed of his blindness believed and worshiped Him. Now these religious leaders with their subtle questions are actually casting the blame on Him! They make it sound as if it is Jesus' fault for not giving enough information, whereas it is their lack of will to believe what God had revealed to them. Well, Jesus has revealed His messiahship to those who will hear, and now He declares it to these religious rulers.

Jesus answered them, I told you, and ye believed not: the works that I do in my Father's name, they bear witness of me.

But ye believe not, because ye are not of my sheep, as I said unto you [John 10:25–26].

Jesus tells them that He has the proofs of His messiahship. His works bear witness to it. He was born in the line of David, according to prophecy. He was introduced by John the Baptist. No man taught as He taught. No man could convict Him of sin. When John the Baptist sent his disciples to find out whether Jesus was the Messiah or whether they should look for another, Jesus told them to go back and tell John the Baptist the things that He was doing. Then John the Baptist would know that He had the credentials of the Messiah. You see, His teaching demonstrated that He was the Messiah, His life demonstrated it, and His miracles demonstrated it. The problem was not in His lack of credentials. The problem was in the unbelieving heart. The fact that they did not believe demonstrated that they were not His sheep. That's the negative side. Now He states the positive side.

My sheep hear my voice, and I know them, and they follow me:

And I give unto them eternal life; and they shall never perish, neither shall any man pluck them out of my hand.

My Father, which gave them me, is greater than all; and no man is able to pluck them out of my Father's hand.

I and my Father are one [John 10:27–30].

His sheep hear His voice. And they follow Him. The brand of ownership on the sheep is obedience. Do you want to know whether a person is saved or not? Then see if he is obeying Christ. Our ears must be open to His voice. "The hearing ear, and the seeing eye, the LORD hath made even both of them" (Prov. 20:12).

"I know them." I'm glad somebody knows me, aren't you? I am sometimes misunderstood, and I have to explain myself to people. However, I never need to explain anything to Him. He knows when I'm putting up an excuse; He knows when I am evading an issue; He understands me. He knows.

"And they follow me." I believe in the eternal security of the believer and in the insecurity of the make-believer. "They follow me"—it's just that simple. If the shepherd called his sheep one morning and started up the hill, and out of five hundred sheep in the sheepfold, one hundred came out and followed him, then I would conclude that those one hundred were his sheep. And I would also conclude that the other four hundred were not his sheep.

"And I give unto them eternal life; and they shall never perish." Friend, when He gives to them eternal life, that means they don't earn it and they don't work for it. He *gives* it to them. Note that it is *eternal* life. It is forever. If it plays out in a week, or in a year, or until they sin, then it is not eternal life after all. They are not really His sheep if the life does not last forever. The sheep may be in danger, but the Shepherd will protect them. They may be scattered, but He will gather them up again. They shall never perish.

May they backslide? Yes. Will they perish? No. The sheep may get into a pigpen, but there has never yet been a sheep in a pigpen that stayed in the pigpen. Sheep and pigs do not live together. The sheep is always a sheep. No man can pluck that sheep out of the Savior's hand. No enemy, no man, no created being can pluck them out of His hand. This is wonderful! One time a fellow gave me the argument that one can jump out of His hand because we are free moral agents. Listen to the passage. It actually says "no created thing shall pluck them out of my hand." He is the Shepherd. He is God. If you think you can jump out, the Father puts His hand right down on you, and you can't do any jumping. Brother, He's got you and you can't get loose. Both hands are the hands of Deity. No created thing can take the sheep out of His hand.

Years ago a Texas rancher told me about sheep. He said he had two thousand sheep, and someone had to be watching them all the time. If two little sheep go over the hill and get half a mile from the flock, they are lost. They cannot find their way back by themselves. The only way in the world they can be safe is for the shepherd to be there. If a wolf would come up and eat one of the little sheep, you'd think the other one would be smart enough to say, "He ate my little brother; so I'll go back over the hill and join the flock." No, he doesn't know where to go. All he does is go "Baa" and run around and wait to be dessert for the wolf. A sheep is stupid. Neither has a sheep any way to defend himself. A sheep can't even outrun his enemy. If a sheep is safe, it is not because the sheep is clever or smart. It is because he has a good shepherd.

When I say to you that He gives me eternal life and I shall never perish, you may accuse me of bragging. No, my friend, I am not bragging on myself; I'm bragging about my Shepherd. I have a wonderful Shepherd. He won't lose any of His sheep. If He starts with one hundred, He will not end with ninety-nine. If one gets lost, He will go out and find it. None will be lost.

Then He says that He and the Father are one. He claims to be God.

Then the Jews took up stones again to stone him.

Jesus answered them, Many good works have I shewed you from my Father; for which of those works do ye stone me?

The Jews answered him, saying, For a good work we stone thee not; but for blasphemy; and because that thou, being a man, makest thyself God [John 10:31–33].

There is one thing that is sure: in that day, those who heard Him understood that He made Himself God. He produced His credentials. There was no way they could deny His miracles. He healed people by the thousands, and there was no denying the evidence. They accused Him of blasphemy. They accused Him of calling Himself God. And do you know, that is exactly what He was doing!

Jesus answered them, Is it not written in your law, I said, Ye are gods?

If he called them gods, unto whom the word of God came, and the scripture cannot be broken;

Say ye of him, whom the Father hath sanctified, and sent into the world, Thou blasphemest; because I said, I am the Son of God?

If I do not the works of my Father, believe me not.

But if I do, though ye believe not me, believe the works: that ye may know, and believe, that the Father is in me, and I in him [John 10:34–38].

Their accusation was that He as a man makes Himself God. He quotes to them Psalm 82:6, "I have said, Ye are gods; and all of you are children of the most High." Men are called to be the children of God, but Jesus is unique because He is the Man "whom the Father hath sanctified." He is the One who has been set apart. He is different from any other man in the world. He has been sent on a mission to the world. He is in the Father and the Father is in Him.

Therefore they sought again to take him: but he escaped out of their hand,

And went away again beyond Jordan into the place where John at first baptized; and there he abode.

And many resorted unto him, and said, John did no miracle: but all things that John spake of this man were true.

And many believed on him there [John 10:39–42].

John the Baptist did no miracles, but he bore a true testimony to the Messiah. Jesus is the Messiah, the Christ. He is the One who was to come. What think ye of Christ? This is the way to test your position. You can't be right in any of the rest unless you are first right in your thinking about Him. What think ye of Christ? If you are His sheep, you will hear His voice. If you are not, you will not hear Him. His voice will be drowned out in the babble of voices speaking to you. His sheep are able to hear the Son of God.

CHAPTER 11

***THEME:** Jesus raises Lazarus from the dead in Bethany (sixth work)*

JESUS RAISES LAZARUS FROM THE DEAD IN BETHANY (Sixth Work)

Let's pause for a moment to get the perspective of John. In the first ten chapters, Christ has revealed Himself in an ever widening circle. This began at the wedding of Cana where there were guests and also His disciples. We are told that His disciples believed on Him. At the Feast of Tabernacles and the Feast of Dedication, the whole nation was before Him. He presented Himself to the nation and He was rejected: His works were rejected in John 5:16; His words were rejected in John 8:58–59; and His Person was rejected in John 10:30–31.

This chapter is a kind of intermission. His public ministry is over and He retires into a private ministry. Centering Himself on individuals, He no longer is reaching out to the nation. The events of this chapter occur between the Feast of Dedication and the Passover which would be sometime between December and April.

The Gospel of John is like climbing up a mountain in that each chapter brings us a little higher than the preceding chapter. Remember that John has told us why he wrote this gospel: "And many other signs truly did Jesus in the presence of his disciples, which are not written in this book: But these are written, that ye might believe that Jesus is the Christ, the Son of God; and that believing ye might have life through his name" (John 20:30–31). Going back to the very beginning: "In the beginning was the Word, and the Word was with God, and the Word was God" (John 1:1). "And the word was made flesh, and dwelt among us" (John 1:14). While He walked among us in the flesh, this great thesis was sustained by miracle and parable and discourse.

Now the supreme question is: Can Jesus raise the dead? The big question in any religion concerns death. Death is a great mystery. And life is a great mystery, but life is practically meaningless if there is no resurrection of the dead. The question to ask of any religion is whether it has power over death.

Liberal theologians long ago threw out the miraculous. They contend that nothing miraculous belongs in the Bible—not because of any scholarly reason, but simply because they don't believe in the miraculous. Today there is a synthetic doctrine that goes something like this: "I believe in a religion of the here and now, not the hereafter. I don't go for pie in the sky by and by. I want a meat and potatoes religion, one that is practical, not theoretical." Now that is something I want also. And in addition, I want a hope.

Although we are given many benefits right here and now, the greatest of all benefits is *eternal* life in Christ Jesus. It is very practical to ask the question: "Will the dead be raised?" Life is so brief. Life's little day compared to eternity is infinitesimal. Recently I conducted the funeral of a very wonderful Christian man—and there sat his wife and mother. Certainly they considered the resurrection very practical. When you stand at a graveside, if you have no hope, you are whistling in the dark and singing in the rain and crying the blues.

I notice that in cults and religions of the day there are all kinds of chicanery and racketeering, but nobody is in the business of raising the dead. Although some of them have claimed they can raise the dead, they never produce the body, the *corpus delicti*. When Jesus healed the sick, it was the body that was healed. When Jesus raised the dead, it was the body that was raised. Many religions promise much for this life, but nothing for the hereafter. That is like taking someone for an airplane ride without knowing how to land the plane. The great hope of the Christian faith is the resurrection of the dead!

The Gospels tell us three incidents of Jesus raising the dead. There was the twelve-year-old girl who had just died. She was a juvenile. There was a young man, whose body was being carried to the cemetery. Then there was Lazarus, possibly a senior citizen, who had been dead four days and had been buried. They were all raised, from every age group.

Allow me to be technical and state that these people were raised from the dead but were not resurrected. Rather, it was a restoration to life. Resurrection is this: ". . . It is sown in corruption; it is raised in incorruption: It is sown in dishonour; it is raised in glory: it is sown in weakness; it is raised in power: It is sown a natural body; it is raised a spiritual body . . ." (1 Cor. 15:42–44). These people were raised from the dead, but none of them were given glorified bodies. They all faced death again. Christ is the firstfruits of them that sleep. His is the only true resurrection—". . . Christ the firstfruits; afterward they that are Christ's at his coming" (1 Cor. 15:23).

While our Lord used different methods to perform His miracles of healing, his method of raising the dead was always the same. He called to them and spoke to them as if they heard Him. Do you know why He did that? Because they heard Him! I think that when He returns with a shout, every one of us will hear his own name because He will call us back from the dead.

Now let's get into the chapter.

Now a certain man was sick, named Lazarus, of Bethany, the town of Mary and her sister Martha.

(It was that Mary which anointed the Lord with ointment, and wiped his feet with her hair, whose brother Lazarus was sick.) [John 11:1–2].

Note that Bethany is the town of Mary. This was written about A.D. 90 and by that time people knew about Mary who had anointed the feet of Jesus with spikenard. The fragrance of the box that she broke still fills this world. Jesus said that her act of devotion would be remembered wherever the gospel was preached. I am of the opinion that many a humble person is breaking an alabaster box of ointment and will have more recognition in heaven than many well-known Christian leaders who receive much publicity down here.

It was the home of Martha. Our Lord had visited there before. Martha had been cumbered and frustrated with her preparations for dinner. Jesus had told her that to sit at His feet and learn of Him is better than being too busy with service.

It was the town of Mary and the home of Martha. There are different gifts. Some women are given a marvelous gift in the home. Talk about women's liberation! I know of no one who is the big boss more than a wife and a mother in her home. She can hustle you out of the kitchen, make you stay out of the refrigerator, and tell you to move when she wants to vacuum. She is in charge of the kitchen and of the whole house. This is the calling of many Christian women. There are others who have an outside ministry. They teach Bible classes and child evangelism classes, and work in the church. Remember, friend, the woman who serves in her home can be serving the Lord and the woman who serves outside her home can be serving the Lord. The Holy Spirit bestows gifts for many types of ministries.

Therefore his sisters sent unto him, saying, Lord, behold, he whom thou lovest is sick [John 11:3].

These are humble folk, and they make no request, no demand of Him. They tell Jesus the problem and let Him decide what to do. So often in prayers I hear the people demanding that the Lord heal the sick. When did God become a Western Union boy? When did He become a waiter to wait upon us or a redcap boy to carry our suitcase? He doesn't do things that way. Mary and Martha knew their Lord! "Lord, behold, he whom thou lovest is sick."

"He whom thou lovest." Lazarus is loved by the Savior. Paul said, "He loved me" (see Gal. 2:20). John called himself the disciple whom Jesus loved. Peter declared that Jesus loves us. And by the way, He loves you and He loves me. Anyone who is a child of God is one whom Jesus loves.

When Jesus heard that, he said, This sickness is not unto death, but for the glory of God, that the Son of God might be glorified thereby [John 11:4].

Jesus, you see, was not in Bethany at the time, and a message was sent to Him.

Some people say that a Christian should never be sick. Is sickness in the will of God? I wish Lazarus were here to tell you about that. Sickness is not a sign that God does not love you. "For all this I considered in my heart even to declare all this, that the righteous, and the wise, and their works, are in the hand of God: no man knoweth either love or hatred by all that is before them" (Eccl. 9:1). In other words, you cannot tell by the circumstances of a man whether God loves him or not. You have no right to judge. "Therefore judge nothing before the time, until the Lord come, who both will bring to light the hidden things of darkness, and will make manifest the counsels of the hearts . . ." (1 Cor. 4:5). Jesus loved Lazarus when he was sick. Not only that, Jesus will let Lazarus die—but He still loves him.

Now Jesus loved Martha, and her sister, and Lazarus.

When he had heard therefore that he was sick, he abode two days still in the same place where he was [John 11:5–6].

He loves you when you are sick, He loves you when you are well, He loves you all the time. You can't keep Him from loving you. You may ask why He lets certain difficulties happen to you. I don't know the reason, but I do know He loves you. He loves you whether or not you are a Christian. You can't keep Him from loving you. You can't stop the sun from shining, but you can get out of the sunshine. And you can put up an umbrella to keep the love of God from shining upon your life.

Because He loves us, we are to come with boldness to present our problems to Him. Boldness means freedom of speech, opening your heart to Him. Boldness does not mean that your requests can be demands of God. Trouble tests our faith and puts us on our knees. Moses cried unto the Lord repeatedly when problems arose in the wilderness wanderings. Hezekiah took the threatening letter from the Assyrians and presented it to the Lord. The disciples of John the Baptist came to the Lord with the heartbreaking news when John was beheaded. My friend, it is down in the valley, even in the valley of the shadow of death, that we must learn to trust Him. He teaches us patience, teaches us that we can rest in Him, teaches us that He works all things well. We need to look beyond the tears, the sorrows, and the trials of life, and see that God has a purpose in everything that happens.

"This sickness is not unto death, but for the glory of God." Jesus permits this to happen because God will get the glory in it. We need to learn that *we* are not the center of the universe—nor is our home, our church, our town. The headquarters of everything are in heaven, and everything is running for *His* glory. Nothing will come into our lives without His permission, and if He permits it, it is going to be for His glory.

I do want you to notice that the Lord loved Martha. Sometimes we are very hard on Martha, very critical of her. The commentaries haven't been kind to her. She was cumbered with much serving and she hadn't learned the best thing, but that did not keep our Lord from loving her.

Does it seem cruel that Jesus let Lazarus die? No, there is a message here for us. The Lord Jesus was not motivated by sentiment, but He was subject to the Father's will. Human sentiment would urge Him to go to Bethany immediately. But He deliberately let Lazarus die. Friend, sometimes He allows our loved ones to die. We need to recognize that He has a reason, and His ways are perfect.

Jesus never moves by sentiment. That is what spoils people and that is how parents spoil their children. He is motivated by love, and that love is for the good of the individual and for the glory of God.

Then after that saith he to his disciples, Let us go into Judaea again.

His disciples say unto him, Master, the Jews of late sought to stone thee; and goest thou thither again? [John 11:7–8].

Don't miss that word *again*. He had been there and had been forced to withdraw. Now He returns and takes His disciples with Him into the danger zone.

Jesus answered, Are there not twelve hours in the day? If any man walk in the day, he stumbleth not, because he seeth the light of this world.

But if a man walk in the night, he stumbleth, because there is no light in him [John 11:9–10].

There are twelve hours in the day, and you can't change that. Because the Father has given the Son a work to do, nothing can stop Him. There is a great principle here. God has given to each man a lifework. You can't extend that for one day any more than you can keep the sun from going down in the afternoon. But, thank God, you are absolutely invulnerable until your work is done. Nobody, not even Satan, can thwart God's purpose in your life if you are following Him. To fail to follow Him is dangerous. Then one is in darkness because *He* is the Light of the World. You can go into the danger zone with Him, and you won't be touched. You will finish your work. But if you stay out in the darkness, if you walk in the darkness, you will stumble. There has been death in Bethany. If there is to be light in that time of darkness, Jesus must go there. He is the Light of the World.

These things said he: and after that he saith unto them, Our friend Lazarus sleepeth; but I go, that I may awake him out of sleep.

Then said his disciples, Lord, if he sleep, he shall do well.

Howbeit Jesus spake of his death: but they thought that he had spoken of taking of rest in sleep.

Then said Jesus unto them plainly, Lazarus is dead.

And I am glad for your sakes that I was not there, to the intent ye may believe; nevertheless let us go unto him [John 11:11–15].

The disciples did not understand what Jesus meant when He said that Lazarus was sleeping. Because many people today do not understand it either, we find people who talk about soul-sleep. Friend, sleep is for the body, never for the soul. This is true of both sleep in this life and the sleep of death. Death means separation. The body of the believer sleeps in the grave, but the spirit goes to be with Christ. For the believer, to be absent from the body is to be present with the Lord (see 2 Cor. 5:8). Jesus is called the firstfruits of them that sleep. Does this mean that Jesus is sleeping somewhere today? Absolutely not. He is in His glorified body. The believer goes immediately to be with the Lord, but the body sleeps until the day of resurrection when the body will be raised.

Death, for the believer, is a sleep for his body. Are you afraid of sleep? You shouldn't be. Sleep is a relief from labor. It is the rest that comes for renewal and preparation for the new day that is coming. There is nothing quite as beautiful as the word *sleep* when it is used for the death of a believer. The body is put to sleep, to be awakened by our Lord. He is the only One who has the alarm clock. He is the only One who can raise the dead. One day He will come and we shall awaken in our new bodies.

The Greek word for resurrection is *anastasis* which means "a standing up." C. S. Lewis, that brilliant Oxford don, ridiculing those who hold that resurrection is spiritual rather than physical, asked, "If it is the spirit that stands up, what position does it take?" There's a question to work over! No, resurrection means a standing up, and it always refers to the body. The soul never dies, nor does the soul ever sleep.

Death is a reality, an awful reality of the body. But, remember, the resurrection is also reality. You see, man leaves off at death. Even in the hospital, there is a finality about death. Doctors will work and work over a patient. Then when he dies, they all stop working. When death comes, they are through. Science is helpless in the presence of death. Where man must leave off, Jesus begins. Resurrection is also reality.

A man in Pasadena told me, "When you die, you die just like a dog." I answered, "Don't you wish that were true?" "But," I said, "if it's not true (and I think that bothers you a little), you're in trouble, aren't you?" He turned away because he didn't want to talk about that. People are afraid of death.

Mrs. McGee and I were in Wichita, Kansas, for a Bible conference, staying at a large motel there. We had dinner before the evening service and the bar room was loud with the "happy hour." When we returned in the evening, word had arrived that the airplane carrying the football team had gone down. The coach and the first line of football players all had been killed. "Happy hour" was like a morgue then. They were silent, without hope.

Then said Thomas, which is called Didymus, unto his fellow-disciples, Let us also go, that we may die with him [John 11:16].

Thomas is a gloom-caster, isn't he? He thinks he is going to die along with Jesus. But, thank God, he was willing to do just that. I believe Thomas meant it, too, just as Simon Peter meant it.

Then when Jesus came, he found that he had lain in the grave four days already.

Now Bethany was nigh unto Jerusalem, about fifteen furlongs off:

And many of the Jews came to Martha and Mary, to comfort them concerning their brother [John 11:17–19].

Bethany is about two miles from the Golden Gate at Jerusalem. Many of the Jews walked from Jerusalem to Bethany to be with Martha and Mary. Apparently they were a prominent family in Bethany and were well known in Jerusalem.

Then Martha, as soon as she heard that Jesus was coming, went and met him: but Mary sat still in the house.

Then said Martha unto Jesus, Lord, if thou hadst been here, my brother had not died.

But I know, that even now, whatsoever thou wilt ask of God, God will give it thee [John 11:20–22].

Martha seems always to be the aggressive type. She is the woman of action. She reveals a wonderful faith but also an impatience and a lack of bending to the will of God. By contrast, Mary is willing to sit at home. She has learned to sit at Jesus' feet.

We can see now that Martha should have been sitting at Jesus' feet a little more. She says, "I know that if You will ask God." Martha, don't you realize that *He* is God? He is God, manifest in the flesh. He has been in your home, sat at your table and has eaten your biscuits, but you didn't realize that He was God, did you? Oh, my friend, how we need to spend time at His feet. How we need to listen.

Jesus saith unto her, Thy brother shall rise again.

Martha saith unto him, I know that he shall rise again in the resurrection at the last day.

Jesus said unto her, I am the resurrection, and the life: he that believeth in me, though he were dead, yet shall he live:

And whosoever liveth and believeth in me shall never die. Believest thou this? [John 11:23–26].

Martha believed in a resurrection. But listen, it makes less demand upon faith to believe that in a future day we shall receive glorified bodies than it does to rest now on the assurance that they that wait upon the Lord shall renew their strength. It is easier to believe that the Lord is coming and the dead will be raised than it is to believe that tomorrow I can live for God. It is so easy to comfort people who are mourning and say, "Well, you'll see your loved ones someday." That doesn't take much faith. It takes a lot of faith to say, "I have just lost my loved one but I am comforted with the assurance that God is with me and He does all things well." You see, although Martha knew from the Old Testament that there would be a resurrection from the dead, she didn't believe that Jesus could help her now.

Jesus says to her, "Martha, don't you know that I *am* the resurrection and the life?" If we have Jesus, we have life. "He that believeth in me, though he were dead" is referring to spiritual death. Though a person is spiritually dead, "yet shall he live." Then He looks into the future and says that the one who has trusted Him shall never die. Life begins at the moment a person accepts the Savior. Whosoever lives and believes in Jesus will never die because Jesus has already died for him. That is, he will never die a penal death for his sins. He will never be separated from God. Then Jesus asks the question: "Believest thou this?"

She saith unto him, Yea, Lord: I believe that thou art the Christ, the Son of

God, which should come into the world [John 11:27].

Martha gives the same confession that Peter gave. She understands that He is the Messiah.

And when she had so said, she went her way, and called Mary her sister secretly, saying, The Master is come, and calleth for thee.

As soon as she heard that, she arose quickly and came unto him.

Now Jesus was not yet come into the town, but was in that place where Martha met him.

The Jews then which were with her in the house, and comforted her, when they saw Mary, that she rose up hastily and went out, followed her, saying, She goeth unto the grave to weep there [John 11:28–31].

Although Martha had told Mary secretly, God will overrule this—the whole crowd will be at the cemetery. They don't know that she is going out to meet Jesus.

Then when Mary was come where Jesus was, and saw him, she fell down at his feet, saying unto him, Lord, if thou hadst been here, my brother had not died [John 11:32].

She was saying along with Martha that if Jesus had been there, her brother would not have died. This is why Jesus will say later on that it was expedient, it was better, for Him to go away. This incident makes it obvious why it was expedient. As long as He was here in the flesh, He was limited geographically. If He were in your town, He couldn't be in my town. If Jesus had not gone away, He could not have sent the Comforter, the Holy Spirit. But now that the Holy Spirit has come, He is everywhere. He indwells every believer today. So the Holy Spirit can be where I am, where you are, and on the other side of the world simultaneously. "Nevertheless I tell you the truth; It is expedient for you that I go away: for if I go not away, the Comforter will not come unto you; but if I depart, I will send him unto you" (John 16:7).

When Jesus therefore saw her weeping, and the Jews also weeping which came with her, he groaned in the spirit, and was troubled,

And said, Where have ye laid him? They said unto him, Lord, come and see.

Jesus wept [John 11:33–35].

If you want to know how God feels about the death of your loved ones, look at this. He groaned in the spirit and was troubled. Death is a frightful thing. And you can be sure that He enters into sympathy with you.

His sympathy was for the living. He knew what He was going to do for the dead. "Jesus wept." While John's gospel is written to show us the deity of Christ, here Jesus is shown in all His humanness. He even asked where Lazarus was laid because He was so human. And here we can see the way God feels at a funeral today. He mingles His tears with ours. He groans within Himself. I get a little impatient with Christians who say one must not cry at a funeral, but one must be a brave Christian. Death is not pretty; it is a terrible thing. Jesus *wept!*

Then said the Jews, Behold how he loved him!

And some of them said, Could not this man, which opened the eyes of the blind, have caused that even this man should not have died? [John 11:36–37].

The Jews missed the point here. He wept, not because He loved Lazarus—He was not weeping for the dead—He wept for those who were living.

You notice that the Jews go back to the incident of healing the blind man. That obviously made a great impression on them.

Jesus therefore again groaning in himself cometh to the grave. It was a cave, and a stone lay upon it.

Jesus said, Take ye away the stone. Martha, the sister of him that was dead, saith unto him, Lord, by this time he stinketh: for he hath been dead four days.

Jesus saith unto her, Said I not unto thee, that, if thou wouldest believe, thou shouldest see the glory of God? [John 11:38–40].

The subject of death is skirted by people today. The undertakers try in every way to make death seem like a pleasant episode. But let us face it very frankly, we can't cover up death by embalming and painting up the face, dressing the body in a good suit of clothes, then placing it in a pretty coffin surrounded by flowers. Although this is done to help soften the shock, death is an awful thing.

Martha said that he had been buried for four

days already and his body would stink; it would be decaying. Someone may think that sounds crude. So is death crude. It is awful. This case is certainly going to require a miracle.

> **Then they took away the stone from the place where the dead was laid. And Jesus lifted up his eyes, and said, Father, I thank thee that thou hast heard me.**
>
> **And I knew that thou hearest me always: but because of the people which stand by I said it, that they may believe that thou hast sent me [John 11:41–42].**

Remember that this whole incident is for the glory of God. Jesus prays audibly to let the people know that what He is going to do is the will of the Father so that the Father will get the glory. He voices His prayer for the benefit of those who are present.

> **And when he thus had spoken, he cried with a loud voice, Lazarus, come forth.**
>
> **And he that was dead came forth, bound hand and foot with graveclothes: and his face was bound about with a napkin. Jesus saith unto them, Loose him, and let him go [John 11:43–44].**

I want to mention here that I think there were multitudes raised from the dead by Jesus Christ. I think there were multitudes who were healed, hundreds of blind people who received their sight. The Gospels record only a few instances for us.

Notice that for Lazarus, life was restored to the old body. He came out still wrapped in all the graveclothes. When our Lord rose from the dead, He left all the graveclothes in place just as they had been wrapped around His body, including the napkin which had been wrapped around his head. He came right out of them. Why? Because He came out in a glorified body. They didn't need to roll away the stone for Jesus to come out. It was rolled away so the people on the outside could look in and see that the tomb was empty. His glorified body could leave the sealed grave and it could also enter a room with all the doors locked.

There is a beautiful picture of salvation in this. We were dead in trespasses and sins, dead to God, and are now made alive to God in Christ Jesus. But, friend, each of us is being held back by those graveclothes. Paul could say, ". . . For what I would, that do I not; but what I hate, that do I. . . . O wretched man that I am! . . ." (Rom. 7:15, 24). This was not an unsaved man talking; this was a believer. Jesus wants us to be free from those graveclothes. He says, "Loose him, and let him go."

> **Then many of the Jews which came to Mary, and had seen the things which Jesus did, believed on him.**
>
> **But some of them went their ways to the Pharisees, and told them what things Jesus had done [John 11:45–46].**

These men cannot ignore this miracle.

It may surprise you to learn that this is the end of the public ministry of Jesus when you see that we are only near the halfway mark in the Gospel of John. His public ministry began when John the Baptist marked Him out as the Lamb of God. It concluded when He raised Lazarus from the dead. John, you see, spent almost as much time on the last forty-eight hours before His death as he did on the first thirty-two years, eleven months, three weeks, and five days of His life. As a matter of fact, this is the pattern shared by all the Gospel writers. They placed the emphasis on the last eight days. There are eighty-nine chapters in the four Gospels. Four of these chapters cover the first thirty years of the life of Jesus and eighty-five chapters the last three years of His life. Of those eighty-five chapters, twenty-seven deal with the last eight days of His life. So about one-third of the gospel records deal with the last few days and place the emphasis on the death and resurrection of Jesus Christ.

Friend, it is a misrepresentation of the gospel if the death and resurrection of Jesus Christ are not preeminent. In fact, that comprises the gospel (see 1 Cor. 15:1–4). The gospel writers did what Paul also did later on. He says, "For I determined not to know any thing among you, save Jesus Christ, and him crucified" (1 Cor. 2:2).

You would think that this crowning miracle would have turned these skeptics to Jesus, but it did not. Our Lord had said previously, you remember, ". . . If they hear not Moses and the prophets, neither will they be persuaded, though one rose from the dead" (Luke 16:31). That is the reason that God does not rend the heavens and come down in spectacular display. That is the reason God does not go about performing miracles today. After the church leaves the earth, during the Great Tribulation Period, and into the Millennium, there will be a period of great miracles, but even that will not convince people. Today we are asked in a quiet way to put our trust in Him even though the mob and the majority turn from Him.

People complain that the crowd isn't going after Jesus. Friend, it never did! He died, He was buried, He rose again from the dead, and that is the gospel. We don't need a miracle. The problem is not in the lack of evidence. The problem is the unbelief of man.

Then gathered the chief priests and the Pharisees a council, and said, What do we? for this man doeth many miracles [John 11:47].

You can see here that the problem for these bloodhounds of hate was not a lack of evidence. His enemies said, "He doeth many miracles." They couldn't deny His miracles.

This is a diabolical group. The chief priests at this time were largely Sadducees who were the "liberals" in that they did not accept miracles or the supernatural—which included resurrection. The Pharisees were the religious conservatives and the political rightists of that day. The two parties were absolutely opposed to each other in every way; yet here they join together in their hatred of Jesus Christ and in their determination to put Him to death. You might label this the first ecumenical movement. If men can get rid of Jesus Christ, they will join with even those of opposing views in their antagonism toward Him. This is the trend of the hour. The majority is attempting to get rid of Christ as He is revealed in the Word of God. It is the minority that accepts Jesus Christ as He is.

If we let him thus alone, all men will believe on him: and the Romans shall come and take away both our place and nation [John 11:48].

They feared there would be a mass turning to Jesus Christ which would bring a revolution. This would provide an occasion for Rome to pounce on them. They moved from a basis of fear. Fear is the motivation which keeps a great many people away from Jesus today. Even in our churches Christians lack the intestinal fortitude to stand on their two feet for the truth of Scripture and for men who teach it as the Word of God.

And one of them, named Caiaphas, being the high priest that same year, said unto them, Ye know nothing at all,

Nor consider that it is expedient for us, that one man should die for the people, and that the whole nation perish not.

And this spake he not of himself: but being high priest that year, he prophesied that Jesus should die for that nation;

And not for that nation only, but that also he should gather together in one the children of God that were scattered abroad [John 11:49–52].

They begin to rationalize and say that Jesus should die rather than the nation die at the hand of Rome. It is interesting to note that although they did succeed in putting Jesus to death, in spite of this, the nation perished when Titus destroyed it in A.D. 70.

We find a strange thing here: Caiaphas' accurate prediction because he was high priest that year! Caiaphas was a scheming politician, and later we will meet his father-in-law, Annas, who was also a mean rascal and the power behind the throne. That Caiaphas had the gift of prophecy should not fool us. Like Balaam in the Old Testament, this rascal could utter a true prophecy.

Then from that day forth they took counsel together for to put him to death.

Jesus therefore walked no more openly among the Jews; but went thence unto a country near to the wilderness, into a city called Ephraim, and there continued with his disciples [John 11:53–54].

This is the beginning of the end, friend. They are openly trying to put Jesus to death and are openly hostile. We don't know exactly where the city Ephraim is. It was probably out in rather wild country.

And the Jews' passover was nigh at hand: and many went out of the country up to Jerusalem before the passover, to purify themselves.

Then sought they for Jesus, and spake among themselves, as they stood in the temple, What think ye, that he will not come to the feast?

Now both the chief priests and the Pharisees had given a commandment, that, if any man knew where he were, he should shew it, that they might take him [John 11:55–57].

The crowds come to Jerusalem to purify themselves before the Passover. As they go through this endless ritual and rub shoulders with each other, there are differences of opinion and talk about Jesus. They wonder whether Jesus will come to the feast this year. They know the Sanhedrin is really after Him. You see, if they will not believe Moses, they will not believe even though one rose from the dead.

At this point John's gospel has reached the breaking point. We are approaching the last week of the earthly life of the Lord Jesus Christ.

CHAPTER 12

THEME: *Witness of Jew and Gentile to Jesus; Jesus comes to Bethany for supper; Jesus comes to Jerusalem—tearful entry; Jesus comes to Greeks; Jesus comes to His hour; Jesus comes to end of His public ministry*

WITNESS OF JEW AND GENTILE TO JESUS

As we come to this twelfth chapter, we are going with Jesus to make a visit to a home, the home of Lazarus, Mary, and Martha of Bethany. In this Gospel of John, He opened His public ministry at a wedding in Cana of Galilee; He closes His public ministry by a visit to this home. Our Lord put an emphasis upon the home, the Christian home, the godly home. Marriage has the blessing of God upon it. So we come now to this lovely picture.

JESUS COMES TO BETHANY FOR SUPPER

Then Jesus six days before the passover came to Bethany, where Lazarus was which had been dead, whom he raised from the dead.

There they made him a supper; and Martha served: but Lazarus was one of them that sat at the table with him.

Then took Mary a pound of ointment of spikenard, very costly, and anointed the feet of Jesus, and wiped his feet with her hair: and the house was filled with the odour of the ointment [John 12:1–3].

In Jerusalem they were plotting and planning His death but, here in Bethany, His friends plan a dinner party for Him. Right in the shadow of the cross, those who loved Him made Him a dinner. We want to study the whole picture of this lovely dinner.

Lazarus, the man who has been raised from the dead, was in fellowship with Christ. Jesus had said, "I am the resurrection, and the life: he that believeth in me, though he were dead, yet shall he live" (John 11:25). This was true of Lazarus in a physical sense. He had been raised from the dead. It is true of you and of me in a spiritual sense. We were dead in trespasses and sins. We had no knowledge of Him nor did we have any fellowship with Him. So for us He said, "And whosoever liveth and believeth in me shall never die" (John 11:26).

What a picture we have here! There is Lazarus alive from the dead and in fellowship with Christ. Then we see Mary sitting at Jesus' feet, growing in grace and in the knowledge of Christ. Then, thirdly, we see Martha serving, putting on a meal. That is her gift and she is exercising it. These are the three essentials in the church today: new life in Christ, worship and adoration, and service. This home at Bethany should be a picture of your church and mine.

All this is in the home where Jesus is with His own. As you know, the church began in the home. It may end in the home. Many of our churches are turning away from God and the things of God. They are no longer places of delightful fellowship and blessing. So perhaps the church will return to homes where true fellowship with Christ will be found.

Then we notice the devotion and adoration, the unutterable attachment and deep affection of this woman, Mary. She anointed the feet of Jesus with costly spikenard and wiped them with her hair. Some people think this is the same story as the harlot who washed Jesus' feet. I think you will have trouble with Mary someday if you think that. She is an altogether different person. The only thing that is the same in both cases is that the hair was used to wipe His feet. The odor of the ointment filled the house. Delightful!

Then saith one of his disciples, Judas Iscariot, Simon's son, which should betray him,

Why was not this ointment sold for three hundred pence, and given to the poor?

This he said, not that he cared for the poor; but because he was a thief, and had the bag, and bare what was put therein [John 12:4–6].

Judas Iscariot is revealing his true nature. He is the treasurer of the group. He doesn't care for the poor; he cares for himself—he is a thief. He was taking some money out on the sly. He wants Mary's money given to the poor so he can handle it and take out his percentage.

May I say to you today, the real test of a Christian, the hard-coin test, is the way he handles his finances. The real test of a church or a Christian organization is the way it handles its finances. Is the money used for the cause for which it was given, or is it shifted and used in some other way?

Three hundred pence was the annual wage of a laboring man of that day. Because the spikenard was too costly for Mary to use on herself, she poured it all out on Jesus. Friend, if we would learn to sit at His feet, we would give more to Him, too. Mary had saved this precious ointment in an alabaster box. It came out of India, where the herbs grow high in the Himalayas, and was very expensive. Do you know why she had bought it and saved it? So that when she died it could be used on her body! Now she pours it all out on Him. This is absolute affection, adoration, and attachment to His Person. The odor of that ointment filled the house, and it still fills the world today.

Then said Jesus, Let her alone: against the day of my burying hath she kept this.

For the poor always ye have with you; but me ye have not always [John 12:7–8].

This is really a remarkable incident. The Lord here reveals that this woman anoints Him to let Him know that she enters into His death. She senses that He is to die for the sins of the world and she anoints Him ahead of time. Matthew recorded that Jesus said that wherever the gospel would be preached, this incident would be told. This is true. Even today the wonderful fragrance of this thing that she did fills the world.

What a contrast we find here between her and Judas Iscariot. Here is where light and darkness are coming together. Judas is the darkness and Mary is the light.

There is an application for us today. Jesus says that the poor are always with us and that He will not always be with us. He is not contradicting His statement that He is with us always, that He will never leave us nor forsake us. What He is saying here is that we can always be of service to the poor—they are always with us—but that our service should not be a substitute for sitting at His feet. There comes a day when it is too late to absorb all He has for us. I get letters saying, "Dr. McGee, I never had Bible teaching; if only I had had Bible teaching when I was young." My friend, learn about Him now. Do not substitute activity for sitting at His feet.

Much people of the Jews therefore knew that he was there: and they came not for Jesus' sake only, but that they might see Lazarus also, whom he had raised from the dead.

But the chief priests consulted that they might put Lazarus also to death;

Because that by reason of him many of the Jews went away, and believed on Jesus [John 12:9–11].

These people are curiosity seekers. The chief priests wanted to get Lazarus out of the way. I personally believe that the people come out of curiosity to see Lazarus rather than to see Jesus and that the faith described here is much like the faith exhibited when Jesus first came up to Jerusalem. Remember that they believed on Him, but He would not commit Himself to them. It was a belief based on curiosity.

JESUS COMES TO JERUSALEM—TEARFUL ENTRY

On the next day much people that were come to the feast, when they heard that Jesus was coming to Jerusalem [John 12:12].

Notice how John gears this One who came out of eternity into the calendar of the world. It is the time before the Feast of the Passover, and the crowd is expectant. Remember that in Matthew's record Jesus was born and sought by the wise men who call Him the King of the Jews. Now, at the end of His ministry, He is again presented as the King of the Jews.

Took branches of palm trees, and went forth to meet him, and cried, Hosanna: Blessed is the King of Israel that cometh in the name of the Lord.

And Jesus, when he had found a young ass, sat thereon; as it is written,

Fear not, daughter of Sion: behold, thy King cometh, sitting on an ass's colt [John 12:13–15].

This is the public offer of Himself as their King and the rulers, of course, reject it. He is no longer mixing among the people and teaching them. That had already ceased. This is now an act which He performs as a fulfillment of prophecy. He is offering Himself to the nation. This is not really a *triumphal* entry. He came in through the sheep gate, quietly, during His public ministry. All through His public ministry, He tended to withdraw from the crowds. Now, when His public ministry is over, He does the most public thing He has ever done. He steps out publicly and presents Himself.

He does this to fulfill prophecy. "As it is written." He rides into Jerusalem to fulfill the Word of God and to fulfill the will of God. John gives us a very brief account of this entry of Jesus, but he does say that it fulfills the prophecy of Zechariah 9:9: "Rejoice greatly, O daughter of Zion: shout, O daughter of Jerusalem: behold, thy King cometh unto thee: he is just, and having salvation; lowly, and riding upon an ass, and upon a colt the foal of an ass." Jesus presents Himself publicly to Jerusalem as the Messiah. They acclaim Him with "Hosanna: Blessed is the King of Israel that cometh in the name of the Lord." What will Israel do with their King? They will crucify Him.

These things understood not his disciples at the first: but when Jesus was glorified, then remembered they that these things were written of him, and that they had done these things unto him [John 12:16].

John is writing this many years later, and he admits that he didn't understand what Jesus was doing that day. Probably he asked James and Peter and Andrew, and they didn't understand either. Mary was the only one who had entered into His death. The others didn't understand until after His death and resurrection. "When Jesus was glorified, then remembered they that these things were written of him."

The people therefore that was with him when he called Lazarus out of his grave, and raised him from the dead, bare record.

For this cause the people also met him, for that they heard that he had done this miracle.

The Pharisees therefore said among themselves, Perceive ye how ye prevail nothing? behold, the world is gone after him [John 12:17–19].

Here is a situation loaded with dynamite. The crowd is enthusiastic because of His miracle; their interest is centered on Lazarus and not on the person of Christ. The Pharisees are out to kill Him. Jerusalem is crowded with people for the feast.

Obviously, Jesus Christ could have had the crown without first going to the cross. However, if He had gone directly to the crown, if He were the ruler today, you and I would never have been saved. He had to go to the cross to save you and me. Although this was a brief moment of triumph before His death, it was not His triumphal entry. In the future when He enters as Lord of lords and King of kings, that will be His triumphal entry.

My favorite painting of the Crucifixion shows three empty crosses. The bodies of the crucified have been taken down from the crosses and lie in the tombs. In the background is a little donkey eating on a palm frond. What a message! The discarded palm branch and the cross are the tokens of His so-called triumphal entry. Where is the crowd that cried, "Hosanna: Blessed is the King of Israel that cometh in the name of the Lord"? They may be the same crowd that on the next day shouted, "Crucify Him!" Now they are gone, and He is in the tomb. You see, He offered Himself to them publicly as their King, but He was rejected.

JESUS COMES TO GREEKS

And there were certain Greeks among them that came up to worship at the feast:

The same came therefore to Philip, which was of Bethsaida of Galilee, and desired him, saying, Sir, we would see Jesus.

Philip cometh and telleth Andrew: and again Andrew and Philip tell Jesus [John 12:20–22].

Apparently Jesus has gone into the temple. Since there is a court for the women and a court for the Gentiles, these Greeks can not go in where Jesus is. Philip has a Greek name and may have spoken Greek, which is probably the reason they came to him. Philip is a modest and retiring fellow and he goes to Andrew for help. Together they bring the Greeks to Jesus.

And Jesus answered them, saying, The hour is come, that the Son of man should be glorified.

Verily, verily, I say unto you, Except a corn of wheat fall into the ground and die, it abideth alone: but if it die, it bringeth forth much fruit [John 12:23–24].

When our Lord says "verily," He is about to say something very important to hear. And when He says, "verily, verily," it is of supreme importance.

He that loveth his life shall lose it; and he that hateth his life in this world shall keep it unto life eternal [John 12:25].

"Jesus answered them"—I think "them" includes both the disciples and the Greeks. It seems that Jesus went out to speak to them. I do not believe He would refuse to come to anyone who was asking for Him.

The Greeks want to see Jesus because they had heard about Him, probably about His miracles, and especially His raising of Lazarus from the dead. Now He directs the attention of the Greeks to His cross. He is in the shadow of the cross. He tells them, "The hour is come." What hour? The hour of crisis for which He came out of eternity and toward which His entire life has moved. You remember that He had said to His mother early in His ministry, "mine hour is not yet come" (John 2:4). Now His hour *is* come. He is going to the cross.

His conception of the cross was far different from that held by the Roman populace. To them it was an instrument of infamy and disgrace and shame. It was the hangman's noose, the electric chair, and the gas chamber. He became obedient to death, even the death of the cross. Why? "Christ hath redeemed us from the curse of the law, being made a curse for us: for it is written, Cursed is every one that hangeth on a tree" (Gal. 3:13). Then on the third day He was raised from the dead and crowned with glory and honor. ". . . for the joy that was set before him [he] endured the cross, despising the shame, and is set down at the right hand of the throne of God" (Heb. 12:2). The glory of God is seen in that cross. That is why He could say that the time had come for Him to be *glorified*. Friend, He was glorified when He died for you and me. He was glorified when He came forth from that tomb. Mercy and pardon and forgiveness are found at that cross.

Then our Lord states a great principle using the physical analogy of a grain of wheat. Although a grain of wheat in the ground dies, it produces the blade, the ear, and the harvest. It must die to bring forth fruit. Many people think they have seen Jesus because they have read the Gospels and they have studied His life. They see the historical Jesus, but they have never seen *Jesus* until they comprehend His death and His resurrection. He died a redemptive death. He gave His life in death so that we might have life. You haven't seen Jesus until you have seen that He is the One who died for you on the cross. He is the One who died for the sins of the world.

This seems a strange thing to be saying to the Greeks who had come to see Him. He is telling them that there is more than just seeing Him physically. The important thing for them to see is that He is going to die. He is going to be put into the ground. When that grain of wheat died, it produced life. He died, but He rose again. That is so important to see.

He goes on to explain a great axiom to the Greeks. There are two kinds of life and they are put in contrast here. There is what is known as the psychological life, the life of the psyche, life that enjoys the things of this world and finds satisfaction in the gratification of the senses. It is the kind of life that really whoops it up down here. "He that loveth his life" refers to this physical, natural life that we have. You can really live it up, drink it up, take drugs, paint the town red, but do you know what is going to happen? One day you are going to die. You'll lose it. I'm sorry, but you will lose it, friend.

I heard of a sensational preacher down in Texas who was asked to preach at the funeral of a rich man of the town who had been a church member but had broken every law of God and man and was living in sin and in drunkenness. This was in the oil section of Texas and a lot of rich people, the fast crowd, the jet set, came to the funeral. Now this preacher did something I wouldn't do, but maybe I should do it, although I never have done it. He preached a gospel message! Then he stepped down to the casket and he preached on what sin will do for an individual and that it will finally send a man to hell. I tell you, the folks were getting uneasy. Then when he invited them to view the remains, he said, "His life is past; he lived it up; he is through. He despised God and he turned his back on Jesus Christ." Then he looked at that crowd and said, "This is the way each one of you is going to end up unless you turn to Jesus Christ." Now, friend, that is making it very plain—maybe a little too plain.

We do need to tell it like it is. This is what our Lord says. "He that loveth his life shall lose it." That is, if you live it up down here, you'll lose it. Then our Lord makes a contrast. "He that hateth his life in this world shall keep it unto life eternal." This means that if you do not live for this world or for the things of this world, you keep your life unto life eternal. And eternal life comes from what? It comes through the death of that grain of wheat that fell into the ground and rose again, the Lord Jesus Christ. That is the way you can save your life—the only way you can save it.

If any man serve me, let him follow me; and where I am, there shall also my servant be: if any man serve me, him will my Father honour [John 12:26].

He tells them to follow Him, and He is on His way to the cross. He promises that where He is, His servants will also be. "If any man serve me, him will my Father honour."

JESUS COMES TO HIS HOUR

Now is my soul troubled; and what shall I say? Father, save me from this hour: but for this cause came I unto this hour [John 12:27].

There is a suffering that is connected with the cross of Christ that you and I cannot comprehend. He didn't suffer at the hands of men only. That was bad enough, but He suffered beyond that. Your sin and my sin were put upon Him. He was ". . . a man of sorrows, and acquainted with grief . . ." (Isa. 53:3) there on the cross. He bore the sin of the world, not His own sin. "Surely he hath borne our griefs, and carried our sorrows . . ." (Isa. 53:4). Our sin was put upon Him. He was made sin for us—not in some academic manner—He actually was made sin for us. "Yet it pleased the LORD to bruise him; he hath put him to grief . . . [He made] his soul an offering for sin" (Isa. 53:10). Although He was holy and undefiled and separate from sinners, He was made sin for you and for me. This involved a suffering that you and I cannot comprehend.

But none of the ransomed ever knew
How deep were the waters crossed;
Or how dark was the night that the Lord
passed through
Ere He found His sheep that was lost.
"The Ninety and Nine"
—Elizabeth C. Clephane

His soul stood in horror; He was aghast before that cross. Yet He had come into the world for the purpose of going to the cross and enduring the shame of it. Also there was glory in the cross, friend. We ought to think more about it and thank Him more. Paul says, "But God forbid that I should glory, save in the cross of our Lord Jesus Christ, by whom the world is crucified unto me, and I unto the world" (Gal. 6:14).

Do you see how this ties in with the two preceding verses? Our Lord is facing the supreme sacrifice—shortly He will give His life as a ransom for the human family. And He has put this challenge to those who are following Him: "He that hateth his life in this world shall keep it unto life eternal. If any man serve me, let him follow me." You can tell where a person is going by the way that person is living. Someone may say, "I thought we are saved by faith—you always emphasize faith rather than works." That's right. I surely do. If you are going to be saved, you will have to put your trust in Him—". . . Believe on the Lord Jesus Christ, and thou shalt be saved . . ." (Acts 16:31). But I want to say that if you truly trust Him, it is going to change your life. If it doesn't change your life, then you aren't really trusting Him.

When I see a Christian who mortgages every dime he has just to own every gadget to live in luxury down here, I wonder how he can be waiting for the Lord to come, and hoping for it with real anticipation. "He that loveth his life shall lose it."

Notice also how this ties in with His saying, "Where I am, there shall also my servant be: if any man serve me, him will my Father honour." It is not a question of the Lord going with us, but of our being where the Lord is. One man said to me, "Well, you know, I'm a member of a liberal church, but I take the Lord with me." My friend, I have news for you. The Lord doesn't go to church there. The Lord is not going to go your way. You are to go where the Lord is.

Our salvation is not cheap. This "hour" is repulsive to our Lord. If it were possible, He would want the Father to spare Him from the horror of being made sin, although He knows this is the reason He came into the world. Then He says, "Father, glorify thy name."

Father, glorify thy name. Then came there a voice from heaven, saying, I have both glorified it, and will glorify it again [John 12:28].

His supreme desire is the glory of God. What a lesson that is for us! We tend to whimper and cry and complain and ask God why He lets unpleasant things happen to us. With Christ, we should learn to say, "Father, through this suffering and through this pain, glorify Thyself."

Heaven couldn't remain silent but had to respond. God answered audibly. Have you noticed that God spoke to Him from out of heaven on three occasions: at the beginning, midway, and at the end of His ministry? Have you noticed that all three occasions are related to the death of Christ? The first was at His baptism when He was identifying Himself with sinful humanity. The second time was at His transfiguration when Elijah, Moses, and the Lord Jesus were talking about His decease which He should accomplish in Jerusalem (see Luke 9:30–31). This third time, at the conclusion of His ministry, the Lord is talking about His death because His hour has come.

The people therefore, that stood by, and heard it, said that it thundered: others said, An angel spake to him.

Jesus answered and said, This voice came not because of me, but for your sakes [John 12:29–30].

Now which group was right? Neither was right. It wasn't an angel; it was the Father speaking to Him. One group did believe it was supernatural; they knew it was articulate. They knew about the ministry of angels in the Old Testament and understood that God's messages for man generally came through "the angel of the Lord." They did not, however, understand that "the angel of the Lord" was the pre-incarnate Christ. They did acknowledge that the voice from heaven brought a message from God.

The other group said it thundered. They gave it a natural explanation. That is the same reaction many people still have today. They say God's Word is full of errors and the miracles recorded can't be accurate. Because they don't believe in them, they say it just "thundered." Some folk who were attending a Bible class where they were listening to my tapes on Revelation were told by a liberal preacher that nobody could understand the Book of Revelation, that it didn't make sense. He revealed his own ignorance because the Book of Revelation is a very logical book and probably the most systematic book in the Bible. But, you see, to him it was thunder. It was just noise.

The Word of God says that His birth was supernatural, His life was filled with miracles, and His death was like a grain of wheat. He didn't stay in the ground, friend; He came up just like the grain of wheat. The liberal who said, "The bones of Jesus sleep somewhere beneath Syrian skies" has a problem on his hands. Where are the bones? Christ's resurrection was not spiritual but actual. It was His body that was raised—His bones just don't happen to be anywhere on earth. Yet, this is the same old gag that has been used down through the years, "it thundered." It is no mark of intelligence to say that. We need spiritual perception and appreciation to hear and to know and to see the Word of God. We need to recognize that the Spirit of God must enlighten us when we come to the Word of God.

Now is the judgment of this world: now shall the prince of this world be cast out.

And I, if I be lifted up from the earth, will draw all men unto me.

This he said, signifying what death he should die [John 12:31–33].

Christ's death on the cross was the judgment of the world and of the prince of this world. That is one of the things the Holy Spirit will bear witness to, according to John 16:7–11. We live in a world that is judged. He came to die a judgment death for the sins of the world. If the world will not accept this, the world is judged.

How is Satan, the prince of this world, cast out? I believe it is done gradually. When Christ died on the cross, I am convinced that Satan did not understand what was happening. What he thought would be a defeat turned out to be a victory. He lost the battle at the cross which is the reason the Lord could say that the prince of this world is cast out. Then in Revelation 12:10 we are told that Satan will be cast out of heaven, which is the second stage. Then in Revelation 20:3, he will be cast into the bottomless pit, and in Revelation 20:10, he will be cast into the lake of fire. That is the last stage of his defeat. At the cross, his doom was sealed. The cross marks the victory of Christ and the defeat of Satan.

Jesus puts the emphasis on His redemptive

death. His death will draw all men unto Him. Those who believe will be saved. Those who reject Him will be lost.

Consider how important it is to lift up Jesus before men, to put the emphasis on His redemptive death. There are multitudes passing by the church today who are not hearing the Word. Think of the laborers, the students, the men in the uniform of our country, the white-collar group, the rich. They do not hear. Jesus, the crucified Lord, is not being lifted up in the churches today. Friend, the gospel needs to be preached, and the gospel is about a Christ who was crucified.

The people answered him, We have heard out of the law that Christ abideth for ever: and how sayest thou, The Son of man must be lifted up? who is this Son of man? [John 12:34].

The crowd is really confused. They say, "When Christ comes, He will reign forever, and now You say that You are not abiding but are going to die." They just did not understand. What was wrong?

Then Jesus said unto them, Yet a little while is the light with you. Walk while ye have the light, lest darkness come upon you: for he that walketh in darkness knoweth not whither he goeth.

While ye have light, believe in the light, that ye may be the children of light. These things spake Jesus, and departed, and did hide himself from them [John 12:35–36].

Jesus now withdraws and this ends His public ministry. He will never appear publicly again until He comes to this earth to establish His Kingdom.

JESUS COMES TO THE END OF HIS PUBLIC MINISTRY

But though he had done so many miracles before them, yet they believed not on him:

That the saying of Esaias the prophet might be fulfilled, which he spake, Lord, who hath believed our report? and to whom hath the arm of the Lord been revealed?

Therefore they could not believe, because that Esaias said again,

He hath blinded their eyes, and hardened their heart; that they should not see with their eyes, nor understand with their heart, and be converted, and I should heal them.

These things said Esaias, when he saw his glory, and spake of him [John 12:37–41].

Now we learn what was wrong. Although they were standing in the presence of the Light of the World, they would not open their eyes. The prophecy of Isaiah was being fulfilled. This quotes the great redemptive chapter of Isaiah 53 which speaks of the death of Christ. Christ's death was presented to them, and they rejected Him. They were blinded to the light which was being presented to them. They were like a man who wakes up in the morning and says to himself, "Today I won't see and I will keep my eyes closed all day." He is just as blind as the man who cannot see. The next quotation is from Isaiah, chapter 6. You may point out that it says, "He hath blinded their eyes, and hardened their heart." That is very true, but this must be taken in its context. Jesus has presented Himself to them as the Messiah and as their King. They have rejected Jesus personally. Now He rejects them! Listen to me carefully. Because they *would* not accept Him, there came the day when they *could* not accept Him. My friend, the most dangerous thing in the world is to hear the gospel and then turn your back on it. If you just go on listening and listening and do not accept it and act upon it, there comes the time when you cannot hear and you cannot see. God is God, and it is He who has the final word.

Nevertheless among the chief rulers also many believed on him; but because of the Pharisees they did not confess him, lest they should be put out of the synagogue:

For they loved the praise of men more than the praise of God [John 12:42–43].

That is unfortunate. They were like secret believers today who are cowards. However, we will find two of these secret believers taking down the body of Jesus from the cross.

Jesus cried and said, He that believeth on me, believeth not on me, but on him that sent me.

And he that seeth me seeth him that sent me.

I am come a light into the world, that whosoever believeth on me should not abide in darkness [John 12:44–46].

Jesus repeats His amazing statement that He is the Light of the World. This is an extension of the time that He opened the eyes of the blind man. He will open the eyes of any who are willing to admit that they are blind and that they need the Light of the world.

And if any man hear my words, and believe not, I judge him not: for I came not to judge the world, but to save the world.

He that rejecteth me, and receiveth not my words, hath one that judgeth him: the word that I have spoken, the same shall judge him in the last day.

For I have not spoken of myself; but the Father which sent me, he gave me a commandment, what I should say, and what I should speak.

And I know that his commandment is life everlasting: whatsoever I speak therefore, even as the Father said unto me, so I speak [John 12:47–50].

Friend, we are going to be judged by the Word of God. We will not be judged by our little good works. We will not be judged by what we think religion is. No, we will be judged by the Word of God. Jesus came the first time as the Savior: "I came not to judge the world, but to save the world." The next time He will come as the Judge. The voice from heaven is still saying to us, ". . . This is my beloved Son . . . hear ye him" (Matt. 17:5).

This concludes this section of the Gospel of John. Men had turned their backs on that voice; they had rejected the King. When they had done this, the King rejected them. He is always the King!

CHAPTER 13

***THEME:** Jesus washes feet of disciples*

We come now to the fourth main division of this gospel. We first studied the prologue, which was the first eighteen verses of chapter 1. Then we had the introduction, which was the remainder of the first chapter. We have seen the Witness of His Works and of His Words from chapters 2 to 12. Now we come to the Witness of Jesus to His Witnesses, chapters 13 to 17.

There is another way in which we could divide this gospel. In the first twelve chapters the subject is *light*. They tell of His public ministry and that He is the Light. The division which we call the Upper Room Discourse is about the subject of *love*. He loves His own. The last part of the gospel, from chapters 18 to 21, is about *life*. He came to bring us life, and that life is in Himself. Our life comes through His death.

The Lord Jesus gave four major discourses. Three of these have already been studied in the Gospel of Matthew: the Sermon on the Mount (Matt. 5–7); the Mystery Parables Discourse (Matt. 13), telling us about the kingdom of heaven; and the Olivet Discourse (Matt. 24; 25). Now we come to the Upper Room Discourse which is recorded in John 13–17.

This discourse is one of the greatest that our Lord ever gave. It is the longest, and it is meaningful for us today because He took His own into the Upper Room and revealed new truths to them. It is still brand new and fresh for us today. There is nothing quite like it. His public ministry has ended, and He has been rejected. Now He talks about His love for us, how we are to live the Christian life, of the provision He has made for us, and of the relationships between Him and those who are His own. As He is on His way to the cross, He has no message for the Pharisees or the religious rulers or the Roman government. This message is for His own.

JESUS WASHES FEET OF DISCIPLES

We come now to a most unusual incident. I wish I could shock you, startle you with it. We hear it so often that we lose the wonder of it. Jesus Christ leaves heaven's glory and comes down to this earth and He takes the place of a slave and washes feet!

In the preceding chapter, you will remember, we saw that the feet of Jesus were anointed. Here, the feet of the disciples are washed. What a difference! As the Savior passed through this sinful world, He contacted no defilement whatsoever. He was holy, harmless, and undefiled. The feet speak of the walk of a person, and the anointing of Jesus' feet with spikenard tells of the sweet savor of the walk of our Lord.

The disciples' feet needed washing! Jesus washed their feet with water, not with blood. That is important to see. I hear many people talking about coming anew to the fountain filled with blood and being cleansed. This dishonors our Lord. The blood of Jesus Christ, God's Son, cleanses us from all sin—past, present, and future—in one application. There is only one sacrifice. "For by one offering he hath perfected for ever them that are sanctified" (Heb. 10:14). When you and I came as sinners to Christ Jesus, it was His shed blood that once and for all cleansed us and gave us a standing before God. But, my friend, we need to be purified along the pilgrim pathway; in our walk through the world we get dirty, and we need washing. We shall see that our Lord washed His disciples' feet for this very definite purpose.

There is a threefold reason given to explain why He washed their feet, and we shall note this as we read.

Now before the feast of the passover, when Jesus knew that his hour was come that he should depart out of this world unto the Father, having loved his own which were in the world, he loved them unto the end.

And supper being ended, the devil having now put into the heart of Judas Iscariot, Simon's son, to betray him [John 13:1–2].

Jesus washed their feet because He knew that He would "depart out of this world." His ministry would continue after He went back to heaven. He has identified Himself with His people, and today He still washes the feet of His disciples. He says that He will depart out of this "world" *(kosmos)*, meaning the world system. It is man's world, a world of sin. It is a civilization that is anti-God and anti-Christ, and it is under judgment. Because He is leaving this world, He washes their feet.

The second reason He does this is that He loved His own. He loved them "unto the end." He is going to the Father because He loved His own. He died to save His own, and He lives to keep them saved. We have a wonderful Savior, and He loves us right on through to the very end. God loves us with an everlasting love; we cannot keep Him from loving us.

The third reason is that another person had entered into the room. There was an uninvited guest present. His name was Satan. We speak of thirteen persons in the Upper Room, but actually, there were fourteen because Satan was there. Satan put into the heart of Judas Iscariot to betray Him. Wherever the Devil gets into Christian work, others are affected and the Lord must wash them. He must wash us if we are to have fellowship with Him.

Notice that this took place at the Feast of the Passover. "Supper being ended" is literally "supper being in progress." This is not the Lord's Supper. Actually John does not even record the Lord's Supper. Why does John omit something so important? I think it is because at the time John wrote, there were already Christians who were making a ritual out of the Lord's Supper. There is a great danger in putting importance on a ritual rather than on the person of Jesus Christ. It is more important to know the Word of God than it is to partake of Communion. There is no blessing in Communion apart from a knowledge of the Word of God. An apologetics professor, whom I had, said that it was Christ in your heart and bread in your tummy. The bread in your tummy won't be there long; Christ in your heart is the essential. I believe this is why John omits telling about the Lord's Supper.

Jesus knowing that the Father had given all things into his hands, and that he was come from God, and went to God [John 13:3].

A better translation would be, "Since Jesus knew that the Father had given all things into His hands, that He was come from God, and that He is going to God." It is restated that what He is doing is because He is returning to the Father. That is important.

He riseth from supper, and laid aside his garments; and took a towel, and girded himself.

After that he poureth water into a basin, and began to wash the disciples' feet, and to wipe them with the towel wherewith he was girded [John 13:4–5].

He lays aside His outer garment; that is, He takes off the robe that He is wearing. Then He takes a linen cloth, and He girds Himself with it. This is such a strange thing which He does.

He takes the place of a servant. He is girded with the towel of service, and He is ready to wash their feet.

In studying Exodus 21, we learn of a law regarding slaves. A Hebrew slave served his master six years, and he could go free on the seventh year. If, during that time, he had taken a wife and had had children, the master would free him but not his family. However, the slave could choose to stay. If he loved his master and his family, he could stay with them. Then the master would back him up to a door post and bore his ear with an awl which would identify him as a voluntary slave forever. Although he could have gone out free, he stayed because of love. Our Lord Jesus came down to this earth, took upon Himself our humanity, and was made in the likeness of a servant. He did all this because He loved us. He could have gone out free, but He died on the cross to provide salvation for us. He did this to establish a wonderful relationship for us and to make it possible for us to have fellowship with Him. He has become a slave because He loves us.

Then cometh he to Simon Peter: and Peter saith unto him, Lord, dost thou wash my feet?

Jesus answered and said unto him, What I do thou knowest not now; but thou shalt know hereafter [John 13:6–7].

Some people say that this is a sacrament and that we should practice foot washing. I see nothing wrong with practicing this if the spiritual meaning is not lost. Others say that this is a lesson in humility and is an example to us. There is nothing wrong with that interpretation, but I do not think it goes deep enough. Peter certainly could see this was an example of humility; yet the Lord said, "What I do thou knowest not now; but thou shalt know hereafter."

Peter saith unto him, Thou shalt never wash my feet. Jesus answered him, If I wash thee not, thou hast no part with me [John 13:8].

What did our Lord mean by that? He meant that without this washing there can be no fellowship with Him. This is the Passover Feast which speaks of His death. He arose from the Passover Feast which speaks of His rising in resurrection and going back to heaven. He is girded with the towel of service and He is saying to us, "If I don't wash you, you'll have no part with me." You cannot have fellowship with Him, service with Him, without the washing.

How does Christ wash us today? "Wherewithal shall a young man cleanse his way? by taking heed thereto according to thy word" (Ps. 119:9). "Now ye are clean through the word which I have spoken unto you" (John 15:3). ". . . even as Christ also loved the church, and gave himself for it; That he might sanctify and cleanse it with the washing of water by the word" (Eph. 5:25–26). It is the Word of God that will keep the believer clean. And when we sin, how are we cleansed? "If we confess our sins, he is faithful and just to forgive us our sins, and to cleanse us from all unrighteousness" (1 John 1:9). Too many people treat sin as a light matter. My friend, may I say to you, the feet speak of the walk, and when you and I become disobedient, we are not walking in His way. That is sin, and that needs to be confessed.

Simon Peter saith unto him, Lord, not my feet only, but also my hands and my head [John 13:9].

He at first pulls his feet up; then when our Lord says he won't have fellowship with Him, he sticks out his feet—big old fisherman's feet—and he holds out his hands—and they must have been strong, calloused hands—and he even held down his head, and said, "Not just my feet, but also wash my hands, wash my head." If it means fellowship, Peter wants all he can get of that.

Jesus saith to him, He that is washed needeth not save to wash his feet, but is clean every whit: and ye are clean, but not all [John 13:10].

Now He says, "He that's washed needeth not to be washed." That doesn't make good sense, does it? The reason it doesn't is that He used two different words and, unfortunately, the translators didn't make that distinction (nor do our more recent translations make the distinction), but they are absolutely two different words. He says, "He that is *louō*." *Louō* means "bathed." *Niptō* is the word translated "wash." "He that is bathed needeth not except to wash his feet."

In those days they went to the public bath for their bathing. Then a man would put on his sandals to come home. In his home was a basin of water for him to wash his feet because they had gotten dirty walking through the streets of the city. Not only was there dirt, but in those days the garbage was thrown into the streets. So even though he had just come from a bath, he had to wash his feet when he entered the house.

Our Lord is teaching that when we came to the cross, when we came to Jesus, we were washed all over. That is the bath, *louō*, regeneration. When we walk through this world, we are defiled and get dirty. We become disobedient, and sin gets into our lives. I do not believe that any believer goes through a day without getting just a little dirty. He says that we cannot have fellowship with Him if we are dirty. So the washing of the feet, *nipto*, is the cleansing in order to restore us to fellowship. "If we say that we have fellowship with him, and walk in darkness, we lie, and do not the truth: But if we walk in the light, as he is in the light, we have fellowship one with another, and the blood of Jesus Christ his Son cleanseth us [keeps on cleaning us] from all sin" (1 John 1:6–7).

Friend, in order to have our feet washed we must first confess our sin. To confess means to agree with God. It means to say the same thing that God says about our sin. One of the hardest things in the world is to get a saint to admit he is a sinner. Coldness, indifference, lack of love, all are seen by God as sin. If we confess, He is faithful and just to forgive. But that is not all. If you are going to have your feet washed, you must put them into the hands of the Savior. That is obedience. We can't just say, "God forgive me, I did wrong," and then go out and do the same thing all over again. That's not getting your feet into the hands of the Savior.

For he knew who should betray him; therefore said he, Ye are not all clean [John 13:11].

Jesus knew that Judas would betray Him. He knew that Judas had not taken a bath. In other words, Judas had never been regenerated. That is why He said they were not all clean.

So after he had washed their feet, and had taken his garments, and was set down again, he said unto them, Know ye what I have done to you?

Ye call me Master and Lord: and ye say well; for so I am.

If I then, your Lord and Master, have washed your feet; ye also ought to wash one another's feet.

For I have given you an example, that ye should do as I have done to you.

Verily, verily, I say unto you, The servant is not greater than his lord; neither he that is sent greater than he that sent him.

If ye know these things, happy are ye if ye do them [John 13:12–17].

If you want joy in your life today, Christian friend, go to Him and confess. This is one of the problems in our Christian congregations today. We may have our heads full of doctrine, but our feet smell. Brother, there is nothing that smells as bad as unwashed feet! Maybe that is the reason some of our services don't smell so good. That is the reason we don't reach more people for Christ. We need to confess in order to have fellowship with Christ.

Jesus said that as He had washed their feet, so they were to wash one another's feet. What does that mean? Paul tells us in Galatians how we are to do that. "Brethren, if a man be overtaken in a fault, ye which are spiritual, restore such an one in the spirit of meekness; considering thyself, lest thou also be tempted" (Gal. 6:1). That is, when a brother in Christ falls into sin, he is to be brought back into fellowship by one who is spiritual. Beating him on the head and criticizing him is not washing his feet, friend. To restore him means to wash his feet. In the church we have all sorts of talent—excellent speakers and beautiful music—but there is no revival. We need foot washing; we need to be cleansed. Before we can wash the feet of a brother, we need first to have the Lord of glory wash our feet. We should come to Him every time that we are dirty and be cleansed by Him.

The psalmist says, "Search me, O God, and know my heart: try me, and know my thoughts: And see if there be any wicked way in me, and lead me in the way everlasting" (Ps. 139:23–24). There is not a one of us who goes through a day without some sin. We need to confess that to the Lord and be cleansed. We are washed by the Word of God. We put our feet into His hands, which means that we are completely yielded to Him. This places us in fellowship with the Lord Jesus. Friend, don't let a single day go by without this fellowship. Don't let sin come in to break this fellowship with Him.

The disciples were like a group of children in that Upper Room. They were frightened, and rightly so. The shadow of the cross had fallen upon that little group.

I speak not of you all: I know whom I have chosen: but that the scripture may

be fulfilled, He that eateth bread with me hath lifted up his heel against me [John 13:18].

Jesus is very careful to tell them that He does not speak of all of them. He has just told them they are happy if they do these things, but there is one man among them who cannot do them. Do you know why? He has not believed. Jesus has already told them that all of them are not clean. Jesus had said, "Ye call me Master and Lord." A master is a teacher and he is to be believed. A lord is to be obeyed. Faith and obedience must go together. Saving, living faith leads to obedience. Judas did not have this faith.

Jesus quotes Psalm 41:9: ". . . which did eat of my bread, hath lifted up his heel against me." He is referring to Judas. It is not a question of this man losing his spiritual life. It is rather a revelation that he never had a spiritual life! He is not a sheep who has become unclean; he is a pig that has returned to its wallowing again, or a dog that has returned to its vomit. That is the picture of Judas Iscariot. Yet, he was there in the Upper Room and this man got his feet washed. He received the washing by the Word of God, and he rejected it totally.

Let us go over this again so it is very clear. The blood of Jesus Christ is the Godward side of His sacrifice. The blood is for the expiation of our sin. The blood has cancelled all my guilt and has washed out that awful, black account which was against me. It has given me a standing before God because it has blotted out all my transgressions. The blood is for penal expiation. The cleansing by the water is the manward aspect of it. This is for our moral purification. After we have our standing before God on the ground of the blood of Jesus Christ, the water of the Word gives us our moral purification in our daily walk.

Now I tell you before it come, that, when it is come to pass, ye may believe that I am he [John 13:19].

Jesus tells them that one of them will "lift up his heel" against Him so that when it happens, they will not be shocked. Then they cannot say it was a pity Jesus didn't know about it. Have you ever noticed that the Lord Jesus is betrayed from the inside? This is still true today. People complain about the sin outside the church, but that doesn't hurt the church. In fact, some of those sinners get saved. The hurt comes when Jesus Christ is betrayed on the inside.

Verily, verily, I say unto you, He that receiveth whomsoever I send receiveth me; and he that receiveth me receiveth him that sent me [John 13:20].

Jesus adds this because Judas had been sent on missions with the rest of the disciples. He had preached and he had healed. "He that receiveth whomsoever I send receiveth me; and he that receiveth me receiveth him that sent me." No one is saved by the faith of the messenger or preacher. We are saved by hearing the Word of God and receiving Christ. If a Western Union boy brings you a telegram that a rich uncle has died and left you a fortune, the fact that the Western Union boy may be a thief doesn't invalidate the message of the telegram, does it?

I knew a preacher who had become an unbeliever. A man who drove me to the train said to me, "Dr. McGee, I am puzzled. I was saved under the ministry of that man. I know I am saved and I know I am a child of God but I am puzzled. How can you explain it?" I showed this man this very text and told him that even Judas had gone out preaching and had won converts, not because he was Judas, but because he had given the message. God will bless His Word. We are saved by hearing the Word.

When Jesus had thus said, he was troubled in spirit, and testified, and said, Verily, verily, I say unto you, that one of you shall betray me.

Then the disciples looked one on another, doubting of whom he spake.

Now there was leaning on Jesus' bosom one of his disciples, whom Jesus loved.

Simon Peter therefore beckoned to him, that he should ask who it should be of whom he spake.

He then lying on Jesus' breast saith unto him, Lord, who is it? [John 13:21–25].

If you think that Jesus was unmoved because Judas was going to betray Him, you are wrong. He was *troubled* in spirit. The disciples were stupefied. You can imagine the shock wave that went over that room. Judas had been so clever that not a person there believed he was the traitor. Each one thought it might be the other, and each one thought it might be himself. Each disciple knew that he was capable of doing the same thing.

I doubt that the little by-play between John

and Peter was noticed by the others. There must have been confusion in the room. Peter was probably farther away from Jesus, and since John was next to Him, Peter signaled to John to ask.

Jesus answered, He it is, to whom I shall give a sop, when I have dipped it. And when he had dipped the sop, he gave it to Judas Iscariot, the son of Simon [John 13:26].

It was the custom for the host at a banquet to take a piece of bread, dip it in the sauce, and present it to the guest of honor. The Lord makes Judas His guest of honor by this gesture. He is extending to him the token of friendship. Judas is at the crossroads. Christ keeps the door open to Judas up to the very last. Even in the garden Jesus will say, ". . . Friend, wherefore art thou come? . . ." (Matt. 26:50)—still keeping the door open for Judas.

Jesus knew what Judas would do. As another has stated it, "foreknowledge is not causation." That is, although the Lord knew what Judas would do, the Lord did not force him to do it. In fact, He offered His friendship to Judas to the very last.

And after the sop Satan entered into him. Then said Jesus unto him, That thou doest, do quickly [John 13:27].

Satan took over this man Judas gradually. I don't think that Satan ever takes a man suddenly. There are many little falls that permit Satan to move in gradually. Then finally he takes over. The Lord gave Judas an opportunity to accept Him, but Judas turned his back on the Lord. Then Satan moved in and took him over completely.

Judas makes his own decision. God never sends a man to hell unless that man first of all sends himself there. You see, God ratifies human decision; God seconds the motion. When a man says that he accepts Christ, God says, "I second it; I receive you." When a man says that he rejects Christ, as Judas did here, God says, "I second the motion."

Now Jesus asks him to leave quickly. Having made his decision, he is not beyond the control of God. In fact, having made his decision, he is compelled to cooperate with God. You see, the religious rulers didn't want to arrest Jesus and crucify Him while the crowds were there during the feast. They wanted to wait until the feast was over. But our Lord tells him to go now and do it quickly. So Judas must go out and tell the leaders that he has been found out, and they must move quickly.

Now no man at the table knew for what intent he spake this unto him [John 13:28].

No one at the table even suspected that Judas was the betrayer.

For some of them thought, because Judas had the bag, that Jesus had said unto him, Buy those things that we have need of against the feast; or, that he should give something to the poor [John 13:29].

Notice that our Lord did not beg for support. They had a treasury, and they carried on their business in a businesslike way. It also tells us that the Lord did not feed them miraculously. They had to go and buy food. They were not some "far out" group. Judas was the treasurer. There is always a temptation in the handling of money—which is equally true today. At the Passover season donations were given to the poor; so the disciples thought this may have been what the Lord asked him to do with the money.

He then having received the sop went immediately out: and it was night [John 13:30].

Notice also that when Judas went out, it was night. Friend, it was eternal night for Judas. It was the Devil's day, and the Devil's day is always like the darkness that descended on Egypt. This man walked out into eternal night.

What God does, He does slowly. What the Devil does, he does quickly. The Devil must move fast because his days are limited. God has all eternity to accomplish His purposes. Often we fail to understand that.

There is now a change in the room. Judas is gone, and our Lord begins to talk to these men. They are frightened. The shadow of the cross is over that little group in the Upper Room. Now our Lord attempts to lift these men from the low plane to the high plane; from the here-and-now to the hereafter; from the material to the eternal; from that which is secular to that which is spiritual. Although Simon Peter interrupts Him, I think Jesus' discourse begins right here and goes on into chapter 14.

Therefore, when he was gone out, Jesus said, Now is the Son of man glorified, and God is glorified in him.

If God be glorified in him, God shall also glorify him in himself, and shall

straightway glorify him [John 13:31–32].

The Lord Jesus is now moving into the spiritual realm. The Son of Man is going to be glorified, and this will be accomplished through His death and resurrection. From the human side the cross looks like shame and defeat, but God is glorified in Him because the salvation of the world will be wrought through the cross.

Little children, yet a little while I am with you. Ye shall seek me: and as I said unto the Jews, Whither I go, ye cannot come; so now I say to you [John 13:33].

Judas is gone now so He can address them as His little children. He is going to the cross, and no one can go to the cross as He did. He suffered alone, and there is a suffering of Christ which you and I cannot fully comprehend.

A new commandment I give unto you, That ye love one another; as I have loved you, that ye also love one another.

By this shall all men know that ye are my disciples, if ye have love one to another [John 13:34–35].

Now He gives to them a new commandment. Some folk would seem to think that He said, "By this shall all men know that ye are my disciples, if you are *fundamental* in the faith." Now friend, I believe in being fundamental in the faith, I believe in the inerrancy of the Word of God, in the verbal, plenary inspiration of the Scriptures, in the deity of the Lord Jesus Christ. I believe that He died on the cross for the expiation of sin; that He died a substitutionary, vicarious death for the sins of the world. I believe He was raised bodily and ascended back into heaven and that He is coming personally to take His church out of the world. But I want to say this, and I want to say it very carefully: believing those things does not convince the unsaved world outside. The world is dying for just a little love. Jesus says that His disciples are to be known for their love.

When I was a boy, my dad died and I went to work to support my mother and sister; so I stayed with two aunts and a bachelor uncle. One aunt was a Baptist and the other a Presbyterian. My uncle was an unbeliever and a beer drinker. Every Sunday he would get up just in time for the noon meal. For dinner every Sunday we heard all the Baptist dirt and the Presbyterian dirt. Years later, when my uncle was in the hospital, one of my aunts wept and asked me, "Vernon, why doesn't he come to Christ?" I almost told her. Friend, may I say, we do not win the lost by being Christian cannibals. "But if ye bite and devour one another, take heed that ye be not consumed one of another" (Gal. 5:15). This is the type of thing that is turning the unsaved away from the church today. This is the reason they don't come in to hear the gospel. They hear the gossip before they can hear the gospel! Do you realize that the most important commandment for a Christian is not to witness, not to serve, but to *love* other believers?

Tertullian writes that the Roman government was disturbed about the early church. Christians were increasing in number by leaps and bounds. Because they wouldn't take even a pinch of incense and put it before the image of the emperor, the Romans felt they might be disloyal. Spies went into the Christian gatherings and came back with a report something like this: "These Christians are very strange people. They meet together in an empty room to worship. They do not have an image. They speak of One by the name of Jesus, who is absent, but whom they seem to be expecting at any time. And my, how they love Him and how they love one another." Now if spies came from an atheistic government to see whether Christianity is genuine and they came to your church, what would be the verdict? Would they go back to report how these Christians love each other?

Simon Peter said unto him, Lord, whither goest thou? Jesus answered him, Whither I go, thou canst not follow me now; but thou shalt follow me afterwards.

Peter said unto him, Lord, why cannot I follow thee now? I will lay down my life for thy sake.

Jesus answered him, Wilt thou lay down thy life for my sake? Verily, verily, I say unto thee, The cock shall not crow, till thou hast denied me thrice [John 13:36–38].

Here is a man who is close to all of us. I believe that if you are a child of God, you would never sell out Jesus as Judas did. The Devil does not have control of you, because the Spirit of God dwells in you. But there isn't a one of us who would not do what Simon Peter did. His problem was not that Satan was in his heart but that he had confidence in his own flesh. I believe that is the problem for all of us.

Peter really loved the Lord. Peter was ready to defend the Lord. Yet the Lord must treat Peter as a juvenile. He is always blundering—I don't believe this man reached mental and spiritual maturity until the Day of Pentecost. The only things he heard of all that Jesus had said was that Jesus was going away. He reacts like a child who says, "Where are you going, Daddy? I want to go, too." His first question is, "Lord, whither goest thou?" His second is, "Lord, why cannot I follow thee now?"

When Jesus answered him, "Whither I go, thou canst not follow me now; but thou shalt follow me afterwards," the only thing that Peter heard was the "now." He is like a child who asks for a cookie. When the mother says he cannot have the cookie now but must wait until after dinner, the child seizes on the "now." He wants the cookie now. He doesn't want to wait until after dinner.

Peter's love for and loyalty to Jesus was sincere. He wanted to follow the Lord wherever He was going. When he said, "I will lay down my life for thy sake," he meant every word of it. He attempted to fight for his Lord, and he cut off the servant's ear. (The reason he got his ear was because he was a fisherman and not a swordsman. He was aiming for his head.) When the Lord told Peter that he would deny Him three times before the cock would crow, it was already dark, and he just couldn't believe he would deny his Lord before the dawn.

What a lesson there is here for us. Peter was overconfident in himself. We should learn from this that we should have no confidence in the flesh. Paul says, ". . . when I am weak, then am I strong" (2 Cor. 12:10). Do you recognize your weakness or do you think you are strong? Someone asked Dwight L. Moody, "Do you have grace enough to die for Jesus?" He answered, "No, He hasn't asked me to do that. But if He asks me to, I know He will give me the grace to do it." That is the answer. Our own flesh is weak, but God will supply our every need.

CHAPTER 14

***THEME:** Jesus comforts His disciples*

Chapter divisions in the Bible are wonderful because they help us find our way around in the Bible, but sometimes the chapter break is at an unfortunate place, as is the case here. What our Lord says at the beginning of chapter 14 is a continuation of what He was saying to Simon Peter in chapter 13.

Simon Peter has just declared that he would lay down his life for Him. Then the Lord Jesus told him that he would deny Him three times by the time the rooster crowed in the morning. We will see later that, when the rooster crowed that morning, Simon Peter had denied Him three times. Still speaking to Simon Peter, our Lord gave this chapter to bring him through that dark night of denial and to bring him back into a right relationship with God. It was given to comfort him. This chapter has cushioned the shock for multitudes of people from that day right down to the present hour.

JESUS COMFORTS HIS DISCIPLES

Let not your heart be troubled: ye believe in God, believe also in me [John 14:1].

People all over the world are seeking comfort at this very moment. They long for peace in their hearts. Jesus alone can bring that comfort, and here He tells the basis for it: "ye believe in God, believe also in me." In the Greek, this can also be an imperative or a command. Believe in God. Believe in Me also.

With the word *believe* we find the preposition *eis* which means "into." When John talks about saving faith, there is always a preposition with it. The faith is not inactive, not passive; it is to believe *into* or to believe *upon* or to believe *in.* It is an active faith, which is trust. If you believe that your car will take you home, how do you get home? By just believing it? No, you believe in it so much that you commit yourself to the car. You get into it and trust that it will get you home. In just such a way you get saved. You believe into Christ; you trust yourself to Him.

"Ye believe in God, believe also in me" is a

clear-cut statement of our Lord that He is God. I know a theology professor who claims that Jesus did not claim deity. I'd like to know what He is saying here in this first verse if He is not making Himself equal with God. His statement makes something very clear right here. To believe in God means you are not an atheist, but to be a *Christian*, you must have personal faith and trust in Christ.

In my Father's house are many mansions: if it were not so, I would have told you. I go to prepare a place for you [John 14:2].

Let's establish, first of all, what the Father's house is; the Father's house is this vast universe that you and I live in today. We are living on one of the very minor, smallest planets. We're just a speck in space. We live in the Father's house.

Sir James Jeans called it the expanding universe. First, men thought of the earth with the stars up there like electric light bulbs screwed in the top of the universe. Then men began to explore and found that we are in a solar system, that we are actually a minor planet going around the sun, and that there are quite a few other planets "tripping the light fantastic" around the sun with us. We, together with other solar systems, are in a galactic system, and when you look up at the Milky Way, you see the other side of our galactic system. Now, friend, ours is only one galactic system. If we could move out far enough, we would find other galactic systems that make ours look like it is just a peanut in space. We are told that our nearest neighbor, Andromeda, is something like 2,000,000 light years away from us. Friend, we won't go to our nearest neighbor of the galactic system to borrow a cup of sugar in the morning, because we won't get back in time for lunch! Even these galactic systems are not the end of space at all. Beyond them, they find what they call quasars. The reason the astronomers call them quasars is because that is a German word meaning they don't know what they are. They have found them through the radio telescopes like they have on the Mojave Desert. They have an even bigger telescope over in England, and they have found that beyond these quasars are other—well, they don't know what they are—so the British have come up with the very fine scientific term, "blops," and so they call them blops! We simply do not know how vast this universe is. It may be an infinite universe. If there is an infinite universe, there must be an infinite God. Maybe God is letting us paint ourselves into a corner so that we will have to acknowledge that He is up there after all!

Our Lord said, "In my Father's house are many mansions." I think there was a wry smile on His face when He said that. He is the One who made them, and He knew how many there were out there. We don't know and may never know. I do not think that God has a vacancy sign hanging out anyplace in this vast universe. I don't mean that human beings are living on other planets. One is enough of little mankind—we are the ones who are in rebellion against God. However, I think this vast universe is filled with created intelligences who are looking at this little earth. This is where they see something unique in the universe. They knew something about God's wisdom and His person and His power, but they knew nothing about His love until the second Person of the Trinity came down to this earth and died on the cross. God so *loved* the world that He gave His only begotten Son! There is a display of God's love on this earth.

You and I think we are pretty valuable. I don't want to offend anybody, friend, but do you know the human race isn't worth saving? God could very easily brush us off this little earth and start over again. He could speak the earth and us out of existence and very little would be missing. But then He wouldn't be demonstrating His love. He would be demonstrating justice and righteousness but not love. God loves us. That is the amazing thing and the most wonderful thing in the world. God loves us! He loves you and me, not because we are worth loving, but He loves us in spite of the fact that we are absolutely, totally depraved. We belong to that kind of human race. If you deny that, look around you. Unless there is something radically wrong with the human family, how could a civilization that reached such heights tumble as far as we have gone in two or three decades?

"In my Father's house are many mansions." For many years I was an ordained Presbyterian preacher, and I lived in what that church calls a "manse," which is a shortened form of *mansion*. I lived in my first manse before I was married. It was a big place with fourteen rooms, and on a clear day you could see the ceiling in the living room. It was cold, and I lived in one corner of a room near the fire. When anybody talks to me about a mansion in the sky, I shudder. The Greek word is *monē* meaning "abiding places." Jesus is saying that this vast universe is filled with abiding places or places to live.

"If it were not so, I would have told you." The Lord Jesus puts His entire reputation on the line here, and you either believe Him or you don't believe Him, my friend. "I go to prepare a place for you." This is quite wonderful. This vast universe is filled with so many places; yet He has gone to prepare a place for those who are His own. I said I think the universe is filled with intelligent creatures. John got a look at some of them in the Book of Revelation, and he was overwhelmed. He said there are a thousand times ten thousand; then he saw more and added thousands of thousands. We are dealing with a tremendous and wonderful God. One can look upon the millions in this world today and wonder whether we will get lost in the shuffle somewhere. But Jesus is up there preparing a place for all of us who belong to Him. No one can occupy it but us.

Years ago a neighbor of mine was one of the men working on the mirror for the 200-inch telescope at Palomar. In grinding the mirror, they missed it the first time by, I think, a millionth of an inch. When they finally got it finished, I kept asking him what they were seeing. Finally, he got tired of my constant questioning and wanted to know why I was so interested. "Well," I said, "you've got that big eye poked in the front window of my Father's house, and I'd like to know what you're seeing, because Jesus is preparing a place for me up there."

And if I go and prepare a place for you, I will come again, and receive you unto myself; that where I am, there ye may be also [John 14:3].

This is the first time in the Bible where you find a mention of God taking anyone off this earth to go out yonder to a place that He has prepared. This was not the hope of the Old Testament saint. God never promised Abraham to take him off yonder to a star. God told him He would make his offspring as numerous as the stars, but the promise to Abraham was to give him an eternal home on this earth. The hope of the Old Testament was for a kingdom down here on this earth in which would dwell peace and righteousness. This is the fulfillment of God's purpose for this earth. Personally, I think the expression "the kingdom of heaven" means the reign of God over this earth. God has said, "Yet have I set my king upon my holy hill of Zion" (Ps. 2:6). That is God's earthly purpose, and He is moving undeviatingly, unhesitatingly, and uncompromisingly toward the day when He puts His own Son upon the throne here on earth. That will be the kingdom of heaven. That is God's earthly purpose; it is the hope of the Old Testament.

The disciples are startled when Jesus reveals that He is going to take a people—beginning with the apostles—off this earth to be with Christ in the place that He is preparing for them. This is the first time it is mentioned, but it is not the last time. Paul talked about it, saying in 1 Thessalonians 4 that the Lord Himself would descend from heaven with a shout. His voice will be like a trumpet and like the sound of an archangel. He is coming to call His own. The dead in Christ will rise first, and then those believers who are still alive will be caught up together to meet the Lord in the air. So shall we ever be with the Lord in that place that He has prepared. John, in Revelation 21, tells us that the city, the new Jerusalem, will come down from God out of heaven. It will be a new city, a new concept in urban dwelling, my friend, and that is where believers, from the apostles on, will dwell throughout eternity.

And whither I go ye know, and the way ye know [John 14:4].

He is lifting these men into the heights, because, you see, there in the Upper Room the shadow of the cross had fallen athwart that company, and sin was knocking at the door of that room demanding its pound of flesh. Our Lord is attempting to lift them from the here-and-now to the hereafter, from the material to the spiritual, from the earthly to the heavenly. Jesus tells them two things: the destination, which is the "where," and the way to go, which is the "how."

Thomas saith unto him, Lord, we know not whither thou goest; and how can we know the way? [John 14:5].

There is an apostle sitting there whom we call doubting Thomas. He seems always to be asking a question or raising a doubt. He had a question mark for a brain, and it took our Lord a long time to make an exclamation mark out of it! I am really glad that he was there and that he asked the question, because it is a good question. I would have wanted to ask it if I had been there. If he hadn't asked the question, we would never have had our Lord's wonderful answer, which is the gospel in a nutshell.

Jesus saith unto him, I am the way, the truth, and the life: no man cometh unto the Father, but by me [John 14:6].

The article in the Greek is an adjective. Jesus said, "I am *the* way." He is not just a person who shows the way, but He, personally, is the way. No church or ceremony can bring you to God. Only Christ can bring you to God. He is the way. Either you have Christ or you don't have Him; either you trust Him or you don't. Also Jesus said that He is *the* truth. He isn't saying that He tells the truth, although He does do that. He *is* the truth! He is the bureau of standards for truth, the very touchstone of truth. And He is *the* life. He isn't simply stating that He is alive. He is the source, the origin of life from the lowest vegetable plane of life to the highest spiritual plane of life.

"No man cometh unto the Father, but by me." He made a dead-end street of all the cults and "isms." He says the *only* way to God is through Him. That is a dogmatic statement! Years ago a student out at UCLA told me he didn't like the Bible because it is filled with dogmatism. I agreed with him that it is. He especially selected this verse and said, "That's dogmatic." I said, "It sure is, but have you realized that it is characteristic of truth to be dogmatic? Truth has to be dogmatic."

I had a teacher who was the most dogmatic, narrow-minded person I've ever met. She insisted that 2 plus 2=4. It didn't make any difference what you had two of—apples or cows or dollars—she always insisted that 2+2=4. She was dogmatic. I have found that the bank I do business with operates on the same principle. Only in my case it is 2 - 2=0, and they are dogmatic about it. Friend, let me say to you that one of the characteristics of truth is its dogmatism.

Now, not all dogmatism is truth—there is a lot of ignorance that is dogmatic. However, that which is truth has to be dogmatic. When I ask directions to go somewhere, I do not want my directions from a man who isn't sure and doesn't know exactly how to get there. I want my directions from one who knows exactly where I'm to turn and how many blocks I'm to go. As I said to this young student, "Millions of people for over nineteen hundred years have been coming to Christ on the basis of His statement, 'I am the way,' and they have found it is accurate, that it has brought them to heaven. Why don't you try it? The Lord Jesus says you are not going to get to heaven except through Him. Why not come through Him and make sure?"

Someday I hope I can thank the apostle Thomas for asking our Lord this question in the Upper Room: "How can we know the way?" Without it we would not have this marvelous answer in John 14:6.

Now there is another interruption. Philip has a question.

If ye had known me, ye should have known my Father also: and from henceforth ye know him, and have seen him.

Philip saith unto him, Lord, shew us the Father, and it sufficeth us [John 14:7–8].

Philip was a very quiet individual, the opposite from loquacious Peter. I think he spoke very seldom. He has a Greek name and some Bible students believe that he was a Greek. However, he could have been Jewish and still have a Greek name. He is a very unusual man because every time we meet him he is bringing someone to Jesus. Remember that he brought Nathanael. I've often wondered about that. Philip was the quiet man and Nathanael was the wisecracker. Philip was the straight man and Nathanael was the humorist. But quiet Philip brings people to Jesus. Remember that the Greeks came to him, wanting to see Jesus. Here he expresses the highest ambition any man can have, the highest desire expressed by any person in the whole Bible, "shew us the Father."

I'd like to ask you a personal question today. What is your desire in life? What is your ultimate goal? Do you want to get rich? Do you want to make a name for yourself? Do you want to educate your children? Do you want to bring them up in the discipline and instruction of the Lord? Our goals may be worthy goals; yet the highest goal is this expressed by Philip, "Lord, shew us the Father."

Jesus saith unto him, Have I been so long time with you, and yet hast thou not known me, Philip? he that hath seen me hath seen the Father; and how sayest thou then, Shew us the Father? [John 14:9].

Philip knew from the Old Testament that Moses had seen the glory of God and that Isaiah had a vision of the glory of God. I don't think that we should interpret Jesus' answer as a rebuke. He tells Philip that He has performed many miracles. Although Philip had not seen the glory of God as Moses or Isaiah did, he had seen Jesus and had witnessed His words and His works. Everything that Philip wished to see, he had seen in Jesus Christ. He had seen God. In Christ there is a much greater revelation of God than anything in the

Old Testament. Philip had the greatest revelation of God because he had seen Him incarnate in flesh and been with Him—in His presence—for three years! Remember that the writer to the Hebrews says that Jesus is the brightness of the Father's glory and the express image of His person (see Heb. 1:3). "He that hath seen me hath seen the Father" does not mean you are seeing the identical Person, but you are seeing the same Person in power, in character, in love, and in everything else. You have seen all you would see in God the Father because "God is a Spirit: and they that worship him must worship him in spirit and in truth" (John 4:24). "No man hath seen God at any time; the only begotten Son, which is in the bosom of the Father, he hath declared him" (John 1:18). It is Jesus Christ whom we see. We are going to spend all eternity with Him. For those of us who love Him, the goal of our lives is to come to know Him.

Believest thou not that I am in the Father, and the Father in me? the words that I speak unto you I speak not of myself: but the Father that dwelleth in me, he doeth the works [John 14:10].

Jesus here points to the testimony of His words and of His works. They are the same. One equals the other. He was perfectly consistent. You see, our problem is to get our words and our works synchronized. We make tremendous statements and give glorious testimonies, but none of us lives a perfect life. This is the reason every Christian should have a time of confession. As we saw in chapter 13, Jesus says that He must wash us so that we may have fellowship with Him. Too many Christians lose their fellowship with God because they think they are all right, but their words and their works are not consistent. This needs to be confessed.

Have you ever noticed that the Lord Jesus never appealed to His own mind and His own will to make a decision? "The words that I speak unto you I speak not of myself: but the Father that dwelleth in me, he doeth the works." When He spoke, it was the will of the Father. All His works were the will of the Father. So He tells Philip that when he heard the words of Jesus, he was hearing the words of the Father and, when he saw the works of Jesus, he was seeing the Father working through Jesus.

You will notice that Jesus has interruptions during His discourse. First it was Peter, then Thomas, and now Philip. But Jesus continues on in His discourse until verse 22 when He is again interrupted.

Believe me that I am in the Father, and the Father in me: or else believe me for the very works' sake [John 14:11].

Jesus says that if you can't believe Him because of His words, then believe Him because of His works. They should convince you.

Verily, verily, I say unto you, He that believeth on me, the works that I do shall he do also; and greater works than these shall he do: because I go unto my Father [John 14:12].

To understand this verse, I should call attention to the fact that the second word *works* is in italics which means that it is not in the better manuscripts but is put in by the translators to fill out the thought. To be accurate, it should read: "the works that I do shall he do also; and greater than these shall he do." When our Lord was down here on this earth, He performed tremendous works and miracles. These apostles to whom He spoke did the same things. They healed the sick and raised the dead. Yet Jesus says that those who believe on Him will do greater. What is the greater thing which they shall do?

Simon Peter, who had denied Him on the night He was arrested, preached a sermon on the Day of Pentecost and 3000 people became believers! I think of the men over the years who have invested their lives in winning men to Christ. I think of missionaries, such as George L. Mackey who went to Uganda. What a missionary he was! Preaching a crucified, risen, glorified, returning Savior so that a hearer may accept Christ and be born again is a greater miracle than healing the sick. Am I right? Which is better: to heal the soul or to heal the body? When Jesus Christ was on earth, He performed the miracle of raising the physical bodies of men, but we have the privilege of preaching Jesus Christ so that men, body and soul, may live eternally. The supreme accomplishment is to bring men and women into a right relationship with God.

How are these greater works done? "Because I go unto my Father." You see, it is *Christ* who is still working, but today He is working through human instrumentality. He works through frail human clay, human flesh. I am amazed that I can give a Bible message over the radio and there are people who turn to Christ. Friend, that is greater. If Jesus Christ were here speaking to people, it would be a great work. When Jesus Christ takes you and me and works through us to reach people, that is greater.

Have you noticed how often Jesus speaks of His Father? The Father is mentioned twenty times in this passage, and it is always the Lord Jesus who mentions Him.

And whatsoever ye shall ask in my name, that will I do, that the Father may be glorified in the Son.

If ye shall ask any thing in my name, I will do it [John 14:13–14].

He continues right on to say that these greater things are the result of prayer. Prayer evangelism is so neglected today. "Whatsoever ye shall ask in my name, that will I do."

These verses have been so misunderstood. A great many people have picked this up like a dog picks up a bone and runs with it. They say they prayed and God just didn't answer their prayer. I've had Christian people tell me that they took that verse at face value. They prayed and God didn't answer their prayer. They ask me what is wrong. I tell them that they are reading something into the verse that is not there at all. They need to keep on reading. This is all tied into one package.

If ye love me, keep my commandments [John 14:15].

Now let us consider what all three of these verses say. What does it mean to ask in the name of Christ? To pray in His Person means to be standing in His place. It means to be fully identified with Him, joined to Christ. It means that you and I are pleading the merits of His blessed Son when we stand before God. We have no standing of our own before God at all. He does not hear my prayer because I am Vernon McGee, and He does not hear your prayer because you are who you are. He hears our prayers when they are in the name of Christ. This is not just a little phrase that we tag on to the end of our prayer closing with "in Jesus' name." Praying in His name is presenting it in His merit and for His glory.

"That will I do, that the Father may be glorified in the Son." A prayer that will enable God to be glorified in the Son is the prayer that He will answer. So, when we pray in the name of Jesus and for the glory of God, we are not praying for something selfishly for ourselves. We are praying for Him. We are praying that the Father may be glorified in the Son.

Also it depends on our obedience to Christ. This promise is given to those who love Him, and the evidence of their love is the keeping of His commandments. Love will be demonstrated by obedience to Christ. An undisciplined Christian cannot say that he loves the Lord Jesus. How are you doing in that area, friend? Do you love Him? Are you keeping His commandments because you love Him today?

Dr. Harry Ironside was sitting on a platform with a young pastor during a meeting one night. A young lady entered the meeting and the pastor told him that she formerly had been an active leader among his members, then had begun to run with the world, and that this was the first time he had seen her in church in months. Dr. Ironside preached on this passage of Scripture that night. She was greatly incensed and came to see him after the meeting. "How dare you tell these people that if you ask anything in the name of Jesus, He will do it!" she fumrd. Dr. Ironside answered, "Why don't you sit down and tell me about it?" She told him that her father had been desperately ill some months before, and while the doctor was up in his room, she had knelt in the living room, claimed that promise, and prayed in Jesus' name for his recovery. When the doctor came down from the room, he told her that her father was dead. "Now," she said, "don't tell me that God keeps His promises!" Dr. Ironside said, "Did you read the next verse, 'If ye love me, keep my commandments'?" Then Dr. Ironside asked her what would happen if she found a check made out to someone else and tried to cash it by signing that name. She said "I would be a forger." So he referred her to this verse, "If ye love me, keep my commandments." Then he asked her, "Have you been doing that?" Instead of replying, she turned red. Then he explained that what she was trying to do was the same thing as trying to cash a check made out to somebody else. We all need to recognize, friend, that obedience to Him is the evidence of our love for Him, and this promise is given to those who love Him.

And I will pray the Father, and he shall give you another Comforter, that he may abide with you for ever;

Even the Spirit of truth; whom the world cannot receive, because it seeth him not, neither knoweth him: but ye know him; for he dwelleth with you, and shall be in you [John 14:16–17].

This is a unique fact of this age in which we are living. The Holy Spirit was here on earth before Pentecost, but on the Day of Pentecost He came to indwell believers. That was the thing which was new.

"Holy" and "Spirit" describe Him, but *Comforter* is His name, if He has a name. It is a very fitting name, as *com* means "along side of" and *fortis* means "strong." He is the strong One who abides with us forever.

He does not say that the world *would not* receive the Spirit of truth. He says the world *cannot* receive Him. Oh, if we could learn this! The Spirit of God can take the Word of God and open it to the believer, but the unsaved man must first believe in Jesus Christ as his Savior. The man of the world cannot see Him because He is seen and worshiped in spirit and truth. He is seen with the spiritual eye. It is only by the Spirit of God that these eyes and ears can be opened to understand the Word of God. The Holy Spirit is the teacher to lead and guide us into truth. Without Him, the Bible becomes a book of history, a book of facts. The Holy Spirit teaches the truths of the Bible. The Holy Spirit has been in the world, but Jesus says that now He "shall be in you."

I will not leave you comfortless: I will come to you [John 14:18].

The Greek word for *comfortless* is *orphanos* which means "orphans." Jesus says that He will not leave us orphans but will come to us in the person of the Holy Spirit.

Yet a little while, and the world seeth me no more; but ye see me: because I live, ye shall live also.

At that day ye shall know that I am in my Father, and ye in me, and I in you [John 14:19–20].

What is "that day?" It is the day you and I are living in. It is the day that began with Pentecost.

"Ye in me, and I in you" is the most profound statement in the Gospel of John or in the whole Bible. They are all monosyllabic words so that a little child can understand them; yet no philosopher can plumb the depths of their meaning. "You in Me"—that is salvation. To be saved means to be in Christ. That is why Peter says that we are saved by baptism. Baptism means identification, and it means to be identified with Christ. God sees everyone as either in Christ or out of Christ. You are either in Him by faith or you are out of Him with your sins still upon you. If you are in Christ, then God sees you in Christ, and His righteousness is your righteousness. You stand complete in Him. "I in you"—is sanctification. That is Christian living down here. Is Christ living in you? Paul says, "I am crucified with Christ: nevertheless I live; yet not I, but Christ liveth in me: and the life which I now live in the flesh I live by the faith of the Son of God, who loved me, and gave himself for me" (Gal. 2:20).

He that hath my commandments, and keepeth them, he it is that loveth me: and he that loveth me shall be loved of my Father, and I will love him, and will manifest myself to him [John 14:21].

Don't say that you love Christ if you are not obeying Him. He is making this very clear here. Jesus is going to manifest Himself to the one who loves Him. Don't think this will be a manifestation by a vision. Later He says that it is the Holy Spirit who will take the things of Jesus and show them to you. Where does He do this? In the Scriptures. That is where Jesus is manifested.

Judas saith unto him, not Iscariot, Lord, how is it that thou wilt manifest thyself unto us, and not unto the world? [John 14:22].

Judas is saying, "Lord, this is wonderful to be here and hear you say these things, but have you forgotten the world?" Here is the first missionary, by the way. The Lord Jesus answers him and His answer is the rest of the chapter.

Jesus answered and said unto him, If a man love me, he will keep my words: and my Father will love him, and we will come unto him, and make our abode with him.

He that loveth me not keepeth not my sayings: and the word which ye hear is not mine, but the Father's which sent me [John 14:23–24].

The way the world is going to find out about the Lord Jesus is through us, and obedience is imperative. Profession is not worth anything. Church membership is not really worth anything. The issue is our love for Him evidenced by our obedience. How about your love for Him? Does it discipline you? Is He real to you? These are the things that are important.

These things have I spoken unto you, being yet present with you.

But the Comforter, which is the Holy Ghost, whom the Father will send in my name, he shall teach you all things, and

bring all things to your remembrance, whatsoever I have said unto you [John 14:25–26].

Jesus hasn't forgotten the world. In fact, He is thinking of the world. He has called these apostles into the Upper Room and has given them the truth so that they might take it to the world in the power of the Holy Spirit. The only way the truth can be given to the world is through these men. John was one of those men, and he has written this Gospel of John for us in the power of the Holy Spirit. Jesus assures them that the Holy Spirit will teach them all things and bring all things to their remembrance. It is evident that He did just that.

Peace I leave with you, my peace I give unto you: not as the world giveth, give I unto you. Let not your heart be troubled, neither let it be afraid [John 14:27].

This verse takes us back to the beginning of this chapter. It is His final word of comfort. The peace He is talking about here is not the peace of sins forgiven. This is the glorious, wonderful peace that comes to the heart of those who are fully yielded to the Lord Jesus Christ. It is the peace of heart and mind of those who are in the will of God.

Ye have heard how I said unto you, I go away, and come again unto you. If ye loved me, ye would rejoice, because I said, I go unto the Father: for my Father is greater than I.

And now I have told you before it come to pass, that, when it is come to pass, ye might believe.

Hereafter I will not talk much with you: for the prince of this world cometh, and hath nothing in me.

But that the world may know that I love the Father; and as the Father gave me commandment, even so I do. Arise, let us go hence [John 14:28–31].

He tells them they should rejoice that He is going away because of the wonderful blessings that will come to them. Jesus Christ was going back to the Father and then He would send the Comforter to them.

He tells them He cannot walk and talk very much more with them, and He didn't—in a few hours He would be arrested and His disciples scattered. The prince of this world was coming. Jesus Christ would have another siege with Satan, which I believe took place in the Garden of Gethsemane. After that, He would go to the cross for the sins of the world. After His ascension, the Comforter would come to indwell believers.

CHAPTER 15

***THEME:** Jesus is genuine Vine; disciples are branches*

This fifteenth chapter is a part of the Upper Room Discourse, although our Lord probably did not speak it in the Upper Room. At least the assumption is that He did not, because the last statement in chapter 14 is, "Arise, let us go hence." Somewhere between the Upper Room and the Garden of Gethsemane our Lord spoke the words found in chapters 15 and 16, then prayed the prayer, recorded in chapter 17, as He entered the garden.

It has been the belief of many expositors that our Lord gave this chapter in a discourse down in the Valley of Kidron or on the side of the Mount of Olives, because we know that at that time there was a vineyard in that area which covered that valley. We also know that it was full moon because it was the time of the Passover. He may well have spoken these words as they walked through the vineyard. It would have been an appropriate place.

Another suggestion has been made by several English expositors—and it is the one I accept—that that night He went by the temple, following the Law as He so meticulously did. The gates would have been open during the Passover nights. Those beautiful gates of the temple were actually a tourist attraction. They had been forged in Greece, floated across the Hellespont, then brought to Jerusalem, and placed in Herod's temple there. The gates were made of bronze and wrought into them was a golden vine. That the vine symbolizes the nation Israel is apparent from the following verses: "Thou hast brought a vine out of Egypt: thou hast cast out the heathen, and planted it. Thou preparedst room before it, and didst cause it to take deep root, and it filled the land" (Ps. 80:8–9). "Now will I sing to my wellbeloved a song of my beloved touching his vineyard. My wellbeloved hath a vineyard in a very fruitful hill. . . . For the vineyard of the LORD of hosts is the house of Israel, and the men of Judah his pleasant plant: and he looked for judgment, but behold oppression; for righteousness, but behold a cry" (Isa. 5:1, 7). "Yet I had planted thee a noble vine, wholly a right seed: how then art thou turned into the degenerate plant of a strange vine unto me?" (Jer. 2:21). "Israel is an empty vine, he bringeth forth fruit unto himself . . ." (Hos. 10:1). It is clear that the vine is a picture of the nation Israel.

Now, friend, our Lord is saying one of the most revolutionary things these men have ever heard. It sounds familiar to us today, but it was strange to their ears. Listen to Him.

JESUS IS GENUINE VINE; DISCIPLES ARE BRANCHES

I am the true vine, and my Father is the husbandman [John 15:1].

The word for *true* here is *alēthinos*, which means "genuine." A thing can be true as over against error and falsehood, or a thing can be true over against that which is a counterfeit. The latter is the way it is used here. We have had this word used in the same way previously in the Gospel of John. John the Baptist was a reflecting light, but Jesus Christ is the *true* Light. Moses gave bread in the wilderness, but Jesus Christ is the *true* Bread. So here Jesus is saying, "I am the true vine, the genuine vine."

These disciples had Jewish concepts and their thought patterns had been governed by the Old Testament. He is telling them now that the nation Israel is not the genuine vine. Their identification with the Jewish nation and the Jewish religion is not the essential thing. "*I* am the genuine vine." The important thing now is for the disciples to be related to Jesus Christ. That was revolutionary!

Our Lord used a marvelous figure of speech, and He made it very clear that it is not your identification with a religion or a ceremony or an organization that is essential. We are to be identified with Christ! We are in Christ by the baptism of the Holy Spirit the moment we trust Christ as our Savior and are born again as a child of God.

"My Father is the husbandman." This, too, is a startling word. In the Old Testament passages and in the parables, God is the owner of the vineyard. Here He is the keeper, the farmer, the One who takes care of the vineyard. Jesus is the genuine Vine, and the Father takes care of Him.

In the Old Testament it is prophesied that the Lord Jesus would grow up before Him as a tender plant and as a root out of the dry ground. Think how often the Father intervened to save Jesus from the Devil who wished to slay Him. The Father is the One who cared for the Vine, and He will care for the branches, too.

The branches must be joined to the Vine. For what purpose? For fruit-bearing. There are three words or phrases which are very important, and we will pick them up as we go along.

Every branch in me that beareth not fruit he taketh away: and every branch that beareth fruit, he purgeth it, that it may bring forth more fruit [John 15:2].

"In me," that is, in Christ, is what it means to be saved. There are tremendous words like propitiation, reconciliation, and redemption that cover particular phases of salvation, but the entire spectrum of salvation is in the phrase "in Christ." There are only two groups of people: those who are in Christ and those who are not in Christ. How do you get "in Christ"? By the new birth. When you trust Christ as Savior, you become a child of God through faith. You are born again by the Spirit of God. The Holy Spirit does something else: He not only indwells you, but He also baptizes you. That is what puts every believer into the body of Christ—"every branch in me."

This passage is directed to believers, to those who are already in Christ. Jesus is not talking about *how* a person gets saved. He is not actually talking about salvation at all in this passage. Rather, He is talking about fruit-bearing, and that is the next word we wish to mark. Fruit is mentioned six times in the first ten verses. We will find as we go further that there are three degrees of fruit-bearing: fruit, more fruit, and much fruit. The whole theme here is fruit-bearing.

"Every branch in me that beareth not fruit he taketh away." Where does He take it? He takes it away from the place of fruit-bearing.

Listen how He describes this in verse 6. (We will come back to verses 3–5 later.)

> **If a man abide not in me, he is cast forth as a branch, and is withered; and men gather them, and cast them into the fire, and they are burned [John 15:6].**

"Oh-oh," somebody says, "that sounds as if you lose your salvation." No, remember this passage is not talking about salvation but about fruit-bearing. It is talking about that which is the *result* of being saved.

First of all, what is the fruit? I do not believe that the fruit mentioned here refers to soul-winning, as so many people seem to think. I believe soul-winning is a by-product but not the fruit itself. The fruit is the fruit of the Spirit. "But the fruit of the Spirit is love, joy, peace, longsuffering, gentleness, goodness, faith, meekness, temperance . . ." (Gal. 5:22–23). This is fruit in the life of the believer. Abiding in Christ will produce effectual prayer, perpetual fruit, and celestial joy:

> **If ye abide in me, and my words abide in you, ye shall ask what ye will, and it shall be done unto you [John 15:7].**

That is prayer effectual.

> **Herein is my Father glorified, that ye bear much fruit; so shall ye be my disciples [John 15:8].**

This is fruit perpetual.

> **These things have I spoken unto you, that my joy might remain in you, and that your joy might be full [John 15:11].**

That is joy celestial.

If a person has such fruit in his life, he will be bringing men into the presence of God by his very life. That, of course, makes soul-winning a by-product.

"Every branch in me that beareth not fruit he taketh away." He wants fruit in our lives. If a branch does not bear fruit, how does He take it away? One of the ways He removes it is by taking such a person away from the place of fruit-bearing. I know many who have been set aside today because they were no longer effective for God. There are ministers like that and there are lay people like that. Removing such a branch does not mean they lose their salvation, but they are taken away from the place of fruit-bearing.

Sometimes this removing from the place of fruit-bearing is by death, physical death. I believe this is what John means in 1 John 5:16 when he says that there is a sin unto death. A Christian can go on sinning until God will remove him from the place of fruit-bearing by death. Ananias and Sapphira were removed by death from the early church, which was a holy church, a fruit-bearing church. These two liars could not stay in that church. I'm afraid they would be very comfortable in some of our churches today, but God would not permit them to remain in the early church.

"Every branch that beareth fruit, he purgeth it, that it may bring forth more fruit." The Greek word is *kathairō*, which means "to cleanse." Some people consider the purging to be pruning, and He does that too, but it really means to cleanse.

There is no doubt that the Lord does some pruning. He moves into our lives and takes out those things that offend, and sometimes it hurts. He removes things that are hindering us. I can speak to that subject and confess that it hurts. I think the Lord was pruning me when He permitted me to have a cancer and allowed it to stay in my body. He prunes out that which hinders our bearing fruit.

One of the reasons so many of God's children get hurt by this method of pruning is that they get so far from God, so far out of fellowship. The closer we are to God, the less it will hurt. I can remember playing hookey from school when I was a boy. We left our books at school and took off for the creek and went fishing. Although we didn't catch any fish, we had a lot of fun. We came in about the time school was out to get our books before going home so our parents wouldn't suspect that we had played hookey. The principal of the school figured we would do this, and when we walked into the room, he walked in right after us and said, "Boys, I'm glad to see you." We had to go to his office and wait while he got his switches. (We'd been through this before.) One of the fellows with me had been through this many times, and he gave me some of the best advice I've ever had. He said that when the principal started switching, we should move a step closer each time instead of backing off. The closer we were to him the less it would hurt. So the first time he hit me, instead of stepping back, I moved right in close to him, and I got so close I was where his fist was, and he wasn't hurting me at all. I have learned that is really good advice when the Lord chastens us also. Whom the Lord *loveth* he chasteneth. His chastening is not a sign that He is against us; He is trying to get fruit out of our lives. We tend to complain and move away from Him, but if we draw close to Him, it won't hurt nearly so much.

However, the "purging" in this verse literally means cleansing. When I was in the Bethlehem area, I saw that in their vineyards they let the grapevines grow on the ground, and they propped them up with a rock. Because the grapes get dirty and pests get on them, they actually go around and wash the grapes before they get ripe. So the Lord comes to our lives; He lifts us up and washes us so that we may bear more fruit. How does He do this?

Now ye are clean through the word which I have spoken unto you [John 15:3].

"Ye are clean through the word." The purging is accomplished by the Word of God. The cleansing power of the Word of God is a wonderful thing. We hear so much today about modern wash-day miracles, but I've never found them to be as miraculous as the claims made for them. The only true wash-day miracle is the cleansing power of the Word of God. "Seeing ye have purified your souls in obeying the truth through the Spirit unto unfeigned love of the brethren, see that ye love one another with a pure heart fervently: Being born again, not of corruptible seed, but of incorruptible, by the word of God, which liveth and abideth for ever" (1 Pet. 1:22–23). We were born again by the Word of God, washed from our sins. Then in our walk down here we get dirty and need the Word of God to cleanse us continually. That is one reason to study the Bible—to be cleansed. "Wherewithal shall a young man cleanse his way? by taking heed thereto according to thy word" (Ps. 119:9).

There are light views among believers today that you can live any kind of life so long as you are fundamental in your belief of salvation by the grace of God. Believe me, God uses the Word of God to reveal to us when we are not walking according to His will. The real test which reveals whether a person is genuine in his relationship to God is whether he is studying the Word of God and whether he is letting it have its way in his life! God intends for us to be obedient to His Word.

"Before I was afflicted I went astray: but now have I kept thy word" (Ps. 119:67). "It is good for me that I have been afflicted; that I might learn thy statutes" (Ps. 119:71). My friend, He uses affliction to bring us to the Word of God that you and I might be made serviceable to Him. I don't think that you will ever be clean before God if you don't study the Word of God. I believe that the people who are really dangerous are the ones who are as active as termites in our churches but who are reluctant to study the Word of God. I consider them the most dangerous element against the Word of God and the cause of Christ in this world. My friend, we need to study the Word of God and apply it to our lives.

Abide in me, and I in you. As the branch cannot bear fruit of itself, except it abide in the vine; no more can ye, except ye abide in me [John 15:4].

We have come to the third word I want you to mark, which is *abide*. To abide in Christ means constant communion with Him all the time. We have just talked of the cleansing power of the Word of God. That is a part of abiding. We must be cleansed daily. There is a story about Spurgeon who stopped in the middle of the street, removed his hat, and prayed. One of his deacons saw this and asked him about it. Mr. Spurgeon said that a cloud had come between him and his Lord and he wanted to remove it immediately; he had stopped to confess his sinful thought. We need to confess our sins to the Lord to abide in Him, to stay in constant communion with Him.

Also to abide in Him, we are to keep His commandments.

If ye keep my commandments, ye shall abide in my love; even as I have kept my Father's commandments, and abide in his love.

Ye are my friends, if ye do whatsoever I command you [John 15:10, 14].

In our hymn books are songs like "Jesus Is a Friend of Mine" and "There's not a Friend like the Lowly Jesus." Friend, let me say this kindly. There is no lowly Jesus today but a glorified Christ at God's right hand. Calling Jesus a friend of mine is sentimental and really wrong. If I would say that the President of the United States is my friend, I bring him down to my level. If he says that I am his friend, that is wonderful. Listen to what Jesus says. "Ye are my friend, if ye do whatsoever I command you." We don't need all this sentimental trash today. We need some honest heart-searching. Are we doing what Jesus has commanded us to do? Obedience is essential to abiding.

As the Father hath loved me, so have I loved you: continue ye in my love [John 15:9].

Abiding is a continuing communion. That is the relationship of branch and vine. I have a 72′ x 123′ ranch here in California on which grow four avocado trees, three orange trees, and one tangerine tree. I have never had to say to the branches that they should abide in the tree or we wouldn't have any fruit. I've never been up in the night to inspect them or come home unexpectedly and found the branches running around away from the tree. They abide and they bear fruit. You think I am being ridiculous. However, many Christians think they can live like the Devil all week and on Saturday night, then come in and serve the Lord on Sunday. I happen to know because I tried that for years. My friend, we must be in constant communion with Him to bear fruit. That means when you wake in the morning, when you are at your desk in the office, when you are driving your car on the streets, you are abiding in constant communion.

I am the vine, ye are the branches: He that abideth in me, and I in him, the same bringeth forth much fruit: for without me ye can do nothing [John 15:5].

Because we have free will, we can break fellowship with God by allowing sin in our life, by stepping out of the will of God, or by worldliness. He wants us to abide so that we bring forth much fruit. You will notice here that there is a similarity to the parable of the sower. Remember that some of the seed fell on good ground and brought forth thirtyfold—that is fruit. Some of the seed brought forth sixty—that is more fruit. Some of the seed brought forth an hundredfold—that is much fruit. God wants us to bear much fruit.

If a man abide not in me, he is cast forth as a branch, and is withered; and men gather them, and cast them into the fire, and they are burned [John 15:6].

Let me say again that this is talking about our fruit-bearing, the product of our salvation. It is not talking about how we are to be saved. Paul uses another illustration for this same thing: "For other foundation can no man lay than that is laid, which is Jesus Christ. Now if any man build upon this foundation gold, silver, precious stones, wood, hay, stubble; Every man's work shall be made manifest: for the day shall declare it, because it shall be revealed by fire; and the fire shall try every man's work of what sort it is." (This is talking about the works of the believers, the fruit in the life of a believer. Fire will purify gold and silver and precious stones and draw off the dross. Wood, hay, and stubble will go up in smoke. That is the same as our verse which says the works will be cast into the fire and burned.) "If any man's work abide which he hath built thereupon, he shall receive a reward" (1 Cor. 3:11–14). I believe that rewards will be given only for the fruit in our lives—and we don't produce the fruit; *He* produces the fruit when we abide in Him.

A branch that is not abiding in Christ "is cast forth as a branch, and is withered; and men gather them, and cast them into the fire, and they are burned." This is amplified by 1 Corinthians 3:15: "If any man's work shall be burned, he shall suffer loss: but he himself shall be saved; yet so as by fire." He may get to heaven smelling as if he had been bought at a fire sale, but he will not lose his salvation.

One of the saddest things is that today the average Christian believes that normal Christian living is failure. They think that bearing much fruit is entirely out of the question and are willing to live on a low plane hoping to produce just a little fruit. Remember that the Lord wants us to produce much fruit.

If ye abide in me, and my words abide in you, ye shall ask what ye will, and it shall be done unto you.

Herein is my Father glorified, that ye bear much fruit; so shall ye be my disciples [John 15:7–8].

This is a marvelous prayer promise, but notice the condition. "If ye abide in me, and my words abide in you" means to be obedient to Him. Then we will have effectual prayer. The whole purpose of the abiding and of the praying is that the Father may have glory. This eliminates prayer for selfish reasons. The issue is fruit-bearing. God is glorified when we do bear fruit.

As the Father hath loved me, so have I loved you: continue ye in my love.

If ye keep my commandments, ye shall abide in my love; even as I have kept my Father's commandments, and abide in his love.

These things have I spoken unto you, that my joy might remain in you, and that your joy might be full [John 15:9–11].

The Lord wants us to have a good time. One of the fruits of the Spirit is to have joy in your life. I am mortally afraid of super-pious Christians who have no humor in their lives, yet walk around with a Bible under their arms. A fruit-bearing Christian will have a lot of fun in this life. There will be fun in going to a Bible study; there will be fun in serving the Lord. A life in fellowship with Christ is a joyous life.

This is my commandment, That ye love one another, as I have loved you [John 15:12].

Remember He is talking to believers in this discourse. We are to love each other as He has loved us! It is sad to see Christians in our churches who tear down each other and gossip about one another. The Spirit of God is not working in such a situation. One can have Bible teaching and still reject this commandment of our Lord. To love as He has loved us is putting it on a very high plane. Only the Spirit of God can produce such love in our lives.

Greater love hath no man than this, that a man lay down his life for his friends [John 15:13].

There is the test.

Ye are my friends, if ye do whatsoever I command you [John 15:14].

The Christian life is not a hit-and-miss proposition. The Christian life is following His instructions, and the instructions are clear. If you follow these instructions, you will bear fruit. He laid down His life for us; He asks us to obey Him. He is our friend because He died for us. We are His friends when we keep His commandments.

He doesn't ask all of us to die for Him. Someone once asked Dwight L. Moody whether he had "dying grace." Mr. Moody replied that he didn't have it, but when He needed it, the Lord would give it to him. And He did.

Henceforth I call you not servants; for the servant knoweth not what his lord doeth: but I have called you friends; for all things that I have heard of my Father I have made known unto you.

Ye have not chosen me, but I have chosen you, and ordained you, that ye should go and bring forth fruit, and that your fruit should remain: that whatsoever ye shall ask of the Father in my name, he may give it you [John 15:15–16].

We are the friends of Jesus if we do whatsoever He has commanded us. Now He tells us that He has opened up His heart to us. God wants to reveal Himself to us. Remember how He searched out Abraham to reveal His plan to him because Abraham was His friend. Now Jesus tells us that He has revealed the things of God to us. That is what a friend does. How many people can you go to and open up your heart? One of the things that should characterize a believer is that you could go to him and tell him your problems and get understanding and help and encouragement from him. This is how we are to love one another.

Now, notice, "Ye have not chosen me, but I have chosen you." A great many people do not like the doctrine of election, but it is wonderful and practical. Many a discouraged Christian has cast himself on the Lord saying, "Lord, you called me and chose me and I'm your child." Dr. G. Campbell Morgan said, "He chose me; therefore I am His responsibility." That is trust!

This little crowd of disciples is going to scatter in a few hours. The Shepherd will be crucified, and the sheep will scatter. At such an hour Jesus tells them, "Ye have not chosen me, but I have chosen you."

A preacher, who had been converted late in life, had been guilty of stealing before he was saved. After he had just started preaching about His Savior and was still a new Christian, he passed a hen house on his way home from church one night. It was a great temptation for him, but he stopped and prayed, "Lord, your property is in danger, and I don't mean the chickens." It is wonderful to call upon the Lord like that.

His great purpose is that we should produce fruit, not just passing fruit, but fruit that will remain. It must all be in His will. If we abide in Him, then we can ask in His name. Answers to our prayers are a pretty good barometer of our spirituality.

He climaxes this section on fruit-bearing by mentioning again that we should love one another.

These things I command you, that ye love one another [John 15:17].

This should be the relationship of believers. There is also a relationship with the world, and now He goes into that subject.

If the world hate you, ye know that it hated me before it hated you.

If ye were of the world, the world would love his own: but because ye are not of

the world, but I have chosen you out of the world, therefore the world hateth you [John 15:18–19].

Notice what will happen if you are a child of God. The world will hate you. I believe that a Christian's popularity can be an indication of how he is representing Christ to the world. I do not believe a Christian can be popular in the world. No Christian has any right to be more popular than Jesus was. Beware of a compromising position in order to be popular. The world will not love a real child of God. The world will love you if you are of the world. You don't have to act oddly or be super-pious. The world will hate you if you are a child of God. This is difficult, especially for young people who want so much to be popular. Let's tell our young people what the Lord says. They are not going to be popular with the world if they are the children of God.

Unfortunately, there are folk in the church today who are not honestly born again, and they will also hate you if you are a child of God. They will hate the preacher if he is true to the Word of God. May I say again, beware of the Christian who is popular with the world.

Remember the word that I said unto you, The servant is not greater than his lord. If they have persecuted me, they will also persecute you; if they have kept my saying, they will keep yours also.

But all these things will they do unto you for my name's sake, because they know not him that sent me.

If I had not come and spoken unto them, they had not had sin: but now they have no cloak for their sin [John 15:20–22].

Don't try to be greater than your Lord. The servant should not be more popular than the Master. Just keep giving out the Word. Those who persecute have two problems: they do not know the Father, and they do not want their sins revealed. Jesus Christ turned the light of heaven upon the souls of men. Whenever one turns on a light, things begin to happen. The rats and snakes and bugs and lizards hate the light and they all run for cover. They will hate the one who turns on the light, too, by the way. Jesus says, "They hated me without a cause." There is no cause for hate in Jesus. The cause is in the sinful hearts of men.

He that hateth me hateth my Father also [John 15:23].

This is an important verse. The world does not hate their *idea* of God, as some vague Someone out yonder. It is Christ they hate. Jesus says when a man hates Him, he is hating God the Father also. You can say you believe in God and be popular. The real test is your relationship and attitude toward Jesus Christ. You cannot be popular and believe in the Lord Jesus Christ, because He is the One who is hated.

If I had not done among them the works which none other man did, they had not had sin: but now have they both seen and hated both me and my Father.

But this cometh to pass, that the word might be fulfilled that is written in their law, They hated me without a cause [John 15:24–25].

Some wag has said, "God created man in His image and now man is creating God in his image." That is the kind of God they want today and the kind of God they think is running the universe. Jesus quotes this as a fulfillment of Psalms 35:19 and 69:4 when He says they hated Him without a cause. They hate Jesus Christ because they have created a false god who is not the God of the Bible.

But when the Comforter is come, whom I will send unto you from the Father, even the Spirit of truth, which proceedeth from the Father, he shall testify of me:

And ye also shall bear witness, because ye have been with me from the beginning [John 15:26–27].

The Holy Spirit bears testimony concerning Christ. If the Lord Jesus Christ is real to you, that is the work of the Holy Spirit. One way to tell whether the Spirit of God is working is whether Christ is being glorified. If the Lord Jesus is not as real to you as you wish He were, ask the Spirit of God to do a work in your heart. We need the reality of Christ in our hearts and lives.

Jesus told these men that they would bear witness to Him, and they certainly did that. It is the witness of John concerning the Lord Jesus Christ that we are studying right now. No one but the apostles could bear such a witness because they had been with Jesus from the beginning.

CHAPTER 16

***THEME:** Jesus will send Holy Spirit during His absence*

This chapter concludes the Upper Room Discourse. We learned in the preceding chapter that His own should love one another. This is a real rebuke to us. It is a rebuke that He must command us to do that. It is a rebuke because it shows that we are not nearly as attractive as we think we are. We need help supernaturally to enable us to love one another. Then He told us that we are to identify with Him which will cause the world to hate us.

Also He told His disciples that if He had not come, they would not have known sin. He did not mean that they did not have their own sins but, that since He had come, their personal sins were as nothing compared to the immeasurable guilt of rejecting the Savior of the world and the Lord of glory.

There are not only degrees of rewards in heaven, but there are degrees of punishment in hell. The person today who hears about Jesus Christ and turns his back on Him is in the same category as Judas Iscariot who in the presence of Christ turned his back upon Him. To reject Him is the greatest sin of all. Jesus warns them about this in the coming chapter.

JESUS WILL SEND HOLY SPIRIT DURING HIS ABSENCE

The chapter begins with Jesus still talking about the hatred of the world.

> **These things have I spoken unto you, that ye should not be offended [John 16:1].**

What things? The things mentioned in chapter 15.

> **They shall put you out of the synagogues: yea, the time cometh, that whosoever killeth you will think that he doeth God service.**

> **And these things will they do unto you, because they have not known the Father, nor me [John 16:2–3].**

The Lord didn't want the apostles to be offended, that is, *scandalized* at what would happen to them. It is characteristic of founders of organizations, and especially of religions, to attempt to present a glorious future for their organizations. The method of the world is to build up the wonderful benefits and to play down the hardships and disadvantages and privations and sacrifices. How different our Lord is!

While it is true that in chapter 14 our Lord told us that He is going to prepare a place for us and that He will receive us unto Himself, He also makes it very clear that if we are going to follow Him down here, it means to forsake all. He said that foxes have holes and birds have nests, but He didn't have a place to lay His head. He said that if we are going to follow Him, we must take up our cross—not *His* cross—*our* own cross, and follow Him. If we suffer with Him down here, we shall reign with Him up there. He was despised and rejected. He was a Man of Sorrows and acquainted with grief. He said His followers are going to be *in* the world but not *of* the world and that the world will hate them. He made all of that very clear. He never said that it would be easy for His followers down here.

The professing church, instead of taking the position of Christ, has gone out into the world, boasting that they are going to convert the world. They, of course, haven't done it in over nineteen hundred years. In their attempt they always try to popularize religion, make it very attractive to the world. You will find that today there are churches using all kinds of devices to attract the ungodly. Today music has come down to the level of the world. They say, "We have to do this to win the world." Who told them they were going to win the world? I'm not talking about liberal churches now—they went off the track years ago—I am talking about fundamental churches. Today fundamental churches are going off the track. In them you will find *enemies* of the Word of God! Although they wouldn't dare attack the Bible, they level their attack against the man who is preaching the Word of God.

There are tragic stories everywhere. I know a deacon in a church who has already destroyed three preachers. One man left broken in health, another simply left the ministry, and the third resigned. I know a minister who is selling second-hand cars. He says he would rather deal with second-hand cars than with second-hand Christians. Friend, if you stand for the Word of God, you will find that the world won't love you. You will experience the hatred that Christ experienced. "These things have I spoken unto you, that ye should not be offended." He is warning them ahead of time in order to strengthen them and let them know what is coming. He loves them right on through to the very end, and He lets them know that He will be with them and that He understands what they are going through.

He knew they would have moments when they would be offended because of Him. He knew that Peter would deny Him that very night. He told His disciples what would happen in order to encourage them and to let them know that He would sustain them through it all. He forewarned them to establish their responsibility to God.

"They shall put you out of the synagogues" means excommunication.

In that day to be excommunicated was the worst that could happen to a religious Jew. It would cost these men to stand for the Lord Jesus Christ. The religious Jews would cast them out. My friend, I'm very candid to say again that if you are standing for Christ, it is going to cost you something.

Jesus again traces the source of the hatred. Because they do not know the Father, they do not know the Lord Jesus Christ. Also this is why the world hates the Word of God. This is why the world hates the genuine believer.

But these things have I told you, that when the time shall come, ye may remember that I told you of them. And these things I said not unto you at the beginning, because I was with you [John 16:4].

He is letting them know what is coming and He is training them for what is to come. The Lord always prepares us, friend. During my years of being a pastor, I have learned that this is God's method. I have learned in my own experience and by watching others that the Lord trains and prepares us for that which lies ahead.

But now I go my way to him that sent me; and none of you asketh me, Whither goest thou? [John 16:5].

It is true that Simon Peter had asked Him where He was going, but Peter had asked the question of a little child. He is saying that none of them has really discerned what is going to take place. None of them has asked intelligently, with spiritual perception.

But because I have said these things unto you, sorrow hath filled your heart [John 16:6].

These men were letting the fact that He was going to leave them absolutely overwhelm them with sorrow. Friend, that is something which Christians today need to avoid. Many Christians let one experience embitter them. They experience some disappointment in an individual or in a church and are overwhelmed by sorrow and turn from God. Some people won't darken the door of a church because they are bitter over some incident in the past. Others who have lost loved ones remain constantly in mourning. This is not the way it should be. We are not to be overcome by sorrow.

Nevertheless I tell you the truth; It is expedient for you that I go away: for if I go not away, the Comforter will not come unto you; but if I depart, I will send him unto you [John 16:7].

"It is expedient for you that I go away"—in other words, it is better for you. Why was it best for the Lord Jesus to leave? I can suggest several reasons and I'm sure you can think of more. One of the reasons is this: His purpose in coming to this world was to die—". . . the Son of man came not to be ministered unto, but to minister, and to give his life a ransom for many" (Mark 10:45). When this was accomplished, He went back to the Father because He had finished the work He was sent to do. Then, there is another reason: when He came to this earth, He took upon Himself our humanity. God is omnipresent, but Jesus limited Himself by becoming a man. That means that, when He was in Galilee, He could not be down in Bethany. Remember that Mary and Martha reminded Him of that when they said that, if He had been there, their brother would not have died. In other words, if the Lord Jesus were in the world today in His human body, He couldn't be here where I am and with you where you are at the same time.

Therefore, He tells them He will send the Holy Spirit to them. The Holy Spirit will be in all places. He is right with me today and He is with you today. Jesus says this is better. He will send the Comforter, the Paraclete, and He will come to us and dwell in us.

When the Holy Spirit comes, He will perform several ministries, one of which He mentions here:

And when he is come, he will reprove the world of sin, and of righteousness, and of judgment:

Of sin, because they believe not on me;

Of righteousness, because I go to my Father, and ye see me no more;

Of judgment, because the prince of this world is judged [John 16:8–11].

The Greek word for "reprove" is *elegchō* which means "to convict." I counted that word used in "The Trial of Socrates," as recorded by Plato, and found it twenty-three times. It is a legal term. When the Holy Spirit is come, He will convict the world in the way a judge or a prosecuting attorney presents evidence to bring a conviction. The Spirit of God wants to present evidence in your heart and in my heart to bring us to a place of conviction, and that, of course, means a place of decision. There must be a conviction before we can turn in faith and trust to Jesus Christ.

In the present ministry of the Holy Spirit in the world, He will convict the world of three things: sin, righteousness, and judgment. Our Lord explains for us what that sin means. "Sin, because they believe not on me." What is the greatest sin in all the world? Murder? No. Who are the greatest sinners in this age? We've had some rascals, haven't we? Every age has had rascals. We might point out Hitler, or Stalin, or Karl Marx, or the Mafia. Well, who is the greatest sinner today? I want to say to you very carefully that *you* could be the greatest sinner living today. You may say, "Now wait a minute, preacher, you can't say that about me! I'm no rascal; I'm a law-abiding citizen." The question is this: Have you accepted Christ? Unbelief is a state and there is no remedy if you refuse to trust Christ. "Of sin, because they believe not on me." If you do not trust Him, you are lost. It is just as simple as that. It is just as important as that. This is a decision that every man must make. The man today, whoever he is, if he is rejecting Jesus Christ, is, in the sight of God, the greatest sinner. Remember that Jesus said, "If I had not come and spoken unto them, they had not had sin: but now they have no cloak for their sin" (John 15:22). Everyone who has ever heard the gospel is responsible for his decision concerning Jesus Christ. To reject Christ is sin.

Secondly, He will convict the world of righteousness. Jesus Christ was delivered for our offenses and was raised again for our justification (see Rom. 4:25). Jesus Christ returned to the Father because He had completed His work here. When He died on the cross, He died a judgment death. He took my guilt and your guilt and He died in our place. He was delivered for our offenses. But He was raised for our justification. He was raised from the dead that you and I might not only have our sins subtracted, but so that we might have His righteousness added. That is very important because you and I need righteousness. It is not enough to have our sins forgiven. We cannot stand in God's presence if we are nothing more than pardoned criminals. Christ has made over to us *His* righteousness. That is the righteousness Paul spoke of: ". . . that I may win Christ, And be found in him, not having mine own righteousness, which is of the law, but that which is through the faith of Christ, the righteousness which is of God by faith" (Phil. 3:8–9). He not only subtracts our sin, but He adds His righteousness. If we are to have any standing before God, we must be in Christ and He is our righteousness. Either we have as much right in heaven as Christ Himself has, or we have no right there at all. He was delivered for our offenses, and He was raised again for our justification (righteousness).

Thirdly, He convicts the world of judgment. Does this mean that judgment is coming some day? No, not in this verse. "Of judgment, because the prince of this world is judged." The prince of this world, Satan, has already been judged. It is difficult for a great many believers to understand that we live in a judged world. One hears people say that they'll take their chances. They act as if they are on trial. My friend, you are not on trial. God has already declared you a lost sinner, and He has already judged you—"For the wages of sin is death; but the gift of God is eternal life through Jesus Christ our Lord" (Rom. 6:23). We live in a world that has already been judged and is like the man waiting in death row for his execution. The judgment against all of us is "Guilty" because all our own righteousnesses are as filthy rags in the sight of God. If we had to stand before God in our own filthy rags, we would not only be ashamed of ourselves, but we would also see how guilty we are.

Remember that Paul reasoned with old Felix concerning judgment to come. That frightened him. Today many people don't like to hear about judgment, and they resent it a great deal. The lost world hates many things about God: for instance, His omnipotence. They don't like the fact that it is His universe and He is running it His way. They don't like it that God saves by grace and that man has already been declared lost. These are the three things of which the Holy Spirit convicts the world today.

I have yet many things to say unto you, but ye cannot bear them now.

Howbeit when he, the Spirit of truth, is come, he will guide you into all truth:

for he shall not speak of himself; but whatsoever he shall hear, that shall he speak: and he will shew you things to come.

He shall glorify me: for he shall receive of mine, and shall shew it unto you [John 16:12–14].

We don't know it all. We are to keep growing in grace and in the knowledge of Him. How can we do it? Just reading the Bible is not the complete answer; the Holy Spirit must be our Teacher as we read.

The Spirit of God is the Spirit of Truth. He will lead and guide you into all truth. He guided the apostles just as the Lord said He would, and we find these truths in the Epistles. The Spirit of God came to these men at Pentecost, and He guided them in the truth both in their preaching and in their writing.

We can see how this was fulfilled in the apostles. The ministry of the Holy Spirit has been to complete the teaching of the Lord Jesus Christ. The Epistles glorify Christ and show Him as the Head of the church. They speak of His coming again to establish His kingdom. The Epistles are the unfolding of the person and ministry of Christ. They also tell of things to come and certainly the Book of Revelation does this.

Notice the seven steps that are here: (1) The Holy Spirit, the Spirit of Truth, has come; (2) He will guide you into all truth; (3) He will not speak of Himself; (4) He shall speak whatsoever He shall hear; (5) He will show you things to come; (6) He shall glorify Jesus; and (7) He shall receive of mine and show it unto you.

Since we have been told these steps, we have a way of testing what we hear and read. I listened to a man on a radio program saying, "We are having a Holy Ghost revival; the Holy Ghost is working; the Holy Ghost is doing this and that." The minute he said all those things, I knew the Holy Ghost was not working. Why? Because the Lord Jesus made it very clear that the Holy Ghost will not speak of Himself. Then how can you tell when the Holy Spirit is working? He will glorify Christ. My friend, when in a meeting or a Bible study you suddenly get a glimpse of the Lord Jesus and He becomes wonderful, very real, and meaningful to you, that is the working of the Holy Spirit. Jesus said, "He shall glorify *me*."

All things that the Father hath are mine: therefore said I, that he shall take of mine, and shall shew it unto you [John 16:15].

Again the Lord Jesus is making Himself equal with God. Whatever the Father has, Jesus has. "He shall take of mine" means He will take the things of God and show them unto us. Only He can do that. ". . . Eye hath not seen, nor ear heard, neither have entered into the heart of man, the things which God hath prepared for them that love him. But God hath revealed them unto us by his Spirit . . ." (1 Cor. 2:9–10). The Spirit is the One who searches the deep things of God and He alone can show these things to us.

A little while, and ye shall not see me: and again, a little while, and ye shall see me, because I go to the Father [John 16:16].

What did He mean? He meant that He would be arrested, and they would be scattered like sheep and separated from Him. He'd be crucified and buried. He would be absent a little while and they wouldn't see Him. On the third day He would come back, and so in a little while they would see Him. This has a fuller, richer, deeper meaning for us today.

Then said some of his disciples among themselves, What is this that he saith unto us, a little while, and ye shall not see me: and again, A little while, and ye shall see me: and, Because I go to the Father?

They said therefore, What is this that he saith, A little while? we cannot tell what he saith.

Now Jesus knew that they were desirous to ask him, and said unto them, Do ye inquire among yourselves of that I said, A little while, and ye shall not see me: and again, a little while, and ye shall see me?

Verily, verily, I say unto you, That ye shall weep and lament, but the world shall rejoice: and ye shall be sorrowful, but your sorrow shall be turned into joy [John 16:17–20].

They didn't know exactly what He meant. There was to be the little while that He was in the grave—that was three days. Then there was to come another "little while" because He would go to the Father (which has been over nineteen hundred years now). He promised not to leave them comfortless, not to leave them orphans. He would be with them in the person of the Holy Spirit. He would take the things of Christ and make them real to them. That is where you and I live today. During these nineteen hundred years the Spirit of God has made Him real to multitudes. They have gone through sorrow; they have known what it is to be hated and to be ridiculed. He has brought them through that. Our sorrow shall be turned into joy.

A woman when she is in travail hath sorrow, because her hour is come: but as soon as she is delivered of the child, she remembereth no more the anguish, for joy that a man is born into the world.

And ye now therefore have sorrow: but I will see you again, and your heart shall rejoice, and your joy no man taketh from you [John 16:21–22].

Regardless of where you are or who you are, if you have accepted Jesus, my friend, you are a child of God. If you are in sorrow and there are tears in your eyes, if you have a broken heart, be assured that joy cometh in the morning. He is going to bring joy into your life. I think that when we get in His presence and look back on this life, if we have any regrets, it will be because we didn't suffer more for Him. The joy of His presence will overwhelm any sorrow we may have had down here.

And in that day ye shall ask me nothing. Verily, verily, I say unto you, Whatsoever ye shall ask the Father in my name, he will give it you.

Hitherto have ye asked nothing in my name: ask, and ye shall receive, that your joy may be full [John 16:23–24].

This is the third time He speaks of praying in His name. We have already seen that "praying in my name" refers to one who is abiding in Him, obeying Him. You cannot simply tag His name on to the end of a request and expect to get what you ask. That is not what He is saying.

Remember that these disciples had never prayed to the Father in the name of Jesus. You and I today are to pray *to* God the Father *in* Jesus' name. Someone may ask whether we can't pray to Jesus. I think you can if you wish to, but why do you rob yourself of an intercessor? Jesus is up there at God's right hand for you, praying for you. That is the reason that we should pray to the Father in the name of Jesus.

These things have I spoken unto you in proverbs: but the time cometh, when I shall no more speak unto you in proverbs, but I shall shew you plainly of the Father.

At that day ye shall ask in my name: and I say not unto you, that I will pray the Father for you:

For the Father himself loveth you, because ye have loved me, and have believed that I came out from God [John 16:25–27].

"The time cometh"—He is nearing His crucifixion, the hour of redemption for which He has come into the world. After that, they are to ask the Father in Jesus' name. He is trying to teach them that the Father is not a hard taskmaster who is reluctant to answer prayer. He is saying in effect, "If you think that I have to ask the Father to be good to you and to be generous to you, you are wrong. The Father Himself loveth you. I don't have to ask Him to love you. He loves you already. The Father isn't hard to get along with. He loves you and that is the reason He will answer your prayer that you pray in My name."

Today God wants to hear and answer prayers, but they must come from the heart of one who loves Christ, and is in fellowship with Him, obeying Him.

I came forth from the Father, and am come into the world: again, I leave the world, and go to the Father [John 16:28].

It is generally conceded that the key verse to the Gospel of John is John 20:30–31, but I would like to put beside it this verse. The eternal Son came into the world for one purpose: to redeem man. When the mission was accomplished, He returned to the Father. This is the movement in the Gospel of John. He has painted a black picture of coming persecution but concludes the chapter with victory.

This verse is bigger than Bethlehem; it is wider than space. It reaches back into eternity, beyond the boundaries of space to the throne of God. Then it speaks of those few moments He spent on this earth. He came in out of eternity; He went back into eternity.

His disciples said unto him, Lo, now speakest thou plainly, and speakest no proverb.

Now are we sure that thou knowest all things, and needest not that any man

should ask thee: by this we believe that thou camest forth from God [John 16:29–30].

It should be plain for us to understand that the Lord Jesus is God manifest in the flesh. There is this great conviction coming over the disciples. They are convinced of the facts. They have seen that He has come forth from the Father and that He has come into the world. He is the Messiah; He is the Savior He claims to be. However, they still do not understand the dark waters of death through which He must pass, nor the door of resurrection and ascension back into the Father's glory. They still don't quite comprehend it. But after nineteen hundred years do we comprehend it?

Jesus answered them, Do ye now believe?

Behold, the hour cometh, yea, is now come, that ye shall be scattered, every man to his own, and shall leave me alone: and yet I am not alone, because the Father is with me [John 16:31–32].

The hour was coming when these men would all scatter. They would leave Him alone; and yet He was not alone "because the Father is with me." That is one of the great mysteries. God was in Christ reconciling the world to Himself (see 2 Cor. 5:19). That is a great truth, and it is also equally true that on the cross Jesus cried out, ". . . My God, my God, why hast thou forsaken me?" (Mark 15:34), which is a quotation from Psalm 22. The explanation is, "But thou art holy, O thou that inhabitest the praises of Israel" (Ps. 22:3). Jesus Christ was made sin for us, friend. There was a rent in the Godhead as well as a rent in the veil. Yet at that very moment, God was in Christ reconciling the world unto Himself.

This is a mystery that the human mind cannot understand. Friends, we do not have enough brains to comprehend the redemption that He wrought on the cross. No wonder God wrapped the mantle of night around that cross as if to say, "You will never be able to enter into what is happening here." I believe that throughout the endless ages of eternity you and I will continually understand something new and wonderful about the death of the Lord Jesus for us. It will cause us to get down on our faces before Him afresh and anew.

These things I have spoken unto you, that in me ye might have peace. In the world ye shall have tribulation: but be of good cheer; I have overcome the world [John 16:33].

Peace. He closes with peace. The child of God can have peace in this life because peace is found in Christ and in no other place. You won't find peace in the church. You won't find peace in Christian service. Peace is found in the person of Jesus Christ.

"In the world ye shall have tribulation." Our Lord made that very clear. There is no peace in the world, only trouble. He was right, wasn't He? But He has overcome the world! His victory is our victory.

I hear so much today about the victorious life. The only One who ever lived a victorious life was Christ. You and I cannot live it. We can let Him live it in us—that is all. When you and I learn to identify ourselves with Him and come into close fellowship with Him, then we will begin to experience the peace of God in our hearts. Also we will be of good cheer. There is trouble in the world but in our lives there will be joy. Peace and joy! How important they are. "These things I have spoken unto you, that in me ye might have peace. In the world ye shall have tribulation: but be of good cheer; I have overcome the world."

CHAPTER 17

***THEME:** The Lord's Prayer—Jesus prays for Himself; Jesus prays for disciples; Jesus prays for His church*

We come now to one of the most remarkable chapters in the Bible. It is the longest prayer in the Bible, although it would take you only three minutes to read it. I think that is a good indication of the length of public prayers. If you can't say all you've got to say in three minutes, then you've got too much to say. I'll be very frank with you. I think brief prayers, thought out right to the point, are more effective than these long, rambling ones we hear. No wonder prayer meetings are as dead as a dodo bird!

The Upper Room Discourse is like climbing a staircase or like climbing a mountain, climaxing in this prayer. I would like to quote to you what others have said about this great chapter.

Matthew Henry: "It is the most remarkable prayer following the most full and consoling discourse ever uttered on the earth."

Martin Luther: "This is truly beyond measure a warm and hearty prayer. He opens the depths of His heart, both in reference to us and to His Father, and He pours them all out. It sounds so honest, so simple. It is so deep, so rich, so wide. No one can fathom it."

Philip Melanchthon, another of the reformers: "There is no voice which has ever been heard, either in heaven or in earth, more exalted, more holy, more fruitful, more sublime than the prayer offered up by the Son to God Himself."

This is the prayer which John Knox read over and over in his lifetime. When he was on his deathbed, his wife asked him, "Where do you want me to read?" He replied, "Read where I first put my anchor down, in the seventeenth chapter of John." We have the record of many others who have read it over and over. Dr. Fisher, who was bishop of Rochester under Henry VIII, had this read as the last portion of Scripture just before his martyrdom.

This is a great portion of Scripture. I feel wholly and totally inadequate to deal with this prayer. It is His high priestly intercession for us. It is a revelation to us of the communication which, I think, constantly passes between the Lord Jesus and the Father in heaven. His entire life was a life of prayer. He began His ministry by going into a solitary place to pray. Often He went up into a mountain to pray and spent the night in prayer. He is our great Intercessor. He prays for you and for me. If you forgot to pray this morning, He didn't. He prayed for you this morning.

God always hears and answers Jesus' prayer just the way He prays it. God answers my prayer also, but not always the way I pray it—sometimes He must answer my prayer with a no, or He may accomplish what I ask by a completely different method or at a different time. However, Jesus said, "Father, I thank thee that thou hast heard me. And I knew that thou hearest me always: but because of the people which stand by I said it, that they may believe that thou hast sent me" (John 11:41–42).

THE LORD'S PRAYER—JESUS PRAYS FOR HIMSELF

I want you to notice that it is not out of line nor even a mark of selfishness to pray for one's self. I believe that when you and I go to God in prayer, we need to get our own hearts and lives right with God. We need to get in tune with heaven, as it were. Every instrument should be tuned up before it is played. Before you and I begin to pray for others, we need to pray for ourselves. That is not selfishness; it is essential.

These words spake Jesus, and lifted up his eyes to heaven, and said, Father, the hour is come; glorify thy Son, that thy Son also may glorify thee [John 17:1].

"These words spake Jesus." Which words? The chapters we have just read, chapters 13–16. Now He stops speaking to the disciples, and He speaks to the Father. Although He is speaking to the Father in this chapter, He is speaking to Him for their benefit—and for our benefit also. He is our great Intercessor today. We may wonder what He is praying for. Well, here it is. This is the Lord's Prayer, the prayer that He prays to the Father.

The prayer in the Sermon on the Mount is not really the Lord's Prayer. It is the prayer that He taught to the disciples. When Jesus begins with "Our Father," He means this for all the believers. However, Jesus calls God "Father" in a different sense. After His resurrection He said to Mary, "I am not yet ascended to my Father: but go to my brethren, and say unto them, I ascend unto my Father, and your Father; and to my God, and your God" (John 20:17). In other words, "I have not yet ascended to *your* Father, yours by the new birth, and to *My* Father, Mine because of My position in the Trinity." Also, it could never be the prayer of Jesus to say, "Forgive us our debts, our sins." He never had any sins. He could not pray that prayer. By the same token, you and I can never pray this prayer of John 17. This is *His* prayer.

Apparently our Lord prayed this prayer as He was walking along. It says that He "lifted up his eyes to heaven," which means that His eyes were open. Of course we can pray without bowing our heads and closing our eyes. We can pray as we walk or as we work or as we drive.

Now notice His prayer. It begins, "Father, the hour is come." What hour? Well, the hour that had been set back yonder in eternity. As He speaks, the clock is striking the hour that was set way back in eternity, because He was the Lamb of God slain before the foundation of the world. It was arranged back there; now "the hour is come." Remember that when He began His ministry at the wedding of Cana, His mother said to Him, "They have no wine." His answer to her was, "Woman, what have I to do with thee? mine hour is not yet come" (John 2:3–4). Now the hour has come, the hour when He will pay for your sins and mine. It is the hour when all the creation of God will see the love of God displayed and lavished as He takes your sins and my sins upon Himself and dies a vicarious, substitutionary, redemptive death for you and for me. And it won't end there; it will go on to the Resurrection.

"The hour is come; glorify thy Son, that thy Son also may glorify thee." The death of Christ will demonstrate that God is not the brutal bully the liberal theologians talk about in the Old Testament, but that He is a loving Father who so loves the world that He gives His only begotten Son. Then the Son will be raised from the dead, ascend back into heaven, and He will be given a name that is above every name, that at the name of Jesus every knee should bow to Him. "Glorify thy Son, that thy Son also may glorify thee." Oh, the wealth of meaning that is here!

As thou hast given him power over all flesh, that he should give eternal life to as many as thou hast given him [John 17:2].

This is a startling statement. He has power over all flesh! He could make this universe and every individual in it bow to Him. He could bring us all into subjection to Him and make robots out of all of us. Although that is the last thing He would want to do, He has the power over all flesh.

The church is God's love gift to Jesus Christ. So He gives eternal life to as many "as thou hast given him." This brings up the question of election and free will, and I don't want to go into that extensively. There are extreme Calvinists and extreme Arminians, and the truth is probably somewhere between the two. If God would somehow reveal to me who are the elect ones, I would give the gospel only to them. But God does not do this. He has said that whosoever will may come. That is a legitimate offer to every person. You have no excuse to offer at all if you will not come to Him. It will be your condemnation that you turned down the offer that God has made to you.

And this is life eternal, that they might know thee the only true God, and Jesus Christ, whom thou hast sent [John 17:3].

Does election shut out certain people? No. Life eternal is to know the only true God and Jesus Christ whom He has sent. Do you have a desire to know the true God and Jesus Christ? Then you are not shut out. You must be one of the elect. He gives eternal life to those who have heard the call and have responded down in their hearts. They have come to Christ of their own free will.

"That they might know thee." It is not the amount of knowledge you have, but the kind of knowledge that is important. It is whom you know. Do you know Jesus Christ? In the same way, it is not the amount of faith you have but the kind of faith that is important. There is a song called "Only Believe." Only believe what? Only believe in the only One, the Lord Jesus Christ. I quote Spurgeon again: "It is not thy joy in Christ that saves thee. It is Christ. It is not thy faith in Christ, though that be the instrument. It is Christ's blood and merit." It is Christ who saves. One can believe in the wrong thing. It is the *object* of faith which is so important. "This is life eternal, that they might know *thee* the only true God, and Jesus Christ." Now faith comes by hearing, hearing the Word of God. What does the Word of God say? The gospel is that Jesus died for our sins, was buried, and rose again. Those are the facts. Our knowledge of the facts and our response to that knowledge is faith. Faith is trusting Christ as our own Savior.

Life eternal is to *know* God and to *know* Jesus Christ. Jesus is His name as Savior, and

Christ is His title—the Messiah, the King of Israel. To know Him means to grow in grace and in the knowledge of Christ. When we move on in the knowledge of the Lord Jesus Christ, we come to the place of assurance. Anyone without the assurance of salvation is either unsaved or is just a babe in Christ. They need to move on to the place where they *know* that they are saved. Life eternal is to know the only genuine God and to know Jesus Christ. This is the reason that the study of the Word of God is so important. Many people stay on the fringe of things and are never sure they are saved.

I have glorified thee on the earth: I have finished the work which thou gavest me to do [John 17:4].

The Lord Jesus is handing in His final report to the Father. He hasn't died on the cross yet; but, as far as God is concerned, He speaks of things which are not as if they are. Future tense for God is just as accurate as past tense. Our Lord Jesus is going to the cross to die and then will rise again. On the cross, He said, "It is finished" (John 19:30). That means our redemption was finished. He has done everything that was necessary. We can put a period there. We cannot add a thing to His finished work. Therefore, the gospel of salvation is not what God is asking you to do, but what God is telling you that He has already done for you. It is your response to that which saves you.

And now, O Father, glorify thou me with thine own self with the glory which I had with thee before the world was [John 17:5].

In Philippians 2, it speaks of Jesus emptying Himself. Some try to teach that He emptied Himself of His deity. John makes it very clear that the Word became flesh. That little baby in Mary's lap is God, and He could have spoken this universe out of existence. He wasn't just 99.9% God; He was, and is, 100% God. So of what did He empty Himself? He emptied Himself of His prerogatives of deity; He laid aside His glory.

At Christmas we make a great deal of the shepherds and the angels and the wise men who came to see Him. Friend, that is not the way it should have been. He is the Lord of glory, and the whole creation should have been there; every human being on the face of the earth should have been there. People will come from all parts of a country and even all parts of the world for the funeral of a great political leader. The whole world should have been at the birth of the Lord of glory when He came to earth. Although He could have claimed such homage, instead He laid aside His glory. Now He is ready to return to heaven, back to the glory.

JESUS PRAYS FOR DISCIPLES

I have manifested thy name unto the men which thou gavest me out of the world: thine they were, and thou gavest them me, and they have kept thy word [John 17:6].

Notice this: "to as many as thou hast given him" (v. 2): "unto the men which thou gavest me . . . and thou gavest them me" (v. 6); "for them which thou hast given me" (v. 9); "whom thou hast given me" (v. 11); and "those that thou gavest me" (v. 12). We are back to the great doctrine of election. Jesus talked to the Father about it. It was a private conversation, but He wanted the disciples to hear it and to know about it. I don't know as much about election as maybe I should know. I've read Hodge, Calvin, Thornwall, Shedd, and Strong on the subject, and they don't seem to know much more about it. The reason we know so little about election is because it is God's side, and there are a lot of things that God knows that we don't know.

It is a wonderful thing to be able to listen to this prayer and to know that Jesus is at God's right hand talking to the Father about us. The Lord Jesus has talked to the Father about you today, if you are one of His.

There is a mystical relationship between the Lord Jesus and His own. They belong to the Father and were given to Jesus Christ. I can't fathom its meaning. What a wonderful relationship!

Now they have known that all things whatsoever thou hast given me are of thee.

For I have given unto them the words which thou gavest me; and they have received them, and have known surely that I came out from thee, and they have believed that thou didst send me [John 17:7–8].

The Lord had given them the Words of the Father. That is important. He had not given them property or money or an automobile, but the Words of the Father. Jesus testifies here that these disciples believed that He came from the Father. They knew who He was. They did not understand His purpose and certainly not His death and resurrection, but they had made tremendous advances during the three years they had been with Him. They knew He had come from God, and they believed that God had sent Him.

I pray for them: I pray not for the world, but for them which thou hast given me; for they are thine [John 17:9].

I will make a startling statement which is no more startling than what He made: Jesus Christ does not pray for the *world* today. His ministry of intercession is for His own who are in the world. He doesn't pray for the world; He *died* for the world. What more could He do for the world? He has sent the Holy Spirit into the world to convict the world of sin, righteousness, and judgment. Jesus Christ prays for His own.

And all mine are thine, and thine are mine; and I am glorified in them [John 17:10].

The whole purpose of our salvation is to bring glory to Jesus Christ.

And now I am no more in the world, but these are in the world, and I come to thee. Holy Father, keep through thine own name those whom thou hast given me, that they may be one, as we are [John 17:11].

He prays for two wonderful things. He prays for us to be kept. You will be kept because you have been sealed by the Holy Spirit and because your Savior is praying for you.

His other request is that we should be one. He prays for the unity of believers. He's not praying for an ecumenical movement or that we all join the same denomination. There has been much wrong teaching about this. First of all, He prays the Father that His own might be one. Notice that He isn't praying to us or to some church authority; He is praying to the Father. And He prays that we should be one "as we are"; that is, as the Father and the Son are one. The Father has answered every prayer of His Son, and He has answered this one. There is an organic unity which God has made. The Holy Spirit takes all true believers and baptizes them into the body of Christ, identifies them in the body of Christ. The disgrace of it all is that down here the believers are pretty well divided. But there is only one true church, and every believer in Jesus Christ is a member of that church. It is called the body of Christ.

While I was with them in the world, I kept them in thy name: those that thou gavest me I have kept, and none of them is lost, but the son of perdition; that the scripture might be fulfilled [John 17:12].

"Those that thou gavest me"—we have election mentioned again. There are certain things which I believe that to me are not contradictory, but they certainly are paradoxical. Election and free will happen to be one of those. I wish you could have met me when I graduated from seminary. I was a smart boy then and I even had the answer to election and free will. But I have a little more sense than I had then, and I realize that we simply do not understand it.

Judas Iscariot is, of course, "the son of perdition." He fulfilled the prophecies concerning him.

And now come I to thee; and these things I speak in the world, that they might have my joy fulfilled in themselves [John 17:13].

Friend, God does not want us to be long-faced, solemn Christians. He came that our lives might be filled with joy—His joy.

I have given them thy word; and the world hath hated them, because they are not of the world, even as I am not of the world [John 17:14].

The Word of God causes problems in the world today. The Bible is the most revolutionary Book in the world. It is revolutionary to teach that you cannot save yourself, that only Christ can save you. And you can't make this world better. Only Jesus Christ can do that. That's revolutionary, and the world doesn't want to hear that. They'd rather plant a few flowers and try to clean up pollution. The problem is that the pollution is in the human heart.

I pray not that thou shouldest take them out of the world, but that thou shouldest keep them from the evil [John 17:15].

This really should read "from the evil *one*." Again it is startling to note that He does not pray that we should be taken out of the world. God gets glory by keeping you and me in the world today. We think of the Rapture as wonderful, and it will be. We think of the Rapture as bringing glory to God, and it will. But let's understand one thing: God gets glory by keeping you and me in the world. If you knew

Vernon McGee like He knows Vernon McGee, you'd know it is a miracle for God to keep me in the world. We long for the Rapture. In Revelation 22:17 it says that the Spirit and the bride say, "Come." The Holy Spirit is weary of this world. He is grieved. He says, "Come." We also are weary, and we who are the bride of Christ say, "Come." But Jesus prays not that we should be taken out of the world, but that we should be kept from the evil one, Satan. And I wouldn't want to be here for a minute if my Lord weren't keeping me from the evil one.

Wouldn't it be wonderful if we could really learn this lesson? We cry and whimper because things are hard down here. Sure they are. He said they would be hard—"but be of good cheer; I have overcome the world" (John 16:33). I suspect that every twenty-four hours there is a great hallelujah meeting in heaven, and the angels say, "Isn't it marvelous that McGee is still being kept. It would be so easy to take him out of the world, but it is a real miracle to keep him in the world." If we could learn that, it would enable us to endure more easily our problems and tensions and difficulties and temptations. The Lord Jesus has prayed to keep us in the world and to protect us from the evil one.

They are not of the world, even as I am not of the world [John 17:16].

The measure in which we as believers realize this, the more completely we fulfill His will and accomplish His purpose.

Sanctify them through thy truth: thy word is truth [John 17:17].

Sanctify means to set apart. The believer is not of the world; he is set apart. The thought has reference to the task rather than the person; it is a commitment to the task. The believer is set apart by the Word of God. That is, the Word reveals the mind of God. As you read the Word, you are led to set yourself apart for a particular ministry. We can serve Him only as we know His Word and are obedient to it.

As thou hast sent me into the world, even so have I also sent them into the world.

And for their sakes I sanctify myself, that they also might be sanctified through the truth [John 17:18–19].

We have been sent out into the world to bear a witness. He sets Himself apart to be identified with us, and we ought to be identified with Him in this world.

JESUS PRAYS FOR HIS CHURCH

Neither pray I for these alone, but for them also which shall believe on me through their word [John 17:20].

He had you and me in mind. Now, many centuries later, we can know our great High Priest is praying for us.

That they all may be one; as thou, Father, art in me, and I in thee, that they also may be one in us: that the world may believe that thou hast sent me [John 17:21].

This prayer has been answered. The church is an organic unity. Believers are one in Christ, for the church is one body. The minute any sinner trusts Christ, that sinner is put into the body of Christ. If believers would manifest that union to the world, the world would be more impressed with Christ. Too often the world sees believers hating each other which may well be one of the reasons they will not accept Christ.

And the glory which thou gavest me I have given them; that they may be one, even as we are one:

I in them, and thou in me, that they may be made perfect in one; and that the world may know that thou hast sent me, and hast loved them, as thou hast loved me [John 17:22–23].

"I in them, and thou in me." How wonderful! Only the Spirit of God can accomplish that. The unity that exists between the Father and the Son is the unity that is to exist between the believer and the Lord Jesus Christ! "And hast loved them, as thou hast loved me"—means that God loves *you* as much as He loves the Lord Jesus Christ. That boggles the mind!

Father, I will that they also, whom thou hast given me, be with me where I am; that they may behold my glory, which thou hast given me: for thou lovedst me before the foundation of the world [John 17:24].

It will be heaven to be with Him in perfect fellowship. I take it that this was God's purpose in creating man. There are other creatures in the universe and on the earth, but God made man a creature with whom He could have fellowship. God created man with a free will; and, even though man sinned, God wants his fellowship. Heaven is going to be wonderful, and it will be important that every one of His sheep is there with Him. Each one will have his contribution to make.

To behold the glory of the Lord Jesus will be the satisfaction of the believer. Moses asked to see the glory of God. Philip asked to see the Father. Sometimes we get a glimpse of glory in a rainbow or a sunset. Think what it will be when we come into His presence and behold His glory! That is the goal to which we are moving.

O righteous Father, the world hath not known thee: but I have known thee, and these have known that thou hast sent me [John 17:25].

Being sent from the Father actually embraces His entire mission of redemption. Anyone who is a believer knows that the Father has sent Him, and the purpose was for Him to die for our sins.

And I have declared unto them thy name, and will declare it: that the love wherewith thou hast loved me may be in them, and I in them [John 17:26].

The last thing He mentions is that His love might be in our hearts and in our lives. We talk so much about grace and about faith, and rightly so; yet the great desire of His heart is that His love should be manifested in the lives of those whom He has redeemed. That should put us down on our faces before Him. My friend, how much of His love is manifested in you?

In review, this is what this prayer says about believers and the world:

1. Given to Christ out of the world (v. 6)
2. Left in the world (v. 11)
3. Not of the world (v. 14)
4. Hated by the world (v. 14)
5. Kept from the evil one (v. 15)
6. Sent into the world (v. 18)
7. Manifested in unity before the world (v. 23)

These are the requests of Christ for His own:

1. Preservation (v. 11)
2. Joy—fullness of the Spirit (v. 13)
3. Deliverance—from evil (v. 15)
4. To be set apart—"sanctify" (v. 17)
5. Unity—"be one"—(this is not union) (v. 21)
6. Fellowship—"be with me" (v. 24)
7. Satisfaction—"behold my glory" (v. 24)

The Lord Jesus Christ is our great High Priest. This is the great truth of the Epistle to the Hebrews. In the Old Testament economy the high priest wore an ephod of beauty and glory, which was joined on each shoulder by two onyx stones with the names of the tribes of Israel engraved on them. Thus he carried the names of the children of Israel with him when he went into the presence of God. This speaks of the strength and power of the high priest. Hebrews 7:25 tells us about Jesus Christ, our High Priest: "Wherefore he is able also to save them to the uttermost that come unto God by him, seeing he ever liveth to make intercession for them." Christ is *able* to save us, you see. He has strength and power.

Also on the breastplate of the high priest were twelve precious stones, arranged three in a row in four rows across his breast. On each was the name of a tribe of Israel. When the high priest went into God's presence wearing the breastplate, he pictured the Lord Jesus Christ who is at the right hand of God interceding for us. The Lord not only carries us on His shoulders, the place of strength and power, but He also carries us on His breast, on His heart, which speaks of His love. He has all power, and He loves us!

CHAPTER 18

***THEME:** Arrest and trial of Jesus—the arrest in Gethsemane; trial before Annas; first denial by Simon Peter; trial before high priest; second denial by Simon Peter; trial before Pilate*

We have now concluded the Upper Room Discourse which began in John 13 and was climaxed with this wonderful prayer of the Lord Jesus in John 17. Augustine made this statement about the discourse: "It is easiest in regards to words but most profound in regards to ideas." That certainly is a true statement.

We come now to the fifth division of this Gospel of John: the witness of Jesus to the world. It includes chapters 18 to 20. We will see in this chapter that He is arrested and taken before the high priest. The presentation here is different from that in the synoptic Gospels (Matthew, Mark, and Luke). The emphasis in those three Gospels is upon the humanity of Christ, His human nature, and upon the sufferings of the Savior. In the first three Gospel records, as He approaches Jerusalem, He says He is going there to die. He mentions His death, His treatment, His abuse in the hands of the Gentiles, and then His bodily resurrection.

In the Gospel of John, the emphasis is upon the deity of the Lord Jesus. He is the God-man in this gospel, and the emphasis here is upon His glory. In His arrest, His death, His resurrection we will see His glory. Remember how often He stated in His discourse that He was returning to the Father. This is in accord with the emphasis on His glory.

THE ARREST IN GETHSEMANE; TRIAL BEFORE ANNAS

When Jesus had spoken these words, he went forth with his disciples over the brook Cedron, where was a garden, into the which he entered, and his disciples [John 18:1].

In these passages we will find a blending of His majesty and His meekness. He seems to have spent His nights under the open sky. Why did He leave Jerusalem and cross the brook Cedron? Apparently He was accustomed to going there.

And Judas also, which betrayed him, knew the place: for Jesus ofttimes resorted thither with his disciples [John 18:2].

Luke tells us in chapter 21:37, "And in the day time he was teaching in the temple; and at night he went out, and abode in the mount that is called the mount of Olives." And again, Luke 22:39: "And he came out, and went, as he was wont, to the mount of Olives. . . ." He would need to cross the brook Cedron.

Our Lord crossed over the brook Cedron after Judas had made his agreement to betray Him. Perhaps you remember another crossing of this same brook by one who was betrayed—King David, when his son Absalom led in a rebellion and Ahithophel, his friend and counsellor, betrayed him.

As far as we can tell, Jesus never spent a night in the city of Jerusalem, in the walled city. The last week of His life, He went to Bethany and stayed with His friends. Even on this last night, He left the walled city to go to the place called the Garden of Gethsemane. He is going to this quiet place in order to give His enemies an opportuntiy to take Him. They wanted to lay hands on Him but, because they were afraid of the people, they wouldn't dare lay hands on Him in the temple or in the streets of Jerusalem.

Notice that John does not include the agony in the garden. John does not record His praying and His extreme suffering. Rather he speaks of the glory. He is putting the emphasis on the deity of Christ, whereas the other gospels emphasize His humanity. You will notice that Jesus will not resist arrest. He is the Lamb of God who offers no resistance. ". . . as a sheep before her shearers is dumb, so he openeth not his mouth" (Isa. 53:7). The dignity of His person at this time is absolutely overwhelming.

Remember in previous incidents, when the enemies of the Lord Jesus tried to close in on Him, He hid Himself. Apparently He could just disappear miraculously. Now, He lays Himself wide open to be taken. This is very important for us to note.

Judas then, having received a band of men and officers from the chief priests and Pharisees, cometh thither with lanterns and torches and weapons [John 18:3].

Luke tells us what He said: ". . . Be ye come out, as against a thief, with swords and staves?" (Luke 22:52). It says that a *band* of men came out. A band is the tenth part of a legion and would consist of approximately five hundred men. Matthew says that a great multitude came with Judas. Why would they come with such a multitude and with swords and clubs? That crowd knew that He had performed miracles, and they thought that, if they would bring along a big enough company of armed men, they could capture Him. Now notice the dignity of our Lord.

Jesus therefore, knowing all things that should come upon him, went forth, and said unto them, Whom seek ye? [John 18:4].

My friend, do you think this is just a poor, weak man who has been trapped by some clever religious rulers and the power of Rome? If He had not yielded Himself, all the weapons those men had would have been absolutely useless and worthless.

They answered him, Jesus of Nazareth. Jesus saith unto them, I am he. And Judas also, which betrayed him, stood with them [John 18:5].

I don't want to pass over this because I wouldn't want you to miss this for anything in the world. They call Him "Jesus of Nazareth." They do not accord Him the dignity that belongs to Him. They refuse to call Him the Christ. Well, it's all right, because Jesus is a name that is above every name. The day is coming when those on earth and even those under the earth, in hell itself, will bow the knee to the name of Jesus. But now, this crowd would not acknowledge Him as the Savior, the Christ, the Son of the living God.

They didn't know Him. The thing that is strange above everything else is that Judas didn't know Him at first. Why didn't Judas know Him? Paul says, "But if our gospel be hid, it is hid to them that are lost: In whom the god of this world hath blinded the minds of them which believe not, lest the light of the glorious gospel of Christ, who is the image of God, should shine unto them" (2 Cor. 4:3–4). We are told that the natural man does not receive the things of the Spirit of God neither can he know them because they are spiritually discerned. I believe that Judas did not know Him because He stood there as the Lord of glory.

As soon then as he had said unto them, I am he, they went backward, and fell to the ground [John 18:6].

"And the Word was made flesh, and dwelt among us, (and we beheld his glory, the glory as of the only begotten of the Father,) full of grace and truth" (John 1:14). Even in this dark hour when He was yielding Himself as the Lamb of God that taketh away the sin of the world, He revealed His deity—and they fell backwards! He revealed to these men that He was absolutely in charge, and they could not arrest Him without His permission. They didn't fall forward to worship Him. They fell backward in fear and in absolute dismay. I think there was utter confusion for a moment there when they fell backward. They are seeing not simply Jesus of Nazareth but the God-man, the Lord of glory.

This fulfills prophecy. "The LORD is my light and my salvation; whom shall I fear? the LORD is the strength of my life; of whom shall I be afraid? When the wicked, even mine enemies and my foes, came upon me to eat up my flesh, they stumbled and fell" (Ps. 27:1–2). This is the God-ward side. Then in Psalm 35:4 we see the man-ward side. "Let them be confounded and put to shame that seek after my soul: let them be turned back and brought to confusion that devise my hurt." Then listen to Psalm 40:14: "Let them be ashamed and confounded together that seek after my soul to destroy it; let them be driven backward and put to shame that wish me evil." What a fulfillment we have here when our Lord for a brief moment reveals His glory to them. They are seeking Jesus of Nazareth. Well, here He is, but He is the Lord of glory.

My friend, whom do you see? Do you know who He is? The unsaved man doesn't know Him. People may even read the Bible and be very religious and very moral and not see that Jesus of Nazareth is the Christ, the Son of the living God.

Then asked he them again, Whom seek ye? And they said, Jesus of Nazareth.

Jesus answered, I have told you that I am he: if therefore ye seek me, let these go their way:

That the saying might be fulfilled, which he spake, Of them which thou gavest me have I lost none [John 18:7–9].

Notice His dignity. He is in charge of everything. He is even telling them whom to arrest and whom not to arrest. There had been the prophecy that the Shepherd would be taken and the sheep scattered, and Jesus had said that He had lost none. The disciples would not be captured. Isn't it interesting that they weren't? One would think they would have been brought in as witnesses or accomplices, but they were not.

Then Simon Peter having a sword drew it, and smote the high priest's servant, and cut off his right ear. The servant's name was Malchus [John 18:10].

Why didn't they arrest Simon Peter for this?

Then said Jesus unto Peter, Put up thy sword into the sheath: the cup which my Father hath given me, shall I not drink it? [John 18:11].

Dr. Luke tells us that Jesus touched the man's ear and healed him. But why didn't they arrest Peter? Because the Lord Jesus said, "You let these men go." He is in command.

Simon Peter, the poor, ignorant fisherman! He probably was really smarting inside. He had asked the Lord why he couldn't go with Him where He was going. He had said he would lay down his life for the Lord, and he meant it. But the Lord had told him that he didn't know himself, that he would deny his Lord that night. Oh, it's so easy to get Christians to dedicate and rededicate their lives to the Lord. Simon Peter would have come forward at every invitation, and he would have meant it. The problem is that we cannot produce this in our own strength. This was Paul's experience, too. He said that to will was present with him, but he couldn't find how to perform it. It is only the power of the Holy Spirit that can produce the life yielded to Christ. I think Peter was smarting inside and thinking, "I'll show Him that I'll die for Him."

Peter's a good fisherman. He can throw a net expertly, but he makes a sorry swordsman. He got an ear when he meant to get a head. Our Lord tells Peter to put up his sword. Earlier, when Jesus advised them to have swords, it was for their protection, not for His defense. Our Lord is yielding Himself into the hands of His captors. He is getting ready, as He says, to drink the cup which His Father has given Him.

There are several "cups" mentioned in the Scriptures. There is the cup of salvation: "I will take the cup of salvation, and call upon the name of the LORD" (Ps. 116:13). Then there is the cup of consolation: ". . . neither shall men give them the cup of consolation to drink for their father or for their mother" (Jer. 16:7). Also there is the cup of joy: "Thou preparest a table before me in the presence of mine enemies: thou anointest my head with oil; my cup runneth over" (Ps. 23:5). This cup which our Lord was to drink was given Him by the Father. It was a dreadful cup, and Jesus prayed in Gethsemane, ". . . O my Father, if it be possible, let this cup pass from me . . ." (Matt. 26:39). This is the cup of judgment He bore for us on the cross. Everyone who turns his back on Jesus Christ must drink that cup of judgment himself. Jesus drank it for us although it was totally repulsive to Him. Remember that He was perfect humanity, absolutely sinless, and yet He drank the hated cup because it was the cup of your sin and my sin. There is still another cup, the cup of judgment which is yet to come on this world. I believe the seven vials or bowls of wrath, which are to be poured upon the wicked as described in Revelation are the fulfillment of this. "Upon the wicked he shall rain snares, fire and brimstone, and an horrible tempest: this shall be the portion of their cup" (Ps. 11:6). This is the cup of His anger. "For thus saith the LORD God of Israel unto me; Take the wine cup of this fury at my hand, and cause all the nations, to whom I send thee, to drink it" (Jer. 25:15).

Notice again what our Lord says to Peter, "Put up thy sword into the sheath: the cup which my Father hath given me, shall I not drink it?" It is not, "He is the judge, and I'm going to drink it by command," but, "Shall I not drink this cup my Father gives me?" There is no willingness higher than that. Let us not get the idea that the Savior did this reluctantly. Hebrews 12:2 says, ". . . who for the joy that was set before him endured the cross, despising the shame, and is set down at the right hand of the throne of God."

Then the band and the captain and officers of the Jews took Jesus, and bound him,

And led him away to Annas first; for he was father in law to Caiaphas, which was the high priest that same year [John 18:12–13].

The religious rulers were the ones who had plotted all this. Because they were afraid of the people, our Lord went outside the city to give them the opportunity they needed to arrest Him. He is going forward in His dignity and in His glory. They took Him and bound Him—which wasn't necessary. He is the Lamb slain from the foundation of the world. He is the sheep before the shearers; He will not offer any resistance.

They led Him away to Annas first. Only John gives us that detail; as apparently he was in a position to see something that the others didn't see. Annas had been the high priest and was probably still in the quarters of the palace of the high priest. Secular history testifies to the fact that Annas was one of the most brilliant, one of the most clever, and one of the most satanic of all the high priests. Caiaphas was the one whom the Roman government accepted, but the real head of the religious group was old Annas. I believe that he was the real leader, a politician who knew how to handle Rome. It is my judgment that it was he who plotted the arrest, the trial, and the crucifixion of Jesus. The entire trial was a mockery, and I think Annas was behind it all.

What an injustice has been done the Jews down through the centuries. They have been blamed for the crime of men like Annas, Caiaphas, and Pilate. I do not take the responsibility for the crimes of Jesse James just because he happened to be an American, do you? Romanism for centuries has called the Jewish people the "Christ-killers," which has been the basis for anti-Semitism in Europe. Yet they are not any more responsible than the Gentiles are. In the final analysis, we all are responsible for His death. He died for the sins of the world. There should be no pointing of the finger at any race or group of people.

Now Caiaphas was he, which gave counsel to the Jews, that it was expedient that one man should die for the people [John 18:14].

I believe John puts this in here to show us that it had already been predetermined that the Lord Jesus was to die. They had already decided that. Old Annas knew how to forge a charge against Jesus to get the death penalty from the Roman authorities. The whole trial was nothing but a mockery.

FIRST DENIAL BY SIMON PETER

And Simon Peter followed Jesus, and so did another disciple: that disciple was known unto the high priest, and went in with Jesus into the palace of the high priest [John 18:15].

That other disciple was John, obviously. John apparently had an "in" with those in Jerusalem, and this enabled him to get a pass for someone else to come in. I want you to see that John apparently was known in these circles, and for John to go in there was no temptation at all. However, it was fatal for Simon Peter to go in there. He was standing on the outside when John got the permission for him to come into the inner court. I want you to see this little byplay at the palace of Caiaphas.

But Peter stood at the door without. Then went out that other disciple, which was known unto the high priest, and spake unto her that kept the door, and brought in Peter [John 18:16].

John had an entree, but Peter is a poor fisherman whom nobody knows, and he can't get in. John tells the girl at the gate that this is a friend of his, and so he brought Peter in. Simon Peter was scared to death. You see, John was at home here, but Simon Peter had never been in that crowd before. Peter has a big mouth, and he just has to talk. Remember the other gospels tell us that the girls spot him as a Galilean because his speech betrays him. He talks too much. He's nervous in there. A little wisp of a girl makes him deny the Lord.

There is an application for us here. You and I have no right to put our little ideas of separation down on another Christian. Another Christian may be able to go where you cannot go. It was wrong for Simon Peter to go in there, but it was not wrong for John.

Then saith the damsel that kept the door unto Peter, Art not thou also one of this man's disciples? He saith, I am not [John 18:17].

She knows the followers of Jesus are there and assumes Peter is one of them. She just asks the question as he is about to go through the gate, "Aren't you one of this man's disciples?" He says, "I am not," and walks on through.

And the servants and officers stood there, who had made a fire of coals; for it was cold: and they warmed themselves: and Peter stood with them, and warmed himself [John 18:18].

Outside the palace grounds the people are gathered—not many at that time of morning, but the guards are there to keep order. They build a fire, and Peter stands with them warming himself.

TRIAL BEFORE HIGH PRIEST

The high priest then asked Jesus of his disciples, and of his doctrine.

Jesus answered him, I spake openly to the world; I ever taught in the synagogue, and in the temple, whither the Jews always resort; and in secret have I said nothing.

Why askest thou me? ask them which heard me, what I have said unto them: behold, they know what I said [John 18:19–21].

The scene shifts back to the trial of the Lord Jesus. Notice the dignity of the Lord Jesus.

And when he had thus spoken, one of the officers which stood by struck Jesus with the palm of his hand, saying, Answerest thou the high priest so?

Jesus answered him, If I have spoken evil, bear witness of the evil: but if well, why smitest thou me? [John 18:22–23].

He is subjected to this kind of humiliation. He is yielding Himself to die for your sin and my sin. However, He does call their attention to the fact that what they are doing is illegal and contrary to the Mosaic Law. They have no witness that He has done evil, and yet they smite Him. They are the ones who are breaking the Law. For one thing, no trial is to begin at night nor end at night. A trial is not to begin and end on the same day. They are not to strike a prisoner who has not yet been proven guilty.

Now Annas had sent him bound unto Caiaphas the high priest [John 18:24].

John puts this little verse in to tell us again that it was Annas who bound Him. Annas is the one who plotted and planned all of this diabolical plot.

SECOND DENIAL BY SIMON PETER

And Simon Peter stood and warmed himself. They said therefore unto him, Art not thou also one of his disciples? He denied it, and said, I am not.

One of the servants of the high priest, being his kinsman whose ear Peter cut off, saith, Did not I see thee in the garden with him?

Peter then denied again: and immediately the cock crew [John 18:25–27].

We learn from the other gospels how Peter went out and wept bitterly. I think that he caught a glimpse of the face of our Lord all bloody and beaten, and he caught His eye. That is when he went out and cried like a baby. You know that if he was arguing with a kinsman of Malchus, he must have been pretty vehement. He denied his Lord. But, thank God, the Lord was on His way to die for him and had already told him that He had prayed so that Peter's faith would not fail.

Why is it that Simon Peter, who did a deed as dastardly as Judas, could make his way back to the Lord? Because he was a child of God, and it broke his heart to know what he had done. A child of God may get far from God, but God is never far from him. You may be dead to God, but God is never dead to you. He is always there and He is always available. The Lord never said to Peter, "I'm sorry, but because you failed Me, I just can't use you anymore." No, He appeared personally to Peter after His resurrection, and He elected Peter to preach the first sermon on the Day of Pentecost. There has never been a sermon like it! Thank God for a Savior and a Lord like that. He will always take you back!

TRIAL BEFORE PILATE

Then led they Jesus from Caiaphas unto the hall of judgment: and it was early; and they themselves went not into the judgment hall, lest they should be defiled; but that they might eat the passover [John 18:28].

There is quite an interesting byplay here that I want you to see. Here we see "religion" and the Person of Jesus Christ side by side. Here is the One who has come to fulfill the Passover. He is going to die on the cross because they are bringing the death sentence against Him. But, because they want to eat the Passover, these men won't go inside the judgment hall. That would pollute them. They will not do that. Are they meticulously religious! Yet they are plotting the death of the very One who is the fulfillment of the Passover! My friend, how this should cause you to search your heart at this time. Are you merely religious or are you joined to the Lord Jesus Christ?

There is another interesting byplay to watch here. The Jews absolutely would not go into the judgment hall and thus contaminate themselves, but they brought Jesus to be taken into the judgment hall to be tried. So there is a change of scene in this drama from outside to inside and inside to outside. Watch it:

"Pilate then went out" (v. 29)

"Then Pilate entered into the judgment hall again" (v. 33)

"And when he had said this, he went out again unto the Jews" (v. 38)

"Then Pilate therefore took Jesus, and scourged him" (John 19:1)

"Pilate therefore went forth again" (John 19:4)

"And went again into the judgment hall" (John 19:9)

"He brought Jesus forth" (John 19:13).

Pilate didn't really like Jerusalem. He liked Caesarea which is on the seacoast and has a lovely beach, very much like Florida. During the feast, He would leave Caesarea and come up to Jerusalem, bringing his soldiers with him. Since he was the Roman governor, he was responsible for keeping order at this time when the Jews gathered from all over the world. That was the reason he was in Jerusalem at this time.

Pilate then went out unto them, and said, What accusation bring ye against this man?

They answered and said unto him, If he were not a malefactor, we would not have delivered him up unto thee.

Then said Pilate unto them, Take ye him, and judge him according to your law. The Jews therefore said unto him, It is not lawful for us to put any man to death:

That the saying of Jesus might be fulfilled, which he spake, signifying what death he should die [John 18:29–32].

Pilate senses that something is wrong and he tries, as we would say, to get off the hook. He tells them to judge Jesus themselves. He couldn't understand what was taking place. The problem was that they wanted the death penalty and they had to admit that they were no longer the rulers and no longer had the authority to exact the death penalty. It is interesting that these men were forced to admit this after they had so arrogantly stated in John 8:33. "We be Abraham's seed, and were never in bondage to any man."

John tells us that this fulfilled what Jesus had prophesied. He had told the disciples that the Jewish religious rulers would condemn Him to death and would deliver Him to the Gentiles. He had predicted this months earlier; now He was here, being brought to Pilate, the representative of Gentile Rome, by the religious rulers who wanted a death sentence. If the Jews had taken Jesus and had put Him to death according to their Law, He would have been stoned to death. Read Psalm 22 again and notice whether it is describing a death by stoning or a death by crucifixion. It is obviously crucifixion, with the piercing of the hands and feet and the agonies of hanging on a cross. The only ones who executed by crucifixion were the Romans. Jesus had to be delivered to the Romans to fulfill Old Testament prophecy.

Then Pilate entered into the judgment hall again, and called Jesus, and said unto him, Art thou the King of the Jews?

Jesus answered him, Sayest thou this thing of thyself, or did others tell it thee of me?

Pilate answered, Am I a Jew? Thine own nation and the chief priests have delivered thee unto me: what hast thou done? [John 18:33–35].

Jesus had appealed to the head of this man, Pilate. He asked him the logical question of where he got his evidence. Pilate sneered at that and said the Jews had brought the accusation. Now Jesus will appeal to this man's heart. Jesus is dealing with him, man to man.

Pilate was dumbfounded. He couldn't believe there was someone claiming to be the king of the Jews and that they would have the audacity to bring such a charge. Pilate is out on a limb and wants to get off. He would like to help Jesus. He is inside the court, alone with Jesus; the Jews are waiting outside because of their scruples about contaminating themselves. Pilate would be happy if Jesus would simply say He is not a king and that would get Pilate off the hook. Who is on trial? Pilate or Jesus?

Jesus answered, My kingdom is not of this world: if my kingdom were of this world, then would my servants fight, that I should not be delivered to the Jews: but now is my kingdom not from hence [John 18:36].

"My kingdom is not of this world." The preposition is the Greek *ek,* meaning "out of." Literally, He said "My kingdom is out of this world." He is not saying that His kingdom is not going to be on this earth someday, as He is going to rule as King of kings and Lord of lords and ". . . the earth shall be full of the knowledge of the LORD, as the waters cover the sea" (Isa. 11:9). But His kingdom is not going to be of this world system. It will not be a power structure built on politics. It will not come through worldly measures. Jesus will not be elected King by either the Democrats or the Republicans or by the United Nations. It is not going to be built by war and turmoil and hatred and bitterness. Pilate, himself, was a crooked politician who bought his job and was a puppet of Rome. He hated the Jews, but he was afraid to offend them because he might lose his job. But Jesus will not come to His kingdom by political maneuvering. Jesus said, "If my kingdom were of this world, then would my servants fight." He was offering no resistance. Peter had tried to defend Him, and Jesus had told him to put his sword in the sheath. He is not building His kingdom out of the present political system.

Friend, the church cannot build His kingdom either. The Bible teaches us clearly that in this present age Christ is gathering out a people for His name (see Acts 15:14). These are the *ekklesia* or the called-out ones, the church. They are called out of the world to live *in* the world but not *of* the world. The time will come when the Lord will completely remove the church from the world. Then, when Christ comes in His kingdom, *He* will establish it!

Pilate therefore said unto him, Art thou a king then? Jesus answered, Thou sayest that I am a king. To this end was I born, and for this cause came I into the world, that I should bear witness unto the truth. Every one that is of the truth heareth my voice [John 18:37].

Pilate is definitely puzzled at this point. Jesus is still pleading with this man. He tells him that an essential of His kingdom is truth. Listen to Psalm 45:1–4: ". . . I speak of the things which I have made touching the king: my tongue is the pen of a ready writer. Thou art fairer than the children of men: grace is poured into thy lips: therefore God hath blessed thee for ever. Gird thy sword upon thy thigh, O most mighty, with thy glory and thy majesty. And in thy majesty ride prosperously because of truth and meekness and righteousness. . . ."

Pilate saith unto him, What is truth? And when he had said this, he went out again unto the Jews, and saith unto them, I find in him no fault at all [John 18:38].

Was Pilate a cynic? Was he simply puzzled? He stood in the presence of the Lord Jesus who was and is the Way, the Truth, and the Life. John tells us later in his gospel that he has written all these things so that we might believe that Jesus is the Christ, the Son of God. Friend, do you ask, "What is truth?" Is He truth to you? Have you faced reality in *Him?*

Again he took Jesus outside and declared, "I find in him no fault at all!"

But ye have a custom, that I should release unto you one at the passover: will ye therefore that I release unto you the King of the Jews? [John 18:39].

He was trying desperately to escape making a decision. "Let me release Jesus to you, and that will settle it."

Then cried they all again, saying, Not this man, but Barabbas. Now Barabbas was a robber [John 18:40].

Pilate didn't dream that these religious rulers would urge the people to demand that Barabbas be released. The contrast between them was too great. The Bible makes it clear that Pilate was assured that Jesus Christ was an innocent man.

"He knew that for envy they had delivered him" (Matt. 27:18).

". . . I am innocent of the blood of this just person . . ." (Matt. 27:24).

"For he knew that the chief priests had delivered him for envy" (Mark 15:10).

"Pilate therefore, willing to release Jesus, spake again to them" (Luke 23:20).

". . . I have found no cause of death in him . . ." (Luke 23:22).

". . . I find in him no fault at all" (John 18:38).

". . . From thenceforth Pilate sought to release him . . ." (John 19:12).

". . . Pilate, when he was determined to let him go" (Acts 3:13).

In spite of all this, Pilate did not have the courage to release Him.

CHAPTER 19

THEME: *Death of Jesus at Golgotha; burial in the tomb of Joseph*

In this chapter we will see a great miscarriage of justice. Rome was noted throughout the world for its justice. On every Roman official's desk there was the little figure of the two-faced god, Janus. One face looked forward and the other face looked backward. (It is from this word that we get the name January for the month that looks back to the old year and forward to the new year.) Janus was to remind the judge to look at both sides of the question. Rome ruled the world for nearly one thousand years. When the Romans took over a people, they promised them good roads, law and order, protection, and peace—but life would be under a dictatorship. Rome ruled with an iron hand. In Roman courts the innocent got justice, and the guilty got justice—not mercy, but justice. The interesting thing that makes this such an anomaly is that the trial of Jesus was one of the greatest miscarriages of justice.

DEATH OF JESUS AT GOLGOTHA

Then Pilate therefore took Jesus, and scourged him.

And the soldiers platted a crown of thorns, and put it on his head, and they put on him a purple robe,

And said, Hail, King of the Jews! and they smote him with their hands [John 19:1–3].

If Jesus was innocent, He should have been turned loose. If He was guilty of the charge brought against Him, He should have been crucified. To scourge Jesus was entirely unlawful and wrong. Pilate did it because he thought this would placate the Jews.

The soldiers took this opportunity to have their fun with Him before He was crucified. When it says "they smote him with their hands," it means they played a cruel Roman game with Him. They could mutilate Him and do anything they wished with Him. All the soldiers would show the prisoner their fists. Then they would blindfold the prisoner and all but one would hit him as hard as they could. Then they would remove the blindfold, and if the prisoner was still conscious he was to guess which soldier did not hit him. Obviously, the prisoner could never guess the right one. They would continue this until they had beaten the prisoner to a pulp. I believe that the Lord Jesus was so mutilated that you would not have recognized Him. "As many were astonied at thee; his visage was so marred more than any man, and his form more than the sons of men" (Isa. 52:14).

Pilate therefore went forth again, and saith unto them, Behold, I bring him forth to you, that ye may know that I find no fault in him.

Then came Jesus forth, wearing the crown of thorns, and the purple robe. And Pilate saith unto them, Behold the man! [John 19:4–5].

Now they come outside again. I think that if you had seen Him then, it would have broken your heart. He had been beaten within an inch of His life. Don't think He looked like the artists picture Him.

"Behold the man!" If you have said only this that Pilate said, you haven't seen Him at all. He is more than a man. He is the Son of God. He is the Savior of the world. John has written these things so that you might believe that Jesus is the Christ, the Son of God, and that believing you might have life in His name.

When the chief priests therefore and officers saw him, they cried out, saying, Crucify him, crucify him. Pilate saith unto them, Take ye him, and crucify him: for I find no fault in him [John 19:6].

It may have been at this point that Pilate called for the basin of water and washed his hands. The water would clean his hands but could not cleanse the guilt of his heart. The oldest creed of the church states that Jesus was crucified under Pontius Pilate.

The Jews answered him, We have a law, and by our law he ought to die, because he made himself the Son of God.

When Pilate therefore heard that saying, he was the more afraid;

And went again into the judgment hall, and saith unto Jesus, Whence art thou? But Jesus gave him no answer [John 19:7–9].

Pilate is not satisfied, and so he takes Him inside again to question Him.

Then saith Pilate unto him, Speakest thou not unto me? knowest thou not that I have power to crucify thee, and have power to release thee?

Jesus answered, Thou couldest have no power at all against me, except it were given thee from above: therefore he that delivered me unto thee hath the greater sin [John 19:10–11].

There are differences of sin and differences of judgment. Those who delivered Jesus to Pilate had the greater sin because they had more light than Pilate did. However, that does not exonerate Pilate at all. He is guilty.

And from thenceforth Pilate sought to release him: but the Jews cried out, saying, If thou let this man go, thou art not Caesar's friend: whosoever maketh himself a king speaketh against Caesar [John 19:12].

From thenceforth Pilate sought to release Him. Because he believed in Him? No. Because he knew that the Lord Jesus was an innocent man.

Jesus is now in the hands of a cheap politician—not the judge of Roman justice that Pilate should have been. These Jewish religious rulers are prepared to report Pilate to Rome accusing him of permitting subversion. That would be treason, and Pilate doesn't want such a charge against him. Pilate will let his political position overrule his justice. It is a terrible thing, even today, when government, whether it be church or state government, gets into the hands of men who are hungry for power and do not regard either God or man.

When Pilate therefore heard that saying, he brought Jesus forth, and sat down in the judgment seat in a place that is called the Pavement, but in the Hebrew, Gabbatha [John 19:13].

The Pavement was the *Lithostrotos*. It was the place of Roman justice. Julius Caesar always carried a moveable one with him so that anywhere he went, the *Lithostrotos* was set up, and there he pronounced his judgments. This Gabbatha is one place in Jerusalem which I think is accurately identifiable. It is about fifteen feet below the present level of the Ecce Homo Street. There is the worn stone which I think may well be the Pavement, the Gabbatha.

And it was the preparation of the passover, and about the sixth hour: and he saith unto the Jews, Behold your King!

But they cried out, Away with him, away with him, crucify him. Pilate saith unto them, Shall I crucify your King? The chief priests answered, We have no king but Caesar [John 19:14–15].

Notice the dignity of the Lord Jesus through all this. Notice that He is not the one on trial. Pilate is forced to a choice. Will it be Jesus Christ or Caesar? The religious leaders are forced to a choice. Will it be Jesus Christ or Caesar? They make their dreadful choice, "We have no king but Caesar." The day will come in the future when they will have to make another choice. Jesus Christ or the Antichrist? Friend, listen; every man must make his choice about Jesus Christ. He says, "He that is not with me is against me . . ." (Matt. 12:30). The minute you make a decision against Christ, you make a decision for "Caesar."

Then delivered he him therefore unto them to be crucified. And they took Jesus, and led him away [John 19:16].

We speak so often of the death and resurrection of Jesus Christ that it becomes almost trite for the average believer. The crucifixion of Jesus Christ is one of the most dastardly, infamous points in history. Yet, this is our redemption. We need to pause here and look at it from various points of view.

From the standpoint of God, the cross is a propitiation. It is the mercy seat where God can extend mercy to you and to me. It is the place where full satisfaction was made, so that a holy, righteous God can reach down and save sinners. The very throne of God, the place of judgment, is transformed into the place of mercy where you and I can find mercy instead of the judgment we deserve. Jesus Christ bore our guilt, and God is satisfied.

From the standpoint of the Lord Jesus, it is a sacrifice. He is the Savior, and He makes Himself an offering for sin. He is a sweet-smelling savor to God. It is also an act of obedience for Him. Paul tells us in Philippians 2:8 that he became obedient to death, even the death of the cross.

From the standpoint of you and me, believers in Christ Jesus, it was a substitution. He took my place and He took your place. He was the sinless One suffering for the sinner. He was the just One suffering for the unjust. "Who his own self bare our sins in his own body on the tree, that we, being dead to sins, should live unto righteousness: by whose stripes ye were healed" (1 Pet. 2:24).

From the standpoint of Satan, it was a triumph and also a defeat. It was a triumph for Satan to bruise the heel of the woman's seed as had been foretold way back in Genesis 3. It was a defeat because the head of Satan is yet to be crushed: ". . . that through death he might destroy him that had the power of death, that is, the devil" (Heb. 2:14).

From the standpoint of the world, the cross is nothing but a brutal murder. They see Jesus of Nazareth. They see the man. They see the injustice.

So they led Him away to be crucified. This fulfills Psalm 94:20–21: "Shall the throne of iniquity have fellowship with thee, which frameth mischief by a law? They gather themselves together against the soul of the righteous, and condemn the innocent blood."

And he bearing his cross went forth into a place called the place of a skull, which is called in the Hebrew Golgotha: Where they crucified him, and two other with him, on either side one, and Jesus in the midst [John 19:17–18].

John does not give us a picture of the Crucifixion. He mentions the place but gives very few details. General Gordon, never satisfied with the spot inside the city walls which is pointed out as Golgotha, decided upon a rocky, skull-like formation outside the city walls, called Gordon's Calvary, which I believe to be the actual Golgotha.

You will recall that every bit of the sin offering was taken outside the camp into a clean place (see Lev. 4:12). Just as the Lord Jesus fulfilled prophecy concerning Himself, so He also fulfills the *types* in the Old Testament. Our sin offering, the Lord Jesus Christ, was taken outside the city. The writer to the Hebrews emphasizes the fact that our Lord suffered outside the gate (see Heb. 13:12).

And Pilate wrote a title, and put it on the cross. And the writing was, JESUS OF NAZARETH THE KING OF THE JEWS [John 19:19].

You will notice that I have made no attempt to harmonize the other gospels with the Gospel of John. They are each different, and each is written for a different purpose. You need to put all four of them together to find the complete statement written on the cross.

This title then read many of the Jews: for the place where Jesus was crucified was nigh to the city: and it was written in Hebrew, and Greek, and Latin.

Then said the chief priests of the Jews to Pilate, Write not, The King of the Jews; but that he said, I am King of the Jews.

Pilate answered, What I have written I have written [John 19:20–22].

It was written in Hebrew, the language of religion. It was written in Greek, the language of culture and education. It was written in Latin, the language of law and order. Thus, it was written for the whole world to see that He died for all. This is the gospel that is to be preached to the world. This is the hope of the world.

Then the soldiers, when they had crucified Jesus, took his garments, and made four parts, to every soldier a part; and also his coat: now the coat was without seam, woven from the top throughout.

They said therefore among themselves, Let us not rend it, but cast lots for it, whose it shall be: that the scripture might be fulfilled, which saith, They parted my raiment among them, and for my vesture they did cast lots. These things therefore the soldiers did [John 19:23–24].

"When they had crucified Jesus." No gospel writer describes the death of Christ. There are things about the cross and the Crucifixion that are hidden from us. God pulls down a veil on many of the details. Darkness covered the land so the people couldn't see. First of all, God is not going to give us morbid details simply to satisfy our idle curiosity. Secondly, there was a transaction between the Father and the Son taking place there. It was a transaction for the sins of the world, which is beyond our comprehension. The only thing that we can do is to accept by faith the forgiveness that is made ours through Christ's death on the cross. That is the only way you and I will ever penetrate that darkness, my friend.

Apparently His garment is a peasant's garment but a good one. Someone had made it for Him. The soldiers cast lots for it—shot dice at the foot of the cross. Although these Romans do not know it, they are fulfilling the Scriptures: "They part my garments among them, and cast lots upon my vesture" (Ps. 22:18).

Now there stood by the cross of Jesus his mother, and his mother's sister,

Mary the wife of Cleophas, and Mary Magdalene.

When Jesus therefore saw his mother, and the disciple standing by, whom he loved, he saith unto his mother, Woman, behold thy son!

Then saith he to the disciple, Behold thy mother! And from that hour that disciple took her unto his own home [John 19:25–27].

Jesus calls Mary, "Woman," just as He had in John 2 at the wedding at Cana. His hour is come. He is to die, but He will rise again. He is to be glorified. His relationship to His mother is to be severed. To her, as well as to us, He is to be the glorified Christ. His resurrection will clear her name forever. Her reputation will be vindicated. But she must come to Christ in faith just as every other believer comes. While He is dying for the sins of the world, He will not neglect her. We know that Mary will be praying with the disciples in the Upper Room after His resurrection (see Acts 1:14), and after that she drops out of the picture. As long as she lived John would keep her in his home and care for her, as the Lord Jesus asked him to do.

After this, Jesus knowing that all things were now accomplished, that the scripture might be fulfilled, saith, I thirst.

Now there was set a vessel full of vinegar: and they filled a sponge with vinegar, and put it upon hyssop, and put it to his mouth.

When Jesus therefore had received the vinegar, he said, It is finished: and he bowed his head, and gave up the ghost [John 19:28–30].

John carefully shows us that Scripture is being fulfilled. There are chapters in the Old Testament which are especially concerned with the Crucifixion. I would list Psalm 22, Genesis 22, Isaiah 53, and Leviticus 16. There are twenty-eight prophecies fulfilled while He was hanging on the cross. "I thirst" is the fulfillment of Psalm 69:21.

"It is finished!" What was finished? Your redemption and my redemption was finished. In His report to the Father He had said, "I have finished the work which thou gavest me to do" (John 17:4).

The Jews therefore, because it was the preparation, that the bodies should not remain upon the cross on the sabbath day, (for that sabbath day was an high day,) besought Pilate that their legs might be broken, and that they might be taken away.

Then came the soldiers, and brake the legs of the first, and of the other which was crucified with him.

But when they came to Jesus, and saw that he was dead already, they brake not his legs:

But one of the soldiers with a spear pierced his side, and forthwith came there out blood and water.

And he that saw it bare record, and his record is true: and he knoweth that he saith true, that ye might believe.

For these things were done, that the scripture should be fulfilled, A bone of him shall not be broken.

And again another scripture saith, They shall look on him whom they pierced [John 19:31–37].

The first prophecy which John mentions was fulfilled. It says "He keepeth all his bones: not one of them is broken" (Ps. 34:20). The second one still awaits fulfillment. ". . . they shall look upon me whom they have pierced, and they shall mourn for him, as one mourneth for his only son . . ." (Zech. 12:10). He has been pierced! That part has been fulfilled. But Zechariah says that He shall return again, and when He comes, then they shall look upon the One whom they have pierced, and they shall mourn for Him.

BURIAL IN THE TOMB OF JOSEPH

We are dealing with facts, the great historical facts of the gospel. What is the gospel? Paul defines it for us. "For I delivered unto you first of all that which I also received, how that Christ died for our sins according to the scriptures; And that he was buried, and that he rose again the third day according to the scriptures" (1 Cor. 15:3–4). These are the central facts of the gospel. Our salvation is based on our relationship to those facts and to the Person of Jesus Christ. Do you trust Him? Do you have faith in what He did for you when He died on the cross? Do you believe that He died a vicarious, substitutionary, redemptive death for you?

And after this Joseph of Arimathaea, being a disciple of Jesus, but secretly

for fear of the Jews, besought Pilate that he might take away the body of Jesus: and Pilate gave him leave. He came therefore, and took the body of Jesus.

And there came also Nicodemus, which at the first came to Jesus by night, and brought a mixture of myrrh and aloes, about an hundred pound weight.

Then took they the body of Jesus, and wound it in linen clothes with the spices, as the manner of the Jews is to bury [John 19:38–40].

The two men who handle the body of Jesus are both prominent men. Joseph of Arimathaea is a rich man, and Nicodemus is the ruler of the Jews who had come to Jesus by night. They were both secret disciples, but now they come out in the open for the first time. Let's not be too critical of these men. They had stayed in the background but, now that the Lord's disciples have all scattered like sheep and gone under cover, these two men come out in the open.

Because the children of Israel had lived in Egypt, some believe that they were the ones who perfected the method of embalming that the Egyptians used. The child of God in the Old Testament as well as the New Testament has always believed that the body will rise again. It is sown in corruption; it will be raised in incorruption. It is sown in weakness; it will be raised in power. It will be a glorified body. For that reason, the child of God has a reverence and a care for the body.

The custom was to use about half the body weight of spices; so we can guess that the Lord Jesus weighed about two hundred pounds. They would prepare the body by rubbing it with myrrh and aloes, then wrapping it with linen strips. That would seal it and keep out the air. They would begin with a finger, then wrap all the fingers that way, then the hand, the arm, and the whole body. In other words, they wrapped the body of the Lord Jesus like a mummy. Now John mentions specifically that they wrapped the body in the linen cloth using the spices, because this is a very important detail for him. You remember that on the Resurrection morning, when John saw the linen lying there and the body not in it, he understood that the Resurrection had taken place, and he believed.

Now in the place where he was crucified there was a garden; and in the garden a new sepulchre, wherein was never man yet laid.

There laid they Jesus therefore because of the Jews' preparation day; for the sepulchre was nigh at hand [John 19:41–42].

They had to hurry because of the approaching Passover, and apparently they didn't get the embalming process completely finished. This explains why the women bought more spices and planned to come to care for the body of the Lord after the feast day.

This moves us into the next glorious chapter.

CHAPTER 20

THEME: *Resurrection of Jesus; appearance to Mary; appearance to the disciples; appearance to Thomas*

This is the Resurrection chapter as it is recorded in John's gospel. The resurrection of Jesus Christ is the very heart-blood of the Christian faith. It is so important that someone has said, "We cannot make too much of the death of Christ, but we can make too little of the resurrection of Christ." That is the thing that is happening today. Theology books, hymns of the church, sermons, all devote great sections to the death of Christ. Too often the resurrection of Christ is observed only on Easter. We should note that the sermons in the New Testament, beginning at Pentecost, have the resurrection of Jesus Christ as their theme.

RESURRECTION OF JESUS

The first day of the week cometh Mary Magdalene early, when it was yet dark, unto the sepulchre, and seeth the stone taken away from the sepulchre [John 20:1].

"The first day of the week," that is, Sunday, Mary Magdalene came to the tomb. When was the Sabbath day changed? This question is often asked by folk who believe we should be observing Saturday as the day of rest and worship. It was changed when Jesus Christ arose from the dead. He was dead during the Sabbath day; He became alive on Sunday. From that time on, believers have been gathering together on the first day of the week. The Sabbath day belongs to the old creation. After God had created everything, He rested on the Sabbath day. Now we have come to the new creation in Christ Jesus. Pentecost occurred on Sunday, the first day of the week. It is interesting that John, the last of the gospel writers, emphasizes that it was the first day of the week when Jesus rose from the dead.

It will be helpful to get in our minds the order of events on this morning of the Resurrection. I quote from a footnote in *The Scofield Reference Bible*, page 1043.

> Three women, Mary Magdalene, and Mary the mother of James, and Salome, start for the sepulchre, followed by other women bearing spices. The three find the stone rolled away, and Mary Magdalene goes to tell the disciples (Lk. 23:55–24:9; John 20:1–2). Mary, the mother of James and Joses, draws nearer the tomb and sees the angel of the Lord (Mt. 28:2). She goes back to meet the other women following with the spices. Meanwhile Peter and John, warned by Mary Magdalene, arrive, look in, and go away (John 20:3–10). Mary Magdalene returns weeping, sees the two angels and then Jesus (John 20:11–18), and goes as He bade her to tell the disciples. Mary (mother of James and Joses), meanwhile, has met the women with the spices and, returning with them, they see the *two* angels (Lk. 24:4–5; Mk. 16:5). They also receive the angelic message, and, going to seek the disciples, are met by Jesus (Mt. 28:8–10).

Mary Magdalene was the one from whom the Lord had cast seven demons. Some Bible students think she was the sinful woman who wiped the feet of Jesus with her hair. This is an assumption which cannot be proved. I take it that she was a person of very high caliber. She was eternally grateful to the Lord for healing her. When she saw the body was not there, she immediately ran to tell John and Peter.

Then she runneth, and cometh to Simon Peter, and to the other disciple, whom Jesus loved, and saith unto them, They have taken away the Lord out of the sepulchre, and we know not where they have laid him [John 20:2].

The disciple "whom Jesus loved" is John. He always refers to himself in this way rather than by name. Any of the disciples, except Judas, could have used this title for himself. You can use it for yourself. Jude 21 says, "Keep yourselves in the love of God, looking for the mercy of our Lord Jesus Christ unto eternal life." Keep yourself in the love of God, because you know that He loves you. You can't keep Him from loving you! It is wonderful to take that position for yourself as John did: "the other disciple, whom Jesus loved."

We find Simon Peter and John together. Apparently John has taken him in. I wonder if some of the other disciples, when they heard of Peter's denial, had pushed him to the outside. Thank God, John took him in at a time when Peter desperately needed someone to befriend him. John, the son of thunder, has become the apostle of love. What a wonderful thing that is.

Mary Magdalene was not expecting the Resurrection. Her thought was that someone had stolen away the Lord's body. Isn't it interesting that the religious rulers would later accuse the disciples of stealing the Lord's body, and that Mary's first thought was that the religious rulers had stolen the Lord's body? (The religious rulers would have given everything in the world if they could have produced the body on that first Sunday!)

Peter therefore went forth, and that other disciple, and came to the sepulchre.

So they ran both together: and the other disciple did outrun Peter, and came first to the sepulchre [John 20:3–4].

Simon Peter and John were not expecting the Resurrection. They probably thought that Mary didn't really see well in the dark. She saw the stone rolled away, became frightened, and ran. Or maybe she went to the wrong tomb. So they rush to the cemetery. Friend, you don't go into a cemetery to look for the living. They were not expecting to find Jesus alive when they rushed to the tomb. They were expecting to find the Lord's body.

This "other disciple" was John. He was a younger man and could outrun Simon Peter.

This confirms tradition that John was probably the youngest of the disciples. I am of the opinion that these men represented quite an age span. John may have been in his late teens.

And he stooping down, and looking in, saw the linen clothes lying; yet went he not in [John 20:5].

What John saw convinced him that Jesus had risen from the dead. He got there first, but because he had a certain amount of reticence and reverence, he didn't go in. He stooped down to look in through the very small entrance that was hewn out of the stone. He saw the evidence that convinced him. It is amazing how God uses little things like this to bring conviction to the hearts of men. Someone has said, "Great doors swing on little hinges." John saw the linen cloth lying there, but the body had gone out of it.

Then cometh Simon Peter following him, and went into the sepulchre, and seeth the linen clothes lie [John 20:6].

Then here comes Simon Peter puffing and blowing. I tell you, it was hard on him to run. Reticence is not one of his qualities; so he goes right into the sepulchre. He, too, sees the linen clothes and the wrapping that was around His head. Remember that Joseph and Nicodemus had wrapped our Lord's body in the linen and had sealed it with the myrrh and aloes, which made a sort of glue to seal in the body. How could the body get out of such an encasement without unwinding all that linen?

Jesus Christ came up out of that tomb just like a seed comes out of the soil. Remember He had said that a grain of corn falls to the ground and remains alone unless it dies. Then new corn will grow out of it. But the old shell of the seed is still in the ground. That is what was left in the tomb—just the old shell that He had been in. He was no longer in that shell. He was alive.

Do you remember that when the Lord Jesus raised Lazarus, he came forth from the grave all wrapped in the graveclothes and the Lord had to tell them to loose Lazarus? Lazarus came out in his old body wrapped in the old graveclothes. The body of Lazarus would have to die again. However, Jesus Christ came forth in a glorified body which will never see death. This is the Resurrection!

And the napkin, that was about his head, not lying with the linen clothes, but wrapped together in a place by itself.

Then went in also that other disciple, which came first to the sepulchre, and he saw, and believed [John 20:7–8].

God carefully records through John another small but important detail. The napkin that was wrapped around His head lay there intact, separate from the linen wound around His body. It was in the shape of the head, lying just as it had been folded around the head. I think this convinced Peter that the Lord had risen. There are three different Greek words used in this passage, and they are all translated as "seeing." This is unfortunate. In verse 5, when John stooped down, looked in and *saw*, the word means *to perceive and understand.* It involves inspection and perceiving. In verse 6, when Peter went in and *saw*, the word used is *theaomai* from which we get our word *theatre.* He viewed it. In verse 8, when John went into the sepulchre and *saw*, it means *to know.* He knew and he believed before he ever saw the risen Christ.

For as yet they knew not the scripture, that he must rise again from the dead.

Then the disciples went away again unto their own home [John 20:9–10].

John tells us something strange. These men had not understood even though Jesus had told them repeatedly that He would rise from the dead, and even though the Old Testament spoke of this. Even today we need the New Testament as sort of a flashlight to go back and interpret the Old Testament. I believe that one of the reasons the Old Testament is not popular is because we do not sufficiently use the New Testament to interpret it.

There are a great many of us today who read the Bible but still do not know certain scriptures. I believe there are two reasons for this. One is that we may read a passage many times and each time see things in the passage that we have never seen before. The Holy Spirit gives us further light as we study and read the passages over and over again. Also I believe that we must experience some of the scriptures to understand their meaning. The trials and sufferings and experiences of life explain their meaning to us. For example, when David wrote that the Lord was his Shepherd, he knew from experience the shepherd-care of God.

APPEARANCE TO MARY

Apparently Mary is the first one to whom the Lord appeared. There are eleven appearances before His ascension and three after His ascension. I think we can surmise from the text that there are others which were not described.

A proverb can be found for all situations. For those who ask why Jesus appeared first to Mary Magdalene, Proverbs 8:17 says: "I love them that love me; and those that seek me early shall find me." She sought Him and she sought Him early.

But Mary stood without at the sepulchre weeping: and as she wept, she stooped down, and looked into the sepulchre,

And seeth two angels in white sitting, the one at the head, and the other at the feet, where the body of Jesus had lain.

And they say unto her, Woman, why weepest thou? She saith unto them, Because they have taken away my Lord, and I know not where they have laid him.

And when she had thus said, she turned herself back, and saw Jesus standing, and knew not that it was Jesus.

Jesus saith unto her, Woman, why weepest thou? whom seekest thou? She, supposing him to be the gardener, saith unto him, Sir, if thou have borne him hence, tell me where thou hast laid him, and I will take him away [John 20:11–15].

Again we are interested in the fact that she does not know Him. Do you know why? She does not believe that He is back from the dead. Unbelief is blind and unbelief is dumb, as in the case of Zacharias. She loves Him, yes, but love must be coupled with faith. She is weeping because she loves Him but also because she does not believe.

How much is the glorified body changed? I don't know, but I don't think the change is so great that this accounts for her lack of recognition of Jesus. I believe that Mary is absolutely single-minded in her grief. Although she sees two angels, this doesn't seem to draw her attention in any particular way. They ask a question, not because they don't know the answer, but because they are trying to arouse some evidence of faith in Mary. She is single-minded in her answer. He is still dead, and the probable answer is that the body has been stolen, as Mary reasons it out. She does not expect to see Christ alive; and, in her unbelief, she does not recognize Him.

Jesus saith unto her, Mary. She turned herself, and saith unto him, Rabboni; which is to say, Master [John 20:16].

When He called her by name, she recognized the voice as only He could speak. I am of the opinion that if the Lord should tarry and all of us go through the doorway of death, our bodies will be raised when He calls us by name someday, just as He called by name those whom He raised from the dead over nineteen hundred years ago.

Jesus saith unto her, Touch me not; for I am not yet ascended to my Father: but go to my brethren, and say unto them, I ascend unto my Father, and your Father; and to my God, and your God [John 20:17].

The Lord told Mary not to touch Him. The word *touch* is *haptomai*, meaning "to hold on." Later, He told the disciples to touch Him. Why this difference? He says to her, "for I am not yet ascended to my Father." This is the reason she should not hold on to Him. So apparently He did ascend to His Father before the appearance to the disciples in the house. I believe that the Lord Jesus presented His blood at the throne of God and that His blood turned the judgment seat into the mercy seat which it is today. That blood was shed for your sin and for my sin. I think the blood will be there throughout all eternity as an eternal testimony of the price He paid for us.

You will notice He was specific in calling God "my Father, and your Father; and to my God, and your God." His relationship to the Father is different from our relationship to Him. We become the sons of God through faith *in* Jesus Christ, while Christ is a member of the Trinity, the eternal Son of God. He made this distinction here.

APPEARANCE TO THE DISCIPLES

Mary Magdalene came and told the disciples that she had seen the Lord, and that he had spoken these things unto her.

Then the same day at evening, being the first day of the week, when the doors were shut where the disciples were assembled for fear of the Jews, came Jesus and stood in the midst, and saith unto them, Peace be unto you [John 20:18–19].

This group of men had scattered when He was crucified, but now, apparently, had regathered and were hidden away in a room because they were frightened. The doors were shut, which actually means they were locked.

Have you noticed that when the supernatural touches the natural the message is always "Peace" or "Fear not"? His word to them now, when His deity touches their humanity, is "Peace." This is the peace that comes from being justified by faith through our Lord Jesus Christ, which gives us peace with God.

Here, you see, they knew Him when they saw Him. These men were frightened, of course. He appeared in His glorified body and came into the room even though the doors were locked. We learn from this that the glorified body is not subject to the laws of the material universe. That is why I believe that when the Rapture occurs and our bodies are changed, there will be no problem for us to meet the Lord in the air.

And when he had so said, he shewed unto them his hands and his side. Then were the disciples glad, when they saw the Lord [John 20:20].

Notice, that even though He has a glorified body, there are the nail prints and the pierced side. There is a strange similarity to that body which had been nailed to the cross. The scars are there. Now I do not think that there will be scars on *our* bodies. I think these scars are on His body because they are the scars He bore for us. He was scarred for us so that you and I might be presented without spot or blemish before Him. He took our sin and this will be the evidence of it throughout eternity.

Then said Jesus to them again, Peace be unto you: as my Father hath sent me, even so send I you [John 20:21].

I do not think the Lord is just repeating Himself. I think this is a different peace here. In verse 19, it was the peace of redemption—peace *with* God. Redemption is now complete. This is the peace described in Matthew 11:28: "Come unto me, all ye that labour and are heavy laden, and I will give you rest." This is the rest of redemption, the peace of redemption.

There is another peace. It is the peace of those who are in fellowship with God and are doing His will. This is the peace described in Matthew 11:29: "Take my yoke upon you, and learn of me; for I am meek and lowly in heart: and ye shall find rest unto your souls."

Redemption is now accomplished. Now Christ sends them out as the Father had sent Him into the world. He had previously mentioned this in His prayer, "As thou hast sent me into the world, even so have I also sent them into the world" (John 17:18).

And when he had said this, he breathed on them, and saith unto them, Receive ye the Holy Ghost [John 20:22].

This period of history is a transition period between law and grace. There is an interval in the life of these men and in the ministry of the Lord Jesus between His death and resurrection and the Day of Pentecost. This is a time unique in the history of the world.

Our Lord had told them about prayer back in Luke 11. He had said that if they would ask, it should be given to them. In verse 13 of that chapter, He says that He is speaking especially of the gift of the Holy Spirit which the heavenly Father would give to them who ask Him. Well, as nearly as we can tell they never asked! In John 14:16 Jesus says, "And I will pray the Father, and he shall give you another Comforter." It is true that Simon Peter showed some discernment when he said that Jesus is the Christ, but it was just a few minutes later that he told Jesus not to go to the cross to die. I personally believe that at the moment our Lord breathed on them, and said, "Receive ye the Holy Ghost," these men were regenerated. Before this, they had not been indwelt by the Spirit of God.

This expression "breathed on them" occurs only one other time in the Bible. In Genesis, God breathed into Adam the breath of life. I believe here that Jesus Christ breathed into these men eternal life by giving them the Spirit of God. This would sustain them and secure them for the interval between His ascension and the coming of the Holy Spirit on Pentecost.

On the Day of Pentecost, the Holy Spirit would come and they would be baptized by the Spirit into the body of Christ. Also they would be indued with power from on high. The church would come into existence on that day. From that time to the present, the Holy Spirit is in the world. He indwells the believer, and He baptizes every believer into the body of Christ.

Whose soever sins ye remit, they are remitted unto them; and whose soever sins ye retain, they are retained [John 20:23].

This is an important verse which is greatly misunderstood. John Calvin writes: "When Christ enjoins the apostles to forgive sins, He does not convey to them what is peculiar to Himself. It belongs to Him to forgive sins. He only enjoins them in His name to proclaim the forgiveness of sins."

Nowhere in the Book of Acts or in the Epistles do we find any instance of an apostle remitting the sins of anyone. They do go everywhere, proclaiming the forgiveness of sins. Let me ask the question: What is it that forgives sins? Even God cannot just arbitrarily forgive sins. Forgiveness of sins is only and alone through the blood of Jesus Christ. Back in the Old Testament, the forgiveness of sins was based on the fact that Christ would come and die. God saved "on credit" in the Old Testament until Christ would come and pay the penalty. Today God forgives our sins when we believe that Christ died for them.

How can you and I remit sins? By telling the gospel! This is the greater work which we shall do. When somebody turned and believed on Jesus while He was here on earth, that was wonderful. But what is staggering is when you or I simply give out the Word of God, and someone is born again and becomes a new creature in Christ Jesus. "Whose soever sins ye remit, they are remitted unto them" happens when you and I proclaim the gospel of the grace of God. That is the most glorious privilege that there is today, my friend.

We have a responsibility. If we do not preach the gospel to the world, their sins will not be remitted. I think we are reaping the penalty for the years we have not taken the gospel to the world. Because we have neglected our responsibility, our boys die in war. Just think, if all the boys we have lost in war had been willing to lose their lives for Christ and be missionaries, how different the world might be! We have the only thing that will bring forgiveness to the world. It is the gospel of Jesus Christ. My friend, what are you doing?

APPEARANCE TO THOMAS

But Thomas, one of the twelve, called Didymus, was not with them when Jesus came [John 20:24].

I can only surmise why Thomas was not there. I think he was a lone wolf and a doubter. He would cast gloom on every situation. I believe the other ten disciples were excitedly talking about Jesus being raised from the dead and Thomas just couldn't believe it.

The other disciples therefore said unto him, We have seen the Lord. But he said unto them, Except I shall see in his hands the print of the nails, and put my finger into the print of the nails, and thrust my hand into his side, I will not believe [John 20:25].

Boy, is he a doubter! He has enough evidence to make him a believer, but he is not. But at least now it appears that he will stay with the other disciples.

My friend, if you are going to grow in grace, you will have to come together with the saints and grow with them. I believe you have to share what you learn from the Word of the Lord. "Not forsaking the assembling of ourselves together, as the manner of some is; but exhorting one another: and so much the more, as ye see the day approaching" (Heb. 10:25). We are to come together so we may grow together.

And after eight days again his disciples were within, and Thomas with them: then came Jesus, the doors being shut, and stood in the midst, and said, Peace be unto you.

Then saith he to Thomas, Reach hither thy finger, and behold my hands; and reach hither thy hand, and thrust it into my side: and be not faithless, but believing.

And Thomas answered and said unto him, My Lord and my God [John 20:26–28].

The record doesn't tell us that he ever reached forth his hand to touch Him. He didn't have to. I know that today there are many people who say, "If only I could see Him, if only I could touch Him, then I would believe." The problem is not with the lack of available evidence of the death and Resurrection. The problem is in the human heart.

God will meet the honest doubt of a man, but I do not think He deals with dishonest doubts. Many people say they can't believe the Bible. They claim their problem is intellectual. Friend, most people will not believe the Bible because of moral problems. A man told me just the other day that he couldn't believe the Old Testament. Later I learned that he is living in adultery. The Old Testament says "Thou shalt not commit adultery" (Exod. 20:14). He doesn't want to believe the Old Testament. However, I am confident that God will always meet an honest doubter.

You will never find a higher testimony to the Lord Jesus than the one given by Thomas.

It is one of the great confessions of Scripture. For a Jew to say "My Lord and my God" is the absolute climax. This comes from the lips of that doubter, Thomas.

Jesus saith unto him, Thomas, because thou hast seen me, thou hast believed: blessed are they that have not seen, and yet have believed [John 20:29].

There is a special blessing on us today who believe the evidence for the death and resurrection of Christ.

And many other signs truly did Jesus in the presence of his disciples, which are not written in this book:

But these are written, that ye might believe that Jesus is the Christ, the Son of God; and that believing ye might have life through his name [John 20: 30–31].

This is the key to the gospel. The Lord did many things that are not recorded. He healed multitudes. I think John also means that He did many other things after His resurrection which are not recorded. John has been selective in his writing of this gospel. He has chosen the material which he has written because he had a definite purpose in mind.

John did not attempt to write a biography of Jesus Christ. He did not even attempt to fill in the life of Christ in areas not covered by the other gospels. He wrote so that you might "believe that Jesus is the Christ, the Son of God; and that believing ye might have life through his name." It is through believing that you receive life and are born again. You become a child of God through faith in the Lord Jesus Christ.

CHAPTER 21

THEME: *Epilogue—Glorification; the resurrected Jesus is still God; Lord of our wills—Directs our service; Lord of our hearts—Motive for service; Lord of our minds—Lack of knowledge no excuse from service*

Chapter 21 is an epilogue. I believe that after John had written his gospel, he added the prologue and the epilogue.

There are three incidents in this chapter. There is the fishing experience on the Sea of Galilee (also called the Sea of Tiberias). It shows the Lord Jesus as the Lord of our wills, and He directs our service. The second incident is the breakfast on the seashore. This shows the Lord Jesus as the Lord of our hearts and presents our love for Him as the motive for service. The third incident is Jesus announcing the death of Simon Peter. It shows the Lord Jesus as the Lord of our minds and teaches that lack of knowledge or variation of circumstance is no excuse from service. The entire chapter reveals to us that the resurrected Jesus is still God.

LORD OF OUR WILLS—DIRECTS OUR SERVICE

After these things Jesus shewed himself again to the disciples at the sea of Tiberias; and on this wise shewed he himself.

There were together Simon Peter, and Thomas called Didymus, and Nathanael of Cana in Galilee, and the sons of Zebedee, and two other of his disciples.

Simon Peter saith unto them, I go a-fishing. They say unto him, We also go with thee. They went forth, and entered into a ship immediately; and that night they caught nothing [John 21:1–3].

This little Sea of Galilee is so much connected with the ministry of our Lord both before and after His resurrection. It is a familiar spot for these men. He had asked them to go up into Galilee and there He would meet them. They have gone there, and they are waiting for Him.

This is an amazing group here. I like to call this the convention of the problem children. Here is Simon Peter, fervent but failing, warm-hearted, yet walking afar off; he is impulsive and impetuous and affectionate. Then here is Thomas, that magnificent skeptic, who has a question mark for a brain; Nathanael, the wisecracker, who was also a doubter at the beginning; the sons of thunder, James and John; and two others who are not named. Perhaps, since this is a crowd of problem children, they represent you and me.

Many worthy commentators condemn these men for going fishing. Well, the Lord did not rebuke them when He appeared to them. They were at Galilee by His commandment. It was springtime, the Passover season. Warm zephyrs from the south made ripples near the shore and whitecaps out on the sea. The surrounding hills were green, and there were wild flowers in profusion. I saw it like that a few days after Easter several years ago, and I imagine it was even more beautiful nineteen hundred years ago. They may have waited and waited for the Lord Jesus to come. Peter would be the one to become impatient, and after pacing back and forth and after looking up and down the shore, would be the one to say, "I go a-fishing." And six others joined him.

They fished all night and caught nothing. This may be the only true fish story that has been told! Dr. Scotts calls it the failure of the experts. Now these men fished all night, and they caught nothing. They had been restless before, and now they are restless and frustrated. It's easy to fish when you catch fish and frustrating when you don't. They knew how to fish—that's the way they made their living—but that night of failure was in the plan and purpose of God for them.

Then morning dawned, and it must have been a glorious morning on the Sea of Galilee. On the morning I was there, I just felt like shouting when I thought of this incident.

But when the morning was now come, Jesus stood on the shore: but the disciples knew not that it was Jesus [John 21:4].

I think this was a normal experience. He was in His glorifed body and He could be recognized; yet they would have been a distance out on the lake, and in the early morning it would be difficult to identify people on the shore.

Then Jesus saith unto them, Children, have ye any meat? They answered him, No [John 21:5].

The word for children is almost like saying, "Sirs." It is not a term of endearment like "Little children" in 1 John. Their answer is a short "No." It's amazing how emphatic one can be and how little one likes to talk about failure. They answer Him, but they don't want to talk about it. If they had caught any fish, they all would have been showing Him how long they were.

This is a question He is bound to ask everyone of us someday: "Did you catch anything? What did you do for men down there on earth?" I hope your answer will not be the same as theirs, "No, we haven't caught a thing."

And he said unto them, Cast the net on the right side of the ship, and ye shall find. They cast therefore, and now they were not able to draw it for the multitude of fishes [John 21:6].

The whole thought here is that He directs the lives of His own. He gives the instructions, and they are to be obeyed. When they fish according to His instruction, the net fills. Notice the net does not break even though it is full. The net is strong—as strong as the gospel of the death, burial, and resurrection of Christ, of which they are witnesses.

Therefore that disciple whom Jesus loved saith unto Peter, It is the Lord. Now when Simon Peter heard that it was the Lord, he girt his fisher's coat unto him, (for he was naked,) and did cast himself into the sea [John 21:7].

John has a spiritual perception that Simon Peter doesn't have. Three years before, Jesus had called them at perhaps the same spot. They had gone back to fishing and the Lord had called them again to fish for the souls of men.

Peter may not have the discernment of John, but have you noticed that at every opportunity he gets close to the Lord? The other men sit in the boat and wait until they get to shore. Not Simon Peter. He can't wait. He wants to be close to his Lord. This man is a wonderful man.

And the other disciples came in a little ship; (for they were not far from land, but as it were two hundred cubits,) dragging the net with fishes.

As soon then as they were come to land, they saw a fire of coals there, and fish laid thereon, and bread.

Jesus saith unto them, Bring of the fish which ye have now caught.

Simon Peter went up, and drew the net to land full of great fishes, an hundred and fifty and three: and for all there were so many, yet was not the net broken [John 21:8–11].

This is the last recorded miracle of our Lord, and the only miracle recorded after His resurrection. This is most important because you and I are concerned about the ministry of Christ after His resurrection. Paul says, ". . . yea, though we have known Christ after the flesh, yet now henceforth know we him no more" (2 Cor. 5:16). We are not joined to the baby in Bethlehem but to a resurrected, living, glorified Christ at God's right hand. This is why His ministry after His resurrection is so vital for us.

There are several things I would like to call to your attention here. Have you noticed that the Lord uses what people have as the basis for His miracles? The disciples are fishing and catch nothing. The Lord Jesus gives them a harvest of fish. At Cana the water pots were empty. The Lord has the pots filled with water and then changes the water to wine. He asks Moses what he has in his hand. Moses says it is a rod, and with that rod, God performs His miracles for Israel. David is faithful as a shepherd with his shepherd's crook, and God gives him a sceptre to hold in his hand. It is interesting that whatever is in your hand, God can use. So many people wish they were somewhere else or in some other circumstances. My friend, if God can't use you right where you are, I don't think He can use you somewhere else.

Besides, have you ever noticed that what God does He does in abundance? The water pots were *full* of wine. There were baskets of food *left over* after the 5,000 had been fed. The nets were *filled* with fish.

Also, notice that although Jesus had fish laid on a bed of coals for their breakfast on the shore of Galilee, He also asks for some of the fish which they had caught. He accepts their service. When they had fished at His command, He accepts what they bring. What blessed fellowship there is in this kind of service!

There was another time when Peter caught a miraculous number of fish, recorded by Luke. It was in the early days of Jesus' ministry, and He was calling Peter to be a fisher of men. That time the net broke. I think Peter was to see that many would follow Jesus, but they would not all be believers. The net would break and many fish would swim away. This time the net did not break but was drawn to land, "full of great fishes." Peter is being called to feed the sheep and feed the lambs. With what? With the Word of God. With the gospel of a risen, glorified Christ. The gospel will not only save, but it will hold. Even in their failures, believers are kept by the power of God through faith.

We see in this incident that Jesus Christ has a purpose for His own. He wants to direct our lives. If we obey, He will bless and have wonderful fellowship with us. He is the Lord of our wills.

LORD OF OUR HEARTS—MOTIVE FOR SERVICE

Jesus saith unto them, Come and dine. And none of the disciples durst ask him, Who art thou? knowing that it was the Lord.

Jesus then cometh, and taketh bread, and giveth them, and fish likewise.

This is now the third time that Jesus shewed himself to his disciples, after that he was risen from the dead [John 21:12–14].

"Come and dine"—what an invitation! Jesus did say, "Go into all the world and preach the gospel" (see Mark 16:15), but He would rather you would come and have breakfast with Him before you go. The lovely part is that the resurrected Lord, God Himself, feeds them. If only we would sit today and let Him feed us! He wants to feed His own.

Now we come to the special interview that He had with Simon Peter.

So when they had dined, Jesus saith to Simon Peter, Simon, son of Jonas, lovest thou me more than these? He saith unto him, Yea, Lord; thou knowest that I love thee. He saith unto him, Feed my lambs.

He saith to him again the second time, Simon, son of Jonas, lovest thou me? He saith unto him, Yea, Lord; thou knowest that I love thee. He saith unto him, Feed my sheep.

He saith unto him the third time, Simon, son of Jonas, lovest thou me? Peter was grieved because he said unto him the third time, Lovest thou me? And he said unto him, Lord, thou knowest all things; thou knowest that I love thee. Jesus saith unto him, Feed my sheep [John 21:15–17].

Our Lord takes Simon Peter and calls this faltering, failing, fumbling disciple to service. We learn one all-important lesson from this interview. Love for the Savior is the prerequisite for service.

Three times our Lord interrogates Simon Peter, and three times he responds. Then we find that three times the Lord Jesus Christ gives him his commission.

Why three times? Dr. Godet suggests that the reason lies in the fact that Simon Peter denied Christ three times, and now He makes him affirm his devotion three times. No doubt that is part of the reason, but there is more.

It is quite interesting to note that Simon Peter, with the other disciples, had been called to the ministry—actually had been called into the apostleship—after a miraculous catch of fish. If you will recall the account of this fishing experience back in the Gospels of Mark and Luke you will refresh your mind in the fact that it was after our Lord took over the directing of their fishing that the nets broke—and after that He made them apostles.

Then you will further recall that Simon Peter lost his commission around a little fire of coals that had been built in the courtyard of the palace of the high priest the night Jesus was arrested. Simon Peter went blundering in there to warm his hands and made the fatal mistake of his life. It was there he denied the Lord three times. He should not have gone there, but he did; and when he did, he committed this base denial.

Is it not an interesting thing that now by the Sea of Galilee, around coals of fire, after a miraculous catch of fish, the Lord Jesus restores his commission to him? Here the Lord puts Simon Peter back into service. What a picture of spiritual beauty!

When our Lord asked Peter the question three times, it looks like repetition, but it is not. While there is a similarity in the questions, no two are identical.

The *first interrogation:* "So when they had dined, Jesus saith to Simon Peter [would that we could read this as our Lord said it that morning!], Simon, son of Jonas, lovest thou me more than these?" There are many who express the desire to have had the privilege of being present at certain great occasions in the life of our Lord—when He performed miracles, etc. Candidly, I am not sure that I would want to go back to that day. However, if I could go back and hear Him speak to Simon Peter by the Sea of Galilee, I would go back gladly.

To begin with, He called him Simon. That is interesting—"Simon, son of Jonas." Why did He call him Simon? You will recall when the Lord Jesus first met this man—Andrew brought him to Jesus. When Jesus beheld him, He said (in effect), "Thou art Simon, son of Jonas, thou shalt be called Cephas, which by interpretation is a stone." *Cephas* is the Aramaic word for "rock man"; in Greek it is *Petros.* And that name clung to him. We find that over in Caesarea Philippi, when he gave that marvelous testimony concerning the Lord Jesus Christ and said, "Thou art that Christ, the Son of the living God" (John 6:69), the Lord Jesus said in effect, "Blessed art thou, Simon [He goes back to his old name], you will be called Peter because you are going to be a rock man from here on. You will be a man who will stand for something, but right now there is still a question." And so the Lord reminds him of his old name.

There are three words in the Greek language that are translated into the English by the one word *love.* Perhaps, my friend, you are not aware of the fact that the English language is a beggar for words. We have the one word *love* and that is about all. You cannot think of another word. Hollywood, today, would give a million dollars for another word. The best they have done is *sex* and that is pretty low. But the Greek language is a language that is versatile; it is flexible. They have three words for this thing called love.

The first word they have is the word *eros.* In the use of this word they degraded the meaning of love. The Greeks degraded the word in this use for they personified it. The fact of the matter is they have made "Eros" a god and put together in combination the names Aphrodite and Eros. Today we know these names better as Venus and Cupid. The latter are the Roman names but they are the same, as the Greeks are the ones who started this idea with Aphrodite and Eros. *Eros* is a word of sensuality and we do believe that the Hollywood word *sex,* that has really been put into high gear today, would best express what the Greeks had in mind. But this word *eros* is never used in the Word of God.

There is another Greek word—it is *phileō,* and it means "friendship." It has to do with the affections and the emotions in human relations at its very best usage. We get our word *philanthropic* from it, and *philadelphia* comes from it—Philadelphia, the city of "brotherly love." And that is a word that is used in Scripture.

But there is yet another word for love. It is *agapaō. Agapaō* is actually the highest and noblest word for love. Dr. Vincent in his *Word Studies* calls it a word of dignity. It is also a divine word, in that it is a word used to speak of the love of God. The Lord Jesus Christ, in His choice of language, passed over the words *eros* and *phileō* and used the word *agapaō* when He was speaking to Simon Peter. He said, "Do you, Simon Peter, love me with all your heart?"

It is wonderful to have the right doctrine and the right creed, but salvation is a love affair. If you do not love Him, there is no affair. "Simon, son of Jonas, lovest thou me more than these?" Love is the supreme word.

Candidly, if it had been left to me I would have chosen *faith* as the supreme word of Christianity. In fact, I would consider *faith* as the supreme word of any religion. But, of course, Scripture answers that right away: "And now abideth faith, hope, charity [love], these three; but the greatest of these is charity [love]" (1 Cor. 13:13). But I'll tell you why I would choose *faith*—it is a greater compliment to be trusted than to be loved. You see, there is many an old rascal today who is being loved by some wonderful girl. Yes, there is. Sometimes it is the other way around also. But, you see, the minute the object proves unworthy, he is no longer trusted. Will you think closely with me for a minute? Simon Peter had failed the Lord. Actually, the Lord could no longer have confidence in him, but He loved him. Oh, how He loved him!

"Greater love hath no man than this, that a man lay down his life for his friends" (John 15:13). While Simon Peter was denying the Lord, the Lord Jesus was on His way to the cross to die for him! Later, Peter wrote in his first epistle, "Who his own self bare our sins in his own body on the tree, that we, being dead to sins, should live unto righteousness: by whose stripes ye were healed" (1 Pet. 2:24).

Now notice that our Lord's first question to Peter is, "Lovest thou me more than these?"

What He is saying is: "Do you love Me more than these men love Me?" You will recall that the Lord Jesus said, the last time they were in the Upper Room, "One of you will deny Me"—Simon doubtless thought, "Yes, I haven't trusted this crowd either. But there is one fellow here upon whom You can depend—You can depend on me." The Lord Jesus said, "Simon, son of Jonas, are you prepared now to say that you love Me more than these other disciples love Me?" That is what He is saying. Now listen to Simon Peter, "Yea, Lord; thou knowest that I love thee." Here Simon came down and would not use the word *agapaō;* he used the word *phileō*. He says, "You know that I have an affection for You."

Why did not Simon Peter use the word our Lord uses? If you want my opinion, this man is through boasting. Never again will he brag of what he will do. Never again will you hear him saying, I am going to do something big for the Lord. For here on he is going to do something big, but he is not going to say anything about it. He comes to the low plain: "I have an affection for You."

Now will you notice the exhortation. Our Lord responds, "Feed my lambs." Let me give you a better translation: "Be grazing my baby lambs"—the word for lambs is diminutive, which means little baby lambs. "Simon Peter, if you love me I want you to go and graze the little baby lambs; I want you to feed them." Many Christians seem to think He said, "Be criticizing My little lambs." But He has not given you that commission, friend. He says feed them.

The *second interrogation:* Will you notice verse 16, "He saith to him again the second time, Simon, son of Jonas, lovest thou me? He saith unto him, Yea, Lord; thou knowest that I love thee. He saith unto him, Feed my sheep." This time our Lord leaves off "more than these." The reason I think He does it is that He is saying, "Maybe, Simon Peter, you cannot boast anymore and say that you love Me more than do the other disciples, but can you not now say that you do love Me?" In this He is helping this man, trying to lift him up to a higher plane. But Simon Peter just cannot. And somehow we admire him for it. We are glad that he is not boasting anymore. Instead he is willing to take a lower position. Listen to his *affirmation:* "Yea, Lord; thou knowest that I have an affection for thee." But he does not attempt to rise higher—he does not dare to do this, for he is afraid to make such a gesture.

The *second exhortation*: Will you notice this second exhortation, which, incidentally, is ours also. "Feed my sheep." Actually it is not that at all, but rather, "Shepherd the sheep"—that is the word that is used. We want you to notice something, and this is interesting: He says, "feed" the little baby lambs but "shepherd or discipline" the sheep. In our day we have this truth in reverse; we want to discipline the young—that is our method, and we feel as if we should "teach" the old folk. My friend, that is not His method. We are to feed the lambs, and shepherd or discipline the older sheep. Do you know why? It is because the little lambs follow the sheep, hence the older sheep must be disciplined.

The *third interrogation:* "He saith unto him the third time, Simon, son of Jonas, lovest thou me?" Christ now adopts the word of Simon Peter when He asks, "Simon Peter, do you really have an *affection* for me?" Our translation does not show it, but our Lord comes down to the statement of Simon Peter here, and Peter is grieved now.

In the *third affirmation*—"Peter was grieved because he said unto him the third time, Lovest thou me? And he said unto him, Lord thou knowest all things; thou knowest that I love thee."

Let us get at the real meaning of this conversation between our Lord and Simon Peter. Peter was grieved, not because the Lord had asked him the question three times, but he was grieved in his heart because the Lord had to come down and stoop to his level in using his word.

But Simon Peter is still not prepared to climb up. He as much as says that the best thing he can do is to say to the Lord that he has an affection for Him and that the Lord knows he has this affection. He is not bragging now for he realizes that the Lord knows his heart—that he has a real affection in his heart for Him.

The *third exhortation* is "Feed my sheep"—here it has the meaning "be grazing my sheep." You see, the sheep need feeding also.

Milton suffered the loss of a friend, a young minister, who was drowned in the Irish Channel, in crossing; and Milton wrote a poem entitled "Lycidas," in which he made this statement: "The hungry sheep look up and are not fed." In this line he was referring to the pulpit in his day—he might well have been writing of a future day which is ours.

Let me impress it upon your heart that the acid test of any man today, either in pulpit or pew, is "Lovest thou me?"

LORD OF OUR MINDS— LACK OF KNOWLEDGE NO EXCUSE FROM SERVICE

Verily, verily, I say unto thee, When thou wast young, thou girdedst thyself, and walkedst whither thou wouldest: but when thou shalt be old, thou shalt stretch forth thy hands, and another shall gird thee, and carry thee whither thou wouldest not.

This spake he, signifying by what death he should glorify God [John 21:18–19a].

Jesus is telling Peter that he is to become a martyr. Peter had said he would lay down his life for the Lord Jesus. Well, that is what he will do.

And when he had spoken this, he saith unto him, Follow me.

Then Peter, turning about, seeth the disciple whom Jesus loved following; which also leaned on his breast at supper, and said, Lord, which is he that betrayeth thee?

Peter seeing him saith to Jesus, Lord, and what shall this man do? [John 21:19b–21].

Isn't this just like this fellow, Simon Peter? He says, "Now you have told me what I am going to do; tell me what John is going to do."

Jesus saith unto him, If I will that he tarry till I come, what is that to thee? follow thou me [John 21:22].

Our Lord is saying, "Look, Simon Peter, you are going to die for me. What John does is none of your business. Even if he lives until I return, that does not affect what you are to do. You follow *Me!*"

Then went this saying abroad among the brethren, that that disciple should not die: yet Jesus said not unto him, He shall not die; but, If I will that he tarry till I come, what is that to thee?

This is the disciple which testifieth of these things, and wrote these things: and we know that his testimony is true [John 21:23–24].

Here is something interesting. Ignorance, or lack of knowledge, is no excuse for not serving the Lord. Some people say they will not serve the Lord if they cannot get all their questions answered. My friend, there are a lot of things that you won't know. There are many things that you don't need to know. There are things that are not your business to know. The important thing is to follow *Him*.

Jesus did not reveal what would happen to John. He simply said that if it were His will for John not to die, that did not affect Peter's service or Peter's obligation to follow Jesus. That is all important for us to see.

Peter wrote in 2 Peter. 1:14: "Knowing that shortly I must put off this my tabernacle, even as our Lord Jesus Christ hath shewed me." Tradition says that he was crucified, but that he asked to be crucified with his head down because he was not worthy to be crucified with his head up, as his Lord had been crucified.

My friend, the Lord Jesus Christ must be the Lord of your mind, the Lord of your heart, and the Lord of your will. If He is not the Lord of all, then He cannot be the Lord of your life.

And there are also many other things which Jesus did, the which, if they should be written every one, I suppose that even the world itself could not contain the books that should be written. Amen [John 21:25].

John is not exaggerating when he says the whole world could not hold the books about Him if it all could be written. The Lord Jesus is the One who died on the cross and rose again from the dead. He is the eternal God, our Savior.

BIBLIOGRAPHY

(Recommended for Further Study)

Gaebelein, Arno C. *The Gospel of John*. Neptune, New Jersey: Loizeaux Brothers, 1925. (Fine exposition.)

Harrison, Everett F. *John: The Gospel of Faith*. Chicago, Illinois: Moody Press, 1962. (A survey.)

Hendriksen, William. *Gospel of John*. Grand Rapids, Michigan: Baker Book House, 1954.

Ironside, H. A. *Addresses on the Gospel of John*. Neptune, New Jersey: Loizeaux Brothers, 1942.

Kelly, William. *An Exposition of the Gospel of John*. Oak Park, Illinois: Bible Truth Publishers, 1898.

Kent, Homer A., Jr. *Fight in the Darkness: Studies in the Gospel of John*. Grand Rapids, Michigan: Baker Book House, 1975. (Excellent for personal or group study.)

Meyer, F. B. *The Gospel of John*. Fort Washington, Pennsylvania: Christian Literature Crusade, n.d. (Devotional.)

Morgan, G. Campbell. *The Gospel According to John*. Old Tappan, New Jersey: Fleming H. Revell Company, n.d.

Pentecost, J. Dwight. *The Words and Works of Jesus Christ*. Grand Rapids, Michigan: Zondervan Publishing House, 1981.

Pentecost, J. Dwight. *The Parables of our Lord*. Grand Rapids, Michigan: Zondervan Publishing House, 1982.

Pink, Arthur W. *The Gospel of John*. Grand Rapids, Michigan: Zondervan Publishing House, 1945. (Comprehensive.)

Robertson, A. T. *Epochs in the Life of the Apostle John*. Grand Rapids, Michigan: Baker Book House, 1935.

Ryle, J. C. *Expository Thoughts on the Gospels*. 4 vols. Grand Rapids, Michigan: Baker Book House, n.d.

Scroggie, W. Graham. *The Gospel of John*. Grand Rapids, Michigan: Zondervan Publishing House, n.d. (Good outlines.)

Tenney, Merrill C. *John: The Gospel of Belief*. Grand Rapids, Michigan: Wm. B. Eerdmans Publishing Co., 1948.

Van Ryn, August. *Meditations in John*. Neptune, New Jersey: Loizeaux Brothers, n.d.

Vine, W. E. *John: His Record of Christ*. Grand Rapids, Michigan: Zondervan Publishing House, 1948.

Vos, Howard F. *Beginnings in the Life of Christ*. Chicago, Illinois: Moody Press, 1975. (Excellent, inexpensive survey.)

The ACTS of the Apostles

INTRODUCTION

The Book of Acts, sometimes called the fifth gospel, is a continuation of the Gospel of Luke. Dr. Luke is the writer, as he states in his introduction (v. 1). Sir William Ramsay, after making a critical study of Luke's writings, declared that Luke was the greatest historian, ancient or modern.

The Book of Acts is remarkable in many ways. It is a bridge between the Gospels and the Epistles. The New Testament without the Book of Acts leaves a great yawning gap. As Dr. Houson puts it, "If the book of Acts were gone, there would be nothing to replace it." The last recorded fact about Jesus in the Gospel of Matthew is the Resurrection, which is recorded in Acts 1. In the Gospel of Mark, the last recorded act of Jesus is the Ascension, which is also recorded in Acts 1. In the Gospel of Luke, the last recorded fact is the promise of the Holy Spirit. That is also in Acts 1. And in the Gospel of John the last recorded fact is the second coming of Christ. You guessed it—that is also in Acts 1. It is as if the four Gospels had been poured into a funnel, and they all come down into this jug of the first chapter of the Book of Acts. Also the great missionary commission, which appears in all four Gospels, is confirmed in the Book of Acts.

The Book of Acts furnishes a ladder on which to place the Epistles. It would be an enriching experience to read them together, as Acts gives the history of the founding of the churches to which the Epistles are directed.

The Book of Acts records the beginning of the church, the birth of the church. The Book of Genesis records the origin of the physical universe. Acts records the origin of the spiritual body which we designate as the *church.*

The theme or key to the Book of Acts is found in 1:8: "But ye shall receive power, after that the Holy Ghost is come upon you: and ye shall be witnesses unto me both in Jerusalem, and in all Judaea, and in Samaria, and unto the uttermost part of the earth."

The book divides naturally according to this key verse. The first seven chapters record the Lord Jesus Christ at work by the Holy Spirit through the apostles in *Jerusalem.* Chapters 8 through 12 record the Lord Jesus Christ at work by the Holy Spirit through the apostles in *Judea* and *Samaria.* The remainder of the book is devoted to the Lord Jesus Christ at work by the Holy Spirit through the apostles unto the *uttermost part of the earth.*

The Book of Acts is not complete. It breaks off with Paul in his own hired house in Rome. It has no proper ending. Do you know why? It is because the Book of Acts is a continuing story. Perhaps the Lord has Dr. Luke up there writing the next chapters now. Perhaps he is recording what you and I do for Christ in the power of the Holy Spirit. I hope so.

Some special features of the Book of Acts are:

1. Prominence of the Lord Jesus Christ. The Lord Jesus has left His disciples now. He is gone. He has ascended in the first chapter of the book. But He is still at work! He has just moved His position, His location. He has moved His headquarters. As long as He was here on this earth, His headquarters were in Capernaum. Now His headquarters are at the right hand of the Father. The Lord Jesus Christ is prominent. He is at work from the vantage place of heaven itself.

2. Prominence of the Holy Spirit. Christ promised to send the Holy Spirit. This promise is mentioned in the Gospel of John four times (John 1:33; 7:37–39; 14:16–17; 20:22). The same promise is given in the Book of Acts (Acts 1:8). You and I are living in the age of the Holy Spirit. The great fact of this age is the indwelling of the Holy Spirit in believers.

3. The power of the church. There is a power in the church, and, of course, this is the working of the Spirit of God. That power of the early church is not manifest in churches today. Why? Because the early church operated on a high spiritual level which has not again been attained in any age since then. However, it is the Holy Spirit working through the believer when any service brings honor and glory to the Lord Jesus Christ.

4. Prominence of the church, visible and invisible. The church is a new institution. It has come into existence in the Book of Acts.

5. Prominence of places. The book begins at Jerusalem and ends in Rome. Sir William

Ramsay checked all the places mentioned by Dr. Luke and found them to be accurate.

6. Prominence of persons. Dr. Luke mentions 110 persons by name, besides the references to multitudes or crowds. I believe that by the end of the first century there were millions of believers in the world. The church had a phenomenal growth in those first two to three hundred years. It certainly has slowed down today, exactly as our Lord said it would.

7. Prominence of the Resurrection. The Resurrection is the center of gospel preaching. In too many churches today, we have one Easter sermon once a year. As a pastor, many times I have featured Easter in August. People would come just to find out what had happened to the preacher. They thought the heat was getting to me. However, in the early church the resurrection of Jesus Christ was the very center and heart of the message, and no sermon was preached without it. The theme of Peter on the Day of Pentecost was the resurrection of Jesus Christ. He explained that what was taking place was because Jesus was now in heaven at the right hand of God and had sent His Holy Spirit into the world. It was all due to the Resurrection. You will find that the Resurrection is the very heart of the messages of Paul.

There are a great many people and preachers who like to "ride a hobby." Some people like to ride the hobby of prophecy; others dwell on the Keswick message or some other facet or phase. Now, if you want to ride a hobby, let me suggest one for you: the resurrection of Jesus Christ. In the early church, every Sunday was Easter, a day to proclaim the Resurrection. "He is risen!" was proclaimed everywhere (see Matt. 27:64).

8. There is a prominence of Peter in the first section of the book and of Paul in the last section. There is a strange omission of the other apostles. God had good reasons, I am sure, for emphasizing the ministry of these two men.

Also there is a human reason. I believe that Dr. Luke was acquainted with the ministries of these two men. He was an associate of Paul.

Some people hold the idea that there was a disagreement between Peter and Paul. Very candidly, I am of the opinion that Dr. Luke and Peter and Paul got together a great many times and had many talks.

The proper title for this historical book has always been a problem. The Bible which I use is the authorized version and there it is called *The Acts of the Apostles*. The Codex Vaticanus and the revised versions also call it *The Acts of the Apostles*. Robert Lee called it *The Acts of the Ascended and Glorified Lord*. The Bantu title is *Words Concerning Deeds*.

I would rather think that the key is given to us in the first two verses of the first chapter. On the basis of this, I would venture a title which is a rather long one: *The Lord Jesus Christ at Work by the Holy Spirit through the Apostles*.

OUTLINE

I. The Lord Jesus Christ at Work by the Holy Spirit through the Apostles in Jerusalem, Chapters 1–7

A. Preparation for the Coming of the Spirit, Chapter 1
   1. Introduction, Chapter 1:1–2
   2. Forty Days Post-Resurrection Ministry of Jesus, Chapter 1:3–8
   3. Ascension and Promise of the Return of Jesus, Chapter 1:9–11
   4. Waiting for the Spirit, Chapter 1:12–14
   5. Appointment of an Apostle, Chapter 1:15–26

B. Day of Pentecost (Bethlehem of the Holy Spirit), Chapter 2
   1. Coming of the Holy Spirit, Chapter 2:1–13
   2. First Sermon in the Church Age by Peter, Chapter 2:14–47

C. First Miracle of the Church; Peter's Second Sermon, Chapter 3
   1. Healing of Lame Man, Chapter 3:1–11
   2. Appealing and Revealing Address of Peter, Chapter 3:12–26
   3. Believing Five Thousand Men (Results), Chapter 4:4

D. First Persecution of the Church; Power of the Holy Spirit, Chapter 4

E. Death of Ananias and Sapphira; Second Persecution, Chapter 5

F. Appointment of Deacons; Witness of Stephen, a Deacon, Chapter 6

G. Stephen's Address and Martyrdom (First Martyr), Chapter 7

II. The Lord Jesus Christ at Work by the Holy Spirit through the Apostles in Judea and Samaria, Chapters 8–12

A. Conversion of Ethiopian Eunuch (Son of Ham), Chapter 8

B. Conversion of Saul of Tarsus (Son of Shem), Chapter 9

C. Conversion of Cornelius, Roman Centurion (Son of Japheth), Chapter 10

D. Peter Defends His Ministry; Gospel Goes to Antioch, Chapter 11

E. Death of James; Arrest of Peter, Chapter 12

III. The Lord Jesus Christ at Work by the Holy Spirit through the Apostles to the Uttermost Part of the Earth, Chapters 13–28

A. First Missionary Journey of Paul, Chapters 13–14

B. Council at Jerusalem, Chapter 15

C. Second Missionary Journey of Paul, Chapters 15:36–16:40

D. Second Missionary Journey (continued) Paul in Thessalonica, Athens, Chapter 17

E. Second Missionary Journey (concluded) Paul in Corinth; Apollos in Ephesus, Chapter 18

F. Third Missionary Journey, Chapters 18:23–21:14 Paul in Ephesus, Chapter 19

G. Third Missionary Journey of Paul (continued), Chapter 20

H. Paul Goes to Jerusalem and Is Arrested, Chapter 21

I. Paul's Defense before the Mob at Jerusalem, Chapter 22

J. Paul's Defense before the Sanhedrin, Chapter 23

K. Paul before Felix, Chapter 24

L. Paul before Festus, Chapter 25

M. Paul before Agrippa, Chapter 26

N. Paul Goes to Rome via Storm and Shipwreck, Chapter 27

O. Paul Arrives in Rome, Chapter 28 *(Last seen preaching to Gentiles)*

CHAPTER 1

THEME: *Preparation for the coming of the Spirit*

As suggested in the Introduction, in my opinion the proper title for the Book of Acts would be: *The Lord Jesus Christ at Work by the Holy Spirit through the Apostles.* And the first seven chapters reveal the Lord Jesus Christ at work by the Holy Spirit through the apostles in *Jerusalem.* The first chapter, which is the preparation for the coming of the Holy Spirit, includes a brief introduction; a resumé of the forty-day post-resurrection ministry of Jesus; His ascension and promise of return; then the apostles waiting for the Spirit, and their appointment of an apostle to take the place of Judas.

INTRODUCTION

The former treatise have I made, O Theophilus, of all that Jesus began both to do and teach,

Until the day in which he was taken up, after that he through the Holy Ghost had given commandments unto the apostles whom he had chosen [Acts 1:1–2].

The "former treatise" was Luke's gospel, which also was directed to *Theophilus*—whose name means "lover of God." I totally reject the idea that just any lover of God is intended. Obviously Luke knew a man by the name of Theophilus, and undoubtedly the name was appropriate—a lover of God. Luke's gospel was "all that Jesus began both to do and teach," and in the Book of Acts Jesus *continues* to do and to teach. Today He is still at it, if I may use that expression, and He will continue on with this present program until He takes His own out of the world.

"Until the day in which he was taken up, *after that* he through the Holy Ghost [Spirit]" makes it clear that just because Jesus was taken up into heaven didn't mean He ceased doing and teaching. But now, from the vantage place of the right hand of God, He is continuing to work through the Holy Spirit. As in the army where commands pass from one man to another, so the Lord Jesus Christ is working through the Holy Spirit; the Holy Spirit operates through the apostles and on out to you and to me where we are today. This is a remarkable statement here.

FORTY DAYS POST-RESURRECTION MINISTRY OF JESUS

Dr. Luke uses one of his periodic sentences here, which continues on through verse 4.

To whom also he shewed himself alive after his passion by many infallible proofs, being seen of them forty days, and speaking of the things pertaining to the kingdom of God [Acts 1:3].

He showed Himself alive by many *infallible* proofs after His suffering and death. There are ten recorded appearances of Jesus after His resurrection. His post-resurrection ministry, as revealed in His appearances, has a more important bearing on the lives of Christians today than does the three year ministry recorded in the Gospels. I have a little book entitled *The Empty Tomb,* which tells of this post-resurrection ministry of the Lord Jesus. Paul stated it this way: "Wherefore henceforth know we no man after the flesh: yea, though we have known Christ after the flesh, yet now henceforth know we him no more" (2 Cor. 5:16).

You and I do not know Him today as the One who walked on this earth over nineteen hundred years ago. We know Him as the one Man in the glory. He is up there right this moment, and He is real. How often the church loses sight of this fact.

Recently a letter came to me from a person who said he had been a church member all his life. He had gone through all the prescribed rituals, and he thought he was a Christian. Then through hearing the Word of God he learned that he didn't even know Jesus. The wonderful discovery for him was that not only did Jesus walk on this earth nineteen hundred years ago, but also He is alive today and is sitting at God's right hand. He came to the living Christ and received Him as Savior and Lord. How wonderful that is! Jesus showed Himself alive by many infallible proofs.

The problem of the unbeliever today is not with the facts but with his own unbelief. The facts are available. I wonder whether anyone doubts that the Battle of Waterloo was an historical event. Very frankly, I believe that Napoleon lived, and I believe that he fought the Battle of Waterloo. But I have very little evidence for it. Actually there is ten thousand times more evidence for the death and resurrection of the Lord Jesus Christ than there is for the Battle of Waterloo, and yet there are people today who say they do not believe it. Where is the problem? The problem is in the heart, the unbelieving heart. There is a natural tendency for man to run away from God just as Adam did. Man turns his back upon God today. If you are an unbeliever, the problem is with *you*. The problem is not in the Word of God. He showed Himself alive by many infallible proofs. You can know if you really want to know. The problem is that you don't want to know. The problem is not in the mind; the problem is in the will.

Let me insert a comment here about the Resurrection. There is a verse which I think has been twisted and distorted. The Lord Jesus Christ said, "And I, if I be lifted up from the earth, will draw all men unto me" (John 12:32). How was He lifted up? He was lifted up in the Resurrection, friend, lifted up from the dead. That is the message. Regardless of how much you talk about Jesus or how lovely you say that He is, the message is that He has been lifted up from the dead. He is risen! The reason that more people are not drawn to Christ is that there is not the preaching of a resurrected Christ. How the Book of Acts puts the emphasis on the resurrection of Jesus Christ!

And, being assembled together with them, commanded them that they should not depart from Jerusalem, but wait for the promise of the Father, which, saith he, ye have heard of me [Acts 1:4].

That's the end of the sentence—these first four verses are all one sentence! The apostles are to wait for the coming of the Holy Spirit. Until that event takes place, His command is to wait.

For John truly baptized with water; but ye shall be baptized with the Holy Ghost not many days hence [Acts 1:5].

The risen Jesus appeared to the apostles and gave them these instructions. He tells them that something is going to happen to them. They are going to be baptized with the Holy Spirit not many days hence. This baptism of the Holy Spirit is the promise of the Father, and Jesus had previously told them about it.

It is very important to point out that this is not talking about water baptism, which is *ritual* baptism. This is the baptism with the Holy Spirit. The baptism of the Holy Spirit is *real* baptism. It is this baptism of the Holy Spirit which places a believer into the body of believers, which we sometimes refer to as the church.

When we get to the second chapter, which tells of the coming of the Holy Spirit on the Day of Pentecost, we will learn that they were filled with the Holy Spirit. Filling was necessary in order that they might serve. The fact that they were filled with the Holy Spirit for service indicates that the other ministries of the Holy Spirit had been performed.

When they therefore were come together, they asked of him, saying, Lord, wilt thou at this time restore again the kingdom to Israel? [Acts 1:6].

You will find that some of the commentators rebuke the apostles for asking this question—they feel the apostles made a mistake. I believe that the answer the Lord gives them indicates they made no mistake. Their question was a legitimate question, a natural question, and one that our Lord answered as such. He did not rebuke them. He did not call it a foolish question.

The apostles were brought up and schooled in the Old Testament. They had waited for the coming of the Messiah. They understood that the Messiah is the One who will establish the kingdom upon this earth. That was their hope. It is still the hope for this earth. God is not through with this earth. God does not intend to sweep this earth under the rug. Although it is small enough to be swept under His rug, He is not going to do that. God has an eternal purpose for the earth. It was the kingdom of God that they talked about, which involves the re-establishment of the house of David. These were the things He talked about after His resurrection—we see in verse 3 that He spoke of things "pertaining to the kingdom of God."

And he said unto them, It is not for you to know the times or the seasons, which the Father hath put in his own power [Acts 1:7].

He let them know, at this particular time, that the kingdom would not be established. Rather, He would call out a people to His name, the church. In chapter 15 of Acts, when the apostles met for the first council in Jerusalem, James pointed out this fact: "Simeon hath declared how God at the first did visit the Gentiles, to take out of them a people for his name. And to this agree the words of the prophets; as it is written, After this I will return, and will build again the tabernacle of David, which is fallen down; and I will build again the ruins thereof, and I will set it up:

That the residue of men might seek after the Lord, and all the Gentiles, upon whom my name is called, saith the Lord, who doeth all these things. Known unto God are all his works from the beginning of the world" (Acts 15:14–18). This is what God is doing today. He is visiting the Gentiles to take out of them a people to His name. That is, God is calling out of the world those people who will trust Christ, and the Holy Spirit baptizes them into the body of believers, the church.

So when the apostles asked Jesus whether He would restore the kingdom "at this time," His answer was that this was not the subject for discussion at that time. Nor is it the subject for discussion today. There are a great many people who say to me, "Don't you think the Lord will be coming soon?" Well, now, I'll let you in on something that is confidential between you and me: I do believe that He is coming soon. However, I don't have any authority to tell you that He is coming soon, because I don't know. Our Lord said it is not for us to know the times or the seasons. That is not the important part for us.

I do believe in prophecy. However, I think one can overemphasize it. To be built up in the faith you need more than a prophetic study.

Then what is our business today? Notice again that the Lord did not rebuke them. Instead, He showed that He had something else in mind. There is something else for us to do. It is not for us to know the times nor the seasons—the Father has put those in His own power—but here is your commission:

But ye shall receive power, after that the Holy Ghost is come upon you: and ye shall be witnesses unto me both in Jerusalem, and in all Judaea, and in Samaria, and unto the uttermost part of the earth [Acts 1:8].

This is the commission that still holds for today. This is not given only to a corporate body, to the church as a body; it is not a corporate commission. This is a very personal command to each believer—personally, privately. This was given to these men even before the Holy Spirit had come and formed the church. It is a direct command for you and for me today. It is our business to get the Word of God out to the world. We can't say that it is up to the church to send missionaries and to give out the gospel, and then sit back and let others do it. The all-important question is whether *you* are getting out the Word of God. Have you gone to the ends of the earth as a witness to the gospel? Or do you support a missionary or a radio program that does? Are you personally involved? Today there are a great many people who want to talk about the times and seasons of His coming, but they don't want to get involved in getting out the Word of God. But that is His commission—not only to the apostles—that is His commission to you and me. I am of the opinion that if the Lord should suddenly appear to you or to me right where we are at this moment, He would not talk about the time of His coming, but He would talk about getting out the gospel. He wants people to be saved. This is our commission.

In order to get this gospel out, we need power. That was His promise: "Ye shall receive power." And we need the leading of the Lord. Although it is our business today to get out the Word of God, there is no power in us, there is no power in the church, but there *is* power in the Holy Spirit. It is the Holy Spirit who moves through an individual or through the church or through a radio program. The question is whether we permit Him to do so. "Ye shall receive power, after that the Holy Ghost is come upon you."

"Ye shall be witnesses unto me." Our witness is to Christ. He is the center of attraction. "In Jerusalem," which applied to us means our hometown, there should be a witness to Christ. "All Judaea" is equivalent to our community; "Samaria" represents the other side of the tracks, the folk we don't associate with. Although we may not meet with these people socially, we are to take the gospel to them. Of course we can't associate with everybody. We can select our friends as everyone else does. That is part of the freedom which we have. There are folk who wouldn't want to associate with us. There are lots of folk who wouldn't want me around; I would crimp their style. But we have both the privilege and the responsibility to get the Word of God out to folk whether or not we associate with them socially.

Finally, this witness to Christ is to go to the uttermost part of the earth. We never should lose sight of the fact that this is the Lord's intention. He has told us if we love Him to keep His commandments. His command is personal. We can't pass this off on the crowd, and say "The church is doing it; so I don't need to get involved." How much are *you* involved, friend? What is *your* witness to Christ?

ASCENSION AND PROMISE OF THE RETURN OF JESUS

And when he had spoken these things, while they beheld, he was taken up; and

a cloud received him out of their sight [Acts 1:9].

The ascension of the Lord Jesus Christ is an important and significant miracle in the ministry of the Lord. This is especially true for our space age when eyes are turned aloft and we are talking about travel in space. Space travel isn't really new. The Lord Jesus took off, and He didn't need a launching pad or a space suit or a missile.

There was a cloud to receive Him. What kind of a cloud was that? Was it a moisture cloud? No, this was the same *shekinah* glory cloud that had filled the tabernacle. In His high priestly prayer He had prayed: "And now, O Father, glorify thou me with thine own self with the glory which I had with thee before the world was" (John 17:5). When He was born into this world, He was wrapped in swaddling clothes. When He left this earth, He was wrapped in glory clouds. This is the way He returned to the Father's right hand.

While the apostles are watching all this, two angels appear to them. They look like men, and they have an important message.

And while they looked stedfastly toward heaven as he went up, behold, two men stood by them in white apparel;

Which also said, Ye men of Galilee, why stand ye gazing up into heaven? this same Jesus, which is taken up from you into heaven, shall so come in like manner as ye have seen him go into heaven [Acts 1:10–11].

It is the glorified Jesus who went up into heaven. This same Jesus, the glorified Jesus, will return in like manner and to the same place. Zechariah 14:4 tells us: "And his feet shall stand in that day upon the mount of Olives, which is before Jerusalem on the east, and the mount of Olives shall cleave in the midst thereof toward the east and toward the west, and there shall be a very great valley; and half of the mountain shall remove toward the north, and half of it toward the south." He took off at that place, and He will come back to that place.

WAITING FOR THE SPIRIT

Then returned they unto Jerusalem from the mount called Olivet, which is from Jerusalem a sabbath day's journey [Acts 1:12].

"A sabbath day's journey," which was less than one mile, kept people pretty much in their location. That was why they would all camp very close to the temple during the feast days when they came to Jerusalem to worship. The Mount of Olives would probably be covered with people camping out, possibly several hundred thousand of them at the time of the feasts. Why? Because they needed to stay within a Sabbath Day's journey of the temple.

And when they were come in, they went up into an upper room, where abode both Peter, and James, and John, and Andrew, Philip, and Thomas, Bartholomew, and Matthew, James the son of Alphaeus, and Simon Zelotes, and Judas the brother of James.

These all continued with one accord in prayer and supplication, with the women, and Mary the mother of Jesus, and with his brethren [Acts 1:13–14].

I rejoice that Mary, the mother of Jesus, was there. Her reputation has now been cleared. At this point it was obvious that Jesus was the Son of God, and virgin born, as she had claimed.

The attitude of the apostles and the other believers was that of oneness, of prayer, and of waiting.

There is no way that we can duplicate this period today. Remember that this is in a time period, a time capsule, between His ascension into heaven and the coming of the Holy Spirit. You and I do not live in that time period. It cannot be duplicated. We are not waiting for the coming of the Holy Spirit; He came over nineteen hundred years ago.

APPOINTMENT OF AN APOSTLE

And in those days Peter stood up in the midst of the disciples, and said, (the number of names together were about an hundred and twenty,)

Men and brethren, this scripture must needs have been fulfilled, which the Holy Ghost by the mouth of David spake before concerning Judas, which was guide to them that took Jesus.

For he was numbered with us, and had obtained part of this ministry.

Now this man purchased a field with the reward of iniquity; and falling headlong, he burst asunder in the midst, and all his bowels gushed out [Acts 1:15–18].

Here is Simon Peter speaking up again. Note that this is *before* the Holy Spirit came at Pentecost. This man needs the filling of the Holy Spirit—and so do you and I.

He certainly gives a vivid picture of Judas, doesn't he?

If you are bothered by a seeming discrepancy here and with Matthew 27:5, the following quotation from *Unger's Bible Dictionary* by Merrill F. Unger (pp. 615–616) will be helpful to you.

> NOTE.—Between these two passages (Matt. 27:5; Acts 1:16-25) there appears at first sight a discrepancy. In Matthew it is stated "He cast down the pieces of silver in the temple and departed, and went and hanged himself." In Acts (ch. 1) another account is given. There it is stated: (1) That instead of throwing the money into the temple he bought a field with it. (2) That instead of hanging himself, "falling headlong, he burst asunder in the midst, and all his bowels gushed out." (3) That for this reason, and not because the priests had bought it with the price of blood, the field was called "Aceldama." The fact would seem to be that Judas hanged himself, probably with his girdle, which either broke or became untied, and threw him heavily forward upon the jagged rocks below, thus inflicting the wound mentioned by Peter in the Acts. The apparent discrepancy in the two accounts as to the disposition of the money may be thus explained: "It was not lawful to take into the temple treasury, for the purchase of sacred things, money that had been unlawfully gained. In such case the Jewish law provided that the money was to be restored to the donor, and, if he insisted on giving it that he should be induced to spend it for something for the public weal. By a fiction of law the money was still considered to be Judas's, and to have been applied by him in the purchase of the well-known 'potter's field'" (Edersheim, *Life of Jesus*, ii, 575).

And it was known unto all the dwellers at Jerusalem; insomuch as that field is called in their proper tongue, Aceldama, that is to say, The field of blood.

For it is written in the book of Psalms, Let his habitation be desolate, and let no man dwell therein: and his bishopric let another take [Acts 1:19–20].

There is always a question about what happened here. Should Simon Peter have held this election to choose a man to take the place of Judas? I don't think so.

Wherefore of these men which have companied with us all the time that the Lord Jesus went in and out among us,

Beginning from the baptism of John, unto that same day that he was taken up from us, must one be ordained to be a witness with us of his resurrection [Acts 1:21–22].

I believe that the election to choose a successor to Judas Iscariot was conducted by Peter without the presence and guidance of the Holy Spirit. The Holy Spirit had not yet been given. Matthias was evidently a good man. He met the requirements of an apostle, which meant he must have seen the resurrected Christ, as that was a necessary requirement.

And they appointed two, Joseph called Barsabas, who was surnamed Justus, and Matthias.

And they prayed, and said, Thou, Lord, which knowest the hearts of all men, shew whether of these two thou hast chosen,

That he may take part of this ministry and apostleship, from which Judas by transgression fell, that he might go to his own place.

And they gave forth their lots; and the lot fell upon Matthias; and he was numbered with the eleven apostles [Acts 1:23–26].

I can't see that this was the leading of the Holy Spirit, nor that it was God's leading in the casting of lots. Is Matthias actually the one who took the place of Judas? I don't think so. I believe that, in His own time, the Lord Jesus himself appointed one to take the place of Judas Iscariot. We don't hear another word about Matthias—nothing is recorded of his ministry. I think the Holy Spirit ignored Matthias. It is my conviction that the man the Lord chose was Paul. You may ask, "Do you have an authority for that statement?" Yes. Listen to Paul as he writes to the Galatian believers: "Paul, an apostle, (not of men, neither by man, but by Jesus Christ, and God the Father, who raised him from the dead;)" (Gal. 1:1). Paul is saying that he was chosen by God the Father and the Lord Jesus Christ. How did He do it? Through the Holy Spirit whom

He had sent into the world. The ministry of Paul certainly justifies the fact that he was the one to take Judas' place. Of course I realize that the majority of good Bible commentators disagree with me, but I am just passing on to you my own conviction.

It is remarkable, and I want to mention again how Acts 1 brings the four Gospels to a focal point. Matthew concludes with the Resurrection, Mark with the Ascension, Luke with the promise of the Holy Spirit, and John with the promise of the Second Coming. Acts 1 brings all four records together and mentions each of them. The four Gospels funnel into Acts, and Acts is the bridge between the Gospels and the Epistles.

CHAPTER 2

***THEME:** The Day of Pentecost*

We can divide this chapter into two sections. The coming of the Holy Spirit is recorded in verses 1–13. The first sermon in the church age, given by the apostle Peter, is recorded in verses 14–47.

COMING OF THE HOLY SPIRIT

And when the day of Pentecost was fully come, they were all with one accord in one place [Acts 2:1].

The words *fully come* could be translated "fulfilled." When the Day of Pentecost was being fulfilled, they were all together in one place.

Pentecost took place fifty days after the Feast of Firstfruits. You may remember in our study in Leviticus that we found that the Feast of Firstfruits speaks of the *resurrection* of Jesus Christ. Christ is the firstfruits—". . . Christ the firstfruits; afterward they that are Christ's at his coming" (1 Cor. 15:23).

The Passover speaks of the *death* of Jesus Christ, we learn from 1 Corinthians 5:7: ". . . For even Christ our passover is sacrificed for us." Since the Passover has been fulfilled in the death of Christ, and the Feast of Firstfruits has been fulfilled in the resurrection of Christ, we believe that the Feast of Pentecost represents something—that is, it is the fulfillment of something. Its fulfillment is the birth of the church, the day the church came into existence.

When the Day of Pentecost "was being fulfilled," or "was fully come," means that this was the fulfillment of the meaning and the purpose for which it was given originally. On Pentecost there was to be a meal offering to the Lord, which was to be presented in two loaves of fine flour baked with leaven (Lev. 23). This was to depict the beginning and origin of the church. It spoke of the coming of the Holy Spirit in the very particular ministry of calling a people out of this world to form the body of Christ, which is the church. Five minutes before the Holy Spirit came on the Day of Pentecost there was no church. Five minutes after the Holy Spirit came on the Day of Pentecost there was a church. In other words, what Bethlehem was to the birth of Christ, Jerusalem on the Day of Pentecost was to the coming of the Holy Spirit. The Holy Spirit became incarnate. He began to baptize believers, which means that the Holy Spirit identified them with Christ as His body here on this earth. "For by one Spirit are we all baptized into one body, whether we be Jews or Gentiles, whether we be bond or free; and have been all made to drink into one Spirit" (1 Cor. 12:13).

The Holy Spirit began to perform a ministry on the Day of Pentecost. The Day of Pentecost was fulfilled on that day. When the Day of Pentecost "was fully come" does not mean it was 12:00 noon or 7:00 in the morning or 2:00 in the afternoon. It means that Pentecost, which Israel had been celebrating for many generations, was fulfilled.

And suddenly there came a sound from heaven as of a rushing mighty wind, and it filled all the house where they were sitting [Acts 2:2].

Now I wish to call your attention to something that is very important. When the Holy Spirit came, He was not visible. However, He made His presence known in two ways. There was an appeal to two of the gates through which all mankind gets his information: the ear-gate and the eye-gate. We hear and we see. The Holy Spirit used both these gates. Through the ear-gate they heard a sound from heaven *as of* a rushing mighty wind. This sound filled the whole house where they were sitting.

Notice that it was not a wind; it was the sound *as of* a wind. It wasn't like the sound of the wind blowing through the treetops. It sounded like a tornado, and I believe that all of Jerusalem could hear it. A friend of my daughter lives in Kansas and went through the experience of a tornado. It did not destroy their home but came within two blocks of it. When she wrote about it to my daughter, she said, "The first thing we noticed was a sound like a thousand freight trains coming into town." Friend, that was a rushing, mighty wind, and that was the sound. It was that kind of sound that they heard on the Day of Pentecost.

And there appeared unto them cloven tongues like as of fire, and it sat upon each of them [Acts 2:3].

Again, I would call your attention to this. The tongues were *like as of* fire. It was not fire, but it looked like fire. This verse would be better translated, "There appeared unto them tongues parting asunder." That is, the tongues were like as a fire and it rested upon each of them. This was the appeal to the eye-gate. So on that Day of Pentecost, when the Holy Spirit came to the church, baptizing them into the body of Christ, there was an appeal to the ear and an appeal to the eye.

This is not to be confused with the baptism of fire. The baptism of fire is judgment which is yet to come. In the Book of Revelation we see the wrath of God revealed from heaven, fire from heaven. That is a baptism of fire. If men will not have the baptism of the Holy Spirit, then they must have the baptism of fire—judgment. The baptism of fire is for those who have rejected Jesus Christ.

I used to go to a prayer meeting which a wonderful preacher attended. I loved that dear brother, although his theology differed from mine in some points. He would always pray that fire would fall on us. And I always canceled out that prayer and said, "Lord, for goodness sake, don't let fire fall on us." Fire, you see, is judgment. Fire burns. That is yet to come. When the Holy Spirit came on the Day of Pentecost they saw something that in appearance looked like fire.

And they were all filled with the Holy Ghost, and began to speak with other tongues, as the Spirit gave them utterance [Acts 2:4].

This verse says they were *filled* with the Holy Spirit. Someone may question the fact that I have been saying they were baptized with the Holy Spirit. Were they? Yes. The Lord Jesus told them they would be. "And, being assembled together with them, commanded them that they should not depart from Jerusalem, but wait for the promise of the Father, which, saith he, ye have heard of me. For John truly baptized with water; but ye shall be baptized with the Holy Ghost not many days hence" (Acts 1:4–5). The very fact that they were filled with the Holy Spirit indicates that all the other ministries of the Holy Spirit to believers in this age had already been performed. They occurred in this order: First, they were *regenerated*. A man must be born again. "Jesus answered, Verily, verily, I say unto thee, Except a man be born of water and of the Spirit, he cannot enter into the kingdom of God" (John 3:5). Secondly, they were *indwelt* by the Spirit of God. "But ye are not in the flesh, but in the Spirit, if so be that the Spirit of God dwell in you. Now if any man have not the Spirit of Christ, he is none of his" (Rom. 8:9). Thirdly, they were *sealed* by the Holy Spirit into an eternal relationship with God. "In whom ye also trusted, after that ye heard the word of truth, the gospel of your salvation: in whom also after that ye believed, ye were sealed with that holy Spirit of promise, Which is the earnest of our inheritance until the redemption of the purchased possession, unto the praise of his glory" (Eph. 1:13–14). And again, "And grieve not the holy Spirit of God, whereby ye are sealed unto the day of redemption" (Eph. 4:30). It is possible to grieve the Spirit of God, but it is not possible to grieve Him away. He seals the believer unto the day of redemption. We are never told to ask for the sealing of the Holy Spirit. It is something which God does "after that ye believed," which is better translated "having believed." Faith in Jesus Christ gives us the sealing of the Holy Spirit unto the day of redemption.

Fourthly, they were *baptized* of the Holy Spirit. This was foretold by John the Baptist (Luke 3:16) and repeated by the Lord Jesus: "For John truly baptized with water; but ye shall be baptized with the Holy Ghost not many days hence" (Acts 1:5). The baptism took place, which placed them in the body of believers. It marked the beginning of the church. Ever since that day every believer in the Lord Jesus Christ is placed into the body of Christ by the baptism of the Holy Spirit. "For by one Spirit are we all baptized into one body, whether we be Jews or Gentiles, whether we be bond or free; and have been all made to drink into one Spirit" (1 Cor. 12:13).

Now when the filling of the Holy Spirit took place on the Day of Pentecost, it indicated that the other four ministries of the Holy Spirit had been accomplished. "And they were all filled with the Holy Ghost." The filling of the Spirit was for service. The *experience* of the Day of Pentecost came from the *filling* of the Holy Spirit (not the baptism of the Holy Spirit). It is still the same today. The filling of the Holy Spirit is for service. This is the only work of the Holy Spirit that we are to do anything about—we are commanded to be filled with the Holy Spirit: "And be not drunk with wine, wherein is excess; but be filled with the Spirit" (Eph. 5:18). Notice that before Pentecost the believers wanted this filling of the Spirit. "These all continued with one accord in prayer and supplication . . ." (Acts 1:14). What would their supplication be about? About the promise of the Lord Jesus that He would send His Holy Spirit to them.

The baptism of the Holy Spirit is not a command given to us. It is not an experience. It is an act of God whereby the believer in Jesus Christ is indwelt by the Spirit of God, sealed unto the day of redemption, and placed into the church, the body of Christ, by the baptism of the Spirit. The filling of the Spirit of God is the enablement for service. We are *commanded* to be filled with the Spirit.

After they were filled with the Holy Spirit, they "began to speak with other tongues, as the Spirit gave them utterance" (v. 4). These "other tongues" are not unknown tongues. There were many tongues spoken by Jews throughout the Roman Empire. These worshipers had come from the different areas of the Roman Empire for the Feast of Pentecost. Remember that all male Jews were required to come to Jerusalem for three of the feasts. They were in Jerusalem because of that, and many of them couldn't speak Hebrew.

That is not unusual. There are many Jews in our country today who cannot speak Hebrew. For years it was a dead language. In Israel today, Hebrew is being spoken again.

Now, my friend, the Day of Pentecost cannot be duplicated. It was a precise point in history. We cannot duplicate it any more than we can duplicate Bethlehem and the birth of Christ at Christmas.

Suppose the wise men had come back to Jerusalem again the next year and had said, "Say, we're looking for the King of the Jews who is born in Bethlehem." Suppose Herod would have said, "Weren't you fellows here last year?" "Yes." "Well, did you find Him?" "Yes." "Well, if He was born in Bethlehem last year, He isn't born there again this year." "Oh, but we had such a wonderful experience here last year, we thought we'd come back and do it all over again." Of course, Herod would have answered, "Look, fellows, you can't duplicate that. He was born in Bethlehem only once."

Just so, friend, you cannot duplicate Pentecost. The Holy Spirit came on the Day of Pentecost. You don't have to beg Him to come or urge Him to come. He is here. The Spirit of God is in the world today. Jesus told us what He would do after He came: "He shall glorify me: for he shall receive of mine, and shall shew it unto you" (John 16:14). We know He is here when He takes the things of Christ and shows them to us. And when we are talking about the things of Christ, the Spirit of God has something that He can work with.

"As the Spirit gave them utterance." These apostles were from Galilee. They couldn't speak all these other languages. But they are speaking them now. The Spirit gave them utterance.

And there were dwelling at Jerusalem Jews, devout men, out of every nation under heaven [Acts 2:5].

They had come from everywhere because of the Feast of Pentecost. This was their reason for being in Jerusalem.

Now when this was noised abroad, the multitude came together, and were confounded, because that every man heard them speak in his own language [Acts 2:6].

A better translation of "when this was noised abroad" is "when this sound having taken place." Because of the sound as of a mighty rushing wind, a multitude came together. I shall never forget here in Pasadena, where I live, the first time we heard a jet plane break the sound barrier. We were all out in our front yards wanting to know where the sound had come from. We had never heard anything like it before. The sound the people of Jerusalem heard had never been heard before; so they came rushing toward it—which may have been to the temple area. Probably all 120 believers were there (Acts 1:15).

The people who rushed there were confounded because every man *heard*—in the Greek the imperfect tense is used, so that it should read, "every man was hearing"—them speak in his own dialect. It was not only that the language of their country was spoken, but each man heard his own dialect as it was spoken in his area of the country.

These men were not talking gibberish. They were not talking in unknown tongues. These men were speaking the dialects of the people in the multitude.

Now there is another aspect which I must mention. Some Bible scholars believe that what is meant here is that the apostles were not speaking in other languages at all, but were speaking in their own Galilean dialect, and the miracle was in the *hearing,* because it says that every man *heard* them speak in his own dialect. Was the miracle that broke down the language barrier in the speaking or in the hearing?

And they were all amazed and marvelled, saying one to another, Behold, are not all these which speak Galilaeans?

And how hear we every man in our own tongue, wherein we were born?

Parthians, and Medes, and Elamites, and the dwellers in Mesopotamia, and in Judaea, and Cappadocia, in Pontus, and Asia,

Phrygia, and Pamphylia, in Egypt, and in the parts of Libya about Cyrene, and strangers of Rome, Jews and proselytes,

Cretes and Arabians, we do hear them speak in our tongues the wonderful works of God [Acts 2:7–11].

Here were people from three continents. Certainly they were of diverse languages and dialects. They each heard these Galileans speak in an understandable dialect. May I say, these were not unknown tongues. They were languages that were understood.

And they were all amazed, and were in doubt, saying one to another, What meaneth this? [Acts 2:12].

They were amazed—*perplexed* would be a better word. They didn't understand what was taking place.

Others mocking said, These men are full of new wine [Acts 2:13].

The literal translation is *sweet wine,* and I understand that is a little more intoxicating. They thought these men were drunk.

Remember that Paul writes: "And be not drunk with wine, wherein is excess; but be filled with the Spirit" (Eph. 5:18). Have you noticed that a drunk man seems to have more power? He certainly is more talkative. Perhaps many of us today need the filling of the Spirit to make us talkative—not to speak in an unknown tongue, but power to speak the gospel to others. That is the kind of tongues movement we need today. And by the way, we need a tongues movement of giving the gospel in the language that the man can understand. That is all important.

What a day Pentecost was! It was the day the Holy Spirit came to call out a body of believers to form the church. The day before Pentecost there was no church. The day after Pentecost there was a church. Just as the Feast of Pentecost in the Old Testament followed fifty days after the Feast of the Firstfruits, so fifty days after the Lord Jesus arose from the dead the Holy Spirit came to call out a body of believers.

Now Simon Peter is going to stand up and answer the mocking taunt that they are full of new wine.

FIRST SERMON IN THE CHURCH AGE, DELIVERED BY PETER

But Peter, standing up with the eleven, lifted up his voice, and said unto them, Ye men of Judaea, and all ye that dwell at Jerusalem, be this known unto you, and hearken to my words:

For these are not drunken, as ye suppose, seeing it is but the third hour of the day [Acts 2:14–15].

Now I think that we need to recognize who the congregation was. These were men of Judea and all that dwell at Jerusalem. In that day Jerusalem was entirely a Jewish city. Pilate and his people had their headquarters in Caesarea, not in Jerusalem. This early church was 100 percent Jewish. It was made up of *Israelites*. We need to recognize that. The church began in Jerusalem, then moved out to Judea, then Samaria, and then to the uttermost parts of the earth. This has been the movement of the church from that day to this. In the Old Testament it was to Jerusalem that the world was to come for worship. Now they are commanded to leave Jerusalem and to take this message to the ends of the earth.

Peter replies to their mockery and ridicule by saying, "This could not be drunkenness, because look at the time of day it is!" This was not an hour when people in that day were drunk. He is talking to the cynic.

Now Peter quotes to them from their own Scripture.

But this is that which was spoken by the prophet Joel [Acts 2:16].

He uses this prophecy as an answer to the cynical, the unbeliever, the mocker. This is his purpose for quoting it. He says, "This is that," which is, *this is similar to* or *this is like that.* He does not say that this is the fulfillment of that which was spoken by the prophet Joel. He is saying, "Why do you think this is something odd or something strange? We have prophecy that says these things are going to come to pass." Peter goes on to quote the prophecy from Joel. I'm glad Simon Peter quoted as much as he did, because he makes it obvious that he was not attempting to say this was fulfilled. Now what is it that is to come?

And it shall come to pass in the last days, saith God, I will pour out of my Spirit upon all flesh: and your sons and your daughters shall prophesy, and your young men shall see visions, and your old men shall dream dreams:

And on my servants and on my handmaidens I will pour out in those days of my Spirit; and they shall prophesy:

And I will shew wonders in heaven above, and signs in the earth beneath; blood, and fire, and vapour of smoke:

The sun shall be turned into darkness, and the moon into blood, before that great and notable day of the Lord come:

And it shall come to pass, that whosoever shall call on the name of the Lord shall be saved [Acts 2:17–21].

I don't think that anyone would claim that on the Day of Pentecost the moon was turned to blood or that the sun was turned to darkness. When Christ was crucified, there was darkness for three hours, but not on the Day of Pentecost. Nor were there wonders of heaven above and signs in the earth beneath. Nor was there blood and fire and a vapor of smoke. Simon Peter quotes this passage to these mockers to show them that the pouring out of the Spirit of God should not be strange to them. Joel had predicted it, and it is going to come to pass.

My friend, Joel 2:28–32 has not been fulfilled to this day. If we turn back to the Book of Joel, we will find that he had a great deal to say about the Day of the Lord. The Day of the Lord will begin with the Great Tribulation Period. It will go on through the Millennium. In three chapters of the Book of Joel the Day of the Lord is mentioned five times. Joel talks about the fact that it is a time of war, a time of judgment upon the earth. That has not yet been fulfilled. It was not fulfilled on the Day of Pentecost.

If we could only see that all Simon Peter is saying in his introduction is, "Now look, this is not strange or contrary. The day is coming when this will be fulfilled. And today we are seeing something similar to it." Now after his introduction, he will move on to his text. Remember he is speaking to men who knew the Old Testament. Don't try to read nineteen hundred years of church history into this. This is just the beginning of the church on the Day of Pentecost. This is the inception of the church. Obviously he is speaking to the Jews—"Ye men of Israel." He doesn't say, "Ye men of Southern California." He is talking to Israelites. Now he is getting down to the nitty gritty. Now he is getting to his subject.

Ye men of Israel, hear these words; Jesus of Nazareth, a man approved of God among you by miracles and wonders and signs, which God did by him in the midst of you, as ye yourselves also know [Acts 2:22].

Now I personally think that miracles and wonders and signs were all different. I believe that miracles were performed for one purpose, wonders for another purpose, and signs for another purpose. Jesus did certain things that were to be signs. Some miracles of healing were performed to prove who He was. And wonders were performed to get the attention of His hearers. These were the three areas in which our Lord moved.

Him, being delivered by the determinate counsel and foreknowledge of God, ye have taken, and by wicked hands have crucified and slain:

Whom God hath raised up, having loosed the pains of death: because it was not possible that he should be holden of it [Acts 2:23–24].

Peter is saying that what has happened was not contrary to God's program. This is not something that took God by surprise. However, he makes it clear that this does not release men from their responsibility. Who is responsible for the crucifixion of Christ? The religious rulers were the ones who began the movement. I would say that they were largely to blame. They moved upon the multitude so that they produced mob action. They also maneuvered the Roman government to execute Him. Remember, friend, He was crucified on a Roman cross. Peter is pointing his finger at his fellow Israelites.

But there is no use in our arguing about who was responsible for His death back at that time. I'll tell you who is responsible for His death. *You* are responsible, and *I* am responsible. It was for my sins and for your sins that He died. Listen to the words of Jesus: "Therefore doth my Father love me, because I lay down my life, that I might take it again. No man taketh it from me, but I lay it down of myself. I have power to lay it down, and I have power to take it again. This commandment have I received of my Father" (John 10:17–18).

Peter is speaking to men who were directly involved in the plot of the Crucifixion, and he says, "Ye have taken, and by wicked hands have crucified and slain."

However, that is not the most important part of his message. He goes on, "Whom God hath raised up, having loosed the pains of death." He preaches the resurrection of Jesus Christ. This is the first sermon ever preached in the church age. This is the beginning. This is the Day of Pentecost. What is his theme? It is *not* the prophecy of Joel, my friend. It is the *resurrection* of the Lord Jesus Christ. Let's not try to change his subject! Now he is going to quote his text. He quotes from Psalm 16:8–10. I am glad he did that because this helps me to understand Psalm 16.

For David speaketh concerning him, I foresaw the Lord always before my face, for he is on my right hand, that I should not be moved:

Therefore did my heart rejoice, and my tongue was glad; moreover also my flesh shall rest in hope:

Because thou wilt not leave my soul in hell, neither wilt thou suffer thine Holy One to see corruption [Acts 2:25–27].

The word *hell* should be "sheol." In that day it was sheol.

Thou hast made known to me the ways of life; thou shalt make me full of joy with thy countenance [Acts 2:28].

In Psalm 16 David is talking about the resurrection of Christ. This has now been fulfilled. The interpretation of this psalm is given by Simon Peter, who is filled with the Holy Spirit.

Men and brethren, let me freely speak unto you of the patriarch David, that he is both dead and buried, and his sepulchre is with us unto this day [Acts 2:29].

Apparently Peter was standing in the temple area. He could point his finger to the sepulchre of David. I have stood in that temple area and I could point my finger up to the top of Mount Zion where David is buried. He is saying, "It is obvious that David wasn't speaking about himself because his bones are right up there on the top of the hill. His grave is there; his body did undergo corruption. He is not speaking of himself but of Someone whom you and I know, Someone who did not see corruption but was raised from the dead."

Therefore being a prophet, and knowing that God had sworn with an oath to him, that of the fruit of his loins, according to the flesh, he would raise up Christ to sit on his throne;

He seeing this before spake of the resurrection of Christ, that his soul was not left in hell, neither his flesh did see corruption [Acts 2:30–31].

This is what David was talking about in Psalm 16. He was speaking of the resurrection of Jesus Christ. You may say, "But I read Psalm 16 and it doesn't say that Jesus Christ will rise from the dead." My friend, here in Acts 2 we have the Holy Spirit's interpretation of this psalm. Now we can go back and read the psalm, knowing that it refers to the resurrection of the Lord Jesus.

What is Simon Peter talking about? His sermon is about the resurrection of Jesus Christ. The first sermon ever preached in the church age was an Easter sermon. And *every* sermon in the early church was an Easter sermon.

This Jesus hath God raised up, whereof we all are witnesses [Acts 2:32].

Now Peter is saying to the crowd there that day, "This that you have seen—that is, the miracle of hearing their own languages spoken by Galileans—has taken place because Jesus was raised from the dead."

Therefore being by the right hand of God exalted, and having received of the Father the promise of the Holy Ghost, he hath shed forth this, which ye now see and hear.

For David is not ascended into the heavens: but he saith himself, The LORD said unto my Lord, Sit thou on my right hand,

Until I make thy foes thy footstool [Acts 2:33–35].

Old Testament saints didn't go to heaven. If any of them had been up in heaven, David would have been there. David did not ascend into heaven. You see, the Old Testament saints are going to be raised to live down on this earth someday. It is the church that will be taken to the New Jerusalem. It is said of the believers today when they die that they are absent from the body and present with the Lord (2 Cor. 5:8)

Now he quotes Psalm 110:1. He is showing them that Jesus is up yonder at the right hand of God. He will be there until He comes back to establish His kingdom. But while He is at the right hand of God, He is still working in the world.

Therefore let all the house of Israel know assuredly, that God hath made that same Jesus, whom ye have crucified, both Lord and Christ [Acts 2:36].

He is preaching the resurrection of Jesus Christ—that Christ died for their sins, but He rose again.

Now when they heard this, they were pricked in their heart, and said unto Peter and to the rest of the apostles, Men and brethren, what shall we do? [Acts 2:37].

The message of Simon Peter brought conviction to them.

Then Peter said unto them, Repent, and be baptized every one of you in the name of Jesus Christ for the remission of sins, and ye shall receive the gift of the Holy Ghost [Acts 2:38].

This is for a pcoplc who had the Word of God, who had heard the message, who knew the prophecies. They had been going along in one direction, which was away from God, even though they had a God-given religion. They are told to repent. They are to turn around and come God's way.

Peter says to them, "Repent, and be baptized." Water baptism would be the evidence that they had repented, that they had come to Christ and had put their trust in Him.

Peter says to them, "Be baptized . . . in the name of Jesus Christ for the remission of sins. This will be an evidence that you have trusted Him for the remission of your sins—rather than bringing a sacrifice to be offered in the temple." You see, their baptism would be a testimony to the fact that Christ is the Lamb of God who takes away the sin of the world.

"And ye shall receive the gift of the Holy Ghost." Anyone who believes, who puts his trust in Jesus Christ, will receive the gift of the Holy Spirit.

For the promise is unto you, and to your children, and to all that are afar off, even as many as the Lord our God shall call [Acts 2:39].

Nineteen hundred years ago you and I were "afar off." He is talking about us here.

And with many other words did he testify and exhort, saying, Save yourselves from this untoward generation [Acts 2:40].

In other words, "Get away from this religion. Turn to Christ."

Then they that gladly received his word were baptized: and the same day there were added unto them about three thousand souls [Acts 2:41].

This is not some preacher's count. These were genuinely born again believers. Here is one place where the figure on the number of converts is absolutely accurate.

THE CHURCH WHICH HAS COME INTO EXISTENCE

And they continued stedfastly in the apostles' doctrine and fellowship, and in breaking of bread, and in prayers [Acts 2:42].

I have a little booklet called the *Spiritual Fingerprints of the Visible Church.* How can you identify a real church? Notice the four marks of identification. First, *They continued stedfastly in the apostles' doctrine.* The mark of a church is not the height of the steeple nor the sound of the bell. It is not whether the pulpit is stationed in the middle or the chancel is divided. The important issue is whether or not they hold to the apostles' doctrine. Correct doctrine was one of the fingerprints of the visible church. Secondly, *fellowship.* They were sharing the things of Christ. The third, *breaking of bread.* Breaking of bread is more than just going through the ritual of the Lord's Supper. It means being brought into a fellowship and a relationship with Christ. The fourth, *prayers*. I'm afraid in the average church today it is a little fingerprint. That is, prayer is the evident weakness of the church. Actually, the greatest asset of any church is prayer.

And fear came upon every soul: and many wonders and signs were done by the apostles [Acts 2:43].

It was the apostles who had the sign gifts.

And all that believed were together, and had all things common;

And sold their possessions and goods, and parted them to all men, as every man had need.

And they, continuing daily with one accord in the temple, and breaking bread from house to house, did eat their meat with gladness and singleness of heart,

Praising God, and having favour with all the people. And the Lord added to the church daily such as should be saved [Acts 2:44–47].

Never has the church been as spiritually strong as it was at that time. This type of living would never work today because we have too many carnal Christians. And, notice, it was the Lord who did the adding to the church.

CHAPTER 3

***THEME:** First miracle of the church; Peter's second sermon*

We are still in the first division of the Book of Acts which shows the Lord Jesus Christ at work by the Holy Spirit through the apostles in Jerusalem. We have seen the birthday of the church on the Day of Pentecost, a day which can never be repeated. There was a church because the Holy Spirit had become incarnate in believers. He was indwelling the believers, and He filled them with His love, power, and blessing for service.

Just as you and I cannot repeat Bethlehem, neither can we repeat Pentecost. But we do need the power of the Holy Spirit today. Thank God, He is in the world, convicting the world, restraining evil in the world. We don't have to seek Him; He is indwelling all believers in the Lord Jesus Christ.

In this third chapter we will find the healing of the lame man, verses 1–11. The appealing and revealing address of Peter is in verses 12–26. The result was five thousand men who believed!

HEALING OF LAME MAN

Now Peter and John went up together into the temple at the hour of prayer, being the ninth hour [Acts 3:1].

This apparently was the time of the evening sacrifice when a priest went in to offer incense with his prayers. We find in the first chapter of Luke that this was the service Zacharias was performing when he went to minister before the golden altar and the angel appeared to him. That golden altar, the altar of incense, speaks of prayer. This was the time of prayer. There would be a great company in the temple area praying at this time.

And a certain man lame from his mother's womb was carried, whom they laid daily at the gate of the temple which is called Beautiful, to ask alms of them that entered into the temple [Acts 3:2].

This man had been born lame. He was brought every day and was put there at the gate of the temple. What a contrast he was to the gate which is called Beautiful. Here was a beautiful gate, and here was a man who was marred. Man can make beautiful things, but man cannot improve himself. Of course, man can do some trimming on the outside. He can cut his hair, have his fingernails manicured, take a bath now and then, and use some deodorant, but man can never change that old nature which he has. This is the contrast we have here—a beautiful gate of the temple and a man lame from his mother's womb.

He was there to beg for alms. This was the way he lived, of course.

Who seeing Peter and John about to go into the temple asked an alms [Acts 3:3].

This shows us that after the Day of Pentecost, Peter and John still went up to the temple to pray. All the believers there in Jerusalem were Israelites or proselytes, and they continued to go to the temple to pray. The poor beggar saw Peter and John, and he hoped that they would be able to give him something.

And Peter, fastening his eyes upon him with John, said, Look on us.

And he gave heed unto them, expecting to receive something of them [Acts 3:4–5].

When these two men gave him this much attention, the beggar looked at them with the certainty that they would give him something.

Then Peter said, Silver and gold have I none; but such as I have give I thee: In the name of Jesus Christ of Nazareth rise up and walk [Acts 3:6].

An incident is told of one of the early saints of the church in Rome who walked in on the pope as he was counting money. Realizing that he had walked in on something which was private, he started to walk out. The pope said to him, "No longer can the church say 'Silver and gold have I none.'" As the saintly man continued walking out, he said, "Neither can the church say to the impotent man, 'Rise up and walk.'"

Today the organized church has wealth. I suppose that if one could put together all the holdings of all the churches, all groups, denominations, and non-denominations across the country, we would find the church wealthier than any other organization. I think it is wealthier than the Standard Oil Company. Yet the church today lacks power.

Now notice what Peter does.

And he took him by the right hand, and lifted him up: and immediately his feet and ankle bones received strength [Acts 3:7].

Remember that Dr. Luke wrote this book. You will notice that when Dr. Luke records a miracle, he gives a great many details which we don't find in some other books. He tells specifically what happened. The weakness had been in the feet and ankle bones of this man.

And he leaping up stood, and walked, and entered with them into the temple, walking, and leaping, and praising God [Acts 3:8].

Friend, don't miss this word *leaping*. It occurs twice in this verse.

This is a very interesting chapter. We will find that Peter is going to offer the kingdom to the nation again because at this time the church is 100 percent Israelite. There are no Gentiles from the outside. The church began with the Jews in Jerusalem. Later, it will go to the ends of the earth. But this, now, is the Jerusalem period.

Don't try to tell me this is another dispensation. We have hyperdispensationalists today who call this another dispensation. It is not different at all. But it is a period of transition. The Lord had said they were to begin at Jerusalem. They were not to begin by going out to the ends of the earth.

Now the kingdom is being offered to Israel again. This will be the final opportunity. What will be some of the identifying marks of the kingdom? Well, one is that the lame shall leap! "Then shall the lame man leap as an hart, and the tongue of the dumb sing: for in the wilderness shall waters break out, and streams in the desert" (Isa. 35:6).

Every instructed Israelite going up to the temple that day marveled at this lame man leaping. They knew this could actually be the beginning of the kingdom. The Messiah had been crucified, raised from the dead, ascended to heaven, and seated at God's right hand. If they would receive Him, He would come again.

And all the people saw him walking and praising God:

And they knew that it was he which sat for alms at the Beautiful gate of the temple: and they were filled with wonder and amazement at that which had happened unto him [Acts 3:9–10].

They saw him. They recognized the man. They caught the significance of this miracle. I'm afraid there are a great many today who haven't caught the significance of this record which Dr. Luke has given us.

And as the lame man which was healed held Peter and John, all the people ran together unto them in the porch that is called Solomon's, greatly wondering [Acts 3:11].

Is this to be the beginning of the kingdom? Great things had happened in Jerusalem during the past few weeks. They had witnessed the crucifixion of Jesus, His resurrection, His ascension, and the Day of Pentecost. They are amazed. What is really taking place?

THE APPEALING AND REVEALING ADDRESS OF PETER

And when Peter saw it, he answered unto the people, Ye men of Israel, why

marvel ye at this? or why look ye so earnestly on us, as though by our own power or holiness we had made this man to walk? [Acts 3:12].

He doesn't say, "Ye men of the United States." He is talking to the men of Israel. This is the Jerusalem period, friend. This is the transition period. The church has not yet moved out to other areas. No one in Rome has heard yet. No one in America has heard. No one in England has heard. This is in Jerusalem.

May I say something kindly? Folk reading the Bible should bring to it the same common sense they use in reading other books. This is God's Book. But it is not some "way out yonder" type of book. It deals with us right where we are, and it communicates so we can understand it.

Peter is very careful to tell them that this miracle was not done in his own power. He is going to direct this Jewish audience back to the Old Testament. He is going to tell them that if they will turn to God, these prophecies can be fulfilled.

Listen to some of the prophecies which these Jewish people knew. "And I will pour upon the house of David, and upon the inhabitants of Jerusalem, the spirit of grace and of supplications: and they shall look upon me whom they have pierced, and they shall mourn for him, as one mourneth for his only son, and shall be in bitterness for him, as one that is in bitterness for his firstborn" (Zech. 12:10). This would be fulfilled if they would turn to Him. It was *not* fulfilled because the nation did not accept the Lord Jesus at that time. They did not repent and turn to Him. Peter will invite them to turn to the Lord Jesus. They will refuse. The time is still to come when this will be fulfilled. Also Ezekiel spoke of the kingdom: "And I will put my spirit within you, and cause you to walk in my statutes, and ye shall keep my judgments, and do them. And ye shall dwell in the land that I gave to your fathers; and ye shall be my people, and I will be your God" (Ezek. 36:27–28). Notice the twelfth chapter of Isaiah, a remarkable chapter—only six verses—that speaks of the worship during the time of the kingdom: "And in that day thou shalt say, O LORD, I will praise thee: though thou wast angry with me, thine anger is turned away, and thou comfortedst me. Behold, God is my salvation; I will trust, and not be afraid: for the LORD JEHOVAH is my strength and my song; he also is become my salvation" (Isa. 12:1–2). Also, as we have mentioned, Isaiah 35:6 told of the lame man leaping as an hart. "And the ransomed of the LORD shall return, and come to Zion with songs and everlasting joy upon their heads: they shall obtain joy and gladness, and sorrow and sighing shall flee away" (Isa. 35:10). They should have seen that this lame man was a miniature, a picture of the whole nation. If they would but turn to God, all these promises would be fulfilled.

The God of Abraham, and of Isaac, and of Jacob, the God of our fathers, hath glorified his Son Jesus; whom ye delivered up, and denied him in the presence of Pilate, when he was determined to let him go.

But ye denied the Holy One and the Just, and desired a murderer to be granted unto you;

And killed the Prince of life, whom God hath raised from the dead; whereof we are witnesses [Acts 3:13–15].

Here he goes again. Simon Peter will never preach a sermon without the mention of the Resurrection. Paul won't either. Unfortunately, today there are many sermons preached without a mention of the Resurrection.

And his name through faith in his name hath made this man strong, whom ye see and know: yea, the faith which is by him hath given him this perfect soundness in the presence of you all [Acts 3:16].

In essence Peter is saying, "Don't you see that man leaping there? That is what they will do in the kingdom. The question is whether or not you want the Messiah to come back. Do you want to receive Him?"

And now, brethren, I wot that through ignorance ye did it, as did also your rulers.

But those things, which God before had shewed by the mouth of all his prophets, that Christ should suffer, he hath so fulfilled [Acts 3:17–18].

Their past deeds call for a course of action. That action is repentance and conversion. This was not a new message to them. "I, even I, am he that blotteth out thy transgressions for mine own sake, and will not remember thy sins" (Isa. 43:25). Listen to Peter's message:

Repent ye therefore, and be converted, that your sins may be blotted out, when the times of refreshing shall come from the presence of the Lord;

And he shall send Jesus Christ, which before was preached unto you [Acts 3:19–20].

If they had accepted Jesus, would He have returned to the earth? The answer, of course, is yes. Peter says He would have. Then what would have been God's program after that? I'll tell you something today that will be a secret just between you and me: I don't know what would have happened. Does that come as a surprise to you? Well, I have news for you. No one else knows either—no one except God. We can ask innumerable "if" questions to which there are no answers. All I know is that the nation did *not* accept Jesus Christ. That is the only answer I know to the "if" question. Any other answer would be only the wildest speculation.

And he shall send Jesus Christ, which before was preached unto you:

Whom the heaven must receive until the times of restitution of all things, which God hath spoken by the mouth of all his holy prophets since the world began [Acts 3:20–21].

Some folk use this verse to bolster their belief that eventually everything and every person will be saved. "The restitution of all things" is the phrase they use. Exactly what are the "all things" which are to be the subject of restitution? In Phillippians 3:8 when Paul said, ". . . I count all things but loss . . ." did he mean all things in God's universe? Obviously not. So here, the "all things" are limited by what follows. "The times of restitution of all things, which God hath spoken by the mouth of all his holy prophets since the world began." The prophets had spoken of the restoration of Israel. Nowhere is there a prophecy of the conversion and restoration of the wicked dead.

For Moses truly said unto the fathers, A prophet shall the Lord your God raise up unto you of your brethren, like unto me; him shall ye hear in all things whatsoever he shall say unto you.

And it shall come to pass, that every soul, which will not hear that prophet, shall be destroyed from among the people [Acts 3:22–23].

The nation of Israel was on the verge of a great judgment. In A.D. 70 Titus, the Roman general, came with his army and destroyed the city. It is estimated that over a million people perished, and the rest were sold into slavery throughout the Roman Empire. Judgment did come upon these people.

Yea, and all the prophets from Samuel and those that follow after, as many as have spoken, have likewise foretold of these days.

Ye are the children of the prophets, and of the covenant which God made with our fathers, saying unto Abraham, And in thy seed shall all the kindreds of the earth be blessed.

Unto you first God, having raised up his Son Jesus, sent him to bless you, in turning away every one of you from his iniquities [Acts 3:24–26].

This is a transition period. They were given their final chance to accept the Messiah. Because they turned down their opportunity to accept the Messiah, later on Paul will come on the scene as the apostle to the Gentiles. What might have happened if they had turned to God is merely speculation. They did not turn to Him. God is never surprised by what man does, and He still works things out according to His plan and purpose.

CHAPTER 4

THEME: *First persecution of the church; power of the Holy Spirit*

This chapter shows the result of Peter's second sermon. Five thousand people were saved. Then the apostles were arrested and put into prison. This was at the instigation of the Sadducees, and the reason for it was the preaching of the resurrection of Jesus Christ.

FIRST PERSECUTION OF THE CHURCH

And as they spake unto the people, the priests, and the captain of the temple, and the Sadducees, came upon them,

Being grieved that they taught the people, and preached through Jesus the resurrection from the dead [Acts 4:1–2].

I want to call your attention to something that is quite startling and interesting to see. Who was it that led in the persecution of the Lord Jesus and finally had Him arrested and put to death? It was the religious rulers, the Pharisees. They were the enemies of Christ as He walked here on earth. Apparently quite a few of the Pharisees were saved. We know that Nicodemus was. Joseph of Arimathea may have been a Pharisee. We know that Saul of Tarsus was one. Apparently there were many others of the Pharisees who were brought to a saving knowledge of the Lord Jesus Christ. After they had gotten rid of Him, their enmity and their spite were over.

Now the Sadducees, who do not believe in resurrection, become the great enemies when the church comes into existence, because the apostles are preaching the resurrection of Jesus Christ.

Let me give you an illustration of this. I have never engaged in any movement or reformation to try to straighten up any of the places where I preached. I never felt that was my job. I was a pastor in downtown Los Angeles for many years. In that town we had movie stars who had their day, but then the stardom disappeared and they became burned-out cinders. Often they would go into some kind of reformation work after their star had gone out. Maybe that was some type of reaction, I don't know. Such a woman called and asked me to serve on a committee that was trying to clean up downtown Los Angeles. I agreed it needed cleaning up, but I told her that I could not serve on the committee. She was amazed. "Aren't you a minister?" she asked. "Aren't you interested in cleaning up Los Angeles?" I answered, "I will not serve on your committee because I don't think you are going about it in the right way." Then I told her what the late Dr. Bob Shuler had told me years ago. He said, "We are called to fish in the fish pond, not to clean up the fish pond." This old world is a place to fish. Jesus said He would make us fishers of men, and the world is the place to fish. We are not called upon to clean up the fish pond. We need to catch the fish and get the fish cleaned up.

I have found that the biggest enemies of the preaching of the gospel are not the liquor folk. The gangsters have never bothered me. Do you know where I had my trouble as a preacher? It was with the so-called religious leaders, the liberals, those who claimed to be born again. They actually became enemies of the preaching of the gospel. It was amazing to me to find out how many of them wanted to destroy my radio ministry. They were our worst antagonists. It was not the gangsters, not the unsaved folk, but these religious leaders. They are the Sadducees of today. They are the ones who deny the supernatural. They deny the Word of God either by their lips or by their lives. That is important to see.

The Sadducees of that day and the "Sadducees" of our day try to make trouble for anyone who preaches the Resurrection. You can preach Jesus, friend. You can make Him a nice, sweet individual, a sort of Casper Milquetoast, and you will not be in trouble. But you are in trouble if you preach Him as the mighty Savior who came down to this earth, denounced sin, died on the cross for the sins of men, and then rose again in mighty power. That is the hated message. When the apostles preached it, the Sadducees arrested them and brought them in to the Sanhedrin.

And they laid hands on them, and put them in hold unto the next day: for it was now eventide.

Howbeit many of them which heard the word believed; and the number of the men was about five thousand [Acts 4:3–4].

All this was happening at Solomon's porch following the sermon which Peter had delivered. If there were five thousand men who believed, how many women and children do you suppose might have believed? This was a whole multitude that turned to Christ.

I have always been reluctant to criticize Simon Peter. You can't help but love the man. He was mightily used of God. This is not an evangelistic meeting where figures are turned in rather carelessly. These are genuine converts. There is nothing like this on record from that day to the present day, and I don't believe it will be exceeded as long as the church is in the world.

And it came to pass on the morrow, that their rulers, and elders, and scribes,

And Annas the high priest, and Caiaphas, and John, and Alexander, and as many as were of the kindred of the high priest, were gathered together at Jerusalem [Acts 4:5–6].

We have met this crowd before. These are the sneaky fellows, Annas and Caiaphas, in the background. These are the two men who condemned Jesus to die.

And when they had set them in the midst, they asked, By what power, or by what name, have ye done this? [Acts 4:7].

Peter and John are brought before the Sanhedrin. The lame man had been healed and Peter had preached his second sermon. The Sanhedrin demands to know by what power and by what name they do these things.

Then Peter, filled with the Holy Ghost, said unto them, Ye rulers of the people, and elders of Israel [Acts 4:8].

Notice that Peter is *filled* with the Holy Spirit. He wasn't baptized by the Holy Spirit at this time—that had already been accomplished. However he was filled with the Holy Spirit. You and I also need the filling of the Holy Spirit. That is something we should seek after; it is something we should devoutly want. Don't tarry and wait for the baptism of the Spirit. They had to tarry and wait until the Day of Pentecost when they were all baptized into one body, but today if you will turn to Jesus Christ, you will be baptized with the Holy Spirit and placed into the body of believers at the very moment you are regenerated.

If we this day be examined of the good deed done to the impotent man, by what means he is made whole;

Be it known unto you all, and to all the people of Israel, that by the name of Jesus Christ of Nazareth, whom ye crucified, whom God raised from the dead, even by him doth this man stand here before you whole [Acts 4:9–10].

Peter does a good job of speaking to these men. Up to this time, every time Peter opened his mouth, he put his foot in it. But this time, I tell you, he has his ". . . feet shod with the preparation of the gospel of peace" (Eph. 6:15). He is filled with the Holy Spirit and he is saying the right thing: "Are we on trial for the good deed we did for the sick man?" That is a searching question!

This is the stone which was set at nought of you builders, which is become the head of the corner [Acts 4:11].

Peter goes on to point out two things about the Lord Jesus. The first is that He was crucified and raised from the dead. The other is that Jesus Christ is the stone. Jesus had said, ". . . Upon this rock I will build my church . . ." (Matt. 16:18). What is the rock? The rock is Christ. Now Peter says, "This is the stone." What is the stone? Is it the church, or is it Simon Peter? No, it is the Lord Jesus Christ of Nazareth. He has become the Head of the corner. This has been accomplished by the Resurrection. Notice that the Resurrection is central to the preaching of the gospel.

Neither is there salvation in any other: for there is none other name under heaven given among men, whereby we must be saved [Acts 4:12].

Go back to the birth of Jesus and the instruction of the angel: ". . . thou shalt call his name JESUS: for he shall save his people from their sins" (Matt. 1:21). He is the Savior. That was His name at the beginning. When you accept the name, you accept all that it implies in the person who is involved. Peter makes it clear, and I want to emphasize that when you come to Him, my friend, you come to Him for salvation. There is no other name under heaven that can save you. The law can't save you. Religion can't save you. A ceremony can't save you. One alone, the name of Jesus, can save you. Jesus is the name of that Person who came down to this earth to save His people from their sins. When any person comes to Him in faith, that person is saved. There is no other place to turn for salvation.

Isn't it interesting that in the long history of this world and all the religions of the world and all the dogmatism that these religions have, not one of them can offer a sure salvation? An uncle of mine was a preacher in a certain church which believes in baptismal regeneration; that is, that you must be baptized to be saved. I asked him this question, "Look, if I get baptized as you say, will that guarantee my salvation?" "No," he said, "it couldn't quite do that." My friend, may I say something to you today? There is none other name under heaven whereby you can be saved. If you come to Him, if you trust Christ, then you are saved. That guarantees your salvation.

That was a great message of Simon Peter's, and this is a fine note to conclude that message to the Sanhedrin.

Now when they saw the boldness of Peter and John, and perceived that they were unlearned and ignorant men, they marvelled; and they took knowledge of them, that they had been with Jesus [Acts 4:13].

"Unlearned and ignorant"—that is, these men hadn't been to a theological seminary. But the Sanhedrin noted that they had been with Jesus. How wonderful to have a life that somehow or other calls attention to Jesus!

And beholding the man which was healed standing with them, they could say nothing against it.

But when they had commanded them to go aside out of the council, they conferred among themselves [Acts 4:14–15].

Were they moved by Peter's speech? No, they were not moved at all.

Saying, What shall we do to these men? for that indeed a notable miracle hath been done by them is manifest to all them that dwell in Jerusalem; and we cannot deny it [Acts 4:16].

Not even the Sadducees of that day could deny that a miracle had been performed. It takes a liberal, living in the twentieth century and removed by several thousand miles, to deny miracles. If you had been there then, you would have had difficulty denying the miracle. The liberals of that day had to say, "We cannot deny a miracle has taken place."

People today say that if they could only see a miracle, they would believe. That is not true. This crowd wouldn't believe, and you have the same human nature as these people had. The problem is not a problem of the mind. It is a problem of the will and of the heart. It is the heart that is desperately wicked. Unbelief is not from a lack of facts; it is the condition of the human heart.

Now they are plotting.

But that it spread no further among the people, let us straitly threaten them, that they speak henceforth to no man in this name.

And they called them, and commanded them not to speak at all nor teach in the name of Jesus [Acts 4:17–18].

Peter and John have an answer for them.

But Peter and John answered and said unto them, Whether it be right in the sight of God to hearken unto you more than unto God, judge ye.

For we cannot but speak the things which we have seen and heard.

So when they had further threatened them, they let them go, finding nothing how they might punish them, because of the people: for all men glorified God for that which was done.

For the man was above forty years old, on whom this miracle of healing was shewed [Acts 4:19–22].

You would think that the men of the Sanhedrin would have been softened by this. They were not. They were hard as nails. Their hearts were hard.

THE POWER OF THE HOLY SPIRIT

And being let go, they went to their own company, and reported all that the chief priests and elders had said unto them.

And when they heard that, they lifted up their voice to God with one accord, and said, Lord, thou art God, which hast made heaven, and earth, and the sea, and all that in them is [Acts 4:23–24].

Peter and John have been released and have returned to the church, and they give their report. Here we have recorded a great meeting of the early church. I do not believe the spiritual condition of the church has ever again been on such a high level. We find the key to this in their prayer. It is more than a prayer; it is a song of praise.

"Lord, Thou art God. Lord, You are the Creator." Friend, I am afraid the church is not sure of that today. The Lord is God. Are you sure that the Lord Jesus is God? Are you? That is most important.

The church is not sure today. The church is fumbling; it has lost its power. The church is always talking of methods, always trying this gimmick and that gimmick to attract people. The church in suburbia and the church in downtown are little more than religious clubs. The church is not a powerhouse anymore.

The early church was sure that Jesus is God. They refer to the second psalm:

Who by the mouth of thy servant David hast said, Why did the heathen rage, and the people imagine vain things?

The kings of the earth stood up, and the rulers were gathered together against the Lord, and against his Christ [Acts 4:25–26].

The beginning of the fulfillment of Psalm 2 was when they crucified Jesus Christ. The hatred of Jesus and of God has been snowballing down through the centuries for nineteen hundred years. It is gathering size and momentum. It will finally break into a mighty crescendo upon this earth in the final rebellion of man against God.

For of a truth against thy holy child Jesus, whom thou hast anointed, both Herod, and Pontius Pilate, with the Gentiles, and the people of Israel, were gathered together,

For to do whatsoever thy hand and thy counsel determined before to be done.

And now, Lord, behold their threatenings: and grant unto thy servants, that with all boldness they may speak thy word [Acts 4:27–29].

I am moved by this. This was a great prayer and praise service. They all were in one accord. Probably they did not all pray at one time, but they were certainly "amen"ing the one who led in prayer. Notice that they did not pray for the persecution to cease. They prayed for the courage to endure it! They asked for power and for boldness to speak. That early church was something different, friend, from the church of our day.

By stretching forth thine hand to heal; and that signs and wonders may be done by the name of thy holy child Jesus [Acts 4:30].

Note the power of the early church.

And when they had prayed, the place was shaken where they were assembled together; and they were all filled with the Holy Ghost, and they spake the word of God with boldness [Acts 4:31].

It was the condition of the church which made this possible.

And the multitude of them that believed were of one heart and of one soul: neither said any of them that aught of the things which he possessed was his own; but they had all things common [Acts 4:32].

This did not last very long. Carnality came into the church very soon.

And with great power gave the apostles witness of the resurrection of the Lord Jesus: and great grace was upon them all [Acts 4:33].

That is the heart of gospel preaching.

Neither was there any among them that lacked: for as many as were possessors of lands or houses sold them, and brought the prices of the things that were sold,

And laid them down at the apostles' feet: and distribution was made unto every man according as he had need.

And Joses, who by the apostles was surnamed Barnabas, (which is, being interpreted, The son of consolation,) a Levite, and of the country of Cyprus,

Having land, sold it, and brought the money, and laid it at the apostles' feet [Acts 4:34–37].

This kind of living could be carried out for a short while because of the spiritual condition of the church. It is nonsense to say that we should put this into effect today. If we tried it, we would have utter chaos. Why? Because there must first be the same high spiritual level, and we don't have that today. Let us be honest and face up to it. We need to come into a closer relationship to the person of Jesus Christ.

We have been introduced to Barnabas. We will hear more of him later.

CHAPTER 5

***THEME:** Death of Ananias and Sapphira; second persecution*

As we come to chapter 5, we are continuing to see the effects of the great sermon that Simon Peter gave. Also we are introduced to the first defection in the church, followed by the death of Ananias and Sapphira—who were Christians, but were not living on the high spiritual level of the early church.

At the end of chapter 4 we were introduced to a man by the name of Barnabas. He will be before us again. He was one of the wonderful saints in the early church, a true man of God. He was the first missionary partner of the apostle Paul when they went into the difficult Galatian area, and yet God marvelously blessed their ministry there.

Barnabas had given quite a sum of money to the church. He had made a generous contribution, and everyone was talking about it. I imagine he received a great deal of publicity for his generosity. Remember that in the early church they had all things common. It reveals the fact that they were on a high spiritual level to be able to do this.

Now the first defection comes in. Having all things common could not continue and did not continue simply because of the carnal nature that is in mankind.

DEATH OF ANANIAS AND SAPPHIRA

> **But a certain man named Ananias, with Sapphira his wife, sold a possession [Acts 5:1].**

It is obvious that they were imitating Barnabas. They saw that he got a certain amount of publicity, and they thought it would be nice if they could get that kind of publicity, too. They wanted it.

I have found that there are people who will give in order to be noticed. I recall a meeting with businessmen in Pasadena when I was a pastor there. We were planning to start a youth organization, and we were asking these men to give donations for the founding of this movement. It was decided that donations would not be made public.

I was informed that one of these men would contribute very little if he were not given the opportunity to speak out publicly to let everybody know how much he was giving. It is quite interesting that he contributed a small amount. After the meeting he confided in one of the men that he had intended to give about ten times that amount, but he had expected to be able to stand up or at least raise his hand to indicate how much he had given. You see, pride is still in human nature today. That was the condition of Ananias and Sapphira.

> **And kept back part of the price, his wife also being privy to it, and brought a certain part, and laid it at the apostles' feet [Acts 5:2].**

There was nothing wrong with the fact that they kept back part of the money. They had a right to do that. The property had been theirs and they had the right to do with the money whatever they wished.

Today, we in the church are under grace. We are not constrained to give any certain amount. Someone may say we ought to give a tithe. In the early church they were giving everything they owned. Ananias and Sapphira did not give all but kept back part of it, which they had a right to do. Their problem, their sin, was that they lied about it. They said they were giving all when actually they were keeping part of it for themselves.

I don't like to have people sing the song that talks about putting "my all" on the altar. Unfortunately, that makes liars out of the people who are singing. We need to be very careful about the songs we sing. A vow to the Lord should never be made lightly.

Ananias and Sapphira said they were laying all on the altar, but they were lying about it.

> **But Peter said, Ananias, why hath Satan filled thine heart to lie to the Holy Ghost, and to keep back part of the price of the land? [Acts 5:3].**

The sin of this man and his wife was that they lied about it.

> **Whiles it remained, was it not thine own? and after it was sold, was it not in thine own power? why hast thou conceived this thing in thine heart? thou hast not lied unto men, but unto God [Acts 5:4].**

There are people today who deny that the Holy Spirit is God. You will notice that Simon Peter believed He was God. First he says, "Ananias, why hath Satan filled thine heart to lie to the Holy Ghost?" Then he says, "Thou hast not lied unto men, but unto God." The Holy Spirit is God.

And Ananias hearing these words fell down, and gave up the ghost: and great fear came on all them that heard these things [Acts 5:5].

There are those today who think that Simon Peter caused the death of this man, Ananias. They even blame him for his death. I want to absolve him of this crime. Simon Peter was probably as much surprised as anyone when Ananias fell down dead. I don't think that he knew at all what was going to happen. Do you know who struck Ananias dead? God did. Do you feel that you want to bring charges against God? Do you want to call the FBI to tell them that God is guilty of murder? May I say to you, if you can give life, you have the right to take it away. This is God's universe. We are God's creatures. We breathe His air. We use bodies that He has given to us. My friend, He can take our bodies any time He wishes to. God is not guilty of a crime. This is *His discipline within the church*. God is the One who is responsible for the death of Ananias and Sapphira.

And the young men arose, wound him up, and carried him out, and buried him.

And it was about the space of three hours after, when his wife, not knowing what was done, came in.

And Peter answered unto her, Tell me whether ye sold the land for so much? And she said, Yea, for so much.

Then Peter said unto her, How is it that ye have agreed together to tempt the Spirit of the Lord? behold, the feet of them which have buried thy husband are at the door, and shall carry thee out [Acts 5:6–9].

Simon Peter knows what will happen to her. He did not know what was going to happen to Ananias, but now it is quite obvious what will happen to this woman.

Then fell she down straightway at his feet, and yielded up the ghost: and the young men came in, and found her dead, and, carrying her forth, buried her by her husband.

And great fear came upon all the church, and upon as many as heard these things [Acts 5:10–11].

There are two things that amaze me about this incident. One is the fact that a lie, such as these two were living, could not exist in the early church. There was a holiness of life in the church. Ananias and Sapphira, although they were saved, lied to the Holy Spirit and were removed from the company of believers. They had committed the sin unto death. "If any man see his brother sin a sin which is not unto death, he shall ask, and he shall give him life for them that sin not unto death. There is a sin unto death: I do not say that he shall pray for it" (1 John 5:16). This was a sin unto death which Ananias and Sapphira committed. This kind of sin could not exist in the early church.

There was defection in the church and it required discipline. However, after this experience the church would never be as pure as it was before. Up until this time they had all things common. This incident almost ruined them. We shall see more of this in the next chapter.

Fear came upon all the church, and fear came upon people who heard of these things. Power would continue in the church, and multitudes would be saved. Yet the church would never be as pure as in those first days of existence.

The other amazing thing is the spiritual discernment of Simon Peter. This also is lacking today.

I was very much amused at a young man who came to me in a Bible class not long ago. He told me he had the gift of discerning of spirits and he could tell truth from error. Then he quoted one of the worst heretics today. I questioned him again about his gift of discernment of spirits, of truth and error, and then asked him whether he approved of the man whom he had just quoted. "Oh yes," he said, "this man speaks the truth." I told him that I didn't believe he had any special gift—he just thought he did.

Today the worst kind of hypocrite can get into our Bible churches. They are not good at coming to Bible studies—I have discovered that, but they can hold offices and even run the church. If those who lied to God in our churches were to drop down dead, we would have a lot of funerals. The undertakers would be doing a land-office business.

And by the hands of the apostles were many signs and wonders wrought among the people; (and they were all with one accord in Solomon's porch.

And of the rest durst no man join himself to them: but the people magnified them.

And believers were the more added to the Lord, multitudes both of men and women.) [Acts 5:12–14].

Notice that the apostles exercise the apostolic gifts. Gifts of healing and gifts of miracles were sign gifts which were given to the apostles. They did many signs among the people.

The discipline in the church had put a fear on the people and had stopped the revival. Yet there were those who were still being saved. Believers were being added to the Lord. We know that by A.D. 300 there were millions of people in the Roman Empire who had turned to Christ.

Insomuch that they brought forth the sick into the streets, and laid them on beds and couches, that at the least the shadow of Peter passing by might overshadow some of them.

There came also a multitude out of the cities round about unto Jerusalem, bringing sick folks, and them which were vexed with unclean spirits: and they were healed every one [Acts 5:15–16].

May I compare this to modern faith healing? Modern faith healers never heal *all* the people who come to them. Have you ever noticed that? The apostles had sign gifts, friend. No one in the church since then has had those gifts. People were healed, every one of them. They emptied the hospitals. This was the power of the early church.

We must remember that at that time there was no written New Testament. The church is built on Jesus Christ—He is the Cornerstone—and the apostles were witnesses to Christ. The sign gifts were given to them to demonstrate the fact that they spoke with God's authority. Today we have a written New Testament as our authority.

THE SECOND PERSECUTION

We have seen that there was discipline within the early church. Now we find that there is persecution from without. When the apostles exercised their gifts, they produced a reaction.

Then the high priest rose up, and all they that were with him, (which is the sect of the Sadducees,) and were filled with indignation,

And laid their hands on the apostles, and put them in the common prison [Acts 5:17–18].

Notice that the Sadducees are leading in the persecution. It was the Pharisees who had led in the persecution against Jesus; it is the Sadducees who lead the persecution against the early church. So the apostles are arrested for the second time and are put into prison.

But the angel of the Lord by night opened the prison doors, and brought them forth, and said [Acts 5:19].

This translation should be "*an* angel" and not "*the* angel." In the Old Testament, *the* angel of the Lord was none other than the preincarnate Christ, but now Christ is the Man in glory at God's right hand, and He is the One who is directing the activity of His apostles. Today, unfortunately, much of the time His hands and His feet are paralyzed because the people in the church are not moving for Him in this world. Jesus Christ wants to move through His church. He wants to move through you and me, if we will permit Him. This is not Christ who appeared here; it was an angel.

Go, stand and speak in the temple to the people all the words of this life.

And when they heard that, they entered into the temple early in the morning, and taught. But the high priest came, and they that were with him, and called the council together, and all the senate of the children of Israel, and sent to the prison to have them brought.

But when the officers came, and found them not in the prison, they returned, and told,

Saying, The prison truly found we shut with all safety, and the keepers standing without before the doors: but when we had opened, we found no man within [Acts 5:20–23].

This is the same sort of thing that happened at the resurrection of Christ. The stone wasn't rolled away to let Jesus out; He was out before the stone was rolled away. The stone was moved to let those on the outside come in. The same thing happened here. The doors did not need to be opened to let the apostles get out. They were out long before the doors were unlocked.

Now when the high priest and the captain of the temple and the chief priests heard these things, they doubted of them whereunto this would grow.

Then came one and told them, saying, Behold, the men whom ye put in prison are standing in the temple, and teaching the people.

Then went the captain with the officers, and brought them without violence: for they feared the people, lest they should have been stoned.

And when they had brought them, they set them before the council: and the high priest asked them,

Saying, Did not we straitly command you that ye should not teach in this name? and, behold, ye have filled Jerusalem with your doctrine, and intend to bring this man's blood upon us [Acts 5:24–28].

People were listening to the apostles. They were good witnesses. They were real missionaries. Jesus had said that the gospel was to go out, first in Jerusalem. We see that this has been done—"Ye have filled Jerusalem with your doctrine."

Then Peter and the other apostles answered and said, We ought to obey God rather than men [Acts 5:29].

The apostles were obeying what their Lord and Master had told them to do. Believers are commanded to obey civil authority—except when it comes in conflict with the commandment of God.

The God of our fathers raised up Jesus, whom ye slew and hanged on a tree [Acts 5:30].

Jesus Christ was hanged on a tree. It was not a nice, smooth piece of timber with a crossbar, as we see it pictured today. It was a tree.

Him hath God exalted with his right hand to be a Prince and a Saviour, for to give repentance to Israel, and forgiveness of sins.

And we are his witnesses of these things; and so is also the Holy Ghost, whom God hath given to them that obey him [Acts 5:31–32].

This is still the message to the nation Israel in Jerusalem today.

When they heard that, they were cut to the heart, and took counsel to slay them.

Then stood there up one in the council, a Pharisee named Gamaliel, a doctor of the law, had in reputation among all the people, and commanded to put the apostles forth a little space [Acts 5: 33–34].

Gamaliel wants the apostles excused so that he can talk to the Sanhedrin. This Gamaliel was an outstanding man and greatly respected. (He was the teacher of the apostle Paul, by the way.)

And said unto them, Ye men of Israel, take heed to yourselves what ye intend to do as touching these men.

For before these days rose up Theudas, boasting himself to be somebody; to whom a number of men, about four hundred, joined themselves: who was slain; and all, as many as obeyed him, were scattered, and brought to nought.

After this man rose up Judas of Galilee in the days of the taxing, and drew away much people after him: he also perished; and all, even as many as obeyed him, were dispersed.

And now I say unto you, Refrain from these men, and let them alone: for if this counsel or this work be of men, it will come to nought [Acts 5:35–38].

He is giving sage advice.

But if it be of God, ye cannot overthrow it; lest haply ye be found even to fight against God [Acts 5:39].

Gamaliel gives examples of men who had started uprisings and had a following, but after they were killed, their followers disbanded. Now he advises them that the same thing will happen to Jesus and His followers.

And to him they agreed: and when they had called the apostles, and beaten them, they commanded that they should not speak in the name of Jesus, and let them go [Acts 5:40].

If these men were innocent, they should have let them go. If these men were guilty, they should have held them and punished them. Beating them and then letting them go was a sorry subterfuge. They should have listened to Gamaliel a little more carefully.

Things aren't much different today. There is that gray line between guilty and not guilty. The courts today let people off by giving them some light sentence. My friend, if a person is guilty, he should be punished. If he is not guilty, he should be let go with no sentence.

And they departed from the presence of the council, rejoicing that they were counted worthy to suffer shame for his name.

And daily in the temple, and in every house, they ceased not to teach and preach Jesus Christ [Acts 5:41–42].

These apostles were marvelous men. They were rejoicing that they could suffer for the Lord Jesus. They continued to teach and to preach Jesus Christ. What is the gospel? It is a Person! It is Jesus Christ.

Do you have Him today? You either do or you don't. You either trust Him, or you do not trust Him. Either He is your Savior, or you do not have a Savior. That is the message. The apostles did not cease to teach and to preach Jesus Christ.

CHAPTER 6

THEME: *The appointment of deacons; witness of Stephen, a deacon*

In this chapter we see the further result of the defection that was in the church. We first saw that defection in the case of Ananias and Sapphira. They were believers who were saved, but they could not remain in the early church with that lie in their lives.

Now the defection we see in this chapter led to the selection of deacons. The chapter continues with the account of one of those deacons, Stephen. He was framed, arrested, and tried.

THE APPOINTMENT OF DEACONS

And in those days, when the number of the disciples was multiplied, there arose a murmuring of the Grecians against the Hebrews, because their widows were neglected in the daily ministration [Acts 6:1].

We need to recognize that this took place early in the history of the church. They had attempted a form of communal living and, actually, it succeeded for a short while. Then carnality entered the church. We saw how Ananias and Sapphira misrepresented their situation. Now we find that there is a murmuring of the Grecians against the Hebrews. This is not a clash between two races. This is not a demonstration of anti-Semitism. The word *Grecians* here means "Hellenists," Greek-speaking Jews. They had a background of Greek culture, while the Hebrews in Jerusalem closely followed the Mosaic Law. Naturally, a misunderstanding developed.

It has been estimated that the number in the church at this time may have been around twenty-five thousand. And we see that this early church was not perfect. We hear people say, "We need to get back to the early church. The early church was power-conscious, and we today are problem-conscious." That is only a half-truth. The early church did have power, but the early church had problems also.

The high plane to which the Spirit had brought the church was interrupted by the intrusion of satanic division and confusion. The sharing of material substance, which first characterized the church, gave way to the selfishness of the old nature. Carnality had come in. The Grecians, who evidently were a minority group, felt neglected and demanded that their widows be given equal consideration with the Hebrews. This communal form of living wasn't working as well as they would have liked. This was brought to the attention of the apostles.

Then the twelve called the multitude of the disciples unto them, and said, It is not reason that we should leave the word of God, and serve tables [Acts 6:2].

The apostles felt that they should not give up the study of the Word of God. They felt it was important for them to continue with that. If they gave up the study of the Word of God and served tables, that would be the undoing of them. They *should* spend their time in prayer and in the study of the Word of God.

It is important for every church to recognize that the minister should have time to study the Word of God and should have time for prayer. Unfortunately, the average church today is looking for a pastor who is an organizer and a promoter, a sort of vice-president to run the church, a manager of some sort. That is unfortunate. As a result the church is suffering today. When I was a pastor in downtown Los Angeles, I had to move my study to my home. I built a special room over the garage for my study. I found out that all I had in the church was an office, not a study. They didn't intend for me to study there. They didn't want me to study there.

Wherefore, brethren, look ye out among you seven men of honest report, full of the Holy Ghost and wisdom, whom we may appoint over this business.

But we will give ourselves continually to prayer, and to the ministry of the word [Acts 6:3–4].

The seven men were to be appointed because a crisis had arisen. The apostles felt it was important that they should not have the burden of this detail so that they could give themselves to prayer and the ministry of the Word.

Now I want you to notice the qualifications of these seven men who are to assume the burden of handling the material substance of the church. I'm afraid this is something which is neglected in the average church today when the deacons are chosen. In fact, I've heard men say they didn't want to be appointed to the spiritual office of an elder but would like to be a deacon to handle the material things.

May I say to you, the office of deacon requires more spirituality and wisdom and prayer than any other office. Now notice the qualifications: These men had to be men of honest report. Their honesty was to be unquestionable. It is really a tragic thing for a church to have a deacon whose honesty is in question so that others—including the pastor—cannot trust him. Such a man should not be in the office of deacon. The second qualification was "full of the Holy Ghost." They were not to be filled with wine but were to be "filled with the [Holy] Spirit" (Eph. 5:18). Thirdly, they were to be men of wisdom. They were to be spiritual men who would be able to make an application of spiritual truth. That was very important. You see, the fact that they were handling material matters was apt to give them a lopsided view of things. So it is most important that deacons should be men who look at things from the spiritual point of view.

We shall see that Stephen was a man who met these qualifications. He had wisdom—"they were not able to resist the wisdom and the spirit by which he spake" (v. 10). He had real conviction. Also he was "full of faith." Not only did he have saving faith but also serving faith—witnessing faith. It wasn't the amount of his faith but the object of his faith that was important. We learn from this same verse that he was full of power. Such were the kind of men chosen as deacons.

But we will give ourselves continually to prayer, and to the ministry of the word [Acts 6:4].

That was the duty of the apostles.

And the saying pleased the whole multitude: and they chose Stephen, a man full of faith and of the Holy Ghost, and Philip, and Prochorus, and Nicanor, and Timon, and Parmenas, and Nicolas a proselyte of Antioch [Acts 6:5].

I can't tell you anything more about the last five men. The first two, Stephen and Philip, will be mentioned again as we go along in the Book of Acts. They were outstanding men in the early church. Although they were to "serve tables," the record of them is that they were spiritual men.

Whom they set before the apostles: and when they had prayed, they laid their hands on them [Acts 6:6].

Now, friends, there is a great deal of hocus-pocus and abracadabra connected with this matter of laying on of hands. A great many people think that some spiritual power is connected to it. They think that putting on the hands communicates something to a person. Frankly, the only thing you can communicate to someone else by the laying on of hands is disease germs. You can pass them on, but you cannot pass on any kind of power.

What is the meaning of the laying on of hands? As we saw in Leviticus, when we were studying the Old Testament sacrifices, the sinner would put his hand on the head of the animal to be sacrificed, which signified that the animal to be offered was taking his place. The offering was identified with the sinner.

When the apostles put their hands on the heads of the deacons, it meant that now the deacons would be partners with them. They were together in this service. It designated that these men were set aside for this office, denoting their fellowship in the things of Christ and their position as representatives for the corporate body of believers.

Notice that this was a social service in

which these men were engaged. The early church took care of its own. I think that should still be true today. The early church had a poverty program, and it included only the members of the church. The church today should also take care of its own.

And the word of God increased; and the number of the disciples multiplied in Jerusalem greatly; and a great company of the priests were obedient to the faith [Acts 6:7].

It is still important in our day for the Word of God to be increasing. Certainly this is the purpose of my radio program. It is my sincere desire that the Word of God may be increased.

Don't miss the fact that many of the priests turned to the Lord. Some of them must have been serving in the temple when the veil was rent in two at the death of Christ. Many of them must have turned to Christ after that experience.

WITNESS OF STEPHEN, A DEACON

Our attention is now drawn to Stephen. He is one of the great men in the early church.

And Stephen, full of faith and power, did great wonders and miracles among the people [Acts 6:8].

Apparently these deacons are one with the apostles in having the sign gifts. They have been brought into a unique position. Because Stephen is a strong witness to the gospel, he incurs the hatred of the Sadducees. False witnesses are brought before the council to accuse Stephen.

Then there arose certain of the synagogue, which is called the synagogue of the Libertines, and Cyrenians, and Alexandrians, and of them of Cilicia and of Asia, disputing with Stephen.

And they were not able to resist the wisdom and the spirit by which he spake.

Then they suborned men, which said, We have heard him speak blasphemous words against Moses, and against God.

And they stirred up the people, and the elders, and the scribes, and came upon him, and caught him, and brought him to the council,

And set up false witnesses, which said, This man ceaseth not to speak blasphemous words against this holy place, and the law:

For we have heard him say, that this Jesus of Nazareth shall destroy this place, and shall change the customs which Moses delivered us.

And all that sat in the council, looking stedfastly on him, saw his face as it had been the face of an angel [Acts 6:9–15].

Stephen is brought before the Sanhedrin, and false witnesses are brought in. The false witnesses tell a half-truth, of course. The Lord Jesus did say that they would destroy this temple and He would raise it up again, but He was speaking of the temple of His body. At His trial, the false witnesses misunderstood that and misrepresented it. So here, they misunderstand Stephen when he says that the temple in Jerusalem will be left desolate. Actually, it was desolate without Christ anyway. And they twist what he is saying about the customs of Moses. Of course men are not saved by the Law but by grace. But salvation in Moses' day was by grace even as it is today. Their accusation is based on only a partial truth.

They see something marvelous in the face of Stephen. This man came closer to being an angel than any man who has ever lived.

CHAPTER 7

***THEME:** Stephen's address and martyrdom*

In this chapter we find Stephen's defense before the council—which is really not a defense. Rather it is a rehearsal of the history of the nation Israel and of their resistance and rebellion against God. He charges the council of being betrayers and murderers of Jesus. That, of course, engenders their bitterest hatred and leads to the stoning of Stephen.

In his inspired survey of the history of the nation, Stephen makes it very clear that there never was a time when the entire nation worshiped God. Yet there was always the believing remnant, a small remnant of true believers—even as there is in our day.

STEPHEN'S ADDRESS

Then said the high priest, Are these things so?

And he said, Men, brethren, and fathers, hearken; The God of glory appeared unto our father Abraham, when he was in Mesopotamia, before he dwelt in Charran [Acts 7:1–2].

They have made an accusation against him. He is questioned as to the truth of the charges. In his response he makes no attempt to clear himself. In fact, he doesn't even mention the charges they have made against him.

What a marvelous beginning. He calls them *brethren.* They are his brethren in the flesh. He calls the older men *fathers*. He is a younger man and shows them this respect. This young man is to become the first martyr in the church.

We sometimes hear it said that Christianity at the beginning was actually a youth movement. It is not altogether inaccurate to state that it was a youth movement. Two men who held as prominent a place as any were Stephen and Saul of Tarsus, whom we will meet soon. These two men had a great deal to do with the shaping of the course of the early church. Both of them were remarkable young men. Both of them were gifted and used by the Holy Spirit. Yet the only time these two young men ever met, they were enemies. The cross divided Stephen and Saul of Tarsus just as truly as it divided the two thieves who were crucified with Jesus. Paul knew what he was saying in 1 Corinthians 1:18: "For the preaching of the cross is to them that perish foolishness; but unto us which are saved it is the power of God." When Saul saw Stephen, he thought Stephen was very foolish.

This address of Stephen is a master stroke. He reviews the history of the nation beginning with Abraham. That is where the history of the nation Israel began. They did not go back any farther. You will find the same thing in the Gospel of Matthew. This book, written to the nation Israel, traces the genealogy of Jesus Christ back to Abraham. If you want to trace it all the way back to Adam, you must turn to the Gospel of Luke. Stephen starts with Abraham, a man of faith.

Even though he traces the resistance and rebellion against God by the nation, still there was always a believing remnant.

This is true today, too. In the organized church, in the visible church which you and I can see, there is a remnant of believers. Not every one in the visible church is a true believer. People may ask, "Do you think So-and-So is a Christian?" The answer is that even though he goes to church and is a church officer, he may not be a Christian. Just as in the nation Israel there was the believing remnant, so in the visible church there is the little remnant of true believers.

Abraham was a man of faith. He believed God, and he obeyed God. Faith always leads to obedience. Stephen starts his narrative with Abraham in Mesopotamia, down in the Tigris-Euphrates valley. That was the place of Abraham's hometown. It was there that God called him.

And said unto him, Get thee out of thy country, and from thy kindred, and come into the land which I shall shew thee [Acts 7:3].

God called Abraham away from his home because it was a home of idolatry.

Then came he out of the land of the Chaldaeans, and dwelt in Charran: and from thence, when his father was dead, he removed him into this land, wherein ye now dwell.

And he gave him none inheritance in it, no, not so much as to set his foot on: yet he promised that he would give it to him for a possession, and to his seed after him, when as yet he had no child [Acts 7:4–5].

He is relating the story of Abraham. This shows the faith of Abraham. God had promised him a child, and God had promised him the land. Although Abraham had neither one, he believed God.

And God spake on this wise, That his seed should sojourn in a strange land; and that they should bring them into bondage, and entreat them evil four hundred years.

And the nation to whom they shall be in bondage will I judge, said God: and after that shall they come forth, and serve me in this place.

And he gave him the covenant of circumcision: and so Abraham begat Isaac, and circumcised him the eighth day; and Isaac begat Jacob; and Jacob begat the twelve patriarchs [Acts 7:6–8].

Stephen goes from Abraham to the patriarchal period. He speaks of the brethren of Joseph, motivated by envy and hatred who sold Joseph into Egypt. But God overruled and used Joseph to save them. What we have here is really the Spirit's interpretation of the Old Testament. That makes this a remarkable section.

And the patriarchs, moved with envy, sold Joseph into Egypt: but God was with him,

And delivered him out of all his afflictions, and gave him favour and wisdom in the sight of Pharaoh king of Egypt; and he made him governor over Egypt and all his house.

Now there came a dearth over all the land of Egypt and Chanaan, and great affliction: and our fathers found no sustenance.

But when Jacob heard that there was corn in Egypt, he sent out our fathers first.

And at the second time Joseph was made known to his brethren; and Joseph's kindred was made known unto Pharaoh.

Then sent Joseph, and called his father Jacob to him, and all his kindred, threescore and fifteen souls.

So Jacob went down into Egypt, and died, he, and our fathers,

And were carried over into Sychem, and laid in the sepulchre that Abraham bought for a sum of money of the sons of Emmor the father of Sychem [Acts 7:9–16].

Now Stephen comes to another period in the history of these people. He is going to remind them of the deliverance out of Egypt. God made Moses the deliverer. And he shows that at first the children of Israel refused to follow Moses and that Moses had trouble with them all the way.

But when the time of the promise drew nigh, which God had sworn to Abraham, the people grew and multiplied in Egypt,

Till another king arose, which knew not Joseph.

The same dealt subtilly with our kindred, and evil entreated our fathers, so that they cast out their young children, to the end they might not live.

In which time Moses was born, and was exceeding fair, and nourished up in his father's house three months:

And when he was cast out, Pharaoh's daughter took him up, and nourished him for her own son [Acts 7:17–21].

The comment which Stephen adds confirms some of the things that we said when we were studying about Moses. If Rameses II was the pharaoh of the oppression, Moses could have been the next pharaoh. Pharaoh's daughter brought him up as her own son. This pharaoh had no sons, so Moses would have been the next in line.

And Moses was learned in all the wisdom of the Egyptians, and was mighty in words and in deeds [Acts 7:22].

Moses was brought up in the wisdom of the Egyptians. The wisdom of the Egyptians is not despised even in our advanced day when we feel that we know about everything. Too often we do not give the Egyptians full credit for what they did know. They had developed mathematics, chemistry, engineering, architecture, and astronomy to a very fine point. They had developed these fields of study in a way that was really remarkable. Look at the pyramids. Look at the colors we find in the tombs, colors which have stood the test of the centuries. They understood about embalming. They had calculated the distance to the sun. My friend, they had a highly developed culture and were not an ignorant people.

Moses had all the advantages of that day,

being raised as the son of Pharaoh's daughter. He was learned in all the wisdom of the Egyptians. He was outstanding. Yet he was not prepared to lead God's people. All the learning of the world of that day did not equip him to lead God's people. All the wisdom that men have today is not enough for them to understand the Word of God. It is too difficult. Why? Because the natural man cannot receive the things of the Spirit of God. These things are foolishness to him and he cannot know them, because they are spiritually discerned (see 1 Cor. 2:14). Although Moses was learned in the wisdom of his day, he was not ready to deliver God's people. So, after forty years of learning in Egypt, God put him out into the desert. There God gave him his B. D. degree, his Backside of the Desert degree, and prepared him to become the deliverer.

And when he was full forty years old, it came into his heart to visit his brethren the children of Israel.

And seeing one of them suffer wrong, he defended him, and avenged him that was oppressed, and smote the Egyptian:

For he supposed his brethren would have understood how that God by his hand would deliver them: but they understood not [Acts 7:23–25].

Notice that Moses did what he considered to be a very fine thing to do. He intended to deliver his brethren. But they didn't understand. Actually, neither did Moses understand. He still was not really ready, and God had to take him out to the desert to train him.

And the next day he shewed himself unto them as they strove, and would have set them at one again, saying, Sirs, ye are brethren; why do ye wrong one to another?

But he that did his neighbour wrong thrust him away, saying, Who made thee a ruler and a judge over us?

Wilt thou kill me, as thou diddest the Egyptian yesterday? [Acts 7:26–28].

Now Moses was frightened.

Then fled Moses at this saying, and was a stranger in the land of Madian, where he begat two sons.

And when forty years were expired, there appeared to him in the wilderness of mount Sina an angel of the Lord in a flame of fire in a bush.

When Moses saw it, he wondered at the sight: and as he drew near to behold it, the voice of the Lord came unto him [Acts 7:29–31].

Moses had wanted to deliver the children of Israel, but he wasn't prepared for it, and the people weren't prepared for him either. They wouldn't accept his leadership. They resisted him. Then *God* called him to be the deliverer.

Saying, I am the God of thy fathers, the God of Abraham, and the God of Isaac, and the God of Jacob. Then Moses trembled, and durst not behold.

Then said the Lord to him, Put off thy shoes from thy feet: for the place where thou standest is holy ground.

I have seen, I have seen the affliction of my people which is in Egypt, and I have heard their groaning, and am come down to deliver them. And now come, I will send thee into Egypt (Acts 7: 32–34].

God told Moses, "I have heard their groaning." He saw their need. That was the reason He delivered them. It was for the same reason that He provided a Savior for you and me. It wasn't because we are such wonderful people. He didn't look down and say, "My, they are so lovely down there. I must go down and save them. They are so sweet, and so kind, and so loving to Me, and so faithful to Me." No! God looked down and saw nothing but corrupt, rotten sinners. We were all lost in iniquity. He loved us in spite of our unloveliness. That is the explanation.

This Moses whom they refused, saying, Who made thee a ruler and a judge? the same did God send to be a ruler and a deliverer by the hand of the angel which appeared to him in the bush [Acts 7:35].

Notice the emphasis that has been placed upon the ministry of the angels in the life of the nation Israel. You will find the ministry of angels prominent throughout Israel's history. God gave the Law to Moses through the ministry of angels.

We hear a lot about the angels at Christmas. Whom were the angels addressing? And for what purpose? They had messages for the people of Israel—for Mary, for Joseph, for Zacharias, and for the shepherds.

God is not sending messages through angels during this period of the church. No angels have appeared around my place. And there have been none appearing to you. If you are seeing angels, you had better make an appointment with a psychiatrist. By contrast, angels did appear and bring messages from God to members of the nation Israel.

Now Stephen goes on to describe the wilderness experience.

He brought them out, after that he had shewed wonders and signs in the land of Egypt, and in the Red sea, and in the wilderness forty years.

This is that Moses, which said unto the children of Israel, A prophet shall the Lord your God raise up unto you of your brethren, like unto me; him shall ye hear.

This is he, that was in the church in the wilderness with the angel which spake to him in the mount Sina, and with our fathers: who received the lively oracles to give unto us [Acts 7:36–38].

The word *church* here does not mean that there was a church in the Old Testament in the same sense that there is a church in the New Testament. The word for church is *ekklésia*, which means "called-out." Even a group called out to mob somebody would be an *ekklésia*, a called-out group. So, Israel in the wilderness was a called-out group. They were called out of Egypt, by God, for a particular purpose.

To whom our fathers would not obey, but thrust him from them, and in their hearts turned back again into Egypt [Acts 7:39].

Israel did not go back to Egypt in a physical, material sense. But in their hearts they went back to Egypt many, many times. In the same way there are many people today who say they deplore certain sins of the world and sins of the flesh. It is always so easy to point the finger at someone else and condemn him for his sin. A question we need to ask ourselves is: Would I *like* to do the same thing? Where is our heart? Israel went back to Egypt in their heart.

Saying unto Aaron, Make us gods to go before us: for as for this Moses, which brought us out of the land of Egypt, we wot not what is become of him [Acts 7:40].

They didn't know what had happened to him, and they didn't care. They had rejected Moses.

And they made a calf in those days, and offered sacrifice unto the idol, and rejoiced in the works of their own hands [Acts 7:41].

Stephen is showing them that Israel has always been rebellious.

Then God turned, and gave them up to worship the host of heaven; as it is written in the book of the prophets, O ye house of Israel, have ye offered to me slain beasts and sacrifices by the space of forty years in the wilderness? [Acts 7:42].

They went into idolatry. That is why Moses (and later Joshua) pleaded with the people to choose God and turn from their idols.

Yea, ye took up the tabernacle of Moloch, and the star of your god Remphan, figures which ye made to worship them: and I will carry you away beyond Babylon.

Our fathers had the tabernacle of witness in the wilderness, as he had appointed, speaking unto Moses, that he should make it according to the fashion that he had seen.

Which also our fathers that came after brought in with Jesus into the possession of the Gentiles, whom God drave out before the face of our fathers, unto the days of David [Acts 7:43–45].

Jesus is the Greek translation of the Hebrew name *Joshua*.

Who found favour before God, and desired to find a tabernacle for the God of Jacob [Acts 7:46].

You see that the temple was David's idea. I have always thought it should be called David's temple even though Solomon built it.

But Solomon built him an house.

Howbeit the most High dwelleth not in temples made with hands; as saith the prophet,

Heaven is my throne, and earth is my footstool: what house will ye build me? saith the Lord: or what is the place of my rest?

Hath not my hand made all these things? [Acts 7:47–50].

Now he comes to his condemnation of the religious rulers of that day.

Ye stiffnecked and uncircumcised in heart and ears, ye do always resist the

Holy Ghost: as your fathers did, so do ye.

Which of the prophets have not your fathers persecuted? and they have slain them which shewed before of the coming of the Just One; of whom ye have been now the betrayers and murderers:

Who have received the law by the disposition of angels, and have not kept it [Acts 7:51–53].

Physically, these men were circumcised, but in their hearts and in their ears, they were uncircumcised. That is, they would not hear God any more than their ancestors down through the years had heard Him.

This is a masterful speech. Stephen reminds them of the deliverance out of Egypt. God made Moses the deliverer, but the children of Israel refused to obey him. The wilderness experience was a series of rebellions against God, brought to a climax in the making of a golden calf. A plague of idolatry broke out again in the land and resulted in the Babylonian captivity. Stephen concludes with Joshua, who led them into the land, and Jesus, who made the way to heaven. He charges that the Law was given to them supernaturally by the ministry of angels, and they did not keep it. Perhaps they knew that the birth of Jesus was announced by angels. Obviously, they have been the betrayers and murderers of Him.

MARTYRDOM OF STEPHEN

Stephen became the first martyr. Also, in this portion of the chapter, we are first introduced to Saul of Tarsus.

When they heard these things, they were cut to the heart, and they gnashed on him with their teeth [Acts 7:54].

How they hated Stephen for saying what he did!

But he, being full of the Holy Ghost, looked up stedfastly into heaven, and saw the glory of God, and Jesus standing on the right hand of God [Acts 7:55].

Since God is a spirit, how can there be a right hand of God? Because at "the right hand of God" indicates the place of prominence, the place of honor. God had promised Jesus Christ that He would glorify Him and give Him a name that is above every name. Jesus Christ is exalted. He is at the right hand of God. In Hebrews 1:3 we are told, ". . . when he had by himself purged our sins, sat down on the right hand of the Majesty on high." The fact that He was *seated* at the right hand of God indicates that His work was completed—our redemption is finished. But that doesn't mean He isn't still working in our behalf. Here He is standing, ready to receive His first martyr.

And said, Behold, I see the heavens opened, and the Son of man standing on the right hand of God.

Then they cried out with a loud voice, and stopped their ears, and ran upon him with one accord,

And cast him out of the city, and stoned him: and the witnesses laid down their clothes at a young man's feet, whose name was Saul [Acts 7:56–58].

These two young men—Stephen and Saul of Tarsus—are together here for the first time, the only time, the last time. They are enemies. They stand on the opposite sides of the cross.

And they stoned Stephen, calling upon God, and saying, Lord Jesus, receive my spirit.

And he kneeled down, and cried with a loud voice, Lord, lay not this sin to their charge. And when he had said this, he fell asleep [Acts 7:59–60].

Stephen falls asleep. Jesus puts his body to sleep to await the Rapture. Stephen goes into the presence of Christ who is standing to meet him. Stephen is the first martyr of the church to go to be with his Lord.

The other young man there that day was a Pharisee, and he thought he had everything. He looked up into heaven when Stephen said that he saw the heavens open. I am sure that Saul looked up longingly and admitted to himself, *I don't see anything, but I'd like to see what he sees. I have an empty heart.* Stephen was a tremendous witness to Saul. Stephen was the one, I believe, who prepared Saul for the appearance of the Lord Jesus on the Damascus road, as we shall see.

CHAPTER 8

***THEME:** Conversion of Ethiopian eunuch (son of Ham)*

We have now arrived at the second major division of the Book of Acts. You remember that we divided the book according to the Lord's commission in Acts 1:8. First they were to witness in Jerusalem. Now we come to the Lord Jesus Christ's work by the Holy Spirit through the apostles in Judea and Samaria. This section of the book includes chapters 8–12.

Chapter 7 concluded with a most unusual scene. It included the two young men who had the greatest influence upon the early church. The one was Stephen, the deacon, the young man who gave up his life, the first martyr in the church. That other was a young Pharisee who had charge of the stoning of Stephen. His name was Saul.

SAUL BECOMES THE CHIEF PERSECUTOR OF THE CHURCH, AND THE CHURCH IS SCATTERED

And Saul was consenting unto his death. And at that time there was a great persecution against the church which was at Jerusalem; and they were all scattered abroad throughout the regions of Judaea and Samaria, except the apostles [Acts 8:1].

Saul was taking the lead in the persecution of Stephen, and he was in the cheering section. Now this young man, Saul of Tarsus, was amazed when he saw the face of Stephen. Stephen was looking into the heavens, and there he saw the Son of Man standing at the right hand of God. Young Saul looked up—he didn't see anything. But, friend, he wished he could. He will see a little later. I believe that Stephen is the one who prepared Saul for the appearance of the Lord Jesus on the Damascus road.

Saul becomes the chief persecutor of the church. This causes the church to scatter. Actually, he does the church a favor. They were all settled down in Jerusalem, and I don't think they would have moved out had it not been for the persecution which Saul of Tarsus instigated.

Judea and Samaria are the next territories which the Lord had told them to enter. Judea surrounds Jerusalem, and Samaria lies to the north of Jerusalem.

And devout men carried Stephen to his burial, and made great lamentation over him [Acts 8:2].

I would like to make a few remarks here about Christian burial. There is a question that comes to us today: Is it right or wrong for Christians to be cremated? There is nothing in the Bible against it. No one will lose salvation by being cremated. However, the burial of a Christian is like sowing seed. It is like putting the body into a motel so it can sleep until the resurrection.

This is the way Paul speaks of it in 1 Thessalonians 4. He speaks of the body as seed in 1 Corinthians 15. You don't burn the seed before you plant it. Neither do you burn a person before you put him into a motel or hotel to go to sleep. Planting the body in the earth like a seed is a testimony—an evidence of your faith in a future resurrection. Undoubtedly the body of Stephen was terribly mutilated. They took him up tenderly and put him in the ground as you would plant a seed. Stephen had gone into the presence of Christ, who was waiting in heaven for him. His body went into the ground to await the resurrection. "So also is the resurrection of the dead. It is sown in corruption; it is raised in incorruption: It is sown in dishonour; it is raised in glory: it is sown in weakness; it is raised in power: it is sown a natural body; it is raised a spiritual body. There is a natural body, and there is a spiritual body" (1 Cor. 15:42–44). I cannot see that cremation sets forth this idea. Rather, this is the picture of real Christian *burial*.

Some people protest that we are running out of space for graves. My friend, this old earth has taken in bodies for thousands of years now, and there is still room.

As for Saul, he made havoc of the church, entering into every house, and haling men and women committed them to prison [Acts 8:3].

This was a young man full of zeal. Remember that he later wrote about himself—"Concerning zeal, persecuting the church . . ." in Philippians 3:6.

Therefore they that were scattered abroad went every where preaching the word [Acts 8:4].

Here we see the effect of the persecution. Actually, it did not hinder the church but furthered the work of the church. Later on, Paul would give this same kind of testimony after he had been put into prison in Rome. "But I would ye should understand, brethren, that the things which happened unto me have fallen out rather unto the furtherance of the gospel" (Phil. 1:12). I do not believe that the church can ever be hurt from the outside. It can be hurt from the inside, as we shall see later in this chapter.

PHILIP BECOMES THE CHIEF WITNESS AFTER THE DEATH OF STEPHEN

We are now introduced to the second deacon whom God used in a marvelous way.

Then Philip went down to the city of Samaria, and preached Christ unto them [Acts 8:5].

The Lord Jesus had said they should be witnessess unto Him in Jerusalem and Judea and Samaria. Now the Word is going to Samaria.

And the people with one accord gave heed unto those things which Philip spake, hearing and seeing the miracles which he did [Acts 8:6].

Stephen had had the sign gifts of the early church, and now we see that Philip had those same gifts. Not everyone had them—only those who were in the places of leadership, those who were taking the Word of God out to the world. There came the day when the sign gifts disappeared. They disappeared after the time of the apostles. By the time the canon of Scripture was complete and established, the credentials of a true man of God was correct doctrine rather than sign gifts.

For unclean spirits, crying with loud voice, came out of many that were possessed with them: and many taken with palsies, and that were lame, were healed.

And there was great joy in that city [Acts 8:7–8].

The gospel has now come to Samaria. Philip is well received in Samaria, and there, of all places, the gospel brings great joy.

Now because the church is growing very fast, there are people actually joining the church who are not believers. Although they are really unbelievers, they make a profession of faith. We will now meet one like that.

SIMON THE SORCERER

But there was a certain man, called Simon, which beforetime in the same city used sorcery, and bewitched the people of Samaria, giving out that himself was some great one [Acts 8:9].

He sets himself up as some great one. We find the same sort of thing today. If someone claims to be a faith healer, that sets him apart, believe me. People may declare that the faith healers are humble. Humility is not manifest in services where a person is supposedly healing people and implying that he is the only person there who has that gift. That is "giving out that himself was some great one," as Simon the sorcerer was doing.

To whom they all gave heed, from the least to the greatest, saying, This man is the great power of God.

And to him they had regard, because that of long time he had bewitched them with sorceries [Acts 8:10–11].

These people felt that Simon the sorcerer was like a god. Just as with these people, there are a great many people who are bewitched today. My friend, do not be bewitched by any man or his power. Even if a man is giving out the Word of God, do not look to the man. Look to the Word of God and check to see if he is presenting it accurately. Look to God. Turn to Him. When we get our eyes on man, we take our eyes off the Lord Jesus Christ. That is what had happened in Samaria.

But when they believed Philip preaching the things concerning the kingdom of God, and the name of Jesus Christ, they were baptized, both men and women [Acts 8:12].

Philip preached the gospel in Samaria, and many men and women believed. Simon came in contact with Philip, and apparently he made a profession of faith under the ministry of Philip. I believe that Simon is the first religious racketeer in the church—but, unfortunately, not the last. He professes to be a believer during the sweeping revival in Samaria under the ministry of Philip.

Then Simon himself believed also: and when he was baptized, he continued with Philip, and wondered, beholding the miracles and signs which were done [Acts 8:13].

Simon believes, he is baptized, and he becomes a friend of Philip. You would certainly think he was a real child of God. However, he is not converted. We will see that there are also others who are professing believers, but they are not born again. They have the head knowledge, they go along with the crowd, but they are not saved. Although they have been baptized with water, they have not been baptized into the church of Jesus Christ by the Holy Spirit.

There are a great many people like that today. I receive many letters from people who have told me that since they have been studying the Bible along with our program, they have begun to examine their faith. Many have come to realize that they have just been following along with someone else and that they have not been genuinely, personally converted. Paul says, "Examine yourselves, whether ye be in the faith; prove your own selves . . ." (2 Cor. 13:5). It is a very good thing to check yourself. See whether you are in the faith or not.

This man Simon had all the outward trappings. He answered that he did believe in Jesus, and so he was baptized. But it was not a genuine faith.

Now when the apostles which were at Jerusalem heard that Samaria had received the word of God, they sent unto them Peter and John:

Who, when they were come down, prayed for them, that they might receive the Holy Ghost:

(For as yet he was fallen upon none of them: only they were baptized in the name of the Lord Jesus.) [Acts 8:14–16].

When the apostles heard that there was a great moving of the Spirit down in Samaria, they sent Peter and John to check on it. They found a great company of professing believers who had not been born again. They had not been baptized into the church by the Holy Spirit. They were not indwelt by the Spirit of God. They were not saved. They had gone through an outward ceremony.

My friend, being baptized with water or going through some other ceremony will not make you a Christian. This gives the background to explain why Simon was able to put over his racket on the others. He liked this idea of performing miracles.

Then laid they their hands on them, and they received the Holy Ghost [Acts 8:17].

It may be that Philip had not told all the facts and conditions of the gospel. It may be that they had not accepted them. At any rate, now they are brought into partnership with the apostles. Now they believe the gospel and they believe in the Lord Jesus Christ. Now the Spirit of God has entered into them. I think this needs to be considered in its historical setting. It was the commission given to the apostles to open up each new area to the gospel. On the Day of Pentecost the gospel was given in Jerusalem. Peter and John are to bring it into Samaria and Judea. Paul is to be the apostle to the Gentiles. Jesus had given this commission. We are now seeing it fulfilled here in Samaria.

And when Simon saw that through laying on of the apostles' hands the Holy Ghost was given, he offered them money,

Saying, Give me also this power, that on whomsoever I lay hands, he may receive the Holy Ghost [Acts 8:18–19].

Simon wanted to pay for the gift. Why? Well, because this man is a religious racketeer. He wants to use it for profit.

How many such claims are made by individuals today! They claim that great miracles take place in their meetings and humbly say they have nothing to do with them. If that is so, why do they permit this type of deception to go on? *Bewitch* is the word used here. There have been religious racketeers around bewitching the multitudes from that day to this.

Persecution from the outside didn't hurt the church. It scattered the believers and actually worked for the furtherance of the gospel. What hurt the church was that people got on the inside, professing to be believers when they were not believers. Always the church is hurt from the inside.

It was the same with the Lord Jesus. He was betrayed from the inside. He was betrayed to His nation by one of His own disciples. His own nation betrayed Him to the Roman Empire, and the Roman Empire crucified Him. Also today He is betrayed within the church.

It is like the wooden horse brought into the city of Troy. The city was impenetrable, it was invulnerable, until that wooden horse got on the inside. The Devil started out by persecuting the church, fighting it from the outside. He found that didn't work. It just spread the gospel. Then he decided to start his work from the inside. That is where he can get in and do damage. How many pastors could testify to that today!

But Peter said unto him, Thy money perish with thee, because thou hast thought that the gift of God may be purchased with money.

Thou hast neither part nor lot in this matter: for thy heart is not right in the sight of God [Acts 8:20–21].

This is the reason we know this man is not converted. Simon Peter declares that his heart is not right with God. He is not converted. His big interest is in the money. That was the important thing to this man.

Repent therefore of this thy wickedness, and pray God, if perhaps the thought of thine heart may be forgiven thee.

For I perceive that thou art in the gall of bitterness, and in the bond of iniquity [Acts 8:22–23].

You can't make it any stronger than the way Simon Peter says it.

Then answered Simon, and said, Pray ye to the Lord for me, that none of these things which ye have spoken come upon me [Acts 8:24].

Simon doesn't ask to be saved. He doesn't ask for prayer for his salvation. He just asks that none of those terrible things happen to him. We do not know if this man ever came to Christ.

And they, when they had testified and preached the word of the Lord, returned to Jerusalem, and preached the gospel in many villages of the Samaritans [Acts 8:25].

The gospel is starting its journey to the ends of the earth. It started in Jerusalem. The apostles were there and a church was established. Soon the center will move to Antioch. Then it will move to Ephesus. Later it will move to Alexandria, then to Rome. Today, I don't think there is any particular center of the church. It has gone to the ends of the earth.

I believe that one of the finest vehicles to get the gospel to the ends of the earth is radio. Through this mechanical means the church can do what has not been accomplished since the first century when the gospel did penetrate to all the known world.

PHILIP AND THE ETHIOPIAN

In chapters 8, 9, and 10 we find the record of three remarkable instances of conversion. I think that these three have been lifted out and given to us particularly for a lesson. Chapter 8 gives the conversion of the Ethiopian eunuch, a son of Ham. Chapter 9 gives the conversion of Saul of Tarsus, a son of Shem. Chapter 10 gives the conversion of Cornelius, a Roman centurion, a son of Japheth. You will recall that the entire human family is divided into these three categories. This was an ethnological and a geographical division made after the Flood. Ham, Shem, and Japheth were the sons of Noah. We find here that the gospel reaches out to representatives of these three divisions of the human family.

You will also notice from these examples that in a conversion three factors must be brought into focus before there can be a conversion. All three of these are evident in these three representative conversions.

1. *The work of the Holy Spirit.* The Holy Spirit had taken this man Philip to Samaria where there had been a great moving of the Spirit of God. Then the Holy Spirit moved him down to Gaza, and again we see His moving in the heart of the Ethiopian eunuch. The Spirit of God had gone ahead to prepare the heart and also to prepare the messenger. This leading of the Spirit of God is absolutely essential. I'm afraid that a great deal of personal work is done in a haphazard manner and without the leading of the Spirit of God. I believe that we ought to make it a matter of definite prayer before we talk to anyone. We should talk to the Lord about the individual before we talk to the individual about the Lord. It is not simply that we need the Holy Spirit to lead us. What we need is for the Spirit of God to go ahead of us and prepare the way, then to call us up to where He is. We want to go where the Spirit of God is moving. This is the first essential in a conversion. We find it true in the conversion of the Ethiopian eunuch and also in the conversion of Saul and of Cornelius.

2. *The Word of God.* "So then faith cometh by hearing, and hearing by the word of God" (Rom. 10:17). The Word of God is the second essential. The Holy Spirit will take the things of Christ and will reveal them to an individual. It is the Spirit of God using the Word of God. But, wait a minute, there must be a human instrument.

3. *The man of God.* The Spirit of God uses the man of God who delivers the Word of God to produce a son of God, one who is born

again. We will see this in the record of the conversion of this Ethiopian eunuch.

The second part of chapter 8 brings us to another part of the ministry of Philip. The gospel had gone to Samaria, and there were many genuine believers. But we also saw that in Samaria evil came into the church in the person of Simon the sorcerer. Now, in contrast to Simon the sorcerer, we come to the experience of Philip with a eunuch from Ethiopia. Philip led this man to Christ, and he became a genuine believer, a wonderful man of God.

And the angel of the Lord spake unto Philip, saying, Arise, and go toward the south unto the way that goeth down from Jerusalem unto Gaza, which is desert [Acts 8:26].

Samaria is an area which lies north of Jerusalem. Now Philip is told to go way down to the south. What we know as the Gaza strip is south, over along the Mediterranean. This was the trade route down into Egypt and Ethiopia. He would probably travel through Jerusalem to get there.

Philip had been speaking to multitudes in Samaria, and now he is sent down to a desert. He is to leave the place where there has been a great moving of the Spirit of God and go into a place, a desert, where there is nobody. However, when he gets there, he finds that God does have someone to whom he is to witness.

And he arose and went: and, behold, a man of Ethiopia, an eunuch of great authority under Candace queen of the Ethiopians, who had the charge of all her treasure, and had come to Jerusalem for to worship,

Was returning, and sitting in his chariot read Esaias the prophet [Acts 8: 27–28].

We read here that this man of Ethiopia had charge of all the treasure of the queen. He was actually the Secretary of the Treasury. He was an official, and a high official of that day. This man was not traveling alone. He had a great retinue of servants and minor officials with him. He wasn't sitting in a chariot with the reins in one hand and a book in the other hand as we see him pictured. This man was sitting back in a chariot, protected from the sun by a canopy. He had a private chauffeur and was riding in style.

He was a citizen of Ethiopia, but he had come to Jerusalem to worship. This indicates that he was a proselyte to Judaism. He had just been to Jerusalem, the center of the Jewish religion. Although Judaism was the God-given religion, he was leaving the city still in the dark. He was reading the prophet Isaiah, but he was not understanding what he was reading.

Then the Spirit said unto Philip, Go near, and join thyself to this chariot [Acts 8:29].

The Holy Spirit is leading, as He must in any conversion. Philip is the man of God whom the Spirit of God is using. The Word of God is already in that chariot, for the Ethiopian is reading from the prophet Isaiah.

And Philip ran thither to him, and heard him read the prophet Esaias, and said, Understandest thou what thou readest? [Acts 8:30].

Philip is a hitchhiker. When he hears what the man is reading, he asks, "Do you understand what you are reading there?" The Ethiopian doesn't; so he stops his retinue and invites Philip to come up and ride with him.

And he said, How can I, except some man should guide me? And he desired Philip that he would come up and sit with him.

The place of the scripture which he read was this, He was led as a sheep to the slaughter; and like a lamb dumb before his shearer, so opened he not his mouth:

In his humiliation his judgment was taken away: and who shall declare his generation? for his life is taken from the earth [Acts 8:31–33].

Where was he reading? You will recognize that this is from the fifty-third chapter of Isaiah. He was reading the seventh and eighth verses. It is obvious that he must have been reading for some time. So it is also obvious that he must have read the preceding verses: "He is despised and rejected of men; a man of sorrows, and acquainted with grief: and we hid as it were our faces from him; he was despised, and we esteemed him not. Surely he hath borne our griefs, and carried our sorrows: yet we did esteem him stricken, smitten of God, and afflicted. But he was wounded for our transgressions, he was bruised for our iniquities: the chastisement of our peace was upon him; and with his stripes we are healed. All we like sheep have gone astray; we have turned every one to his own way; and the LORD hath laid on him the iniquity of us all" (Isa. 53:3–6).

And the eunuch answered Philip, and said, I pray thee, of whom speaketh the prophet this? of himself, or of some other man? [Acts 8:34].

What a marvelous place to begin! When the Spirit of God leads, how wonderfully everything opens up! He will take the things of Christ and make them clear.

Then Philip opened his mouth, and began at the same scripture, and preached unto him Jesus [Acts 8:35].

The Holy Spirit will use the Word of God.

I do not believe that people can be converted by hearing a song. The song may affect a person emotionally and influence the will to make a decision for Christ. However, if the Word of God is not in it, there can be no true conversion. It requires the Word of God. How important that is!

Simon Peter, whom God used so wonderfully in the conversion of multitudes, makes it very clear that the Word of God must be involved if a person is saved. He wrote in his first epistle: "Being born again, not of corruptible seed, but of incorruptible, by the word of God, which liveth and abideth for ever. For all flesh is as grass, and all the glory of man as the flower of grass. The grass withereth, and the flower thereof falleth away: But the word of the Lord endureth for ever. And this is the word which by the gospel is preached unto you" (1 Pet. 1:23–25).

When the Spirit of God uses the Word of God, what is going to happen? These men were in the chariot, discussing the Word of God. Philip was telling the eunuch about Jesus.

And as they went on their way, they came unto a certain water: and the eunuch said, See, here is water; what doth hinder me to be baptized?

And Philip said, If thou believest with all thine heart, thou mayest. And he answered and said, I believe that Jesus Christ is the Son of God [Acts 8:36–37].

Remember that Philip had had an experience with Simon the sorcerer up there in Samaria. He is not about to have a repetition of that. When this man asks for water baptism, Philip wants to be very sure that he believes with all his heart.

And he commanded the chariot to stand still: and they went down both into the water, both Philip and the eunuch; and he baptized him.

And when they were come up out of the water, the Spirit of the Lord caught away Philip, that the eunuch saw him no more: and he went on his way rejoicing [Acts 8:38–39].

Philip is snatched off the page of Scripture. He is not needed here anymore. The Ethiopian rides off the pages of Scripture in his chariot. He went on his way, rejoicing. Now what about this man? The first great church was not in the United States, nor was it in Europe, nor was it in Jerusalem, nor was it in Asia Minor. The first great church was in northern Africa. The Ethiopian evidently went back and, through his witness and his influence, a church was begun there. You would find it very profitable to read about the early church in North Africa.

Now what about Philip?

But Philip was found at Azotus: and passing through he preached in all the cities, till he came to Caesarea [Acts 8:40].

Azotus is Ashdod, which is over in the Gaza strip. To reach Caesarea, he would have gone through Joppa. Tel Aviv is there today. So he went, preaching the gospel along the coast up to Caesarea. The gospel has gone to Judea and to Samaria and is moving out. The eunuch has carried it down to Ethiopia. Philip is carrying it along the coast to Caesarea.

CHAPTER 9

***THEME:** Conversion of Saul of Tarsus (son of Shem)*

This chapter tells about another remarkable conversion. The conversion of the Ethiopian eunuch was in a chariot; the conversion of Saul of Tarsus was down in the dust. Probably he was riding a little donkey when he went up to Damascus, and he was knocked right down into the dust.

When we get to the Book of Philippians, we shall look at the theological, psychological, and philosophical aspects of the conversion of Saul of Tarsus. Here, we are dealing with the facts of what actually happened on the road to Damascus.

THE CONVERSION OF SAUL OF TARSUS

And Saul, yet breathing out threatenings and slaughter against the disciples of the Lord, went unto the high priest,

And desired of him letters to Damascus to the synagogues, that if he found any of this way, whether they were men or women, he might bring them bound unto Jerusalem [Acts 9:1–2].

When the persecution broke out in Jerusalem, the church went underground. The apostles remained in Jerusalem, but many of the others were scattered—we found Philip up in Samaria and along the Mediterranean coast. The thing that triggered it was the stoning of Stephen, followed by persecution.

The other religious leaders in Jerusalem were satisfied after they had run the Christians out of Jerusalem. They were willing to let it stay at that point. But not Saul of Tarsus! He was the one who was breathing out threatenings and slaughter. He hated Jesus Christ. I do not think that the Lord Jesus Christ ever has had an enemy greater than this man Saul of Tarsus. He went to the high priest and said, "Look, I've heard that a group of them have run off up there to Damascus, and I'm going after them." The fact of the matter is that he intended to ferret them out, anywhere they went. His goal was to exterminate the Christians.

And as he journeyed, he came near Damascus: and suddenly there shined round about him a light from heaven:

And he fell to the earth, and heard a voice saying unto him, Saul, Saul, why persecutest thou me? [Acts 9:3–4].

Paul will recount this incident twice more in the Book of Acts. In fact, Paul never tired of telling about his conversion. We find him going over it again in his Epistle to the Philippians where he gets right down to the heart of the matter and tells what really happened to him. Here we are simply given the facts. He will go over them again when he gives his testimony before King Agrippa—that is a masterpiece.

And he said, Who art thou, Lord? And the Lord said, I am Jesus whom thou persecutest: it is hard for thee to kick against the pricks [Acts 9:5].

Will you notice, here, the ignorance of Saul? He was possibly the most brilliant man of his day. He was probably a graduate of the University of Tarsus, the greatest Greek university of that day. He was a student in the school of Gamaliel, the Hebrew scholar. He was trained in the details of the Jewish religion. But he did not know the Lord Jesus Christ. "Who art thou, Lord?" Friend, to know *Him* is life. Saul didn't know Him!

And he trembling and astonished said, Lord, what wilt thou have me to do? And the Lord said unto him, Arise, and go into the city, and it shall be told thee what thou must do [Acts 9:6].

Saul is right down in the dust on that road to Damascus. This is a remarkable conversion. He immediately reveals his conversion. This man who hated the Lord Jesus, who did everything he could against Him, now calls Him "Lord." And he asks what the Lord would have him do. He is ready to do the bidding of the Lord. He has been completely changed. "Wherefore by their fruits ye shall know them" (Matt. 7:20). We can surely tell what has happened to this man.

And the men which journeyed with him stood speechless, hearing a voice, but seeing no man [Acts 9:7].

Later on it says that they didn't hear. Is this a conflict? No, they heard a voice but that was all. They couldn't understand what was said. It didn't make any sense to them. They didn't see anyone. There was no one for them to see. They were speechless with amazement. We shall see this in more detail in Acts 22 and 26.

And Saul arose from the earth; and when his eyes were opened, he saw no man: but they led him by the hand, and brought him into Damascus.

And he was three days without sight, and neither did eat nor drink [Acts 9:8–9].

This man was blinded by the light that he had seen from heaven. Here was a man who was puzzled as much as any man has ever been. Some people jump up and down when they are converted. Some shout for joy. Not Saul of Tarsus. There never was a man as confused as he was. Had we met him on one of those three days in Damascus and had we asked him what had happened to him, his answer would have been, "I don't know." But he is going to find out.

And there was a certain disciple at Damascus, named Ananias; and to him said the Lord in a vision, Ananias. And he said, Behold, I am here, Lord.

And the Lord said unto him, Arise, and go into the street which is called Straight, and inquire in the house of Judas for one called Saul, of Tarsus: for, behold, he prayeth,

And hath seen in a vision a man named Ananias coming in, and putting his hand on him, that he might receive his sight [Acts 9:10–12].

Saul of Tarsus, a brilliant young man, is sitting in darkness and confusion. The Spirit of God comes to another man, Ananias, and sends him over to Saul of Tarsus.

Then Ananias answered, Lord, I have heard by many of this man, how much evil he hath done to thy saints at Jerusalem:

And here he hath authority from the chief priests to bind all that call on thy name.

But the Lord said unto him, Go thy way: for he is a chosen vessel unto me, to bear my name before the Gentiles, and kings, and the children of Israel:

For I will shew him how great things he must suffer for my name's sake [Acts 9:13–16].

God states two reasons for calling Saul. He was God's chosen vessel for two things. First, he was to bear the name of Jesus. Notice that he is not called a *witness* as the disciples were. Although Paul may have seen Jesus at His crucifixion, he had not walked with Him in the days of His flesh. He really knew nothing about Him until that day on the road to Damascus. Now he is to bear that name. That is the same name we are to bear today, the name of Jesus.

He is to bear that name before three different groups: Gentiles, kings, and the children of Israel. Gentiles are first on the list. Paul will be the great Apostle to the Gentiles. Then to kings—he will appear before kings, probably including Nero himself, and then to the nation Israel. When Paul goes into a city, he always will begin in the Jewish synagogue. The synagogue will be his springboard to put him into the community, into the life of the city. From there he will reach the Gentiles. But he will go to the Jews first.

Secondly, the Lord said He will show Saul how great things he must suffer for His name's sake. He is chosen to suffer for Jesus Christ. In my judgment, there has never been anyone else who has suffered for the Lord as Paul the apostle suffered. None of us dare say, "I'm suffering more than anyone else. Why does God let this happen to me?" We may be suffering or we may think we are suffering more than we are. At any rate, none of us suffer as Paul the apostle suffered for the Lord.

Now as we look back on this remarkable conversion, you may remember that I said conversion requires the Holy Spirit using the Word of God through a man of God. Does this prove true in the conversion of Saul of Tarsus?

The Lord Jesus appeared to Saul personally. Before the Lord Jesus left His disciples, He told them that He was going away but that He would not leave them orphans. He promised them that He would send His Holy Spirit, and this is what the Spirit would do: "He shall glorify me: for he shall receive of mine, and shall shew it unto you. All things that the Father hath are mine: therefore said I, that he shall take of mine, and shall shew it unto you" (John 16:14–15). Now I think that when our resurrected Lord appeared to Saul personally, the Spirit of God opened his eyes spiritually and closed them physically so that he might see the Lord Jesus. So the Holy Spirit was definitely at work.

How about the Word of God? How was that used in the conversion of Paul? Saul of Tarsus was a Pharisee. He knew a great deal about the Word of God. In fact, if there ever has been anyone saturated with the Word of God, he was Saul of Tarsus. When reading his epistles, it becomes obvious that he was very familiar with the Old Testament. The Holy Spirit and the Word of God were operative in Saul's conversion.

How can one say that God used a man of God as the human instrument to reach Saul? Although a man of God was not present at the time, I believe the man whom the Lord used to reach Saul was none other than Stephen. These two young men, Saul and Stephen, met only once, and that was when Saul stood with those who killed him. Stephen had looked up into the heavens and said, "I see heaven open and Jesus standing there!" (see Acts 7:56). Saul of Tarsus looked up into the heavens and couldn't see anything. Then he looked into the face of Stephen and he knew that Stephen was actually seeing something. I believe that Saul actually hoped that the heavens would open and that he, too, could have a vision of God. And he did on the Damascus road. It was Jesus Christ who was revealed to him.

I believe that God uses a human instrument in the conversion of every individual, although that individual may not be present at the moment of the conversion. That is the reason you and I should cast our influence for the Lord Jesus Christ at all times.

Recenty I received a letter from a man who is a barber. A certain man had been his customer for twenty years. One time when the customer got out of the chair and was paying for his haircut, he asked the barber, "Have you ever heard Dr. McGee on the radio?" The barber said he had not; so the customer walked over to his radio and turned it to the station on which we can be heard in that town. He said, "Every morning at eight o'clock! You listen to him!" That was the last time these two men saw each other. The customer died suddenly within a day or so. You can guess the end of the story. The barber started listening to the program. He had been listening to it for over two years when he wrote to me. He has come to know Jesus Christ as his Savior. The human instrument in his conversion was his old customer.

Dr. C. I. Scofield is the man who edited the Scofield Bible. Before his conversion he was an outstanding international lawyer, but he had the problem of being a very heavy drinker. He had a godly mother who prayed for him continually. She died before Dr. Scofield was converted. On one occasion Dr. Lewis Sperry Chafer was praying with Dr. Scofield. He told us that he heard Dr. Scofield say, "Lord, if my mother doesn't know that I have been converted, would You please tell her so?" God uses a human instrument in the conversion of every person, although that person may not be present at the moment of conversion. I don't think a person can be converted without a human instrument. So why don't *you* be an instrument? That doesn't mean you have to get a person to his knees; it does mean that you get the good news of Jesus Christ to him. There will not be a real conversion without a man of God using the Word of God, directed by the Spirit of God.

Now, going back to Saul of Tarsus where we left him in Damascus, he is still sitting in solitary blindness, praying. Brilliant young man that he is, he is still somewhat confused since his conversion. So the Spirit of God appeared to Ananias and sent him over to help him.

And Ananias went his way, and entered into the house; and putting his hands on him said, Brother Saul, the Lord, even Jesus, that appeared unto thee in the way as thou camest, hath sent me, that thou mightest receive thy sight, and be filled with the Holy Ghost [Acts 9:17].

What a change! He is still Saul of Tarsus, but now he is *Brother* Saul. He is not the enemy. He is a brother. Any person who loves the Lord Jesus Christ is a brother to any other believer. Unfortunately, I must add that brothers don't always act like brothers.

Saul is to receive his physical sight. Also, he is to be filled with the Holy Spirit. He is to be filled with the Holy Spirit for service. This is the experience which reveals itself in the life of the believer. He was baptized with the Holy Spirit on the Damascus road. In other words, he was saved on the Damascus road. But it wasn't until this man Ananias came to him that he was filled with the Holy Spirit. He is going to become a witness for the Lord Jesus. He will receive his physical sight and his spiritual sight.

And immediately there fell from his eyes as it had been scales: and he received sight forthwith, and arose, and was baptized [Acts 9:18].

Now he is baptized with water as a sign and seal of his conversion. The water had nothing to do with his salvation. He had been baptized by the Holy Spirit—that is, he had been saved on the Damascus road. When Ananias had laid his hands on him, he had been filled with the Holy Spirit for service. And now he is baptized with water.

And when he had received meat, he was strengthened. Then was Saul certain days with the disciples which were at Damascus [Acts 9:19].

SAUL BEGINS TO WITNESS AT DAMASCUS

And straightway he preached Christ in the synagogues, that he is the Son of God [Acts 9:20].

Saul of Tarsus begins to witness immediately. Why? Because he is filled with the Holy Spirit. He began to preach "Christ in the synagogues, that he is the Son of God."

Friend, you must know who Christ is before you can believe what He did. He died to pay the penalty for your sins. It is because He is the Son of God that He could die for your sins. I couldn't die for your sins; you couldn't die for mine. No human being can die a redemptive death for another human being. Only Christ could do this, because He is the Son of God. So Saul began to preach that Christ is the Son of God. That is the first thing you must know.

But all that heard him were amazed, and said; Is not this he that destroyed them which called on this name in Jerusalem, and came hither for that intent, that he might bring them bound unto the chief priests?

But Saul increased the more in strength, and confounded the Jews which dwelt at Damascus, proving that this is very Christ [Acts 9:21–22].

The "very Christ" means the *very Messiah.* Saul confounded the Jews by preaching this. Saul of Tarsus is number one in several departments. He is number one in suffering; he is number one as a missionary. I think he is also number one in his I.Q.—he was a brilliant man. He was able to confound those who attempted to tackle him intellectually.

And after that many days were fulfilled, the Jews took counsel to kill him:

But their laying await was known of Saul. And they watched the gates day and night to kill him.

Then the disciples took him by night, and let him down by the wall in a basket [Acts 9:23–25].

When the Jews couldn't win by argument, they resorted to another tactic, which was to eliminate the enemy.

I'm sure it must have been quite a thrilling experience to have been let down over the wall in a basket. Yet we never read anywhere in the New Testament that Paul toured the Roman Empire giving a lecture on the subject, "Over the Wall in a Basket." That ought to be a lesson for a great many folk who deal in sensationalism today. Here is a man who has had a most remarkable experience, but he has something more important to present.

We must never let our *experience* get in the way of presenting Christ. We must never let our *person* get in the way of the Person of Christ. Sometimes I hear the very pious prayer, "Hide the preacher behind the cross." No, friend, that is not what he needs. Rather, we should pray, "Help the preacher to present Christ in such a way that the Spirit of God can take the things of Christ and show them to us. Help him to present Christ!" This was Paul's method.

SAUL IN JERUSALEM

And when Saul was come to Jerusalem, he assayed to join himself to the disciples: but they were all afraid of him, and believed not that he was a disciple [Acts 9:26].

They thought this was a deception on the part of Saul of Tarsus, that he was worming his way in. They were experiencing persecution. And they probably had heard of Simon the sorcerer and the tactics he used in Samaria.

But Barnabas took him, and brought him to the apostles, and declared unto them how he had seen the Lord in the way, and that he had spoken to him, and how he had preached boldly at Damascus in the name of Jesus [Acts 9:27].

Good old Barnabus, whose very name means the "son of consolation and comfort"! He comes over and puts his arm around Saul. What a blessing he was to him! How we still need people who will put their arms around some new Christian and will help that new Christian along. Barnabas becomes the sponsor of Saul.

And he was with them coming in and going out at Jerusalem [Acts 9:28].

Paul is accepted into the assembly at Jerusalem and joins forces with the Jerusalem church.

And he spake boldly in the name of the Lord Jesus, and disputed against the

Grecians: but they went about to slay him [Acts 9:29].

These are not Greeks. They are Israelites who have a Greek background. They had been brought up outside Israel somewhere in the Greek world. The witness of Saul was so powerful that they concluded the only way to get rid of his effectiveness was to eliminate him, to kill him.

Which when the brethren knew, they brought him down to Caesarea, and sent him forth to Tarsus [Acts 9:30].

Paul goes to his hometown. He probably went back home to tell his father and mother, brothers and sisters, and other relatives about Christ. We know nothing about them. Paul never talks about his family—with one exception. In Romans 16 he mentions some folk who are related to him.

Then had the churches rest throughout all Judaea and Galilee and Samaria, and were edified; and walking in the fear of the Lord, and in the comfort of the Holy Ghost, were multiplied [Acts 9:31].

The church continued to grow. The gospel went into Judea, Galilee, and Samaria. It will start to go to the ends of the earth very shortly.

PETER'S MINISTRY IN LYDDA AND JOPPA

And it came to pass, as Peter passed throughout all quarters, he came down also to the saints which dwelt at Lydda.

And there he found a certain man named Aeneas, which had kept his bed eight years, and was sick of the palsy.

And Peter said unto him, Aeneas, Jesus Christ maketh thee whole: arise, and make thy bed. And he arose immediately.

And all that dwelt at Lydda and Saron saw him, and turned to the Lord [Acts 9:32–35].

Because Peter was an apostle, he had the sign gifts of an apostle.

Now there was at Joppa a certain disciple named Tabitha, which by interpretation is called Dorcas: this woman was full of good works and almsdeeds which she did [Acts 9:36].

This woman was engaged in social service. She had the gift of sewing. Do you mean to tell me that sewing is a gift of the Holy Spirit? Yes, it was for this woman. Many people today are seeking for some exciting, fleshly gift such as speaking in tongues. May I suggest seeking a gift that is practical? I say very carefully and kindly, "Dear sister, learn to sew."

Sewing was the gift of Dorcas. I doubt that she ever spoke at a missionary meeting or taught a women's Bible class. I don't think she ever had such an opportunity because she was one of the early saints. But she did a lot of wonderful things for folk.

And it came to pass in those days, that she was sick, and died: whom when they had washed, they laid her in an upper chamber [Acts 9:37].

Notice how the Christians prepared for burial in that day.

And forasmuch as Lydda was nigh to Joppa, and the disciples had heard that Peter was there, they sent unto him two men, desiring him that he would not delay to come to them [Acts 9:38].

They sent word from Joppa to Lydda that a very wonderful woman in the church there in Joppa had died. They apparently believed that Simon Peter could raise her from the dead. At least they asked him to come down.

Then Peter arose and went with them. When he was come, they brought him into the upper chamber: and all the widows stood by him weeping, and shewing the coats and garments which Dorcas made, while she was with them [Acts 9:39].

You will notice that it was the widows who conducted this fashion show. They were all showing off the garments that Dorcas had made. Why did the widows do it? Because they were poor. They wouldn't have had any clothes if it had not been for Dorcas. She had sewn their clothes for them. This was her ministry. Sewing was her gift of the Holy Spirit.

But Peter put them all forth, and kneeled down, and prayed; and turning him to the body said, Tabitha, arise. And she opened her eyes: and when she saw Peter, she sat up.

And he gave her his hand, and lifted her up, and when he had called the saints and widows, presented her alive [Acts 9:40–41].

Here is an example of the exercise of a sign gift. We have in the Book of Acts, the historical book of the church, the ministries of Simon Peter who was an apostle and of Paul who was an apostle. Simon Peter was a minister to his own people; yet he was the one to open the door for the Gentiles. Saul of Tarsus became the apostle Paul, and he was the Apostle to the Gentiles. The record states that each one raised a person from the dead. Quite possibly they raised others, but these are recorded to show that these men had sign gifts. They could perform miracles. They could heal the sick. They could raise the dead. These were the marks, the evidences of an apostle. They were apostolic gifts. Paul says that the apostles are the foundation of the church in the sense that the church is built on them. They are the ones who put down the New Testament on which the church is actually built.

Today we do not need sign gifts. The issue today is doctrine. At the end of the era of New Testament writings, the apostle John wrote his epistles. Listen to his instructions for detecting deceivers: "If there come any unto you, and bring not this doctrine, receive him not into your house, neither bid him God speed: For he that biddeth him God speed is partaker of his evil deeds" (2 John 10–11).

Toward the end of Paul's own ministry the record clearly shows that Paul did not exercise the gift of healing. For instance, notice that he left Trophimus at Miletum sick (2 Tim. 4:20). Why did not Paul heal his friend Trophimus? Paul, you see, had come to the end of his ministry, and the sign gifts even then were beginning to disappear from the church. At the beginning of Paul's ministry, nothing of the New Testament had been written. Paul himself wrote the second book of the New Testament. When he went into a new territory with his message, what was his authority? He had no authority except sign gifts. However, after the New Testament was in written form, the emphasis shifted from sign gifts to correct doctrine. Paul warns that if a man does not have correct doctrine—even if he is an angel from heaven—you should not receive him. "But though we, or an angel from heaven, preach any other gospel unto you than that which we have preached unto you, let him be accursed" (Gal. 1:8).

However, in these early days of the church, the apostles' sign gifts were important. Notice the reaction of those who heard of Dorcas being restored to life.

And it was known throughout all Joppa; and many believed in the Lord [Acts 9:42].

The sign gifts were used to confirm to them the gospel of grace.

And it came to pass, that he tarried many days in Joppa with one Simon a tanner [Acts 9:43].

A tanner used acid to tan his animal hides. It really made the place quite odoriferous. When I was in Joppa, we were shown the place where Simon Peter is said to have stayed. Joppa is a rather picturesque village right on the water's edge, and the tanner's house was down there. The house looks old enough to have been there that long. So this may well have been the place where Simon Peter stayed.

CHAPTER 10

THEME: *Conversion of Cornelius, the Roman centurion (son of Japheth)*

Chapter 10 continues the record of the ministry of Simon Peter. Later Peter will pass from the scene, and the history will continue with the ministry of the apostle Paul. Although Paul is the Apostle to the Gentiles, Peter opened the door to the Gentiles by entering the home of Cornelius and presenting salvation through Christ to his household.

CORNELIUS' VISION

There was a certain man in Caesarea called Cornelius, a centurion of the band called the Italian band [Acts 10:1].

Remember that Paul had been in Caesarea (Acts 9:30) and probably some of the other apostles had been preaching the gospel along the coast. Tel Aviv is really a part of old Joppa. As one travels up the coast from Joppa, the next place of any size is Caesarea, which was really a Roman city. It was the place where Pilate lived. The governor and those who ruled the land stayed there. This is where Cornelius was stationed. He was a centurion, which means he was a commander of a hundred soldiers in the Roman army. The Italian band was a cohort of Roman soldiers recruited in Italy.

A devout man, and one that feared God with all his house, which gave much alms to the people, and prayed to God alway [Acts 10:2].

He was "a devout man." That means his worship was rightly directed. He recognized his dependence upon that which is divine. Remember that even a pagan can have devotion and a deep conviction to his gods. Sometimes we wish that Christians today had more devotion and conviction.

He was a devout man and "one that feared God." He was not a Jewish proselyte in the strict sense of the term, but gravitated toward Judaism and could be called a "proselyte of the Gate." Today we might say that he was a man who lived in the neighborhood, attended church on special occasions, was friendly toward the church, but was not actually a Christian. That could have been Cornelius. He feared God.

He "gave much alms to the people" means he gave many gifts of charity to the Jewish people. The nation Israel has always laid great stress upon giving. God had taught them this in the Old Testament. We speak of the tithe, but it is obvious from the Mosaic system that they actually gave three tenths. They gave for the running of the government (which was a theocracy at the beginning), they gave for the maintenance of the temple, and they gave a tenth of all that they produced. So they have been a giving, generous people.

It is interesting that even today many of our eleemosynary, that is, charitable foundations, were established by Jews. There is no group of people in our day that gives as generously as does the Jewish community in its support of the nation of Israel. They are a very generous people.

Cornelius "prayed to God alway." This centurion took his needs to God. He needed to have more light. He wanted it. He probably didn't really know too much about prayer, but he prayed.

He saw in a vision evidently about the ninth hour of the day an angel of God coming in to him, and saying unto him, Cornelius [Acts 10:3].

This centurion was an officer in the Roman army, a career officer, and a man of influence. Also he had a tremendous influence on his own household, as we shall see. He was a good man to all outward observation. In America today he would pass for a Christian, a Christian of the highest degree, an outstanding man. But he actually was not a Christian. He had not even heard the gospel.

He is an example of a man who lived up to the light which he had. John 1:9 says this of Jesus: "That was the true Light, which lighteth every man that cometh into the world." This centurion had not met Jesus Christ nor come into His presence, but he was living up to the light that he had. Paul is referring to those who do not live by the light they have in Romans 1:19–20: "Because that which may be known of God is manifest in them; for God hath shewed it unto them. For the invisible things of him from the creation of the world are clearly seen, being understood by the things that are made, even his eternal power and Godhead; so that they are without excuse." This is God's answer to that oft-repeated question, "What about the poor pagan, that 'good' heathen, who wants to know God but never had a chance? Is he lost?" The answer is that God will get light to such a person. God will enable him to hear the gospel. Now how will God get the gospel to Cornelius? The barriers seem insurmountable. The church at this time—and for the first eight years—was exclusively Jewish.

These Christian Jews were still going to the temple and observing many Jewish customs. They could do that under grace because they were *trusting* Christ. Then the gospel broke over into Samaria. The Jews in Jerusalem were surprised, but they recognized the hand of God in this. Now how is God going to open the door of the gospel to the Gentiles?

Paul is to be the great missionary to the Gentiles, but God has Paul out in the desert in Arabia, training him there. It is Simon Peter who must open the door to the Gentiles. God used perhaps the most prejudiced and religious bigot, the greatest extremist of the day. Obviously, the Holy Spirit directed every move in getting the gospel to the Gentiles. My friend, all genuine Christian work is directed by the Holy Spirit. No other work amounts to anything. The Holy Spirit had to work in the heart of the Gentile; the Holy Spirit had to work in the heart of the Jew. The Holy Spirit directed the bringing of the gospel to the gentile world.

And when he looked on him, he was afraid, and said, What is it, Lord? And he said unto him, Thy prayers and thine alms are come up for a memorial before God [Acts 10:4].

An angel of God appeared to Cornelius in a vision. He was not dreaming but was given this vision while he was praying.

Now I do want you to notice that there are certain things that do count before God. These are things which can in no way merit salvation, but they are things which God notes. The prayers of Cornelius and his alms had come up for a memorial before God, and God brought the gospel to him. Wherever there is a man who seeks after God as Cornelius did, that man is going to hear the gospel of the grace of God. God will see that he gets it.

And now send men to Joppa, and call for one Simon, whose surname is Peter:

He lodgeth with one Simon a tanner, whose house is by the sea side: he shall tell thee what thou oughtest to do [Acts 10:5–6].

The angel tells him where to find Peter. He doesn't need more of an address. The odor of those hides down in that vat will lead them to the right place!

And when the angel which spake unto Cornelius was departed, he called two of his household servants, and a devout soldier of them that waited on him continually;

And when he had declared all these things unto them, he sent them to Joppa [Acts 10:7–8].

These men won't have any trouble finding the tanner's house. While they are on their way, God must prepare Simon Peter.

PETER'S VISION

On the morrow, as they went on their journey, and drew nigh unto the city, Peter went up upon the housetop to pray about the sixth hour [Acts 10:9].

It is absolutely necessary for God to prepare Simon Peter. You see, Simon Peter didn't have the breadth that Paul had. Although he didn't have the background or the training that Paul had, God can use him differently. I believe it is a tremendous mistake to think that every person has to be poured into the same mold for God to use him.

And he became very hungry, and would have eaten: but while they made ready, he fell into a trance,

And saw heaven opened, and a certain vessel descending unto him, as it had been a great sheet knit at the four corners, and let down to the earth:

Wherein were all manner of fourfooted beasts of the earth, and wild beasts, and creeping things, and fowls of the air [Acts 10:10–12].

Notice that there were beasts, all kinds of birds, and all kinds of bugs.

And there came a voice to him, Rise, Peter; kill, and eat.

But Peter said, Not so, Lord; for I have never eaten any thing that is common or unclean [Acts 10:13–14].

While Peter is wondering what this means, a voice speaks to him. Isn't it interesting that he calls Him, "Lord," but he doesn't obey what the Lord tells him to do?

Now don't miss this. Here is a man who is on this side of the Day of Pentecost. He is living in this age of grace when it makes no difference whether we eat meat or whether we don't eat meat. However, Peter is still abiding by the Mosaic system and he is not eating anything that is ceremonially unclean. He is sincere and honest about it. Someone may say that he ought to be broad-minded and eat everything. Well, you see that the Lord is teaching him that he is no longer under the Mosaic system and is free to eat anything. Today the big problem is that some people decide they don't want to eat meat and then they try to put everyone else under that same system. My friend, under grace you can eat meat or not eat meat. That is your business. Eating some certain food may give you indigestion, but it certainly will not change your relationship with the Lord.

And the voice spake unto him again the second time, What God hath cleansed, that call not thou common [Acts 10:15].

What God has made clean, don't you call unclean. You can eat anything because God has said so.

This was done thrice: and the vessel was received up again into heaven [Acts 10:16].

Peter was left wondering what it was all about.

Now while Peter doubted in himself what this vision which he had seen should mean, behold, the men which were sent from Cornelius had made inquiry for Simon's house, and stood before the gate,

And called, and asked whether Simon, which was surnamed Peter, were lodged there.

While Peter thought on the vision, the Spirit said unto him, Behold, three men seek thee.

Arise therefore, and get thee down, and go with them, doubting nothing: for I have sent them.

Then Peter went down to the men which were sent unto him from Cornelius; and said, Behold, I am he whom ye seek: what is the cause wherefore ye are come?

And they said, Cornelius the centurion, a just man, and one that feareth God, and of good report among all the nation of the Jews, was warned from God by an holy angel to send for thee into his house, and to hear words of thee [Acts 10:17–22].

Simon Peter is to go to Caesarea. This little delegation from Cornelius gives an explanation to him, then extends an invitation to come with them to the house of Cornelius.

THE CONVERSION OF CORNELIUS

Then called he them in, and lodged them. And on the morrow Peter went away with them, and certain brethren from Joppa accompanied him.

And the morrow after they entered into Caesarea. And Cornelius waited for them, and had called together his kinsmen and near friends.

And as Peter was coming in, Cornelius met him, and fell down at his feet, and worshipped him [Acts 10:23–25].

We can see that Cornelius had quite an influence on his family and friends. He has called them together for this occasion. Also we can see that Cornelius is still a pagan, a heathen. When he is instructed by an angel to send for Simon Peter, he concludes that this man must really be important; so he falls down and worships Peter.

It is interesting to see Simon Peter's reaction to this. Friend, Simon Peter would never have let you get down to kiss his big toe. He just wouldn't permit it.

But Peter took him up, saying, Stand up; I myself also am a man [Acts 10:26].

Peter reached down and pulled him to his feet and said, "Stand up; I myself also am a *man.*" I like the way he did that.

And as he talked with him, he went in, and found many that were come together.

And he said unto them, Ye know how that it is an unlawful thing for a man that is a Jew to keep company, or come unto one of another nation; but God

hath shewed me that I should not call any man common or unclean [Acts 10:27–28].

Peter stepped into the house. What a step that was! It was the first time that Peter had ever been in a gentile house. He still is really a little baffled at God's command to go there.

He violates the first rule of homiletics when he begins his message with an apology. What he says is not a friendly thing to say. In fact, it is an insult. In essence, he said, "If you really want to know how I felt about this, well, I just didn't want to come. I've never been in the home of a Gentile before. Never before have I gone into a place that is unclean!" But he does go on to add, "Even though I have never before been in an unclean home, God has told me not to call any man unclean. We are all sinners and we are all savable." How would you feel, especially if you are a lady who is a housekeeper, if some visitor came into your home and his first words were, "I am coming into your home, which I consider dirty"? You wouldn't exactly respond with a warm, friendly feeling, would you? Yet this is the substance of what Simon Peter said.

Because God had showed him that there was neither clean nor unclean, he continues his message.

Therefore came I unto you without gainsaying, as soon as I was sent for: I ask therefore for what intent ye have sent for me? [Acts 10:29].

This amazes me. Why would Simon Peter ask that question? Why didn't he immediately begin to tell them about Jesus Christ? Well, you see, the Spirit of God is in charge here, and He keeps Peter from rushing right into this.

This should be an important lesson for us. So often we are rather brisk and even crude in our witnessing. Because we find it difficult to witness, generally when we do it, we are very amateurish about it. We do it so abruptly and in such a way that often it offends people.

We need to be led by the Spirit of God. I personally believe that the finest kind of evangelism today is prayer evangelism. I mean that we should begin by praying for an individual. Then the day will come when we need to put legs on the prayer. Ask God to lead you. Friend, I *know* that He will lead you. If you have been praying for a loved one, or a friend, or a stranger, don't just go to him in your own strength and in the power of the flesh. If you do, you will fail. Let God be the One to lead you.

Let me share with you one of my first experiences of witnessing. When I was a student in college, I was very zealous to be a witness for God, but I was rather timid about it, and, very frankly, I wanted to be sure I had the leading of the Holy Spirit. I didn't have any money for bus or train fare, so I did a lot of hitchhiking. One time when I was out on the highway, a man in a brand new Model A Ford drove by and stopped fifty yards past me. Then he motioned for me to come on and get in. He said that he always looked over a hitchhiker before he picked one up. He introduced himself and told me he was a salesman for drug companies. He asked where I was going and I told him it was to Memphis. Well, he was going all the way to Memphis and he would be glad to take me all the way, but he did need to stop at several drug stores on the way to get his orders from them. Obviously, that was fine with me.

As we rode along, we talked of everything under the sun. Under my breath I was praying, "Lord, I'd like to witness to this man, but You will have to open the door for me. I'm not going to broach the subject because if I do, he'll think he has some religious nut in the car with him. If *I* open the door, *he* will probably open the car door and tell me to get out." So we rode along some more and just talked and talked. Finally he asked me whether I'd mind driving for him. Of course, I would love to drive that new car; so I did. He sat there and relaxed.

We got about sixty miles from Memphis and we had run out of conversation. There was a lull, and I was still praying, "Lord, we're getting near Memphis and there still hasn't been a door open for me. I'm not going to open it because I'm afraid he'll throw me out. You open the door for me if You want me to witness." We rode on for about ten more minutes, and then out of a clear sky he said, "You know, my wife and I went to church yesterday." He looked at me and laughed, and I laughed. Then he said, "I don't go very often. But that preacher said the funniest thing. He said Jesus was coming to this earth again. What do you think about that?"

Well, friend, I told him. Then I told him all about the first coming of the Lord Jesus. Finally I said, "The second coming of Christ means nothing to you now. You've got to come to Christ and accept what He did for you the first time He came if you are to have an interest in His second coming." This man was wide open. He drove me to the dormitory where I stayed at the college. He parked there and said, "I want to see you again." So I just blurted out, "Wouldn't you like to accept Christ as your Savior?" He said, "I sure would." I told him he could do that right there in the car. So we bowed our heads in prayer. I prayed and then asked him to pray, and he accepted Christ. Now I'll be honest with you, I would never have opened my mouth if the Lord hadn't prompted him to open up the conversation. We need to be led by the Spirit. The Holy Spirit had prepared his heart, and his conversion was genuine. The first sermon I preached after I was ordained in Nashville, as I looked down at the congregation, I noticed this man and his wife. He just sat there and smiled. Afterward I invited him to join my church. He said they had already joined a good church over in another part of town. He and his wife had become active Christians. What a wonderful experience that was!

We ought to be very careful in our witnessing that we are being led by the Spirit of God. Simon Peter does not walk right in and begin lecturing or preaching. He first finds out what is going on. "Why have you called for me? Why did you send these men for me?"

And Cornelius said, Four days ago I was fasting until this hour; and at the ninth hour I prayed in my house, and, behold, a man stood before me in bright clothing,

And said, Cornelius, thy prayer is heard, and thine alms are had in remembrance in the sight of God.

Send therefore to Joppa, and call hither Simon, whose surname is Peter; he is lodged in the house of one Simon a tanner by the sea side: who, when he cometh, shall speak unto thee.

Immediately therefore I sent to thee; and thou hast well done that thou art come. Now therefore are we all here present before God, to hear all things that are commanded thee of God [Acts 10:30–33].

Cornelius tells him, "I really don't know why I sent for you, except that God told me to send for Simon Peter. You must have some message for me."

Then Peter opened his mouth, and said, Of a truth I perceive that God is no respecter of persons:

But in every nation he that feareth him, and worketh righteousness, is accepted with him.

The word which God sent unto the children of Israel, preaching peace by Jesus Christ: (he is Lord of all:)

That word, I say, ye know, which was published throughout all Judaea, and began from Galilee, after the baptism which John preached [Acts 10:34–37].

Apparently Cornelius and those assembled with him would have heard certain basic facts about Jesus of Nazareth and also about the ministry of John the Baptist.

How God anointed Jesus of Nazareth with the Holy Ghost and with power: who went about doing good, and healing all that were oppressed of the devil; for God was with him.

And we are witnesses of all things which he did both in the land of the Jews, and in Jerusalem; whom they slew and hanged on a tree:

Him God raised up the third day, and shewed him openly [Acts 10:38–40].

Notice carefully what Simon Peter does. He presents the facts concerning Jesus Christ, assuming there are some of the incidents which they already know. He makes it very clear to them that this Jesus was crucified on a tree and that He rose again on the third day. God raised Him and showed Him openly. This is the gospel. Nothing short of that will do.

This past Christmas I received many cards on which were printed the rather well-known message, "One Solitary Life." It is very fine, there is no question about that. It is very readable, but there is a strange omission—a solitary omission in it. The most important fact is not recorded. It records that Jesus died, even mentions that He was buried, but completely leaves out His resurrection. Friend, there is not a single sermon preached, as recorded in the Book of Acts, that does not mention the resurrection of Jesus Christ. That is the very heart of the gospel. Until that is preached, the gospel has not been preached. Jesus Christ died, He was buried, He rose again from the dead. Those are the historical facts. Your relationship to a *risen* Savior determines your eternal destiny. He died for our sins according to the Scriptures, and He was *raised* again for our justification (Rom. 4:25).

Not to all the people, but unto witnesses chosen before of God, even to us, who did eat and drink with him after he rose from the dead.

And he commanded us to preach unto the people, and to testify that it is he which was ordained of God to be the Judge of quick and dead.

To him give all the prophets witness, that through his name whosoever believeth in him shall receive remission of sins [Acts 10:41–43].

You may remember that I have pointed out Peter's weaknesses and his faults. I actually rejoice in the fact that Peter was so human and so like another fellow I know very well by the name of McGee. But the important thing is that Peter preached the gospel. Here is the gospel: Jesus Christ died, He has risen, and whoever believes in Him shall receive remission of sins. If we do not tell people that message, we are not telling them the gospel.

While Peter yet spake these words, the Holy Ghost fell on all them which heard the word.

And they of the circumcision which believed were astonished, as many as came with Peter, because that on the Gentiles also was poured out the gift of the Holy Ghost.

For they heard them speak with tongues, and magnify God. Then answered Peter,

Can any man forbid water, that these should not be baptized, which have received the Holy Ghost as well as we?

And he commanded them to be baptized in the name of the Lord. Then prayed they him to tarry certain days [Acts 10:44–48].

This incident has been called the Gentile Pentecost. Peter was astonished that the Gentiles should receive the Holy Spirit. This outpouring of the Holy Spirit was made audible by their speaking in tongues. The tongues were an evidence to Simon Peter and the others with him that God would save the Gentiles and would give to them His Holy Spirit. Peter later relates this as evidence that these Gentiles had believed on the Lord Jesus Christ and that God had granted repentance unto life also to the Gentiles (Acts 11:17–18). In Acts 15:7–11 Peter again refers to this incident, declaring that it proves that the Holy Ghost has been given to the Gentiles and that they are saved through the grace of the Lord Jesus Christ just as are the Jews. It is hard for us to realize the great barrier that existed between Jew and Gentile. The Jews of that day simply could not believe that Gentiles were going to be saved—in spite of the fact that the Lord had told them this was to be so. Then the Gentiles at Cornelius' house are baptized in water.

Again let me call your attention to the fact that the Book of Acts records three representative conversions. The Ethiopian eunuch was a son of Ham. Saul of Tarsus was a son of Shem. Cornelius was a son of Japheth. In each instance the Holy Spirit moved, using a man of God and the Word of God.

CHAPTER 11

***THEME:** Peter defends his ministry; gospel goes to Antioch*

Peter recounts the events in connection with the conversion of Gentiles in the home of Cornelius. The news that the Gentiles had received the Word of God did not seem to bring any joy to the church in Jerusalem. They demand of Peter an explanation of his conduct, so Peter must defend his ministry—which is really difficult for Simon Peter, as he himself feels apologetic about it.

Antioch becomes the center of the gentile church.

PETER DEFENDS HIS MINISTRY

And the apostles and brethren that were in Judaea heard that the Gentiles had also received the word of God.

And when Peter was come up to Jerusalem, they that were of the circumcision contended with him,

Saying, Thou wentest in to men uncircumcised, and didst eat with them [Acts 11:1–3].

There was doubt and division. We need to understand that to the Jews the action of Simon Peter was a terrible thing. In fact, if we could have talked to Simon Peter a month before this, he also would have said it was a terrible thing to do. Actually, Peter gives them an apology. He makes it clear that he didn't want to do it at all, but that the Spirit of God was in the whole episode.

But Peter rehearsed the matter from the beginning, and expounded it by order unto them, saying,

I was in the city of Joppa praying: and in a trance I saw a vision, A certain vessel descend, as it had been a great sheet, let down from heaven by four corners; and it came even to me:

Upon the which when I had fastened mine eyes, I considered, and saw fourfooted beasts of the earth, and wild beasts, and creeping things, and fowls of the air [Acts 11:4–6].

Listen to his account. He is still amazed at God's command.

And I heard a voice saying unto me, Arise, Peter; slay and eat.

But I said, Not so, Lord: for nothing common or unclean hath at any time entered into my mouth.

But the voice answered me again from heaven, What God hath cleansed, that call not thou common.

And this was done three times: and all were drawn up again into heaven [Acts 11:7–10].

The word for "drawn up" indicates all were suddenly withdrawn into heaven.

And, behold, immediately there were three men already come unto the house where I was, sent from Caesarea unto me.

And the Spirit bade me go with them, nothing doubting. Moreover these six brethren accompanied me, and we entered into the man's house:

And he shewed us how he had seen an angel in his house, which stood and said unto him, Send men to Joppa, and call for Simon, whose surname is Peter;

Who shall tell thee words, whereby thou and all thy house shall be saved.

And as I began to speak, the Holy Ghost fell on them, as on us at the beginning [Acts 11:11–15].

Now Simon Peter tells what went through his mind.

Then remembered I the word of the Lord, how that he said, John indeed baptized with water; but ye shall be baptized with the Holy Ghost.

Forasmuch then as God gave them the like gift as he did unto us, who believed on the Lord Jesus Christ; what was I, that I could withstand God? [Acts 11:16–17].

The purpose of the tongues was to give evidence to Simon Peter that the Holy Spirit had actually "fallen on them." How else would he have known that they had been baptized by the Holy Spirit which placed them in the body of believers?

When they heard these things, they held their peace, and glorified God, saying, Then hath God also to the Gentiles granted repentance unto life [Acts 11:18].

Even the Judaizers had to shut their mouths now. They had nothing more to say in objection, because this obviously was of God. So they glorified God. This was a great day—the door had been opened to the Gentiles! We see now that the stage is being set for the gospel to move out to the ends of the earth.

GOSPEL GOES TO ANTIOCH

Now they which were scattered abroad upon the persecution that arose about Stephen travelled as far as Phenice, and Cyprus, and Antioch, preaching the word to none but unto the Jews only.

And some of them were men of Cyprus and Cyrene, which, when they were come to Antioch, spake unto the Grecians, preaching the Lord Jesus [Acts 11:19–20].

The "Grecians," you will remember, are Jews who spoke Greek and were Greek in their customs. So far, you will notice, the preaching has been to Jews only.

And the hand of the Lord was with them: and a great number believed, and turned unto the Lord.

Then tidings of these things came unto the ears of the church which was in

Jerusalem: and they sent forth Barnabas, that he should go as far as Antioch [Acts 11:21–22].

There is a great moving of the Spirit of God in Antioch, and the church in Jerusalem hears about it. So the Jerusalem church sends Barnabas to Antioch. We are going to see now that Antioch becomes the second center of the church. In fact, the center actually shifts from Jerusalem to Antioch.

Who, when he came, and had seen the grace of God, was glad, and exhorted them all, that with purpose of heart they would cleave unto the Lord.

For he was a good man, and full of the Holy Ghost and of faith: and much people was added unto the Lord [Acts 11:23–24].

This is a wonderful thing that is said about Barnabas. He was a good man, full of the Holy Spirit, and full of faith. And, my friend, there is no reason why every Christian shouldn't be a good person.

Barnabas became the pastor of the church there. He began "exhorting," which would be preaching and teaching. And the congregation grew, for "much people was added unto the Lord." As the church grew, it became evident to Barnabas that he needed an assistant pastor, and he knew where to get a good one.

Then departed Barnabas to Tarsus, for to seek Saul:

And when he had found him, he brought him unto Antioch. And it came to pass, that a whole year they assembled themselves with the church, and taught much people. And the disciples were called Christians first in Antioch [Acts 11:25–26].

Barnabas had to go find Saul and bring him with him. I detect in this that Saul was a little reluctant to come. He held back.

It was here that believers in the Lord Jesus Christ were first called "Christians." I do not think this was a term of ridicule. I think it simply meant that these were the ones who were the followers of Christ, they were *Christians*. It is an excellent name.

And in these days came prophets from Jerusalem unto Antioch.

And there stood up one of them named Agabus, and signified by the Spirit that there should be great dearth throughout all the world: which came to pass in the days of Claudius Caesar.

Then the disciples, every man according to his ability, determined to send relief unto the brethren which dwelt in Judaea:

Which also they did, and sent it to the elders by the hands of Barnabas and Saul [Acts 11:27–30].

The incident that is recorded here is also verified in secular history. There was a general famine, but the effect was especially felt in Jerusalem where the church had been persecuted, decimated, and hurt. They were in dire need during this time. It is wonderful to see the fraternal spirit, the bond of love, that held the early church together. The other believers sent help to the troubled church in Jerusalem.

We remember that Saul had been one of those who had wasted the church in Jerusalem by his relentless persecution of them. How wonderful it is to see that by his own hands a transformed Saul now brings *relief* to that same church. That is Christianity in shoe leather, my friend. That is the way it ought to be.

CHAPTER 12

***THEME:** Death of James; arrest of Peter*

In this chapter persecution strikes through Herod Agrippa I. James is executed and Peter is imprisoned—but is miraculously delivered. Herod dies by a judgment of God. Although persecution comes, the church grows and the Word of God is multiplied.

DEATH OF JAMES

Now about that time Herod the king stretched forth his hands to vex certain of the church [Acts 12:1].

"Herod the king" is Herod Agrippa I, grandson of Herod the Great (who attempted to put the Lord Jesus to death at the time of His birth). There never was a family more at enmity against God. As far as we know, not a single member of the Herod family ever really turned to God.

You will recall that up to this point the persecution against the church had been largely from the religious rulers, the Sadducees in particular. Now it moves into the realm of government. Persecution swings from religion to politics. Perhaps Herod did this to gain favor with certain influential groups. We know that he stretched forth his hands to vex certain of the church. The word *vexed* is hardly adequate to describe what he did. He carried on a brutal, unfeeling persecution of the church.

And he killed James the brother of John with the sword [Acts 12:2].

The fact is stated so bluntly—he killed James with the sword. James becomes another martyr in the church. He is the second martyr who is named. I am of the opinion that there had been many others who had already died for the name of the Lord Jesus.

And because he saw it pleased the Jews, he proceeded further to take Peter also. (Then were the days of unleavened bread.) [Acts 12:3].

James is slain, but Peter will be miraculously preserved in all of this. Here we find an example of the sovereign will of God moving in the church. I'm sure there were many who asked, "Why in the world was James put to death and Peter permitted to live? Why would God do that?" Many ask that same question today. The answer is that this is the sovereign will of God. He still moves like this in the contemporary church. I have been in the ministry for many years, and I have seen the Lord reach in and take certain wonderful members out of the church by death. And then there are others whom He has left. Why would He do that? If He had asked me, from my viewpoint as the pastor, I would say that He took the wrong one and He left the wrong one! But life and death are in the hands of a sovereign God. When you and I rebel against His decision, it is simply too bad for us. This is His universe, not ours. It is God's church, not ours. The hand of a sovereign God moves in the church.

James apparently was one of the heads of the church in Jerusalem. God permits Herod to slay him. Peter must have been a leader, too. God permits him to live.

And when he had apprehended him, he put him in prison, and delivered him to four quaternions of soldiers to keep him; intending after Easter to bring him forth to the people [Acts 12:4].

The word *Easter* should be "Passover." Actually, they are at the same time because you remember that Jesus ate the meal with His disciples just before He was crucified. However, the Jews in Jerusalem at this time would have been celebrating the Passover and not Easter.

He really put Peter under guard here. The guard is strengthened and enlarged. *Four quaternions* of soldiers to keep this man! Wouldn't you say that he suspected someone would try to deliver Peter?

PETER'S DELIVERANCE

Peter therefore was kept in prison: but prayer was made without ceasing of the church unto God for him [Acts 12:5].

Another translation would be "but prayer was made earnestly of the church unto God for him." They didn't come before God with a kind of grocery-list prayer. They went before God and earnestly prayed that this man Simon Peter be delivered. Their hearts were in their prayers.

And when Herod would have brought him forth, the same night Peter was sleeping between two soldiers, bound with two chains: and the keepers before the door kept the prison [Acts 12:6].

How could Simon Peter sleep between two soldiers? Remember that he went to sleep also in the Garden of Gethsemane. I would say that Simon Peter was not troubled with insomnia. He didn't have any difficulty sleeping. It seems he could sleep just about any place and any time. What a wonderful confidence he must have had in God to be able to sleep between these two soldiers!

And, behold, the angel of the Lord came upon him, and a light shined in the prison: and he smote Peter on the side, and raised him up, saying, Arise up quickly. And his chains fell off from his hands.

And the angel said unto him, Gird thyself, and bind on thy sandals. And so he did. And he saith unto him, Cast thy garment about thee, and follow me.

And he went out, and followed him; and wist not that it was true which was done by the angel; but thought he saw a vision [Acts 12:7–9].

The angel tells him to do a very reasonable thing—get dressed. There was nothing in the way of alarm, just sensible directions. Peter thought the whole thing was a dream, and he would have walked out of there without his shoes!

When they were past the first and the second ward, they came unto the iron gate that leadeth unto the city; which opened to them of his own accord: and they went out, and passed on through one street; and forthwith the angel departed from him [Acts 12:10].

They certainly had enough guards to keep Peter in prison. I really think that they expected something like this. You remember that the Lord Jesus had come forth from the grave. That was a source of real embarrassment to them. They do not intend to let something like that happen to them again. So they more than doubled the guard.

Remember that the church in Jerusalem is praying for Simon Peter while this is happening. As soon as Peter is out of danger, the angel lets Peter go on his own.

Let me call attention to the fact that the translation in verse 7 should be *an* angel of the Lord and not *the* angel of the Lord. *The* angel of the Lord in the Old Testament referred to the preincarnate Christ. Jesus Christ is now at God's right hand in His glorified body. It was not the Lord Jesus who came down to deliver Peter. It was an angel whom the Lord Jesus had sent. The prayers of the church are definitely answered.

And when Peter was come to himself, he said, Now I know of a surety, that the Lord hath sent his angel, and hath delivered me out of the hand of Herod, and from all the expectation of the people of the Jews [Acts 12:11].

Peter immediately recognizes that God has delivered him.

And when he had considered the thing, he came to the house of Mary the mother of John, whose surname was Mark; where many were gathered together praying [Acts 12:12].

The church at this particular time, and for about a hundred and fifty years after this, did not have church buildings. Today, when we talk of a church, we usually mean a building. We say, "The First So-and-So church is on the corner of Main and So-and-So." Actually, that is not a church at all; it is a building in which the church meets. The church is the body of believers. At the beginning the church never met in a public building. They had none. They met in homes.

Now Mary, the mother of John Mark, apparently was a woman of means and had a home large enough for the church to meet there. They were gathered together praying for Simon Peter to be delivered.

And as Peter knocked at the door of the gate, a damsel came to hearken, named Rhoda [Acts 12:13].

"To hearken" means that she came to the door to listen. These were days of persecution. It was important to know who was knocking. *Rhoda* means "rose"; she was probably a servant girl.

And when she knew Peter's voice, she opened not the gate for gladness, but ran in, and told how Peter stood before the gate [Acts 12:14].

She forgot all about opening the gate, you see. She was so excited that she just left him standing there at the gate while she rushed back in to the people who were praying.

And they said unto her, Thou art mad. But she constantly affirmed that it was even so. Then said they, It is his angel [Acts 12:15].

When she tells them Peter is at the gate, they tell her she is crazy. "No," she tells them, "Peter is at the gate." "Well, did you see him?" "No, I didn't open the gate but I heard him, and I know his voice." "Oh," they say, "it's his spirit." The word *angel* is *pneuma*, which really means "spirit" rather than angel. They are not saying that he has a guardian angel. They think it is his spirit. In other words, they think Peter is dead, that he has been slain by Herod.

It is interesting that while the church is praying for Simon Peter to be delivered, he is delivered; but when it happens, they don't believe it. They think he has been slain and it is his spirit which has appeared.

It is a great comfort to me that the early church, with all of its tremendous spiritual power, did not believe that their prayers had been answered on this occasion. They didn't believe that Simon Peter had actually been delivered. Isn't that same thing true of us so many times? When we do have an answer to our prayer, we rejoice and talk about it as if we are really surprised. And we are surprised—to be honest, we really didn't expect an answer. Yet God heard and answered our prayer. How gracious He is!

"But Peter continued knocking." That's just like Peter. Nobody's opening the gate because they don't believe their prayers have been answered—they are in there arguing whether it is Peter or whether it is his spirit. Peter wants in and he is about to knock that gate down!

But Peter continued knocking: and when they had opened the door, and saw him, they were astonished.

But he, beckoning unto them with the hand to hold their peace, declared unto them how the Lord had brought him out of the prison. And he said, Go shew these things unto James, and to the brethren. And he departed, and went into another place [Acts 12:16–17].

They just couldn't believe their eyes. They just couldn't believe that their prayers had been answered.

Now Peter got out of town. Since God had miraculously delivered him, couldn't God have miraculously kept him safe in Jerusalem? Shouldn't Peter have said, "I'm just going to stick around. God has delivered me out of prison and I know He can keep me"? Of course, God could keep him. But God expects us to use our common sense. Sometimes what looks like a tremendous faith in God is actually tempting God. Even after God has done some wonderful or miraculous thing for you and for me, He still expects us to use our common sense.

Now as soon as it was day, there was no small stir among the soldiers, what was become of Peter [Acts 12:18].

Notice that Dr. Luke uses the diminutive—"no small stir." When he says there was no small stir, believe me, he means there was a mighty big stir. Also in chapter 15 of Acts, when Judaism came into the church, Dr. Luke says they had "no small dissension." He means they had a regular knock-down-drag-out. They had a real fight, a regular donnybrook. But Dr. Luke always uses that very gracious and gentle diminutive—"no small stir" and "no small dissension."

When the soldiers found what had happened and realized that Simon Peter was gone, I think they called out half the army. They must have made a house-to-house search. Maybe they threw a guard around the city to prevent his escape. There was no small stir according to Dr. Luke. I'll say not! There was a mighty big stir.

And when Herod had sought for him, and found him not, he examined the keepers, and commanded that they should be put to death. And he went down from Judaea to Caesarea, and there abode [Acts 12:19].

Herod is cold-blooded and he is hardhearted. He has no regard for human life. By executing the guards, he is saying to the world that he does not believe Peter's escape was an act of God. He is holding his men responsible. He executes all the soldiers who were guarding Peter. Then he goes down to Caesarea, which is a resort area on the Mediterranean. Pilate enjoyed it down there, and many of the Roman rulers stayed down there. Actually, it was the Roman headquarters. Romans, like Pilate, didn't care for Jerusalem. They certainly didn't love Jerusalem as King David had. So now Herod beats it down to Caesarea to have a little vacation.

DEATH OF HEROD

Now we will see that God holds Herod responsible for the light He has given him.

And Herod was highly displeased with them of Tyre and Sidon: but they came with one accord to him, and, having made Blastus the king's chamberlain

their friend, desired peace; because their country was nourished by the king's country [Acts 12:20].

Tyre and Sidon did business with Herod and when he was displeased, this hurt the economy of Tyre and Sidon. So they came down to make an overture to Herod.

And upon a set day Herod, arrayed in royal apparel, sat upon his throne, and made an oration unto them [Acts 12:21].

Herod was pompous and lifted up by pride. He was also a pleasing speaker. He was the kind of politician who would have been elected no matter what party he would run for.

Herod is one of the men who is a miniature of Antichrist. John tells us this in 1 John 2:18: "Little children, it is the last time: and as ye have heard that antichrist shall come, even now are there many antichrists; whereby we know that it is the last time." The people hail him as a deity.

And the people gave a shout, saying, It is the voice of a god, and not of a man.

And immediately the angel of the Lord smote him, because he gave not God the glory: and he was eaten of worms, and gave up the ghost [Acts 12:22–23].

Friend, God will not share His glory with anyone. "I am the LORD: that is my name: and my glory will I not give to another, neither my praise to graven images" (Isa. 42:8). Herod refused to glorify God through the miracle of Peter's escape from prison. And now he is willing to let the people deify *him*! God judges him. God is jealous of His glory. What a lesson we have here!

Now one would think that with all this persecution taking place the poor church would be destroyed and disappear.

But the word of God grew and multiplied [Acts 12:24].

Persecution didn't hurt the church at all.

And Barnabas and Saul returned from Jerusalem, when they had fulfilled their ministry, and took with them John, whose surname was Mark [Acts 12:25].

John Mark goes back to Antioch with Barnabas and Saul. Remember that they had been down in Jerusalem with the gift to the church there.

We have come now to the end of the second period of the Book of Acts. The gospel has gone into Judea and Samaria. Beginning with the next chapter we will see the movement of the gospel to the uttermost part of the earth. We are still in that movement today. I hope that you and I are both involved in it.

CHAPTERS 13–14

***THEME:* First missionary journey of Paul**

We come now to the final major division of the Book of Acts. It is the Lord Jesus Christ at work by the Holy Spirit through the apostles to the uttermost part of the earth. The section includes chapters 13–28.

You will remember that the key to the book is the fact that Jesus said, "Ye shall be witnesses unto me" (Acts 1:8). This was not a command to the church as a corporate body but to you and me individually. This witness was to go out to Jerusalem, then to Judea and Samaria, and then to the uttermost part of the earth. During the Jerusalem period we saw that the gospel went to the Jews, and the church was 100 percent Jewish—no Gentiles. During the next period we saw the gospel go to the Samaritans and we saw the conversion of some Gentiles. Now the gospel moves out officially on its way to the ends of the earth.

On its way to the ends of the earth the gospel came to my ancestors and to your ancestors. Today you and I are the beneficiaries of the fact that someone went down the road of this world to bring the gospel to the ends of the earth. You and I ought to be in the business of taking the gospel down beyond where we are to some who have not heard.

In this surge of the gospel beyond the boundaries of Israel we find that Paul becomes the dominant leader and Peter disappears from the scene. God had used him mightily. Now Paul is the dominant one whom God will use.

As you will see by the map on page 570, Paul begins his journey with Barnabas. The first stop is the island of Cyprus, the home of Barnabas. They cross the island, then set sail from Paphos to go over to Perga in Pamphylia. Then they enter the interior of Asia Minor, which is now Turkey, and go into the Galatian country. They visit Antioch, Iconium, Lystra, and Derbe; then they return through Attalia, and then sail back to Antioch.

BARNABAS AND PAUL SENT OUT FROM ANTIOCH

Now there were in the church that was at Antioch certain prophets and teachers; as Barnabas, and Simeon that was called Niger, and Lucius of Cyrene, and Manaen, which had been brought up with Herod the tetrarch, and Saul.

As they ministered to the Lord, and fasted, the Holy Ghost said, Separate me Barnabas and Saul for the work whereunto I have called them [Acts 13:1–2].

You will notice as they begin their ministry it is "Barnabas and Saul." They will not be very far into the first missionary journey until Saul's name is changed to Paul. It is soon evident that Paul becomes the leader and the chief spokesman; then this team is called "Paul and Barnabas."

And when they had fasted and prayed, and laid their hands on them, they sent them away [Acts 13:3].

These men are now set aside as missionaries. Did you notice the church that sent them forth into the world? It was not the church in Jerusalem. I say to you very candidly, the church in Jerusalem was not a missionary church. The church in Antioch had the missionary vision. They fasted and prayed because of their earnestness and their desire for the will of God.

They laid their hands on these two missionaries they were sending out. We still do that today to our missionaries. Why? Is it that we are imparting something to them? I'm afraid all that we can impart to someone by laying our hands on them is whatever disease germ we have on our hands. The laying on of hands is a means of identifying, of declaring that we are partners with that one. So the Christians in Antioch are indicating by placing their hands on them that they are in a partnership with Paul and Barnabas in the enterprise of getting out the Word of God. They are sending these men out as their representatives. They will minister at home while Paul and Barnabas go to the regions beyond.

So they, being sent forth by the Holy Ghost, departed unto Seleucia; and from thence they sailed to Cyprus [Acts 13:4].

The important thing is that they are sent forth by the Holy Spirit. They will be led by the Holy Spirit of God. They went down to the seacoast town of Seleucia and sailed from there.

And when they were at Salamis, they preached the word of God in the synagogues of the Jews: and they had also John to their minister [Acts 13:5].

Notice that they had John Mark along with them.

From the very beginning Paul adopts a method which he followed through his entire ministry. He always used the Jewish synagogue as the springboard from which he preached the gospel. A friend of mine was criticized for going to speak in a synagogue. This man preached the gospel, I can assure you. I reminded his critic that Paul always went first to the synagogue to preach. If he was going to find fault with my friend, he would also have to find fault with the method of the apostle Paul.

OPPOSITION AT PAPHOS

And when they had gone through the isle unto Paphos, they found a certain sorcerer, a false prophet, a Jew, whose name was Bar-jesus [Acts 13:6].

It would appear that their ministry didn't have much success at Salamis. At least no record is given of any fruit from their ministry. They cross over the Isle of Cyprus to the other side of the island. In Paphos they encounter this opposition, which is actually satanic, through a sorcerer who had a tremendous influence on the Roman deputy, the governor of that island, Sergius Paulus.

Which was with the deputy of the country, Sergius Paulus, a prudent man; who called for Barnabas and Saul, and desired to hear the word of God.

But Elymas the sorcerer (for so is his name by interpretation) withstood

them, seeking to turn away the deputy from the faith [Acts 13:7–8].

This is satanic opposition. This man had the governor under his influence. Unfortunately there are a great many rulers today who are under the influence of all kinds of cultism which is in opposition to the Word of God and in opposition to the gospel.

Then Saul, (who also is called Paul,) filled with the Holy Ghost, set his eyes on him [Acts 13:9].

Here his name is changed. Why was he called Paul? The name *Paul* means "small or little." Some think that he took that name as an act of humility, that he no longer wanted to bear the proud name of Saul. It is possible he took the name of the governor, Sergius Paulus, who was his first convert.

And said, O full of all subtilty and all mischief, thou child of the devil, thou enemy of all righteousness, wilt thou not cease to pervert the right ways of the Lord? [Acts 13:10].

Paul may have been a mild man in some ways, but I tell you, when he encountered this kind of opposition, he denounced it with all his being. He recognized it as satanic and he denounced it. I think we ought to do the same today.

And now, behold, the hand of the Lord is upon thee, and thou shalt be blind, not seeing the sun for a season. And immediately there fell on him a mist and a darkness; and he went about seeking some to lead him by the hand [Acts 13:11].

He was already in spiritual darkness. Now he is put into physical darkness as well.

Then the deputy, when he saw what was done, believed, being astonished at the doctrine of the Lord [Acts 13:12].

I call your attention to the fact that Paul had the sign gifts of an apostle. When he went over there to Paphos, he couldn't ask them to turn to the New Testament. There was no New Testament for him to preach from or for them to turn to. He couldn't preach from the Epistle to the Romans because he hadn't written it yet. They couldn't turn to the Gospel of John because John hadn't written it yet. So how will they recognize his authority? It is by the sign gifts. Today, the New Testament is written. We are now given a different way to recognize authority. "If there come any unto you, and bring not this doctrine, receive him not into your house, neither bid him God speed" (2 John 10). This doctrine is in the Word of God, in the New Testament.

Probably the sorcerer had been doing some fancy tricks by the power of Satan. In that day a false prophet could probably heal and perform other miracles by the power of Satan.

Paul has his authority from the Lord Jesus Christ. He absolutely dominates the sorcerer by his message of the gospel of the Lord Jesus Christ. Sergius Paulus comes to the light. He has been in spiritual darkness but now believes and is astonished at the doctrine of the Lord.

Now when Paul and his company loosed from Paphos, they came to Perga in Pamphylia: and John departing from them returned to Jerusalem [Acts 13:13].

That is all Dr. Luke says; he mildly records the fact of John Mark's departure. He doesn't issue a tirade against him. We will learn later that John Mark actually deserted. He showed a yellow streak and ran home to mommy. Remember that his mother was a prominent member of the church in Jerusalem and that her home was the place of meeting for the church there. When he reached Perga and got a look into the interior of Asia Minor—the paganism and the physical dangers and hardships that were there—he decided that he hadn't been called as a missionary. He heads in another direction, and that direction is home.

Later on we will find that Paul refuses to take John Mark on another missionary journey. In fact, Paul and Barnabas disagree so violently over the issue of taking along John Mark that Paul and Barnabas finally separated. Paul went one way and Barnabas went another way. Paul was wrong about John Mark. God didn't throw him overboard because of his failure. Thank God, He doesn't throw us overboard because of our failure either. He gave John Mark another chance. Later on Paul was big enough to admit he had been wrong, and when he was close to his death, he actually asked for John Mark to come to him. "Only Luke is with me. Take Mark, and bring him with thee: for he is profitable to me for the ministry" (2 Tim. 4:11). This is the John Mark who wrote the Gospel of Mark. He made good. Thank God, He gives us a second chance!

However here at the beginning John Mark is a failure. He left them and returned to Jerusalem. Meanwhile Paul and Barnabas go into the interior of Asia Minor.

PAUL'S SERMON AT ANTIOCH

But when they departed from Perga, they came to Antioch in Pisidia, and went into the synagogue on the sabbath day, and sat down.

And after the reading of the law and the prophets the rulers of the synagogue sent unto them, saying, Ye men and brethren, if ye have any word of exhortation for the people, say on [Acts 13:14–15].

Paul follows his method of going first to the synagogue. Jews were scattered throughout the Roman Empire, and they established synagogues in the cities in which they had settled. When visitors would come from Jerusalem, since they would want word from the religious center, they would invite the visitor to say something. This always afforded a marvelous opportunity for the apostle Paul. He certainly took advantage of it here.

This sermon which Paul preached in Antioch of Pisidia is one of the great sermons, in my opinion; yet it is generally passed by today. It is the first recorded sermon of Paul, preached in the synagogue on the Sabbath day. When they asked Paul whether he would like to say something, you can be sure that he wanted to say something. That was his whole reason for being there.

Then Paul stood up, and beckoning with his hand said, Men of Israel, and ye that fear God, give audience [Acts 13:16].

One would conclude from this introduction that there were some visitors there—probably Gentile proselytes.

The God of this people of Israel chose our fathers, and exalted the people when they dwelt as strangers in the land of Egypt, and with an high arm brought he them out of it.

And about the time of forty years suffered he their manners in the wilderness.

And when he had destroyed seven nations in the land of Chanaan, he divided their land to them by lot.

And after that he gave unto them judges about the space of four hundred and fifty years, until Samuel the prophet [Acts 13:17–20].

Notice that Paul is doing the same thing that Stephen did before the Sanhedrin. He recounts Israel's history as a nation.

And afterward they desired a king: and God gave unto them Saul the son of Cis, a man of the tribe of Benjamin, by the space of forty years.

And when he had removed him, he raised up unto them David to be their king; to whom also he gave testimony, and said, I have found David the son of Jesse, a man after mine own heart, which shall fulfil all my will.

Of this man's seed hath God according to his promise raised unto Israel a Saviour, Jesus [Acts 13:21–23].

After recounting their history, he will present to them the person of the Savior.

When John had first preached before his coming the baptism of repentance to all the people of Israel.

And as John fulfilled his course, he said, Whom think ye that I am? I am not he. But, behold, there cometh one after me, whose shoes of his feet I am not worthy to loose.

Men and brethren, children of the stock of Abraham, and whosoever among you feareth God, to you is the word of this salvation sent [Acts 13:24–26].

These people apparently had heard of John the Baptist. Now Paul will get down to the nitty-gritty.

For they that dwell at Jerusalem, and their rulers, because they knew him not, nor yet the voices of the prophets which are read every sabbath day, they have fulfilled them in condemning him.

And though they found no cause of death in him, yet desired they Pilate that he should be slain [Acts 13:27–28].

As Paul is reviewing their history, he is pointing out that all this was done as a fulfillment of prophecy. They were fulfilling the prophets at the very same time they were reading them! They read without understanding what they were reading.

And when they had fulfilled all that was written of him, they took him down

from the tree, and laid him in a sepulchre.

But God raised him from the dead:

And he was seen many days of them which came up with him from Galilee to Jerusalem, who are his witnesses unto the people [Acts 13:29–31].

You will notice that the core, the heart of every sermon preached in the New Testament, is the death and resurrection of Jesus Christ. That is the message. Simon Peter preached it; now Paul the apostle preaches it. There is not the slightest disagreement in the message of these two men. Don't tell me these two men disagreed. They did not!

And we declare unto you glad tidings, how that the promise which was made unto the fathers,

God hath fulfilled the same unto us their children, in that he hath raised up Jesus again; as it is also written in the second psalm, Thou art my Son, this day have I begotten thee [Acts 13:32–33].

This Old Testament reference, Psalm 2:7, does not refer to the *birth* of Christ; it refers to the *resurrection* of Christ. "This day have I begotten thee"—not begotten in the Virgin Birth but actually in the resurrection from the dead.

And as concerning that he raised him up from the dead, now no more to return to corruption, he said on this wise, I will give you the sure mercies of David.

Wherefore he saith also in another psalm, Thou shalt not suffer thine Holy One to see corruption [Acts 13:34–35].

Paul enlarges upon the Resurrection. He is citing the same that Simon Peter did on the Day of Pentecost.

For David, after he had served his own generation by the will of God, fell on sleep, and was laid unto his fathers, and saw corruption:

But he, whom God raised again, saw no corruption.

Be it known unto you therefore, men and brethren, that through this man is preached unto you the forgiveness of sins:

And by him all that believe are justified from all things, from which ye could not be justified by the law of Moses [Acts 13:36–39].

Now he is pinning this thing down. He is explaining the significance of the death and resurrection of Jesus Christ. He is actually asking them for a decision to believe on the Lord Jesus.

Beware therefore, lest that come upon you, which is spoken of in the prophets;

Behold, ye despisers, and wonder, and perish: for I work a work in your days, a work which ye shall in no wise believe, though a man declare it unto you [Acts 13:40–41].

Here is his appeal to them. He urges them not to reject the message.

And when the Jews were gone out of the synagogue, the Gentiles besought that these words might be preached to them the next sabbath [Acts 13:42].

There were Gentiles there who said, "We would like to hear this same message."

Now when the congregation was broken up, many of the Jews and religious proselytes followed Paul and Barnabas: who, speaking to them, persuaded them to continue in the grace of God.

And the next sabbath day came almost the whole city together to hear the word of God [Acts 13:43–44].

There must have been much discussion of Paul's message. The next Sabbath day almost the entire city was there to hear Paul preach.

But when the Jews saw the multitudes, they were filled with envy, and spake against those things which were spoken by Paul, contradicting and blaspheming [Acts 13:45].

This time there was a big commotion because the leading religious rulers of the synagogue opposed Paul and Barnabas.

Then Paul and Barnabas waxed bold, and said, It was necessary that the word of God should first have been spoken to you: but seeing ye put it from you, and judge yourselves unworthy of everlasting life, lo, we turn to the Gentiles.

For so hath the Lord commanded us, saying, I have set thee to be a light of the Gentiles, that thou shouldest be for salvation unto the ends of the earth.

And when the Gentiles heard this, they were glad, and glorified the word of the Lord: and as many as were ordained to eternal life believed.

And the word of the Lord was published throughout all the region [Acts 13: 46–49].

Here is the recurring pattern. The gospel is preached to the Jews first; they reject it; so they turn to the Gentiles with the good news.

But the Jews stirred up the devout and honourable women, and the chief men of the city, and raised persecution against Paul and Barnabas, and expelled them out of their coasts [Acts 13:50].

They were run out of town; they actually were forced to leave the town.

But they shook off the dust of their feet against them, and came unto Iconium.

And the disciples were filled with joy, and with the Holy Ghost [Acts 13:51–52].

Notice the condition of those who were converted. They were filled with joy, and they were filled with the Holy Ghost.

GALATIAN COUNTRY

Now in chapter 14 Paul and Barnabas face the almost impenetrable paganism of Galatia. I personally believe that the Galatian field was the hardest mission field that Paul ever entered. You need only to read the Epistle to the Galatians to discover that. Galatians was the harshest epistle that Paul wrote. He wrote it to a group of people who had a spiritual bent in the wrong direction. They were constantly going off the track. He visited those churches more than any others.

Let me give you this brief background of the Galatian country which Paul is entering on this first missionary journey. The people for whom the province was named were Gauls, a Celtic tribe from the same stock which inhabited France. In the fourth century B.C. they invaded the Roman Empire and sacked Rome. Later they crossed into Greece and captured Delphi in 280 B.C. At the invitation of Nikomedes I, King of Bithynia, they crossed over into Asia Minor to help him in a civil war. They were a warlike people and soon established themselves in Asia Minor. In 189 B.C. they were made subjects of the Roman Empire and became a province. Their boundaries varied, and for many years they retained their customs and language. The churches which Paul established on this first missionary journey were included at one time in the territory of Galatia, so this is the name which Paul would normally give to these churches.

The people were blond orientals. These Gallic Celts had much of the same temperament and characteristics of the majority of the

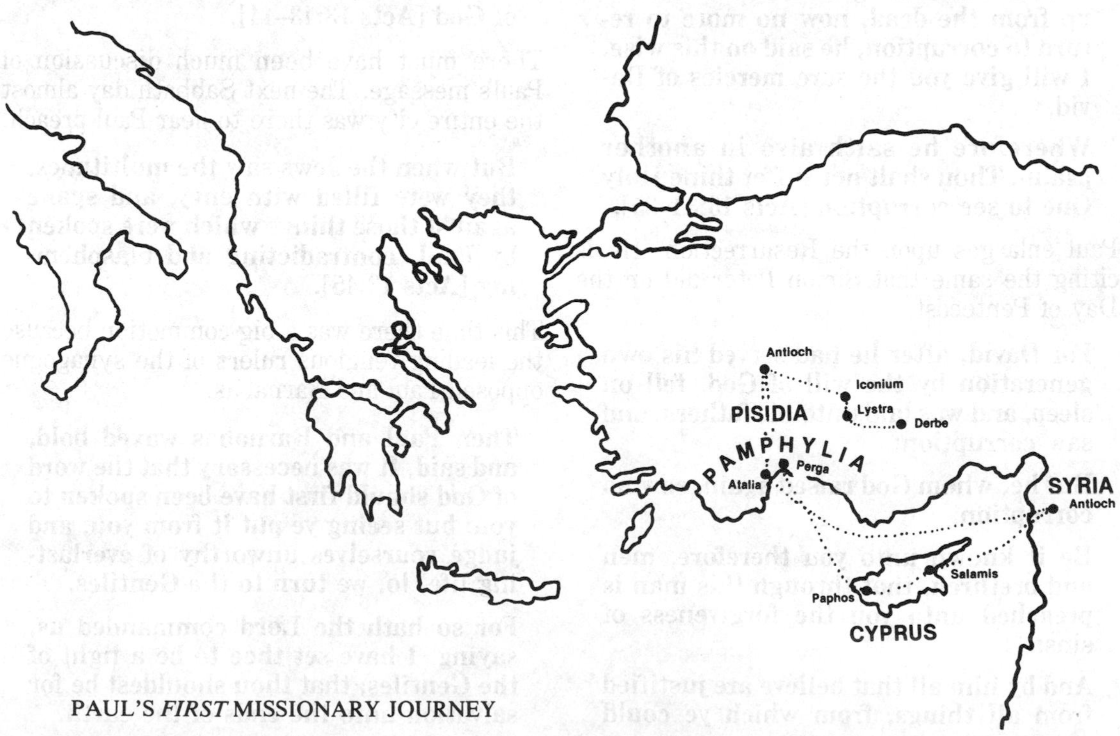

PAUL'S *FIRST* MISSIONARY JOURNEY

American population, which came out of that same stock in Europe and the British Isles. Caesar had this to say of them: "The infirmity of the Gauls is that they are fickle in their resolves, fond of change, and not to be trusted." Another writer of that period described them as "frank, impetuous, impressible, eminently intelligent, fond of show, but extremely inconstant, the fruit of excessive vanity." Paul wrote them a very harsh letter because they needed that kind of letter. The majority of the people in the United States are like them. That is the reason so many cults and "isms" have begun in this country. We are a fickle people. One day we follow one leader, and the next day we follow someone else. It is amazing to watch the polls of our political candidates. If they make one statement, one slip of the tongue, the entire population shifts from them to someone else. We are a fickle people—very much like the Galatians.

All of this should make this section especially interesting to us. Martin Luther used the Epistle to the Galatians for the Reformation because it was written to folk who are like we are.

THE WORK IN ICONIUM

And it came to pass in Iconium, that they went both together into the synagogue of the Jews, and so spake, that a great multitude both of the Jews and also of the Greeks believed [Acts 14:1].

If you follow the journey on a map, you will notice that they crossed over the length of the island of Cyprus, and then sailed to Perga in Pamphylia. Then they traveled up into the country of Antioch, Iconium, Lystra, and Derbe. These are the cities of Galatia. So they are now in the heartland of Asia Minor.

But the unbelieving Jews stirred up the Gentiles, and made their minds evil affected against the brethren.

Long time therefore abode they speaking boldly in the Lord, which gave testimony unto the word of his grace, and granted signs and wonders to be done by their hands.

But the multitude of the city was divided: and part held with the Jews, and part with the apostles [Acts 14:2–4].

Paul and Barnabas cause quite a division in the city. You must remember that Paul and Barnabas are both Jews. They always went to the Jews first and used the synagogue as a springboard to get to the Gentiles.

And when there was an assault made both of the Gentiles, and also of the Jews with their rulers, to use them despitefully, and to stone them,

They were ware of it, and fled unto Lystra and Derbe, cities of Lycaonia, and unto the region that lieth round about:

And there they preached the gospel [Acts 14:5–7].

Because they didn't get a very good reception in Iconium, they fled to Lystra and Derbe. However, we know that they came back through Iconium so there must have been some believers there.

THE EVENTS AT LYSTRA

And there sat a certain man at Lystra, impotent in his feet, being a cripple from his mother's womb, who never had walked:

The same heard Paul speak: who stedfastly beholding him, and perceiving that he had faith to be healed,

Said with a loud voice, Stand upright on thy feet. And he leaped and walked [Acts 14:8–10].

As we have seen, Paul and Barnabas had the gifts of an apostle, the sign gifts. They came into these places without any New Testament with the message of the gospel. What were their credentials? How could they prove their message was from God? The sign gifts were their credentials—they needed them. Today we have the entire Bible, and what people need today is to study this Bible and to learn what it has to say. If only we could get people to do that!

The other day I played golf with a very affable, generous, bighearted man. He is an unsaved man, and he told me very candidly that he was chasing around. Mutual friends had asked me to play with him. I attempted to talk with him about the gospel. He knew the facts of the gospel as well as I do. And you know something else? He believed them. He said he believed that Jesus died and rose again, and he believed that if he put his trust in Jesus, He would save him. So I asked him why he didn't do that. Then he began to mention names, names of certain men whose lives just didn't measure up to their profession of faith. So I said to him, "For goodness sake get your eyes off men. In the first century the apostles performed miracles and men got their eyes on the apostles. So it was necessary to get their eyes off the apostles and turn them to the Book which presents the Lord Jesus Christ. You need to get your eyes on the Word of God and learn what God says today. He tells us that the important thing is our personal relationship with God through Jesus Christ. All those other men you mention will not even enter into the picture when you stand before the Lord Jesus someday. The only question will be your personal relationship to Jesus Christ as it is revealed in the Word of God. Go to the Word of God." I'll be very frank with you, I didn't really get very far with this man. He did say that I had given him a new approach; he had never heard it that way before. He thought maybe he would try it. I encouraged him again to get his eyes off other Christians, because we all have feet of clay.

The people at Lystra were looking to Paul and Barnabas.

> **And when the people saw what Paul had done, they lifted up their voices, saying in the speech of Lycaonia, The gods are come down to us in the likeness of men [Acts 14:11].**

The man had real faith to be healed. When Paul told him to stand upright on his feet, he leaped and walked. Remember that the people in the area were pagan, heathen people. When they saw what Paul had done, they began to shout that the gods had come down in the likeness of men. Their eyes were on Paul and Barnabas. They were really excited about them.

> **And they called Barnabas, Jupiter; and Paul, Mercurius, because he was the chief speaker.**

> **Then the priest of Jupiter, which was before their city, brought oxen and garlands unto the gates, and would have done sacrifice with the people [Acts 14:12–13].**

Paul is the leader of the team, the chief speaker, and the people want to make them gods. They bring garlands and sacrifice and are ready to worship them. Fickle! Does it remind you of someone else? In America it is a baseball player one year, then a politician, then a football star, then another politician. By the following year they are all forgotten, and it is someone else new. It is the same way with the preachers. One can preach the Word of God and everyone will acclaim him as a wonderful preacher. Then the next day they are ready to crucify him.

> **Which when the apostles, Barnabas and Paul, heard of, they rent their clothes, and ran in among the people, crying out,**

> **And saying, Sirs, why do ye these things? We also are men of like passions with you, and preach unto you that ye should turn from these vanities unto the living God, which made heaven, and earth, and the sea, and all things that are therein:**

> **Who in times past suffered all nations to walk in their own ways [Acts 14: 14–16].**

Paul and Barnabas are not only startled and amazed that these people want to worship them, but they are completely shocked. They rush in among them, shouting, "We are human beings like you are!" You will remember that Peter had to say the same thing to Cornelius when Cornelius bowed down to him to worship him.

Certainly none of us is to bow down to worship any man. A Christian is not to be so obsequious that he gets down to lick the boots of anyone. Unfortunately, even in Christian work, we find some people who want others to bow to them. How tragic that is.

> **Nevertheless he left not himself without witness, in that he did good, and gave us rain from heaven, and fruitful seasons, filling our hearts with food and gladness.**

> **And with these sayings scarce restrained they the people, that they had not done sacrifice unto them [Acts 14:17–18].**

He is attempting to turn their attention to the living God who is the Creator. He wants to draw them away from their heathen, pagan idols and the mythology of the Greeks.

> **And there came thither certain Jews from Antioch and Iconium, who persuaded the people, and, having stoned Paul, drew him out of the city, supposing he had been dead [Acts 14:19].**

How amazing this is. Such fickle people! One day they are ready to worship Paul and Barnabas as gods. The next day they stone Paul to death.

(How like Americans—we follow fads. One time it is the hula hoop. Then it is the miniskirt. We simply follow one fad after another.)

They stoned Paul and dragged him out of

the city "supposing he had been dead." Do you think he was dead? I'll tell you what I think. I think he was dead. Later Paul writes of the experience he had: "I knew a man in Christ above fourteen years ago, (whether in the body, I cannot tell; or whether out of the body, I cannot tell: God knoweth;) such an one caught up to the third heaven. And I knew such a man, (whether in the body, or out of the body, I cannot tell: God knoweth;) How that he was caught up into paradise, and heard unspeakable words, which it is not lawful for a man to utter" (2 Cor. 12:2–4). Who was that man? It was Paul himself. "And lest I should be exalted above measure through the abundance of the revelations, there was given to me a thorn in the flesh, the messenger of Satan to buffet me, lest I should be exalted above measure" (2 Cor. 12:7). I don't think that crowd left him there half dead; I think they left him dead. I believe that God raised him from the dead.

Why would God permit this stoning? Galatians 6:7 tells us: "Be not deceived; God is not mocked: for whatsoever a man soweth, that shall he also reap." Paul reaped what he had sowed. He had ordered the stoning of Stephen. Maybe someone will object that now he is converted. Yes, but even after conversion we will reap whatsoever we have sown. This is a law of nature as well as a law operating in our lives. We shall reap whatever we sow. Because Saul took part in the stoning of Stephen, years later the same thing happened to him.

Howbeit, as the disciples stood round about him, he rose up, and came into the city: and the next day he departed with Barnabas to Derbe [Acts 14:20].

This is miraculous. A man who has been stoned would be brutally wounded. Paul rose up, and the very next day he was able to travel. This is a miracle whether or not he was actually raised from the dead.

And when they had preached the gospel to that city, and had taught many, they returned again to Lystra, and to Iconium, and Antioch,

Confirming the souls of the disciples, and exhorting them to continue in the faith, and that we must through much tribulation enter into the kingdom of God [Acts 14:21–22].

If you are following the map, you will notice that Derbe is the pivotal point. It is the end of the line. At this point they turn back and retrace their steps through Lystra, Iconium, and Antioch.

And when they had ordained them elders in every church, and had prayed with fasting, they commended them to the Lord, on whom they believed [Acts 14:23].

They return through Pisidia and Pamphylia, and preached again in Perga. Then they go to Attalia, and sail from that port back to Antioch.

And thence sailed to Antioch, from whence they had been recommended to the grace of God for the work which they fulfilled.

And when they were come, and had gathered the church together, they rehearsed all that God had done with them, and how he had opened the door of faith unto the Gentiles.

And there they abode long time with the disciples [Acts 14:26–28].

Paul and Barnabas return to Antioch to give a report of the work because this is the church that had sent them out. They revealed that God had now definitely opened the door of the gospel to Gentiles. When the gospel started out, the churches were comprised entirely of Hebrews. Then they became partially Gentile. And now the gospel is going definitely to the Gentiles. Now the churches in Asia Minor are comprised entirely of Gentiles. Although there may also have been some Jews in these churches, it seems that in most places the Jews rejected the gospel and the Gentiles received it.

CHAPTER 15

THEME: *The council at Jerusalem*

Now that the first missionary journey of Paul and Barnabas has been completed and the churches which they established in the Galatian country are 100 percent gentile, the church faces its first great crisis.

In Judea many of the Hebrew converts are Pharisees who have no intention of giving up the Mosaic system. They assert that the Gentiles must also come into the church through the Mosaic system. In fact, they believe that Gentiles are not saved until they are circumcised.

The news of this contention reaches the church in Jerusalem. The apostles must now face up to the question. What course is the church to take? So in Jerusalem the first church council convenes to resolve the matter.

Down through history you will find that there have been other church councils that have decided other great issues, such as the validity and the inerrancy of the Scriptures. Another council decided upon the deity of Christ and the fact that He is both God and man. And there have been other important councils when differences arose in the church. Some folk may think that we need a council in our day. We certainly do. However, I am afraid there could never be an agreement because too many churches are far removed from the person of Christ. A council that cannot meet around the person of Christ is not actually a *church* council because the Lord Jesus Christ is the very center of the church. The issue is not one of ritual, or of membership, or of ceremony. The central issue is that of one's personal relationship to Jesus Christ. Unfortunately, people who are personally far removed from Christ and who do not experience fellowship with Him want to argue about ritual. Oh, they may carry a big Bible under their arms, go to church on Sunday and sing the hymns lustily, but on Monday the Lord Jesus is far removed from them.

Friend, the Lord Jesus should occupy the very center of our lives. We should think of Him constantly. We should not see a sunset without thinking of the One who made it. He should be brought into our daily living, into all situations of life, our tensions and our anxieties.

Now let's turn our attention to this council at Jerusalem. It is an outstanding group which has come together here. These men have convened in order to consider this great issue: law versus grace, or law versus liberty.

THE QUESTION OF CIRCUMCISION

And certain men which came down from Judaea taught the brethren, and said, Except ye be circumcised after the manner of Moses, ye cannot be saved [Acts 15:1].

Here is the crux of the issue. It is not simply a question of whether one should be circumcised or not, whether one should eat meat or not. The question is: Must one do any of these things *in order to be saved*? Now we will move on and penetrate a little deeper into their problem.

When therefore Paul and Barnabas had no small dissension and disputation with them, they determined that Paul and Barnabas, and certain other of them, should go up to Jerusalem unto the apostles and elders about this question [Acts 15:2].

Again I call attention to Dr. Luke's use of the diminutive. "No small dissension" really means they had a regular donnybrook! It was a heated debate.

We need to realize here that it is really the gospel which is under question at this council. The Epistle to the Galatians gives us a full explanation of the council.

The gospel is used in two senses in the New Testament. First of all, there are the *facts* of the gospel. These are absolutely basic and essential. Paul gives those facts in the first five verses of 1 Corinthians 15. It is the death, the burial, and the resurrection of the Lord Jesus Christ. "Moreover, brethren, I declare unto you the gospel which I preached unto you, which also ye have received, and wherein ye stand; By which also ye are saved, if ye keep in memory what I preached unto you, unless ye have believed in vain. For I delivered unto you first of all that which I also received, how that Christ died for our sins according to the scriptures; And that he was buried, and that he rose again the third day according to the scriptures: And that he was seen of Cephas, then of the twelve." These are the facts of the gospel, and they concern the person of Christ. I move on down to 1 Corinthians 15:15–17: "Yea, and we are found false witnesses of God; because we have testified of God that he raised up Christ: whom he raised not up, if so be that the dead rise not. For if the dead rise not, then is not Christ raised: And if Christ be not raised, your faith is vain; ye are yet in your sins." Face up to it, my friend; if Christ is not raised from the dead, then there is no gospel at all. But thanks be to God, ". . . now is Christ risen from the dead, and become the firstfruits of them that slept" (1 Cor. 15:20). The facts of the gospel are the death, burial, and resurrection of Christ.

The second sense of the gospel is the *interpretation* of the facts. It is this interpretation which is the basic truth in the Epistle to the Galatians. That is the crux of the whole matter at this first council at Jerusalem. Thus the gospel also hinges on this fact which Paul states in Galatians 3:22: "But the scripture hath concluded all under sin, that the promise by faith of Jesus Christ might be given to them that believe." What must one do to be saved? Nothing more nor less than *believe*. Again in Galatians 2:15–16: "We who are Jews by nature, and not sinners of the Gentiles, Knowing that a man is not justified by the works of the law, but by the faith of Jesus Christ, even we have believed in Jesus Christ, that we might be justified by the faith of Christ, and not by the works of the law: for by the works of the law shall no flesh be justified." That is important to see.

The Judaizers of that day were different from the liberal of today. The liberal will actually deny the facts of the gospel. He will deny the physical resurrection of Christ. Some go so far as to say that Jesus Christ is just a myth, that He never lived or died. Most of them do not try to upset history quite to that extent. However, they deny that Jesus died *for our sins*.

In the first century the Judaizers did not deny the facts of the gospel—there simply were too many witnesses. Paul says that over five hundred people saw the risen Christ at one time. My friend, if you get five hundred witnesses into any law court, you will win your case! Also the apostles were witnesses to the risen Christ. They were there to testify to it. The facts of the gospel were not under question by the Judaizers.

The contention arose over the *interpretation* of those facts. What did Christ do for you on the cross? Is the work of Christ adequate to save you? Do you need to go through some ritual or something else in order to be saved? Must you go through the Law? These are the questions they were asking.

Now let's return to Acts 15 and go with Paul and Barnabas up to Jerusalem.

And being brought on their way by the church, they passed through Phenice and Samaria, declaring the conversion of the Gentiles: and they caused great joy unto all the brethren.

And when they were come to Jerusalem, they were received of the church, and of the apostles and elders, and they declared all things that God had done with them [Acts 15:3–4].

Paul and Barnabas give a report to the church in Jerusalem just as they had done to the church in Antioch. They tell them, "We have preached the gospel, and men and women over in the Galatian country have trusted Christ. They know nothing about Mosaic Law. They trusted Christ and were saved."

But there rose up certain of the sect of the Pharisees which believed, saying, That it was needful to circumcise them, and to command them to keep the law of Moses [Acts 15:5].

They wanted to add something to the gospel. Friend, whenever you add something to the gospel, you no longer have the gospel but you have a religion. You no longer have the gospel of Jesus Christ. The only approach that you can make to Jesus Christ is by faith. We must all come to Him by faith. He won't let us come any other way. Jesus said, ". . . I am the way, the truth, and the life: no man cometh unto the Father, but by me" (John 14:6). He's bottled the whole world into this. There is only one question God asks the lost world: "What do you do with My Son who died for you?" God doesn't give us some little Sunday school lesson by saying, "I want you to be a good boy. I want you to join a church. I want you to go through this and that ritual." That kind of teaching is only for an insipid *religion*. It does not come from God. God is saying, "My Son died for you. What will you do with Him?" The answer to that question will determine your eternal destiny. This is the issue being discussed at the council in Jerusalem. This is really exciting.

And the apostles and elders came together for to consider of this matter [Acts 15:6].

THE DECISION OF THE COUNCIL

The apostles and elders had come together to argue this thing out. The disputes were hot and heavy. A decision must be made and Simon Peter is the first one to express his decision.

And when there had been much disputing, Peter rose up, and said unto them, Men and brethren, ye know how that a good while ago God made choice among us, that the Gentiles by my mouth should hear the word of the gospel, and believe [Acts 15:7].

I don't think that this is the first time Peter spoke. If he had been quiet through all that time of disputing, it certainly would not have been consistent with his character. No, I'm of the opinion that he had already put in his two bits worth before this. But now he is going to sum up the whole thing. This is not a new decision for Peter. Peter had already declared this same thing at the time of the conversion of Cornelius. Remember that Peter himself had been shocked by the truth of it. He was told to go into the home of a Gentile and preach the gospel without the Law. The people were uncircumcised, they didn't follow the Mosaic system, they ate pork—and yet they were saved!

The council would listen to Simon Peter because he was narrow-minded—I don't say this in an ugly way—I mean that he was a Jew of the Jews. He himself said he had never eaten anything unclean, and he wouldn't have thought of entering the home of a Gentile. He stuck as close to the Mosaic system as any man could. So if Peter spoke up, they would listen.

Now he testifies that the Gentiles had heard the gospel from his mouth, and they had believed. You mean they were actually saved? Yes, they were saved by grace. Peter himself had to learn that salvation is not decided by whether one eats meat or doesn't eat meat, whether one eats pork or doesn't eat pork. Salvation is not dependent on our observation of the Sabbath, or Sunday, or any other day. Salvation is by grace through faith. We are free to choose what we wish to do about these other things. We have freedom in that connection.

And God, which knoweth the hearts, bare them witness, giving them the Holy Ghost, even as he did unto us;

And put no difference between us and them, purifying their hearts by faith [Acts 15:8–9].

Does Peter say that God purified their hearts by keeping the Law? No! By going through a ceremony? No! By joining a church? No! By *faith.* Peter said, "I went into the home of Cornelius. I gave them the facts of the gospel. They believed and were saved—the Holy Ghost came upon them just as He had come to us in Jerusalem."

My friend, this is always the only way of salvation. It is by faith. You don't have to do anything to merit your salvation. Jesus Christ did it all for you nineteen hundred years ago. All God asks you to do is to accept His Son who died for you.

Now therefore why tempt ye God, to put a yoke upon the neck of the disciples, which neither our fathers nor we were able to bear? [Acts 15:10].

Simon Peter makes a tremendous admission here. He says that neither they nor their fathers kept the Law. I have said this many times before, and I will say it many, many times more: God has never saved anybody through the keeping of the Law. Do you know why? There has never been a person who has kept it. God saves on one basis and one basis only: faith in the death and resurrection of the Lord Jesus Christ.

Before the time of Christ, men brought a sacrifice to God. They brought that sacrifice by faith. Abel understood that the little lamb could never take away sin. He understood that the little lamb pointed to the One whom God had told his mother about. He had said that the Seed of the woman would come and would bruise the head of the serpent (Gen. 3:15). Abel believed that. He believed God. He was saved by faith.

So Simon Peter says, "To tell the truth—why don't we admit it—we can't keep the Law." You see, there is nothing more hypocritical than to pretend that you are living life on a high spiritual plane, that you are living by the Sermon on the Mount and you are keeping God's Law. There is no use pretending.

I wish I could look you in the eye and ask you, "Why don't you admit that you are a lost sinner? Why don't you confess that you do not please God, that you have no capacity for Him? Why don't you come to God as a sinner and trust Christ as your Savior?" He will receive you! ". . . him that cometh to me I will in no wise cast out" (John 6:37). That is the way I came to the Lord. Everybody I have ever met who has been saved has come to Him in that way. Saul of Tarsus came like that. The Ethiopian eunuch came like that. All who have come to Christ have come like that.

But we believe that through the grace of the Lord Jesus Christ we shall be saved, even as they [Acts 15:11].

Simon Peter puts it so nicely. The Jews must be saved in exactly the same way that the Gentiles are saved. I'm pretty sure that Simon Peter still didn't eat pork at this time, but he implies, "I'm not saved because I don't eat pork; I'm saved because I have trusted Christ." He is saved by the grace of God.

Then all the multitude kept silence, and gave audience to Barnabas and Paul, declaring what miracles and wonders God had wrought among the Gentiles by them [Acts 15:12].

What a story they had to tell! I wish I could have sat in on the council of Jerusalem. Especially I wish I could have heard these two men tell their experiences in the Galatian country.

The next man to get up to speak will be James. I want to stop here for a moment to explain that this was not James, the brother of John, as he had already died a martyr's death (Acts 12:2). There is some question as to who this James was. We know that he became the leader of the church in Jerusalem. He has already been mentioned as a leader by Peter in Acts 12:17. This may have been James, the son of Alphaeus, one of the twelve (Matt. 10:3). However, the tradition of the church from the early church fathers has identified this man as James, the half brother of our Lord (Matt. 13:55), the same one who wrote the Epistle of James.

I should stop here to make another remark. I believe that the proper way to study the Book of Acts is to study it along with the Epistles. For example, we have already mentioned the Epistle to the Galatians, and during the study of Acts 13 and 14 would be a good time to read that Epistle. At this point in Acts 15 it would be appropriate to study the Epistle of James.

James is going to sum up the thinking of this council at Jerusalem, and He will put down God's program for the future.

We need to remember that these men stood with their noses pressed right up to the window of the opening of a new dispensation. The church had been brought into existence at Pentecost; it was still very new, in its infancy. Some people still do not understand that we live in the age of grace, the period of the church. So let us not be too critical of these men who stood on the threshold of this new age.

And after they had held their peace, James answered, saying, Men and brethren, hearken unto me [Acts 15:13].

I take it that after Simon Peter spoke and after Paul and Barnabas gave their report, there was silence because no one had anything to say. Even the Judaizers were silenced by the reports of what had taken place.

When James speaks to the crowd on that day, he asks them to "hearken," that is, to really listen. What he has to say is very important. So he means that you and I should listen to him, too. Probably all of us should spend more time listening to God and less time doing the talking. Well, now let's listen.

Simeon hath declared how God at the first did visit the Gentiles, to take out of them a people for his name [Acts 15:14].

James completely agrees with Peter. They state the plan of God for today. Is God saving the whole world? No. Is God bringing in His kingdom? No. Then what is God doing today? He is visiting the Gentiles to take out of them a people for His name. We learn in Revelation that standing before the throne of God there will be those of every tribe and tongue and people and nation. The Word of God is to go out into the world. There will be opposition to it and there will be apostasy, but the Word of God is to go out to all the world because God is calling out a people for His name.

This is why I am so anxious to get out the Word of God. Right now there are people of every color, every clime, every condition, every race, and practically every nation who hear Bible teaching by radio. We broadcast on stations that pretty well circle the globe. Thank God we can use this means to get out the Word of God. What does God do with that Word? He is calling out a people for His name. Not everyone who hears believes the Word. Not everyone accepts the good news of Jesus Christ. But of those who hear, God calls out a people for His name. Underline verse 14 in your Bible—I have it circled in mine. God is visiting the Gentiles to take out of them a people for His name. I am so thankful that He has given me the opportunity to tell people about salvation in the Lord Jesus Christ and to teach them the Word of God.

And to this agree the words of the prophets; as it is written [Acts 15:15].

Do you think this new age is contrary to the teaching of the Old Testament? Well, it is not. The words of the prophets agree to this.

Now James begins to quote a prophet (see Amos 9:11–12). "After this," which in the prophecy is "in that day." What does it mean? After what? After God has called out a people for His name. God today is calling out individuals for His name. They become a part of the church, the body of believers. The day is coming when God will remove His church from this world—this we call the Rapture. It is the next event on the agenda of God. After this—after His church has left the earth—

After this I will return, and will build again the tabernacle of David, which is fallen down; and I will build again the ruins thereof, and I will set it up [Acts 15:16].

The tabernacle of David is fallen down—there's no doubt about that. There is no one around from the line of David. The only One who has that claim is sitting at the right hand of God at this very moment. But God is going to build it again. He is going to send Jesus back. God says to His Son: "But to which of the angels said he at any time, Sit on my right hand, until I make thine enemies thy footstool?" (Heb. 1:13). God is bringing all the enemies of Christ to be put under His feet. The rebellion is going to be over one of these days. Until the day when He sends Jesus back, the Spirit of God is saying, "Kiss the Son, lest he be angry, and ye perish from the way, when his wrath is kindled but a little. Blessed are all they that put their trust in him" (Ps. 2:12).

The program of God is clearly outlined. He is calling a people out of the world now. His second step with the world will be to build again the line of David. That is, he will reestablish the Davidic rule over Israel.

That the residue of men might seek after the Lord, and all the Gentiles, upon whom my name is called, saith the Lord, who doeth all these things [Acts 15:17].

Today He is calling a people out of the Gentiles. However, in that day there will be a great turning to God. This will be after the church has left this world. These are the ones who will enter the kingdom. The "residue of men might seek after the Lord" and "all the Gentiles, upon whom my name is called" will turn to the Lord. This, then, will be the third step in God's program.

Known unto God are all his works from the beginning of the world [Acts 15:18].

James has been doing the summing up. He understands that there is a definite program which God is following. Now James is ready to hand down his decision, and it is a very important decision.

Wherefore my sentence is, that we trouble not them, which from among the Gentiles are turned to God:

But that we write unto them, that they abstain from pollutions of idols, and from fornication, and from things strangled, and from blood [Acts 15:19–20].

The decision is that Gentiles who have turned to God are not to be put under the Mosaic system. However, they are going to ask the Gentiles to do certain things out of courtesy. They will ask them to abstain from pollutions of idols. The reason this is so specifically mentioned will come up again in 1 Corinthians in the section about eating meat. The situation was that the gentile world of that day worshiped idols, and in a city like Corinth, for example, the people would take their best animals and offer them to their pagan gods. They were very clever about this. They would take the animal in and make an offering of it, and the gods, which were "spiritual," ate the "spiritual" animal. Then the people would take the meat and sell it in the meat markets at the heathen temples. That was the place to buy the best steaks in that day—the filet mignon and the porterhouse and New York cuts.

The Gentiles were not offended by this. They had always bought their meat at these markets, and it was not a matter of conscience for them. However, for the Israelite Christian this would be very offensive. They had been brought up and trained not to eat anything that had been offered to an idol. So the thought here is that the Gentile who invites a Jewish brother over for dinner should not offend him by serving him something that had been offered to idols. So this request was not a matter of putting the Gentiles under Mosaic Law. It was a request that they should not do something which would be very offensive to their Jewish brothers.

They were also requested to abstain from fornication. Again, we need to understand the background to see why this is specifically mentioned. Adultery was so common among the Gentiles in that day that the conscience had been dulled. In fact, adultery was actually a part of the religious rite. The Gentiles who had become Christians were to "abstain from fornication."

In America we are going back to paganism today. Folk talk about a new morality. Friend, what they call new morality is old paganism. Our ancestors came out of the forest half naked, eating raw meat, and indulging in gross immorality. There is nothing new about the "new" morality!

Also, the Jerusalem council asked the gentile Christians to abstain from things strangled and from blood, which would be very offensive to their Jewish brothers. This again was a matter of courtesy.

For Moses of old time hath in every city them that preach him, being read in the synagogues every sabbath day [Acts 15:21].

I think we should review what James has said. He fits the church into the program of the prophets although the church is not a subject of prophecy. God is taking out of the Gentiles a people for His name today. Then the program of the prophets will follow.

1. "After this" means after the church is taken out of the world. "I will return" (v. 16) is the second coming of Christ described in Revelation 19.

2. He "will build again the ruins" of the house of David that today has fallen down (v. 16).

3. When Christ returns, there will be a way for the remainder of men to "seek after the Lord" (v. 17).

4. Then *all* the Gentiles will be in the kingdom "in that day" (Amos 9:11).

The important contrast is between "out of them (Gentiles)" (v. 14) and "all the Gentiles" (v. 17).

THE DECISION OF THE COUNCIL IS ANNOUNCED

Then pleased it the apostles and elders, with the whole church, to send chosen men of their own company to Antioch with Paul and Barnabas; namely, Judas surnamed Barsabas, and Silas, chief men among the brethren:

And they wrote letters by them after this manner; The apostles and elders and brethren send greeting unto the brethren which are of the Gentiles in Antioch and Syria and Cilicia [Acts 15:22–23].

There are some new men mentioned here. Silas will be the partner of Paul on the next journey. Notice the love that is demonstrated in this letter. They wrote to the Gentiles who had turned to God and they called them "the brethren which are of the Gentiles."

Forasmuch as we have heard, that certain which went out from us have troubled you with words, subverting your souls, saying, Ye must be circumcised, and keep the law: to whom we gave no such commandment [Acts 15:24].

These people who had gone out, the Judaizers, had no authority from the church in Jerusalem. In fact, we can say that anyone who tries to put a believer under the Law today is not doing it on the authority of the Word of God.

It seemed good unto us, being assembled with one accord, to send chosen men unto you with our beloved Barnabas and Paul [Acts 15:25].

Isn't this a lovely expression?

Men that have hazarded their lives for the name of our Lord Jesus Christ [Acts 15:26].

The church sends out men who have been tested, men who have hazarded their lives. Friend, how much have you suffered for Him? What has it cost you? Have you paid a price in order to get out the Word of God?

We have sent therefore Judas and Silas, who shall also tell you the same things by mouth [Acts 15:27].

You can see that if they had sent only Barnabas and Paul the people might have said, "Well, of course, these two men would bring back that kind of a report." So they send along Judas and Silas in order to confirm the fact that this was the decision of the council.

For it seemed good to the Holy Ghost, and to us, to lay upon you no greater burden than these necessary things [Acts 15:28].

"It seemed good to the Holy Ghost, and to us"—the Holy Spirit was guiding and directing them in this decision.

That ye abstain from meats offered to idols, and from blood, and from things strangled, and from fornication: from which if ye keep yourselves, ye shall do well. Fare ye well [Acts 15:29].

That is the report. That is all they have to say to them. Gentile believers are not required to meet any of the demands of the Mosaic system, but they are to exercise courtesy to those who do—especially in the area of meats offered to idols, and of course they are not to commit fornication.

So when they were dismissed, they came to Antioch: and when they had gathered the multitude together, they delivered the epistle:

Which when they had read, they rejoiced for the consolation [Acts 15:30–31].

There is consolation and comfort in the gospel; there is nothing but condemnation in the Law. The Law condemns. The Law is a mirror. When I look in it, I say, "Oh, McGee, you are ugly! You have fallen short of the glory of God." But the gospel says, "Come on to God. He wants to receive you. He will save you by His grace." It is a comfort, you see.

And Judas and Silas, being prophets also themselves, exhorted the brethren with many words, and confirmed them.

And after they had tarried there a space, they were let go in peace from the brethren unto the apostles.

Notwithstanding it pleased Silas to abide there still [Acts 15:32–34].

It is evident that Paul and Silas got along well together. Silas must have liked Paul and enjoyed working with him. So he stayed there at the church in Antioch. He must have been excited about working with these gentile believers. At any rate, he stayed.

Paul also and Barnabas continued in Antioch, teaching and preaching the word of the Lord, with many others also [Acts 15:35].

Paul and Barnabas were actually the pastors of the church there.

PLANS FOR A SECOND MISSIONARY JOURNEY

And some days after Paul said unto Barnabas, Let us go again and visit our brethren in every city where we have preached the word of the Lord, and see how they do [Acts 15:36].

Paul had a concern for the churches, a genuine concern for the believers. Knowing how fickle the Galatians were, he thought it would be a good idea to go back again and to visit those churches.

And Barnabas determined to take with them John, whose surname was Mark [Acts 15:37].

We know Barnabas as a very generous, gracious fellow. He is eager to give John Mark another chance. But I want to note that when he has made up his mind, he is hardheaded. Remember that both these men were human. Paul and Barnabas each took a stand and would not budge.

But Paul thought not good to take him with them, who departed from them from Pamphylia, and went not with them to the work [Acts 15:38].

Paul had his convictions also. Barnabas wants to take John Mark along, and Paul will not do it. Well, I'm glad these two brethren had this little altercation because it teaches me that these men were human and that even the saints can disagree without being disagreeable. They didn't break up anything. They did not split the church and form two different churches in Antioch. They just disagreed. It's all right to disagree with some of the brethren.

And the contention was so sharp between them, that they departed asunder one from the other: and so Barnabas took Mark, and sailed unto Cyprus [Acts 15:39].

The account does not follow Barnabas any longer. He went to Cyprus and there he had a great ministry. Barnabas had come from Cyprus; it was his home. He had a desire to take the gospel to his own people. We know from tradition that he had a great ministry there, and from Cyprus a great ministry was carried on in North Africa.

At this point Barnabas sails off the pages of the Scriptures. The Bible does not give us information about his ministry. From here on we are going to follow Paul.

And Paul chose Silas, and departed, being recommended by the brethren unto the grace of God.

And he went through Syria and Cilicia, confirming the churches [Acts 15:40–41].

The church now has two great mission projects where before they had only one. Barnabas is going in one direction and Paul is going another. This is God's method. God will use both these men. Paul now has Silas with him, and the brethren recommended them "unto the grace of God."

PAUL'S *SECOND* MISSIONARY JOURNEY

CHAPTER 16

***THEME:** The second missionary journey of Paul*

The final verse of chapter 15 actually told of the beginning of the journey. Paul and Silas "went through Syria and Cilicia, confirming the churches." From there *they* will go up into the Galatian country. *Paul* will visit the Galatian churches because that is where the problem had arisen with the Judaizers. The Epistle to the Galatians is Paul's letter to them, sternly warning them about being led astray by those who are trying to put them under the Mosaic system. It is his strongest declaration and defense of the doctrine of justification by faith. Not only is a sinner saved by grace through faith, but the saved sinner lives by grace. Grace is a way *to* life and a way *of* life.

Again let me suggest that you follow Paul's journey on the map. You will find that traveling with Paul is a very thrilling experience. On this second missionary journey we will go with him to Europe (after he has received the vision of the man in Macedonia). We will see that he arrives in Philippi where he ends up in the local jail. At midnight Paul and Silas pray and sing praises! An earthquake shakes the jail, the doors are opened, and the jailer opens his heart to receive Christ as Savior.

PAUL REVISITS THE CHURCHES OF GALATIA

Then came he to Derbe and Lystra: and, behold, a certain disciple was there, named Timotheus, the son of a certain woman, which was a Jewess, and believed; but his father was a Greek:

Which was well reported of by the brethren that were at Lystra and Iconium [Acts 16:1 2].

Paul first comes to Derbe, then over to Lystra where he finds this young man Timotheus. Paul knew his mother and his grandmother, and he had turned this young man to the Lord on his first trip. So Paul takes him with him. The team is now Paul, Silas, and Timothy.

Him would Paul have to go forth with him; and took and circumcised him because of the Jews which were in those quarters: for they knew all that his father was a Greek [Acts 16:3].

I want to note carefully the method of the apostle Paul. When he went up to Jerusalem, he took along Titus, a Gentile, who wasn't circumcised—and Paul wasn't about to have him circumcised. However, now Paul wants to take along Timothy as a fellow missionary. He wants Timothy to go out to reach people for Christ. Since he doesn't want any kind of argument or any reason for offense, he has Timothy circumcised. This is not because there is any merit in circumcision, but because he doesn't want it to be an issue. This is what Paul wrote in 1 Corinthians 9:19–20: "For though I be free from all men, yet have I made myself servant unto all, that I might gain the more. And unto the Jews I became as a Jew, that I might gain the Jews; to them that are under the law, as under the law, that I might gain them that are under the law." Paul did this in order to break down all arguments.

Sometimes people come to me and say they want to join a certain church but that church has a different idea of baptism than they hold. They ask if they should be baptized and join the church anyway. So I ask them, "Is the church a good Bible-teaching church? Does it teach salvation only and alone through faith in the Lord Jesus Christ? Is it a place where you can serve, and be blessed, and grow in grace and in the knowledge of the truth?" If they can answer yes to these questions, then I tell them to go ahead and be baptized and affiliate with that church. There are fundamentals of faith in which there can be no deviation. However, there are forms and rituals which are not essential to salvation, and I believe there is a great deal of elasticity in these areas. This was Paul's feeling. Certainly circumcision had no bearing on Timothy's salvation, but the rite was performed so that the ministry of Timothy with the Jews would not be handicapped.

And as they went through the cities, they delivered them the decrees for to keep, that were ordained of the apostles and elders which were at Jerusalem.

And so were the churches established in the faith, and increased in number daily [Acts 16:4–5].

Paul has another tremendous ministry in Galatia. Not only does he visit the churches which had been founded the first time, but multitudes in other places turn to Christ. New churches are formed and there is an increase in number daily.

PAUL GOES TO PHILIPPI

Now when they had gone throughout Phrygia and the region of Galatia, and were forbidden of the Holy Ghost to preach the word in Asia [Acts 16:6].

Galatia includes all this area. I am of the opinion that Paul moved into the northern part of the country at this particular point. The province of Asia is down south where Ephesus is. In fact, Ephesus was the chief city of the province of Asia. Paul may have been planning to make a circuit through Asia Minor. This was a heavily populated area in that day, and it was really the center of Greek culture. This was a great commercial area, a great political area, a great educational area. Paul would make a great circle by going through the Galatian country, then Phrygia, then south into the province of Asia, and then back again to Antioch to report to the home church.

The Spirit of God had something else in mind. We are told that the Holy Spirit forbade him to preach the Word down in Asia. That is really amazing, isn't it? Paul wanted to go there, and the Spirit of God wanted the Word of God given out, but the Spirit wanted Paul in a different place at this time. So Paul naturally thought that if he could not go south, he would go north. Bithynia was in the north, along the Black Sea. That also was a large population center, and there was a very heavy concentration of Hebrews in that area. This section is in Turkey today.

After they were come to Mysia, they assayed to go into Bithynia: but the Spirit suffered them not [Acts 16:7].

The Spirit forbade them to go south into the province of Asia. Then the Spirit of God forbade them to go north into Bithynia. He has come from the east. Where will he go? Well, there is only one direction left and that is west. You see, it was not Horace Greeley of *The New York Tribune* who first said, "Go west, young man, go west." Instead it was the Spirit of God speaking to the apostle Paul!

So Paul kept going west until he came to Troas. He had to stop there because from that point he would need a ship to continue. Paul couldn't imagine what he was to do or where he was to go from that point.

And they passing by Mysia came down to Troas [Acts 16:8].

I think that if we had met Paul during the time of his delay in Troas, we could have asked him, "Paul, where are you going?" I'm sure his reply would have been, "I don't know." I'm afraid our next statement would have been something like this: "Now brother Paul, do you mean that the great Apostle of the Gentiles doesn't know where he is going next? Surely you must know the will of God for your life." Then we would have sat down for a nice long lecture on how to determine the will of God in his life. My, I've read so many books on that subject—it's too bad Paul didn't have one of those books with him at that time! Paul does not know the will of God. Why? Because the *Spirit of God* is leading him. Paul is simply waiting. It is going to take a mighty movement to get Paul out of Asia and move him over into Europe.

And a vision appeared to Paul in the night; There stood a man of Macedonia, and prayed him, saying, Come over into Macedonia, and help us [Acts 16:9].

This is Paul's call into Macedonia. Now Macedonia is across the Aegean Sea, over in Europe. Paul is in Asia. The gospel is going to cross from Asia into Europe. The Spirit of God is moving him in that direction.

I do not know why Paul was not moved east to China. All I know is that the Spirit of God moved him west to Europe. I thank God that this is the direction he went. At that particular time my ancestors, from one side of the family, were roaming in the forests of Germany. They were pagan and they were evil, worshiping all kinds of idols. They were a low, heathen people. The other side of my family came from Scotland and perhaps my ancestors were already in Scotland at that time or came there a little later. At any rate, I am told they were the dirtiest, filthiest savages that have ever been on the topside of this earth. I thank God the gospel went to Europe to reach my people over there.

Now maybe you are smiling, thinking that your ancestors were very superior to mine. Well, you can wipe that smile off your face because your ancestors probably were living in the cave right next door to mine! They were just as dirty and just as filthy as mine were. Thank God the gospel crossed over into Europe. This was a great and significant crossing.

And after he had seen the vision, immediately we endeavoured to go into Macedonia, assuredly gathering that the Lord had called us for to preach the gospel unto them [Acts 16:10].

Note it says "we endeavored to go." We have never had "we" before. It has always been "they" or "them" or "he" or "him." What about "we"? Well, Dr. Luke has now joined the party. It is really quite a party now—in fact, it is a quartet. There may have been others along also, but we have four who are named: Paul, Silas, Timothy, and Dr. Luke. This is quite a delegation that crossed over into Europe.

Therefore loosing from Troas, we came with a straight course to Samothracia, and the next day to Neapolis [Acts 16:11].

Neapolis is just inland a little from the coast.

And from thence to Philippi, which is the chief city of that part of Macedonia, and a colony: and we were in that city abiding certain days [Acts 16:12].

Philippi was a colony in Macedonia, which means it was a Roman colony. This would be where the Roman governor resided. These people had Roman customs and they spoke Latin. It would be a city where they would "do as the Romans do."

This is their first destination in Europe. Paul went to a strategic center to begin his ministry in Europe. That alone makes the church in Philippi a remarkable church. For other reasons, which we will learn when we get to the Epistle to the Philippians, we will see that this church was close to the heart of Paul. This was the church which loved him; and Paul loved this church. There were wonderful saints in this church, as we shall see.

PAUL'S MINISTRY IN PHILIPPI

And on the sabbath we went out of the city by a river side, where prayer was wont to be made; and we sat down, and spake unto the women which resorted thither [Acts 16:13].

Just outside the city, down by the river, there was a prayer meeting. I wonder whether that prayer meeting had anything to do with Paul coming over to Europe and the vision of the man of Macedonia! We will find that the "man of Macedonia" is a woman by the name of Lydia who was holding this prayer meeting.

And a certain woman named Lydia, a seller of purple, of the city of Thyatira, which worshipped God, heard us: whose heart the Lord opened, that she attended unto the things which were spoken of Paul [Acts 16:14].

Thyatira is over in Asia Minor. It is the place where one of the seven churches was located which received admonition from our Lord in the second chapter of the Book of Revelation. This woman had come from over there. She worshiped the living and true God, but she had very little knowledge.

Lydia was a remarkable person. She was a dominant person and a leader. Apparently she was the leader of the prayer meeting. She will be the first convert to Christ in Europe.

And when she was baptized, and her household, she besought us, saying, If ye have judged me to be faithful to the Lord, come into my house, and abide there. And she constrained us [Acts 16:15].

We do not know anything about Mr. Lydia, but he must have been around there somewhere. There are families like that, you know, where the woman is the dominant one in the family. Apparently that was the way it was in the family of Lydia. Thank God she was that kind of woman because her entire household turned to God through her witness. And now we find Paul and his group staying at her home and boarding there. I would assume she was a person of means and was able to take care of them.

And it came to pass, as we went to prayer, a certain damsel possessed with a spirit of divination met us, which brought her masters much gain by soothsaying [Acts 16:16].

Don't think this was just foolish superstition. This girl was possessed by a demon. We are seeing a resurgence of demonism in our own day. I have before me now a letter from a Christian woman in El Paso, Texas. She got tied up in spiritism by just fooling around with it, not thinking that it was dangerous. She has quite a story. It was hearing the Word of God through our radio program that delivered her from it. She cried out to God, and He delivered her. Demonism is a reality. This girl in Paul's day was demon possessed. She was a slave girl and her masters were using her to make a big profit. The Mafia had already begun in those days.

The same followed Paul and us, and cried, saying, These men are the servants of the most high God, which shew unto us the way of salvation.

And this did she many days. But Paul, being grieved, turned and said to the spirit, I command thee in the name of Jesus Christ to come out of her. And he came out the same hour.

And when her masters saw that the hope of their gains was gone, they caught Paul and Silas, and drew them into the marketplace unto the rulers [Acts 16:17–19].

Paul was able to cast out the demon in the name of the Lord Jesus Christ. This dried up the profit her masters were making, and you know that, if you touch a man's pocketbook, he will begin to move. So now these men really turn against Paul and his group.

And brought them to the magistrates, saying, These men, being Jews, do exceedingly trouble our city,

And teach customs, which are not lawful for us to receive, neither to observe, being Romans [Acts 16:20–21].

Remember that Philippi was a Roman colony and practiced Roman idolatry. Paul and his men were charged with trying to change things. Of course the real issue was that the girl's masters had lost their source of income.

And the multitude rose up together against them: and the magistrates rent off their clothes, and commanded to beat them.

And when they had laid many stripes upon them, they cast them into prison, charging the jailer to keep them safely:

Who, having received such a charge, thrust them into the inner prison, and made their feet fast in the stocks [Acts 16:22–24].

These men are beaten, their backs are lacerated, and they are locked into the stocks.

And at midnight Paul and Silas prayed, and sang praises unto God: and the prisoners heard them [Acts 16:25].

What a wonderful thing it is that these men were singing praises unto God while they were in such a miserable situation. No wonder the doors were shaken loose!

And suddenly there was a great earthquake, so that the foundations of the prison were shaken: and immediately all the doors were opened, and every one's bands were loosed.

And the keeper of the prison awaking out of his sleep, and seeing the prison doors open, he drew out his sword, and

would have killed himself, supposing that the prisoners had been fled [Acts 16:26–27].

Let's look at this Philippian jailer for a moment. He was responsible for those prisoners. He naturally assumed that if the doors were open and the chains lying loose, the prisoners would be gone. He would be responsible for their escape and would have to forfeit his own life. So he stands there, poised, ready to fall on his own sword. When a man is in a position like that, he thinks about eternity. This man did just that, as his question to Paul indicates.

But Paul cried with a loud voice, saying, Do thyself no harm: for we are all here.

Then he called for a light, and sprang in, and came trembling, and fell down before Paul and Silas,

And brought them out, and said, Sirs, what must I do to be saved? [Acts 16:28–30].

He had looked into eternity. He knew that he was a lost man.

And they said, Believe on the Lord Jesus Christ, and thou shalt be saved, and thy house [Acts 16:31].

How can a man be saved? By believing on the Lord Jesus Christ. Could he believe for someone else? No. Believe on the Lord Jesus Christ and thou shalt be saved, and if thy household believes on the Lord Jesus Christ, they shall be saved also. That is the meaning here.

And they spake unto him the word of the Lord, and to all that were in his house.

And he took them the same hour of the night, and washed their stripes; and was baptized, he and all his, straightway [Acts 16:32–33].

What a difference! He had put the stripes on these men. Now he washes their stripes. He is a changed man.

And when he had brought them into his house, he set meat before them, and rejoiced, believing in God with all his house [Acts 16:34].

All in one night they were flogged, thrown into jail, freed by the direct intervention of God, and now they are being royally entertained in the home of these rejoicing young converts!

And when it was day, the magistrates sent the sergeants, saying, Let those men go.

And the keeper of the prison told this saying to Paul, The magistrates have sent to let you go: now therefore depart, and go in peace [Acts 16:35–36].

You see, they realize that what they had done was illegal. Now they are issuing orders to free the prisoners and get them out of town. However, Paul objects. He says that he will not leave under such circumstances.

But Paul said unto them, They have beaten us openly uncondemned, being Romans, and have cast us into prison; and now do they thrust us out privily? nay verily; but let them come themselves and fetch us out [Acts 16:37].

Of course Paul's reason for insisting upon a public recognition of their innocence was to protect the new believers whom he would soon be leaving there in Philippi.

And the sergeants told these words unto the magistrates: and they feared, when they heard that they were Romans.

And they came and besought them, and brought them out, and desired them to depart out of the city.

And they went out of the prison, and entered into the house of Lydia: and when they had seen the brethren, they comforted them, and departed [Acts 16:38–40].

CHAPTER 17

THEME: *The second missionary journey of Paul continued (Paul in Thessalonica, Berea, and Athens)*

REMARKS

In this chapter we continue with Paul on his second missionary journey. In chapter 16 we were with him when he crossed over into Europe, a memorable, significant, revolutionary crossing. It brought the gospel to the ancestors of many of us, who were by no means a superior people. Actually, God chooses the weak things of this world just to let the world know that it is all because of His sovereign grace and not because of merit. We thank Him for sending the gospel over into Europe.

We went with Paul first to Philippi where he received some rough treatment. Yet, a little church came into existence in that town. When we study the Epistle to that church, we will find that it was closer to the apostle Paul than any other church or any other group of believers.

Now he continues on his journey. I hope you will follow this on the map. You will notice that he goes to Thessalonica and Berea, still traveling westward into Macedonia, then south to Athens. Thessalonica will be his next significant stop for missionary activity.

PAUL'S MINISTRY IN THESSALONICA

Now when they had passed through Amphipolis and Apollonia, they came to Thessalonica, where was a synagogue of the Jews [Acts 17:1].

As we have noted before, Paul used the synagogue as a springboard to get into a city or a community. This would lead him to the devout Jews of the city, and some of those Jews would believe. Never did all of them believe, but some of them did. In fact, most of them would reject him and this would push him right out to the Gentiles. Then some of the Gentiles believed. This is how a church would come into existence, a local church composed of Jews and Gentiles.

Amphipolis was also called "Nine Ways," which name suggests its importance both strategically and commercially. Most cities are built on the pattern of a square, but this was like a roundhouse and the wall around it was round. It was an important station on the Via Egnatia, a Roman road which was the prominent thoroughfare through that area. It was five hundred miles from the Hellespont to Dyrrhachium on the Adriatic by this road. This would be the highway which the Roman army would use. This was the route the traders would travel. And now here come some missionaries on this road going to Thessalonica. Apollonia was another town on this same Egnatian Road.

Thessalonica was thirty-eight miles west of Apollonia on the Egnatian Road. It was inland but it was a seaport because three rivers flowed into the sea from there. It was a prominent city of that day, another Roman colony. Cassander rebuilt it in about 315 B.C. and it is thought that he named it after Thessalonica, the stepsister of Alexander the Great. There are some warm springs there and the earlier name of the town was Therma or Therme. Cassander was one of the generals of Alexander the Great, and he took over the rule of that area after the death of Alexander. At the time of Paul, however, the city was a Roman colony.

And Paul, as his manner was, went in unto them, and three sabbath days reasoned with them out of the scriptures,

Opening and alleging, that Christ must needs have suffered, and risen again from the dead; and that this Jesus, whom I preach unto you, is Christ [Acts 17:2–3].

Paul followed his usual custom of first preaching in the synagogue. He was there only three sabbaths, which means that he could not have been there longer than a month. In that limited period of time he did his missionary work. Believers came to Christ, a local church was organized, and Paul taught them. In that brief time he taught them all the great doctrines of Scripture, including the doctrine of the Rapture of the church—we know this from his First Epistle to the Thessalonians which was the first Epistle that Paul wrote. Paul had quite a ministry there in one month's time!

Now note his message. He was "opening and alleging"—that is, from the Old Testament Scriptures—"that Christ must needs have suffered." He preached the death and resurrection of Jesus Christ, showing that this was necessary, as set forth in the Old Testament. Friend, you will not find a message given in the Book of Acts either by Peter or by Paul in which the Resurrection is not the heart of the message.

Today we find so often that the Resurrection

just doesn't seem to be the heart of the message. What we talk about today is the cross—even in fundamental circles. But, my friend, we have a living Christ today. Someone has put it this way: "There is a Man in the glory but the church has lost sight of Him." The Lord Jesus Christ is yonder at God's right hand at this very moment. That is very important. It is one thing to talk about the historical death of Christ nineteen hundred years ago and His resurrection on the third day, but the question is: How are you related to it? That was Paul's great theme in the Galatian epistle. Is it meaningful to you that Christ died and that He rose again? Are you related today to that living Christ? How has this been meshed and geared into your life?

Today we have conservatism in the church and we have liberalism in the church and, very candidly, neither group seems to be getting through to *Him*. Why not? Well, because every Sunday should be an Easter—on the first day of the week He came back from the dead! It is important to mention the resurrection of Christ because we are talking about the Man in the glory.

Unfortunately, that just doesn't seem to be the emphasis. Pastors don't emphasize it because seminaries don't emphasize it. Take down any theology book and study it—Strong's, Shedd's, Thornwall's, Hodge's, and you will find that all of them have a long section on the death of Christ. That's very important; thank God they have a long section on that. But they have a short section, just a few pages on the Resurrection. I think they missed the boat there. I think they should have put in a long section about the resurrection of Christ. That was the basis of New Testament preaching. I'm emphasizing this because it is very important. Paul was in Thessalonica only three Sabbath days, and the resurrection of Christ was his message.

Notice their reception of Him.

And some of them believed, and consorted with Paul and Silas; and of the devout Greeks a great multitude, and of the chief women not a few [Acts 17:4].

Some of them believed. That always happens when you give out the Word of God. Some of them believe. Also some of them won't believe. The minority believe; the majority will not.

When Dr. Luke says "of the chief women not a few," he is using his usual understatement and means that a large number of prominent women came to the Lord. How wonderful!

But the Jews which believed not, moved with envy, took unto them certain lewd fellows of the baser sort, and gathered a company, and set all the city on an uproar, and assaulted the house of Jason, and sought to bring them out to the people [Acts 17:5].

Unfortunately, we also have some "lewd fellows of the baser sort" in our churches today.

And when they found them not, they drew Jason and certain brethren unto the rulers of the city, crying, These that have turned the world upside down are come hither also [Acts 17:6].

Now don't put that down as an oratorical gesture or hyperbole. When they said that these men were turning the world upside down, that is exactly what they meant. When Christianity penetrated that old Roman Empire it was a revolution. It had a tremendous effect.

Today we don't see much revolution except in the wrong direction. It's too bad we can't have a great revolution of turning back to the Lord Jesus Christ and to the Word of God. Our country is a country filled with hypocrisy. We pretend that we are a Christian nation. We pretend that our leaders are Christian, that all the politicians are Christians, that everyone is a Christian. Friend, we are one of the most pagan nations this world has ever known. Christianity today is mostly a pretense. We need to recognize that we need to get back to the Word of God and to the living Christ. How important that is!

Whom Jason hath received: and these all do contrary to the decrees of Caesar, saying that there is another king, one Jesus.

And they troubled the people and the rulers of the city, when they heard these things.

And when they had taken security of Jason, and of the other, they let them go [Acts 17:7–9].

Remember that this was a Roman colony, which was operated according to Caesar's dictates. "They had taken security of Jason" means that he had to make bond.

PAUL'S MINISTRY AT BEREA

And the brethren immediately sent away Paul and Silas by night unto Berea: who coming thither went into the synagogue of the Jews [Acts 17:10].

You would think that all this would dampen the enthusiasm of Paul, that it would slow him down. It didn't slow him one bit and he is still going. He goes to Berea, which is a town down closer to the coast.

These were more noble than those in Thessalonica, in that they received the word with all readiness of mind, and searched the scriptures daily, whether those things were so [Acts 17:11].

These people were reasonable. They searched the Scriptures, and there came into existence a church in Berea. We don't hear much about that church. It is interesting that the strongest churches arose where the persecution was the greatest. One of the troubles today is that the church is not being persecuted. In fact, the church is just taken for granted. The average Christian is just a person to be taken for granted. It wasn't that way in the first century.

Therefore many of them believed; also of honourable women which were Greeks, and of men, not a few [Acts 17:12].

Here goes Dr. Luke again with his diminutive "not a few." Why doesn't he say a great crowd of men and honorable women believed? When he says, "Not a few," he means it was a multitude.

But when the Jews of Thessalonica had knowledge that the word of God was preached of Paul at Berea, they came thither also, and stirred up the people.

And then immediately the brethren sent away Paul to go as it were to the sea: but Silas and Timotheus abode there still [Acts 17:13–14].

Paul continues on his way without the other members of his team.

PAUL'S MINISTRY AT ATHENS

And they that conducted Paul brought him unto Athens: and receiving a commandment unto Silas and Timotheus for to come to him with all speed, they departed [Acts 17:15].

Paul goes to Athens. He will wait for Silas and Timotheus there. He probably had said to them, "You go back to check on the believers in Thessalonica and see how the church is progressing there, and check on the believers in Berea; then join me in Athens."

Now while Paul waited for them at Athens, his spirit was stirred in him, when he saw the city wholly given to idolatry [Acts 17:16].

Athens was the cultural center of the world. In fact, when one thinks of Athens, one thinks about culture. Yet it was a city filled with idolatry.

Therefore disputed he in the synagogue with the Jews, and with the devout persons, and in the market daily with them that met with him [Acts 17:17].

When I was in Athens, I went down to that market. It is right at the foot of the Acropolis. I can imagine Paul walking up and down there. He was a tentmaker, you know, and I think he sold a few tents while he was there. While he was selling the tents, he was talking about the Lord Jesus Christ. The people began to get interested.

Then certain philosophers of the Epicureans, and of the Stoics, encountered him. And some said, What will this babbler say? other some, He seemeth to be a setter forth of strange gods: because he preached unto them Jesus and the resurrection [Acts 17:18].

The philosophy of the Epicureans was more or less hedonistic. The Stoics, a group who believed in restraint, were what we today call stoical. The Epicureans believed that you go the limit, and in that way you could overcome the flesh. They thought that you should give the flesh all that it wants. If it wants liquor, drink all you can hold. Concerning sex, believe me, the Epicureans could really join in the "new morality," which was nothing new for them. By contrast, the Stoics believed that the body should be held under control.

Philosophers of both groups come to Paul to hear what he has to say. Paul has been doing a lot of talking and they call him a babbler. His subject is something new to them. Jesus and the idea of resurrection are to them "strange gods."

I hear people say today that Paul got his idea from Platonism. They say he didn't really believe in the bodily resurrection but in a platonic idea of a spiritual resurrection. It was more or less the influence of an individual permeating through society. This is the life after death. One still hears that type of thing today. It is found in liberalism, and it is nothing in the world but old Greek philosophy. But these Greeks, philosophers as they were, didn't quite understand Paul. I think Paul was a little too deep for them. Philosophy had gone to seed in Athens at this particular time. However, they wanted to hear him.

And they took him, and brought him unto Areopagus, saying, May we know what this new doctrine, whereof thou speakest, is? [Acts 17:19].

The Areopagus is a very peculiar formation of rock on top of which the Parthenon and the buildings connected with it stand. Frankly, it is a very lovely setting, beautiful buildings and beautiful statues, but a city wholly given over to idolatry. It is up from the market place of the city and Paul is brought there to speak. Probably every preacher who visits there reads Paul's sermon from the top of Mars' Hill. When I was there another preacher began to read it, and since I didn't like the way he was reading it, I went way over to the other side of the rock. I sat with my Bible and read it silently. It was a thrilling experience.

Now these Greek philosophers say to him, "May we know what this new doctrine, whereof thou speakest is?" They want to know more about it. They are completely in the dark. They are worse off than the Galatians or the people in Philippi and Thessalonica. Why? Because they think they know something. The very hardest people in the world to reach with the Word of God and the gospel are church members because they think they don't need it. They think the gospel is for the man on skid row and for some of their friends. Some church members can be mean and sinful and yet not recognize they really need a Savior, not only to save them from sin, but also to make their lives count for God.

For thou bringest certain strange things to our ears: we would know therefore what these things mean.

(For all the Athenians and strangers which were there spent their time in nothing else, but either to tell, or to hear some new thing.) [Acts 17:20–21].

In this same way America is going to seed today. Have you ever listened to the talk shows? They are boring to tears. Everyone is trying to come up with something new. Each one is trying to say something novel. They try so hard to say something smart, something sophisticated; yet it is the same old story. Athens tried the same thing.

There must have been quite a bunch of loafers back in Athens. They didn't work—they didn't do anything. They just talked, propounding new theories and new ideas. The human family seems to reach that place of sophistication. They think they know something when they don't. They don't know the most important fact in the whole universe.

There are those who say that Paul failed on Mars' Hill, that he fell flat on his face at Athens. I totally disagree with that. I believe this was one of the greatest messages that Paul ever preached.

Then Paul stood in the midst of Mars' hill, and said, Ye men of Athens, I perceive that in all things ye are too superstitious [Acts 17:22].

He begins his message quite formally, "Ye men of Athens." Then he says, "I perceive . . . ye are too superstitious." The word *superstitious* is wholly inadequate to say what Paul really means. He is saying that he perceives they are in all things too religious. The Athenians were very religious. Athens was filled with idols. There was no end to the pantheon of gods which the Athenians and the Greeks had. There were gods small and gods great; they had a god for practically everything. That is what Paul is saying. They were too religious.

I sometimes hear people ask, "Why should we send missionaries to foreign countries? Those people have their religion." I suppose that when Paul went down to Athens, somebody said, "Why are you going down there? They have religion." I am sure Paul would have answered, "That's their problem; they have too much religion." A preacher friend of mine said many years ago, "When I came to Christ, I lost my religion." There are a great many folk in our churches today who need to lose their religion so they can find Christ. That is the great problem. Some folk say, "People are too bad to be saved." The real problem is that people are too good to be saved. They think they are religious and worthy and good. My friend, we are to take the gospel to all because all men are lost without Christ, which is the reason Paul went to Athens. The Athenians needed to hear the message of the gospel.

Notice that in Athens Paul did not go to a synagogue. He had no springboard in Athens. He begins his masterly address to "Ye men of Athens." After he makes the observation that they are too religious, he continues:

For as I passed by, and beheld your devotions, I found an altar with this inscription, TO THE UNKNOWN GOD. Whom therefore ye ignorantly worship, him declare I unto you [Acts 17:23].

"I . . . beheld your devotions." He saw their objects of worship. He noted their altars and their idols and their temples. In fact, that very beautiful temple called the Parthenon was a temple built to Athena, the virgin goddess of the Athenians. There were idols all around. Paul said, "I observed all of this, and amidst the idols I found an altar inscribed to the unknown god."

Now an altar to the unknown god could mean that the Athenians were broad-minded. They didn't want to leave anyone out. If someone had come to Athens and said, "How is it you don't have an altar to my god?" they would have answered, "Well, this altar is really to your god." That way any stranger could come to worship at the altar to the unknown god, believing it was built for his god.

Or it could mean that they recognized there is a God whom they did not know. Many pagan folk recognize that behind their idolatry is a living and true God. They know nothing about Him, and they do not know how to approach Him. They have traditions that back in the dim and distant past their ancestors did worship Him. This could have been the case with the Athenians.

Paul uses this as the springboard for his message. He says he wants to talk to them about this unknown God. He says he wants to tell them about the God whom they don't know. Perhaps that is not as diplomatic as his first approach. After all, the Athenians thought they knew everything. This crowd of philosophers met in Athens and talked back and forth, as philosophers do on college campuses today. And now Paul begins to talk to them about the God they do not know. Who is He? Well, first of all, He is the God of creation.

God that made the world and all things therein, seeing that he is Lord of heaven and earth, dwelleth not in temples made with hands [Acts 17:24].

God had made very clear all the way through the Old Testament—even when He gave to Israel the pattern for the tabernacle and the temple—that He did not dwell in one geographical spot. Solomon acknowledged this in his prayer at the dedication of the temple: "But will God indeed dwell on the earth? behold, the heaven and heaven of heavens cannot contain thee; how much less this house that I have builded?" (1 Kings 8:27). These men in the Old Testament recognized that God the Creator, the living God, could not live in a building that had been made by man. Man lives in a universe that God has made. Why does man get the idea that he can build a building for God to live in?

Neither is worshipped with men's hands, as though he needed any thing, seeing he giveth to all life, and breath, and all things [Acts 17:25].

Here is a masterly stroke by Paul. He tells them,"God doesn't need anything from you. You built an altar to Him; you bring offerings to feed Him"—they wanted this unknown God to know that they were thinking of Him. Now Paul says, "God doesn't need anything from you! God is on the giving end. He gives you life. He gives you your breath. He has given you the sun, the moon, and the stars. He has given you all things." These Athenians worshiped the sun. They said that Apollo came dragging his chariot across the sky every day. Paul says that the sun is something that God has made, and it is a gift for you. The Creator is the living God. He is the One who has given you everything. By the way, He gives you salvation also. He not only gives you physical things but also gives you spiritual gifts.

And hath made of one blood all nations of men for to dwell on all the face of the earth, and hath determined the times before appointed, and the bounds of their habitation [Acts 17:26].

So much has been made of this "one blood" business that I think we need to dissipate any wrong notions here. A better translation is, "He made from one every nation of mankind." God has made one humanity. This verse is not talking about brotherhood. The only brotherhood which Scripture knows is the brotherhood of those who are in Christ Jesus. Perhaps I should amend that by saying there is a brotherhood of sin. We all are sinners. Paul's statement that God "hath determined the times before appointed, and the bounds of their habitation" is fascinating.

Not only is He the God who created the universe and who created human beings, but it is interesting to note that He also put them in certain geographical locations.

My doctor is a cancer specialist and he has told me to stay out of the sun here in California because I am a blonde. There seems to be even a medical reason why God put the darker races where the sun shines and put the light-skinned races up north where there is not so much sun. So some of us who are blonde and light-skinned need to be very careful about too much exposure to the sun. God is the One who has determined the geographical locations for

His creatures. I guess some of my ancestors should have stayed where they belonged. Maybe I'm kind of out of place here in California, but I'm glad to be here and I try to be careful about protecting myself from too much sunshine. Now that is just a little sideline as an illustration.

God has put nations in certain places. It is interesting that the thing that has produced the wars of the past is that nations don't want to stay where they belong; they want someone else's territory. That has been the ultimate cause for every war that has ever been fought.

That they should seek the Lord, if haply they might feel after him, and find him, though he be not far from every one of us [Acts 17:27].

This phrase "feel after him" has the idea of groping after Him. Man is not really searching for the living and true God, but he is searching for a god. He is willing to put up an idol and worship it. Man is not necessarily looking for the living and true God, but he is on a search.

For in him we live, and move, and have our being; as certain also of your own poets have said, For we are also his offspring [Acts 17:28].

He does not call them sons of God but the offspring of God. He is referring to creation and the relationship to God through creation. By the way, this is not pantheism that he is stating here. He is not saying that everything is God. He says that in God we live and move and have our being but that God is beyond this created universe.

Paul quotes to them from their own poets. One of the poets he quoted was Arastus who lived about 270 B.C. He was a Stoic from Cilicia. He began a poem with an invocation to Zeus in which he said that "we too are his offspring." Cleanthes was another poet who lived about 300 B.C. He also wrote a hymn to Zeus and speaks of the fact that "we are his offspring." Paul means, of course, that we are God's creatures.

Forasmuch then as we are the offspring of God, we ought not to think that the Godhead is like unto gold, or silver, or stone, graven by art and man's device [Acts 17:29].

In other words, he says we ought not to be idolaters. He has shown God to be the Creator. Now he will present Him as the Redeemer.

And the times of this ignorance God winked at; but now commandeth all men everywhere to repent [Acts 17:30].

There was a time when God shut His eyes to paganism. Now light has come into the world. God asks men everywhere to turn to Him. Light creates responsibility. Now God is commanding all men everywhere to repent.

He has presented God as the Creator in His past work. He shows God as the Redeemer in His present work. Now he shows God as the Judge in His future work.

Because he hath appointed a day, in the which he will judge the world in righteousness by that man whom he hath ordained; whereof he hath given assurance unto all men, in that he hath raised him from the dead [Acts 17:31].

When God judges, it will be right. Judgment will be through a Judge who has nail-pierced hands, the One who has been raised from the dead. Paul always presents the resurrection of Jesus Christ. The resurrection of Jesus Christ from the dead is a declaration to all men. It is by this that God assures all men there will be a judgment.

And when they heard of the resurrection of the dead, some mocked: and others said, We will hear thee again of this matter [Acts 17:32].

Do you know why they mocked? Because Platonism denied the resurrection of the dead. That was one of the marks of Platonism. It denied the physical resurrection. When you hear people today talk about a *spiritual* resurrection but denying the *physical* resurrection, you are hearing Platonic philosophy rather than scriptural teaching. Paul taught the physical resurrection from the dead. So when they heard of the resurrection of the dead, some mocked.

So Paul departed from among them [Acts 17:33].

Some critics have said that Paul failed at Athens. He didn't fail, friend. There will always be those who mock at the gospel. But there will also be those who believe.

Howbeit certain men clave unto him, and believed: among the which was Dionysius the Areopagite, and a woman named Damaris, and others with them [Acts 17:34].

There was quite an aggregation of converts in the city of Athens. When Paul went to a place and preached the gospel, he had converts. He didn't fail. He succeeded. Wherever the Word of God is preached, there will be those who will listen and believe.

CHAPTER 18

THEME: *The second missionary journey of Paul continued (Paul in Corinth; Apollos in Ephesus)*

We are still on the second missionary journey of Paul. He is in Athens alone waiting for Timothy and Silas to come and join him and to bring reports from the churches in Berea and in Thessalonica. After his missionary thrust in Athens Paul goes on his journey to Corinth.

THE MINISTRY OF PAUL AT CORINTH

After these things Paul departed from Athens, and came to Corinth [Acts 18:1].

I have made the trip from Athens to Corinth by bus. Paul probably walked it. It would take a long time to walk that distance although it would be a beautiful walk. I enjoyed the scenery more since I was riding than I would have if I had been walking, I assure you. It goes past the site where the Battle of Salamis was fought at sea. This is where the Persian fleet was destroyed. There are other historical places along that way before arriving at Corinth.

In our study of the Epistle to the Corinthians, we will see the reason Paul wrote as he did to the believers at Corinth.

For now let me say that the city of Corinth was probably the most wicked city of that day. It was the Hollywood and the Las Vegas of the Roman Empire. It was the place where you could go to live it up. Sex and drink and all other sensual pleasures were there. In Corinth today one can see the remains of a great Roman bath. That is where they went to sober up. In the distance is the temple that was dedicated to Aphrodite (or Venus) in which there were a thousand so-called vestal virgins. They were anything but virgins; they were prostitutes—sex was a religion. Corinth was one of the most wicked cities of the day. Also there were two tremendous theatres there. People came from all over the empire to the city of Corinth.

Paul came to Corinth on his second missionary journey and again on his third journey. I believe it was here where Paul had one of his most effective ministries. It is my judgment that in Corinth and in Ephesus Paul had his greatest ministries. Ephesus was a religious center; Corinth was a sin center. Both cities were great commercial centers.

Now notice what Paul does on his first visit to Corinth.

And found a certain Jew named Aquila, born in Pontus, lately come from Italy, with his wife Priscilla; (because that Claudius had commanded all Jews to depart from Rome:) and came unto them [Acts 18:2].

In the city of Corinth he found this Jewish couple, recently come from Rome. The reason they had left Rome was because of anti-Semitism which had rolled like a wave over the earth. During the days of the Roman Empire this happened several times. At this time Claudius commanded all Jews to leave Rome. Among those who got out of Rome was a very wonderful couple, Aquila and Priscilla.

And because he was of the same craft, he abode with them, and wrought: for by their occupation they were tentmakers [Acts 18:3].

Aquila had come there because they were in business. They opened up their shop, and one day there came to their shop a little Jew who had traveled all the way from Antioch. They got acquainted and they invited Paul to stay with them.

What do you suppose they talked about? Well, Paul led them to the Lord. In the synagogue there were others who also turned to the Lord. However, there was also great opposition against Paul among the Jews.

And he reasoned in the synagogue every sabbath, and persuaded the Jews and the Greeks.

And when Silas and Timotheus were come from Macedonia, Paul was pressed in the spirit, and testified to the Jews that Jesus was Christ [Acts 18:4–5].

Paul had waited in Athens for Timothy and Silas to come, but they didn't show up. Now they come to him in Corinth and bring the report from the churches in Macedonia. When we get to the first Thessalonian Epistle, we will find that Paul wrote it during this period, after he had received Timothy's report.

Now he feels that he must speak out, and he testifies that Jesus is the Messiah.

And when they opposed themselves, and blasphemed, he shook his raiment, and said unto them, Your blood be upon your own heads; I am clean: from henceforth I will go unto the Gentiles [Acts 18:6].

Apparently it was at this time that Paul made the break that took him to the Gentile world. It would seem that from this point Paul's ministry was largely to the Gentiles. We will find that true in Ephesus and less obviously in Rome.

And he departed thence, and entered into a certain man's house, named Justus, one that worshipped God, whose house joined hard to the synagogue.

And Crispus, the chief ruler of the synagogue, believed on the Lord with all his house; and many of the Corinthians hearing believed, and were baptized [Acts 18:7–8].

Paul spent about eighteen months in the city of Corinth where he had a tremendous ministry. When the Jews oppose him, he turns to the Gentiles. We find now that the Lord speaks to Paul because he is coming into a great new dimension of his missionary endeavor.

Then spake the Lord to Paul in the night by a vision, Be not afraid, but speak, and hold not thy peace:

For I am with thee, and no man shall set on thee to hurt thee: for I have much people in this city [Acts 18:9–10].

Corinth was about the last place that you would expect the Lord to "have much people." I have been through Las Vegas quite a few times. I'll be honest with you—when I look at that crowd, I wouldn't get the impression that the Lord might have people there. If the Lord were to say to me, "I have much people in this city," I wouldn't question the Lord, but it surely would be the opposite from my own impression.

Paul had already been in Corinth for quite a while, and I am sure that he was wondering about that city. I'm of the opinion that when he received this opposition, he was ready to leave and go somewhere else. However, the Lord Himself steps in and detains Paul. He tells him, "I have much people in this city."

And he continued there a year and six months, teaching the word of God among them [Acts 18:11].

After Paul has had several months of ministry in Corinth, again opposition will arise.

And when Gallio was the deputy of Achaia, the Jews made insurrection with one accord against Paul, and brought him to the judgment seat [Acts 18:12].

This "judgment seat" is the Bema seat. It is the Bema that Paul talks about in the Epistle to the Corinthians. I have been there and I have sat on the ruins of the Bema seat in Corinth. They brought Paul to the Bema seat, the judgment seat, and there they brought the charge against him.

Saying, This fellow persuadeth men to worship God contrary to the law [Acts 18:13].

They didn't mean contrary to the law of the Roman Empire or contrary to the law of Corinth. They meant contrary to the law of the Mosaic system.

And when Paul was now about to open his mouth, Gallio said unto the Jews, If it were a matter of wrong or wicked lewdness, O ye Jews, reason would that I should bear with you:

But if it be a question of words and names, and of your law, look ye to it; for I will be no judge of such matters.

And he drave them from the judgment seat.

Then all the Greeks took Sosthenes, the chief ruler of the synagogue, and beat him before the judgment seat. And Gallio cared for none of those things [Acts 18:14–17].

I have read and heard Bible expositors condemn this man Gallio in no uncertain terms.

He is pictured as an unfeeling typical judge of that day. I want to say something for the defense of Gallio. I thank God for him, and I personally think that he took the right position. I'll tell you what I mean by that. He is probably the first person who made a decision between church and state. Gallio said that if the matter was concerning religion or about some religious thing, then they should take it and handle it themselves. He was a Roman magistrate and he was concerned with enforcing Roman law. But when the case did not involve Roman law, he would not interfere. He told them to handle religious matters themselves. He adopted a "hands off" policy. I like Gallio. He separated church and state. He would not interfere with Paul preaching in the city of Corinth. Corinth was a city of freedom, including religious freedom. Since the issue had to do with religion, he asked them to settle it themselves.

Now I want to say this: I wish the Supreme Court of the United States would adopt the same policy. I wish they would adopt a "hands off" policy when it comes to matters of religion. What right does a group of secular men have to come along and make a decision that you can't have prayer in the schools? If a community wants prayer in their school, then they should have prayer in their school. If they are not having prayer in school, then the state should not force prayer in school. We claim to have freedom of speech and freedom of religion in our land. The unfortunate thing is that our freedoms are often curtailed. They are abused and misdirected. Under the guise of separating church and state, the freedom of religion is actually curtailed. If we are going to separate church and state, then the state should keep its nose out of that which refers to the church.

If this man Gallio were running for office, I would vote for him. I think we need men with this kind of vision. It says Gallio cared for none of those things. Of course not! He is a secular magistrate. He is not going to try to settle an argument about differences in doctrine. That's not his business, and he'll stay out of it. I would vote for him.

PAUL SAILS FOR ANTIOCH

And Paul after this tarried there yet a good while, and then took his leave of the brethren, and sailed thence into Syria, and with him Priscilla and Aquila; having shorn his head in Cenchrea: for he had a vow [Acts 18:18].

There are a great many folk who find fault with Paul because he made a vow. They say that this is the man who preached that we are not under Law but we are under grace, and so he should not have made a vow. Anyone who says this about Paul is actually making a little law for Paul. Such folk are saying that Paul is to do things their way. Under grace, friend, if you want to make a vow, you can make it. And if you do not want to make a vow, you don't have to. Paul didn't force anyone else to make a vow. In fact, he said emphatically that no one has to do that. But if Paul wants to make a vow, that is his business. That is the marvelous freedom that we have in the grace of God today.

There are some super-saints who form little cliques and make laws for the Christian. They say we can't do this and we can't do that. May I say to you very candidly that our relationship is to the Lord Jesus Christ, and it is a love affair. If we love Him, of course we will not do anything that will break our fellowship with Him. Don't insist that I go through your little wicket gate; I am to follow Him. He shows me what I can and cannot do in order to maintain fellowship with Him.

If one wishes to eat meat, there is freedom to eat meat. If one wishes to observe a certain day, there is freedom to observe it. "Whether therefore ye eat, or drink, or whatsoever ye do, do all to the glory of God" (1 Cor. 10:31). The important thing is to do all to the glory of God. Eating meat will not commend you to God and neither will abstaining from meat commend you to God.

Let's not find fault with Paul here. Poor Gallio and Paul surely do get in trouble with their critics right in this particular passage. I want to defend both of them.

Paul is now returning from his second missionary journey. He has made Corinth the terminus of his journey and now he is going back to Antioch. He sails from Cenchrea, which is the seaport over on the east side. There is a canal through the Corinthian peninsula today, but there was none in that day. They would actually pull the boats overland. I have a picture taken to show the rocks that are worn by the boats which were pulled over the isthmus to the other side. Cenchrea was the port of Corinth on the eastward side. Paul goes there with Aquila and Priscilla, and they take ship there. He is not going westward any farther; he is sailing for home.

And he came to Ephesus, and left them there: but he himself entered into the

synagogue, and reasoned with the Jews [Acts 18:19].

You remember that when he came out on this second journey, the Spirit of God would not allow him to come down to Ephesus. Now, on his way back, he stops at Ephesus but he does not stay there very long.

When they desired him to tarry longer time with them, he consented not;
But bade them farewell, saying, I must by all means keep this feast that cometh in Jerusalem: but I will return again unto you, if God will. And he sailed from Ephesus [Acts 18:20–21].

Again someone may ask what business Paul has in keeping feasts. Remember his background. He is a Jew like Simon Peter. He has the background of the Mosaic system. He knows a lot of his friends will be in Jerusalem for the feast. He wants to go up to witness to them. He feels that he must by all means keep this feast that is coming in Jerusalem. He is under grace. If he wants to do that, that is his business.

However, he did see that there was a great door open in Ephesus. He has the heart of a missionary, and he wants to return to them. Ephesus was one of the great cities of the Roman Empire.

And when he had landed at Caesarea, and gone up, and saluted the church, he went down to Antioch [Acts 18:22].

He landed at Caesarea. Caesarea and Joppa were the ports from which one could go up to Jerusalem. He went to Jerusalem and gave his report there. Then he went back up north to his home church which was in Antioch. This concludes the second missionary journey of Paul.

Notice that it isn't long before he starts out on his third journey.

And after he had spent some time there, he departed, and went over all the country of Galatia and Phrygia in order, strengthening all the disciples [Acts 18:23].

This is now his third trip through the Galatian country. We will find that he will go to Ephesus on his third missionary journey. He is going to have a great ministry there. But right now someone else has come into Ephesus. He is Apollos, another great preacher in the early church. He is not as well known as Paul, but we can learn a great deal about him.

APOLLOS IN EPHESUS

And a certain Jew named Apollos, born at Alexandria, an eloquent man, and mighty in the scriptures, came to Ephesus [Acts 18:24].

Apollos was a Jew, which meant he had the background of the Mosaic Law. His name, *Apollos*, is Greek. So he was a Hellenist of the Diaspora. He hadn't been born in Greece or in that area of Macedonia; he was born at Alexandria in North Africa. Alexandria, founded by Alexander the Great, was one of the great centers of Greek culture. A great university was there and it had one of the finest libraries in the world. It was there that a Greek version of the Old Testament, the Septuagint, was made. There was a Jewish temple in Alexandria. The great center of the early church moved from Jerusalem and Antioch to Alexandria, and it remained important for several centuries of early church history. Athanasius, Tertullian, and Augustine, three great men of the early church, came from there. Philo, a contemporary of Apollos, mingled Greek philosophy with Judaism. This combined Platonism and Judaism. Apollos was obviously influenced by this background.

We are told that he was "an eloquent man," a great preacher. Also he was "mighty in the scriptures," which means he was well trained in the Old Testament.

This man was instructed in the way of the Lord; and being fervent in the spirit, he spake and taught diligently the things of the Lord, knowing only the baptism of John [Acts 18:25].

That he had been "instructed in the way of the Lord" means he had an education by word of mouth not by revelation. And he was "fervent in the spirit"—not the Holy Spirit. He had a passion for the things of God. This is the Holy Spirit's testimony about him. Frankly, friend, he was a great man, an outstanding man.

Apollos spoke and taught "diligently the things of the Lord." He taught everything that he had learned, but he knew only about the baptism of John. He couldn't go any further than that. He had not heard of Jesus.

And he began to speak boldly in the synagogue: whom when Aquila and Priscilla had heard, they took him unto them, and expounded unto him the way of God more perfectly [Acts 18:26].

They invited Apollos home for dinner after the service. They realized that his information was very limited; so they told him about Jesus.

And when he was disposed to pass into Achaia, the brethren wrote, exhorting the disciples to receive him: who, when he was come, helped them much which had believed through grace [Acts 18:27].

Apollos was a brilliant man, but up until the time that Aquila and Priscilla took him home for dinner, he didn't know the gospel of the grace of God. Here is a case where a woman helped a preacher a great deal. She taught him something that he didn't know.

For he mightily convinced the Jews, and that publicly, shewing by the scriptures that Jesus was Christ [Acts 18:28].

"He mightily convinced" the Jews, showing them by the Scriptures that Jesus was Christ. He had taught zealously the things of the Old Testament up through the ministry of John the Baptist. He knew nothing beyond the baptism of John. Aquila and Priscilla had the privilege of bringing him up to date and also to conversion. He then went to Achaia, visiting the churches in Greece, including Corinth and Athens, preaching Jesus as the Messiah and Savior.

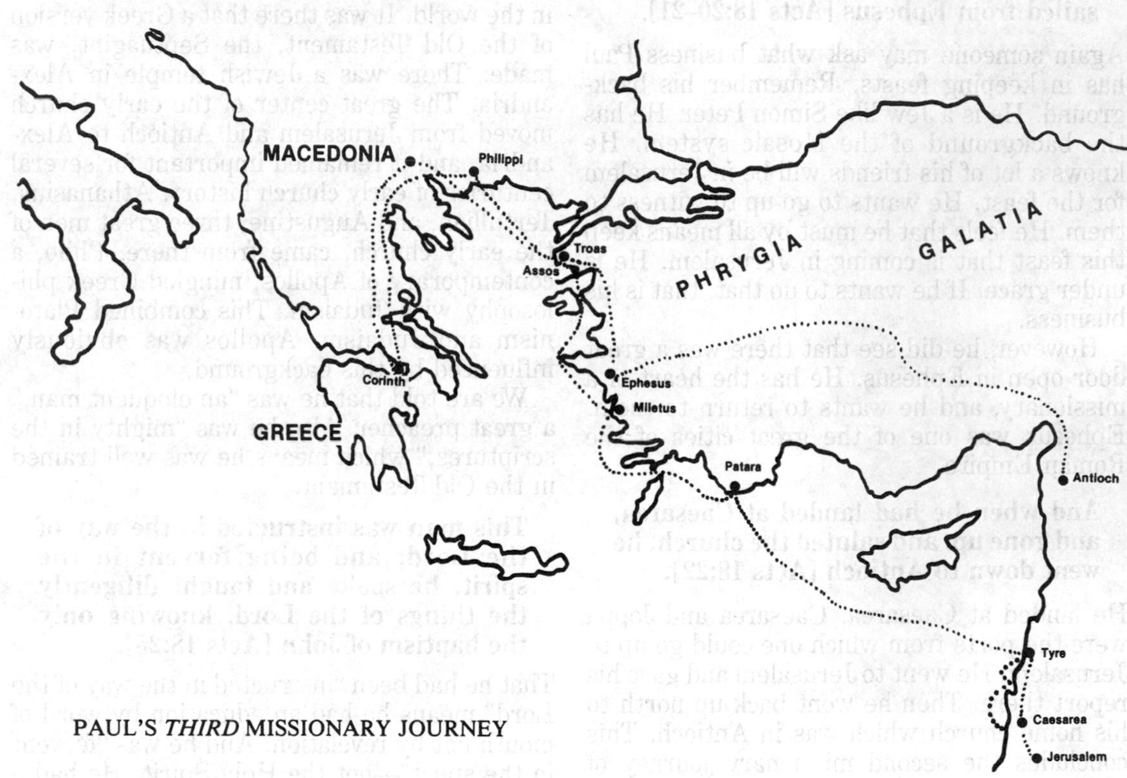

PAUL'S *THIRD* MISSIONARY JOURNEY

CHAPTER 19

***THEME:** Third missionary journey of Paul (Paul in Ephesus)*

Paul's third missionary journey began in the previous chapter at verse 23 when he left Antioch. In this chapter he retraces part of his first and second missionary journeys. Then he comes to Ephesus where he speaks daily in the school of Tyrannus for two years. Paul performs miracles which lead to the march against him led by Demetrius and his fellow silversmiths. The mob is quieted by the town clerk who urges them to appeal to the law rather than resorting to violence.

PAUL'S MINISTRY IN EPHESUS

And it came to pass, that, while Apollos was at Corinth, Paul having passed through the upper coasts came to Ephesus: and finding certain disciples,

He said unto them, Have ye received the Holy Ghost since ye believed? And they said unto him, We have not so much as heard whether there be any Holy Ghost [Acts 19:1–2].

You will remember that Paul had come through Ephesus on his return trip from his second missionary journey and had told them that he would come back to them if God so willed. He had not stayed in Ephesus previously and had had no ministry there. Now he returns to Ephesus, but he has been preceded there by that great preacher, Apollos. You recall that Apollos did not know anything about the death and resurrection of Jesus Christ until Aquila and Priscilla had talked to him. All he had been preaching was the baptism of John, which was as far as his knowledge went. As a result of this, the people who had heard his preaching had been instructed only as far as the baptism of John and had not even heard of the Holy Spirit. Paul detected that.

"Have ye received the Holy Ghost *since* ye believed?" is a poor translation. Both verbs *receive* and *believe*, are in the same tense. The American Standard Version translates the verse more accurately: "Did ye receive the Holy Spirit when ye believed?" Paul is asking them, "When you believed, did you receive the Holy Spirit?" Their response was that they had not even heard that there was a Holy Spirit. They had been instructed up to the baptism of John. They had not been taught about the Lord Jesus and didn't know anything about Pentecost.

And he said unto them, Unto what then were ye baptized? And they said, Unto John's baptism [Acts 19:3].

You see that these people were baptized, but they were not saved. They had not received the Holy Spirit because they were not saved. Friend, the moment you trust Christ you are regenerated by the Spirit of God, you are indwelt by the Spirit of God, you are sealed by the Spirit of God, and you are baptized into the body of believers by the Spirit of God. This happens the moment you believe and trust Christ. Paul detected that this had not happened to these people. Now Paul explains to them that they must trust the Lord Jesus to be saved. They respond to his message and many believe.

Then said Paul, John verily baptized with the baptism of repentance, saying unto the people, that they should believe on him which should come after him, that is, on Christ Jesus.

When they heard this, they were baptized in the name of the Lord Jesus [Acts 19:4–5].

The baptism of John was a "baptism of repentance." It was a preparation for the coming of the Lord Jesus Christ. Now the people turn to Christ and are saved. They did not get saved under Apollos because he didn't even know about Christ when he preached to them. Some people interpret this passage to mean that they had been saved, and then later when Paul came they received the Holy Spirit. That is not true, as you can see.

And when Paul had laid his hands upon them, the Holy Ghost came on them; and they spake with tongues, and prophesied.

And all the men were about twelve [Acts 19:6–7].

These men could now speak the gospel in other languages—in tongues that could be understood. Ephesus was a polyglot city of the Roman Empire. There were many languages spoken there, just as there had been in Jerusalem on the Day of Pentecost. East and West met all along that coast. It was a great city of that day. These men were now able to give the good news of Christ to the entire city.

Notice there were twelve men. This was the beginning of the ministry at Ephesus. Paul had a great ministry in Corinth and an even greater ministry in Ephesus.

And he went into the synagogue, and spake boldly for the space of three months, disputing and persuading the things concerning the kingdom of God.

But when divers were hardened, and believed not, but spake evil of that way before the multitude, he departed from them, and separated the disciples, disputing daily in the school of one Tyrannus.

And this continued by the space of two years; so that all they which dwelt in Asia heard the word of the Lord Jesus, both Jews and Greeks [Acts 19:8–10].

Paul had to leave the synagogue because there was a great deal of opposition to him. He moved his place of operation and did his speaking daily in the school of Tyrannus.

What was this school of Tyrannus? Well, it was a school that was conducted for the Ephesians. They had a siesta in the middle of the day, probably for two or three hours. Paul, I imagine, rented the space and at siesta time, in the middle of the day, he preached the Word of God for a period of two years. As a result, the whole province of Asia heard the Word of God, both the Jews and the Greeks.

This gives us some concept of how the Word of God was growing in that day. Apparently from this vantage point the church in Colosse came into existence. You see, Paul wrote to the Colossians as he did to the Romans before he had visited them. Yet he was the founder of those churches. How could this be? By the simple fact that from the school of Tyrannus the gospel sounded forth—it went out everywhere. When the Corinthians wanted Paul to come over to them, he wrote to them, "For I will not see you now by the way; but I trust to tarry a while with you, if the Lord permit. But I will tarry at Ephesus until Pentecost. For a great door and effectual is opened unto me, and there are many adversaries" (1 Cor. 16:7–9). For two years the gospel sounded out so that everyone had heard it in the province of Asia. Probably the seven churches of Asia Minor came into existence through the preaching of Paul the apostle here at Ephesus. This may have been where he had his greatest ministry.

And God wrought special miracles by the hands of Paul [Acts 19:11].

There are different words used in the Greek which our Bible translates as miracles. Here the word for "miracle" is *dunamis* from which we get our word *dynamite.* It means "an act of power." God wrought special powers by the hands of Paul. He is exercising the gifts of an apostle.

This was a great religious center, possibly more than Athens or any other place. The great temple of Diana was there, and the worship connected with it was satanic to the very core. Now in order to meet that kind of opposition, God granted to Paul some special powers.

So that from his body were brought unto the sick handkerchiefs or aprons, and the diseases departed from them, and the evil spirits went out of them [Acts 19:12].

What were these handkerchiefs and aprons which are mentioned here? Well, actually we could call them sweat cloths. Paul used them as he worked. Remember that he was a tentmaker and this was in a warm climate. While he was working, he would be perspiring. He would use these cloths, these handkerchiefs and aprons, to wipe his brow. They were dirty. They had his perspiration from his body on them. People would come and pick up these dirty cloths and would be healed of their diseases! In that area there were the mystery religions which used white garments and emphasized that everything must be very clean and white. Everything had to be just so. It seems that God was rebuking all of that sort of thing. He used these dirty, sweaty cloths to heal people.

This reveals the special power that was granted to the apostle Paul. As far as I know, this is the only incident like this that ever took place—including the day in which we live. It is almost blasphemous for anyone to send out a little handkerchief and claim there is a power in it. Paul's handkerchief was an old sweat cloth. God used that to rebuke the heathen, pagan religions of that day. Diseases were healed and evil spirits went out of them when they picked up these dirty, sweaty cloths.

Then certain of the vagabond Jews, exorcists, took upon them to call over them which had evil spirits the name of the Lord Jesus, saying, We adjure you by Jesus whom Paul preacheth [Acts 19:13].

When they saw what Paul did, they tried to duplicate it. Now a specific incident will be related.

And there were seven sons of one Sceva, a Jew, and chief of the priests, which did so.

And the evil spirit answered and said, Jesus I know, and Paul I know; but who are ye? [Acts 19:14–15].

Notice that these were priests. The priests had actually gone into this type of thing. The Greek word here for "know" is *ginōskō.* It does not imply a knowledge by faith. It means simply that the evil spirit knows who Jesus is.

And the man in whom the evil spirit was leaped on them, and overcame them, and prevailed against them, so that they fled out of that house naked and wounded [Acts 19:16].

The attempt of the sons of Sceva to try to duplicate the miracles of Paul backfired. It backfired to their humiliation and hurt and apparently was a great embarrassment for them.

And this was known to all the Jews and Greeks also dwelling at Ephesus; and fear fell on them all, and the name of the Lord Jesus was magnified [Acts 19:17].

You can see the effect that this had. It caused the name of the Lord Jesus to be spread through that entire pagan city. Ephesus was a great city, and it was shaken by this.

The miracles which Paul and the other apostles performed were not the type of thing that one hears about today. For many years there have been stories of miracles being performed in Los Angeles and in Southern California, but they made no dent or impression on this great pagan city. The miracles of Paul shook Ephesus to its very foundation. The name of the Lord Jesus was magnified through them.

And many that believed came, and confessed, and shewed their deeds.

Many of them also which used curious arts brought their books together, and burned them before all men: and they counted the price of them, and found it fifty thousand pieces of silver [Acts 19:18–19].

That would be about $8,000.00 U.S. currency before inflation. That is quite a bonfire, by the way, an $8,000.00 bonfire! That's what they had in Ephesus.

So mightily grew the word of God and prevailed.

After these things were ended, Paul purposed in the spirit, when he had passed through Macedonia and Achaia, to go to Jerusalem, saying, After I have been there, I must also see Rome [Acts 19:20–21].

"After these things were ended"—that is, these experiences which Dr. Luke has recorded here—it apparently was Paul's intention to go to Rome on this missionary journey. The interesting thing is that he did go to Rome, but not the way he had planned to go.

So he sent into Macedonia two of them that ministered unto him, Timotheus and Erastus; but he himself stayed in Asia for a season [Acts 19:22].

This is the time that he wrote to the Corinthians. Apparently Timothy and Erastus took the letter to deliver it. Although it was addressed to the Corinthians, the letter would reach the people in Macedonia, which would include Philippi and Thessalonica, and also the churches in Achaia, which would include Athens and Corinth. It was in this letter that Paul wrote that a great and effectual door was open for him in Ephesus but that there were many adversaries. We can see now that the adversaries were satanic. This was a center of pagan religion and of Satan worship. The Satan worship we see today is not something new at all.

And the same time there arose no small stir about that way [Acts 19:23].

Christianity had no name for the churches at that time—certainly no denominational name. It was simply called "that way." It was a new way, that is certain. The way was the Lord Jesus who Himself said, ". . . I am the way, the truth, and the life: no man cometh unto the Father, but by me" (John 14:6).

For a certain man named Demetrius, a silversmith, which made silver shrines for Diana, brought no small gain unto the craftsmen [Acts 19:24].

The temple of Diana was a great pagan temple, and it was the center of business. It was the bank of that day. It was also the center of sin. Gross immorality took place around it. It is true that religion can go to a lower level than anything else. That temple was one of the seven wonders of the ancient world, the largest Greek temple that was ever built. It was beautiful and was adorned with works of art, but the image of Diana or Artemis was hideous. It was not the Diana of the Greeks, a graceful image, but was the crude, many-breasted, oriental Diana. They were selling those silver images, and it was big business. Paul's ministry was interfering with it.

Whom he called together with the workmen of like occupation, and said, Sirs, ye know that by this craft we have our wealth.

Moreover ye see and hear, that not alone at Ephesus, but almost throughout all Asia, this Paul hath persuaded and turned away much people, saying that they be no gods, which are made with hands:

So that not only this our craft is in danger to be set at nought; but also that the temple of the great goddess Diana should be despised, and her magnificence should be destroyed, whom all Asia and the world worshippeth [Acts 19:25–27].

You can see that the uproar of the silversmiths led by Demetrius was centered, actually, around their bread and butter. They made those little images and sold them, and they were doing very well. There would be many people come to the temple of Diana in Ephesus since it was one of the seven wonders of the ancient world. So these men were getting rich by selling these images. I tell you again, you cannot step on a man's pocketbook without hearing him say, "Ouch!"

The worship of Diana had spread throughout Asia. Ephesus was a center of commerce and a center of religion and a center of worship. It was a center for the Oriental and the Occidental, a place where East and West did meet—the worst in both came to Ephesus.

And when they heard these sayings, they were full of wrath, and cried out, saying, Great is Diana of the Ephesians [Acts 19:28].

They went around the city with their placards shouting, "Great is Diana of the Ephesians."

And the whole city was filled with confusion: and having caught Gaius and Aristarchus, men of Macedonia, Paul's companions in travel, they rushed with one accord into the theatre.

And when Paul would have entered in unto the people, the disciples suffered him not [Acts 19:29–30].

Paul would have been mobbed, of course. He would absolutely have been killed. He already had one experience like that over in the Galatian country when he was stoned in Lystra.

And certain of the chief of Asia, which were his friends, sent unto him, desiring him that he would not adventure himself into the theatre [Acts 19:31].

This is a mob action which is taking place. "The chief of Asia" were political or religious officials, called Asiarchs, who advised Paul against trying to address the mob. They told him it would be foolish and wouldn't do a bit of good for him to get into the mob.

Some therefore cried one thing, and some another: for the assembly was confused; and the more part knew not wherefore they were come together.

And they drew Alexander out of the multitude, the Jews putting him forward. And Alexander beckoned with the hand, and would have made his defence unto the people [Acts 19:32–33].

Alexander was probably a convert who was with Paul.

But when they knew that he was a Jew, all with one voice about the space of two hours cried out, Great is Diana of the Ephesians [Acts 19:34].

This was typical mob action. Many of them didn't even know why they were gathered together. However, notice that they do not grant freedom of speech to anyone else. They would not permit Alexander to speak because *they* wanted to run around and squeal, "Great is Diana of the Ephesians."

And when the townclerk had appeased the people, he said, Ye men of Ephesus, what man is there that knoweth not how that the city of the Ephesians is a worshipper of the great goddess Diana, and of the image which fell down from Jupiter?

Seeing then that these things cannot be spoken against, ye ought to be quiet, and to do nothing rashly [Acts 19:35–36].

The townclerk was, of course, a local official who told them that they were making too much out of this whole thing. He says, "Look at this great temple and at the great Diana. Nothing could happen to them. Nothing could be said against them!" Now, of course, they have been in ruins for nearly two thousand years.

For ye have brought hither these men, which are neither robbers of churches, nor yet blasphemers of your goddess.

Wherefore if Demetrius, and the craftsmen which are with him, have a matter against any man, the law is open, and there are deputies: let them implead one another [Acts 19:37–38].

He is saying that if the silversmiths want to make a legal charge, the court is open.

But if ye inquire any thing concerning other matters, it shall be determined in a lawful assembly.

For we are in danger to be called in question for this day's uproar, there being no cause whereby we may give an account of this concourse.

And when he had thus spoken, he dismissed the assembly [Acts 19:39–41].

He told them that if they had some issue to bring up, they should all sit down and have an orderly meeting. They were to put down their placards and quit their shouting and running around. They were actually in danger of being accused of rioting. Riots are not something new, friend. This whole scene sounds very up to date.

He dismissed the crowd. When he called their attention to what they were actually doing, the crowd broke up and the people went home. Paul's ministry in Ephesus is over now. He leaves Ephesus and goes back to Macedonia.

CHAPTER 20

***THEME:** Third missionary journey of Paul concluded*

After Paul's experience in Ephesus, he continues on to Macedonia, to Philippi, back to Troas, and to Miletus. The elders of the church in Ephesus meet him in Miletus and they have a tender reunion and a touching farewell.

PAUL GOES INTO MACEDONIA

And after the uproar was ceased, Paul called unto him the disciples, and embraced them, and departed for to go into Macedonia.

And when he had gone over those parts, and had given them much exhortation, he came into Greece [Acts 20:1–2].

This means that he revisited Athens and Corinth.

And there abode three months. And when the Jews laid wait for him, as he was about to sail into Syria, he purposed to return through Macedonia.

And there accompanied him into Asia Sopater of Berea; and of the Thessalonians, Aristarchus and Secundus; and Gaius of Derbe, and Timotheus; and of Asia, Tychicus and Trophimus [Acts 20:3–4].

The men named are all believers who had come to Christ under the ministry of Paul. He has quite a delegation now. These men have become missionaries.

We need to recognize that when Paul went through Greece and Macedonia, he visited all the churches which he had founded there. He would have stopped at Athens and Corinth, at Thessalonica and Berea and Philippi. So he retraced his steps and visited all the churches that were in Europe—or at least in the European section of his third journey.

PAUL AT TROAS

You may remember that Troas was the springboard from which Paul leaped into Europe on his second missionary journey. Now he comes back to Troas on his last missionary journey.

These going before tarried for us at Troas [Acts 20:5].

The "us" indicates that Dr. Luke is still with Paul while the others go ahead of them to Troas.

This is quite a group of men, missionaries, who worked with Paul. I take it that these men had been traveling with Paul before. When Paul would have a ministry in a place like Corinth, probably these men would radiate out and have a ministry in the countryside and the small towns. We read in the Epistle to the Colossians about the fact that the Word of God had sounded out in that day to the whole world. That sounds unbelievable, but it was true. It was no oratorical gesture. Of course "the whole world" means the Roman world because that was the world of that day. The Word of God had spread throughout the Roman world. We get some insight here and recognize that there were other people working with the apostles. Acts traces the work of Peter and Paul as the dominant ones—Peter as the Apostle to the Jews and Paul as the Apostle to the Gentiles. What we have here in the Book of Acts is a very limited account of the missionary work that was going on.

And we sailed away from Philippi after the days of unleavened bread, and came unto them to Troas in five days; where we abode seven days [Acts 20:6].

It is interesting that the trip that took them five days to make can now be made by tourists in about fifty minutes. How different transportation is today! Transportation is more efficient, but our ministry is certainly not as effective.

> **And upon the first day of the week, when the disciples came together to break bread, Paul preached unto them, ready to depart on the morrow; and continued his speech until midnight [Acts 20:7].**

There are several things I want to say about this verse. I want you to note that it was upon the first day of the week that they came together. Where we have a record of the day on which the early church met, it was always the first day of the week. Paul tells the Corinthians that they are to bring their gifts on the first day of the week (see 1 Cor. 16:2). In our verse in Acts here it says that "when the disciples came together to break bread" it was "upon the *first* day of the week." This means that they celebrated the Lord's Supper on Sunday. It was on this day that Paul preached to them. The early church met on the first day of the week. That was the important day because it was the day when Jesus came back from the dead. Under the old creation the seventh day was the important day, the Sabbath day. That belongs to the old creation. On the Sabbath day Jesus was dead, inside the tomb. On the first day of the week He came forth. We meet on that day because we are now joined to a living Christ. That is the testimony of the first day of the week.

Now the other thing that interests me about this verse is that Paul was going to leave them the next day; so he preached all the way to midnight. Now, I do not know any congregation that would listen to me until midnight. I'm of the opinion that there aren't many preachers who would preach until midnight in these days in which we live. However, this is Paul's last visit. It is a tender meeting. He is getting ready to leave and he will not be back. This gives him an excuse to preach that long.

I tell congregations very frankly that I'm a long-winded preacher. I'm known as that. I love to teach the Word of God. I have a system of homiletics that I never learned in the seminary. I picked it up myself—in fact, I got it from a cigarette commercial. This is it: It's not how long you make it but how you make it long. I believe in making it long; my scriptural authority for it is that Paul did it. He spoke until midnight. You can't help but smile at that.

> **And there were many lights in the upper chamber, where they were gathered together [Acts 20:8].**

They had the place all lighted up. These early Christians didn't stay up until midnight whooping it up, but they were still up at midnight listening to the Word of God and praising Him. May I say to you that we have let the world take away from us the fun that we ought to be having today with the things of God. So if your preacher goes a little overtime, friend, be patient with him. However, I think midnight was a little long for the apostle Paul to preach, because look what happened here.

> **And there sat in a window a certain young man named Eutychus, being fallen into a deep sleep: and as Paul was long preaching, he sunk down with sleep, and fell down from the third loft, and was taken up dead [Acts 20:9].**

A friend of mine who preached up in the country of middle Tennessee invited me to come there to hold some meetings in his church. In the summertime they would have quite protracted meetings at this Bible conference. It was interesting that in the back of the church there was a place for several pallets. When a little fellow would go to sleep, the mother holding him would simply get up and take him to the back of the room and put him down on the pallet. When another little fellow would go to sleep, his mother would get up with him and do the same thing. There would be six or more children asleep in the back of that church. One night after several mothers had put their children down on the pallet, my friend interrupted his message and remarked, "I'm a better preacher than the apostle Paul! Paul preached until midnight and he put only one to sleep. I'm preaching here until about nine o'clock and I've already put four to sleep!"

I confess that Paul's experience has always been a comfort to me. When I look out at the congregation and see some brother or sister out there sound asleep, I say to myself, "It's all right. Just let them sleep. Paul put them to sleep, too."

Can't you just see this Eutychus? It says that "he sunk down with sleep." He was sound asleep, and I can imagine that he was snoring. He fell from the third loft—which means he was higher than the second floor. It is no longer a laughable experience. If this had been the end, it would have been a tragedy. But notice what happens.

And Paul went down, and fell on him, and embracing him said, Trouble not yourselves; for his life is in him.

When he therefore was come up again, and had broken bread, and eaten, and talked a long while, even till break of day, so he departed.

And they brought the young man alive, and were not a little comforted [Acts 20:10–12].

Paul raised this boy from the dead. You will remember also that Simon Peter raised Dorcas from the dead. This was a gift that belonged to the apostles. After the canon of Scripture was established, the sign gifts were not manifested—they disappeared from the church. When Dr. Luke writes that they "were not a little comforted," he means they were really thrilled that this precious young man had been raised from the dead and was back in their midst. And now Paul continues to preach through the night even until daybreak. What a rebuke that is to us! In some churches there is a chorus of complaint if a pastor preaches ten or even five minutes longer than usual. These early believers sat up all night listening to Paul. I know someone is going to say, "If I could listen to Paul, I'd listen all night, too." Probably Paul was nothing more than a humble preacher of the gospel. We do know that Apollos was an eloquent man, but that is not said of Paul. These believers simply wanted to hear the Word of God. How wonderful that is!

PAUL AT MILETUS

And we went before to ship, and sailed unto Assos, there intending to take in Paul: for so had he appointed, minding himself to go afoot [Acts 20:13].

Now they are traveling again. Dr. Luke and others of the group sailed to Assos but Paul traveled on foot. Why do you suppose Paul did that? Well, I'm sure it was so that he could witness along the way. I think as he walked, there were many places along the way where he would stop to witness to people.

And when he met with us at Assos, we took him in, and came to Mitylene.

And we sailed thence, and came the next day over against Chios; and the next day we arrived at Samos, and tarried at Trogyllium; and the next day we came to Miletus [Acts 20:14–15].

Now there is a good exercise in pronunciation as well as a little study in geography. I hope you will follow on a map these journeys of Paul. They make a nice little travelog.

For Paul had determined to sail by Ephesus, because he would not spend the time in Asia: for he hasted, if it were possible for him, to be at Jerusalem the day of Pentecost [Acts 20:16].

Paul wants to be in Jerusalem for the feast of Pentecost; so he is in a hurry. However, he was determined not to miss Ephesus. He stops at Miletus which is the port of Ephesus.

And from Miletus he sent to Ephesus, and called the elders of the church [Acts 20:17].

A good map will show you that Ephesus was actually a little inland. The river there slowly filled up the harbor at Ephesus. Today the city of Ephesus is actually inland about two or three miles from the water's edge. A great part of the city is as much as five miles inland. Miletus is right down on the coast. Paul sent for the elders of Ephesus to come to Miletus to meet him there.

And when they were come to him, he said unto them, Ye know, from the first day that I came into Asia, after what manner I have been with you at all seasons,

Serving the Lord with all humility of mind, and with many tears, and temptations, which befell me by the lying in wait of the Jews:

And how I kept back nothing that was profitable unto you, but have shewed you, and have taught you publicly, and from house to house,

Testifying both to the Jews, and also to the Greeks, repentance toward God, and faith toward our Lord Jesus Christ [Acts 20:18–21].

Paul was a faithful witness for Jesus Christ. He pulled no punches. He could declare that he had given them the Word of God, the total Word of God. I am not the first one to have a through the Bible program—Paul taught it all. He gave to them the full counsel of God. He was faithful even in the face of opposition by the religious rulers of the Jews.

And now, behold, I go bound in the spirit unto Jerusalem, not knowing the things that shall befall me there:

Save that the Holy Ghost witnesseth in every city, saying that bonds and afflictions abide me.

But none of these things move me, neither count I my life dear unto myself, so that I might finish my course with joy, and the ministry, which I have received of the Lord Jesus, to testify the gospel of the grace of God [Acts 20:22–24].

Here is a point over which many great teachers of the Bible differ. Some of my good friends in the ministry and many good, authoritative Bible teachers believe that Paul made a mistake in going to Jerusalem. They think that he should not have gone. However, this testimony which Paul gives is very clear. I believe that he was entirely in the will of God in going to Jerusalem. He is saying in effect, "I am going to Jerusalem. I am bound in the spirit because everywhere I have gone, the Spirit of God has shown me that bonds and affliction await me in Jerusalem." Now that is different from Acts 16 when he was forbidden by the Spirit of God to preach in Asia. In fact God simply put up roadblocks which directed him to Europe. There is no roadblock here. Rather the Spirit of God is revealing to Paul what he will be walking into when he reaches Jerusalem. Paul makes it clear that he realizes he will suffer if he goes to Jerusalem. He says, "I don't count my life dear. I'm willing to lay down my life for Jesus." He wanted to bring the gift to the poor saints in Jerusalem in his own hands. In his swan song Paul wrote, "I have finished my course." I think Paul touched all the bases. Jerusalem was one of those bases.

And now, behold, I know that ye all, among whom I have gone preaching the kingdom of God, shall see my face no more.

Wherefore I take you to record this day, that I am pure from the blood of all men.

For I have not shunned to declare unto you all the counsel of God [Acts 20:25–27].

Paul knew that he would not see these folk again in this life. Paul also knew that he had honestly given to them the entire counsel of God.

As I write this, I am a retired preacher. I have made many blunders and have failed in many ways. But as I look back on my ministry, I can say truthfully that when I stood in the pulpit, I declared the Word of God as I saw it. I have the deep satisfaction of knowing that if I went back to any pulpit which I have held, I haven't a thing to add to what I have already said. I don't mean I couldn't say it in a better way, but the important thing is that I declared the whole counsel of God. I have always believed that the important issue is to get out the entire Word of God.

Take heed therefore unto yourselves, and to all the flock, over the which the Holy Ghost hath made you overseers, to feed the church of God, which he hath purchased with his own blood [Acts 20:28].

This is the business of the officers of the church. They are not to run the church, but they are to see that the church is fed the Word of God.

For I know this, that after my departing shall grievous wolves enter in among you, not sparing the flock.

Also of your own selves shall men arise, speaking perverse things, to draw away disciples after them [Acts 20:29–30].

Friend, I have seen that happen. The Devil wants to get into a church where the Bible has been taught. He would like to wreck a radio ministry that is teaching the Word of God. The Devil is not our friend; he is our enemy. He wants to stop the teaching of God's Word. Paul warned them at Ephesus that this would happen to them. He tells them there will be little termites right in their midst who will really cause trouble for them.

Therefore watch, and remember, that by the space of three years I ceased not to warn every one night and day with tears.

And now, brethren, I commend you to God, and to the word of his grace, which is able to build you up, and to give you an inheritance among all them which are sanctified [Acts 20:31–32].

He commends them to God and to the Word of His grace. That is what we can do whenever we leave our people.

I have coveted no man's silver, or gold, or apparel.

Yea, ye yourselves know, that these hands have ministered unto my necessities, and to them that were with me [Acts 20:33–34].

Paul was not covetous of money. He worked in order to support himself and those who were with him.

I have shewed you all things, how that so labouring ye ought to support the weak, and to remember the words of the Lord Jesus, how he said, It is more blessed to give than to receive.

And when he had thus spoken, he kneeled down, and prayed with them all.

And they all wept sore, and fell on Paul's neck, and kissed him,

Sorrowing most of all for the words which he spake, that they should see his face no more. And they accompanied him unto the ship [Acts 20:35–38].

This is a tender meeting between Paul and the elders of the church in Ephesus. These men love Paul and he loves them. It is difficult for them to let him go, knowing that they will not see him again in this life. They bid him a touching farewell.

CHAPTER 21

***THEME:** Paul goes to Jerusalem and is arrested*

Paul has made three missionary journeys. He is returning now, and it is almost like a wonderful victory march as he comes back into the city of Jerusalem. But along the way warnings are coming to him. He knows that trouble awaits him in Jerusalem.

Chapter 20 concluded with the tender meeting he had with the Ephesian elders at Miletus. Now he boards ship for the voyage that will return him to Israel.

PAUL AT TYRE

And it came to pass, that after we were gotten from them, and had launched, we came with a straight course unto Coos, and the day following unto Rhodes, and from thence unto Patara:

And finding a ship sailing over unto Phenicia, we went aboard, and set forth [Acts 21:1–2].

Are you following him? He took a ship at Miletus and they sailed down to the southern coast of Asia Minor to Patara. There they changed ships. Now he is headed for Tyre on the seacoast north of Caesarea. It was actually on the coast of Israel in what was ancient Phoenicia. Today that is Lebanon.

Now when we had discovered Cyprus, we left it on the left hand, and sailed into Syria, and landed at Tyre: for there the ship was to unlade her burden [Acts 21:3].

I love the way this is expressed here. I think the translators of our Authorized Version have captured something that the modern translations just miss. They "discovered Cyprus" on the left hand is a way of saying that as they were sailing towards Tyre, Cyprus loomed up in the distance on their left-hand side. Of course it doesn't mean that they were the first people to discover Cyprus. They saw the island and were near enough to recognize it, but they did not stop there. They were on their way to Tyre, a great commercial center which had been there since ancient times.

And finding disciples, we tarried there seven days: who said to Paul through the Spirit, that he should not go up to Jerusalem [Acts 21:4].

This is the verse used by those Bible teachers who feel that Paul made a great mistake when he went up to Jerusalem. It shows that these men spoke to Paul through the Holy Spirit. If I understand this correctly, the Spirit of God is not going to contradict Himself. I believe He is saying the same thing here that He had said before. Paul is not to go up to Jerusalem unless he is prepared to make the required sacrifice. Paul keeps saying that he is willing to make the sacrifice. He is perfectly willing to lay down his life for the Lord Jesus. That is the way I think it should be understood.

For several reasons I do not believe that Paul stepped out of the will of God when he went up to Jerusalem. He had a sentimental reason for going there, but it was a good reason. He was carrying the offering from the gentile Christians to the suffering saints in Jerusalem. He wanted to present this to the church in Jerusalem with his own hands, because it was his hands that at one time had wasted the church in Jerusalem. He had been partly responsible for the state of penury in which the saints in Jerusalem found themselves. Paul did not want to send some representative to Jerusalem; he wanted to go to Jerusalem himself.

Another reason I do not believe that Paul stepped out of the will of God is because of his writings later on. When Paul was in prison in Rome, the church at Philippi sent to him an expression of their sympathy. They loved him and they sympathized with his condition. But Paul wrote to them, "But I would ye should understand, brethren, that the things which happened unto me have fallen out rather unto the furtherance of the gospel" (Phil. 1:12). Because what happened to Paul did not hinder the spread of the gospel, I do not believe that Paul was out of the will of God.

Furthermore, you remember that when the Lord appeared to Ananias and told him to go to Paul after his conversion, He said to Ananias, ". . . Go thy way: for he is a chosen vessel unto me, to bear my name before the Gentiles, and kings, and the children of Israel: For I will shew him how great things he must suffer for my name's sake" (Acts 9:15–16). Up to this point in our study of Acts, Paul has not appeared before kings and rulers, but we know it is in the will of God that he should do so. In the next chapters we will find that he does go before kings. He will testify before King Agrippa. It is probable that he appeared before Nero in Rome. We know for certain that he reached those who were in Caesar's household because he sent greetings from them in his Epistle to the Philippians (4:22), which was written while he was a prisoner in Rome.

Finally, as I have already mentioned, in 2 Timothy 4:7 Paul writes, ". . . I have finished my course. . . ." This was written at the end of his life. It seems to me that he would not say that if for a time he had stepped out of the will of God. I must confess that as I look back over my own ministry, I am confident that I stepped out of the will of God for a brief time. I didn't do it purposely. I did it ignorantly. I did it in a headstrong manner. I think the Lord has a way of making these things up to us. But I do not think that Paul at the end of his life could write that he had finished his course if he had been out of the will of God.

I have spent some time on this because there is controversy over it. I have several very good friends in the ministry who do not agree with my point of view, but we are still friends. I love these brethren in the Lord. I just tease them and say I hope they will see the light someday. As one of them said to me, "When we get in the presence of the Lord, we will all be in agreement."

And when we had accomplished those days, we departed and went our way; and they all brought us on our way, with wives and children, till we were out of the city: and we kneeled down on the shore, and prayed [Acts 21:5].

Again, this is a lovely thing that Paul did here. Paul and the people with him kneeled down there on the shore and prayed.

Friend, the best position to be in while praying is kneeling. However, you can pray in any posture and anywhere. Since I drive a great deal, I have learned to pray in the car. (When you drive the freeways of Southern California, you had better learn to pray!) But the most appropriate posture when we come into the presence of Almighty God is to kneel.

And when we had taken our leave one of another, we took ship; and they returned home again.

And when we had finished our course from Tyre, we came to Ptolemais, and saluted the brethren, and abode with them one day [Acts 21:6–7].

I have often wondered why Paul didn't stay there longer than that. You will notice the marvelous reception given to him and the number of believers in all these various places at that time. There must have been millions of believers in the Roman Empire by the end of the first century.

PAUL AT CAESAREA

And the next day we that were of Paul's company departed, and came unto Caesarea: and we entered into the house of Philip the evangelist, which was one of the seven; and abode with him [Acts 21:8].

Paul is traveling down the coastline going from one place to another. I have driven that route by bus. Since there was no bus running in Paul's day, I'm sure that he walked this route. And what a ministry he had! Think of the believers that he met on the way. He had a real ministry and a real opportunity.

As I have been going from church to church, from town to town, from city to city, from place to place, ministering the Word of God, it is a great encouragement to see what God is doing in the lives of folk. When I was a pastor, I had to keep my nose to the grindstone, and I developed an Elijah complex—"I'm the only one left. I'm all by myself. I am the only one standing for you, Lord." Friend, if you could go over the ground I have been over in the past year, it would thrill your heart to know the number of wonderful churches, wonderful Christian works, wonderful Christian homes, wonderful Christian believers that there are in this country and in other countries of the world. It has been a real thrill to my own heart to meet these believers. Undoubtedly this was also the experience of Paul.

And the same man had four daughters, virgins, which did prophesy [Acts 21:9].

Philip was an *evangelist*. The word literally means "one who announces good tidings." This verse shows that women did occupy a prominent place in the church. These particular women had the gift of prophecy. The New Testament had not been written as yet; so the gift of prophecy was needed in the early church.

And as we tarried there many days, there came down from Judaea a certain prophet, named Agabus.

And when he was come unto us, he took Paul's girdle, and bound his own hands and feet, and said, Thus saith the Holy Ghost, So shall the Jews at Jerusalem bind the man that owneth this girdle, and shall deliver him into the hands of the Gentiles [Acts 21:10–11].

The Holy Spirit is revealing to Paul what will happen to him when he goes up to Jerusalem. It is as though He is saying, "Paul, this is what you are going to face. Are you willing to do it?" God doesn't want Paul to feel that He let him stumble unwittingly into a trap. Paul knows what awaits him, and he still is perfectly willing to go. Actually, this prophet is not telling him anything new. Back in chapter 20, when he was still in Asia Minor, he already knew that bonds and afflictions waited for him.

And when we heard these things, both we, and they of that place, besought him not to go up to Jerusalem.

Then Paul answered, What mean ye to weep and to break mine heart? for I am ready not to be bound only, but also to die at Jerusalem for the name of the Lord Jesus [Acts 21:12–13].

Remember that this is Dr. Luke writing. He and the others didn't want to see Paul go to Jerusalem. The Spirit of God is revealing to Paul that he is going to be bound. Paul is not only willing to be bound but is also willing to die for Jesus in Jerusalem. He asks the believers not to cry and to break his heart. It is touching here to see the concern of the believers for the apostle Paul. My, how they loved him!

And when he would not be persuaded, we ceased, saying, The will of the Lord be done [Acts 21:14].

And I think the will of the Lord was done.

PAUL AT JERUSALEM

And after those days we took up our carriages, and went up to Jerusalem.

There went with us also certain of the disciples of Caesarea, and brought with them one Mnason of Cyprus, an old disciple, with whom we should lodge.

And when we were come to Jerusalem, the brethren received us gladly [Acts 21:15–17].

Notice that when the apostle Paul came to Jerusalem, the church that was there received him gladly.

And the day following Paul went in with us unto James; and all the elders were present [Acts 21:18].

What a glorious reception by the church in Jerusalem! He is a veteran now, friend. He has been in the ministry of the Lord Jesus Christ, and he bears in his body the marks of the Lord Jesus.

And when he had saluted them, he declared particularly what things God had wrought among the Gentiles by his ministry.

And when they heard it, they glorified the Lord, and said unto him, Thou seest, brother, how many thousands of Jews there are which believe; and they are all zealous of the law:

And they are informed of thee, that thou teachest all the Jews which are

among the Gentiles to forsake Moses, saying that they ought not to circumcise their children, neither to walk after the customs [Acts 21:19–21].

The Jews twisted a little what Paul was actually doing. Paul did not really teach the things that they claimed he was teaching.

We come now to another interesting passage about which good Bible expositors offer different explanations. Was Paul out or in the will of God when he went to Jerusalem and took a Jewish vow that evidently involved a sacrifice?

The believers here in Jerusalem speak of the thousands of Jewish converts to Christ. These Jews who had found their completion in Jesus Christ had not forsaken the Mosaic Law. However, they could not insist that Gentiles must come under the Law. On the other hand, Gentiles could not insist that the Jews forsake the *practices* of the Law—*provided they were not trusting it for salvation*. Those who insist that the grace of God did not force the Gentiles to keep the Mosaic Law seem to forget that the same grace permits the Jew to continue in its *precepts* if he feels it is the will of God.

For example, we know that Peter had eaten nothing contrary to Mosaic Law until he visited Paul in Antioch. Also, Jewish believers had an abhorrence of eating anything that had been sacrificed to idols. This did not bother the conscience of the Gentile. However, if the eating of such meat offended the conscience of another believer and caused him to stumble, then it was wrong. Paul makes it very clear that meat does not commend us to God. "But meat commendeth us not to God: for neither, if we eat, are we the better; neither, if we eat not, are we the worse" (1 Cor. 8:8).

Paul also wrote that if a person was brought up under certain customs, the grace of God allows him to follow those customs after he has accepted the Lord Jesus as his Savior. "But as God hath distributed to every man, as the Lord hath called every one, so let him walk. And so ordain I in all churches. Is any man called being circumcised? let him not become uncircumcised. Is any called in uncircumcision? Let him not be circumcised. Circumcision is nothing, and uncircumcision is nothing, but the keeping of the commandments of God. Let every man abide in the same calling wherein he was called" (1 Cor. 7:17–20).

Paul applies this principle in winning people for Christ. "For though I be free from all men, yet have I made myself servant unto all, that I might gain the more. And unto the Jews I became as a Jew, that I might gain the Jews; to them that are under the law, as under the law, that I might gain them that are under the law; To them that are without law, as without law, (being not without law to God, but under the law to Christ,) that I might gain them that are without law. To the weak became I as weak, that I might gain the weak: I am made all things to all men, that I might by all means save some. And this I do for the gospel's sake, that I might be partaker thereof with you" (1 Cor. 9:19–23). I do not think that we should criticize Paul for what he does here in Jerusalem. Grace permitted Paul to take a Jewish vow to win the Jews. If he had been a Gentile, it would have been questionable for him to adopt a foreign custom.

With that as a background, we understand Paul's action.

What is it therefore? the multitude must needs come together: for they will hear that thou art come.

Do therefore this that we say to thee: We have four men which have a vow on them;

Them take, and purify thyself with them, and be at charges with them, that they may shave their heads: and all may know that those things, whereof they were informed concerning thee, are nothing; but that thou thyself also walkest orderly, and keepest the law.

As touching the Gentiles which believe, we have written and concluded that they observe no such thing, save only that they keep themselves from things offered to idols, and from blood, and from strangled, and from fornication.

Then Paul took the men, and the next day purifying himself with them entered into the temple, to signify the accomplishment of the days of purification, until that an offering should be offered for every one of them [Acts 21:22–26].

Now what should Paul do? He has arrived at Jerusalem and has been given a royal reception by the church. He has given them the gift from the gentile churches. They have listened to his report and rejoiced in the way God has saved the Gentiles. Now they turn to Paul and tell him that there are thousands of Jews in Jerusalem who are trusting Christ and have accepted Him as their Messiah and Savior.

None of them want to have a division in the church. There is only one church of Jesus Christ, not a Jewish church and a gentile church. A Jew who comes to Jesus Christ does not stop being a Jew. So they say to Paul, "Look, you are a Jew. That is your background. And you want to win the Jews for Christ." Paul says, "I sure do!" So they say, "Since you are a Jew, it wouldn't hurt you to go with these four Jewish men who have made a vow. They have shaved their heads and are going into the temple. Would you go along with them?" Paul says, "Sure."

Paul didn't take this vow because he was commanded to do so. He took this vow because he wanted to win these people.

Friend, you don't have to take a vow. But if you want to take a vow, you can. If you want to shave your head with a vow, that is your business. If you want to take a vow and let your hair grow long, that is your business. It is all right with the Lord. Under grace you have a right to do these things. Under grace you have the right to make a vow if you want to do so—just so you understand that you are not *saved* by what you do but by the grace of God.

PAUL IN THE TEMPLE AT JERUSALEM

And when the seven days were almost ended, the Jews which were of Asia, when they saw him in the temple, stirred up all the people, and laid hands on him,

Crying out, Men of Israel, help: This is the man, that teacheth all men every where against the people, and the law, and this place: and further brought Greeks also into the temple, and hath polluted this holy place [Acts 21:27–28].

As mobs generally do, this mob acts on assumption and misinformation.

(For they had seen before with him in the city Trophimus an Ephesian, whom they supposed that Paul had brought into the temple.) [Acts 21:29].

Here we find this distinction that we need to make. Paul, a Jew, brought up in that tradition, went to the temple when he came to Jerusalem. Trophimus who was a Gentile Ephesian, apparently a convert through the ministry of Paul, when he was in Jerusalem with Paul, would have no inclination to go to the temple or take part in any ritual in the temple. That was not part of his background. Under grace he could have if he had wanted to. This is what I mean by our freedom under grace. Of course Paul knew that the vow he was taking had no bearing on his salvation. Both Jew and Gentile are saved only and alone by the grace of God through Jesus Christ.

Paul's vow probably included fasting and eating certain foods. That was a part of his background. Today as I travel around, I find that a great many Christians are diet faddists. It always amazes me to find how many there are. They are constantly telling me their advice about what this or that diet will do for me. May I say that the only difference a diet will make is in your physical body. A diet will not commend you to God. Under grace you can go on a diet or not go on a diet. It may have something to do with your health and your physical condition. It has nothing to do with your relationship to God. Oh, if God's people could only learn that!

And all the city was moved, and the people ran together: and they took Paul, and drew him out of the temple: and forthwith the doors were shut.

And as they went about to kill him, tidings came unto the chief captain of the band, that all Jerusalem was in an uproar.

Who immediately took soldiers and centurions, and ran down unto them: and when they saw the chief captain and the soldiers, they left beating of Paul [Acts 21:30–32].

Notice their bitterness and hatred of Paul. They hate him because he is teaching that one does not need to go through the Mosaic system to be saved. Paul is right in following one of the customs of his people if he wants to do it. He is trying to win his own people. Although it didn't accomplish the purpose that he had in mind, I think it accomplished a God-given purpose.

The mob would have killed Paul if the captain and the soldiers had not intervened.

PAUL BOUND IN CHAINS

Then the chief captain came near, and took him, and commanded him to be bound with two chains; and demanded who he was, and what he had done [Acts 21:33].

This captain did not know Paul at all. He didn't cry out, "Oh, this is Paul, the great Apostle to the Gentiles." He wasn't looking upon him like that at all. He didn't know who he was and actually thought that he had committed some crime; so he put him in chains.

And some cried one thing, some another, among the multitude: and when he could not know the certainty for the tumult, he commanded him to be carried into the castle.

And when he came upon the stairs, so it was, that he was borne of the soldiers for the violence of the people.

For the multitude of the people followed after, crying, Away with him [Acts 21:34–36].

Since the captain couldn't learn anything from the mob, he took Paul to the castle in order to find out what the charge was against him. The mob was not willing to settle for anything less than the death of Paul.

And as Paul was to be led into the castle, he said unto the chief captain, May I speak unto thee? Who said, Canst thou speak Greek? [Acts 21:37].

The captain was amazed. He thought that he had bound a common criminal, but this man speaks fluent Greek. The captain understood that because he was a foreign emissary.

Art not thou that Egyptian, which before these days madest an uproar, and leddest out into the wilderness four thousand men that were murderers? [Acts 21:38].

He thought that Paul was a mob leader, one of the protesters taking a mob out into the country.

But Paul said, I am a man which am a Jew of Tarsus, a city in Cilicia, a citizen of no mean city: and, I beseech thee, suffer me to speak unto the people [Acts 21:39].

Paul speaks Greek, but he informs the captain that he is a Jew. When the captain learns who Paul is, he says, "Well, sure. I didn't know who you were. Go ahead and speak to them."

And when he had given him licence, Paul stood on the stairs, and beckoned with the hand unto the people. And when there was made a great silence, he spake unto them in the Hebrew tongue, saying [Acts 21:40].

Although Paul speaks to the captain in Greek, when he addresses this Jewish mob, he speaks in their native tongue, Hebrew. And the minute he begins to address them in Hebrew, the language they love and understand, they listen to him.

CHAPTER 22

***THEME:** Paul's defense before the mob at Jerusalem*

This chapter gives Paul's message before the mob. He recounts his encounter with Christ and his subsequent experience which brought him to Jerusalem. Then Paul appeals to his Roman citizenship to deliver himself from the awful whipping of a prisoner.

Let us listen to Paul. Here is a great message of the apostle Paul.

PAUL'S DEFENSE BEFORE THE MOB

Men, brethren, and fathers, hear ye my defence which I make now unto you [Acts 22:1].

"Men?" Yes. "Brethren?" Yes, they belong to the same race. Yet these brethren want to kill him. Is he being sarcastic? No, because then he shows respect for the elder men, "and fathers."

(And when they heard that he spake in the Hebrew tongue to them, they kept the more silence: and he saith,) [Acts 22:2].

The minute he begins to speak in Hebrew, they become quiet. It is like a raging wind suddenly dying down, like calming the waves of the seas. They are listening to a man who is one of them. He begins with his personal history.

I am verily a man which am a Jew, born in Tarsus, a city in Cilicia, yet brought up in this city at the feet of Gamaliel,

and taught according to the perfect manner of the law of the fathers, and was zealous toward God, as ye all are this day [Acts 22:3].

Paul is being persecuted by the Jewish leaders, by the religious leaders of that day. Paul shows them that he had been one of them—he had been a Pharisee. One of the reasons he has so much sympathy for them and is so loving toward them is that he knows exactly how they feel. He is giving them his background because he wants to win them for Christ.

Paul had a tremendous background. Tarsus was actually the center of Greek learning of that day. The finest Greek university in Paul's day was in Tarsus, not in Athens or Corinth, which had passed their zeniths. Tarsus was a thriving Greek city and an educational center.

Undoubtedly Paul had been brought up in that university in Tarsus and had a Greek background, but he had also been in Jerusalem where he had studied under Gamaliel. They are listening to him now.

And I persecuted this way unto the death, binding and delivering into prisons both men and women [Acts 22:4].

Notice that Paul calls it "this way" again. He doesn't mention the church or the followers of Christ or Christians. He uses the term which they understand and which he understands. I think "this way" is still a good term to use. What is "this way?" Well, it is the Way, the Truth, and the Life. It is the person of the Lord Jesus.

He is saying to them, "Listen, I have the same background you folk have. I persecuted 'this way.' I know how you feel. I did the same thing."

As also the high priest doth bear me witness, and all the estate of the elders: from whom also I received letters unto the brethren, and went to Damascus, to bring them which were there bound unto Jerusalem, for to be punished.

And it came to pass, that, as I made my journey, and was come nigh unto Damascus about noon, suddenly there shone from heaven a great light round about me.

And I fell unto the ground, and heard a voice saying unto me, Saul, Saul, why persecutest thou me? [Acts 22:5–7].

Paul is telling them his experience.

And I answered, Who art thou, Lord? And he said unto me, I am Jesus of Nazareth, whom thou persecutest [Acts 22:8].

I think you could have heard a pin drop in that crowd now.

And they that were with me saw indeed the light, and were afraid; but they heard not the voice of him that spake to me [Acts 22:9].

I want to stop to notice something here. If you will recall where we read about the conversion of Saul of Tarsus, it says, "And the men which journeyed with him stood speechless, hearing a voice, but seeing no man" (Acts 9:7). Here Paul says, "But they heard not the voice of him that spake to me." This looks like it might be a contradiction, and it is something which the critic likes to pounce on.

Actually, there is no contradiction at all. The men heard a voice—they heard the sound, but they did not understand what the voice said nor did they know whose voice it was. They simply heard a voice.

And I said, What shall I do, Lord? And the Lord said unto me, Arise, and go into Damascus; and there it shall be told thee of all things which are appointed for thee to do.

And when I could not see for the glory of that light, being led by the hand of them that were with me, I came into Damascus.

And one Ananias, a devout man according to the law, having a good report of all the Jews which dwelt there,

Came unto me, and stood, and said unto me, Brother Saul, receive thy sight. And the same hour I looked up upon him.

And he said, The God of our fathers hath chosen thee, that thou shouldest know his will, and see that Just One, and shouldest hear the voice of his mouth.

For thou shalt be his witness unto all men of what thou hast seen and heard [Acts 22:10–15].

Notice that Paul had been given a private interview with the Lord Jesus. I believe that the Lord talked with him and taught him when he spent time out on that Arabian desert.

And now why tarriest thou? arise, and be baptized, and wash away thy sins, calling on the name of the Lord.

And it came to pass, that, when I was come again to Jerusalem, even while I prayed in the temple, I was in a trance;

And saw him saying unto me, Make haste, and get thee quickly out of Jerusalem: for they will not receive thy testimony concerning me.

And I said, Lord, they know that I imprisoned and beat in every synagogue them that believed on thee:

And when the blood of thy martyr Stephen was shed, I also was standing by, and consenting unto his death, and kept the raiment of them that slew him [Acts 22:16–20].

Paul never forgot that he had been present at the stoning of Stephen and actually had had charge over it. It left an indelible impression on his mind and prepared him for his own conversion.

And he said unto me, Depart: for I will send thee far hence unto the Gentiles.

And they gave him audience unto this word, and then lifted up their voices, and said, Away with such a fellow from the earth: for it is not fit that he should live [Acts 22:21–22].

Paul mentions the Gentiles because he has been out in the gentile world speaking to them about Jesus Christ. The Jews know that. The minute he mentions the Gentiles, it is just like lighting a fuse. They will hear him no longer.

And as they cried out, and cast off their clothes, and threw dust into the air,

The chief captain commanded him to be brought into the castle, and bade that he should be examined by scourging; that he might know wherefore they cried so against him [Acts 22:23–24].

You see, when Paul lapsed over into the Hebrew tongue and spoke to the mob in Hebrew, the captain stood there not able to comprehend what he was saying. The captain simply could not grasp what was happening nor could he understand the problem. All he could do when the mob broke into this rage was to take Paul inside the castle. He thought that since Paul was a prisoner, he would find out the truth about the whole matter by whipping him.

PAUL APPEALS TO HIS ROMAN CITIZENSHIP

And as they bound him with thongs, Paul said unto the centurion that stood by, Is it lawful for you to scourge a man that is a Roman, and uncondemned? [Acts 22:25].

Paul is being misunderstood all the way around. The Jews thought he had brought Trophimus into the temple, and he hadn't done that. The captain thought he was an Egyptian who was a riot leader, and he wasn't that man. Notice who he is. He is a Hebrew who can speak fluent Greek. Also, he is a Roman citizen. He now appeals to that citizenship to escape the scourging of a prisoner.

When the centurion heard that, he went and told the chief captain, saying, Take heed what thou doest: for this man is a Roman.

Then the chief captain came, and said unto him, Tell me, art thou a Roman? He said, Yea.

And the chief captain answered, With a great sum obtained I this freedom. And Paul said, But I was free born [Acts 22:26–28].

This captain, you see, was an ex-slave. He had saved his money or somehow he got the money to buy his freedom. He has advanced in the Roman army so that now he is a captain. He is amazed that he has a prisoner who is a Roman citizen who was born free.

Then straightway they departed from him which should have examined him: and the chief captain also was afraid, after he knew that he was a Roman, and because he had bound him.

On the morrow, because he would have known the certainty wherefore he was accused of the Jews, he loosed him from his bands, and commanded the chief priests and all their council to appear, and brought Paul down, and set him before them [Acts 22:29–30].

The captain finds that he has a remarkable man on his hands. He is a learned man who speaks Greek. He is not a common crook by any means. He is a Jew, but he is also a Roman citizen. The captain says, "I am not going to treat Paul like a common criminal. We will have a hearing to find out what the charges are against him." So the captain arranged a hearing before the chief priests and all their council.

Notice that Paul had many assets which made him suitable to be the missionary to the Roman Empire. He had a world view. Greek training had prepared him as the cosmic Christian. He was trained in the Mosaic system, which prepared him to interpret it in the light of the coming of Christ and His redemptive death and resurrection. Not the least of his assets was his Roman citizenship which finally opened the door for him to visit Rome.

CHAPTER 23

***THEME:** Paul's defense before the Sanhedrin*

Paul is now a prisoner, and we will follow his life as a prisoner. From this point on we find Paul giving a defense of himself and his ministry. He will appear before several rulers. Because the Jews are plotting his death, he will be taken down to Caesarea. He will spend about two years there in prison before he finally appeals and is sent to Rome.

You recall we have mentioned that there has always been some controversy, some difference of opinion, as to whether or not Paul should have gone to Jerusalem. Was he in the will of God when he did this? I contend that he was entirely in the will of God. I think that as we move on we will find again and again that Paul is in the will of God. It is true that he has been arrested, and it is true that he is having a rough time, but that does not mean that he is not in God's will.

As we go along we can see the hand of God in the life of this man. The same One who moved in the life of Paul wants to move in your life and in my life today. That is the glory and wonder of it all, friend. Right down here where you and I walk in a commonplace way, God is moving in our lives. In one way we are living a very humble existence and many of us today have a very simple, routine life. Yet God is concerned and interested in us. God wants to give us that leading and guiding that you and I need for today in the complexity that faces us in our contemporary culture. Believe me, we need that help today. There is no question that we need God on the scene.

A great many people go to the extremes today. They are trying to have some great emotional or revolutionary experience such as Paul had. I don't think that we need to do that. As a matter of fact, I doubt that you or I will have some great experience. It is by simple faith that one comes to Christ. We are to trust Him and to walk with Him. He will give the leading, the guidance, and direction in our everyday lives.

We have seen how the Roman captain arrested Paul and put him in prison and was going to beat him. He refrained from doing that when he learned that Paul was a Roman citizen. He was amazed to find that Paul was a Jew who could speak Greek and was a Roman citizen. Paul was a highly educated, cosmopolitan gentleman.

Now the Sanhedrin, composed of the religious rulers, wants to try him. Paul makes a futile attempt here to explain his position and his conduct to the Sanhedrin. The Lord encourages Paul. Then we see that the plot to murder Paul leads to his transfer to Caesarea for trial before Felix. This is a remarkable section and a very thrilling account of the experiences of Paul as a prisoner for Jesus Christ.

PAUL'S DEFENSE BEFORE THE SANHEDRIN

And Paul, earnestly beholding the council, said, Men and brethren, I have lived in all good conscience before God until this day.

And the high priest Ananias commanded them that stood by him to smite him on the mouth [Acts 23:1–2].

Paul is before the Sanhedrin. The chief priest and the council are there. The rudeness of the high priest is appalling. He was not about to let Paul speak until he was ready to hear him.

Then said Paul unto him, God shall smite thee, thou whited wall: for sittest thou to judge me after the law, and commandest me to be smitten contrary to the law? [Acts 23:3].

Under Roman law no man was to be punished until judgment had been handed in. Just because a man is arrested and accused of a certain crime does not grant liberty to those who had arrested him to abuse him. In that day the Roman law actually granted a great deal of justice. However, this incident and the trial of Jesus make us recognize that even the Roman law could be twisted and turned. Justice is dependent upon the one who is executing the law.

In our day there are a great many people who feel that if we change our form of government, or at least if we change our party from the one that is in power—whichever it may be—this will give us a solution to all our problems. It has never solved our problems in the past. The men who began our system of government had a great consciousness of God. Although a man like Thomas Jefferson was a deist and could not be called a born-again believer, he had a conviction that the Bible was the Word of God and he respected it. We don't find that in our leadership today, and yet we wonder why the system won't work. We think we need to change the system. Do you know what we need? We need to change men's hearts. It is man that needs changing, not the system.

The high priest orders Paul smitten on the mouth, and Paul speaks out against him very strongly. This should dispel the idea that Paul was some sort of pantywaist. The concept that humility makes a person a sort of Mr. Milquetoast is all wrong. Actually, humility and meekness mean that you submit yourself to the will of God, regardless of the cost. Paul is a meek man and a humble man, but he is not about to take injustice lying down. He calls this man a whited wall. "While you are judging me according to the Mosaic Law, you are breaking the Law yourself." That reveals that Paul also knew the Law. A man cannot be condemned or punished before judgment has been handed down.

And they that stood by said, Revilest thou God's high priest? [Acts 23:4].

Paul didn't know this man was the high priest. Certainly he would recognize the high priest on sight. Before his conversion he had been a Pharisee in Jerusalem. I think this is another evidence that Paul had an eye disease and didn't see too well. As we go in the Epistles, we will find other statements which indicate that Paul had trouble with his vision.

Then said Paul, I wist not, brethren, that he was the high priest: for it is written, Thou shalt not speak evil of the ruler of thy people [Acts 23:5].

Paul knew the Law. He knew every detail of it. He knew that the Law said that rulers were to be respected.

This is something else that we have forgotten today. I personally believe that the president of the United States, regardless of who he is or how bad he is, ought never to be made a subject of a cartoon. He should not be ridiculed because of the position he holds. We should respect the office. We as human beings need to respect authority. Paul wrote: "Render therefore to all their dues: tribute to whom tribute is due; custom to whom custom; fear to whom fear; honour to whom honour" (Rom. 13:7). It is interesting that he wrote this at a time when Nero was on the throne in Rome, and Nero was a madman.

But when Paul perceived that the one part were Sadducees, and the other Pharisees, he cried out in the council, Men and brethren, I am a Pharisee, the son of a Pharisee: of the hope and resurrection of the dead I am called in question [Acts 23:6].

We are getting more of Paul's background. His father had also been a Pharisee, probably a wealthy and influential man.

Paul uses the discord between two parties to further his own defense. The issue here is not the resurrection of Jesus Christ. It is simply that the Pharisees believed in the resurrection of the dead and had this hope, while the Sadducees did not. So Paul turns the trial into a theological argument between the "fundamentalists" and the "liberals." That is easy to do. There never has been a time when you couldn't get these two groups at each other's throats! That is what Paul is doing here.

And when he had so said, there arose a dissension between the Pharisees and the Sadducees: and the multitude was divided.

For the Sadducees say that there is no resurrection, neither angel, nor spirit: but the Pharisees confess both.

And there arose a great cry: and the scribes that were of the Pharisees' part arose, and strove, saying, We find no evil in this man: but if a spirit or an angel hath spoken to him, let us not fight against God [Acts 23:7–9].

The Pharisees now come to Paul's defense. When they find out he is a Pharisee, they rally around him to defend him.

And when there arose a great dissension, the chief captain, fearing lest Paul should have been pulled in pieces of them, commanded the soldiers to go down, and to take him by force from among them, and to bring him into the castle [Acts 23:10].

This is the first time that Dr. Luke says there was "a great dissension." Knowing how he uses understatements, I am of the opinion this is the worst dissension recorded in the Book of Acts concerning any group. Paul's life is so in danger again that the Roman captain reaches in and saves him from the angry Sanhedrin. While I have defended Gallio's concept of the separation of church and state, the state is protecting the apostle Paul at this point, which is quite proper. So the chief captain rescues Paul again without learning the real nature of the hatred against Paul.

THE LORD APPEARS TO PAUL

And the night following the Lord stood by him, and said, Be of good cheer, Paul: for as thou hast testified of me in Jerusalem, so must thou bear witness also at Rome [Acts 23:11].

This again shows that Paul was not out of the will of God in going to Jerusalem. The Spirit of God had warned Paul that he could expect bonds and difficulties if he went to Jerusalem. In spite of this, Paul had gone to Jerusalem and had witnessed for the Lord Jesus in that city. Now God tells him that just as he has testified in Jerusalem so he will also bear witness in Rome. This is God's method. Paul had never had such an opportunity to witness in Jerusalem before. Now God is going to give him the opportunity to witness in Rome. It is God's will that he should go to Rome also.

It is important to note that there is no rebuke to Paul from the Lord. He doesn't say, "Look, Paul, I told you not to go to Jerusalem because you would get in trouble there." Rather, the Lord encourages him. He is using this means to get Paul over to Rome.

THE PLOT AGAINST PAUL

And when it was day, certain of the Jews banded together, and bound themselves under a curse, saying that they would neither eat nor drink till they had killed Paul [Acts 23:12].

I imagine they got pretty hungry and thirsty before this was all over!

And they were more than forty which had made this conspiracy.

And they came to the chief priests and elders, and said, We have bound ourselves under a great curse, that we will eat nothing until we have slain Paul.

Now therefore ye with the council signify to the chief captain that he bring him down unto you to-morrow, as though ye would inquire something more perfectly concerning him: and we, or ever he come near, are ready to kill him [Acts 23:13–15].

This is the plot to put Paul to death. It's well that the Lord Himself has made it very clear to Paul that He has a different plan for him; he is going to Rome.

And when Paul's sister's son heard of their lying in wait, he went and entered into the castle, and told Paul.

Then Paul called one of the centurions unto him, and said, Bring this young man unto the chief captain: for he hath a certain thing to tell him.

So he took him, and brought him to the chief captain, and said, Paul the prisoner called me unto him, and prayed me to bring this young man unto thee, who hath something to say unto thee [Acts 23:16–18].

Paul is exerting his right as a Roman citizen, which he has a perfect right to do. Also, we learn more about Paul's family. We see that he has a sister who lives with her family in Jerusalem.

Then the chief captain took him by the hand, and went with him aside privately, and asked him, What is that thou hast to tell me?

And he said, The Jews have agreed to desire thee that thou wouldest bring down Paul to-morrow into the council, as though they would inquire somewhat of him more perfectly.

But do not thou yield unto them: for there lie in wait for him of them more than forty men, which have bound themselves with an oath, that they will neither eat nor drink till they have killed him: and now are they ready, looking for a promise from thee.

So the chief captain then let the young man depart, and charged him, See thou

tell no man that thou hast shewed these things to me [Acts 23:19–22].

In this way the captain is alerted to the plot against Paul.

Let's stop to note something here. I find today that there is a group of super-pious folk, very sincere and very well-meaning, which tells me I should not go to a doctor concerning my cancer or other illnesses but that I should trust the Lord to heal me. Well, I certainly do trust the Lord; I have turned my case over to the Great Physician, and I believe He provides doctors. It would have been a simple thing for Paul to have told his nephew, "Thanks for telling me the news, but I'm trusting the Lord—so you can go back home." But we find here that Paul used the privileges of his Roman citizenship which were available to him. Obviously the Lord provides these means and He expects us to use them. This in no way means that we are not trusting Him. Rather, we are trusting God to use the methods and the means to accomplish His purpose.

PAUL SENT TO CAESAREA

The chief captain goes into action. To be forewarned is to be forearmed.

And he called unto him two centurions, saying, Make ready two hundred soldiers to go to Caesarea, and horsemen threescore and ten, and spearmen two hundred, at the third hour of the night [Acts 23:23].

A centurion, you remember, had one hundred soldiers under him.

And provide them beasts, that they may set Paul on, and bring him safe unto Felix the governor [Acts 23:24].

This is quite an army that is going to escort Paul down to Caesarea. Is this what one calls trusting the Lord? Of course it is the captain who has ordered it, but Paul has called for this type of protection from him. Certainly Paul is in the will of God in doing this. It certainly reveals the danger that Paul was in. There is no doubt that the Jews had every intention to put him to death.

He is sending Paul to Caesarea to appear before Felix, the governor. The Roman governors had their headquarters in Caesarea and only occasionally went up to Jerusalem. Pilate had had his headquarters there. The ruins of that Roman city are still there today. It has a lovely situation on the coast.

I can understand why those Romans would rather live in Caesarea than in Jerusalem. The climate was delightful when I was there, and I got very cold in Jerusalem.

Paul is to be sent to Felix in Caesarea. This will remove Paul from the danger in Jerusalem.

And he wrote a letter after this manner [Acts 23:25].

Although Dr. Luke may have had the actual letter, when he says the letter was "after this manner" it probably means that he didn't have access to the letter but is giving us the sense of it.

Claudius Lysias unto the most excellent governor Felix sendeth greeting [Acts 23:26].

Notice the formal manner of address. In those days they didn't sign letters as we do today. They put their name at the beginning of the letter rather than at the end of the letter.

This man was taken of the Jews, and should have been killed of them: then came I with an army, and rescued him, having understood that he was a Roman [Acts 23:27].

The captain in Jerusalem wants the governor in Caesarea to know that he is performing his duty. He is protecting Roman citizens.

And when I would have known the cause wherefore they accused him, I brought him forth into their council:

Whom I perceived to be accused of questions of their law, but to have nothing laid to his charge worthy of death or of bonds [Acts 23:28–29].

It is clear that Claudius Lysias never did know exactly what the charge was against Paul. He knew it pertained to their law. Under Roman law Paul was not guilty of anything worthy of death or of imprisonment.

And when it was told me how that the Jews laid wait for the man, I sent straightway to thee, and gave commandment to his accusers also to say before thee what they had against him. Farewell.

Then the soldiers, as it was commanded them, took Paul, and brought him by night to Antipatris.

On the morrow they left the horsemen to go with him, and returned to the castle:

Who, when they came to Caesarea, and delivered the epistle to the governor, presented Paul also before him.

And when the governor had read the letter, he asked of what province he was. And when he understood that he was of Cilicia;

I will hear thee, said he, when thine accusers are also come. And he commanded him to be kept in Herod's judgment hall [Acts 23:30–35].

We will find that his accusers were quick to come down to Caesarea. They didn't hesitate to follow Paul. As we move along, I think you will detect that Paul is not defending himself as much as he is witnessing for Christ. The Lord Jesus had said he would witness before governors and rulers and kings. He is being brought before them. This is God's method. Paul is in the will of God, and God is carrying out His purpose.

CHAPTER 24

THEME: *Paul before Felix*

This chapter opens and closes with Paul a prisoner in Caesarea. As we have seen, he was brought here secretly from Jerusalem to elude the Jews who had plotted his murder.

Candidly, Paul had failed in gaining the sympathies of his brethren for the gospel ministry in which he was engaged. I suspect that there was a time of mental depression and discouragement for him, because the Lord came to him in the night to give him encouragement (Acts 23:11). He told His faithful servant that he would witness to Him in Rome also. The Lord did not promise him that it would be easy. Many trying experiences and hardships were immediately before him. In fact, from here to his final martyrdom there was nothing but peril and danger—actually that had been the pattern since the day he was let down in a basket over the wall at Damascus.

In this chapter we will learn that the high priest Ananias and the elders come down from Jerusalem to accuse Paul before Felix. Paul is accused of sedition, rebellion, and profaning the temple.

PAUL BEFORE FELIX

And after five days Ananias the high priest descended with the elders, and with a certain orator named Tertullus, who informed the governor against Paul [Acts 24:1].

The accusers didn't waste time. They came down after five days in order to press charges against Paul. They brought with them a man named Tertullus who would act as the prosecuting attorney. He was a clever and well-prepared man. The charge he brought was very well prepared, too. It was brief and to the point. I think he did the best he could with the charges he had.

And when he was called forth, Tertullus began to accuse him, saying, Seeing that by thee we enjoy great quietness, and that very worthy deeds are done unto this nation by thy providence [Acts 24:2].

He starts out with flattery in his address to Felix. This had nothing in the world to do with the charge against Paul.

We accept it always, and in all places, most noble Felix, with all thankfulness [Acts 24:3].

Believe me, he is really buttering up the governor.

Notwithstanding, that I be not further tedious unto thee, I pray thee that thou wouldest hear us of thy clemency a few words.

For we have found this man a pestilent fellow, and a mover of sedition among all the Jews throughout the world, and a ringleader of the sect of the Nazarenes [Acts 24:4–5].

He calls Paul a mover of sedition. He couldn't prove that, of course.

Who also hath gone about to profane the temple: whom we took, and would have judged according to our law.

But the chief captain Lysias came upon us, and with great violence took him away out of our hands,

Commanding his accusers to come unto thee: by examining of whom thyself mayest take knowledge of all these things, whereof we accuse him.

And the Jews also assented, saying that these things were so [Acts 24:6–9].

The "Jews" are the religious rulers who came down to press charges.

Notice he makes subtle insinuations about the way the chief captain handled the case. He cannot charge him with dereliction of duty, but there is a faint breath of criticism to the governor. He says the Jews could have handled this case adequately themselves. He has nothing but flattery for Felix, unjust charges against Paul, and subtle insinuations against Claudius Lysias.

So the charges against Paul are that he is a mover of sedition, he is a leader of a rebellious sect, and he has profaned the temple. Tertullus presents these charges for the religious rulers. Now Paul makes his defense before Felix.

Then Paul, after that the governor had beckoned unto him to speak, answered, Forasmuch as I know that thou hast been of many years a judge unto this nation, I do the more cheerfully answer for myself:

Because that thou mayest understand, that there are yet but twelve days since I went up to Jerusalem for to worship [Acts 24:10–11].

Paul is saying that he is delighted to present his case before Felix. He knows that Felix has been a judge of the people for a long time, which means that Felix understands their customs. So what Paul is going to say will not be something that will be strange or foreign to Felix.

And they neither found me in the temple disputing with any man, neither raising up the people, neither in the synagogues, nor in the city:

Neither can they prove the things whereof they now accuse me.

But this I confess unto thee, that after the way which they call heresy, so worship I the God of my fathers, believing all things which are written in the law and in the prophets [Acts 24:12–14].

Since Felix understands the customs of the Jews, Paul tells him that he went up to Jerusalem to worship according to their custom. In substance he says, "I am in agreement with my nation. Only I must confess that the way in which I worship God is to them heresy." But Paul makes it clear that the way he worships is according to the message to the fathers, that is, the Old Testament.

And have hope toward God, which they themselves also allow, that there shall be a resurrection of the dead, both of the just and unjust [Acts 24:15].

Have you noticed that the Resurrection is the very center of Christianity? It has been from the very beginning, friend. "What think ye of Christ?" is always the test. Did He die for your sins? Was He raised from the dead? Paul immediately comes to the core: the Resurrection.

And herein do I exercise myself, to have always a conscience void of offence toward God, and toward men [Acts 24:16].

Paul testifies that what he has done, he has done for the sake of his conscience.

Now after many years I came to bring alms to my nation, and offerings [Acts 24:17].

Paul came to bring to the church in Jerusalem the gifts which he had been gathering on his third missionary journey. I have a notion it was a substantial gift which the gentile believers sent to Jerusalem, and Paul wanted to bring that gift with his own hands.

Whereupon certain Jews from Asia found me purified in the temple, neither with multitude, nor with tumult.

Who ought to have been here before thee, and object, if they had aught against me [Acts 24:18–19].

The real accusers, if there were any at all, are not even present. The charge that Tertullus makes is that Paul had been stirring up people in the temple. Why don't the people who were being stirred up testify against Paul? They aren't there, and Paul calls attention to it.

Or else let these same here say, if they have found any evil doing in me, while I stood before the council [Acts 24:20].

"Let them tell you about my appearance before the Sanhedrin. Did they find that I had done anything evil? Let them give testimony about that."

Except it be for this one voice, that I cried standing among them, Touching the resurrection of the dead I am called in question by you this day [Acts 24:21].

He tells Felix again that the real issue is the Resurrection. The Resurrection is the very heart of the gospel message. Christ died for our sins, was buried, and was raised again on the third day. In fact, I think of Christianity as an arch supported by two pillars. One pillar is the death of Christ and the other pillar is the resurrection of Christ. Without one or the other the arch would fall.

And when Felix heard these things, having more perfect knowledge of that way, he deferred them, and said, When Lysias the chief captain shall come down, I will know the uttermost of your matter [Acts 24:22].

Felix had been hearing about "that way"; he knew the death and resurrection of Christ was being preached. He realized that Paul was the expert, that Paul was the man who could tell him all about it. So he deferred the Jews because he wanted to have another hearing with Paul about this matter. He told the Jews he would wait until Lysias could come down, and then he could get the real story about what had happened to Paul. Apparently he could make no decision from the contradictory testimony that was offered here. Tertullus was making certain accusations. Paul said the real issue was the Resurrection. So he defers judgment.

And he commanded a centurion to keep Paul, and to let him have liberty, and that he should forbid none of his acquaintance to minister or come unto him [Acts 24:23].

Actually, Felix should have freed Paul. However, he was a politician, an astute politician. He does give Paul a great deal of liberty while still keeping him a prisoner.

FELIX HAS PAUL IN FOR A PRIVATE AUDIENCE

And after certain days, when Felix came with his wife Drusilla, which was a Jewess, he sent for Paul, and heard him concerning the faith in Christ.

And as he reasoned of righteousness, temperance, and judgment to come, Felix trembled, and answered, Go thy way for this time; when I have a convenient season, I will call for thee [Acts 24:24–25].

A sinner will never have "a convenient season" to hear the gospel.

This man Felix already knew something about the gospel, or "the Way," which is synonymous with what we today call Christianity or the Christian faith. I personally would like to see the name "the Way" restored because *Christianity*, as it is used today, is a most abused word and has lost its real meaning.

I heard a man, actually a good preacher, say the other day that we live in a Christian nation. My friend, we don't live in a Christian nation! This country is not Christian by any stretch of the imagination. We have a lot of church members, but the number of real Christians composes a small minority today.

Felix called Paul in to explain to him the gospel which had induced this entire situation. He called Paul in "and heard him concerning the faith in Christ." Some Bible teachers caption this section "Paul's Defense Before Felix." I disagree with that. Paul was not defending himself here. What he was doing in this second appearance before Felix was witnessing to him, trying to win this man for Christ.

The scriptural record does not present this man Felix in the bad light that secular history does. I would like you to know what a rascal he really was. To know the man, we must turn to the record of that day. Felix was a freed slave who through cruelty and brutality had forged to the front. He was a man given to pleasure and licentiousness. By the way, his very name means "pleasure." The Roman historian, Tacitus, says this concerning him: "Through all cruelty and licentiousness he exercised the authority of a king with the spirit of a slave." This was the man into whose hands Paul was placed. Yet the Scripture does not condemn him.

His wife Drusilla sat there alongside him. Again secular history turns the spotlight on her for us. She was a daughter of Herod Agrippa I. Her father killed the apostle James—we have already seen that in Acts 12:1–2. The great uncle of this woman had slain John the Baptist. Her great grandfather tried to kill the Lord Jesus Christ.

This couple of rascals, Felix and Drusilla, are in an exalted position. They probably would never have attended a church in which the gospel was preached, nor would they have gone to hear Paul the apostle if he had come to town to preach. Yet here are these two who have this great opportunity given to them under the most favorable circumstances. They have a private interview with the greatest preacher of the grace of God that the world has ever known. God gives them a private sermon. Their palace becomes a church and their thrones become almost a mourner's bench. Oh, the wonder of the grace of God to give these two a chance! The hour of salvation struck for them. The door of the kingdom was opened and they had their opportunity to enter. This is in fulfillment of the verse in the second psalm: "Be wise now therefore, O ye kings: be instructed, ye judges of the earth" (Ps. 2:10). It appears that they heard Paul with a great deal of interest. I think Felix would have liked to have made a decision for Christ. But he didn't make that decision. He wanted to wait for a convenient season. My friend, the sinner will never have a convenient season to hear the gospel. Man does not set the time; God does.

Paul reasoned with him of righteousness, temperance, and judgment to come. This makes a very good sermon, by the way. Righteousness here is, I think, the righteousness of the Law, which man cannot attain. In other words, the Law reveals that man is a sinner, and he cannot even present a legal righteousness that would be acceptable to God. A sinner must have a standing of legal righteousness before God and he cannot provide it for himself. So God provides it for him in Christ Jesus. That is the "robe" of righteousness which comes down like a garment over those who put their trust in Christ. That is the righteousness "Even the righteousness of God which is by faith of Jesus Christ unto all and upon all them that believe: for there is no difference" (Rom. 3:22). Paul reasoned with this man about the righteousness of the Law which he could not meet and the righteousness which Christ provides the sinner who puts his trust in Him. Then Paul talked of temperance, which is self-control. Felix was a man mastered by passion and cruelty. These two, Felix and Drusilla, great sinners, living in sin, did not know what real freedom was. Then Paul spoke about the judgment to come, which is the final judgment at the Great White Throne of Revelation 20:11–15.

Friend, today your sins are either on you or they are on Christ. If your sins are on Christ, if you have put your trust in Him, then He paid the penalty for your sins over nineteen hundred years ago. They do not lie ahead of you for judgment in the future. But if your sins today are still on you, then there is yet a judgment to come. People don't like to hear about judgment to come.

Felix and Drusilla did not like to hear about it either. But if your sins are not on Christ, that is, if you have not trusted Him as your Savior, then you are going to come up for judgment. You can close this book right now, but that doesn't alter a thing. You cannot escape the fact that you are coming up for judgment.

Very few preachers touch on this subject. Those who still teach the Bible are the only ones who mention it at all, and most preachers soft-pedal it. I received a letter from a college professor in Virginia who wrote, "I listened to you and I was about ready to tune you out when I found out you were a hell-fire and damnation preacher. But I noticed that you didn't handle it in a crude way, and then I noticed that you did offer salvation; so I continued to listen to you." Hell-fire and damnation is a pretty good subject if it is used to lead one to Christ, friend. But it should never be used alone without the message of salvation which we have in Christ Jesus.

It is interesting to observe Felix here. When Paul had to appear before Felix, Ananias the high priest with the elders and with the great orator Tertullus came to bring their charges against him. Felix could immediately see that they had no real charge. He should have let Paul go free. But Felix was most of all a politician and did not want to antagonize the Jews. He did not do what was right but did what was politically expedient. Then Felix had this private interview with Paul, and Paul apparently really touched him. Yet he delayed his decision and postponed the day.

It has been proven out in the history of the human family for nineteen hundred years that folk can keep postponing making a decision for Christ until they come to the place where they cannot make a decision for Him at all. That is the reason that most decisions for Christ are made by young people—we ought to try to reach young people for Christ. Also this is the reason a person need not think that because he is getting older he is becoming smarter. Older people just become more hardened to the gospel. Years ago I heard the late Dr. George Truett, a great prince of the pulpit in Dallas, Texas, tell an incident that illustrates this fact. It was at the celebration of his fiftieth anniversary that a lawyer friend, who was not a Christian, came to him. He said,

"George, you and I came here to Dallas at the same time. You were a young preacher and I was a young lawyer. I must confess that when I first heard you, I was moved a great deal by your sermons. Very frankly, there were nights when I couldn't sleep. As the years wore on, the day came when I could listen to you and *enjoy* hearing you. Your message didn't disturb me at all. And you're a much greater preacher today than you were at the beginning." The lawyer chuckled about it. He didn't realize how tragic it was. He didn't realize the place to which he had actually come. "Go thy way for this time; when I have a convenient season, I will call for thee," said Felix. That time never came for Felix. That time never came for the lawyer in Dallas. That time does not come for a great many people who postpone receiving Christ.

He hoped also that money should have been given him of Paul, that he might loose him: wherefore he sent for him the oftener, and communed with him [Acts 24:26].

He was a clever politician and also a crook, by the way. He hoped that he would be bribed and then he would have let Paul go free.

But after two years Porcius Festus came into Felix' room: and Felix, willing to shew the Jews a pleasure, left Paul bound [Acts 24:27].

Felix played politics to the very end. He left Paul in prison. Again we say that Roman justice was no better than the men who executed it. Either Paul was guilty or he was not guilty. If guilty of treason, he should have been put to death. If not guilty, he should have been freed. One or the other should have been done. Under no circumstances should he have been left in prison for two years.

CHAPTER 25

THEME: *Paul before Festus*

Paul had been unjustly kept in prison for two years. Festus is the new governor who followed Felix. Now Paul will appear before this new governor.

We have seen Paul before the mob on the steps of the castle in Jerusalem. We have seen him before the Sanhedrin. We have seen him before Felix and then in private interview with Felix and his wife Drusilla. Apparently there were other meetings. Now he will appear before Festus. Later he will appear before Agrippa. Paul appeared before all these rulers and it must have been a tedious time for Paul, something to try his patience. However, I'm sure that he rejoiced in the opportunity given him to testify before the high political figures of the Roman Empire. Remember that when the Lord Jesus had apprehended Paul on the Damascus road, He had said, ". . . he is a chosen vessel unto me, to bear my name before the Gentiles, and kings, and the children of Israel" (Acts 9:15). Paul is moving according to God's plan and program.

Each time Paul tells about what the Lord Jesus had done for him, and he tells it with a great deal of conviction and enthusiasm. Paul witnesses a good confession of Jesus Christ. Although Felix trembled as he listened, the rascality and cupidity and covetousness of this man triumphed. He had his chance. He sent for Paul many times but he wanted a bribe, not salvation.

Those two years that Paul languished in prison are silent years in the life of Paul. Perhaps he chafed under it all. We don't know. We do know that the hand of God was manifested in all this, and His purposes were carried out. How comforting this can be for us when our activity seemingly comes to a standstill.

PAUL APPEARS BEFORE FESTUS

Now when Festus was come into the province, after three days he ascended from Caesarea to Jerusalem.

Then the high priest and the chief of the Jews informed him against Paul, and besought him,

And desired favour against him, that he would send for him to Jerusalem, laying wait in the way to kill him.

But Festus answered, that Paul should be kept at Caesarea, and that he himself would depart shortly thither [Acts 25:1–4].

It seems that Festus understood the situation. I'm of the opinion that Felix told him about Paul's imprisonment, and I think he explained the circumstances. I'm sure he told Festus that he had brought him to Caesarea to protect him from being put to death by the Jews. So when Festus gets word from the Jews that they want Paul in Jerusalem, he says, "Oh, I won't bring him down here. I'm going back to Caesarea myself. I'm not going to stay around in Jerusalem." Here was another Roman who preferred Caesarea to Jerusalem.

The enemies of Paul certainly didn't waste any time getting to the new governor to try to get a judgment against Paul. I don't know whether Festus was actually aware of their plan to ambush the party and kill Paul. I think he was, but it doesn't really say that he knew about it. However, he refused to accede to their demands and requested instead that they come to Caesarea to bring charges.

Let them therefore, said he, which among you are able, go down with me, and accuse this man, if there be any wickedness in him.

And when he had tarried among them more than ten days, he went down unto Caesarea; and the next day sitting on the judgment seat commanded Paul to be brought.

And when he was come, the Jews which came down from Jerusalem stood round about, and laid many and grievous complaints against Paul, which they could not prove [Acts 25:5–7].

Paul is again called upon to defend himself against the accusations of the Jews. However it provides an opportunity to present the gospel to Festus.

While he answered for himself, Neither against the law of the Jews, neither against the temple, nor yet against Caesar, have I offended any thing at all.

But Festus, willing to do the Jews a pleasure, answered Paul, and said, Wilt thou go up to Jerusalem, and there be judged of these things before me? [Acts 25:8–9].

This Festus is another rascal. Paul is not only in the midst of a den of thieves, he is in the midst of a bunch of rascals.

Then said Paul, I stand at Caesar's judgment seat, where I ought to be judged: to the Jews have I done no wrong, as thou very well knowest [Acts 25:10].

There are some people who think that Paul made a mistake here, that he should never have appealed to Caesar. They think he should simply have let his case rest with Festus. Friend, don't you see that Festus was going to use Paul for his own political ends? Festus was going to take Paul back to Jerusalem. Perhaps Festus was receiving bribes from the Jews who had come from Jerusalem. I am reluctant to criticize Paul. I don't think that he made a mistake here. Paul was a Roman citizen and he exercised his rights as a citizen, which was the normal and the right thing for him to do. Going back to Jerusalem would have surely meant death for him. He doesn't purposely make himself a martyr. In fact, he did what he could to avoid martyrdom.

Friend, there are a people today who wear a hair shirt—and God didn't give it to them. In other words, they like to take the position of a martyr. I've had a number of people who have told me that I should rejoice that I have a cancer because now I can suffer for Christ and maybe die for Christ. Well, I can tell you, I don't feel that way about it. I want to get rid of the cancer. I want to live. I think a person is depressed spiritually and mentally if he wants to put on a hair shirt and lie on a cold slab. Martin Luther tried that and he found it didn't accomplish anything.

You will remember that two years before this the Lord had appeared to Paul and had promised him a trip to Rome (Acts 23:11). That's what is taking place. He went to Rome by the will of God. He was in chains—but the Lord hadn't told him *how* he would get to Rome. This was God's method for him. When Paul wrote to the Romans, he told them that he was praying to be able to come to Rome and he asked them to pray that he might be able to come (Rom. 1:9–10; 15:30–32). I believe he went to Rome by the will of God.

For if I be an offender, or have committed any thing worthy of death, I refuse not to die: but if there be none of these things whereof these accuse me, no man may deliver me unto them. I appeal unto Caesar [Acts 25:11].

I detect a note of impatience here. Rome was noted for its justice, and Paul respected authority. However, Paul is not getting justice, and so he makes a legal appeal. God intended that Paul use his rights as a Roman citizen. It is very interesting for us to observe that God leads some people in one way and leads others in another way. Some of the others could not claim the protection of Roman citizenship.

I knew a wonderful Christian man and wife whom the Lord had blessed in a material way. They had built a lovely home, a home in which it was always a delight to visit. The man told me that he felt under conviction because he had a lovely home, and he wanted to open his home and use it for Christian witnessing and testimony as much as possible. So I asked him, "Did you ever stop to think that God blessed you materially and gave you such a nice home because He knew you were the kind of a man who would use his home for Him?" Then I said to him, "You just go ahead and fall into a sweet sleep every night, knowing that you are in the will of God and thanking Him for that lovely home." Now the Lord didn't give me that kind of a home because evidently He doesn't intend for me to use my home for that type of thing.

What has the Lord done for you, friend? Whatever it is, you should use it for Him. If you are in a political position, you should use that position for Him. If the Lord has put something in your hand, use it for Him. Remember that Moses had a rod in his hand—just a rod, but he was to use it for God. That is the whole thought here. Paul had his Roman citizenship. It was a rod in his hand. He's going to use it, use it for God. I don't think that Paul made a mistake here.

Then Festus, when he had conferred with the council, answered, Hast thou appealed unto Caesar? unto Caesar shalt thou go [Acts 25:12].

Festus is forced to concur with Paul at this point. He cannot prevent Paul from going to Rome to the court of Caesar.

KING AGRIPPA AND BERNICE COME TO VISIT FESTUS

And after certain days king Agrippa and Bernice came unto Caesarea to salute Festus [Acts 25:13].

Festus had just come into office as the new governor; so the king comes over for a visit. I have a notion these politicians work together. They all belong to the same party.

And when they had been there many days, Festus declared Paul's cause unto the king, saying, There is a certain man left in bonds by Felix:

About whom, when I was at Jerusalem, the chief priests and the elders of the Jews informed me, desiring to have judgment against him [Acts 25:14–15].

Agrippa and Bernice stayed there quite a long time. Dr. Luke calls it "many days." Finally they ran out of conversation. Even a king and a governor finally run out of things to talk about. When there was a lull in the conversation, Festus said, "Oh, by the way, I should tell you about a prisoner that we have here. It's a rather odd, unusual case. His name is Paul and he was arrested and brought down here by Felix. Felix left him for me. I'd like you to hear him."

To whom I answered, It is not the manner of the Romans to deliver any man to die, before that he which is accused have the accusers face to face, and have licence to answer for himself concerning the crime laid against him [Acts 25:16].

I'd like to call your attention to this. We sometimes think that Roman law was not just because we have seen how it went awry in the case of the Lord Jesus and also in the case of the apostle Paul. However this was not because of the law but because of the crooked politicians. We still operate under the principle of Roman law that no man is to be sentenced until he has been brought into the presence of his accusers and his crime be established.

Therefore, when they were come hither, without any delay on the morrow I sat on the judgment seat, and commanded the man to be brought forth.

Against whom when the accusers stood up, they brought none accusation of such things as I supposed:

But had certain questions against him of their own superstition, and of one Jesus, which was dead, whom Paul affirmed to be alive [Acts 25:17–19].

The issue is always the same: it is the Resurrection. We see from this that Paul had witnessed to the resurrection of Jesus Christ so that Festus knew about it.

And because I doubted of such manner of questions, I asked him whether he

would go to Jerusalem, and there be judged of these matters.

But when Paul had appealed to be reserved unto the hearing of Augustus, I commanded him to be kept till I might send him to Caesar.

Then Agrippa said unto Festus, I would also hear the man myself. To-morrow, said he, thou shalt hear him [Acts 25:20–22].

Actually, Festus was in a sort of hot seat here. The charge against Paul was sedition and for that he should die, but he had committed no crimes. Now Paul has appealed to Caesar. What are you going to do with a prisoner like that? So he asked Agrippa to help him out.

I'm of the opinion that Agrippa had previously heard about Paul and was actually anxious to hear him. He wanted to know more about the charges and he wanted to hear what Paul would have to say. So they arranged for a meeting.

It is interesting to see how this meeting was arranged by a king and a governor. Yet all the while they were actually fulfilling prophecy even though they were unaware of this. Paul is to appear before kings, as the Lord had said.

THE HEARING BEFORE FESTUS AND AGRIPPA

And on the morrow, when Agrippa was come, and Bernice, with great pomp, and was entered into the place of hearing, with the chief captains, and principal men of the city, at Festus' commandment Paul was brought forth [Acts 25:23].

What a scene this was! Wherever did a preacher have a greater audience than this man? The setting is dramatic with great pomp and ceremony. Paul appears in chains before this august company of rulers and kings. Festus is asking Agrippa to help him frame a charge against Paul to send him to Caesar.

And Festus said, King Agrippa, and all men which are here present with us, ye see this man, about whom all the multitude of the Jews have dealt with me, both at Jerusalem, and also here, crying that he ought not to live any longer.

But when I found that he had committed nothing worthy of death, and that he himself hath appealed to Augustus, I have determined to send him.

Of whom I have no certain thing to write unto my lord. Wherefore I have brought him forth before you, and specially before thee, O king Agrippa, that, after examination had, I might have somewhat to write.

For it seemeth to me unreasonable to send a prisoner, and not withal to signify the crimes laid against him [Acts 25:24–27].

Paul uses this opportunity to preach one of the greatest sermons ever recorded.

CHAPTER 26

***THEME:** Paul before Agrippa*

This testimony of Paul is not a defense of himself. It is a declaration of the gospel with the evident purpose of winning Agrippa and the others present to Christ. This is a dramatic scene, and this chapter is one of the greatest pieces of literature, either secular or inspired.

This chapter was marvelous to me even before I was saved. When I was a young man, I was connected with a little theater. You know that everybody at some time wants to be an actor, and I had the foolish notion that I could become one. The director suggested that I memorize chapter 26 of the Book of Acts. She didn't give me the Bible, but this chapter was printed in some other book and I memorized it from that. I must say that it has always had a tremendous effect upon me.

PAUL'S TESTIMONY BEFORE AGRIPPA

Then Agrippa said unto Paul, Thou art permitted to speak for thyself. Then

Paul stretched forth the hand, and answered for himself [Acts 26:1].

The appearance of Paul before Agrippa is, in my judgment, the high point in the entire ministry of this apostle. It is a fulfillment of the prophecy that he should appear before kings and rulers. Undoubtedly it was God's will that he should come before King Agrippa. I have already indicated that this made a profound impression on me when I memorized it. I must confess that it had some effect upon my decision later on to study for the ministry.

There are several features about this chapter that we ought to note before we get into Paul's message before King Agrippa. First of all, I want to make it clear again that Paul is not on trial. This is not a court trial. Paul is not making a defense before Agrippa. He is preaching the gospel. In view of the fact that this great apostle had appealed to Cacsar, not even King Agrippa could condemn him, and he is certainly out of the hands of Governor Festus, as the final verse of this chapter confirms: "Then said Agrippa unto Festus, This man might have been set at liberty, if he had not appealed unto Caesar" (v. 32). They no longer had the authority to condemn him. Neither could they set him free. They are helpless. So Paul is not attempting to make a defense. Rather he is trying to win these men for Christ.

This was not a trial, but it was a public appearance of Paul before King Agrippa and the court so that they might learn firsthand from the apostle what "that way" really is. You see, everyone was talking about *The Way.* Someone would ask another, "Say, have you heard this new thing about *The Way*?" The other would reply "Well, I have heard some things about it. It is something new going around. What's it all about?" I would imagine that even Festus and Agrippa had some sort of exchange like that. Agrippa would have said, "I've been hearing about this but I'd like to know more about it. We ought to get it from an expert." Therefore they have this public appearance to explain *The Way.* I think this was one of the most splendid opportunities that any minister ever had to preach Christ. There has never again been an opportunity quite like this.

This was an occasion filled with pagan pomp and pageantry. It was a state function filled with fanfare and the blowing of trumpets. There was the tapestry and tinsel. The function was attended by all the prominent personages of that section and the prestige of Rome. It must have been a scramble for people to be able to attend this occasion. The purple of Agrippa and the pearls of Bernice were in evidence. There were the gold braid and the brass hats of the Roman Empire. The elect and the elite, the intelligentsia and the sophisticates had all turned out in full regalia. There would be the pride and ostentation and the dignity and display which only Rome could put on parade in that day.

Notice again how Dr. Luke records it: "And on the morrow, when Agrippa was come, and Bernice, with great pomp, and was entered into the place of hearing, with the chief captains, and principal men of the city, at Festus' commandment Paul was brought forth" (Acts 25:23).

This stirs the imagination. I trust that somehow we can picture this scene before us as we listen to the message of Paul. This elaborate gathering is for just one purpose: to hear from a notable prisoner by the name of Paul. He is the one who has already been over the greater part of the Roman Empire, certainly the eastern part of it, preaching *The Way.*

When the door of that great throne room swings open, a prisoner in chains is ushered into this colorful scene. He is dressed in the garb of a prisoner, and he is chained to two guards. He is unimpressive in his personal appearance. This is the man who teaches and preaches the death, the burial, and the resurrection of Christ for men because they are sinners and need a Savior. This is the one who can speak with authority about the new *Way.* And they will listen to this man because he knows how to speak and because he is an intelligent man. The light of heaven is on his face. He is no longer Saul of Tarsus but Paul the apostle. What a contrast he is to that gay, giddy crowd of nobility gathered there!

Festus told how the Jews had tried to kill Paul. My, how they hated him, and yet they had no real charge against him. That whole crowd looked at Paul, and I rather think that he looked over the whole crowd.

Paul is not a scintillating personality. Some liberal has called him, "Pestiferous Paul." Well, you can call him that if you want to. Maybe in the Roman Empire that is what they thought of him. Remember that the Lord Jesus had said, "If the world hate you, ye know that it hated me before it hated you" (John 15:18). This man is true to the Lord Jesus, so the world will hate him.

I do not think, frankly, that Paul was physically attractive. Yet he had the dynamic kind of attraction which the grace of God gives to a man. He was energized by the Holy Spirit. Oh, that you and I might be able to say with Paul, "I am crucified with Christ: nevertheless I live; yet not I, but Christ liveth in me: and the life which I now live in the flesh I live by the faith of the Son of God, who loved me, and gave himself for me" (Gal. 2:20).

Now let's turn our eyes from the glitter and the glamour of the occasion to the two men who stand out in this assembly: Agrippa and Paul. What a contrast! One of them is in purple, the other is in prison garb. One is on a throne, the other is in shackles. One wears a crown, the other is in chains. Agrippa is a king, but in the slavery of sin. Paul is a chained prisoner, rejoicing in the freedom of sins forgiven and liberty in Christ. Agrippa is an earthly king who could not free Paul nor himself. Paul is an ambassador of the King who had freed him and who could free Agrippa from the damning effects of sin.

We need to remember that King Agrippa was a member of the family of Herod. He belonged to the rottenest family that I know anything about. It is the worst family that is mentioned in the Bible. I think old Ahab and Jezebel were like Sunday school kids compared to the Herod family. You know the old bromide about giving the Devil his due. Well, let's give the Herods their due. Agrippa was an intelligent man and a great man in many respects in spite of his background. He knew the Mosaic Law, that is, he knew the letter of it. Paul rejoiced in this because it gave him an opportunity to speak to a man who was instructed and who would understand the nature of the charges.

As I have said before, I can't help but believe that Paul was getting a little impatient during those two years of incarceration. He had appeared before the mob in Jerusalem, before the captain, then before Felix (publicly, then privately many times), then he appeared before Festus. Now he must appear before Agrippa. None of these other men fully understood the background of the charges against Paul. Neither did they understand the gospel. This is true even of the Roman captain in Jerusalem. It is amazing that these people could have lived in that area, been exposed to Christians, have heard the apostle Paul, and still not really have understood. Yet that was the situation.

Paul's plea to Agrippa to turn to Christ is magnificent. It is logical and it is intelligent. Rather than being a defense, it is a declaration of the gospel.

I think myself happy, king Agrippa, because I shall answer for myself this day before thee touching all the things whereof I am accused of the Jews:

Especially because I know thee to be expert in all customs and questions which are among the Jews: wherefore I beseech thee to hear me patiently [Acts 26:2–3].

Paul is now speaking to a man who understands what he is talking about. Agrippa is an intelligent man, he knows the Mosaic Law, and he understands the Jewish background. Paul really rejoices in this opportunity to speak to such an instructed man who will understand the true nature of the case. Paul likewise is well instructed in the Mosaic Law, but Paul has met Christ. Now the Law has a new meaning for him. The soul of Paul is flooded with a new light. Now he sees that Christ is the end of the Law for righteousness. Now he knows that God has supplied that which He had demanded. He knows that God is good and that through Christ God is gracious. Paul wants King Agrippa to know this. There is a consummate passion filling the soul of the apostle as he speaks. I think this is his masterpiece. His message on Mars' Hill is great, but it does not compare at all to this message.

Although there were probably several hundred people present to hear this message, Paul is speaking to only one man, King Agrippa. Paul is trying to win this man for Christ.

Paul starts with a very courteous introduction, telling Agrippa how he rejoices in this opportunity. Then he proceeds to give King Agrippa a brief sketch of his youth and background. Then he tells of his conversion. Finally he makes his attempt to reach the man for Christ.

Now first of all I am going to ask you to read this entire message without interruption. Actually it tells its own story. Then I shall make some comments about it.

I think myself happy, king Agrippa, because I shall answer for myself this day before thee touching all the things whereof I am accused of the Jews:

Especially because I know thee to be expert in all customs and questions which are among the Jews: wherefore I beseech thee to hear me patiently.

My manner of life from my youth, which was at the first among mine own nation at Jerusalem, know all the Jews;

Which knew me from the beginning, if they would testify, that after the most straitest sect of our religion I lived a Pharisee.

And now I stand and am judged for the hope of the promise made of God unto our fathers:

Unto which promise our twelve tribes, instantly serving God day and night, hope to come. For which hope's sake, king Agrippa, I am accused of the Jews.

Why should it be thought a thing incredible with you, that God should raise the dead?

I verily thought with myself, that I ought to do many things contrary to the name of Jesus of Nazareth.

Which thing I also did in Jerusalem: and many of the saints did I shut up in prison, having received authority from the chief priests; and when they were put to death, I gave my voice against them.

And I punished them oft in every synagogue, and compelled them to blaspheme; and being exceedingly mad against them, I persecuted them even unto strange cities.

Whereupon as I went to Damascus with authority and commission from the chief priests,

At midday, O king, I saw in the way a light from heaven, above the brightness of the sun, shining round about me and them which journeyed with me.

And when we were all fallen to the earth, I heard a voice speaking unto me, and saying in the Hebrew tongue, Saul, Saul, why persecutest thou me? it is hard for thee to kick against the pricks.

And I said, Who art thou, Lord? And he said, I am Jesus whom thou persecutest.

But rise, and stand upon thy feet: for I have appeared unto thee for this purpose, to make thee a minister and a witness both of these things which thou hast seen, and of those things in the which I will appear unto thee;

Delivering thee from the people, and from the Gentiles, unto whom now I send thee,

To open their eyes, and to turn them from darkness to light, and from the power of Satan unto God, that they may receive forgiveness of sins, and inheritance among them which are sanctified by faith that is in me.

Whereupon, O king Agrippa, I was not disobedient unto the heavenly vision:

But shewed first unto them of Damascus, and at Jerusalem, and throughout all the coasts of Judaea, and then to the Gentiles, that they should repent and turn to God, and do works meet for repentance.

For these causes the Jews caught me in the temple, and went about to kill me.

Having therefore obtained help of God, I continue unto this day, witnessing both to small and great, saying none other things than those which the prophets and Moses did say should come:

That Christ should suffer, and that he should be the first that should rise from the dead, and should shew light unto the people, and to the Gentiles [Acts 26:2–23].

After Paul gives a simple explanation of his conduct, which was the natural outcome of his background, he goes on to tell how he lived a Pharisee, and then of the experience he had on the Damascus road.

He said, "I thought I should do many things contrary to the name of Jesus of Nazareth." The Lord Jesus has never had an enemy more bitter and brutal than Saul of Tarsus. He had an inveterate hatred of Jesus Christ and of the gospel. He tells how he wasted the church in Jerusalem and how he shut up many of the saints in prison. This is one reason he could endure two years of prison and such abuse from the religious leaders. He had been one of them. He knew exactly how they felt.

Then in verse 13 he recounts his experience on the Damascus road, how the Lord Jesus waylays him, how he falls to the ground and hears Jesus speak to him. Then Paul realizes he is going against the will of God. Many years later, as he was writing to the Philippians about this experience he said, "But what things were gain to me, those I counted loss for Christ. Yea doubtless, and I count all things but loss for the excellency of the knowledge of Christ Jesus my Lord: for whom I have suffered the loss of all things, and do count them but dung, that I may win Christ" (Phil. 3:7–8). A revolution really took place in his life. He had trusted religion, but when he met Jesus Christ, he got rid of all his religion. What was gain he counted loss. Jesus Christ, whom he had hated above everything else, became for him the most wonderful Person in his life.

Then Paul describes for Festus and King Agrippa the reality of the vision he had. The Lord commissioned him to preach to the Gentiles and promised to deliver him from them. That was a telling blow since there he stands before these two powerful Gentiles who cannot touch him because he has appealed to Caesar—and yet he is able to preach the gospel to them!

Beginning with verse 19, Paul tells his response to the vision that he had. "Whereupon, O king Agrippa, I was not disobedient unto the heavenly vision." The implication is, "What else could I have done. Wouldn't you have done the same thing?"

From the beginning Paul is making it clear that *The Way* is a development and fulfillment of the Old Testament. "Having therefore obtained help of God, I continue unto this day, witnessing both to small and great, saying none other things than those which the prophets and Moses did say should come" (v. 22). It is not contrary to the Old Testament.

Now Paul presents the gospel to this man King Agrippa—and all the crowd assembled there that day heard it. "That Christ should suffer, and that he should be the first that should rise from the dead, and should shew light unto the people, and to the Gentiles" (v. 23). I think Paul emphasized that word *Gentiles* because the king was a Gentile. Notice that he has presented the gospel: that Christ died for our sins, that He was buried, and that He rose again. Paul as always emphasized the Resurrection. Friend, we should never preach the death of Christ without also preaching about His resurrection. Paul confronts that august assembly with the fact that God has intruded into the history of man and that God has done something for man. God demonstrated His love—God so loved the world that He gave His Son.

Suddenly there is an interruption. Evidently Governor Festus is on a hot seat.

And as he thus spake for himself, Festus said with a loud voice, Paul, thou art beside thyself; much learning doth make thee mad.

But he said, I am not mad, most noble Festus; but speak forth the words of truth and soberness [Acts 26:24–25].

It seems unfortunate that Paul is interrupted at this point. But notice how courteously Paul answers him. Certainly his calm response demonstrates that he is not a madman and he is not a fanatic.

In our day, friend, there are many witnesses, especially ministers, who are so afraid that they won't appear intellectual, but will be considered fanatical, that they do not declare the great truths of the gospel. Friend, we ought to be willing to take the place of madmen—but not act like them. We should present the gospel soberly as Paul did.

Notice that having answered Governor Festus, Paul went right back to King Agrippa with the question.

For the king knoweth of these things, before whom also I speak freely: for I am persuaded that none of these things are hidden from him; for this thing was not done in a corner.

King Agrippa, believest thou the prophets? I know that thou believest [Acts 26:26–27].

It is possible to believe the facts without them being meaningful to you. You may know the facts of the gospel—that Jesus died for your sins and rose again—but your relationship to these facts is the thing that is essential.

Then Agrippa said unto Paul, Almost thou persuadest me to be a Christian.

And Paul said, I would to God, that not only thou, but also all that hear me this day, were both almost, and altogether such as I am, except these bonds [Acts 26:28–29].

Agrippa was an intelligent man. He answered, "Almost thou persuadest me to be a Christian." Friend, do you know that you can almost be a Christian and then be lost for time and eternity? How tragic that is! "Almost" will not do. It must be all or nothing. Either you accept Christ or you don't accept Christ. No theologian can probe the depths of salvation and its meaning. Yet it is simple enough for ordinary folk like most of us to understand. Either you have Christ or you don't have

Christ. Either you trust Christ or you don't trust Christ. Either He is your Savior or He is not your Savior. It is one of the two. There is no such thing as a middle ground. It cannot be *almost*. It must be all.

Paul answered, "I would to God, that not only thou, but also all that hear me this day, were both almost, and altogether such as I am, except these bonds." Paul is saying that he longs for them to have a relationship to Christ and be like he is—except for the chains. He wouldn't want chains on anyone. This is the man who had been a proud and zealous Pharisee. This is the man who a few years before bound Christians in chains and put them to death. Now his attitude is different. He wants all people to become Christians and to have a vital and personal relationship with Jesus Christ.

One cannot help but be struck by the mighty transformation that had taken place in Saul of Tarsus. What is the explanation? It is that Jesus was *alive*! He was back from the dead. This is why Paul said very early in his testimony before Agrippa, "Why should it be thought a thing incredible with you, that God should raise the dead?" There is nothing unreasonable about that. Nineteen hundred years of man's development in knowledge in many fields makes the Resurrection even more credible in our day. Actually, it should be easier for you to believe in the Resurrection than it was for folk in that day.

Since Jesus is back from the dead, there is another and coming judgment. There is another throne, and Jesus is seated upon it. And there is another prisoner—the prisoner is you or me. Either you have bowed to Him and accepted Him as your Lord and Savior, or you will be accountable to Him in that day. The Resurrection is very important to the unsaved man as well as to the saved man.

And when he had thus spoken, the king rose up, and the governor, and Bernice, and they that sat with them:

And when they were gone aside, they talked between themselves, saying, This man doeth nothing worthy of death or of bonds.

Then said Agrippa unto Festus, This man might have been set at liberty, if he had not appealed unto Caesar [Acts 26:30–32].

It is obvious that Paul is going to Rome now. We have mentioned before that there are those who question whether Paul did the right thing when he appealed to Caesar. Some feel that Paul made a mistake. I don't think it was a mistake at all.

In the Epistle to the Romans Paul expressed his longing to go to Rome. "Making request, if by any means now at length I might have a prosperous journey by the will of God to come unto you. For I long to see you, that I may impart unto you some spiritual gift, to the end ye may be established" (Rom. 1:10–11).

He is going to Rome all right. You may question whether or not he had a "prosperous journey." I have a friend in the ministry who ran a series of messages for young people (which were tremendous, by the way), and the title of the series was "Paul's Prosperous Journey to Rome." It was a prosperous journey in that it was the will of God that he should go to Rome.

CHAPTER 27

***THEME:** Paul goes to Rome via storm and shipwreck*

This sea voyage might reasonably be called Paul's fourth missionary journey. He was just as active when he went to Rome, he exercised the same latitude, he made as many contacts, and he witnessed just as faithfully as he had on his other journeys. Chains did not hinder him even though he made this entire journey in chains. He is the one who said "Wherein I suffer trouble, as an evildoer, even unto bonds; but the word of God is not bound" (2 Tim. 2:9). Also he wrote to the Philippians that the things which happened to him worked out for the furtherance of the gospel (Phil. 1:12).

God is in all of this, friend. The trip this time will be a little different from the others. It is to be made at the expense of the Roman government because he is Rome's prisoner. This is the fulfillment of Paul's prayer that he might come to Rome.

When Paul appealed his case to Caesar, he was moved out of the jurisdiction of Festus, the governor, and King Agrippa. As King Agrippa had said after hearing his case, "This man might have been set at liberty, if he had not appealed unto Caesar" (Acts 26:32). They couldn't do anything about it now; they must send Paul to Rome.

In chapter 27 of Acts we have the record of his voyage to Rome. What we have here might be called the log of the ship. This chapter of Acts has been considered the finest description of a sea voyage in the ancient world that is on record today. Sir William Ramsay made a study of Dr. Luke's writing, and he considers this a masterpiece and the most accurate that has ever been written. So we are coming to another great chapter in the Bible, as you can see.

Those of you who have studied Caesar in Latin may recall the account of the building of a bridge. That has always been a passage that stands out in the memory of all who study Latin because there are so many new words that pertain to the building of a bridge. This chapter in the Greek corresponds to it because there are many technical terms which Dr. Luke uses to describe this voyage.

Let's take off now with the apostle Paul. We're going to take a sea voyage to Rome. This is the final and most exciting travelog in the Book of Acts.

PAUL'S PROSPEROUS JOURNEY TO ROME

And when it was determined that we should sail into Italy, they delivered Paul and certain other prisoners unto one named Julius, a centurion of Augustus' band [Acts 27:1].

This is the beginning of the voyage to Italy. Paul, along with other prisoners, is put in the charge of a centurion by the name of Julius. I would think it safe to say that Paul was the only one of the prisoners who was a Roman citizen. Probably the others were criminals who were sent to Rome for execution. Many of them would become gladiators and would be fed to the wild beasts. In that day there was a constant stream of human life from all corners of the empire that was being fed into the mall of this public vice there in the Colosseum in Rome. These prisoners would be utterly hopeless men. What an opportunity this gave Paul to bring the gospel of hope to this class of men. You will remember that the Lord Jesus Himself said that one of the reasons He came was to set the prisoners free—free spiritually, delivered from their sins and delivered from their guilt.

This centurion, Julius, was a very courteous pagan, as we shall see.

And entering into a ship of Adramyttium, we launched, meaning to sail by the coasts of Asia; one Aristarchus, a Macedonian of Thessalonica, being with us [Acts 27:2].

Again, it will be a help if you will follow this voyage on a map. You will notice that now they are going up the coast of Israel. In other words, they don't sail directly out to sea from the point of departure and then arrive at Rome. The ship hovers close to the coastline and goes up the coast of Israel.

And the next day we touched at Sidon. And Julius courteously entreated Paul, and gave him liberty to go unto his friends to refresh himself [Acts 27:3].

Sidon is a familiar place to us. Tyre and Sidon are up on the coast in Phoenicia in what is now the country of Lebanon.

Notice the liberty that is granted to the apostle Paul. I am of the opinion that here is a Roman official whom Paul reached with the gospel. His treatment of Paul is gracious. Even the great apostle Paul needed the fellowship and refreshment of Christian brethren. None of us are immune to that. We need the understanding and encouragement of one another.

And when we had launched from thence, we sailed under Cyprus, because the winds were contrary [Acts 27:4].

"Under Cyprus" actually means that they came all the way down south of Cyprus, which indicates they were encountering some north winds.

And when we had sailed over the sea of Cilicia and Pamphylia, we came to Myra, a city of Lycia [Acts 27:5].

We've been with Paul over this water before. They are sailing along the southern coast of Asia Minor, hovering close to the shore along there.

And there the centurion found a ship of Alexandria sailing into Italy; and he put us therein [Acts 27:6].

If you check on your map, you will see that Myra is sort of a jumping-off place. This was the place at which they changed ships. The centurion found a ship of Alexandria, which means it had come up from northern Africa and was sailing to Italy.

And when we had sailed slowly many days, and scarce were come over against Cnidus, the wind not suffering us, we sailed under Crete, over against Salmone;

And, hardly passing it, came unto a place which is called The fair havens; nigh whereunto was the city of Lasea [Acts 27:7–8].

They were headed for the island of Crete. Apparently they were still having difficulty sailing. Contrary winds were the great difficulty for sailing vessels of that day. They passed on the south side of the island and came to Lasea, which is on the south shore of Crete.

Now when much time was spent, and when sailing was now dangerous, because the fast was now already past, Paul admonished them [Acts 27:9].

This means that it was late in the season and that winter was coming on. They had been hoping to get to Rome before the stormy season. It is interesting to note that Paul takes a moral ascendancy at this point. When the sailing became dangerous, Paul admonished them.

And said unto them, Sirs, I perceive that this voyage will be with hurt and much damage, not only of the lading and ship, but also of our lives.

Nevertheless the centurion believed the master and the owner of the ship, more than those things which were spoken by Paul [Acts 27:10–11].

One can certainly understand the centurion. After all, you would expect the captain of the ship to know more about sailing than Paul.

We see Paul under a real testing here. He certainly stands out. He makes a suggestion which, they will find later, should have been followed. The spiritual superiority of Paul is evident at this point. There is no confusion in the life of Paul, no uncertainty, no frustration. He is what would be called a poised personality. Paul knew the way he was going. "This one thing I do" was his declaration when he got to Rome. We can observe these qualities in his behavior, throughout the voyage. Paul lived his life as a man in touch with God.

And because the haven was not commodious to winter in, the more part advised to depart thence also, if by any means they might attain to Phenice, and there to winter; which is an haven of Crete, and lieth toward the south-west and north-west [Acts 27:12].

Crete is an island that lies off the coast of Asia Minor and also off the coast of Greece. It is the largest island and contains several good harbors.

Events are going to prove that Paul was right. Throughout this voyage the captain, the soldiers, and the sailors were depending on human speculation alone. Paul was looking to God.

And when the south wind blew softly, supposing that they had obtained their purpose, loosing thence, they sailed close by Crete [Acts 27:13].

To them the voyage was guesswork. The south wind blew softly, so they "supposed." The captain was a man who looked to self and to the wisdom of men. Paul was looking to God. Later on Paul would tell these men, "I believe God" (v. 25). Notice he would not say that he believed *in* God, but "I believe God."

Life is a great sea and our lives are little boats. We can sail our boats by human supposition if we so choose. Friend, there is a storm blowing out there, a bit of a gale. The tragedy is that, amid confusion, world chaos, and darkness, most men are still guessing. There are a thousand human plans for building a better world. Yet everywhere we look we see failure. We need men who *know* God. It was Gladstone who said, "The mark of a great statesman is a man who knows the way God is going for the next fifty years." We don't seem to find many such men around today.

THE STORM

But not long after there arose against it a tempestuous wind, called Euroclydon [Acts 27:14].

What is Euroclydon? Dr. Luke is using a very technical navigational term of that day. It has to do with the north wind, and it actually came north by east. In other words, the storm came down out of Europe. This was wintertime and the stormy season. It was a "tempestuous wind" and it is in this storm that Paul and all those on the ship with him are caught.

Now I want to stop here to point out something very interesting. You will remember that when Paul was in Ephesus, which was a time of triumph for the gospel, he expressed a great desire to visit Rome. It was the great yearning of his heart. "After these things were ended, Paul purposed in the spirit, when he had passed through Macedonia and Achaia, to go to Jerusalem, saying, After I have been there, I must also see Rome" (Acts 19:21). The hour of darkness came for Paul in Jerusalem. It looked as if he would never see Rome at all. In that hour of darkness, despair, and defeat, God appeared to him to reassure him. "And the night following the Lord stood by him, and said, Be of good cheer, Paul: for as thou hast testified of me in Jerusalem, so must thou bear witness also at Rome" (Acts 23:11). The Lord had assured Paul that he would go to Rome.

And when the ship was caught, and could not bear up into the wind, we let her drive.

And running under a certain island which is called Clauda, we had much work to come by the boat:

Which when they had taken up, they used helps, undergirding the ship; and, fearing lest they should fall into the quicksands, strake sail, and so were driven.

And we being exceedingly tossed with a tempest, the next day they lightened the ship [Acts 27:15–18].

They were out there in the Mediterranean Sea being driven westward from the island of Crete. It looked very much as if they would be wrecked on the little island of Clauda, which, by the way, is a very small island south of Crete. They had to let the wind take the ship. They threw all the cargo overboard to lighten the ship.

And the third day we cast out with our own hands the tackling of the ship [Acts 27:19].

They completely stripped the ship of everything that had any weight.

And when neither sun nor stars in many days appeared, and no small tempest lay on us, all hope that we should be saved was then taken away [Acts 27:20].

Dr. Luke says that "no small tempest" lay on them. We have already seen how Dr. Luke likes to use the diminutive like this. He means that it was really a terrible storm. In fact, they did not think they would escape from it alive. It was in the storm that the voice of the Lord was heard through the lips of Paul.

After fourteen days of wave and wind, the folk on the ship felt that they would not come through alive. They felt like this was it. However, the Lord had appeared to Paul and assured him that he was going to see Rome. With this assurance Paul was able to stand out above the others.

But after long abstinence Paul stood forth in the midst of them, and said, Sirs, ye should have hearkened unto me, and not have loosed from Crete, and to have gained this harm and loss.

And now I exhort you to be of good cheer: for there shall be no loss of any man's life among you, but of the ship.

For there stood by me this night the angel of God, whose I am, and whom I serve,

Saying, Fear not, Paul; thou must be brought before Caesar: and, lo, God hath given thee all them that sail with thee.

Wherefore, sirs, be of good cheer: for I believe God, that it shall be even as it was told me.

Howbeit we must be cast upon a certain island [Acts 27:21–26].

You can understand that this was a very encouraging word to all those who were on board the ship. In fact, it was the only thing they had to hold onto. Notice the wonderful testimony of the apostle Paul: "Whose I am, and whom I serve." His confidence was in God: "Be of good cheer: for I believe God, that it shall be even as it was told me."

It was revealed to Paul that they would be cast upon an island. We will learn later that the island was Melita, which is just south of Sicily. So they had traveled quite a distance across the Mediterranean from the island of Crete. Melita is the island we know today as Malta.

But when the fourteenth night was come, as we were driven up and down in Adria, about midnight the shipmen deemed that they drew near to some country [Acts 27:27].

"Adria" is the Adriatic Sea. The Adriatic Sea lies between Italy and Macedonia or Greece. Apparently they have been driven up and down the Adriatic in the storm, passing between Crete and Sicily. They are out in the deep, out in the open sea. On the fourteenth night about midnight it becomes apparent that they are being driven near some land.

And sounded, and found it twenty fathoms: and when they had gone a little further, they sounded again, and found it fifteen fathoms.

Then fearing lest we should have fallen upon rocks, they cast four anchors out of the stern, and wished for the day [Acts 27:28–29].

Their sounding showed that they were moving in closer to the land. Each sounding showed that the water was becoming more shallow.

Perhaps I should mention here that I have heard sermons on "Four Anchors," and those anchors have been labeled about everything under the sun. Let us not fall into the trap of trying to spiritualize something which is very practical and very realistic. These men were in a ship and they were approaching land. Since they didn't want to be cast upon the rocks, they threw out four anchors. It required all four to hold the ship. If you started to guess how many anchors it would take to hold you or to hold me, you would be trying to spiritualize this passage. In my judgment, that is a very foolish way to handle the Word of God.

And as the shipmen were about to flee out of the ship, when they had let down the boat into the sea, under colour as though they would have cast anchors out of the foreship,

Paul said to the centurion and to the soldiers, Except these abide in the ship, ye cannot be saved [Acts 27:30–31].

The crew was trying to abandon the ship, you see. They acted as if they were dropping anchor, but actually they were going overboard. They were leaving a sinking ship as the rats leave it. They were doing something which they should never have done.

Paul tells the centurion that the only assurance of safety is for all to remain with the ship. Paul has put his trust in God. What a wonderful thing it is to trust the Word of God. The angel of God had told Paul that he and the men would be saved. But they couldn't be saved their way. They must be saved God's way. God's way was for them to stay with the ship. It was a question of believing that God would save them or not believing and taking matters into their own hands. Paul had told them that he believed God. And he tells them that if they want to be saved, all will need to stay on board the ship.

Then the soldiers cut off the ropes of the boat, and let her fall off [Acts 27:32].

Paul has given the information to the centurion. The centurion is beginning to listen to Paul now. He gives the command and the soldiers cut the ropes to the life boats. Now everyone must stay on board.

And while the day was coming on, Paul besought them all to take meat, saying, This day is the fourteenth day that ye have tarried and continued fasting, having taken nothing.

Wherefore I pray you to take some meat: for this is for your health: for there shall not an hair fall from the head of any of you [Acts 27:33–34].

You know very well, fourteen days of fasting would weaken even the hardiest men. Now Paul urges them all to eat. Apparently they had all fasted. The pagans had fasted because they were scared to death. Paul and the Christians may have fasted because they were doing it unto the Lord. Now they are near land and they all need their strength to make it to shore. So Paul uses sanctified sanity in the Lord's service. He uses good sense.

In Christian work we need just good, common, sanctified sense more than in any other area of life. How foolish people can be and at the same time excuse it by saying they are simply trusting the Lord. My friend, the Lord expects us to use some common sense.

And when he had thus spoken, he took bread, and gave thanks to God in presence of them all: and when he had broken it, he began to eat [Acts 27:35].

Paul gave thanks to God in the presence of them all. This again is a wonderful testimony. This is Paul's prosperous journey to Rome. Perhaps you are saying, "It doesn't sound very prosperous to me! It seems to me he is out of the will of God!" No, my friend, Paul is not out of the will of God.

Do you remember another instance back in the Gospels when the Lord Jesus put His own disciples into a boat one night and sent them across the Sea of Galilee? He told them to go to the other side, and on the way over a storm arose on the sea. He sent them right into a storm. Now don't say that Jesus didn't know the storm was coming. He deliberately sent them into the storm! He is God. He knew about the storm, and He knew what He was doing. I personally believe that oftentimes the Lord deliberately sends us into a storm. We need to remember that we can be in the storm and still be in the will of God. He has never said we will miss the storms of life, but He has promised us that we will make the harbor. And He will be right there with us through the storm. That is the comfort that should come to the child of God in the time of the storm.

Then were they all of good cheer, and they also took some meat.

And we were in all in the ship two hundred threescore and sixteen souls [Acts 27:36–37].

There were 276 people on board—so it was a sizable ship.

And when they had eaten enough, they lightened the ship, and cast out the wheat into the sea [Acts 27:38].

They had previously thrown all the cargo overboard. Now they throw all their food overboard.

And when it was day, they knew not the land: but they discovered a certain creek with a shore, into the which they were minded, if it were possible, to thrust in the ship.

And when they had taken up the anchors, they committed themselves unto the sea, and loosed the rudder bands, and hoisted up the mainsail to the wind, and made toward shore.

And falling into a place where two seas met, they ran the ship aground; and the forepart stuck fast, and remained unmoveable, but the hinder part was broken with the violence of the waves.

And the soldiers' counsel was to kill the prisoners, lest any of them should swim out, and escape.

But the centurion, willing to save Paul, kept them from their purpose; and commanded that they which could swim should cast themselves first into the sea, and get to land:

And the rest, some on boards, and some on broken pieces of the ship. And so it came to pass, that they escaped all safe to land [Acts 27:39–44].

Their landing could be considered miraculous, although I am not going to insist that it was a miracle. However, God certainly fulfilled His promise that Paul and all the 276 people on the ship would get to land safely.

CHAPTER 28

THEME: *Paul arrives in Rome*

This, our final study in the Book of Acts, follows Paul from Melita to Rome. When Paul arrives in Rome, he ministers first to Jews and then to Gentiles. The narrative is not concluded but breaks off with Paul preaching in Rome. The acts of the Holy Spirit have not been finished even in our day. The Book of Acts will end with the Rapture.

THE LANDING ON MELITA

And when they were escaped, then they knew that the island was called Melita [Acts 28:1].

This is the island which we know today as Malta. The bay where this took place is known today as Saint Paul's Bay. This is a very interesting place to those of us who lived during World War II when this island made the headlines at the very beginning of the conflict. It was the most bombed spot of the war because it was in a strategic position. At that time General Darby was the general and the governor of the island. He was a Christian and a worthy successor to the apostle Paul. He said that he had no notion of surrendering. I think it is interesting to be reading about Paul landing at this bay and to realize that General Darby had command on that same island.

Certainly in the incident of this shipwreck and the landing of Paul on the island of Melita we see the providence of God in the life of the apostle Paul. All of this is recorded for our learning.

And the barbarous people shewed us no little kindness: for they kindled a fire, and received us every one, because of the present rain, and because of the cold [Acts 28:2].

It may cause us to smile a little that Dr. Luke labels the natives of the island "barbarous people." The word *barbarian* was used to describe one who did not speak Greek. It does not imply tribal savagery. Here we have another instance of the kindness and the courtesy of pagans. Remember that there are 276 people who have landed on this little island. Out of this crowd, many are criminals who are being sent to Rome for punishment. Yet we find this wonderful compassion and helpfulness on the part of people who are pagans. We find in the Book of Jonah another instance of this same thing when the pagan sailors tried to spare Jonah. They didn't want to throw him overboard even though he had told them they should do it. They tried to bring the ship to land but found out they couldn't do it. Sometimes pagan folk are more gracious than the folk who are religious.

And when Paul had gathered a bundle of sticks, and laid them on the fire, there came a viper out of the heat, and fastened on his hand [Acts 28:3].

You remember that at the end of the Gospel of Mark there is this promise: "And these signs shall follow them that believe; In my name shall they cast out devils; they shall speak with new tongues; They shall take up serpents; and if they drink any deadly thing, it shall not hurt them; they shall lay hands on the sick, and they shall recover" (Mark 16:17–18). I believe that these signs were confined to that time before the New Testament was completed when the believers needed the sign gifts to substantiate the message of the gospel.

My advice to you today is not to deliberately pick up a rattlesnake. I lived in Tennessee for many years and I have never known an authentic case where someone picked up a rattlesnake during a meeting, was bitten, and was unaffected by the venom of the snake. Most of them die. Those who live through it almost die. The venom has a tremendous effect upon them.

May I point out something else. Paul did not deliberately pick up this viper. Paul was not tempting God. I consider this another evidence that Paul's ". . . thorn in the flesh . . ." (2 Cor. 12:7) was eye trouble. (I'll develop that when we get to the Epistle to the Galatians.) Paul couldn't see very well. When he picked up some sticks, there was a viper on the sticks and Paul just didn't see it.

There is another interesting sidelight to the apostle Paul that I want you to notice here: the great apostle Paul gathered sticks. These people on the island had been very gracious to them. They had accepted the 276 strangers who landed there. It was cold and rainy, and they had started a big fire to help warm these people who had come in from the sea. When the fire began to go down, Paul went out to gather a bundle of sticks. This should dispel any notion that Paul was a lazy preacher. He himself tells us that he practiced his trade as a tentmaker so that he would not be a burden to the church. Obviously he was not afraid of work.

When Paul threw the sticks onto the fire, the viper would naturally crawl away from the fire. The viper not only bit Paul but actually fastened onto his hand.

And when the barbarians saw the venomous beast hang on his hand, they said among themselves, No doubt this man is a murderer, whom, though he hath escaped the sea, yet vengeance suffereth not to live [Acts 28:4].

The Greek word here for "vengeance" is *dike* which actually would be better translated "justice." "Yet justice suffereth not to live." In other words, they felt that Paul was guilty of a great crime, and justice was catching up with him. He had escaped from the sea but now he would surely die of the venom. Very frankly, I think they sat down to watch what would happen to him. They expected that any moment he would begin to show swelling in his hand and arm, then would fall down dead. They knew by sad experience, as that is what had happened to their own people. They expected it to happen to Paul.

Notice that these pagans did have a sense of justice. They assumed that Paul was a murderer and that he deserved punishment. In such a circumstance today, folk would be helping the criminal to get back out to sea to escape being punished. This incident shows that throughout the Roman Empire there was a sense of justice. Pagan Rome made that contribution to the world. Rome was noted for justice, not mercy. Sins were not forgiven. If you broke the law, you paid the penalty. Under the iron heel of Rome the world was crying for mercy. This was a preparation for the coming of Christ who came as the Savior from sin—that mankind might know the mercy and forgiveness of God.

And he shook off the beast into the fire, and felt no harm.

Howbeit they looked when he should have swollen, or fallen down dead suddenly: but after they had looked a great while, and saw no harm come to him, they changed their minds, and said that he was a god [Acts 28:5–6].

The promise of God in Mark 16:18 was fulfilled in Paul's experience. He suffered no ill effects from the venom. When folk today deliberately pick up snakes and claim that promise as their protection, they are far afield from what God had in mind.

When they saw that no harm came to Paul, they decided that he certainly could not be a criminal but was instead a god. Although they were equally as wrong in this judgment, it did give Paul a very important contact on the Island of Melita here.

In the same quarters were possessions of the chief man of the island, whose name was Publius; who received us, and lodged us three days courteously.

And it came to pass, that the father of Publius lay sick of a fever and of a bloody flux: to whom Paul entered in, and prayed, and laid his hands on him, and healed him [Acts 28:7–8].

Paul was now exercising his gift as an apostle. He entered in and he prayed. Apparently he did not pray for the man; he prayed for himself. That is, he prayed to determine the will of God. Was this man to be healed through Paul? That is what he prayed to know.

So when this was done, others also, which had diseases in the island, came, and were healed:

Who also honoured us with many honours; and when we departed, they laded us with such things as were necessary [Acts 28:9–10].

The question has been raised whether or not Paul preached the gospel in Melita. There are those who believe that this is one place where Paul did not preach. This is an instance where I think the Holy Spirit expects us to use ordinary common sense. Of course, he preached the gospel. We are coming to the end of the book, and the incident is related in a very brief and blunt manner. By now Dr. Luke expects us to know what Paul would do. Remember that Paul is the man who wrote, "For I determined not to know any thing among you, save Jesus Christ, and him crucified" (1 Cor. 2:2). With the apostles, healing was God's witness that the gospel they preached was from Him. It is very important for us to realize that Paul preached the gospel and that the healing was the result of it. It was the evidence of the truth he was preaching. I think it can be only a normal inference that Paul did exactly the same here as he did everywhere he went.

THE VOYAGE CONTINUES

And after three months we departed in a ship of Alexandria, which had wintered in the isle, whose sign was Castor and Pollux [Acts 28:11].

Since Paul stayed in Melita for three months, it is evident that the few verses given to us here are not the complete story of his ministry on that island. Therefore, I think we can be sure that Paul preached the gospel.

"Castor and Pollux," the sign of their ship, were gods of the Romans. There is still a pillar to them in the Roman Forum.

And landing at Syracuse, we tarried there three days.

And from thence we fetched a compass, and came to Rhegium: and after one day the south wind blew, and we came the next day to Puteoli [Acts 28:12–13].

The storm is over. The Euroclydon, that tempestuous wind from the north, is passed. Now there is a south wind blowing again.

Where we found brethren, and were desired to tarry with them seven days: and so we went toward Rome.

And from thence, when the brethren heard of us, they came to meet us as far as Appii forum, and The three taverns: whom when Paul saw, he thanked God, and took courage [Acts 28:14–15].

Paul is now on the Appian Way. Again we see how important the encouragement of believers was to the apostle Paul.

PAUL IN ROME

And when we came to Rome, the centurion delivered the prisoners to the captain of the guard: but Paul was suffered to dwell by himself with a soldier that kept him [Acts 28:16].

Paul apparently had the freedom to live in a house, but he was always guarded by a soldier. In fact, different soldiers took turns on guard duty.

And it came to pass, that after three days Paul called the chief of the Jews together: and when they were come together, he said unto them, Men and brethren, though I have committed nothing against the people, or customs of our fathers, yet was I delivered prisoner from Jerusalem into the hands of the Romans.

Who, when they had examined me, would have let me go, because there was no cause of death in me.

But when the Jews spake against it, I was constrained to appeal unto Caesar; not that I had aught to accuse my nation of.

For this cause therefore have I called for you, to see you, and to speak with you: because that for the hope of Israel I am bound with this chain [Acts 28:17–20].

We see Paul following his usual pattern of approaching the Jews first. He explains to them why he has been brought to Rome.

And they said unto him, We neither received letters out of Judaea concerning thee, neither any of the brethren that came shewed or spake any harm of thee.

But we desire to hear of thee what thou thinkest: for as concerning this sect, we know that every where it is spoken against.

And when they had appointed him a day, there came many to him into his lodging; to whom he expounded and testified the kingdom of God, persuading them concerning Jesus, both out of the law of Moses, and out of the prophets, from morning till evening.

And some believed the things which were spoken, and some believed not [Acts 28:21–24].

We see here the kind of liberty that Paul had as a prisoner. Apparently he could have quite large crowds come to his home. However, there was always a soldier on guard to watch him.

Again we see that the apostle Paul used his background in the Old Testament to persuade the Jews concerning Jesus. As always, there was the double response to the message. Some believed, but others did not.

And when they agreed not among themselves, they departed, after that Paul had spoken one word, Well spake the Holy Ghost by Esaias the prophet unto our fathers,

Saying, Go unto this people, and say, Hearing ye shall hear, and shall not understand; and seeing ye shall see, and not perceive:

For the heart of this people is waxed gross, and their ears are dull of hearing, and their eyes have they closed; lest they should see with their eyes, and hear with their ears, and understand with their heart, and should be converted, and I should heal them.

Be it known therefore unto you, that the salvation of God is sent unto the Gentiles, and that they will hear it.

And when he had said these words, the Jews departed, and had great reasoning among themselves.

And Paul dwelt two whole years in his own hired house, and received all that came in unto him,

Preaching the kingdom of God, and teaching those things which concern the Lord Jesus Christ, with all confidence, no man forbidding him [Acts 28:25–31].

The Book of Acts tells of the beginning of the movement of the gospel to the ends of the earth. Remember that in the Garden of Eden man doubted God and that led to disobedience. The way back to God is by faith, ". . . for obedience to the faith . . ." as Paul says in Romans 1:5. So we find in that day that some believed the gospel and some did not.

The Book of Acts ends with Paul "preaching the kingdom of God, and teaching those things which concern the Lord Jesus Christ, with all confidence." The record is not concluded. The Holy Spirit continues to work today. The acts of the Holy Spirit have not been finished even in our day. The Book of Acts will end with the Rapture, the coming of Christ for His own. The work of the church has not yet been completed; it is a continuing story. What you and I have done in the power of the Holy Spirit will be included in that record.

BIBLIOGRAPHY

(Recommended for Further Study)

Alexander, J. A. *The Acts of the Apostles*. Carlisle, Pennsylvania: The Banner of Truth Trust, 1875.

Conybeare, W. J. and Howson, J. S. *The Life and Epistles of St. Paul*. Grand Rapids, Michigan: William B. Eerdmans Pub. Co., 1855. (A classic work.)

Eims, Leroy. *Disciples in Action*. Wheaton, Illinois: Victor Books, 1981.

Frank, Harry Thomas, editor. *Hammond's Atlas of the Bible Lands*. Wheaton, Illinois: Scripture Press Publications, 1977. (Inexpensive atlas with splendid maps.)

Gaebelein, Arno C. *The Acts of the Apostles*. Neptune, New Jersey: Loizeaux Brothers, 1912. (A fine interpretation.)

Heading, John. *Acts: A Study in New Testament Christianity*. Kansas City, Kansas: Walterick Publishers.

Hiebert, D. Edmond. *Personalities Around Paul*. Chicago, Illinois: Moody Press, 1973. (Rich studies of people in contact with the Apostle Paul.)

Ironside, H. A. *Lectures on the Book of Acts*. Neptune, New Jersey: Loizeaux Brothers, 1943. (Especially good for young Christians.)

Jensen, Irving L. *Acts: An Inductive Study*. Chicago, Illinois: Moody Press, 1968.

Kelly, William. *An Exposition of the Acts of the Apostles*. Addison, Illinois: Bible Truth Publishers, 1890.

Kent, Homer A., Jr. *Jerusalem to Rome: Studies in the Book of Acts*. Grand Rapids: Baker Book House, 1974. (A splendid work for individual or group study.)

Morgan, G. Campbell. *The Acts of the Apostles*. Old Tappan, New Jersey: Fleming H. Revell Co., 1924.

Rackham, R. B. *The Acts of the Apostles*. Grand Rapids, Michigan: Baker Book House, 1901. (A detailed study.)

Robertson, A. T. *Epochs in the Life of Paul*. Grand Rapids, Michigan: Baker Book House, 1909.

Ryrie, Charles D. *The Acts of the Apostles*. Chicago, Illinois: Moody Press, 1961. (A fine, inexpensive survey.)

Scroggie, W. Graham. *The Acts of the Apostles*. Grand Rapids, Michigan: Zondervan Publishing House, n.d. (Splendid outlines.)

Thomas, W. H. Griffith. *Outline Studies in the Acts of the Apostles*. Grand Rapids, Michigan: William B. Eerdmans Publishing Co., 1956.

Vaughan, Curtis. *Acts*. Grand Rapids, Michigan: Zondervan Publishing House, 1974.

Vos, Howard F. *Beginnings in Bible Archeology*. Chicago, Illinois: Moody Press, 1973.

The Epistle to the

ROMANS

INTRODUCTION

Let me say just a word concerning Paul the apostle. With his writings we actually come now to a different method of revelation. God has used many ways to communicate to man. He gave the Pentateuch—the Law—through Moses. He gave history, He gave poetry, and He gave prophecy. He gave the Gospels, and now we come to a new section: the Epistles, the majority of which were written by Paul.

Adolf Deissmann tried to make a distinction between epistles and letters. Having examined the papyri that were found at Oxyrhynchus in Egypt, he made a decision between literary and nonliterary documents, placing the Epistles of Paul in the latter category, thereby making them letters rather than epistles. However, a great many scholars today think this is an entirely false division.

These letters that we have—these epistles—are so warm and so personal that, as far as you and I are concerned, it is just as if they came by special delivery mail to us today. The Lord is speaking to us personally in each one of these very wonderful letters that Paul and the other apostles wrote to the churches. Nevertheless, Romans contains the great gospel manifesto for the world. To Paul the gospel was the great ecumenical movement and Rome was the center of that world for which Christ died. Paul's Epistle to the Romans is both an epistle and a letter.

Paul made this statement in Romans 15:15–16, "Nevertheless, brethren, I have written the more boldly unto you in some sort, as putting you in mind, because of the grace that is given to me of God, That I should be the minister of Jesus Christ to the Gentiles, ministering the gospel of God, that the offering up of the Gentiles might be acceptable, being sanctified by the Holy Ghost." Paul made it very clear here that he was the apostle to the Gentiles. He also made it clear that Simon Peter was the apostle to the nation Israel. For instance, in Galatians he said, "(For he that wrought effectually in Peter to the apostleship of the circumcision, the same was mighty in me toward the Gentiles:) And when James, Cephas, and John, who seemed to be pillars, perceived the grace that was given unto me, they gave to me and Barnabas the right hands of fellowship; that we should go unto the heathen, and they unto the circumcision" (Gal. 2:8–9). Therefore you see that Paul was peculiarly the apostle to the Gentiles. When you read the last chapter of Romans and see all those people that Paul knew, you will find that most of them were Gentiles. The church in Rome was largely a gentile church.

Paul also made the point that, if somebody else had founded the church in Rome, he would never have gone there. Instead, he said that he was eager to go there. "So as much as in me is, I am ready to preach the gospel to you that are at Rome also" (Rom. 1:15). He wanted to go to Rome to preach the gospel. In Acts 26 Paul recounted to Agrippa the message the Lord gave to him when He appeared to him: "Delivering thee from the people, and from the Gentiles, unto whom now I send thee, To open their eyes, and turn them from darkness to light, and from the power of Satan unto God, that they may receive forgiveness of sins, and inheritance among them which are sanctified by faith that is in me" (Acts 26: 17–18).

Further, Paul would never have gone to Rome, although he was eager to go, if anyone else had preached the gospel there ahead of him. In Romans 15:20 he said, "Yea, so have I strived to preach the gospel, not where Christ was named, lest I should build upon another man's foundation." Paul, my friend, just didn't go where another apostle had been. We can conclude, therefore, that no other apostle had been to Rome.

Now that leads me to say a word about Rome, and the question is: Who founded the church in Rome? I am going to make a rather unusual statement here: Paul is the one who founded the church in Rome, and he founded it, as it were, by "long distance" and used the "remote control" of an apostle to write and guide its course.

Let me make this very clear. You see, Rome was a tremendous city. Paul had never been there, no other apostle had been there, and yet a church came into existence. How did it come into existence? Well, Paul, as he moved throughout the Roman Empire, won men and women to Christ. Rome had a strong drawing power, and many people were in Rome who had met Paul throughout the Roman Empire.

You might ask, "Do you know that?" Oh, yes, we have a very striking example of that in Acts where we find Paul going to Corinth. "After these things Paul departed from Athens, and came to Corinth; And found a certain Jew named Aquila, born in Pontus, lately come from Italy, with his wife Priscilla; (because that Claudius had commanded all Jews to depart from Rome:) and came unto them. And because he was of the same craft, he abode with them, and wrought: for by their occupation they were tentmakers" (Acts 18:1–3). Paul had met Aquila and Priscilla—their home was in Rome, but there had been a wave of anti-Semitism; Claudius the emperor had persecuted them, and this couple had left Rome. They went to Corinth. We find later that they went with Paul to Ephesus and became real witnesses for Christ. Then, when Paul wrote the Epistle to the Romans, they had returned to Rome, and Paul sent greetings to them. We do have this very personal word in Acts concerning this couple. What about the others? Well, Paul did know them. That means he had also met them somewhere and had led them to Christ. Paul was the founder of the church at Rome by "long distance"—by leading folk to Christ who later gravitated to Rome.

Paul knew Rome although he had not been inside her city limits at the time of the writing of the Roman epistle. Rome was like a great ship passing in the night, casting up waves that broke on distant shores. Her influence was like a radio broadcast, penetrating every corner and crevice of the empire. Paul had visited Roman colonies such as Philippi and Thessalonica, and there he had seen Roman customs, laws, languages, styles, and culture on exhibit. He had walked on Roman roads, had met Roman soldiers on the highways and in the marketplaces, and he had slept in Roman jails. Paul had appeared before Roman magistrates, and he had enjoyed the benefits of Roman citizenship. You see, Paul knew all about Rome although he was yet to visit there. From the vantage point of the world's capital, he was to preach the global gospel to a lost world that God loved so much that He gave His Son to die, that whosoever believed on Him might not perish but have eternal life.

Rome was like a great magnet: It drew men and women from the ends of the then-known world to its center. As Paul and the other apostles crisscrossed in the hinterland of this colossal empire, they brought multitudes to the foot of the cross. Churches were established in most of the great cities of this empire. In the course of time, many Christians were drawn to the center of this great juggernaut. The saying that "all roads lead to Rome" was more than just a bromide. As Christians congregated in this great metropolis, a visible church came into existence. Probably no individual man established the church in Rome. Converts of Paul and the other apostles from the fringe of the empire went to Rome, and a local church was established by them. Certainly, Peter did not estabish the church or have anything to do with it, as his sermon on Pentecost and following sermons were directed to Israelites only. Not until the conversion of Cornelius was Peter convinced that Gentiles were included in the body of believers.

Summarizing, we have found that Paul is the one writing to the Romans. He was to visit Rome later, although he knew it very well already. And Paul was the founder of the church in Rome.

As we approach this great epistle, I feel totally inadequate because of its great theme, which is the righteousness of God. It is a message that I have attempted over the years to proclaim. And it is the message, by the way, that the world today as a whole does not want to hear, nor does it want to accept it. The world likes to hear, friend, about the glory of mankind. It likes to have mankind rather than God exalted. Now I am convinced in my own mind that any ministry today that attempts to teach the glory of man—which does not present the total depravity of the human family and does not reveal that man is totally corrupt and is a ruined creature, any teaching that does not deal with this great truth—will not lift mankind, nor will it offer a remedy. The only remedy for man's sin is the perfect remedy that we have in Christ, that which God has provided for a lost race. This is the great message of Romans.

Friend, may I say to you that the thief on the cross had been declared unfit to live in the Roman Empire and was being executed. But the Lord Jesus said that He was going to make him fit for heaven and told him, ". . . Today shalt thou be with me in paradise" (Luke 23:43). God takes lost sinners—like I am, like you are—and He brings them into the family of God and makes them sons of God. And He does it because of Christ's death upon the cross—not because there is any merit in *us* whatsoever. This is the great message of Romans.

It was Godet, the Swiss commentator, who said that the Reformation was certainly the work of the Epistle to the Romans (and that of

Galatians also) and that it is probable that every great spiritual renovation in the church will always be linked both in cause and in effect to a deeper knowledge of this book. It was Martin Luther who wrote that the Epistle to the Romans is "the true masterpiece of the New Testament and the very purest Gospel, which is well worthy and deserving that a Christian man should not only learn it by heart, word for word, but also that he should daily deal with it as the daily bread of men's souls. It can never be too much or too well read or studied; and the more it is handled, the more precious it becomes, and the better it tastes."

Chrysostom, one of the early church fathers, had the epistle read to him twice a week. And it was Coleridge who said that the Epistle to the Romans was the most profound writing that exists. Further, we find that one of the great scientists turned to this book, and he found that it gave a real faith. This man, Michael Faraday, was asked on his death bed by a reporter, "What are your speculations now?" Faraday said, "I have no speculations. My faith is firmly fixed in Christ my Savior who died for me, and who has made a way for me to go to heaven."

May I say to you, this is the epistle that transformed that Bedford tinker by the name of John Bunyan. A few years ago I walked through the cemetery where he is buried, and I thought of what that man had done and said. You know, he was no intellectual giant, nor was he a poet, but he wrote a book that has been exceeded in sales by only one other, the Bible. That book is Bunyan's *Pilgrim's Progress*. It is a story of a sinner saved by grace, and that sinner was John Bunyan. And the record of history is that this man read and studied the Epistle to the Romans, and he told its profound story in his own life's story, the story of Pilgrim—that he came to the cross, that the burden of sin rolled off, and that he began that journey to the Celestial City.

Let me urge you to do something that will pay you amazing dividends: read the Book of Romans, and read it regularly. This epistle requires all the mental make-up we have, and in addition, it must be bathed in prayer and supplication so that the Holy Spirit can teach us. Yet every Christian should make an effort to know Romans, for this book will ground the believer in the faith.

OUTLINE

I. Doctrinal, Chapters 1–8
("Faith")

A. Justification of the Sinner, Chapters 1:1–5:11

1. Introduction, Chapter 1:1–17
   - (a) Paul's Personal Greeting, Chapter 1:1–7
   - (b) Paul's Personal Purpose, Chapter 1:8–13
   - (c) Paul's Three "I Am's," Chapter 1:14–17
     (Key verses, 16–17—the revelation of the righteousness of God)
2. Revelation of the Sin of Man, Chapters 1:18–3:20
   (This is "Sinnerama." Universal fact: Man is a sinner. Ecumenical movement is away from God. Axiom: World is guilty before God—all need righteousness.)
   - (a) Revelation of the Wrath of God against Sin of Man, Chapter 1:18–32
     - (1) Natural Revelation of God (Original Version), Chapter 1:18–20
     - (2) Subnatural Response of Man (Reversion), Chapter 1:21–23
     - (3) Unnatural Retrogression of Man (Perversion), Chapter 1:24–27
     - (4) Supernatural Requittal of God (Inversion), Chapter 1:28–32
   - (b) Revelation of the Sin of Good People, Chapter 2:1–16
     (Respectable people need righteousness.)
   - (c) Revelation of the Sin of Israel Under Law, Chapters 2:17–3:8
   - (d) Revelation of the Universality of Sin, Chapter 3:9–20
     - (1) Judge's Verdict of Guilty against Mankind, Chapter 3:9–12
       (Man cannot remove guilt.)
     - (2) Great Physician's Diagnosis of Mankind, Chapter 3:13–18
       (Man cannot change his nature. Man has incurable disease.)
     - (3) Purpose of the Law, Chapter 3:19–20
       (Law reveals sin, not salvation. Last word "sin," 3:20.)
3. Revelation of the Righteousness of God (Righteousness Provided), Chapters 3:21–5:11
   (Righteousness of God defined—not the character of God nor self-righteousness of man)
   - (a) Justification by Faith Explained, Chapter 3:21–31
     (Definition: *Justification is the act of God that declares a sinner righteous by faith on the merit of Christ's sacrifice. It is the addition of the righteousness of Christ as well as the subtraction of sins.*)
     (Propitiation—"mercy seat" (Heb. 9:5); Redemption—to pay a price for deliverance. Propitiation is toward God. Redemption is toward sin.)
   - (b) Justification by Faith Illustrated, Chapter 4:1–25
     (Demonstration—Abraham and David)
   - (c) Justification by Faith—Results Derived, Chapter 5:1–11
     Eight benefits:
     - (1) Peace—verse 1
     - (2) Access—verse 2
     - (3) Hope—verse 2
     - (4) Patience—Fruit of Tribulations—verse 3
     - (5) Love—verse 5
     - (6) Holy Spirit—verse 5
     - (7) Deliverance from the Great Tribulation—verse 9
     - (8) Joy—verse 11
       (Reconciliation is toward man. Definition: Change from enmity to friendship. Justification by faith is an act of God which is permanent.)

B. Sanctification of the Saint, Chapters 5:12–8:39
  1. Potential Sanctification, Chapter 5:12–21
     (Federal headship, of Adam and Christ)
     (a) Headship of Adam, Chapter 5:12–14
         (Death—Sin)
     (b) Headship of Christ, Chapter 5:15–17
         (Life—Righteousness)
     (c) Offense of Adam vs. Righteousness of Christ, Chapter 5:18–21
         (Disobedience vs. Obedience; Judgment vs. Free Gift; Sin vs. Grace; Condemnation vs. Justification)
  2. Positional Sanctification, Chapter 6:1–10
     (Union with Christ in His death and resurrection, the basis of deliverance from sin)
  3. Practical Sanctification, Chapter 6:11–23
     (Obedience to God leads to the experience of deliverance from sin.)
  4. Powerless Sanctification, Chapter 7:1–25
     (a) Shackles of a Saved Soul, Chapter 7:1–14
         (Spiritual Emancipation)
     (b) Struggle of a Saved Soul, Chapter 7:15–25
         (Civil War—No good in old nature, no power in new nature)
  5. God's New Provision for Sanctification, Chapter 8:1–39
     (Powerful Sanctification)
     (a) New Law: Holy Spirit vs. Law, Chapter 8:1–4
     (b) New Struggle: Holy Spirit vs. Flesh, Chapter 8:5–13
     (c) New Man, Son of God: Holy Spirit and Spirit of Man, Chapter 8:14–17
     (d) New Creation: Old vs. New; Bondage vs. Liberty, Chapter 8:18–22
     (e) New Body: Groaning vs. Redeemed Body, Chapter 8:23–27
         (The Holy Spirit helps us in our present bodies.)
     (f) New Purpose of God, Chapter 8:28–34
         (God's purpose guarantees the salvation of sinners.)
     (g) New Security of the Believer, Chapter 8:35–39
         (God's love guarantees the security of the believer.)

II. Dispensational, Chapters 9–11
("Hope")

A. God's Past Dealings with Israel, Chapter 9
  1. Israel Defined, Chapter 9:1–5
  2. Israel Identified, Chapter 9:6–13
  3. Choice of Israel in the Sovereign Purpose of God, Chapter 9:14–24
  4. Choice of Gentiles in the Scriptural Prophecies of God, Chapter 9:25–33

B. God's Present Purpose with Israel, Chapter 10
  1. Present State of Israel—Lost, Chapter, 10:1–4
     (Reason: Christ is the end of the law for righteousness.)
  2. Present Standing of Israel—Same as Gentiles, Chapter 10:5–12
     ("For there is no difference")
  3. Present Salvation for Both Jew and Gentile—Hear and Believe the Gospel, Chapter 10:13–21

C. God's Future Purpose with Israel—Remnant Regathered as a Nation and Redeemed, Chapter 11
  1. Remnant of Israel Finding Salvation, Chapter 11:1–6
  2. Remainder of Israel Blinded, Chapter 11:7–12
  3. Reason for Setting Aside the Nation Israel—Salvation of the Gentiles, Chapter 11:13–21
  4. Restoration of Nation Israel—Greater Blessing, Chapter 11:22–32
  5. Reason for Restoring the Nation Israel, Chapter 11:33–36
     (Locked in the riches of the wisdom of God)

III. Duty, Chapters 12–16
("Love")
- A. Service of "the Son of God," Chapters 12–13
  1. Relationship to God ("Present—Yield"), Chapter 12:1–2
  2. Relationship to Gifts of the Spirit, Chapter 12:3–8
  3. Relationship to Other Believers, Chapter 12:9–16
  4. Relationship to Unbelievers, Chapter 12:17–21
  5. Relationship to Government, Chapter 13:1–7
  6. Relationship to Neighbors, Chapter 13:8–14
- B. Separation of "the Sons of God," Chapters 14–16
  1. Relationship to Weak Believers, Chapters 14:1–15:3
     (Three Principles of Conduct for Christians)
     (a) Conviction, Chapter 14:5
     (b) Conscience, Chapter 14:22
     (c) Consideration, Chapter 15:1–2
  2. Relationship of Jews and Gentiles as Believers, Chapter 15:4–13
     (Racial Relationships)
  3. Relationship of Paul to Romans and Gentiles Generally, Chapter 15:14–33
     (The Gospel and Gentiles, Chapter 15:16)
  4. Relationship of Christians to One Another Demonstrated, Chapter 16:1–27
     (Thirty-five persons mentioned by name—mutual love and tender affection)

CHAPTER 1

THEME: *Paul's personal greetings; Paul's purpose; Paul's three "I ams"; a natural revelation of God; subnatural response of man; unnatural retrogression of man*

This opening chapter is an inclusive as it embraces the introduction, the missionary motives of the great apostle, the definition of the gospel, and the condition of man in sin which necessitates the gospel. This chapter furnishes the tempo for the entire epistle.

Romans teaches the total depravity of man. Man is irrevocably and hopelessly lost. He must have the righteousness of God since he has none of his own.

It is interesting to note that this great document of Christian doctrine, which was addressed to the church at Rome to keep it from heresy, did not accomplish its purpose. The Roman church moved the farthest from the faith which is set forth in the Epistle to the Romans. It is an illustration of the truth of this epistle that man does not understand, neither does he seek after God.

Verses 16 and 17 have long been recognized as the key to the epistle. These two verses should be memorized and the meaning of each word digested. The words will be dealt with individually when we come to them.

PAUL'S PERSONAL GREETINGS

Paul, a servant of Jesus Christ, called to be an apostle, separated unto the gospel of God [Rom. 1:1].

The name *Paul* comes from the Latin *Paulus*, meaning "little." (He was Saul of Tarsus but was also called Paul as indicated by Acts 13:9.)

Paul identified himself to the Romans in the very beginning as a slave, or *doulos*, of the Lord Jesus Christ. He took the position of a servant willingly. The Lord Jesus Christ loved us and gave Himself for us, but He never makes us His slaves. You must come voluntarily to Him and make yourself His slave. He will never force you to serve Him. He said even to Jerusalem, "O Jerusalem, Jerusalem, which killest the prophets, and stonest them that are sent unto thee; how often would I have gathered thy children together, as a hen doth gather her brood under her wings, and ye would not!" (Luke 13:34). On another occasion our Lord said, "And ye will not come to me, that ye might have life" (John 5:40). It is wonderful beyond measure that you have the privilege of making yourself a bondslave to the Lord Jesus Christ. You must do it on your own; He will not force you.

On the road to Damascus, the Lord said to Paul, "Saul, Saul, why persecutest thou me?" And Paul replied, "Who art thou, Lord?" He said, "I am Jesus whom thou persecutest." It was at this moment that Paul came to know Him as his Savior. Then Paul's question was, "What wilt thou have me to do?" (see Acts 9:4–6). This is when Paul made himself a bondslave of the Lord Jesus Christ.

"Paul, a servant of Jesus Christ, called to be an apostle"—the infinitive of the verb "to be" is not in the original manuscripts. Paul was a "called" apostle—*called* is an adjective—he means that he is that kind of an apostle. It was not his decision that made him an apostle. It was God's decision, and God called him. Paul first made himself a bondslave of Christ, and now he is a called apostle, a witness for the Lord Jesus Christ. One whom He has chosen is the only kind of servant God will use. There are too many men in the ministry today whom God has not called. Paul could say, ". . . woe is unto me, if I preach not the gospel!" (1 Cor. 9:16). You may remember that Jeremiah was called when he was a child (Jer. 1:4–10). God said of the false prophets, "I have not sent these prophets, yet they ran: I have not spoken to them, yet they prophesied" (Jer. 23:21). Jeremiah was a called prophet, and Paul was a called apostle.

Paul says that he is an apostle, which means "one who is sent." Our Lord said that he that is sent [apostle] is not greater than he that sent him (see John 13:16). The same word occurs again in Philippians 2:25. The word has the technical meaning in the New Testament of one chosen by the Lord Jesus to declare the gospel. He must be a witness of the resurrected Christ. Paul said that the resurrected Christ had appeared to him. "And last of all he was seen of me also, as of one born out of due time" (1 Cor. 15:8). Then Paul asks the rhetorical question, "Am I not an apostle? am I not free? have I not seen Jesus Christ our Lord? . . ." (1 Cor. 9:1).

Another evidence that Paul was an apostle was that he had what we call "sign gifts." He said that he could speak in other languages, other tongues. I believe that when he went through the Galatian country, for instance, into that area along the Aegean Sea where there were so many Greek cities and tribes in which unfamiliar languages were spoken, Paul was able to speak the language of each tribe as he came among them. He had the apostolic gift of tongues. Also he had the gift of healing, a gift that I do not believe is in existence today. When God heals in our day, He does it directly. I tell folk that I take my case directly to the Great Physician, not to one of the interns. I know that God heals, but He does not give that *gift* to men in our day. However, Paul had the gift of healing; he was an apostle. He could also raise the dead. We have records of both Peter and Paul raising the dead. They were apostles.

Now, Paul is a bondslave of Jesus Christ; he is a called apostle; and he is "separated unto the gospel of God." Notice that "separated" is used with the preposition *unto*, not *from*. He was separated unto the gospel of God.

The word *separated* is a marvelous word. There are several words that have almost an opposite meaning. For instance, there is the word *cleave*. An object can cleave to something or an object can be cleaved asunder. One time *cleave* can mean to join together and another time it can mean to separate. Paul was a separated Christian, but he was separated *to* something, not *from* something. I am afraid that many Christians today are only separated from something. When I hear some people talk, I get the idea that they are doing a spiritual striptease. They say, "I don't do this and I don't do that anymore." Well, my friend, *unto* what are you separated? Paul tells us that the Thessalonians turned to God from idols. They did not get up in a testimonial meeting and say, "We do not go to the temple of Apollo anymore." There was no need to say that because they were separated unto the Lord Jesus Christ. A Christian who is separated *from* something and not separated *unto* Christ will have a barren life. His life will be without joy, and he will become critical and sometimes cynical. A phrase in the marriage ceremony I use says, "Do you promise to love and to keep yourself unto her (or him) and no one else?" This is separation unto one person. That is what marriage is. Imagine a fellow on the first night of his honeymoon saying to his new bride, "I have a girl friend in this town. I think I will go to see her." There are many Christians who practice that kind of "separation"! If you are separated unto Christ, you will have a life that appeals rather than one that turns people off. A little Chinese girl once said, "Christians are salt. Salt makes you thirsty." Think it over, friend. Do you make anyone thirsty for Christ, the Water of Life?

The word *separated* is the Greek word *aphorizō*, the same word from which we get our word *horizon*. I have noticed when taking off on a plane that the horizon becomes enlarged. I remember a flight from Athens, Greece. When we took off, I tried to see the Acropolis and the ocean, but I could not see a thing. We had not gone far when I could see the ocean, the Acropolis, the outer islands, and the mountains. The higher we flew, the wider was the horizon. It is wonderful to be separated unto Christ because He brings you to the place where your horizons are enlarged. This is what Paul is talking about in 1 Corinthians 13:11 when he says, "When I was a child, I spake as a child, I understood as a child, I thought as a child: but when I became a man, I put away childish things."

I can recall a time in my early boyhood when I used to play house. Because there was a bunch of girls in the neighborhood and only a couple of boys, in order to play, we played house with the girls. There came a day, friend, when I outgrew that stuff, and I went outside and played baseball. The girls would say, "Let's play house." I would reply, "No, I am playing first base on the team. I am not interested in playing house anymore." I had a new horizon. Today I am not only uninterested in playing baseball, I *can't* play baseball. But I am interested in something else. My horizons have widened. And, friend, when you are separated unto Christ, it doesn't mean you become little and narrow. Rather, life broadens out to include innumerable thrilling and wonderful experiences.

Now notice that Paul says he is separated unto "the gospel of *God*." In other words, man did not create the gospel. When you and I arrived on the scene, the gospel had been in existence for over nineteen hundred years. He didn't wait until we got here to see if we had a better plan. It is God's gospel. We can take it or leave it. The gospel was originated by God.

(Which he had promised afore by his prophets in the holy scriptures,) [Rom. 1:2].

The gospel is not brand new. It was promised by His prophets all the way through the Old Testament. It is a message that God loves mankind and that God presents a way of saving mankind. It brings us into a love relationship. He loves us and gave Himself for us. How wonderful!

Verses 2–6 form a parenthesis which gives a

definition of the gospel. First of all, it is all about Jesus Christ.

Concerning his Son Jesus Christ our Lord, which was made of the seed of David according to the flesh [Rom. 1:3].

The word *concerning* is the little Greek preposition *peri*—used also in *periscope* and *perimeter*—and means "that which encircles." The gospel is all about Jesus Christ. It is what He has done. It is "concerning his Son Jesus Christ our Lord."

We have His full title here. He is the Son of God, and He is Jesus Christ our Lord. That is His wonderful name. We often hear today that we need the religion of Jesus. My friend, He had no religion. He didn't need one—He is God. What we need today is to have a religion that is *about* Jesus, that surrounds Him, that is all about what He has done. Jesus Christ actually is God. He cannot worship; He is to be worshiped. Somebody objects, "But He prayed." Yes, because He took the place of humanity. He prayed as a means of accommodation. For instance, at the grave of Lazarus the Bible says, ". . . Jesus lifted up his eyes, and said, Father, I thank thee that thou hast heard me. And I knew that thou hearest me always: but because of the people which stand by I said it, that they may believe that thou hast sent me" (John 11:41–42). My friend, He prayed to help our faith, but He is the Lord Jesus Christ.

Notice that He also is of the seed (the sperm) of David, according to the flesh. This is the humanity of Jesus. He is virgin born because He is declared—horizoned out to be—the Son of God with power.

And declared to be the Son of God with power, according to the spirit of holiness, by the resurrection from the dead [Rom. 1:4].

You see, the Resurrection did not make Him the Son of God; it simply revealed who He was.

Declared is from the same Greek word *horizo*, which we have seen before. Jesus is declared, He is horizoned, the Son of God. This gives us the perfect humanity of Christ and the perfect deity of Christ. One of the oldest creeds in the church states that He is very man of very man and that He is very God of very God. And Paul said it before the creed was written. Here it is. Jesus Christ is not any more man because He is God, and He is not any less God because He is man. He is God-man.

He is declared to be the Son of God "according to the spirit of holiness." This could mean the human spirit of Jesus, but I personally believe the reference is to the Holy Spirit. I believe the Trinity is in view here.

Now notice that He is declared to be the Son of God "by the resurrection from the dead." The Resurrection proves everything. It is Resurrection that sets Him forth as the Son of God. As you read through the Bible you will discover that the Lord Jesus Christ is presented in the power of His resurrection. First He is seen in the days of His flesh, walking upon the earth, despised and rejected of men. He is seen even in weakness as He sits down to rest at a well and as He sleeps through a storm on the sea. And He finally is brought to ignominy and shame and death upon a cross. Although He was a Man of Sorrows and acquainted with grief, there came a time when He was raised from the dead. His resurrection proves that He was accurate when He said, ". . . Ye are from beneath; I am from above: ye are of this world; I am not of this world" (John 8:23). The days of walking along the dusty roads of Israel are over now; He has come back from the dead in mighty power. His resurrection proves His virgin birth. He is the Son of God with power.

Then there is another great truth here. We see Christ, resurrected and presently seated at the right hand of God in the heavens, interceding today for believers and giving them power and comfort. There is a Man in the glory, but the church has lost sight of Him. We need to recover our awareness of Him. Are you having personal contact with the living Christ today?

Also the resurrection of Christ insures that He will return to this earth as the Judge and as the King of kings and Lord of lords. He will put down sin, and He will reign in righteousness on this earth. He will judge mankind, as Paul said to those glib, sophisticated Athenian philosophers, ". . . we ought not to think that the Godhead is like unto gold, or silver, or stone, graven by art and man's device. And the times of this ignorance God winked at; but now commandeth all men everywhere to repent: because he hath appointed a day, in which he will judge the world in righteousness by that man whom he hath ordained; whereof he hath given assurance unto all men, in that he hath raised him from the dead" (Acts 17:29–31). It is a most solemn fact that because Jesus Christ came back from the dead, you will have to stand before Him someday. Will you stand before Him as one who has trusted Him as your Savior, or will you stand before Him to be judged? If you have not received Him as your Savior, the condemnation of God must be upon you. You cannot stand before Him in your own righteousness. You must be condemned to a lost eternity unless you trust Him as your Savior. The Resurrection is the guarantee that each one of us is going to have to face the Lord Jesus Christ.

By whom we have received grace and apostleship, for obedience to the faith among all nations, for his name [Rom. 1:5].

"Grace and apostleship" are significant terms. "Grace" is God's method of salvation. None of us could ever have been saved if God had not been gracious. Although "apostleship" referred specifically to Paul and the others who were technically apostles, *every* believer is a "sent one." The word in the Greek is *apostolē*, meaning "a sending forth." Every believer should be a witness, one sent forth with a message. What are you doing to get the Word of God out in these days? That is the business of those who have received grace and apostleship.

For the "obedience to the faith among all nations, for his name"—this epistle opens with obedience and closes with obedience. In the final chapter Paul says, "For your obedience is come abroad unto all men" (Rom. 16:19), also "made known to all nations for the obedience of faith" (Rom. 16:26). Obedience to the faith is very important to God. God saves us by faith, not by works; but after He has saved us, He wants to talk to us about our works, about our obedience to Him. I hear many people talk about believing in Jesus, then they live like the Devil and seem to be serving him. My friend, saving faith makes you obedient to Jesus Christ.

Is there a difference in faith? There surely is. The difference is in the object of your faith. For example, I believe in George Washington. I consider him a great man, our first president, the father of our country. Also, I believe in Jesus Christ. Now my faith in George Washington has never done anything for me. It has nothing to do with my salvation and has very little effect upon my life. But my faith in the Lord Jesus Christ is quite different. "Saving faith" brings us to the place where we *surrender* to the Son of God who loves us and gave Himself for us. While correct doctrine is very important, there is a discipline and a *doing* that goes with it. You can't be the salt of the earth without combining both of them. By the way, have you ever considered that salt is composed of sodium and chloride, and each taken by itself would poison you? However, when they are combined, they form a very useful ingredient. Believing and doing go together, my friend, to make us the salt of the earth. My favorite hymn has always been "Trust and Obey," by Rev. J. H. Sammis.

But we never can prove
The delights of His love,
Until all on the altar we lay,
For the favor He shows,
And the joy He bestows,
Are for them who will trust and obey.

Trust and obey, for there's no other way
To be happy in Jesus, but to trust and
obey.

Among whom are ye also the called of Jesus Christ [Rom. 1:6].

The called are the elect. Who are the called? Well, they are those who have heard. The Lord Jesus made it clear when He said, "My sheep hear my voice, and I know them, and they follow me" (John 10:27). If you are following someone or something else, you haven't heard Him, you are not one of His sheep. The ones who hear and follow Him are the called ones. Let's not argue about election. It is as simple as this: He calls, and you answer. If you have answered, you are among the elect, one of "the called of Jesus Christ." Paul assures the Roman Christians that they are called-ones.

This concludes the profound parenthesis in the introduction to this letter to the Romans. Dr. James Stifler calls our attention to four features of this parenthesis: Paul has a message in accord with the Scriptures; the message is from the risen Christ; the message is universal; and the message is for the obedience to the faith.

Now Paul returns to the introduction proper.

To all that be in Rome, beloved of God, called to be saints: Grace to you and peace from God our Father, and the Lord Jesus Christ [Rom. 1:7].

"Beloved of God"—isn't that lovely? God loved those believers in Rome. When I was there not long ago, there was a strike going on, and I found it a little difficult to love anybody as I was carrying my own suitcases up to my room and unable to get any kind of service—even a taxi. But God loves us. How wonderful!

"Called to be saints" should be simply "called saints"—the verb *to be* is not in the better manuscripts. They were "called saints" and this is the name for every believer. A saint is not one who has been exalted; a saint is one who exalts Jesus Christ. A person becomes a saint when Jesus Christ becomes his Savior. There are only two classes of people in the world: the saints and the ain'ts. If you are not an ain't, then you're a saint. And if you are a saint, you have trusted Christ. It is not your character that makes you a saint, it's your faith in Jesus Christ and the fact that you are set apart for Him. As Paul said of himself in the beginning, he was a bondslave of Jesus Christ.

"Grace and peace" constitute the formal introduction in all of Paul's letters. Grace *(charis)* was the Gentile form of greeting, while peace *(shalom)* was the Jewish form of greeting. Paul combined them.

PAUL'S PURPOSE

First, I thank my God through Jesus Christ for you all, that your faith is spoken of throughout the whole world [Rom. 1:8].

Word had filtered out throughout the empire that many in Rome were turning to Christ—so much so that it disturbed the emperors. Later on, persecution began. Paul mentions here that their faith was spoken of throughout the whole world.

I wonder about your group, your church. Has anybody heard about your personal testimony? What is it worth today? My, what a testimony this church in Rome had at the beginning!

For God is my witness, whom I serve with my spirit in the gospel of his Son, that without ceasing I make mention of you always in my prayers [Rom. 1:9].

"The gospel of his Son"—in the first verse Paul called it "the gospel of God," and later he will call it his gospel.

"Without ceasing I make mention of you always in my prayers." Paul had a long prayer list. When I was teaching in a Bible institute, I gave the students the assignment of recording each time Paul said he was praying for somebody. Many of the students were deeply impressed at the length of Paul's prayer list. He says here that he prayed without ceasing for the Roman believers.

Making request, if by any means now at length I might have a prosperous journey by the will of God to come unto you [Rom. 1:10].

Paul is praying for a "prosperous journey" to come to Rome. When we read about his journey in the Book of Acts, it doesn't look exactly prosperous—he went as a prisoner, he got into a terrific storm at sea, the ship was lost, and he was bitten by a viper when he made it to land. Yet it was a prosperous journey.

He says he wants to come to Rome "by the will of God." I believe he went there by the *will* of God.

For I long to see you, that I may impart unto you some spiritual gift, to the end ye may be established [Rom. 1:11].

He wants to come to Rome to teach the Word of God. Paul loved to teach the Word of God. When a preacher does not want to teach the Word of God, he becomes a clergyman, he becomes an administrator, he becomes a promoter, but he is not a minister of the Word anymore. I know several men in this position. One man said, "I don't enjoy preaching anymore." I said, "For goodness sake, get out of the ministry. You have no business in the ministry if you don't love to teach the Word of God!"

That is, that I may be comforted together with you by the mutual faith both of you and me [Rom. 1:12].

In other words, Paul would communicate something, but the believers in Rome would also communicate something to him. They would be mutually blessed in the Word. Not too long ago I had the privilege of speaking to a conference of over a thousand students. I laid it on the line for those folks and was a little hard on them at the beginning. Then I saw how wonderfully they responded, and it opened my eyes to a new world. I left that conference singing praises to God for the privilege of being there. While I was ministering to them, they were ministering to me. This is what Paul is talking about here.

Now I would not have you ignorant, brethren, that oftentimes I purposed to come unto you, (but was let hitherto,) that I might have some fruit among you also, even as among other Gentiles [Rom. 1:13].

He was hindered from coming to them, although he longed to come. Many of these folks were his converts, as he had led them to Christ when he had met them in different parts of the Roman Empire. His desire to have "fruit among you" probably does not refer to soul winning, but to the fruit of the Spirit in the lives of believers (see Gal. 5:22–23).

PAUL'S THREE "I AMS"

I am debtor both to the Greeks, and to the Barbarians; both to the wise, and to the unwise [Rom. 1:14].

"To the Greeks, and to the Barbarians" was the Greek division of all mankind. The Greeks were cultured, educated, and civilized. The barbarians were those whom we label pagan and heathen today. Actually, it is a false division, but it encompasses all mankind and was understood by Romans.

Paul said, "I am debtor both to the Greeks, and to the Barbarians." How did he become indebted? Did he run up a bill for neckties and shoes (that is what Rome is famous for today) and forget to pay the bill? No, he had had no business transaction with these people. However, he had had a personal transaction with Jesus Christ which put him in debt to every man, because the grace of God had been so bountifully bestowed upon him. Paul was in debt to a lost world. I hear Christians say, "I pay my honest debts." Do you? Not until *every person* has heard the gospel of Jesus Christ have you and I paid our honest debts. One day I was driving with a preacher friend of mine in the interior of Turkey. (Turkey is closed to the gospel—a person can get into trouble even propagandizing there.) As we were driving along, we came to a little town in which all of the signs were in Turkish, and we felt very much like strangers in a strange land. Then way down at the end of the street we saw a big sign which read: "*Coca-Cola.*" I said to my friend, "Is it not interesting that *Coca-Cola* in just a few years has done a better job of advertising and getting out its message than has been done with the gospel in over nineteen hundred years?" We have not paid our debt, friend, until all have heard the good news, and multitudes have not yet heard. Paul says, "I am debtor," and that was another reason he wanted to come to Rome.

Then Paul has another "I am."

So, as much as in me is, I am ready to preach the gospel to you that are at Rome also [Rom. 1:15].

Paul has said that he is a debtor; now he says he is ready to pay. In other words, Paul says, "My side is ready." In *The Epistle to the Romans* Dr. James Stifler writes, "He is a master of his purpose, but not of his circumstances." He is not only ready, he is eager to preach it. Oh, how we need that enthusiasm and high anticipation of getting out the Word of God!

In the next verse we have the third "I am" of Paul. Also verses 16 and 17 give us the key to this great Epistle to the Romans.

For I am not ashamed of the gospel of Christ: for it is the power of God unto salvation to every one that believeth; to the Jew first, and also to the Greek [Rom. 1:16].

"I am not ashamed of the gospel" ("of Christ" is not in the better manuscripts). Paul says, "I am debtor. . . . I am ready. . . . I am not ashamed." I'm debtor—that is admission; I am ready—remission; I am not ashamed—submission. These are the three "missions" of Paul: admission, remission, and submission.

Why did Paul say, "I am not ashamed of the gospel"? As I walked down the streets of Ephesus and looked at the ruins of marble temples, I realized that there was not a church building in Ephesus in the first century. In Ephesus was one of the seven wonders of the ancient world, the gorgeous temple of Diana (or Artemis), but there was no church building. I suppose there were folk in Rome who were saying, "Well, brother Paul hasn't come to Rome because he is just preaching a message geared for poor people. The message he preaches is without prestige; there are no great temples connected with it. He would be ashamed to bring it to an important place like Rome." So Paul says, "I am not ashamed of the gospel."

Now why is Paul not ashamed of the gospel? "It is the power of God"! The Greek word translated "power" is *dunamis*, from which we get our word *dynamite*. It is *dunamis* power! It is the kind of power Dr. Marvin R. Vincent calls divine energy! In itself the gospel has power, innate power.

It has power for a very definite thing: "It is the power of God unto salvation." That is the end and the effect of the gospel. "Salvation" is the all-inclusive term of the gospel, and it simply means "deliverance." It embraces everything from justification to glorification. It is both an act and a process. It is equally true that I *have been* saved, I *am being* saved, and I *shall be* saved.

The gospel is "to the Jew first, and also to the Greek." It's to everyone. It includes the entire human race, irrespective of racial or religious barriers. And it is personal; it is directed to every individual—"whosoever will may come."

It is universal in scope, but it is limited to "every one that believeth." This statement wraps up election and free will in one package. The only way of procuring salvation is by personal faith.

"To the Jew first, and also to the Greek" does not imply that the Jew has top priority to the gospel today. The important thing is to make sure the Jew is on a par with the Gentile as far as evangelism is concerned. Chronologically the gospel went to the Jew first. If you had been in Jerusalem on the Day of Pentecost, you would have seen an altogether Jewish meeting. And Paul in his missionary journeys took the gospel first to the Jewish synagogue, but in Acts 13:46 we are told, "Then Paul and Barnabas waxed bold, and said, It was necessary that the word of God should first have been spoken to you: but seeing ye put it from you, and judge yourselves unworthy of everlasting life, lo, we turn to the Gentiles." The gospel began in Jerusalem, a Jewish city, then spread to Judea, Samaria, and to the ends of the earth.

Dr. Stifler calls our attention to three very pertinent truths in this verse: the effect of the gospel—salvation; the extent—it is worldwide—to everyone; the condition—faith in Jesus Christ.

For therein is the righteousness of God revealed from faith to faith: as it is written, The just shall live by faith [Rom. 1:17].

"A righteousness from God is being revealed" is a literal translation. It should not be *the* righteousness of God, because that would be His attribute, and God is not sharing His attribute with anyone. It is *a* righteousness, and it is from God; it is not man's righteousness. God has already said that He will not accept the righteousness of man, for the righteousness of man is as filthy rags in His sight according to Isaiah 64:6. Paul is talking about the imputed righteousness of Christ. God places a lost sinner in Christ, and He sees him in Christ. The believer is absolutely accepted because of what Christ has done for him. The only method of procuring this righteousness is by faith. It is a by-faith righteousness. You can't work for it; you can't make a deposit on it; you can't buy it. You can do nothing but accept it by faith. "And be found in him, not having mine own righteousness, which is of the law, but that which is through the faith of Christ, the righteousness which is of God by faith" (Phil. 3:9).

The word for "righteousness" is *dikaiosune.* This word occurs ninety-two times in the New Testament, thirty-six times in Romans. The phrase "a righteousness from God" occurs eight times in this epistle. The root word *dike* means simply "right." *Justice* and *justify* come from the same word. "To be right" is the primary meaning, which is the antonym of sin. Dr. Cremer gives this apt definition: "It is the state commanded by God and standing the test of His judgment; the character and acts of a man approved of Him, in virtue of which the man corresponds with Him and His will as His ideal and standard." The righteousness he is talking about is what God demands, and it is what God provides—it is a righteousness that is from God.

"From faith to faith" simply means out of faith into faith. God saves you by faith, you live by faith, you die by faith, and you'll be in heaven by faith. Let me use a homely illustration. Quite a few years ago I was born deep in the heart of Texas. When I was born, my mother said the doctor lifted me up by my heels, gave me a whack, and I let out a cry that could be heard on all four borders of that great state. I was born into a world of atmosphere and that whack started me breathing. From that day to this I have been breathing atmosphere. From air to air, from oxygen to oxygen. Much later, in the state of Oklahoma, I was born again. I was saved by faith, and from that time on it has been by faith—from faith to faith.

"As it is written" refers to Habakkuk 2:4, where the statement is made, ". . . the just shall live by his faith." This is quoted in three great epistles of the New Testament: Romans, Galatians, and Hebrews.

"The just shall live by faith"—justification by faith means that a sinner who trusts Christ is not only pardoned because Christ died, but he also stands before God complete in Christ. It means not only subtraction of sin, but addition of righteousness. He "was delivered for our offences, and was raised again for our justification" (Rom. 4:25)—that we might stand before God complete in Christ.

The act of God in justification by faith is not an arbitrary decision on His part. He does not disregard His holiness and His justice. Since God saves us by grace, this means that there is no merit in us. He saves us on no other ground than that we trust Jesus. God is in danger of impugning His own justice if the penalty is not paid. He is not going to open the back door to heaven and slip sinners in under cover of darkness. But because He loves you, Christ died for you to make a way. The Lord Jesus Christ is the way to heaven. Since Christ paid the penalty for our sin, salvation is ours "through faith in his blood" (Rom. 3:25). The hymn writer is correct—

> Jesus paid it all,
> All to Him I owe;
> Sin had left a crimson stain,
> He washed it white as snow.

This concludes Paul's introduction. Now he begins a new section in which he reveals the sin of man. My friend, this is "sinnerama." The universal fact is that man is a sinner. The ecumenical movement is always *away* from God. We can put down the axiom that the world is guilty before God; all need righteousness. In this section Paul is not attempting to prove that man is a sinner. If you attempt to read it that way, you will miss the point. All Paul is doing is stating the fact that man is a sinner. He not only shows that there is a revelation of the righteousness of God, but that there is also the revelation of the *wrath* of God against the sin of man.

A NATURAL REVELATION OF GOD

For the wrath of God is revealed from heaven against all ungodliness and unrighteousness of men, who hold the truth in unrighteousness [Rom. 1:18].

"The *wrath* of God is revealed." Actually, if you want to know what salvation really is, you have to know how bad sin is. Stifler says, "Sin is the measure of salvation." The wrath of God is God's feeling, not His punishment of sin. It is His holy anger. Wrath is the antithesis of righteousness, and it is used here as a correlative.

"Is being revealed" is God's answer to those who assert that the Old Testament presents a God of wrath, while the New Testament presents a God of love. There is a continuous revelation of the wrath of God in both the Old Testament and New Testament. It is revealed in our contemporary society. This is God's constant and insistent displeasure with evil. He changes not. God is merciful, not because He is lenient with the sinner, but because Christ died. The gospel has not changed God's attitude toward sin. The gospel has made it possible to accept the sinner. The sinner must have either the righteousness or the wrath of God. Both are revealed from heaven. And you can see it on every hand. If you want to know how bad sin is, look at the cases of venereal diseases today. You don't get by with sin, my friend. I won't give personal illustrations, but I have been a pastor long enough to see again and again the judgment of God upon sin. It is revealed from heaven. Also there will be a *final* judgment.

"Against all ungodliness"—ungodliness is that which is against God. It is that which denies the character of God. Oh, the irreligiousness of today! There are multitudes of people who disregard the very existence of God—that is a *state* of the soul. That is sin.

"Unrighteousness" is against man. Ungodliness is against God, but unrighteousness is against man. What does that mean? It is the denial of the rule of God. It is the *action* of the soul. That man who gets drunk, goes out on the freeway, breaks the traffic laws, and kills someone—that man is unrighteous. He is sinning against man. Another example is the man who is dishonest in his business dealings. God hates man's unrighteousness. He will judge it.

"Who holds the truth in unrighteousness" is literally to hold down, suppress the truth in unrighteousness. The wrath of God is revealed against folk who do this.

Because that which may be known of God is manifest in them; for God hath shewed it unto them [Rom. 1:19].

There is an original revelation from God.

For the invisible things of him from the creation of the world are clearly seen, being understood by the things that are made, even his eternal power and Godhead; so that they are without excuse [Rom. 1:20].

This universe in which you and I live tells two things about God: His person and His power. This has been clearly seen from the time the world was created. How can invisible things be seen? Paul makes this a paradox purposely to impress upon his readers that the "dim light of nature" is a man-made falsehood. Creation is a clear light of revelation. It is the primary revelation. The psalmist said, "When I consider thy heavens, the work of thy fingers, the moon and the stars, which thou hast ordained" (Ps. 8:3). Also "The heavens declare the glory of God; and the firmament sheweth his handiwork" (Ps. 19:1).

"His eternal power and Godhead"—His eternal power and deity, power and Person. Creation reveals the unchangeable power and existence of God. Paul said this, ". . . he left not himself without witness, in that he did good, and gave us rain from heaven, and fruitful seasons, filling our hearts with food and gladness" (Acts 14:17). And because all of us are the offspring (not the sons) of God, Paul said, "Forasmuch then as we are the offspring of God, we ought not to think that the Godhead is like unto gold, or silver, or stone, graven by art and man's device" (Acts 17:29). Dr. James Denny writes, "There is that within man which so catches the meaning of all that is without as to issue in an instinctive knowledge of God." I think the most ridiculous position man can hold is that of atheism. It is illogical and senseless. When the psalmist said, "The fool hath said in his heart, There is no God" (Ps. 14:1), the word for *fool* means "insane." A man is insane when he denies the existence of God.

"So that they are without excuse." Creation so clearly reveals God that man is without excuse. This section reveals the historical basis of man's sin. It did not come about through ignorance. It was willful rebellion in the presence of clear light.

SUBNATURAL RESPONSE OF MAN

If you examine the next few verses carefully, you will see that there are seven steps which mankind took downward from the Garden of Eden.

> **Because that, when they knew God, they glorified him not as God, neither were thankful; but became vain in their imaginations, and their foolish heart was darkened.**
>
> **Professing themselves to be wise, they became fools,**
>
> **And changed the glory of the uncorruptible God into an image made like to corruptible man, and to birds, and fourfooted beasts, and creeping things [Rom. 1:21–23].**

There is no such thing as man moving upward. These verses contradict the hypothesis of evolution. Man is not improving physically, morally, intellectually, or spiritually. The pull is downward. Of course this contradicts all the anthologies of religion that start with man in a very primitive condition as a caveman with very little intellectual qualities and move him up intellectually and begin moving him toward God. This is absolute error. Man is moving away from God, and right now the world is probably farther from God than at any time in its history. The fact of the matter is that every primitive tribe has a tradition that way back in the beginning their ancestors knew God. Dr. Vincent in *Word Studies in the New Testament* says, "I think it may be proved from facts that any given people, down to the lowest savages, has at any period of its life known far more than it has done: known quite enough to have enabled it to have got on comfortably, thriven and developed, if it had only done what no man does, all that it knew it ought to do and could do." No people have ever lived up to the light that they have had. Although they had a knowledge of God, they moved away from Him.

"They glorified him not as God." They did not give Him His rightful place, and man became self-sufficient. In our day man has made the announcement that God is dead. In the beginning the human family did not suggest that God was dead, they simply turned their backs upon Him and made man their god.

"Neither were thankful." Ingratitude is one of the worst sins there is. You recall that the Lord Jesus healed ten lepers, but only one returned to thank Him. Only ten percent were thankful, and I believe it is less than that today.

"Became vain in their imaginations"—they even concocted a theory of evolution.

"Their foolish heart was darkened." They moved into the darkness of paganism. You see living proof of this as you walk down the streets of Cairo in Egypt or of Istanbul in Turkey. In fact, all you have to do is walk down the streets of Los Angeles to know that man's foolish heart is darkened.

"Professing themselves to be wise, they became fools." The wisdom of man is foolishness with God. Man searches for truth through logical reasoning but arrives at a philosophy that is foolish in God's sight.

"And changed the glory of the uncorruptible God into an image made like to corruptible man, and to birds, and fourfooted beasts, and creeping things." Have you noted that the unsaved world has made caricatures of God? Look at the images and the idols of the heathen. I was aware of this during my visit to the ruins of the ancient city of Ephesus. That city in the Roman Empire reached probably the highest degree of culture in civilization that any city has ever reached. Yet at the heart of that city was one of the most horrible images imaginable, enshrined in the temple of Artemis, one of the seven wonders of the ancient world. Called also Diana, she was not the lovely image you see in Greek sculptures. She is like the Oriental Cybele, the mother goddess, the many-breasted one. She had a trident in one hand and in the other a club—she was a mean one. That is the idea the most cultured, civilized people had of God! She was a female principal, and gross immorality took place around her temple, and dishonesty of the worst sort. They had turned the glory of the uncorruptible God into the likeness of an image of corruptible man. Actually, idolatry is a cartoon of God; it is a slander and a slur against Him. Personally I do not like to see pictures of Jesus, as Paul said that we know Him no longer after the flesh (see 2 Cor. 5:16). He is the glorified Christ. He is not that picture you have hanging on your wall, my friend. If He came into your room, you would fall on your face before Him. He is the glorified Christ today. Don't slur our God by having a picture of Him! The Greeks made their gods like men; the Assyrians and the Egyptians and the Babylonians made their gods like beasts and birds and creeping things. I walked through the museum in Cairo and looked at some of the gods they had made. They are not very flattering representations, I can assure you.

Man did not begin in idolatry. The savage of today is very unlike primitive man. Primitive man was monotheistic; idolatry was introduced later. In the Word of God the first record we have of idolatry is in connection with Rachel stealing her father's idols (Gen. 31). Man descended downward; he did not develop upward. Religiously man has departed from God. Sir William Ramsay, who was once a belligerent unbeliever, wrote in *The Cities of Paul:* "For my own part, I confess that my experience and reading show nothing to confirm the modern assumptions in religious history, and a great deal to confirm Paul. Whatever evidence exists, with the rarest exceptions, the history of religion among men is a history of degeneration. . . . Is it not the fact of human history that man, standing alone, degenerates; and that he progresses only where there is in him so much sympathy with and devotion to the Divine life as to keep the social body pure and sweet and healthy?" My friend, the reason today there is failure in our poverty programs and health programs and other social programs is because of gross immorality and a turning away from God. They say, "We want to be practical, and we do not want to introduce religion." That's the problem. The only *practical* thing for man to do is to return to the living and true God.

UNNATURAL RETROGRESSION OF MAN

Now we see the results of man's revolution against God. In the remainder of this chapter it says three times that God gave them up.

Wherefore God also gave them up to uncleanness through the lusts of their own hearts, to dishonour their own bodies between themselves [Rom. 1:24].

Man's degeneration is measured by his perversion of sex. While many churches in our day are espousing sex perversion instead of condemning it, God says He has given them up. Idolatry and gross immorality are the bitter fruits of rejecting God's revelation.

"God gave them up" is literally *God handed them over*—it is positive, not a passive attitude.

Who changed the truth of God into a lie, and worshipped and served the creature more than the Creator, who is blessed for ever. Amen [Rom. 1:25].

"Who exchanged the true God for the lie." The suggestion is that they turned from God to Satan, the author of the lie and the father of idolatry. This is idolatry which led to the lowest depths of moral degradation.

For this cause God gave them up unto vile affections: for even their women did change the natural use into that which is against nature:

And likewise also the men, leaving the natural use of the woman, burned in their lust one toward another; men with men working that which is unseemly, and receiving in themselves that recompence of their error which was meet [Rom. 1:26–27].

These are passions of dishonor and disgrace and depravity—regardless of what public opinion is today. Perversion entered into Greek life, and it brought Greece down to the dust. Go over there and look at Greece today. The glory has passed away. Why? These were their sins.

And even as they did not like to rctain God in their knowledge, God gave them over to a reprobate mind, to do those things which are not convenient [Rom. 1:28].

Anybody who tells me that he can be a child of God and live in perversion, live in the thick mire of our contemporary permissiveness, is not kidding anyone but himself. If he will come to Christ, he can have deliverance.

The next three verses list a frightful brood of sins which follow man's rebellion against God.

Being filled with all unrighteousness, fornication, wickedness, covetousness, maliciousness; full of envy, murder, debate, deceit, malignity; whisperers,

Backbiters, haters of God, despiteful, proud boasters, inventors of evil things, disobedient to parents,

Without understanding, covenantbreakers, without natural affection, implacable, unmerciful [Rom. 1:29–31].

In my book *Reasoning Through Romans,* I define these sins, but it is enough to say here that this is what the human family is doing today. I used to tell the students in my classes to buy any of our metropolitan daily newspapers, sit down, and find a headline for every sin that is mentioned here. This is the condition, not only of Cairo, not only of Calcutta, not only of Peking, but also of the United States today. How much longer will God tolerate it and be patient with us? He has judged great nations in the past who have gone in this direction.

Who knowing the judgment of God, that they which commit such things are worthy of death, not only do the same, but have pleasure in them that do them [Rom. 1:32].

Man has a revelation from God, but he flagrantly flaunts it by defying the judgment of God against such sins. He continues to practice them and applauds and approves those who do the same.

CHAPTER 2

***THEME:** God will judge self-righteous and religious people*

In this chapter Paul is showing that God will judge self-righteous and religious people. There are many people like the man on the top of the hill who looks down at the man at the bottom of the hill and says, "Something should be done for that poor fellow. We ought to start a mission down there. We should start giving him soup and clothes and a shower bath. I am living on the top of the hill, and I do not need anything." The hurdle to meet the demands of God is just as high on top of the hill as it is at the bottom of the hill. The only difference is that the man at the bottom of the hill will probably see his need sooner than the man at the top of the hill. Religious people, self-righteous people, and so-called good people need a Savior. In chapter 2 Paul sets down certain principles by which God is going to judge "good" people. Chapter 1 reveals the unrighteousness of man, and chapter 2 reveals the self-righteousness of man.

Therefore thou art inexcusable, O man, whosoever thou art that judgest: for wherein thou judgest another, thou condemnest thyself; for thou that judgest doest the same things [Rom. 2:1].

This puts before us the very important issue of this chapter. It's well to keep in mind here that Paul is not talking about salvation. He is talking about *sin* and the basis on which God will judge men. These principles of judgment are not the basis of salvation; they are the basis of judgment. I don't know about you, but I wouldn't want to be judged by them. I thank God for a Savior today, and Scripture presents the gospel as the only means of attaining eternal life. To reject the Son of God immediately brings upon a person the judgment of God, and the only verdict here is guilty. "He that hath the Son hath life; and he that hath not the Son of God hath not life" (1 John 5:12). And He says, "Verily, verily, I say unto you, He that heareth my word, and believeth on him that sent me, hath everlasting life, and shall not come into condemnation; but is passed from death unto life" (John 5:24). And then listen to the Lord Jesus after that marvelous, wonderful John 3:16—we generally stop there—but He continues. "For God sent not his Son into the world to condemn the world; but that the world through him might be saved. He that believeth on him is not condemned: but he that believeth not is condemned already, because he hath not believed in the name of the only begotten Son of God" (John 3:17–18). Also, "He that believeth on the Son hath everlasting life: and he that believeth not the Son shall not see life; but the wrath of God abideth on him" (John 3:36). So today these folk who do not have Christ are *lost*. You may be a religious person, you might be a good person, but without Christ, my friend, you're lost.

"Thou art inexcusable, O man"—"man" is the Greek *anthrope*, a generic term meaning both men and women. It includes both Jews and Gentiles and refers to mankind in general.

"Whosoever thou art that judgest." He passes now from the general to that which is specific, from the masses to the individual person. And he addresses any person of the human race, but he limits it to those who judge others. Now, the word here for "judge" carries the thought of judging with an adverse verdict. It can be translated, "Whosoever thou art that *condemnest* another." Therefore this raises the question: What should be the attitude of a believer today toward this awful, horrible group who are mentioned in Romans 1? It should be this: We should want them to get saved; we should try to get the gospel to them; they are poor, lost creatures. It should be as the hymn writer, Fanny Crosby, expressed it:

Rescue the perishing,
Care for the dying,
Snatch them in pity from sin and the grave;
Weep o'er the erring ones,
Lift up the fallen,
Tell them of Jesus, the mighty to save.

This should be our attitude, while making it clear that they need to be saved and delivered from perversion and immorality.

"For thou that judgest doest the same things" may give a wrong impression. "Same" is the Greek *auta*, and the meaning is not identical things, but things that are as bad in God's sight as the awful, depraved acts of the heathen which are offensive to the cultured and refined sinner.

Let me illustrate this. I heard a man who is not saved say that he didn't believe that hell could be heated hot enough for Hitler. My friend, he is sitting in judgment. He is taking the place of God. And you and I are sitting in judgment on those who are not on our plane. We use society's standards today, and it varies. If someone does not measure up to the standard of your little group, you condemn him. I know some churches where members can get by with lying, with being gossipers, and with being dishonest, but they couldn't get by with smoking a cigarette! They would be condemned for that. My friend, when you judge other people, you are assuming the position of judge. God is saying that by the same token that you have the right to judge other people by your standards, He has the right to judge you by His standards. If we could see ourselves as God sees us, we could see that we are obnoxious; we are repugnant! What contribution can you and I make to heaven? Would we adorn the place? I get the impression from some people that heaven is going to be a better place when they get there—yet the earth has not been a better place since they have been here! My friend, you try to deny God the same privilege you have of sitting in judgment on others. Well, God is going to judge *you*, and He won't judge you by your standards, but by *His* standards. Does that begin to move you? It ought to, because I have found that we don't come up to God's standards.

Now Paul puts down the principles by which God will judge the refined and cultured sinner. Here is the first great principle.

But we are sure that the judgment of God is according to truth against them which commit such things [Rom. 2:2].

In other words, he says, "We *know* that the judgment of God is according to reality." There are so many folk today, including church members, who live in a world of unreality. They do not want to hear the truth of the gospel. Now, I hear a great many pious folk who say, "Oh, I do want to study the Bible." And then when they get into the Word of God, they find what John found in the Book of Revelation when he began to see the judgments of God. When he first started out, it was thrilling, it was "sweet in his mouth." But when he ate that little book, it gave him indigestion, it was "bitter in his belly" (see Rev. 10:9–10). And there are a great many Christians today, who say they want Bible study, but they don't want reality. They do not want to hear the truth. "We know that the judgment of God is according to reality [the factual condition of man] against them which commit such things."

Now keep in mind that these are principles of *judgment*, not principles of salvation. Man has an inherent knowledge that he must be judged by a higher power. The coming judgment of God is something every man out of Christ either dreads or denies. The Scripture is very clear on judgment. Paul said to the Athenians, "Because he hath appointed a day, in the which he will judge the world in righteousness by that man whom he hath ordained; whereof he hath given assurance unto all men, in that he hath raised him from the dead" (Acts 17:31). And Paul reasoned, you remember, with Felix about righteousness and self-control and judgment to come. And it frightened this fellow, Felix. In fact, he didn't want to hear another sermon. The judgment of God is in contrast with man's judgment. Man does not have all the facts and his judgment is partial and prejudiced. God's judgment takes in all the facts. God knows the actual state of man—just what he is. And on that basis He will judge him.

As a boy, I used to pick cotton—and I wasn't very good at it. I'd bring in a sack of cotton to be weighed, and they only weighed what I brought in. The man weighing the cotton didn't ask me where I picked it or how I picked it or to whom it belonged; he just weighed it. ". . . Thou art weighed in the balances . . ." (Dan. 5:27), is God's word to every man that boasts of his morality. I think the great delusion of the cultured person is that the depraved person must be judged, but he's confident that he will escape because he's different. Most people believe Hitler and Stalin ought to be judged, but they think they should escape. God will judge man for what he is in *His* sight. Do you want to stand before God on that basis? I don't.

And thinkest thou this, O man, that judgest them which do such things, and doest the same, that thou shalt escape the judgment of God? [Rom. 2:3].

Robert Govett has called attention to the *four* ways of escape which are open to the man who breaks human laws:

1. His offence will not be discovered.
2. He may escape beyond the jurisdiction of the court.
3. After arrest, there may be some legal technicality which will cause a breakdown of the legal procedure.
4. After conviction, he may escape from prison and stay under cover.

None of these avenues of escape are open to man in regard to divine judgment. Your offenses will be discovered. You cannot go beyond God's jurisdiction. There will be no legal technicality. You will never be able to escape from prison. The writer of Hebrews asked, "How shall we escape, if we neglect so great salvation . . . ?" (Heb. 2:3).

Or despisest thou the riches of his goodness and forbearance and longsuffering; not knowing that the goodness of God leadeth thee to repentance? [Rom. 2:4].

We ought to recognize today that the *goodness* of God is something that ought to bring us to our knees before Him. But instead of that, it drives men from God. The psalmist was disturbed by the way the wicked could prosper. God didn't seem to do anything to them. In Psalm 73, he says, "For I was envious at the foolish, when I saw the prosperity of the wicked. For there are no bands in their death: but their strength is firm. They are not in trouble as other men; neither are they plagued like other men. . . . They set their mouth against the heavens, and their tongue walketh through the earth. . . . Until I went into the sanctuary of God; then understood I their end" (Ps. 73:3–5, 9, 17). They will face God's judgment, my friend.

And, by the way, if you're a lost man, don't think I am the sort of preacher that tries to take everything away from you. If you haven't trusted Christ and your only hope is in this life, brother, you had better suck this earth like it is an orange and get all you can out of it. Drink all you can, sin all you can, because you won't have anything in the next life. You had better get it while you are here if that's the way you want to live. Eat, drink, and be merry. Tomorrow you die. My friend, you need a Savior. And the goodness of God ought to lead you to Him.

But after thy hardness and impenitent heart treasurest up unto thyself wrath against the day of wrath and revelation of the righteous judgment of God [Rom. 2:5].

If you are not saved, let me say this to you: you *know* God has been good to you. God has blessed you. Think of the multitudes of folk on this earth who have nothing, who are literally starving to death. And here you are, a wicked man, living on top of the world. Do you think God is not going to judge you? Do you think that you are going to escape? My friend, the very goodness of God ought to lead you to repentance.

As we come to verse 6, we see the second great principle.

Who will render to every man according to his deeds [Rom. 2:6].

He shall reward every man according to his works. Absolute justice is the criterion of the judgment or rewards. Man's deeds stand before God in His holy light. No man in his right mind wants to be judged on this basis. Remember Cornelius—he was a good man, but he was lost.

To them who by patient continuance in well-doing seek for glory and honour and immortality, eternal life [Rom. 2:7].

Let's keep in mind that under this second principle, a way of life is not the subject. Rather, a way of life is the basis of judgment. The "do-gooder" will be judged according to his works. John said, "And I saw the dead, small and great, stand before God; and the books were opened: and another book was opened, which is the book of life: and the dead were judged out of those things which were written in the books, according to their works" (Rev. 20:12). The man who wants to work for eternal life may do so. He will be judged according to his deeds, but he is warned that they will avail nothing. "And whosoever was not found written in the book of life was cast into the lake of fire" (Rev. 20:15). Trusting Christ as Savior puts your name in the "book of life." Eternal life is not a reward for effort; it is a gift to those who trust Christ.

Now notice the third principle of judgment.

For there is no respect of persons with God [Rom. 2:11].

This was also a great principle of the Old Testament. "For the LORD your God is God of gods, and Lord of lords, a great God, a mighty, and a terrible, which regardeth not persons, nor taketh reward" (Deut. 10:17). Simon Peter discovered this when he went into the home of Cornelius. "Then Peter opened his mouth, and said, Of a truth I perceive that God is no respecter of persons" (Acts 10:34). God plays no favorites. He has no pets. All men are alike before Him. Justice is blindfolded, not because she is blind, but that she may not see men in either silk or rags; all must appear alike. Church membership, a good family, being an outstanding citizen, or having a fundamental creed give no advantage before God at all. Do you have a Savior, or don't you? That is the all-important issue.

For as many as have sinned without law shall also perish without law: and as many as have sinned in the law shall be judged by the law [Rom. 2:12].

This is another great principle by which God is going to judge. Notice how it is expressed in the next verse.

(For not the hearers of the law are just before God, but the doers of the law shall be justified [Rom. 2:13].

I hear it said that the heathen are lost because they haven't heard of Christ and haven't accepted Him. My friend, they are lost because they are sinners. That's the condition of all mankind. Men are not *saved* by the light they have; they are *judged* by the light they have.

"For not the hearers of the law are just before God"—many folk seem to think that if they just *approve* the Sermon on the Mount, they are saved.

Now here is the fifth principle.

Which shew the work of the law written in their hearts, their conscience also bearing witness, and their thoughts the mean while accusing or else excusing one another;) [Rom. 2:15].

God can and will judge the heathen by his own conscience. Some folk think because the heathen do not have the revelation of God that they will escape God's judgment. But the fact is that they are not living up to the light they have. God will judge them on that basis.

In the day when God shall judge the secrets of men by Jesus Christ according to my gospel [Rom. 2:16].

We have a false idea today that because we happen to be good folk, that is, we think we are, that we'll be saved. God is going to *judge* the do-gooders. And He will judge them by Jesus Christ who said that if a man looks upon a woman to lust after her, he is guilty of adultery (see Matt. 5:27–28). This is only one example of the secrets of the human heart. Do you want the secrets of your heart brought out—not the lovely things you have said, but the dirty little thoughts that come to you? This should cause all of us to flee to Jesus to save us!

God is going to judge religious people, the Jews in particular, because theirs was a God-given religion.

Behold, thou art called a Jew, and restest in the law, and makest thy boast of God.

And knowest his will, and approvest the things that are more excellent, being instructed out of the law [Rom. 2:17–18].

Religion was no longer a crutch for this man. It caused him to be proud and self-sufficient. Light created an added responsibility, which brought a greater condemnation. The Jew had ten advantages over the Gentiles, which are listed in these verses. The first five are what he *was:* (1) Bears the name Jew; (2) rests upon the Law; (3) boasts in God; (4) knows the will of God; (5) proves the things which are more excellent, being instructed out of the Law.

And art confident that thou thyself art a guide of the blind, a light of them which are in darkness,

An instructor of the foolish, a teacher of babes, which hast the form of knowledge and of the truth in the law [Rom. 2:19–20].

The last five personal privileges of the Jew are what he *did:* (1) Art persuaded that thou thyself art a guide of the blind; (2) a light of them that are in darkness; (3) a corrector of the thoughtless or immature; (4) a teacher of babes or proselytes; and (5) having in the law the outward form of knowledge and truth.

Now here is Paul's question:

Thou therefore which teachest another, teachest thou not thyself? thou that preachest a man should not steal, dost thou steal?

Thou that sayest a man should not commit adultery, dost thou commit adultery? thou that abhorrest idols, dost thou commit sacrilege? [Rom. 2:21–22].

Paul mentions three common sins: (1) immorality—sin against others; (2) sensuality—sin against self; and (3) idolatry—sin against God.

"Teachest thou not thyself?" In other words, "Do you practice what you preach?" For many of us our preaching is better than our living.

"Dost thou commit sacrilege?"—or "Do you rob temples?" When the Jew was in Babylonian captivity, he took "the gold cure," and, as far as I can tell, he was never given to idolatry after that. However, he didn't mind handling merchandise that came from heathen temples and selling it in his business. Today there are certain Christians who handle merchandise in their business (in order to make money) that they would condemn in their church.

Now the three sins that Paul mentions—immorality, sensuality, and idolatry—he had dealt with in inverse order in chapter 1. Idolatry was the terrible climax for the Jew; he could go no lower than that. I wonder if you and I make a mockery of the person of Christ. Someone has put the question in poetic language:

> The gospel is written a chapter a day
> By deeds that you do and words that you say.
> Men read what you say, whether faithless or true.
> Say, what is the gospel according to you?

Now he deals with something that is extremely vital.

For circumcision verily profiteth, if thou keep the law: but if thou be a breaker of the law, thy circumcision is made uncircumcision [Rom. 2:25].

Circumcision was the badge of the Mosiac system—and that's all it was. There was no merit in the rite itself. That badge indicated that the man believed the Mosaic Law. Now for them to be transgressors of the Law brought circumcision into disrepute. That which should have been sacred, became profane.

This thought can be applied to our church sacraments. Water baptism is rightly a sacrament of the church, *if* it is the outward expression of a work of God in the heart. But it is a mockery if the person who is baptized gives no evidence of salvation. This also can be said of church membership. The lives of some church members make membership a mockery.

Listen to Paul as he continues:

Therefore if the uncircumcision keep the righteousness of the law, shall not his uncircumcision be counted for circumcision? [Rom. 2:26].

To use another figure of speech, if my wife loses her wedding ring, that does not mean she becomes unmarried. Marriage is more than a wedding ring, although the ring may be the symbol of it.

And shall not uncircumcision which is by nature, if it fulfil the law, judge thee, who by the letter and circumcision dost transgress the law? [Rom. 2:27].

Using again the illustration of a wedding ring, to wear a wedding ring speaks of something sacred. But to be unfaithful to that which it stands for makes the wedding ring a disgrace. On one occasion when I was in a motel in another city, I saw a man who was a deacon in a church, sitting at a table, having a very friendly talk with a very beautiful young lady who was not his wife. The thing that impressed me was that as his hand hung over the side of the table, the light was shining on his wedding ring, making it stand out. I thought, what a mockery! When the man saw me, he was embarrassed, of course. But, you see, the wedding ring was meaningless.

The point Paul is making here is that circumcision should stand for something.

But he is a Jew, which is one inwardly; and circumcision is that of the heart, in the spirit, and not in the letter; whose praise is not of men, but of God [Rom. 2:29].

The Mosaic Law had already stated that circumcision was of the heart. Listen to Moses in Deuteronomy 10:16: "Circumcise therefore the foreskin of your heart, and be no more stiff-necked."

CHAPTER 3

***THEME:** Availability of a righteousness from God*

What advantage then hath the Jew? or what profit is there of circumcision? [Rom. 3:1].

"Profit" means that which is surplus, that which is excess, and the question has to do with the outward badge of God's special covenant with the Jews, circumcision.

It looks as if Paul is in danger of erasing a distinction which God has made. The question is, if Jew and Gentile are on the same footing before God, what then is the supposed advantage of the Jew and what good is circumcision?

Let me give you a statement of Dr. James Stifler: "If circumcision in itself does not give righteousness, if uncircumcision does not preclude it, what profit was there ever in it? A distinction that God made among men seems, after all, not to be one." Now, this is the same question, I think, that we hear today. I get it because the gospel that I preach says that church membership has no advantage for salvation, that any rite or ritual you go through is meaningless as far as salvation is concerned. God has the world shut up to a cross. He's not asking you to join anything or do anything. What God is asking the lost sinner to do is to believe on the Lord Jesus Christ, and he shall be saved. And until a person answers that question, then God hasn't anything else to say to him. After he's saved, then God probably will talk to him about church membership and about baptism. We hear people say today, "Well, doesn't my church, my creed, my membership, my baptism help toward my salvation?" The answer is no, it doesn't help you toward salvation. But if you are saved, then these things are a badge, and these things are a means of communicating to the world who you are. But if you're not measuring up, then your church membership and your baptism are a disgrace; and instead of being sacred they become profane.

Now Paul is going to answer the question: What advantage then did the Jews have?

Much every way: chiefly, because that unto them were committed the oracles of God [Rom. 3:2].

Paul is saying, "Yes, the Jew has an advantage." The advantage, however, created a responsibility. We need to note carefully the advantage the Jew had because there is a great deal of confusion in this area. I know men who are teaching in theological seminaries who make no distinction between Judaism in the Old Testament and the church in the New Testament. Paul is making it clear that God not only gave to the nation Israel the oracles of God—they were the ones who communicated the Word of God—but in the Word of God was something special for them. God is not through with the nation Israel. I always test a theologian at that particular point: Does God have a future for Israel? My friend, if God doesn't have a future for Israel, I don't think He has a future for you either or for that theological professor. All God's promises are in the same Word of God. God is going to make good John 3:16, and God is also going to make good His covenant with Abraham in chapter 12 of Genesis. Listen again to Dr. Stifler as he is speaking of Israel: "His advantage was not that God sowed Judaism and the world reaped Christianity. That blots out Judaism. It was first of all 'that unto them were committed to the oracles of God,' not that they were made a mere Bible depositary, but that God gave them, as Jews, promises, not yet fulfilled, and peculiarly their own. The Old Testament, the record of its oracles, contains not one promise either of or to the church as an organization. It does not predict a church; it foreshadows a kingdom in which the Jew shall be head and not lose his national distinction as he does in the church." Now, friend, I think that's one of the most important and profound statements that has been made concerning the Word of God. At this point "great" theologians differ. Dr. Adolph Saphir was a converted Jew, and he made this tremendous, pointed statement: "The view that is so prevalent, that Israel is a shadow of the church, and now that the type is fulfilled vanishes from our horizon, is altogether unscriptural. Israel is not the shadow fulfilled and absorbed *in the church*, but the *basis* on which the church rests." Friend, that is an important comment, and that's what Paul is saying here—that the Jew has a great advantage. God has a future for him, and his faithlessness will not destroy God's promise. Listen to Paul:

For what if some did not believe? shall their unbelief make the faith of God without effect? [Rom. 3:3].

"If some were without faith" is a better translation. Shall their lack of faith cancel out the faithfulness of God? This is another objection that would be put up, and Paul meets this by going back to the first. Now if the advantage of the Jew did not serve the intended purpose, does this not mean God's faithfulness to His people is annulled? The Jew failed; doesn't that mean God failed? No. God's promise to send Israel the Redeemer was not defeated by their willful disobedience and rejection. All His promises for the future of the nation will be fulfilled to His glory in spite of their unbelief. Now, my friend, you may not like that, but I personally thank God that His promises to me do not depend on my faithfulness. If it had depended on me, I would have been lost long ago. Thank God for *His* faithfulness!

God forbid: yea, let God be true, but every man a liar; as it is written, That thou mightest be justified in thy sayings, and mightest overcome when thou art judged [Rom. 3:4].

In other words, the unbeliever that raises this question is a liar and God is going to make him out to be a liar someday. Why? Because the faithfulness of God is true and cannot be changed. How important that is! John says, "He that believeth on the Son of God hath the witness in himself: he that believeth not God hath made him a liar; because he believeth not the record that God gave of his Son" (1 John 5:10). How bad is it not to believe that God gave His Son to die for you? Well, I'll tell you how bad it is: You make God a liar. That's what you do when you reject His Son.

But if our unrighteousness commend the righteousness of God, what shall we say? Is God unrighteous who taketh vengeance? (I speak as a man) [Rom. 3:5].

By some subtle sophistry it might be argued that since the nation's unbelief merely puts in contrast the faithfulness of God, God is not just to punish that which brings greater glory to Himself. A better translation would be: "Is God unjust who visiteth with wrath by judging" these people? Now this is the severest criticism that Paul faced in preaching the gospel of the grace of God. If God uses sin to get glory to Himself, then He should not punish the sinner. This, of course, was used by some as an excuse for sinning. We'll find this again in Romans 6:1 and will deal with it then. Paul asks the question in such a way in the Greek as to demand a negative answer. God is not unjust. He says, "I speak as a man." That doesn't mean that Paul is not writing this particular passage by inspiration, but rather that he is presenting this question from the finite and human standpoint.

Now, the whole point is this: if my unrighteousness reveals the marvelous, wonderfully infinite faithfulness of God in the grace of God, then has God a right to judge me? That's what Paul is asking here. This makes it very clear that the unsaved world in Paul's day understood that Paul was preaching salvation by the grace of God. How wonderful!

God forbid: for then how shall God judge the world? [Rom. 3:6].

If God would have no right to judge us because our sin merely reveals the grace of God, then God would have no right to judge any person, you see, because they would reveal something of the common grace of God.

Paul's answer is again an emphatic and categorical denial of any such premise that God is unjust. The argument here is that if this particular sin merely enhances the glory of God and the grace of God, then all sin would do the same. Therefore, God would not be able to judge the world. He would abdicate His throne as Judge of all the earth. This specious argument would say that Hitler ought not to be judged. And whoever you are—even if you are an unbeliever—you *do* believe that some people ought to be judged. Now, you may not think that *you* ought to be, but you believe *somebody* ought to be judged. Everyone believes that. We have that innate sense within us today, and God has put it there.

For if the truth of God hath more abounded through my lie unto his glory; why yet am I also judged as a sinner? [Rom. 3:7].

The lie here means moral falsehood. Each individual could claim exemption from the judgment of God because his sin had advanced the glory of God.

And not rather, (as we be slanderously reported, and as some affirm that we say,) Let us do evil, that good may come? whose damnation is just [Rom. 3:8].

In this verse Paul drives his argument to its logical, yet untenable conclusion. This is called an *argumentum ad absurdum.* If sin magnifies the glory of God, then the more sin the more glory. Some had falsely accused Paul of teaching this absurdity. It was ridiculous, for it was Paul who insisted that God must judge sin. As surely as there is sin there must be judgment. You see, this facetious type of argument which Paul has met here makes a Robespierre a saint in the name of utilitarianism. It's the old bromide that the end justifies the means.

Now we come to this section where we have the accusation of "guilty" by God against mankind. Paul is going to conclude this section on sin by bringing mankind up before the Judge of all the earth. And the accusation of "guilty" is made by God against all mankind—both Jew and Gentile, black and white, male and female, rich and poor. It doesn't make any difference who we are; if we belong to the human race, you and I stand guilty before God. And then Paul is going to take us to God's clinic. It's a real spiritual clinic, and the Great Physician is going to look at us. We see that there are fourteen different charges made; six of them before the Judge and the other eight before the Great Physician who says we're sick. In fact, we're sick nigh unto death. To tell the truth, we are dead in trespasses and sin. That is our condition.

What then? are we better than they? No, in no wise: for we have before proved both Jews and Gentiles, that they are all under sin [Rom. 3:9].

Now Paul doesn't mean "proved" here. That word is a little too strong; it does not have quite that shade of meaning, because Paul is not trying to prove man a sinner. Rather, he is showing that God judges sin. He assumes man is a sinner, and you don't have to assume it—it is evident. He is merely stating that which is very obvious today. The better word is *charged*—"for we have before *charged* both Jews and Gentiles, that they are all under sin." He is just stating the case, by the way, that it doesn't make any difference who we are today—high or low, rich or poor, good or bad—we're all under sin.

Now it's very important to understand what it means to be "under sin." Man is a sinner four different ways. God is giving man four strikes (in baseball you get only three). (1) Man is a sinner by act. (2) Man is a sinner by nature. Sinning does not make a sinner; we sin because we are sinners. (3) Man is a sinner by imputation. We'll see that later in this epistle. (4) The estate of man is under sin. We all are under sin—the entire human family.

This is the first charge:

As it is written, There is none righteous, no, not one [Rom. 3:10].

This should read, "It is written *that* there is none righteous, no, not one," because it is a free rendering of Psalm 14:1 where David makes the positive statement that "none . . . doeth good." "Doeth good" and righteousness are the same.

What does it mean to be righteous? Well, it means to be right. Right with whom? We are to be right with God. And if we are going to be right with God, it is a little different from being right with your fellow man. When we have differences with friends, we may or may not be to blame, but we have to reach some sort of compromise. But if we are going to be right with God, we are going to play according to His rules. Actually, you can't play games with Him. You see, God's salvation is a take it or leave it proposition. God is not forcing anybody to take His salvation. You don't have to be saved. You can turn it down. God says, "This is My universe. You're living on My little world, using My sunshine and My water and My air, and I have worked out a plan of salvation that is true to My character and My nature. My plan and My program is the one that's going to be carried out. You're a sinner, and I want to save you because I love you. Now here it is. Take it or leave it." That's what God is saying to a lost world. This is what He is saying to you. Have you accepted it? Well, I want you to know that I have accepted it. To be right with God, then, means to accept His salvation.

When I was in school, I had a professor of sociology who really enjoyed batting that little ball around, saying, "Who is right? Who is going to make the rules?" Well, I know one thing: that professor is not going to make the rules. I know something else: I am not going to make the rules, and you are not going to make the rules either. God makes the rules. Take it or leave it. That is God's plan; that is God's program. There is none who is righteous, none right with God. But He has worked out a plan. No one has done good according to God's standard, according to God's method. That is the Judge's first charge.

The second charge is this:

There is none that understandeth, there is none that seeketh after God [Rom. 3:11].

In other words, there is none who acts on the knowledge that he has. No one is the person he would like to be.

The third charge:

"There is none that seeketh after God." God is not concealed today. God is not playing hide and seek with man. He has revealed Himself. You remember that Paul told the Athenians, the philosophers on Mars' Hill: "And the times of this ignorance God winked at; but now commandeth all men everywhere to repent" (Acts 17:30). He is not winking at sin today. God is out in the open telling man that he is a sinner and offering him salvation. And His salvation is clear, you see. That's what He is saying here. And there is none that seeks after God. The anthologies of religion say man is out looking for God—how fallacious they are! It's claimed that in the evolutionary process religion is man's search for God. Well, actually, is religion man's search for God? No. That's not what the Bible teaches. Believe me, man hasn't found out very much about God on his own. He hasn't advanced very far in that direction, because he's going the wrong way. He's going away from God.

Then the fourth charge that He makes is:

They are all gone out of the way, they are together become unprofitable; there is none that doeth good, no, not one [Rom. 3:12].

They've detoured. They left the way they knew was right. And primitive tribes have an ancient tradition that way back at one time their forefathers knew the living and true God. My friend, if you are honest, you know that you are not doing what you ought to do. Furthermore, you are not going to do it, although you know what it is. You have gone out of the way. Man has deviated from the way. This is the fourth charge that God makes.

The fifth charge is: "they are together become unprofitable." The word *unprofitable* suggests overripe, spoiled fruit. It could be translated, "they have altogether become sour." I am very fond of fruit, especially the papaya. But when it passes the ripe state and becomes rotten, there is nothing quite as bad as that. Mankind is not lush fruit; he is corrupt fruit. That is what the Judge of all the earth is saying.

The sixth charge: "there is none that doeth good, no, not one." This is a triple negative. Mankind is like a group of travelers who have gone in the opposite direction from the right one, and not one can help the others. Our Lord said to the religious leaders of His day, "You are blind leaders of the blind" (see Matt. 15:14). That is what the Judge of all the earth says about you and about me and about everyone on the face of the earth.

Now Paul transfers us over to God's clinic into the hands of the Great Physician. This is a spiritual clinic, and the Great Physician says that we are spiritually sick.

Their throat is an open sepulchre; with their tongues they have used deceit; the poison of asps is under their lips [Rom. 3:13].

When you go to the doctor, what's the first thing that he says to you? Well, I have to go in for a regular check-up because of the fact that I apparently have cancer in my system, and I report regularly in case of an outbreak. Well, it is a ritual for me to go in, and I sit down in the little room where he does his examination. Do you know the first thing that he says to me? "Open your mouth." Then he takes a little wooden stick and pushes it around in my mouth, and he looks at my throat. Likewise God, the Lord Jesus, the Great Physician, does that with mankind. Do you know what He says? "Their throat is an open sepulchre." Have you ever smelled decaying human flesh? When a little girl in Nashville was kidnapped many years ago, the sheriff of the county was a member and a deacon in my church. He called me up and told me they had found the body of a little girl, and they were going out to exhume it. He wanted to know if I wanted to go with them. I got to the place where they had taken the body out—it had been buried several days—and the body was corrupt. Oh, it was terrible! I've never been as sick in my life as I was at the odor of corrupt human flesh. I always think of that in connection with this verse.

When God looks down at you, friend, He doesn't say what a sweet, fine little boy or girl you are. God says you smell like an open grave! Someone, I think it was Mel Trotter, said, "If we could see ourselves as God sees us, we couldn't even *stand* ourselves!" Well, that is what Paul is saying here.

And "with their tongues they have used deceit." That's number two. And the second thing my doctor says to me (after he looks at my throat) is, "Stick out your tongue!" That's what the Great Physician says to the human family. "Stick out your tongue." And when God looks at the tongue of mankind—that means your tongue and mine—do you know what He says? "The poison of asps is under their lips." There's a snake house and a place for reptiles in the zoo in San Diego, California, which I have been through several times. As I look at the vicious fangs of those diamondback rattlers, I think of the poison that is there. Friend, right now, if you go and look in the mirror, you will see a tongue that is far more dangerous than any diamondback rattlesnake. He can't hurt your reputation at all. He can kill your body, but he can't hurt your reputation. *You* have a tongue that you can use to ruin the reputation of someone else. You can ruin the fair name of some woman. You can ruin the reputation of some man. I think today the most vicious thing in some of our churches is the gossip that is carried on. I actually advised someone not too long ago not to join a certain church, because I happen to know that some of the worst gossips in the world are in that church. And I want to tell you they have slaughtered the reputation of many individuals. Do you know who they are? They are the so-called spiritual crowd. I call them the spiritual snobs, because that's what they are. With their tongues they use deceit, and "the poison of asps [adder's poison] is under their lips." Oh, how vicious the human tongue is! How terrible it can be.

Whose mouth is full of cursing and bitterness [Rom. 3:14].

This is the fourth thing the Great Physician says about man. His mouth is full of cursing and deceit and fraud; under his tongue is mischief and vanity. Also he is prone to curse. And if you listen to what is being said today, you know that cursing is in the vocabulary of all men, whether he is a ditch digger or a college professor. They're better at using profanity than they are at any other language. A man challenged this verse one time when I was a pastor in downtown Los Angeles. He didn't believe it was true. So I said to him, "Let's test it. You and I will walk out here to the corner, and the first man who comes by, whoever he is, you punch him in the mouth and see what comes out. I guarantee that it will be as God says."

Then God says the fifth thing.

Their feet are swift to shed blood [Rom. 3:15].

Isaiah 59:7 gives the unabridged version: "Their feet run to evil, and they make haste to shed innocent blood: their thoughts are thoughts of iniquity; wasting and destruction are in their paths." What a picture this is of mankind—"Their feet are swift to shed blood."

Destruction and misery are in their ways [Rom. 3:16].

Man leaves desolation and distress behind him. This is included in Isaiah 59:7 which we have quoted.

And the way of peace have they not known [Rom. 3:17].

Man does not know the way of peace. Look about you in the world today. After all these years man is still talking about peace, but he hasn't found it. Just read your newspaper, my friend; there is no peace in this world.

There is no fear of God before their eyes [Rom. 3:18].

Paul seems to sum up all of man's sin in this final statement. He has no fear of God at all. Man is living as if God does not exist. Man actually defies God. What a picture this gives of mankind!

Now we come to the final thing Paul has to say about sin. Because there are still those who will say, "Well, we have the Law and we'll keep the Law. We will hold onto it."

Now we know that what things soever the law saith, it saith to them who are under the law: that every mouth may be stopped, and all the world may become guilty before God [Rom. 3:19].

Man cannot attain righteousness by the Mosaic Law. It is as if mankind in desperation grabbed for the Law as the proverbial straw when drowning. The Law won't lift him up. Actually, it does the opposite. To hold onto the Law is like a man jumping out of an airplane, and instead of taking a parachute, he takes a sack of cement with him. Well, believe me, the Law will pull you down. It condemns man. It's a ministration of death.

Therefore by the deeds of the law there shall no flesh be justified in his sight: for by the law is the knowledge of sin [Rom. 3:20].

Now, I challenge any person today who believes that you have to keep the Law to be saved to take this verse and explain it. "Therefore by the deeds of the law there shall no flesh be justified in his sight." And "justified" means to be declared righteous, to be saved, to meet God's standards. You can never do it, my beloved. It's absolutely impossible for mankind to do. "By the deeds of the law there shall no flesh be justified." Then what is the purpose of the Law? "By the law is the knowledge of sin." Rather than providing a salvation for man, the Law reveals man to be a sinner.

Between verses 20 and 21 there is a "Grand Canyon" division. We move out of the night into the day. Now Paul begins to speak of God's wonderful salvation. He will talk about justification by faith, which will be explained in the remainder of the chapter.

AVAILABILITY OF A RIGHTEOUSNESS FROM GOD

But now the righteousness of God without the law is manifested, being witnessed by the law and the prophets [Rom. 3:21].

"The righteousness of God" should be *a* righteousness of God, since the article is absent in the Greek. This "righteousness" is not an attribute of God—He says that He will not share His glory with another—nor is it the righteousness of man. God has already said that ". . . our righteousnesses are as filthy rags . . ." (Isa. 64:6), and God is not taking in dirty laundry. Then what righteousness is Paul speaking of? It is the righteousness which God provides. Christ has become our righteousness. "But of him are ye in Christ Jesus, who of God is made unto us wisdom and righteousness, and sanctification, and redemption" (1 Cor. 1:30). Also we are told in 2 Corinthians 5:21: "For he hath made him to be sin for us, who knew no sin; that we might be made the righteousness of God in him." It is very important for us to recognize that God is the One who provides this righteousness. It's not something that you and I can work out, but rather it is something that God has provided for us. A righteousness that God demands, God also provides.

This is a righteousness that is apart from the Law. That is, you can't get it, my friend, by doing something or keeping something—not even God's law. You can't keep the Law to begin with. God can't save you by law for the very simple reason that you can't measure up to it. God can't accept imperfection, and you and I cannot provide perfection. Therefore, He cannot save us by law. "Being witnessed by the law and the prophets" means that the Law bore witness to it in that at the very center of the Mosaic system was a tabernacle where bloody sacrifices were offered which pointed to Christ. Also the prophets witnessed to it when they spoke of the coming of Christ, His death and resurrection. For example, Isaiah prophesied, "All we like sheep have gone astray; we have turned every one to his own way; and the LORD hath laid on him the iniquity of us all. . . . Yet it pleased the LORD to bruise him; he hath put him to grief: when thou shalt make his soul an offering for sin, he shall see his seed, he shall prolong his days, and the pleasure of the LORD shall prosper in his hand" (Isa. 53:6, 10).

Both the Law and the prophets witnessed to this righteousness that God would provide in Christ.

Even the righteousness of God which is by faith of Jesus Christ unto all and upon all them that believe: for there is no difference [Rom. 3:22].

When I was a young preacher I thought that the grace of God had to go way down to reach the bad sinners but didn't have to go down so far to reach others who weren't so bad. But now I know that God's grace has to go all the way to the bottom to get all of us. Each one of us is completely lost outside of Christ. Either you are absolutely saved in Christ, or you are completely lost outside of Christ. All of us need the righteousness of Christ. There is no difference.

The righteousness of Christ comes to us through our faith in Christ. Great men of the past have given some apt definitions of this righteousness. William Cunningham wrote: "Under law God required righteousness from man. Under grace, He gives righteousness to man. The righteousness of God is that righteousness which God's righteousness requires

Him to require." That is a deep definition, but it is a good one. The great Dr. Charles Hodge has given this definition: "That righteousness of which God is the author which is of avail before Him, which meets and secures His approval." Then Dr. Brooks gives this definition: "That righteousness which the Father required, the Son became, and the Holy Spirit convinces of, and faith secures." Dr. Moorehead writes: "The sum total of all that God commands, demands, approves, and Himself provides." I don't believe it can be said any better than the way these men have said it.

Now this righteousness, as we have seen, is secured by faith, not by works. Let's look at these verses together.

Even the righteousness of God which is by faith of Jesus Christ unto all and upon all them that believe: for there is no difference:

For all have sinned, and come short of the glory of God [Rom. 3:22–23].

Let me give you a free rendering of these verses: Even the righteousness from God which is obtained by faith in Jesus Christ unto all and upon all that believe: for there is no distinction: for all have sinned and fall short of the glory [approval] of God. That this righteousness is by faith, not by works, the Lord Jesus made clear when they asked Him, ". . . What shall we do, that we might work the works of God?" Jesus answered and said unto them, "This is the work of God, that ye believe on him whom he hath sent" (John 6:28–29). And the important thing about securing this righteousness of God is not that there's any merit in your faith or that there's merit in just believing. Because, actually, faith is not a work on your part. The *object* of faith is the important thing. Spurgeon put it like this: "It's not thy hope in Christ which saves you. It's Christ. It's not thy joy in Christ that saves you. It is Christ. And it is not thy faith in Christ that saves you, though that be the instrument, it is Christ's blood and merit." Now, friend, that's very important to nail in our thinking.

And that righteousness is like a garment. It is available *to* all, but it only comes *upon* all that believe. And then he says that it's needed by everyone: "For all have sinned, and come short of the glory of God." Now that doesn't mean that there is not a difference in sinners. Let me illustrate this with a very homely illustration. Let's suppose that we folk here in California play a game called "Jumping to Catalina." Catalina Island is out in the Pacific Ocean at least fifteen or twenty miles from the shore of California. We will go down to the pier in Santa Monica, and we will take a big running jump, and we'll see who can jump to Catalina. Somebody's going to say, "That's an impossible jump!" Frankly, no one has jumped it, but it's a lot of fun playing the game. Suppose you and I play the game. You may be able to jump farther than I can jump, but you will miss Catalina. And the fellow who jumps the farthest gets the wettest and has to swim farther back to shore. Of course, nobody could jump to Catalina. Some are better than others, but it's rather childish to play a game like that and say, "I jumped farther than you did. I'm better than you are, and I'm better than half the church members." Suppose you are—and you may well be—but what difference does that make? You have not come up to the glory of God.

Being justified freely by his grace through the redemption that is in Christ Jesus [Rom. 3:24].

"Freely" is the Greek word *dōrean*, translated in John 15:25 "without a cause." Our Lord Jesus said that they hated Him freely, without a cause—there was no basis for it. Now Paul is saying, "Being justified freely—without a cause." There is no explanation in us. God doesn't say, "Oh, they are such wonderful people, I'll have to do something for them!" As we have seen before, there is nothing in us that would call out the grace of God, other than our great *need*. We are justified without a cause. It is by His grace, which means that there is no merit on our part. Grace is unmerited favor; it is love in action.

It is "through the redemption that is in Christ Jesus." Redemption is always connected with the grace of God. The reason that God can save you and me is that Christ redeemed us, He paid a price. He died upon a cross to make it available to us. You see, justification by faith is actually more than subtraction of our sins—that is, forgiveness. It is the addition of the righteousness of Christ. In other words, we are not merely restored to Adam's former position, but now we are placed *in Christ* where we shall be throughout the endless ages of eternity the sons of God!

John Bunyan was driven almost to distraction because he realized that he was such a great sinner with no righteousness of his own. And he said at that time, "When God showed me John Bunyan as God saw John Bunyan, I no longer confessed I was a sinner, but I confessed that I was sin from the crown of my head to the sole of my feet. I was full of sin." And Bunyan struggled with the problem of how he could stand in God's presence even with his sins forgiven. Where could he gain a standing before God? And so, walking through the cornfields one night, as he wrestled with this problem, the words of Paul (who was another great sinner, who called himself the chief of sinners) came to him, and his burden rolled off his shoulders. The word from Paul was Philippians 3:9: "And be found in him, not having mine own righteousness, which is of the law, but that which is through the faith of Christ, the righteousness which is of God by faith." And when you read Bunyan's *Pilgrim's Progress*, you're reading actually the story of Bunyan's life. And you remember, when Pilgrim came with that great burden on his shoulders through the Slough of Despond, he didn't know what to do until finally he came to the cross, and there the burden rolled off, and he trusted Christ as his Savior.

"By his grace" is the way God saves us. This is the fountain from which flow down the living waters of God in this age of grace. And so, because of what God has done—sending His Son to die—God is able to save by grace. And Paul in Ephesians 2:4–5 says, "But God, who is rich in mercy [that means He has plenty of it], for his great love wherewith he loved us, Even when we were dead in sins, hath quickened us together with Christ, (by grace ye are saved;)." And Dr. Newell said of that grace, "The grace of God is infinite love operating by an infinite means—the sacrifice of Christ; and an infinite freedom, unhindered, now, by the temporary restrictions of the law." Today a holy God is free to reach down to meet your needs. How wonderful it is to know a holy God is *free* to save those who will trust Christ. Dr. Newell again said, "Everything connected with God's salvation is glad in bestowment, infinite in extent, and unchangeable in its character." And it's all available, and only available, in Christ Jesus. He alone could pay the price. As Peter put it to the nation Israel, "Neither is there salvation in any other: for there is none other name under heaven given among men, whereby we must be saved" (Acts 4:12).

Whom God hath set forth to be a propitiation through faith in his blood, to declare his righteousness for the remission of sins that are past, through the forbearance of God;

To declare, I say, at this time his righteousness: that he might be just, and the justifier of him which believeth in Jesus [Rom. 3:25–26].

Notice it is "faith in his blood." That blood speaks of His life—". . . without shedding of blood is no remission" (Heb. 9:22). And I tell you, when you put a knife in the body of a man and the blood pours out, that man is a dead man because "the life of the flesh is in the blood." And the life of Jesus Christ was *given*. That blood is a very precious thing according to Simon Peter.

Now, these two verses are filled with words that are jawbreakers: propitiation, righteousness, remission. Although they are difficult words, don't be too frightened of them, because when we boil them down to our size, we find that in these two verses we have what Calvin called the very marrow of theology. Calvin also wrote: "There is not probably in the whole Bible a passage which sets forth more profoundly the righteousness of God in Christ."

"God hath set forth"—God is the sole architect of salvation, and He is the One today who is able to save. You and I cannot save; no religion can save; no church can save. Paul said to the Corinthians, "And all things are of God, who hath reconciled us to himself by Jesus Christ . . ." (2 Cor. 5:18). *He* did it. Now, He is giving to us the *ministry* of reconciliation, and so all that the holy God is asking you and me to do today is to be reconciled to Him. You don't have to do anything to soften God's heart. I have a friend who was an evangelist for years, and he always liked to get people to cry. I used to ask him how many tears you'd have to shed to soften God's heart. "Oh," he said, "don't be ridiculous." I told him, "I'm not being ridiculous. *You* are. You say you've got to come down to the altar and shed some tears." My friend, God's heart is already soft. All you have to do is come. He is reconciled to you. He says to you, "Be ye reconciled to God." Christ has been "set forth"; that is, He has been exhibited or displayed.

"To be a propitiation" points back to the time over nineteen hundred years ago when Christ was set forth as the Savior. You will recall that the veil of the temple hid the mercy seat and only the high priest could go in past that veil. But today Christ has been set before us as the mercy seat. Speaking of the mercy seat, the writer of Hebrews says, "And over it the cherubims of glory shadowing the mercyseat . . ." (Heb. 9:5)—the Greek word for mercy seat, *hilasterion,* is the same word translated "propitiation." Christ has been set forth as the mercy seat. You recall that the poor publican cried out, because he needed a mercy seat, ". . . God be merciful to me a sinner" (Luke 18:13), which literally is, "God, if there were only a mercy seat for me, a poor publican, to come to!" You see, when a Jew became a publican, he cut himself off from the temple and from the mercy seat that was there. Paul is saying that now there is on display a mercy seat—God hath set forth Christ to be a propitiation through faith in His blood. It is wonderful to know that we have a holy God who in joy and in satisfaction and delight can hold out to the world today a mercy seat.

And God doesn't reluctantly save you. If you come, He saves you wholeheartedly, abundantly. Some folk tell me that after I am saved I still have to search and pray and tarry for something more. My friend, when I came to Jesus, I got *everything* (see Eph. 1:3). Oh, how good He was! He didn't hold back anything. And He says to come, He can accept you. ". . . him that cometh to me I will in no wise cast out" (John 6:37). Actually, you and I were shut out from a holy God. But the way now has been opened up for us by His blood.

"To declare his righteousness for the remission of sins that are past." That doesn't mean your sins and my sins of the past; it means the sins of those who lived before the cross. You see, back in the Old Testament, they brought a little lamb. And I'm sure you don't take a little lamb to church to sacrifice. Today it would be sinful to do that. But back then, before Christ came, it was required; the Law required it. Now, that little lamb pointed to the coming of Christ. No one back in those days believed that the little lamb could take away sins. I don't think any of them did. Suppose you had been there when Abel brought a little lamb to God, "Abel, do you think this little lamb is going to take away your sin?" He would have told you no. And you would have said, "Then why did you bring it?" His answer would have been, "God required it. God commanded us to bring it." Hebrews 11:4 tells us "By faith Abel offered unto God a more excellent sacrifice than Cain. . . ." In other words, he did it by revelation, because "faith cometh by hearing, and hearing by the word of God" (Rom. 10:17). The only way Abel could have brought that sacrifice by faith was for God to have told him to bring it. And that is what God did.

You might have said to Abel, "Specifically what do you think God has in mind?" And I think he would have said this, "Well, God has told my mother that there's coming a Savior. We don't know when, but until He comes, we're to do this because we're to come by faith." And so the "sins that are past" means that up to the time when Christ died, God saved on *credit*. God did not save Abraham because he brought a sacrifice. God never saved any of them because they brought a sacrifice. A sacrifice pointed to Christ. When Christ came, He paid for *all* the sins of the past and also for the sins this side of the cross.

"To declare, I say, at this time his righteousness: that he might be just, and the justifier of him which believeth in Jesus." On this side of the cross we don't bring a sacrifice, but we are to trust in Christ and His blood.

Now Paul raises a question:

Where is boasting then? It is excluded. By what law? of works? Nay: but by the law of faith [Rom. 3:27].

If God is saving by faith in Christ and not by your merit, your works, then where is boasting? What is it that you and I have to crow about? We can't even boast of the fact that we're fundamental in doctrine. We have nothing to glory in today. Paul asks, "Where is boasting then?" And he answers the question he raises.

"It is excluded. By what law? of works? Nay: but by the law of faith." The word *law* in the first instance is not restricted to the Old Testament Law but means the *principle* of law—any law, anything that you think you can do. The second reference to *law* excludes the Old Testament Law and means simply a rule or principle of faith. In other words, God has the human race not on the merit system, but on the basis of simply believing what He has done for us. Therefore, it excludes boasting.

Therefore we conclude that a man is justified by faith without the deeds of the law [Rom. 3:28].

This is not a conclusion that Paul is coming to or even a summing up of what he has said. Rather, he is giving an explanation of why boasting is excluded. Why is boasting excluded? Man is justified by faith.

Now Paul not only drives the nail in, he turns the board over and clinches it. Listen to him:

Is he the God of the Jews only? is he not also of the Gentiles? Yes, of the Gentiles also [Rom. 3:29].

In other words, does God belong to the Jews alone and not also to the Gentiles? And Paul says, "Yes, to the Gentiles also." Now, listen to this. This is a very cogent argument. Paul says, "If justification is by the law, then God *does* belong to the Jews. But if justification is by faith, then He is the God of both Jews and Gentiles." Now, notice the logic of this. If the Jew persisted in this position, then there must be two Gods—one for the Jews, one for the Gentiles. But the Jew would not allow this. He was a monotheist, that is, he believed in one God. Probably the greatest statement that ever was given to the nation Israel was Deuteronomy 6:4, "Hear, O Israel: Jehovah, our Elohim is one Jehovah" (literal translation mine). That was the clarion message He gave in the pagan world before Christ came.

Seeing it is one God, which shall justify the circumcision by faith, and uncircumcision through faith [Rom. 3:30].

In other words, there's only one God. And in the Old Testament, He gave man the Law. Man failed. God didn't save them by their keeping the Law; salvation was always by the sacrifice which man brought in faith, pointing to the coming of the Lord Jesus Christ.

Do we then make void the law through faith? God forbid: yea, we establish the law [Rom. 3:31].

The reference to the Law, I think, brings in another meaning of this word. It is not restricted to the Mosaic system here. Neither does it refer to just any law. Rather, it refers to the entire Old Testament revelation. "Faith" excluded the works of the Law. But did it abrogate the entire Old Testament revelation? Of course not! Paul will demonstrate in the next chapter by Old Testament illustrations of two men, Abraham and David, that it did not exclude that. These two key men, outstanding men, were saved, not by law but by faith. To begin with, Abraham was born and lived and died four hundred years before the Law was ever given. Abraham did not live on the basis of the Mosaic Law since it was not yet given in his day. God saved him on a different basis, which is *by faith.* And somebody says, "Well, then what about David?" Now, very honestly, do you think David could have been saved by keeping the Law? Of course he couldn't. The Old Testament made it very clear that David *broke* the Law. And yet God saved him. How? Well, He saved him by faith. David trusted God and believed God. Even in his sin, he came in confession to God. God accepted him and saved him by faith.

Today, my friend, when you and I will take the position that we're sinners and come to God and trust Christ as our Savior—regardless of who we are, where we are, how we are or when we are—God will save us. For God today has put man on one basis and one basis alone. His question is, what will you do with My Son who died for you on the cross?

CHAPTER 4

***THEME:** Abraham; David; Abraham justified by faith*

In this great section of justification by faith, we have seen the doctrine. Paul has vividly stated that man is a sinner. Then he revealed that God provides a righteousness for sinners, and justification by faith has been explained. Now he will illustrate this truth with two men out of the Old Testament: Abraham and David.

In Paul's day Abraham and David were probably held in higher esteem by the nation Israel than any other two whose lives are recorded in the Old Testament. Abraham was the founder of the Hebrew race, and David was their greatest king. Paul uses these two Old Testament worthies as illustrations to establish his statement in chapter 3 that there is concord and agreement between the Law and the gospel. Although they represent two diametrically opposed systems, neither contradicts nor conflicts with the other. And they are not mutually exclusive. Even under the Law and before the Law, faith was God's sole requirement. Abraham, before the Law, was justified by faith. And David, under the Law, sang of justification by faith. Paul is not presenting some strange new doctrine which cancels out the Old Testament and leaves the Jew afloat on the sea of life holding onto an anchor rather than being in a lifeboat. Paul is showing that Abraham and David are in the same lifeboat, which he is offering his own people in his day, labeled "justification by faith." The Law was a pedagogue—it took the man under Law by the hand to lead him to the Lord Jesus Christ.

ABRAHAM

Now we see in the first five verses that Abraham was justified by faith.

What shall we say then that Abraham our father, as pertaining to the flesh, hath found? [Rom. 4:1].

Let's rearrange the modifiers and phrases to help us follow the thought of Paul: Therefore, what shall we say that Abraham, our first father, has found according to the flesh, that is, by natural human effort? The *therefore* that opens this chapter connects this argument with what Paul has been talking about back in the third chapter. The gospel excludes boasting and establishes the Law, as we have seen. Abraham and David confirm Paul in this thesis.

Paul uses the idiomatic phrase "What shall we say?" here and in the other argumentative portions of this epistle. In the first division, Paul did not attempt to prove or argue that man is a sinner. For this reason we did not find this phrase there. Also in the last section of this epistle, which is practical, it is entirely omitted.

"Abraham, our first father" reveals that the nation Israel began with Abraham. "First father," I think, is a peculiar expression. It reveals the importance attached to Abraham, who was first chronologically and also first in importance. Many years ago when I was a pastor in Nashville, several friends that I had known before I studied for the ministry—they were Jewish friends—invited me to come up one evening to speak to a group in the Young Men's Hebrew Association. So I spoke to them on the glories of the Mosaic Law. I was amazed to find that they reckoned their ancestry from Abraham—they never went past Abraham. Quite a few of their questions revealed that, and finally I asked them some questions. I asked, "Don't you count Noah or Adam in the line?" These young Jewish friends laughed and said, "No, we stop with Abraham. He's our first father."

"Pertaining to the flesh" could modify *Abraham*, or it could modify the verb *has found*. What has he found according to the flesh? Abraham has found that Abraham's works according to the flesh did not produce boasting but produced shame and confusion. That was Abraham's works. He had nothing to boast of. Oh, don't misunderstand; I think Abraham was a great man, and especially in that matter of Lot. He wouldn't let the kings of Sodom and Gomorrah reward him. But in another section Abraham didn't believe God, and he ran down to Egypt. This matter of that little Egyptian maid that he got and the son that came from her, these are things that are not to be boasted of by Abraham.

Now notice how Paul develops this.

For if Abraham were justified by works, he hath whereof to glory; but not before God [Rom. 4:2].

If Abraham were justified (declared to be righteous) by works—that is, the works of the flesh "he hath whereof to glory," but not before God. He can glory in self, but he cannot glory before God. It was assumed that Abraham had good works that counted before God. And the fact of the matter is that Abraham had many good works. But the startling thing was to discover that these good works were not the ground of salvation but were the result of his salvation and the result of being justified by faith. You see, James and Paul did not contradict each other when James said, "Was not Abraham our father justified by works, when he had offered Isaac his son upon the altar?" (James 2:21). The works that James described are not the works of the flesh under the Law, because Abraham wasn't under the Law. They were works of faith. Abraham believed God, and he offered up Isaac. But did he actually do it? No, God stopped him and would not let him go through with it. Why? Because it was wrong. You see, Paul and James quote the same verse: Abraham believed God, and He counted it unto him for righteousness (cf. Gen. 15:6; James 2:23; Rom. 4:3). But James goes to the end of Abraham's life, to the time that he offered up Isaac. Abraham stood on the same ground on which the weakest sinner stands. Granted that he did have works in which to boast, but he could never boast before God, because God does not accept the works of the flesh. The works of the flesh cannot stand before His holiness, and certainly Abraham's works were tinctured.

For what saith the scripture? Abraham believed God, and it was counted unto him for righteousness [Rom. 4:3].

Paul appeals to the Scripture as final authority. He even personifies it here—the Scripture is God speaking. What does the Scripture say? There is no other authority to which he can appeal. It was Dr. Benjamin Warfield who made this statement: "The Bible is the Word of God in such a way that whatever the Bible says *God* says."

How I wish that more men who claim to be evangelical really believed the Word of God—that it *is* the Word of God, that it is God speaking. Paul quotes from the Old Testament directly about sixty times in this epistle. This quotation is, of course, from Genesis 15:6: "And he believed in the LORD; and he counted it to him for righteousness." Paul is saying, "Hear what the Scripture says; God is speaking to you in His Word." How tremendous this is.

This promise was given to Abraham at a time when he raised a question with God: ". . . what wilt thou give me, seeing I go childless . . . ?" (Gen. 15:2). God gave him no assurance other than a confirmation of the promise that his seed would be like the stars. In other words, Abraham simply believed God. He took the naked Word of God at face value, and he rested in it. Newell puts it like this: "There was no honor, no merit, in Abraham believing the faithful God, who cannot lie. The honor was God's. When Abraham believed God, he did the one thing that a man can do without doing anything! God made the statement, the promise, and God undertook to fulfill it. Abraham believed in his heart that God told the truth. There was no effort here. Abraham's faith was not an act, but an attitude. His heart was turned completely away from himself to God and His promise. This left God free to fulfill that promise. Faith was neither a meritorious act by Abraham, nor a change of character or nature in Abraham; he simply believed God would accomplish what He had promised: 'In thee shall all the families of the earth be blessed' (Gen. 12:3)." How wonderful! "Counted unto him for righteousness." God counted, reckoned, it to him. God put it to Abraham's account. He imputed it over to him for righteousness. It was not righteousness, but that is how God reckoned it.

Now to him that worketh is the reward not reckoned of grace, but of debt.

But to him that worketh not, but believeth on him that justifieth the ungodly, his faith is counted for righteousness [Rom. 4:4–5].

It is a general rule that a workman is paid wages for the services that he renders. A man works for so much an hour, or he is paid so much for a particular job. Obviously Abraham was not a workman, for he did not earn what he received. His salvation was received on the only other basis, and that was undeserved favor—by the grace of God—and he believed God. "But to him that worketh not"—that is, there is nothing that you can do that will merit salvation. But you believe on Him, that is, on God, who declares the ungodly righteous. And the only kind of people God is saving are unrighteous people. Somebody says, "You mean that He doesn't save good people?" Well, do you want to name one? God will save any man who is good. But Scripture, as we've already seen, says, "There is none righteous, no, not one" (Rom. 3:10). This is according to God's standard, not according to my little standard or your standard. If you want to name somebody who is good, you will make God out a liar. Are you prepared to do that? And, of course, you would have to prove your point.

"His faith is counted for righteousness." Faith is the only condition. God accepts faith in lieu of works. There is no merit in faith, but it is the only way of receiving that which God freely offers. Faith honors God and secures righteousness for man. God put down righteousness in Abraham's account to his credit. His faith counted for what it was not—a righteousness from God. This is important to see.

DAVID

Even as David also describeth the blessedness of the man, unto whom God imputeth righteousness without works [Rom. 4:6].

David lived under the Law—Abraham did not because no law had been given during his lifetime. The Mosaic system didn't come along until four hundred years later. However, although David lived under the Law, David could never be saved under the Law. And therefore David described the blessedness that God reckons righteousness without works—because David had no works. The works that he had were evil. And therefore righteousness must be totally apart and separate from works. Righteousness must come on an entirely different principle.

Saying, Blessed are they whose iniquities are forgiven, and whose sins are covered [Rom. 4:7].

This is a direct quotation from Psalm 32, verses 1 and 2. And this is one of the great penitential psalms of David—Psalm 51 is the other one. These verses are the outcome of David's great sin and his confession and acceptance which followed.

"Blessed are they whose iniquities are forgiven." Are you one of the blessed ones today? Well, I'm glad to be in that company, in that number. "Blessed" expresses, oh, that glorious, wonderful joy of sins forgiven! This is the greatest statement of all, and David knew this by experience.

"Iniquities" is lawlessness. David deliberately broke the law. He didn't do it ignorantly. He knew what he did, and he was forgiven.

"Are forgiven" refers to a definite and complete act of remission. A hard-boiled judge may under certain circumstances remit sins. But this speaks of the tenderness of God by taking the sinner into His arms of love and receiving him with affection. His sins are covered. How? Because Jesus Christ died and shed His blood, my friend.

Blessed is the man to whom the Lord will not impute sin [Rom. 4:8].

In other words, joyful is the man whose sin the Lord will not put to his account. David was a great sinner. And God put away his sin, as Nathan informed him. Nathan said to David, ". . . The LORD also hath put away thy sin; thou shalt not die" (2 Sam. 12:13). Nevertheless, David was chastened. David set his own penalty when he responded to Nathan's account of the rich man who took the poor man's ewe lamb: "And he shall restore the lamb fourfold . . ." (2 Sam. 12:6). Four of David's children were killed—the child of Bathsheba, Amnon his firstborn, Absalom, and Adonijah. Sorrow plagued David all the days of his life. David's guilt was not put on his account, though—Another bore it for him. Little wonder that he could say, "Joyful is the man whose sin the Lord will in no wise put to his account."

ABRAHAM JUSTIFIED BY FAITH

Cometh this blessedness then upon the circumcision only, or upon the uncircumcision also? for we say that faith was reckoned to Abraham for righteousness [Rom. 4:9].

The argument now returns to Abraham to illustrate that justification is universal. Since David has spoken of the joy of the man under law who has been forgiven, the answer of the Jew would be that David belonged to the circumcision and only the circumcision could expect this joy. For this reason Paul returns to Abraham to show that Abraham was justified before the Law was given and also before he was circumcised.

How was it then reckoned? when he was in circumcision, or in uncircumcision? Not in circumcision, but in uncircumcision [Rom. 4:10].

God made the promise to him, and he believed God long before there was any kind of agreement made at all—other than that God said He would do it. Abraham believed the naked Word of God.

And he received the sign of circumcision, a seal of the righteousness of the faith which he had yet being uncircumcised: that he might be the father of all them that believe, though they be not circumcised; that righteousness might be imputed unto them also:

And the father of circumcision to them who are not of the circumcision only, but who also walk in the steps of that faith of our father Abraham, which he had being yet uncircumcised.

For the promise, that he should be the heir of the world, was not to Abraham, or to his seed, through the law, but through the righteousness of faith [Rom. 4:11–13].

God made that promise to Abraham long before circumcision was introduced. Abraham just believed God; that's all.

For if they which are of the law be heirs, faith is made void, and the promise made of none effect:

Because the law worketh wrath: for where no law is, there is no transgression.

Therefore it is of faith, that it might be by grace [Rom. 4:14–16a].

You see, God saved Abraham by faith alone.

Now notice something else here. Abraham was justified actually by faith in the resurrection.

And being not weak in faith, he considered not his own body now dead, when he was about an hundred years old, neither yet the deadness of Sarah's womb [Rom. 4:19].

There is no merit in faith itself. You see, there was nothing around Abraham in which he could trust—nothing that he could feel, nothing that he could see, *nothing*. All he did was believe God. That's important.

He staggered not at the promise of God through unbelief; but was strong in faith, giving glory to God [Rom. 4:20].

He was not double-minded. That's the whole thought here. He looked away from his circumstances to the promise. He believed the promise, in spite of the fact that the circumstances nullified it. He put confidence in the promise because of the One who gave it, thus giving worship to God. You see, man was created to glorify God, but by disobedience he did the opposite. And, my friend, the only way *you* can glorify God is to believe Him.

And being fully persuaded that, what he had promised, he was able also to perform [Rom. 4:21].

"Fully persuaded" means that he was filled brimful. There was no room for doubt.

And therefore it was imputed to him for righteousness [Rom. 4:22].

This faith in the resurrection—life from the dead—is what God accepted from Abraham in lieu of his own righteousness, which he did not have. God declared Abraham righteous for his faith in the promise of God to raise up a son out of the tomb of death, that is, the womb of Sarah. God promises eternal life to those who believe that He raised up His own Son from the tomb of Joseph of Arimathaea, the place of death.

Now it was not written for his sake alone, that it was imputed to him;

But for us also, to whom it shall be imputed, if we believe on him that raised up Jesus our Lord from the dead [Rom. 4:23–24].

The womb of Sarah was a tomb. It was a place of death. But out of that came life. Abraham believed God. And this is what the Lord Jesus meant when He said, "Your father Abraham rejoiced to see my day: and he saw it, and was glad" (John 8:56).

Who was delivered for our offences, and was raised again for our justification [Rom. 4:25].

That is faith, not only in the death of Christ, but also in His resurrection. Matthew Henry put it like this: "In Christ's death He paid our debt; in His resurrection He took out our acquittance." God justifies those who believe in the death and resurrection of Christ. How wonderful this is! Have you gone that far with God? Do you believe Him?

CHAPTER 5

THEME: *Benefits of salvation; sanctification of the saint*

As we come to the fifth chapter of Romans, we find Paul answering one of the questions that would naturally arise in the minds of those who had read his epistle to this point. He has told us that we have been saved by the redemption that we have in Christ, the redemption that had been purchased at tremendous price upon the cross. It delivers us from the guilt of sin so that the sin question has been settled. This means that we will not come before God for judgment which will determine our salvation. It means that an eternal home is waiting for those who have trusted Christ. Now the question Paul will answer is: What about the here and now?

I have heard liberal preachers say, "I do not believe in a religion of the hereafter; I believe in a religion of the here and now." In San Francisco in the early days of the "hippie" movement, I was talking to a young vagrant on a street corner, and he didn't want to hear about Christianity. He said, "That's 'pie in the sky by and by' religion, and I don't care for that." And so I said to this young fellow, "Then you believe in getting your pie here and now and not by and by?" He said, "That's right." I told him that it didn't look to me like he was getting very much pie in the here and now, and he admitted that he wasn't. So I said, "Well, it is tragic indeed to miss the pie here and now, and miss it hereafter also."

Paul now is going to show that there are certain benefits that accrue to the believer right here and now when he trusts Christ, when he's been justified by faith in the redemption that we have in Christ. And actually these are benefits that the world is very much concerned about, and would like to have them.

Many people are spending a great deal of money today trying to attain the things that are the present benefits of every believer. That doesn't mean that all believers are enjoying them. However, God has them on the table for you, and all you have to do is reach over and take them (see Eph. 1:3).

BENEFITS OF SALVATION

1. Peace

Therefore being justified by faith, we have peace with God through our Lord Jesus Christ [Rom. 5:1].

"Therefore being justified by faith" refers to the one act of faith the moment we trust Christ.

"We have peace with God through our Lord Jesus Christ."

The Bible mentions several kinds of peace. First, there's world peace. The United Nations has worked for it as the old League of Nations did. They didn't get anywhere in the past, and they're not getting anywhere today. As I write this, a great many people believe that if you protest loudly enough you can bring peace to the world by human manipulation or psychological gyrations. Well, my friend, as long as there is sin in the hearts of men, there never will be peace in the world—not until the Prince of Peace comes. Christ will bring peace on this earth. But world peace is not the kind of peace that Paul is talking about here.

Then there is that peace which is known as tranquility of soul. That is the peace to which the Lord Jesus referred when He said to His disciples, "Peace I leave with you, my peace I give unto you: not as the world giveth, give I unto you . . ." (John 14:27). This is a peace that comes to certain believers who have trusted Christ and who are resting in Him and who are doing His will. I wish I could say that I experience this peace all the time. I do not. I recognize that it is available for every believer today. I suppose I am like most believers in that I have up and down experiences. There are times when this peace floods my soul, and it is wonderful. But there are times when I am under pressure or under tension or when I am weary and this peace somehow eludes me. However, Paul is not referring to the peace of personal tranquility.

Then there is a third kind of peace which Paul mentions to the Philippian believers—"the peace that passeth all understanding" (see Phil. 4:7). Well, since it passes all understanding, I certainly don't know what it is, and I have a notion that you don't know either.

The peace Paul is talking about, which he lists as the first benefit of salvation, is "peace *with God* through our Lord Jesus Christ." This is the peace that comes to the soul of one who has trusted Christ as Savior and knows that God no longer has any charge against him, that he is no longer guilty. He knows that God, who had to be against him in the past, is now *for* him. He knows that he has a salvation that is permanent and eternal. This is the peace that comes because of sins forgiven and because everything is right between you and God. You will notice that Paul mentions again and again that we have peace through the blood of Jesus Christ, which means that everything is all right between our soul and God. That is wonderful peace!

This was explained to me by a wonderful pastor when I was a young boy in my teens. He said that when man sinned in the Garden of Eden, not only did man run away from God—and found himself alienated from the life of God, with no capacity for God and no inclination to turn to Him—but God also had to turn away from man. Then when Christ died on the cross, God turned around, so that now a holy God can say to a lost sinner, "Come." His arms are outstretched. He says, "Come unto me, all ye that labour and are heavy laden, and I will rest you" (Matt. 11:28, literal translation mine). This is peace, the rest of redemption.

My friend, God is reconciled. You don't have to do anything to reconcile Him, as we have seen. A great many people think that you have to shed tears to reconcile God. You don't need tears to soften the heart of God! You don't have to do anything. Because Christ died on the cross, God is reconciled today. The message of the gospel is, "Be *ye* reconciled to God." The next move is *yours*. When you accept His salvation, then you experience peace that your sins have been forgiven.

There are a great many people who pillow their heads at night, not knowing what it is to have peace in their hearts. Oh, how many weary souls today are laboring with a guilt complex and would love to go somewhere to have that guilt removed from their souls! A Christian psychologist told me several years ago, "The only place you can have a guilt complex removed is at the cross of Christ." Peace is the first wonderful benefit that accrues to the child of God.

2. Access

By whom also we have access by faith into this grace wherein we stand, and rejoice in hope of the glory of God [Rom. 5:2].

"Access" means that you and I have access to God in prayer. It's wonderful to have someone to go to and talk to about yourself and about your problems and about your friends and your loved ones. Today we as children of God have access to a heavenly Father who will listen to us here and who does answer our prayer. Now, that doesn't mean He answers it the way you want it answered, but He always hears you, and sometimes He shows He is a good Heavenly Father by saying no. He will answer according to His wisdom, not according to our will. You will notice that we have access by faith into this grace wherein we stand.

3. Hope

"And rejoice in *hope* of the glory of God" is the third benefit. The hope that is mentioned here is the hope that the Scriptures hold out. Paul said to a young preacher by the name of Titus, "Looking for that blessed hope, and the glorious appearing of the great God and our Saviour Jesus Christ" (Titus 2:13). (I don't think looking for the Great Tribulation is very much of a hope. I'm certainly not looking for it because that would be a dread rather than a hope.) To look for the Lord to come and take His church out of this world, that's a glorious hope, and it will take place at His appearing.

Now, the child of God has this hope. That means he has a future. He has something to look forward to. You and I are living in a day when man has all the comforts of life in an affluent society, but the interesting thing is, he has no future. James Reston, one of the reporters and editors of *The New York Times*, several years ago made the statement that in Washington there is a feeling that the problems have so mounted and multiplied that man is totally incapable of solving the problems of this world. The Word of God, you know, goes along with that—I suppose that was one time that *The New York Times* and the Bible agreed. What a dark outlook is being given to us today, and the band can play and you can wave the flag all you want, but you'd better face facts: there's a cancer in the body politic. One of the last statements that Bernard Shaw made before his death was that he had pinned his hopes on atheism, but he had found that atheism did not solve the problems of the world. Then he made this remarkable comment, "You are looking at an atheist who has lost his faith." When an atheist loses his faith, he has nothing in the world to hold onto.

The world today is looking for a hope, looking for a future. This explains the restlessness that is throughout the world, and I think it explains a great many of the movements of the present moment. I believe it has driven a great many folk to alcohol and drug addiction and down other avenues that are dead-end streets. Why? Because they've lost hope of the future.

Well, the child of God has a hope, a blessed hope. And he knows that all things are going to work together for good (see Rom. 8:28). He knows that nothing is going to separate him from the love of God (see Rom. 8:39). How wonderful that hope is, the blessed hope of the church.

4. Triumph in troubles

And not only so, but we glory in tribulations also: knowing that tribulation worketh patience;

And patience, experience; and experience, hope [Rom. 5:3–4].

In other words, we *joy* in troubles, knowing that trouble works patience—patience doesn't come automatically—and patience, experience; and experience, hope.

It is quite interesting to see the three words that are associated with trouble. One is joy, another is hope, and the third is patience. God has to work that into us although it is a fruit of the Holy Spirit. In other words, it takes trouble to bring out the best in the believer's life. The only way God can get fruit out of the life of the believer is by pruning the branches. The world does it differently. If you, as an unbeliever, are in a nice, comfortable situation and have no troubles, then you can have fun, you can also be patient, and you may have a little hope as you go along. But that is not the way it is with the child of God. Actually, trouble produces these fruits in our lives.

5. Love of God

And hope maketh not ashamed; because the love of God is shed abroad in our hearts by the Holy Ghost which is given unto us [Rom. 5:5].

"The love of God is shed abroad in our hearts" doesn't mean our love for God; it means God's love for us. And this love is made real by the Holy Spirit who is given to us.

6. The Holy Spirit

This is the first time in the Epistle to the Romans that the ministry of the Holy Spirit is mentioned. This is only a reference to Him in this list of present benefits. We will not come to the ministry of the Holy Spirit until we get to chapter 8 of Romans where He is mentioned more than twenty times. Here we are simply told that the Holy Spirit is given to every believer—not to only some believers, but to all believers. Even to the Corinthians Paul wrote, "What? know ye not that your body is the temple of the Holy Ghost which is in you, which ye have of God, and ye are not your own?" (1 Cor. 6:19). The Corinthian believers were certainly a carnal lot—in fact, Paul called them babes in Christ—yet the Holy Spirit indwelt them. That's wonderful! I'm glad that, when I came to Christ, I got everything God offers in salvation.

And it is the Holy Spirit who actualizes, or makes real, the love of God in the hearts of believers—that is, God's love for us. Today we need to be conscious of the fact that God loves us. How people need to be assured of that in their lives! Only the Spirit of God can make real to us God's love.

Now notice how Paul explains the love of God.

For when we were yet without strength, in due time Christ died for the ungodly [Rom. 5:6].

Christ died for the ungodly—not for the good boys and girls, but for ungodly sinners—those who actually were His enemies, who hated Him, to whom He said when they were crucifying Him, ". . . Father, forgive them; for they know not what they do . . ." (Luke 23:34). And, friend, you and I were numbered with the ungodly.

A few years ago I talked to a young man who had *love* written on his cap, on his funny coat, on his trousers, and even on his shoes! I asked him why. He said, "Why, man, God is love." I agreed with that. Then he said, "God saved me by His love." I replied, "I disagree with that. God does not save you by His love."

Now that seems startling to a great many folk even today. But actually, friend, God does not save you by His love. You see, God is more than love; He is holy and He is righteous. God cannot open the back door of heaven and slip sinners in under the cover of darkness, and He can't let down the bars of heaven and bring sinners in. If He does that, He's no better than a crooked judge who lets a criminal off. God has to do something for the guilt of sinners. There must be judgment, you see. However, God does love us. Regardless of who you are or what you have done, God loves you. It is wrong to say to children, "If you are mean, Willie, or if you do what is wrong, God won't love you." The interesting thing is that God will love little Willie, regardless of what he does. And He loves *you*. You can't keep God from loving you. Now you can get to the place that you do not experience the love of God. For instance, you can't keep the sun from shining, but you can get out of the sunshine. You can put up an umbrella of sin, an umbrella of indifference, an umbrella of stepping out of the will of God, which will keep His love from shining on you. Although all these things will remove you from experiencing God's love, He still loves you.

As I was talking to this young fellow with *love* written on his clothing, I asked him to show me a verse in the Bible that said God saves us by love. Of course he didn't know any. I said, "The Word of God says, 'For by grace are ye saved through faith; and that not of yourselves: it is the gift of God' (Eph. 2:8). God saves us by His grace, not by His love. 'God so loved the world' that He saved the world? Oh, no—He couldn't. A holy God has to be true to His character. But He did this: '. . . God so loved the world, that he gave his only begotten Son, that whosoever believeth in him should not perish, but have everlasting life' (John 3:16)."

God has demonstrated His love for you, my friend, in that He gave His Son to die for you. He paid the penalty for your sin, and our holy God now can save you if you come His way. Of course, you'll have to come *His* way. There is a mistaken idea today that you can come to Him your way. This isn't your universe; it's *His* universe. You and I don't make the rules. *He* makes the rules. And He says that no man comes to Him except through Christ (see John 14:6).

Now notice how he continues.

For scarcely for a righteous man will one die: yet peradventure for a good man some would even dare to die [Rom. 5:7].

Do you know any folk who would die for you? Could you put upon the fingers of one hand those who would be willing to die for you? By the way, could you put upon one finger those who love you enough to die for you? Well, you certainly could put it upon one finger, because God loved you enough to send His Son to die for you. And if it were necessary, He would appear today to die for you again, if it would take that to save you. He loves you that much.

But God commendeth his love toward us, in that, while we were yet sinners, Christ died for us [Rom. 5:8].

He died for you and me. That is where God revealed His love. And God doesn't save us by love. He now saves us by grace because the guilt of sin has been removed by the death of Christ, and He can hold out His arms and save you today.

7. Deliverance from wrath

Much more then, being now justified by his blood, we shall be saved from wrath through him [Rom. 5:9].

The "wrath" mentioned here is what the prophets spoke of: "That day is a day of wrath, a day of trouble and distress, a day of wasteness and desolation, a day of darkness and gloominess, a day of clouds and thick darkness" (Zeph. 1:15). What is the great day of wrath? It is what the Lord Jesus called the Great Tribulation. And Paul tells believers that we shall be "saved from wrath." We have been saved from the penalty of sin; He is constantly saving us today from the power of sin; and He is going to save us in the future from the presence of sin. That means that every believer will leave this earth at the Rapture. We will escape that day of wrath, not because we are worthy, but because we have been saved by the grace of God. We have been saved by grace; we live by the grace of God; and ten billion years from today we will still be in heaven by the grace of God. We are saved from wrath through Him—through Christ.

For if, when we were enemies, we were reconciled to God by the death of his Son, much more, being reconciled, we shall be saved by his life [Rom. 5:10].

You see, He died down here to save us; He lives up yonder to keep us saved.

8. Joy

And not only so, but we also joy in God through our Lord Jesus Christ, by whom we have now received the atonement [Rom. 5:11].

We joy in God! I think this is one of the most wonderful statements we have in Scripture. It means that right now, wherever you are, whatever your problems are, my friend, you can joy, rejoice, in God. Just think of it! You can rejoice that He lives and that He is who He is. You can rejoice because He has provided a salvation for us and is willing to save us sinners and bring us into His presence someday. He has worked out a plan to save us because of His love for us. Isn't that enough to make you rejoice? Oh, the child of God should have joy in his heart. He doesn't need to go around smiling like a Cheshire cat, but he certainly ought to have a joyful heart. I love the song, "Let's Just Praise the Lord." These are the eight wonderful benefits of salvation. Let's just praise the Lord!

SANCTIFICATION OF THE SAINT

We have seen the salvation of the sinner; now we are coming to the sanctification of the saint. In salvation we are declared righteous, but God wants to do more than declare a person righteous. Justification does not *make* a person righteous. It means that before God's holy court, before the bar of heaven, a lost sinner is now declared righteous, but his heart has not been changed. My friend, if you think God intends to leave a sinner in his sin, you are wrong. God wants to make us the kind of folk we should be. So God also has a plan in salvation whereby He not only *declares* a sinner righteous, but He is also going to *make* a sinner righteous. That is, God provides a way that a sinner may grow in grace and become sanctified (set apart) for God.

The remainder of this chapter is labeled potential sanctification. Now let me warn you that you may find this difficult to understand and difficult to accept.

In potential sanctification we have what is known as the federal headship of Adam and Christ.

HEADSHIP OF ADAM

Wherefore, as by one man sin entered into the world, and death by sin; and so death passed upon all men, for that all have sinned [Rom. 5:12].

Let me give you my own translation of this verse, which may bring out the meaning a little better: "On this account (the plan of salvation for all by one Redeemer) just as through one man sin entered (as a principle) into the world, and death through sin, and so death spread throughout upon all men on the ground of the fact that all sinned."

Now we need to understand that the sin we're talking about is the sin of Adam, that first sin of Adam—not his second one or his third one or his fourth one—his first sin of disobedience in the Garden of Eden, which brought death upon all of his offspring.

Now that brings me back to consider something that is very important: You and I are sinners, as we have said, in four different ways. (1) We are sinners because we commit acts of sin. Also, (2) we're sinners by nature (sin doesn't make us sinners, but we sin because we have that nature). (3) We are in the state of sin. God has declared the entire human family under sin. (4) Finally, you and I are also sinners by imputation. That is, Adam acted for the human race because he was the head of it.

It is on the basis of the federal headship of Adam that now God is able through the federal headship of Christ to save those who will trust Christ. This is what theologians have labeled the federal headship. Adam and Christ are representatives of the human race. Adam is the *natural* head of the human race. By the way, I accept that. I saw a bumper sticker that interested me a great deal. It read, "My ancestors were human—sorry about yours." This lays in the dust the idea that you can be a Christian, believing the Word of God, and also accept the theory of evolution. Adam is the head of the human family. That is what Paul is saying here—he is the natural head. And his one act of disobedience plunged his entire offspring into sin. We are all made sinners by Adam's sin.

First, let's see what this does not mean. It does not refer to the fact that we have a sinful nature inherited from Adam. It is true that I got a sinful nature from my father, and he from his father, and on back. Also, I passed on that nature to my child and to my grandchildren. The first grandchild was such a wonderful little fellow, I was beginning to doubt the total depravity of man. But as he began growing up, he began to manifest this depraved nature. Now I have a second grandson, a redheaded boy, and does he have a temper! Now I am convinced again of the total depravity of man. I have seen a manifestation in those two little fellows of a nature they got from their grandmother (I think!). Although you and I do have sinful natures and do pass them on to our offspring, this particular verse does not refer to that fact.

Also, the verse before us that says "all have sinned" does not mean that we are guilty of a sinful act. Of course, we are guilty, but that is not what the verse is talking about.

Now let's see what it *does* mean. It does refer to the fact that we are so vitally connected with the first father of the human race that before we even had a human nature, before we had committed a sin, even before we were born, we were sinners in Adam.

Maybe you don't like that. But God says that that is the way it is. We see it illustrated in Hebrews 7:9, "And as I may so say, Levi also, who receiveth tithes, payed tithes in Abraham." That is, long before Levi was even born, he paid tithes to Melchisedec. How could he do it? "For he was yet in the loins of his father, when Melchisedec met him" (Heb. 7:10). In just such a way, Adam's sin was imputed to us. What Adam did, we did. God could put all of us in a Garden of Eden and give us the same test He gave to Adam. Do you think you would do any better with your sinful nature than Adam did without a sinful nature? I don't think so. We might as well accept the fact that Adam's one act of disobedience made all of us sinners.

Now let me give you a personal illustration. My grandfather lived in Northern Ireland although he was Scottish. Even in his day they were fighting, and he didn't like it. So he emigrated to the United States. Now, what my grandfather did, I did. When he left Northern Ireland, I left Northern Ireland. And I thank God he left. I really appreciate what Grandpa did for me! What he did, I did because I was in him. The reason I was born in America is because of what he had done.

In this same way Adam's sin is imputed to us.

We have already seen that the righteousness of Christ is imputed to us by the death of Christ. Christ is the head of a new race, a new redeemed man, and the church is His body, a new creation. The hymn writer put it accurately: "The Church's one foundation is Jesus Christ her Lord. She is His new creation by water and the word." The church *is* a new creation, a new race. This is what Paul says, "And so it is written, The first man Adam was made a living soul; the last Adam was made a quickening spirit. . . . The first man is of the earth, earthy: the second man is the Lord from heaven" (1 Cor. 15:45,47). Now, there will not be a third Adam, for Christ is the *last* Adam. There will be the third and fourth and myriads of *men* because Christ is the second man, but He's not the second Adam. He is the *last* Adam. He is the *head* of a new race. That is something that is preliminary.

As we go through this section, we will notice an expression that is very meaningful. It is "much more." What Paul is going to say is that we have "much more" in Christ than we *lost* in Adam. That expression occurred in verse 9, "Much more then, being now justified by his blood, we shall be saved from wrath through him." And in verse 10, "Much more, being reconciled, we shall be saved by his life." There is a great deal of "much more" in this section. In 1 Corinthians 15, verses 21–22, I read this, "For since by man came death, by man came also the resurrection of the dead. For as in Adam all die, even so in Christ shall all be made alive." Now, death came by Adam. And if you want proof that the first sin of Adam was a representative act, consider why a little infant will die when that little child has not committed a sinful act. Well, that little infant belongs to the race of Adam. In Adam all die. You see, God did not create man to die. God had something better in store for man and does today.

Now, with that thought in mind, let's move on to verse 13.

(For until the law sin was in the world: but sin is not imputed when there is no law [Rom. 5:13].

From Adam to Moses sin was in the world, but at that time sin was not a transgression; it was merely rebellion against God. I think this is the reason God did not exact the death penalty from Cain when he murdered his brother. I cannot think of a deed more dastardly than what he did, but at that time God had not yet said, "Thou shalt not kill" (Exod. 20:13). Actually, God put a mark on Cain to protect him. A little later on you find that one of the sons of Cain, Lamech, tells why he killed a man. He says, "I have slain a man to my wounding, and a young man to my hurt. If Cain shall be avenged sevenfold, truly Lamech seventy and sevenfold" (Gen. 4:23–24). You see, Lamech had a reason. Also, that generation that was destroyed at the Flood was saturated with sin. They were incurable incorrigibles. "And God saw that the wickedness of man was great in the earth, and that every imagination of the thoughts of his heart was only evil continually" (Gen. 6:5). But not one of them broke the Ten Commandments—because there were no Ten Commandments then. But they were judged because they were sinners. And, friend, that answers the question about the heathen being lost who haven't heard the gospel. The answer is that all men belong to a lost race. It may be difficult for you and me to accept this fact, but you and I have been born into a lost race. We're not a lovely people. We are not the product of evolution—onward and upward forever with everything getting better. You and I belong to a lost race, and we need to be redeemed. Even the very thoughtlife of man is alienated from God.

Somebody may say, "Then I think God is obligated to save all of us." No, He is not. Suppose that you could go down to an old marshy lake covered with scum where there are hundreds of turtles, and you take a turtle out of there. And you teach this turtle to fly. Then this turtle goes back to the lake and says to the other turtles, "Wouldn't you like to learn to fly?" I think they'd laugh at the turtle. They'd say, "No! we like it down here. We don't want to learn to fly." And that is the condition of lost mankind today. People don't want to be saved. People are lost, alienated from God. Now, that's a great truth that does not soak into our minds easily, because we have that lost nature. We just love to think that we're wonderful people. But we are *not*, my friend.

Nevertheless death reigned from Adam to Moses, even over them that had not sinned after the similitude of Adam's transgression, who is the figure of him that was to come [Rom. 5:14].

Paul is personifying death. He speaks of the fact that death reigned like a king from Adam to Moses. Although he had not broken the Ten Commandments—because they hadn't yet been given—man was yet a sinner.

The word *death* is used in a threefold way in Scripture. There is what is known as physical death. That refers only to the body, and it means a separation of the spirit from the body. This death comes to man because of Adam's sin. Also, there is spiritual death, which is separation from and rebellion against God. And we inherit this nature from Adam, by the way. We are alienated from God, and we are dead in trespasses and sins (see Eph. 2:1). That is the picture that Scripture presents. Then there is eternal death. That is the third death that Scripture speaks of, and it is eternal separation from God. And, unless man is redeemed, eternal death inevitably follows (see Rev. 21:8).

Adam is here definitely declared to be a type of Christ—"who is the figure" or "he is the type of him who was to come." That is, Adam is a type of Christ.

HEADSHIP OF CHRIST

But not as the offence, so also is the free gift. For if through the offence of one many be dead, much more the grace of God, and the gift by grace, which is by one man, Jesus Christ, hath abounded unto many [Rom. 5:15].

We have "much more" in Christ. Today we are looking forward to something more wonderful than the Garden of Eden. As the writer of Hebrews tells us, "These all died in faith, not having received the promises, but having seen them afar off, and were persuaded of them, and embraced them, and confessed that they were strangers and pilgrims on the earth" (Heb. 11:13).

And not as it was by one that sinned, so is the gift: for the judgment was by one to condemnation, but the free gift is of many offences unto justification [Rom. 5:16].

Now I recognize that this is a difficult section, and this is one of the most difficult passages. To simplify it, all this section means is this: one transgression plunged the race into sin; and one act of obedience and the death of Christ upon the cross makes it possible for lost man to be saved.

For if by one man's offence death reigned by one; much more they which receive abundance of grace and of the gift of righteousness shall reign in life by one, Jesus Christ) [Rom. 5:17].

Paul has previously stated (v. 14) that death reigns as king. Death came to the throne by one man who committed only one offense—that is, the original sin, the one act, involved the race. Here Paul presents another kingdom which is superior to the kingdom of death. It is the kingdom of life. It is offered to the subjects of the kingdom of death through the superabundance of grace. Man has only to receive it. The King of the kingdom of life is Jesus Christ. The gift comes through Him.

Therefore as by the offence of one judgment came upon all men to condemnation; even so by the righteousness of one the free gift came upon all men unto justification of life [Rom. 5:18].

This is the underlying principle of the imputation of sin and the imputation of righteousness. This is the doctrine of the federal headship of the race in Adam and Christ.

For as by one man's disobedience many were made sinners, so by the obedience of one shall many be made righteous [Rom. 5:19].

Here Paul sums up his argument on federal headship: Adam's one act of disobedience made all sinners—not just possessors of a sin nature, but guilty of the act of sin. Christ's obedience—His death and resurrection—makes it possible for God to declare righteous the sinner who believes in Him.

Moreover the law entered, that the offence might abound. But where sin abounded, grace did much more abound [Rom. 5:20].

When God gave the Law, He gave with it a sacrificial system. Then later on Christ came to fulfill that part of it also. In other words, God has given to the human race, a lost race, an opportunity to be delivered from the guilt of sins—not the nature of sin. You and I will have that old sin nature throughout our lives.

That as sin hath reigned unto death, even so might grace reign through righteousness unto eternal life by Jesus Christ our Lord [Rom. 5:21].

"As sin hath reigned unto death"—you and I are living in a world where sin reigns. Do you want to know who is king of the earth today? Well, Scripture tells us that Satan is the prince. He is the one who goes up and down this earth seeking whom he may devour (see 1 Pet. 5:8). "Sin hath reigned unto death," and the cemeteries are still being filled because of that.

"Even so might grace reign through righteousness unto eternal life by Jesus Christ our Lord." He is calling out a people—out of a lost race—and He is "teaching turtles to fly" if they want to. However, the turtle nature doesn't want to fly. Man is alienated from God; he has a sin nature. Now God offers salvation to a lost race.

The claims of God's righteousness are fully met in the death of Christ. The kingdom is fully and firmly established on the cross of Christ. All other ground is sinking sand. The believing sinner now has eternal life by being united to the last Adam, the raised and glorified Savior. This makes possible the sanctification of the saved sinner, which is the theme of the next chapter.

CHAPTER 6

THEME: *Positional sanctification; practical sanctification*

We discovered in chapter 5 that sin has come through the headship of Adam and that sanctification comes through the headship of Christ. Because of the natural headship of Adam, sin was imputed to the human family. But there is another head of the human family, and that is Christ. He brings life and righteousness. He removes the guilt of sin from us. And on that basis, He can move into the lives of those who trust in Him and begin to make them righteous. That is, He can begin to make them *good*.

Now here in chapter 6 we begin with what I have labeled "positional sanctification."

Let me say a word about this matter of sanctification. There is a difference between justification and sanctification. These are two words from the Bible, my friend, that you ought to cozy up to and get acquainted with. There is a difference between merely being saved from sin and being made the type of folk we should be because we are separated unto God.

Identification with Christ for justification is also the grounds of our sanctification. We are in Christ. These are two different subjects, but they are not mutually exclusive. Justification is the foundation on which all the superstructure of sanctification rests.

Now let me put it like this: justification is an *act*; sanctification is a *work*. Justification took place the moment you trusted Christ—you were declared righteous; the guilt was removed. Then God began a work in you that will continue throughout your life. I believe in instantaneous salvation, but sanctification is a lifelong process. In other words, justification is the means; sanctification is the end. Justification is *for* us; sanctification is *in* us. Justification *declares* the sinner righteous; sanctification *makes* the sinner righteous. Justification removes the *guilt* and *penalty* of sin; sanctification removes the *growth* and the *power* of sin.

God is both an exterior and interior decorator. He is an exterior decorator in that He enables us to stand before Him because He has paid the penalty and removed the guilt of sin from us. But He is also an interior decorator. He moves into our hearts and lives by the power of the Holy Spirit to make us the kind of Christians we should be. God does not leave us in sin when He saves us.

This does not imply that sanctification is a duty that is derived from justification. It is a fact that proceeds from it, or rather, both justification and sanctification flow from being in Christ, crucified and risen. The sinner appropriates Christ by faith for both his salvation and his sanctification. We're told in 1 Corinthians 1:30, "But of him are ye in Christ Jesus, who of God is made unto us wisdom, and righteousness, and sanctification, and redemption."

Up to chapter 6, Paul does not discuss the *holy life* of the saint. From chapter 6 on, Paul does not discuss the salvation of the sinner. He wasn't talking about the saint and the life he is to live when he was discussing salvation. Now he *is* discussing that. Therefore, the subject of this chapter is the ability of God to make sinners, whom He has declared righteous, actually righteous. He shows that the justified sinner cannot continue in sin because he died and rose again in Christ. To continue in sin leads to slavery to sin and is the additional reason for not continuing in sin. The believer has a new nature now, and he is to obey God. This section delivers us from the prevalent idea today that a believer can do as he pleases. Union with Christ in His death and resurrection means that He is now our Lord and our Master. He gives us freedom, but that freedom is not license, as we are going to see.

POSITIONAL SANCTIFICATION

What shall we say then? Shall we continue in sin, that grace may abound? [Rom. 6:1].

Paul is being argumentative. He wasn't, you remember, when he was discussing sin. Rather, he was stating facts. He wasn't trying to prove anything. He just looked at life in the raw, right down where the rubber meets the road, and said that we are all sinners. However, now he uses this idiomatic question which opens this chapter, and he is argumentative. In the Greek the question is asked in such a way that there is only one answer. He precedes the question with "What shall we say then?" After you see God's wonderful salvation, what can you say to it? Our only fitting response is hallelujah! What else can you say to God's wonderful salvation? Now Paul's argumentative question is this: "Shall we continue in sin, that grace may abound?"

And this, my friend, is God's answer to the

question of whether, after we are saved, we can continue to live in sin. The answer is, "God forbid" or "perish the thought!" or "may it never be!"

God forbid. How shall we, that are dead to sin, live any longer therein? [Rom. 6:2].

The very fact that Paul is asking this question makes it obvious that he understood justification to mean a *declaration* of righteousness; that it did not mean to *make* a person good, but to *declare* a person good. Justification means that the guilt or the penalty of sin is removed, not the power of sin in this life.

Now he is going to talk about removing the *power* of sin. If God has declared you to be righteous and has removed the guilt of your sin, then, my friend, you cannot continue in sin. The answer is, "God forbid!"

"How shall we, that are dead to sin"—this is something that is misunderstood. We are never *dead* to sin as long as we are in this life. The literal translation is, "How shall we who have *died* to sin." Note this distinction. That means we died in the person of our substitute, Jesus Christ. We died to sin in Christ. But we are never *dead* to sin. Any honest person knows he never reaches the place where he is dead to sin. He does reach the place where he wants to live for God, but he recognizes he still has that old sin nature.

It is verses like that that have led a group of sincere folk, whom I call super-duper saints—I hope I'm not being unfair to them—to feel they have reached an exalted plane where they do not commit sin. One such group is a branch of those who teach the "victorious life." They feel they have reached the pinnacle of perfection. There are different brands of these, I know, but one group was especially obnoxious several years ago in Southern California. One young man approached me following a morning worship service, and he asked, "Are you living the victorious life?" I think I shocked him when I said, "No, I'm not!" Then I asked him, "Are you?" Well, he beat around the bush and didn't want to give me a direct answer. He said he tried to. And I said, "Wait a minute, that's not the question. You asked me if I am living it, and I said no. Now you answer me yes or no." And to this good day he hasn't answered me. Like most of them, he was a very anemic-looking young fellow; I suspected he was a fugitive from a blood bank. He continued arguing his case. "Well, doesn't the Scripture say, 'I am crucified with Christ?' and doesn't it say that we are dead to sin?" I said, "No, that is not what the Scriptures say. We *died* to sin in Christ—that's our position—but we are never dead to sin in this life. You have a sinful nature; I have a sinful nature; and we'll have it as long as we are in this life." He persisted, "Then what does it mean when it says we are crucified with Christ?" So I told him, "When Christ died over nineteen hundred years ago, that is when we died. We died in Him, and we were raised in Him, and we are joined now to a living Christ. This is the great truth that is there. I don't know about you, but I'm not able to crucify myself. The very interesting thing is that you can kill yourself in a variety of ways—by poison, with a gun, by jumping off a building—but you cannot crucify yourself. Maybe you can drive the nails into one hand on a cross, but how are you going to fasten the other hand to the cross? You cannot do it. How are you going to crucify yourself? You cannot do it. My young friend, you were crucified over nineteen hundred years ago when Christ died."

Know ye not, that so many of us as were baptized into Jesus Christ were baptized into this death? [Rom. 6:3].

This again is a verse that has been misunderstood. If you find water in this verse, you have missed the meaning.

Many years ago the late Dr. William L. Pettingill was conducting a conference in the church I was pastoring, and as I was driving him back to the hotel after a service, I said, "Dr. Pettingill, did I understand you to say there is no water in the sixth chapter of Romans?" (I should add that he was the strongest "immersionist" I have ever met in my life.) He laughed and said, "No, that's not exactly what I said. I said that if all you see in Romans 6 is water, you have missed the point." I said, "Well, if you go that far, that is wonderful for me because it confirms the great truth that is here."

What did Paul mean by the word *baptize* in this third verse? I do not think he refers to water baptism primarily. Don't misunderstand me; I believe in water baptism, and I believe that immersion best sets forth what is taught here. But actually he is talking about identification with Christ. You see, the translators did not translate the Greek word *baptizō*, they merely transliterated it. That is, they just spelled the Greek word out in English, because *baptizō* has so many meanings. In my Greek lexicon there are about twenty meanings for this word. Actually *baptizō* could refer to dyeing your hair. In fact, there was a group in Asia Minor who dyed their hair purple; and they belonged to a *baptizō* group. But here in Romans 6:3 Paul is speaking about identification with Jesus Christ. We were baptized or identified into His death. In 1 Corinthians 12:13 Paul says, "For by one Spirit are we all baptized into one body. . . ." We are identified in the death of Christ, as Paul will explain in the next verse.

Now Paul is going to say that there are three things essential to our sanctification. Two of them are positional; one of them is very practical. For the two that are positional, we are to *know* something. Every gadget that you buy has instructions with it. When I buy a toy for one of my grandsons, I take it out of the box, and I try to follow instructions for assembling it—and sometimes it is very difficult for me to do. Well, living the Christian life is such an important thing that it comes with instructions. There are certain things we are to know. We are to know that when Christ died over nineteen hundred years ago, we were identified with Him. Let me make it personal. Nineteen hundred years ago, they led me outside of an oriental city by the name of Jerusalem. By the way, I stood at that spot not too long ago. I looked up to Gordon's Calvary, the Place of the Skull, Golgotha. I tried to visualize the One who died there. When He died there over nineteen hundred years ago, He took Vernon McGee there. I was the one who was guilty. He was not guilty. Don't argue with me about whether the Jews crucified Christ—He died on the Roman cross—but let's not argue that. My sin put Him up there, and your sin put Him up there, my friend. We were identified with Jesus Christ. That is something that we should know, and it is very important for us to know. We're identified with Him.

Now Paul will amplify this:

Therefore we are buried with him by baptism into death: that like as Christ was raised up from the dead by the glory of the Father, even so we also should walk in newness of life [Rom. 6:4].

"We are buried with him by baptism into death"—just as we are identified with Christ in His death, likewise are we identified with Christ in His resurrection. We are joined today to a living Christ. In other words, our sins have already been judged; we are already raised; and we are yonder seated with Christ in the heavenlies. My friend, there are only two places for your sins: either they were on Christ when He died for you over nineteen hundred years ago—because you have trusted Him as your Savior—or they are on you today, and judgment is ahead for you. There is no third place for them.

"We are buried with him by baptism [identification] into [His] death." Frankly, although I was reared a Presbyterian, I think that immersion is a more accurate type of this identification. I think the Spirit's baptism is the real baptism. Water is the ritual baptism, but I do think that immersion sets forth the great spiritual truth that is here. This is the reason a child of God should be baptized in water in our day. It is a testimony that he is joined to the living Christ. That is all important.

What did Peter mean when he said in 1 Peter 3:21, ". . . baptism doth also now save us . . ."? How does it save us? Well, in the preceding verse he talks about eight souls who were saved in the ark. They went through the waters of judgment inside the ark. The folk in the water were those who were outside the ark, and they were drowned. The eight people in the ark didn't get wet at all—yet Peter says they were saved by baptism. Obviously the word *baptism* has nothing to do with water in this instance; rather it means identification. They were identified with the ark. They had believed God, and they had gotten into the ark. God saw that little boat floating on the surface of the water. Now today God sees Christ; He doesn't see Vernon McGee because I am in Christ. He is my ark today. Christ went down into the waters of death, and we are in Christ. And we are raised with Him. We are joined to Him. This is important. Don't miss it. If you do, you will miss one of the greatest truths of the Christian life.

For if we have been planted together in the likeness of his death, we shall be also in the likeness of his resurrection [Rom. 6:5].

In other words, if we are united by being grafted together in the likeness of His death, we shall be also united by growth—grafted, vitally connected—in the likeness of His resurrection. We actually share the life of Christ somewhat as a limb grafted into a tree shares the life of the tree. The life of Christ is our life now.

Knowing this, that our old man is crucified with him, that the body of sin might be destroyed, that henceforth we should not serve sin [Rom. 6:6].

"Knowing this"—these are things we know.

When Paul says your "old man" is crucified with Him, he doesn't mean your father; he means your old nature is crucified with Him. "That the body of sin might be destroyed"—the word *destroyed* is *katargeo*, meaning "to make of none effect, to be paralyzed or canceled or nullified"—"that henceforth we should not serve sin." Paul is not saying that the old nature is eradicated. He is saying that since the old man was crucified, the body of sin has been put out of business, so that from now on we should not be in bondage to sin.

For he that is dead is freed from sin [Rom. 6:7].

For he who died is declared righteous from sin. He is acquitted. That is his position.

Now if we be dead with Christ, we believe that we shall also live with him [Rom. 6:8].

If we died with Christ, we believe that we shall also be living with Him both here and hereafter. We share His resurrection life today, and we will be raised from the dead someday.

Knowing that Christ being raised from the dead dieth no more; death hath no more dominion over him [Rom. 6:9].

"Knowing"—this is something else we are to know.

"He ever liveth" is the victor's chorus. The glorified Christ says, "I am he that liveth, and was dead; and, behold, I am alive for evermore, Amen; and have the keys of hell and of death" (Rev. 1:18). The Resurrection opens up eternity to Christ, and it will open up eternity to those who will trust Him.

For in that he died, he died unto sin once: but in that he liveth, he liveth unto God [Rom. 6:10].

He died one time, but He is alive today. And He ever lives to make intercession for those who are His. Because of this, He can save you right through to the uttermost.

Now we come to the second thing that we as believers are to reckon on.

Likewise reckon ye also yourselves to be dead indeed unto sin, but alive unto God through Jesus Christ our Lord. [Rom. 6:11].

"Reckon" doesn't mean I "reckon" or "suppose," as some of us Texans use it. Rather, we are to *count* on the fact that we are dead unto sin and alive unto God. We are to reckon (count on it) that our old nature lay in Joseph's tomb over nineteen hundred years ago, but when Christ came back from the dead, we came back from the dead in Him. This is something to count on.

Let not sin therefore reign in your mortal body, that ye should obey it in the lusts thereof [Rom. 6:12].

That is, don't let sin keep on reigning in your body, that you should obey the desires of the body.

PRACTICAL SANCTIFICATION

We have seen that sanctification is positional. That means we are to know something. We are to know God's method of making a sinner the kind of person He wants him to be. While justification merely declared him righteous, removed the *guilt* of sin, it did not change him in his life. It gave him a new nature. Now he is to know that he was buried with Christ and raised with Him. God wants him to live in the power of the Holy Spirit. The believer is joined to the living Christ. He is to reckon on that fact; he is to count on it. He is to consider it as true. You see, God saved us by faith, and we are to live by faith. Many of us, and that includes this poor preacher, have trusted Him for salvation, but are we trusting Him in our daily living? We are to live by faith.

Now we come to that which is very practical indeed. You are to yield yourself or present yourself to God.

Neither yield ye your members as instruments of unrighteousness unto sin: but yield yourselves unto God, as those that are alive from the dead, and your members as instruments of righteousness unto God [Rom. 6:13].

Yield is the same word as *present* in Romans 12:1: "I beseech you therefore, brethren, by the mercies of God, that ye present your bodies a living sacrifice, holy, acceptable unto God. . . ." This is a presentation of yourself for service. *Yield* is the same word, and it means "to present yourself." The idea of the surrendered life or the yielded life sounds colorless to so many people. We talk about surrendering and at the same time living the victorious life, and they seem to be a contradition of terms. I like the word *present* much better—"Neither present ye your members as instruments of unrighteousness unto sin." The reason most of us get into trouble is because we yield ourselves to the old nature. By an act of the will we can yield ourselves to do God's will through the new nature.

A little girl fell out of bed one night and began to cry. Her mother rushed into her bedroom, picked her up, put her back in bed, and asked her, "Honey, why did you fall out of bed?" And she said, "I think I stayed too close to the place where I got in." And that's the reason a great many of us fall, my friend. It is because we are actually yielding ourselves to the old nature. We're following the dictates of the old nature; that is what gets us into trouble.

Although we will not get rid of that old nature in this life, we are told now, "Yield yourselves unto God." Just as you yield yourself to do sin, you are to yield yourself unto God "as those that are alive from the dead." You're now alive in Christ. You have a new nature. You've been born again.

"And your members as instruments of righteousness unto God" deals with that which is specific and particular. What is your real problem, friend? I know what mine is. What about yours? Whatever that specific thing is, yield it to God. A bad temper? Well, take that to Him and talk to Him about it. What about a gossipy tongue? A dear lady who attended a "tongues meeting" was asked if she wanted to speak in tongues. She exclaimed, "Oh, my no. I'd like to lose about forty feet off the one I have now!" If your tongue is your problem, yield it to God. And by the way, in this day in which we are living, what about immorality? Sex is the big subject of the hour. My, everybody's getting in on the act today. Is that your sin? Well, you're to yield yourself to God—your members "as instruments of righteousness unto God." And don't tell me you can't do it. You can do it through the power of the Holy Spirit.

For sin shall not have dominion over you: for ye are not under the law, but under grace [Rom. 6:14].

The Law was given to control the old nature. As a believer, you are not to live by the old nature. You have a new nature, and you are to yield yourself or present yourself to God. What a glorious, wonderful privilege it is to present ourselves to Him!

What then? shall we sin, because we are not under the law, but under grace? God forbid [Rom. 6:15].

Let me give my translation of this verse, which may be helpful: What then? Shall we sin, because we are not under law, but under grace? (Should we commit an act of sin? For you are no more under law, but under grace.) Away with the thought (perish the thought). The form of the question is put differently here than it was back in verse 1. Paul has demonstrated in the past fourteen verses that God's method of sanctification is on the same basis as justification; it is by faith, faith that God can do it. You and I *cannot* do it. When we learn that we cannot live the Christian life, we have learned a great lesson. Then we are prepared to let Him live it through us.

Paul's question here is whether there should be an assist given to grace to accomplish its high and holy end. In other words, the natural man thinks there ought to be some laws, rules, or regulations given. In the course of the church's history we have had all kinds of groups that have come up with rules for living the Christian life. There were the Puritans, a wonderful group of folk, and we owe a great deal to them, but they had a strict observance of the Sabbath day (they called Sunday the Sabbath, which, of course, it is not). A strict observance of Sunday was an obsession with them. We have a carry-over of that today. There are a great number of groups who put down certain rules for a believer. Some of our fundamental people have made, not ten commandments, but about twenty new commandments. If the believer does certain things and refrains from doing certain other things, he is living the Christian life. This is the reason, friend, that I oppose the idea that you can become a wonderful Christian by taking some of these short courses being offered today. That's not the way you are to do it. We have a girl in our office who took a course, and, oh, she was enthusiastic. But you ought to see her today. She is really in a depression. Why? Because she tried to do it by rules and did not let Christ do it.

The Christian life is not following certain rules; you can follow rules and regulations and still not be living the Christian life. Somebody asks, "Then what is the Christian life?" The Christian life is to be *obedient* unto *Christ.* It means communication with Christ. My friend, do you love Him? That's the important thing. He says, "If ye *love* me, keep my commandments" (John 14:15, italics mine). Identification with Christ is positional sanctification, as we have seen. That is basic. But obedience to Christ is the *experience* of sanctification, and that is practical sanctification. It is just as simple as that, my friend. It is not *how* you walk, but *where* you walk—are you walking in the light, walking in fellowship with Christ? Sin will break the fellowship, of course, and then we are to confess our sin. The Lord Jesus said to Peter yonder in the Upper Room, "If I wash you not, you have no part with me" (see John 13:8). We don't have fellowship with Him unless we confess our sins to Him as we go along. Our part is confession; His part is cleansing (see 1 John 1:9). The important thing for you and me is to have fellowship with the Lord Jesus Christ and to obey Him. Then we will be living the Christian life.

Vincent once said to Godet, "There is a subtle poison which insinuates itself into the heart even of the best Christian; it is the temptation to say: Let us sin, not that grace may abound, but because it abounds." You see, there are many Christians today who say, "I am saved, and I can do as I please." My friend, if you have been saved by grace, you cannot do as you please, as we shall see in the eighth chapter of Romans.

In his letter to the Galatian believers, Paul makes it clear that there are three ways in which you can live: (1) You can live by law; (2) you can live by license; (3) you can live by liberty. To live by law, everyone puts down some principle. I read of a movie star who said that his whole life was given to sex—that's his law; he lives by that. Regardless of who you are, if you are living by law, you are living by the old nature. Then, the other extreme which Paul is guarding against here, is license. If you are a child of God, you can't do as you please; you have to do as Christ pleases. You must be obedient to the Lord Jesus Christ, present yourself to Him. This is practical, a great deal more practical than you may realize.

Know ye not, that to whom ye yield yourselves servants to obey, his servants ye are to whom ye obey: whether of sin unto death, or of obedience unto righteousness? [Rom 6:16].

"Know ye not"—when Paul says this, we can be sure that we believers *don't* know, and we need to know.

"To whom ye yield yourselves servants to obey, his servants ye are." Every person who is living is a bond servant to someone or something. I heard a contemporary commentator observe that every person obeys some person or some thing. That is true. You could even be obeying Satan himself. Because of our very natures, we are servants or slaves to something or to somebody.

Now Paul is saying here that the one who is our master is the one whom we obey. If you obey sin, then that is your master. Don't say Christ is your master if you are living in sin; He is *not* your master. He brings you into the place of liberty. "If the Son therefore shall make you free, ye shall be free indeed" (John 8:36)—free to do what? You will be free to live for Him, free to obey Him. And the Lord Jesus said again, ". . . Verily, verily, I say unto you. Whosoever committeth sin is the servant of sin" (John 8:34). Now let me use a very homely illustration. There is a very swanky club across the street from the church I served in downtown Los Angeles. It is made up of rich men, and I'm told that it costs several thousand dollars to join this club. If you belong to it, you probably own a Cadillac and have a chauffeur. Well, one day as I looked out the window, I saw a group of chauffeurs standing around talking, and there were several Cadillacs parked there. It was after lunch. Finally, I saw a very distinguished-looking gentleman come out of the club; he made a motion and said something. I couldn't hear what he said, but I saw one of the chauffeurs leave the group of about fifteen men. He went over, opened the door of the car, the distinguished-looking man got in, then he went around, got in the driver's seat and drove off. Now, I came to a very profound conclusion: that chauffeur was the servant or the employee of the man who called him. I don't think those other fourteen chauffeurs were employed by the man in the car because they didn't obey him. Only the man who obeyed him was working for him. He obeyed him because that man was his master. This is what Paul is saying. Regardless of who you are, whomever you obey, whatever you obey, that is your master. You are obeying something or someone.

Now that brings us to a personal question. Is Christ really our master today? Just because you don't murder, you don't lie, you don't do other things the Mosaic Law prohibits, doesn't mean you are living the Christian life. It may mean you are living a good life, but that is all. The Christian life is one where we obey Christ.

But God be thanked, that ye were the servants of sin, but ye have obeyed from the heart that form of doctrine which was delivered you [Rom 6:17].

In other words, when you were in the world, when you were lost, you obeyed sin. It was natural for you to do that. A man may live such an exemplary life that the chamber of commerce presents him with a medal and a loving cup and makes him the citizen of the year. I overheard such a man talking one time after he had been presented with the cup as the outstanding citizen of a certain community. The language of this man was the foulest language I had ever heard. He may be the outstanding citizen of that community, but it's quite obvious whom he's obeying. He is obeying the Devil! The fact that you obey Christ is the thing that is important.

Now, another thing that we need to understand is that, when you have been saved, you have a new nature that *can* obey Christ. Paul went through the experience, as we shall see in the next chapter, of being a new Christian and discovering that there was no good in his old nature. Paul says, "I know that in me (that is, in my flesh,) dwelleth no good thing" (Rom. 7:18). Although many of us have not discovered this, there is no *good* in us; the old nature has no good in it. You can do a lot to improve it, but you sure can't make it good.

The second startling fact is this: there is no power in the new nature. That's where most of us make our mistake. We think that because we are now Christians, we can walk on top of the world. We can't. We are just as weak as we've ever been before. This is the reason that we have to walk by faith and in the power of the Holy Spirit. Only the Spirit of God can produce the Christian life, as we shall see.

Being then made free from sin, ye became the servants of righteousness [Rom. 6:18].

We have been liberated. In other words, He has made it possible for us to live the Christian life. It does not mean that sin has been eradicated or removed. It does mean that now we can live for God.

I speak after the manner of men because of the infirmity of your flesh: for as ye have yielded your members servants to uncleanness and to iniquity unto iniquity; even so now yield your members servants to righteousness unto holiness [Rom. 6:19].

Let me give you my translation of this verse: I speak in human terms on account of the difficulties of apprehension or the weakness of your human nature; for as you presented or yielded your members slaves for the practice of impurity and to lawlessness; even so now present your members slaves to righteousness.

Paul explains here, I think, why he uses the term *servants*. He half-way apologizes in the last verse for using it. Slavery was common in the Roman Empire. Out of the 120 million people in the Roman Empire, one half were slaves. Many Christians were slaves. And the little Epistle to Philemon reveals that freedom was a prized possession and difficult to obtain. Now Paul uses this familiar metaphor which he describes as "human terms"—"I'm speaking to you in human terms." He doesn't mean he is not speaking by inspiration, but he is speaking in a manner which we will understand. And we will understand by these human terms that we are actually slaves.

Now, the religious rulers were insulted when the Lord suggested that they were slaves of sin. Remember the Lord Jesus said to those Jews that believed on Him, ". . . If ye continue in my word, then are ye my disciples indeed; And ye shall know the truth, and the truth shall make you free. They answered him, We be Abraham's seed, and were never in bondage to any man: how sayest thou, Ye shall be made free? Jesus answered them, Verily, verily, I say unto you, Whosoever committeth sin is the servant of sin" (John 8:31–34). Oh, how many men and women today are slaves of sin! Observe the tragedy of our young people who have rebelled against the rules and regulations of the establishment and who have been destroyed by the thousands by drugs and alcohol! You may be delivered from one group with its rules and regulations, but if you don't turn to Christ, you may be getting out of the frying pan and into the fire. What is happening in our culture today is one of the saddest things of our contemporary age. The Lord Jesus says that when you commit sin, you are the servant of sin.

For when ye were the servants of sin, ye were free from righteousness [Rom. 6:20].

That is, you didn't think of serving Christ then; you weren't interested in that. You were free from Him.

What fruit had ye then in those things whereof ye are now ashamed? for the end of those things is death [Rom. 6:21].

You were not only free from Christ, you were fruitless. You did as you pleased. The only fruit was shame. Actually, it was not real freedom, it was license. Do you want to go back to the old life?

I receive scores of letters from young people who were formerly known as "hippies" and have turned to Christ. They are ashamed of that old life. When you drop into sin, does it break your heart? The difference between a child of God and a child of the Devil is that a child of the Devil just loves doing what the Devil wants done. But to the child of God it is a heartbreak.

But now being made free from sin, and become servants to God, ye have your fruit unto holiness, and the end everlasting life [Rom. 6:22].

He sets before believers now the golden and glad prospect that is theirs as slaves of God. They are freed from sin which leads to death, and they can have fruit which will abide into eternity. Life eternal is in contrast to death. An illustration of this is seen in the lives of pioneer missionaries. I think of the group of young people, some of them still in their teens, who went out to the Hawaiian Islands in 1819. They gave their lives gladly, joyfully, to the service of Christ. (They have been maligned in recent years. Oh, how the godless tourist loves to hear them ridiculed!) But they laid the foundation for the greatest revival that has taken place since Pentecost—more people were won to Christ per capita. I never grow weary of hearing their story. They had fruit, my friend. How wonderful it was!

Now Paul concludes this section:

For the wages of sin is death; but the gift of God is eternal life through Jesus Christ our Lord [Rom. 6:23].

The Devil is the paymaster, and he will see to it that you get paid. If you work for him, the wages of sin is death. But the gift of God is eternal life. And you will receive that gift by faith.

You are saved by faith. You are to live by faith. You are to walk moment by moment by faith. You cannot live for God by yourself any more than you can save yourself. It requires constant dependence upon Him, looking to the Lord Jesus Christ by the power of the Spirit.

CHAPTER 7

***THEME:** Shackles of a saved soul; struggle of a saved soul*

The theme of sanctification began in the latter part of chapter 5 where it was "potential sanctification." Then in chapter 6 we saw "positional sanctification"; that is, identification with Christ in His death and resurrection. We are to reckon on that, present ourselves to Him, and trust him to live the Christian life through us.

Now in the chapter before us there are two subjects: the shackles of a saved soul and the struggle of a saved soul. The Law cannot produce sanctification in the life of the believer; it merely shackles it. Neither can the believer produce sanctification in his life by depending on the desire of the new nature. Just to say you want to live for Christ won't get you anywhere. You need to present yourself to Him, recognizing that you are joined to the living Christ.

The importance of this chapter cannot be overemphasized. Let me give you a quotation from Dr. Griffith Thomas: "Dr. Alexander Whyte once said that whenever a new book on Romans comes out and is sent to him by its publisher for consideration, he at once turns to the comments on chapter VII, and according to the view taken of that important section he decides on the value of the entire work." Then Dr. Frederic Godet makes this bold statement: "But it is a hundred to one when a reader does not find the Apostle Paul logical, that he is not understanding his thought." Paul is certainly logical all through this chapter.

When I was a young man, a very wonderful itinerant Bible teacher, who was a great blessing to multitudes of folk, was a great help to me. He was never a pastor, and he taught that we are to detour around the seventh chapter of Romans; we are not to live there. We are to get into the eighth chapter of Romans. For several years I taught that philosophy also. But I have now been a pastor for a long time, and I have come to the conclusion that we are not to miss the seventh chapter of Romans. I am sure that many a pastor wishes his church members would get into the seventh of Romans, because the man who gets into the seventh of Romans will get into the eighth of Romans. I am of the opinion that the way into the eighth chapter is through the seventh chapter—at least that is the route most of us take. Well, you are not to detour around it, because if you do, you are not on the direct route. It reminds me of a jingle:

To dwell above
With the saints in love—
Oh, that will be glory!
But to stay below
With the saints I know—
That's another story!

In this "struggle of a saved soul" a believer reaches out and grabs a straw. Sometimes that straw is the Mosaic Law. And he finds that he has gotten hold, not of a straw, nor even of a life preserver, but actually of a sack of cement, and it is pulling him under. He can't live that way. As a result, multitudes of the saints accept defeat as normal Christian living. There are many saints who are satisfied to continue on the low level of a sad, shoddy, sloppy life. God doesn't want us to come that route.

The "powerless sanctification" of this chapter shows us the way we are *not* to live. Many years ago a cartoon appeared in a daily paper—when it was popular to make things and repair things yourself—showing a mild-mannered man in a "Do-It-Yourself Shop." His hands were bandaged, and one arm was in a sling. He was asking the clerk behind the counter, "Do you have any undo-it-yourself kits?" Today we as believers need to know that *we* cannot live the Christian life; we need to learn that we cannot do it ourselves. In fact, we need an undo-it-yourself kit; that is, we need to turn our lives over to the Spirit of God, yield to Him, and let Him do for us what we cannot do ourselves.

The Mosaic Law is where many Christians go to try to find Christian living. Now Paul is going to show that the Mosaic Law has no claim on the believer. Actually, the Law condemned man to die; it was a ministration of condemnation (see 2 Cor. 3:9). You don't contact the judge who sentenced you to die and ask him how you are going to live!

SHACKLES OF A SAVED SOUL

Know ye not, brethren, (for I speak to them that know the law,) how that the law hath dominion over a man as long as he liveth? [Rom. 7:1].

"Know ye not" is an expression that occurs again and again in the writings of Paul. Putting it into the positive, it is, "Are you so ignorant?" When Paul says, "Know ye not," you may be sure that the brethren did not know.

"I speak to them that know the law." The Mosaic Law had had over a millennium's trial with God's chosen people in a land that was favorable and adaptable to the keeping of the Law—the Law was not only given to a people but to a land. Yet Israel did not keep the Law. Remember that Stephen in his defense said that they had ". . . received the law by the disposition of angels, and have not kept it" (Acts 7:53). Peter calls it a yoke "which neither our fathers nor we were able to bear" (Acts 15:10).

Now Paul will give an illustration that I think is a great one. Unfortunately folk try to draw from it rules for marriage and divorce. But Paul is not talking about marriage and divorce here. Rather, he is illustrating by a well-established and stated law that a wife is bound to a living husband and that death frees her from the status of wife.

For the woman which hath an husband is bound by the law to her husband so long as he liveth; but if the husband be dead, she is loosed from the law of her husband [Rom. 7:2].

A wife is bound to her husband as long as he lives, but when the husband dies, she is completely discharged from the law of her husband. In other words, if he is dead, she is no longer married to him.

So then if, while her husband liveth, she be married to another man, she shall be called an adulteress: but if her husband be dead, she is free from that law; so that she is no adulteress, though she be married to another man [Rom. 7:3].

Some folk insist that divorce and remarriage is not permitted under any circumstances according to this verse. We need to thoroughly understand the background. What would happen under the Mosaic Law if a man or woman were unfaithful in marriage? Suppose a woman is married to a man who is a philanderer, and he is unfaithful to her. What happens? He is stoned to death. When the old boy is lying under a pile of stones, she is free to marry another, of course. In our day we cannot apply the Mosaic Law—we can't stone to death the unfaithful. And Paul is not giving us instructions on divorce and remarriage here; he will do that elsewhere. The point Paul is making here is that when a woman's husband dies, she is no longer a wife, she is a single woman again. This is, I think, a universal principle among civilized people. There are heathen people who put the wife to death when the husband dies, but civilized folk have never followed that practice.

Paul goes on to amplify the law of husband and wife. He brings into sharp focus her status in the case that her husband is alive and again in the case that the husband is dead.

Wherefore, my brethren, ye also are become dead to the law by the body of Christ; that ye should be married to another, even to him who is raised from the dead, that we should bring forth fruit unto God [Rom. 7:4].

In other words: Accordingly, my brethren, you (old Adamic nature) also were done to death as to the Law; the Law was killed to you by means of the body of Christ; that you should be married to another, even to Him who rose from the dead, that we might bear fruit unto God.

The wife represents the believer in Christ. The second husband represents Christ. We are joined to Him. But who is the first husband?

Let's see what some have said. Dr. William Sanday interprets him as the old state before conversion: "The (first) Husband—the old state before conversion to Christianity." Dr. Stifler concludes that the first husband is Christ crucified. Dr. William R. Newell held that the first husband set forth Adam and our position in him.

Personally, I consider the latter the best interpretation, because all the way through this section, beginning at chapter 5 where there were two headships—Adam and Christ—we have seen the first Adam and the last Adam, the first man and the second man. We are joined to Adam through the old Adamic nature. The Law was given to control the old Adamic nature, but it failed through the infirmity of the flesh. The Law actually became a millstone around the neck of the Israelite. It never lifted him up, but it kept him in slavery for fifteen hundred years. Its demands had to be met, but man could not meet them. It was indeed a ministration of condemnation. If the Gentile had to adopt the Law when he became a believer, there was no hope for him either. Paul says that Christ died in His body, we are identified with Christ in His death, and now we are dead to the Law and the Law is dead to us. That first husband is Adam, and we are no longer joined to him. Now we are joined to the living Christ. We died with Him and we have been raised with Him. He is the second husband, the living Christ, who enables us to bear fruit. We know Christ no longer after the flesh; it is the *resurrected* Christ we are joined to. The Law is not given to the new man in Christ—old things have passed away and all things have become new (see 2 Cor. 5:17). The believer is not under law but under grace—this is the *ipso facto* statement of Scripture. Believer, *believe* it! It is so, for God says it!

Now let me illustrate this with a very ridiculous illustration that I heard when I was a student in seminary down in Georgia. Back in the antebellum days, before the Civil War, there was a plantation owner, a very fine, handsome man married to a beautiful woman, and they lived happily in a lovely home. Then he became sick and died suddenly. It was a great heartbreak to her, for she loved him dearly, and she did a strange and morbid thing. She had his body embalmed, placed in a sitting position in a chair in an air-tight glass case, and situated in the great hallway of her lovely southern home. The minute you opened the door, you were looking at him. Well, her friends realized that this wouldn't do, so they urged her to go away and travel for awhile. So she went North, then traveled abroad for almost two years. During that time she met another man, fell in love with him and married him. On their honeymoon they came to her plantation home. The new bridegroom did as a new bridegroom is supposed to do, he picked her up and carried her over the threshold. When he put her down, he was staring into the face of a man in a glass case. He said to his bride, "Who is *that*?" Well, she had forgotten about him. She told him that he was her first husband. They both decided it was time to bury him, which was the proper thing to do. She was married to a new man; the old man was dead. Now I confess that that is a ridiculous story; I sometimes wonder if it really ever happened. Whether or not the story is true, it *is* true that there are many believers today who have dug up the Law—in fact, they have never buried the Law. They have the Law sitting in a glass case, and they are trying to live by the Law in the strength of the old Adamic nature! How ridiculous! The believer is joined to the living Christ today, and the Christian's life is to please Him. Oh, how important that is. I can't overemphasize it.

For when we were in the flesh, the motions of sins, which were by the law, did work in our members to bring forth fruit unto death [Rom. 7:5].

Face this squarely, my friend. Are you able in your own strength to keep the Law? The Law was a straitjacket put on the flesh to control it. The flesh rebelled and chafed under the irksome restraint of the Law. The flesh had no capacity or desire to follow the injunctions of the Law. The flesh broke out of the restraint imposed by law and therefore brought down the irrevocable penalty for breaking the Law, which is death.

But now we are delivered from the law, that being dead wherein we were held; that we should serve in newness of spirit, and not in the oldness of the letter [Rom. 7:6].

"But now we are delivered from the law" means *discharged* or *annulled* from the law. Notice the paradoxes in this section. In verse 4 it was having died, they bear fruit; here in verse 6 they have been discharged, yet they serve. Today we are to serve Him, not on the basis or the motive, "I ought to do it," but now, "I delight to do it because I want to please Christ." The believer is set free, but now in love he gives himself to the Savior as he never could do under the Law. Note this little bit of verse I used to carry in my Bible when I was a student in college and seminary:

I do not work my soul to save;
That work my Lord hath done.
But I will work like any slave
For love of God's dear Son.

We serve Christ because we love Him. Our Lord asked Simon Peter the direct question, ". . . Lovest thou me? . . ." (John 21:17). That is the question that faces you and me. God's question to the lost world is: "What will you do with My Son who died for you?" However, His question to the believer is: "Lovest thou me?"

The Christian life is Christ living His life through us today. We can't do it ourselves, nor can we do it by the law. There is nothing wrong with the law—let's understand that—the problem is with us.

What shall we say then? Is the law sin? God forbid. Nay, I had not known sin, but by the law: for I had not known lust, except the law had said, Thou shalt not covet.

But sin, taking occasion by the commandment, wrought in me all manner of concupiscence. For without the law sin was dead [Rom. 7:7–8].

Let me try to bring out the meaning a little more clearly: What shall we say then? Is the Law sin? Away with the thought! On the contrary, I should not have been conscious of sin, except through law; for I had not known illicit desire (coveting). But sin, getting a start through the commandment, produced in me all manner of illicit desire. For apart from the Law sin is dead.

Paul, you recall, began his argument way back in the sixth chapter of Romans with this expression, "What shall we say then? Shall we continue in sin?" Now again he says, "What shall we say then? Is the Law sin?" In the first part of this chapter Paul seems to be saying that law and sin are on a par. If release from sin means release from law, then are they not the same? Paul clarifies this. He says, "Perish the thought!" Paul will now show that the Law is good; it reveals God's will. The difficulty is not with the Law; the difficulty is with us. The flesh is at fault.

Paul becomes very personal in the remainder of this chapter. Notice that he uses the first person pronouns: *I*, *me* and *myself;* they are used forty-seven times in this section. The experience is the struggle Paul had within himself. He tried to live for God in the power of his new nature. He found it was impossible. The Law revealed to Paul the exceeding sinfulness of sin. The Law was an X-ray of his heart. That is what the Law will do for you if you put it down on your life. The Word of God is called a mirror; it reveals what we are. If you have a spot on your face, the mirror will show it to you, but it can't remove the spot. However, God has a place to remove it:

There is a fountain filled with blood
Drawn from Immanuel's veins;
And sinners, plunged beneath that flood,
Lose all their guilty stains.

The Law reveals the exceeding sinfulness of sin. The Law is not at fault, but the old Adamic nature is the culprit. The admonition of prohibition contained in the Law makes clear the weakness of the flesh. It shows we are sinners.

Here in California a test was made some time ago. A mirror was put in a very prominent public place, and the test was to see if men or women looked at themselves more. I felt it was an unnecessary test; I could have told them that women looked at themselves more. But unfortunately, the test proved otherwise. We all like to see ourselves. We all like to look in a mirror—except one: the Word of God. We don't like to look in that one because it reveals us as sinners, horrible, lost sinners.

For I was alive without the law once: but when the commandment came, sin revived, and I died [Rom. 7:9].

The Law is a ministry of condemnation. The Law can do nothing but condemn us.

And the commandment, which was ordained to life, I found to be unto death [Rom. 7:10].

Oh, the tragedy of the person who seeks to live by the Law! It does not lead him to life. While it is true that God had said, "This do and thou shalt live" (see Deut. 8:1), the doing of it was the difficulty. The fault was not in the Law, but in the one who thought the Law would bring life and power. It did neither. It merely revealed the weakness, inability, and the sin of mankind. If there had been a law which could have given life, God would have given it (see Gal. 3:21). But life and Christian living do not come by the Law.

Let me illustrate this. A car is a very useful thing. But a car in the hands of an incapable driver can be a danger and a menace. In fact, it can be a death-dealing instrument. The fault is not with the car; the fault is with the driver. The problem is man; he is the culprit.

For sin, taking occasion by the commandment, deceived me, and by it slew me [Rom. 7:11].

Sin is personified again here and is a tempter. Sin tempts every man outside the Garden of Eden relative to himself and God. In the Garden of Eden Satan made man believe that God could not be trusted and that man was able to become god, apart from God. Sin, like a Pied Piper, leads the children of men into believing that they can keep the Law and that God is not needed. This is the false trail that he has been talking about, which leads to death. It was ordained to life, Paul says, and he found it led him to death. Sin at last will kill, for the Law did bring the knowledge of sin, and man is without excuse. Again, the difficulty is not with the Law, but within man.

Wherefore the law is holy, and the commandment holy, and just, and good [Rom. 7:12].

The problem is a human problem. Man is the "x" in the equation of life. He is the uncertain one, the one who cannot be trusted.

Was then that which is good made death unto me? God forbid. But sin, that it might appear sin, working death in me by that which is good; that sin by the commandment might become exceeding sinful [Rom. 7:13].

Is this a strange paradox? Is it a perversion of a good thing? The commandment was totally incapable of communicating life. Man must have recourse to help from the outside, because the commandment intensified the awfulness of sin.

For we know that the law is spiritual: but I am carnal, sold under sin [Rom. 7:14].

This is Paul's testimony.

"We know" was the general agreement among believers. The Law is spiritual in the sense that it was given by the Holy Spirit and is part of the Word of God. In other words, that is an expression in Scripture. For example, the Rock is called spiritual in 1 Corinthians 10:4, for it was produced by the Holy Spirit. Israel in the wilderness had spiritual meat and spiritual drink in this sense—that is, the Spirit of God provided it.

"But I am carnal." This means, "I am in the flesh [Greek *sarkinos*]." It does not mean the meat on the bones of the body. This body of ours is neutral and can be used for that which is either good or bad. It is like the automobile I referred to. Carnality refers to this old human mind and spirit and nature which occupies and uses the flesh so that actually the flesh itself is contaminated with sin. (For example, look upon the face of a baby and then look at the face fifty years later. Sin has written indelible lines even upon the surface of the body.) Flesh is inert and has no capabilities or possibilities toward God. It is dominated by a sinful nature, the ramifications of which reach into the inmost recesses of the body and mind. The frontal lobe of the brain is merely an instrument to devise evil. The motor neurons are ready to spring into evil excesses. The heart of man is desperately wicked. He wants to do the things that are evil, and the body responds.

Paul describes his pitiful plight as a slave sold to a Simon Legree taskmaster with a whiplash of evil.

STRUGGLE OF A SAVED SOUL

For that which I do I allow not: for what I would, that do I not; but what I hate, that do I [Rom. 7:15].

Here we have the conflict of two natures, the old nature and the new nature. There are definitely two "I's" in this section. The first "I" is the old nature as he asserts his rights.

"For what I would" is what the new nature wants to do. "That do I not"—the old nature rebels and won't do it. "But what I hate"—the new nature hates it—"that do I"; the old nature goes right ahead and does it.

Do you have the experience of this struggle in your Christian life? Do you do something, then hate yourself because you have done it? And you cry out, "God, oh how I've failed You!" I think every child of God has this experience. Paul is speaking of his own experience in this section. Apparently there were three periods in his life. First he was a proud Pharisee under the Mosaic system, kidding himself by bringing the sacrifices and doing other things which he thought would make him right with God. But the Law was condemning him all the while. Then the second period began when he met Christ on the Damascus Road. This proud young Pharisee turned to Christ as his Savior, but he still felt he could live the Christian life. His new nature said, "I am now going to live for God!" But he failed and was in the arena of struggle and failure for a time. I do not know how long it lasted—probably it was not long. There came a day when there was victory, but Paul did not win it; Christ did. Paul learned that it was a matter of yielding, presenting himself and letting the Spirit of God live the Christian life through him.

If then I do that which I would not, I consent unto the law that it is good [Rom. 7:16].

When the old nature breaks the commandment (in this instance it was coveting), then the new nature agrees with the law that coveting is wrong. Paul was not fighting the Law because he broke it. He was agreeing as a believer that the Law was good.

Now then it is no more I that do it, but sin that dwelleth in me [Rom. 7:17].

In other words: It is no longer I (new nature) who am working it out, but sin (the old nature) living in me. You see, Paul still had the old nature.

For I know that in me (that is, in my flesh,) dwelleth no good thing: for to will is present with me; but how to perform that which is good I find not [Rom. 7:18].

Paul learned two things in this struggle, and they are something that many of us believers need to learn. "In me (that old nature we have been talking about) dwells no good thing." Have you learned that? Have you found there is no good in you? Oh, how many of us Christians feel that we in the flesh can do something that will please God! Many believers who never find out otherwise become as busy as termites and are having about the same effect in many of our churches. They are busy as bees, but they aren't making any honey! They get on committees, they are chairmen of boards, they try to run the church, and they think they are pleasing God. Although they are busy, they have no vital connection with the person of Christ. His life is not being lived through them. They are attempting to do it in their own strength by the flesh. They haven't learned what Paul learned: "I know that in me (that is, in my flesh,) dwelleth no good thing."

Let me make it personal. Anything that Vernon McGee does in the flesh, God *hates*. God won't have it; God can't use it. When it is of the flesh, it is *no good*. Have you learned that? That is a great lesson. The Lord Jesus said, "That which is born of the flesh is flesh . . ." (John 3:6) (and that is all it will ever be), but "Whosoever is born of God doth not commit sin . . . " (1 John 3:9). My, how wonderful that is! We are given a new nature, and that new nature will not commit sin. I assure you that the new nature won't commit sin. When I sin, it is the old nature. The new nature won't do it; the new nature just *hates* sin. That new nature won't let me sleep at night; it says, "Look, you are wrong. You have to make it right!"

Paul found out something else that is very important for us to learn: "for to will is present with me; but how to perform that which is good I find not." He found there is no *good* in the old nature and there is no *power* in the new nature. The new nature wants to serve God, but the carnal man is at enmity against God; it is not subject to the law of God, neither indeed can be (see Rom. 8:7). But the new nature has no power.

I remember when I started out, oh, I was going to live for God! That's when I fell on my face, and I have never fallen harder than I did then. I thought I could do it myself. But I found there was no power in the new nature. And that is the reason that an evangelist can always get response in a meeting. I'm afraid ninety percent of the decisions that are made in our churches today have been made by Christians who have been living in defeat in their Christian lives. What they are really saying is, "I want to live for God. I want to do better." Often an evangelist in a meeting says, "All of you that want to live for God, put up your hand. All of you today that want to come closer to God, put up your hand. Those of you who want to commit your life to God, come forward." The minute an evangelist says that, he's got me. That is what I want to do. That new nature of mine says, "I sure would like to live for God." But there is no power in it. That is what multitudes of believers fail to recognize. There have been folk who have been coming forward for years, and that's all they have been doing—just coming forward! They never make any progress. Oh, how they need to understand this truth!

For the good that I would I do not: but the evil which I would not, that I do [Rom. 7:19].

Have you experienced this?

Now if I do that I would not, it is no more I that do it, but sin that dwelleth in me [Rom. 7:20].

It is that old nature, my friend, that is causing us trouble.

I find then a law, that, when I would do good, evil is present with me [Rom. 7:21].

When you are attempting to serve God in the Spirit, have you discovered that the old nature is right there to bring evil? Perhaps an evil thought will come into your mind. Every child of God, regardless of his state, must admit that in every act and in every moment evil is present with him. Failure to recognize this will eventually lead to shipwreck in the Christian life.

For I delight in the law of God after the inward man [Rom. 7:22].

"The inward man" is the new nature.

But I see another law in my members, warring against the law of my mind, and bringing me into captivity to the law of sin which is in my members [Rom. 7:23].

You see, you don't get rid of the old nature when you are saved. And yet there is no power in your new nature. "I see a different law" is the enmity of the old nature against God. It causes the child of God who is honest to cry out, as Paul cried:

O wretched man that I am! who shall deliver me from the body of this death? [Rom 7:24].

This is not an unsaved man who is crying, "O wretched man that I am"; this is a saved man. The word *wretched* carries with it the note of exhaustion because of the struggle. "Who is going to deliver me?" He is helpless. His shoulders are pinned to the floor—he has been wrestled down. Like old Jacob, he has been crippled. He is calling for help from the outside.

I thank God through Jesus Christ our Lord. So then with the mind I myself serve the law of God; but with the flesh the law of sin [Rom. 7:25].

"I thank God [who gives deliverance] through Jesus Christ our Lord." This is the answer to Paul's SOS. God has provided deliverance. It introduces chapter 8 in which the deliverance is given in detail. Both salvation and sanctification come through Christ; He has provided everything we need.

> Run, run and do, the Law commands
> But gives me neither feet nor hands.
> Better news the Gospel brings,
> It bids me fly and gives me wings.

CHAPTER 8

***THEME:** The new man; the new creation; the new body; new purpose*

This chapter brings us to the conclusion of sanctification. In fact, it presents three great subjects: sanctification, security, and no separation from God. Here it is powerful sanctification in contrast to powerless sanctification. In this chapter we are going to see God's new provision for our sanctification.

While inadequacy has been my feeling all the way through this epistle, especially here I feel totally incapable of dealing with these great truths. This is such a glorious and wonderful epistle that all we can do is merely stand as Moses did at the burning bush with our feet unshod and our head uncovered, not fully realizing or recognizing the glory and wonder of it all.

Chapter 8 is the high-water mark in Romans. This fact is generally conceded by all interpreters of this great epistle. Spencer said, "If Holy Scripture were a ring and the epistle to the Romans its precious stone, chapter eight would be the sparkling point of the jewel." Godet labeled it, "this incomparable chapter." Someone has added, "We enter this chapter with no condemnation, we close with no separation and in between all things work together for good to those that love God."

My friend, how could you have it any better than that? We find that there is to be given to the child of God in this life joy and peace. He is to live for God in the very presence of sin. Sin is *not* to dictate his life's program. It has already been shown that there is nothing in the justified sinner that can produce this ideal state. We have seen that the new nature has no power and the old nature has no good. Then how is a child of God to live for God? Paul cried out for outside help, "O wretched man that I am! who shall deliver me from the body of this death?" (Rom. 7:24). In other words, who is going to enable me to live for God?

Paul concluded chapter 7 by saying, "I thank God through Jesus Christ our Lord. So then with the mind I myself serve the law of God; but with the flesh the law of sin." Now chapter 8 will give us the modus operandi; that is, the means by which the victory is secured.

This chapter introduces us to the work of the Holy Spirit in sanctification. The Holy Spirit is mentioned nineteen times in this chapter. Up to chapter 8 there were only two casual references (see Rom. 5:5; 7:6). In this epistle we see the work of the Blessed Trinity:

God the Father in creation (Rom. 1:1—3:20)
God the Son in salvation (Rom. 3:21—7:25)
God the Holy Spirit in sanctification (Rom. 8:1-39)

Now here in chapter 8 we see the Holy Spirit and real sanctification. A life that is pleasing to God must be lived in the power of the Holy Spirit. As Paul said to the Ephesian believers, "And be not drunk with wine, wherein is excess; but be filled with the Spirit" (Eph. 5:18). Sanctification is the work of the Holy Spirit in the regenerated life of a believer, delivering the believer from the power of sin—even in the very presence of sin—and performing all God's will in the life of the believer.

Godet labels the first eleven verses "The Victory of the Holy Spirit over Sin and Death."

There is therefore now no condemnation to them which are in Christ Jesus, who walk not after the flesh, but after the Spirit [Rom. 8:1].

"Who walk not after the flesh, but after the Spirit" does not really belong in this verse. Apparently some scribe picked it up from verse 4 where it belongs. The literal rendering is: "Therefore now, not one condemnation." This is the inspired statement that, in spite of the failure that Paul experienced in chapter 7, he did not lose his salvation. There is no condemnation to those who are in Christ Jesus. However, he wasn't enjoying the Christian life—he was a failure, and he was a wretched man. God wanted him to have joy in his life. Now how is he to have this? Notice the next verse.

For the law of the Spirit of life in Christ Jesus hath made me free from the law of sin and death [Rom. 8:2].

This is a very important statement. This little word *for* occurs seventeen times in this chapter. Because it is the cement that holds the chapter together, it is a word that requires real mental effort. We need to follow the logic of the apostle Paul. One of the great expositors of Romans said that if you do not find Paul logical, you are not following him aright.

"The law of the Spirit" means not only a principle of law, but also the authority which is exercised by the Spirit.

"The Spirit of life" means the Holy Spirit who brings life because He essentially is life. He is the Spirit of life.

"In Christ Jesus" means that the Holy Spirit is in complete union with Christ Jesus. Because the believer shares the life of Christ, He liberates the believers.

"The law of sin and death" is the authority that sin had over our old nature, ending in complete severance of fellowship with God. That new nature could not break the shackles at all. Only the coming of a higher authority and power could accomplish this, namely the Holy Spirit. The Holy Spirit operates upon the new nature, which is vitally joined to the life of Christ. The man in Romans 7, who was joined to the body of the dead, is now joined to the living Christ also.

For what the law could not do, in that it was weak through the flesh, God sending his own Son in the likeness of sinful

flesh, and for sin, condemned sin in the flesh:

That the righteousness of the law might be fulfilled in us, who walk not after the flesh, but after the Spirit [Rom. 8:3–4].

We have here the whole crux of the matter. Let me give my translation, which may bring out several things we need to understand. "For the thing impossible for the Law in which it was powerless through the flesh, God, having sent His own Son in the likeness of the flesh of sin, and in regard to sin, He condemned the sin in the flesh; in order that the justification (the righteous result) of the Law might be fulfilled in us, who walk not according to flesh but according to Spirit."

It was impossible for the Law to produce righteousness in man. This is not the fault of the Law. The fault lay in man and the sin in his flesh. The Law was totally incapable of producing any good thing in man. Paul could say, "For I know that in me (that is, in my flesh,) dwelleth no good thing" (Rom. 7:18). And, friend, that is Scripture, and that is accurate. Man is totally depraved. That doesn't mean only the man across the street or down in the next block from you, nor does it mean only some person who is living in overt sin; it means *you* and it means *me*. The Holy Spirit is now able to do the impossible. The Holy Spirit can produce a holy life in weak and sinful flesh. Let me illustrate this truth by using a very homely incident. Suppose a housewife puts a roast in the oven right after breakfast because she is going to serve it for the noon meal. The telephone rings. It is Mrs. Joe Dokes on the phone. Mrs. Dokes begins with "Have you heard?" Well, the housewife hasn't heard, but she would like to; so she pulls up a chair. (Someone has defined a woman as one who draws up a chair when answering a telephone.) Mrs. Dokes has a lot to tell, and about an hour goes by. Finally our good housewife says, "Oh, Mrs. Dokes, you'll have to excuse me. I smell the roast—its burning!" She hangs up the phone, rushes to the kitchen, and opens the oven. Then she gets a fork and puts it down in the roast to lift it up, but it won't hold. She can't lift it out. She tries again, closer to the bone, but still it won't hold. So she gets a spatula. She puts the spatula under the roast and lifts it out. You see, what the fork could not do, in that it was weak through the flesh, the spatula is able to do. Now, there is nothing wrong with the fork—it was a good fork. But it couldn't hold the flesh because something was wrong with the flesh—it was overcooked. The spatula does what the fork could not do.

The Law is like the fork in that it was weak through the flesh. It just won't lift us up; it *can't* lift us up. But a new principle is introduced: the Holy Spirit. What the Law could not do, the Holy Spirit is able to do. Therefore, you and I are to live the Christian life on this new principle. We are not to try to lift ourselves up by our own bootstraps. We'll never make it that way, my friend. We make resolutions and say, "I'm going to do better"—all of us have said that. But did we ever do better? Didn't we do the same old things?

God is able to do this new impossible thing by sending His very own Son, His own nature in the likeness of sinful flesh. Christ had the same kind of flesh that we have, apart from sin. Notice how the writer to the Hebrews puts it: "Forasmuch then as the children are partakers of flesh and blood, he also himself likewise took part of the same; that through death he might destroy him that had the power of death, that is, the devil. . . . For verily he took not on him the nature of angels; but he took on him the seed of Abraham. Wherefore in all things it behoved him to be made like unto his brethren, that he might be a merciful and faithful high priest in things pertaining to God, to make reconciliation for the sins of the people" (Heb. 2:14, 16–17). Also he says, "For such an high priest became us, who is holy, harmless, undefiled, separate from sinners, and made higher than the heavens" (Heb. 7:26). Then he says, "Wherefore when he cometh into the world, he saith, Sacrifice and offering thou wouldest not, but a body hast thou prepared me" (Heb. 10:5).

This was God's way of getting at the roots of sin in our bodies, minds, and spirits. He could condemn and execute sinful flesh on the cross so that it had no more rights in human beings. God was able to deal with sin itself—Christ was identified with us—what condescension! Sin has been condemned in these bodies of ours. It has not been removed, in spite of the belief of some very sincere people. These bodies are to be redeemed—". . . raised a spiritual body . . . " (1 Cor. 15:44). Today, the Holy Spirit is the Deliverer from sin in the body. A great many people think it would be wonderful if Christ would come and take us out of this world of sin—and that would be wonderful. I wish He would come right now. However, there is something éven more wonderful than that. It is this: He enables you and me to live the Christian life right where we are today in this old world of sin. That is *more* wonderful. Our Lord Jesus said in His high priestly prayer, "I pray not that thou shouldest take them out of the world, but that thou shouldest keep them from the evil" (John 17:15). Down here is where the victory is.

"That the righteousness of the law might be fulfilled"—this is the passive voice. It means that the Holy Spirit produces a life of obedience which the Law commanded but could not produce. The Holy Spirit furnishes the power; the decision is ours.

The next verse introduces us to a new struggle. It is not for us to do the fighting. Now it is the Holy Spirit versus the flesh.

For they that are after the flesh do mind the things of the flesh; but they that are after the Spirit the things of the Spirit [Rom. 8:5].

"Do mind the things of the flesh." When I was holding a meeting in Middle Tennessee after I was first ordained, I was invited to dinner in a lovely country home. The housewife had prepared some wonderful fried chicken. When we were already sitting at the table, she went out to call her little boy again. After she'd called him several times, she came in and said, "That young'un won't *mind* me." And what she meant was, "That young one will not obey me." Paul, you see, sounds like a good Southerner because he uses this word, "they *mind* the things of the flesh." We have seen that before in the sixth chapter of Romans. My friend, if you live habitually in the flesh and obey the things of the flesh, and the new nature doesn't rebuke you, you must not have a new nature—because "they that are after the Spirit [*mind*] the things of the Spirit." A believer has been given a new nature, and now he can yield himself to the new nature. And this is an act of the will. This is the new struggle that's brought to our attention. "The flesh" describes the natural man. The Lord Jesus said, "That which is born of the flesh is flesh"—it will always be flesh. God has no program to change the flesh. Rather He brings in something new: "and that which is born of the Spirit is spirit" (John 3:6).

A new struggle is brought to our attention. It is no longer the new nature or the believer striving for mastery over sin in the body; it is the Holy Spirit striving against the old nature. The little boy coming home from school was being beaten up by a big bully. He was on the bottom, and the big bully was pounding him very heavily. Then he looked up from his defeated position on the bottom, and he saw his big brother coming. The big brother took care of the bully while the little fellow crawled up on a stump and rubbed his bruises. The believer has the Holy Spirit to deal with the flesh, that big bully. I learned a long time ago that I can't overcome it. So I have to turn it over to Somebody who can. The Holy Spirit indwells believers. He wants to do that for us, and He can!

"They that are after the flesh" describes the natural man. Paul paints his picture in Ephesians 2:1–3. "And you hath he quickened, who were dead in trespasses and sins: Wherein in time past ye walked according to the course of this world, according to the prince of the power of the air, the spirit that now worketh in the children of disobedience: Among whom also we all had our conversation in times past in the lusts of our flesh, fulfilling the desires of the flesh and of the mind; and were by nature the children of wrath, even as others." This was the condition of all of us until we were saved.

And the "flesh" includes the mind. "And you, that were sometime alienated and enemies in your mind by wicked works, yet now hath he reconciled" (Col. 1:21). It includes the total personality which is completely alienated from God.

The natural man strives and even sets his heart upon the things of the flesh. Here is his diet: "Now the works of the flesh are manifest, which are these; adultery, fornication, uncleanness, lasciviousness, idolatry, witchcraft, hatred, variance, emulations, wrath, strife, seditions, heresies, envyings, murders, drunkenness, revellings, and such like: of the which I tell you before, as I have also told you in time past, that they which do such things shall not inherit the kingdom of God" (Gal. 5:19–21). It is an ugly brood!

In Colossians Paul says: "But now ye also put off all these; anger, wrath, malice, blasphemy, filthy communication out of your mouth. Lie not one to another, seeing that ye have put off the old man with his deeds" (Col. 3:8–9). The Lord Jesus said: "For out of the heart proceed evil thoughts, murders, adulteries, fornications, thefts, false witness, blasphemies" (Matt. 15:19).

It is humiliating but true that the child of God retains this old Adamic nature. It means defeat and death to live by the flesh. No child of God can be happy in living for the things of the flesh. The prodigal son may get into the pig pen, but he will never be content to stay there. He is bound to say, "I will arise and go to my father."

"They that are after the Spirit" are born

again, regenerated and indwelt by the Spirit of God. They love the things of Christ. "If ye then be risen with Christ, seek those things which are above, where Christ sitteth on the right hand of God. Set your affection on things above, not on things on the earth" (Col. 3:1–2). And Paul says, "Put on therefore, as the elect of God, holy and beloved, bowels of mercies, kindness, humbleness of mind, meekness, longsuffering" (Col. 3:12). These are just some of the things for which the child of God longs. You and I cannot do these things by effort. It is only as we let the Spirit of God work in our lives that they will appear.

Here is another great principle.

For to be carnally minded is death; but to be spiritually minded is life and peace [Rom. 8:6].

"For to be carnally minded" means that you are separated from fellowship with God and that flesh is death here and now. The Spirit who indwells the believer brings life and peace. When we sin, we are to come to Him in confession and let Him wash us. This restores us to fellowship.

The "life" He offers speaks of full satisfaction and the exercise of one's total abilities. Oh, to live life at its fullest and best! Many people think they are really living today, but it is a shoddy substitute for the life God wants to provide.

"Peace" means the experience of tranquility and well-being regarding the present and future. Oh, my beloved, how you and I need to get into that territory!

There is one thing for sure: if you are living in the flesh, and you are a child of God, you are *not* having fellowship with God. You *can't*. The Lord Jesus in the Upper Room said to Simon Peter, ". . . If I wash thee not, thou hast no part with me" (John 13:8). Now, my friend, He meant that. He will not fellowship with you or with me if we are committing sin and are continuing to live in the flesh. "Well," somebody says, "what are we to do?" Do what Simon Peter had to do—he stuck out his feet and let the Lord wash them. And you and I need to go to Him in confession. First John 1:9 tells us, "If we confess our sins." Who is "we"? We Christians. "He is faithful and just . . ." when He does it, because it will take the blood of Christ, my friend. You and I do not know how wicked the old nature is. And we need to go to Him for cleansing.

The English poet, John Donne, using the mythological story of the labors of Hercules—where that strong man of the ancient world was confronted with the task of cleaning out the Augean stables—illustrates this important truth. Though Hercules was able to perform the task, Donne shows that man cannot clean the much greater filth of the human heart. He writes:

> Lord I confess that Thou alone are able
> To purify this Augean stable.
> Be the seas water, and all the land soap
> Yet if Thy blood not wash me—there's no hope.

The blood of Jesus Christ, God's Son, keeps on cleansing us from all sin" (see 1 John 1:7). This old nature is totally depraved. God has no plan to redeem it. He gives us a new nature. And you and I can't live for God in that old nature. If you continue to live in that old nature, you must not be a child of God. Somebody says, "Then if a child of God sins, what's the difference between him and the lost man?" The difference is simply this: when the lost man goes out at night and paints the town red, he comes back and says, "I'll get a bigger brush and a bigger bucket of paint next time; wow, I want to live it up!" While the child of God, if he does a thing like that, will cry out to God, "Oh, God, I hate myself for what I've done!" And this idea today that you can somehow train your old nature, and live in it, is false. That's the thing that leads to legalism. Legalists—well, I call them Priscilla Goodbodies and Goody-goody-gumdrops, those sweet lovely people who are trying to control the flesh—they are so pious! I want to tell you, they are the worst gossips you have ever met.

Dr. Newell has put down some very interesting statements which I would like to pass on to you. "To hope to do better is to fail to see yourself in Christ only." You say, "I hope to do better." You *know* you're not. You need to see yourself in Christ today and realize that only the Spirit of God moving through you can accomplish this. And then Newell says again, "To be disappointed with yourself means you believed in yourself." Somebody says, "Oh, I'm so disappointed in myself." Well, you had better be disappointed in yourself. You know no good thing is going to come out of the flesh, friend. Stop believing in yourself, and believe that the Spirit of God today can enable you through the new nature to live for God. Also Newell says, "To be discouraged is unbelief." Somebody says, "Oh, I'm so discouraged." My friend, that means you don't believe God. God has a purpose and a plan, a blessing for you. And you need to lay hold of it. Here is another statement: "To be proud is to be blind." We have no standing before God in ourselves. Oh, my friend, see yourself as God sees you. Here is the final gem: "The lack of divine blessing comes from unbelief, not a failure of devotion." I am sick and weary of these super-duper pious, "dedicated" Christians who talk about their devotion. My friend, the lack of divine blessing comes because we do not *believe* God. It is not because of a lack of devotion. Oh, to believe God today! Now, real devotion arises not from man's will to show it, but from the discovery that blessing has been received from God while we were yet unworthy and undevoted. Nothing I get from God has come through my devotion. I haven't anything to offer Him. It comes because of His marvelous grace. And I've seen these folk who preach "devotion" troop down to dedicate their lives in services. I got so sick and tired of seeing that same crowd come down—and you could not trust them, my friend. They were liars. They were dishonest. They were gossips, and they would crucify you. May I say to you, you do not need to dedicate yourself. What you need today is to *believe* God can do something and you can't do anything. Now, somebody says, "That's pretty strong." I hope that it is. I intend for it to be that way, because Paul is making it very clear here. The carnal mind is *enmity* against God.

Because the carnal mind is enmity against God: for it is not subject to the law of God, neither indeed can be.

So then they that are in the flesh cannot please God [Rom. 8:7–8].

This verse reveals how hopelessly incorrigible and utterly destitute the flesh really is. It is a spiritual anarchist. This demolishes any theory that there is a divine spark in man and that somehow he has a secret bent toward God. The truth is that man is the enemy of God. He is not only dead in trespasses and sins but active in rebellion against God. Man will even become religious in order to stay away from the living and true God and the person of Jesus Christ. Man in his natural condition, if taken to heaven, would start a revolution, and he would have a protest meeting going on before the sun went down! Jacob, in his natural condition, engaged in a wrestling match. He did not seek it, but he fought back when God wrestled with him. It wasn't until he yielded that he won, my friend.

Anything that the flesh produces is not acceptable to God. The so-called good work, the civilization, the culture, and man's vaunted progress are all a stench in the nostrils of God. The religious works of church people done in the lukewarmness of the flesh make Christ sick to His stomach (see Rev. 3:15–16).

I wonder if we are willing to accept God's estimation of our human boasting. This is a terrible picture of man; but it is accurate. Yet there is deliverance in the Spirit of God. Are you willing, my friend, to turn it over to the Holy Spirit and quit trusting that weak, sinful nature that you have? That is the question.

But ye are not in the flesh, but in the Spirit, if so be that the Spirit of God dwell in you. Now if any man have not the Spirit of Christ, he is none of his [Rom. 8:9].

This first "if" is not casting a doubt over the Roman believers' salvation. They are saved. Let me give you a literal translation: "But you are not in the flesh, but in the Spirit *since* the Spirit of God really dwells in you." That is the real test. But if anyone has "not the Spirit of Christ, he is none of his." The true mark of a born-again believer and a genuine Christian is that he is indwelt by the Spirit of God. Even Paul could say to the carnal Corinthians: "What? know ye not that your body is the temple of the Holy Ghost which is in you, which ye have of God, and ye are not your own?" (1 Cor. 6:19). When Paul went to Ephesus the first time, he missed something; he missed the distinguishing mark of the believer. So he asked, "Did you receive the Holy Spirit when you believed?" They didn't even know what he was talking about. So he asked them, ". . . Unto what then were ye baptized? And they said, Unto John's baptism" (Acts 19:3). Well, John's baptism was unto repentance; it was not to faith in Jesus Christ. So he preached Christ to them. Then they received Him and were baptized in His name (see Acts 19:5). A believer is a new creation. Do you love Him? Do you want to serve Him? Are these things uppermost in your mind and heart? Or are you in rebellion against God?

And if Christ be in you, the body is dead because of sin; but the Spirit is life because of righteousness [Rom. 8:10].

In other words: Now if Christ be in you, the body indeed is dead on account of sin; but the Spirit is life because of righteousness. He is saying here that you and I are in Christ, and since we are in Him, when He died, we died. And we are to reckon on this, as we have already been told. Also we are to yield, that is, *present* our bodies to Him. Don't say you can't do this—that is not the language of a believer. Paul could say, "I am crucified with Christ: nevertheless I live; yet not I, but Christ liveth in me: and the life which I now live in the flesh I live by the faith of the Son of God, who loved me, and gave himself for me" (Gal. 2:20).

If you today are not conscious of the presence of the Spirit of God in your life and if you do not have a desire to serve God, then it would be well to do as Paul suggests, "Examine yourselves, whether ye be in the faith; prove your own selves. Know ye not your own selves, how that Jesus Christ is in you, except ye be reprobates?" (2 Cor. 13:5). The Lord wants us to *know* that we are in Christ. "To whom God would make known what is the riches of the glory of this mystery among the Gentiles; which is Christ in you, the hope of glory" (Col. 1:27).

If you are not sure that Christ is in you, He extends this invitation: "Behold, I stand at the door, and knock: if any man hear my voice, and open the door, I will come in to him, and will sup with him, and he with me" (Rev. 3:20). Is your door open? Has He come into you? My friend, the body has been put in the place of death. This is something the child of God should reckon on. And he should turn over his life to the Spirit of God, saying very definitely, "I cannot do it, Lord, but You can do it through me."

But if the Spirit of him that raised up Jesus from the dead dwell in you, he that raised up Christ from the dead shall also quicken your mortal bodies by his Spirit that dwelleth in you [Rom. 8:11].

These bodies that you and I have will be put in the grave one of these days, if the Lord tarries. However, the indwelling Holy Spirit is our assurance that our bodies will be raised from the dead (2 Cor. 5:1–4). Because Christ was raised from the dead, we shall be raised from the dead. The Holy Spirit will deliver us from the "body of his death"—this old nature.

Therefore, brethren, we are debtors, not to the flesh, to live after the flesh [Rom. 8:12].

In other words, we are not to live according to the flesh. God created man body, mind, and spirit. When man sinned, his spirit died to God. Remember that God had warned, "But of the tree of the knowledge of good and evil, thou shalt not eat of it: for in the day that thou eatest thereof thou shalt surely die" (Gen. 2:17). After Adam ate of the fruit, he lived several hundred years—physically; but spiritually he died immediately. Man was turned upside down. The body, the old nature, the flesh became dominant. Today man is dead spiritually. Regeneration means that you are turned right side up, that you are born again spiritually, and that you have a nature which wants to serve God.

Oh, my friend, to stay close to Christ is the important thing. You can be active in Christian work, as active as a termite, yet Christ can be in outer space as far as you are concerned. The natural man says he owes it to his flesh to satisfy it. He may rationalize his dishonesty by saying, "A man has to eat." A movie star has said, "I live for sex, and I have to have my needs met." We hear this today on every hand. Satisfying the old nature has plunged our nation into the grossest immorality! But God says that we as believers are not debtors to the flesh. My friend, the flesh—and we all have it—is a low-down, dirty rascal. And we don't owe it anything.

For if ye live after the flesh, ye shall die: but if ye through the Spirit do mortify the deeds of the body, ye shall live [Rom. 8:13].

"For if ye live after the flesh, ye shall die"—die to God. That is, you have no fellowship with Him. I am not talking about a theory; if you are a child of God, you know this from experience. If you are a child of God and you have unconfessed sin in your life, do you *want* to go to church? Do you *want* to read your Bible? Do you *want* to pray? Of course you don't. You are separated from God.

"But if ye through the Spirit"—you can't do it yourself—"do mortify the deeds of the body, ye shall live." Let's be practical now. What is *your* problem today? Liquor? Drugs? Sex? You may say, "I don't have those problems!" Then how about your thought-life? How about your tongue? Do you gossip? Do you tell the truth? Whatever your problem is, why don't you confess it to God, then turn it over to the Holy Spirit? My friend, if you deal with it in reality, you won't need to crawl up on the psychiatrist's couch. He won't help you. He can shift your guilt complex to another area, but he can't get rid of it. Only Christ can remove it; He is in that business. He says, "Come unto me, all ye that labour and are heavy laden, and I will *rest* you" so that you will know what it is to have sins forgiven (see Matt. 11:28).

THE NEW MAN

We come now to a new section concerning the new nature of man.

For as many as are led by the Spirit of God, they are the sons of God [Rom. 8:14].

That makes sense, doesn't it? God does not drive His sheep; He leads them. When our Lord told of the safety and security of the sheep, He made it clear that they were not *forced* into the will of His hand and that of the Father. He said, "My sheep hear my voice, and I know them [*and I drive them out!* Oh, no] and they follow me" (John 10:27). They are the ones who are safe and secure; they follow Him. They are led by the Spirit of God. They hear His voice because they have a new nature, and they follow Him.

I have been preaching the Word of God for a long time. I have found that those who are His sheep will hear His voice. The others—they hated me and wanted to get rid of me. Why? They were not His sheep. The Lord Jesus said, "If the world hate you, ye know that it hated me before it hated you" (John 15:18). A young pastor came to me and said, "I'm having all kinds of trouble!" I asked, "Who is giving you trouble?" He said, "My church officers and my Sunday school teachers." So I asked him what he had been doing. He said, "Well, I've been preaching the Bible, following your Thru the Bible method." I said to him, "Well, thank God. You will find that a lot of your folk are not really His sheep." Friend, His sheep will follow Him—they have to because they are *His*, you see. That's what Paul is saying here.

For ye have not received the spirit of bondage again to fear; but ye have received the Spirit of adoption, whereby we cry, Abba, Father [Rom. 8:15].

"Ye have not received the spirit of bondage again to fear"—there is not that spirit of fear within you, wondering about your spiritual condition, unhappy, and despondent. Instead, you are filled with joy because you are His child. And the Spirit of God wells up within you, saying, "Abba, Father."

The word *Abba* is an untranslated Aramaic word. The translators of the first English Bibles, who had great reverence for the Word of God, who believed it was indeed the Word of God, would not translate it. *Abba* is a very personal word that could be translated "My Daddy." We don't use this word in reference to God because of the danger of becoming overly familiar with Him. But it expresses a heart-cry, especially in times of trouble.

The Spirit itself beareth witness with our spirit, that we are the children of God [Rom. 8:16].

I found this true the first time I went to the hospital for cancer surgery. I turned my face to the wall, like old Hezekiah did, and said, "Lord, I've been in this hospital many times. I've patted the hands of folk and had prayer with them, and told them, 'Oh, you trust the Lord; He will see you through.' Lord, I have told *them* that, but this is the first time *I've* been in here. Now I want to know whether it is true or not. I want You to make it real to me. If You are my Father, I want to *know* it." And, my friend, He made it real. At a time like that the Spirit of God cries out, "Abba, Father"—it just wells up within you. How sweet it is to trust Him, turn yourself over to Him.

And if children, then heirs; heirs of God, and joint-heirs with Christ; if so be that we suffer with him, that we may be also glorified together [Rom. 8:17].

"If so be" assures the fact that the child of God will suffer with Him. I believe it could be translated "*since* we suffer with Him." I don't think the "if" is as important as some folk make it out to be.

My friend, what are you enduring for Him today? Whatever it is, Paul makes it clear that it is just a light thing we are going through now. But there is a weighty thing, an "eternal weight of glory" that is coming someday. In eternity we will wish that we had suffered a little more for Him, because that is the way He schools and trains us. "For whom the Lord loveth he chasteneth, and scourgeth every son whom he receiveth" (Heb. 12:6).

THE NEW CREATION

This brings us to a new division in this eighth chapter of Romans.

Not only the bodies of believers are to be redeemed, but we're going to find out that this entire physical universe, this earth on which you and I live, is to be redeemed. That is the purpose of God. In fact we're trading in this old earth for a new earth, a new model, brand new, wherein there will be no sin. No curse of sin will ever come upon it again. That is something that is quite wonderful. Someone said to me not long ago, "I believe that healing is in the Atonement." I think I shocked the person when I said, "I believe that too. Not only is healing in the Atonement, but a new body is in the Atonement, and a new world is in the atonement of Christ. But we don't have it yet." The political parties and the United Nations have been trying to bring in a new world for years, but we certainly do not have these yet. But Christ is going to bring it in someday through His redemption. And then I'm going to get a new body. I'm looking forward to that. This one I've got is wearing out, and I want to trade it in for a new one. And that's coming. And healing—I'll grant that it is in the Atonement, but I don't have all of that yet. I still have cancer.

For I reckon that the sufferings of this present time are not worthy to be compared with the glory which shall be revealed in us [Rom. 8:18].

"I reckon" means that Paul calculates, counts upon, both the debit and credit side of the ledger of life.

"The sufferings of this present time" are the common lot of all believers. This generation, which is enjoying more creature comforts than any other in history, frowns upon this statement, but even present-day Christians cannot escape suffering.

For the earnest expectation of the creature waiteth for the manifestation of the sons of God [Rom. 8:19].

Let me give my translation of this verse: For the creation, watching with outstretched head (head erect), is waiting (sighing) for the revelation of the sons of God.

The world is not waiting for the sunrise of evolution's pipe dream. The pipe dream of evolution will never come true. However, creation is waiting "for the manifestation of the sons of God." Creation is like a veiled statue today. When the sons of God have removed the outward covering of this flesh, creation also will be unveiled. What a glorious day that will be!

For the creature was made subject to vanity, not willingly, but by reason of him who hath subjected the same in hope [Rom. 8:20].

"For the creation was subjected to vanity"—*vanity* means "failure, decay, something that is perishable."

"Not willingly" means not of its own will, but because of Him who subjected it on the basis of hope. King Solomon, who was quite a pessimist, by the way, wrote: "All the rivers run into the sea; yet the sea is not full; unto the place from whence the rivers come, thither they return again" (Eccl. 1:7). There is a weary round of repetition. The rivers run into the sea, and the Lord has quite a hydraulic pump that pumps the water right out of the ocean, and with His good transportation system, the wind moves the clouds across the dry land, and here comes the rain again. It fills the rivers, and the rivers run into the sea. There is a monotony about nature; you see it on every hand. Nature is waiting for the promised manifestation, the unveiling.

"Creation was subjected to vanity" because God made it that way. The curse of sin came upon man in Adam's disobedience, but the physical world also came under the curse. Remember that God said to Adam, "Thorns also and thistles shall it bring forth to thee; and thou shalt eat the herb of the field; In the sweat of thy face shalt thou eat bread . . ." (Gen. 3:18–19). I enjoy going out to the Hawaiian Islands; I know of no place quite as delightful. Yet on a golf course in that "paradise" I found—of all things—thorns! I knocked a ball out in the rough there, out in the lava, and I have never seen as many thorns as were there. I have a pair of shoes that have thorns in them to this good day—I can't get them all out. Even in that paradise there are thorns. There is a curse on creation.

Because the creature itself also shall be delivered from the bondage of corruption into the glorious liberty of the children of God [Rom. 8:21].

Man has a dying body. As someone has said, "The moment He gives us life, He begins to take it away from us." And there is death and decay yonder in nature. Go out in the beautiful forest, and there you see a tree lying dead, corrupt, rotting. That's nature. And you catch the stench of the decaying bodies of dead animals.

For we know that the whole creation groaneth and travaileth in pain together until now [Rom. 8:22].

Browning in his *Pippa Passes* writes.

God's in His Heaven—
All's right with the world.

The Christian knows that that is not true. God is in His heaven all right, but all is not right with the world. The Word of God is more realistic: "How do the beasts groan! the herds of cattle are perplexed, because they have no pasture; yea, the flocks of sheep are made desolate" (Joel 1:18).

Some have called our attention to the fact that nature sings in a minor key. The wind blowing through the pine trees on a mountainside and the breaking of the surf on some lonely shore—both emit the same sob. The music of trees has been recorded, and it is doleful. The startled cry of some frightened animal or bird pierces the night air and chills the blood. Surely nature bears audible testimony to the accuracy of Scripture. Godet quotes Schelling in this connection, "Nature, with its melancholy chorus, resembles a bride who, at the very moment when she is fully attired for the marriage, saw the bridegroom die. She still stands with her fresh crown and in her bridal dress but her eyes are full of tears."

It is accurate to say that "nature is groaning."

THE NEW BODY

And not only they, but ourselves also, which have the firstfruits of the Spirit, even we ourselves groan within ourselves, waiting for the adoption, to wit, the redemption of our body [Rom. 8:23].

Not only does nature groan, but the believer is in harmony with nature. This verse is devastating to those who propose the theory that the mark of a Christian is a perennially smiling face. They contend that a Christian should be a cross between a Cheshire cat and a house-to-house salesman. A Christian should grin—at all times? Smile your troubles away is good for Rotary, but it is not the Christian method.

We groan within these bodies. Some years ago when I began to move into middle age, I would come down the steps in the morning groaning because my knees were hurting. My wife told me I ought not to groan! I told her it is scriptural to groan. Paul says, "For in this we groan, earnestly desiring to be clothed upon with our house which is from heaven" (2 Cor. 5:2). Also the psalmist wrote, "I am weary with my groaning; all the night make I my bed to swim; I water my couch with my tears" (Ps. 6:6). Our Lord Jesus did some weeping also. Although I believe He was a joyful person, there were times when He wept. In these bodies we groan.

For we are saved by hope: but hope that is seen is not hope: for what a man seeth, why doth he yet hope for? [Rom. 8:24].

"We are saved by hope" speaks of the work of Christ for us on the cross and our faith in Him. But that is not all. We have a redeemed body coming up in the future.

But if we hope for that we see not, then do we with patience wait for it [Rom. 8:25].

You see, faith, hope, and love are the vital parts of the believer's life. There would be no hope if all were realized. Someday hope will pass away in realization. In fact, both faith and hope will pass away in the glory which shall be revealed in us. Only love abides.

Likewise the Spirit also helpeth our infirmities: for we know not what we should pray for as we ought: but the Spirit itself maketh intercession for us with groanings which cannot be uttered [Rom. 8:26].

Years ago when the late Dr. A. C. Gaebelein was speaking, a very enthusiastic member of the congregation kept interrupting with loud amens. That annoyed Dr. Gaebelein. Finally, he told him, "Brother, the Scripture says that the *Spirit* maketh intercession for us with groanings which cannot be uttered—so don't you utter them if it's the Spirit of God." We didn't even know how we ought to pray; but the Spirit of God will make intercession with groanings which cannot be uttered.

Have you gone to God sometimes in prayer when you actually did not know what to pray for? All you could do was just go to Him and say, "Father." You could not ask anything because you didn't know what to ask for. At times like this the Spirit "helpeth our infirmities." How wonderful that is!

And he that searcheth the hearts knoweth what is the mind of the Spirit, because he maketh intercession for the saints according to the will of God [Rom. 8:27].

Now, if I go to God in prayer and say, "Look, Lord, I want You to do it this way," That's the way I usually do it, and I may not get the answer the way I prayed. But it's wonderful sometimes to go to the Lord and say, "Lord, I don't know what to ask for. I don't know what to say. But I'm coming to You as Your child. And I want Your *will* done." And the Spirit of God then will make intercession for us according to the will of God. My, again, how wonderful that is!

NEW PURPOSE

We come now to the new purpose of God. If Romans is the greatest book of the

Bible, and chapter 8 is the high-water mark, then verse 28 is the pinnacle. God's purpose guarantees the salvation of sinners, and the next three verses give the "ascending process of salvation," as William Sanday calls it.

And we know that all things work together for good to them that love God, to them who are the called according to his purpose [Rom. 8:28].

I have translated it this way: But we know (with divine knowledge) that for those who love God, all things are working together for good, even to them who are called-ones according to His purpose.

The late Dr. Reuben A. Torrey (I had the privilege of being pastor for twenty-one years of the church that he founded) was a great man of God, greatly abused and misunderstood. He knew the meaning of this verse, and he called it a soft pillow for a tired heart. Many of us have pillowed our heads on Romans 8:28. We know the whole creation is groaning, but we also know something else: all things are working together for good—even the groanings.

"We know" is used five times in Romans, and "know" is used thirteen times. It refers to that which is the common knowledge of the Christian, that is, that which the Holy Spirit makes real. "Knowledge puffeth up, but love edifieth" (see 1 Cor. 8:1), and this is the knowledge that only the Spirit of God can make real to our hearts. Charles Spurgeon used to say, "I do not need anyone to tell me how honey tastes; I *know*." And I can say, my friend, that I *know* God loves me. I don't need to argue that point; I *know* it.

"For those who love God" is the fraternity pin of the believer. "For in Jesus Christ neither circumcision availeth any thing, nor uncircumcision [that is, there is no badge]; but faith which worketh by love" (Gal. 5:6). Love is the mark. The apostle John put it like this: "Herein is love, not that we loved God, but that he loved us, and sent his Son to be the propitiation [the mercy seat] for our sins. Beloved, if God so loved us, we ought also to love one another. No man hath seen God at any time. If we love one another, God dwelleth in us, and his love is perfected in us. Hereby know we that we dwell in him, and he in us, because he hath given us of his Spirit. And we have seen and do testify that the Father sent the Son to be the Saviour of the world. Whosoever shall confess that Jesus is the Son of God, God dwelleth in him, and he in God. And we have known and believed the love that God hath to us. God is love; and he that dwelleth in love dwelleth in God, and God in him" (1 John 4:10–16). My friend, you are going to have trouble believing that God loves you, and you will have difficulty loving God, if you are hating other Christians. "We love him, because he first loved us" (1 John 4:19). And the apostle Peter said: "Whom having not seen, ye love; in whom, though now ye see him not, yet believing, ye rejoice with joy unspeakable and full of glory" (1 Pet. 1:8). The thing that will bring joy and brightness into your life is the sincere love of God.

"All things"—good and bad; bright and dark; sweet and bitter; easy and hard; happy and sad; prosperity and poverty; health and sickness; calm and storm; comfort and suffering; life and death.

"Are working together for good" is causative and means that God is working all things—there are no accidents. You remember that Joseph could look back over his life, a life that had been filled with vicissitudes, disappointments, and sufferings, yet he could say to his brethren—who were responsible for his misfortune—". . . ye thought evil against me; but God meant it unto good . . ." (Gen. 50:20). And I am confident that we as children of God will be able to look back over our lives someday and say, "All of this worked out for good." Job could say, "Though he slay me, yet will I trust in him . . ." (Job 13:15). That is the kind of faith in God we need, friend. We know that He is going to make things work out for good because He's the One who is motivating it. He's the One who is energizing it.

However, we often cry out, as Jeremiah did, "Why did you let me see trouble?" (see Jer. 11:14). It was during the San Francisco earthquake many years ago that a saint of God walked out into the scene of destruction and debris and actually smiled. A friend asked her, "How can you smile at a time like this?" Her reply was, "I rejoice that I have a God who can shake the world!" How wonderful to be able to face life—and death—unafraid. I think of Paul who could face the future without flinching. He said to his friends, ". . . What mean ye to weep and to break mine heart? for I am ready not to be bound only, but also to die at Jerusalem for the name of the Lord Jesus" (Acts 21:13). Many of us would like to come to that place of total commitment to Him.

Now notice that all things are working together for good for them "who are the called" ones, and it is "according to his purpose." This is something that is hard for a great many people to swallow. "The called" are those who not only have received an invitation, they have accepted it. And they were born from above. They know experimentally the love of God. Paul describes three groups of people, and I think they are the three groups that are in the world today: "But we preach Christ crucified, unto the Jews a stumblingblock, and unto the Greeks foolishness; But unto them which are called, both Jews and Greeks, Christ the power of God, and the wisdom of God" (1 Cor. 1:23–24). (1) The Jews trusted in religion, rite and ritual. To them the cross was a stumblingblock. (2) The Greeks (the Gentiles) trusted in philosophy and human wisdom. To them the cross was foolishness. (3) "The called" were a group out of both Jews and Greeks who were chosen not because of their religion or wisdom. God called them. To them the cross was the *dynamite* of God unto salvation. "The called" heard God's call. That is important.

Let me go back to my illustration of the turtles. Suppose you go down to a swamp, and there are ten turtles. You say to the turtles, "I'd like to teach you to fly." Nine of them say, "We're not interested. We like it down here; we feel comfortable in this environment." One turtle says, "Yes, I'd like to fly." *That* is the one which is called, and that is the one which is taught to fly. Now that doesn't have anything in the world to do with the other turtles. They are turtles because they are turtles. My friend, the lost are *lost* because they want it that way. There is not a person on topside of this world that is being forced to be lost. They are lost because they have chosen to be lost.

A boy down in my southland years ago wanted to join a church. So the deacons were examining him. They asked, "How did you get saved?" His answer was, "God did His part, and I did my part." They thought there was something wrong with his doctrine, so they questioned further. "What was God's part and what was your part?" His explanation was a good one. He said, "God's part was the saving, and my part was the sinning. I done run from Him as fast as my sinful heart and rebellious legs could take me. He done took out after me till he run me down." My friend, that is the way I got saved also.

This does not destroy or disturb the fact that "whosoever will may come" and "whosoever believeth." Henry Ward Beecher quaintly put it, "The elect are the whosoever wills and the non-elect are the whosoever won'ts." And it is all according to His purpose. And, my friend, if you have not yet got your mind reconciled to God's purpose and to God's will, it is time you are doing that, because this is His universe. He made it. I don't know why He made a round earth instead of a square one—He didn't ask me how I wanted it—He made it round because *He* wanted it round. My friend, His purpose is going to be carried out, and He has the wisdom and the power to carry it out. Whatever God does is right. Don't you criticize God and say He has no right to save whoever wants to be saved. He has the right to do it. He is just and He is loving, and anything my God does is right.

There was a great theologian in the past by the name of Simeon. In his sermons on Romans 8 he said there were three reasons why he preached on the doctrine of election: It laid the axe at the root of pride, presumption, and despair. I like that. My friend, there is no place for human pride in the doctrine of election. It is God's work, His wisdom, and His purpose that is being carried out. The will of God comes down out of eternity past like a great steamroller. Don't think you can stop it. In fact, you had better get on and ride.

For whom he did foreknow, he also did predestinate to be conformed to the image of his Son, that he might be the firstborn among many brethren.

Moreover whom he did predestinate, them he also called: and whom he called, them he also justified: and whom he justified, them he also glorified [Rom. 8:29–30].

"For" refers back to verse 28 to remind us that he is not talking about anybody being elected to be *lost,* but he is speaking of "the called," the predestined ones. Predestination never has any reference to the lost. You will never find it used in connection with them. If you ever hear someone talk about being predestined to be lost, you know he is not being scriptural.

Predestination means that, when God saves you, He is going to see you through. Whom He foreknew, He predestinated, and whom He predestinated, He called, and whom He called, He justified, and whom He justified, He glorified. In other words, this amazing section is on *sanctification*—yet Paul does not even mention being sanctified. Why? Because sanctification is the work of God in the heart and life of the believer. This is God's eternal purpose. It just simply means this: When the Lord—who is the Great Shepherd of the Sheep, the Good Shepherd of the Sheep, and Chief Shepherd of the Sheep—starts out with one hundred sheep, He's going to come home with one hundred sheep; He will not lose one of them. You may remember that our Lord gave a parable about this, recorded in Luke 15. There was a shepherd, a good shepherd, who represents the Lord Jesus. One little old sheep got lost, got away. You would think He might say, "Well, let him go. We've got ninety-nine of them safe in the fold. That's a good percentage." Anyone raising sheep knows that if you get to market with a little over fifty percent of those that are born, you're doing well. But this is an unusual shepherd. He is not satisfied with ninety-nine. If He justifies one hundred sheep, He's going to glorify one hundred sheep. I'll make this rather personal. Someday He will be counting them in—"One, two, three, four, five . . . ninety-seven, ninety-eight, ninety-nine—where in the world is Vernon McGee? Well, it looks like he didn't make it. We'll let him go because a great many people didn't think he was going to make it anyway." My friend, thank God He won't let him go. That shepherd is going after him. The doctrine of election means that the Lord will be coming home with *one hundred* sheep! This is not a frightful doctrine; it is a wonderful doctrine. It means that Vernon McGee's going to be there; and it means you are going to be there, my friend, if you have trusted Christ. This is a most comforting doctrine in these uncertain days in which we live.

What shall we then say to these things? If God be for us, who can be against us? [Rom. 8:31].

"What shall we then say to these things?" My answer is, "What can I say? This is so wonderful I have nothing to add!"

"Who can be against us?" God is on our side. Nobody will be able to bring a charge against us in His presence.

He that spared not his own Son, but delivered him up for us all, how shall he not with him also freely give us all things? [Rom. 8:32].

How wonderful that is! He did not spare His Son. He spared Abraham's son, but not His own. Since He gave His Son to die for us, He will give us all things that we need. Somebody may say, "But I may not be able to hold out." He is going to do that for you—He will *hold you*. His sheep are safe, my friend. It is not because they are smart sheep. A rancher in San Angelo, Texas, who raises sheep, told me, "Sheep are stupid!" Also they are defenseless. They don't have sharp claws or fangs to protect themselves. They can't even run very fast. They are little old helpless animals. If a little old sheep stands up and sings, "Safe am I," is that sheep safe? Yes. Smart sheep? No, stupid. That little sheep is safe because he has a wonderful Shepherd.

"How shall he not with him also freely give us all things?" Dwight L. Moody illustrated it somewhat like this: Suppose I go into the finest jewelry store in the land, and they bring out the loveliest diamond, and the owner says, "It's yours!" And I say, "You don't mean that you are giving me this valuable diamond!" He says, "Yes. I am giving it to you." If he gave it to me, do you think I would hesitate asking him for a piece of brown wrapping paper to wrap it up and take it home with me? My friend, since God gave his *Son* to die for you, don't you know that He is going to give you everything that is necessary in this life and in the life to come?

Who shall lay any thing to the charge of God's elect? It is God that justifieth. Who is he that condemneth? It is Christ that died, yea rather, that is risen again, who is even at the right hand of God, who also maketh intercession for us [Rom. 8:33–34].

God's elect are justified sinners. God has placed His throne behind them. Who is going to condemn them? Nobody can condemn them. Why? "It is Christ that died, yea rather, that is risen again."

Christ has removed all condemnation, and the believer is secure because of the fourfold work of Christ: (1) Christ died for us—He was delivered for our offenses; (2) Christ was raised from the dead, raised for our justification; (3) He is on the right hand of God. He is up there right now, my friend. He is the living Christ. Do you need Him? Why don't you appeal to Him? (4) He maketh intercession for us. Did you pray for yourself this morning? You should have. But if you missed praying, He didn't. He prayed for you. How wonderful! This fourfold work of Christ is the reason that nobody can lay anything to the charge of God's elect.

Who shall separate us from the love of Christ? shall tribulation, or distress, or persecution, or famine, or nakedness, or peril, or sword? [Rom. 8:35].

He mentions everything imaginable here.

Is it possible that "tribulation" or trouble can separate us? No, my friend, because He won't let it. "Distress or anguish?" Oh, you may think God has let you down, but He hasn't. "Persecution"—and this means legal persecution. It means there are those who will carry on a campaign against you. But that will not separate you from the love of Christ. "Or famine, or nakedness, or peril, or sword?" By the way, this is a brief biography of Paul's life. He knows from experience that these will not separate you from Christ's love.

As it is written, For thy sake we are killed all the day long; we are accounted as sheep for the slaughter [Rom. 8:36].

This is a quotation from Psalm 44:22: "yea, for thy sake are we killed all the day long; we are counted as sheep for the slaughter." This is a frightful picture of the saints in this day of grace. I believe with all my heart that this is the attitude of a satanic system toward the child of God even in this hour. Also the history of the church reveals this. My friend, if you stand for God today, it will cost you something.

My first job, as a kid about fifteen years old, was in an abatoir, a slaughterhouse. I worked right next to the man who took a sharp knife and cut the sheep's throat. To see animals slaughtered by the hundreds was a frightful spectacle. I got so sick I had to go outside and sit in the fresh air.

And, friend, it is sickening to see what is happening to some of the saints of God in our day. But even this will not separate us from the love of God.

Nay, in all these things we are more than conquerors through him that loved us [Rom. 8:37].

How can a sheep for the slaughter be more than a conqueror? This is another wonderful paradox of the Christian faith. What does it mean to be more than a conqueror? It means to have assistance from Another who gets the victory for us, who never lets us be defeated. The victory belongs to Christ; not to us. The victorious life is not our life. It is His life.

For I am persuaded, that neither death, nor life, nor angels, nor principalities, nor powers, nor things present, nor things to come,

Nor height, nor depth, nor any other creature, shall be able to separate us from the love of God, which is in Christ Jesus our Lord [Rom. 8:38–39].

"For I am persuaded" means that he *knows.*

"Death" cannot separate us—in fact, it will take us into His presence. The response of many of the early Christian martyrs when they were threatened with death was, "Thank you, you will transport me right into the presence of my Savior." You can't hurt people like that.

"Life"—often it is more difficult to face life than to face death. But life's temptations, failures, disappointments, uncertainties, and sufferings will not separate us from the love of God that is in Christ our Lord.

"Angels"—and I think he means fallen angels—"principalities and powers" are spiritual enemies of the believer (see Eph. 6:12).

"Things present" means present circumstances.

"Things to come" refers to the future.

"Nor height, nor depth" may refer to the space age in which we live.

"Any other created thing" would include anything else you want to mention. Absolutely nothing can separate us from the love of God which is centered in Christ.

My friend, salvation is a love story. We love Him because He first loved us. Nothing can separate us from that. We entered this chapter with no condemnation; we conclude it with no separation; and in between all things work together for good. Can you improve on this, friend? This is wonderful!

CHAPTER 9

***THEME:** Israel defined; Israel identified; the choice of Israel is in the sovereign purpose of God; the choice of Gentiles in the scriptural prophecies*

We have now come to the second major division of this epistle. Romans chapters 1–8 is *doctrinal*. Romans chapters 9–11 is *dispensational*. Romans chapters 12–16 is *duty*. The first eight chapters of Romans emphasize *faith*. Chapters 9–11 emphasize *hope*. Chapters 12–16 emphasize *love*. There is another way to view Romans: The first section deals with *salvation;* the second section with *segregation;* and the last section with *service*.

Paul has concluded the first eight chapters of Romans, and he has put salvation on a broad basis, because the entire human race is lost. "For all have sinned, and come short of the glory of God" (Rom. 3:23). God has made salvation available to everyone on one basis alone—faith in the Lord Jesus Christ. Paul is now ready to discuss the second major division.

Some have attempted to dismiss this section by labeling it an appendix. Others minimize its importance by terming it a parenthesis and not actually pertinent. However, it is not only pertinent, it is vital to the logic and doctrine of the epistle.

There is a sense in which chapters 8 and 12 can be joined together as two boxcars. But Paul was not making up a freight train when he wrote Romans. Romans is not a freight train but a flowing stream. Chapters 9–11 can no more be removed than you can take out the middle section of the Mississippi River without causing havoc. Griffith Thomas writes, "The chapters 9-10-11 are an integral part of the epistle and are essential to its true interpretation."

There are certain grand particulars which reveal the significance of this section. They are: The psychological factor; the historical factor; the doctrinal factor.

The psychological factor has to do with the personal experience of the apostle Paul. It is not entirely accurate to state that Romans comes from the head of the apostle and Galatians comes from his heart. The heart of Paul is laid bare in the opening of chapter 9—and in fact, throughout this section. There is a great gap between chapter 8 and chapter 9. Chapter 8 closes on the high plane of triumph and joy in the prospect of no separation from the love of God in Christ Jesus our Lord. Chapter 9 opens on the low plane of despair and sorrow. Obviously a change of subject matter brought about this heartbreak in the apostle. This we shall observe when we consider the text.

The historical factor takes into account the unique position and problem in Paul's day. Modern interpretation has largely failed to take into consideration this factor. The present-day church is for the most part Gentile, and the Jewish background has been all but forgotten. Men assume that the Old Testament promises are merged and dissolved into the church. The arbitrary assumption is that the church is heir to the prophecies of the Old Testament and that God is through with the nation Israel.

Some time ago a Christian organization held a prophetic congress in Jerusalem. It was rather amusing because a meeting that was to be so important ended up as a "tempest in a teapot." Many writers who covered the congress said that the city of Jerusalem did not even know that it was taking place. It is interesting to compare this congress with the Council at Jerusalem in Acts 15 when the whole city was shaken. Half of those present in the congress had no place for the nation Israel in God's plan for the future. They felt that God was through with Israel. If that were true, why did they go to Jerusalem to hold a prophetic congress? They could have gone just as well to Scappoose, Oregon, or Muleshoe, Texas. God is *not* by any means through with Israel, as we shall see. Stifler states this view:

> It has been tacitly assumed in Christian interpretation that Judaism's day is over; that an elect, leveling church built on faith in Christ was the intent of the law and the prophets; and that it was the duty of all Jews to drop their peculiarities and come into the church. Such an assumption the Jews ascribed to Paul. It is strangely forgotten that the mother church in Jerusalem and Judaea never had a Gentile within its fold, that none could have been admitted, and that every member of that primitive body of tens of thousands was zealous of the law (Acts 21:20). They accepted Jesus as the Messiah, but abandoned none of their Old Testament customs and hopes. Christianity has suffered not a little in the continuous at-

tempt to interpret it not from the Jewish, but from the Gentile point of view. The church in Jerusalem, and not the church in Antioch or Ephesus or Rome, furnishes the only sufficient historic outlook (James M. Stifler, *The Epistle To the Romans*, p. 162).

My friend, it is a very narrow view to assume that God is through with the nation Israel. Paul's answer to, "Hath God cast away his people?" is a sharp negative: "God forbid" (Rom. 11:1). He is going to show that the promises that God made to the nation Israel are going to be fulfilled to that nation. Also he will show that God has made certain promises to the church, and today He is calling out an elect people, both Jew and Gentile, to form the church. This is exactly the conclusion to which the Council at Jerusalem came (Acts 15). This is actually the crux of the interpretation of prophecy: "And after they had held their peace, James answered, saying, Men and brethren, hearken unto me: Simeon hath declared how God at the first did visit the Gentiles, to take out of them a people for his name. And to this agree the words of the prophets; as it is written, After this I will return, and will build again the tabernacle of David, which is fallen down; and I will build again the ruins thereof, and I will set it up: That the residue of men might seek after the Lord, and all the Gentiles, upon whom my name is called, saith the Lord, who doeth all these things. Known unto God are his works from the beginning of the world" (Acts 15: 13–18).

James is making it very plain that God is calling out a people to His name. When He concludes this, He will remove the church from the earth and will turn again to Israel. But even at that time, God is not through with Gentiles. We are told that all the saved Gentiles at that time will enter the kingdom with Israel, and God's kingdom will be set up on this earth. This historical factor cannot be ignored.

The doctrinal factor concerns the right dispensational interpretation and the sovereign purposes of God. Paul has traced in the first eight chapters the great subjects of sin, salvation, and sanctification—all the way from grace to glory. In this age, nationality, ritual, and ceremonies have no weight before God. Faith is the *only* item which God accepts from man. Any person, regardless of race or condition, can find mercy. This *does* seem to level out the very distinctions made in the Old Testament. But Paul is going to answer that, and he begins by the rhetorical question: "Hath God cast away his people?" (Rom. 11:1). The answer, of course, is that He has not. Paul began this epistle, you remember, by saying that the gospel is "to the Jew first" (Rom. 1:16), which I think means that chronologically it was given to the Jew first.

Chapter 9–11 is a very important section. It may not deal with Christian doctrine, but it deals with the eschatological, that is, the prophetic, section of the Bible that reveals God is not through with Israel.

Now as we begin chapter 9, notice that this has to do with God's *past* dealings with Israel. In chapter 10 we will see God's *present* dealings with Israel and, in chapter 11, God's *future* dealings with Israel as a nation. God's reason for dealing with the nation in the past did not derive from their exceptional qualities or superior efforts. On the contrary, all of God's actions are found in His own sovereign will. He functions through mercy in His dealings with Israel and all others—with you and me. Luther's statement affords a fitting introduction to this chapter. "Who hath not known passion, cross, and travail of death cannot treat of foreknowledge (election of grace) without injury and inward enmity toward God. Wherefore take heed that thou drink not wine while thou art yet a sucking babe." This is strong medicine we are going to look at here.

ISRAEL DEFINED

I say the truth in Christ, I lie not, my conscience also bearing me witness in the Holy Ghost [Rom. 9:1].

Let me give you my translation of this verse: I speak the truth in Christ, I do not lie, my conscience in the Holy Spirit bearing witness with me.

This seems to be a very formal introduction coming from the apostle Paul, but you must remember that at the time he wrote this he was accused of being an enemy of his own people. We are told in Acts 23:12, "And when it was day, certain of the Jews banded together, and bound themselves under a curse, saying that they would neither eat nor drink till they had killed Paul." Now Paul uses an expression that is a favorite with him: "I tell the truth, I do not lie."

That I have great heaviness and continual sorrow in my heart [Rom. 9:2].

It is impossible for us to appreciate adequately the anguish of this great apostle for his own nation. His patience in the presence of their persistent persecution is an indication of it. He knew how they felt toward Christ and toward Christianity, for he once felt that way himself. He had been a Pharisee, a leader; he longed for them to come to Christ as he had.

For I could wish that myself were accursed from Christ for my brethren, my kinsmen according to the flesh [Rom. 9:3].

I'd like to give you a different translation of this: For I was wishing (but it is not possible) that I myself were accursed (devoted to destruction) from the Christ for the sake of my brethren, my kinsmen according to the flesh.

The verse presents a real problem in translation. If you want a free translation, here it is: For I was once myself accursed from Christ as my brethren, my kinsman according to the flesh.

Frankly, I do not understand Paul at all, if our Authorized Version has translated it accurately. Paul has just said in chapter 8 that nothing can separate us from the love of God, which is in Christ Jesus. Now Paul says, "I wish I were accursed." That is idle wishing, Paul. You can't be accursed—you just told us that. This, then is just an oratorical gesture; you are not sincere when you say a thing like this.

However, the apostle Paul is always sincere. He didn't use oratorical gestures. So I believe he is saying, "For I was once myself accursed from Christ just like my brethren. I know I cannot be accursed, and I want them to come to know Christ and be in my present position." Professor J. A. Bengel said, "It is not easy to estimate the measure of love in a Moses and a Paul." Moses expressed the same sentiment in Exodus 32:31–32, "And Moses returned unto the LORD, and said, Oh, this people have sinned a great sin, and have made them gods of gold. Yet now, if thou wilt forgive their sin—; and if not, blot me, I pray thee, out of thy book which thou hast written."

Who are Israelites; to whom pertaineth the adoption, and the glory, and the covenants, and the giving of the law, and the service of God, and the promises;

Whose are the fathers, and of whom as concerning the flesh Christ came, who is over all, God blessed for ever. Amen [Rom. 9:4–5].

Paul raises the question: Who are Israelites? There are eight things that identify Israelites:

1. *The Adoption.* The adoption was national and pertained to the national entity, not to separate individuals. The *only* nation that God ever called His "son" is the nation Israel: "And thou shalt say unto Pharaoh, Thus saith the LORD, Israel is my son, even my firstborn" (Exod. 4:22). Again in Deuteronomy 7:6 "For thou art an holy people unto the LORD thy God: the LORD thy God hath chosen thee to be a special people unto himself, above all people that are upon the face of the earth." Either God meant this or He did not mean it. And if He didn't mean it, then I don't know why you believe in John 3:16—both promises are in the same Book. I believe John 3:16, and I believe Deuteronomy 7:6. He said "When Israel was a child, then I loved him, and called my son out of Egypt" (Hos. 11:1). God speaks of the nation—not just an individual—the *nation* of Israel as being His son. He never said that of any other people. The *adoption* belongs to Israel.

2. *The Glory.* This was the physical presence of God with them as manifested in the tabernacle and later in the temple. Exodus 40:35 reveals, "And Moses was not able to enter into the tent of the congregation, because the cloud abode thereon, and the glory of the LORD filled the tabernacle." The children of Israel are the only people who have ever had the visible presence of God. There is no visible presence of God today. We need to remember that fact.

Many years ago there was an evangelist who put up a tent in Southern California. He bragged that you could see angels walking on top of the tent and that you could see angels inside the tent. The minute he made a statement like that I knew there was something radically wrong. I also knew there was an explanation, and there was—the man died an alcoholic. I imagine that, after two or three drinks, you could see angels walking on tents, and he probably did. But only Israel truly had the visible presence of God. The church does not have it. Why? Because the Spirit of God indwells every believer, making real the living Christ who is at God's right hand.

3. *The Covenants.* God has made certain covenants with the nation Israel that He intends to carry out. Many of them He has already carried out. He said He would make them a blessing to all people. He said to David that this One would come in his line. All of this has been fulfilled in the Lord Jesus Christ. God made many covenants with Israel—with Abraham, with David, with the nation—which He has not made with any other people. To Israel belong the covenants.

4. *The Law.* The Mosaic Law was given to the nation Israel. "Now therefore, if ye will obey my voice indeed, and keep my covenant, then ye shall be a peculiar treasure unto me above all people: for all the earth is mine" (Exod. 19:5). Then God says in Exodus 31:13, "Speak thou also unto the children of Israel, saying, Verily my sabbaths ye shall keep: for it is a sign between me and you throughout your generations; that ye may know that I am the LORD that doth sanctify you." This is for the nation Israel, you see.

I have been asked, "Why don't you keep the Sabbath day?" I do not keep it because I am not a member of the nation Israel. Others have asked me, "Did God ever change the Sabbath day?" God has not changed the Sabbath, but He has sure changed us. We are in Christ, and that is a new relationship. He gave the Mosaic Law to Israel.

5. *The Service of God.* This had to do with the worship of the tabernacle and temple. They were to be a kingdom of priests. "And ye shall be unto me a kingdom of priests, and an holy nation. These are the words which thou shalt speak unto the children of Israel" (Exod. 19:6). The nation failed God, but God did not give up His purpose that they should be priests. God took the tribe of Levi and gave them the responsibility of serving and caring for the tabernacle and, later on, the temple. In the future, in the millennial kingdom the nation Israel will once again be God's priests upon the earth.

6. *The Promises.* The Old Testament abounds with promises made to these people. God told Joshua, "Moses my servant is dead; now therefore arise, go over this Jordan, thou, and all this people, unto the land which I do give to them, even to the children of Israel" (Josh. 1:2). The children of Israel were to possess the land. I was over there some time ago, but I didn't cross the Jordan because it wasn't safe—probably someone would have shot at me. Several years ago I did cross the Jordan River, but not because God gave a command to Joshua and the people of Israel. I have never felt that any of the land of Palestine belonged to me. The land is beginning to bloom like a rose, but much of that land is still barren. It will be a beautiful land again when the Lord Jesus comes to rule. It has never been my land, and it never will be. The land of Palestine was given strictly to the Jews.

7. *The Fathers.* This refers primarily to Abraham, Isaac, and Jacob.

8. *Christ the Messiah.* He came according to the flesh. When He came to this earth, He was a Jew. The woman at the well called Him a *Jew* (see John 4:9). Paul is careful to say that we know Him no longer after the flesh: "Wherefore henceforth know we no man after the flesh: yea, though we have known Christ after the flesh, yet now henceforth know we him no more" (2 Cor. 5:16). Paul identifies Jesus as God, and to Paul He is the God-Man. John 1:14 tells us, "And the Word was made flesh, and dwelt among us, (and we beheld his glory, the glory as of the only begotten of the Father,) full of grace and truth." Christ came as a human babe to the nation Israel. The woman at the well identified Him as a Jew, and I think she was in a better position to say who He was than some scholar in New York City sitting in a swivel chair in a musty library.

Perhaps "Christ the Messiah" should be separated from the other seven features because it is greater than all the others. "For verily he took not on him the nature of angels; but he took on him the seed of Abraham" (Heb. 2:16).

ISRAEL IDENTIFIED

The Israel of another time period has already been defined. Now let us identify them in Paul's day and in our day also.

Not as though the word of God hath taken none effect. For they are not all Israel, which are of Israel [Rom. 9:6].

This is a strange expression. In other words, not all the offspring, the natural offspring of Israel, are the real Israel. The Jew in Paul's day raised the question as to why the Jew had not wholeheartedly accepted Christ since theirs was an elect nation. Is not this failure on God's part? Paul partially dealt with this problem at the beginning of Romans 3. Now Paul is going to make a distinction between the natural offspring of Jacob and the spiritual offspring. Always there has been a remnant, and that remnant, whether natural or not natural, has been a spiritual offspring. This is a distinction within the nation Israel, and he is not including Gentiles here at all. The failure was not God's; but the people had failed. God's promises were unconditional.

Neither, because they are the seed of Abraham, are they all children: but, In Isaac shall thy seed be called [Rom. 9:7].

This verse is a devastating blow to the argument of those who were attempting to stand against Paul. If the "seed" were reckoned on natural birth alone, then the Ishmaelites,

Midianites, and Edomites would be included. A fine Arab man in Jericho said to me several years ago, "I want you to know that I am a son of Abraham." I could not argue against that. He *was* a son of Abraham. These others were all the physical offspring of Abraham. To be the natural offspring of Abraham was no assurance that a person was a child of promise.

You will recall what the Jews said to the Lord Jesus on one occasion, ". . . Abraham is our father. Jesus said unto them, If ye were Abraham's children, ye would do the works of Abraham." Then the Lord continued saying, "Ye are of your father the devil, and the lusts of your father ye will do. He was a murderer from the beginning, and abode not in the truth, because there is no truth in him. When he speaketh a lie, he speaketh of his own: for he is a lair, and the father of it" (John 8:39, 44).

That is, They which are the children of the flesh, these are not the children of God: but the children of the promise are counted for the seed [Rom. 9:8].

The apostle Paul makes a clear distinction between the elect and the nonelect in the nation Israel. "The children of the flesh" are not the children of God. "The children of the *promise*" are the ones counted for the seed. In Acts 21:20 Dr. Luke tells us, "And when they heard it, they glorified the Lord, and said unto him, Thou seest, brother, how many thousands of Jews there are which believe; and they are all zealous of the law." There were in Israel *thousands* of Jews who turned to Christ after His death and resurrection. They were the *elect*, and Paul always called them "Israel." When we come to the Book of the Revelation where our Lord was speaking to the churches (the turn of the first century), He says to them in effect, "They do not even belong to a synagogue that worships Me any longer; it is a synagogue that worships Satan" (see Rev. 2:9; 3:9).

For this is the word of promise, At this time will I come, and Sarah shall have a son [Rom. 9:9].

The children of the promise are not those who believed something—Isaac did not *believe* before he was born! Isaac was the promised seed. God promised, and God made good.

Now we are coming to some strong statements.

And not only this; but when Rebecca also had conceived by one, even by our father Isaac [Rom. 9:10].

Isaac and Rebecca are likewise given as an illustration of this principle of the divine election.

(For the children being not yet born, neither having done any good or evil, that the purpose of God according to election might stand, not of works, but of him that calleth;) [Rom. 9:11].

Although this verse is in parentheses, its truth is of supreme importance. Some explanation may be offered for God's rejection of Ishmael, but that is not possible in the case of Isaac and Rebecca's children—those boys were twins! God rejected the line of primogeniture, that is, of the first born, and chose the younger son. At that time Jacob had done no good, and Esau had done no evil. It does not rest upon birth—that was identical—and it does not rest upon their character or their works. Paul makes the entire choice rest upon "the *purpose* of *God* according to election." He further qualifies his statement that it is not of works, but rests upon God who calls. However, the calling in this verse is not to salvation.

It was said unto her, The elder shall serve the younger [Rom. 9:12].

This is a quotation from Genesis 25:23, which was given before the two boys were born. "And the LORD said unto her, Two nations are in thy womb, and two manner of people shall be separated from thy bowels; and the one people shall be stronger than the other people; and the elder shall serve the younger."

As it is written, Jacob have I loved, but Esau have I hated [Rom. 9:13].

This is a quotation from the last book in the Old Testament (see Mal. 1:2–3). This statement was not made until the two boys had lived their lives and two nations had come from them, which was about two thousand years later, and much history had been made. A student once said to Dr. Griffith Thomas that he was having trouble with this passage because he could not understand why God hated Esau. Dr. Thomas answered, "I am having a problem with that passage too, but mine is different. I do not understand why God *loved* Jacob." That is the big problem. It is easy to see why God rejected Esau, friend. He was a rascal; he was a godless fellow, filled with pride, and from him came a nation that wanted to live without God and turned their backs upon Him. I can understand why God rejected Esau, but not why He chose Jacob.

The Bible tells us that He made His choice according to His sovereign will.

THE CHOICE OF ISRAEL IS IN THE SOVEREIGN PURPOSE OF GOD

What shall we say then? Is there unrighteousness with God? God forbid [Rom. 9:14].

What will we say to this? Is there injustice with God? Perish the thought! Let it not be. The answer is a resounding *no*!

The natural man rebels against the sovereignty of God. If anything is left to God to make the choice, man immediately concludes that there is injustice. Why is that?

There are people today who have applauded some of the presidents we have had during the 1960s and 1970s. Apparently—I don't know if we will ever get the truth—there have been bad judgments made during their terms in office, and as a result thousands of our boys have died. Yet one of those men received more votes than any man who has run for president. The remarkable thing is that we often do not question the judgments of men, but we do question the judgments of God.

My friend, although we cannot intrude into the mysterious dealings of God, we can trust Him to act in justice. We cannot avoid the doctrine of election, nor can we reconcile God's sovereign election with man's free will. Both are true. Let's keep in mind that this is His universe. He is sovereign. I am but a little creature on earth, and He could take away the breath from me in the next moment. Do I have the audacity to stand on my two feet, look Him in the face, and question what He does? That would be rebellion of the worst sort. I bow to my Creator and my Redeemer, knowing that whatever choice He makes is right. By the way, if you do not like what He does, perhaps you should move out of His universe and start one of your own so you can make your own rules. But as long as you live in God's universe, you will have to play according to His rules. Little man needs to bow his stiff neck and stubborn knees before Almighty God and say, "There is no unrighteousness with Thee" (see John 7:18).

For he saith to Moses, I will have mercy on whom I will have mercy, and I will have compassion on whom I will have compassion [Rom. 9:15].

Moses, you recall, wanted to see the glory of God. God said in effect, "I'll show it to you Moses, but I'll not show it to you because you are Moses." Now, Moses was a very important person. He was leading the children of Israel through the wilderness. God says, "I will have compassion on whom I will have compassion. I will do this for you, not because you are Moses, but because I am God!" Do you know why God saved me? It was not because I am Vernon McGee but because He is God. He made the choice, and I bow before Him.

So then it is not of him that willeth, nor of him that runneth, but of God that sheweth mercy [Rom. 9:16].

God's mercy is not extended as a recognition of human will, nor is it a reward of human work. Human-willing and human-working are not motivating causes of God's actions. Man thinks that his decision and his effort cause God to look with favor upon him. Stifler states it succinctly when he says, "Willing and running may indicate the possession of grace, but they are not the originating cause" (*The Epistle to the Romans*, p. 172). God extends mercy, and He does it because he is *God*, my friend. Who are we to question Him? I bow before Him today.

For the scripture saith unto Pharaoh, Even for this same purpose have I raised thee up, that I might shew my power in thee, and that my name might be declared throughout all the earth.

Therefore hath he mercy on whom he will have mercy, and whom he will he hardeneth [Rom. 9:17–18].

God says that He used Pharaoh. "But," you may say, "he was not elected." No, he sure wasn't. Just think of the opportunities God gave him. Pharaoh would have said, "I am Pharaoh. I make the decisions around here. I reject the request to let the people of Israel go." God says, "You may think you won't, but you are going to let them go." God's will prevails. When the Scriptures say that God hardened Pharaoh's heart, it means that God forced Pharaoh to make the decision that was in his heart. God forced him to do the thing he wanted to do. There never will be a person in hell who did not choose to be there, my friend. You are the one who makes your own decision.

Thou wilt say then unto me, Why doth he yet find fault? For who hath resisted his will? [Rom. 9:19].

This is the reasoning of the natural man: If God hardened the heart of Pharaoh, why should He find fault with Pharaoh? Wasn't he accomplishing God's purpose?

Nay but, O man, who art thou that repliest against God? Shall the thing formed say to him that formed it, Why hast thou made me thus? [Rom. 9:20].

Human reasoning is not the answer to the problem. The answer is found only in the mystery and majesty of God's sovereignty. Faith leaves it there and accepts it in humble obedience. Unbelief rebels against it and continues on under the very wrath and judgment of the God it questions.

Johann Peter Lange has well stated it: "When man goes the length of making himself a god whom he affects to bind by his own rights, God then puts on His majesty, and appears in all His reality as a free God, before whom man is nothing, like the clay in the hand of the potter. Such was Paul's attitude when acting as God's advocate in his suit with Jewish Pharisaism. This is the reason why he expresses only *one side* of the truth."

You cannot put one little star in motion;
You cannot shape one single forest leaf,
Nor fling a mountain up, nor sink an ocean,
Presumptuous pigmy, large with unbelief!
You cannot bring one down of regal splendor,
Nor bid the day to shadowy twilight fall,
Nor send the pale moon forth with radiance tender;
And dare you doubt the One who has done it all?

—Sherman A. Nagel, Sr.

The important thing is that God is *God*, and little man won't change that.

In the next few verses Paul uses the illustration of the potter and the clay. God is the Potter and we are clay. God took man out of the dust of the earth and formed him. He didn't start with a monkey—man made a monkey of himself, but God didn't make him like that. God took man from the dust of the ground. The psalmist says, ". . . he remembereth that we are dust" (Ps. 103:14). We forget this sometimes. As some wag has said, when dust gets stuck on itself, it is mud. Abraham took his correct position before God when he said, ". . . Behold now, I have taken upon me to speak unto the Lord, which am but dust and ashes" (Gen. 18:27).

Hath not the potter power over the clay, of the same lump to make one vessel unto honour, and another unto dishonour? [Rom. 9:21].

God reaches into the same lump of humanity and takes out some clay to form Moses. Again, He reaches in and takes out of the same lump the clay to make Pharaoh. It was all ugly, unlovely, sightless, and sinful clay at the beginning. His mercy makes a vessel "unto honour"; that is, a vessel for honorable use. It is the Potter's right to make another vessel for "dishonour" or common use.

What if God, willing to shew his wrath, and to make his power known, endured with much longsuffering the vessels of wrath fitted to destruction.

And that he might make known the riches of his glory on the vessels of mercy, which he had afore prepared unto glory,

Even us, whom he hath called, not of the Jews only, but also of the Gentiles? [Rom. 9:22–24].

Paul has already established the fact that God is free to act in the mystery and majesty of His sovereignty. Now Paul shows that God deals in patience and mercy even with the vessels of wrath. God did not fit them for destruction; the rebellion and sin of the clay made them ripe for judgment. God would have been right in exercising immediate judgment, but He dealt with these vessels, not as lifeless clay, but as creatures with a free will. He gave them ample opportunity to reveal any inclination they might have of obeying God. Although God hates sin and must judge it in a most final manner, His mercy is constantly going out to the creatures involved.

God suggests that the "vessels of wrath" are the Jewish nation, which was destroyed in A.D. 70. Jesus, you recall, announced this destruction, but He wept over the city, and He prayed, ". . . Father, forgive them . . ." (Luke 23:34). When the final judgment came in A.D. 70, God saved a remnant. These were "vessels of mercy."

THE CHOICE OF GENTILES IN THE SCRIPTURAL PROPHECIES

This is the final division of the chapter. Paul has made it very clear that the nation Israel was chosen by the sovereign will of God, not because of their merit. God not only chose a nation and not only saved those in that nation who turned to Him—and it's a remnant always—but among the Gentiles He is calling out a people today to His name.

As he saith also in Osee, I will call them my people, which were not my people; and her beloved, which was not beloved.

And it shall come to pass, that in the place where it was said unto them, Ye are not my people; there shall they be called the children of the living God [Rom. 9:25–26].

"Osee" is the Greek name of the prophet Hosea. This is a quotation from Hosea 2:23, and it refers to the nation Israel. Peter refers this prophecy to the believing remnant in his day which perpetuated the nation. To his people who had turned to Christ, he says, "But ye are a chosen generation, a royal priesthood, an holy nation, a peculiar people; that ye should shew forth the praises of him who hath called you out of darkness into his marvellous light: Which in time past were not a people, but are now the people of God: which had not obtained mercy, but now have obtained mercy" (1 Pet. 2:9–10).

The second prophecy (v. 26) is from Hosea 1:10 and refers to Gentiles anyplace on the earth who turn to Christ now and in the future. As James put it: "That the residue of men might seek after the Lord, and all the Gentiles, upon whom my name is called, saith the Lord, who doeth all these things" (Acts 15:17).

And so God reached into Europe. He did not send the gospel into Europe because the people there were superior. Some members of the white race seem to think that they are superior people. They are not. The Chinese were way ahead of my ancestors in Paul's day. My ancestors—and perhaps yours—were there in the forests of Europe. A branch of my family was over in Scotland. I am told they were the dirtiest, filthiest savages who have ever been on this earth. Do you think God carried the gospel to them because they were superior? They were anything but that. "It is not of him that willeth, nor of him that runneth, but of God that sheweth mercy" (v. 16). I thank Him for that—how wonderful it is!

Esaias also crieth concerning Israel, Though the number of the children of Israel be as the sand of the sea, a remnant shall be saved:

For he will finish the work, and cut it short in righteousness: because a short work will the Lord make upon the earth [Rom. 9:27–28].

A literal translation would be: Isaiah also cried in anguish over Israel, if the number of the sons of Israel be as the sand of the sea, the remnant only shall be saved; for He [the Lord] will execute His word upon the earth, finishing and cutting it short in righteousness.

The quotation Paul uses is from Isaiah 10:22–23. Only a remnant of Israel will be saved in the Great Tribulation Period. If you want to see the percentage, there are approximately fifteen million Jews today. In the Great Tribulation Period we know that only 144,000 Jews will be sealed—that is a small ratio. While I do believe others will be saved during that period, 144,000 will be His witnesses, and a small remnant will be saved. It has always been only a remnant with them, and it is only a remnant with Gentiles. Now don't ask me why—it is God that shows mercy. If He saved only *one*, it would reveal the mercy of God, because none of us deserve His mercy.

And as Esaias said before, Except the Lord of Sabaoth had left us a seed, we had been as Sodoma, and been made like unto Gomorrha [Rom. 9:29].

In this verse Paul is quoting from Isaiah 1:9. This is a startling statement, but it is a fitting climax to the sovereignty of God. Even the elect nation would have been like Sodom and Gomorrah in depravity and rebellion to God if He had not intervened in sovereign mercy and recovered a remnant. What an indictment of proud Pharisaism and proud church membership today! Only God's *mercy* keeps any of us from going to hell, my beloved.

What shall we say then? That the Gentiles, which followed not after righteousness, have attained to righteousness, even the righteousness which is of faith [Rom. 9:30].

This is a thrilling statement. Gentiles, without willing or working, found righteousness in Christ because *God* worked and *God* willed it. The Old Testament Scriptures had prophesied it. As we have seen, Isaiah had said that Gentiles were to be saved.

But Israel, which followed after the law of righteousness, hath not attained to the law of righteousness [Rom. 9:31].

In other words, Israel, pursuing after a law which should give righteousness, did not arrive at such a law. This is a terrifying statement. The Jews tried to produce a righteousness of their own through the Mosaic system. They didn't produce it—look at the nation today. Religious people are the most difficult people to reach with the gospel—church members, who think they are good enough to be saved.

You will never be able to reconcile the sovereignty of God and the responsibility of man. But Paul is making it very clear here that if you are going to be saved it is *your* responsibility. It is "whosoever will may come" (see Mark 8:34) and ". . . him that cometh to me I will in no wise cast out" (John 6:37). You can come; don't stand on the sidelines and say, "I'm not elected." But I have never heard of anybody being elected who didn't run for office. If you *want* to be saved, you are the elect. If you don't, you're not. And that is all I know about it. I cannot reconcile election and free will. I have come to the place in the sunset of my life that I can say that God is sovereign, and He is going to do this according to His will. And His will is right—there is no unrighteousness with Him. He won't make a mistake. Men make mistakes; men in government make mistakes, yet people believe in them. My friend, why don't you believe in God? He is righteous, He is good, and whatever He does it right.

Wherefore? Because they sought it not by faith, but as it were by the works of the law. For they stumbled at that stumblingstone;

As it is written, Behold, I lay in Sion a stumblingstone and rock of offence: and whosoever believeth on him shall not be ashamed [Rom. 9:32–33].

The quotation here is from both Isaiah 8:14 and Isaiah 28:16. The Jews stumbled. To the Gentile the cross is foolishness. The one who believes, either Jew or Gentile, will be saved. The humble mind will come in simple faith. The natural man will still try to produce salvation by some natural process. He will try to reconcile the sovereignty of God and the responsibility of man as if the puny mind of man is capable and infallible.

CHAPTER 10

***THEME:** Present state of Israel; present standing of Israel; present salvation for both Jew and Gentile*

We have seen the present state of Israel; they are lost. And that is their condition today. They are lost just as the Gentiles are lost. The reason is that Christ is the end of the law of righteousness.

Now Paul turns from the sovereignty of God to the responsibility of man. He began this thought in the concluding verses of chapter 9.

PRESENT STATE OF ISRAEL

Brethren, my heart's desire and prayer to God for Israel is, that they might be saved [Rom. 10:1].

They are responsible, you see; they are responsible to God. Our Lord has said to them, "For the days shall come upon thee, that thine enemies shall cast a trench about thee, and compass thee round, and keep thee in on every side, And shall lay thee even with the ground, and thy children within thee; and they shall not leave in thee one stone upon another; because thou knewest not the time of thy visitation" (Luke 19:43–44). That is the condition of the nation over there today. They are surrounded by nations that want to push them into the sea. Why? You can blame the Arab, you can blame Russia, you can blame everybody. You can blame God if you want to, because He says the reason they are in such a state—unable to have peace—is that they did not recognize their time of visitation. So Paul says, "My heart's desire and prayer to God for Israel is, that they might be saved." Now notice the three great features in His statement:

1. Israel, with all they possessed (see Rom. 9:4–5) of religion, were not saved. May I say that probably 75 percent of church members are not saved. They are just members of a religious club. They are in rebellion against God in that they will not accept the righteousness God offers in Christ. You can be religious and *lost.* Israel had a God-given religion, but they needed to be saved. They had religion but not righteousness. They had more than any other nation, but they were lost. Paul's desire was that Israel might be saved.

2. Israel was savable. Bengel says, "Paul would not have prayed had they been altogether reprobate." They were savable. Who would have thought that my ancestors in the forests of Germany were savable? They were as heathen as anyone could possibly be. Yet at that time the Chinese had a civilization. Why didn't the missionaries go in that direction? Why didn't the apostles say, "Let's not bother with those pagan Gentiles; they are not even savable"? Pagan Gentiles were savable, and the Jews were savable also.

3. They are on the same plane before God today as Gentiles and should be evangelized as any other people without Christ. There is no difference today. "For all have sinned, and come short of the glory of God" (Rom. 3:23). The idea of a superior race or an inferior race is ridiculous. The ground at the foot of the cross is all level. Whoever you are, your social position, your church membership, your good works, or the color of your skin will not help you. Without Christ you are a hell-doomed sinner. God is just and righteous when He says that to you. Perhaps you say, "I don't like what that preacher said." Well, it is actually what God said, my friend. God is putting it in neon lights here. He doesn't want you to miss it.

There are those today who believe that the gospel ought to go to Israel first. I think Paul meant that chronologically it went to the Jew first. For the first few years in the city of Jerusalem and in all Israel there was not a Gentile saved. The church was 100 percent Jewish. Although I do not believe we are told to evangelize the Jew first in our day, I certainly do believe that the Jew should not be left out. He is in the plan and purpose of God, and he should have the gospel. I disagree with a man like the late Dr. Reinhold Niebuhr, a recent liberal theologian, who is reported to have said (by *Time* magazine in 1958), "Do not try to convert Jews . . . Jews may find God more readily in their own faith than in Christianity." He maintains this viewpoint, so he says, "especially because of the guilt they are likely to feel if they become Christians." However, coming to Christ is the way to get rid of guilt. They should have the gospel—all people should have it. God is prepared to show mercy today.

For I bear them record that they have a zeal of God, but not according to knowledge [Rom. 10:2].

I know some churches, friend, where the members are as busy as termites. On Monday night they play basketball. On Tuesday night it is football. On Wednesday night it is volleyball. On Thursday night it is baseball. On Friday night they just "have a ball." They have something going on every night. They have a "zeal of God"—they like to do it all in the name of Jesus. But all they have is religion. My friend, do you have Christ? Have you accepted the righteousness that God offers in Christ Jesus? You cannot be saved on any other basis. You have to be *perfect* to go to heaven, and I have news for you: you are not perfect. Neither am I perfect. But I am going to heaven because Jesus died for me, was buried, and rose again from the dead. He was delivered for my offenses and was raised for my justification. He is my righteousness. I will go to heaven one day because He took my place. Is Jesus Christ your Savior? Forget your church membership for awhile. I do not mean to minimize your membership, but do not trust it for salvation. The average church today is as dead as a dodo bird. A fellow said to me some time ago concerning the church, "I would just as soon go out and play golf on Sunday." Knowing the church he attended, I understood how he felt. In fact, I believe he could be more spiritual out on the golf course than he could be in a service in that church. The point is that he should find a church that is really preaching *Christ*. Oh, how wonderful He is! How important it is to have a *personal* relationship to Him.

For they being ignorant of God's righteousness, and going about to establish their own righteousness, have not submitted themselves unto the righteousness of God [Rom. 10:3].

This was true of Israel, and it is true of the average church member today. Dr. Griffith Thomas commented on this lack of discernment. "Is it not marvellous that people can read the Bible and all the time fail to see its essential teaching and its personal application to themselves? There is scarcely anything more surprising and saddening than the presence of intellectual knowledge of God's Word with an utter failure to appreciate its spiritual meaning and force." I have seen men, officers of the church, who carry such big Bibles under their arms that they leaned in that direction when they walked down the street. I watched them for twenty-one years and saw no spiritual growth. They just did not grow. They had no discernment whatsoever. So many church people have no real discernment of what it really means to be saved.

For Christ is the end of the law for righteousness to every one that believeth [Rom. 10:4].

"Christ is the end of the law" means He is the *goal*. Our Lord made it clear. He said in effect, "I didn't come to patch up an old garment; I came to give you a new garment—the robe of My righteousness" (see Matt. 9:16). The Mosaic Law was given to lead men to Christ; it wasn't given to save men. Paul said to the Galatian believers that ". . . the law was our schoolmaster to bring us unto Christ, that we might be justified by faith" (Gal. 3:24). The Law was not given to save us, but to show us that we needed to be saved. It takes us by the hand, brings us to the cross of Christ, and says, "Little fellow, you need a Savior." The Law came to an end in Christ. "Christ is become of no effect unto you, whosoever of you are justified by the law; ye are fallen from grace" (Gal. 5:4). William R. Newell (*Romans Verse by Verse*, p. 393) made the statement: "The Law is no more a rule of life than it is a means of righteousness." It is for *everyone* that *believes*, which suggests both the freeness and universality of salvation. "Every one"—universal. "Believeth"—oh, the freeness of it! Why don't you accept it?

PRESENT STANDING OF ISRAEL

For Moses describeth the righteousness which is of the law, That the man which doeth those things shall live by them [Rom. 10:5].

Granted that you could attain a righteousness in the law, it would be your *own* righteousness, not God's righteousness. It could never measure up to His.

But the righteousness which is of faith speaketh on this wise, Say not in thine heart, Who shall ascend into heaven? (that is, to bring Christ down from above:) [Rom. 10:6].

He talks about ascending up to heaven to bring it down, or going down to hell and bringing it up. My friend, the righteousness that Paul is talking about—he quotes from Deuteronomy 30:11–14—is *available*!

Or, Who shall descend into the deep? (that is, to bring up Christ again from the dead.) [Rom. 10:7].

You don't have to make a trip anywhere to get it.

But what saith it? The word is nigh thee, even in thy mouth, and in thy heart: that is, the word of faith, which we preach [Rom. 10:8].

It is available right where you are sitting. A great many folk think they have to go to an altar in some sort of meeting to be saved. But salvation is available to you right where you are now.

That if thou shalt confess with thy mouth the Lord Jesus, and shalt believe in thine heart that God hath raised him from the dead, thou shalt be saved.

For with the heart man believeth unto righteousness; and with the mouth confession is made unto salvation [Rom. 10:9–10].

There are many folk who maintain that a believer has to make a public confession of faith. That is not what Paul is saying here. It does not mean to go forward in a public meeting. In the church I served for twenty-one years I saw many people come forward, but they were not all saved. Paul is not saying that you have to make a public confession.

Paul is saying that man needs to bring into agreement his confession and his life. The mouth and the heart should be in harmony, saying the same thing. It is with the heart that you believe. Your "heart" means your total personality, your entire being. You see, there are some folk who say something with their mouths—they give lip service to God—but their hearts are far from Him. When you make a public confession, you be dead sure that your heart is right along with you; that you are not just saying idle words that mean nothing to you personally. If there is confession without faith, it is due either to self-deception or to hypocrisy. If there is faith without confession, it may be cowardice. It seems to me that Paul is saying here that James is accurate, ". . . faith without works is dead" (James 2:20). If you are going to work your mouth, be sure you have faith in your heart, my friend.

"Believe in thine heart that God hath raised him from the dead" means that the resurrection of Christ is the heart of the gospel. As Paul said earlier, He "was delivered for our offences, and was raised again for our justification" (Rom. 4:25).

For the scripture saith, Whosoever believeth on him shall not be ashamed [Rom. 10:11].

Paul is quoting from Isaiah 28:16: "Therefore thus saith the Lord GOD, Behold, I lay in Zion for a foundation a stone, a tried stone, a precious corner stone, a sure foundation: he that believeth shall not make haste." The difference in our translation is not due to Paul's changing the quotation. Rather, the word for *confound* and *make haste* is the same. It means to flee because of fear. Paul is quoting Isaiah to enforce his previous statement that the "by faith righteousness" is taught in other passages of the Old Testament. This passage also shows the universal character of salvation in the word *whosoever*.

For there is no difference between the Jew and the Greek: for the same Lord over all is rich unto all that call upon him [Rom. 10:12].

There is no distinction between the Jew and the Greek (or Gentile)—all have sinned and come short of the glory of God. All, if they are to be saved, must come the same way to Christ. The Lord Jesus said, ". . . no man cometh unto the Father, but by me" (John 14:6). You can't come to Him by the Old Testament ritual or by the Mosaic Law. Salvation is offered to all people on the same basis of mercy—by faith. Hear and believe the gospel.

PRESENT SALVATION FOR BOTH JEW AND GENTILE

For whosoever shall call upon the name of the Lord shall be saved [Rom. 10:13].

This is a remarkable statement, which Paul draws from the Old Testament (see Joel 2:32), to enforce his argument that salvation is by faith. This makes it very clear that both Jew and Gentile are to call on the Lord. To "call upon the name of the Lord" means to believe in the Lord Jesus Christ.

How then shall they call on him in whom they have not believed? and how shall they believe in him of whom they have not heard? and how shall they hear without a preacher?

And how shall they preach, except they be sent? as it is written, How beautiful are the feet of them that preach the gospel of peace, and bring glad tidings of good things! [Rom. 10:14–15].

It is necessary to understand Paul's position in order to appreciate these verses. The Jews, his own people, hated the apostle Paul even though they applauded Saul, the Pharisee. He is showing the logic of his position. They rejected his claim, or the right of any of the apostles, to proclaim a gospel that omitted the Mosaic system which had degenerated into Pharisaism.

Paul shows that there must be messengers of the gospel who have credentials from God. Paul, you recall, began this epistle with the claim that he was a called apostle of Jesus Christ (see Rom. 1:1). There follows a logical sequence. Preachers must be sent in order for people to hear that they might believe, for they would not know how to call upon God. Paul pinpoints all on *believing*. This, therefore, necessitated his ministry.

Paul clinches this bit of logic with a quotation from Isaiah 52:7 which says: "How beautiful upon the mountains are the feet of him that bringeth good tidings, that publisheth peace; that bringeth good tidings of good, that publisheth salvation; that saith unto Zion, Thy God reigneth!" This quotation precedes the marvelous fifty-third chapter of Isaiah, which is a prophecy of Christ's death and resurrection. He opened it with the prophet's query, ". . . Who hath believed our report? . . ." (Isa. 53:1). The law of Moses surely was not glad tidings of good things, but it was a ministration of death.

We are told here that the feet of those who bear glad tidings are beautiful. I believe that my radio program is important, and I am giving the rest of my life to it. I feel it is important to get God's Word out to needy people. One day I was making tapes for the program in my bare feet. I looked at them and concluded that they are not beautiful. There is nothing about feet that causes them to be an object of beauty. But God calls beautiful the feet of His called-ones and His sent-messengers—beautiful. Johann Peter Lange has an appropriate word on this: "In their running and hastening, in their scaling obstructing mountains, they are the symbols of the earnestly-desired, winged movement and appearance of the Gospel itself." That is one of the reasons I love the opportunity provided by radio today. We can scale mountains, go over the plains, reach over the vast expanses of water, and go into the inner recesses of the earth with the gospel. We can go into homes, automobiles, and places of business. We have been even in barrooms with the gospel by radio. It is wonderful to get out the Word of God. It is wonderful to have feet that the Lord calls beautiful!

But they have not all obeyed the gospel. For Esaias saith, Lord, who hath believed our report? [Rom. 10:16].

While we are amazed at the great number of

folk who tell us that they have received Christ because of our ministry, when we look at the total picture, it is a very small minority. Who *has* believed our report? Not very many.

So then faith cometh by hearing, and hearing by the word of God [Rom. 10:17].

Oh, this is so important! Faith does not come by preaching philosophy or psychology or some political nostrum; it comes by preaching the *Word of God*. Until you hear the Word of God, you cannot be saved, my friend.

But I say, Have they not heard? Yes verily, their sound went into all the earth, and their words unto the ends of the world [Rom. 10:18].

While I am not saying that Paul has reference to radio, it certainly applies to radio broadcasting. Radio is a marvelous way of getting God's Word to the ends of the world.

But I say, Did not Israel know? First Moses saith, I will provoke you to jealousy by them that are no people, and by a foolish nation I will anger you [Rom. 10:19].

Paul is quoting from Deuteronomy 32:21. Today God is calling out a people from among Gentiles. Paul will develop this thought in the next chapter.

But Esaias is very bold, and saith, I was found of them that sought me not; I was made manifest unto them that asked not after me [Rom. 10:20].

Paul quotes from Isaiah 65:1: "I am sought of them that asked not for me; I am found of them that sought me not: I said, Behold me, behold me, unto a nation that was not called by my name." Even Isaiah predicted gentile salvation. The Gentiles in darkness were finding Christ. What excuse could Israel who had the Old Testament Scriptures offer? They are entirely without excuse.

But to Israel he saith, All day long I have stretched forth my hands unto a disobedient and gainsaying people [Rom. 10:21].

Have you ever stopped to think how tiresome it is to hold your hands out for a long period of time? Try it sometime and see how long you can do it. It is one of the most tiring things in the world. When Moses held up his hands in prayer to God for Israel's victory in battle, Aaron and Hur had to prop up his hands because he got so tired holding them up (see Exod. 17:9–12). But God says, "I have been holding out My hands to a disobedient people" (see Isa. 65:2). No one knows how gracious God has been to the nation Israel.

Stephen's final word to this nation is revealing: "Ye stiffnecked and uncircumcised in heart and ears, ye do always resist the Holy Ghost: as your fathers did, so do ye. Which of the prophets have not your fathers persecuted? and they have slain them which shewed before of the coming of the Just One; of whom ye have been now the betrayers and murderers: Who have received the law by the disposition of angels, and have not kept it" (Acts 7:51–53). This is not confined to Israel. It could be said today that God is holding out His hands to a gainsaying world. I marvel at the patience of God. I do not mean to be irreverant, but if I were running the show on this little earth down here, I would make a lot of changes. I would move in like a bulldozer! But God is just holding out His hands to our gainsaying world.

CHAPTER 11

***THEME:** Remnant of Israel finding salvation; remainder of Israel blinded; reason for setting aside the nation Israel; restoration of the nation Israel*

We will see that God has a future purpose with Israel. In chapter 9 we saw God's *past* dealings with Israel. In chapter 10 we saw God's *present* dealings with Israel: a remnant of Israel is finding salvation. Perhaps you are saying, "Well, it must be a very small remnant." It is larger than you might think it is. It is estimated that there are about fifteen million Jews throughout the world, and the percentage of those who are believers is probably much higher than that of the gentile world with its four billion people.

We have seen that the nation rejected Christ and the "by faith" righteousness of God in Christ which was offered to them. And now God has rejected them temporarily as a nation. Two questions naturally arise: Has God permanently rejected them as a nation? In other words, does the nation of Israel have a future? Secondly, are all the promises of the Old Testament nullified by the rejection of Israel? Remember that God had promised primacy to Israel in the Old Testament. He had said they would be the head, not the tail, of the nations (see Deut. 28:13). My friend, all the promises of the Old Testament will have a literal fulfillment. Paul will make that clear.

REMNANT OF ISRAEL FINDING SALVATION

I say then, Hath God cast away his people? God forbid. For I also am an Israelite, of the seed of Abraham, of the tribe of Benjamin [Rom. 11:1].

What people is Paul talking about? *Israel.* In case the amillennialist might miss this, Paul is very specific. Paul himself is present proof. He is a true Israelite of genuine stock. He is descended from Abraham; he is from one of the twelve tribes of Israel, Benjamin, one of the two tribes that never seceded from the nation. He was 100 percent Israelite.

"God forbid" is more accurately, *Let it not be!* It is a strong negative. Even the form of the question demands a negative answer. God has not cast away Israel as a nation.

God hath not cast away his people which he foreknew. Wot ye not what the scripture saith of Elias? how he maketh intercession to God against Israel, saying, Lord, they have killed thy prophets, and digged down thine altars; and I am left alone, and they seek my life [Rom. 11:2–3].

Paul uses old Elijah as an illustration, and he makes a good one. Elijah stood for God, and he stood alone. How I admire that man standing alone for God against 450 prophets of Baal. And Elijah goes to the Lord to complain. He says, "Lord, I am all alone; I am the only one left." God says, "Wait a minute, you think you are alone, but you are not."

But what saith the answer of God unto him? I have reserved to myself seven thousand men, who have not bowed the knee to the image of Baal [Rom. 11:4].

Elijah was totally unaware that God had been working in the hearts of seven thousand men. If there were seven thousand men who had not bowed the knee to Baal, then it follows that there were about twice as many women who did not bow the knee either, if you go by percentages. For the northern kingdom this was a sizable remnant in the day of Ahab and Jezebel.

Even so then at this present time also there is a remnant according to the election of grace [Rom. 11:5].

God always had a remnant in Israel. That remnant today is composed of those Jews who have come to Christ. This is the reason Paul will say later that all Israel is not Israel.

And if by grace, then is it no more of works: otherwise grace is no more grace. But if it be of works, then is it no more grace: otherwise work is no more work [Rom. 11:6].

In other words, grace and works represent two mutually exclusive systems. They are diametrically opposed to each other. The remnant at this time is composed of those who are not saved by works or by merit; they are saved by the grace of God. The future purpose of God—from the day Paul wrote down to the present—concerns those who will accept Christ.

What about those who do not accept Christ? Well, the remainder of Israel is hardened.

REMAINDER OF ISRAEL BLINDED

It is important to notice that they were hardened because they failed; they did not fail because they were hardened. A lot of folk get the cart before the horse—in fact, they get the horse *in* the cart, and it doesn't belong there!

What then? Israel hath not obtained that which he seeketh for; but the election hath obtained it, and the rest were blinded [Rom. 11:7].

Did they fail to come to Christ because they had been blinded? Oh, no. They had been exposed to the gospel as no other people have been exposed to it. God said, "All day long have I stretched forth my hands unto a disobedient and gainsaying people" (Rom. 10:21). He has been patient with them. Now they are blinded because they would not accept the light He gave them.

(According as it is written, God hath given them the spirit of slumber, eyes that they should not see, and ears that they should not hear;) unto this day [Rom. 11:8].

They had rejected, you see. When a man rejects, he becomes the most difficult to reach with the grace of God.

And David saith, Let their table be made a snare, and a trap, and a stumblingblock, and a recompence unto them [Rom. 11:9].

This is a quotation from Psalm 69:22 which says, "Let their table become a snare before them: and that which should have been for their welfare, let it become a trap." The table has reference to feasting, which is representative of material prosperity. The children of Israel had great feasts at which they were actually guests of God—they did not invite God to their feasts as the pagans did—rather, God invited them. The Passover was a notable example. The thought here is that they were feasting in a conceited confidence which was entirely pagan. Their carnal security deceived them as to their true spiritual ruin. They trusted the things they ate without any true confidence in God. My friend, this is the condition at the present moment of multitudes of church members. They come to the Lord's Supper without a spiritual understanding.

Let their eyes be darkened that they may not see, and bow down their back alway [Rom. 11:10].

God gives light in order that men might see, but if they are blind, they will not see. The light reveals the blindness of multitudes today. I am amazed that so many intelligent people do not seem to understand what the Bible is all about.

REASON FOR SETTING ASIDE THE NATION ISRAEL

The nation Israel was set aside for the salvation of the Gentiles. Paul deals with this in the following section.

I say then, Have they stumbled that they should fall? God forbid: but rather through their fall salvation is come unto the Gentiles, for to provoke them to jealousy [Rom. 11:11].

In other words: I say then, did they stumble in order that they might fall? Away with the thought—that's not it. But by their false step, salvation has come to the Gentiles, to provoke Israel to jealousy.

Now Paul opens this verse with the same engaging inquiry as he did verse 1. Do you remember that he raised the question, "Hath God cast away his people?" (v. 1). Rejection is only partial and temporary. His question is, "Have they stumbled in such a way that they will not rise again?" The answer is an emphatic negative. Their fall has enabled God through His providence to open the gates of salvation *wide* to the Gentiles. The Jew will see the reality of salvation of the Gentiles, that they are experiencing the blessings of God which the Jew thought could come only to him. This should move him to emulation, not jealousy as we define it. In our trips to Israel, we have had several guides who were Jewish. They were puzzled that we were so interested in things that are Jewish in the nation Israel. They marveled at that. I have visited other countries and enjoyed them. I enjoyed England because some of my ancestors came from that area. In Egypt I saw the pyramids and that great hunk of rock there, and now that I have seen it, I don't want to see it again. But I have an interest in Israel that is not equaled in any other nation. The Jewish people don't understand this. One Jewish guide talked to me about it. He said, "I want to know why these things are so important to you."

Now if the fall of them be the riches of the world, and the diminishing of them the riches of the Gentiles; how much more their fulness? [Rom. 11:12].

Israel has been set aside; that is, God is not dealing with them as a nation at this time. When God does begin to deal with them, they won't have any problem with the Arab—that conflict will be completely resolved. Israel will not live in fear, because God has made it very clear that every man is going to dwell in peace and tranquility. "But they shall sit every man under his vine and under his fig tree; and none shall make them afraid: for the mouth of the LORD of hosts hath spoken it" (Mic. 4:4).

Now since their setting aside has brought the grace of God to Gentiles, what about the grace of God toward the Gentiles after the Jews are received again? It will be multiplied. James made this clear at that great council at Jerusalem. He said that God is calling out from among Gentiles a people for His name just as He is calling out Israelites. Then God says, "After this I will return, and will build again the tabernacle of David, which is fallen down; and I will build again the ruins thereof, and I will set it up: That the residue of men might seek after the Lord, and all the Gentiles, upon whom my name is called, saith the Lord, who doeth all these things" (Acts 15: 16–17). This is my reason for periodically making a statement—that sometimes puzzles folk—that the greatest "revival" took place on this earth before the church got here. (I use the word *revival* in the popular sense of a turning to God.) A man by the name of Jonah went into the city of Nineveh and saw the entire city turn to God. It is true that there was a great turning to God on the Day of Pentecost (which marks the beginning of the church), but what was the percentage? Pentecost was a feast in Jerusalem to which all male Israelites were required to go—there must have been several hundred thousand Jews in the environs of Jerusalem. How many were saved? Well, judging from the record, there were probably about ten thousand who were saved after the first few days of preaching. That is actually a small percentage. And the greatest revival since then took place in the Hawaiian Islands. The percentage there was probably 50 percent. But that was small in comparison to the days of Jonah. And I believe that the greatest revival will take place after the church leaves this earth. Actually, the church has not done too well. I believe that after the church has been raptured, multitudes of Gentiles will turn to God—not only in the Great Tribulation Period, but in the Millennium. Gentile nations will enter the Millennium, and a great many of them are going to like the rule of Christ, and they will turn to God during that period. I believe this with all my heart.

For I speak to you Gentiles, inasmuch as I am the apostle of the Gentiles, I magnify mine office:

If by any means I may provoke to emulation them which are my flesh, and might save some of them [Rom. 11:13–14].

Perhaps my translation will help you in the understanding of these two verses: "But I speak to you, the Gentiles. Inasmuch, then, as I [Paul] am an apostle of Gentiles, I glorify my ministry, if by any means I may move to emulation, that is, provoke to jealousy them of my flesh, and may save some of them."

In other words, Paul says, in effect, "I am an apostle to the Gentiles, and I rejoice in that. But as I preach to the Gentiles, I hope it will move many of my own people to turn to Christ also." Paul, you remember, wrote to the Corinthians, "And unto the Jews I became as a Jew, that I might gain the Jews; to them that are under the law, as under the law, that I might gain them that are under the law" (1 Cor. 9:20).

This is the reason Paul went to Jerusalem with his head shaven and under an oath—he was trying to win his people to Christ. Should he have done this since he lived under grace? Living under grace means that he could do it if he wanted to. In his letter to the Corinthians he continued, "To them that are without law, as without law, (being not without law to God, but under the law to Christ,) that I might gain them that are without law" (1 Cor. 9:21). In other words, he was obeying Christ. Then Paul says, "To the weak became I as weak, that I might gain the weak: I am made all things to all men, that I might by all means save some" (1 Cor. 9:22). He was first of all fulfilling his office as an apostle to the Gentiles, and in so doing, he was trying to move his Jewish brethren to turn to Christ. Some turned to Christ—only a few—but some. In all of this Paul was fulfilling his ministry, and God was accomplishing His purpose in this age with both Jew and Gentile.

I understand the satisfaction Paul felt in doing what God had called him to do. God has a place for you, my friend. He may want you to get busy and teach a Sunday school class, do personal work, or reach people through a business enterprise. Or He may want you to support another who is really getting out the Word of God. Whatever it is, you will experience great satisfaction in doing what you are confident God has called you to do.

For if the casting away of them be the reconciling of the world, what shall the receiving of them be, but life from the dead? [Rom. 11:15].

It is wonderful to anticipate the future. I think the greatest days are ahead of us. From man's point of view, the future is dark. Man has gotten his world in a mess. I felt sorry for a businessman to whom I was talking in Hawaii. We started chatting on the golf course. He told me that he was a businessman from Chicago—a vice-president of some concern. Obviously he had money, but, oh, how pessimistic he was about the future. Many thinking people are very pessimistic about the future of our civilization. But my God is on the throne, and He is going to straighten it out. The greatest days are yet in the future. Oh, the glorious future a child of God has. If I were not a dignified preacher, I would say *Hallelujah*!

For if the firstfruit be holy, the lump is also holy: and if the root be holy, so are the branches [Rom. 11:16].

You may recall that in the Book of Numbers, God said, "Of the first of your dough ye shall give unto the LORD an heave offering in your generations" (Num. 15:21). "Dough," of course, is bread dough! A part of the dough was offered to God as a token that all of it was acceptable.

The "firstfruit" evidently refers to the origin of the nation: Abraham, Isaac, and Jacob. "Holy" has no reference to any moral quality, but to the fact that it was set apart for God. Now if the firstfruit, or the first dough—that little bit of dough—was set apart for God, what about the whole harvest? Since Abraham, Isaac, and Jacob were set apart for God, what about the nation? It all belongs to God, you see. God is not through with the nation Israel.

And if some of the branches be broken off, and thou, being a wild olive tree, wert grafted in among them, and with them partakest of the root and fatness of the olive tree [Rom. 11:17].

You and I benefit because of the nation Israel. That is the reason I could never be anti-Semitic. I owe too much to them as a nation.

Boast not against the branches. But if thou boast, thou bearest not the root, but the root thee.

Thou wilt say then, The branches were broken off, that I might be grafted in [Rom. 11:18–19].

The "olive tree" is a picture of the nation Israel, and the "wild olive" is the church. Everything you and I have is rooted in the fact that God called Abraham, Isaac, and Jacob and that out of the nation Israel He brought Jesus Christ, our Savior and our Lord.

Well; because of unbelief they were broken off, and thou standest by faith. Be not highminded, but fear [Rom. 11:20].

The important thing is that they were set aside because of their unbelief. Oh, my Christian friend, you do not stand before God on your merit, your church membership, or your good life. You stand on one basis alone: your faith in Jesus Christ.

Now Paul gives a word of warning.

For if God spared not the natural branches, take heed lest he also spare not thee [Rom. 11:21].

Since God did not spare the nation Israel when they apostatized, the argument is that He will not spare an apostate church. I am more and more convinced that the church which is based on a philosophy or ritual or some sort of gyroflection—the type of church which was designated in the third chapter of the Book of Revelation as the church of Laodicea—will go into the Great Tribulation. As Dr. George Gill used to say, "Some churches will meet on the Sunday morning after the Rapture, and they won't miss a member." That's Laodicea.

In contrast to this, He says to the church of Philadelphia, "Because thou hast kept the word of my patience, I also will keep thee from the hour of temptation [that is, the Tribulation], which shall come upon all the world, to try them that dwell upon the earth" (Rev. 3:10). He promised to keep from the Tribulation that church which has an open door before it and is getting out the Word of God. My friend, I belong to that church; I hope you do also. It is an invisible body of believers. This is the church that will be taken to meet Christ at the time of the Rapture, which precedes the Great Tribulation.

RESTORATION OF THE NATION ISRAEL

Now we shall see that the restoration of the nation Israel will bring the greatest blessing.

Behold therefore the goodness and severity of God: on them which fell, severity; but toward thee, goodness, if thou continue in his goodness: otherwise thou also shalt be cut off [Rom. 11:22].

These are stern words. Paul calls upon the Gentiles to behold two examples. Rejected Israel reveals the severity of God, but to the Gentiles who have turned to God, the benevolent goodness of God is revealed. These two sides of God need to be revealed today: the judgment of God against the rejection of Christ and against sin, and the grace of God to those that will trust Christ.

Paul did not have the complete picture of the severity of God toward Israel. The history of Israel in the destruction of Jerusalem in A.D. 70 and all that succeeded it is a terrifying story. My friend, let's not trifle with the grace of God. It is grace which has brought us into the family of God and granted us so many privileges. After over nineteen hundred years the gentile church is as much a failure, if not more so, than Israel.

And they also, if they abide not still in unbelief, shall be grafted in: for God is able to graft them in again [Rom. 11:23].

Since God accepted Gentiles who had no merit, surely God can restore Israel who likewise has no merit.

"Again" is the key word. God will again restore Israel. The Old Testament makes it very clear that Israel is going to turn to God again. As an example, read Jeremiah 23:3–8, which is one of the many remarkable prophecies of the restoration of Israel. Zechariah speaks of this: "And I will pour upon the house of David, and upon the inhabitants of Jerusalem, the spirit of grace and of supplications: and they shall look upon me whom they have pierced, and they shall mourn for him, as one mourneth for his only son, and shall be in bitterness for him, as one that is in bitterness for his firstborn" (Zech. 12:10). This will be the great Day of Atonement. They will turn to God in repentance, and God will save them just as He saves us—by His marvelous, infinite mercy and grace.

For if thou wert cut out of the olive tree which is wild by nature, and wert grafted contrary to nature into a good olive tree: how much more shall these, which be the natural branches, be grafted into their own olive tree? [Rom. 11:24].

Paul continues the illustration of the olive tree. The olive tree is Israel with Abraham as the root. Some of the branches were cut off. The nation, as such, was rejected. God grafted in Gentiles, but not by their becoming Jewish proselytes, which would mean they would have to adopt the Old Testament ritual. Rather, He cut off Israel and grafted in the church—including both Jew and Gentile—directly and immediately upon Abraham by faith. If God could and did do that, it is reasonable to conclude that He can and will take the natural branches and graft them in again. In other words, He will not cast Israel away permanently.

For I would not, brethren, that ye should be ignorant of this mystery, lest ye should be wise in your own conceits; that blindness in part is happened to Israel, until the fulness of the Gentiles be come in [Rom. 11:25].

"The fulness of the Gentiles" began with the calling out of the church. "Simeon hath declared how God at the first did visit the Gentiles, to take out of them a people for his name" (Acts 15:14). It will continue until the Rapture of the church. Blindness and hardening of Israel will continue as long as the church is present in the world.

The word *mystery* needs a word of explanation. In the ancient world of Paul's day there were mystery religions. Today it applies in a popular way to a story that has an unrevealed plot or person. It is used in Scripture in neither of these ways. In the New Testament the word is used to refer to that which had been concealed but is now revealed. The mystery here is the identification of the fulness of thc Gentiles, which was not a subject of revelation in the Old Testament.

And so all Israel shall be saved: as it is written, There shall come out of Sion the Deliverer, and shall turn away ungodliness from Jacob:

For this is my covenant unto them, when I shall take away their sins [Rom. 11:26–27].

When Paul says "all Israel shall be saved," he does not mean every individual Israelite will be saved. It is the *nation* he has before us in this chapter. In every age, only a remnant is saved. The quotation Paul uses is from Isaiah 59:20 in the Old Testament: "And the Redeemer shall come to Zion, and unto them that turn from transgression in Jacob, saith the

LORD." The message to the individual is that he or she will have to "turn from transgression" to the Lord. There will be a remnant that will turn to Him. All of *them* will be saved. He speaks of the saved remnant as the nation Israel.

There is always only a remnant that is saved. There was a remnant in Elijah's day; there was a remnant in David's day; there was a remnant in Paul's day; there is a remnant in our day; and there will be a remnant during the Great Tribulation Period.

As concerning the gospel, they are enemies for your sakes: but as touching the election, they are beloved for the fathers' sakes.

For the gifts and calling of God are without repentance [Rom. 11:28–29].

In other words, with reference to the gospel, they are enemies for your sakes; but with reference to the election, they are beloved for the sake of the fathers. For the gifts of grace and the calling of God are without repentance—without a change of mind. Paul is summing up the preceding discussion. There have been two lines of thought which are seemingly in conflict and contradictory, although both are true. In the first place, Israel is regarded as an enemy for the sake of the Gentiles—that is, so the gospel can go to the Gentiles. On the other hand, they are beloved for the sake of Abraham, Isaac, and Jacob. Therefore, a Christian cannot indulge in any form of anti-Semitism—that is a point I have made before, and I continue to make it.

The failure of Israel and our failure likewise do not alter the plan and purpose of God.

"The gifts" are not natural gifts, but the word has to do with grace.

The "calling" is not an invitation, but it is the effectual calling of God, which is "without repentance." In other words, God is not asking even repentance from an unsaved person. The "calling of God" does not require any human movement. From God's viewpoint it is without man's repentance or change of mind. Some folk think they have to shed tears in order to be saved. Now certainly the shedding of tears could be a by-product of an emotional person who turns to Christ, but the tears have nothing in the world to do with your salvation. It is your faith in Christ that saves you. And neither is your faith meritorious. It is Christ who is meritorious. Your faith enables you to lay hold of Him.

For as ye in times past have not believed God, yet have now obtained mercy through their unbelief:

Even so have these also now not believed, that through your mercy they also may obtain mercy [Rom. 11:30–31].

You see, Paul is writing to Gentiles—the church in Rome was largely composed of Gentile believers. By this time, many Gentiles were being saved. He is drawing a contrast here between the nation of Israel and the Gentiles. In times past, the Gentiles did not believe, but now a remnant of the Gentiles have "obtained mercy." During this same time period Israel as a nation, which formerly believed, does not now believe. Paul puts down the principle by which God saves both Jew and Gentile: it is by *mercy*. Just as God showed mercy to the Gentiles, He will show mercy to the nation Israel.

For God hath concluded them all in unbelief, that he might have mercy upon all [Rom. 11:32].

Both Jew and Gentile are in the stubborn state of rebellion and aggravated unbelief. Because of this, by *grace* we are saved, through faith; and that not of ourselves, it is the gift of God; not of works, lest any of us should boast (see Eph. 2:8–9).

REASON FOR RESTORING THE NATION ISRAEL

What is the reason that the nation Israel will be restored? Well, that is locked in the riches of the wisdom of God. My friend, let's rest on the fact that what God is doing is wise, it is right, and it is the best that can be done. You and I have an old nature that questions God when He makes a decision. I have heard many Christians say, "Why are the heathen lost when they haven't heard the gospel? God has no right to condemn them!" My friend, God has every right imaginable. He is *God*. And what He is doing is right. If you don't think it is right, your thinking is wrong. And if you don't think He is being smart, you are wrong. God is not stupid. You and I may be stupid, but God is not. Oh, how we need to recognize this!

O the depth of the riches both of the wisdom and knowledge of God! how unsearchable are his judgments, and his ways past finding out! [Rom. 11:33].

Paul has come to the place of recognizing the wisdom and the glory of all that he has been discussing.

Godet's statement on this section is worth quoting: "Like a traveller who has reached the summit of an Alpine ascent, the apostle turns and contemplates. Depths are at his feet, but waves of light illumine them, and there spreads all around an immense horizon which his eye commands."

This section is pure praise and is no argument at all, yet it is the greatest argument of all. If we do not understand the *why* of God's dealings with Israel, with the Gentiles, and with ourselves, it is not because there is not a good and sufficient reason. The difficulty is with our inability to comprehend the wisdom and ways of God. "But the natural man receiveth not the things of the Spirit of God: for they are foolishness unto him: neither can he know them, because they are spiritually discerned" (1 Cor. 2:14).

Once, while driving back from Texas to California, my little girl developed a fever of 104 degrees. I took her to a hospital in Phoenix, Arizona. She did not understand why I had taken her to the hospital, especially when the doctor probed around and actually made her cry. She said, "Daddy, why did you bring me here?" She did not understand that, since she was sick, I was doing the wisest thing I could do under the circumstances and that I was doing it because I loved her. Oh, my friend, God is doing what is best for us. We may not understand the things that happen to us, but we must believe that it is for our good that God allows them. We are like little children, and we cannot understand God's ways. Our circumstances may not always seem to be good, but they come from the "depth of the riches both of the wisdom and knowledge of God." God says to us, "For my thoughts are not your thoughts, neither are your ways my ways, saith the LORD. For as the heavens are higher than the earth, so are my ways higher than your ways, and my thoughts than your thoughts" (Isa. 55:8–9). Oh, how we need to recognize this fact.

For who hath known the mind of the Lord? or who hath been his counsellor?

Or who hath first given to him, and it shall be recompensed unto him again? [Rom. 11:34–35].

These questions that we have here are simple enough, but the answer is not so easy.

"Who hath known the mind of the Lord?" Well, no one knows the mind of the Lord—that's the answer. It was Paul's *ambition* to know Him. He says, "That I may know him, and the power of his resurrection, and the fellowship of his sufferings, being made conformable unto his death" (Phil. 3:10).

"Who hath been his counsellor?" No one can advise God. I have seen a lot of church boards that felt they were really giving God good advice, but He doesn't need it. Have you noticed that the Lord Jesus never asked for advice when He was here on earth? One time—before feeding the five thousand—He asked Philip, ". . . Whence shall we buy bread, that these may eat?" Why did He ask that question? "And this he said to prove him: for he himself knew what he would do" (John 6:5–6). He didn't need Philip's advice. The fact of the matter is, he didn't use His disciples' advice. They said, "Send them away." He said, "You give them something to eat." My friend, God does not ask for advice, although a lot of folk want to give Him advice today.

"Who hath first given to him?" Have you ever really given anything to God which put Him in the awkward position of owing you something? If you were able to give God something, He would owe you something. What do you have that He hasn't already given you? I think one reason many of us are so poor is simply because we return to Him so little of what he has given us. To tell the truth, God says He won't be in debt to anybody. When somebody gives Him something, He turns around and gives him more. Years ago someone asked a financier in Philadelphia, a wonderful Christian man, "How is it that you have such wealth, and yet you give away so much?" The financier replied, "Well, I shovel it out, and God shovels it in; and God's shovel is bigger than my shovel!" Oh, my friend, most of us are not giving God a chance to use His shovel! We cannot do anything for Him—He will give us back more than we give to Him.

For of him, and through him, and to him, are all things: to whom be glory for ever. Amen [Rom. 11:36].

This just lifts me to the heights. Let me give you my translation: Because out of Him, and through Him, and unto Him are all things. To Him be the glory unto the ages. Amen.

Alford labeled this verse "the sublimest apostrophe existing even in the pages of inspiration itself."

"Out of Him" means God is the all-sufficient cause and source of everything.

"Through Him" means God is the mighty

sustainer and worker. ". . . My Father worketh hitherto, and I work," Jesus said (John 5:17).

"Unto Him" means God must call every creature to account to Him. All things flow toward God.

"To whom be glory"—the glory belongs to Him in all ages. Are we robbing God of His glory by taking credit for things we have no business to claim? The glory belongs to Him.

Oh, my friend, what a section of Scripture we have been in, and we leave it reluctantly.

CHAPTER 12

THEME: *Relationship to God; relationship to gifts of the Spirit; relationship to other believers; relationship to unbelievers*

This is the beginning of the final division in the Book of Romans. As you recall, the first eight chapters were doctrinal; the next three chapters were dispensational; now the emphasis in this last section is duty. We come now to the practical application of the theological arguments that Paul has placed before us. Here the gospel walks in shoe leather—and that is where I like it to walk.

In the first part of Romans the reader saw displayed the helmet of salvation and the shield of faith. But in this last section, the feet are shod with the preparation of the gospel of peace. We are to *stand* in the battle; we are to *walk* in our life; we are to *run* in the race.

Someone may suggest that we have already studied the practical application in the section on sanctification. There the gospel walked in shoe leather, it is true, but there is a sharp distinction in these two sections. Under "sanctification" we were dealing with Christian *character*; in this section we are dealing with Christian *conduct*. There it was the *inner* man; here it is the *outward* man. There it was the *condition* of the Christian; here it is the *consecration* of the Christian. There it was who the Christian *is*; here it is what he *does*. We have seen the *privileges* of grace; we now consider the *precepts* of grace. Enunciation of the way of life must be followed by evidences of life. Announcement of justification by faith must be augmented by activity of life.

There is something else we should note as we proceed into this last section. The conduct of the Christian must be expressed in this world by his relationship to those with whom he comes in contact, and these relationships must be regulated in some way. It is so easy to put down rules of conduct, but Paul is not doing that. He has delivered us from the Mosaic Law, and he did not deliver us in order to put us under another legal system. There are a lot of Christians who call themselves separated Christians because they don't do this, they don't do that, and they don't do about fifteen other things. I wish they would *do* something, by the way. I have found that those folk have gossipy tongues—you had better watch them. They ought to recognize that the child of God is *not* given rules and regulations. However, Paul puts down great principles that are to guide the believer. The Holy Spirit is giving the believer a road map of life, showing the curves but not the speed limit. He identifies the motels and eating places which he recommends without commanding the believer to stop at any certain one. Detours are clearly marked, and there is a warning to avoid them. The city of Vanity Fair is named, and the routes of exit are clearly marked. The believer is told to leave without being given the exact route by which to leave—there are several routes.

We are coming down the mountain top of Romans 8–11; we leave the pinnacle of Romans 11:33–36, and we now plunge down to the plane of duty—and it is *plain* duty. This is where we all live and move and have our being.

RELATIONSHIP TO GOD

I beseech you therefore, brethren, by the mercies of God, that ye present your bodies a living sacrifice, holy, acceptable unto God, which is your reasonable service [Rom. 12:1].

In other words: Therefore, I beg of you, brethren, by the mercies of God that you yield your bodies—your total personalities—a living sacrifice, set apart for God, well-pleasing to God, which is your rational or spiritual service.

Notice that the "therefore" ties it into everything that has come before it. Although it has immediate connection with that which has just preceded it, I am of the opinion that Paul is gathering up the whole epistle when he says, "Therefore."

"I beg of you" is the language of grace, not law. There is no thunder here from Mount Sinai. Moses commanded; Paul exhorts. Could Paul have commanded? Well, he told Philemon that he could have given him a command, but he didn't. Paul doesn't command; he says, "I beg of you."

"By the mercies of God"—the plural is a Hebraism, denoting an abundance of mercy. God is rich in mercy; God has plenty of it, my friend. He has had to use a lot of it for me, but He still has plenty of it for you. "Mercy" means compassion, pity, and the tenderness of God. His compassions never fail.

We are called upon to "present"—to yield. This is the same word we had, you recall, back in chapter 6. Although some expositors suggest that there it refers to the mind while here it refers to the will, I think it is a false distinction. The appeal in both instances is to the will. In the sixth chapter, the way to Christian character is to yield to Him. Here yielding is the way to Christian consecration and conduct.

He says to yield "your bodies," your total personalities. The body is the instrument through which we express ourselves. The mind, the affections, the will, and the Holy Spirit can use the body.

Vincent has assembled the following Scriptures which reveal this wide latitude. We are told to glorify God in our bodies. "For ye are bought with a price: therefore glorify God in your body, and in your spirit, which are God's" (1 Cor. 6:20). "According to my earnest expectation and my hope, that in nothing I shall be ashamed, but that with all boldness, as always, so now also Christ shall be magnified in my body, whether it be by life, or by death" (Phil. 1:20). "Always bearing about in the body the dying of the Lord Jesus, that the life also of Jesus might be made manifest in our body" (2 Cor. 4:10).

By an act of the will we place our total personalities at the disposal of God.

This is our "reasonable service," our rational service, and it is well-pleasing to God.

And be not conformed to this world: but be ye transformed by the renewing of your mind, that ye may prove what is that good, and acceptable, and perfect, will of God [Rom. 12:2].

Kenneth S. Wuest has an excellent translation—actually an interpretation—of this verse: "And stop assuming an outward expression that does not come from within you and is not representative of what you are in your inner being, but is patterned after this age; but change your outward expression to one that comes from within and is representative of your inner being, by the renewing of your mind, resulting in your putting to the test what is the will of God, the good and well-pleasing, and complete will, and having found that it meets specifications, placing your approval upon it" (*Romans in the Greek New Testament*, p. 290).

Although this is rather elaborate, it is exactly what Paul is saying in this passage of Scripture. Paul is urging the believer not to fashion his life and conduct by those around him, even those in the church.

I know two or three groups of folk who, when they come together in a meeting, assume a front that is not real at all. They are super pious. Oh, I tell you, when they meet on Sunday night, you would think they had just had their halos shined. They are not normal and they are not natural. Yet if you want to hear the meanest and dirtiest gossip, you meet with that group! The child of God ought not to be like that. We ought to be normal and natural—or probably I should say, normal and *super*natural. It is so easy to play a part. That is what the word *hypocrite* really means. *Hupokrites* is the Greek word for actors. They were playing a part. *Hupokrites* means to answer back. In acting it means to get your cue and to say the right thing at the right time. In our daily lives hypocrisy is to seem to be something that we are not. I have learned over the years that some folk who flatter you to your face, smile, and pat you on the back can be your worst enemies. They are dangerous to be with. It was Shakespeare who said something about the world being a stage and that every man must play a part. This is not true of the believer. He must be genuine because the Holy Spirit is working from within, transforming his life by "renewing" the mind.

Again and again Paul calls attention to this. To the Corinthians he said, "But we all, with open face beholding as in a glass the glory of the Lord, are changed into the same image from glory to glory, even as by the Spirit of the Lord" (2 Cor. 3:18). Also to Titus he said,

"Not by works of righteousness which we have done, but according to his mercy he saved us, by the washing of regeneration, and renewing of the Holy Ghost" (Titus 3:5).

By permitting the Spirit of God to renew the mind, the believer will be able to test the will of God and find it good. The minute that you and I assume a pose and pretend to be something we are not, it is impossible for us to determine the will of God for our lives. By yielding, the will of God for the life of the believer becomes good and fits the believer's will exactly. It's first good, and then it is acceptable, and finally it is perfect, in that the believer's will and God's will are equal to each other. My friend, you can't improve on that kind of a situation. Paul could say, "I can do all things." Where? "Through Christ which strengtheneth me" (Phil. 4:13). The believer can do all things that are in God's will. It is wonderful not to have to *act* the part of being Christian, but just be natural and let the Spirit of God move and work through you. Handley C. G. Moule (*The Epistle to the Romans*, p. 335) has put it like this:

I would not have the restless will
That hurries to and fro,
Seeking for some great thing to do
Or secret thing to know;
I would be treated as a child,
And guided where I go.

Oh, to reach the place of just turning this over to the Lord! Paul begs us to do this. This is the way of happiness. This is the way of joy. This is the way of fullness in your life. If you are in a church or in a group of play actors, for God's sake get away from it and try to live a normal Christian life where you can be genuine. A man said to me the other day, "My wife and I have quit going to such and such a group." I asked why. He told me, "We just got tired of going to a place where you almost have to assume something that you are not. Everyone there is being absolutely abnormal. The way I found out was that I had an occasion to meet a super pious member of the group in a place of business. I hardly recognized the man—his manner and everything about him was different." He was "conformed to the world" when he was not with the pious group. Oh, to be a normal Christian and enjoy God's blessing.

RELATIONSHIP TO GIFTS OF THE SPIRIT

For I say, through the grace given unto me, to every man that is among you, not to think of himself more highly than he ought to think; but to think soberly, according as God hath dealt to every man the measure of faith [Rom. 12:3].

This is my translation: For I am saying through the grace given to me, to everyone among you, not to be thinking of himself more highly than that which is necessary to think, but to think wisely of one's self, even as God has divided a measure of faith to each one.

My translation may have lost something of that pungent statement: "not to think of himself more highly than he ought to think." I imagine that when Paul wrote this, there was a whimsical smile on his face, because there are a great many Christians who are ambitious, who feel that they must have positions of prominence. And I have found out in Christian work that a great many folk in the church want to hold an office. If you want to be a successful pastor today and get a bunch of folk working like termites, you create a great many offices, committees, boards, and have presidents, chairmen, and heads of organizations. You will get a lot of people working who would never work on any other basis. Why? Because they think more highly of themselves than they ought to think.

What we need to do, as Paul says here, is "to think soberly." He says that we ought not try to advance ourselves in Christian circles. There is the ever-present danger of the believer overestimating his ability and his character and his gifts. We need to have a correct estimation of ourselves in relationship to other members of the church.

When I became pastor of certain churches, I was invited to serve as a board member of certain organizations. Finally I was serving on about a dozen or fifteen boards, and I was really a *bored* member. I was bored for the simple reason that I don't have gifts for that type of thing. To begin with, I don't have the patience to sit and listen to pages of "minutes" that take hours to read. And the second thing is that I just don't like to sit in a board meeting and listen to a group of incompetent men discuss spiritual matters. It took me a long time to find out I didn't have the kind of gift that would make me helpful in such situations, and I was killing myself going to board meetings. The Christian life became a round of being bored. Finally one day I came to myself, like the prodigal son, and I sat down and wrote twelve or more letters of resignation. That was one of the happiest days of my life.

And today I am not on anybody's board. I have several friends who say to me, "Oh, won't you be on my board?" I say, "No, I wouldn't help you. I have no gift for it. I'm for you, I'll even pray for you, but I cannot be on your board." My friend, we are not to think of ourselves more highly than we ought to think. We need to recognize our inabilities and do the things *God* wants us to do. It is a joy to get into the slot where God wants you to be!

For as we have many members in one body, and all members have not the same office:

So we, being many, are one body in Christ, and every one members one of another [Rom. 12:4–5].

This is the first time that Paul has introduced the great theme of the church as the body of Christ. This is the primary subject in Paul's letter to the Corinthians, Ephesians, and Colossians. The church as the body of Christ is to function as a body. This means that the many members do not have the same gifts. You may have a gift that I could never exercise. There are many members in the body, hundreds of members, and therefore hundreds of gifts. I do not think Paul ever gave a complete list of all the gifts because every time he dealt with gifts of the Spirit he always brought up new gifts which he had not mentioned in previous lists. I am sure the Spirit of God led him to do that.

Having then gifts differing according to the grace that is given to us, whether prophecy, let us prophesy according to the proportion of faith [Rom. 12:6].

"Gifts" is the Greek word *charismata*, which comes from the same stem as the word for grace. It can be translated as "grace" or "free gift" and is what the Spirit of God gives you. He gave to the church men who had the gift of a prophet, or a teacher, etc.

"Having then gifts"—each member of the body of Christ has a gift and a function to perform.

"Differing" means that the gifts differ; it does not mean that some folk do not have a gift. Every individual in the church has a gift. And the gift is part and parcel of the grace of God to us. When God saves you and puts you in the body of believers, you are to function. You are not to function as a machine, but as a member of a body, a living organization. When the gift is exercised, it is confirmed by the power of the Holy Spirit. Every believer needs to test his gift. If you feel that you have a certain gift and you are using it, you ought to test it. Analyze your effectiveness: Are you really a blessing to folk? Are you building up the church? Or are you dividing the church?

"Prophecy" here does not refer to prediction but to any message from God. Notice that prophecy is to be done in "proportion" (this is a mathematical term) to God's provision of the faith and the power to match the gift.

Or ministry, let us wait on our ministering: or he that teacheth, on teaching [Rom. 12:7].

"Ministering" is performing an act of service, referring to a manifold ministry with practical implications. There are multitudinous forms for service in the body of believers which this gift covers—setting up chairs and giving out songbooks is a ministry. Some folk do not have a gift of speaking, but they do have a gift of service. I know one dear lady who can put on a dinner that will make everybody happy. And I believe in church dinners; if you look at me, you will know I have been to quite a few of them—and many that this lady put on. That is her gift, and I've told her that. She would never make a good president of the missionary society, and you wouldn't want her to sing in the choir, but if you want to put on a church dinner for some purpose, she is the one to get. "Ministering" includes many gifts, my friend.

Or he that exhorteth, on exhortation: he that giveth, let him do it with simplicity; he that ruleth, with diligence; he that sheweth mercy, with cheerfulness [Rom. 12:8].

"Exhortation" is the Greek word *paraklésis*, literally "a calling near" or "a calling for." In other words, exhortation is comfort. Some folk have the gift of being able to comfort. I know one pastor who is not a preacher—he knows he is not—but if I were sick or had lost a loved one, he is the man I would want to come to visit me. He can comfort.

"He that giveth" is he that shares his earthly possessions. God may have given you a gift of making money—and that *is* a gift. I know several Christian businessmen who have the Midas touch. That is their gift.

"He that ruleth, with diligence" refers to the gift of leadership. There are certain men who are leaders, and they need to exercise their gift in the church so that everything might be done decently and in order. The business of the church requires a man with the gift of administration.

"He that sheweth mercy" indicates the gift of performing acts of kindness. For instance, there are some believers who can bring a sunbeam into a sickroom, while others cast a spell of gloom.

RELATIONSHIP TO OTHER BELIEVERS

Let love be without dissimulation. Abhor that which is evil; cleave to that which is good [Rom. 12:9].

"Let love be without dissimulation"—that is, without hypocrisy. Don't pat another believer on the back and say something that you don't mean. Let love be without hypocrisy.

"Abhor that which is evil" means to express your hatred of that which is evil. When you find something wrong in the church, bring it to the attention of the proper authorities. If you are on the board of directors and you find things are being done which are not honest, you are to stand up for the truth. There are too many Mr. Milquetoasts and Priscilla Goodbodies, these sweet folk who haven't the intestinal fortitude to stand for that which is honorable. This is the reason many good, fundamental churches are in trouble today. We need men and women with backbone to express their hatred for that which is evil.

"Cleave to that which is good." *Cleave* means to stick like adhesive tape, to be welded or cemented together with the good things. The believer should always be identified with good things rather than shady or questionable practices.

Be kindly affectioned one to another with brotherly love; in honour preferring one another;

Not slothful in business; fervent in spirit; serving the Lord [Rom. 12:10–11].

My, how wonderful these things are: have a code of honor, and be aglow with the Spirit of God. Never flag in zeal—have a zeal for the things of God.

"Be kindly affectioned one to another with brotherly love." In other words, as to your brotherly love, have family affection one to another. Farrar puts it in this language, "Love the brethren in the faith as though they were brethren in blood." For example, three men are sitting together. Two of the men are identical twins; one twin is a Christian and the other is not. Sitting with these men is a believer from Africa. His culture, background, and language are all different. The color of his skin is different, but he knows the Lord as Savior. The Christian twin is actually closer to the man from Africa than he is to his twin brother. My friend, you ought to be nicer to your fellow believer because you will have to live with him throughout eternity. You had better start getting along now and practice putting up with his peculiar ways. However, he will have a new body then, and he will be rid of his old nature—and you will also! It will make it better for both of you.

"Not slothful in business" is better translated "never flag in zeal." It has nothing to do with business. Luther gives it this translation: "In regard to zeal be not lazy."

"Fervent in spirit," or aglow with the Spirit suggests that our zeal and enthusiasm should be under the control of the Holy Spirit.

"Serving the Lord" points everything in Christian conduct toward this focal point.

Rejoicing in hope; patient in tribulation; continuing instant in prayer;

Distributing to the necessity of saints; given to hospitality.

Bless them which persecute you: bless, and curse not [Rom. 12:12–14].

"Rejoicing in hope" should be the portion of the believer. The circumstances of the believer may not warrant rejoicing. The contrary may be true. But he sees the future, and in hope projects himself into other circumstances which are more favorable. I think of a brother down in my Southland years ago. In a church service they were giving favorite Scripture verses. He stood and said that his favorite verse was "It came to pass." Everyone looked puzzled. The preacher stood up and said, "Brother, how in the world can 'It came to pass' be your favorite?" His answer was, "When I have trouble, and when I have problems, I like to read that verse, 'It came to pass,' and I know that my trouble or my problem has come to pass; it hasn't come to stay." He was looking for a new day out there, and that is what Paul has in mind when he says, "rejoicing in hope."

"Continuing instant in prayer" is to be a man or woman of prayer.

"Distributing to the necessity of saints" means sharing the necessities of life with needy believers. A great many churches make a great deal of having a fund for the poor, but how much do they use it? God expects us to share what He has given to us with fellow believers who are in need.

"Given to hospitality" means actually to *pursue* hospitality. That is, we are to seek out other believers to whom we can extend hospitality. There may be a person in your neighborhood or even in your church who is introverted and retiring yet longs for Christian fellowship. We are to look him up and extend our fellowship to him.

"Bless them which persecute you" seems to be a needless injunction for believers. Surely one believer would not persecute another—or would he? It is difficult to bless a man who is kicking you! But we are to bless and "curse not."

Rejoice with them that do rejoice, and weep with them that weep.

Be of the same mind one toward another. Mind not high things, but condescend to men of low estate. Be not wise in your own conceits [Rom. 12:15–16].

"Rejoice with them that do rejoice." The world's motto is "Laugh and the world laughs with you; weep and you weep alone." But that is not true of the believer. We are to enter into the joys and sorrows of other believers. Weep with those who weep.

"Be of the same mind one toward another" doesn't mean uniformity of thought but that we are to have the mind of Christ.

Believers ought to enter emotionally into the lives of other believers. I think that is something that makes genuine Christians so wonderful.

"Mind not high things, but condescend to men of low estate." My friend, let's not be afraid of associating with humble men and things of low estate. Paul said to the Philippians, "Let this mind be in you, which was also in Christ Jesus" (Phil. 2:5)—what kind of a mind did Christ have? A humble mind.

"Be not wise in your own conceits." In other words, stop being wise in your own opinion. What an injunction that is! A great many of the saints think they are spiritual giants, but they are not. Solomon, who was a man with wisdom from God, gave a very interesting injunction: "Seest thou a man wise in his own conceit? there is more hope of a fool than of him" (Prov. 26:12). I wouldn't dare say a thing like that, but Solomon said it.

RELATIONSHIP TO UNBELIEVERS

You and I live in a world of unbelievers. What is to be our relationship with them?

Recompense to no man evil for evil. Provide things honest in the sight of all men.

If it be possible, as much as lieth in you, live peaceably with all men [Rom. 12:17–18].

"Recompense to no man evil for evil." The suggestion is that the believer may expect evil at the hands of the world. However, we are not to strike back.

"Provide things honest in the sight of all men." There is nothing that can hurt the cause of Christ more than a dishonest Christian. The non-Christian is not concerned about the doctrine you hold—whether you are a premillennialist or whether you believe in election or free will. However, he does want to know if you are truthful or not, and he does want to know if you pay your honest debts. Are you a person that a man can depend upon? Providing things honest in the sight of all men is a lot better than giving out tracts, my friend. Let me illustrate this. Some years ago in Memphis, Tennessee, a Christian handed a man a tract. "What is this?" asked the man. The Christian replied, "It is a tract and I want you to read it." "I don't read," the man replied, "but I will tell you what I will do—I will watch your tracks!" Oh, how accurate that is! The world is watching the tracks that you make, not the tracts you give out. Don't misunderstand me; giving out gospel tracts is important. But you had better have a life that will back them up when you give out tracts.

"If it be possible, as much as lieth in you, live peaceably"—I love this because there are people that you just cannot get along with; they won't let you get along with them. A dear lady who lived alone, a wonderful Christian, called me one day in deep concern because she had a neighbor whom she couldn't get along with, and she wondered if I would come and talk with the neighbor. As I was driving out there, I was thinking that since this lady had been living alone, although she was a Christian, she might be a little difficult herself. So I went out and talked to her neighbor. Well, the neighbor told me what she thought of *me* as well as this dear lady. I went back to this wonderful Christian and said, "I don't think you need to worry anymore if you can't get along with her. Nobody can get along with that woman. The Bible says 'as much as lieth in you'; it doesn't say you *have* to get along with her. Just do the best you can."

Dearly beloved, avenge not yourselves, but rather give place unto wrath: for it is written, Vengeance is mine; I will repay, saith the Lord.

Therefore if thine enemy hunger, feed him; if he thirst, give him drink: for in so doing thou shalt heap coals of fire on his head [Rom. 12:19–20].

This is one of the greatest principles you will find in the Word of God, yet it is the most difficult thing for a child of God to do. When somebody hits you on one cheek, it is difficult to turn the other cheek. I am like the Irishman who was hit on one cheek, and he got up and turned the other cheek. This time the fellow hit him so hard, he knocked him down. Then the Irishman got up and beat the stuffings out of the other fellow. Somebody asked him, "Why in the world did you do that? You turned the other cheek; why didn't you leave it like that?" "Well," he said, "the Bible says to turn your cheek, and I had only one other cheek to turn. The Lord didn't tell me what to do after that, so I did what *I* thought I ought to do." That is what most of us do. We find it difficult not to hit back. But the minute you and I take the matter into our own hands and attempt to work the thing out by hitting back as hard as we can, we have taken the matter out of God's control, and we are no longer walking by faith. God is saying to us, "You walk by faith with Me, and let Me handle the matter for you, because I will handle it in a just manner. If this person has injured you, I'll take care of him." You and I can turn these matters over to the Lord, and we ought to do that. I can tell you what to do, but I confess that I find it most difficult to do myself. But there have been one or two times when I have turned it over to the Lord, and I have been amazed at how well He handled it. He does it a lot better than I do it.

There was a man, an officer in one of the churches I served, who did me a great injury, a terrible injury. My first thought was to clobber him, but I remembered this passage of Scripture. I went to the Lord and said, "Lord, I'd like to hit back and I can, but I don't think I will. I'll turn him over to You, and I expect you to handle him." Well, I saw that man the other day. I have never looked at a person who is as unhappy as that man is. He has *troubles*, friend. The Lord has taken him to the woodshed and whipped him within an inch of his life. When I looked into that man's face, I couldn't help but feel sorry for him. I wish I could say that I turn all of these matters over to the Lord, but I confess that sometimes I hit back.

Be not overcome of evil, but overcome evil with good [Rom. 12:21].

In other words, stop being overcome of evil; overcome evil by means of good. As the believer walks through this evil world with its satanic system, he cannot fight it. If you attempt to fight this satanic system, my friend, it will whip you. You cannot adopt the same worldly tactics of hate and revenge. If you do, you can be assured of defeat.

"Overcome evil with good." God has given the believer the "good," which is the Holy Spirit. He is to walk in the Spirit. "This I say then, Walk in the Spirit, and ye shall not fulfil the lust of the flesh" (Gal. 5:16). Paul goes on to say, "If we live in the Spirit, let us also walk in the Spirit" (Gal. 5:25).

CHAPTER 13

THEME: *Relationship to government; relationship to neighbors*

As we come to chapter 13, we still are talking about the service of the sons of God. We are going to see that the believer has citizenship in heaven, but he also is a citizen in the world down here, which gives him a twofold responsibility. If there is a conflict between the two always our first responsibility is to our Lord in heaven.

The Lord Jesus made it very clear that we have a responsibility to human government. You remember that He was asked by His enemies, "Is it lawful to pay tribute to Caesar, or not?" He asked them to show Him a coin—He wanted to teach them from something they themselves had, and also I don't think He had a coin in His pocket that day. He didn't have much while He was down here in this world. He asked them whose superscription and whose image was on that coin. They said, "Caesar's." Then He made this significant statement, ". . . Render therefore unto Caesar the things which be Caesar's, and unto God the things which be God's" (Luke 20:25).

Governments are ordained of God, and He

gave them certain authority. At the very beginning of human government He said, "Whoso sheddeth man's blood, by man shall his blood be shed: for in the image of God made he man" (Gen. 9:6). God has a regard for human life; it is precious in His sight. You have no right to take another human life. If you do, you are to forfeit your own life. Our contemporary society feels differently about it and makes the criminal the hero and the honest man the villain. We live in a day when evil is called good and good is called evil. However, believers have a responsibility to human government. In fact, Paul said to a young preacher, "I exhort therefore, that, first of all, supplications, prayers, intercessions, and giving of thanks, be made for all men; For kings, and for all that are in authority; that we may lead a quiet and peaceable life in all godliness and honesty. For this is good and acceptable in the sight of God our Saviour." (1 Tim. 2:1–3). By the way, *we* are to pray for those in authority, not leave it to the preacher on Sunday morning.

The duty of the believer as a citizen of heaven is spiritual. The duty of a believer as a citizen under a government is secular. These two are separate functions, and to combine them is to fail to keep church and state separate and distinct.

The Jew in Paul's day was reluctant to bow before the proud Roman state. Jewry had fomented disturbances in the city of Rome, and as a result Claudius had banished them on one occasion. The proud Pharisees rejected the Roman authorities in Palestine in their desire to restore the government to the nation of Israel; it was they who masterminded the encounter with Jesus and raised the issue, "Is it lawful to give tribute unto Caesar, or not?" The implications smacked of revolution, as you can see. It is well to remember that the authorities in Paul's day were mad and murderous. Nero was on the throne of Rome, and there was Pilate and Herod—all a bunch of rascals, yet he said that believers were to obey those in authority.

RELATIONSHIP TO GOVERNMENT

Let every soul be subject unto the higher powers. For there is no power but of God: the powers that be are ordained of God [Rom. 13:1].

We are to submit ourselves to governmental authorities for the very simple reason that they are ordained of God. It is true that the kingdoms of this world belong to Satan and that injustice and corruption abound in all governments; yet God still has control. History is the monotonous account of how a government flourished for a time in pomp and pride and then was brought to ruin and rubble. Why? Because corruption and lawlessness became rampant. As it did, God brought the government to an end. God still rules—even over this earth. God has not abdicated His throne; He is riding triumphantly in His own chariot. Neither is He disturbed about what is happening on this earth.

You will recall that when Uzziah, king of Judah, died, Isaiah was disturbed and very much discouraged. Uzziah had been a good king, and Isaiah thought the government would disintegrate after he was gone. So Isaiah went into the temple, which is a good place to go at a time like that. He came into God's presence, and He saw the Lord sitting upon the throne, high and lifted up. In other words, God had not abdicated. Uzziah was dead, but God was not dead. God was still on the throne.

Now the allegiance of the Christian is to *that* throne. And his relationship to his government on earth is submission.

Whosoever therefore resisteth the power, resisteth the ordinance of God: and they that resist shall receive to themselves damnation [Rom. 13:2].

In other words, anyone resisting the authority is resisting the ordinance of God. And those resisting shall receive for themselves judgment.

The principle stated in verse 1 raised many questions which the following verses amplify and explain. This verse seems to preclude the possibility of a believer having any part in rebellion or revolution. What about it? James Stifler cites the examples of Cromwell and Washington. Both of those men led a revolution. Stifler offers no solution. I am not sure I have one either, but I am going to do the best I can to solve this. The believer has opposed bad government and supported good government on the theory that good government is the one ordained of God. The believer is for law and order, as over against lawlessness. He is for honesty and justice, as over against corruption and rank injustice. At great moments of crisis in history—and that's where we are today—the believers have had difficult decisions to make.

I want to briefly give you my viewpoint, and I believe that it will coincide with history. During these last days, which I believe we are in right now, lawlessness abounds. The believer must oppose it; he must not be a part of it, even when it is in his own government. We need to beware of those who would change our government under the guise of improving it. Remember John the Baptist was beheaded by Herod, Jesus was crucified under Pontius Pilate, James, the brother of John, was slain with the sword of Herod, and Paul was put to death by Nero. Yet Paul says, "Whosoever therefore resisteth the power, resisteth the ordinance of God: and they that resist shall receive to themselves damnation" (v. 2). Therefore, Christianity never became a movement to improve government, help society, or clean up the town. The gospel was the power of God unto salvation of the individual. Paul never went around telling about the deplorable conditions of Roman jails—and he knew them well from the inside. When visiting Rome, my wife and I went to the Mamertine prison, and I got claustrophobia down there. I said to my wife, "Let's get out of here!" But Paul couldn't get out; they kept him down in that damp, dark prison. Remember he wrote to Timothy, "Bring my cloak with you" (see 2 Tim. 4:13)—he was getting cold down there.

It is very difficult to say that we are to obey a corrupt government. I am not impressed by these men—preacher or politician—who are running up the American flag and singing the national anthem as promotion for themselves. And behind it is corruption. Frankly, I feel resentful when I hear of certain government officials and certain wealthy men in positions of power who pay no taxes at all when I have a heavy tax burden. There is corruption in government from the top to the bottom, and it is not confined to one party. These unsaved, godless men who are in positions of government actually do not understand the American system. You see, the men who made our laws had a Bible background. I don't know that Thomas Jefferson was a Christian—he was a deist—but he had great respect for the Word of God. Many of those men were outstanding Christians—John Hancock, whose name is first on the Declaration of Independence, was a real Christian. However, in our day the government is corrupt. I go to the civic centers in our cities, and I see fine buildings, costing millions of dollars, which have been built by contractors who are friends of the politicians. Also I see poverty areas. While both parties talk about eliminating poverty, the poverty remains. Oh, corruption is there. What's wrong? Well, the thing wrong is the human heart.

What is the Christian to do? My business is to get out the Word of God, and my business is to obey the law. That is what Paul is saying here. Christianity is not a movement to improve government or to help society clean up the town. It is to preach a gospel that is the power of God unto salvation which will bring into existence individuals like the men who signed the Declaration of Independence and gave us a government of laws.

My friend, nothing is wrong with our form of government; there is something wrong with the individuals who are in positions of power. A professor in the history department of the University of Michigan summed it up well when he said, "America is in the hands of those who do not understand the spiritual heritage that we have."

For rulers are not a terror to good works, but to the evil. Wilt thou then not be afraid of the power? do that which is good, and thou shalt have praise of the same:

For he is the minister of God to thee for good. But if thou do that which is evil, be afraid; for he beareth not the sword in vain: for he is the minister of God, a revenger to execute wrath upon him that doeth evil [Rom. 13:3–4].

The government is to maintain law and order. When it does not do that, it has failed. I feel that a Christian should be opposed to the breakdown of law and order. We are to respect our rulers who are enforcing the law. I have great respect for our army, although it is honeycombed with corruption. I have great respect for police officers, although I know they make mistakes.

Wherefore ye must needs be subject, not only for wrath, but also for conscience sake [Rom. 13:5].

Christians are to obey the law not only because we'll be judged and have to pay a fine if we don't, but obey for conscience sake.

For for this cause pay ye tribute also: for they are God's ministers, attending continually upon this very thing [Rom. 13:6].

Although we may resent the way our tax money is being used, we are to pay taxes anyway.

In this verse the word for minister is one from which we get our word *liturgy*. It is strictly religious and is the same word used of angels in Hebrews 1:14 where they are called ministering spirits. This means that the ruler occupies a divinely-appointed office. He has no religious function, of course, but he holds a God-appointed office. That makes me pay my taxes, although I resent doing so.

We need today a heaven-sent revival. I am sick and tired of those who are shedding crocodile tears. They remind me of Lewis Carroll's brilliant satire, *Alice in Wonderland.* You remember that the Walrus and the Carpenter in this story were walking along the seashore weeping because there was so much sand and not enough oysters. They kept on eating and eating and weeping and weeping. What a picture of corruption! But in all of this the believer should submit to his government.

Render therefore to all their dues: tribute to whom tribute is due; custom to whom custom; fear to whom fear; honour to whom honour [Rom. 13:7].

Although there may be unworthy men in the office, we are to respect the office. When I was in the army, I was told to salute the uniform. There were some folk in that uniform that I didn't care about saluting, but I saluted the uniform. We are to show respect for authority. A Christian will be the best citizen although his citizenship is in heaven.

RELATIONSHIP TO NEIGHBORS

Owe no man any thing, but to love one another: for he that loveth another hath fulfilled the law [Rom. 13:8].

Did you borrow your neighbor's lawnmower? Take it back to him. Housewife, did you borrow a cup of sugar from your neighbor? Return it, please. Owe no one anything. In this we find Paul saying that the believer is positively to owe no man anything but love. This is a great principle to guide Christians in installment purchasing. You may ask, "Do you think we should turn in our credit cards?" No, but you had better be able to see your way clear in order to pay your debts.

The believer always owes the debt of love to his neighbor. That does not necessarily mean the man next door, but all people with whom you come in contact. This love is not some sentimental thing. I get a little disturbed when I hear liberalism continually talk about love, love, love. How do you reveal love?

For this, Thou shalt not commit adultery, Thou shalt not kill, Thou shalt not steal, Thou shalt not bear false witness, Thou shalt not covet; and if there be any other commandment, it is briefly comprehended in this saying, namely, Thou shalt love thy neighbor as thyself [Rom. 13:9].

"Thou shalt not commit adultery." Now don't tell me that you love someone and are committing adultery with that one. You can call that love if you want to, but it is nothing in the world but sex. It is licentiousness, it is fornication, and it is *sin* in God's sight. God hasn't changed His mind about it.

"Thou shalt not kill." You can kill a person in more ways than pulling a trigger of a gun. You can destroy them by ruining their reputation.

"Thou shalt not steal." If you love, you won't get something dishonestly.

"Thou shalt not covet." When your neighbor drives up in a new automobile, how do you feel about it? Sometimes we say, "I wish we had the car and they had one just like it." What we really mean is that we would rather have that car than see them have it.

Paul is saying that our love for our neighbor is revealed in what we do rather than in what we say. He is not putting the Christian back under the Law; he is saying that love manifests itself in not committing adultery, not killing, not stealing, not coveting. You can talk about love all you want to, but if you commit these acts against your neighbor, you have no love for him.

Love worketh no ill to his neighbour: therefore love is the fulfilling of the law [Rom. 13:10].

Loving your neighbor is the fullness of the law. This love, let me repeat, is the fruit of the Spirit.

And that, knowing the time, that now it is high time to awake out of sleep: for now is our salvation nearer than when we believed.

The night is far spent, the day is at hand: let us therefore cast off the works of darkness, and let us put on the armour of light [Rom. 13:11–12].

Paul said this nineteen hundred years ago, and certainly we ought to say it with a little more urgency in this day in which we are living. Let me give you my translation: And this—seeing that ye know the time or the season, that now it is the hour for you to wake out of sleep, for now is our salvation nearer than when we believed. The night is passing, it is far spent, and the day is at hand; let us therefore cast off the works of darkness, and let us put on the armor of light.

In this closing section an alarm clock goes off to waken believers who have gone to sleep in the world and have forgotten this added incentive for yielding their total personalities to God. My friend, this is not the time for the child of God to live for the things of this world. I think many a rich Christian is going to be embarrassed when the Lord comes. How big will your bank account be, my friend? Are you using your time and what you possess for God? I beseech you therefore, brethren, by the mercies of God, that ye yield your total personalities—all you are, all you have—to God. This is rational. This is reasonable. This is what you are supposed to be doing, Christian friend.

If we really are looking for the return of Christ, it will purify our lives. "And every man that hath this hope in him purifieth himself, even as he is pure" (1 John 3:3). These fellows who get divorces and live like the world, then talk about being premillennial and pretribulational and looking for the imminent coming of Christ, are not being honest. The apostle John says that that man is a liar! Let us wake up, my friend. Let us live for *God* in this hour!

Let us walk honestly, as in the day; not in rioting and drunkenness, not in chambering and wantonness, not in strife and envying [Rom. 13:13].

In other words, let us walk honorably as those in the day; not in revelings and drunkenness, not in sexual intercourse and dissolute abandon, not in strife and jealousy.

We hear a great deal about night life. The believer is identified with day life. He walks as one who belongs to the day.

But put ye on the Lord Jesus Christ, and make not provision for the flesh, to fulfil the lusts thereof [Rom. 13:14].

Oh, how many believers are making every provision for the flesh but are making no provision to go into His presence. My friend, I beg you to put Christ first in your life and to get out the Word of God. This is all important.

CHAPTER 14

THEME: *Conviction; conscience*

This chapter brings us to a new section, the final division in the Epistle to the Romans. It is: the separation of the "sons of God." What do we mean by separation? Frankly, I am tired of "separated" and "dedicated" Christians who are not separated or really dedicated.

There are two areas of Christian conduct. In one area the Bible is very clear, as we saw in the preceding chapter. The duty of the Christian to the state is submission. He is to obey the laws of the land, he is to pay his taxes, and he is to show respect to those in authority. Also chapter 13 was specific on a believer's relationship to his neighbor: He is to pay his bills; he is not to commit adultery, kill, steal, bear false witness, or covet what another has. In fact, he is to love his neighbor as himself. The believer is to be honest, and he is to avoid reveling and drunkenness, strife, and jealousy. The Bible is very clear on these things.

However, there is another area of Christian conduct on which the Bible has no clear word. Let me mention only two things: the use of tobacco and mixed bathing (that is, both sexes swimming together). If you don't think these are questionable, let me give you an illustration out of my own experience. My wife was reared in Texas in a Southern Baptist church. She was brought up by a mother and father and pastor who believed that mixed bathing was sinful. Then when she came to California, you can't imagine the shock she had the first time she went down to the beach with the young people from our church—even in those days they weren't wearing much. My wife was in a state of shock for twenty-four hours after that! She had never seen anything like it. However, in the area from which she came the use of tobacco was not frowned upon. The officers of her church smoked; in fact, her pastor smoked. When she came to California, she found that using tobacco was taboo. If you were a Christian, you did not smoke.

Is mixed bathing all right in one place and wrong in another place? Is smoking right in one place and wrong in another place? I am sure that the hair on the back of the necks of some of the saints is standing on end, and they are thinking, *Dr. McGee you ought to give a lecture against smoking, and you let this subject of mixed bathing alone.* Let me assure you that I am not condemning either one, nor am I condoning either one. I'm not going to stick out my neck on questionable things any farther than Paul stuck out his neck.

In this section Paul puts down principles of conduct for Christians relative to questionable matters. He gives us three guidelines: conviction, conscience, and consideration. A Christian should have a conviction about what he does. *Conviction* means "that which anticipates." Does he look forward to what he is going to do in high anticipation and enthusiasm? The second guideline is conscience. Does he look back on what he has done, wondering if he were right or wrong? Or does he even hate himself for what he has done? The third guideline is consideration for others. Are other people adversely affected by what he does? These three guidelines give us principles of conduct for our Christian lives.

In our day there are actually two extreme viewpoints about this matter of Christian conduct in questionable matters. And it has created an artificial atmosphere in which one is to live the Christian life. As a result we have abnormal or subnormal Christians in these extreme areas. One extreme position has no wall of separation from the world; the lives of these folk are carbon copies of the unsaved man of the world. Their lives are no different from what they were before their so-called conversion. They indulge in all forms of worldly amusement. They go everywhere the world goes, and they spend their time and energy in activities that have no spiritual profit. There are certain passages of Scripture that have no meaning for them at all. For example: "Brethren, be followers together of me, and mark them which walk so as ye have us for an ensample. (For many walk, of whom I have told you often, and now tell you even weeping, that they are the enemies of the cross of Christ: Whose end is destruction, whose God is their belly, and whose glory is in their shame, who mind earthly things.)" (Phil. 3:17–19). There are other folk who do not indulge in any form of worldly amusements, yet they are as worldly as they can possibly be. They gorge and gormandize themselves. They don't get drunk, but they certainly overeat. Also they over talk—they are great gossips. They even tell questionable stories.

Again let me quote Paul: "Finally, brethren, whatsoever things are true, whatsoever things are honest, whatsoever things are just, whatsoever things are pure, whatsoever things are lovely, whatsoever things are of good report; if there be any virtue, and if there be any praise, think on these things" (Phil. 4:8). My friend, your thought life is bound to affect your conduct sooner or later. What you keep thinking about you will eventually do. I have found that a great many Christians think about a temptation for a long time before they actually submit to it. This sort of thing is done by a great many so-called Christians. Paul seemed to question whether or not they were Christians, because they lived exactly as the worldling lived.

Now there is a second group that is extreme in the opposite direction. They have reduced the Christian life to a series of negatives. Paul warned the Colossian believers against the group that was characterized by "Touch not; taste not; handle not" (Col. 2:21). These folk rejoice in salvation by grace and deliverance from the Mosaic Law, but they immediately make a new set of ten commandments—only they usually double that number. They become very self-centered, very critical, and very proud. These are the ones that Paul labels "weak in the faith" (v. 1), by the way. And they are the folk who have become very "separated."

The following letter which I received several years ago illustrates the sad state of one who adopts this position.

> I've returned to California after a year of full-time Christian service in Ohio and an extended trip east. But I've come back almost spiritually shipwrecked! Have been a Christian for three and one-half years and until recently was able to give a glowing testimony about being saved out of Unity.
>
> But lately, I've been so dead that Christ seems way up there, and I'm way down here. I have all the negative virtues of a Christian (don't smoke, drink, play cards, attend movies, use makeup), but those things do not make a happy Christian! My friends tell me I'm becoming bitter—and oh, I don't want that to happen!
>
> Before becoming a Christian, I was very ambitious, worked hard for whatever I believed in (and incidentally I was listed in *Who's Who*)—but now I wonder what's the use? The world is going from bad to worse. Everything is heading for disaster, and the only hope is to wait for the return of the Lord Jesus Christ.

Now, my friend, this person was in a terrible condition! Notice how "separated" she was, but this kind of separation will not bring joy in the life.

Somewhere between these two extreme viewpoints of questionable matters in Christian conduct the believer is to walk. These are the Scylla and Charybdis through which the believer must sail his little bark on the sea of life.

I have given a great deal of space to these preliminary remarks because I know there are many puzzled Christians who will be helped by what Paul has for us in this important chapter.

Him that is weak in the faith receive ye, but not to doubtful disputations [Rom. 14:1].

To put it another way: Now, the one who is weak in faith, receive him into your fellowship, but not with the view of passing judgment upon his scruples—that is, upon his conduct and upon his viewpoint.

"Now" connects this chapter to what has preceded it. The law of love will now go into action. Having condemned things (in the last part of Romans 13) which are immoral and obviously wrong, like killing, committing adultery, stealing, bearing false witness, and coveting, Paul now warns against the danger of condemning questionable matters which are not expressly forbidden in Scripture.

"The one who is weak in the faith" does not mean one who is weak in the great truths of the gospel—the facts of faith—but rather it refers to the abstract quality of faith. It means the faith of the weak falters and hesitates about matters of conduct. He does not know what he should do relative to certain things. This one is to be received into the fellowship of believers with open arms. You may not agree with him, but you are to receive him if he is a believer in Jesus Christ. You are not to receive him in order to start an argument about questionable things. One group of believers is not to sit in judgment upon another group of believers about questionable matters of Christian conduct. Some things are not expressly condemned in Scripture, but some believers separate themselves from these things. And if they want to do this, that's their business. These things are not to separate believers. *The Scofield Reference Bible* has a very helpful note on this verse—"The church has no authority to decide questions of personal liberty in things not expressly forbidden in Scripture."

For one believeth that he may eat all things: another, who is weak, eateth herbs [Rom. 14:2].

This verse may hurt the extreme separationist. The *strong* brother in the faith is the one eating all things; the *weak* brother is the vegetarian. The strong brother realizes that Jesus made all meats clean, "cleansing all meats" (see Mark 7:19). After the Flood God gave all meats to be eaten according to Genesis 9:3, "Every moving thing that liveth shall be meat for you; even as the green herb have I given you all things."

God made a distinction between clean and unclean animals for the nation Israel. The instructed believer knows this does not apply to him, for the apostle says in 1 Corinthians 8:8, "But meat commendeth us not to God: for neither, if we eat, are we the better; neither, if we eat not, are we the worse." You remember that Peter was given a practical lesson about this subject on the housetop of Simon the tanner in Joppa (see Acts 10:9–16). Peter was proud of the fact that he had not eaten anything unclean. Boy, was he separated, and he was proud of it! The Holy Spirit said to him, ". . . What God hath cleansed, that call not thou common" (Acts 10:15).

Paul could eat meat without his conscience bothering him, but Peter had scruples about it. The weak believer who has a background of eating vegetables finds eating meat repugnant to him.

What is the principle? One can eat meat and the other cannot eat meat. By the grace of God one is not to eat meat and the other is to eat meat. Now listen to Paul:

Let not him that eateth despise him that eateth not; and let not him which eateth not judge him that eateth: for God hath received him [Rom. 14:3].

I recognize that I am wrong when I condemn these extreme separationists. If they want to be that way, candidly, that is their business. The thing that upsets me is that they want to straighten *me* out. I know I need straightening out, but they are not the crowd to do it, I'm sure of that. One group is not to condemn the other. If you believe that you should not eat meat (he uses meat as an example, but this could apply to anything else not expressly forbidden in Scripture), then you should not eat meat, my friend. But if you believe that you can eat meat, then you go ahead and eat meat.

Who art thou that judgest another man's servant? to his own master he

standeth or falleth. Yea, he shall be holden up: for God is able to make him stand [Rom. 14:4].

This is devastating. Paul asks, "What right have you to judge another man's servant?" What right have you, Christian friend, to sit in judgment on another Christian's conduct when it involves something that is questionable? Are you God? Is that person accountable to you? Paul says, "He is not accountable to you. He is accountable to *God*. He is going to stand before his own Master."

Can you imagine being a dinner guest in someone's home, and the servant brings in cold biscuits. You say to the servant, "What's the big idea of bringing me cold biscuits?" And you chide—in our common colloquialism, *bawl out*—the servant! May I say to you, there would be an awkward silence in that home. That person is not *your* servant. Maybe she should not have served cold biscuits, but it is not your place to say so. I have a notion that the lady of the house will go back to the kitchen and will tend to the matter.

Now maybe you disapprove of my conduct in one of these doubtful areas. I don't have to account to you; you are not my master. I am responsible to Jesus Christ. He is my Master.

CONVICTION

Paul gives us now the first great principle of conduct for Christians:

One man esteemeth one day above another: another esteemeth every day alike. Let every man be fully persuaded in his own mind [Rom. 14:5].

"Fully persuaded" means to be convinced, to be assured in your own mind.

Now Paul changes his illustration from diet to the *day* question. Some people insist that the Lord's Day is different. Some observe Sunday as the Lord's Day and others observe Saturday. It is not the *day* that should be different, but the *believer*. The particular day is not the important thing. Paul said, "Let no man therefore judge you in meat, or in drink, or in respect of an holyday, or of the new moon, or of the sabbath days" (Col. 2:16). Don't you tell me what day I am to observe. I'm not responsible to you; I am responsible to the Lord Jesus. He is my Master.

When I was a student in seminary, I was in a denomination in the South that were strict Sabbatarians—Sunday was their sabbath, as they called it. And they didn't believe in traveling on Sunday. I used to take a train to Augusta, Georgia, to preach, and I left on Saturday evening. Some of the officers of the church wanted to know what time the train got into Augusta! Well, it got in early Sunday morning, and one man said to me, "Doesn't that disturb you?" I said, "It doesn't disturb me at all." Now, I respect that man, and I don't think he ought to travel on Sunday. But when I am traveling from one speaking engagement to another, and it is necessary to travel on Sunday, I do it without the slightest compunction. Paul says that whatever we do, we should be fully persuaded, convinced, and assured in our own mind that it is the right thing to do.

"Let every man be fully persuaded in his own mind" means literally he is to be filled to the brim—mind, heart, will, and the total personality. A believer should do only those things to which he can give himself fully and without reserve. My friend, whatever you do for God, you should do with enthusiasm. I think it is sinful the way some people go to church on Sunday. Can you imagine people going to a football game when the alma mater is playing with that same lackluster attitude they have when they attend church? Personally, I don't go to football games because I think they are a waste of time. But I don't criticize other folk for going—that's their business. But when I go to play golf, I go with enthusiasm. And whatever I do for the Lord, I do with enthusiasm. I teach the Bible because I *love* to teach it. I would rather do it than anything I know of. One of the reasons church work is bogged down as it is today is that there is a lack of enthusiasm. A man is asked to teach a Sunday school class, and he says, "Oh, if you can't get anybody else, I'll take it." Then don't take it, brother, if that is the way you feel. It would be better for the class to have no teacher than a disinterested, unenthusiastic teacher. Some people are actually committing sin by doing church work! The first great principle is: "Let every man be fully persuaded in his own mind."

Now let's bring this principle over to questionable things. Frequently folk, especially young folk, ask me if doing this or that is wrong. I say, "Well, for you I think it is wrong, but for me it's all right." Of course they ask me what I mean by that. I tell them, "I have no question about it. If I wanted to do it, I would do it with enthusiasm. The point is, you have a question about it. 'Let every man be fully persuaded in his own mind.' You wouldn't have come and asked me the question if you had been persuaded in your own mind." My friend, this is a great guiding principle: if you have a question in your mind about something you are doing—whatever it is—for you it is wrong. It might not be wrong for me, but it is certainly wrong for you.

You recall that Simon Peter followed the Lord afar off after He was arrested. Peter went that night into the judgment hall of the high priest. I sat in the hotel in Jerusalem in the old city on the side of the Valley of Kidron one morning. When the morning sun had come up, it set that whole city ablaze across the Kidron Valley. Over there is a church called the Church of the Cock Crowing. It is situated on the spot where the high priest's judgment hall was located—that's where Caiaphas had his home. And that is the place to which Simon Peter came and where he denied three times that he knew the Lord. I am convinced that Simon Peter should not have gone there that night. On the other hand, John, who apparently had a home in Jerusalem and was known in the palace of the high priest, went there and did not deny his Lord. It was all right for John to be there, but it was wrong for Simon Peter. Simon Peter was the weak brother, you see.

Today it is the weak brother who is the "separated" brother. That may seem strange to you. But the people who set up a little legal system of "dos" and "don'ts" bear watching. They are the weak ones. When I was a student in seminary, I used to have a water fight on Saturday night in the seminary dorm. One of the students would gather together two or three of the super-duper saints, and they would pray for us. (I always hoped he would pray that I would win!) We were pretty rough fellows. One night we soaked all the rugs, and we almost got booted out of the place. But this young fellow was a model student. About fifteen years later, I sat down with him and his wife and begged him not to leave her. He told me he had to. I said, "Why?" His reply was this, "Because I have a little daughter by a woman out in Australia, and I want to marry her." He posed as a super-duper saint, but actually he was a weak brother.

Questionable amusements are wrong for the believer if they are questionable to him. If he can participate in them and maintain a close relationship to Christ, they are not wrong for him. Let me tell you a little story in this connection. Many years ago in Tennessee a young lady went to her pastor with the question, "Do you think it is wrong for a Christian to dance?" He said to her, "Anywhere you can take Jesus Christ with you is all right to go." That made her angry. She said, "Well, I can take Him to the dance." The pastor said, "Then go ahead." So she went to the dance. A boy whom she had not met before cut in on her and danced with her. She had determined to take Jesus Christ with her, so she asked him, "Are you a Christian?" He said, "No." Wanting to make conversation with her, he asked, "Are you a Christian?" She said, "Yes." And this is what the unbeliever said, "Then what are you doing *here*?" After she got home that night she decided that maybe she couldn't take the Lord Jesus Christ there after all.

He that regardeth the day, regardeth it unto the Lord; and he that regardeth not the day, to the Lord he doth not regard it. He that eateth, eateth to the Lord, for he giveth God thanks; and he that eateth not, to the Lord he eateth not, and giveth God thanks [Rom. 14:6].

Maybe you play golf on Sunday. If you can take Jesus Christ with you, if you can stop out on the ninth hole and have a prayer meeting with the foursome you are playing with, that would be fine. But what will the foursome playing behind you think when their game is interrupted in this way? When they see you are praying, one of them will say, "What in the world are *they* doing out here on Sunday morning?"

The important thing to note is that the day is to be "regarded" or *observed* unto the Lord.

Also, the one who eats meat gives thanks to God from his heart. The one who does not eat meat gives thanks to God from his heart. It is not what is on the table, but what is in the heart that is noted by God. It is the heart attitude that conditions Christian conduct.

For none of us liveth to himself, and no man dieth to himself.

For whether we live, we live unto the Lord; and whether we die, we die unto the Lord: whether we live therefore, or die, we are the Lord's.

For to this end Christ both died, and rose, and revived, that he might be Lord both of the dead and living [Rom. 14:7–9].

"None of us liveth to himself, and no man dieth to himself" is generally quoted as a proof text that our lives affect others. However, that thought is not in this passage. The fact is that we as Christians cannot live our lives apart from Christ. Whether you live, you will have to live to Him; whether you die, you will have to die to Him. Our Christian conduct is not gauged by the foods spread out on the table, but by the fact that our lives are spread out before Him. That is the important thing. One day we are going to have to give an account of the things we have done in this life. "For we must all appear before the judgment seat of Christ; that every one may receive the things done in his body, according to that he hath done, whether it be good or bad" (2 Cor. 5:10). At that time it will not be a question of the meat you had on the table; it will be the question of your relationship to Him when you sat down at that table. You can be godless without meat; and you can be godless with meat, of course.

Christ's death and resurrection are given as grounds for Him to exercise lordship over both the dead and the living:

But why dost thou judge thy brother? or why dost thou set at nought thy brother? for we shall all stand before the judgment seat of Christ.

For it is written, As I live, saith the Lord, every knee shall bow to me, and every tongue shall confess to God.

So then every one of us shall give account of himself to God [Rom. 14:10–12].

"Why dost thou judge thy brother?" You remember that the Lord Jesus said to that bunch of Pharisees who wanted to stone an adulterous woman, ". . . He that is without sin among you, let him first cast a stone at her" (John 8:7). And not one of those boys threw any stones that day. My friend, you and I need to recognize that we have to give account of *ourselves* to Him. I'll be honest with you, that disturbs me a little. I am wondering how I am going to tell Him about certain things. So I can't sit in judgment upon you; I'm worried about Vernon McGee.

Let us not therefore judge one another any more: but judge this rather, that no man put a stumblingblock or an occasion to fall in his brother's way [Rom. 14:13].

Paul is going to develop the thought that our conduct has to be for the sake of the weak brother. If I am traveling in the same car with a fellow who believes he should not travel on Sunday, I'm going to have to stay with him—not because I agree with him, but for the sake of a weak brother.

I know, and am persuaded by the Lord Jesus, that there is nothing unclean of itself: but to him that esteemeth any thing to be unclean, to him it is unclean.

But if thy brother be grieved with thy meat, now walkest thou not charitably. Destroy not him with thy meat, for whom Christ died [Rom. 14:14–15].

Since Christ was willing to die for that weak brother, certainly we ought to be willing to refrain from eating something or doing something that would hurt him in his Christian walk.

Let not then your good be evil spoken of [Rom. 14:16].

In other words, liberty does not mean license. The believer is to *use* his liberty, not *abuse* it. We are always to keep in mind how our conduct will affect weaker Christians.

For the kingdom of God is not meat and drink; but righteousness, and peace, and joy in the Holy Ghost [Rom. 14:17].

This is the only reference in this epistle to the kingdom of God. I do not believe the "kingdom of God" is synonymous with the kingdom of heaven in Matthew's gospel, which finds its final fruition in the millennial and messianic kingdom here on earth. I believe that the kingdom of God embraces all that is in God's created universe, which, of course, includes the church. It is broader and larger and includes God's reign over all His creation. Lange's definition is satisfactory: "The heavenly sphere of life in which God's word and Spirit govern, and whose organ on earth is the Church." This was our Lord's use of the term. "Jesus answered and said unto him, Verily, verily, I say unto thee, Except a man be born again, he cannot see the kingdom of God" (John 3:3). Well, that is the heavenly sphere of life in which God's Word and Spirit govern. As Stifler has said (*The Epistle to the Romans*, p. 245), "God rules everywhere, but there is a realm where he governs by spiritual forces or laws alone"—which is in the area of the life of the believer. Man is totally incapable of seeing or entering this kingdom without the new birth. This kingdom has nothing to do with eating or drinking, fasting, no meat on Friday, no pork, or a vegetarian diet. These things just do not enter into it.

"Righteousness" in this verse means the same as it does in chapters 1 and 3. It means to be right with God; it means a life lived well-pleasing to Him.

"Holy Ghost" apparently goes with righteousness and refers, not to our standing, but to our walk—we are to walk in the Spirit. It is practical rather than theological. It is moral rather than oral. It is a righteousness in the Holy Spirit rather than righteousness in Christ.

"Joy" is the fruit of the Holy Spirit in the lives of believers. Unfortunately, it is often absent from the lives of believers. There should be joy in our lives. This doesn't mean you have to run around smiling like a Cheshire cat, but it does mean you are to have a joyful feeling deep in your heart.

For he that in these things serveth Christ is acceptable to God, and approved of men [Rom. 14:18].

Although, of course, there will be a literal kingdom on this earth, he is talking here about the spiritual realm that you enter by the new birth. Christ is not served by eating and drinking, but our service to Him must pertain to righteousness, peace, and joy in the Holy Spirit. In these things a believer is well pleasing to God and approved of men.

"Approved of men" does not mean that men will get in your cheering section and applaud you because you are a believer. They may even persecute you. But underneath, men do approve of genuine believers, while they despise and reject that which is hypocritical and phony.

This is a great principle of conduct. The walk and talk of the believer should please God and meet the approval of the conscience of men.

Let us therefore follow after the things which make for peace, and things wherewith one may edify another [Rom. 14:19].

This is a twofold exhortation. To "follow after the things which make for peace" is to eagerly pursue this course of action. The believer is to make a definite effort to avoid the use of food or any physical thing which offends a Christian brother. This would be the negative aspect of the exhortation. The positive aspect is to press toward the mark of spiritual values: righteousness, peace, and joy in the Holy Spirit. These are the things which build up the believer.

For meat destroy not the work of God. All things indeed are pure; but it is evil for that man who eateth with offence [Rom. 14:20].

On account of food, do not tear down the work of God. Of course the believer has the liberty to eat meat or abstain from it—but neither will commend him to God. We are not to tear down the work of God in the heart of some weak believer for the sake of some physical gratification. That old bromide is active: one man's porridge is another man's poison. Esau, for instance, had no regard for God or for his birthright. He exchanged it for a bowl of soup. Well, don't sell your birthright just to satisfy your appetite.

It is good neither to eat flesh, nor to drink wine, nor any thing whereby thy brother stumbleth, or is offended, or is made weak [Rom. 14:21].

Paul returns to these two points: eating and drinking. Then he goes beyond them with the sweeping statement: *nor anything*. Anything that is questionable and is a matter of conscience for a weak brother becomes wrong for the strong one.

CONSCIENCE

Now verse 22 gives us the second great principle of Christian conduct.

Hast thou faith? have it to thyself before God. Happy is he that condemneth not himself in that thing which he alloweth [Rom. 14:22].

Let me give you my translation of this verse: The faith which thou hast, have thou thyself in the sight of God. Happy is the man who condemneth not himself in the things which he approves—that which he does.

This is the second principle of conduct for Christians. He has already dealt with the aspect of conviction. As we look toward doing something for God, we ask ourselves the questions: Will it be right for me to do this? Can I do it with excitement and anticipation and joy? Now this second exhortation looks back at what has been done. Happy is the man who does not condemn himself in what he has done. The believer should be able to look back upon his conduct without any qualms of conscience.

Let me use an illustration, and I trust you will not misunderstand it. I have been asked the question: "Can a Christian get drunk?" The answer is yes. The prodigal son in Luke 15 was a *son* out in the far country. I am confident that he got drunk in addition to a few other things, but he was always a son. Then what was the difference between him and the pigs? The difference was that none of those pigs said, "I will arise and go to my father." You see, as the prodigal son was there with the pigs, he said to himself, *I hate it here, and I'm going to get out of this. I am going back to my father and confess what a sinner I am.* What, then, is the difference between the Christian who gets drunk and the non-Christian who gets drunk? The difference is simply this: the next morning the man of the world will get up with a headache, put an ice pack on it, and say, "Boy, I sure had a big time! I'm going to get a bigger bucket of paint and a bigger paint brush, and I am really going to paint the town red the next time!" But what will the child of God do? When he wakes up the next morning with a head as big as a barrel, he drops down by the side of his bed and cries, "Oh, God, I hate myself! I don't want to do that again." He confesses his sins to God. And the interesting thing is there is no record that the prodigal son went back to the pig pen. He didn't like it there. That is the difference between a believer and an unbeliever. "Happy is he that condemneth not himself in that thing which he alloweth."

My Christian friend, do you look back and hate yourself for what you have done? That is your conscience condemning you. Regardless of what it was and regardless of how many other people do the same thing, for you it was *wrong*. You might have even been in a church (and a church can be a very dangerous place because Satan is there—he goes to church every Sunday morning, and he goes to the best churches). Do you come home from church and say, "I could bite my tongue off. I wish I hadn't said what I did." Well, you should not have said it. "Happy is he that condemneth not himself in that thing which he alloweth."

And he that doubteth is damned if he eat, because he eateth not of faith: for whatsoever is not of faith is sin [Rom. 14:23].

"Whatsoever is not of faith is sin." My friend, you are to believe in what you are doing. If you don't believe in it, you should not be doing it. Here is a new definition of sin for the believer: Any line of conduct or any act which is not the outflow of faith becomes sin. This is the Holy Spirit's answer to questionable things. As the believer is saved by faith, just so the believer is to walk by faith.

CHAPTER 15

THEME: *Consideration of the weak brother; consolidation of Jews and Gentiles in one body; continuation of Paul's personal testimony*

We have been looking at the great principles of conduct for the Christian. In the preceding chapter we have seen two of these principles: conviction and conscience. Now we see the third: consideration of the weak brother, a thought which is continued from chapter 14. In the first three verses the subject is separation. Then we shall see the consolidation of Jews and Gentiles in one body to glorify God, and finally the continuation of Paul's personal testimony as the apostle to the Gentiles and to the Romans in particular. This chapter concludes the major argument of the Epistle to the Romans. In the final chapter, Paul will lapse back to personal relationships.

A remark needs to be made here that radical higher criticism has questioned the authenticity of these last two chapters of Romans. Without any valid reason or documentary evidence, the Pauline authorship of these two chapters was rejected. Baur's school led in this objection. Today the Pauline authorship is established, and we may conclude with this statement from Kerr in his *Introduction to New Testament Study*, "Despite these objections, the integrity of the epistle as it now stands is certain."

CONSIDERATION OF THE WEAK BROTHER

We then that are strong ought to bear the infirmities of the weak, and not to please ourselves [Rom. 15:1].

This is the third and last guiding principle which should govern the conduct of Christians. When you invite a Christian over to your house who doesn't believe in dancing, don't put on a square dance for him, because you will offend him. Now maybe you can square dance, but I cannot. Why? Because there are certain things I very definitely feel I cannot do because of a consideration of others. Neither have I been inside a motion picture theater in years—I can't even remember the last time I went. Somebody says, "Oh, you are one of those separated fellows who doesn't believe you can go to movies." Maybe you can go—I'm not judging you if you do—but I cannot. One of the reasons is right here: consideration of the weak brother. "We that are strong" I feel applies to me. I feel that I could go without losing my fellowship with the Lord—I'm sure that many of these movies would disgust me today, to tell the truth. But a weak brother might be strongly influenced and his relationship to Christ actually damaged by certain movies. So we who are strong ought to bear the infirmities of the weak.

Paul identifies himself with the strong ones, and he insists that these should show consideration for the feelings and prejudices of the weak believers. He wrote to the Corinthians, "Wherefore, if meat make my brother to offend, I will eat no flesh while the world standeth, lest I make my brother to offend" (1 Cor. 8:13). In other words, Paul said, "I can eat meat. I love a good pork roast. But I will not eat it if it is going to offend my brother." Also Paul wrote, "Let no man seek his own, but every man another's wealth" (1 Cor. 10:24). Seek the interests of the other man. "Bear ye one another's burdens, and so fulfil the law of Christ" (Gal. 6:2).

Let every one of us please his neighbour for his good to edification [Rom. 15:2].

"For his good to edification" means with a view to his building up. The objective of all Christian conduct is the edification of our neighbor. Of course our neighbor is not to be pleased to his detriment or loss. Paul said, "For though I be free from all men, yet have I made myself servant unto all, that I might gain the more. And unto the Jews I became as a Jew, that I might gain the Jews . . ." (1 Cor. 9:19–20). A great many people criticize Paul and cannot understand why he would take a Jewish oath, shave his head, and go to Jerusalem to the temple. You will understand it if you understand what Paul is saying here: "And unto the Jews I became as a Jew, that I might gain the Jews; to them that are under the law, as under the law, that I might gain them that are under the law" (1 Cor. 9:20).

Now let's keep in mind that we are still in the area of questionable things, things that are not mentioned in Scripture as wrong. Going back to the example of the movies. Would I ever go to a movie? Yes, if I thought by so doing I could win someone for Christ. You may ask, "How far can you carry this?" Well, I know a group that went into a burlesque show to witness. I think they were in the wrong place. I know a girl who started going to nightclubs and drinking with her friends, thinking she could witness to them. But she became an alcoholic, and she didn't win anybody. I can show you from Scripture that these things are wrong.

However, because the Scripture is silent on many things in our contemporary society, we have been given these great guidelines, three principles of separation: (1) Conviction. Whatever we do is to be done with enthusiasm because we are persuaded in our own minds that it is what God wants us to do. (2) Conscience. Our conduct should be such that we do not look back upon it with qualms of conscience. (3) Consideration. We should show consideration for the feelings and prejudices of the weak believers.

For even Christ pleased not himself; but, as it is written, The reproaches of them that reproached thee fell on me [Rom. 15:3].

The quotation here is from Psalm 69:9. This is an imprecatory psalm and also one of the great messianic psalms. Christ never put His own interest and pleasures first. Stifler thinks that Christ is presented here as an argument rather than as an example. In *The Epistle to the Romans* (p. 250) he writes, "The Scriptures are not in the habit of holding up Christ as an example, for men are neither saved nor sanctified by an example." Always when Christ is given as an example it is in connection with the redeeming grace of God.

CONSOLIDATION OF JEWS AND GENTILES IN ONE BODY

Paul now begins to talk about the fact that Jews and Gentiles are in one body to glorify God.

For whatsoever things were written aforetime were written for our learn-

ing, that we through patience and comfort of the scriptures might have hope [Rom. 15:4].

The Old Testament, therefore, does have a definite application to believers today. I frequently receive letters from folk who say, "I didn't know the Old Testament was so practical," or, "I had not realized that the Old Testament had such meaning for us today. I did not know it spoke of Christ as it does." Paul here says that it was written for "our learning."

In my opinion, the greatest sin in the church of Jesus Christ in this generation is ignorance of the Word of God. Many times I have heard a church officer say, "Well, I don't know much about the Bible, but . . ." and then he gives his opinion, which often actually contradicts the Word of God! Why doesn't he know much about the Bible? These things were written aforetime for our learning. God wants you to *know* His Word. As an officer of the church, are you boasting that you are ignorant of the Word of God? Well, you had better get down to business and find out what God has said to you in His Word. Ignorance of the Bible is the greatest sin of the hour—in and out of the church. Paul says these things were written for your learning.

What will a knowledge of the Bible do for you? "That we through patience and comfort of the scriptures might have hope." The Word of God imparts patience, comfort, and hope.

You won't find any hope in the daily newspaper. You won't find any hope in modern literature. Look at any field and see if you can find any hope. There is none whatsoever. It is dark and dismal when you look out at this world today. My friend, the only place you can find real hope is in the Word of God.

I was in the state of Washington, speaking at a Bible conference, and it rained and rained and rained. Then it rained some more. Oh, how dark and dismal the days were! For our flight back home we went to the airport, and it was still raining. The plane took off and went up through a heavy layer of cloud. In a few moments we broke out into the light—the sun was shining up there. Oh, how beautiful it was. Less than a mile up, the sun was shining. Here we had been living like a bunch of gophers in all that rain. Now, don't misunderstand me—Washington needs all that rain to grow that lush vegetation and beautiful trees. But because I live in Southern California, I am used to sunshine, and I love it.

There are a great many Christians today who are living down beneath the clouds. The Lord says, "Come on up here and get in the sunshine of hope!" That is what the Bible will do for you, my friend. Paul wrote to the Corinthians: "Now all these things happened unto them for ensamples: and they are written for our admonition, upon whom the ends of the world are come" (1 Cor. 10:11). When I was teaching the life of David, scores of people told me what an encouragement David was to them. One person said that he was going through a very dark period in his life and that the study in the life of David delivered him from suicide. Well, that is the reason God put these things in His Word. God put David's sin on display—and it wasn't very nice—but God paints mankind exactly as he is for our *learning*. Everything in the Old Testament is written for our learning and to give us patience and to give us comfort and to bring hope into our lives.

Now the God of patience and consolation grant you to be likeminded one toward another according to Christ Jesus [Rom. 15:5].

Paul pauses here to pray that the blessings which are channeled only through the Word of God might have their effect upon both Jews and Gentiles in the body of Christ; not that they should see eye to eye with each other on meats and drink—they won't—but that they might demonstrate that they are one in love and consideration one of another.

That ye may with one mind and one mouth glorify God, even the Father of our Lord Jesus Christ [Rom. 15:6].

There should be such a harmony in their praise that they reveal the unity of believers. When I was a boy in West Texas, we had a Methodist church on one corner, a Baptist church on another corner, and a Presbyterian church on the third corner. A story was told that one night the Methodists were singing, "Will there be any stars in my crown?" And the Presbyterians were singing, "No, not one; no, not one." And the Baptists were singing, "Oh, that will be glory for me." Well, that is just a story. I'm sure it never worked out that way, but sometimes it actually looks like that. However, if the Baptists and Methodists and Presbyterians are really believers (just to be a member of one of these denominations doesn't make you a believer, by the way), all three could sit down and sing the doxology together: "Praise God from whom all blessings flow." That is the testimony we should give to the world.

Wherefore receive ye one another, as Christ also received us to the glory of God [Rom. 15:7].

Let me give you my translation of this: Wherefore receive ye one another, even as Christ also received *you* to the glory of God.

God receives man—both strong and weak, high and low, Jew and Gentile—on the simple acceptance of Christ. Now let both the strong and the weak receive each other in fellowship. The glory of *God* is the supreme objective.

A man said to me the other day, "Since you are very critical of the Pentecostal point of view, why is it that Pentecostal brethren are friendly toward you and actually invite you to speak in their churches?" I said, "Well, the reason is that they have more of the grace of God than I have." A recent letter from a Pentecostal pastor read, "We agree on too many things to let one or two differences separate us." When we agree on the major doctrines of the faith, though we may differ on minor points, we need to receive one another, as Christ also received us to the glory of God. Although I disagree with Pentecostal brethren on the matter of tongues, I see no reason why I should break fellowship with them. I just pray they will see it as I see it. And the very interesting thing is that one of these days, when we are in His presence, we will agree. In fact, all will agree with me. Do you know why? Because I am going to have to change a whole lot of things also. All of us will be changed, changed into His image and His likeness. Then all of us will agree. In view of that fact, we had better concentrate on the areas in which there is agreement now.

Now I say that Jesus Christ was a minister of the circumcision for the truth of God, to confirm the promises made unto the fathers:

And that the Gentiles might glorify God for his mercy; as it is written, For this cause I will confess to thee among the Gentiles, and sing unto thy name [Rom. 15:8–9].

When the Lord Jesus Christ came into this world, He came as "a minister of the circumcision"—this is the only time it is mentioned. His ministry was confined to the nation Israel. He frankly said so Himself: "But he answered and said, I am not sent but unto the lost sheep of the house of Israel" (Matt. 15:24). Also He directed His disciples: "But go rather to the lost sheep of the house of Israel" (Matt. 10:6). Christ came to earth about nineteen hundred years ago. He came in this capacity to confirm the promises made to Abraham, Isaac, and Jacob. God said that from the loins of Abraham He would bring One who would be a blessing to the world. Christ came to be a blessing to both Jew and Gentile. "And when eight days were accomplished for the circumcising of the child, his name was called JESUS, which was so named of the angel before he was conceived in the womb" (Luke 2:21). He could not have been "Jesus" unless He had been born in the line of Abraham and David and unless He followed the Law. They called Him Jesus after He was circumcised. He came to fulfill the entire Mosaic system. "But when the fulness of the time was come, God sent forth his Son, made of a woman, made under the law, To redeem them that were under the law, that we might receive the adoption of sons" (Gal. 4:4–5). Salvation came to Israel through Christ in confirming and fulfilling the truth of the Old Testament promises. Also by this method salvation was brought to the Gentiles. The Gentiles' only claim was upon the mercy of God. No promise was ever made to *their* fathers. I do not know who my father was, way back in the beginning in the forests of Germany and in Scotland. I do not know his name. But I do know that God never made any promise to him. He did, however, make a promise to Abraham, Isaac, and Jacob. Christ came to confirm the truth of the promises made to the fathers of the Jews, and He also came that the Gentiles might obtain mercy. In this the Gentiles are to glorify God. I thank God that He brought the gospel to my ancestors. They were pagan and savage and had done nothing to merit God's grace.

"As it is written" introduces four quotations from the Old Testament that show that the Gentiles are to praise God.

"For this cause I will confess to thee among the Gentiles, and sing unto thy name" is a quotation from Psalm 18:49. Christ is praising God through the Gentiles, which implies their conversion.

And again he saith, Rejoice, ye Gentiles, with his people [Rom. 15:10].

This quotation is from Deuteronomy 32:43. It concludes the song of Moses, which is a prophetic recitation of the history of the nation Israel until the coming of the millennial kingdom. Here the Gentiles are invited to join Israel in praise to God.

And again, Praise the Lord, all ye Gentiles; and laud him, all ye people [Rom. 15:11].

This is a quotation from the briefest psalm (see Ps. 117:1). It is an invitation to the Gentiles to join Israel in praise to God. It is interesting to note the occurrence of the word *all* twice in this brief quotation.

And again, Esaias saith, There shall be a root of Jesse, and he that shall rise to reign over the Gentiles; in him shall the Gentiles trust [Rom. 15:12].

This quotation is from Isaiah 11:10. Though the Messiah is from the line of David, He is to rule over the Gentiles. Obviously it was the clear intention of God that the Gentiles should come to Christ. Some had come to Christ in Paul's day, and they were the firstfruits of even a greater day. Remember that Paul was writing to the Romans, and the Roman church was largely a gentile church, as are our churches today.

Now the God of hope fill you with all joy and peace in believing, that ye may abound in hope, through the power of the Holy Ghost [Rom. 15:13].

"The God of hope" is a new title for God which is thrilling. The believing heart finds here the Rock of Ages who is the shelter in the time of storm. "The God of hope fill you with all joy and peace in believing." This is what a study of Romans should do for you. I trust it has given you joy and peace and that it has strengthened your faith. I trust it has brought hope and power into your life, my friend.

This is the benediction that concludes the doctrinal section of the Epistle to the Romans.

CONTINUATION OF PAUL'S PERSONAL TESTIMONY

At this point Paul resumes his personal testimony as an apostle to the Gentiles. You remember that he began this epistle in a very personal manner. Now he leaves the doctrinal section, and he picks up that personal note with which he began the epistle, in which he expressed the desire to visit Rome. "Now at length I might have a prosperous journey by the will of God to come unto you" (Rom. 1:10). Now listen to him.

And I myself also am persuaded of you, my brethren, that ye also are full of goodness, filled with all knowledge, able also to admonish one another [Rom. 15:14].

This, I think, is one of the loveliest passages. Paul is offering in this verse a gentle apology for his frankness and boldness in speaking to the Romans in the doctrinal section. It was not because they were lacking in goodness and knowledge, but rather because they possessed these qualities that Paul was able to be so explicit. Isn't that wonderful? He gave us the Epistle to the Romans so that he could talk to us about these important issues. My friend, an understanding of the Epistle to the Romans is an essential part of your Christian growth. Every Christian should make an effort to know Romans, for this book will ground the believer in the faith. Paul is being very humble and sweet about his exhortations in this epistle. He is not lording it over God's heritage.

Nevertheless, brethren, I have written the more boldly unto you in some sort, as putting you in mind, because of the grace that is given to me of God,

That I should be the minister of Jesus Christ to the Gentiles, ministering the gospel of God, that the offering up of the Gentiles might be acceptable, being sanctified by the Holy Ghost [Rom. 15:15–16].

When Paul says, "I have written," he is referring to this Epistle to the Romans. He is explaining the fact of his boldness by reminding the Romans that he is the apostle to the Gentiles. On the basis of this God-appointed office, which came to him through the grace of God, he is exercising that office in writing as he does to the Romans. He is ministering to them. This statement gives added weight to the inspiration of the writings of Paul. He adopts the language of the Levitical temple worship in describing himself as a minister preaching the gospel.

The Gentiles are "acceptable"—apart from the Law or any religion—through Jesus Christ as preached by Paul.

"Sanctified"—the Holy Spirit indwelt the gentile believers, beginning with Cornelius. The sanctifying work of the Holy Spirit begins with Jew and Gentile the *moment* of regeneration when the Spirit of God takes up His abode within the believer. Paul gave the gospel, but God gave the Holy Spirit when they believed. It must be kept in mind that Paul was the apostle to the Gentiles in a very special sense. As a high priest, Paul offered up the Gentiles, making an offering unto God. It is difficult for us today to fathom the full significance of all this, and yet we as Gentiles have entered into all that this implies. My friend, if you have never thanked God for the apostle Paul, you should thank Him right now. God gave Paul to us. For this reason we should read his Epistle to the Romans.

I have therefore whereof I may glory through Jesus Christ in those things which pertain to God [Rom. 15:17].

Paul had written boldly to the Romans and was rather apologetic about it because he recognized that these saints in Rome probably did not need his instructions. In spite of this, however, he wrote with confidence to them. There is no personal assumption in this. He is a servant of Christ Jesus and is doing His will. This is important to see. There is one thing that should never characterize a servant of God, and that is pride. We should never become officious, but rather take the position that we are merely serving the Lord Jesus Christ, and He is the One in charge.

For I will not dare to speak of any of those things which Christ hath not wrought by me, to make the Gentiles obedient, by word and deed,

Through mighty signs and wonders, by the power of the Spirit of God; so that from Jerusalem, and round about unto Illyricum, I have fully preached the gospel of Christ [Rom. 15:18–19].

Paul is saying something very important in this passage. If we are to understand Paul, and especially whether he or Peter founded the church at Rome, we must pay close attention to what he says here. Paul is saying, "I will not take credit for the work of God that is being done by others—especially among the Gentiles." Of course he couldn't take credit for what was accomplished on the Day of Pentecost, which was the beginning of the ministry that resulted in the gospel going to the Gentiles. He couldn't take credit for the gospel going to the first Gentiles. It was Simon Peter who took the gospel to the home of Cornelius. Paul will speak only of those things which Christ wrought by him. He had a peculiar ministry as the apostle to the Gentiles.

"Through mighty signs and wonders," which were the credentials of the apostles and the ministers in the early church. These were given to establish the church on the right foundation before a word of the New Testament had been written. Paul, speaking to the Ephesian believers, says that they ". . . are built upon the foundation of the apostles and prophets, Jesus Christ himself being the chief corner stone" (Eph. 2:20). He does not intend to say that the apostles are the foundation. There is no foundation but Christ: "For other foundation can no man lay than that is laid, which is Jesus Christ" (1 Cor. 3:11). But the apostles are the ones who put down the foundation of Jesus Christ. That is what Paul is saying here.

Paul says that the gospel of Christ had come through him "unto Illyricum." Illyricum was a province of the Roman Empire next to Italy. It extended to the Adriatic Sea and the Danube River. Paul, you see, had preached by this time from Jerusalem to the province next to Rome. He had not quite reached Rome. By the way, we have no record of Paul's journey in this area. Undoubtedly he went many places that are not detailed for us. There are those who believe that Paul went to Spain. I believe this epistle reveals that he did go to Spain, and I think he also went to Great Britain because he covered the Roman Empire, as we shall see.

Yea, so have I strived to preach the gospel, not where Christ was named, lest I should build upon another man's foundation:

But as it is written, To whom he was not spoken of, they shall see: and they that have not heard shall understand [Rom. 15:20–21].

Perhaps my translation will make these verses a little clearer: Indeed, in this way having made it my ambition to preach the gospel, not where Christ was named, in order that I might not be building upon another man's foundation: but as it is written, They shall see, those to whom there came no tidings of Him, and those who have not heard shall understand.

It was a point of honor with Paul—not competition—which caused him to go as a pioneer where the gospel had not been preached. Paul had a peculiar ministry. Paul did not minister where a church already existed or where others had gone. He was a true missionary, which is the meaning of the word *evangelist* in the New Testament. Paul never had a committee to do the groundwork ahead of him. When Paul entered a town, he was not given a welcome. The mayor did not greet him. If anyone greeted him, it was usually the chief of police, who generally arrested him and put him in jail. Since the apostles laid the foundation, the believers would have to be very careful to discern who the apostles were and to whom they were listening. Paul had the credentials God had given to the apostles. It is said of Paul and Barnabas, "Long time therefore abode they speaking boldly in the Lord, which gave testimony unto the word of his grace, and granted signs and wonders to be done by their hands" (Acts 14:3). You see, these were the marks of the apostles and the early preachers of the gospel. They did not come with a New Testament in their hands—it hadn't been written yet. They came with these credentials: mighty "signs and wonders."

Of course the day came when signs and wonders were no longer the identifying mark. The apostle John, near the end of his long life, wrote; "If there come any unto you, and bring not this doctrine, receive him not into your house, neither bid him God speed" (2 John 10). Correct doctrine was the identifying mark for a man of God even then. And today the identifying mark is correct doctrine, not signs and wonders.

A tragic movement is going on at this writing. Coming to my desk is literally a flood of letters from people who are being carried away by fanaticism, by wrong teaching, and by false doctrine. Although there is a movement of the Holy Spirit today, there is also a movement of the Devil. Satan is busy. A great many people are being carried away and trapped by incorrect teaching. Paul has been so careful to emphasize the fact that the kingdom of God is not meat and drink. Well, the kingdom of God is not signs and wonders either. It is not any of these outward things. The kingdom of God just happens to be *righteousness*. I hear of groups meeting and indulging in all kinds of sexual rites—not living for God at all—yet talking about certain signs that they demonstrate, such as speaking in tongues. My friend, it had better be a *clean* tongue. If the Lord has come into your life, He will clean you up. A clean tongue and one that declares the Word of God accurately is what a great many folk need today. Paul always ministered where the gospel had not previously gone. He was a true evangelist, a true missionary.

Since Paul said that he did not go where the gospel had been preached before, who is the founder of the church in Rome? He makes it very clear, both in his introduction and at this point, that he is the founder of the church in Rome.

In Romans 16 we will be introduced to a group of people in Rome whom Paul knew. The record tells us that Paul led them to the Lord. He reached these people out in the Roman Empire and many of them gravitated to Rome. There they met together around the person of the Lord Jesus. I am sure they talked many times about their beloved pastor, Paul. He founded the church, not by going there in person, but by remote control—you might say, by spiritual radar.

"To whom he was not spoken of, they shall see: and they that have not heard shall understand" seems to be Paul's life verse as a missionary. It is a quotation of Isaiah 52:15 from the Septuagint version. Paul was thrilled to go and preach the gospel to those who were spiritually blind. After Paul had preached, some brother would say, "I understand, brother Paul. I will accept Christ as my Savior." My friend, there is no thrill equal to presenting Christ and having people turn to Him.

For which cause also I have been much hindered from coming to you [Rom. 15:22].

When Paul says that he had been "much hindered," you may be sure of one thing: he was *much* hindered. Many roadblocks had been put in his way.

But now having no more place in these parts, and having a great desire these many years to come unto you;

Whensoever I take my journey into Spain, I will come to you: for I trust to see you in my journey, and to be brought on my way thitherward by you, if first I be somewhat filled with your company [Rom. 15:23–24].

Paul makes it clear that he wants to take the gospel way out yonder and that he is coming to Rome. Now he says something unusually strange: "But now having no more place in these parts." There is a question about what Paul meant by this. Was he saying that there was no longer an opportunity to preach the gospel in the section of the Roman Empire where he was at that time? Had the doors completely closed to him? Had everyone been saved? Had every nook and cranny been evangelized? I used to take the position that the answer was "no" to these questions. However, now that I have visited the sites of the seven churches of Asia Minor, I'm not sure that I was right, because Paul and the other witnesses had been faithful, and the gospel had been sounded out through that entire area. The Word had gone out. Dr. Luke says that everyone, both Jew and Gentile, had heard the gospel. This does not mean that they all had turned to Christ, but they all had heard. Now Paul is looking for new territory. He has his eyes on the frontier of the empire. He says, "Whensoever I take my journey into Spain, I will come to you." In other words, Rome was not his destination. He wanted to go to Spain. He had come from one end of the Roman Empire, and he wanted to go to the other end of the Roman Empire. He says, "For I trust to see you in my journey, and to be brought on my way thitherward by you." You see, Rome was not his terminal. He wanted to go all the way to the other end of the empire.

The question is: Did Paul ever go to Spain? If he did, we have no record of it. But neither have we a record of his journey to Illyricum; we would not know he had been there if he had not mentioned it in verse 19. Personally I believe that Paul did go to Spain and to the rest of the Roman Empire. My reason is a statement that he made when he came to the end of his life. He said, "I have fought a good fight, I have finished my course, I have kept the faith" (2 Tim. 4:7). Paul said he had finished his course. I don't think he would have said that if he had not been to Spain, because Spain was on his itinerary.

Paul wanted to go to Spain and he also wanted to go to Jerusalem.

But now I go unto Jerusalem to minister unto the saints.

For it hath pleased them of Macedonia and Achaia to make a certain contribution for the poor saints which are at Jerusalem [Rom. 15:25–26].

He wanted to go to Jerusalem to take a gift to the poor saints there, and he wanted to take it with his own hands. Why? Because with his own hands he had "wasted" the church at Jerusalem; he had led in the persecution of the believers in Jerusalem. Now it was in the heart of this great apostle to make up for that by taking a gift to them.

"A certain contribution." The Greek word which is translated "contribution" is *koinōnia*, meaning "a fellowship." This word was used for everything that believers could share: Christ, the Word, prayer, the Lord's Supper, and material gifts. Christians have fellowship with God, with Christ, and with one another when they give. Fellowship is not just patting somebody on the back. The knife and fork clubs meet every week, and that *is* fellowship as far as they are concerned. But for a believer, fellowship is sharing the things of Christ. Paul is talking here about going to Jerusalem where previously he had persecuted the church. Now he wants to have fellowship with them; he wants to take a gift to them. In Acts we have the historical record of this: Paul said, "Now after many years I came to bring alms to my nation, and offerings" (Acts 24:17). This collection was very important to Paul. We find him writing about it in 2 Corinthians—in fact, chapters 8 and 9 deal with it.

It hath pleased them verily; and their debtors they are. For if the Gentiles have been made partakers of their spiritual things, their duty is also to minister unto them in carnal things [Rom. 15:27].

Paul makes it clear that it was a freewill offering. "Every man according as he purposeth in his heart, so let him give; not grudgingly, or of necessity: for God loveth a cheerful giver" (2 Cor. 9:7). This is the offering Paul collected. Paul makes it very clear that it not only was a freewill offering (they couldn't give any other way to please God), but he also enforces the fact that they had a moral obligation and debt to pay. The Gentiles had received the gospel from Israel. Our Lord Jesus said, "Ye worship ye know not what: we know what we worship: for salvation is of the Jews" (John 4:22). You see, the gospel began in Jerusalem. Macedonia and Achaia were *obligated* to Jerusalem. Now some of the saints in Jerusalem were having financial difficulties, evidently because of persecution. Macedonia and Achaia could now pay a spiritual debt in the coin of the realm. This is foreign missions in reverse! It is the missionary church helping the home church. This very thing may take place in our nation, by the way, in the not too far distant future!

When therefore I have performed this, and have sealed to them this fruit, I will come by you into Spain [Rom. 15:28].

You can see that this gift was on the heart of the great apostle Paul—notice the zeal he had in taking it to Jerusalem. That trip, of course, placed him into the hands of his enemies who had him arrested. I disagree with some of my brethren who believe that Paul was out of the will of God during this time. I maintain that Paul was absolutely in the will of God when he went up to Jerusalem, as we have seen in the Book of Acts.

"And have sealed to them this fruit" is an awkward phrase for us and could mean no more than that he wanted a receipt for the offering. He secured to them the gift. It probably means that he wanted the Jerusalem church to see some fruits of their missionary efforts. I personally believe that if you are going to contribute money to some cause, you ought to know what it is doing. The area of Christian giving is one of grave danger today. I do not believe, Christian friend, that you should give to any work unless you know two things about it: (1) what it is doing, and (2) is it getting out the Word of God in a way that is effectual in hearts and lives?

And I am sure that, when I come unto you, I shall come in the fulness of the blessing of the gospel of Christ [Rom. 15:29].

This is Paul's stamp of approval on his prosperous journey to Rome. He went there according to the will of God and in the fulness of his apostolic office. God gave him divine insight into this trip. Paul is not out of the will of God in going to Jerusalem. Neither was he out of the will of God in going to Rome. It may not look like a prosperous journey, but God used it that way. It is very easy for God's children, when trouble comes and things look dark and doubtful, to say, "I must be out of the will of God." My friend, just because you have trouble and disturbed feelings does not mean that you are out of God's will. In fact, it may definitely mean you are in His will. If you are living in perfect calm today and nothing is happening, the chances are you are not in His will.

Now I beseech you, brethren, for the Lord Jesus Christ's sake, and for the love of the Spirit, that ye strive together with me in your prayers to God for me [Rom. 15:30].

I have been dwelling a long time in this area. One reason is that this is a personal area, and Paul is laying bare his heart. The second reason is that we are seeing how Christianity functioned in the first century. We are seeing the practical side of Christianity. In the first part of Romans Paul gave us doctrine. Now Paul is putting that doctrine into practice.

This is one of the most solemn, earnest, and serious appeals of Paul for prayer that we find in the Bible. He says, "I beg of you, brethren, through our Lord Jesus Christ, and through the love of the Spirit, that ye strive intensely with me in your prayers to God on behalf of me." Paul recognizes that he is facing danger and has come to a crisis in his ministry. Enemies are on every hand. Paul had reason to fear, as succeeding events proved. He is asking for prayer in a very wonderful way, "through our Lord Jesus Christ." Paul realized that everything that was to come to him had to come through Jesus Christ. He asked the believers in Rome to join with him in prayer. He says, "I want all of you to pray through Christ—He is our great Intercessor—go through Him to God on my behalf."

By "through the love of the Spirit" he means that love is the fruit of the Spirit which joins all believers together. And, friend, we ought to pray for each other.

"That ye strive intensely for me." The Greek word for *strive* is tremendous. We get our English word *agonize* from it. Paul is saying, "Agonize with me."

"On behalf of me"—he is asking for prayer for his personal safety that he might come in "the fulness of the blessing of the gospel of Christ." Oh, my friend, how we need to pray like this—not just praying by rote or by going over our prayer list hurriedly. For the apostle Paul prayer was with great agony, great exercise of soul. He laid hold of God. This kind of praying is so desperately needed today! You and I *need* people who know how to pray for us.

That I may be delivered from them that do not believe in Judaea; and that my service which I have for Jerusalem may be accepted of the saints [Rom. 15:31].

In other words, this is Paul's prayer request, and it is twofold. His life was in jeopardy from unbelievers in Judea, the religious rulers. He wanted to be delivered from them. Secondly, the church in Jerusalem might be hesitant in accepting a gift from Gentiles, and he wanted them to accept it. My friend, both requests were answered. Somebody says, "Yes, but he was arrested." Right, but he was immediately put into the hands of the Romans and was enabled to appear before kings, and finally he actually appeared before the Caesar in Rome, which was the fulfillment of the will of God for the apostle Paul.

That I may come unto you with joy by the will of God, and may with you be refreshed [Rom. 15:32].

This is the conclusion of Paul's prayer request. The prayer was answered: his life was spared, the church in Jerusalem accepted the gift, he did come with joy to Rome—in spite of the fact that he spent two years in jail at Caesarea, was shipwrecked on the way, and when he arrived in Rome he was in chains. Yet Paul came in the joy of the Holy Spirit. Oh, how all of us need that kind of joy in our lives!

Did Paul find rest and refreshment in Rome? Well, the answer is debatable. He did find all this and more beyond Rome and Spain when he entered the presence of Christ. He wrote near the end of his life to Timothy, his son in the faith: "For I am now ready to be offered, and the time of my departure is at hand. I have fought a good fight, I have finished my course, I have kept the faith: Henceforth there is laid up for me a crown of righteousness, which the Lord, the righteous judge, shall give me at that day: and not to me only, but unto all them also that love his appearing" (2 Tim. 4:6–8).

This chapter concludes with Paul's benediction:

Now the God of peace be with you all. Amen [Rom. 15:33].

"The God of peace" shows that Paul experienced peace in prison, in chains, in storm, and in shipwreck. I pray that you and I might have that kind of peace in our lives.

CHAPTER 16

THEME: *Commendation of Phebe; Christians in Rome greeted; conduct toward other Christians; Christians with Paul send greetings; concluding benediction*

In this final chapter of Romans the gospel walks in shoe leather in the first century of the Roman Empire. It thrills my heart to know that in the pagan Roman Empire there were Christians, witnesses for Christ, walking down the streets of those cities with the joy of the Lord in their hearts. I consider this one of the most revealing chapters that we have in the Epistle to the Romans. Paul has left the mountain peaks of doctrine to come down to the pavements of Rome. Here we see Christianity in action. The great doctrines which Paul proclaimed are not missiles for outer space. They are vehicles which actually operated on Roman roads. The gospel was translated into life and reality. This remarkable chapter should not be omitted or neglected in any study of Romans. William R. Newell has well said, "The sixteenth chapter is neglected by many to their own loss" (*Romans Verse by Verse*, p. 548).

There are thirty-five persons mentioned by name in this chapter. All were either believers living in Rome or they were believers who were with the apostle Paul—he was probably in Corinth when he wrote this epistle. There is expressed a mutual love and tender affection which was a contradiction of Roman philosophy and practice. (Also, it is rather unlike some churches today!) These Christians were different. Little wonder that Rome marveled at these folk and exclaimed, "My, how these Christians love each other!"

COMMENDATION OF PHEBE

The chapter begins with a commendation of Phebe, the woman who brought this epistle to Rome.

I commend unto you Phebe our sister, which is a servant of the church which is at Cenchrea:

That ye receive her in the Lord, as becometh saints, and that ye assist her in whatsoever business she hath need of you: for she hath been a succourer of many, and of myself also [Rom. 16:1–2].

Phebe is the first believer mentioned in this, another catalog of the heroes of the faith. She was a Gentile, as her name indicates. As I have already stated, there were many Gentiles in the church at Rome. She was named for the Greek goddess, Artemis or Diana, who in Greek mythology was the goddess of the moon, as her brother, Apollo, was the god of the sun. Many believers adopted new names at baptism, but Phebe kept her heathen name for some reason.

Phebe was the bearer of the Epistle to the Romans. Apparently she was a very prominent woman in the church, which means she was a woman of ability. She is called a "servant of the church which is at Cenchrea." Cenchrea is the eastern seaport of Corinth. When I stood at the ruins of ancient Corinth, I looked down and saw in the distance Cenchrea. On that clear day, it looked much closer than the eight or nine miles it is said to be. Apparently Paul wrote the Epistle to the Romans while he was at Corinth, and Phebe, who may have been a woman of means or engaged in business, took it with her to Rome. She is called a servant of the church, which means she was a deaconess. The Greek word *diakonos* is the same word used for deacon. It reveals the fact that women occupied a very prominent place in the early church.

It is my feeling that we would not be seeing women today occupying the position of pastors in the church (which is forbidden by Scripture) if they had been given their rightful position in the church. I think they should be deaconesses in the church and that they should sit on an equality with any other board of the church. The church needs some of the insights and sensibilities that women possess. God has made a woman finer than a man, just as a watch is finer than an automobile. She has been given a sense that man doesn't have. For instance, she can watch a woman who is a complete stranger to her, and in five minutes she knows a great deal about her simply by observing her dress and her manner. Those of us who belong to the male side of the human race appear stupid at a time like that. We can see if she is good looking or not, but that is the extent of our observation. The church needs the insight that a woman has.

Paul apparently put into Phebe's hand this Epistle to the Romans rather than trusting it to public transportation. Rome did have mail service, but it was slow. Paul, you see, is going back to Jerusalem, and Phebe brings his epistle with her to Rome.

"I commend unto you Phebe our sister"—Paul commends her to the believers there at Rome. She is the first woman mentioned in this final chapter.

CHRISTIANS IN ROME GREETED

Now Paul sends his greetings to quite a list of Christian folk.

Greet Priscilla and Aquila my helpers in Christ Jesus:

Who have for my life laid down their own necks: unto whom not only I give thanks, but also all the churches of the Gentiles [Rom. 16:3–4].

At this time there were gentile churches, you see, and I believe the church at Rome was largely gentile, made up of many races. It was integrated for sure.

"Priscilla and Aquila" were a Jewish couple. How had Paul met them, and in what way were they his helpers? Well, there had been a wave of anti-Semitism that had swept over the city of Rome, and Priscilla and Aquila had had to leave. They came to the city of Corinth while Paul was there and set up shop. Corinth was a good commercial center, and Paul was also plying his trade there. Since they were all tentmakers, this drew them together (see Acts 18:1–3), and Paul led them to the Lord. Then they were with Paul at Ephesus. Perhaps they had gone over there to open up a branch store. In Acts 18:26, we find that they were able to be helpful to Apollos: "And he [Apollos] began to speak boldly in the synagogue: whom when Aquila and Priscilla had heard, they took him unto them, and expounded unto him the way of God more perfectly." Notice that when we first meet them it is "Aquila and Priscilla." Now here in Romans it is Priscilla and Aquila. Why are the names reversed? Well, I think here is a case when the woman became dominant in spiritual matters. Spiritually she became the leader, although they were both outstanding workers for Christ.

Likewise greet the church that is in their house. Salute my well-beloved Epaenetus, who is the firstfruits of Achaia unto Christ [Rom. 16:5].

The local church met in private homes at the very beginning. (See Acts 12:12; 1 Cor. 16:19; Col. 4:15; Philem. 2.) Sanday writes, "There is no decisive evidence until the third century of the existence of special buildings used for churches." It is the belief of many folk today, and I have found this belief for years, that the church which began in the home will return to meeting in the home. Many of these great big buildings we call churches, with great steeples on them, are nothing more than a pile of brick, stone, and mortar. They are mausoleums, not living churches that contain a real, living body of believers. The church was never intended to be spoken of as a building. For the first three centuries the church was the body of believers and met in homes like that of Aquila and Priscilla.

Epaenetus is a Greek name meaning "praised." Evidently he was Paul's first convert in the Roman province of Achaia.

Greet Mary, who bestowed much labour on us [Rom. 16:6].

Mary is a Jewish name, the same as Miriam, meaning "rebelliousness." She "bestowed much labour on us" means that she labored to the point of exhaustion. What a change had taken place in her life! Before becoming a believer, she was in rebellion, but now she "knocks herself out" for the sake of other believers, because she is now obedient to Christ.

Salute Andronicus and Junia, my kinsmen, and my fellowprisoners, who are of note among the apostles, who also were in Christ before me [Rom. 16:7].

Andronicus is a Greek name, and the name has been identified with a slave.

Junia is a Roman name and can be either masculine or feminine. Paul calls them "my fellow countrymen," which may mean that they belonged to the tribe of Benjamin as did Paul. It does not necessarily mean close blood relationship.

Paul says, they were "my fellow prisoners." Evidently Paul had met them in one of the numerous prisons of the Roman Empire. These two were well-known to the apostles and were held in high regard by them. Paul had not led them to Christ, as is the natural assumption, for they were in Christ before he was.

The church in Rome was founded by Paul under most unusual circumstances. He had met Aquila and Priscilla in the Corinthian agora, the marketplace, and then he met these two men in jail. These had then gone to Rome and formed the church there.

Greet Amplias my beloved in the Lord.

Salute Urbane, our helper in Christ, and Stachys my beloved [Rom. 16:8–9].

Amplias is a common slave name and occurs in the tombs of the early Christians in the catacombs, always in a place of honor. He evidently was one of Paul's converts and dear to his heart.

Urbane means "city bred." In other words, his name actually means "city-slicker." This was also a common slave name, and it may mean that he was brought up in the city rather than in the country. He is identified as a real worker among believers.

Stachys has been found listed in the royal household. It is a masculine name. He was beloved not only to Paul but to the church.

Salute Apelles approved in Christ. Salute them which are of Aristobulus' household [Rom. 16:10].

Apelles is the approved one. His is either a Greek or a Jewish name—the name was a common one among the Jews. He had stood some outstanding test. Tradition identifies him as bishop either of Smyrna or Heracleia.

Aristobulus has been identified by Bishop Lightfoot as the grandson of Herod the Great. Or possibly he was a slave who took the name of his master—we can't be sure of this.

Salute Herodion my kinsman. Greet them that be of the household of Narcissus, which are in the Lord [Rom. 16:11].

Herodion was evidently a Jew, as Paul calls him a fellow countryman. The name suggests the Herod family. He may have been a slave who adopted the name of the family to which he belonged.

Narcissus is the name of a well-known freedman put to death by Agrippina. The one whose name appears here was probably a slave who formerly belonged to him and had taken his name.

Salute Tryphena and Tryphosa, who labour in the Lord. Salute the beloved Persis, which laboured much in the Lord [Rom. 16:12].

Tryphena and Tryphosa are euphonious names that mean "delicate" and "dainty." I imagine these two little ladies were old maid sisters who came to know Christ. They may have been women of means, and they had supported the apostle Paul. Paul says that they labored "in the Lord"—they were real workers in the church at Rome.

"The beloved Persis" is another woman who "laboured *much* in the Lord." *Persis* is the name of a freedwoman, and her position may have enabled her to do more than the preceding two sisters.

Salute Rufus chosen in the Lord, and his mother and mine [Rom. 16:13].

Although this man seems to stand in the shadows in this chapter, actually we can know a great deal about him—even to the color of his hair! His name means "red." *Red* was the name by which he was called. However, there were many red-haired folk; it was not his hair that made him unusual. The thing that marks him out is the phrase that follows, "chosen in the Lord." I love that. "But," you may say, "were not the others in this chapter chosen in the Lord also?" Yes, they were all wonderful saints, but this man was outstanding. Perhaps a better translation would be "distinguished in the Lord." He was a great saint of God.

That Rufus was prominent in the church is inferred in the reference to his father. When

John Mark wrote his gospel, he wrote it primarily for the Romans. In it he mentions the incident of a man by the name of Simon carrying the cross of Christ. "And they compel one Simon a Cyrenian, who passed by, coming out of the country, the father of Alexander and Rufus, to bear his cross" (Mark 15:21). The Roman soldiers that day saw Jesus falling under the cross. Looking over the crowd they shouted, "Here!" to a big double-fisted fellow, Simon of Cyrene. "You come here and carry it." And carry it he did—an act that has made him immortal. John Mark, writing to Rome, identifies Simon for them by adding, "the father of Alexander and Rufus"—all the saints at Rome would know Rufus because he was outstanding in the church.

Will you notice further that Paul's greeting includes the mother of Rufus. "Salute Rufus . . . and his mother and mine." While we know nothing of the mother of Paul the apostle and nothing of his father, we learn here of a godly woman in the city of Jerusalem, the wife of Simon the Cyrenian, who was like a mother to the apostle Paul. You may recall that the first time Paul came to Jerusalem following his conversion, the Christians feared him. They were unconvinced that this powerful Pharisee was genuine; they suspected trickery. Yet the mother of Rufus took Paul in, "You just come in and stay with Rufus in his room." Looking back to that time, Paul writes concerning her, "She is Rufus' mother, but she is mine also." What a lovely tribute to this warmhearted Christian mother!

Salute Asyncritus, Phlegon, Hermas, Patrobas, Hermes, and the brethren which are with them [Rom. 16:14].

These are all just names to us, but Paul knew them. Probably he had led them to Christ.

Salute Philologus, and Julia, Nereus, and his sister, and Olympas, and all the saints which are with them [Rom. 16:15].

Here is another group of believers who were in the church there in Rome.

CONDUCT TOWARD OTHER CHRISTIANS

Salute one another with an holy kiss. The churches of Christ salute you [Rom. 16:16].

This was the formal greeting in Paul's time—I don't recommend it for today!

Now I beseech you, brethren, mark them which cause divisions and offences contrary to the doctrine which ye have learned; and avoid them.

For they that are such serve not our Lord Jesus Christ, but their own belly; and by good words and fair speeches deceive the hearts of the simple [Rom. 16:17–18].

Paul puts in this word of warning. We would do well to heed this warning also, my beloved.

For your obedience is come abroad unto all men. I am glad therefore on your behalf: but yet I would have you wise unto that which is good, and simple concerning evil [Rom. 16:19].

You see, their faith came abroad also, but the faith is manifested in obedience.

"Wise unto that which is good" means they must be instructed in the Word of God.

"Simple concerning evil" means without admixture of evil. To the Corinthians Paul said, "Brethren, be not children in understanding: howbeit in malice be ye children, but in understanding be men" (1 Cor. 14:20).

And the God of peace shall bruise Satan under your feet shortly. The grace of our Lord Jesus Christ be with you. Amen [Rom. 16:20].

It is "the God of peace" who will put down Satan shortly. In the meantime we are to resist the Devil, be sober and vigilant.

CHRISTIANS WITH PAUL SEND GREETINGS

Now Paul sends greetings from those who were with him as he was writing this Epistle to the Romans.

Timotheus my workfellow, and Lucius, and Jason, and Sosipater, my kinsmen, salute you [Rom. 16:21].

All of these were companions of Paul. They send greetings to their fellow believers in Rome.

I Tertius, who wrote this epistle, salute you in the Lord [Rom. 16:22].

Paul, you see, had an amanuensis, a secretary, to write his letters. (The Epistle to the Galatians is the exception.)

Gaius mine host, and of the whole church, saluteth you. Erastus the chamberlain of the city saluteth you, and Quartus a brother [Rom. 16:23].

Paul was staying in the home of Gaius, and Gaius wanted to send his salutations also.

The grace of our Lord Jesus Christ be with you all. Amen [Rom. 16:24].

BENEDICTION

Now to him that is of power to stablish you according to my gospel, and the preaching of Jesus Christ, according to the revelation of the mystery, which was kept secret since the world began [Rom. 16:25].

"The mystery" means that it had not been revealed in the Old Testament. It refers to the present age when God is taking both Jew and Gentile and fashioning them into one body, the church.

But now is made manifest, and by the scriptures of the prophets, according to the commandment of the everlasting God, made known to all nations for the obedience of faith [Rom. 16:26].

Here we see the obedience of faith. When you trust Christ, you will obey Him, my friend. The Lord Jesus said, "My sheep hear my voice, and I know them, and they follow me" (John 10:27). Obedience is the work and fruit of faith.

My favorite hymn is "Trust and Obey" by John H. Sammis:

When we walk with the Lord
In the Light of His Word,
What a glory He sheds on our way!
While we do His good will,
He abides with us still,
And with all who will trust and obey.

Then in fellowship sweet
We will sit at His feet,
Or we'll walk by His side in the way;
What He says we will do,
Where He sends we will go—
Never fear, only trust and obey.

Trust and obey, for there's no other way
To be happy in Jesus, but to trust and obey.

To God only wise, be glory through Jesus Christ for ever. Amen [Rom. 16:27].

BIBLIOGRAPHY

(Recommended for Further Study)

Barnhouse, Donald Grey. *Romans*. 4 vols. Grand Rapids, Michigan: Wm. B. Eerdmans Publishing Co., 1952–1960. (Expositions of Bible doctrines, taking the Epistle to the Romans as a point of departure.)

DeHaan, Richard W. *The World on Trial: Studies in Romans*. Grand Rapids, Michigan: Zondervan Publishing House, 1970.

Epp, Theodore H. *How God Makes Bad Men Good: Studies in Romans*. Lincoln, Nebraska: Back to the Bible Broadcast, 1978.

Hendriksen, William. *The Epistle to the Romans*. Grand Rapids, Michigan: Baker Book House, 1980.

Hodge, Charles. *Commentary on the Epistle to the Romans*. Grand Rapids, Michigan: Wm. B. Eerdmans Publishing Co., 1886.

Hoyt, Herman A. *The First Christian Theology: Studies in Romans*. Grand Rapids, Michigan: Baker Book House, 1977. (Good for group study.)

Ironside, H. A. *Lectures on Romans*. Neptune, New Jersey: Loizeaux Brothers, n.d. (Especially fine for young Christians.)

Jensen, Irving R. *Romans: Self-Study Guide*. Chicago, Illinois: Moody Press, n.d.

Johnson, Alan F. *Romans: The Freedom Letter*. Chicago, Illinois: Moody Press, 1974.

Kelly, William. *Notes on Romans*. Addison, Illinois: Bible Truth Publishers, 1873.

Luther, Martin. *Commentary on Romans*. 1516 Reprint. Grand Rapids, Michigan: Kregel Publications, 1976.

McClain, Alva J. *Romans: The Gospel of God's Grace*. Chicago, Illinois: Moody Press, 1942.

McGee, J. Vernon. *Reasoning Through Romans*. 2 vols. Pasadena, California: Thru the Bible Books, 1959.

Moule, Handley, C. G. *The Epistle to the Romans*. Fort Washington, Pennsylvania: Christian Literature Crusade, n.d. (See note below.)

Moule, Handley C. G. *Studies in Romans*. Grand Rapids, Michigan: Kregel Publications, 1892. (Originally appeared in the Cambridge Bible for Schools and Colleges. These two books by Moule complement each other and are both excellent.)

Murray, John. *Romans*. Grand Rapids, Michigan: Wm. B. Eerdmans Publishing Co., 1965. (For advanced students.)

Newell, William R. *Romans Verse by Verse*. Chicago, Illinois: Moody Press, 1938. (An excellent study.)

Philips, John. *Exploring Romans*. Chicago, Illinois: Moody Press, 1969.

Stifler, James. *The Epistle to the Romans*. Chicago, Illinois: Moody Press, 1897.

Thomas, W. H. Griffith. *The Book of Romans*. Grand Rapids, Michigan: Wm. B. Eerdmans Publishing Co., 1946. (Fine interpretation.)

Vine, W. E. *Romans*. Grand Rapids, Michigan: Zondervan Publishing House, 1950.

Wuest, Kenneth S. *Romans in the Greek New Testament for English Readers*. Grand Rapids, Michigan: Wm. B. Eerdmans Publishing Co., 1955.

Wiersbe, Warren W. *Be Right. (Romans)*. Wheaton, Illinois: Victor Books, 1977.